SPORT...

The third millennium | Le troisième millénaire

1890
1990

100 Years after the Visit of Pierre De Coubertin to North America
100 ans après la visite de Pierre De Coubertin en Amérique du Nord

SPORT...

The third millennium | Le troisième millénaire

Edited by | Édité par

Fernand Landry
Marc Landry
Magdeleine Yerlès

Proceedings of the
International Symposium
Québec City, Canada
May 21-25, 1990

Compte rendu du
Symposium international
Québec, Canada
21-25 mai 1990

Under the Distinguished Patronage
of the International Olympic Committee

Sous le haut patronage
du Comité international olympique

LES PRESSES DE L'UNIVERSITÉ LAVAL
Sainte-Foy, 1991

Données de catalogage avant publication (Canada)

Sport... the third millennium: proceedings of the International Symposium, Quebec City, Canada, May 21-25, 1990 — Sport... le troisième millénaire: compte rendu du Symposium international, Québec, Canada, 21-25 mai 1990

Texte en anglais et en français.

Comprend des références bibliographiques et des index.

"Under the distinguished patronage of the International Olympic Committee — Sous le haut patronage du Comité international olympique".

ISBN 2-7637-7267-6

1. Sports - Aspect social - Congrès. 2. Sports - Philosophie - Congrès. 3. Jeux olympiques - Congrès. 4. Coubertin, Pierre de, 1863-1937 - Congrès. 5. Mass media et sports - Congrès. 6. Sports - Politique gouvernementale - Congrès. I. Landry, Fernand, 1930-   . II. Landry, Marc, 1956-   . III. Yerlès, Magdeleine, 1943-   . IV. Comité international olympique. V. Titre: Sport... le troisième millénaire.

GV576.S66 1991   796   C91-096942-6F

Données de catalogage avant publication (Canada)

Sport... the third millennium: proceedings of the International Symposium, Quebec City, Canada, May 21-25, 1990 — Sport... le troisième millénaire: compte rendu du Symposium international, Québec, Canada, 21-25 mai 1990

Text in English and French.

Includes bibliographical references and indexes.

"Under the distinguished patronage of the International Olympic Committee — Sous le haut patronage du Comité international olympique".

ISBN 2-7637-7267-6

1. Sports - Social aspects - Congresses. 2. Sports - Philosophy - Congresses. 3. Olympic games - Congresses. 4. Coubertin, Pierre de, 1863-1937 - Congresses. 5. Mass media and sports - Congresses. 6. Sports and state - Congresses. I. Landry, Fernand, 1930-   . II. Landry, Marc, 1956-   . III. Yerlès, Magdeleine, 1943-   . IV. International Olympic Committee. V. Title: Sport... le troisième millénaire.

GV576.S66 1991   796   C91-096942-6E

Conception graphique
>   Norman Dupuis

Photocomposition
>   Composition MARIKA inc.

Photographies
>   Service des relations publiques, Université Laval
>   (hors texte); Luc Noppen (hors texte)

Résumés, traductions, choix des citations et indexation
>   Fernand Landry, Marc Landry, Magdeleine Yerlès

Révision finale des épreuves et de la mise en pages
>   Michelle Fleury

Conception graphique du logo du Symposium
>   Jean-Pierre Labeau

Dedicatio

To three giants of olympic education, scholars, teachers and administrators of the International Olympic Academy

À trois géants de l'éducation olympique, experts, enseignants et administrateurs de l'Académie internationale olympique

NIKOS NISSIOTIS†
President / Président
1977-1986

OTTO SZYMICZEK†
Dean / Doyen
1961-1990

KLEANTIS PALEOLOGOS†
Scholar / Expert
1961-1990

Together, they contributed more than 70 years of faithful, devoted and competent services to the study of the olympic phenomenon, ancient as well as modern, and to the diffusion of the olympic ideals

À eux trois, ils ont consacré plus de 70 années de services loyaux, dévoués et compétents à l'étude du phénomène olympique ancien et moderne ainsi qu'à la diffusion de l'idéal olympique

Table
of Contents

Table
des matières

Sport, Culture and Society:
Heritage, Ideologies and Challenges

Sport, culture et société:
Héritage, idéologies et controverses

Official Opening Ceremonies
Quebec City
May 21th, 1990

Ouverture officielle du Symposium
Québec
le 21 mai 1990

Message by the President of the International Olympic Committee

The International Symposium *Sport... the Third Millennium*, which took place in Quebec from the 21st to the 25th of May 1990, marked the one hundredth anniversary of the visit to Canada by the founder of modern Olympism, Baron Pierre de Coubertin, and offered an opportunity to reflect upon sport as a social and cultural phenomenon as well as a fundamental right of every human being.

As the Olympic centenary and the year 2000 approach, sport and the Olympic Movement are enjoying enormous prestige, and play an essential role in the peaceful development of human society and education. However, the scale and importance of this prestige and social role create within Olympism and sport a certain vulnerability. Their supporters must protect them against this by taking a stance with regard to the future of this philosophy of life and social phenomenon, and by devoting serious study to the way we would like sport united with culture to develop. This is precisely what the *Sport... the Third Millennium* International Symposium did by bringing together scholars and scientists as well as representatives from the fields of education, the media and culture in general to study and discuss the history of sport; the opinions and ideas held on it; its controversies; the dangers which threaten it; the obligations society has towards sport; the possible consequences of the development of sport as the third millennium draws near; and the aspirations of the Olympic Movement. It is extremely important to publicize the ideas and opinions which were expressed together with the results of this event so that it can be followed up. The Official Report of this Symposium will play a key role in this respect.

On behalf of the International Olympic Committee, of which I have the honour to be President, and the whole Olympic Movement, I should like to thank all the participants and organizers of the *Sport ... the Third Millennium* International Symposium for their very important work and for the results achieved.

Mot d'introduction du Président du Comité international olympique

Le Symposium international *Sport... le troisième millénaire* qui s'est tenu à Québec du 21 au 25 mai 1990, a marqué le centenaire de la visite au Canada du Baron Pierre de Coubertin, fondateur de l'Olympisme moderne, et a fourni une occasion rêvée de réfléchir au sport comme phénomène social et de culture ainsi que comme droit fondamental de tout être humain.

À l'approche du centenaire olympique et de l'an 2000, le sport et le Mouvement olympique jouissent d'un prestige énorme et jouent un rôle essentiel dans l'éducation et le développement pacifique de toute la société. Cependant, l'importance même de ce prestige et de ce rôle social les rend vulnérables; les sympathisants de l'Olympisme et du sport ont donc l'obligation de les protéger en prenant position sur le futur de cette philosophie de vie et de ce phénomène social, et en réfléchissant d'une façon approfondie aux destins désirables du sport uni à la culture. C'est justement ce qu'a fait le Symposium international *Sport... le troisième millénaire*, qui a réuni des savants et des scientifiques du sport ainsi que des représentants de l'éducation, des mass media et de la culture en général pour étudier, entre autres, l'histoire du sport, les opinions et les idées qui le décrivent, ses controverses, les dangers qui le menacent, les obligations de la société envers le sport, les conséquences possibles des destins du sport à l'approche du troisième millénaire ainsi que les aspirations du Mouvement olympique. Je juge important de faire connaître les opinions qui ont été exprimées ainsi que les résultats de cette réunion pour que cette dernière puisse avoir des suites. Le rapport officiel de ce Symposium jouera un rôle crucial à cet effet.

Au nom du Comité International Olympique que j'ai l'honneur de présider et au nom de tout le Mouvement olympique, je voudrais remercier tous les participants et organisateurs du Symposium pour leur très important travail ainsi que pour les résultats obtenus.

Juan Antonio | SAMARANCH

The Organizing Committee
Le Comité d'organisation

EX OFFICIO MEMBERS
MEMBRES DE DROIT

Michel GERVAIS
Recteur
Université Laval

Roland ARPIN
Directeur général
Musée de la civilisation, Québec

Richard W. POUND
Vice-Président
International Olympic Committee,
Comité international olympique

EXECUTIVE
EXÉCUTIF

Fernand LANDRY
Président
Université Laval

Magdeleine YERLÈS
Université Laval

Michel-M. BONNEAU
Université Laval

MEMBERS
MEMBRES

Henri DORION
Musée de la civilisation, Québec

Michelle FLEURY
Université Laval

Jacques SAMSON
Université Laval

A. Edward WALL
McGill University

ADVISORS
CONSEILLERS

R. Gerald GLASSFORD
University of Alberta   (CAN)

Ommo GRUPE
Universität Tübingen   (FRG)

Bernard JEU
Université de Lille   (FRA)

John J. MACALOON
University of Chicago   (USA)

Donald MACINTOSH
Queen's University   (CAN)

Major Sponsors   *Les commanditaires majeurs*

Canadä   Québec

The organizing Committee wishes to acknowledge the kind cooperation of a number of representatives of the private sector in the pursuit of the academic objectives of the Quebec City International Symposium

Le Comité d'organisation tient à exprimer sa haute appréciation à un certain nombre de représentants de l'entreprise privée qui ont endossé et appuyé généreusement la poursuite des objectifs académiques du Symposium international de Québec.

John H. Bennett, Senior Vice President, VISA U.S.A. Inc., San Francisco, USA; Roger F. Woodward, President, VISA CANADA ASSOCIATION, Toronto, CAN; Gary P. Hite, Vice President, International Sports, The COCA-COLA COMPANY, Atlanta, USA; John M. Barr, Director, Corporate Sponsorships and Events, EASTMAN KODAK COMPANY, Rochester, USA; Robert W. Foulkes, Vice President Public Affairs, William W. Brand, Vice President, Marketing and Development and Gaston Beauregard, Senior Vice President Eastern Region, PETRO-CANADA, Calgary, CAN; Gordon G. Hendren, Christopher Lang & Associates and Olympic Torch Scholarship Fund, Toronto, CAN.

Acknowledgements   Remerciements

The Organizing Committee wishes to express its deepest gratitude to the international, Canadian and Quebec agencies and organizations which have provided the financial, scientific, cultural and professional support and services necessary for the planning and conduct of the Symposium and associated events.

INTERNATIONAL

- The International Olympic Committee
- Olympic Solidarity
- The United Nations Educational, Scientific and Cultural Organization (UNESCO)
- The International Council of Sport Science and Physical Education (CIEPSS-ICSSPE, N.G.O. Status A, UNESCO)
- The International Pierre de Coubertin Committee
- Visa
- Coca-Cola
- Eastman Kodak

CANADIAN

- Government of Canada
  - External Affairs
  - Secretary of State
  - Fitness and Amateur Sport
- Petro-Canada: Olympic Torch Scholarship Fund
- Royal Canadian Mint
- Canada Post Corporation
- Canadian Olympic Association
- Canadian Council of University Physical Education Administrators
- Tilden
- IBM

Le Comité d'organisation tient à exprimer ses remerciements les plus sincères aux instances internationales, canadiennes et québécoises qui lui ont procuré les appuis financiers, scientifiques, culturels et professionnels nécessaires à la planification et au déroulement du Symposium.

INSTANCES INTERNATIONALES

- Le Comité international olympique
- Solidarité olympique
- L'Organisation des nations-unies pour l'éducation, la science et la culture (UNESCO)
- Le Conseil international pour l'éducation physique et la science du sport (CIEPSS-ICSSPE, O.n.g. Statut A, UNESCO)
- Le Comité international Pierre de Coubertin
- Visa
- Coca-Cola
- Eastman Kodak

INSTANCES CANADIENNES

- Le Gouvernement du Canada
  - Affaires extérieures Canada
  - Secrétariat d'État du Canada
  - Condition physique et Sport amateur
- Pétro-Canada: Fonds de bourses d'études du flambeau olympique
- Monnaie Royale du Canada
- La Société canadienne des postes
- L'Association olympique canadienne
- Le Conseil canadien des administrateurs universitaires en éducation physique
- Tilden
- IBM

QUEBEC

- Government of Quebec
  - Ministère des Affaires internationales
  - Secrétariat aux Affaires intergouvernementales canadiennes
  - Ministère de la Justice
  - Ministère de l'Enseignement supérieur et de la Science
  - Ministère de l'Industrie, du Commerce et de la Technologie
  - Ministère du Loisir, de la Chasse et de la Pêche
  - Ministère du Tourisme
  - Ministère des Communications
- Musée de la civilisation, Quebec City
- Laurentienne-Vie
- Quebec Urban Community
  - Tourism and Convention Bureau
  - Transport Commission
- The City of Quebec
  - Office of the Mayor
- Université Laval
  - Le Secrétaire général
  - Faculté des sciences de l'éducation
  - Département d'éducation physique
  - Extension de l'enseignement
  - Service des relations publiques
  - Service des ressources pédagogiques

INSTANCES QUÉBÉCOISES

- Le Gouvernement du Québec
  - Ministère des Affaires internationales
  - Secrétariat aux Affaires intergouvernementales canadiennes
  - Ministère de la Justice
  - Ministère de l'Enseignement supérieur et de la Science
  - Ministère de l'Industrie, du Commerce et de la Technologie
  - Ministère du Loisir, de la Chasse et de la Pêche
  - Ministère du Tourisme
  - Ministère des Communications
- Le Musée de la civilisation, Québec
- Laurentienne-Vie
- Communauté Urbaine de Québec
  - Office du tourisme et des congrès
  - Commission des transports
- La Ville de Québec
  - Le Cabinet du Maire
- L'Université Laval
  - Le Secrétaire général
  - Faculté des sciences de l'éducation
  - Département d'éducation physique
  - Extension de l'enseignement
  - Service des relations publiques
  - Service des ressources pédagogiques

The Organizing Committee also extends its deepest gratitude to all the individuals who in the last two years have worked behind the scenes in a competent and generous manner: Suzanne Bibeau, Marie-Thérèse Bonneau, Jacques Boudreau, France Dumont, Jean Fortin, Georgette Gagnon, Charles Garon, Anne M. Hillmer, Monique Landry, Jean Lavoie, Robert Marois, Ginette Martel, Jocelyne Paré, Jean-Guy Racicot, amongst others.

Sincere thanks are given to a number of guests and participants who have graciously accepted the invitation of the Organizing Committee to chair the work sessions: Anthony DW (GBR), Bard C (CAN), Barney RK (CAN), Brand WW (CAN), Cantelon H (CAN), Chu Fook-Wing (HGK), Crosswhite P (AUS), Defrantz AL (IOC), De Koninck JM (CAN), De Wachter F (BEL), Dion Y (COA-CAN), Donnelly P (CAN), Drolet GR (CAN), Duerkop D (COA-CAN), Duplessis S (CAN), Fleury M (CAN), Foulkes RW (CAN), Freeman WH (USA), Gebauer G (FRG), Glassford RG (CAN), Glen-Haig MA (IOC), Grenier J (COA-CAN),

La gratitude du Comité d'organisation s'étend à toutes les personnes qui, au cours des deux dernières années, et trop souvent dans l'ombre, ont apporté leur efficace et généreuse collaboration, entre autres: Suzanne Bibeau, Marie-Thérèse Bonneau, Jacques Boudreau, France Dumont, Jean Fortin, Georgette Gagnon, Charles Garon, Anne M. Hillmer, Monique Landry, Jean Lavoie, Robert Marois, Ginette Martel, Jocelyne Paré, Jean-Guy Racicot.

Des remerciements sont aussi exprimés à l'intention des nombreux invités et participants qui ont avec la plus grande bienveillance accepté de présider les sessions de travail: Anthony DW (GBR), Bard C (CAN), Barney RK (CAN), Brand WW (CAN), Cantelon H (CAN), Chu Fook-Wing (HGK), Crosswhite P (AUS), Defrantz AL (CIO), De Koninck JM (CAN), De Wachter F (BEL), Dion Y (AOC-CAN), Donnelly P (CAN), Drolet GR (CAN), Duerkop D (AOC-CAN), Duplessis S (CAN), Fleury M (CAN), Foulkes RW (CAN), Freeman WH (USA), Gebauer G (FRG), Glassford RG (CAN), Glen-Haig MA (CIO), Grenier J

Gruneau R (CAN), Henderson P (CAN), Hindmarch R (COA-CAN), Hoffman A (CAN), Isava-Fonseca F (IOC), Jeu B (FRA), Jobling IF (AUS), Keyes ME (CAN), Laferrière T (CAN), Laplante L (CAN), Larson JF (USA), Leblanc C (CAN), Letheren CA (IOC-COA-CAN), Loy JW (USA), MacAloon JJ (USA), Macintosh D (CAN), Marcotte G (CAN), Ndiaye AD (SEN), Paillou N (FRA), Park RJ (USA), Plourde G (CAN), Pound RW (ICO), Rail G (CAN), Rivenburgh N (USA), Rodichenko V (URS), Samson J (CAN), San Giovanni LF (USA), Schneider AJ (CAN), Smith M (CAN), Thomas CE (USA), Toner V (CAN), Tripps DG (USA), Walker LT (USA), Wall AE (CAN), Weis K (FRG), Worrall J (IOC).

(AOC-CAN), Gruneau R (CAN), Henderson P (CAN), Hindmarch R (AOC-CAN), Hoffman A (CAN), Isava-Fonseca F (CIO), Jeu B (FRA), Jobling IF (AUS), Keyes ME (CAN), Laferrière T (CAN), Laplante L (CAN), Larson JF (USA), Leblanc C (CAN), Letheren CA (CIO-AOC-CAN), Loy JW (USA), MacAloon JJ (USA), Macintosh D (CAN), Marcotte G (CAN), Ndiaye AD (SEN), Paillou N (FRA), Park RJ (USA), Plourde G (CAN), Pound RW (CIO), Rail G (CAN), Rivenburgh N (USA), Rodichenko V (URS), Samson J (CAN), San Giovanni LF (USA), Schneider AJ (CAN), Smith M (CAN), Thomas CE (USA), Toner V (CAN), Tripps DG (USA), Walker LT (USA), Wall AE (CAN), Weis K (FRG), Worrall J (CIO).

Notice   Avertissement

By decision of the Organizing Committee, *French* and *English* were adopted as the two official languages of the Quebec City International Symposium *Sport... the Third Millennium*, May 1990.

In these Proceedings, a number of papers and Editors' Notes are given in the two languages. The various individual communications that deal with the theme and/or sub-themes appear *in the language in which they were presented. Abstracts* in the other language, and/or Editors' notes in the two official languages accompany the key-note addresses and panel presentations made at the invitation of the Organizing Committee. The free papers, however, are not accompanied by abstracts.

The opinion expressed and the data shown in these Proceedings by the various authors are entirely their own and, as such, do not necessarily represent the views of the Organizing Committee, the sponsors, l'Université Laval, the International Olympic Committe, or the organizations which had graciously given their patronage to the Quebec City Symposium.

Les langues *française* et *anglaise* furent adoptées par le Comité d'organisation comme langues officielles du Symposium international de Québec *Sport... le troisième millénaire*, qui eut lieu en mai 1990.

De ce fait, les conférences et communications apparaissent au présent Rapport officiel chacune *dans sa langue de présentation*. Un certain nombre de notes des éditeurs sont toutefois rédigées dans les deux langues. Des *abrégés* dans la langue autre que celle de la présentation accompagnent les conférences principales ainsi que les exposés des panelistes invités(es) par le Comité d'organisation. Les communications libres, toutefois, ne sont pas accompagnées d'un abrégé.

Les opinions émises, les analyses et les données figurant au présent Rapport officiel relèvent de la responsabilité des auteurs et, de ce fait, ne représentent pas nécessairement les vues du Comité d'organisation, des commanditaires, de l'Université Laval, du Comité international olympique, ou de l'un ou l'autre des organismes qui avaient gracieusement accordé leur patronage au Symposium de Québec.

PREFACE

The Occasion

By an Order in Council dated July 17, 1889, Pierre de Coubertin was conferred with the mission to visit a number of universities and colleges of the United States and Canada, in order to study their general organization as well as to examine the operations "of the athletic associations founded by the youth of these two countries".

It was during the Autumn of 1889 that Pierre de Coubertin visited the cities of Montreal and Quebec. He took advantage of that opportunity to visit McGill and Laval Universities. The extensive information collected and the observations which he made during his trip to North America were assembled and published in the form of an official report[1] presented to the Honorable Armand Fallières, then minister of France's Department of Public Instruction.

The accounts of Coubertin's visit indicate how he was greatly impressed at the time by the co-penetration of diverse influences which were evolving in North America at the end of the last century in the areas of general education, physical education, sports, and more broadly speaking, lifestyle and various forms of behavior.

One of the practical consequences of this influence was undoubtedly to strengthen Coubertin in his resolve—to work on the reform of the pedagogical views in France;—to use the invention of modern sports to give an "international reinforcement" to a renewed humanism and approach to education and teaching. Less than three years later, during a conference at the Sorbonne, on the 25th of November 1892, Pierre de Coubertin announced the forthcoming "restoration of the Olympic Games".

The destinies of the two branches of the Coubertinian achievement progressed at very different rates during the Twentieth Century. It was his idea of the renewal of the Olympic Games which was to develop with astonishing speed and with world-wide consequences.

Despite generally favorable advocacy given to the overall phenomenon in the four corners of the world, Olympism, the Olympic Movement and the Olympic Games now face increasingly sustained questioning especially at the time of the celebration of a new Olympiad. Where is sports heading to? Is its expansion irreversible? What are its paradoxes, its grandeurs, its miseries? Behind the rapid escalation of its successes, given the present controversies, how to distinguish between the essential and the unessential?

At the time of Coubertin's visit to Canada, in 1889, no one could have foreseen such a rapid globalization of the sports phenomenon, or its continuity, or indeed the far reaching cultural effects of the idea which had germinated in the mind of the wellknown renovator.

---

1. Coubertin Pierre de (1890). Universités Trans-Atlantiques. Paris: Hachette, 389 p.

PRÉFACE

L'occasion

Par un arrêté ministériel du 17 juillet 1889, Pierre de Coubertin se voyait confier la mission de visiter un certain nombre d'universités et de collèges, aux États-Unis et au Canada, afin d'y étudier l'organisation générale comme aussi d'y examiner le fonctionnement «des associations athlétiques fondées par les jeunes gens de ces deux pays».

C'est au cours de l'automne 1889 que Pierre de Coubertin a visité les villes de Montréal et de Québec. Il n'a pas manqué de se rendre aux Universités McGill et Laval. Les nombreux renseignements qu'il a recueillis et les observations qu'il a faites à l'époque de son voyage en Amérique du Nord ont été colligés et publiés par la suite sous la forme d'un rapport officiel[1] présenté à monsieur Armand Fallières, alors ministre de l'Instruction publique de France.

Le compte-rendu de la visite de Coubertin laisse voir combien ce dernier a été impressionné à l'époque par la co-pénétration d'influences diverses qui s'élaborait en Amérique du Nord à la fin du siècle dernier en matière d'éducation générale, d'éducation physique, de conception du sport, et, d'une manière plus globale, de façons de se comporter.

L'une des conséquences pratiques de cette influence a nul doute été de confirmer Coubertin dans sa résolution — de travailler à la réforme de la pensée pédagogique en France; — de se servir de l'invention du sport moderne pour donner un «contrefort international» à un humanisme et à un enseignement renouvelés. Moins de trois ans plus tard, à l'occasion d'une conférence à la Sorbonne, le 25 novembre 1892, Pierre de Coubertin annonçait le prochain «rétablissement des Jeux olympiques».

Les destins des deux branches de l'œuvre coubertinienne ont progressé à des vitesses fort différentes au cours du XXe siècle. C'est la rénovation des Jeux olympiques qui allait se développer avec une rapidité étonnante et des conséquences mondiales.

Malgré des vents plutôt favorables à l'ensemble du phénomène dans tous les coins du monde, l'Olympisme, le Mouvement olympique et les Jeux olympiques doivent faire face à des questionnements sans cesse plus soutenus, à chaque célébration d'une Olympiade. Où va le sport? Sa montée est-elle irréversible? Quels sont ses paradoxes, ses grandeurs, ses misères? Derrière l'escalade efficace de ses succès, devant les controverses de l'heure, comment distinguer l'essentiel de l'inessentiel?

À l'époque de la visite de Coubertin au Canada, en 1889, nul n'aurait pu prévoir une planétisation si rapide du phénomène sportif, pas plus d'ailleurs que la continuité et le rayonnement de l'idée directrice qui germait déjà dans le cerveau du célèbre rénovateur.

---

1. Coubertin Pierre de (1890). Universités Trans-Atlantiques. Paris: Hachette, 389 p.

In more ways than one, the Olympic Movement has solid roots in North and Central America. The Americans have participated in the first Games of the modern era, while the National Olympic Committee of Canada (COA-AOC) was founded in 1904, and that of Mexico in 1923. In addition, the generous and for the most part enthusiastic support given by the citizens of these neighboring countries to the grand quadrennial sporting manifestation does not have its equal in the Olympic annals. On the whole, the Summer Games (Games of the Olympiad) and the Winter Games have been held on nine occasions in North and Central America: six times in the United States, twice on Canadian soil, and once in Mexico. And it is in North America that again will be celebrated the Games of the Olympiad, this time the XXVth, which will mark the First Centennial of the Modern Olympic Movement.

In the broad perspective of Laval University's mandate and tradition for community services on the Quebec, Canadian and international scenes, the centennial commemorating the visit of Pierre de Coubertin to Canada affords a unique opportunity to initiate an in-depth reflection on the becoming of sports and on its overall usefulness within and between societies.

Nature of the Symposium

An initiative and a joint project of the Department of Physical Education and of the Department of Continuing Education of Laval University, the Symposium purported to be inter-disciplinary and international in scope, taking into account the universal interdependence of the structures and forces which exert pressure on competitive sport, and in particular on the Olympic Movement, as complex and influencial phenomena and systems.

The concepts of *Sports, Culture and Society: Heritage, Ideologies and Controversies* have served in the determination of the central theme of the Symposium as well as in the development of its eighteen sub-themes.

The Symposium's central theme was thus to be a comprehensive reflection on the contemporary sports phenomenon. Scholars, scientists and representatives of various social institutions and groups (including sport) were asked to contribute to the program, with the specific intent to:

– shed light on the origins, development and progress of the universal characteristics of the sporting heritage;

– review the analyses of the various systems of ideas which attempt to describe, explain, interpret or justify contemporary sport;

– analyze and debate a number of problems and issues in sports and highlight the more contentious elements, contradictory values and paradoxes between the culture of sport and society at large;

– analyze and debate the responsibilities which sport has towards society.

The various key-note addresses, presentations, discussions, seminars and other activities were intended not only for the academic circles, but also for the sports community, the media, as well as the public in general. Converging, differing and even opposing viewpoints, as expressed by various speakers in the course of the program, were welcome without necessarily being endorsed by the members of the Organizing Committee or Laval University.

Observers and critics of the sports phenomenon have long recognized that play, games, sport and high performance athletics possess personal, social and global political dimensions which go well beyond the sporting act or exploit and

À plus d'un point de vue, le Mouvement olympique a de fortes racines en Amérique du Nord et Centrale. Les américains ont participé aux premiers Jeux de l'ère moderne, cependant que le Comité national olympique du Canada (COA-AOC) fut créé en 1904 et celui du Mexique en 1923. Par surcroît, le soutien généreux et dans l'ensemble enthousiaste que les citoyens de ces pays voisins ont accordé à la grande manifestation sportive quadriennale n'a guère son égal dans les annales olympiques. Au total, les Jeux de l'Olympiade (jeux d'été) et les Jeux d'hiver ont été célébrés à neuf reprises en Amérique du Nord et Centrale: six fois aux États-Unis, deux fois en sol canadien, une fois au Mexique. Et c'est en sol américain que seront célébrés, en 1996 à Atlanta, les Jeux de la XXVe Olympiade, ceux qui marqueront le premier centenaire du Mouvement olympique moderne.

Dans la perspective des responsabilités et de la tradition de service de l'Université Laval sur les scènes québécoise, canadienne et internationale, le centenaire de la visite de Pierre de Coubertin au Canada constitue un moment favorable à une réflexion en profondeur sur le devenir du sport et sur son utilité sociale.

Nature du Symposium

L'initiative du projet revient au Département d'éducation physique ainsi qu'à l'Extension de l'enseignement de l'Université Laval. Il fut jugé dès le départ que le Symposium méritait d'être inter-disciplinaire et d'envergure internationale, en raison même de l'interdépendance universelle des structures et des forces qui marquent présentement le sport de compétition et, plus particulièrement encore le sport olympique, en tant que systèmes complexes et influents.

Les concepts de *Sport, Culture et Société: Héritage, Idéologies et Controverses* servirent à l'élaboration du thème principal et des dix-huit sous-thèmes du Symposium.

L'objectif central du Symposium fut donc celui d'être une réflexion approfondie sur le sport contemporain. Des scientifiques et des savants, des représentants d'organismes et institutions variés (incluant ceux du sport) ont été appelés à contribuer au programme, plus spécialement dans l'intention

– de mettre en lumière les origines, le développement et les cheminements des universaux de l'héritage en cause;

– de faire le point sur les analyses des systèmes d'idées qui décrivent, expliquent, interprètent ou justifient le sport contemporain;

– d'analyser et de débattre des controverses du sport et de souligner les éléments tensionnels, les valeurs contradictoires et les paradoxes entre culture sportive et société;

– d'analyser et de débattre des redevances du sport envers la société.

Les conférences, les entretiens, les séminaires et les activités complémentaires s'adressaient non seulement aux communautés universitaires internationales, mais aussi au monde du sport, à celui des media et au public en général. Les points de vue divergents ou même opposés ont été agréés sans pour autant être cautionnés dans leur substance par le Comité d'organisation ou par l'Université Laval.

Les observateurs et les critiques du phénomène du sport reconnaissent depuis longtemps au jeu, au sport et à la haute performance athlétique des dimensions personnelles, sociales et politiques universelles qui dépassent carré-

basically have to do with a kind a renewed possibility for self-development and social achievement.

Compulsions of a purely biological order, means of identification or of self-expression, the conscious or unconscious search for experimentation or for personal or collective gain, are but a few of the motives for involvement in sport. Their roots can be traced in the deepest recesses of one's individuality, as well as to certain extra-personal considerations that have to do with the rapid development of technological societies and their associated value systems. By feedback, these considerations contribute on the one hand to the affirmation and expression of the sporting phenomenon and, on the other hand, to its alienation. Under many and varied aspects and in complex ways indeed, the practice of sport (and to a larger extent high performance sport) consequently overlaps into the world of education, health and well-being, work and leisure, marketing and publicity, communications and business, arts and culture, as well as international relations and politics.

And the Coubertinian idea of 1894...?

In this immense constellation which characterizes competitive sport at the world level, one could say that the Olympic Games continue to shine as a star of the highest magnitude. For reasons that are evident, the Olympic Movement enjoys enormous prestige. It has become doubtful, however, as to whether all the institutions that support the olympic ideology do it with the same purposes, integrity and respect as was originally proposed by Coubertin. Rather unscrupulously, success at the Olympic Games is often and increasingly used as a powerful and efficient means to acquire notoriety, prestige and influence. It is a matter of common observation that the relentless pursuit of excellence in the Olympic Games, by legions of athletes from the four corners of the globe, has been at times subject to non-equivocal attempts to illustrate, defend or propagate to a world audience a vision or a given philosophy of man, society and existence.

Nonetheless, the Olympic Movement continues to expand. Scores of people estimate that the olympic ideology continues to prevail in many ways and on many fronts, as a positive and universal social reality. In that perspective, the Olympic Movement can be considered as one of the institutions of international prestige and character which has best succeeded in its mission, despite the many obstacles, since the turn of the century.

One of the centripetal forces which contributes to giving the phenomenon of the Olympic Games an internal coherence stems from the very nature of competitive sport. In general terms, it can be characterized by the pursuit of excellence and the quest for victory within a framework dominated by intense competitiveness, involvement and effort. In this perspective, high performance sport becomes a particular form of endeavor aimed at "self-improvement" which operates in artificial situations indeed, but nonetheless requires ever-increasing degrees of fitness, dedication, effort, motivation, perseverance, self-sacrifice, respect of the rights and dignity of the adversary: in brief, non-equivocal characteristics and qualities of a physical, psycho-social and even spiritual nature. Athletic activities, in particular those which figure prominently in the Olympic Games, give their participants a unique opportunity to reach relative levels of perfection, to go beyond that which has already been achieved by others. In this way, top athletes become, for better or for worse, concrete images of the levels of perfection man is capable of achieving.

In a kind of joyous spiral, the performance levels targetted by incumbents are literally dictated by the champions. The ever-increasing levels of performance

ment le geste ou l'exploit et qui ont trait, au fond, à une sorte de possibilité pour l'être humain de s'accomplir, aussi et par cette voie.

Pulsion d'ordre purement biologique, mode d'identification ou d'expression de la personne, recherche inconsciente ou consciente d'expériences ou de bénéfices personnels ou collectifs, autant de raisons de «faire du sport» qui trouvent racine au plus profond de l'individualité de chacun, mais auxquelles se surimpriment des considérations impersonnelles qui renvoient à l'évolution rapide de sociétés technologiques et qui, par rétroaction, contribuent tantôt à l'affirmation et à l'expression du phénomène, tantôt aussi à son aliénation. Sous une multitude de formes et dans les ramifications les plus complexes, la pratique du sport (et à plus forte raison encore celle du sport de haute performance) se trouve ainsi et de toute évidence imbriquée dans le monde de l'éducation, de la santé et du bien-être, du travail et du loisir, du marketing et de la publicité, des communications et des affaires, de l'art et de la culture, sans oublier bien sûr celui des relations internationales et de la politique.

Et l'idéologie coubertinienne de 1894...?

Dans cette immense constellation que constitue le sport de compétition à l'échelle mondiale, on peut dire que les Jeux olympiques brillent toujours comme l'étoile de la plus grande magnitude. Pour des raisons évidentes, le Mouvement olympique jouit d'un prestige énorme. Il est devenu douteux cependant que la totalité des institutions qui le supportent le fassent dans le respect intégral de l'idéologie proposée par Coubertin. Sans trop de scrupules, on s'en sert aussi et de plus en plus comme un moyen puissant et efficace pour acquérir de la visibilité, du prestige et de l'influence. Il peut être observé que la poursuite résolue de l'excellence aux Jeux olympiques par des légions d'athlètes de tous les coins du globe se voit souvent assujettie à des tentatives non-équivoques d'illustrer, de défendre ou de propager à la face du monde une vision et une philosophie donnée de l'homme, de la société et de l'existence.

Malgré tout, le Mouvement olympique va son chemin. Nombreux sont ceux et celles qui estiment que l'idéologie olympique a prévalu de plusieurs manières et sur plusieurs fronts, en tant que réalité sociale positive à l'échelle universelle. Certains sont même d'avis que le Mouvement olympique peut être considéré comme l'une des institutions à caractère et à prestige international qui ait le mieux réussi, dans sa mission et en dépit des obstacles, depuis le tournant du siècle.

L'une des forces centripètes qui contribue à donner aux Jeux olympiques une systématique interne découle de la nature même de la haute compétition sportive. En gros, cette dernière se caractérise par la poursuite de l'excellence et la recherche de la victoire dans des cadres où dominent l'intensité de l'engagement, de l'implication et de l'effort. Sous cet angle, la haute performance devient une sorte d'entreprise d'«auto-perfectionnement» qui a cours dans des situations artificielles, il est vrai, mais qui exige néanmoins et à des degrés sans cesse plus élevés, aptitudes, engagement, efforts, motivation, persévérance, renoncement, respect des droits et de la dignité de l'adversaire, bref, des traits et des qualités à caractère physique, psycho-social et même spirituel non-équivoques. Le sport de haute performance, entre autres les spécialités qui figurent au programme des Jeux olympiques, fournit donc à ses adeptes des occasions uniques d'atteindre des paliers de perfection relative, de surpasser sans cesse le «déjà fait». Ainsi, les athlètes de pointe deviennent, bon an mal an, autant d'images concrètes des degrés de perfection dont l'humain se rend capable.

Dans cette sorte de joyeuse spirale, le niveau de performance du champion dicte carrément le niveau-cible aux aspirants. Le niveau montant de performance

of these incumbents then become a menace for the champion, who in turn has no alternative but to raise his/her own level, otherwise he/she must quickly relinquish position. The overall requirement levels needed for athletic (including "olympic") success thus tend to increase even higher and further as the number of incumbents grows within a given reference group. Under these circumstances, it is understandable that as the requirements for top-level physical and psychological performances increase, so to do the needs for greater incentives and support, and for ever more attractive or valorizing gratifications, whether tangible or symbolic.

This stated, it is clear that the importance (or the overly exaggerated importance) which is ultimately bestowed on sporting (and olympic) success within a given culture and, consequently, on the social strategies devised to produce, establish and increase it in the eyes of the world, ultimately results in a kind of "totalisation" process of the production means. Observations on the reality and the major controversies at the Seoul Games suffice to show that education, science, technology, finance and politics (of course in varying degrees) are among the contributing forces. The effect of such a situation is to:

– provoke (by feedback) the continuing escalation of the total costs and of the socio-economico-cultural significance of sporting success;

– create a new competitive dimension, the one between sporting systems at the international level and, evidently, between the socio-political and economic regimes which support them.

Under such conditions, it appears unrealistic to contend that sport (just as culture in general) is (or can remain) independent from economic considerations, science, high technology, and politics.

The tension, the drama, the attraction of the *Citius, Altius, Fortius*, at the ultimate limits of muscular activity, continue nonetheless to be modified, permuted through the will, imagination and creativity of the athletes themselves as much as by the combined effect of science, economics and politics. In the end it is the athletes, and not the systems, which function at the limits of "possibility", each in his/her own specialty. As a consequence, one of the most fundamental values of high performance sport is that of demonstrating the reciprocity relationship between "the possible" and "the real". In this fundamental attraction indeed seems to reside the charm as well as the universal and transcendental popularity of high performance sport. This is possibly the force which tends to give the coherence, both necessary and sufficient, to the continuity of both the Olympic Movement and the Olympic Games.

Towards a new equilibrium?

If the first half of the 20th century was witness to the globalization of competitive sport as a "system", it seems that the last quarter will for its part have been marked by the liberalization and generalization of the practice of physical activities as a means of self-realization and self-expression aimed at personal well-being, health and adaptation to one's environment. The upward spiral of budgets and the analyses of cost-effectiveness in the areas of public health and welfare have in fact provoked new and important questioning of (and changes in) governmental policies. Preventive measures have gained, and continue to gain public favor as virtually everywhere in the world health and welfare costs soar incessantly upwards.

de ces derniers devient par la suite menaçant pour le champion, lequel à son tour n'a d'autre choix que celui d'élever son propre niveau, sans quoi il doit vite céder la place. Le niveau des exigences totales de la réussite sportive (incluant l'«olympique») tend ainsi et par surcroît à augmenter dans la mesure où s'élargit le nombre des aspirants dans un groupe de référence donné. Dans cette perspective, l'on comprendra que plus hautes se situent les exigences physiques et psychiques de la performance, plus élevés doivent être les incitations et les appuis, et plus attirants ou valorisants aussi tendent à devenir les gratifications, qu'elles soient tangibles ou symboliques.

Cela étant, il est clair que l'importance (ou la sur-importance) que l'on accorde au succès sportif (et olympique) dans une culture donnée et, par voie de conséquence, à l'ensemble des solutions sociales que l'on imagine pour le produire, l'établir à la face du monde et l'accroître, aboutit nécessairement à une sorte de «totalisation» des moyens d'entreprise. L'observation de la réalité et la grande controverse de Séoul montrent vite que l'éducation, la science, la technologie, la finance et la politique se trouvent dans les faits (mais à des degrés divers) mis à contribution. Une telle situation a pour effet :

– de provoquer (par rétroaction) l'escalade continue des coûts totaux et de la signification socio-culturelle du succès sportif ;

– d'engendrer une nouvelle dimension de la compétiton, celle-là entre les systèmes sportifs à l'échelle internationale, et, bien sûr, entre les régimes socio-politiques et économiques qui les sous-tendent.

Dans une telle conjoncture, il n'est guère réaliste de prétendre que le sport (comme d'ailleurs la culture en général) est (ou peut demeurer) indépendant de la politique, de l'économique, de la science et de la haute technologie.

La tension, le drame, l'attrait du *Citius, Altius, Fortius*, à l'extrémité où l'activité musculaire a ultimement cours, n'en continuent pas moins d'être continuellement modifiés, permutés par la volonté des athlètes, leur imagination et leur créativité propre, autant et sinon plus, peut-être, que par l'effet combiné de la science, de l'économique et du politique. Car au fond ce sont les athlètes eux-mêmes, et non les systèmes, qui fonctionnent aux confins du «possible», chacun/chacune dans sa spécialité. Ainsi, l'une des valeurs les plus fondamentales du sport de haut niveau est celle de pouvoir mettre en évidence (autant pour l'athlète que pour le spectateur) les relations d'effets réciproques entre «le possible» et «le réel». En cela semble résider l'attrait fondamental, le charme et la popularité universelle et transcendante de la haute performance sportive. En cela réside la force qui tend à conserver au Mouvement et aux Jeux olympiques la cohérence nécessaire et suffisante à leur continuité.

Vers un nouvel équilibre ?

Si la première partie du XXe siècle a été témoin de la planétisation de la compétition sportive en tant que système, il semble bien que le dernier quart aura pour sa part été marqué par la libéralisation et la généralisation de la pratique des activités physiques comme moyen de réalisation et d'expression de soi comme aussi en vue du bien-être, de la santé et de l'adaptation à l'environnement. L'augmentation en spirale des budgets et les analyses de coûts-bénéfices en matière de bien-être social et de santé publique ont en effet provoqué des changements importants de politiques gouvernementales. Les mesures préventives ont gagné et gagnent toujours plus de faveur face à l'épineux problème de l'augmentation en flèche des coûts de recouvrement de la santé, où que ce soit, semble-t-il, dans le monde.

In the mosaic of means recognized as having the potential to influence health and well-being, both individual and collective, physical activity continues to gain in popularity and prestige. Traditionally, most everywhere, government interest in the practice of physical activities by the citizenry was in the past concentrated in two areas:—exercise and sports-training within the educational system;—competitive sport of national and international character. This vision now seems a thing of the past. Taxpayers, governments and public administrators, the physical education and sport federations and associations, leisure, recreation and outdoor organizations, youth agencies, employer groups, unions, medical, para-medical and health organizations, the mass media, the business community and private corporations, are manifesting an unprecedented interest all in that which pertains to the free and open practice of a wide spectrum of physical activities (including sport), each attempting in its own way to offer new advice and services to the population. In principle, as in practice, it seems that the agencies which have long been devoted to promoting elite sports and which traditionally have drained such a large portion of public and corporate funds, will in the future be expected to share a greater part of the latter. The obvious implication is that this becomes a progressive challenge to the kind of privileged situation in which high profile sports have placed themselves over the past decades. In the industrialized countries, at least in those said to be pluralistic-liberal, the symbolic function of high performance sport is increasingly subjected to open criticism, especially as concerns the social accountability of the entire sport-system. The sharing of resources and clientele is creating new dilemmas and would lead to better and more balanced approaches, programs and services in the not too distant future.

The Organizing Committee of the Quebec City International Symposium sincerely hopes that its efforts will have contributed to an in depth reflexion on the fascinating contemporary sports phenomenon. It also sincerely hopes that the results of the work of those who participated in the event, and the present Official Proceedings, will have a positive influence on the future of sport, as we draw near the third millennium.

The Editors

Fernand Landry   *Marc Landry*   *Magdeleine Yerlès*

Quebec, June 1991

Dans la mosaïque des moyens d'action reconnus comme pouvant influer sur la santé et le bien-être individuels et collectifs, l'activité physique gagne sans arrêt du rang et du prestige. Par tradition, l'intérêt des autorités gouvernementales à l'égard de la pratique des activités physiques s'était résumé dans le passé au soutien de l'éducation physique et sportive dans le système éducatif et à celui du sport de compétition à caractère national et international. Ce temps semble bel et bien révolu. Les contribuables, les gouvernements et les fonctionnaires, les fédérations et associations d'éducation physique et de sport, les organismes de loisir, de récréation, de plein-air, les agences de jeunesse, le patronat, les syndicats, les organisations médicales, para-médicales et de santé publique, les mass-média, le monde des affaires et l'entreprise privée, manifestent un intérêt sans précédent à l'égard de la question de la pratique libre d'un large éventail d'activités physiques et sportives, chacun s'efforçant à sa façon d'offrir de nouveaux avis ou services inédits à la population. En principe comme en pratique, il semble donc que les agences qui sont vouées depuis si longtemps à la promotion du sport d'élite et qui drainent par tradition et encore de nos jours une si large part des fonds publics et privés, seront dans l'avenir appelées à partager une plus large part de ces derniers. On assiste en effet un peu partout à un challenge déclaré et sérieux de la situation en quelque sorte privilégiée dans laquelle le sport d'élite s'est placé au cours des dernières décades. Dans les pays industrialisés, du moins dans ceux qui sont caractérisés par une société de type dit libéral, la fonction symbolique du sport d'élite est de plus en plus soumise à une sévère critique sociale. Le partage des ressources et de la clientèle prend ainsi l'allure de dilemmes nouveaux sinon de confrontations inaccoutumées.

Le Comité d'organisation du Symposium international de Québec ose croire que ses efforts auront contribué à une réflexion approfondie sur le fascinant phénomène du sport contemporain, et que le résultat du travail des personnes présentes lors de l'événement, comme aussi le présent Rapport officiel, influeront de manière positive sur les choix sociaux et le cours des choses, au tournant du troisième millénaire.

Les éditeurs

Fernand Landry   *Marc Landry*   *Magdeleine Yerlès*

Québec, juin 1991

[...] De quatre ans en quatre ans, le vingtième siècle verrait ainsi cette [jeunesse universelle] se réunir successivement près des grandes capitales du monde pour y lutter de force et d'adresse et s'y disputer le rameau symbolique. Oh! sans doute il y a beaucoup d'obstacles à franchir pour en arriver là; il y a, nous venons de le voir, les coutumes, les traditions, les instincts de race et toutes les particularités que la vie sportive emprunte au climat, à la législation, aux circonstances... Mais notez bien qu'il n'y a qu'à consentir, ça et là, quelques sacrifices de détail et à faire montre d'un peu de bonne volonté... Modernes, très modernes, seront ces jeux olympiques restaurés: il n'est pas question de se vêtir de maillots roses pour courir dans un stade de carton; et ceux qui entrevoient déjà les théories blanches gravissant solennellement, aux sons retrouvés de l'Hymne à Apollon, quelque colline sacrée, ceux-là en sont pour leurs frais d'imagination. Point de trépieds, ni d'encens: ces belles choses sont mortes et les choses mortes ne revivent pas; l'idée seule peut revivre, appropriée aux besoins et aux goûts du siècle. De l'antiquité nous ne prétendons rétablir qu'une chose, la trêve, la très sainte!... que consentaient les nations grecques pour contempler la jeunesse et l'avenir.

Coubertin P de (1894) Le rétablissement des Jeux olympiques. Revue de Paris, 15 juin, p 184

Sport, Culture and Society:
Heritage, Ideologies and Challenges

Sport, culture et société :
héritage, idéologies et controverses

Official Opening Ceremonies

Quebec City
May 21th, 1990

Ouverture officielle du symposium

Québec
le 21 mai 1990

-

Speech Allocution
by the President of du Président
the Organizing Committee du Comité d'organisation

Fernand Landry

Monsieur le Ministre Rémillard,
Monsieur le Président Samaranch,
Monsieur le Secrétaire d'État à la Jeunesse et au sport de la France,
Monsieur le Recteur,
Madame la Représentante du Gouvernement du Canada,
Distingués invités d'honneur,
Mesdames, messieurs,

Mes collègues du Comité d'organisation se joignent à moi pour vous souhaiter la plus chaleureuse des bienvenues à notre Symposium International.

Je m'empresse de remercier de tout cœur le président Samaranch d'avoir endossé nos objectifs et de nous honorer de sa présence à Québec.

Notre profonde gratitude s'étend aussi:

– aux Gouvernements du Canada et du Québec;
– au recteur de l'Université Laval, le Dr Michel Gervais, qui nous a encouragés et soutenus avec la plus grande bienveillance, et dont l'institution est l'hôte académique du Symposium;
– à nos quatre commanditaires majeurs (dont je souligne avec grand plaisir la présence des représentants officiels sur cette scène) sans la collaboration desquels notre programme académique n'aurait pu avoir la présente ampleur;

Enfin, un merci très spécial;

– à l'UNESCO;
– au Conseil international pour l'éducation physique et la science du sport;
– au Comité international Pierre de Coubertin;
– à l'Association olympique canadienne et au Conseil canadien des administrateurs universitaires en éducation physique et sport, pour les patronages scientifique et professionnel accordés.

C'est François Mauriac qui a dit du siècle présent : « ... cet étrange siècle du sport... »

Ce XXe siècle qui a connu l'expansion phénoménale du sport et de l'Olympisme moderne, idée généreuse de Pierre de Coubertin dont les caractéristiques essentielles étaient au départ pour lui et sont toujours pour le Mouvement olympique actuel :

– la poursuite de l'excellence,

– le fair-play,

– le désintéressement des bénéfices matériels,

– le rejet de la discrimination sous toutes ses formes,

– enfin, la promotion du respect mutuel, de la coopération et de la paix entre individus, peuples et nations.

Le sport est devenu, sans l'ombre d'un doute, un fait social universel. Sous les formes les plus diverses, le voilà propagé dans tous les continents. On compte aujourd'hui pas moins de 167 comités nationaux olympiques sur 170 états-nations ! On ne s'étonne pas non plus de trouver le sport si répandu dans les pays en voie de développement où on le considère comme une force de cohésion pouvant servir la nation dans sa lutte pour l'existence et le développement. Jeu, sport, haute performance, des biens communs de l'humanité, certes, mais des réalités qui laissent plusieurs d'entre nous perplexes en raison même de l'ampleur sans cesse grandissante du phénomène.

Malgré des vents plutôt favorables à l'ensemble du mouvement dans tous les coins du monde, le sport (surtout le sport d'élite) semble soumis à des questionnements soutenus, plus particulièrement à chaque nouvelle célébration d'une Olympiade. Où va le sport ? Où va le Mouvement olympique ? L'expansion des Jeux est-elle irréversible ? Quelles sont les vraies valeurs universelles du sport, ses grandeurs, ses misères, ses paradoxes ? Derrière l'escalade du succès des Jeux olympiques, devant l'urgence des besoins et des demandes de l'ensemble des citoyens, dans la vie de tous les jours, comment distinguer l'essentiel de l'accessoire ? Bref, en quoi le sport peut-il demeurer centré sur la prééminence de l'humain, et, à sa manière, être utile socialement, et pour tous ?

In choosing the central theme of the Symposium, *Sport, Culture and Society*, exactly one hundred years after the visit of Pierre de Coubertin to North America, the Organizing Committee has proposed to analyze, highlight, and debate questions and issues that have relevance to the relationships between the culture of sport and society at large. It is the hope of our Organizing Committee that the presentations, discussions and debates will shed light on the progression of the sporting heritage.

A bilingual symposium may be a new experience for many of you, dear colleagues and friends. There are here representatives from more than 30 nations. In that respect, I feel that I must seize the opportunity for asking kindly, in the name of the highest academic ideals, for your understanding, your tolerance, your patience. Simultaneous interpretation services will be provided at each of our thematic sessions. It is the belief of our Scientific Commission that we will all grow stronger academically and culturally in this kind of exercise, which, I am sure, will turn out to be a pleasant and enriching experience.

Mesdames et messieurs, chers amis, à tous les participants et à toutes les participantes du Symposium International de Québec, je souhaite bonnes présentations, et de fructueuses discussions.

À ceux et à celles qui ne sont pas d'ici, je dis : puisse la joie de vivre au Québec vous pénétrer et vous faire chaud au cœur !

Speech Allocution
by the Representative du Représentant
of the City of Quebec de la Ville de Québec

Pierre Mainguy

Monsieur le Président,
Monsieur le Ministre,
Monsieur le Président du Comité international olympique,
Monsieur le Recteur,
Mesdames, Messieurs,

Au nom de la Ville de Québec, il me fait plaisir de vous accueillir dans notre ville à l'occasion de ce prestigieux symposium *Sport... le troisième millénaire.*

En effet, après ces nombreuses années d'expansion des activités sportives, pourquoi ne pas s'arrêter pour réfléchir sur cette réalité si populaire et si importante de notre monde moderne ?

Le sport déborde le sport. Songeons à toute la place qu'il prend dans l'activité économique ; aux droits de télévision considérables, aux coûts de construction des immenses stades modernes ; aux salaires incroyables versés aux vedettes. Le sport est devenu une chaîne de production fort complexe. Cette activité a aussi gagné ses lettres de noblesse chez les universitaires, où l'on retrouve maintenant des scientifiques de l'activité physique. On pratique le sport avec des outils de précision. Le sport est enfin un phénomène social étudié par les sociologues et psychologues sociaux ; et j'irais jusqu'à dire qu'il est un phénomène de culture de masse.

Et pourquoi, pour faire le point sur le sport, ne pas s'arrêter dans la ville de Québec, déclarée il y a quelques années par l'UNESCO, joyau du patrimoine mondial ? Nous espérons que votre réflexion collective vous laissera quand même le temps, au cours des prochains jours, de vous familiariser avec notre capitale, la plus ancienne ville d'Amérique du Nord.

J'aimerais particulièrement souhaiter la bienvenue aujourd'hui à monsieur Juan Antonio Samaranch, président du CIO, dont la visite à Québec n'est pas sans nous rappeler celle, il y a 100 ans, du baron Pierre de Coubertin. Nous osons croire que ces années ne furent pas «Cent ans de solitude», *Cien años de Soledad*, pour paraphraser Gabriel Garcia Marquez, mais «Cent années de solidarité», *Cien años de Solidaridad* entre le Mouvement olympique international et le Mouvement olympique canadien et québécois.

Je vous souhaite à tous et toutes bon congrès et bon séjour chez nous.

Speech by the President of the Canadian Olympic Association

Allocution de la Présidente de l'Association olympique canadienne

Carol Anne Letheren

Chairman Landry,
Honoured Guests,
Friends and Colleagues,

It is a pleasure to represent the Canadian Olympic Association at this event.

Au nom de l'Association, je remercie tout particulièrement monsieur Fernand Landry et ses collègues du Comité d'organisation pour la créativité et la diligence dont ils ont fait preuve dans la préparation et l'organisation de ce Symposium international qui a pour titre «*Sport... le troisième millénaire — Sport... the Third Millennium*».

The Canadian Olympic Association recognizes the need for such gatherings and deliberations, particularly at this time in world history when rapid changes of significant scope and magnitude are occuring around us, each of them susceptible of having an impact on sport, and thus on the youth of the world through sport.

We have noted the range of topics that will be covered during the Symposium, and we are certainly encouraged by the breadth of issues that will be addressed and debated during the next days, including the matters of ethics and technology which were so preeminent during our days in Seoul.

We congratulate the Organizing Committee in putting such an event together, and we wish all of the participants a very stimulating exploration over the days ahead.

Speech by the Minister of Youth and Sport, France

Allocution du Secrétaire d'État chargé de la Jeunesse et des Sports de la France

Roger Bambuck

Monsieur le Président,
Monsieur le Ministre,
Monsieur le Président du Comité international olympique,
Monsieur le Recteur,
Distingués invités,
Mesdames, Messieurs,

1890. Pierre de Coubertin, de retour de sa tournée nord-américaine pour promouvoir les valeurs humanistes héritées de nos ancêtres les Grecs, souligne la liberté dont jouissent Canada britannique et Canada français. 1990. Nous assistons aux aspirations de liberté dans tous les pays, et en particulier dans les pays de l'est. Nous assistons à la mise en doute des idéologies les plus ancrées, nous assistons à la contestation des structures de toutes les sociétés, nous assistons à la montée des angoisses devant l'avenir, en particulier devant l'avenir de l'environnement. Nous assistons également à l'avènement d'une culture planétaire intégrant toutes les autres cultures.

Le Mouvement olympique, le mouvement sportif, ont une voie très étroite à suivre entre tous ces questionnements, entre les nationalismes et les égoïsmes. Coubertin était nationaliste, dans le sens traditionnel du terme, quand il pensait que les athlètes devaient représenter leur nation. Coubertin était humaniste, quand il pensait que les athlètes sont facteurs de progrès pour la société, quand il pensait que seul un homme libre peut atteindre son plein épanouissement. Il est relayé en cela par le poète et auteur français Jean Giraudoux, pour qui le sport est l'art qui libère l'homme de lui-même, c'est-à-dire de son inconscient, et de sa culture pour être créatif.

La proposition d'une vision différente des choses et des gens marquera le siècle prochain. L'homme du XXIe siècle sera un être social, mais à l'échelle planétaire, par sa capacité à créer, à créer le mouvement, à créer la technique, à créer de nouvelles relations entre les hommes, à créer des mythes, à interpréter les symboles. Il sera en cela exemplaire dans l'histoire de l'humanité. Il fera la promotion de l'homme. L'homme du XXIe siècle mettra en évidence ce vieil adage du sport, qui voudrait que la meilleure leçon du sport soit d'être seul avec soi-même mais avec l'aide des autres. Nous serons obligés de développer une société plus solidaire qui respecte et qui partage, qui partage le sport qui doit à tous les sports, qui doit au sport-pour-tous, pour que nous puissions atteindre un échange inter-culturel véritable au travers des sports, du sport olympique certes, des sports occidentaux, mais aussi de tous les sports traditionnels qui sont l'expression d'une adéquation entre l'homme et sa société, entre l'homme et sa nation. Les États, parce qu'ils sont le miroir et le reflet de tout un groupe, ont cette grande responsabilité.

Le droit à l'éducation recouvre la pratique du sport. L'institution éducative doit apprendre à mieux connaître le sport, à mieux appréhender ses promesses et ses dangers. Parmi les dangers, le dopage en est un exemple, mythe moderne du Dr Faust où l'homme pour garder sa jeunesse ou pour conquérir des médailles perçoit l'obligation de vendre son âme au diable. L'argent, en est un autre exemple, l'argent qui désolidarise l'athlète de la société en le rendant égoïste. La politique, qui opprime. La violence, qui sanctionne l'échec de l'éducation. Pour que la pratique du sport tienne ses promesses, il faut que nous apprenions à redécouvrir et à apprendre l'éthique, l'éthique comme morale des comportements. Seule l'éthique peut nous apprendre à vivre avec un sport de plus en plus tourné vers le spectacle.

C'est une très belle idée que d'avoir associé à ce Symposium *Sport... le troisième millénaire* le centième anniversaire du voyage de Pierre de Coubertin en Amérique du Nord. Beaucoup de questions vont être débattues aujourd'hui et pendant les jours qui viennent et elles ne sont pas toutes du même ordre. Mais faute de les résoudre les unes après les autres nous risquons de voir que le sport soit dénaturé. Je souhaite que tous les participants à ce Symposium fassent preuve, comme Coubertin, d'une totale disponibilité face à l'avenir, et préparent les évolutions qui feront du sport un phénomène majeur dans la société mondiale du XXIe siècle. A vous qui êtes des acteurs privilégiés dans les différents secteurs des sciences du sport, il vous appartient par la qualité de vos informations, par la pertinence et la rigueur scientifique de vos travaux de bien éclairer et de baliser les dangers. Ainsi la saine démocratie que Coubertin voulait voir pénétrer les stades sera l'œuvre des sportifs du troisième millénaire. Il me reste à vous souhaiter à tous de fructueux travaux. Je suis convaincu qu'ils contribueront non seulement à entretenir, mais à propager la flamme de l'idéal que Pierre de Coubertin nous a légué.

Speech by the President of the International Olympic Committee

Allocution du Président du Comité international olympique

Juan Antonio Samaranch

Monsieur le Président du Comité d'organisation,
Monsieur le Ministre,
Monsieur le Secrétaire d'État,
Monsieur le Recteur,
Mesdames, Messieurs et chers Collègues,

Comme Président du Comité international olympique, je me dois de féliciter les organisateurs de ce Symposium international *Sport ... le troisième millénaire*, tenu à l'occasion du centenaire de la visite en Amérique du Nord de notre fondateur, le Baron Pierre de Coubertin. Le Comité international olympique n'a pas hésité à accorder son patronage à cet événement et environ dix pour cent des membres du Comité sont ici présents. Cela confirme l'importance du Symposium de Québec aux yeux du Comité international olympique.

Je me permets de considérer ce Symposium de mai 1990 comme le premier des événements destinés à célébrer le centenaire de la création de l'Olympisme moderne, de la création aussi du Mouvement olympique et de notre Comité international olympique. Les célébrations vont continuer pendant toute cette décennie avec, entre autres, la tenue d'un Congrès olympique à Paris, en 1994, soit un siècle exactement après celui qui fut tenu à la Sorbonne à l'initiative de notre fondateur, Pierre de Coubertin.

Les discours précédents ont souligné l'importance du sport et du Mouvement olympique dans le monde d'aujourd'hui. Oui, nous sommes conscients de cette importance du sport dans la société, et cette importance manifeste tient au fait que nous sommes à l'écoute de la société d'aujourd'hui. Nous comprenons très bien l'ensemble des besoins et nous sommes conscients d'être partie prenante de la société moderne et, particulièrement, d'être solidaires des visées de l'institution éducative. Lors d'un séjour récent en Afrique, et alors que j'adressais quelques mots à mes hôtes, j'ai mentionné qu'à mon avis, et compte tenu de l'expérience accumulée au cours de mes voyages, la plus grande richesse d'un pays n'est pas d'avoir des gisements de pétrole ou d'or, mais bien celle de pouvoir offrir une solide éducation à sa jeunesse. Au pays qui investit dans l'éducation de sa jeunesse appartient l'avenir. Et je souligne qu'une grande partie de cette éducation trouve des assises dans le sport, comme aussi dans l'Idée et le Mouvement olympiques.

Je sais que, parmi vous, nombreux sont ceux et celles qui conçoivent le sport dans l'esprit de l'Olympisme; je puis vous assurer que les portes du Comité international olympique vous sont grandes ouvertes, nous avons en effet grand besoin de vous. Nous avons besoin de vous parce que vous savez mieux que quiconque illustrer notre philosophie, et défendre le devoir que nous avons de contribuer à une formation humaniste de la jeunesse. Je l'ai souvent dit, et je le répète ici aujourd'hui: ce sont les liens étroits qui existent entre sport et culture qui définissent le mieux l'Olympisme. C'est pourquoi je suis heureux, à titre de représentant du Mouvement olympique, de me trouver au Canada, à Québec et à l'Université Laval pour y discuter de l'avenir du sport. Discuter de cet avenir, c'est avant tout travailler à l'avenir de la jeunesse. Je souhaite à tous et à toutes un fructueux Symposium.

Speech by the Minister of Justice, Attorney General and Minister for Canadian Intergovernmental Affairs

Allocution du ministre de la Justice, procureur général et ministre délégué aux Affaires intergouvernementales canadiennes

Gil Rémillard

Monsieur le Président du Comité international olympique,
Monsieur le Président du Comité organisateur du symposium,
Monsieur le Secrétaire d'État à la jeunesse et au sport de la France,
Madame la Députée fédérale de Louis-Hébert,
Madame la Présidente de l'Association olympique canadienne,
Monsieur le Président de Monnaie royale canadienne,
Monsieur le Représentant du Maire de la Ville de Québec,
Messieurs les Représentants des commanditaires,
Distingués invités d'honneur,

C'est un grand plaisir pour moi d'être présent parmi vous afin de procéder à l'inauguration du symposium de grande qualité qui vous réunira au cours des prochains jours. Je sais combien d'énergie exige l'organisation d'un tel événement et je désire féliciter sincèrement le comité organisateur.

Le Gouvernement du Québec était fort heureux de contribuer financièrement à la tenue d'un tel symposium. Le sport constitue aujourd'hui un fait social universel, propagé dans tous les continents. Puisque la pratique du sport est intrinsèquement liée au monde de l'éducation, des sciences, de la culture, de l'administration ou des médias, le Gouvernement du Québec considère qu'il a le rôle, voire la responsabilité, d'encourager des forums pluridisciplinaires comme le vôtre. Nous sommes assurés que vos discussions seront constructives et qu'elles soulèveront des questions importantes pour le présent comme pour l'avenir de la société québécoise.

Depuis près de vingt ans plus particulièrement, on a assisté à l'échelle internationale à une démocratisation de l'activité sportive. Ce phénomène a permis à nos sociétés de promouvoir ce moyen de réalisation et d'expression de soi, et d'encourager l'être humain à se préoccuper de son bien-être, de sa santé et de son environnement. Les Gouvernements, les Fédérations et Associations sportives, les groupes syndicaux et patronaux, les organisations médicales et les médias reconnaissent la nécessité d'encourager la pratique libérale du sport et de fournir les moyens pour le faire.

Parallèlement à la promotion de l'activité sportive à titre de loisir, chacune des nations se fait un honneur de développer le sport d'élite. Plus que jamais toutefois, nous constatons que les balises du concept de haute performance athlétique sont difficiles à délimiter. D'une part, le succès de l'athlète est le produit de l'intensité de son engagement, de sa persévérance et de ses efforts. D'autre part, l'État s'enorgueillit souvent de ces succès pour mieux exploiter son hégémonie, sa visibilité et son influence.

Nous célébrons cette année le 100e anniversaire de la venue du Baron Pierre de Coubertin au Canada. Cet illustre personnage prônait une idéologie dont nous aurions intérêt à nous rappeler aujourd'hui. En parlant du jeune adulte dont la force de caractère, le potentiel et l'ambition l'ont amené à atteindre le degré d'excellence politique, Pierre de Coubertin avait dit:

> [...] celui-là est l'homme vraiment fort dont la volonté se trouve assez puissante pour s'imposer à soi-même et imposer à la collectivité un arrêt dans la poursuite des intérêts ou des passions, et de domination et de possession, si légitimes soient ils [...]

Les plus récents événements sportifs internationaux nous ont hélas démontré que des athlètes, entraîneurs, organisateurs du sport et même certains gouvernements peuvent être tentés de s'appuyer sur la science et la technologie pour accroître artificiellement le succès de l'athlète et ainsi satisfaire les préoccupations étatiques de propager à travers le monde une image de vainqueur. Il est temps de revenir aux sources et à l'enseignement de Pierre de Coubertin. Nous avons eu droit, au cours des dernières années, à un débat international sur ces questions d'éthique dans le sport. En 1988, le Canada était l'hôte de la première conférence mondiale permanente sur l'antidopage dans le sport. Il avait alors été décidé de préparer une stratégie et un plan favorisant une campagne antidopage internationale. Depuis, de nombreux États de tous les continents, l'Unesco, le Comité international olympique ainsi que divers organismes scientifiques s'emploient à unir leur forces et connaissances pour étudier le problème à fond et trouver des solutions rationnelles au problème et adaptées aux réalités du troisième millénaire. Par ailleurs, la Commission Dubin a étudié pendant de nombreux mois les différents aspects de la question et devrait sous peu soumettre ses recommandations au gouvernement canadien. Nous constatons donc que la première pierre est posée, encore faut-il poursuivre ces discussions afin de permettre au sport de retrouver toute la pureté qui lui revient.

Je ne voudrais terminer cette allocution sans rendre hommage au Président du Comité international olympique, Monsieur Juan Antonio Samaranch, qui recevra cette semaine des mains du Recteur de l'Université Laval un doctorat *honoris causa*. Nous savons tous que Monsieur Samaranch est un diplomate de grande envergure et se veut être un défenseur inconditionnel des grands principes dont nous avons hérité de Pierre de Coubertin: fraternité, amitié, compréhension mutuelle, développement égal des qualités physiques et morales. Sa présence au sein du Comité international olympique nous assure que nos espoirs de retrouver le sens profond de l'Olympisme ne sont pas vains.

Je déclare donc ouvert le Symposium international *Sport... le troisième millénaire*.

Lectures at the invitation
of the Organizing Committee

Conférences présentées à l'invitation
du Comité d'organisation

Sport, Culture and Society

*From the Anthropological Meanings of the Sporting Phenomenon,
to the Influences of 20th Century Economics and Politics on
Sport's Present and Future Institutions and Manifestations*

Sport, culture et société

*Des racines du sport dans la poétique et l'imaginaire, aux
influences de l'économique et du politique sur l'institution
sportive, ses manifestations, et leur avenir*

The Poetic and Political Functions of Sport; Contemporary Sport Seen in the Perspective of the Global Society

The author advances that one is faithful to the memory of Pierre de Coubertin and his Olympic idea, when one purports to make as passionate a plea as his was, a century ago, in favor of the place of sport at the heart of education and culture. On the contrary, it would be showing disrespect for Coubertin, if one would be satisfied with simply and mechanically repeating his words, his earnest, patient, and untiring exhortations. For the world, indeed, has changed tremendously since Coubertin's days. In the first part of the presentation, sport is described as an integral part of humanism. Fundamentally, it aims at contributing to the valorization of human beings, whatever the cultural differences. In this sense sport is part of the fiber of culture, it comprises more than the mere facts, actions, and results of games and matches. Its objects, implications and consequences extend much further than the fury and vehemence of physical confrontation or violence on the field. Sport hinges upon esthetics through the sentiments and passions that it provokes and raises. From this angle sport is tradition, heritage. Its echoees reach as far back as the earliest recorded history of mankind, and beyond. In the author's view, the poetics of sport is founded on anthropological considerations that reflect the cosmogonic scenarios present in all cultures. In subtle and stylized ways, sport reproduces and re-enacts the struggles, accomplishments and tragedies of human existence. The second part of the presentation underscores the notion of sport as a society within a society. Sport depends upon society, yet it has characteristics, a structure, and a life of its own. Societies, in general, pass laws to curtail confrontations and violence; sport, paradoxically, appears to propose the opposite. People meet and freely agree, on the basis of specific rules and as strangely as it may seem, for the specific and unequivocal purpose of confronting each other violently. Sport is in fact a sort of counter-society. The author then advances that the notion of the autonomy of the sporting movement is nowadays fundamental to its existence and further development. He describes how, in the actual facts of life, the reality of the relationships between the sporting and global societies is constantly shifting, changing. Thus, there exists a dialectics through which both societies are at one and the same time drawn apart as well as together. Inevitably, sport will continue to be observed, analyzed and judged, morally and politically. It has been and will continue to be both extalled and condemned. Yet, as the author indicates sport is neither worse nor better, ethically, than the very society of which it is a part. Paradoxically also, the sporting society, through its universal behavior codes and efficient international structures, appears to come closer to realizing the universal goals and ideals of international understanding and humanism, than do indeed many contemporary social systems. Given the astounding successes of high-performance sport on the intra- and international scenes, it was expected that the sporting movement would tend to fall under the heavy influence of economics and politics. From that angle, sport, as a counter-society, becomes in its turn countered by two powerful societal forces: it is the paradox of the double negation. Irremediably, the pressures and tensions are here to stay. Each partner, so to speak, needs the other: sport needs the global society; the latter also needs the former. The last part of the author's presentation deals with the universal dimensions and repercussions of modern (including olympic) sport. Sport has become an informal yet surprisingly revealing indicator of change, on the national and international scales. On account of its immense popularity and high visibility, sport is increasingly used as an open window through which one can observe and even question a number of socio-economic principles, policies, strategies and/or inequalities, note the rejoicing signs of a newly admitted complementarity of world cultures, and witness an unequivocal betterment of international relations.

La double fonction poétique et politique du sport ; rapport de ce dernier à la société universelle

Bernard Jeu †

Monsieur le Président du Comité international olympique,
Messieurs les Ministres,
Monsieur le Recteur,
Monsieur le Président du Comité d'organisation,
Mesdames, Messieurs,

Mes premiers mots sont tout naturellement pour rendre hommage à Pierre de Coubertin. Il nous laisse une œuvre. Il nous laisse un message. Nous saluons en lui le rénovateur des Jeux dans la période moderne. Nous saluons en lui également l'un des pionniers de la pensée sportive. Pierre de Coubertin constitue la référence incontournable. C'est à juste titre que le Professeur MacAloon parle de lui comme du « grand symbole[1] ». En faisant cette référence à Pierre de Coubertin, nous nous inscrivons dans une continuité. Mais nous nous engageons dans cette continuité de façon active. C'est l'occasion pour nous de réfléchir sur le sens du sport à l'aube du troisième millénaire. Car ce n'est pas en effet être infidèle à Coubertin, mais bien au contraire lui témoigner le plus grand respect que de suivre son exemple et de nous efforcer à notre tour d'apporter des éléments de compréhension et des modèles explicatifs à cette idée et à ce grand fait mondial que sont devenus l'Olympisme et le Mouvement olympique.

Pour ma part, je voudrais apporter une contribution à cet effort en soulignant trois thèmes de réflexion[2, 3]. Le premier s'articule autour de la notion d'*héritage*. Nous assumons des choses anciennes. Nous les vivons. Nous les transmettons. Ce que je voudrais souligner, c'est que le sport est une *poétique* appuyée sur une *anthropologie*. Le second s'articule autour de la notion d'*autonomie*. Le sport est une société au sein de la société. Il en dépend. Il ne s'y réduit pas. Ce que je voudrais souligner cette fois, c'est que le sport est une contre-société contredite. Il existe une dialectique qui oppose et qui rapproche en même

1890
1990

Bernard Jeu, Faculté de Philosophie, Université de Lille III; Président, Centre Lillois de recherche en analyse du sport, Lille, France.
† Décédé/Deceased 91.08.15

temps la *société sportive* et la *société globale*. Le troisième évoque la dimension *mondiale* et *universelle* du sport. Le sport symbolise avec l'histoire. Le sport est un *indicateur de changement*. Il est à l'image de l'évolution du monde. Nous pouvons nous interroger à travers lui sur l'économie, la complémentarité des cultures et les relations internationales.

Le sport: une poétique appuyée sur une anthropologie

La formule peut surprendre et la démarche paraître insolite. En fait, mon propos est tout simplement de constater une évidence. Pour la grande masse des sportifs qui vivent intensément le sport, comme pour ceux qui un peu partout se passionnent pour lui, le regardent sur les écrans de télévision et en lisent les comptes rendus dans la presse, la compétition est perçue comme une belle histoire, quelque chose qui sort de la grisaille, qui fait rêver. On est dans l'extraordinaire. On parle d'exploit. Et les livres s'intitulent tout naturellement la fabuleuse histoire du tennis, la fabuleuse histoire du football, la fabuleuse histoire du golf. Dans le sport l'histoire et la fable se confondent. Bref il existe une fonction *poétique* du sport. Cette fonction poétique du sport est d'ailleurs parfaitement ressentie par la littérature et les poètes. Déjà Homère en écrivait. Il n'est pas le seul. Il y aurait Simonide, Bacchylide, Pindare chez les Grecs, Virgile chez les Romains. Et il en va de même dans la modernité. Je cite au hasard Montherlant, Giraudoux, Blondin, Sillitoe, Buzzati. Rien de nouveau donc. Ce que je veux mettre en évidence, c'est que la fonction poétique du sport est essentielle. Ce qu'il faudrait pouvoir réussir, c'est faire pour l'univers du sport ce que Propp[4] a fait pour l'univers du conte. Le sport a en effet ses personnages stylisés, sa mythologie, son scénario immuable, ses métaphores révélatrices[5, 6].

Tout de suite nous découvririons des archaïsmes et, derrière ces archaïsmes, des archétypes[7]. On retrouverait facilement la séquence de la *fuite*, de la *poursuite* et du *sacrifice*. Dans le cyclisme, le peloton chasse les échappés. Dans le soccer, l'avant-centre est abattu à la limite de la surface de réparation. Un suspense s'organise. Le sport est un mimodrame. On le vit intensément. Des passions s'investissent. On peut alors penser aux formules de Freud dans *Totem et Tabou*[8], lorsqu'il parlait des origines de la tragédie et lorsqu'il évoquait la bande des frères et la grande fête primitive de l'humanité. Il suffit de traduire et de penser aux supporters qui regardent les champions. Il est évident que quelque chose d'important se passe. Nous vivons au niveau du sacré. Nous devinons toute une puissance sous-jacente de l'imaginaire. Il semble bien que les profondeurs de l'inconscient nous renvoient aux profondeurs de l'histoire.

C'est pourquoi, dans notre effort d'explication, nous sommes poussés vers l'anthropologie. Ce n'est d'ailleurs pas non plus une démarche nouvelle. Depuis longtemps déjà les ethnologues ont remarqué que les jeux populaires traditionnels — la soule, la paume, la crosse — ces jeux qui ont inspiré les structures des grands sports modernes, sont eux-mêmes d'anciennes cérémonies religieuses dégradées, désacralisées. Ainsi une ligne presque directe semble-t-elle s'établir entre compétitions sportives d'aujourd'hui et compétitions rituelles d'autrefois[9]. Ces compétitions rituelles, bien entendu, nous les connaissons. Elles sont nombreuses. La mythologie les évoque. La littérature les mentionne. L'ethnologie les étudie[10, 11].

Certaines sont *funéraires*. C'est le cas des jeux célébrés en l'honneur de Patrocle au chant XXIII de l'*Iliade* d'Homère. Achille est le juge-arbitre et le sponsor parce qu'il conduit le deuil de son ami Patrocle. Mais des jeux sont célébrés aussi pour les funérailles d'Amarynkée, d'Oedipe, d'Azan. D'autres sont *initiatiques*[12]. Un adolescent doit satisfaire à son temps d'épreuve. On raconte dans la Bible que Jacob doit lutter toute la nuit contre un dieu. D'autres encore sont *matrimoniales*. C'est la course ou la lutte pour l'épouse. On connaît, dans la mythologie grecque, l'histoire d'Atalante. On connaît l'histoire d'Hippodamie. Bref, les trois grands moments de la vie sociale — *mort, entrée dans la société, mariage* — sont ainsi scandés, rythmés par la compétition rituelle.

Mais il faut faire un pas de plus. Il y a aussi une dimension *métaphysique* qui donne son sens à tout l'ensemble. Peut-être les diverses compétitions rituelles ne sont-elles que l'image éclatée d'une autre compétition plus haute, plus fondamentale, plus profonde, plus importante, où s'opposent les forces de *mort* et les forces de *vie* de l'univers[13]. Imaginons aux approches de l'hiver une tribu qui voit le soleil décliner et perdre de sa force. Le monde va-t-il disparaître? La tribu va-t-elle périr? Faute de mieux, la réponse sera d'ordre magique. On va s'efforcer de *simuler* et de *stimuler* — c'est la définition même de ce qu'on appelle la magie sympathique — ce drame que vit l'univers, cette lutte des forces de l'ordre et des forces du désordre. On va aider la nature à accomplir son cycle et à renaître d'elle-même. La compétition rituelle aura valeur *cosmogonique*. Elle joue et rejoue inlassablement le scénario de la création du monde.

Tout cela peut nous paraître lointain. Et pourtant nous sommes bien proche de ce qui se passe aujourd'hui dans l'enceinte sportive. Regardez un terrain de football. La sémiologie nous invite à décoder les systèmes de signes. Le lieu de l'épreuve, c'est l'enfer. Les buts sont les portes de l'enfer. La balle, c'est l'âme du jeu. Les joueurs sont les héros de cette mythologie. Il s'agit de sortir l'âme de l'enfer et de sauver la tribu[14]. Regardez un terrain de tennis. Nous pourrions nous contenter de décrire géométriquement les espaces: un filet sépare ce qu'une balle réunit. Mais en y regardant d'un peu plus près nous verrions que le filet reproduit la vieille séparation symbolique du monde des vivants et du monde des morts. Chacun veut renvoyer la balle, son âme, de l'autre côté du filet, dans le monde des vivants ou, ce qui revient au même, l'âme de l'autre dans le monde des morts.

On prendra garde cependant à une différence essentielle. Le sport a introduit la *symétrie*. Les joueurs partent à zéro; les coureurs partent sur la même ligne. La symétrie dissimule ce que le scénario simule. De ce fait, jusqu'à la fin de la course, jusqu'à la fin de l'échange, jusqu'à la fin de la partie, on ne peut pas savoir qui est le sacrificateur, qui est le sacrifié, puisque les deux équipes, puisque les deux joueurs sont symétriquement opposés. Nous côtoyons sans nous en rendre compte les cosmogonies anciennes. Le sport hérite d'un imaginaire. Nos compétitions sportives d'aujourd'hui renvoient aux compétitions rituelles d'autrefois[15]. Nous rejouons inlassablement, sans même le savoir, le scénario de la création du monde tel que le concevaient nombre de religions primitives. Et j'imagine volontiers un anthropologue extraterrestre qui débarque de son engin spatial et qui télégraphie ses premières impressions. Je le vois expliquant que les Terriens pratiquent un culte du ballon, toutes races et tous régimes confondus. Ils écoutent debout les hymnes de leurs tribus. Puis ils se livrent à une lutte ardente, tandis que les fidèles sur les gradins psalmodient des refrains et scandent des cris de toutes sortes destinés à relever leur ardeur[16]. Il ne ferait pas de doute pour ce visiteur insolite — c'était l'objet de cette première partie — que le sport est une réalité culturelle qui puise au plus profond de notre passé. Le sport *est* un héritage.

Le sport: une contre-société contredite

Nous avons envisagé le sport comme une *poétique*. Nous l'envisageons maintenant comme une *politique*. Prenons acte du fait que le sport s'exerce dans le cadre d'institutions permanentes. Les sportifs se regroupent en clubs et en fédérations. Bref le sport se présente comme une société *dans* la société. La chose n'est pas difficile à faire admettre. C'est l'évidence même. Le sport, en fait, n'a pu se construire, se développer que sous la forme d'une société. Mais je veux avancer que le sport, de nos jours, est une *contre-société contredite*[17].

Le problème qui se pose à nous est celui du statut de la société sportive dont nous venons de voir qu'elle est ludique et archaïsante. Elle a des propriétés, des spécificités. Elle ne peut pas se réduire à la société globale d'aujourd'hui. Ce qui est moins remarqué en revanche, c'est qu'il s'agit d'une société *construite à l'envers*. En général, toutes les sociétés font des lois pour lutter, en dernière analyse, contre la violence. Le sport, lui, accepte d'entrée le principe de l'affrontement. Dans le sport, on se rencontre même *tout exprès* pour s'affronter. Le Scythe Anacharsis, dans l'Antiquité, l'un des sept sages de la Grèce, avait déjà noté ce caractère *juridiquement paradoxal* de la société sportive. Il faisait semblant de s'en étonner. Les Grecs font des lois contre la violence, disait-il, et ils s'empressent de couronner les athlètes qui se sont donné les plus furieux coups de poing. Il ironisait. L'huile rend fou, affirmait-il. On lui demandait pourquoi. Parce que les athlètes, après s'en être frottés, se jettent furieusement les uns contre les autres[18]. On notera cependant que cette violence *acceptée* est une violence *réglée, codifiée, organisée*. Ce n'est donc plus véritablement «la violence». Cela change tout et c'est même tout ce qui fait la différence entre une rixe et un combat de boxe. Dans le premier cas, on se bat parce qu'on *n'est pas* d'accord. Dans le second cas, on se bat parce qu'*on est* d'accord. Les gendarmes qui interrompirent, dit-on, les premiers combats de boxe ne faisaient pas cette différence. Ils estimèrent nécessaire d'intervenir et procédèrent à des arrestations pour coups et blessures réciproques.

Donc la règle est de s'affronter et le sport, en apparence du moins, fait tout *le contraire* de la société. Et c'est un premier sujet d'étonnement. Mais, chose étrange, en prenant ainsi le contrepied de la société globale, la société sportive, deuxième sujet d'étonnement, réalise l'idéal que poursuit *sans y parvenir* la société globale. Son institution s'achève en fédérations internationales qui sont des sociétés universelles. On peut donc parler de *contre-société*. La société sportive n'est pas seulement une société historiquement décalée, ludique et archaïsante. Elle est aussi une société juridiquement inversée. On peut même parler de contre-société idéale puisqu'elle réalise un idéal qui est celui de la société réelle, l'idéal d'universalité.

L'analyse ne s'arrête pas là. Ce serait trop peu de dire que c'est une contre-société *idéale*. Il faut ajouter aussitôt que c'est une contre-société *contredite*. Le sport, en effet, émerge *de* la société globale et continue de se situer *dans* la société globale. Il en dépend par son recrutement et par son financement. Et celle-ci va tenter de la récupérer pour la faire fonctionner à ses propres fins, commerciales ou politiques. La contre-société sportive va être *contredite* par la société globale. Le processus est de toute façon inévitable. Il est lié à l'importance croissante du sport. Le sport est désormais phénomène connu et reconnu. Il existe aux yeux de la société. L'économie et la politique vont nécessairement s'intéresser à lui. Du coup, la contre-société sportive tend à être récupérée. Nous sommes entrés dans une procédure de double négation. Un mécanisme subtil se constitue. Un rapport tensionnel va se construire entre les deux sociétés. Chacune dit et contredit. Chacune a besoin de l'autre. Chacune essaie de circonvenir l'autre. Leurs principes de fonctionnement ne coïncident pas. Une dialectique s'instaure. Et c'est dans l'intervalle de cette dialectique que l'autonomie du mouvement sportif prend tout son sens. Précisons tout de suite qu'autonomie ne veut pas dire indépendance. Le sport ne peut pas se prétendre indépendant de la société. Pas plus qu'un être humain ne peut être indépendant de la nourriture qu'il mange ni de l'air qu'il respire. Pas plus qu'une automobile ne peut être indépendante de l'essence qu'on verse dans son réservoir. Le sport lui-aussi possède son propre principe de fonctionnement. Il ne se réduit pas, bien qu'il en dépende, à la société globale, à son économie, à sa politique. *Il a sa propre raison d'être*. Le combat que soutient la société sportive pour le maintien de son autonomie n'est pas une simple vue de l'esprit. Il est de l'ordre du fait. À titre d'exemple, on remarquera que le mouvement sportif a passablement bien réussi à préserver son autonomie lors des boycotts successifs de Moscou et de Los Angeles, face à chacune des deux superpuissances du monde. Le degré d'autonomie du sport découle donc logiquement de la dialectique d'une société contredite dont nous venons de décrire, en gros, le mécanisme. Nous verrons maintenant que cette dialectique, à son tour, résulte des spécificités irréductibles de la société ludique et archaïsante.

Le sport: un fait mondial

J'ai présenté ci-avant deux idées qui me paraissent essentielles pour comprendre la logique de fonctionnement du système sportif. La première se situe au niveau de la *rencontre sportive*, de son émotion, de son imaginaire. C'est le cœur même du sport. C'en est la poétique. Nous touchons là à l'esthétique essentielle du sport. Nous sommes dans le tragique. Et ce tragique plonge ses racines dans la préhistoire des humains.

La seconde idée se situe au niveau de la *société sportive*, de sa spécificité, de son originalité. C'est la carapace du sport, sa colonne vertébrale. Il s'agit de l'institution. Nous touchons à la politique. C'est une société inversée, ludique, archaïque, tribale. Mais elle est terriblement efficace dans son fonctionnement.

Il reste une troisième approche. Le sport est devenu un fait mondial. Nous devons l'examiner *au niveau planétaire*. C'est là que nous le voyons dans ses ultimes développements. Nous l'y voyons aux prises avec la société globale en ses aspects les plus globalisants. Bien sûr, rien de ce que nous avons décrit jusqu'ici ne disparaît. L'imaginaire et l'émotion y sont toujours omniprésents. Ils y ont même pris des dimensions gigantesques et insoupçonnées jusque là. De même, les sociétés sportives n'ont pas non plus disparu. Au contraire, elles aussi ont pris de la puissance: elles ont nom fédérations internationales. Mais la société globale sous sa forme politique, sous sa forme économique et sous sa forme médiatique éprouve un intérêt de plus en plus fort pour ce monde du sport parvenu à un haut niveau de développement et de visibilité. *Sport* mondial et *politique* mondiale sont alors dans un rapport d'interaction[19, 20]. Et le sport peut devenir *un indicateur de changement* de la société globale, anticipation et reflet de grandes évolutions. On peut citer en exemple le tennis de table, connu par la fameuse diplomatie de ping-pong, ouvrant symboliquement des relations entre les USA et la Chine. Depuis de longues années, ce sport qui regroupe plus de 130 fédérations nationales, voit paradoxalement se rencontrer dans les championnats d'Asie et les championnats du monde les équipes représentatives des deux Corée et celles de Taïwan, Hong-Kong et de la Chine Populaire.

On souligne souvent de façon négative l'entrée en force de l'argent dans le sport. D'où les diatribes moralisantes et les propos pessimistes sur l'avenir du sport. Il serait parfaitement inutile de s'en indigner. Tout le moralisme passéiste et nostalgique n'y pourra rien. Voyons-y plutôt la conséquence de la *réussite* du sport. Il n'y a rien d'inquiétant au fait que les pouvoirs sportifs aient à composer avec les hommes d'affaires, aussi longtemps du moins que les choses pourront se faire sur la base de contrats égaux et loyaux entre le sport et ses partenaires intéressés. Rien d'inquiétant non plus, bien au contraire, dans la disparition d'un amateurisme anachronique, qui n'était, de toute manière, qu'une fiction. Réjouissons-nous plutôt, comme d'un fait positif, de l'abandon d'une hypocrisie trop longtemps entretenue. Étonnons-nous plutôt qu'on ait pu si longtemps donner au professionnalisme dans le sport une connotation péjorative, alors qu'en musique, par exemple, il a toujours paru évident qu'un virtuose professionnel était supérieur à un musicien amateur.

Là où l'inquiétude pourrait commencer, en revanche, c'est quand on se met à subordonner la logique sportive traditionnelle à celle des media et des intérêts financiers qui s'associent à ces derniers. Car il semble bien que nombre de sports ont maintenant tendance à faire évoluer leurs règlements pour mieux correspondre aux exigences des média, surtout celles de la télévision. Mais là encore l'inquiétude doit être tempérée. L'adaptation aux réalités économiques n'est pas forcément trahison de la logique du sport. On peut même y voir une stimulation nouvelle. Ne tirons pas de conclusions trop hâtives.

Ce n'est pas dans ces directions trop voyantes qu'il convient d'orienter l'essentiel de la réflexion sur les rapports du sport et de l'économie. Il serait préférable d'insister sur le fait que le sport, si on l'observe mondialement, est devenu un redoutable *dénonciateur* des inégalités planétaires. Ce que nous remarquons, en effet, c'est que les différents continents ne sont pas sur un même pied d'égalité sportive. Un tel fait n'est pas à l'honneur du sport et encore moins de la société qui l'environne. Mais la participation des divers continents dans l'organisation des grands jeux symbolise parfaitement avec les réalités économiques. Et l'imperfection du sport souligne ici l'imperfection du monde. C'est surtout sur ce point, semble-t-il, que devrait porter une réflexion *morale* et *politique* du sport, lorsque l'on aborde le domaine de l'argent et de l'économie. Il n'est pas possible d'y affirmer le principe olympique de l'universel sans être confronté immédiatement au concept de justice.

Indicateur de changement : le détour serait intéressant aussi du côté d'une philosophie comparée des cultures. L'Orient rencontre, reçoit l'Occident et se compare à lui[21]. C'était particulièrement le cas lors des Jeux de Séoul. Tous les continents, géographiquement définis, sont présents aux Jeux, bien entendu. Mais, culturellement, il y a les trois grandes traditions de l'Occident, de l'Inde et de la Chine. L'Amérique, l'Afrique, l'Océanie, en vertu des événements de leur histoire, appartiennent à l'esprit d'Occident. L'Inde jouant un rôle moindre que l'Extrême-Orient sur la scène sportive internationale, il reste en face à face l'Orient et l'Occident. Deux grandes traditions culturelles prennent la mesure l'une de l'autre sur le terrain de la pratique et de l'organisation du sport. Ce que le sport met alors en relief, c'est une *opposition*, une *complémentarité* et finalement une *unité* profonde des cultures. Car les choses finissent par se rejoindre. *Opposition* : l'Occident accepte et valorise l'affrontement, la dialectique et l'histoire ; l'Orient valorise la non-différenciation, la nature et l'instinct. *Complémentarité* : l'Occident apporte l'analyse, la technique et la science ; l'Orient souligne, avec le Zen, l'insuffisance de l'analyse et de la technique et leur préfère une compréhension totale, globale et subite mais aléatoire. Chacune de ces démarches unilatérales a ses limites. *Unité* : de telles approches s'influencent réciproquement ; nous sommes sur la même planète et nous vivons la même histoire.

Une simple remarque cursive sur un point bien particulier. L'Occident, recherchant un supplément d'âme, s'est intéressé aux arts martiaux d'Orient pour le message de sagesse dont ils étaient supposés porteurs. Mais l'Orient, dans ces mêmes disciplines, a développé, par une sorte de croisement des valeurs des uns et des autres, l'esprit compétitif qui semblait jusqu'alors l'apanage de l'Occident. Dans le premier cas, nous pensons à l'aïkido surtout. Dans le second cas, ce sera le judo. À l'origine Jigoro Kano, l'exact correspondant asiatique de Coubertin, prônait des valeurs éducatives, nationalistes. Tout cela a été dépassé par le gigantesque et incontournable développement du sport international moderne. Il y a un troisième cas intéressant, celui du kendo. Ce sport risque de suivre la même évolution que le judo.

Les savoirs analytiques et les techniques ne garantissent jamais le sens. J'ai battu un record. Mais que vais-je faire de ce temps que j'ai gagné ? Et n'en ai-je pas trop perdu préalablement pour remplir les conditions de ce gain ? Bien entendu, les significations sont ailleurs. C'est l'homme qui est la mesure de toutes choses. Il décide de se dépasser dans toutes les dimensions possibles de l'homme ou il prétend, à l'inverse, qu'un tel dépassement n'a pas de sens. Il apparaît ainsi que la rencontre de l'Orient et de l'Occident s'effectue sur le mode de la *communication* et de l'*échange*. Chacun peut emprunter à l'autre. Chacun apporte sa contribution complémentaire. Tout ce jeu de l'*identité* et de la *différence* constitue, cela va de soi, un enrichissement. Et le sport mondial est ici encore un parfait indicateur de la société universelle, à la fois une et multiple. Indicateur du changement toujours : nous nous devons encore de nous tourner, sur un plan cette fois purement politique, du côté des relations internationales. Les Jeux olympiques de Séoul nous sont apparus avec évidence comme la fin symbolique de la guerre froide. La Corée a été, en cette occasion, le lieu privilégié de cette confrontation dont nous parlions — culturellement essentielle — entre l'Orient et l'Occident. Mais elle a été aussi le lieu d'apaisement entre l'Est et l'Ouest. Et sur le plan purement sportif, elle pouvait se proclamer, après Moscou, après Los Angeles, la ville des premiers Jeux sans boycott. Cette circonstance illustre on ne peut mieux la fonction pacificatrice que l'on a toujours voulu accorder aux Jeux. Ici encore et toujours, le sport est un indicateur fidèle du mouvement de la société globale.

En guise de conclusion, trois mots : fierté, modestie, optimisme

Fierté d'abord, parce que nous assumons un héritage. Nous reproduisons des formes anciennes du comportement. Nous leur conférons des significations nouvelles. Et nous inventons même dans le sport des structures inédites de sociabilité. Nos clubs, à l'évidence, sont des cellules fortement intégrées, de caractère quasi-tribal. Ainsi, le sport fonctionne à la fois comme un *conservatoire* d'usages anciens et un *laboratoire* de réalités nouvelles. *Conservatoire* : nous arrachons à l'oubli des procédures archaïques. *Laboratoire* : les fédérations sont de l'universel se réalisant à l'échelle planétaire.

Modestie ensuite. Parfois nous portons un peu vite des jugements de valeur. Sachons nous rappeler que le monde n'a pas attendu pour exister qu'on vienne lui dire comment il devrait être. Respectons la réalité. Respectons cette grande création collective qu'est le sport. Et ne soyons pas exigeants au point de demander au sport d'être meilleur que la société dont il fait partie.

Optimisme enfin. On lance périodiquement des cris d'alarme. Pourquoi supposer toujours le sport si fragile ? Pourquoi les générations futures auraient-elles moins de lucidité ou de générosité que celles d'autrefois ? Et pourquoi l'absurde aurait-il plus de titre à se maintenir dans l'existence que ce qui est rationnel et raisonnable ? Fierté, modestie, optimisme, la route pour nous se trouve toute tracée. La règle est claire. Efforçons-nous de déchiffrer « le sens ». C'est le sens qui rend efficace notre action. Nous le chercherons, suivant en cela l'exemple de Coubertin, dans le rapport du sport avec l'histoire et la culture. Nous y rencontrerons immanquablement l'humanisme. Le reste nous sera donné par surcroît.

NOTES ET BIBLIOGRAPHIE

1. MacAloon JJ (1981) This great symbol: Pierre de Coubertin and the origins of the modern Olympic Games. Chicago: University of Chicago Press

2. Jeu B (1987) Analyse du sport. Paris: Presses Universitaires de France [Dans ce texte, le sport est décrit et analysé dans l'ordre de ses raisons: poétique, historique, morale et politique. L'auteur y insiste sur la logique d'une création qui se développe dans l'ordre du temps, d'une institution qui naît, se développe, se transforme, habitée par des émotions profondes dont le sens aujourd'hui dépend de ceux et celles qui le pratiquent]

3. Jeu B (1985) De la vraie nature du sport. Paris: Vigot [Le texte produit au Centre Lillois de recherche en analyse du sport se veut un essai de déduction générale des catégories sportives]

4. Propp V (1928) Morphologie du conte. (Traduction du russe) Paris: Seuil 1970 [L'auteur, par analogies, traite de l'univers à décoder des personnages du sport]

5. Eliade M (1957) Mythes, rêves et mystères. Paris: Gallimard

6. Frazer JG (1912) Le rameau d'or. Tome I. Le roi magicien dans la société primitive. Paris: Laffont [Réédition de The Golden Bough: a study in magic and religion (1980) London: Macmillan. Le texte contient des analyses fort intéressantes sur les combats opposant rois et challengers]

7. Eliade M (1964) Traité d'histoire des religions. Paris: Payot [L'auteur traite amplement de la nostalgie des origines et de la répétition des archétypes]

8. Freud S (1947) Totem et tabou: interprétation par la psychanalyse de la vie sociale des peuples primitifs. Paris: Payot [Une phrase de Freud utile à l'analyse des origines du sport: «Une déformation qu'on pourrait dire hypocrite et raffinée d'événements véritablement historiques»]

9. Augé M (1982) Football: de l'histoire sociale à l'anthropologie religieuse. Le Débat 19 59-67

10. Huizinga J (1950) Homo Ludens. Boston: Beacon [En référence à la notion de jeu comme constituant de la culture]

11. Jeu B (1977) Le sport, l'émotion, l'espace. Paris: Vigot [Il s'agit d'un essai sur la classification des sports et de ses rapports avec la pensée mythique]

12. Eliade M (1976) Initiation, rites, sociétés secrètes: naissances mystiques, essai sur quelques types d'initiation. Paris: Gallimard

13. Jeu B (1972) Toute-puissance, immortalité ou les arrières-pensées du sport. Ethno-psychologie 27 15-37

14. Jeu B (1981) L'émergence de l'institution sportive à partir des rituels de la tribalité. Proceedings of the 9th International HISPA Congress Lisbon April 4-10

15. Serres M (1979) Le culte du ballon ovale. Le Monde 4-5 mars [Dans l'article du philosophe français bien connu, on peut lire, au sujet de la rumeur du stade, «Ecoutez donc la marée humaine hurler. Voici l'écho ou la reprise du plus enfoui des archaïsmes. Cette cérémonie est religieuse, j'entends par religion des choses oubliées depuis toujours, des choses barbares, sauvages, qui n'ont peut-être jamais eu de mots dans aucune langue, et qui nous viennent de nos commencements, sans texte»]

16. Morris D (1981) La tribu du football [Traduction de The soccer tribe. London: Jonathan Cape. Dans ce texte, l'auteur traite en détail de la structure tribale du sport: «Très vite il devint clair que tout centre d'activité de football — tout club de football — était organisé comme une petite tribu, avec son territoire tribal, ses ancêtres de la tribu, ses docteurs miracles, ses héros...»]

17. Jeu B (1973) La contre-société sportive et ses contradictions. Esprit 428 391-416

18. Diogène L (1965) Vie, doctrines et sentences des philosophes illustres. Tome 1. Vie d'Anarcharsis p 87sq [L'édition originale de l'ouvrage remonte à la période 200-500 Apr JC; il se dégage de la lecture de l'auteur que le caractère juridiquement paradoxal du sport était déjà perçu et fort discuté dans l'Antiquité]

19. Dubech L (1930) Où va le sport? Paris: Librairie de la revue française [Au sujet du sport comme contre-société contredite, le critique littéraire français dira sur le sport, en particulier international, dans ses rapports avec l'argent et la politique: «Le sport doit ignorer la politique. Mais la politique n'ignore pas le sport»]

20. Guttmann A (1984) The Games must go on: Avery Brundage and the Olympic Movement. New York: Columbia University Press

21. Jeu B (1987) op cit 120-27

Tournants de deux siècles:
sport et aspects politiques des relations inter-culturelles

L'auteur rappelle le double objectif du Symposium de Québec (pour plusieurs en apparence dissociés) — commémorer la visite de Pierre de Coubertin en Amérique du nord, — réfléchir sur l'avenir du sport à l'approche du troisième millénaire. Il souligne la conjoncture socio-politique qui prévalait au tournant du XIXe siècle et le fait, également, que les grands événements qui marquent la présente et rapide évolution socio-économico-politique, à l'échelle mondiale, eurent été inimaginables, il y a à peine cent ans. Il explique que pour les réformateurs et idéalistes de fin de siècle précédent, il eut été impossible de prévoir la place énorme qu'occupent actuellement le sport et le Mouvement olympique dans l'économie et la politique aux échelles intra- et internationale, comme aussi dans les préoccupations de tous les jours de tant de citoyens dans tous les coins de la planète. Il fait allusion à l'influence et à la qualité du leadership récent du Comité international olympique en ce qui a trait aux questions et problèmes de relations et de diplomatie internationales qui se sont trouvés associés à la préparation des Jeux de Séoul. Il souligne à cet effet le caractère tout à fait particulier des relations géo-politiques mises en branle à l'occasion de la célébration de la XXIVe Olympiade lesquelles, à son avis, sont devenues dorénavant indissociables des grands événements culturels internationaux. Dans la première grande division de sa présentation, l'auteur traite de la méconnaissance des liens existants entre sport et politique. Il pose la question de savoir si les Jeux olympiques de Séoul n'ont pas sonné le glas de cette créance de longue date et bien occidentale en une séparation véritable entre le sport et la politique. Or, selon l'auteur, cette distinction n'a même pas existé dans l'esprit de Pierre de Coubertin lui-même qui, dès l'origine de son projet, n'avait surtout pas hésité à placer ce dernier dans un cadre politique, celui des interfaces entre l'extension de la démocratie, la réforme de l'éducation, et le sport. Par la suite, l'auteur décrit la montée progressive du sport moderne et des Jeux olympiques et de leurs effets politico-culturels compensatoires, plus spécialement au cours des années 1920 et 30, qui furent si lourdement marquées par des intérêts, des vues et des actes si divergents en matière de politique internationale, incluant deux guerres dévastatrices. Malgré la menace nucléaire et la Guerre froide, le développement du sport s'est maintenu et même accéléré au cours des années 60 et 70, porté par la vague de décolonisation, d'extension des droits de l'homme et d'un accès sans cesse plus libéral au bien-être social. L'Idée olympique n'en est pas moins aux prises aujourd'hui, souligne l'auteur, avec les aspirations internationales des élites politiques, celles des financiers, des mass media et des représentants de diverses formes d'entrepreneurship technologique. À ce stade de sa présentation, l'auteur recommande la plus grande vigilance à ceux et celles qui gèrent la chose sportive internationale. Il suggère de ne pas laisser les savants et les scientifiques à l'extérieur du débat qu'il importe autant de faire porter sur la signification et les valeurs socio-culturelles du sport d'élite internationale, qu'il est urgent de le protéger contre les abus, excès ou déviations. Dans la deuxième grande division de sa présentation, l'auteur traite d'un fusionnement graduel des notions de catégorie politique et de catégorie culturelle. Des exemples sont tirés à cet effet des efforts et de la réussite sportive et culturelle éclatante des Jeux de Séoul et de la philosophie empreinte de compréhension internationale et de générosité qui les a animés, rendant le concept de l'Olympisme et les Jeux olympiques, vraiment partie intégrante du système mondial d'interrelations et d'interdépendance. Dans la dernière partie de sa présentation, l'auteur aborde la nécessité d'un paradigme nouveau en matière de relations interculturelles, lequel permettrait et assurerait tout à la fois la protection des valeurs, leur différenciation et leur transmission dans un système global moins homogénéisant et moins hégémonisant. L'auteur se dit d'avis que le respect et la gestion de la vaste complexité interculturelle contemporaine devront se situer bien au centre des préoccupations de la nouvelle génération de leaders du sport international et olympique. De toute évidence, selon l'auteur, cette fonction exigera des connaissances et un savoir faire nouveaux et élevés aux plans de la diplomatie et du doigté géo-politique, comme aussi une vision des choses beaucoup plus pluraliste que celle qui a servi jusqu'à maintenant de toile de fond à l'humanisme occidental. L'analyse et l'entendement des nouvelles réalités interculturelles et des fonctions désormais élargies du sport (et partant du Mouvement olympique) se doivent de porter au-delà des notions conservatrices de nation, de région et même de science.

The Turn of Two Centuries: Sport and the Politics of Intercultural Relations

John J. MacAloon

Mr. President Samaranch,
Monsieur le Recteur de l'Université Laval,
Municipal, provincial, and federal Officials of Canada,
IOC members and leaders of international sport,
Ladies and Gentlemen,

As a foreigner and one with no other claim to your attention than his scholarly activity, my gratitude to the Organizing Committee is particularly acute for the opportunity of addressing you on this occasion. I am likewise honored to follow my distinguished colleague Bernard Jeu, and to hope that my remarks will attain such clarity, while reversing his procedure and ascending from earth to heaven, as a 19th century European social theorist much in today's news once put it.

Moments of epic change are rare in human history. Rarer still are those which the subjects of that history are able to recognize as they are occurring. We meet at such an extraordinary moment. The majority of persons alive on this earth and in this room, including the present speaker, have never drawn an adult breath outside the Cold War atmosphere. That environment has threatened us day-by-day with thermonuclear destruction, not merely the belligerents but every human being, no matter how geographically distant or morally repelled by the conflict. While the bombs remain, today we watch with elated fascination and nervous uncertainty as this order of things disappears before our very eyes.

Those of us privileged by our association with olympic sport to be active in Korea between 1986 and 1988 received earlier warning of this dramatic transformation than many of our fellow citizens, for whom events in Central Europe brought the news. I refer not simply to the co-participation in Seoul of so many nations from both sides of the Great Divide, as extraordinary as was that

1890
1990

John J. MacAloon, Social Science Graduate Division, The University of Chicago, Illinois, USA.

achievement on the part of international authorities, the organizing committee, and the Korean nation. Nor do I refer only to the IOC-led negotiations between the two Koreas—a policy whose authors are present in this room—though, in my judgment, it was the greatest single act of diplomacy and statesmanship in olympic history, one whose fruits will continue to be harvested in future years. Rather, it was the totality of geopolitical relations of Seoul—not merely set in motion by the Games or framing them, but absolutely inseparable from them—that deserves our thoughtful reflection.

Sport and Politics: Uncommon Understandings of a Common Relation

The first point to consider is whether the recent Olympic Games did not finally *put paid to the categorical opposition between politics and sport* which has been so taken-for-granted a part of our dominant discourse of sport that we almost stopped recognizing its strange peculiarities. This cultural epistemology is not now, nor has it ever been, universal. It is fundamentally a Western European and North American phenomenon, distinguishing and often isolating these regions from the rest of the world's civilizations. For Them, in contrast to Us, a generic divorce between politics and sport (more broadly, culture) appears both senseless and dehumanizing, at best a romantic vision with practical benefits, at worst an imperialist internationalism, as Hoberman has styled it.

The Foundational Logic

Moreoever, this mode of thinking is not even universal in the modern histories of the West or of the Olympic Movement. For instance, you will not find it in Coubertin's foundational works, such as *Universités transatlantiques* or "La philosophie de l'histoire des États-Unis" which issued from his voyage to Canada and the United States, whose centennial we meet to commemorate. That inquiry was, of course, commissioned by a French government ministry. But more importantly, in his writings Coubertin moves among observations on political history, political conditions, institutions of higher learning, physical education, and sport initiatives without betraying the slightest sense of any essential division, incommensurability, or alienation among these realms of social life.

Indeed, it is the political category which frames everything else. This is clear in Coubertin's general preoccupations with relations among democracy, education, and sport—the last being his distinctive addition to the problematic of Tocqueville, whom he self-consciously imitated—and with national *rénovation*, which Coubertin recognized as "the great idea which dominates transatlantic civilization [. . .] never to be lost from sight[1]". The same pattern organizes each account of particular North American places and communities. For example, in a passage of contrast between English and French Canada, he begins by commenting on the "marvelous" political wisdom of the Francophones in the face of the "cruelties exercised against them and the injustices to which they've had to submit" from the Anglophones, while twice refusing "the United States come to conquer and to liberate them". French Canadians preferred instead to "keep themselves united to their persecutors" in a federal state "infinitely more inclusive and better constituted than that of the United States". "One seeks in vain in the history of the world", Coubertin continues, "a second example of so remarkable a political consciousness". Only with this context set, does the author then proceed to discuss education as the key variable in the French Canadian future and to mention its "clear and indubitable" deficiencies in comparison to the English model, including, of course, in matters of physical education and liberal character-building[2].

That political circumstances and conflicts with political elites and institutions offered practical and ideological dangers to the nascent international sport movement was a fact of which Coubertin was already eminently aware. He came to North America in the aftermath of his battles at home with the left-wing nationalist Paschal Grousset, and a hundred lesser skirmishes had already been fought. And he was on his way to a confrontation in Athens with the right-wing nationalist Charles Maurras which would set the terms of the debate that continues today over whether nations are brought into closer communication or are repelled by one another through the medium of sports competition[3]. None of this, however, led Coubertin or his contemporaries, even the most bourgeois among them, to a categorical disjunction between sport and politics, any conception of them as constitutionally separate, mutually exclusive, and automatically hostile spheres, much less to the rhetoric of sport as an anti-politics, which over the course of many years has grown familiar to our own ears. Far from it.

Sport's direct engagement with the great political questions and movements of its times remained for Coubertin the source of its importance at least equal to, if not surpassing, its presumed effects on individual health, psychological and moral development. Mutual respect among different peoples through sport—which Coubertin promoted "in default of a common faith impossible to realize in the modern world" and as lying between tolerance, a "purely negative virtue" really signifying "passive indifference", and the *fraternité* and love of the French revolutionaries and religious utopians, which he consigned to children and the angels[4]—depended absolutely on political engagement rather than some rejection of all that is political. The latter move would be not only destructive of international understanding but profoundly anti-democratic.

In words that should give many international sportspersons pause today, he wrote in 1898 (in an American magazine and surely thinking of his visit here): "In order to understand a country it is not enough to see it live; its present state must be compared with its recent past [. . .] For this history is indispensable, and especially the political history of the present century [. . .] I would like to say that it is regrettable that one should visit a country before he has made such a study[5]." Coubertin himself, for example in his ignorance about modern Greece when he went there, did not always live up to his own principles, but that does not detract from their merit. Indeed, the very things we in the West today find most troublesome about his views at the time—unwillingness to separate sporting from military virtues, complicity in sport as a virility cult at the reactionary expense of women and as a "civilizing" device used against colonialized peoples—are testimony to this late 19th century understanding of sport and political affairs as inseparably and desirably interconnected, regardless of the practical difficulties thus occasioned.

World Wars, Olympism, and the Political Category

What happened to alter this dominant view, to bring to the fore in the 1920s and 30s a new rhetoric of politics as distant from and poisonous to sport, of sport as an alternative to politics, a compensation for politics, indeed as an anti-politics? There were surely many factors, not least of which was the development of sport itself, its increasing penetration throughout the social orders and cultural representations of more and more societies, bringing more political, economic, and social interests, actors, and conflicts into the game. Among sports leaders and ideologues of the time, one can already note a certain weariness and wariness, far different from the optimism and spirit of renovation which carried their predecessors across the *fin-de-siècle*. But above all, it was World War I, the "war to end all wars", that shattered the dreams of post-Enlightenment rationality, of perpetual progress, of social harmony, and beneficent science, revealing the mad darkness in the heart of Europe herself, undercutting all her claims to moral and cultural superiority, and introducing into the minds of her greatest and her smallest such suspicions as Weber expressed in the famous "Iron Cage" passage of *The Protestant Ethic*, quoting the poet: "Specialists without spirit, sensualists without heart; this nullity imagines that it has attained a level of civilization never before achieved[6]."

Less well remembered is a line preceding this, where Weber remarks that particularly in the United States, "the pursuit of wealth, stripped of its religious and ethical meaning, tends to become associated with purely mundane passions, which often actually give it the character of sport[7]". Thus was marked the migration of the category of sport away from that of politics: in the United States—where this development was to reach its zenith—toward the luring economic category; in Europe away from the horror of the Great War, which the politicians and the corruption of political institutions were felt to have brought on, and toward the category of "moral culture".

Of course, in the gay 1920s, efforts were made to recapture and display the old confidences. In sport, one thinks especially of the photos of Coubertin striding happily through the Paris olympic stadium in 1924, in the company of statesmen, political elites, and even the intellectuals, who had rallied one last time before departing sport forever. But in Giraudoux's *Maximes sur le sport*, the most famous literary product of that interlude, the new dualism was firmly announced: "Dans les périodes de guerre, les Jeux olympiques sont une trêve. Dans les époques pacifiques, une vraie guerre;" "Le sport crée à l'intérieur de chaque patrie des patries locales, toutes ennemies." (And he might have added with Democratic Worker's Sport Movements and Bolshevism in mind, "à travers des patries"). The new logic of the individual in faceless mass society made its appearance as well, as Giraudoux, under the sign of the trenches, wrote hauntingly and ambiguously: "Le sport délimite notre corps de la masse terriblement vague des autres corps[8]."

Such social darkness never fully descended on Coubertin, though the Great War had touched him directly too. His own political vision was still expanding; he was still struggling to learn, to renovate himself. In 1923, he wrote against the European belief in African inferiority, in a passage that contains a new anthropological concept of culture and, therefore, of sport as a medium of intercultural education. "That which is important above all is to penetrate the family organization which distinguishes [African peoples], their conception of life, and the secrets of the beliefs they profess. On this last point it seems that fanaticism is foreign to their nature, and that, when it does appear, the responsibility for it lies with whites[9]." But in the context of this general reversal of, or at least new reticence about, which peoples were to be assigned to the categories "civilized" and "savage", a new note of wishing for a general quarantine between politics and sport slips into Coubertin's later writings too, works increasingly memoirist or philosophical. In a text addressing American and French proposals for a boycott of the Berlin Olympic Games, Coubertin tried to mediate the two positions by distinguishing between "the visage" and "the soul" of an institution like the Olympic Games and the natural but regrettable pressure of "electoral interests" and political "passions of the moment" as against the deep and desirable politics of "general history" and "human evolution[10]". As is well-known, Coubertin was no better prepared than most younger sport leaders to understand what a Faustian bargain had been struck with the Games of 1936, held on the eve of still more terrible destruction. Though it remains difficult to apply to the particular case of Berlin even today, Coubertin's dualistic formulation of the general sport and politics relation came to dominate the practical discourse of later sports leaders and publics. In sum, we may recall that in 1889 and 1890, as Coubertin traveled through and contemplated North America, Heinrich Schlie- mann and Cardinal Newman died, and Hitler, Molotov, Eisenhower, and De Gaulle each was born. In 1936, the intermediate historical world Coubertin had occupied came to its end.

Naziism, World War II, and the Holocaust meant that international sport, rightly or wrongly, would forever be tied in public memory to Berlin. Coupled with the unprecedented conditions of the post-war period, when two powerful nations came into possession of atomic weapons and the world's best athletic teams and one into control of 40% of the world's gross national product, it is hardly surprising that the ideology of separation of sport from politics became a commonplace, nor that the American IOC president and erstwhile Berliner Avery Brundage should set himself up as the apostle of this view. Its dualism became inescapable contradiction, but to be sympathetic for a moment—if not with the man then with the theory—it represented an illusion in Freud's technical sense. A powerful wish-fulfillment was registered here that there be some arena where human beings could get on with the project of coming to understand and abide with one another away from the machinations of those with their fingers on the neo-colonialist cash registers and the nuclear triggers which now changed everything.

Nuclear Weapons, The Cold War, and Schizophrenic Illusion

The counter-evidence to the illusion was, of course, so evident to everyone that there is no need to dwell upon it. This is the history that we have left behind just yesterday, and its schizophrenic discourse is still too much with us in some parts and communities of the world. Many Western publics, journalists, and academics scoffed at the claims of sport's political disengagement and innocent victimage while simultaneously complaining that sport has grown "too political, too commercial", thus betraying their own participation in the illusion. Because of Cold War pressures in the 1960s and 70s, but also because of other important developments in the world such as decolonization, domestic human rights and social welfare movements, the advent of television, and the birth of the sporting goods and sportswear industries—now the 22nd largest industry in the United States and accounting for 3% to 5% of British and French GNP—sport took on greater importance for a greater number of governments. The proliferation of national Sports Ministries and the fear of a UNESCO intrusion into the Olympic Movement offered serious challenges to an IOC rightly concerned with maintaining its independence and its historical uniqueness as an institution that was international before it was national. Dangerously, these threats of governmental and political-bloc takeovers occurred at just the moment when, especially in the English-speaking countries, the inaccurate image of the IOC as a club of doddering *déclassés* or *parvenus* white men ignorant of the world was at its strongest.

We are all aware of both the reforms of the past decade and the residual threats to the Olympic Idea and the international aspirations of the Movement from political elites, corporate capital, entertainment media, and the pharmacological and technological entrepreneurs within sport itself. These more subtle forms of inequality, exploitation, and domination come paired with new opportunities to expand the proper missions of sport, the agony and the ecstasy of the present situation. Watching the present olympic leadership steer its fine line in enormously complex circumstances has had the merit of opening up our discourse once again about the mutual integration of sport, whose social and cultural importance increases, and political institutions and processes which bear primary respon-sibility for the quality of life for millions of human beings, indeed for whether they will be permitted to live at all. As we contemplate present developments in world alignments, in Eastern Europe and within our own countries, we are reminded once again that only the rich, powerful, unthreatened, or massively deluded few can afford to be contemptuous of or isolated from politics. Sport cannot afford it either and still maintain its claims to being a human liberation movement.

But a new complication has arisen which both counters and complements this trend, one which brings us back to the meaning of Seoul. An enormous political and diplomatic complexity and sensitivity are now required to bring a Games into being at all, much less one which accomplished geopolitically what Seoul did. As a necessary and unavoidable consequence, much of this labor must be conducted in secret. A different kind of sports leadership is required for this task than was ever so much the case before. The irony is that their most difficult diplomatic accomplishments must remain outside the public eye and thus may neither be credited nor contribute to the reunderstanding of sport itself as a political process. The very silence required of top sports officials interferes with the capacity of sport to serve its highest mission of public education in international and intercultural relations. It introduces new barriers between top international and government-connected national sport leaders and those at the civic and local levels, who are expected to understand and support policies and priorities which may be communicated to them in only the vaguest of terms, if at all. Sports scholars, especially those who specialize in contemporary international, political, and cultural relations, find themselves held once again at a distance from sport leaders, who understandably fear the scholarly ethos of analyzing and publishing all important information. This is doubly destructive in that sport leaders deny themselves the professional expertise of scholars in these areas, and scholars are less able to free themselves and their audiences of the old discourses, which trivialize the achievements and political significance of the Olympic Movement. Treated like journalists, sport scholars are tempted to act like them. Finally, the secret aspects of the new sports diplomacy leave olympic leaders unchecked by any public scrutiny of the associations they maintain, the decisions they reach, and the directions to which they commit the entire Olympic Movement.

We must consider this growing dilemma now, when the results of Seoul have been so universally positive and the IOC's demonstration of diplomatic sensitivity and initiative proved sufficient to gain the trust of world political leaders, drawing them into common engagement in processes of ending the Cold War, which we all support. President Gorbatchev's Vladivostok declaration on the eve of the Opening Ceremonies and the unaccustomed forbearances on the part of Washington are key emblems of this accomplishment. Both indicated the erosion of a certain superpower exceptionalism, that vain and hegemonic refusal to acknowledge full embeddedness in the same system of interdependencies which condition the actions of other nations. Hosting the transnational sport community has frequently and abidingly—beginning with the first modern Olympic Games of 1896—altered the political landscape of the host nation. On the domestic front in South Korea, by all informed observations, political reforms equally admired by socialist and liberal democratic foreigners were accelerated by the olympic process. Undoubtedly sport, both international and domestic, must remain vigilant against political interventions and interferences which do not serve the goals of Olympism. But neither this cause nor public appreciation for the positive world impact of sport today will any longer be served by maintaining a discourse of necessary and categorical antagonisms and separations between sport and politics. This way of speaking, to repeat a key point, leads the majority of world cultures and less privileged segments of our own societies to continue to fear that the Olympic Movement is a really Euro-American elite and not a truly multicultural system of institutions and practices.

Power, Culture, and Communication

Here we arrive at the second overriding challenge for our reflection on the situation of sport at our own *fin-de-siècle*, another profound epistemological shift. Appearing everywhere today, popularly as well as among humanist and human scientific elites, is *a fundamental fusing of the political category with the culture category*, a new understanding of the relations between power and social meaning. Power itself, where it is not maintained solely by terror, is increasingly recognizable as a matter of languages and representations. Professor Jeu has thoughtfully exposed how the semantic properties of sport necessarily generate a politics and a poetics. It may no longer be easy or desirable to enforce a boundary between these categories. In Huizinga's words, sport like all forms of serious play either "represents a contest or else becomes a contest for the best representation of something[11]". Sport is above all a cultural performance system for the generation of symbols and meanings, and the vast economic and political interests that accrue to it do so as a consequence. There is no autonomous realm of political or economic action which stands outside or independent of the cultural languages by which it is constituted and communicated. Power is a contest for meaning, just as meanings are a contest for power.

The IOC-encouraged negotiations between South and North Korea offer an important example of this principle and its challenges it introduces for the sport movement. Though the IOC was resistant for constitutional reasons to such language, the negotiations were understood by the principals, the Western press, and public opinion as being about, in the English phrase, the possibility of "co-hosting" the Games. And, insofar as the substance of the discussions has been made public, the issues included such essentially legal, financial, technological, and political issues as the number of contests and rituals that might be held in the North, the distribution of television monies, the opening of the border to the olympic family, visa requirements, and so on, issues which in the end proved too intractable to solve. Despite this outcome, these efforts were a huge diplomatic success with regard to smoothing the way for participation of most of the fraternal socialist countries, transforming the image of the IOC itself, ameliorating security fears, and providing a setting for extra-olympic political contacts essential to changing the world.

But paradoxically, these successes were least appreciated among segments of the South Korean population most devoted to reunification and suspicious of the superpowers and the ROK government for maintaining the division for their own geopolitical interests. The paradox is largely explained in the realm of language, indeed in the simple matter of translation. The expression "co-hosting" was, as my colleague Kang Shin-pyo and I discovered, regularly translated into Korean as *kong dong che*, a phrase with profoundly different meanings and intensities than the English one. *Kong dong che* denotes "belonging in the social world", "family and communal solidarity", the "sharing of good and friendly feelings", "welcoming respect, warmth, and openness to one another", thus connoting fundamental concepts of the entire Korean and East Asian sociocultural order.

Thus, official statements and press announcements that the Games could not be co-hosted came out in Korean not as assertions of fact about technical or legal difficulties but as statements that the olympic authorities were literally refusing to have a Games of communal and friendly feeling and were denying the deepest aspirations and conceptions of identity of the Korean people by setting the North Koreans beyond the border of humanity. By this cultural mistranslation, the progressive actions of the international sport and geopolitical and local government authorities in service of Korean nationalism and ending the Cold War were received as the very opposite, a rejection of and an insult to the national sentiment in favor of the old propaganda! Sadly, the effect was strongest among Korean groups whose devotion to human rights most closely parallels that of the Olympic Movement. I have discovered no evidence that the IOC leaders and consultants were aware of how their actions became subject to this understandable and avoidable distortion, or that SLOOC and South Korean government officials, operating in both languages, appreciated the situation and acted, as they could have, to ameliorate it. This cultural misunderstanding, in turn, has strong impact on political processes, from the breadth of Korean public support for the Games to Koreans' estimation of the sincerity and legitimacy of their own new government and of European, Soviet, and American authorities' intentions to abandon imperialist tendencies in favor of Korean human rights of self-determination.

This one example points out quite clearly how, if politics, sport, culture, and language are not thought of as separate in other segments of the global system, the West can maintain the separation after the fashion of its dominant discourses of political economy and universal humanism only at great cost to its self-understanding as well as its understanding of others. A multitude of further instances could be brought forward, especially in regard to the crucial matter of olympic ceremonies where the project of constructing and communicating diverse cultures to one another in ways both compelling but guarded against consequential misunderstandings is most self-conscious and delicate. The new complexities of our world situation and the new sensitivities demanded of sport leaders points to the need for new kinds of expert consultants for the deepest commitment of Olympism to intercultural understanding and mutual respect to proceed in the 21st century. Whether through a new IOC commission or in some other form, cultural scientists must be assembled to contribute the same level of expertise now available to the Olympic Movement through the reform of commissions concerned with press, television, financial, and legal matters.

Global and Local in the "World System"

The complete interpenetration of the global and domestic aspects of the recent Olympic Games reveals to us a third general dimension of the new world situation which will grow increasingly apparent as we enter the next century. Our familiar dichotomy between the international and the local no longer has very much meaning. Few indeed are the struggles of local communities to define their indentities and ameliorate their conditions which are not mediated by a conscious awareness and appeal to transnational forms and conditions. *Mutatis mutandis*, what is typically termed "the world system" is less and less comprehensible without direct reference to the mediations, intentions, and struggles of the particular communities which constitute that system. No one contemplating current events in Central Europe can fail to appreciate these new recognitions. We must struggle to abandon ways of thinking that hide from us the fact that we are all cosmopolitans and locals at the same time, and in Sept-Îles as fully as in Montréal, Timisoara as in Bucharest, in Jiangmen City as much as Tienamen Square, and on the Sepik River as much as in Port Moresby. Indeed, just as our explicit conceptions of the world order can at times be our most parochial conceptions, so too our struggles for local identity may engage our most substantive awarenesses of transnational and global interconnections.

In the summer Olympic Games of Barcelona, we shall see this paradigm played out again in spectacular fashion for both hosts and guests, as the deployment of imageries of the new Europe in the new world system will be mediated by the *catalanista/espanolista* opposition, just as all parties to the formation of local identities in Spain will formulate their claims in part on the logic and in the language of a constructed international order. Nor—as we anticipate a unified German team, conflicts over separate delegations for nationalities now vigorously seeking their independence from current states, and struggles for recognition within NOCs between representatives of the old and the new political orders—will such dramas be limited to the host country. Indeed, this process is not even restricted to national identity formations or top class sport staged before a maximum audience. It just as thoroughly organizes experience and meaning in local contexts and communities: for women seeking equality in American collegiate and Canadian civic sport; for Poles and Soviets demanding redistribution of resources from elite to public sport-for-all; for Korean and Chinese athletes seeking their due in systems not used to heroes and heroines issuing from the less privileged social strata.

Recognition of politics and culture as entwined discursive formations and of the international and the local as mutually constituting phenomena are features of what is today labelled "post-modernism" among intellectual elites, not only in Paris, London, and New York, but also in Buenos Aires, Bombay, Lagos, and Seoul where olympic ceremonies planners referred as often to Derrida and Lyotard as to Monk Wonhyo, Yi Yul-gok, or King Sejong. Such labels, however, specify an attitude toward history not always so different from the notions of linear progress and development they are meant to supplant. While it is clear that we are living through the end of an era and the onset of a period of massive change that draws our eyes firmly and more hopefully toward the future, we need be suspicious of vain and fashionable formulae that would seduce us into believing that the past is fully dead and buried. This is particularly the case for us North Americans, more especially still for us Americans, whose dominant ethos in such matters was articulated in that great culture-bearer Henry Ford's maxim that "History is Bunk". Our contemporary challenge of how to estimate history itself recurs in the very design of this conference.

Do We Live in the Nineteenth Century?

Under present geopolitical circumstances, it would not be surprising if some delegates detected an apparent contradiction in being summoned to reflect simultaneously on sport in the 21st century, just before its turn, and on Coubertin's visit to these shores just before the turn of the 20th century. Is there not something odd, or merely academic, in being asked to contemplate simultaneously the arrival of an international order which we are now, and not altogether regrettably, in the act of leaving behind? I have tried to suggest, through an admittedly inadequate narrative, that we can only appreciate our present situation through situating it as a chapter in an ongoing story of the modern world. We must, in Foucault's expression, construct the history of the present. The past is indeed another country, but it is likewise our own. Grappling with it is a powerful means of help in the struggle to occupy the present world of cultural Others. And perhaps we have a special relationship precisely with that world of the last turn of the century, a dramatic and wondrous structural relation this time, a kind of fearful synchrony, revealed in many ways, for example by the fact that the 1880s were the scene of the first wave of feminism and the 1980s the second, or that these dates mark the opening and the closing of what some have called the "American Century."

Consider, please, the following sketch of the global situation.

Continental Europe is claiming a still more powerful position in the world system by seeking to temper national antagonisms through a variety of multilateral treaties, intergovernmental organizations, articulations of common cultural identity, and increased flows of people, information, and goods. German political unification, British standoffishness, and French ambivalence provide one set of uncertainties with regard to this general trend. In Central Europe, popular liberation movements and the weakening of regional political forms and compacts provide another set of opportunities and dilemmas. In both Western and Central Europe, perceived incongruities between existing cultural and political boundaries — taking most dramatic form in a variety of nationalist separatism—threaten to compromise vertically the efforts of state governments and leaders to reach out to and cooperate with one another horizontally.

The Russias and the Americas stand in ambiguous relation to this new Europe. While jealous of their own political power and revolutionary independence, and wishing to claim that they have developed unique ways of life of equal world-historical significance to European ones, they nevertheless find strategic reasons to assert shared cultural descent, race, religions, economic forms, and tastes in education, literature, and the plastic arts. While gratified by the cultural deference implied in claims by Russians and Americans to belong to a common European house, many Europeans remain dubious of the cultural level of these rude and unsophisticated materialists and wary of their potential military and economic impact on Europe's own aspirations. In reaction to being kept perpetually in the status of "candidate members" to European civilization and to valuing their own experimental tendencies toward radical egalitarianism over Europe's hidebound class and status hierarchies, North Americans and Russians become newly able, situationally at least, to overcome their own otherwise substantial ideological and cultural differences.

As in Europe herself, separatist movements complexify this picture—the Francophones in Canada and Georgians or Ukrainians in Greater Russia. And even in their absence, populations in all the Americas as in all the Russias must mediate their identities through choices about thinking longitudinally—New Worldism in the one place, pan-Slavism or religious Orthodoxy, in the other—versus thinking latitudinally, with Western Europe as a continuing reference point. In addition, internal population entwined with the histories of other empires—say, the Spanish or the Ottoman—or of involuntarily transported labor—former slaves, conscripts, and guest workers of other colors, religions and cultures—struggle to make and have made for them their own complex choices of identity, hostility, and allegiance.

Meanwhile Asia, particularly East Asia, is being reborn, on its own rather than Western colonial terms. Asian nationalist intellectuals and pedagogues have been so successful that every Chinese school child repeats that his rich civilization is 7000, every Korean 5000, and every Japanese 2600 years-old, older in each case than that of Europe which claims spiritual descent from classical Greece. At the same time, Asian efforts at regional cooperation to compete globally with Europe and America remain bedeviled by racist nationalisms, memories of invasion and exploitation of Asian by Asian, and persistent struggles for hierarchical domination in the cultural field. Polities remain unstable in the absence of a consensual concept of legitimacy that must somehow lie both between and beyond Western forms (liberal or Marxist) and indigenous dynastic models.

Amidst this unleashing of economic and political force in the Northern Hemisphere, other areas of the world—black Africa, portions of Central and South America, South Asia, and Oceania—are left out of the action. While their own elites are cosmopolitanized, the majority feel themselves to languish in a perpetual halfway house of poverty, famine, political disorganization, and dependency, between their past cultural riches—ever more valorized at home and studied, admired, and appropriated in Euro-America—and the chimerical promises of each "new world order" proclaimed in the North. From the perspective of cultures practiced in seeing European *laissez faire* capitalism and Marxist socialism as two sides of the same foreign coin, settling of differences in the North can appear nothing more than new strategies for expropriating the rest of humanity.

Like any snapshot, this one may be judged too bold or too blurry. But I offer it to a different end than mere *vraisemblance*. You will surely have taken it as a depiction of our world of the late 20th century, but, wonder of wonders, it describes just as precisely the world of the 1880s and 90s, when Coubertin arrived in North America on his mission of inquiry.

Of course the correspondences lie, as we anthropologists say, in the domain of structure: not in the identity of the historical terms but in relational similarities among their clear differences. In the years 1889 and 1890, as Coubertin made his rounds, France, Britain, and Germany were preoccupied among themselves with carving up Africa and Asia into colonial spheres of domination, whereas in 1989-1990, it is the distribution of continental market shares and the future of NATO which chiefly concern them. A century ago, inter-European domestic agreements—in weights and measures, customs and banking, postal, railroad and telegraph services, and a host of scientific, cultural, and civic organizations (including in the new domain of sport)—took the form of insistent recognition of nation-state distinction and autonomy, with cooperation on that basis alone. Today, in the European Community context, the terms of the discussion have greatly reversed themselves into a debate about which national prerogatives to preserve in a discourse of union.

As Coubertin journeyed, the Kaiser judged Chancellor Bismarck's work of unification finished and dismissed him, just as the German Social Democrats were adopting a Marxist program at the Erfurt Congress. Today, it is Chancellor Kohl who intends to be the new Bismarck, ironically on a ground laid for him by Social Democrats whose adjustments to their political heritage have proved insufficient to deliver to them the moment. With regard to France, we can recall that Boulanger fled and the first May Day celebration took place in Paris, just as the *rallié* aristocrat Coubertin followed Tocqueville and before him Crèvecoeur in contemplating the future of French society through the lens of the American. Today, we wonder whether *cohabitation* will remain a *de facto* feature of French political life, regardless of the parties in power, or whether internationalization, the emasculation of the grand socialist/capitalist opposition, and the impatience of the young with the hierarchical insularities of their elders will not lead, as they did in Coubertin's time, to some quite different France.

It is worth recalling that Crèvecoeur, the Frenchman whom I mentioned, gave the United States its dominant metaphor for itself, the social melting pot. (Canadians prefer the significantly different metaphor of the multicultural mosaic). Throughout the 19th century and forward to Myrdal's epic work *The American Dilemma*, Europeans including Coubertin have both fascinated and distanced themselves from North Americans over the racial and ethnic integration question. Today, we have another historic reversal, wondering which North American will appear to write *The European Dilemma* over the same issues in Britain, France, Germany, and even Central Europe and Scandinavia.

In Latin America, as Coubertin traveled in Canada, Brazil was proclaimed a Republic, Uruguay was developing the first stable two-party democracy in the hemisphere, and there were more sports clubs in Montevideo than there were in Paris. Today South America struggles to emerge from the ruins of its proud political achievements, to throw off the burden of its crushing foreign debt, and to turn once again toward Europe and in new ways toward the Far East, away from the order imposed upon it from the north by the Monroe Doctrine and its Cold War consequents.

In the Far East of the 1880s and 1990s, the challenge of the West posed itself above all in political and military terms, as the Americans penetrated Japan, the Germans and British occupied China, and the Union Indo-Chinoise was declared by France in the same year Chiang Kai-shek was born. In this destabilized world, old regional hostilities were unleashed under the new banner of driving off the Western barbarians, as emblemized by the Japanese occupation of Seoul and by Port Arthur. Today, save in parts of Southeast Asia still reorganizing after the defeat of the French and the Americans, the fighting has largely stopped. For Japan, Korea, and the "Little Tigers", economic competition with the West has become the privileged means of achieving national sovereignty and restarting the domestic process of cultural and political revitalization interrupted by the foreigners at the last turn of the century. China struggles to choose between joining this process and her ancient conviction of cultural superiority and hegemony.

Sport and the Paradigm of
Contemporary Intercultural Relations

In the late 19th century, the root paradigm that still organizes intercultural relations was laid down. These illustrations of structural symmetry, Coubertin's journey, indeed the very design of the Olympic Games all remind us of it. Though we sometimes speak, as did our ancestors, of global interconnection and of national and sub-national cultural differentiation as opposing processes—indeed of the first as erasing the second—this has never been the case. Versions of such historical evolutionism and modernization theory are not merely ethnocentric but utterly deceptive as to the facts. Beginning in the 1950s and 60s, with the coming into being of so many "new nations", of the atomic weapons, and the new communications technologies, the paradox began to be explicity recognized that *the processes of global interconnection and cultural differentiation occur everywhere simultaneously.* Far from being opposed, they are two sides of the same historical coin; paradox has become paradigm[12].

The linkages we assemble into something called "the world system" are absolutely dependent upon the simultaneous claims and activities of the world's peoples to generate unique identities for themselves, to differentiate themselves equally from their neighbors and distant others. Being a nation, having a culture, are the chief requirements for claiming a rightful and autonomous place in the global system. Just so, identifying and articulating a communicable cultural identity for one's group depends upon the availability of forms supplied by the transnational community. As in human language, so in the international human order, differentiation and articulation are two sides of the same coin. If there is a key difference from prior periods today, it is the indigenous self-consciousness of the process[13]. No group, no matter where they are located or how peripheral to Northern Hemisphere centers of power they might be, any longer needs outsiders, including anthropologists, to inform them that they have a distinctive culture worth representing and preserving. And as we see today in the mutual accompaniment of democratization and revived nationalism in Central and Eastern Europe, the process of constructing cultural identities is not only eminently political but is the very stuff of politics.

The Olympic Games are one, indeed one of the most important sources of such transnational forms for constituting differentiated identities. To be a nation recognized by others and realistic to themselves, a people must march in the Olympic Games Opening Ceremonies procession. To march in those ceremonies, a people must enter into communication and conformity with the requirements of transnational olympic organizations and participate in the more universalizing forms of sport. But common practices need not entail common meanings—that was the error of modernization theory, liberal and Marxist—and how peoples decode their common activity in the Olympic Games remains probably more not less various, not to mention more politically lively, than ever. The very same paradigm works itself out within nations and in infranational sport systems too. *It is this global process, not some supposed homogenization or hegemonization, which joins the cosmopolitan and the local into a truly world system.* This is the position which humanity has reached and which should frame and organize all our reflections not only on the future of sport but on the general future of humankind.

Perhaps you will permit me to conclude in a way that is both personal and situational. My first visit to Québec in a sports context was for the Olympic Scientific Congress of 1976. That event was organized by Fernand Landry and his colleagues with the same self-sacrificing devotion they have brought to the enormous task of this symposium on *Sport... The Third Millennium.* One evening in 1976, we were treated to a reading by the Québécois poet Gilles Vigneault. Permit me to close with some lines of his which evoke, with far more beauty and resonance, the themes I have tried to articulate.

De mon grand pays solitaire
Je crie avant que de me taire
À tous les hommes de la terre
Ma maison c'est votre maison
Entre mes quatre murs de glace
Je mets mon temps et mon espace
À préparer le feu la place
Pour les humains de l'horizon
Car les humains sont de ma race
(Mon pays)

NOTES AND REFERENCES

1. Coubertin P de (1898) La philosophie de l'histoire des États-Unis. Revue Bleue 35 4 juin p 3

2. Coubertin P de (1890) Universités transatlantiques. Paris: Hachette p 133-36. In Müller N, Comité international olympique (eds) (1986) Pierre de Coubertin. Textes choisis. Tome I Révélation. Zürich: Weidmann p 124-25

3. See MacAloon JJ (1981) This Great Symbol: Pierre de Coubertin and the origins of the modern Olympic Games. Chicago: University of Chicago Press p 109-13, 153-63, 216-69

4. Coubertin P de (1915) Le respect mutuel. Paris: Alcan p 14-15

5. Coubertin P de (1898) Does cosmopolitan life lead to international friendliness? American Monthly Review of Reviews 17 p 433

6. Weber M (1930) The protestant ethic and the spirit of capitalism. London: Allen and Unwin p 182

7. Ibid. In the accompanying footnote Weber points to the business spirit of record-setting—"That beats everything!"—as the principle of connection between sport and managerial capitalism. It is interesting to note that among the new economic powers of East Asia, the business ethos is dominated by national measures of success and long-term development of market share in contrast to the short-term profitability of individual sectors or firms. Similarly in sport, record-setting holds little interest in comparison with the moral and historical meanings of victory itself.

8. Giraudoux J (1928) Maximes sur le sport. Paris: Grasset

9. For analysis from a cultural anthropological point of view of the Olympic project with regard to successive historical concepts of culture, see MacAloon "Intercultural Education and Olympic Sport" Montreal and Ottawa: Canadian Olympic Association/Olympic Academy of Canada 1986. Ommo Grupe's paper in this book "Identity, Legitimacy, Sense and Non-Sense of Modern Sport as a Cultural Phenomenon" treats the same relationship from the perspective of European critical philosophy.

10. Coubertin P de (1936) L'Olympisme et la politique. La revue sportive illustrée 32 p 38. In Müller N, Comité international olympique (eds) (1986) Pierre de Coubertin. Textes choisis. Tome II Olympisme. Zürich: Weidmann p 440-41

11. Huizinga J (1950) Homo Ludens. Boston: Beacon p 13

12. The epic struggle between these two points of view dominated and enlivened the 1989 Olympic Anniversary Congress in Seoul and the prior Korean Academic, and the Olympics and Cultural Exchange Congresses [The proceedings of this last meeting have been published as Kang S-p, MacAloon JJ, DaMatta R (eds): The Olympics and cultural exchange in the world system. Seoul: Hanyang University Institute for Ethnological Studies, 1988]. Revealingly and sadly, the theme was almost absent from the Olympic Scientific Congress itself, a condition created by the dominance of the bio-medical and sports technical fields at the expense of the human sciences. One trusts that the organizers of academic meetings in Barcelona to accompany the Games of 1992 will follow the Korean model of providing opportunities for experts in all disciplines and perspectives to reflect on the global situation and will struggle not to allow the official scientific congress to continue its trend toward one-sided and reactionary parochialism.

13. As Marshall Sahlins stressed in his keynote address to the Seoul Olympiad Anniversary Conference in Seoul: "China Reconstructing or Vice Versa: Humiliation as a stage of Economic Development, with comments on Cultural Diversity in the Modern World System". In Koh B-i (1990) Toward one world beyond all barriers. Vol. I Keynote speeches; cultural exchange and cultural nationalism. The Seoul Olympiad Anniversary Conference. Seoul Olympic Sports Promotion Foundation. Seoul: Poong Nam p 78-96

The Olympic Games, Communications Technologies and Cultural Exchange

On the Presentation, Interpretation and Meaning of Multicultural Performances (such as the Olympic Games) as an Import-Export Medium and in the Translation of Culture

Les Jeux olympiques, les techniques de communication et les échanges culturels

Sur la présentation, l'interprétation et la signifiance des Jeux olympiques en tant que produit d'exportation-importation et en tant que médium de translation de culture

A Note
by Professor MacAloon and the Editors

Note
du professeur MacAloon et des éditeurs

The panel presentations on "The Olympic Games, Communications Technologies and Cultural Exchange" used the 1988 Games of Seoul, and in particular selected episodes from the Opening Ceremony telecast in three nations, to explore the manner in which culture is presented, interpreted and translated through globally televised multicultural performances. The format of the panel itself incorporated elements of televised presentation. During the introduction by Professor **MacAloon** and the subsequent presentations by each of the panel members [Professors **Kang** (KOR), **de Moragas** (ESP), and **Larson** (USA)], a bank of video monitors was used to simultaneously show, *without sound*, how three different national telecasts—the Korean Broadcasting System (KBS) domestic broadcast in Korea, Spanish Television (TVE) in Spain, and NBC Television in the United States—covered each of three selected episodes from the Opening Ceremony. During the presentation by Professor **Larson**, one excerpt from the NBC telecast was however shown *with sound*:

Episode 14	Entry of the torch into the stadium and lighting of the cauldron
Episode [18,19]	Prayer of blessing, *Cha-il* dance and *Hwakwan* dance
Episode 20	*Hondon* (Chaos)

The use of videotaped excerpts from the Opening Ceremony telecasts showed some rather striking differences in the three televised constructions of the event, ranging from the faithfulness of KBS to the international television signal and the intent of those who planned the ceremony to the major departures and additions imposed by NBC in its telecast. Obviously, the nature and importance of such telecast excerpts is less easily conveyed in printed proceedings such as this volume. However, it may assist the reader to know that comments by the panelists were largely based on each of the following papers, in the order they are presented hereafter.

The initial paper by Professor **Kang** was presented against the backdrop of visual excerpts from the KBS telecast of the Opening Ceremony. As his paper suggests, not only these selected episodes, but the entire experience of the Seoul Olympic Games, can be better understood if interpreted through Korean *Dae-Dae* cultural grammar.

The second paper formed the basis for comments by Professor **de Moragas**. He analyzed the discourse constructed by Spanish Television (TVE), with a particular emphasis on the verbal component of the telecast.

Les présentations qui ont été faites sur le thème «Les Jeux olympiques, les techniques de communications et les échanges culturels» ont porté directement sur les Jeux de Séoul, notamment sur des épisodes particuliers de la Cérémonie d'ouverture tels qu'ils furent télédiffusés dans trois pays différents. L'objectif poursuivi était celui d'analyser la manière par laquelle certains aspects de la culture se trouvent présentés, interprétés ou rendus au cours de pareils événements multi-culturels diffusés à l'échelle mondiale. Au moment du Symposium, des éléments télévisuels furent incorporés aux diverses présentations. Au cours de l'introduction du sujet par le professeur **MacAloon**, comme aussi en accompagnement des présentations faites par les professeurs **Kang** (KOR), **de Moragas** (ESP), et **Larson** (USA), une série de moniteurs vidéo illustrait aux personnes présentes (sans la *bande sonore* toutefois) la manière par laquelle trois réseaux nationaux de télédiffusion avaient couvert trois épisodes particuliers de la Cérémonie d'ouverture: le Korean Broadcasting System (KBS), pour la Corée; le Réseau national de télédiffusion espagnol (TVE), pour l'Espagne; la NBC Television, pour les USA. Par ailleurs, la *bande sonore* fut utilisée pour illustrer une partie de la présentation du professeur **Larson**.

Épisode 14	Entrée de la torche dans le stade et allumage de la vasque
Épisode [18,19]	La prière, la danse *Cha-il* et la danse *Hwakwan*
Épisode 20	*Hondon* (le chaos)

L'analyse des extraits vidéos en question a révélé qu'il y avait eu des différences frappantes dans la construction du message télédiffusé en provenance de Séoul. Le réseau KBS est resté fidèle en tout point à la substance du signal de transmission optique international, et de ce fait aux perspectives d'intention de ceux qui avaient conçu et planifié le contenu même de la Cérémonie d'ouverture. Le réseau NBC, pour sa part, s'est permis des déviations et des ajouts d'importance. De toute évidence, le présent rapport écrit ne se prête guère à une description poussée de l'analyse des extraits des vidéos concernés. Le lecteur remarquera cependant que dans leurs textes et leurs commentaires, les trois auteurs sont restés centrés sur l'objectif proposé.

La présentation du professeur **Kang** a porté sur les extraits vidéos de la KBS. Il souligne à l'évidence que non seulement les trois épisodes choisis, mais l'ensemble même de l'expérience de Séoul s'interprète parfaitement par l'intermédiaire de la grammaire culturelle coréenne du *Dae-Dae*.

The third presentation was by Professor **Larson**. He explored the nature of coverage by NBC television, the dominant commercial broadcaster in Seoul, with particular attention to commercial breaks, specially produced background features, and their implications for olympic broadcasting policy.

As a follow-up to these papers, the reader will find 1– a listing of all story units (episodes) in the complete Opening Ceremony telecasts, 2– transcriptions of the KBS, TVE and NBC commentary for the episodes analyzed in the panel, and 3– three tables which broaden the comparison and examine themes touched on by commentators for several international broadcasters, including the three already referred to. The analysis of themes was presented by Professor **Rivenburgh** (USA). The discussion session which ensued in the afternoon was co-chaired at the Quebec City Symposium by Professor **Rivenburgh** and Canadian free-lance journalist **Laurent Laplante**.

La deuxième présentation, celle du professeur **de Moragas**, porte plus spécialement sur l'analyse du discours verbal transmis en Espagne par la TVE.

Enfin, la présentation du professeur **Larson** traite pour sa part du travail de la NBC, avec un accent particulier sur les pauses commerciales et autres ajouts, avec ce que cela implique au plan d'une éventuelle politique de télédiffusion des choses olympiques.

À la suite des trois présentations, le lecteur intéressé trouvera: 1– une liste de tous les épisodes qui ont constitué la substance du signal visuel et sonore de l'entière Cérémonie d'ouverture; 2– la transmission exacte des commentaires KBS, TVE et NBC pour les trois épisodes traités par les conférenciers principaux; 3– trois tableaux où se trouvent sommairement analysés les commentaires d'un certain nombre de télédiffuseurs internationaux additionnels. L'analyse du professeur **Rivenburgh** complète le traitement du sujet. Au moment du Symposium de Québec, cette présentation a servi d'introduction à la séance de discussion qui suivit les conférences des professeurs **Kang**, **Moragas** et **Larson** et qui fut co-présidée par le Dr **Rivenburgh** et le journaliste canadien **Laurent Laplante**.

[...] For, as every serious study of intercultural exchange has shown, it is simply a fact—a basic law of history, applicable to every department of life—that materials carried from any time past to a time present, or from one culture to another, shed their values at the culture portal and thereafter either become mere curiosities, or undergo a sea change through a process of creative misunderstanding [...]

Campbell Joseph (1968) Creative mythology. New York: Penguin Books. Chapter 3: The word behind the words, p 137 [in 1976 edition]

The Seoul Olympic Games and Dae-Dae Cultural Grammar

Kang Shin-pyo

The meanings of the Seoul Olympic Games are manifold and still in the process of being discovered and articulated. There can be no question in a short paper of doing justice to them. Some general facts of the Korean historical and social context became widely known throughout the world because of the 1988 Summer Olympic Games. Koreans have not yet fully recovered from the bitter experiences of the Japanese colonialization (1910-45) and a destructive civil war (1950-53). Today the nation remains divided under an armistice agreement still insured by the presence of United Nations forces. Hence, Korea has not yet fully attained its independence. In the self-estimation of most Koreans, the nation is considered small and still emergent, neither the so-called "Hermit Kingdom" of the past nor yet a full player on the world stage. At the same time Korea's phenomenal economic growth since the 1960s and external recognition of such development achievements as the *Saemul undong* (New Village Movement) encouraged Koreans in their hope of organizing something of worldwide significance and in the process changing Korea's self-image from "Third World" to a "First World" country.

Well-publicized difficulties at previous Olympic Games left Korea in the fortuitous position of having only Nagoya as a serious rival for the privilege of hosting the 1988 Games. South Korea was also fortunate in being chosen as host of the 1986 Asian Games, in competition with north Korea, which gave Seoul the chance to prepare facilities and to gain experience for 1988. These opportunities were accompanied by their share of domestic controversy. Many Koreans perceived the initial offer of Seoul as olympic host to be too closely associated with the military-inspired governments of the late Park Chung-hee and Chun Du-hwan. After award of the Games, many local anti-olympic campaigns were mounted, some with considerable militancy[1]. Talk about co-hosting the Games with the north presented echoes of the Cold War, and calls for reunification of the divided peninsula assumed greater prominence among the populace. These developments were well-publicized internationally and threatened to reinforce the

Shin-pyo Kang, Institute for Ethnological Studies, Department of Cultural Anthropology, Hanyang University, Ansan, Korea.

foreign view of Korea as a land of war, political strife, and military dictatorship. Korean experiments with economic reform and political democratization, themselves hastened by hosting the Olympic Games, were placed into additional tension and sometimes undervalued because of these conflicts. Meanwhile Korea's strong cultural tradition remained hidden behind a curtain both domestically and internationally. In the end, all these difficulties were overcome, with the exception of north Korean participation. Whatever their social stations and political attitudes, south Koreans eventually united in wishing for olympic success as an important moment in the nation's history.

The eventual success of the Seoul Olympic Games became manifest to all who participated, and an atmosphere of general satisfaction seems to have pervaded the world audience. Only now, however, are we beginning to appreciate the impact of the Seoul Games in such matters as hastening the end of the Cold War, altering the situation between north and south Korea, transforming the Korean people's view of themselves, and increasing the diplomatic prestige of the Olympic Movement and the IOC[2]. The Olympic Games played a great role in the reinvention and revitalization of traditional Korean culture. Obviously, a great volume of cultural imagery and information was transmitted between East and West through this occasion, but the problem of estimating in a scholarly way the degree and value of this intercultural communication is a complex and ongoing challenge[3]. Intercultural communication is no simple matter of conveying neutral and context-independent information between various points on the globe. Encoding cultural messages into public texts, transmitting them through the filtering and reinterpretive agencies of highly culture-bound broadcast and print media, and finally the decoding of meanings by mass audiences through local schemes and communities of interpretation are processes involving the fundamental anthropological problem of translation of culture.

The purpose of this thematic session here in Quebec is to expose and explore aspects of this process by considering some successes and failures of intercultural communication between Korea and other parts of the world in the context of the Olympic Games Opening Ceremonies. A comparative focus will be placed on two segments of the ceremonies: the entry of Sohn Kee-chung with the olympic flame, a part of the official ceremony mandated by the IOC; and the segment stretching from the *Kang-bok* and *Cha-il* dances through the *Hondon* (Chaos) and *Taekwando* displays, part of the Korean cultural performances designed by the SLOOC. These segments will be contextualized in the overall intentions of the Korean scenographers and organizers[4], then an analysis will follow from the point of view of Korean culture. Korean meanings encoded into these performances can then be compared and contrasted with the meanings presented and decoded by a number of Western national television agencies, which my colleagues will subsequently discuss.

However, a complex cultural performance like the Seoul Opening Ceremonies is not a mere catalogue or congeries of independent scenes and cultural items, any more than spoken language is a mere lexicon of words. One cannot analyze symbolic systems, or follow a translation and communication process, without close attention to the underlying grammatical rules by which units of signification are consciously or unconsciously composed into meaningful utterances. It is the special task of the anthropologist to expose these underlying cultural codes. This presentation begins with a general depiction of the Korean *Dae-dae* cultural grammar, then its operation is shown in the overall logic and selected segments of the Opening Ceremony. It is emphasized that Dae-dae cultural grammar formed the backbone in the management of the olympic event from conception to completion. This is not to suggest that the olympic spectacle witnessed in Seoul was not without powerful constitutive elements best understood by cultural grammars imported from outside Korea. Indeed, the olympic institution itself represented unfamiliar territory for Koreans. However, the Olympic Games took on unique significance after being placed on Korean soil. The key to grasping this significance is found by understanding Dae-dae cultural grammar, which itself is not to be taken as something static but is always in a creative process of becoming.

Dae-dae Cultural Grammar

There is a well-known story by Chuang Tzu. In it he dreamed he was a butterfly. Waking, he asked himself whether, if a few moments earlier he was a man dreaming of being a butterfly, he could not now be a butterfly dreaming of being a man. Which, he asked himself, was the reality? The message of the story is that actuality is less important than the way of thinking, of constructing and breaking down ideas. In just this way, Koreans do not give an either/or construction: they prefer "yes and no" to "yes or no." In effect, "yes" sometimes means "no" and "no" sometimes means "yes". This is *Dae-dae* (McCune-Reischauer romanization, *Taedae*) cultural grammar, which may also be translated into English as the "Con/Pro" logical organization of being, thought, and action.

Korean culture has three principal aspects: hierarchy, group, and drama-ritual. Hierarchy emphasizes an orderly rank of seniority in which the higher morally encompasses the lower. Superordinate and subordinate stand in complementary position[5]. For example, the authority of the senior businessman, politician, or teacher is ideally dependent upon his moral sincerity in favor of the group as a whole. Groupness emphasizes membership and creates a kind of family which, in turn, generates responsibility. For example, at New Year, every Korean gains one year despite his or her actual birth date, a practice which creates age-sets. Ritual drama prescribes appropriate behavior toward members of the group for the sake of harmony. Thus, for example, a son has the right to withhold the truth from the father to avoid unnecessary worry on the latter's part. In ritual drama, "no" and "yes", "con" and "pro", go together.

Western sport prefers clear winners and losers, yet in Korean tradition, winners are also losers and losers winners, depending on the context and occasion. For the sake of the group, individuals may take the role of loser and vice versa[6]. This kind of logic is fundamental to Korean practice and performance but is largely incompatible with the Western Aristotelian tradition. In Korean culture, performance becomes transformative, with its own peculiar grammar underpined by the three cultural aspects. The dramatic ritual of performance allows the group to grow or become smaller, and it transforms hierarchical positions. Man is the key here, as agent, practitioner, transformer, and "Awakened Man". Human beings have a mind and a body, matching dream, vision, and ideal to performance and practice[7]. Fear of failure is absent here, because failure is not a concern in the moment of practice[8]. Failure itself is viewed as a stepping stone in the process of endless practice toward completion, life as a continuous evolution to its own conclusion.

To explain further, reference is made to China. Chinese philosophy creates harmony through an orderly hierarchy of opposing but equally essential and complementary constituent components. Harmony comes from the oscillation between two poles, commonly expressed as *yin* (*um* in Korean) and *yang*, such that the dialectic of interaction involves the resolution of conflict. That binary conflict is expressed in terms of man and universe, heaven and earth, Being and non-Being, male and female, self and others, *li* (form) and *chi* (content), *hsing* (reason) and *ching* (emotion), knowledge and conduct, one and many, good and evil, and so on, patterns of thought laid down during the Zhou dynasty (1100-220 BC). Scholars have variously accounted for the roots of this mode of thought.

Some have pointed to a pre-existing social dualism between rural and urban as witnessed in the Shang archaeological record. Urbanites were sometimes explained as having a different racial origin than peasants and there was little common ground between high and low cultures[9]. For his part, Eberhard explains the dual society in terms of religion (the formalistic and almost abstract heavenly way as against popular demonic belief), literature (dry annalistic-statistical court records as against earthy folksongs and tales), law (moral code of the nobility against the criminal code of the peasants), and settlement (location of an ownership or property)[10]. Gernet focuses on the division among the peasants, isolating male and female distinctions on both the temporal and spatial levels[11]. Whatever the precise history of these views, taken together we can see that there is posited a profound metaphorical relationship between social regularity and the dualistic principle of categorical classification. This world view is neatly represented by *yin* and *yang*, a "dualism of ideology", a balance and harmony that provides an all-inclusive schema showing how "yes" can be "no" and vice versa in the related Korean cultural code[12].

History itself is not a universal factual given but a contextualized understanding constructed according to determinate cultural codes. As mentioned above, a world audience came to know certain "facts" about the changing Korean social order: that Korea has moved or is moving from dynasty to republic, from agrarian to industrial economy, from a rural to an urban society, from extended to nuclear family groups, from hierarchical to egalitarian relationships, from ascribed to achieved status, and, even, from family to individual. But the overall story is quite different when it is constructed according to a logic of linear "progress" or "modernization"—as in Western cultural commonsense, academic sociology, and among some Korean groups these days—than when the account is composed according to Dae-dae cultural grammar.

The latter sort of account stresses transformations of hierarchical relations seeking balanced complementarity and reciprocity in contexts of unequal power. Three historical moments of transformation have been previously identified in which Koreans were forced to accept and adjust to a new world order imposed upon them from outside[13]. The basal stage one can call "Korea in East Asia", or perhaps more correctly "Korea in China", which allowed for the continuation of the Confucian relation with her huge and immediate neighbor to the geographical west. Then from 1876 to 1905, Korea began to open her frontiers, finally signing a protectorate agreement that would lead to her annexation by Japan. "Korea in Transition" under Japanese rule coincided with a forced opening to that other West, that is to Europe. Again, a struggle was made to see the Western way as a complement to the Eastern tradition, as Korean powers welcomed Western materialism while rejecting Western learning. Liberation from the Japanese in 1945 brought on the third moment, "Korea in the World", or perhaps better, "Korea in America". A bitter civil war, turmoil in student rebellion (1960), military coups, and finally the 1987 summer of discontent marked attempts to match economic growth with political reordering. Korea is now entering a new transformation in her history, one in which she ventures out into the world without the constraints imposed upon her by the USA and the USSR. Hosting the Olympic Games allowed Koreans the opportunity to reflect on their own place in the world system. It remains difficult, nonetheless, for Koreans to comprehend the new world order in which they live. Yet the more they understand the West and can reproduce its points of view, the more Koreans value their own unique traditions. This double process was apparent in the making of the olympic ceremonies.

Codes and Performances

In the preparation of the scenarios for the opening and closing ceremonies, literally hundreds of scholars and artists were invited to participate in order to realize "*Saegye nun Seoul ro, Seoul un Saegye ro*", The World to Seoul, Seoul to the World. For over three years, they studied, reviewed, and analyzed ceremonies which had accompanied previous Olympic Games in other countries. It was felt that the Olympic Games are less a national matter than an international event; hence lessons were to be learned from past hosts. It became apparent that the main issue was how to synthesize a universalizing cultural code with particular cultural codes[14]. Those involved had to determine what was the particular Korean cultural code that would provide the basic guiding logic and principles. Whereas anthropologists normally look for underlying cultural codes which are largely unconscious in operation and practice, here they were to create and even "invent" the scenario culture. At the same time, it is probably beyond the capacities of even such a dedicated and resourceful army of scholars, artists, and cultural specialists to produce out of whole cloth a logic of cultural representation that would have sufficient depth and would be both coherent and persuasive to Korean audiences. Whether drawn from cultural repertoires widely accepted as "traditional" or created afresh through a process of *bricolage*, particular performances and the symbolic forms which composed them had certainly to be arranged and altered to fit the radically novel situation of the Opening Ceremony, the stadium site, open-air choreography, television constraints, international expectations, and so on. The issue is rather the grammatical code that would draw these various components into an ordered unity, acutely depicting and performing, at this more fundamental level, the character of Korea's cultural heritage.

The code which was mobilized, in a combination of self-conscious reflection and unconscious emergence, was the code of *Dae-dae*[15]. It was hardly the only cultural code engaged in these ceremonies. As Kapferer has strongly pointed out, in non complex literate civilization today, and perhaps in no society whatever, is there only one ontology or deep cultural grammar operating[16]. Logics labelled "Western" for convenience now have Korean proveniences as well, and as already pointed out, the scenarists of the olympic ceremonies found it necessary and desirable to accommodate them. Indeed, some of the planners thought to do so through an explicitly "post-modernist" strategy, Derrida and Lyotard being sometimes cited in discussions as frequently as the great scholars in Korean tradition[17]. At the same time, Dae-dae was not just one code among others. Because of the specific properties of its logic, it served as a kind of metacode in drawing "the Olympic" and "the Korean" into relations of contrast, complementarity, and harmony, a claim that shall now be demonstrated with specific examples.

Saegye nun Seoul ro, Seoul un Saegye ro

The overall theme of the Seoul Olympic Games, the ideal to be accomplished, was "Harmony and Progress". Here one sees a complementary pair. Harmony means "space", the synchronic and paradigmatic dimension. Progress means "time", the diachronic, syntagmatic dimension. This binary set is composed according to a *yin/yang* logic, setting the issue for Korea and the world of creating a balance and a synthesis between harmony and progress. A second binary pair, Seoul/World, forms the center of complex semantic relations in the official motto of the Olympic Games. "Seoul Toward World, World Toward Seoul". Alternative English translations of the motto bring out the creative doubleness of the Korean verb form and the optative, subjunctive, and imperative possibilities of mood. "Let Seoul Come/Go Out to the World, Let the World Come/Go Out to Seoul"; or, from the point of view of Korean speakers, "Bring the World to Seoul, Send Seoul Out Into the World". In Dae-dae grammar, going and coming, bringing and sending are not opposed but two aspects of the same dialectical process. In the olympic and historical context, the Seoul/World pair is associated with further oppositions seeking mediation in the new order of things.

Seoul	**World**
Particularity	Universality
National History and Culture	Global History and Culture
"The Third World"	"The Advanced World"
Reality (Within the Barrier)	Ideal (Beyond all Barriers)

"Beyond all Barriers" was the title and the organizing theme of the Olympic Games Opening Ceremonies, whose scenario sought through Dae-dae cultural code to bring olympic universality and Korean particularity into dynamic, dialectical reciprocity and emergent harmony. To further appreciate how the various episodes of the ceremony were related grammatically and syntactically from a Korean point of view, an additional general feature of Dae-dae logic must be indicated. *Yang* and *yin* stand to one another as template to transformation. In *Figure 1*, this process is illustrated visually in the form of Korea's national *taeguk* symbol, omnipresent in the ceremonies as a kind of code key reminding all of the logic organizing them. Each template (*yang*), for example in a particular ceremony scene, calls out and joins with its transformation (*yin*), which in turn serves as template for a subsequent scene which incorporates its own transformation, and so on, in an endless series of transformations which are nonetheless harmonically balanced at each moment. Thus is created the simultaneous impression of movement and non-movement, or better, movement in non-movement and non-movement in movement, which is an essential feature of Korean aesthetics and their underlying ontologies, here especially Mahayana Buddhism. Also included in *Figure 1* is a more complete structural diagram of this East Asian cultural grammar, the full explication of which may be found in my book[18].

The Entry of the Olympic Flame into the Stadium

The arrival of the Olympic *song hwa* (sacred fire) is both the culmination of the earlier ritual process of the Greek flame-lighting and the torch relay across the host country and the high point of the official part of the Olympic Opening Ceremony in the stadium. A majority of Koreans watched the television coverage of the initial ceremony at Ancient Olympia in Greece, where the bringing down of the fire from Heaven to Earth through the medium of a female spiritual figure, the priestess of Hera, happened to match Korean cultural conceptions quite neatly. In Athens, the fire was handed over by Greek officials to a Korean delegation composed of representatives of all social strata and a famous Korean art troupe. Listening to the thousands of Greeks assembled in the Panathenaic stadium shouting "Korea-Seoul" led Korean commentators and audiences to search for connections between the Balkan and Korean peninsulas, two areas from opposite sides of the earth. The difference between East and West compares to the difference between day and night. As the Earth is round, one nation has daylight while the other has night, a constant cycling of life activity. Just as Ancient Greece was a point where East and West met, where Middle Eastern and Chinese wisdom were transmitted to Europe and European culture to the East, so too Korea has served and continues to serve as a crossroads between Asia and the West.

By representing the Hellenistic roots of European civilization, the olympic flame came to symbolize a kind of Western essence for Koreans, an essence now

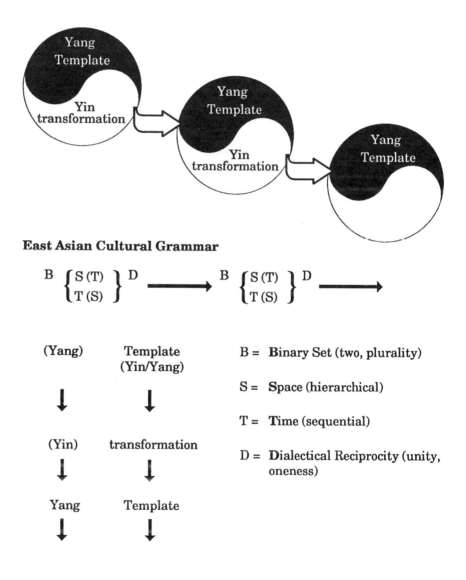

Figure 1.   Structural elements and significance of the **Dae-Dae** Cultural Grammar

willingly entrusted to Korea and accepted by her gratefully in equal partnership. Lingering Greek resentment of the American treatment of the flame on the occasion of the previous Los Angeles Olympic Games added a situational factor with Korean resonances as well. In 1988, this process of mutually respectful cooperation between East and West, Korea and Greece, could be seen in paired contrast with the earlier invasion of Korea by Western capitalism, iron ships and weaponry, followed by Christianity which treated the tradition of ancestor worship as superstition and thereby sought to destroy an integral East Asian cultural tradition. Koreans were reminded that the original Olympic Games were destroyed by the colonization of Greece from her west by Romans and Christians. Additional space/time complementarities and transformations were set into the logical motion of Dae-dae, for example, relations between the past measured in millennia and the changes of the late 20th century measured in decades, years, and days. Greek civilization, coming along Alexander's route along the Silk Road, took a hundred years to reach the center of Korean civilization, Kyongju and the Sokkuram Grotto. Now the flame as a symbol of Western civilization arrived on Korean soil overnight by airplane and was carried to these same centers by Korean torchbearers. As the olympic fire and flame ritual were Koreanized, Koreans were reminded of their past sufferings, of what adapting to the West had meant, and yet of how they had triumphed: the West need no longer represent military strength, but intercultural cooperation, peace, and harmony among civilizations newly portrayed as complementary and even equal[19].

In Seoul, the organizers faced the challenge of respecting and celebrating the universalizing olympic meanings of the sacred flame and the IOC's rigid protocol for its stadium arrival while at the same time adapting it through the Korean cultural code organizing the ceremony as a whole. As the flame had descended vertically from Heaven to Earth and then had been carried horizontally across the land of and by Human Society, so the linkages and boundary-openings between these three traditional Korean cosmological spaces and principles were continued and elaborated in new transformations in the stadium. The torch was carried into the arena by the "highly respected senior" (Korean Broadcast System commentary) Sohn Kee-chung, marathon gold medalist at the 1936 Berlin Olympic Games and nationalist hero for his powerful protest against the Japanese emblems he was forced to wear and listen to on the victory stand because of the colonial occupation. In the Seoul Opening Ceremonies, Mr. Sohn passed the torch to Lim Chun-ae, the young nineteen-year-old girl who was triple gold medalist at the 1986 Asian Games and was here "representing the female athletes of the country (*uri nara*)". Relations between senior/junior, male/female, past suffering/bright future, destruction/construction, imperialized and enslaved, Korea/free and autonomous Korea, were set into *yang/um* binary complementarity as well as into historical succession by the handing on of the torch from one generation to the next.

As the flame circled the stadium, the Korean broadcast commentary reproduced and emphasized the Dae-dae relation of dialectical contrast between the processes of destructive purification and constructive harmonization and blessing, the complementary relation between going out and coming in we saw earlier in discussing the olympic motto. "[The *song hwa* has] appeared in front of our eyes. The Sacred Flame, it will burn as a sacred flame ignited in every one of our hearts. The Sacred Flame will burn out evil and injustice, division and conflict, corruption and misfortune. It will bring goodness and peace, harmony and progress, prosperity, happiness, and material well-being".

Then, in the way of Dae-dae outlined above, a further transformation of these symbolic relations was achieved. It is visually diagrammed in *Figure 2*. The triad of Heaven, Earth, and Man was joined with and transformed into another triad. President Park Seh-jik of the SLOOC had always emphasized that Seoul must be the Olympic Games of academics, sport, and art, so as to be a Games of "total culture".

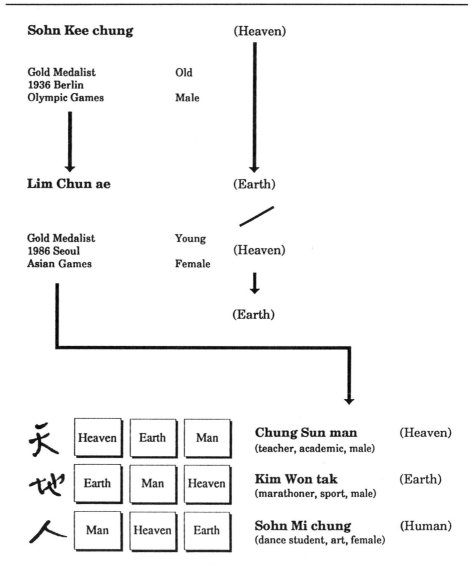

Figure 2. The **Dae-Dae** Cultural Grammar depicted in the episode of the Olympic Torch Relay: heaven, earth, human beings; academia, sports, arts.

At the base of the torch brazier, "designed by Mr. Kim Soo-keun . . . [in] the shape of the Korean traditional candle holder", Lim Chun-ae handed the flame to three torchbearers who would light the cauldron in unison. These were: Chung Sun-man (rural middle school teacher, academic, male), Kim Won-tak (marathoner/employee, sport, male), and Sohn Mi-chung (Korean traditional dance student, art, female). Next, as the KBS commentator solemnly described it: "The three are going up in a circular lift, twelve meters in diameter, climbing a stand twenty meters high as if they are going to heaven". The movement of the flame in Human hands back from Earth toward the Heaven from whence it came, thus symbolically completing its journey through traditional Korean cosmology, was in this way seamlessly joined with the wonders of modern technology, the contemporary pride in "firsts" ("the first time in olympic history that three participated in the kindling of the flame"), and the ooh-and-aah surprise and awe required by the modern spectacle for stadium and television audiences alike[20].

That the torch stand with its innovative mechanical apparatus itself further represented a joining of social elites and ordinary Koreans in sincere common effort was made plain in the later publication of Park Seh-jik's olympic memoirs in a series of newspaper articles. In the fifth installment, he recounted the efforts of the factory workers who made the flame pillar: "Fifteen men abstained from alcohol and made the pillar for the olympic fire at an iron foundry. Every day and night they worked... people volunteered for extended shifts". Park quotes his own words to the workers:

> Indeed, all of you have much work to do. Talking about the Olympics may seem to you as if it is talk of great and magnificent things for splendid and great people to take part in. But this is not the whole story. Little things put together, including the thing you are working on now, create the Olympics. Of all the Olympic facilities and constructions, the making of this most sacred pillar for the Olympic fire on this foundry's dirt floor has the deepest meaning. I ask you to make it with the utmost sincerity[21].

While President Park's commentaries on "The Ceremonies: An Integration of Heaven, Earth, and Man" were published after the event, Western broadcasters and press journalists were provided in advance with a detailed scenario containing these exegeses and interpretations of the ceremonies by the scholars and artists who designed them[22]. My colleagues on this panel will describe the degree to which foreign broadcasters chose to communicate these Korean explanations to their Western audiences, or instead substituted their own interpretations. As you consider these research results, you are urged to keep in mind the difference between explaining particular vignettes and symbols and communicating the cultural code which organized them into a whole from the Korean point of view.

Understandably, the KBS broadcasters stuck quite closely to the scenarists own interpretations. This was not only because they were "official", "authoritative", and "scholarly" but also because the deep Dae-dae cultural grammar in its three aspects of hierarchy, groupness, and ritual drama was—at some level and among the other cultural codes present—recognizable and comprehensible to KBS broadcasters as Koreans. As the cameras focused on the olympic flame billowing from the cauldron toward the sky, the announcer concluded the segment by saying: "The global village stage, the epic drama performed by the entire global family. Its highlight is the kindling of the Sacred Flame. The Sacred Flame is focusing everyone's eyes on one point and also bringing everyone's mind and spirit into one mind and spirit. Now we must all be one. Now we must all be together". Again, this is Dae-dae, the generation of the one from the many and unity from diversity through a series of transformations of binary oppositions, here reaching out to encompass not only a particular ground of common Korean understanding but also the idioms of a universalizing global culture embodied in the Olympic Games. For a moment, in other words, the World/Seoul opposition is transcended.

But, as prescribed by Dae-dae logic, things rest only for a moment and then the process begins again. Being begets becoming, as moving beyond boundaries begets a new awareness of boundaries, as *yang* begets *yin*. The conclusion, with the flame-lighting, of the "official" olympic part of the ceremonies begins again the host country's cultural performances, the boundary between the two being marked by the exit of the assembled athletes from the stadium. From the project of discovering and representing the Korean in the Olympic, the challenge for the ceremonies designers shifts to representing the Global in the Korean. And the challenge for foreign broadcasters and mass media consumers shifts to seeing and understanding something deeper and more substantive than "pretty dances and folklore" in these representations of Korean culture.

A New Dawn and Chaos

The segment called "A Great Day"—with its *Kang-bok* (Blessings from Heaven), *Cha-il* (Sunshade), and *Hwagwanmu* (Flower Crown) dances, the parachutists descent, and the *Hondon* (Chaos) performance—reproduces in various keys the paradigmatic code of Heaven, Earth, and Man. At the same time, the active opening of the boundaries and mediation among these realms is composed into a syntagmatic narrative of a cosmological drama. The KBS announcer's first comment invokes a mythological state of being: "At the beginning when the world opened, a great day when all mankind lived together peacefully is depicted in this scene. This [*kang-bok*] dance is praying for heavenly blessing and expressing earthly joy upon receiving mysterious forces from heaven". The announcer immediately proceeds to name the choreographers and composer and to identify the 800 dancers as students from the Yeungdeungpo Girls' High School, thus juxtaposing primordial time and contemporary time, transhistorical cultural imagery on the level of the ritual code and the creative invention of tradition on the level of the historical performance.

These temporal contrasts and complementarities are joined with spatial ones according to the formula of Dae-dae logic diagrammed in *Figure 1*. Prayers go up to Heaven from a joyful Earth through the agency of the female dancers. Blessings then come down from Heaven to Earth in the form of the male parachutists, bearing the colors of traditional Korean shamanic ritual which happen also to be the colors of the rings in the olympic emblem. The parachutists are not only Korean but multinational, and they land to form the olympic rings with a first surrounding circle of all-Korean female dancers, which is in turn encompassed by the ring of multinational stadium spectators both male and female, which is in turn encompassed by the wider circle of the global television audience. In these symbolic ways, the global, the national, and the local are once again placed into moving harmony through transformative association with the Heaven, Earth, and Man triad through the agency of Dae-dae cultural grammar. Human society is representationally cosmologized, while a traditional Korean cosmology is revitalized under contemporary and particular social conditions. "Korean Fantasia", the musical accompaniment to the parachutists' descent from Heaven, joins Korean idioms with Western symphonic form and incorporates themes from the Korean national anthem. Korean national aspirations and political independence are thus marked and asserted in a way which represents them as in harmony with the global order represented by the olympic gathering. Just as the nationalist aspirations of a particular society are encompassed within a world of nations, so too the military references of the parachutes, skyjumpers, and helicopters are performatively domesticated and encompassed by civil society represented by the dancers who flowingly engulf them on the field.

This leads to another visual and semantic transformation, this time of high technology to local festivity, physical danger to domestic sociability. As the KBS announcer said: "Eight hundred *Cha-il* dancers are performing a Blessing Dance, welcoming the high-altitude skydivers. The parachutes are seemingly transformed into *Cha-il* [sunshades] by the dancers' blue sheets [of cloth]. Whenever, there is a festival, we prepare for it with *Cha-il*. A billowing *Cha-il* means heavenly blessing and represents the excitement of man's mind brought about by the festival. The entire field is full with blowing *Cha-il*, like a sea of *Cha-il*". Though not mentioned by the KBS announcers, the scenario exegesis provided to all broadcasters clearly mentions a further reference intended by the designers. The *Cha-il* were intended additionally to evoke the smaller cloths with which Koreans wrap and carry parcels, an ubiquitous feature of Korean everyday life. Thus through the material symbol of squares of cloth, the interpenetration of ritual drama and everyday life was carried out through the mediation of popular festivity.

The Flower Crown Dance (*hwagwanmu*) which followed in the sequence reproduces the configuration of space/time meanings all over again, but in another transformation of context. *Hwagwanmu* is a court dance, probably Korea's most famous and most performed, invoking the past of dynastic kingship as well as the present Korean efforts at cultural preservation and revitalization. Again, the KBS announcer marks this paired relation by first identifying by name the present choreographers and composer of the dance, and the dancers themselves by their school affiliation. (In Korean practice, these public acknowledgements always convey the competitive struggle for distinction and honor). Then he proceeds to point out that: "Hwagwan dance as a court dance is characterized by its strong emphasis on ritual and self-control. The costumes, hair decorations, and various props of the dancers express the typical decorative traditions. The colors used in the dance come from the traditional color combination in *Tanchung* (red and blue), *Samtaeguk* (Triple Taichi), and *Saekdong* (Children's multicolored dress)".

The court dance was usually performed around the king, who mediates between Heaven and Earth in traditional conception. Without the one mediating person, there can be no synthesis of two opposite poles. The highly stylized movement of the dance and music invoke the dignity and richness of Korea's recorded cultural history, thus standing in conceptual juxtaposition to the fantasized primordial time which opened the whole segment while moving its narrative along. Of course, the king is today absent, and thus the past is once more juxtaposed with the present, destruction with construction, an abiding cultural code with the search for a new model of political legitimacy in contemporary Korea. Again, in Dae-dae form, struggle and order, yes and no, are conceived not in either/or relation but as dialectical aspects of the same process of transformation.

The following *Hondon* performance, quite unique in olympic ceremonial history, transforms these relationships by turning them inside out. In *Hwagwanmu*, struggle is concealed within stylized ritual order; in *Hondon*, order is hidden with chaos. The KBS commentator announces this change in the narrative context of the overall performative construction. "Now the Golden Ages are gone, the Age of Chaos is coming where discord and conflict are dominant". Tranquility is smashed by dancers, mostly male, racing madly around carrying affixed to poles "838 masks consisting of 108 various kinds from 60 different countries", even breaking the boundaries between performers and audience by running up into the stands. "This masked dance", the announcer continues, "symbolizes chaotic dances representing respectively good and evil, love and hatred, creation and destruction, and antagonism and division emanating from different values and personalities. Discord emerged from conflict among different ideologies, ethnicity, and sex".

Openly acknowledged here are the powerful boundaries, discords, misunderstandings, and dangers among all the different cultures brought together into common activity in the Olympic Games, the other side of the olympic project of harmony and peace, the realism necessarily to be paired with the idealism. For Koreans, the performance invokes all the invasions from outside in past history, the darker and more terrifying sides of opening the country to the world in the context of the Olympic Games, and more generally the doubts and fears of the new world Koreans must now enter and be entered by. Even aestheticized in a cultural performance, this episode is a daring acknowledgement of the dangers and difficulties of the projects of global intercultural communication and of "Seoul to the World, The World To Seoul". But Dae-dae demands that darkness be dramatically represented with light, evil with good, chaos with harmony, destruction with construction, otherwise true completion and unity cannot be achieved.

Dae-dae grammar also shows the way out of the chaos. If *Hondon* forms the *yin* transformation of the *yang* template of the previous representations of cosmic and global harmony, in the next transformation *Hondon* becomes the *yang* template calling out its own *yin* complement in a new balance. At the very top of the stadium, new masks rise to look down on the dance, taking top place in a vertical hierarchy. The KBS announcer points them out as the cameras focus upward: "Above the roof of the stadium, the typical Korean masks, Chuyong (the legendary figure in the Shilla Kingdom), Mukchung (Buddhist monk), Maldooki (young man), Yangban (traditional upper class), Halmi (grandmother), Toryung (upper class youth) and Musam (servant) are watching. Over the fence they are watching us while we are also watching the mask dance". Here many meanings are assembled through deployment in Dae-dae form of the categorical pair watching/being watched. Unmoving, much larger than the other masks, and situated hierarchically above them, the roof masks are comfortingly familiar features of the mask dances of traditional Korean folk culture. They assert a confidence in the power of indigenous Korean culture to domesticate, contain, and encompass the shock of invasion by and new relations with so many strange and foreign cultures. Added to the conflict between nation and inter-nation is now the above-nation which mediates and begins to bring harmony once again to the chaos. The roof masks also belong with the field masks as together opposed to and watching all the people from different ideologies, ethnicities, and sexes, an assertion perhaps of the power of universally shared cultural forms—indigenous ones like masks, emergent ones like the Olympic Games—to balance social division and overcome it in a new, higher-order for transcending boundaries. As the announcer comments to the Korean television audience, "The world of chaos is waning. Our will is toward overcoming this chaos".

The Challenge of Intercultural Communication

Of course, the Opening Ceremony did not end here. The next episode was the mass taekwando performance, presented as returning order to human chaos and representing the breaking of political, ideological, and social boundaries, "the brick walls" as the scenario puts it, in the dramatic form of the taekwandoists, old and young, male and female, smashing hundreds of boards. This performance introduced further transformations of semantic relations between Korea and the world, sport and art, discipline and creativity again according to the logic of Korean Dae-dae cultural grammar deployed alongside, but also as a metacode organizing and perhaps even encompassing, other logics more familiar to Westerners.

In these ceremonies, Koreans interpreted the new olympic world to themselves while at the same time inventively portraying the new situation of Korea in the world. The representations by which this was accomplished were a mix of scholarly and artistic adaptation, invention, bricolage, and historicism. In so doing, Koreans remobilized and revitalized their traditional cultural code as the main mechanism by which diverse cultural elements were combined into a coherent, beautiful, and moving whole, impressive to outsiders and recognizable to insiders. I have tried to show in the analysis of selected performance episodes how Dae-dae cultural grammar provided the logic of coherence linking the various segments into a whole that was unified structurally and paradigmatically as well as narratively and syntagmatically.

The ceremonies designers sought to create an event that was first and foremost international, while creatively accommodating national and transnational meanings within it. What remains is to estimate how foreign broadcasters responded to these messages, what they were willing or able to perceive, understand, and communicate to their respective audiences. How much of the explicitly Korean character of the performance came into focus in foreign coverage? How much use did foreign media make of the carefully prepared scenario interpretation provided to them in advance by the Korean organizers? Did broadcasters translate the ceremonies into their own cultural codes and idioms to such a degree that their commentaries suppressed and replaced Koreans' attempts to translate and communicate their culture to the world? In more technical and sophisticated ways, one must look for patterns in the complex project of translation and mistranslation of culture. For example, was narrative emphasized at the expense of structure, melody over harmony? Did foreign broadcasters recognize the presence of a distinct East Asian cultural code in the performance, or did they treat it as perfectly transparent to Western logics alone? How with reference to the Korean meanings did Western national broadcasts differ from one another?

These questions bear an importance beyond the communication of the Seoul Games alone. Only by such comparative research can the success of the Olympic Movement in intercultural communication and mutual understanding, its highest aims, truly be evaluated. Translation and communication of cultures will be of increasing importance in the new world order. Through the Opening Ceremonies, Koreans offered an alternative cultural code to peoples both East and West, North and South, for coping with the many problems of the 21st century. In considering whether the mass media contribute to or interfere with the process of exchange of cultural resources, one should not forget that television audiences are not passive consumers of the interpretations broadcasters explicitly provide. Audiences bring their own resources to decoding the messages inherent in what they see and hear through the media. Perhaps the mass appeal of the Seoul Olympic Games Opening Ceremonies to world audiences was based in part on their recognition of and interest in the presence of a different cultural code, even where broadcasters themselves failed to articulate it.

NOTES AND REFERENCES

1. Mulling C (1990) Dissidents' critique of the 1988 Seoul Olympics. In Koh B-i (ed) Toward one world beyond all barriers. Vol I Keynote speeches; Cultural exchange and Cultural Nationalism. The Seoul Olympiad Anniversary Conference. Seoul Olympic Sports Promotion Foundation. Seoul: Poong Nam p 394-407

2. See MacAloon [this volume]

3. Kang S-p, MacAloon JJ, DaMatta R (eds) (1988) The Olympics and cultural exchange. Seoul: Hanyang University Institute for Ethnological Studies. Koh B-i (ed) (1990) Toward one world beyond all barriers. Vol I II III The Seoul Olympiad Anniversary Conference. Seoul Olympic Sports Promotion Foundation. Seoul: Poong Nam. [A further volume of papers by international scholars collaborating on this topic is in preparation: MacAloon JJ, Kang S-p (eds) The 1988 Seoul Olympic Games: intercultural perspectives]

4. For a detailed account, see Walker Dilling M (1990) The familiar and the foreign: music as medium of exchange in the Seoul olympic ceremonies. In Koh B-i (ed) (1990) Toward one world beyond all barriers. Vol I Keynote speeches; Cultural exchange and Cultural Nationalism. The Seoul Olympiad Anniversary Conference. Seoul Olympic Sports Promotion Foundation. Seoul: Poong Nam p 357-77. Also see Kim M-h (1988) The aesthetic character of the Olympic Opening and Closing Ceremonies. In Hand in hand, beyond all barriers. Seoul: Korean Broadcasting System (1988). ["Kae-P'yehwoe Shik ui Mihakchok Songgyok," Son e Son Chapko, Pyogul Nomoso. Seoul: Hanguk Pangsong Saopdan (1988)]

5. This understanding of hierarchy is thus quite different from the commonsense meaning of simple inequality given the term in Western cultures. See Kapferer B (1988) Legends of people, myths of state. Washington: Smithsonian Institution Press

6. Kang S-p (1988) Korean culture, the olympic and world order. In Kang S-p, MacAloon JJ, DaMatta R (eds) The Olympics and cultural exchange. Seoul: Hanyang University Institute for Ethnological Studies p 97-99

7. Turner V (1977) The ritual process. Ithaca: Cornell University Press

8. Brown R (1964) Discussion of the conference. In Romney AK, D'Andrade RG (eds) Transcultural studies in cognition. American Anthropologist 66 II 243-53

9. Gernet J (1968) Ancient China: from the beginning to the Empire. Berkeley: University of California Press. Chang K-c (1968) The archeology of ancient China. New Haven: Yale University Press. Granet M (1959) Danse et légendes de la Chine ancienne. Paris: Presses Universitaires de France

10. Eberhard W (1965) Conquerors and rulers: social forces in medieval China. Leiden: Brill

11. Gernet J (1968) op cit p 51-52

12. Kang S-p (1972) The East Asian culture and its transformation in the West. Seoul: Seoul National University American Studies Institute

13. Kang S-p (1988) op cit p 86-91

14. Kim M-h (1988) op cit

15. Our position, therefore, is neither exactly that of "the modernity of tradition" [eg Rudolph L, Rudolph S (1984) The modernity of tradition: political development in India. Chicago: University of Chicago Press] nor that of "the invention of tradition" [eg Hobsbawm E, Ranger T (eds) (1983) The invention of tradition. Cambridge: Cambridge University Press], neither of which consider the level of cultural codes and ontologies while preserving in different ways the opposition between culture authentic and invented. For other recent anthropological attempts to break out of this straightjacket, see Wagner R (1981) The invention of culture. Chicago: Chicago University Press. Herzfeld M (1982) Ours once more: folklore, ideology, and the making of modern Greece. Austin: University of Texas Press. Kapferer B (1988) op cit

16. Kapferer B (1988) op cit p 3-48

17. Walker Dilling M (1990) op cit

18. Kang S-p (1972) op cit

19. My colleague John MacAloon and I made a special study of the Korean torch relays for the Asian Games in 1986 and the Olympic Games in 1988, traveling day after day with the flame as it made its progress around the Korean peninsula. Our analysis of the Koreanization of this Western ritual form and its connection with the social and political transformation of Korea will be the subject of a separate monograph [in preparation]

20. See MacAloon JJ (1984) Olympic Games and the theory of spectacle in modern societies. In MacAloon JJ (ed) Rite, drama, spectacle, festival: rehearsals toward a theory of culture performance. Philadelphia: ISHI Press. [In MacAloon's categories, the special achievement of the designers of the Seoul Opening Ceremonies was their successful integration of the performance genres of ritual and spectacle]

21. Translated by the present author from the Korean text. A slightly different translation will be found in the English version in Park S-j (1990) The stories of Seoul Olympics. Seoul: Chosun-Ilbo p 14-15

22. Seoul Olympic Organizing Committee (1988) Beyond all barriers: the opening and closing ceremonies. Seoul: SLOOC

Spanish Television (TVE)
and the Coverage of the Opening Ceremony
of the 1988 Seoul Olympic Games

Miquel de Moragas i Spà

This presentation deals with the Spanish Television (TVE) coverage of some episodes from the Seoul Olympic Games Opening Ceremony. It is part of an international comparative study of television coverage of that Ceremony[1]. The main subject of the present report is the verbal component of the television discourse. Accordingly, a transcript of the relevant portions of audio commentary is presented further on. Of necessity, the verbal discourse is discussed in the context of visual elements and natural sound which form the other major components of the telecast. The sample analyzed consists of four fragments, with a total duration of 27 minutes 12 seconds, selected from the approximately three-hour Opening Ceremony. They are: "The Lighting of the Olympic Flame," [Episode #14] "Prayer of Blessing and *Cha-il* Dance," [Episode #18] *"Hwakwan* Dance," [Episode #19] and *Hondon* (Chaos) [Episode #20]."

The content analysis of open and complex discourses, such as the one which concerns us here, should begin by establishing specific semantic fields which permit the subsequent interpretation of their multiple meanings. In this instance we have arrived at these semantic fields through a double procedure:

– from the text itself, enumerating and ordering all the thematic references which appear in the verbal discourse of the sample under analysis.

– from experiences that are external to the text, proposing a semantic field for the evaluative interpretation of the (Olympic) event under analysis.

This double approximation is essential in order to be able to recognize not only what is said in the text but also what is not said in it.

After determining the four fragments of the opening ceremony which were to be studied and making a transcription of the verbal discourse we proceeded to a

Miquel de Moragas i Spà, Center for Olympic Studies and University of Barcelona, Barcelona, Spain.

preliminary identification and quantification of the basic components of the sound track. They fall into the following categories, as detailed in *Table 1*:

– Verbal discourse
  – scripted
  – impromptu
– Straight sound without superimposed verbal material
– Commercial advertizing.

TABLE 1

**Quantification of components of auditory discourse
Seoul Olympic Games Opening Ceremony
Spanish Television (TVE)**

Selected fragments or episodes # 14, # 18, # 19, # 20	Duration Minutes/seconds		%	
# 14 The lighting of the olympic flame				
Verbal discourse	4:57		87.3	
Scripted (following scenario)		1:39		(33.3)
Impromptu		3:18		(66.7)
Direct sound	0:43		12.6	
Total for the episode	5:40			
# 18 Prayer of Blessing				
Verbal discourse	5:52		57.4	
Scripted (following scenario)		1:39		(28.0)
Impromptu		4:13		(72.0)
Direct sound	4:21		42.6	
Total for the episode	10:13			
# 19 Hwakwan				
Verbal discourse	0:56		13.4	
Scripted (following scenario)		0:40		(71.0)
Impromptu		0:16		(29.0)
Direct sound	6:02		86.6	
Total for the episode	6:58			
# 20 Chaos				
Verbal discourse	2:23		55.0	
Scripted (following scenario)		0:33		(23.0)
Impromptu		1:50		(77.0)
Direct sound	1:58		45.0	
Total for the episode	4:21			
Summary				
Verbal discourse	14:08		52.0	
Scripted (following scenario)		4:31		(32.0)
Impromptu		9:37		(68.0)
Direct sound	3:04		48.0	
Advertising	0:0		0:0	
Total for the episodes	**27:12**			

Note: The quantification of these periods was obtained by statistical extrapolation of the time taken to read the text; the results are therefore only approximate.

Having established these preliminary blocks, and after a process of several phases in which thematic hypotheses were set up and verified, we achieved a thematic classification, shown in *Table 2*, which we consider valid for each and every utterance in the discourse.

TABLE 2

**Thematic classification of the verbal discourse
Seoul Olympic Games Opening Ceremony
Spanish Television (TVE)**

Themes/sub-themes of relevance to 1988 Seoul Opening Ceremony	Number of references		
	Sub-theme	Total	%
1. Olympic/Olympism		7	8.4
Olympism: anecdotal and subordinate			
Olympic flame	1		
Olympic symbols			
Seoul 88 symbol	1		
Olympic rings	1		
Olympic torch			
Bearers of the flame	1		
Manner of arrival (in Korea)	1		
Greek origin	1		
Ascent to flame-holder by lift	1		
2. Korea/Korean		11	13.3
Korea, destination of the torch	1		
Toponyms, proper names	5		
Koreans			
Bearer of the torch	1		
Maker of the cauldron	1		
Parachutists	2		
Attitude of spectators	1		
3. Development of spectacle		41	49.4
Trivial anecdotes	13		
Surprises of the spectacle	2		
Comparison with rehearsal	4		
Announcing scenes (as scenario)	4		
Impressiveness of spectacle			
Dimensions of cauldron	1		
Number of cameras	2		
Technology of spectacle	5		
Participants in spectacle			
Aviators and parachutists	5		
Others	2		
Organisation	3		
4. Presenters		9	10.8
Previous experience of presenter	4		
Complacency	4		
Television images	1		
5. History of the Olympics		2	2.4
Epics with national reference	1		
Epics without national reference	1		
6. Cultural aspects		11	13.3
Western culture (technology)	1		
Significance of scenes (from scenario)	4		
Interpretation "sui generis"	6		
7. International relations		2	2.4
United States (parachutists)	2		
Total	**83**		

It has been possible, therefore, to classify the whole sample under seven basic themes:

1 Olympic/Olympism, 2 Korea/Korean, 3 Development of the spectacle, 4 References to the commentators themselves, 5 History of the Games, 6 Cultural aspects, 7 International relations.

These basic themes subsume a total of 25 sub-themes.

A Proposed Semantic Field for the Evaluative Interpretation of an Olympic Event

The aim of our analysis was to shed light on the adaptation of the television discourse of the Opening Ceremony to the values or countervalues attributed to Olympism in contemporary society. For this it was necessary to analyse the text proper, yet also to analyse thematic absences in the text.

Given the limits of the sample, the results obtained on "what the text does not say" have to be considered as only indicative. However, a study of a fragment of such significance in the olympic symbolism as the entry of the torch and lighting of the flame allows us to extrapolate results to the whole of the television coverage of the olympic events. The analysis at least enables us to discover some of the basic structures of the production of the discourse and some especially significant absences. For this purpose we propose a semantic field which contains eight major themes, relating to the cultural values of sport and the Olympic Games in modern society[2] (*Table 3*).

TABLE 3

**Semantic field of cultural values of Olympic Games
Some elements for a comparative international content-
analysis of the Television coverage of the Opening Ceremony**

Culture

- National/Infranational culture
- National/Infranational language(s)
- Community values
- Religious values
- Music
- Fine/Performing Arts
- etc.

Host City

- Organizational aspects
- Administrative aspects
- Hospitality
- etc.

Sportsmanship

- Sport and fair-play
- Impartiality in sport
- Sport and violence
- etc.

Internationalism

- The idea of consensus
- The idea of fraternity
- The idea of solidarity
- The idea of mutual understanding and respect
- The idea of peace
- etc.

Sport and Society

- Athletes and the supra-normal
- Athletes and health
- Sport and sponsorship
- Sport and entertainment
- Sport and gender
- etc.

Structure and Themes of the Auditory Discourse

The discourse of Spanish Television (TVE) had the following broad characteristics:

– total absence of commercials (0%);

– important presence of direct sound, from the stadium without commentary or superpositions (48% of total time);

– basic distinction between two forms of content in the verbal discourse: "impromptu discourse" and "scripted discourse".

By "scripted discourse" we mean that which uses the official scenario to interpret or present the spectacle[3]. The time devoted to this form of discourse represents 16.6% of the total analysed and 32% of the total verbal discourse. By "impromptu discourse" we mean that which does not use the official scenario for the spectacle, and which evolves spontaneously through association of ideas and is relaxed, informal or trivial in style. The time devoted to this discourse represents 35% of the total analyzed and up to 68% of the total verbal discourse.

Table 2 shows the themes dealt with in the discourse. In quantitative terms the most common thematic area is that relating to the development of the spectacle, with 41 references, representing 49% of the total discourse. Of these, 19 (23%) are unimportant comments and 13 (15.6%) are admiring references to the technology of the spectacle. The second most common themes are references to "Korea/Korean" and to "cultural aspects". Their importance however is only relative. The references to "Korea/Korean", a total of 11 (13.3%), are descriptive and non-evaluative. The references to "cultural aspects", also a total of 11 (13.3%), are especially weak in genuinely cultural content. Six of them have been qualified as "sui generis" because they were judged void of a cultural basis.

The great absence from the discourse analyzed is precisely "Olympism", with only 7 references (8.4%). These limited references are either anecdotal and subordinate, or purely descriptive (torch, symbol) without evaluative or historical reference. References to the presenters themselves and to the station (TVE), 9 references (10.8%), outnumber those to "Olympism". In *Table 3*, we propose a semantic field for assessing the presence or absence of some of the chief positive values of Olympism and sport. For this purpose we propose five "items", with various sub-categories: "Culture", "Internationalism", "Host City", "Sport and Society", "Sportsmanship". It turns out then that in the analysis of the verbal discourse no explicit reference to any of these semantic fields can be found, and there are only a few references to the folklore of the local culture, which we do not classify as evaluative since they are confined to describing the movements of the performers, or an occasional irrelevant comment, supposedly humorous, on the hairstyle of the dancers.

Conclusions and Recommendations

With respect to the content-analysis

Limited references to Olympism: the references to Olympism were very limited. When they appeared they were associated with trivial or descriptive concerns. In the analyzed sample there was not a single reference to the universal values of Olympism.

Scant attention to Korean culture: positive evaluations or evaluative references were focussed on and limited to the wonders of technology and there was no comment on or evaluation of the cultural or aesthetic considerations of the spectacle. The television coverage did not contribute to the interpretation of human cultures as plural phenomena. Western culture was taken as the measure of all culture.

Neither fraternity nor internationalism: despite what was proposed by the scenario of the opening ceremony, the television commentators did not use the opportunity of emphasizing fraternity and internationalism.

Triviality of the impromptu discourse: the greater part of the verbal discourse consisted of content evoked by the impromptu discourse, which was, in the main, trivial and anecdotal.

Which respect to the overall structure of the discourse

More interest in Spanish Television (TVE) than in Spain: in the fragments analyzed no reference could be found to Spain; on the other hand, various self-congratulatory references to the television cameras (TVE) could be identified, and the part played by the presenters was stressed.

Presentation and description, but no interpretation of the scenes: the commentators, and especially the female commentator, announced the various phases of the ceremony. At other moments the development of the spectacle was described, with the aid of the scenario. But these presentations and comments did not usually go beyond the descriptive level, even when they repeated Korean toponyms and names. One could also emphasize the lack of interpretative comments to enable Spanish viewers to understand concepts formulated from the viewpoint of a Korean culture which was alien and unknown to most viewers.

Lack of commercial breaks: it is important to emphasize the absence of commercial breaks on TVE during the long transmission of the Opening Ceremony. This absence of breaks is due partly to the time of transmission, early morning in Spain, but also to the general criteria of European television for events of this nature.

Direct image and sound: the most effective part of the TVE transmission was precisely its long silences. It should be emphasized that up to 48% of the transmission time was devoted to direct sound. These periods without commentary coincided with the moments of greatest beauty in the spectacle. Thanks to these silences the Spanish audience, without assistance but also without interruption from the commentators, was able to interpret freely the polysemy of the ceremony.

Implications for a future olympic broadcasting policy

Competent journalists: the commentary on an event of such complexity as an Opening Ceremony should be entrusted to a professional team which is competent in various fields, principally the history of the Olympic Movement, international relations, and the culture of the host country.

Guides for the ceremony: the organizing committees should provide accredited journalists with both complete versions and brief summaries of the programme for the ceremony, with capsular information on the content and principal significance of each scene.

Regulated spaces for publicity: although Spanish Television dit not include any commercial break during the transmission of the Opening Ceremony in Seoul, the nature of international television makes it necessary to plan suitable spaces for publicity which will not interfere with the proper substance and logic of the spectacle.

It is strongly recommended that the entities responsible for the Opening Ceremony—IOC, OGOC—establish minimum norms for the transmission of the ceremonies, to avoid their devaluation or distortion by forms of television logic which may be alien to the ideals and values of Olympism.

NOTES AND REFERENCES

1. This study forms part of the international comparative study directed by Professor John MacAloon with parts presented at this Quebec City Symposium *Sport... The Third Millennium*.

2. This is an adaptation of my proposal put forward in de Moragas i Spà M (1990) Mass media, olympic values and the Opening Ceremony. In Koh B-i (ed) Toward one world beyond all barriers. Vol I Keynote speeches; Cultural exchange and Cultural Nationalism. The Seoul Olympiad Anniversary Conference. Seoul Olympic Sports Promotion Foundation. Seoul: Poong Nam p 455-473

3. It is important to note the existence and availability of an ample dossier provided by the organization of the Games to all accredited journalists. Seoul Olympic Organizing Committee (1988) Scenario for the Opening and Closing Ceremonies. Commentary for broadcast and press materials. Seoul: SLOOC

Commercial Imperatives:
NBC's Construction
of the Seoul Olympic Games
Opening Ceremony

James F. Larson

This analysis deals with NBC Television's construction of selected episodes from the Seoul Olympic Games Opening Ceremony. The four hour NBC telecast was broadcast live beginning at 8:00 p.m. in the Eastern time zones of the US, an "advantage" for viewers that was duly noted by co-anchor Bryant Gumble in the opening minutes of the program.

The NBC telecast assumes a special importance among all of the international broadcasts that comprised the global television spectacle for several reasons. First, as the largest rights-holder, NBC paid 302 million dollars for the exclusive rights to televise the Games to its US audience, approximately three-quarters of the total rights fees paid for the Seoul Olympic Games. With such commercial dominance came certain prerogatives and priorities for NBC *vis-à-vis* the host broadcaster, KBS/SORTO and other international broadcasting organizations in the process of planning and shaping both its own opening ceremony telecast and the international television signal. Second, as an American commercial television network, NBC presented an important contrast as concerns the task of broadcasting operations that were government controlled, non-commercial or less commercially oriented in their approach to the telecasts of the Seoul Olympic Games. Third, the NBC telecast is of particular interest in retrospect because of the public controversy over the network's coverage which surfaced in Korea during the Games. Several separate occurences fed into anti-NBC and anti-American sentiment. One was NBC's coverage of the boxing incident in which Korean team officials attacked a referee and a losing Korean boxer staged a 67-minute sit-in protest in the ring. Many Koreans viewed the coverage as overly extensive and harsh in tone. Another was the network's coverage of the alleged theft of a lion mask from a hotel bar by two US swimmers[1].

The analysis addresses most directly the content of selected episodes of the NBC telecast, but does so with the intent of drawing better inferences about the construction of the television of the Games and the new roles of such

1890
1990

James F. Larson, School of Communications, University of Washington, Seattle, Washington, USA.

constructions in contemporary cultural exchange. The paper concludes with a discussion of several direct implications for a broadcasting policy with respect to the Olympic Games.

The Olympic Games as Media-constructed Spectacle

The attractiveness of conceptual perspectives which view phenomena as media constructed realities increases in proportion to the pervasiveness of media as epitomized today by the global reach of television. For example, Edelman chooses to view politics as a continual construction and reconstruction of social problems, crises, enemies, and leaders by the media and influential publics[2]. The same epistemological approach can and ought to be applied more widely to the contemporary Olympic Games. By all measures, the proportions of the televised spectacle have come to dwarf those of the spectacle as experienced by the athletes, officials and spectators physically present for the Games. Although precise estimates are difficult, the Seoul Olympic Games Opening Ceremony was unquestionably viewed by the largest audience to date in the history of television, possibly exceeding one billion[3]. Perhaps the most telling indicator is that of the number of broadcast personnel in Seoul. Foreign and domestic holders of broadcast rights assembled 10 360 accredited staff members to televise the Seoul Olympic Games[4]. Together with a smaller number of representatives of other media, they exceeded the total count of athletes and officials participating in the games. In these and other respects, the Seoul Olympic Games tested the upper limits for the size of international broadcast operations.

Negotiation of a Third Culture

This approach to the Olympic Games as a media-constructed spectacle draws on Tehranian's observation that human communication always involves the transformation of meaning in a cultural medium through which sender and receiver communicate. In intercultural communication, the sender and receiver "[. . .] often have to negotiate on the invention of a third meaning system, a third culture, in order to communicate. In reality, this has led to a global transcultural communication system that borrows heavily from the dominant world cultures[5]."

The modern Olympic Games represent such a system as does broadcasting more generally. It is now well recognized by communication researchers that Anglo-American media have exerted a strong influence on the development of broadcasting organizations, routines and norms around the world. In similar fashion, it appears that the television of the Olympic Games may reflect the strong influence of those American networks which have covered the Games in recent years.

The Main Actors or "Publics" Involved

As in political communication more generally, media constructions of Olympic Ceremonies and sport are created by television and the other media through the efforts of concerned "publics" or constituencies. In Seoul, the most influential of these actors were the International Olympic Committee (IOC), the Seoul Olympic Organizing Committee (SLOOC), the host broadcaster (KBS/SORTO), and as noted above, the international broadcasters led by NBC.

The IOC increasingly recognizes the power of television as a transcultural meaning system and attempts to control certain aspects of that system. The Olympic Charter dictates that the IOC shall secure the widest possible audience for the Olympic Games. It also declares that all of the central visual symbols of the Olympic Movement are the property of the IOC and directs that the international television signal be produced "[. . .] in an objective and universal manner so as not to concentrate on athletes from one or several countries, but rather to cover the events with the impartiality required by an international audience[6]".

In short, the planning and construction of the NBC's Opening Ceremony telecast as a third culture or meaning system was a negotiated process involving the IOC and its interests in conveying certain universal olympic symbols, the host city with its interest in portraying Korea and its culture to the world, and NBC with its own requirements and the American audience in mind. Key questions revolve around an assessment of which parts of the telecast were "global" as reflected in the international television signal (visual coverage with natural sound) and which were more "localized" by NBC to suit the American culture and its commercial imperatives.

The NBC Construction of Selected Episodes of the Opening Ceremony

The Seoul Olympic Games Opening Ceremony was from its inception planned with an integral role for television in mind. It was principally through television that Korea would show "Seoul to the World." Several episodes, in particular, highlight the important role of the medium.

Sohn Kee-chung Enters the Stadium

Although relatively short in duration, the entry of the olympic torch into the main stadium carried by Sohn Kee-chung was infused with symbolism and was, from a political communication perspective, one of the most powerful moments in the global telecast from Seoul. Unlike most other telecasts which relied on the international television signal, NBC's coverage must be described in the context of the opening quarter-hour of the entire telecast which placed heavy emphasis on building up suspense and providing background for the entry of the olympic torch into the stadium.

The Opening Ceremony telecast by NBC started with hosts Bryant Gumbel and Dick Enberg setting the scene and discussing such topics as the weather, security and the record-setting attendance at the Games. After the first commercial break, less than nine minutes into the telecast, they asked the question of who would carry the olympic torch into the stadium and then introduced two "Olympics Past" features. The first of these ran under two minutes in length and told the story of former olympic weightlifting medalist Kim Sung-jip. The second was 4 minutes 13 seconds in length and traced the story of Sohn Kee-chung and how he won the olympic marathon in 1936, competing as a Japanese subject and with a Japanese name because Korea was then under colonial rule. The feature used rather extensive footage from the 1936 marathon race and the medal ceremony, with Sohn describing his emotions then, his personal insistence on always using and signing his Korean name, and his continuing campaign to have his name corrected in the olympic record books. The spot showed Sohn "up close and personal", concluding with a scene of him exercising near a Buddhist temple in the mountains near Seoul. At the conclusion of the feature, Dick Enberg let viewers in on the secret that Sohn Kee-chung would indeed carry the torch into the stadium.

By designing the first quarter hour of its telecast as it did, NBC aimed at building suspense while providing its viewers with knowledge about an important element of the ceremony. In line with the general analysis of television ceremonial events suggested by Dayan and Katz[7], it provided viewers with a certain sense of cultural continuity and depth that even some present in the olympic stadium did not share.

The actual entry of Sohn with the torch occurred much later in the ceremony, allowing NBC to make repeated short references to it. Just minutes before the entry, the co-hosts switched to Bob Costas at the International Broadcast Center who interviewed Gina Hemphill, granddaughter of Jesse Owens. She had carried the olympic torch on its final lap during the 1984 Los Angeles Opening Ceremony and was asked about her recollections of that.

Prayer of Blessing, *Cha-il* Dance, *Hwakwan* Dance

A 12-minute segment of the Opening Ceremony called *A Great Day* consisted of several components. It began with a short *Prayer of Blessing* and the longer (almost seven minute) *Cha-il Dance* involving 800 dancers in traditional Korean costumes. During these segments an international team of sports parachutists formed the olympic rings in the sky, landed in the stadium and again formed the rings on the ground. This was followed by the 5-minute *Hwakwan (Flower Crown) Dance*, an example of a traditional Korean court dance from the Yi Dynasty era performed by 1 500 young women in traditional dress.

NBC gave extensive coverage to the parachutists, in the air and upon landing, but chose to cover very little else from this entire twelve-minute segment. Their coverage began by cutting to a studio interview with NBC commentators and former Olympians Dwight Stones and Mary Lou Retton. They discussed their experiences in previous Olympic Games Opening Ceremonies, but without any direct reference to Seoul. After a commercial break, co-host Bryant Gumbel engaged in a discussion with Tom Brokaw about security outside the stadium. During their talk, they several times appeared together on a split screen and the *Cha-il* dancers showed up in the distance behind Gumbel while the dance music provided background sound. Apart from this incidental or background glimpse, the *Cha-il* dance was largely ignored visually by NBC. The only verbal reference to it was Bryant Gumbel's comment following a commercial break, "Back in Seoul. An awful lot more action, a great deal of pageantry and color [. . .] but let's go to Tom Brokaw in our NBC pagoda".

Following the Gumbel-Brokaw discussion of security, NBC switched to its coverage of the descending parachutists and stayed with it for more than five minutes during which there were only occasional and incidental visual shots of the dancers on the field. The descent of the sports parachutists was accompanied by a lengthy and stirring rendition by orchestra and chorus of variations on the South Korean national anthem. For Korean audiences and for those who know Korea well the music evoked a strong sense of patriotic and even nationalistic pride. For the American viewing audience and probably for others around the world, the meaning of the music was different. As noted by Dayan and Katz, the secondary audiences who view televised media events around the world see a ritual formally similar to the primary audiences in the host city and nation, but semantically different. In their words, "The British watch royalty. Foreigners watch England[8]."

Hondon (Chaos)

NBC covered just over two out of five minutes from the *Hondon* episode which involved 846 performers wearing and carrying masks of traditional Korea and from other nations of the world. The masks were very large and colorful, with some being carried on poles and with 20 immense balloon masks popping up over the stadium roof. It would appear that the size, color and movement of the masks in this episode led NBC to give relatively more attention to it than to the preceding dances. The commentators also had a bit more to say about this segment including Bryant Gumbel's comment that "In case you're wondering, there is no mask representing the US out there. The Olympic Games Ceremonies organizers were not able to find a mask that they felt was indigenous to American folk history, not even, they said, in American Indian folklore".

Implications for a Future Broadcasting Policy
of the Olympic Games

Analysis of NBC's coverage of these episodes from the Opening Ceremony in Seoul helps to clarify several issues that ought to be considered in the development of future broadcasting policies. First, it lends some weight to suggestions that the Opening and Closing Ceremonies of the Olympic Games be telecast without commercial interruption[9]. NBC's telecast of the ceremony was interrupted 25 times for nearly 52 minutes of commercials, and another 21 times for newsbreaks, interviews, and "Olympic Chronicles" or "Olympics Past" segments averaging 3 minutes 3 seconds in length[10].

The majority of both commercial and other segments cut into NBC's coverage of cultural performances and the entry of the athletes, rather than detracting from the central olympic rituals. In this process, the cultural narrative contained in the ceremony and the international television signal was replaced for US viewers with a narrative that would better meet the imperatives of a commercial broadcaster. This suggests a second policy issue of whether rights holders should be required to provide a higher level of coverage devoted to the cultural background of the country where the Olympic Games are being staged[11]. However, some of NBC's departures from the international television signal, such as the "Olympics Past" segment on Sohn Kee-chung show television in the more positive role of affording viewers a sense of historical and cultural depth that otherwise would be missing from the telecast. Given the present requirements of rights holders and the dominance of the US network, such background pieces, produced at considerable cost, are viewed only by a US audience. This situation poses a third major issue for a future olympic broadcasting policy. Should prospective Olympic Ceremonies be planned even more completely than those in Seoul with television in mind, by incorporating breaks for planned telecast of cultural or historical information?

While coverage of the parachutists in the Opening Ceremony used television dramatically to convey breaking barriers of space, future ceremonies might routinely break barriers of time and space by incorporating televised segments of an historical and cultural nature. As to the spatial barriers we might easily imagine scenarios that might link geographically more separate locations within a ceremony than the main stadium, the sky above it, and the Han River nearby. The idea of linking different cities or regions of a country via satellite as part of an olympic ceremony might eventually come into conflict with the host city concept in the Olympic Movement, but as with the issues already discussed it illustrates the catalytic role of television in today's Olympic Games.

Finally, a related policy concern has to do with the financing of productions that provide cultural and historical background and pooling arrangements to ensure broader global telecast of such features. The IOC may wish to require large rights holders to share such programming with other broadcasters or engage in co-production of them. The growth of international television is already creating pressures in such a direction. In its final report on television broadcasting operations, the Seoul Olympic Organizing Committee noted that requests by major broadcasters such as NBC for exclusive commentator positions, security systems, transportation, and catering were excessive and it suggested that regional broadcasting unions play an increased role as coordinators[12]. All of the foregoing policy questions stem from the continued growth of television and its correspondingly greater influence on the Olympic Games as a media-constructed global spectacle. They were all brought into clearer focus by the experience in Seoul and are part of a broader agenda that promises to better define the nature of international sport in the next century.

NOTES AND REFERENCES

1. Lee S-c (1990) Lessons and achievements of the Seoul Olympics. In Koh B-i (ed) Toward one world beyond all barriers. Vol II Harmony through human movement; Culture and communication. The Seoul Olympiad Anniversary Conference. Seoul Olympic Sports Promotion Foundation. Seoul: Poong Nam p 200-13

2. Edelman M (1988) Constructing the political spectacle. Chicago: The University of Chicago Press

3. Based on host broadcaster (KBS/SORTO) estimates and those of industry observers

4. Seoul Olympic Organizing Committee (1989) Report on television broadcasting operations for the Games of the XXIVth Olympiad p 21-23

5. Tehranian M (1989) Is comparative communication theory possible/desirable? Paper presented at the Annual Conference of the International Communication Association San Francisco May 25-29

6. International Olympic Committee (1984) Olympic Charter. Appendix II Lausanne: International Olympic Committee p 103

7. Dayan D Katz E (1987) Television ceremonial events. In Berger AA (ed) Television in society. New Brunswick: Transaction Books

8. Ibid p 44

9. Kidd B (1989) The Olympic Movement and the sports-media complex. Proceedings of the conference on the Olympic Movement and the mass media: past, present and future issues. Calgary: Hurford p 1-8

10. Larson JF, Rivenburgh N (in press) Televised constructions of the Seoul Olympic Opening Ceremony in Australia, the United Kingdom and the United States. In MacAloon JJ (ed) The 1988 Seoul Olympics: intercultural perspectives. Urbana: University of Illinois Press

11. See Kidd B (1989) op cit and also Lee J-w (1990) The symbiosis of modern Olympics and mass media: policy concerns for Olympism. In Koh B-i (ed) Toward one world beyond all barriers. Vol II Harmony through human movement; Culture and communication. The Seoul Olympiad Anniversary Conference. Seoul Olympic Sports Promotion Foundation. Seoul: Poong Nam p 179-85

12. Seoul Olympic Organizing Committee (1989) op cit

Editor's Note   ## Note des éditeurs

The documents in this sub-section served both to illustrate the presentations of panelists **Kang**, **Moragas**, and **Larson** (above), and as supplementary information and guidelines for the ensuing discussion session co-chaired by **Rivenburgh-Laplante**:

– a Table-form overview of the Story Units in the Opening Ceremonies;

– a Table-form transcription of KBS, TVE and NBC commentaries of four selected episodes of the Opening Ceremony;

– Three tables encompassing comparative broadcast commentaries of selected Opening Ceremony episodes in various national broadcasting systems;

– a brief paper by Professor **Rivenburg** which served to initiate and summarize the discussion scssion.

Les documents qui se trouvent à la présente section ont servi au cours des conférences des panelistes **Kang**, **Moragas** et **Larson** (ci-avant), et aussi comme renseignements d'appoint pour la période de discussion ouverte qui a suivi les présentations des panelistes et qui a été co-présidée par le Dr **Rivenburgh** et le journaliste **Laplante**:

– sous forme de Tableau, une description générale des épisodes qui ont constitué la trame de la Cérémonie d'ouverture;

– également sous forme de Tableau la transcription intégrale des commentaires transmis sur les réseaux KBS, TVE et NBC, au cours de quatre épisodes donnés de la Cérémonie d'ouverture;

– trois Tableaux comparatifs des commentaires transmis sur un certain nombre de réseaux nationaux de télédiffusion au cours de certains épisodes de la Cérémonie d'ouverture;

– un bref document du Dr. Rivenburgh, lequel a servi de toile de fond à la session de discussion.

An Overview of the Story Units in the 1988 Seoul Olympic Games Cultural Manifestations and Official Opening Ceremony Telecasts

Category*	Num-bering	Episode	Approximate duration (min)	Descriptive remarks
B	—	Pre-boat Parade	—	Not part of official cultural manifestations
C	1	**Han River Boat Parade**	10	The Stadium looms at the river's edge; the river connects directly with the sea; the 5 oceans and 6 continents are symbolically attracted to Seoul
		Greeting the Sun	[~20]	Four distinct yet closely interrelated parts
C	2	Part 1 Passage at Dawn	6	Stadium becomes focal point of a re-creation of the world
C	3	Part 2 Dragon Drum Procession	4	Dragon drum represents beating human hearts gathering around "World Tree" which in turn symbolizes union of heaven and earth
C	4	Part 3 Heaven, Earth and Man	4	Greek and Korean nymphs express symbolic and joyful meeting of West and East in Seoul witnessed by the entire world
C	5	Part 4 Light of Genesis	6	Figure of "first light" by 1 500 dancers is gradually transformed to spell "Welcome" to the world
O	6	**Olympic Fanfare**	1	Trumpeters play, MC calls attention to beginning of official part of Opening Ceremonies
O	7	**Introduction and entry of Korea's President Roh Tae-woo**	1	The President is accompanied by Mrs Roh
C	8	**O-So-O-Se-Yo**	5	1 100 dancers form Olympic Rings, Games' Logo, and then fan out into "Welcome emblem"
O	9	**Entry of the Athletes and Officials**	60	Flag bearers and delegations from 161 NOCs enter and parade in order of Korean alphabet
O	10	**Speech by President Park Seh-jik**	2	Chief executive officer of SLOOC pronounces speech of circumstance
O	11	**Welcoming Address by HE JA Samaranch**	2	President of IOC invites President Roh to proclaim official opening
O	12	**Opening Proclamation**	2	President of Korea, Roh Tae-woo, declares open the Games of the XXIVth Olympiad, Seoul, 1988
O	13	**Hoisting of Olympic Flag**	8	Accompanied by a release of 2 400 perfectly white doves symbolizing universal yearning for peace and freedom
O	14	**Lighting of Sacred Flame**	5	4 163 km from Olympia to Seoul in 21 days; the last of some 1 500 runners, renown Sohn Kee-chung enters stadium; torch is relayed and 4 other selected Koreans participate in kindling of flame
O	15	**Olympic Oaths**	5	Korean representatives of athletes and judges take the oaths

[continued]

Category*	Num-bering	Episode	Approx-imate duration (min)	Descriptive remarks
O	16	**National Anthem, Republic of Korea**	2	
O	17	**Athletes' Departure**	15	
		A Great Day	[~12]	Two distinct parts
C	18	Part 1 Prayer of Blessing, *Cha-il* Dance	7	800 dancers pray toward the sky, 76 parachutists fall from the sky forming olympic rings
C	19	Part 2 *Hwakwan* Dance	5	Flower crown dance by 1 500 women celebrating happy moments of human history
C	20	**Chaos**	5	Choreography of 800 masks, of 148 kinds, from 60 countries; a critique of modern civilization: discord between ideologies, races, sexes
C	21	**Beyond all Barriers**	5	As an antithesis to chaos and barriers, 1 008 taekwondo champions figuratively express in unisson the constructive power of patience, self control and moral strength
C	22	**Silence**	1	Expectation of a new life; in absolute silence lone Korean child crosses field rolling silver hoop representing the hopes of humanity
C	23	**New Sprouts**	5	1 200 children enter and play games symbolizing continually renewed life transcending time and space
C	24	**Harmony**	7	Konori Folk Game by 1 450 participants symbolizing transcendance and union of Yin and Yang
C	25	**One World**	7	6 000 figurants representing flowers, plants, animal life, people of all age-categories and nations symbolically come together and dance hand-in-hand
B	26	Commercials	~ *	
B	27	Newsbreaks	~	
B	28	Olympic Chronicle	~	NBC
B	29	Olympic Past	~	NBC
B	30	Commentator on location or in broadcast center	~	
B	31	Interviews, live shots and/or films	~	But not a Chronicle
B	32	Commentary after end of the Opening Ceremony	~	

* O   Part of official Olympic Games Opening Ceremony.
  C   Cultural manifestation or performance engineered by the SLOOC.
  B   Broadcastor—added segment.
  ~   Segment or episode of variable duration.

Contrast of Korean, Spanish and American Commentaries
During Four Selected Episodes of the Cultural Manifestations
and Official Opening Ceremonies, 1988 Seoul Olympic Games:
Episodes # 14, # 18, # 19, # 20

KBS Commentary — KOR [Original in the *Korean* language. Translation/adaptation by Professor Kang Shin-pyo]	TVE Commentary — ESP [Original in the *Spanish* language. Translation/adaptation by Professor Miquel de Moragas i Spà]	NBC Commentary — USA [Original in the *English* language. Adaptation by Professor John J. MacAloon]

Note from the Editors: In his presentation of the transcript which follows, Professor Kang Shin-pyo chose to focus strictly on the substance of the commentary; the name(s) of the commentator(s) were thus omitted with a view of drawing the reader's attention more specifically to the intended content of the SLOOC scenario	Legend:
	OV Olga Viza
	         TVE Commentator
	MP Matias Prats
	         TVE Commentator
	[ ] Note by Professor Miquel de
	         Moragas i Spa inserted
		Legend:
		DE Dick Enberg,
		              NBC Commentator
		BG Bryant Gumbel,
		              NBC Commentator
		DS Dwight Stones,
		              former Olympian
		MR Mary Lou Retton,
		              former Olympian
		TB Tom Brokaw,
		              NBC Anchorman
		CO Unidentified,
		              NBC Commentator
		CE Christ Evert,
		              international Tennis star
		[ ] Note by Professor
		              John MacAloon inserted

EPISODE # 14 Entry and Lighting of the Olympic Flame
Approximate duration: 5 min

KBS — KOR	TVE — ESP	NBC — USA
*"The Sacred Flame is now entering. . . Highly respected senior citizen Sohn Kee-chung, gold medalist in the marathon at the 1936 Berlin Games, is entering with the Sacred Flame. Athlete Lim Chun-ae is receiving the Sacred Flame. Nineteen years old. University student from Ewha Women's University. Representing the female athletes in Korea's [**Uri Nara**] middle and long distance running. Triple gold medalist in the 1988 Asian Games. She was given the honorary role of being the final torch relay runner in the XXIVth Seoul Olympic Games".* *"Last August 23rd at the Temple of Hera, the Sacred Flame was ignited by the chief priestess, Didaskalou, by way of the sun's rays with the assistance of the 16 priestesses. The Sacred Flame passed through Greece, was flown to Cheju Island via Bangkok on August 27th. And during the past 21 nights and 22 days it passed 61 cities, 41 ku [**urban districts**], and 85 kun [**rural districts**] throughout Korea. It's appeared in front of our eyes. The Sacred Flame, it will burn as a sacred flame ignited in every one of our hearts. The*	OV *"Here we have the torch carried by Sohn Kee-chung, a veteran Korean athlete and winner of a medal in the 1936 Berlin Olympic Games. The electronic panel of the stadium is featuring shots of his performance in the Berlin Games where he won the gold medal. He's handing the torch over to Lim Chun-ae, Lim Chun-ae, famous for her outstanding performance in the Asian Games celebrated here in 1986. The big question is: who will light the olympic flame?"* MP *"And the next question is: will they allow her to pass? There she goes!"* OV *"The bright flame is shedding a trail of smoke. I don't know if they will let her pass. . . !"* MP *They have formed the classic tunnel".* OV *"The torch was lit in the Hera temple on August 11th and arrived on Korean soil on August 27th. To be precise, it landed on the island of Cheju,*	[ ] **NBC, in the opening moments of its telecast, presented a three minute studio-produced segment on Sohn Kee-chung, sympathetically detailing the events of 1936, his subsequent struggles and experiences, and his present triumph. For NBC, Sohn was the most focused upon individual, indeed the hero of the Opening Ceremonies, his life treated as a metaphor for the collective history of Korea.** DE *"There he is. Sohn Kee-chung approaching the tunnel".* BG *"When he bursts into the stadium, there will be a burst of emotion".* DE *"This gives you a chill, the 1936 Games, 52 years ago. He still runs daily, he's very fit at the age of 76".* BG *"5 400 white doves of peace being released, a lovely sight here in Seoul. The tradition started in 1920 in Antwerp".*

Continued

EPISODE # 14 *continued*

KBS Commentary — KOR	TVE Commentary — ESP	NBC Commentary — USA
Sacred Flame will burn out evil and injustice, division, and conflicts, corruption and misfortune. It will bring goodness and peace, harmony and progress, prosperity, happiness and material well-being. Now, it will be carried around the track and passed on to the final three who will in unison kindle the flame atop the olympic cauldron".	*from which point it has covered 4 167 km, passing through 21 cities and changing hands 20 972 times. It is going to be her! How will she light the olympic flame? Look! The doves have settled on the cauldron".*	*DE* "And there is Sohn Kee-chung! Is he thrilled! He's a man of great pride".
	MP "And..."	*BG* "He'll be handing to Lim Chun-ae, a girl from a poor area, unknown, but they found her and she won the 800, 1 500, and 3 000 meters in the Asian Games. Eventually she'll hand the flame to a trio of youngsters".
"The three are representing: academia, Mr. Chung Sun-man, middle school teacher on the small island at the southern tip of the Korean Peninsula; sport, Mr. Kin Won-tak, marathoner; and the arts, Miss Sohn Mi-chung, student of Seoul Art High School majoring in the traditional dance. The three are going up in a circular lift, twelve meters in diameter, climbing a stand twenty meters high as if they are ascending into heaven. First time in olympic history three participated in the kindling of the flame. Chung Sun-man, middle school teacher in Soheuksan Island, born 1958, his wife is also a kindergarten teacher in Mokpo. Kim Won-tak, Korean marathoner, employed at Tongyang Nylon Company, 24 years of age, champion at the 1985 Chosun Ilbo marathon competition. Sohn Mi-chung, born 1970, student at Seoul Art High School, majoring in traditional dance, represents the arts".	*MP-OV* "Somebody must shoo them away".	
	MP "The poor doves. Because any moment now..."	*DE* "Of all the ceremonies in sport, this may be the most dramatic of all".
	OV "How will the Flame be lit? Will the cauldron be lowered? Will it be ignited? There are four athletes at the foot of the cauldron. Chung Sun-man, Kim Won-tak, Song Mi-chung. The rumour that three athletes would ascend all the way to the top is now confirmed".	*BG* "As she completes her lap, she will hand off to a trio of cauldron lighters, and it is a measure of the priorities of the Republic of Korea that the common element among the three is that they all have something to do with education. One is an elementary school teacher, one is a graduate student, and one is a high school student in this land where education is so valued, so prized, and where the literacy rate is so high".
	MP "But we didn't see this in the dress rehearsal".	
	MP "It is one of the surprises, a pleasant surprise! During the rehearsal we observed how the flame would be lit and we must admit that it was not the normal procedure for an olympic flame lighting ceremony".	*DE* "98%. Here they are, three quite ordinary people. [**Gives their names**]. They have some system we haven't seen in operation yet [**to raise the torchbearers to the cauldron**]".
"The global village stage, the epic drama performed by the entire global family. Its highlight is the kindling of the Sacred Flame. The Sacred Flame is focusing everyone's eyes on one point, it also brings everyone's mind and spirit into one mind and spirit. Now we must all be one. Now we must all be together. In the blue sky above five airplanes are celebrating with five colored streams of smoke in their wake".	*OV* "For the first time in history the olympic flame is being raised in a, in quotes, lift, and the doves are still on the holder! The cauldron, that is to say, the tower of the torch stand is 22 meters high".	*BG* "Oh my goodness! This is something we haven't seen!"
	MP "It weight 33 tons. It was designed by the Korean Space Group and gifted by Rinay Korea, a Korean manufacturer of gas ovens".	*DE* "Pigeons, or doves, provide a... well... thank goodness [**they've flown off the cauldron**] As the flame is lit, five jets fly overhead to the applause of the athletes and the 100 000 here in the stadium. Quite a sight... And it's not over yet. After the oaths we'll have the skydivers. They have their own special treat in store for us".
"The cauldron is 22 meters high and 5,5 meters in diameter, designed by Mr. Kim Soo-keun. The conception of the design is after the shape of the Korean traditional candle holder".	*OV* "I don't know if you will be able to appreciate this, but two of the flames are red, one is saffron, the others are red. Even the smoke won't scare the doves away! They're still perched there".	
	MP "This was the most classic and certainly the best way to light the olympic flame. Five jets trailing the colours of the Seoul '88 emblem have just painted the sky above the stadium, while the three athletes who lit the olympic flame are slowly descending".	*BG* "We've got a lot more ahead".

EPISODE # 18 Prayer of Blessing, *Cha-il* Dance
Approximate duration: 7 min

KBS Commentary — KOR	TVE Commentary — ESP		NBC Commentary — USA	
"'At the beginning when the world opened; a great day it was when all mankind lived together peacefully, is depicted in this scene. This dance epitomizes praying for heavenly blessing and expressing earthly joy upon receiving mysterious forces from heaven. Kim Baek-bong, principal choreographer; Kim Mal-ae, co-choreographer; and Kim Ilee-cho, composer. Eight-hundred Yeungdeungpo Girl's High School students are participating in the performance".	MP	*"The athletes are leaving the field".*	BG	*"Back in Seoul, the athletes are leaving the infield.* [**There will be TV**] *monitors outside for them to watch* [**the rest**]*".*
	OG	*"Here come the 800 dancers dressed in blue and white to interpret the dance called Cha-il".*	DE	*"Looking forward to what we have seen in the rehearsal: a traditional battle, a rural battle involving a huge ropes* [**Sic. Ko-nori**]*, and the taekwando... "*
	MP	*"The item itself is titled «A marvelous day»".*		
"It's Korea's high-altitude, 22-member Black Eagle skydiving team. They are falling from an altitude of 4 000 meters, from heaven into the main stadium".	OV	*"The great day".*	BG	*"Oh, the Go Go, the... uh... uh... Go battle. That will be coming up in a little bit. There's still quite a show to follow here. We've got some parachutists, some taekwando specialists, and an awful lot of color and pageantry. As we watch the athletes depart, let's go back to the IBC* [**International Broadcast Center**]*".*
	[ ]	**Musical sequence.** *"This programme is being broadcast live from the olympic stadium in Seoul. It is 12:55 in the afternoon and there is still a long half hour of ceremony left".*		
"Next, 55 foreign members of the International Skydivers Association are making the five rings of the olympic emblem in the heavens. KBS is transmitting this scene to you through the use of two special cameras".	MP	*"Thanks for the details. We must sit down or those behind us will complain. Let us pay attention to the dance on the stadium field".*		
	OV	*"And the sky where Korean TV has still not focussed its cameras whereas ours has on 54 members of the International Parachutists Association who are descending from a height of 4 000 meters. There are an additional 22 Korean parachutists. There they are".*	[ ]	**Cut to studio interview with NBC commentators and american former olympians Dwight Stones (DS) and Mary Lou Retton (MR) (Condensed).**
"They are descending directly into the main stadium, with an opening of only 830 meters in circumference, from 4 000 meters above".			CO	*"Did these ceremonies mean anything special to you. Munich, Montreal, LA... compare them".*
"Eight-hundred Cha-il dancers are performing a Blessing Dance, welcoming the high-altitude skydivers. The parachutes are seemingly transformed into Cha-il [**sunshades**] *by the dancer's blue sheets".*	MP	*"But they have arrived before their scheduled time".*	DS	*"When I was 18... then the slendor and pageantry of Munich was* [**sic**] *so awe-inspiring".* [**Comment on Montreal, when expected to win**] *"When you walk into the stadium, it's an unimaginable feeling.* [**LA**] *was the best of the three feelings".*
	OV	*"They had to arrive now. What incomparable precision! They are not ahead of time".*		
"Whenever there is a festival, Koreans prepare for it with Cha-il. A blowing Cha-il means heavenly blessing and represents the excitement of man's mind brought about by the festival. The entire field is full with blowing Cha-il, it's like a sea of Cha-il".	MP	*"I think they have come too early because..."*	CO	*"Mary Lou Retton, you were just 16"* [**in LA**]*. "Were you able to fully appreciate the pageantry and the scope of what you were involved in?"*
	OV	*"The dancers are going through their routine faster".*	MR	*"When we marched into the stadium, I truly appreciated that these were the Olympics".* [**Further comment on LA**]
	MP	*"In the rehearsal, the dancers were already out of the stadium. This time they've had to go much faster. It's probably one of the few western touches of this ceremony".*	DS	*"Ceremonies may be best for those who are not medal contenders".* [**Further expression of feeling bad for those who miss the Opening Ceremonies because of proximate competition**]
	OV	*"54 American parachutists, 22 Korean and 100 000 spectators watching the sky".*		

Continued

EPISODE # 18 *continued*

KBS Commentary — KOR	TVE Commentary — ESP	NBC Commentary — USA
	MP *"The parachutists are descending on earth bringing with them divine blessings. That is the significance of this scene. What absolute precision! Look! They are going to form the five olympic rings as they plummet. I hope they can do it. They have only a few seconds. They have jumped from a height of 4 000 meters".*	[ ] **Cut To Commercial Break (Including George Bush campaign commercial).**
	OV *"One of them has a camera on the helmet. The picture is not very clear".*	BG *"Back in Seoul. An awful lot more action, a great deal of pageantry and color... "* [**Cha-il dancers briefly visible coming out on the field**] *"But let's go to Tom Brokaw in our NBC pagoda... "*
	MP *"That can be forgiven, can't it?"*	[ ] **Cut To Brokaw in "Pagoda" Studio outside the stadium**
	OV *"That's the view from 3 000 meters!"*	TB-BG [**Discussion of security, its necessity, and possible unevenness, and relaxation as the Games open**]
	MP *"Perfect! There we are down below. That's where they have to descend".*	TB *"Some say Pyongyang's relationship with Beijing and Moscow will keep the North Koreans from trying anything..."* [**The North Koreans**] *"say any trouble will be the fault of the US and South Korea. It's a tricky situation for the North Koreans".*
	[ ] **Musical sequence.**	
	MP *"Order, synchronization and perfect landings, wouldn't you say?"*	*"*[**U.S. military maneuvers are**] *pretty considerable."* [**They've**] *"made clear to North Korea and outside terrorists that they're fooling around not just with* [**South**] *Korean police but the might of the U.S. military".*
	OV *"Indeed!"*	
	MP *"The other day, we almost had a very serious accident when one of the parachutes did not open up completely. Fortunately the parachutist did not touch down at too great a speed. However, he has not been able to participate today due to a wrist fracture".*	[ ] **Cha-il dance visually and verbally ignored. Only NBC talking heads on screen. In audio background, performance music (Korean Fantasia) can be heard.**
	[ ] **Musical sequence.**	
	MP *"This second group of parachutists is American. The former were Koreans and these are from the USA".*	[ ] **Cut Back to Pictures of Ceremony (parachutists in the sky)**
	OV *"There's the one with the camera! There's none left in the sky".*	BG *"OK, Tom, thanks very much, we'll be coming back to you in just a little bit. But as you can see our parachutists are taking over the infield right now, parachutists not only from Korea, but a great deal of them, Dick, from the United States also".*
	MP *"That's what you call getting a perfect picture. He had... "*	
	MP-OV *"Two cameras!"*	
	MP *"Two parachutists with two cameras! I really don't know how many cameras there are, they're innumerable".*	
	OV *"A different version of the olympic rings has been formed by the parachutists on the ground".*	
	[ ] **Musical sequence.**	

Continued

EPISODE # 18 *continued*

KBS Commentary — KOR	TVE Commentary — ESP	NBC Commentary — USA
	MP "*This is called Cha-il. Cha-il floats in the wind and symbolises the divine benediction, the happiness of the festivities and the joy of all men. It forms a part of the celebrations in all Korean festivals. By the way, the rhythm and melody of the traditional music is being played on western wind and string instruments*". [ ] **Musical sequence.**	DE "*Seventy-six are the total number, Bryant, and they've been descending from 13 000 feet, 54 foreign, 22 Korean parachutists. And there, the climax, in the colors of the Olympics, red, green, black, yellow, blue, one on the shoulders of another, or seemingly so. You see the finale of this jump, and just as they arrive in the stadium, they'll release*" [**Visual of the column of five jumpers, a demi-climax, not the real finale**] "*Meanwhile, high above, after forming the olympic rings... Look at this!... Up at about 11 000 feet... that's a live shot obviously... we're having*" [**transmission**] "*trouble... And now, that image! With Seoul and the olympic complex below... Oh, My!*" BG "*We had promised a show that broke all barriers, and certainly the barrier that would normally lie above the stadium floor is certainly well-broken by these gentlemen*". DE "*It really symbolically is very well thought out. The idea of using the river, of using the sky, that we're not constricted to just the arena, this is an experience for all of Korea. Look at that... shot!*" [ ] **Of jumpers flying in the five ring, taken from camera mounted on helmet of jumper above them, with the round stadium the target far below** BG "*Uh... Look at that shot!*" DE "*And once they land in the center of this huge olympic stadium, they'll transpose those rings again on the infield. As with the river festival, this communicates the notion of unrestricted space. It converts a modern instrument, a parachute above the stadium, into a traditional symbol*". [**Did not say which one**] "*All that's left now are the parachutists that are in the olympic ring colors who will reform*"

Continued

EPISODE # 18 *continued*

KBS Commentary — KOR	TVE Commentary — ESP	NBC Commentary — USA
		those rings, you'll see them dropping now... You know sport parachuting is making a bid to become an Olympic demonstration sport in 1992. No thank you, I'm not signing up!"
		[ ] **Comparatively long silence.**
		BG *"Fabulous!"*
		[ ] **Comparatively long silence.**
		DE *"And"* [**now lands**] *"the rainbow cameraman parachutist, camera mounted on helmet,"* [**who**] *"gave you those spectacular shots... He was the last to leave the helicopter... Bravo!"*
		BG *"As we continue here in Seoul, we'll go to some commercial messages, then your local news break. We'll be back".*
		[ ] **Cut to Commercials before parachutists have formed olympic rings on stadium floor and are encompassed by female Cha-il dancers, transforming their own kerchiefs.**

EPISODE # 19 Hwakwan Dance (The Flower Crown Dance)
Approximate duration: 5 min

KBS Commentary — KOR	TVE Commentary — ESP		NBC Commentary — USA	
"The Flower Crown Dance is celebrating the Ancient Golden Ages when Heaven was harmonious with Earth. The dance is an expression of an age when human beings enjoyed the happiest of times". *"Kim Baek-bong, principal choreographer; Mon In-sook and Kim Liyun-sook, associate choreographers; and Kim Hee-cho, composer. One-thousand four-hundred and fifty students from Kyunghee University, Taedong Commercial High School and Yeumkwang Commercial Girl's High School are participating in the performance. Hwakwan dance as a court dance is characterized by its strong emphasis on ritual and self-control. The costume, hair decorations and various props of the dancers express the typical decorative traditions. The colors used in the dance come from the traditional color combination in Tan-chung* [**red and blue**], *Sam-Tae-keuk* [**Triple Taichi**], *and Saekdong* [**Children multicolor dress**]".	OV MP OV [ ] OV	*"Here are the 1 500 young male and female dancers who will be interpreting the Hwakwan Dance, a courtly dance that symbolises the harmony between Heaven and Earth at the beginning of man's history. It is a beautiful dance, and what beautiful robes!"* *"And the hairstyles! As you can see all appreciate now. It certainly is a royal dance".* *"It is 500 years old, dating from the time of the Tsing dynasty.* **Musical sequence.** *"You have witnessed the flower of the crown, the Hwakwan Dance".*	[ ] [ ] BG [ ] CO CE CO CE	**Cut to local newsbreak (Lead story in Chicago: hurricane Gilbert making US landfall)** **Cut to commercials** **[Brief screen visual of Hwakwan Dance, three-quarters through the performance]** *"Back in Seoul, it's shortly after 6:00 in the afternoon. This is the Flower Crown Dance, a performance designed to showcase the beauty of Korea's traditional arts and culture, The Program continues. Right now, a chance to meet one of the Olympians, the winningest tennis player man or woman".* **Cut to talking head interview with Christ Evert (CE), outside the stadium.** *"Does this compare at all with Wimbledon, say? What was the Opening Ceremony like for you?"* *"It was unbelievable, it was fantastic. You know... it's... I mean... It's just a great feeling to mix with these other athletes, whether they're amateurs or professionals, and the spirit and the patriotism you feel out there is just unbelievable. In tennis, being an individual sport, you miss out on that a lot".* *"Does it compare to Wimbledon?"* *"Well, you're mixing with people more, so I think it means a lot more, it's a deeper feeling. And I'm sure at the end of the day, when the gold medals and the silver medals are handed out and you're standing up there, I think it could compare just as much with a Wimbledon".*
			[ ] [ ] BG [ ]	**Cut back to stadium.** **Brief visual shot, without comment, of chrysanthemum formation. Talk continues about Chris Evert's career trajectory and competitive chances.** *"We'll be back to these Olympic Games".* **Cut to commercials.**

EPISODE # 20 Chaos
Approximate duration: 5 min

KBS Commentary — KOR	TVE Commentary — ESP		NBC Commentary — USA	
"Now the Golden Ages are gone, the Age of Chaos is coming where discord and conflict are dominant". *"Song Bum, principal choreographer; Kin Boh-hee, co-choreographer; and Kim Chung-kil, composer. Eight-hundred and forty-six dancers from the National Dance Group, the National Korean Music Academy, Sunbong Dance Group, Chungang University and Hanyang University are performing with 838 masks consisting of 198 various kinds from 60 different countries. This mask dance symbolizes chaotic dances representing respectively, good and evil, love and hatred, creation and destruction, and antagonism and division emanating from different values and personalities. Discords emerged from conflict among different ideologies, ethnicities and the sexes".* *"Some masks rise up at the top of a pole to watch the dancing around. Above the roof of the stadium, the typical Korean masks, the legendary figure in Shilla Kingdom [*__Chŭyong__*], Buddhist monk [*__Mŭkchung__*], young man [*__Maldooki__*], upper class [*__Yangban__*], grandmother [*__Halmi__*], upper class youth [*__Toryung__*], and servant [*__Mŭsam__*] are watching. Over the fence they are watching us while we are also watching the mask dance".* *"The world of chaos is waning. Our will is now toward overcoming this chaos".*	*MP* *OV* *MP* [ ] *OV*	*"This item is called Chaos. The ideological discord of races, of men and women. The spread of good and evil, of love and hatred, of creation and destruction are expressed through 800 masks of 148 different types representing 60 countries. It is a criticism of modern civilisation. The world is peopled with innumerable faces, the mask is yet another human face".* *"This dance has begun 10 minutes behind schedule, a schedule that was being strictly kept until, naturally, the March Past. The ceremony could easily stretch to 2:15 korean standard time".* *"From ancient times until today, indescribable and innumerable masks have been fashioned. Counting the number and the types of masks that have existed and those that are still to be seen would be as arduous a task as explaining human history. And unravelling the significance of these masks would be almost as complicated as trying to understand the human heart".* **Musical sequence.** *"And to crown it all, 20 balloons shaped like masks have appeared over the stadium to contemplate the dance of Silence, while a sparse circle of fire-works frames the field".*	*BG* *DE* [ ]	*"Back in Seoul, we've reached that part of the Opening Ceremonies known as Hondon, or "Confusion", the peace and harmony represented by the crown dancers has been replaced by the confusion of traditional masks, the masks representing countries around the world. This particular element of the show is meant to represent the disruption, the conflict, and the chaos that exists [*__sic__*] in the world. In case you're wondering, there is no mask representing the US out there. The olympic ceremonies organizers were not able to find a mask that they felt was indigenous to American folk history, not even, they said, in American Indian folklore".* *"Well, just as we look down on the masks, Bryant, they're looking at us from the rim of the stadium. As the dancers go every-which-way, the large scoreboard up there has a single word, «Chaos». The chaos is about to be replaced by the discipline of taekwondo. Quite a show to come, stay with us".* **Cut to commercials.**

Editors' Note

Note des éditeurs

The three (3) following tables are presented by authors **Rivenburgh** and **Larson** and Editors **Landry-Landry-Yerlès** for the purpose of facilitating an inter-broadcaster comparison of *subject treatment* of three (3) selected episodes from the international television signal originated and provided by KBS, as host broadcaster of the 1988 Seoul Olympic Games. The reader is referred to the preceding *Overview of Story Units* for a perspective of the substance and/or orientation of the various episodes of the cultural manifestation and official Opening Ceremonies. The content analysis of the three tables focuses on Episodes #14, #19 and #20.

Les trois (3) tableaux qui suivent ont été conçus et préparés par les auteurs **Rivenburgh** et **Larson** ainsi que par l'équipe des éditeurs **Landry**, **Landry** et **Yerlès**. Ils ont pour objectif de mettre en relief comment certains diffuseurs internationaux branchés sur le signal vidéo de la KBS ont traité le contenu de trois des épisodes particuliers du programme des manifestations culturelles et de la Cérémonie d'ouverture officielle [Épisodes #14, #19, #20]. On est prié de se référer au tableau ci-avant (intitulé «*An overview of the story units...*») pour une liste sommaire des épisodes qui ont constitué la substance de l'entière Cérémonie d'ouverture.

TABLE 1

Comparative Broadcast Commentary of the Hwakwan Dance
[Episode # 19]

Items/substance from SLOOC "Scenario for the Opening and Closing Ceremonies"	Countries/National Broadcasting Systems								
	KOR KBS	CHN CCTV	USA NBC	NZL —	GBR BBC	FRG ZDF	AUS TEN	ESP TVE	CAN SRC
Flower crown by name	✔		✔	✔	✔	✔	✔	✔	
1500 dancers	✔	✔			✔	✔		✔	✔
Harmony with the earth	✔							✔	✔
Age of happiness	✔	✔		✔	✔				✔
Name of composer	✔								
Court dance	✔			✔	✔	✔	✔	✔	✔
Traditional Korean dance	✔		✔	✔	✔		✔		✔
Crown has five beads					✔		✔		
Long sleeves				✔			✔		
From the Yi Dynasty				✔	✔★	✔	✔	✔	
Last Korean Dynasty						✔			
Colors bright				✔		✔			✔
Colors traditional	✔					✔			✔
Reason for the calm				✔	✔	✔	✔		✔
Prelude to history	✔							✔	✔
Korean drums									
Peony dance						✔			
Additional broadcaster comments									
Dancers' schools	✔					✔			
Beautiful dance		✔	✔	✔				✔	✔
Music				✔					
Modern Korea				1		2,3	4,5,6		7

★ Does not specify "Yi" Dynasty by name.
1 Reference to modern hairstyles.
2 Interrogation as to: "can today's youth relate to this?"
3 Reference to two types of Korean dance; peasant and court.
4 Reference to Gates of Peace in Seoul having the same design.
5 Reference to importance of Korea's image to the world.
6 Reference to Korean naval hero.
7 Reference to dance as representing spirit of Korea further described as epitomizing the patience and endurance that has marked their 5000-year history.

TABLE 2

**Comparative Broadcast Commentary of the Hondon (Chaos)
[Episode # 20]**

Items/substance from SLOOC "Scenario for the Opening and Closing Ceremonies"	Countries/National Broadcasting Systems							
	KOR KBS	CHN CCTV	USA NBC	NZL —	GBR BBC	ESP TVE	AUS TEN	CAN SRC
Use the word "Chaos"	✔	✔	✔	✔	✔	✔	✔	✔
Confusion, strife	✔		✔		✔	✔	✔	✔
Blend of modern/traditional								
Critical of modern civilization	✔				✔	✔		✔
846 masks, 60 nations	✔	✔			✔	✔	✔	✔
Good/bad, love/hate, etc.	✔				✔	✔	✔	✔
Balloon masks (large)	✔		✔	✔	✔	✔		✔
Stadium as a stage	✔						✔	
Country-specific masks	✔		✔	✔	✔		✔★	✔
Choreographer, etc.	✔							
Additional broadcaster comments								
Where performers are from	✔							
Fireworks				✔	✔	✔		
Masks as cultural symbols						✔	1	2,3
Difficult to comprehend culture							✔	

★   Commentator jokes that US mask "should be of Ronald McDonald".
1   Reference to Korean people as fond of masks.
2   Reference to task of explaining masks is "as difficult as explaining history of man".
3   Reference to music of accompaniment.

TABLE 3

Comparative Broadcast Commentary of the Entrance of Mr. Sohn Kee-chung into the Stadium
[Episode # 14]

Items/substance from SLOOC "Scenario for the Opening and Closing Ceremonies"	Countries/National Broadcasting Systems							
	KOR KBS	CHN CCTV	USA NBC	NZL —	GBR BBC	ESP TVE	AUS TEN	CAN SRC
76 years old		✓	✓	✓	✓		✓	✓
1936 games	✓	✓	✓	✓	✓	✓	✓	✓
Gold medalist	✓	✓	F	✓	✓	✓	✓	
Marathon	✓		F	✓	✓		✓	
Annexation by Japan			F	✓	✓		✓	✓
Japanese name			F	✓	✓		✓★	
Forced to use			F	✓			✓	✓
Status in Korea	✓		F	✓		✓		✓
Berlin location	✓		F	✓		✓	✓	✓
Others			F 1,2	3	3			4

F NBC inserted a video feature on Sohn Kee-chung just prior to his entrance into the stadium; much of NBC's commentary about Mr. Sohn was part of that segment.

★ They did not actually say the Japanese name of Mr. Sohn.

1 Reference to Mr. Sohn's excitement at carrying the torch into the Olympic Stadium of Seoul.

2 Reference to Mr. Sohn as feeling proud at that very special moment.

3 Quotes from Sohn Kee-chung.

4 Winning time for the 1936 marathon won by Mr. Sohn.

Learning about Korea – Or Did We?
A Multi-Nation Comparison of Televised Cultural Coverage of the Seoul Olympic Opening Ceremony

Nancy Rivenburgh

The panel presentations on "The Olympic Games, communications technologies and cultural exchange," represented in the preceding papers, touched on a variety of topics pertaining to the Opening Ceremony of the 1988 Seoul Olympic Games. These ranged from the intrusion of commercials into Opening Ceremony broadcasts to the understanding—or misunderstanding—of the Korean cultural meanings imbedded in the program itself.

Common to all the presentations is the conceptualization of the modern Olympic Games Opening Ceremony as a media-constructed event meticulously planned and produced with worldwide television audiences in mind. In the case of Seoul, each national broadcaster or broadcasting union had access to the KBS international television feed—comprised of visuals, graphics, and natural sound— to use or edit at will. In some cases, broadcasters altered the feed by editing in their own live footage from extra cameras or inserting prepackaged video segments such as NBC's "Olympic Chronicles" or necessary commercial breaks. In all cases, the broadcasters added their own commentary to the coverage of the Opening Ceremony.

The result, as the preceding analyses and transcripts of US, Spanish, and Korean broadcasts demonstrate, was not a single Opening Ceremony as planned by the host organizers, but a multiplicity of Opening Ceremonies broadcast around the world; each was constructed in unique ways depending on the commercial obligations, financial resources, geopolitical or cultural perspectives of the various broadcasting networks. In some cases, as with the commercial/non-commercial distinction between national broadcaster (*e.g.*, the BBC and NBC), the resulting broadcasts were vastly different in structure and format. In other cases, depending on a broadcast nation's geographic location or international political relations, program content very likely differed in focus on, or understanding of, South Korea and other nations of the world.

1890
1990

Nancy Rivenburgh, School of Communications, University of Washington, Seattle, Washington, USA.

The three tables preceding this section expand upon the analyses of Korean, Spanish, and US coverage by Professors Kang, de Moragas i Spà and Larson by presenting a brief sample of data from a larger, on-going comparative study taking place at the University of Washington, with the assistance of colleagues elsewhere, which compares 12 countries' television coverage of the Opening Ceremony of the Seoul Olympic Games. These particular tables encompass the same three segments discussed by the panel—the Hwakwan dance, the Hondon segment, and the Entrance of Sohn Kee-chung—and add a summary of transcripts from the Federal Republic of Germany's (ZDF), Chinese (CCTV), New Zealand, British (BBC), Canadian (french language network: Société Radio-Canada-SRC)), and Australian (TEN) broadcasts to the US, Korea, and Spanish data. The data in the tables deal with the nature or the commentary both across broadcasters and against background information provided by the Korean hosts.

Prior to the Opening Ceremony, all international broadcasters received a guide document, "Scenario for the Opening and Closing Ceremonies" produced by the Seoul Olympic Organizing Committee (SLOOC). This document provided an optional script as well as indepth explanatory notes concerning Korean cultural and historical significance and olympic meaning for all segments of the ceremony. While none of the broadcasters read the suggested script verbatim all paraphrased selected cultural or historical facts from the text in varying levels of detail. In *Tables* 1 and 2, one can compare the information from the "Scenario" each broadcaster chose to use in its live commentary of the Hwakwan dance and of the Hondon. The same comparative data in *Table* 3 have to do with the commentaries of the entrance of Sohn Kee-chung into the stadium. The choice of Sohn Kee-chung to carry the torch into the stadium was intended as a "surprise" and therefore had not been included in the printed "Scenario."

One can see, for example, that during the Hwakwan dance the BBC commented on 8 of about 17 primary contextual "facts" included in the SLOOC document. By contrast, China's CCTV mentioned only 2 facts from the text provided (*Table* 1) and spent the balance of the segment silent (natural sound only). In the case of NBC, there was also sparse commentary but for wholly different reasons. In the NBC broadcast, the beginning of the Hwakwan dance was missed altogether due to a commercial break. Bryant Gumbel then explained that this was "a performance designed to showcase the beauty of Korea's traditional arts and culture" at which time the network cut to a live interview with Chris Evert Mills outside the stadium, followed by another commercial break. In all, NBC spent only 26 seconds on this nearly 7-minute cultural performance.

The German broadcast attempted to explore contemporary Korea while viewing traditional Hwakwan dance. As an example, one commentator asked a Korean-born colleague assisting with the broadcast whether today's Korean youth were in a position to relate to the traditional aspects of the Opening Ceremony. Although the answer received was "no, they can't", the audience was informed of a renewed interest in South Korea for reviving cultural traditions and finding ways to integrate them into its modern society. Commentators from New Zealand and Australia also attempted to relate the traditional performance to a modern South Korea.

Although not apparent from the tables, it was the British and French Canadian commentators who most closely followed the somewhat lyrical tone of the "Scenario" as provided to the broadcasters by the SLOOC. As in the Hondon (or Chaos) segment, both the BBC and SRC commentators covered the segment both in Korean and olympic terms explaining its intended criticism of modern civilization and symbolic expression of the futility of human conflict. The Australian commentators were for their part exuberant about Korean culture and Olympism. The tone and substance of their commentaries can be said to be consistent with scholarly work on media events to the fact that broadcasts associated with extraordinary events tend to strike a tone of high drama and reverence. Across all the western broadcasts, there was also a lack of descriptive precision as the commentators found it difficult to translate Korean culture and history, as referenced in the SLOOC document, into terms or symbols readily familiar to their own audiences. The result was that they tended toward descriptive laziness, refered to the dances simply as "traditional" or glossed over several hundreds of years of history by saying it was a period "of the arts" in Korea. Some Australian commentators "confessed" that Korean culture "is difficult to under-stand."

The western broadcasters clearly enjoyed the story of Sohn Kee-chung, as demonstrated by how much of the story was told by each network (*Table* 3). This particular entrance of the olympic torch into the stadium included all the elements known to appeal to western programming tastes, including individual spirit and honor, heroism, and the triumph of "right" over a historical "wrong." To the western broadcasters—in particular NBC, SRC, TEN and New Zealand networks—it was a great story with a beginning, middle, and climatic end. The Chinese commentator, on the other hand, chose not to tell the story. As for the Koreans, of course, they already knew it well.

While several more specific comparisons and observations could be made concerning the above mentioned segments, the analyses inevitably bring us back to the broader questions posed by the sub-theme of this session on the "Olympic Games, communications technologies, and cultural exchange". For example, can the similarities one finds across national broadcasts give weight to the notion of "third cultures", or "global media communities," where olympic symbol systems or media formats could be shared, and understood, across diverse cultures? Or, are the implications of this multiplicity of broadcast constructions such that one must reconsider the ability of diverse nations and cultures to ever truly cooperate in an interdependent world? The comparison of the broadcast commentaries to the SLOOC document begs the question of television's ability—or willingness—to translate meanings and values from one culture to another. Or, are the media—despite their global reach—doomed to wear the same cultural blinders that characterize their national audiences? That is, can the Olympic Games as a media event really increase international understanding? This leads one directly to the question of how these and related studies might provide feedback to the International Olympic Committee and Olympic Games Organizing Committees to assist in future policy formation. Meaningful answers to such questions require continued research and thoughtful analysis at many levels, in many forms, and certainly from all corners of the world.

Il est d'ordinaire assez difficile, de savoir pourquoi et comment une idée nait – se dégage du flot des autres idées qui attendent leur réalisation – prend un corps et devient un fait. Mais tel n'est pas le cas pour les Jeux Olympiques. L'idée de leur rétablissement n'était pas une fantaisie: c'était l'aboutissement logique d'un grand mouvement. [. . .] En même temps les grandes inventions, le chemin de fer et le télégraphe ont rapproché les distances et les hommes se sont mis à vivre d'une existence nouvelle ; les races se sont pénétrées les unes les autres, elles ont appris à se mieux connaître et tout de suite elles ont aimé à se comparer entre elles. Ce que l'une accomplissait, l'autre voulait à son tour le tenter [. . .] Comment les athlètes n'auraient ils pas cherché à se rencontrer alors que l'émulation est la base même de l'athlétisme, et presque sa raison d'être? Cela est arrivé en effet [. . .] peu à peu, l'internationalisme s'est glissé sous le sport, avivant l'intérêt, agrandissant la sphère d'action. Le rétablissement des Jeux Olympiques devenait possible. En y réfléchissant, il m'apparut même comme nécessaire. [. . .]

Coubertin P de (1896) Les Jeux Olympiques de 1896. Rapport officiel, 2e partie. Athènes/Paris p 1-2

[. . .] Des États-Unis le sport est revenu en Europe [. . .]

Coubertin P de (1894) Le rétablissement des Jeux olympiques. La Revue de Paris, 15 juin p 176

Cross-Influences
in the Revival
and Development
of Olympic Sport

Influences inter-culturelles
dans la rénovation
et le développement
du sport olympique

Mythes et voile de brume entourant la rénovation
des Jeux olympiques au siècle dernier

D'entrée en matière, l'auteur cite les paroles prononcées par Coubertin en 1934, à l'occasion du 40ᵉ anniversaire du rétablissement des Jeux olympiques, trois ans avant sa mort. Coubertin avançait alors que l'Olympisme et les Jeux olympiques étaient nés à la façon de Minerve, tout de go et en leur pleine maturité. L'auteur exprime son étonnement devant l'assertion de Coubertin qu'il trouve pour le moins exagérée. Il propose un tour d'horizon pour démontrer que les Jeux olympiques modernes dont on impute la rénovation à Coubertin ont des antécédents historiques réels qui leur découvrent des ancêtres ; par surcroît les Jeux ont eu une enfance et sont passés, au cours du XIXᵉ siècle, par une période de tâtonnements. Dans la première partie de sa présentation, l'auteur rappelle que c'est en 1890 que Coubertin visita Brookes à Much Wenlock, c'est-à-dire à l'époque de sa vie où il semblait beaucoup plus préoccupé de questions d'éducation générale, d'éducation physique et de sport qu'il ne l'était de Jeux olympiques. C'est donc en 1890 que Coubertin, grâce à sa visite à Much Wenlock et grâce aussi à l'information qu'il reçut sur place de la part de Brookes, devient informé de deux efforts authentiques de rénovation de Jeux olympiques nationaux : – en Grèce, à Athènes, sous le leadership du philanthrope Evangelis Zappas ; – en Angleterre, à Much Wenlock, fondés par William Penny Brookes qui besognait en fait à cette œuvre depuis déjà quarante ans. Qui plus est, des liens s'étaient tissés entre les Jeux olympiques nationaux d'Athènes et ceux de Much Wenlock, grâce à l'initiative de Brookes. C'est même ce dernier qui en 1880, soit dix ans avant la visite que lui fit Coubertin, avait proposé que des Jeux olympiques internationaux soient rétablis en sol grec. Sur la base de ce qui précède, l'auteur se dit d'avis que Coubertin a fait siennes les idées de Brookes plutôt qu'il n'a conçu lui-même et surtout à lui seul, comme il l'a prétendu subséquemment, l'idée de la rénovation des Jeux olympiques. Dans la deuxième partie de sa présentation, l'auteur démontre que les racines de l'idée de la rénovation des Jeux olympiques remontent en Grèce à 1835, et que ce serait le Grec Panagiotis Soutsos qui, le premier, en aurait fait la suggestion à son gouvernement. L'auteur décrit par la suite des événements en date de 1837 et 1838, en Grèce, lesquels montrent à l'évidence une montée de l'intérêt général et gouvernemental à l'égard de la rénovation des Jeux olympiques. Il décrit par la suite les efforts de Brookes, qui, déjà en 1840 et en 1850, avait lancé son mouvement. Il montre que Brookes avait pris contact avec le mouvement grec dès 1860, soit dans l'année qui suivit les Jeux olympiques d'Athènes de 1859. Une description est faite de l'importante initiative que prit Brookes, en 1860, à l'effet d'établir une rotation des villes hôtes pour ses jeux ; cette tendance allait, selon l'auteur, marquer l'avenir des jeux. Par la suite, il est fait état des difficultés qui marquèrent, en Angleterre, l'histoire des Jeux nationaux à compter de 1866, en raison de la conception bourgeoise de l'amateurisme à laquelle Brookes s'objecta sa vie durant. Après une description de l'importance des Jeux olympiques grecs de 1870 et de 1875, l'auteur avance qu'à compter de la dernière date et grâce à Brookes et à ses relations avec la Grèce, on venait à toutes fins utiles d'assister à la véritable naissance d'un mouvement olympique international. Dans la dernière partie de sa présentation, l'auteur décrit la situation qui prévalait au moment où, de 1892 à 1894, Coubertin prit les choses en main. Zappas était décédé, les Jeux grecs de 1888 avaient été annulés, Brookes se faisait vieux et sa santé chancelait. Encouragé par Brookes, Coubertin alla de l'avant, organisa son congrès de 1894, lequel, à certains point de vues avait l'allure d'un écran de fumée. Sans se faire de scrupules en rendant à César ce qui appartient à César, Coubertin lança, sans plus, l'idée de la rénovation des Jeux olympiques. En guise de conclusion, l'auteur se dit d'avis que Coubertin n'a pas été fidèle à l'histoire ni au travail, ni à la réputation de ceux qui avant lui, comme Zappas et Brookes, entre autres, avaient tant donné d'eux-mêmes. Pour l'auteur, Coubertin mérite certes le titre de sauveur des Jeux olympiques modernes ; le titre de rénovateur appartient cependant de droit historique à Zappas et à Brookes.

Myths and Mist Surrounding the Revival of the Olympic Games: the Hidden Story

David C. Young

In a private letter to Bill Henry, in July 1934, Coubertin wrote:

[. . .] It has been said that Olympism was 'in the air' and likely to be revived somehow or other. It was not[1].

Just earlier, on June 23, 1934, on the occasion of the celebration of the 40th anniversary of the re-establishment of the Olympic Games, Coubertin had said:

[. . .] Vainement, des perfidies ultérieures s'exerceront-elles à faire prédominer la notion d'une création incertaine dont les étapes se seraient succédées timidement au hasard des circonstances. La vérité est différente. L'Olympisme est né cette fois tout équipé, comme Minerve! — avec son programme complet et sa géographie intégrale; la planète entière serait son domaine[2].

In mythology Latin Minerva, the Greek Athena, was born from the head of her father, Zeus, fully adult, fully armed, and ready to go—no mother, no childhood. Coubertin here implies that Olympism was born out of his own head, with no other parent, no childhood. But were the modern Olympic Games born solely out of his head? Was he really their only parent? Was there really no "Olympism" in the air before Coubertin? No childhood? Coubertin's claims here appear amazingly exaggerated. Others, such as MacAloon and Redmond, have explored some of the antecedents of the olympic phenomenon[3]. In this presentation, I shall not retread their ground, but rather focus only on those games that have a linear relation to the present Olympic Games. And I will argue for other fathers, and a childhood as well.

In 1890 Coubertin went to Much Wenlock, England, to visit William Penny Brookes. What took him there was not his interest in the Olympic Games; it was his interest in general education, physical education, and sport, a favorite topic with Brookes at the time. But once in Much Wenlock, the Baron stumbled midstream into the olympic revival movement, already half a century old, aging and ailing. That is to say, that in 1890 in England, Coubertin unexpectedly met with the movement that led to the modern international Olympic Games, the very movement that Coubertin later claimed he founded himself—singlehandedly.

1890
1990

David C. Young, Classics Department, University of Florida, Gainsville, Florida, USA

To make it clear that I do not just point to sporadic olympic revivals before Coubertin ("pseudo-Olympics", to use Redmond's term), I shall preview my remarks. My *thesis* is this. There were, in the last half of the 19th century, two serious and significant national olympic revivals. The one was in Greece, founded by Evangelis Zappas. The other was in England, founded by William Penny Brookes. Several olympic meetings took place in both countries. These two revivals became interconnected; and, in 1880, Brookes proposed that international Olympic Games be re-established on Greek soil. Brookes' proposal for international Olympic Games had supporters—and opponents—in both England and Greece. When Coubertin visited him in 1890, Brookes was eighty-one years old and a hardened veteran of an olympic campaign of forty years. He had almost given up; he was indeed ready to pass the torch. Brookes told Coubertin (then twenty-seven) all about the olympic movement of the time, including his proposal for international Olympic Games. When Coubertin learned of the olympic movement in 1890, he joined it. The torch can be said to have passed from Brookes to Coubertin, and Coubertin indeed appears to have espoused most of Brookes' ideas after acknowledging them succinctly in his 1890 article in La Revue Athlétique[4], and also making an indirect allusion to Zappas' Games in Greece and the influence of Brookes upon them[5]. Through his and others' efforts, the movement succeeded, and created the modern Olympic Games. But the Baron did not further acknowledge the work of his predecessors in the movement, so that he would be viewed as the *rénovateur*, the originator and sole source[6] of the modern olympic revival, thus contradicting his own statement of 1890[7].

This thesis is not all mine alone; I mention especially Rühl and Neumüller of Cologne. Most of my information on Brookes and England comes from their recent work. Further, Kivroglou has done a paper on the first Zappas Olympics, 1859. These studies, along with my own work on the Zappas olympic series, the 1894 Paris Congress, and Demetrios Vikelas, provide a wealth of new, documented data on the origins of the modern Olympic Games[8]. I must emphasize that some of my concepts have been suggested by Dr. Rühl on the basis of recently uncovered archival material; it is not simply a new interpretation of the already existing sources.

Where to begin? I suggest in 1835 in modern Greece, a new nation has just freed itself from Turkish rule. That year the government received a memo suggesting that the ancient Olympic Games be revived and held annually, in a four-year rotation among four Greek cities, including Athens. The memo was written, it seems, by a Greek named Panagiotis Soutsos[9]. We shall return to Soutsos shortly. This 1835 memo failed to revive the Games; but perhaps it did help to induce the 1837 law published by Greece's new King, Otto of Bavaria. In January 1837 Otto passed a law establishing a "Committee for the Encouragement of National Industry" mandated to form a national gathering, with contests and money prizes in three categories, agriculture, industry, and the athletic games of ancient Greece: "discus, javelin, long jump, footraces, wrestling, and chariot racing". But Otto did not use the words "Olympic" or "revival". He probably thought more in terms of the Munich Oktoberfest of his native Bavaria[10]. And Otto's national festival did not take place (not until 1859—when it was called "Olympiad I").

Another seed of the present Olympic Movement was soon planted at Olympia, Greece, A.D. 1838. That is not a sentimental choice. On March 25, 1838, the people of Letrini, near Ancient Olympia, proposed to revive the Olympic Games there, and "recall those happy times" of Antiquity as part of the "rebirth of Greece". This olympic revival would be held every four years on March 25 (the starting date of the Greek War for Independence). "This way the celebration of the national festival would be genuinely Greek"—that apparently a reference to King Otto's law[11]. They appointed a five-man committee to pursue their proposal. One member, Pavlos Giannopoulos, as we shall later see, had a career in the olympic revival movement that spanned at least 37 years, approaching those of Coubertin and Brookes. But this committee, too, seems to have failed. Seven years later, in 1845, before an audience of 15 000 people, Panagiotis Soutsos delivered a speech in which was advocated again the olympic revival in Greece, but still to no avail[12].

In the meantime, in England, the seed of the other olympic revival had been planted by Brookes in Much Wenlock. In 1840 Brookes founded The Wenlock Agricultural Reading Society. Its principal activity over the next decade was to collect books for the working class, farmers and laborers, to read. Brookes' interest in the working class would last all his life. Ironically, it also helped to cause his later British National Olympic Movement to run aground—and lead to the international movement, instead. In 1850 Brookes founded the "Olympian Class", that is, a "sub-section" of the Reading Society, and arranged for annual athletic games, with cash prizes for the victors. He called the sub-section "Olympian" because he admired the ancient Greek Games. Along with mediaeval tilting at the ring, these "annual meetings of the Olympian Class of the Wenlock Agricultural Reading Society" featured real athletics from their start in 1850: cricket, quoits, foot-ball, and modern track and field. These "meetings"—Brookes did not yet call them "Olympic Games"—were held throughout the 1850s[13]. But in 1860, there were significant changes. For then Brookes had fallen under the influence of the 1859 Zappas olympic revival in Greece. We must now go back to Greece, to the man named Zappas.

Evangelis Zappas was an unschooled Greek, born in 1800 in a small village now part of Albania. After fighting in the Greek War of Independence, he moved to Romania, where he became very wealthy as a landowner and businessman. He never set foot in Athens. In early 1856[14], Zappas proposed to the Greek government a permanent revival of the ancient Olympic Games, with cash prizes for the victors; he would pay for it all. For months no response came from Athens[15]. On July 13 a strange article appeared in a Greek newspaper: the author was Panagiotis Soutsos, the subject, the Olympic Games. Soutsos writes of the 1835 memo proposing an annual "revival of the Olympic Games", and of his own 1845 speech advocating the same idea, while he recommended that other things such as "economic goods" be exhibited at the same time as the Games—an apparent concession to King Otto's 1837 law[16]. Yet Soutsos' article was not titled "Olympic Games", but "Evangelis Zappas", the man who, Soutsos said, was willing to pay for the entire olympic revival. It seems clear that Zappas had contacted Soutsos about the government's failure to respond. Just as Soutsos' article went to press, an answer finally came from Athens. It came from Alexandros Rangavis, King Otto's Foreign Minister. Rangavis later paraphrased his response:

> I thanked Zappas for his [. . .] splendid idea; but told him also that times have changed since Antiquity. Today, nations do not become distinguished, as then, by having the best athletes and runners, but the champions in industry, handiwork, and agriculture. I suggested that he found [. . .] Industrial Olympic Games[17].

Rangavis, a former classics professor, is the first of many Greek intellectuals who for decades formed an anti-athletic clique that finally ran the Greek Olympic Movement aground. He and Zappas began a correspondence. Zappas agreed to "Industrial Olympics"—but still wanted ancient Olympic Athletic Games, as well. He wanted the ancient Panathenaic stadium in Athens restored as their site, rebuilt with marble seats and all. He agreed to fund a building nearby, for the industrial exhibits. He gave money and said he would give more. The organization of the olympic meeting was given to King Otto's "Committee for the Encouragement of National Industry", established in 1837. Rangavis, with extensive Zappas funds earmarked to restore the stadium in marble, refused even to buy the property on which the ancient stadium lay. Nonetheless, in Athens in 1859, Olympic Games took place in three areas, industry, agriculture—and athletics: footraces, discus, javelin, wrestling, jumps, and a pole climb. These athletic Olympic Games could easily be termed the first modern Olympic Games of the present tradition. But it was far from a great festival.

I have already written on the 1859 Olympic Games themselves[18]. I here give a one-word summary: "C–", 3 or 4 points on a scale of 10. It was not Zappas' fault, but the organizers'. There would be no more Olympic Games in Athens until 1870. I should like to add only one item to my earlier account. The winner of the 1859 distance race received a cash prize of ten British pounds from the "Olympian Class of the Much Wenlock Agricultural Reading Society of England". Brookes had obviously learned of the coming 1859 Greek Olympic Games. He had induced the Much Wenlock Olympian Class to send ten pounds to Athens, a prize for the victor at "Tilting at the Ring", a favorite at Wenlock. The Greeks had no such event, so they gave the prize to the winner of the 1859 distance race, Petros Velissariou. When Brookes learned of this disposition of his prize, he immediately made Velissariou an Honorary Member of "The Wenlock Olympian Society". For he had just changed the name of his group. The Chairman of the 1859 Athens Olympic Committee, Theocharis, too, was made as an Honorary Olympian at Wenlock.

The 1859 Athens Olympic Games, as Rühl has shown, profoundly changed Brookes' activity, making it far more "olympic" even in such details as the awards ceremonies. Armed with the Athens program before he set the 1859 Much Wenlock Games, he introduced the javelin to England that year. But 1859 was the last annual meeting of the "Olympian Class". In 1860 Brookes severed his group from the Agricultural Reading Society, and renamed it the "Wenlock Olympian Society" (hereafter WOS). And, though still interested in the working man, he seemed bitten by the bug of the olympic movement that had developed in Greece[19].

In 1860 Brookes sent various letters to the Greeks, one a letter to Theocharis, another to King Otto. I do not know all their contents. The letter to Theocharis probably concerned Velissariou's prize and his own election to Wenlock membership. Brookes wrote to King Otto that he had founded the Olympian Class at Wenlock "in humble imitation of the example of the ancient Greeks". But even more interesting is an exchange of letters between Brookes and Charilaos Trikoupis, a young Greek politician apparently then in the Greek embassy in London[20]; for thirty-four years later, Trikoupis would be the bane of the olympic movement, and almost end the long common dream of Brookes, Zappas, and Coubertin in a single day. We shall come to Trikoupis later. And around England Brookes sent a flurry of programs for the new "Wenlock Olympian Games". In May 1860, just months after the first Zappas Games, he told the new WOS that five cities of their county, Shropshire, agreed to annual regional games, "Shropshire Olympics", which would rotate about the major cities of the county. It seems mere coincidence that Brookes' proposal for rotating sites in Shropshire recalled Soutsos' first notion of rotating the Olympic Games in Greece. But Brookes' idea was destined to transform into our own system; for example, Moscow, Los Angeles, Seoul, and Barcelona. It was thus Brookes' idea before it was Coubertin's. Four of these Shropshire County Olympics actually took place: 1860 (Much Wenlock), 1861 (Wellington), 1862 (Much Wenlock), and 1864 (Shrewsbury). They too were serious athletic meetings, most events being those standard to track and field[21]. They ended because Brookes had more important things to do—and Olympism was in the air.

In 1862 another series of Olympic Games sprang up in Liverpool, with John Hulley as their co-founder. It is almost certain that the Liverpudlian Olympics were inspired by Brookes' activity, as it is certain Brookes was inspired by the 1859 Zappas Games in Greece[22]. Hulley's meetings in Liverpool, too, were serious athletic contests, but did not last long. They were held in 1862, 1863—the best of the set, with more than 12 000 spectators and national competitors—and 1864[23]. But Hulley, too, had more important things to do.

In 1865 he and Brookes formed the National Olympian Association, or NOA. Brookes' olympic movement had advanced from the local to the national level. The NOA proposed to hold their annual national Olympic Games, "in rotation in the principal cities and towns of England[24]". We are one step closer to Coubertin's "ambulatory international Olympics Games". Hardly known to olympic history, the NOA held six national Olympic Games in England, from 1866-1883. For its first Olympic Games, the NOA thought big: London in 1866. Their announcement, when it reached London in 1865, panicked the upper class gentlemen athletes of London and Oxbridge; the sporting world would never be the same. These gentlemen athletes of southern England quickly formed a counter-olympic movement to foil these "provincials" from Liverpool. The class and regional prejudices of the southern aristocracy outweighed any sympathy they might have had for the hallowed name from Ancient Greece.

The southern athletes founded an elitist club, the Amateur Athletic Club, or AAC—the first time the word *amateur* appeared in a name. The AAC later became the AAA, Amateur Athletic Association. Lovesey, historian of the AAA, wrote: "It has been said that the AAC prospectus, published in February 1866, bears signs of having been cobbled together to thwart the National Olympian Association[25]." The AAC enrolled the best athletes in southern England and quickly produced the first amateur Championships several months before the first national Olympic Games were staged. All but a few of its members then boycotted Brookes' NOA Games in July. For Brookes would not exclude working class athletes; the AAC did. But the first national Olympian Games in London, July 1866, were a success. They included swimming events as well as track and field. And the steeplechase event appeared for the first time in history. Athletes from all over England competed, and 10 000 spectators watched. Newspaper judgments were, in the main, very favorable. An Oxford newspaper called Brookes "the father of the Olympian Movement". But the AAC boycott had put a damper on the affair[26].

The second national Olympic Games were held in Birmingham the next year. As earlier, the Games were open only to amateurs; but Brookes and the NOA still refused to define "amateur" as the AAC wanted. The aristocratic AAC wanted all amateur meetings to exclude explicitly any applicant who worked as a "mechanic, artisan, or labourer". Brookes would not. The AAC boycotted him again. The olympians competing at Birmingham came from all over England, including London, but not many from the AAC. There was a good crowd. The 1867 British National Games were also a success[27]. But things started to deteriorate the next year. The 1868 Olympic Games were first scheduled for Manchester; but there were few sign-ups, and the Games moved to Wellington, a small town in Shropshire. Few first-rate athletes came. The AAC had succeeded in rebuffing Brookes' national Olympic Movement, which was now headed downhill[28]. There would be no more NOA Games for six years; and then, in 1874, they would be held in Much Wenlock. The British National Olympic Movement was sick, if not dead.

Just as the movement began to founder in England, it got new life in Greece. King Otto was long gone. The Greeks had ousted him in 1862 for his tyrannical ways[29]. Their allies rewarded them with a Danish teenager, King George the First, instead. Zappas was also long dead. He had passed away in 1865. But in his will Zappas had left a huge sum for the permanent revival of the Olympic Games—and the restoration of the marble stadium in Athens. A new "Committee of the Olympics" was formed. In turmoil, Greece could not organize further Olympic Games until 1870. But then they held Games of the first order, an "A–" if not an "A". On the 1870 Athens Olympic Games, too, I have written elsewhere[30]; I shall thus only summarize. Although most of the money was spent on the agri-industrial competitions, the ancient stadium was excavated, cleared, and well prepared for the athletic events. There were no marble seats, but in that stadium 30 000 spectators watched Greek athletes from all over the Greek world, the poor ones subsidized by the state, contend for cash prizes and olympic glory. There was perfect order in the stadium and stands, and at the end almost everyone sung the praises of Zappas, called now "the founder of the Olympics[31]".

But the anti-athletic clique had fumed, just before the 1870 Games, that bodily excellence was no longer of value: since guns had been invented, physical prowess meant nothing on the battle-field. After the Games, it found another reason to carp. Taking its cue from the elitist rules of the AAC in London, it complained that athletes from the working class had been allowed to compete and had won. Some Athenian professors asked that in future Olympic Games, competition be limited to youth from the "cultured class". Elitist amateurism had thwarted the Olympic Movement in England, and now it thwarted it in Greece. The government listened to the intellectual clique's call for class-exclusive amateurism. Entry in the next edition of the Zappas Olympic Games, 1875, was limited to "the cultured class", namely, students at the university[32].

Again, I summarize. The 1875 Olympic Games, too, were held in the ancient Panathenaic stadium. But entry was restricted to amateurs, *i.e.*, youth of the "upper class". There were fewer contestants, and a smaller crowd than at the successful 1870 Games. Even worse, these upper class boys made a joke out of the competitions. The newspapers criticized these Olympic Games so severely that the main coach left town. They can be given a "D" rating[33]. But the 1875 Olympic Games contain a wonderful missing link between the Letrini committee, charged to pursue the olympic idea at Ancient Olympia in 1838, and the Barcelona Olympic Games of 1992. His name is Pavlos Giannopoulos. Giannopoulos was a member of that Letrini committee that had conceived the olympic idea in 1838. In 1875, he was Vice President of the Greek Olympic Organizing Committee. And in the official 1875 report he proudly noted that the olympic idea had become international: that "Dr. Brookes in Wenlock, England, has founded Olympic Games, and he warmly greeted our first Olympiad in 1859[34]." From the 1838 Letrini committee, through the Olympic Games of 1859, 1870, 1875, and now the Olympic Games in Wenlock, England—all those things concerned Giannopoulos. Therefore he, too, should be reckoned a member of the Olympic Movement, from 1838 to 1875. How many other unsung members of the movement there may also be[35].

The renewed Zappas series in Greece apparently inspired Brookes to try to restore life to his own national Olympic Games, which the NOA now scheduled for nearby Shrewsbury in 1877, the fifth British National Olympic Games. The 1875 Athens Olympic Games clearly inspired Brookes to renew his contacts with Greece. *The result was, in fact, the birth of the International Olympic Movement.*

Through the Greek ambassador in London, John Gennadius, Brookes asked King George of Greece to donate a cup to the winner of the pentathlon at these fifth British National Olympic Games in 1877. King George complied, and gave the cup "from the King of the Hellenes" to "the winner of the pentathlon in the English Modern Olympic Games". But top-flight athletes did not come; the prize went to a local law-student. In fact the gift of King George's cup was the most notable event of the 1877 British National Olympic Games, allowing Brookes to claim that "the monarch of Greece takes a lively interest in our modern Olympian Games[36]".

A curious entry in the 1880 Wenlock financial ledger notes that Socrates Parasyrakes donated a pound to the Wenlock Olympic Society[37]. And then it happened. In 1880 Brookes proposed the creation of an "International Olympian Festival in Athens": "The proposal has been favorably received by Greek residents in England, and will, no doubt, be cordially responded to by the authorities at Athens, and by the principal athletic societies of Great Britain [...] athletes of other nations, contending in the time-consecrated stadium at Athens[38]."

In June 1881 a Greek language newspaper in Trieste reported: "Dr. Brookes [. . .] is endeavoring to organize an International Olympian Festival, to be held in Athens, [. . .] we have no doubt that the Greek Government will give every facility for its realization[39]." But by 1881 the Greek Olympic Committee, dominated by the anti-athletic faction, was refusing even to hold national Olympic Games, to say nothing of international Games. It decided instead to spend Zappas' money on a fancy building, ostensibly for the industrial exhibits of the Olympics[40].

In 1883, Gennadius wrote Brookes a temporizing letter: "I feel grateful to you regarding your proposal to re-establish Olympic Games [. . .] I am sure that the Greeks would view that with great approval[41]." In 1886 Mr. Alexander, the Greek ambassador to the United States, wrote to Brookes, and in 1887, so did Gennadius, again. I do not know the contents, but most likely they concerned Brookes' idea of Athens international Olympic Games[42]. The next year, 1888, Paschal Grousset, proposed "the inauguration of French Olympic Games[43]". Olympism was in the air, even if Coubertin later denied it. The Greek Olympic Committee announced the opening of the new building, the "Zappeion", and scheduled Industrial Olympics there, Athletic Olympics in the stadium. The Industrial Games were indeed held for the first and last time in the Zappeion. But the Olympic Committee, now entirely in the hands of the anti-athletic clique and chaired by Stephanos Dragoumis, smugly and silently canceled the Athletic Olympic Games. (Later Dragoumis tried to stop the 1896 Olympic Games, too.) When Phokianos, coach at the 1875 Games heard that the 1888 Athletic Olympic Games were canceled, he decided to hold them himself in 1889 in his tiny gym, contests for the upper class alone. Spectators could attend by invitation only. First, the Greek people, to whom Zappas had given the revived Games, were excluded from competition. Now they could not even watch. That was a good thing; for as the Games began, the upper class athletes ran amuck in the crowd, frightening women and creating chaos. The Games were cancelled almost as they began[44]. So the 1888 (1889) Olympic Games may deserve a clear "F" rating. But the Greek Olympic Movement just gets an "I", for "Incomplete".

The next year the 1890 Wenlock Olympian Games took place in May, as usual. By 1890 Brookes' Olympic Games were just a shadow of their former selves. In the early years Brookes' Games had attracted good athletes. But now there were scores of athletic meetings around England, held under the auspices of the AAA. The best athletes did not come to Wenlock now. Brookes' Society was in financial straits. The crowds were down—thousands had dwindled into a couple of hundred for 1890. Coubertin was not one of them. He visited Wenlock in autumn. For he had, as yet, no known interest in the Olympic Games, only in physical education and sport. But when Coubertin did come in October, Brookes, wanting to show the Baron his festival, staged a special Autumn "Olympian" meeting. Coubertin admired the opening ceremonies, the award ceremonies, the pomp and trappings of Brookes' Olympic Games[45]. MacAloon has already suggested that their counterparts in the present Olympic Games were Coubertin's borrowings from Brookes[46].

But what else did Coubertin borrow from Brookes? To state it flatly: the olympic idea was borrowed directly from Brookes and indirectly from Zappas; for Brookes' olympic idea had in turn been heavily influenced by Zappas' olympic idea, and his modern Greek Games. These things are all inextricably bound together. Coubertin's visit to Much Wenlock and his own writings indicate that Brookes had indeed informed Coubertin of the history of the olympic movement and with the Greeks' and his own (Brookes) role in it. Coubertin himself admits that Brookes told him at least the following items: 1– that Brookes had sent a prize to Greece in the time of King Otto, a prize to be given in athletic contests named "Olympics[47]"; 2– that King George of Greece had sent a prize for the pentathlon victor in one of Brookes' olympic festivals[48]; 3– that Brookes had already caused "Olympian Festivals" (*i.e.*, the British National Olympic Games) to be held in Birmingham,

Shrewsbury, and Wellington[49]; 4– that Brookes had proposed that international Olympic Games be held in Greece[50].

Without question, Coubertin knew from Brookes that there had been an olympic revival movement in both Greece and England, that Olympic Games had in fact been held in both those countries, and that Brookes himself had proposed that international Olympic Games be begun in Athens. I cannot, therefore, view Coubertin as the man who first had the idea of a modern olympic revival. Zappas had already been called "founder of the Olympic Games", and Brookes "the father of the Olympian Movement". I submit that Coubertin is neither the "founder" nor the "father" of the modern Olympic Games. Rather, I think, he is its "savior", savior of the Olympic Idea, savior of the Olympic Movement. I explain. Here was the state of the Olympic Movement when the young Coubertin joined it in 1890. In Greece, an olympic movement begun half a century earlier appeared to have run an unsuccessful course. The 1870 Olympic Games, viewed by 30 000 spectators in the ancient Panathenaic stadium, had been a high point. But the anti-athletic faction had always made sure that industry eclipsed athletics. It now wholly controlled the Olympic Committee and its money, thwarting Zappas' wills—his desire and his testament—by refusing to hold further editions of the revived Olympic Games.

In England, Brookes too had had some success in reviving the Olympic Games. But he had turned his attention to physical education, because the elitist clubs ran his national Olympic Movement aground, and his calls to Greece for international Olympic Games had been ignored[51]. Brookes—probably along with Zappas the real founder of the modern Games—was aging and ailing, ready to pass the torch to a successor. In 1892, two years after his visit with Brookes, Coubertin acted as if he had a wholly novel idea. He had at the time never been in Greece. But inspired, he claimed, by many "spiritual" walks around Ancient Olympia, he proposed to his colleagues in Paris this "novel" idea: "the restoration of the Olympic Games". Coubertin claimed that the idea was so novel that it wholly baffled his audience. If one knows the previous history of the Olympic Movement, the Baron's assertions here are actually amazing[52].

The next year, 1893, Coubertin scheduled an International Athletic Congress for Paris, June 1894. I have already written on the famous June 1894 Congress, and on the events just before it met[53]. I summarize. By April, 1894, Coubertin had hardly advertised his congress, and almost no delegates had signed up for June. But then something happened in Greece. In early April Coubertin's friend, Charles Waldstein, at the Baron's request, "laid the question before the Greek royal family". Waldstein had a long audience with Constantine, heir to the Greek throne. In mid-April Waldstein wrote Coubertin that Prince Constantine would be an Honorary Member of his Paris Congress[54]. Waldstein, too, was enrolled. That same month, then, Coubertin sent out a flurry of invitations for his congress in June, along with a request that delegates send ahead their opinions on amateurism and the revival of the Olympic Games. In May Brookes got his invitation. Failing health, he told Coubertin, would keep him from Paris. But on May 22 1894, he responded on both Congress topics. On the Olympic Games, he recommended that Greece be the permanent site; but he was willing to accept a rotating pattern:

> This has long been a cherished idea of mine so far as making Greece the centre, but the plan of your Congress [...] is a really superb one and deserving of [...] support [...] [I approve the idea of] the establishment of an international Olympian Association and the arrangement that such gatherings shall be held, in rotation, in or near the Capitals of all nations joining in the movement[55].

That concept of rotation, first conceived by Soutsos and implemented in Brookes' Shropshire Games, Coubertin embraced and presented as if it were his own. The same is true of Brookes' ideas on amateurism[56]; they became part of the

Olympic Games, ratified by Coubertin's 1894 Congress. But MacAloon and others have already written on that congress, and its public history is rather well known[57]. I shall focus on what took place behind the scenes. Brookes deeply believed in the international Olympic Movement that he had founded, and if Coubertin were willing to take over and succeed, he was willing to compromise. He wanted him to succeed. So, on Coubertin's behalf, he called on what he thought were some old friends in Greece. On June 11, several days before the Paris Congress, Brookes wrote to Charilaos Trikoupis. He and Brookes had exchanged letters some thirty years before, when Trikoupis was a young Greek diplomat. Now he was the Prime Minister. Brookes addresses him as "Your Excellency":

> I have taken the liberty of forwarding to you a report of the Wenlock Olympian Society, an institution which I established 44 years ago. [. . .] My friend, Baron Pierre de Coubertin of Paris, and the other advocates of physical education, myself among their number, are exerting ourselves to promote international Olympian festivals, and I earnestly hope they will be successful, and be honoured by the patronage of His Majesty, The King of the Hellenes. The remembrance of my correspondence with Sir Thos. Wyse and yourself relative to the Olympian Games at Athens in Nov. 1859 [. . .] is a source of great pleasure to me[58].

What Trikoupis' first reaction was, we do not know–only his later reaction.

About the same time, a strange event happened in Paris—strange at least as told by Demetrios Vikelas, soon to become first President of the IOC. Vikelas, a Greek citizen born in Greece, had spent virtually all his adult life living in England and France as a businessman and author. According to Vikelas[59], in early June 1894 he received at his Paris home a certificate making him a member of an Athens athletic club; and letters from friends, asking him to represent that club at Coubertin's Paris Congress a few days away. Vikelas, who had never had anything to do with athletics, claims he had never before heard of the Athenian athletic club, nor of Coubertin, nor of the Paris Congress. But he went, as a favor to his friends. There, "as if by previous agreement", he was elected chairman of the Congress' sub-committee on the Olympic Games. A couple of days later he became the first President of the IOC; for when he, all on his own, he writes, on the last day, June 23, decided to propose to begin the Olympic Games at Athens, it was approved by acclamation. The last item here, that it was Vikelas' idea to propose Athens for 1896, is not true. Ignored for too long, the minutes of that 1894 Congress prove that several days before, the delegates had voted to begin in London, 1896[60]. Coubertin immediatly proposed Athens instead. When they voted for London, anyway, the Baron simply tabled their motion. Vikelas did not, on that first occasion, support Coubertin's Athens motion. Later that day, the Baron sent a telegram to King George in Greece. The King replied, in response to Coubertin's "question", with his "thanks" to the Congress, and best wishes for the re-establishment of the Olympic Games[61]. What was Coubertin's question? Why was King George thanking the Congress—before Athens had been publicly mentioned as the site? Why was the non-athletic Vikelas so suddenly pressed into service, and "as if pre-arranged" made chair of the Olympic sub-committee? Why did Coubertin insist on Athens, when the delegates voted for London? Why did both Coubertin and Vikelas lie about the proposal of Athens, saying it was first heard from Vikelas on that final day, June 23, when the minutes show it was Coubertin's motion, days before, on June 19[62]? All this makes little sense.

I make a hypothesis, which, if substantiated, would solve these questions. The analysis of the information points to a single answer: namely, that Coubertin and the Greek Royal family—Constantine in particular—had already agreed to hold the first International Olympic Games in Athens before Coubertin's Paris congress even met[63]. MacAloon has suggested that the congress was mostly show. I suspect it was all show as Coubertin almost admits himself[64]. When Coubertin asked Waldstein "to lay the question before the Royal Family of Greece", what was the question? Was it just the broad question of an olympic revival? Or was it more specific: Will Greece host Olympic Games in 1896? Was it Coubertin's idea, Brookes', Constantine's, or Waldstein's? One thing seems certain, the "Athens in 1896" idea was not a June 1894 invention of Demetrios Vikelas, as one has been led to believe. But Vikelas, now President of the IOC, was the man charged to carry it out.

In October 1894 Vikelas went to Athens to work with the Zappas Olympic Committee, which he assumed would form the local Olympic Organizing Committee. Coubertin was to join him soon—the Baron's first trip to Greece. Vikelas scheduled a meeting with Dragoumis' Olympic Committee, but suddenly learned that his wife was dying in Paris. He left for France. Coubertin soon arrived alone, at the mercy of Greek politics. He got Crown Prince Constantine to agree to preside over the organizing committee. But he got a resounding "No" from Trikoupis on the question whether the Games would even be held. Dragoumis, head of the Olympic Committee and a political ally of Trikoupis, told Coubertin there would be no Games. What Coubertin perhaps did not know then—but later found out to his chagrin—was that Prince Constantine and Trikoupis were bitter political enemies. Constantine had even marched in a street demonstration against Trikoupis! When Dragoumis told the Baron that his Olympic Committee would do nothing for the Games, Coubertin said he would form his own Greek organizing committee. Dragoumis gave him a meeting room in the Zappeion, and some Greeks' names, as Coubertin requested. But Dragoumis had played a trick on the Baron: the people whose names he gave were either out of town or anti-royalist. When Coubertin convened this group, he announced that Prince Constantine would be their president; the committee agreed to host the Games and—as soon as Coubertin left town—it dissolved itself.

Now Vikelas returned after his wife was buried: no Coubertin, no committee. He and Constantine began anew, formed another committee, and started plans for the 1896 Games. Both were excellent administrators, and fanned pro-olympic opinion among the people. It spread to parliament. There Trikoupis and Dragoumis opposed the Games that Coubertin and Vikelas proposed, but they were rebuffed by others who claimed that these Games were the fulfillment of Zappas' dream. Trikoupis was soon voted out of office, and Olympic Games preparations proceeded apace.

I shorten a long story[65]. Coubertin, occupied writing a French history book and preparing for marriage, switched his interests away from the lost interest in the Olympic Games. He refused to come to Athens to help, did very little for the 1896 preparations. At one point, it seems, he even tried to resign from the IOC. Vikelas refused to accept his resignation. He, Constantine, and the Greek organizing committee, despite all the odds and bad weather, produced an excellent edition of the first international Olympic Games. The Greek Louis won the first marathon, and so on. The 1896 Games were a success. But Brookes did not live to see his dream come true. He died a few months too soon, in July 1895, joining Zappas in Olympic mist.

In 1883, shortly after proposing that the Olympic Games be revived on an international scale, Brookes had said:

> I often think of a remark of O'Connell's that 'There are but two classes in the world; one to hammer, and the other to be hammered at.' So I shall hammer on in the belief that others will succeed me who will strike with more effect[66].

NOTES AND REFERENCES

1. Private letter from Coubertin to Bill Henry, dated July 27, 1934

2. Coubertin P de (1934) Quarante années d'Olympisme 1894-1934. Le Sport Suisse, 30ᵉ année, 4 juillet. In Müller N, Comité international olympique (eds) Pierre de Coubertin. Textes Choisis. Tome II Olympisme. Zürich: Weidmann p 347. References 1 and 2 are both quoted in Henry B, Yeomans PH (1984) An approved history of the Olympic Games. Los Angeles: Southern California Committee for the Olympic Games (1984 edition updated by Patricia Yeomans; first edition 1948 p 19). *Editors' Note:* an incorrect translation of Coubertin's words appears to have been made somewhere. Examples: «Vainement des *perfidies ultérieures* s'exerceront-elles à faire prédominer la notion [...]» was translated as "Vainly, *perfidious outsiders* [...]"; also, «L'Olympisme est né *cette fois* tout équipé, comme Minerve [...]» was translated with the «cette fois» = "this time" left out (Emphasis added)].

3. MacAloon JJ (1981) This great symbol: Pierre de Coubertin and the modern Olympic Games. Chicago: University of Chicago Press. Redmond G (1988) Toward modern revival of the Olympic Games: the various "pseudo-Olympics" of the 19th century. In Segrave J, Chu D (eds) The Olympic Games in transition. Champaign: Human Kinetics p 71-87

4. Coubertin P de (1890) Les jeux olympiques à Much Wenlock: une page de l'histoire de l'athlétisme. La Revue Athlétique 1ᵉʳᵉ année 25 déc. no 12 p 706 «[...] Much Wenlock est un bourg du Shropshire, comté sur les confins du pays de Galles et si les jeux olympiques que la Grèce moderne n'a pas su ressusciter y revivent aujourd'hui, ce n'est pas à un Hellène qu'on en est redevable, mais bien au Dr. W.P. Brookes. C'est lui qui les inaugura il y a 40 ans et lui encore, âgé maintenant de 82 ans, mais toujours alerte et vigoureux, qui les organise et les anime». [...] In Müller N, Comité international olympique (eds) Pierre de Coubertin. Textes Choisis. Tome II Olympisme. Zürich: Weidmann p 78

5. Ibid [...] «Une tentative plus audacieuse encore eut la Grèce pour théatre [...]» (p 712); «[...] le Dr Brookes qui a entretenu une volumineuse correspondance avec tous ceux qu'il a crus favorables à sa cause, le Dr Brookes écrivit au Roi des Hellènes et fit si bien que sa Majesté donna une magnifique coupe pour le concours de Wenlock et favorisa le rétablissement à Athènes des jeux olympiques» (p 712); [...] «J'ai vu dans les annales de Wenlock les résultats de ce concours et les noms des lauréats. Depuis lors, oncques n'a entendu parler des jeux olympiques à Athènes» (p 712); [...] «On a crié, pesté, lutté contre ce développement de l'athlétisme, mais les contradicteurs ont été noyés par la marée montante et nous qui croyons cette marée salutaire et féconde, nous ferons tout pour accroître sa force et pour qu'elle submerge les obstacles qui, en France aujourd'hui, comme en Angleterre jadis, lui sont opposées» (p 707). In Müller N, Comité international olympique (eds) Pierre de Coubertin. Textes Choisis. Tome II Olympisme. Zürich: Weidmann p 83, 84, 84, 80

6. Coubertin P de (1896) Les Jeux Olympiques de 1896. In Les Jeux olympiques: 776 av JC—1896. Rapport officiel, Deuxième partie: Athènes: Beck. [...] «Pour moi j'en revendique hautement la paternité et je veux ici remercier de plus, ceux qui m'ont aidé à la mener à bien» (p 60) In Müller N, Comité international olympique (eds) Pierre de Coubertin. Textes Choisis. Tome II Olympisme. Zürich: Weidmann p 128

7. Coubertin P de (1890) op cit [...] «Mais quand on recherchera pour les fixer les origines de ce mouvement d'une si colossale amplitude, il ne suffira pas d'en retracer les lignes centrales. A certaines époques, *certaines idées parcourent le monde* et elles se propagent comme de véritables épidémies; il est bien difficile de les *monopoliser au profit d'un seul* et l'on découvre généralement que sans être entendus et s'être mis d'accord *plusieurs hommes ont travaillé simultanément à la même œuvre en des lieux différents*» (p 708). In Müller N, Comité international olympique (eds) Pierre de Coubertin. Textes Choisis. Tome II Olympisme. Zürich: Weidmann p 80 (Emphasis added)

8. Rühl J (1989) L'idéal de l'amateurisme et l'influence de la Grèce sur les "Jeux olympiques" à Much Wenlock; Paper delivered at the HISPA Meeting, Olympia, Greece. Neumüller B (1985) Die Geschichte der Much Wenlock Games; Unpublished Diplomarbeit, Deutsche Sporthochschule Köln. Kivroglou A (1981) Die Bemühungen

von Ewangelos Sappas um die Wiederereinführung der Olympischen Spiele in Griechenland unter besonderer Berücksichtigung der Spiele von 1859; Unpublished Diplomarbeit, Deutsche Sporthochschule Köln. Young DC (1984) The olympic myth of Greek amateur athletics. Chicago: Ares. Young DC (1987) The origins of the modern Olympics: a new version. International Journal of the History of Sport 4 271-300. Young DC (1988) Demetrios Vikelas, first president of the IOC. Stadion: International Zeitschrift für Geschichte des Sports 14 85-102

9. Article by Panagiotis Soutsos in the Athens newspaper, ''Ηλιος (Ilios), July 13, 1856, p 2. Kivroglou, op cit p 25, interprets Soutsos' words differently: "Nach Soutsos [in an article in Ilios, July 13, 1856] war dieses Angebot [Zappas' wish to finance a re-establishment of the Olympic Games] die Verwirklichung einer Idee, die im Jahr 1835 ein Komitee aufgebracht hatte—Soutsos war Mitglied dieses Komitees—die auch vom damaligen Innenminister, Ionnis Koletis, akzeptiert worden war". But in my own transcription of this article, I find nothing about a committee. And I would translate Soutsos' first paragraph thus: "In 1835 we wrote a memo, which [...] Kolettis accepted, concerning the revival of the Olympic Games [...]". Perhaps the "editorial we" (regularly means "I" in Soutsos' works) misled Kivroglou to conclude there was a committee.

10. The 1835 memo suggested 25 March—Greek Independance Day—for the revived Olympic Games; Otto's 1837 law specified October as the time of the Greek national festival.

11. Ioannis Chrysafis Οἱ σύγχρονοι διεθνεῖς Ὀλυμπιακοὶ Ἀγῶνες, Athens: Hellenic Olympic Committee, 1930, 18. The text of the 1838 proposal from Letrini is reproduced in the Δελτίον τῆς Ἱστορικῆς καὶ Ἐθνολογικῆς Ἑταιρείας τῆς Ἑλλάδος 9 (1926) 566-67

12. ''Ηλιος, 13 July 1856 p 2. Soutsos there prints the text of his 1845 speech, which, he says was "published in the news-papers"; 1845 Greek newspapers are difficult to find, and I have seen no pre-1856 version.

13. Neumüller B (1985) op cit p 39-94

14. Chrysafis I (1930) op cit p 24 says "1858" and I followed him (Young DC (1987) op cit p 274) wrongly, in view of the original 1856 documents in Kivroglou. In fact, Zappas actually proposed that the first revived Olympic Games take place in 1857 (Kivroglou A (1981) op cit)

15. Kivroglou A (1981) op cit p 27 with relevant documents. Alexandros Rangavis (who, as Foreign Minister, received Zappas' offer and carried on elaborate correspondance with him; below) implies that Zappas got the idea from reading Soutsos' article Ἀπομνημονεύματα [Memoirs], II [Athens, 1895], p 377). Since Soutsos' article postdates Zappas' original proposal (below)—and is titled "Evangelis Zappas"—it cannot have been this article; but Rangavis' wording misled me (Young DC (1987) op cit p 273-74) and Kivroglou A (1981) op cit p 26

16. Soutsos P (1856) op cit p 2; see note 12 above

17. Rangavis published at least three different paraphrases of his own letter. I follow the earliest version (from Ὑπομνηματικοὶ Σημείωσις [Berlin], July 9/21, 1886; reprinted in Μέγα Ἑλληνικὸν Βιογραφικὸν Λεξικόν [Athens; not dated but 1962], sv Zappas, Evangelis, p 396); for there Rangavis admits that Zappas forced him to compromise by adding athletics to the proposed Olympic program. In another version (in his Ἀπομνημονεύματα [Memoirs], II [Athens, 1895], p 377, which Kivroglou A (1981) op cit p 29-30 follows) it appears that Rangavis offered the compromise himself; and Rangavis says he wrote: "[Nations become distinguished] not by physical strength and ability but through intellectual activity and development". The third version as in Ἑστία, 10 January, 1888 p 17

18. Young DC (1987) op cit p 274-75; Young DC (1984) op cit p 30, 39 I corrected some errors in previous reports of these games (but myself mislocated them at the Plateia Kotzia)

19. Rühl J (1989) op cit p 8-9; Neumüller B (1981) op cit p 95-97, 102-05

20. These letters are merely listed (with no text or analysis) as documents in Neumüller B (1981) op cit p 302. Some of the letter to King Otto is reproduced in Neumüller B (1981) op cit p 101

21. Neumüller B (1981) op cit p 97-100

22. The 1862 Games in Liverpool featured an essay contest on the phrase "mens sana in corpore sano"—a favorite motto of WP Brookes see Redmond G (1988) op cit p 79; Neumüller B (1981) op cit p 240

23. A few more Liverpudlian Olympics were held, last in 1867, organized by another group, the Athletic Society of Great Britain. See Neumüller B (1981) op cit p 109; Redmond G (1988) op cit p 76

24. Neumüller B (1981) op cit p 120, 114, 116-17. A third founding member, with Hulley and Brookes, was EG Ravenstein, a devotee of German Turner traditions and President of the German Gymnastic Society of London.

25. Lovesey P (1979) The official centenary history of the Amateur Athletic Association. Enfield: p 21 [in Neumüller B (1981) op cit p 122]

26. Neumüller B (1981) op cit p 116-29

27. Ibid p 132-37

28. Ibid p 142-44

29. Kousoulas DG (1974) Modern Greece: profile of a nation. New York: Scribner's Sons p 40

30. Young DC (1987) op cit p 275-77; Young DC (1984) op cit p 30-32

31. Chrestides D (1872) (ed) Ὀλύμπια τοῦ 1870, II. Athens: Government Press p 218 sq

32. Young DC (1987) op cit p 277; Young DC (1984) op cit p 32-34

33. Fuller accounts in Young DC (1987) op cit p 277-78; Young DC (1984) op cit p 33-37, 40

34. Ὀλύμπια τοῦ 1875 (Official Committee Report) Athens: Government Press, not dated (1876) p 192

35. Another interesting connection: the 1870 Olympic Committee Report (Ὀλύμπια τοῦ 1870, above, note 31), p 170 lists Julius Ennig as Gymnasiarch (coach) for those games; Demetrios Vikelas, first president of the IOC, as a child studied under Ennig (Vikelas, Ἡ Ζωή μου, Athens: Ὠφέλιμα βιβλία, 1908, p 116-17)

36. Rühl J (1989) op cit p 10; Neumüller B (1981) op cit p 180-83, 302, document no 108

37. Neumüller B (1981) op cit p 288, no 409

38. Wenlock Olympian Society. Address of the Committee of 1880, Jan 21, 1881 (minute book 2 p 52; from Neumüller B (1981) op cit p 200); Brookes, it seems, had already sounded out, or been contacted by, some Greeks (Parasyrakes? Gennadius?) about the question of international Olympic Games.

39. Κλειώ, 14/25 June, 1881 p 4. Neumüller B (1981) op cit p 201 reproduces part of an English translation found among Brookes' papers. Neumüller further believes (288, no 409) that the author of the Κλειώ piece—signed "S.P."—is the same Socrates Parasyrakes who had, the previous year, donated a pound to Wenlock. But the article was no doubt written by S. Papandonopoulos, whom the newspaper masthead lists as its London correspondent.

40. Young DC (1987) op cit p 278

41. Rühl, J (1989) op cit, who cites the WOS minute book II.89, and a letter dated October 11, 1883. The English here is my translation of Rühl's French translation of a (no doubt) English original. Cf Neumüller B (1981) op cit p 302, document no 109; p 217-18

42. Alexander later helped to provide an American team for the 1896 Athens Olympic Games: see Young DC (1987) op cit p 298 n 66

43. MacAloon JJ (1981) op cit p 111

44. Young DC (1987) op cit p 278-79

45. Coubertin P de (1890) op cit. Coubertin, writing about Brookes' Olympic Games says: [. . .] «l'épisode que je veux vous conter ne sera pas l'un des moins curieux dans ces annales de l'athlétisme. Ce qui le caractérise, c'est le voile de poésie qui l'enveloppe et le parfum d'antiquité qui s'en échappe» (p 708). In Müller N, Comité international

olympique (eds) Pierre de Coubertin. Textes Choisis. Tome II Olympisme. Zürich: Weidmann p 80

46. MacAloon JJ (1981) op cit p 147-50; Neumüller B (1981) op cit p 230-49; see Mandell R (1976) The First Modern Olympics. Berkeley: University of California Press p 77

47. Coubertin P de (1909) Le comité, la ligue et l'union. In Une campagne de vingt-et-un ans 1887-1908. Paris: Librairie de l'Éducation physique p 53; Coubertin here misrepresents (see Young DC (1987) op cit p 287): "Malheureusement, l'épreuve ne se renouvela pas". Coubertin knew his statement was false; *l'épreuve se renouvela* several times.

48. Coubertin P de (1897) A typical Englishman: Dr WP Brookes of Wenlock in Shropshire. The Review of Reviews XV 62-65. (The title-page of that particular number of the Review had for a title: "A Typical Englishman: Dr WP Brookes, and His British Olympic Games. By Baron Pierre de Coubertin. Illustrated"). [...] "His Majesty [King George] presented to the Wenlock Association, as a prize for the Pentathlon, a cup of the value of 10 £, and was of course honored by the dedication of a tree" [...] p 65

49. Coubertin P de (1890) op cit. The Baron refers only indirectly and not by name to the first British National Olympic Games in London: [...] «un essai fut bien tenté vers 1866 pour étendre et généraliser les jeux olympiques. Un festival eut lieu cette année-là au Palais de Cristal. Il fut renouvelé l'année suivante à Birmingham, puis à Shrewsbury, si j'ai bonne mémoire» p 712. Coubertin P de (1897) op cit. The Baron again does not mention by name the first British National Olympic Games in London, obviously a noteworthy event in a major city. Instead, Coubertin refers to the interest of the Greek minister at the English court who read an account of the "Olympian Festival" in the London papers and [...] "communicated with the managers of the [Olympian] festival inquiring whether any memento of an occasion so interesting to a descendant of the ancient Greeks could be furnished to him for transmission to his sovereign". [...] p 65

50. Coubertin P de (1897) op cit [...] "Dr Brookes even endeavored to promote a festival in Athens; many young Englishmen, he thought, would gladly avail themselves of such an opportunity of visiting the classic land. But the proposal was declined by the Greek government. A festival of this kind could hardly be planned as long as the Paris Congress had not met to reorganize and revive the Olympian games on a permanent and broader scale. Dr. Brookes lived long enough to see this work done, and stood on that occasion among our most hearty supporters" p 65

51. MacAloon JJ (1981) op cit p 150 speculates that "The real reason why this proposal [Brookes' proposal for international Olympics in Athens] was refused was that the Greeks already had their own Olympic Games" (p 150). That is not wholly correct; the reason was because the Greek anti-athletic faction controlled the Olympic Committee.

52. Coubertin P de (1909) op cit p 90

53. Young DC (1987) op cit p 280-86; Young DC (1984) op cit p 60-67; Young DC (1988) op cit; Vikelas op cit p 89-90

54. Coubertin P de (1909) op cit p 94

55. Letter dated May 22, 1894; Neumüller B (1981) op cit p 253 (with no 528). Neumüller works from a copy, unsuccessful, he says in seeking the original at the IOC Archives in Lausanne in 1983. In 1985 I saw a photocopy of this letter in the IOC Library at Lausanne.

56. On the topic of amateurism, Brookes had been the first to refuse to define "amateur" in terms of social class. His views in this respect, never accepted by the majority of English amateur clubs, were, as Rühl has noted, adopted in practice by Coubertin's congress. Rühl gives an excellent account of the long history of Brookes' experience with the amateur question in his English games. Rühl J (1989) op cit p 8 suggests that the experience, and Brookes' communications on the matter to Coubertin, strongly influenced the amateur rules which became the first IOC rules; and that Coubertin was remiss in not giving Brookes the credit: "Après comparaison des deux lettres de Brookes et des résultats de Paris, il est sûr et certain que Coubertin était informé jusque dans les moindres détails des débats approfondis de Brookes sur le problème de l'amateurisme et des activités olympiques. Ne pas le nommer plus tard était plus qu'un acte acte inamical". Coubertin's Mémoires olympiques (1932) Lausanne: Bureau international de pédagogie sportive, begins with 1892 and makes no mention of Brookes.

57. Macaloon JJ (1981) op cit p 164-74; Mandell R (1976) op cit p 85-91. I have tried to revise what I see as inaccuracies in those histories: see note 53 above

58. Unpublished letter in the Gennadius Library, Athens; see Young DC (1987) op cit p 280 with n 48

59. Vikelas D (1895) Οἱ διεθνεῖς 'Ολυμπιακοὶ 'Αγῶνες. 'Εστία Εἰκωνογραφημένη 7 May 145-50

60. Minutes of the 1894 Congress; see Young DC (1987) op cit p 272; Vikelas D (1895) p 90

61. Coubertin P de (1894) Circulaire du 15 janvier 1894. Bulletin du Comité international des Jeux Olympiques. July p 3. In Müller N, Comité international olympique (eds) Pierre de Coubertin. Textes Choisis. Tome II Olympisme. Zürich: Weidmann p 104

62. In one account, Coubertin states that it was Vikelas who first proposed to begin with Athens (Bulletin du Comité international des Jeux Olympiques. July 1894 p 1). Elsewhere he claims it was his own idea (Une campagne de vingt-et-un ans p 98). The Baron's contradictory reports on this matter have confused olympic historians in the past (including me). The 1894 minutes now prove it was Coubertin's proposal before it was Vikelas'.

63. I argue this case more fully in Young DC (1987) op cit p 280-85

64. Coubertin P de (1931) Mémoires olympiques. [. . .] «Mais pour moi, le Congrès projeté avait, avant tout, cette importance de me constituer un précieux paravent» (p 8).[1976 edition by the International Olympic Committee, Lausanne]

65. A fuller version in Young DC (1987) op cit p 283-90

66. The Shrewsbury Chronicle 6 June, 1883. In Neumüller B (1981) op cit p 209

Influence du sport américain sur le sport européen
et sur le Mouvement olympique

L'auteur rappelle que c'est au cours du XIXe siècle que tant d'Européens ont émigré vers l'Amérique du Nord, à la recherche de la liberté politique, sociale ou religieuse, comme aussi pour tenter d'y faire fortune. On désignait à l'époque le Nouveau Monde par l'expression «Amérique» qui s'appliquait autant au Canada qu'aux États-Unis d'Amérique (USA). Dans le langage de tous les jours, cependant, l'expression «Amérique» en vint vite à ne s'appliquer qu'aux USA. L'auteur souligne aussi que les historiens, de manière générale, s'accordent à dire que c'est au cours de la période qui s'étend des années 1890 jusqu'à la fin de la guerre 1914-18 que les USA ont affirmé leur rôle international en tant que puissance politique, militaire et sociale. Par surcroît, de l'avis de l'auteur, la même période a été marquée par une augmentation appréciable de l'implication et du succès des Américains en matière d'échanges culturels internationaux. Les succès des Américains, entre autres sur le nouveau théâtre des Jeux olympiques, ont été tels que l'approche américaine en matière d'éducation physique et de pratiques sportives n'a pas tardé à servir de modèle à imiter pour plusieurs pays d'Europe Centrale, plus particulièrement ceux de langue et de culture allemandes, comme les monarchies de Prusse et d'Autriche-Hongrie. L'auteur démontre ensuite comment le modèle américain de la chose sportive a supplanté celui qui avait été importé de l'Angleterre. Parmi les facteurs qui ont contribué à cette mutation, l'auteur avance trois faits: – la culture physique selon le système des «Turners» allemands était devenue trop rigide et stéréotypée pour plaire aux jeunes; – le projet de la tenue des Jeux olympiques à Berlin, en 1916, avait provoqué de nouvelles attentes auprès du public; – les performances des athlètes allemands et autrichiens s'étaient avérées médiocres, depuis les Jeux d'Athènes, tout particulièrement dans les disciplines sportives classiques comme l'athlétisme. L'auteur décrit par la suite les initiatives et le leadership exercés par les pays germanophones dans l'envoi aux USA de délégations chargées d'étudier, d'analyser et d'importer les idées, les approches et les méthodes américaines en matière d'éducation physique, de sport, et de sciences du sport. La contribution de Carl Diem à cet effet est soulignée par l'auteur. Les efforts ont porté, entre autres, – sur le développement de stratégies d'implantation des caractéristiques du système américain dans les sociétés austro-hongroises; – sur l'adoption, par les Européens, de l'idée que l'entraînement athlétique à l'américaine pourrait servir, avec l'aide des Américains eux-mêmes, autant à la préparation d'équipes olympiques qu'à l'éducation générale et à la formation spécialisée des entraîneurs; – sur l'importation en Europe du mouvement américain de développement et d'implantation des terrains de jeux et des parcs communautaires désigné par l'expression «The Spirit of Chicago»; – sur l'imitation et l'importation d'initiatives américaines d'ordre scientifique et technologique, comme éléments constitutifs d'une nouvelle science du sport. Dans la partie suivante de sa présentation, l'auteur décrit les principales déductions faites par les analystes européens sur la supériorité des formes culturelles développées par les anciens Européens dans le Nouveau Monde: – le système américain a su intégrer en un tout cohérent un large modèle qui va des sports de masse au sport d'élite; – les Américains ont su intégrer l'éducation générale à la formation spécialisée, dans la préparation de leurs entraîneurs sportifs; – «The Spirit of Chicago» mérite carrément d'être imité comme mouvement de promotion de la pratique des activités physiques et comme stratégie d'implantation de réseaux d'installations et d'équipements sportifs à la portée des usagers sans frais d'utilisation; – les foires internationales du début du XXe siècle sont d'excellentes occasions d'illustrer des initiatives scientifico-techniques associées à l'éducation physique et au sport. Sur ce dernier point l'auteur élabore sur l'influence toute spéciale des Américains dans le domaine du développement de l'instrumentation technique visant à mesurer la capacité de travail et un large éventail de dimensions corporelles (anthropométrie) associées au rendement physique, sportif, ainsi qu'à la haute performance. L'auteur conclut que les exemples, les attitudes et l'influence des Américains, à la fin du XIXe siècle et dans les premières décades du siècle présent ont été marquants sur l'évolution des pratiques qui avaient cours en Europe en matière d'éducation physique, de sport, de services récréatifs publics et de sport d'élite.

The Impact of North-American Sport on European Sport and the Olympic Movement

Dietrich R. Quanz

Historians generally agree that the United States of America (USA) established its role as political, military and industrial world power between 1890 and the end of World War I. People to-day speak about "America" and mean the USA, whilst Europeans, at the turn of the century, diffusely joined Canada and the USA when they referred to "America". Many Europeans emigrated to the New World in the 1900s, in search of personal fortune, political, religious or social freedom, as an alternative to the Old World. Conversely, North-Americans re-emerged on various international stages of the 19th century intensifying cultural exchanges with a new self-confidence and a seemingly self-evident superiority.

On the olympic world platform the Americans scored continuing hits that tended to make their approach stand out as a model right next to the antique ones in countries such as those run by the Prussian and Austro-Hungarian monarchies. In this context the empirical-philological question is irrelevant as to whether the portraits of American physical education and sport correspond to the facts. With respect to intercultural influences, their use and function as models were rather decisive. As the rising Olympic Movement developed in Central Europe, there was an upsurge of the American sport model which took the formerly held position of the English sportimport (*Figure 1* [2,3]).

Oliver[3] attributes the *mondial* role of the Americans to their scientific-technological progress in fields like industry, engineering, trade and agriculture. The Europeans themselves had had a platform for comparison between those areas since London 1851: the World('s) Fairs. Torn between global and patriotic ideals, the Olympic Games also emerged as celebrations of modern progress entailing an immediate manifestation of human ability in a competitive situation between national cultures. American universities played an equally important role in the exhibitions of products, methods and sporting competitions.

Dietrich R. Quanz, Deutsche Sporthochschule, Cologne, Federal Republic of Germany.

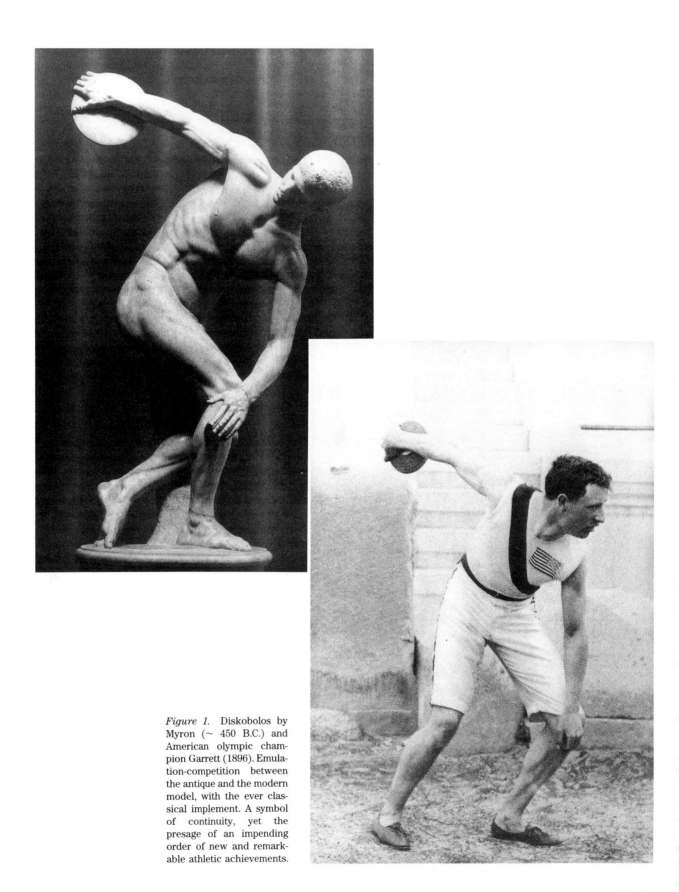

Figure 1. Diskobolos by Myron (∼ 450 B.C.) and American olympic champion Garrett (1896). Emulation-competition between the antique and the modern model, with the ever classical implement. A symbol of continuity, yet the presage of an impending order of new and remarkable athletic achievements.

In examining the period of the first five Olympiads, I shall concentrate on the European turn to the American cultivation of physical education and sport, a turn brought about by the new olympic enthusiasm. In the German-speaking monarchies there were ample reasons for focusing on new concepts of physical education.

1.   Physical Culture under the influence of the German "Turners" had grown rather dull and stylized in most gymnasiums with teacher-governed-regulated calisthenics or apparatus exercises. Pupils and students yearned at the time for free movement, games and sports (*Figure 2*[4,5]).

2.   It had been proposed that the Olympic Games be held in Berlin since the year 1906; in the end, they had been planned for 1916[6]. This situation created a national awakening as to the efficiency of the German physical education system. This was overlapped by Coubertin's universal expectation, as stated in Berlin in 1909, that the Scandinavian-Germanic Period 1912-1916 should bring "strict and intellectual discipline" to the Olympic Games, and furthermore enrichment through links between sport, science and art[7].

3.   An obstacle however to this expected glory was the lack of experience of German and Austrian athletes in athletic events, the "true olympic sport", termed as such on account of ancient athletics. This modern type of central olympic sports required new instructors indeed.

With the growth of nationalistic tendencies within Europe, it must have come as a relief that the olympic sport ideals of the New World could be imported for the simple reason that they had shown considerable evidence of effectiveness. The actions undertaken in the German-speaking monarchies show astonishing similarities. 1– Both countries sent persons in systematic tours throughout North-America with the task of concentrating their observations on schools and universities. 2– Both countries employed American coaches in view of the Olympic Games of 1916. 3– The reform intentions in both countries were focussed on a new concept of physical education open to American sport and receding from mere bodily specialization and perfectness. Hence, since that period the term "sport" has gradually become a synonym for "physical education" in Germany.

In German books and magazines, at the turn of the century, numerous accounts relating to North-America's history of civilization (the so-called cultural history) appeared that featured articles on the sport- and health movement. In addition, reformist magazines such as "Köperliche Erziehung" (in Austria), "Sport im Bild" and "Sport im Wort" (in both countries), and also periodicals such as athletic yearbooks, began to be published[8,9].

Undoubtedly, the most prominent figure in the German opening to American influence was Carl Diem (1882-1962). Evidence of this can be found in his study trips in the context of the German Olympic Movement, his two books about the USA in 1914[10] and 1930[11], his guest lectures at Los Angeles (1932), his emphasis on the universal historical importance of American Sport (1923[12], 1960[13]) and, basic to his theory on the teaching of sports, his thesis to the fact that the modern theory of physical education (or its synonym "sport") bore its roots in the USA at the turn of the century and was thus well apt to take the place of the antiquated and rigid system in place in Europe[14].

Four avenues for incoming American influences may be distinguished, which are however closely intertwined: 1– Genuine attempts at characterizing physical education and sport in the educational system and life of the Americans and, subsequently, at developing strategies for introducing them into the German and Austro-Hungarian societies. 2– The idea of associating athletic training and life-style, with American help, as a method of preparation for the Olympic Games and a basis for the general education of sport instructors and for building a theory

Figure 2. An example of "Turnen" in the German schools around 1900 (**Top**); this type of "physical education" was prevalent throughout German speaking middle Europe in the period 1900-1918 (**Bottom**).

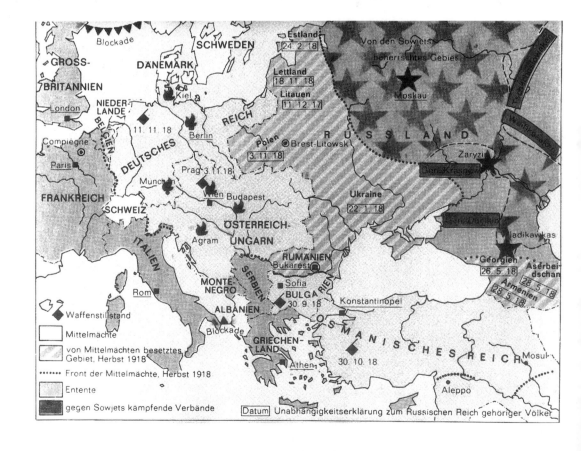

of training. 3– The park- and playground-movement of American communities and the "Spirit of Chicago" in Mid-Europe as "Sport-for-all, around the corner, within natural surroundings". 4– American incentives for scientific-technological analyses and applications to sport as contributions to the rise of sport sciences. Many Europeans were convinced that the four areas could explain the Americans' olympic successes which extended much further than mere results. A German study-commission in 1913 starts with a comparison of achievements in the Olympic Games. The victories earned by the Americans in the course of the Olympic Games from 1896 to 1912, in relation to the number of competitions, are compared to those won by the German athletes. Carl Diem, then Secretary General for the Games that were scheduled for Berlin in 1916, completed this table[15] (*Figure 3*) showing the unquestionable global superiority of the Americans; he emphasized two aspects extending beyond competition and results. Firstly, the statistics were limited to athletics and swimming, as these disciplines, according to Diem, demonstrated "primary human powers". Hence the global aspect of athletic training was emphasized, namely, that running, jumping, throwing and swimming should serve as a basis for physical education for all human individuals; these disciplines should thus receive a special educational status. For Diem, it was the competitive sport of athletics that constituted the essence of physical education: the development of overall human strength and power, a concept that extends to other cultural implications and consequences. Secondly, Diem gave to the statistics a biblical motto: "Thus you will recognize them by their fruits" (Matt. 7, 16-23). Victories and records were judged relevant only as results and indications of previous efforts which are valuable preparatory activities in themselves. Like true Christianity revealing itself in brotherly love, olympic victories were to be harvested as by-products of genuine improvements in various aspects of life-style, including the physical. A general theory of physical education and its links with olympic events were thus the basis for Diem's examination of American sport. His question was: *how* do the Americans do it? For Diem, the answer had to lie within the cultural forms which the former Europeans had developed in the New World of America.

American Physical Education and Sport as an Integrative Model

A general picture of American physical culture and sport emerged at the turn of this century as a model for the integration of mass-sport and elite sport. European observers since St. Louis were unanimous in their reports: the Americans had developed a modern physical culture approach and system for their male and female youth, which obviously was producing positive effects up to late adolescence as an integral part of the "american way of life": general games and sports activities for the masses serving also as a basis for high performance and olympic victories, without undue emphasis on the selection process (*Figure 4*).

Government subsidies and private sponsors had been put to contribution in the USA with a view of building a comprehensive system of physical education and sport: public playgrounds in cities and towns, professional sport instructors and adequate compulsory and elective sport in schools and universities with competitions and magnificent training- and spectator-facilities. The physical education curriculum emphasized stimulating games and sports education as well as individual developmental exercises facilitating gradual increases in performance; this constituted a broader and a better basis than the previous emphasis on strictly competition in a particular discipline. At the time, American life-style began to feature an inclination to competitiveness in sport and a gradual shift from personal activity to enthusiastic spectatorship. Excesses such as the "six days"

„An ihren Früchten sollt ihr sie erkennen."

Olympische Spiele

Athletik und Schwimmen.*)

Athen 1896.

Amerika . 9 Siege von 18 Kämpfen
Deutschland 1 Sieg

Paris 1900.

Amerika . 16 Siege von 24 Kämpfen
Deutschland 2 „

St. Louis 1904.

Amerika . 31 Siege von 38 Kämpfen
Deutschland 4 „

Athen 1906.

Amerika . 12 Siege von 31 Kämpfen
Deutschland 2 „

London 1908.

Amerika . 16 Siege von 36 Kämpfen
Deutschland 1 Sieg

Stockholm 1912.

Amerika . 16 Siege von 50 Kämpfen
Deutschland 3 „

*) Die Beschränkung auf obige Sports ist erfolgt, weil sie unmittelbarer Ausdruck menschlicher Kraft sind.

"You shall recognize them by their fruits"

Olympic Games

Athletics and Swimming*

Athens 1896

America - 9 winners in 18 events
Germany - 1 winner

Paris 1900

America - 16 winners in 24 events
Germany - 2 winners

St-Louis 1904

America - 31 winners in 38 events
Germany - 4 winners

Athens 1906

America - 12 winners in 31 events
Germany - 2 winners

London 1908

America - 16 winners in 36 events
Germany - 1 winner

Stockholm 1912

America - 16 winners in 50 events
Germany - 3 winners

* The account has been limited to the two sports in question since they manifestly indicate human physical power.

Figure 3. Carl Diem's comparison of American and German successes at the Olympic Games, between the years 1896-1912.

Figure 4. American communities tended to offer a wide spectrum of exercise and festive-type competitive activities emphasizing joyful individual achievement for both girls (**Top**) and boys (**Bottom**). Playground festivals, New York, 1913.

were criticized, but were not judged an integral part of the educational system. Physical education and competitive sport rather aimed at character formation *i.e.*, at a balance between education of the individual will and social responsibility or fair-play in society. For the Americans, sport was thus an attitude toward life and an enjoyment of life. This double potential of modern sport made it an even more potentiating educational medium.

On the very basis of the anticipated multi-faceted effects or benefits of sports, the American friend of Pierre de Coubertin, William Sloane, found reasons for higher payments to sport instructors in comparison to other teachers, as expressed during his guest lecture in Berlin in 1913. Among the European reporters of the St. Louis World's Fair and Olympic Games of 1904 were two German experts: Willibald Gebhardt, the German NOC Founder and IOC Member, and the more sceptical physician F.A. Schmidt, from the German Play Movement, both members of the International Committee for Physical Education which had been founded by the Olympic Movement at Paris in 1900[16,17,18].

In 1904, the Austrian Minister of Education officially sent the royal school headmaster Franz Kemeny from Budapest on a study trip concerning the American physical education system. Kemeny was then an IOC Member (1894 to 1907). At the World Exhibition in St. Louis, Kemeny got an insight into the mandate and objectives of the Department of Physical Culture then directed by James E. Sullivan, a man both engaged in the promotion of competitive sport, school sport, the playground movement, yet also employed in a Spalding sporting manufacturing branch. In his official memorandum, Kemeny concludes on the indispensability of a general approach to hygienic physical education. He presented ten central ideas for the implementation of the American "sportextension" as "sport-for-all" in Austro-Hungary[19]. Ten years later, even stronger accents in favor of a competitive system as an integral part of physical education were voiced by the Olympic Committee's German-American-Delegation headed by Diem and organized by Sullivan. In a series of 11 recommandations, the delegation calls upon the State, communities, universities, schools, sport organizations and potential private sponsors to use the "American model" to build playgrounds, commence supervision by sport instructors, carry out sportive school gymnastics and intramural sport, along with the organization of a competitive system for various sport disciplines in clubs and federations. The key to American olympic successes was not special institutions, but rather a games-, sport- and competition-culture valued by the public and society as a whole. The examples put forth were not a call to "Americanization"; they were simply calls for the integration of the *positive* aspects of the American approach within the terms of the European means. The discussions conjured up by such demands are easily imagined. In principle, the modern idea of a sportive physical culture entailed the necessity of intensive biological and psychological preparation for training and competition as well as the usefullness of preserving general fitness throughout life. In the view of the Americans, athletics had a double role: on the one hand a foundation for all sports, and on the other a special discipline in itself.

American athletics developed as a domain of the American universities. Their students impressed the Europeans from the first Olympic Games onward, even in the disciplines of the Ancient Games. It is the American exchange students who demonstrated the practical art of running methods, running tactics or hurdle techniques. Bernett has described this situation of sportimport[20]. In the 1870s an English-American sportclub in Dresden was already carrying out athletic competitions. After the Olympic Games at Athens in 1896, the student Cushing demonstrated athletics at their best in Munich. Ten years later the olympic champion and world record holder Lightbody was a member of the Berlin Sportclub, where the princes of the imperial family also trained. American students also reported on athletics and American university sport in German magazines.

The German olympic athletes Doerry, Runge and Weinstein, in contact with American athletes, presented reports and instructions on techniques and training accompanied by action photographs of the "champions". The German medical student and olympic prospect Brustmann initiated "scientific" analyses (as he called them) of athletic techniques in relation to an ideal body type at Athens in 1906. In his books on athletics, "Olympischer Sport", (Olympic Sport, 1910) and "Olympisches Trainierbuch", (Olympic Training Book, 1912) the American olympic champions such as Sheridan, Hahn and Lightbody were used to demonstrate techniques thus attesting of the reputation of the "American" (as opposed to the "English") training methods[21,22] (*Figure 5*[21,23]).

In the autumn of 1913, Germans and Austrians independently travelled through North-America in search of olympic caliber coaches. Dr. Otto Herschmann hired the decathlete and hurdling champion Alexander Copland for Vienna[24]. Carl Diem also hired the four-time olympic champion of 1900 Alvin Kraenzlein for Berlin. One can postulate that as the latter had been of German origin, his successes after he had come to the USA must have been thought to have been due to the "American" methods. Kraenzlein's "Olympic courses", in the new Berlin Stadium were apparently short-termed for the 1916 olympic candidates. But they nonetheless contained, besides athletic practice, courses in the theory of an hygienic-ascetic life-style along with seminars given by German lecturers dealing with the humanistic principles of sport. The effort was directed towards "competitive sport-for-all" in which the German Heir Prince apparently took part, and which distinctly aimed at the education of sports instructors, the eventual leaders of the German mass-sport movement grounded on the conviction that athletics led to the unfolding of human abilities. The intended functions obviously overlap. These olympic courses were the foundations of the diploma courses created by the German College for Physical Education at Berlin in the 1920s[25].

The "Spirit of Chicago"

The demand for the "playground around the corner", as the Mayor of Boston formulated the principle for outdoor games and sport in town parks to Carl Diem in 1913, is still important to-day in the Federal Republic of Germany. The Europeans have adopted three criteria from the American early park- and playground movement: 1- the aspect of social politics and national education; 2- the aspect of park- and garden-architecture in town development; and 3- an interest in nationwide games and sport facilities, including the construction of indoor training halls and multi-purpose sports arenas. Contemporary Europeans continue to interpret the slogan "Spirit of Chicago", as stemming from metropolitan park politics and professionally organized and free of charge public use of facilities. The Chicago nexus of town-garden concept and recreation offered in "baby-carriage distances" were judged ideal for Europe as they were in North-America itself. Roosevelt is reported to have said that Chicago should be proud to have "carried out one of the greatest public deeds ever made by an American town[26]" (*Figure 6*[25,31]). The social political propaganda in Germany and Austria concerning the American public parks started around 1909 with Ernst Schultze[27,28,29,30]. He wrote various socio-political articles on North-America including some on the effect of public parks on criminal statistics[31]. In 1912, he began a series of articles in the Austrian magazine "Köperliche Erziehung" illustrated by many photographs graciously offered by the Chicago Park Association[32]. The British Board of Education also published a special report authored by W. Wood, in 1913[33]. The architectural propaganda on the American public parks commenced for its part after the analyses made by architect Werner Hegemann. He had been a student of Otto March, who, following the Athens Olympic Games in 1906, was in charge of the first German Stadium project in Berlin in view of the 1916 Olympic Games. In 1911 Hegemann published a park book in the form of a catalogue, abundantly

Figure 5. American athletic methods contrasted with traditional English approaches in Germany. **Top:** American A. Kraenzlein (center) coaching the Prussian Prince (1914). **Bottom:** American (left) vs English (right) hurdling technique (1910).

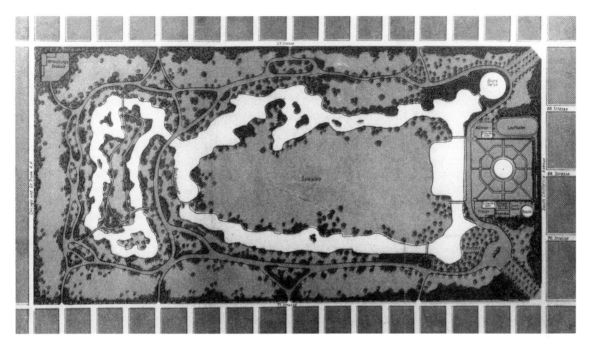

Figure 6. The "Spirit of Chicago", as reported in German-Austrian Publications. **Top:** Plan of the Market Park in South Chicago (~ 1914), encircled by apartment blocks. **Bottom:** Large-size public pool in an industrial sector of Chicago (~ 1912).

illustrated with American park-, playground- and sport facilities, for an exhibition which toured many German towns. Of Chicago alone, the catalogue contained as many as 11 park plans[34].

The sport-political propaganda for the playground movement was carried out by the German olympic movement itself, which favoured a controlled development based on American examples with municipal responsibility. As a follow-up to the study trip of 1913, playgrounds were given priority in the 11 demands made. In 1914, the German National Committee for the Olympic Games published a guide for town sportfields development, which advocated public swimming pools and sports facilities, club houses and leisure centres featuring Hegemann's pictures of American towns as examples. The German communities did in fact take up the challenge and built spacious park- and sport facilities in the 1920s. The democratic impulse of the park- and playground movement was based on a sports policy extending to every citizen. This policy was part of a broad concept of physical education and a supplement to university athletics for the gifted.

American Influences in the Development of German Sport Sciences

Scientific exchange, like sport, knows no frontier and is open to influences from all countries. An important role in this field may be attributed to the 19th century international exhibitions. The year 1911 saw the International Hygiene Exhibition in Dresden which focussed on questions of human health and was referred to as the World Health Fair. On that occasion, the German Olympic Movement for the first time displayed itself outside the olympic domain with its own sport exhibit, the central item of which was a sports laboratory for athletic research in a model athletics stadium. The American universities at the turn of the century were already featuring laboratories with instrumentation for body measurements. This was known to the people responsible for the Dresden Exhibition such as F.A. Schmidt, who had been to St. Louis, and Prof. Zuntz from the agricultural University at Berlin, who was scientifically involved with America[35,36]. Thus it is no surprising that about 10 American laboratories and university gymnasia were represented at Dresden. The catalogue described their work which encompassed both sportive and scientific aspects. From the many exhibits, one could point out both a bicycle-ergometer with electric braking power built by Atwater and Benedict and a universal apparatus for the measurement of muscular exertion manufactured by Kellogg from Battle Creek. Tracks of the founder of the German NOC W. Gebhardt lead to the Kellogg Battle Creek Sanatorium after the Chicago Exhibition in 1893, where he acquired a solar-light bath for his Therapeutic Institute in Berlin, which was also used by athletes. In the overall efforts to build a scientific body of knowledge and a modern theory of physical education, the Americans can be said to have markedly stimulated—the development of laboratory techniques and methods;—the use of anthropometric measurements with and for physical education students. The Europeans attempted to deduce from the above scientifically derived normative models of superior body types for various categories of athletic activities (*Figure 7*[36,37]).

The impact of laboratory methods on the triumphant march of the Americans in athletics, at the turn of the century, has been impressively depicted by Oliver[38]: not scientific or technical discoveries of importance, but a generally applicable method of observation coupled with inventiveness. Laboratories in university institutes for physical education had been observed and described by travellers to St. Louis, to other exhibitions and to universities. In 1903, the German NOC discussed the possibility of creating an institute for body measurements in conjunction with a scientific training centre, on the basis of the American approach and principles. At Athens, in 1906, a German stadium laboratory

Figure 7. Elements of olympic success: laboratory equipment and anthropometry. **Top:** electro-magnetic braking bicycle-ergometer by Atwater-Benedict on exhibit at Dresden World Health Fair. **Bottom:** Tall-slender body-type favored by Americans for athletics, and exemplified by Princeton students at Athens Olympic Games of 1896.

conducted heart research with technical equipment and attempted to correlate fitness (capability) to heart size in American sprinters.

In the field of body measurements, the Europeans regarded Dudley Allen Sargent of Harvard University as the authority. German athletes and "Turners" began to value the rationale for individual body parameters attainable through calisthenics and sport activities in compulsory university sports programs which the Olympic authorities simultaneously demanded for German universities. The ideal body type pictured by American athletes in European magazines was described by Carl Diem thus: "tall, erect figure, broad shoulders, arching breast, sturdy back, fleshy but slim muscles and muscular straight legs". This sportively successful body type was judged scientifically appropriate and was thus to be produced by the modern sportive physical education in Europe.

Conclusion

In the period before and especially around the turn of the 20th century, an intensive sport-related cultural exchange between the USA and Middle Europe was noticeable. Exhibitions, study trips, university student- and teacher-exchanges and the Olympic Games themselves were instruments used by the Europeans to deduce and import pedagogical and olympic knowhow. "American sportsmanship" corresponded to the idealized role and the athletic body composition of the American students. This import led to new standards for a theory of physical education and its related interpretation of the modern Olympic Movement and Games. The American ideals thus replaced the Antique and English models. The Europeans copied the approaches which they judged were responsible for American successes in physical education, sport and the Olympic Games: – the pedagogical and social system underlying the park- and playground movement; – the academic and scientific approach to sport as a broad concept of physical education and sport as instruments of self-development; – the important role of track and field athletics as a basic element of physical education and as the true essence of olympic sport; – the extension of mass-sport as a natural basis for the gradual unfolding of olympic talent and performance levels.

NOTES AND REFERENCES

1. Fellmann B, Scheyhing H (1972) (eds) 100 Jahre deutsche Ausgrabungen in Olympia. München: Prestel-Verlag (Fig 1)

2. Schmidt FA (1899) Unser Körper. Handbuch der Anatomie, Physiologie und Hygiene der Leibesübungen. Leipzig: Voigtländer Verlag (Fig 1)

3. Oliver JW (1959) Geschichte der amerikanischen Technik. Düsseldorf (History of American technic. New York: Ronald Press 1956)

4. Quanz DR et al (1987) Bock auf Schulsport - Ein Schulfach im Wandel der Zeiten. Ausstellungskatalog. Recklinghausen Ruhrfestspiele "Woche des Sports" (Fig 2)

5. Kinder H, Hilgemann W (1966) DTV-Atlas zur Weltgeschichte. Karten und chronologischer Abriss II. München: Deutscher Taschenbuch-verlag (Fig 2)

6. Lennartz K (1978) Die VI Olympischen Spiele Berlin 1916. Carl-Diem-Institut, Köln: Barz u. Beienburg

7. Mallwitz A (1909) Das Deutsche Stadion im Grunewald. Berlin: Verlag für Volkshygiene und Medizin Berlin 1909 (Pierre de Coubertin 1909, p 11-14)

8. Quanz DR (1986) Studien zu Bild und Funktion des amerikanischen Sports in der deutschen Sportentwicklung. In Spitzer G Schmidt D (eds) Sport zwischen Eigenständigkeit und Fremdbestimmung. Pädagogische und historische Beiträge aus der Sportwissenschaft. Schorndorf: Hofmann p 129-44

9. Editorial (1913) Der IV internationale Schulhygiene-Kongress Buffalo. Amerika 25-30 August. In Körperliche Erziehung 9 p 267

10. Diem C (1914) Sport und Körperschulung in Amerika. Bericht über eine Sport-Studienreise nach den Vereinigten Staaten im August-September 1913. Berlin: Deutscher Reichsausschuss für Olympische Spiele (Fig 3, Fig 4)

11. Diem C (1930) Sport in Amerika. Ergebnisse einer Studienreise. Berlin: Weidmannsche Buchhandlung

12. Diem C (1923) Amerika. In Diem - Mallwitz - Neuendorff (eds) Handbuch der Leibesübungen, Bd I. Berlin: Weidmannsche Buchhandlung p 324

13. Diem C (1960) Weltgeschichte des Sports und der Leibeserziehung. Stuttgart: Cotta Verlag

14. Diem C (1961) Modern principles of physical education and their American origin. Citation for honorary Dr of Letters (litt D). Autumn Convocation, George Williams College

15. Diem C, Berner M (1914) Städtische Sportanlagen. Ein Wegweiser für den Bau von Spiel - und Sportgelegenheiten. Ed. im Auftrage des Deutschen Reichsausschusses für Olympische Spiele. Berlin: Verlag der BZ am Mittag 1914 (Fig 6)

16. Gebhardt W (1970) Der Sport auf der Weltausstellung in St-Louis (1903). In Carl-Diem-Institut (ed) Dokumente zur Frühgeschichte der Olympischen Spiele. Köln: Barz u. Beienburg p 154-59

17. Schmidt FA (1905) Spiel und Leibesübungen auf der Weltausstellung in St-Louis. Reiseerinnerungen und Eindrücke. In Jahrbuch für Volks- und Jugendspiele 14 p 91-106

18. Hamer E (1971) Willibald Gebhardt 1861-1921. Beiträge zum olympischen Gedanken. Carl-Diem-Institut (ed). Köln: Barz u. Beienburg

19. Kemeny F (1905) Das körperliche Erziehungswesen in den Vereinigten Staaten. In Körperliche Erziehung I p 192-96

20. Bernett H (1987) Leichtathletik im geschichtlichen Wandel. Schorndorf: Hofmann

21. Brustmann M (1910) Olympischer Sport. Theorie, Technik, Training und Taktik der olympischen Sportzweige. Berlin: Verlag "Kraft und Schönheit" (Fig 5)

22. Brustmann M (1912) Olympisches Trainierbuch. Berlin: Verlag Illustrierter Sport

23. Maegerlein H (1980) 100 Jahre Sportfotografie. Frankfurt: Limpert Verlag (Fig 5)

24. Pimmer V (1914) Der neue amerikanische Olympiatrainer Alexander Copland in Wien. In Körperliche Erziehung p 67-70

25. Diem C (1942) Die ersten Olympia-Kurse. In Olympische Flamme. Das Buch vom Sport, Bd II Sinn. Berlin: Deutscher Archiv Verlag p 351-352

26. Hegemann W (1911) Ein Parkbuch. Amerikanische Parkanlagen. Zierparks, Nutzparks, Aussen-und Innenparks, Nationalparks, Park-Zweckverbände. Gelegentlich der Wanderausstellung von Bildern und Plänen amerikanischer Parkanlagen. Berlin: Verlag von Ernst Wasmuth

27. Schultze E (1909) Amerikanische Volksparke. Reihe "Kultur und Fortschritt" Vol 259-260. Neue Folge der Sammlung sozialer Fortschritt. Hefte für Volkswirtschaft, Sozialpolitik, Frauenfragen, Rechtspflege und Kulturinteressen. Leipzig: Felix Dietrich

28. Schultze E (1909) Die Spielplatzbewegung in den Vereinigten Staaten. In Soziale Korrespondenz 2 Februar

29. Rasser EO (1911) Mehr Spiel - und Sportplätze für das Jugend- und Volksleben. In Körperkultur 6 p 223-27

30. Stecher WA (1911) Spielplätze in Philadelphia. In Körpererziehung 7 p 52-56

31. Schultze E (1913) Parkpolitik und Jugendpflege. In Jahrbuch für Volks- und Jugendspiele 22 p 82-97

32. Schultze E (1912) Amerikanische Volksparke. In Körperliche Erziehung 8 p 291-98, 355-65, 376a (Fig 6)

33. Wood W (1913) The playground movement in America and its relation to public education. London: Eyre and Spottiswoode Ltd. Educational pamphlets no 27 Board of Education. Office of Special Inquiries and Reports

34. Hegemann W (1911) op cit

35. Zuntz N (1910) Sportliche und hygienische Eindrücke einer Amerikareise. In Körperkultur 5 9-10

36. Zuntz N et al (1911) Sonderkatalog der Abteilung Sportausstellung der Internationalen Hygiene-Ausstellung Dresden 1911. Dresden: Verlag der IHA (Fig 7)

37. Hueppe F (1922) Hygiene der Körperübungen. Leipzig: Verlag Hirzel (Fig 7)

38. Oliver JW (1959) op cit

The Sport Culture and the Sportization of Culture: a Search for 21st Century Values and Norms

Identity, Legitimacy, Sense and Non-Sense
of Modern Sport as a Cultural Phenomenon.
Does 20th Century Elite (Olympic) Sport Bear
the Imprint of Universal Values and Norms?
The 21st Century: a New Age of Sport?
An Analysis of Mutations in Motives, Attitudes,
and Values Associated with Sport

Culture sportive et sportisation de la culture: à la recherche de valeurs et de normes nouvelles à l'approche de l'an 2000

Identité, légitimité, sens et contre-sens du sport moderne
en tant que phénomène de culture.
Le sport d'élite (olympique) moderne est-il porteur
de valeurs vraiment universelles?
Le XXIᵉ siècle: un nouvel âge du sport?
Une analyse de la mutation des mobiles de participation,
des attitudes et des valeurs associés à la pratique sportive

Culture sportive et sportisation de la culture : identité, légitimité, sens et contre-sens du sport moderne en tant que phénomène de culture

La présentation comporte quatre parties principales. La première a une dominante historique et constitue un rappel des principes de l'Olympisme moderne et des idées de Pierre de Coubertin sur le sujet. Dans sa deuxième partie, l'auteur brosse un tableau du cheminement qu'a fait le sport avant d'être considéré à plein titre comme partie constituante de la culture. Dans un troisième temps, l'auteur traite de la transformation du concept même de la culture dans le sens où cette dernière est en voie de sportisation cependant que les frontières du domaine traditionnel du sport, pour leur part, deviennent plus floues. Enfin, dans la dernière partie de sa présentation, l'auteur trace un certain nombre de voies dans lesquelles le sport mériterait, selon lui, d'être orienté. En ce qui a trait à l'Olympisme coubertinien, l'auteur souligne que les principes ou caractéristiques en sont avant tout philosophiques et éducatifs. Il procède par la suite à une description de cinq des valeurs traditionnelles qui sous-tendent le concept de l'Olympisme moderne : – l'idéal d'un développement harmonieux du corps et de l'esprit ; – le développement de la personne par la poursuite de l'excellence ; – la discipline personnelle et un désintéressement à l'égard des gains matériels ; – l'acceptation inconditionnelle des règles du sport ; enfin, – la promotion de la compréhension internationale et de la paix par l'entremise du sport. L'auteur s'empresse d'ajouter que dans la réalité, on ne fait pas toujours et partout honneur aux valeurs énumérées. Coubertin fut le premier à admettre la chose, tout en gardant la profonde conviction que le sport moderne allait offrir au vingtième siècle de nouveaux horizons et des idéaux concrets aux plans de l'éducation, de l'affranchissement social et de la croissance morale. L'auteur démontre par la suite que pendant longtemps il y a eu de la résistance à considérer le sport comme une dimension significative de la culture. À son avis, la tendance fut au contraire celle de juger le sport comme une forme d'anti-culture. Pas de place pour les trivialités du sport dans un concept restreint, normatif et élitiste de la culture. Cette dernière, longtemps, ne fut que l'apanage du petit nombre et son domaine se limitait aux formes classiques du théâtre, de la littérature, de la musique et de l'art en général. Mais le sport moderne n'a jamais accepté le rejet. Au fil de son premier siècle d'existence, il a sans cesse gagné du rang et du prestige. Ironie du sport, selon l'auteur, ce sont ceux-là même qui ont refusé d'admettre les origines profondément éducatives, culturelles et religieuses du sport dans l'Antiquité, qui se voient aujourd'hui confrontés à leur propre ignorance. Les choses ont en effet changé ; le sport est devenu un phénomène social et culturel de première importance, tant par les expressions si concrètes et présentes que constituent les Jeux olympiques et les grands championnats du monde, que par le phénomène du sport de masse et celui d'une participation plus libre que jamais aux activités physiques, par des citoyens et des citoyennes de tous les âges et de toutes les couches sociales, et cela dans le monde entier. Les changements politiques, économiques et sociaux des dernières décades ont provoqué, au dire de l'auteur, un éclatement des notions de culture et de sport. L'effet net de cet état de choses a été, de part et d'autre, d'embrouiller les principes et les valeurs. Dans la partie suivante de sa présentation, l'auteur décrit comment et en quoi le concept de la culture s'est élargi, au point même d'être devenu ambigu. De nos jours, tout fait partie de la culture ; tout est devenu culture. Dans une perspective semblable, il est évident que le sport ne saurait être exclu ou retranché du mouvement d'ensemble. Le dynamisme nouveau de la culture sportive est par la suite décrit, au plan de la variété des mobiles et des formes de participation comme aussi des organismes qui le soutiennent, en font la promotion, ou encore s'en servent à des fins de prestige personnel, sociales, économiques ou politiques. L'auteur souligne que le sport n'est plus le lot exclusif des athlètes ; cette dimension demeure et s'amplifie, il est vrai. Mais il semble aussi que la sportivité soit devenue l'une des marques caractéristiques du citoyen d'aujourd'hui, de son mode de vie, et de la mode tout court. De là le danger, selon l'auteur, d'un effritement des valeurs et d'une banalisation des coutumes, des usages et symboles. L'auteur termine sa présentation en discutant du bien-fondé de conserver le relief des valeurs fondamentales ou classiques de l'Olympisme et du sport dans au moins deux des grandes dimensions de leur contexte de réalisation. La première a trait à la poursuite de l'excellence et aux questions d'éthique auxquelles l'athlète, le système sportif et la société toute entière se trouvent confrontés, à l'époque hyper-compétitive actuelle. La deuxième constitue un plaidoyer en faveur non seulement de la préservation, mais aussi du développement de la diversité dans le sport. Pour l'auteur, il est tout aussi important de conserver et d'illustrer l'identité des cultures qu'il ne l'est de rapprocher les peuples et les nations les unes des autres. La diversité des cultures ludiques et sportives, de l'avis de l'auteur, est susceptible d'aider le sport à éviter de devenir trop uniformisé et de ce fait monotone et ennuyeux. Ainsi, le sport contribuera-t-il à la compréhension internationale et à la démonstration de sa valeur et de son utilité culturelles.

The Sport Culture
and the Sportization of Culture:
Identity, Legitimacy, Sense, and Nonsense
of Modern Sport as a Cultural Phenomenon

Ommo Grupe

The theme and intent of this presentation have urged me to use four complementary approaches in its treatment. The first is an historical one: looking back to the main principles of Olympism and the ideas of Pierre de Coubertin. The second deals with the long-lasting endeavour of sport to achieve—on the basis of these principles—cultural acceptance and valuation. The third concerns the transformation of culture, the changing of sport and olympic principles which means more exactly the "*sportification*" of culture and the "*de-sportification*" of sport. In the fourth part, a suggestion is made as to the direction in which the future development of sport should go.

The "Classical" Meaning of Sport:
Educational and "Olympic"

This Symposium is held in commemoration of Pierre de Coubertin's first visit to North America one hundred years ago. However, it is not only in his memory that we are meeting here. It is also to analyze Coubertin's ideas in order to identify those elements which should be preserved today, because there is good reason to believe that they may provide a sound foundation for the course of sport into the Third Millennium. Therefore, I should first like to discuss Coubertin's ideas and the basic elements of Olympism, as he shaped them and as they further developed into a modern, yet venerably traditional cultural philosophy of sport *i.e.*, the classical meaning of sport.

The standard response to the question of this meaning is an educational one, or, in a broader sense, a philosophical one. It is taken for granted that the cultural and educational meanings of sport should come to fruition on the basis of clear value-orientations. Five fundamental values appear of special significance.

Ommo Grupe, Institute of Sport Sciences, University of Tübingen, Tübingen, Federal Republic of Germany.

1– The principle of unity of body and soul and the ideal of an harmonious education: sport and all those engaged in it, especially athletes, are expected to follow this ideal. Olympism is grounded on the spirit of "harmony" of man, not on the principle of exercises strictly for the body. Olympism is, in the words of Coubertin, the "essence" of a "distinct culture of the body". Athletic "muscular training" therefore needs to be fitted into a broader ethical context.

2– The aim of human self-development by way of athletic achievement: sporting activities are not to be confined to the concern for athletic performance, they should always "aim at bringing the human to perfection", at the "enhancement of man", the moulding of his character, in brief at his education. According to Coubertin, it is essential in sport, not only to "develop the body", but to fulfill the "task of moral perfection". Striving for athletic achievement is a means of shaping and developing oneself.

3– The ideal of amateurism as a form of self-discipline: this ideal was understood as self-commitment and was supposed to lend sport a "noble and chivalrous character". For the athlete, the pursuit of such a goal represented a "process of purification", a moral self-exercise, a form of secularized asceticism. Amateurism, according to Diem, was an appeal to the "conscience of sport". In general terms, the issue at stake was at first to protect sport against the spirit of "profit-mindedness", but as Coubertin said, it is also a matter of preventing the "athlete of Olympia" from becoming a "Circus gladiator". Coubertin feared professionalism although he had indeed anticipated the difficulties which the amateur rule would later cause.

4– The voluntary adherance to sport rules, principles and codes of conduct, keeping rules, observing the principle of fairness, renouncing unjustified advantages, declining material gains—all means of elevating sport to a higher and more demanding, indeed really cultural level. According to Diem, an "athlete has to be a master of a nobler life and not a servant of profit". "Olympic education" is a "school" of practical "chivalry"; it provides the opportunity to learn not only that success is "achieved through will and perseverance", but also that it "is consecrated only through honesty and fairness". It is only in this way that the impetus of "youth to compare their strength is elevated into the sphere of culture"; and only if sport is faithful to its values will it be capable of playing a role in modern education, and of promoting "social pacification". Only in this way, said Coubertin, will sport reach beyond the circle of a privileged few and be able to unfold its broad cultural and educational potential. It is with the above criteria that Coubertin and Diem distinguished sport from simple physical training, idle pastime or irrelevant pleasure.

5– The peace ideal of sport: one of Coubertin's central concepts, which can be found in his political and educational essays rather than in his writings on sport, deals with the need for peace between peoples and nations. For Coubertin, the peace ideal did not contradict the principle of athletic achievement and competition. On the contrary, sport in general and especially international meets and sport festivals, such as the Olympic Games, were explicitly envisaged as parts of the efforts for active peace, international understanding and contact—in a spirit of "mutual respect[1]"—between people of different races, creeds, and ideologies.

Only when it exhibits the above fundamental values, should sport be judged a valuable part of culture. In the light of this interpretation, Olympism, which represents a particular ideology of sport, may be seen as a cultural attitude and a moral approach, offering to those who engage in it guidelines for their sport activities, and beyond the latter, for their entire life. In its quest for a high cultural status and recognition as a part of culture, sport may derive from Olympism standards, norms, meanings and orientations.

The reality of sport, however, is often at odds with fundamental principles. This was well known, even to Coubertin. High aims were frequently used as window dressing to achieve public justification and to obtain cultural recognition. Indeed also, some of the values attributed to sport proved to be grounds for the expression of a double standard of morals. Frequently, athletes transgressed rules, violated the amateur ethos, or accepted money more greedily than laurel wreaths; and neither did at times officials, judges and referees, nor even the Olympians themselves, resist manifestations of racism, nationalism, and political intent.

It should come as no surprise that numerous critics, over the years, have questioned the cultural and educational importance of sport. They pointed to its weaknesses and imperfections, to its political use and abuse. In their eyes, the contention that sport was capable of eliminating intra-or international differences, of overcoming class barriers, and of promoting peace, was just as much a delusion as the assumption that the arduous athletic path would lead to educationally ennobled sportsmen and sportswomen. Nevertheless, a century ago, sport seemed to many, especially to Coubertin, a means and a symbol of educational, social and cultural progress, a hopeful and new horizon of individual and even of social liberation. Those who would follow the light emanating from its ideals, would be offered a new opportunity for moral growth. And indeed, many made use of the opportunity; for them, sport became a new tool for self-awareness and self-realization.

During the first decades of modern sport development, this kind of concept of Olympic sport was however understood only by a small number of individuals, and by no means did it instantly meet with widespread acceptance. On the contrary, a long process of discussion and controversy was required, before general approval was achieved. Nonetheless, in the traditional concept of culture and education, sport and physical activities in general, even though they were nicely adorned with Coubertin's ideals, found no place and were rejected as culturally valueless.

The Struggle of Sport for Cultural Recognition: The Olympic Ideals as a Justification Motif

For decades, sport was not perceived as cultural achievement, or as an expression of modern culture. It was, on the contrary, taken by many as a sign of cultural decline. Culture, in the eyes of most people, was something "superior" and special. It mainly belonged to the "upper classes"; the latter determined what was to be admitted into the domain of culture. Such privilege was not conceded to those barbaric forms of behaviour diffused from England in the latter part of the 19th century, which nonetheless fascinated young people, in particular, and, what was worse, claimed to be a new and valuable cultural asset[2].

The concept of culture underlying the traditional understanding of culture is normative. Sport, in its effort to win cultural recognition, for example as part of education and science, whether in the academic training of physical education teachers, or in the perspective of public health, again and again was judged on the basis of the above normative concept and often repudiated. Culture stood for drama, literature and poetry, classical music and art, not for sporting activities. By means of such a concept of culture, it was easy to justify the marginalization of sport. What had it to offer in terms of cultural quality? Nothing! It was sufficient to look into noisy football stadia, untidy boxing arenas, sweaty locker rooms, to read sport reports, observe bawling spectators or the disproportionate bodies of some athletes, in order to recognize an absence of "culture". Thorstein Veblen, the American sociologist, the German writer Friedrich Georg Jünger, and many other representatives of the normative concept of culture painted this grotesque picture.

Play (which according to the internationally renowned Dutch cultural philosopher and historian Johan Huizinga, *is* at the origin of culture), was believed to have vanished from sport; sport, therefore, had lost its dignity and had nothing to do with culture, in its "true" sense[3].

Not surprisingly, the representatives of sport were not willing to accept this rejection. For almost a whole century they struggled against a concept of culture which they felt was restrictive and derogatory. Their defense consisted of converting the critique of sport into a critique of the critics of sport. In the traditions of Western civilisation, sport's defenders were quick to find an arsenal of arguments. The "ignorants" who denied cultural values to sport, were in their turn confronted. Physical education and sport, as was readily demonstrated, had always been part of cultural life. Philosophers had commented positively on them, poets had directed their attention to them, composers had written music to their glory. Homer, Pindar, Herodous, Plato, Plutarch, Lucian, and Pausanias had all praised the value of athletic achievement; great educators—from Rousseau, Pestalozzi and Froebel to Makarenko and Dewey—had looked upon physical education as an integral and important part of education. And there were also the "glorious" Olympic Games of the Ancient Greeks, to the tradition of which the modern games could lay claim. All this tended to silence the critics; those who had looked at sport and sportsmen as lacking in culture, were now judged as lacking themselves in culture[4]. The irony was that sport, which again and again in the course of its history had to struggle against an exclusive and often class-bound concept of culture, did not hesitate, in the interest of its reputation and legitimization, to use the very normative concept of culture which had long denied the claim of sport to be recognized as a cultural heritage.

Fortunately, this situation has changed radically in the last decades. Despite some reservations, sport has become a worldwide cultural phenomenon. Its public image is fashioned not only by the prestigious Olympic Games and by glittering world championships in a myriad of disciplines, but also by mass sport, sport-for-all, sport for the aged, and sport for the handicapped. This development is not only due to changing political and social conditions and new economic and media interests, but also to internal qualitative changes and transformations. For one, the concept of culture has undergone a fundamental change; secondly, sport has produced and developed a specific culture of its own which reaches far beyond the kind of sport traditionally organized in clubs and associations; and thirdly, sport-related meanings and behavior-patterns have extended deeply into everyday cultural life, a process which is called "*sportization*" or "*sportification*". The net effect has not only accelerated the expansion of sport—it has also blurred its classical principles and traditional values.

A New Notion of Culture and a Different Interpretation of Sport: Is the Olympic Ideal Obsolete?

In the course of the last decades, the notion of culture has undergone a worldwide, radical change. By now, almost all expressions of human life are considered to be a part of culture. The very concept of culture has become irridescent and ambiguous: one talks about political culture, love and/or sex culture, about the culture of science, of the media and of pop music, about economic culture and dining culture, about the culture of Sunday, of peace, of leisure, about bar culture, youth culture, and fan culture, even about international scholarly conference culture, and the culture of this historical City of Quebec, our host city. Among these different "cultures", the term "sport culture" is enjoying a quite remarkable boom. Whatever happens in bed or kitchen, in the street, in the concert hall or on the sports field—everything is considered equally to form part of cultural life. Culture in its old and largely normative sense is being levelled, "flattened", "planified" as some will argue. An all-embracing and at the same time vague concept of culture has prevailed and now covers almost every human activity; it no longer indicates which one is, for example, valuable or which one is not[5].

In this perspective, sport has obviously also become a part of culture. This was not achieved, however, by deliberately leaving behind the faults and exaggerations of the past or by a pious process of purification. Nothing of the kind occurred. What happened was that as a different cultural concept emerged and formed a new umbrella, sport was seen in a different light than before and, unexpectedly and without new merits of its own, found itself an element of this newly-conceived culture. This transformation of the cultural concept was not the only cause, however. There are also other ways in which sport has become a cultural phenomenon. Two additional developments merit consideration: – the development of a specific sport culture; – the "sportization" of cultural life in general.

Specificity of the Sport Culture

Today, more and more people partake in sport activities, both actively and passively. Especially during the last two decades, the growth of sport has been phenomenal. This was not only the case in the highly industrialized and affluent countries; the number of participants in sport activities has increased considerably all over the world, as has the number of sports, sport facilities, clubs, physical education teachers, coaches, and officials. The expansion of sport has taken on new features. Apart from the classical sport organizations, numerous commercial sport agencies are now offering a wide variety of services. The number of fitness and exercise studios, of sport schools and of health institutes is increasing everywhere. Opportunities are also offered by business and industry, tourist agencies, churches, municipal authorities, hotels, governmental and para-governmental agencies. In addition, there are individual excursions into athletic adventures: wild-water canoeists, hang-glider pilots, long-distance runners, sailers, skiers, surfers and mountaineers search for excitement and experience in what sociologist Norbert Elias calls seeking for excitement in an unexciting and uneventful society. Avid sportsmen and women migrate weekly and during their vacation periods to the sites of their athletic passions.

Interestingly also, many people set out on a space-saving and ecologically impeccable journey into their own innermost soul in order to discover their "true identity". With the help of yoga, tai-chi and other techniques of exercise, relaxation and movement, they descend as deeply as they can into their physical and psychical depths (or sometimes shallows), in order to find the happiness they believe is concealed in their own body. This too, is understood by many as "sport[6]".

In tandem with sport organized in associations, clubs, and schools (which for many decades held a monopoly on sport activities), there is thus a new sport culture which goes far beyond conventional sport, and which differs not only in its structural and organizational patterns, but also in its concepts and values. Explicitly, it makes an unequivocal statement under the label of the "alternative". Meanwhile, it has become common practice to speak of sport as a culture of its own. Hans Lenk, philosophy professor and Olympic rowing gold medalist, has reduced this development to a formula: "The idea of sport is formed culturally and socially: sport is a cultural phenomenon on a natural biological basis[7]". But the extent to which today's sport affects us, reaches even further. Insatiably, sport occupies our TV programs for days at a time. No daily newspaper appears without a sport section, radio stations transmit extensive sport programs. Commercial advertizing uses images from the sphere of sport; it does so even for products which have nothing to do with sport and are judged harmful to health, such as alcohol and smoking. Sport has opened up lucrative markets and nowadays absorbs large portions of media entertainment.

Sport-related and quasi-sport-related motives form the behavior, interests, and preferences of many people even outside of sport. Sportswear is worn not only for jogging, but also in the laboratory, even in concert and congress halls and in church. Athletic "fitness" is taken as an indicator of youthfulness and vitality; it is judged desirable in employment and in everyday life as well. "Fair-play" is expected not only on the sports field, but also in the political arena and in the business world. "Sports-mindedness" or "sportivity", as motives, are spreading into many spheres of life; they affect all social strata and age levels, and—as the French sociologist, Pierre Bourdieu has shown—frequently are used to emphasize social differences between people by means of appropriate clothing, discreet symbols and little animals[8].

Against the background of this cultural development, it is understandable that today's sport is no longer just a concern of athletes. It indeed also influences the behavior of those who are satisfied with just wearing a sporting outfit. "To be", or to "pretend to be", a sportive type is now part of individual life style. To exercise one's body is no longer considered—as it frequently was in the past—a stupid body cult. Exercise has even become a kind of moral imperative. The new sport and body ideal is being propagated everywhere: in health and family journals and men's and women's magazines, in TV programs and videotapes; Sidney Rome, Jane Fonda and Denise Austen are delivering the message in their own specific and lucrative way. To act sportingly, to be fit and sun-tanned, to be health-conscious—all this is becoming a behavioral standard which no longer requires special justification. Justification is rather expected of those who remain abstinent from physical activities or disapprove of them. Furthermore, participation motives and behavioral patterns have become more diversified. For many people, achievement, competition, and companionship are no longer the primary motivation for activities. Instead, they are interested in their well-being, entertainment, fun and pleasure. They wish to take care of their individuality, of their health and body, and to attain the youthful image presented for consumer acceptance through large-scale advertizing. They want pleasure and fun, not asceticism and strenuous competition. Some bathe in reflected athletic glory by just sitting in VIP-sections and watch athletes at work. Athletic achievement, in comparison, is not in great demand. "More pleasure than achievement" is the title of a book recently published in the Federal Republic of Germany[9]. The new culture of sport is turning into a culture, which has already been labelled the "entertainment sport culture" or "fun culture".

The Sportization of Culture

A characteristic feature of this development is that the motif of "sports-mindedness" or sportivity, which for a long time was typical of club and association sport, is distancing itself from sport: today, everyone can be a sporting type individual without having to be an athlete, belong to a sports club, or even practise "real" sport. The traditional concept which linked "sports-mindedness" to fairness, companionship, achievement orientation and competitiveness, remains valid but only to a limited extent. The classical ethics of sport are losing their normative profile. Today, the elements which people are looking for in sport, are not necessarily found in clubs and associations; in addition, specific club and association values are not necessarily relevant to one's individual sporting activity. "Sports-mindedness" means more, and frequently something else, than physical exercise and athletic achievement; it stands for life-style, and for many people it has become an important behavioral standard in their everyday culture.

Sport as a cultural phenomenon reaches far beyond the traditional boundaries of sport itself, it is the expression of a new understanding of culture. This process has been called the "sportization" of culture and it means that sport-related values, norms and models of behavior have penetrated deeply into the cultural life courses. This situation leads to an increase in the influence of those organizations and institutions which offer and disseminate sport-related sense-patterns. No longer are sport organizations the only entities concerned; media, business, and political institutions are also involved. This is historically new, and—no matter whether desirable or not—it is a striking characteristic of a new understanding of both sport and culture which is spreading into many countries around the world and which affects leisure time, entertainment and amusement, consumer goods and services. Not only has sport been "received in the holy shrine of culture", as one critic puts it, but "culture itself has turned sportive[10]". Followers and fans of sport have therefore ceased to look for cultural-philosophical justifications for what they are doing. However, this does not mean that the value concepts of classical sport have become irrelevant. But today's sportization of culture goes hand in hand with the de-sportization of traditional sport. The traditional profile of sport is becoming increasingly more informal and unrestricted; new values gain acceptance. The clarity of the hitherto prevailing idea of sport and of its principles is fading. Olympic patterns of meaning and behavior orientation are no longer followed consistently; even the word "olympic" is joyously used—and sometimes misused—for many purposes including commercial publicity. The sport culture, as a unity and a uniform idea of sport has ceased to exist[11]. As a consequence also, the arguments which for decades were used to distinguish sport from culture have lost their validity. Normatively determined differences between sport and culture are no longer valid. A vague concept of culture now encompasses everything, sport included. This means that sport is no longer confronted with the earlier challenge of setting and meeting high standards and goals, in order to be accepted as a real part of culture, and at the same time avoiding everything which could have disqualified it as a mere body and performance cult. If everything *is* culture, then why should sport of all things have to distinguish itself as particularly valuable, by means of its exceptional quality and a specific set of ethics?

As the Third Millennium Draws Near: Some Olympic Perspectives

The topic we have been asked to treat is how can sport, on its way into the next millennium, be provided with those standards of meaning and guidelines which will prevent it from becoming culturally insignificant? A descriptive or positivistic concept of culture is hardly suited to answer this question. Such a concept may provide a charming description of that colorful mixture of the trivial and the extraordinary, the commonplace and the pretentious, the annoying and the aesthetic, between which man's life (even in sport) takes place, but in the long run, such descriptions will remain neutral. Culture begs to go beyond indifferent descriptions. Culture is also a design, a vision, a perspective for social life and development, frequently even conceived as contrast and contradiction. It is an outline of the ideals of a better, freer, and more vivid and satisfying life, and it implies endeavors to realize human dreams and aspirations. This also applies to the culture of sport. What would that sport look like?

History has shown that the development of sport has always been stimulated (not in the least) by cultural criticism. When people began, around the turn of the century, to take their stiff and gloomy clothes off, when, despite protest from honorable citizens they bared their bodies partially or completely, and somewhat bashfully exposed them to the sun and the wind, when people tried to get away from the dust and the noise of the factories, from the stuffy air of offices, and from the confinement of sit-still schools, it *was* sport which abetted their efforts. Sport afforded the opportunity to live more naturally and more freely, to enjoy nature and the companionship of like-minded men and women, and to experience in a hitherto unknown way movement, play, performance and competition. Even though from today's point of view some of their attitudes and activities seem to have been silly or exaggerated, in *those* days the escape into sport was indeed an entry into a new culture. The newly gained freedom of movement became a piece of real freedom. Sport was experienced as something different and better than the prevailing culture, which was felt to be restrictive and rigid. In that sense, the history of sport is not only an expression of man's quest for progress and modernity, it also is a new culture born out of critical ambitions, a kind of "counter-" or "anti-culture". More than ever before, sport is a solid part of our cultural landscape. Its traditional values—the ideas of equal opportunity, fairness, achievement, health, companionship, and internationalism—certainly still exist, but they are now affected by numerous other social influences which may impede their effectiveness: the insatiable and constantly stimulated desire for entertainment, tension and fun, the tendency for narcissistic self-presentation, and the constant drive for success and economic profit. Although this reflects general contemporary trends and, to a certain extent, the "feeling of life" of many people, it does not reveal all of the essence of that which sport stands for. We therefore need to remind ourselves of what *else* sport is, or *can be*, and reflect on how it can be made more colorful, honest, lively, charming, relaxed, gentle, peaceful, open, and humane, and, thus also more Olympic than it frequently shows itself to be today. This does not imply depriving sport of its freedom, risks and suspense, or converting it into one of these instruments of public morality or social hygiene. But it should assist sport in chanelling its unrestrained growth and in correcting its objectionable developments. This will only be possible if sport conveys a better image of itself, and if it offers not only pleasure and fun, but also appeals to people in ways which go beyond the pleasure motive.

Today, however, the realization of the authentic possibilities of sport is constantly threatened by negative developments: for example, excessive competition, discrimination against the less successful, over-emphasis on winning, tacit approval of aggression, clandestine tolerance of rule infringements and performance manipulation, utilization of sport as a media spectacle and advertizing medium, dependence on politics and economic interests. In these cases, sport is losing something of its authentic potential. One must however admit that according to the prevailing culture concept this, too, is part of *culture*. Nonetheless, it should not be considered as desirable or as culturally enriching. For this reason, it is necessary to preserve and adhere to those patterns of meaning which are compatible with the classical fundamental values. We can even say that against the background of today's social and societal developments, these classical meaning patterns are especially relevant and opportune. Two messages of sport are of particular importance in this context.

The first is related to the achievement-oriented and competitive principles of sport, *i.e.*, to the classical educational motif of self-perfection. The American philosopher Paul Weiss has called this the "concern for excellence[12]". In view of the anticipated developments in sport, this principle needs to be particularly cultivated, an endeavor which will be successful if the pursuit of athletic achievement is guided by—the recognition of the opponent as a partner;—the concept of equality, and,—the renunciation of illicit means. Only then will the fundamental values of sport prevail, even though in today's suspense and pleasure-oriented sport culture this may be difficult to convey. Only then will athletic achievement serve as an incentive for those who practice sport to work on and challenge themselves, and deserve to be presented as role models to the youth. If the self-perfection motif is preserved in this sense, it will lead to the just recognition of extraordinary performances. Exceptional skills are not only convincing in and by themselves; they also guard against mediocrity, simplicity and insignificance, and are thus in a special way formative elements of culture. They convert competitive sport into an exploration of human limits *under fixed rules*, with its implied cultural feature that not everything which is possible is allowed by the prevailing rules. Although sporting excellence is in a certain way unlimited by boundaries (which explains its universal attractiveness) it is at times, as Coubertin puts it, extravagant. Its achievements have become models of voluntary and self-determined activity and also of rule-guided action *per se*. It is in this capacity that they are especially important in a culture which puts a strong emphasis on tension, fun, and entertainment, yet which may be threatened by "consumer passivism and the total dominance of the mass media", as Lenk has noted[13]. The olympic achievement motif today has yet another significance—one which is part of the ideals of freedom, progress and equality which have been spreading since the second half of the 19th century. In many parts of the world and for many people, these ideals have so far not been redeemed. In our age of individualism, athletic achievement should not only stand as personal self-realization; it should also be seen as a unique model of fair and equal achievement and, thus, as conducive to man's quest for just participation in the material and immaterial cultural and social commodities of the modern world.

The second message is related to the need for preserving the diversity of sport, and even more, to the need to specifically stimulate such a diversity in a multicultural world. As countries and nations draw more and more together, yet on the other hand, tend to preserve its cultural identity for the sake of their own future, sport is certainly a field in which it will be necessary to learn that cultural differences not only have to be accepted, but also are an enrichment to be cultivated and cherished in a spirit of mutual understanding and active tolerance. It is therefore appropriate to deal carefully with the existing diversity of sport, which has numerous and deep roots in the history and cultures of mankind. Diversity needs to be developed creatively, and its links with music, art, and dance need to be strengthened. Through this diversity people will find their individual way to health, self-realization, a holistic life approach and personal identity. Diversity is an expression of human imagination, phantasy, and inventiveness, a sign of both cultural individuality and community. And diversity will prevent sport from becoming boring, gray and drab. It is to its spectrum of colors, forms, exercises, activities and traditions, that the sport culture owes its charm and richness, not to monochromatic dullness and monotony. Diversity in sport merges well with its old and yet highly modern values of peace, tolerance, understanding and internationalism. These characteristics reflect a universal idea which deserves to be promoted. In a world in which distances are dwindling, continents are drawing nearer, and a global communication network is tying everything together, but in which a global or a common society is still in want, sport offers a great chance. Its language, symbols and rules, unlike those in many other social and cultural fields, are universally understood. It is in this way that sport tends to create solidarity between people, and it does so right across national, political and ideological barriers, and even in spite of religious, racial and sexual differences and discrimination. Sport provides a concrete mechanism for peaceful cooperation instead of militant confrontation.

Diversity and achievement, individual self-perfection and multi-cultural communication, are not meaning patterns and objectives which exclude each other. Instead, they need to be explicitly related. In its future development, the new sport culture will have to cover different and perhaps even contradictory concepts of meaning in which competitive and social dimensions may be developed simultaneously and preserved in a tolerant manner. But this will not take place automatically. It involves effort, sometimes controversy. Those who practice sport, the institutions of sport, the national and international organizations and, last but not least, the International Olympic Committee, all bear responsibility for protecting the ideals of fairness, achievement, and equality, for denouncing aggression and violence, ensuring plurality and tolerance in the inter-cultural sport dialogue, and developing a sport culture to which all, and not just the privileged, have access.

Sport is frequently called a mirror of culture and society. But it is more than just a mirror; it represents also hopes and perspectives. This is especially true in the perspective of the radical political and economic changes taking place in the world, but also against the background of the experience of war and violence, and the awareness of the threats to peace, nature and the environment, the discrepancies in technological development, and of undeserved poverty, social injustice and unnecessary sufferings and death, all of which determine historical consciousness as the end of the century draws near. Sport may assist mankind in moving together by practicing solidarity, and in developing models for more peaceful relations, active tolerance, diversity, and for settling conflicts according to rules while seeking achievement under fair-play conditions. Coubertin spoke about these objectives decades ago, but they are still to be fully realized. One hundred years after his visit to North America, sport, in its authentic form, is still an element of hope and promise. If hope and promise are to become reality, we shall have to emphasize the culturally ambitious side of sport and indeed concentrate more on its educational and social possibilities—this is where the challenge lies on this short stretch to the next millennium.

NOTES AND REFERENCES

1. The presentation of the fundamental values of Olympism and the quotations are based on the following works edited by the Carl Diem Institut in Cologne: Coubertin P de (1967) Der Olympische Gedanke. Reden und Aufsätze. Schorndorf: Hofmann; Coubertin P de (1988) Die gegenseitige Achtung (Le respect mutuel) St Augustin: Richarz; Diem C (1967) Der Olympische Gedanke. Reden und Aufsätze. Schorndorf: Hofmann. For further references cf: Coubertin P de (1968). Textes choisis. Tome I-II Zürich: Weidmann and Diem C (1982) Ausgewählte Schriften (3 vols). St Augustin: Richarz

2. For a detailed discussion of this controversy, see Grupe O (1987) Sport als Kultur. Zürich: Interfrom

3. Suggested readings: Veblen T (1981) Theorie der feinen Leute. München: DTV [original work New York, 1899]; Jünger FG (1953) Die Perfektion der Technik. Frankfurt: Klostermann p 146-55; Huizinga J (1987) Homo Ludens. Vom Ursprung der Kultur im Spiel. Reinbek: Rowolt; Adorno TW (1976) Prismen. Kulturkritik und Gesellschaft. Frankfurt: Suhrkamp p 75 sq

4. See for example some of the works of Carl Diem: Persönlichkeit und Körpererziehung. Berlin: Weidmannsche Buchhandlung (1924); Asiatische Reiterspiele. Hildesheim: Olms (original work Berlin, 1941); Ewiges Olympia. Quellen zum Olympischen Gedanken. Ratingen: Henn Verlag (original Minden, 1948); Poesie des Sports. Stuttgart: Olympischer Verlag (1957)

5. See for example the articles in Neidhardt F et al (ed) (1968) Kultur und Gesellschaft. Kölner Zeitschrift für Soziologie und Sozialpsychologie. Special issue no 27; Tenbruck FH (1989) Die kulturellen Grundlagen der Gesellschaft. Opladen: Westdeutscher Verlag

6. See Elias N, Dunning E (1986) Quest for excitement: sport and leisure in the civilizing process. Oxford: Blackwell; Liebau E (1989) "In-Form-Sein" als Erziehungsziel? Pädagogische Überlegungen zur Sportkultur. Sportwissenschaft 19 139-55

7. The quotation is taken from Lenk H: "Den wirklichen Gipfel werde ich nie erreichen". Kulturphilosophische Bemerkungen zu Erlebnis und Eroberung im extremen Alpinismus. In Berg (1985) Alpenvereinsjahrbuch p 106. As regards the development and sociological analysis of subcultures in sport, see McPherson BD, Curtis JE, Loy JW (1989) The social significance of sport: an introduction to the sociology of sport. Champaign: Human Kinetics p 249-78

8. Bourdieu P (1985) Historische und soziale Voraussetzungen modernen Sports. Merkur 35 575-90

9. Opaschowski HW (1987) Sport in der Freizeit. Mehr Lust als Leistung. Auf dem Weg zu einem neuen Sportverständnis. Hamburg: BAT. See also Heinemann K, Dietrich K (eds) (1989) Der nicht-sportliche Sport. Schorndorf: Hofmann

10. Nutt H (1988) Hauptsache Sport. Merkur 38 p 245. Regarding the issue of the sportization of culture, see Kaschuba W (1989) Sportivität: Die Karriere eines neuen Leitwertes. Sportwissenschaft 19 154-71

11. Regarding this discussion in the Federal Republic of Germany, see Heinemann K (1983) Einführung in die Soziologie des Sports. Schorndorf: Hofmann; Jütting DH (1987) Zukunftsperspektiven des Sports. In Deutsche Gesellschaft für Freizeit (ed) Freizeit, Sport, Bewegungen. Erkrath: Rigodon p 100-04; Jütting DH (1989) Die Differenzierung des Sports und die Beteiligung der Lebensalter. In Deutsche Vereinigung für Sportwissenschaft (ed) Bewegungswelt von Kindern und Jugendlichen. Schorndorf: Hofmann p 311-18; Digel H (1986) Über den Wandel der Werte in Gesellschaft, Freizeit und Sport. In Deutscher Sportbund (ed) Die Zukunft des Sports. Materialen zum Kongress "Menschen im Sport 2000". Schorndorf: Hofmann p 14-44. On the question of de-sportization see also Rittner V (1985) Sport und Gesundheit. Zur Ausdifferenzierung des Gesundheitsmotivs im Sport. Sportwissenschaft 15 136-54

12. Weiss P (1969) Sport—a philosophic inquiry. London: Feffer & Simons

13. Lenk H (1983) Eigenleistung. Plädoyer für eine positive Leistungskultur. Zürich: Interfrom. See also Galtung J (1984) Sport and international understanding: sport as carrier of deep culture and structure. In Ilmarinen M (ed) Sport and international understanding. Berlin: Springer p 12-19

Le système sportif comme métaphore du système du monde

L'auteur propose une analyse du phénomène du sport sur la base de variables à caractère sociologique. Pour les fins de sa présentation, il classifie les sports comme individuels ou d'équipe et selon qu'ils sont principalement actifs ou inter-actifs, chaque combinaison étant porteuse d'une signification sociale particulière. Il analyse brièvement les programmes des Jeux de l'Olympiade et des Jeux d'Hiver et souligne que les spécialités sportives de la combinaison «individuel-actif» comptent pour 36% des premiers et 66% des seconds, des reflets non équivoques, à son avis, de la tradition individualiste grecque. Même si le message social que porte le sport paraît en plusieurs sens mixte, il n'en demeure pas moins, au fond, celui de la valeur fondamentale qu'on attribue à l'esprit de compétition. De l'avis de l'auteur, l'élément de la coopération, dans le sport moderne, n'apparaît que comme un moyen pour parvenir aux fins les plus élevées de la compétition: on coopère pour se faire compétition plutôt que l'on ne se fait compétition pour la coopération. Le fait également que les deux-tiers des sports olympiques actuels soient de type individuel souligne pour l'auteur une forme d'individualisme caractéristique des personnes de sexe male et principalement issues des classes favorisées, lesquelles sont par surcroît hautement compétitives. L'auteur ajoute que cet état de choses et d'esprit est également celui qui prévaut de manière tout à fait caractéristique dans deux des principales institutions sociales occidentales, l'État et la Corporation, toutes deux fortement compétitives, particulièrement sur la scène internationale. L'auteur procède à une analyse de cinq des grands facteurs qui façonnent les rapports sociaux au XXe siècle. Le culte du corps, tel qu'on peut l'observer dans le sport moderne, se trouve en effet fortement marqué de stéréotypes associés aux concepts de l'âge, du sexe, des classes sociales, de la race, de la nation. Le sport d'élite moderne est décrit par la suite comme porteur d'un message bien particulier, celui du schème de valeurs fondamentales et de modèles de comportements occidentaux. Dans cette perspective, on ne devrait pas se surprendre du fait que 5 des 167 Comités nationaux olympiques se sont approprié jusqu'à ce jour 85% du succès (décompte des médailles) aux Jeux olympiques d'été, depuis leur rénovation en 1896. Il appert donc que le sport d'élite moderne a irradié du «centre» (l'Occident) vers la «périphérie» (le reste du monde). En raison même de la popularité et de l'ubiquité de la compétition sportive, il semble bien aussi que le sport soit devenu l'un des plus puissants moyens de transfert de structures sociales et de culture qu'ait connu l'humanité jusqu'à maintenant. Le sport moderne, incluant l'olympique et tel qu'il se trouve exporté partout dans le monde, a tous les traits caractéristiques de la cosmologie occidentale expansionniste. L'auteur décrit ces traits comme relevant de la conception même de l'espace, du temps, de la connaissance, de la nature, des relations entre deux ou plusieurs personnes. Dans la dernière partie de sa présentation, l'auteur analyse l'idée sportive dominante dans six des grandes puissances qui sont en voie de créer le nouveau monde multipolaire de demain: les États-Unis, l'Union Soviétique, la Communauté Européenne, le Japon, la Chine, les Indes. Il explique que même si la compétitivité se retrouve partout au cœur du sport national favori, il n'en existe pas moins des différences énormes dans les attitudes fondamentales et les comportements à l'égard de la compétition et, par voie de conséquence, à l'égard des comportements des six puissances en matière de politique internationale. À l'aide de la métaphore de la compétition sportive, l'auteur fait une projection de ce que seront la place et le taux de succès de chacune des six puissances en question dans le monde réel de la politique internationale, au cours des prochaines décades. En guide de conclusion, il pose la question de savoir ce que deviendrait le monde de demain si les relations internationales entre les puissances globales ou régionales devenaient imprégnées d'un esprit de coopération plutôt que de rester marquées au sceau de la compétitivité qui les caractérise présentement et de façon si profonde autant que très particulière.

The Sport System as a Metaphor for the World System

Johan Galtung

Sport as a Social Message

Sport can be classified many ways; for instance in terms of the aspects of the human body most utilized (strength, speed, coordination, or all of them) and the type of criterion used to measure the achievement (distance, weight, time, numbers). For social analysis, however, social variables are more useful. So the focus here will be on individual vs team sports, and on whether the sport is active or interactive. Both are competitive. In interactive sport individuals or teams are competing directly with each other; in active sports they are competing indirectly by comparing their scores on some criterion variable. Both are *active*, an important and very positive characteristic of sports in general. But they are active in different ways, and each one of the four combinations indicated carries a different social message.

Of the 25 summer olympic sports at present 16 are individual sports and 9 team sports, meaning about two-thirds individual; reflecting the Greek individualist tradition[1]. They divide equally into 12 active and 13 interactive, with a low correlation ($Q = .44$) between the two dimensions. The 6 winter olympic sports divide into 4 individual and 2 team sports, (bobsleigh, ice hockey), and 5 active and 1 interactive (hockey). In the "individual, active" combination we get 9 or 36% of the summer sports, but 66% of the winter sports.

The *social* message is mixed. The *basic* message is *competition*. But there is also the cooperation of the team sports since the team is more (maybe sometimes less) than the sum of the individual performances. Of the total of 31 olympic sports 12 or one-third are team sports. But that element of cooperation is a means to the higher end of competition. And that also applies to cooperation to organize the games, and the cooperation fostered by the rules surrounding the games, the rules of *fair play* with all their implications. Behind or beyond it all the essence of the whole exercise is clear: to provide a stage for competition. We are dealing with *cooperation* to *compete* rather than *competition* to *cooperate*. The two-thirds prevalence of individual sports underlines male, upper class, com-

1890
1990

Johan Galtung, Professor of Peace Studies, College of Social Sciences, University of Hawaï, Honolulu, Hawaï, USA.

petitive individualism even more forcefully. What does this remind us of? Of the two basic pillars in the western social formation, of course: the *state* and the *corporation*, both of them eminently competitive, particularly internationally; but also based on considerable team-work on the inside. In their wake have followed wars[2] and exploitation, combining in the figure of colonialism, now dying. But imperialism in a broader sense is very healthy as witnessed by the activities of the Trilateral countries, the United States, Japan and the European Community countries. In other words, olympic sports should provide good training for devoted work for state and capital. For the people these institutions are supposed to serve, the *civil society*, much less competitive, at least internationally, olympic sports may carry the wrong message.

The Social Function of Sport as a Metaphor

Let us now try to understand the consequences of competitive olympic sports in the light of the social message. One way of doing this would be to reflect on the consequence of sports on the major divides of humankind: age, gender, race, class and nation. Sports relate in very different ways to these five; all of them socially important, probably among the major factors shaping society in the 20th century.

The relation to the category of *age* is marginalization to the extent of bordering on the fascist. There is a cult of the body, meaning the body mainly of those from 18-25, in some sports less, in some more. The very young and the very old are excluded from olympic sports although provisions are made in sport as general mass culture of the 20th century. This goes further than the bias in favor of the middle-aged in our society in general; only the younger ranges of the middle-aged are included. The message is crystal clear: only they are valid. The children have the advantage that they may qualify later; the old do not even do that but are highly expendable from this particular sports angle. Could there be a relation between this message and the many movements to "help" the old pass away, through euthanasia, assisted suicide, suicide? With sports adding "you too easily get tired" to society's clear stamp, "you are already retired?"

The approach to *gender* is different but not necessarily much better. The basic idea is to have two parallel tracks for men and women in some, potentially all sports. As a consequence not only is the division in male and female branches of humankind reinforced, but with a clear ranking; you girls cannot compete with the boys anyhow, so have your own little games. How do we know? It is reminiscent of efforts to set nutrition standard for the people in Third world countries, fixing lower minima for, say, small girls in the tropical countries, arguing that they need less because they are so small. The circularity of the argument should be obvious to all, in sports as well as in nutrition. However, what has been said so far is only the reinforcement of patriarchal structure. More important would be the way in which olympic sports inculcate male, even macho, values of competition rather than cooperation, solidarity and compassion. It is as if male society has the suspicion that there are such values high on the agenda of women and wonder how they can change the code, making them more like men, down to male levels in egocentric focus on individual achievement and competition!

When it comes to *race*, however, I think the report card is more positive. Of course, we then have to abstract race away from class and nation, visioning situations where sports people of different races but from the same class and nation compete within a framework of *fair-play*. Under these conditions it seems to me that olympic sports have contributed to equality and social justice. Nonwhites have been tested by whites with white standards and found not only not wanting but often superior to the whites like the famous Jesse Owens case in the infamous Berlin Olympic Games of 1936. But the argument about competitive values still holds.

How about *class*? The relation is complex. No doubt, just as for race and to some extent for gender sports provide a mobility ladder, a move upwards, at least into the limelight. But one thing is for sports to be a model of social mobility, quite another is transfer of real mobility. Sports organizers, except for the highest levels, sports journalist/commentators and dealers in sports hardware may have honorable professions, but not socially very high ones. Sports could also be a sidetrack in the sense of not only being parallel, but leading to nowhere, an *Abstellgleis*.

The interactive team sports—basketball, baseball, football, handball, volleyball and hockey (summer and winter)—may certainly also play a role not only for working class cooperation. Somebody should try to find out whether there is any spill-over in, for instance, trade union organization. My guess would be not, since the mobility channels above would deflect organizational talent in other directions; provided the former star does not get too desperate about no longer being in the limelight and starts self-immolation with alcohol, drugs, etc. instead.

Then there is another problem for which it would be interesting to have the empirical answer. Could it be that the middle and upper classes have reconquered sports that became working class preserves simply by upgrading the players? Easy access to colleges, scholarships etc. do not change the sports but change the players, probably making sports increasingly a student (if only undergraduate student) activity. The working class aspect, so clear in, say, European football would disappear the US way.

We then come to *nation* where the conclusions again are rather clear. Of the 25 summer sports only 1 is non-Western, judo. Clearly the olympic exercise is basically a one-way flow. However, again the inculcation of values is more important. In another context I have argued that this kind of sports serves as a carrier of Western cosmology, by reinforcing the West as a center of the world from which things originate, in which the power resides, and to which the medals will flow[3]. Thus, five countries alone of 167 participating National Olympic Committees account for 85% of the medals thus far won at the Games of the Olympiad, and these countries are all Western: the Club of Five (soon to become the Club of Four): United States, Soviet Union, United Kingdom, Federal Republic of Germany and German Democratic Republic[4].

There are deeper aspects of the hidden message: a Western time concept complete with crisis, catharsis (victory) or apocalypse (defeat); a way of reducing knowledge of societies and human beings to teams and individuals with their measurable "results" on one narrow dimension; the dominion over nature which is cemented and disciplined to serve as a stage, like the human body of the competitors; the reinforcement of verticality coming out of the competition; and, finally, the new God, also in three letters: WIN. For winning is not everything as Lombardi once said, but the only thing. But could this competition not lead to peace? Look at the list of the four nations above: the most belligerent countries in our century. If this leads to peace, it must be "in the longer run". At best sports are irrelevant, at worst they reinforce nationalism and general bellicist (as opposed to pacifist) behavior[5].

To return to the point of departure: sports is *activity*, and it must have provided millions with things to do, at least with their bodies. But the form and content of this activity is very far from socially neutral, and far from beneficial. Except, that is, from the narrow angles of competitive states and competitive corporations, heading for mega-bangs and mega-bucks, and certainly making use of olympic mega-games for both purposes.

Sports and National Character

Let us now explore this theme a little further through the hypothesis that a nation will *not* choose its favorite sports at random. There will be some relation to national character, even to the point that we might risk trying "tell me your favorite sport, and I will tell you who you are!" In so doing, maybe sport becomes a metaphor also for world society?

What comes first, sport or national character? Most people would probably vote in favor of the latter, seeing national character, not to mention civilizational character, as some kind of constant condition serving as a filter for selecting sports, even creating sports rather than vice versa. Not true.

Thus, what happens when there is massive export of sports, radiating from Western centers, following old colonial trade and control lines, into the last little corner of the world, leaving cricket bats, soccer fields, racing tracks, courts of all sorts and what not behind? Could that not have an impact on national, even civilizational character? And could it not be that this impact is particularly important, because (a) so many people are affected, if not as participants at least as observers, imbibing both *structure* and *culture*; (b) people are affected at very early, impregnable stages of their lives, leaving *imprints* that may well be indelible; (c) there is some kind of *equalizer* at work with sports for both genders, all age groups, all races, all classes, all nations; and (d) the media culture serves as a great *multiplier*?

In short, we are probably dealing with one of the most powerful transfer mechanisms for culture and structure ever known to humankind. It is essentially based on a universal language, *body language*, meaning that it transcends linguistic borders having no need for translators. There is no need for literacy either, the message is not mediated through the written word, meaning that *sportization* transcends a number of class borders. Increasingly being open to women, sports becomes a homogenizer of the same magnitude as evangelism—which, incidentally, followed the same pathways through the world and also offered something regardless of man or woman, Greek or Jew. And increasingly being available to children, the older, the handicapped, sport must be one of the most universally shared pursuits in the world.

Of course, to paraphrase a very often paraphrased phrase attributed to Marx "the leading sport is the sport of the leading people", meaning elite sports, and more particularly the sports of the Olympic Games. Presumably sports, like human rights, are "universal", meaning that the Center has managed to get Periphery acceptance, at least from the center in the Periphery, the people most likely to serve on local committees for Olympic Games (like on Red Cross Committees). That suggests three ways of producing universal sports: – by having sports, like so much else, flow from the Center to the Periphery;– by having the Center adopt Periphery sports and from there to the rest of the world;– or by some Periphery country making it to the Center, then leaving its sport imprint on the rest of the world. We still live in a world where *universal = Western,* and the *limes* of the British Empire, today the Commonwealth (no longer "British") can be better understood as the perimeter of cricket than as the perimeter of the English language. Sports like anything else carries the sociocultural code of the senders. As mentioned above the argument can certainly be made that sports from the West serve as fully fledged carriers of the combination typical for expansionist occidental cosmology:

SPACE: causal flow from Center to Periphery
TIME: building progress to climax, make-or-break
KNOWLEDGE: controlled experiments, equal opportunity
NATURE: overcoming nature, breaking records

PERSON-PERSON: vertical + individualist = competitive
TRANSPERSONAL: WIN is "the only thing"; a new name for GOD.

Engage in Western sports and you become a Westerner, in a much deeper sense than being accepted into the sports leagues. Universal sports, like universal human rights, are ways of occidentalizing the world. Far from bearing the imprint of universal values, whatever that is, Western values and norms are propagated through sports; including perspectives on space and time and above all the value of competition and ranking of people, combined with equality of opportunity, competition with rules, the famous "fair-play".

Here I shall take that for granted and rather explore some of the consequences. And the first consequence is obvious: let us be counterfactual, not denying in any sense the significance of games, of joy, of Leistung[6], doing your best, using brain, using body, using the two together. Let us imagine that instead of competitive games the world had focussed on cooperative games.

The anthropological literature is filled with examples. I have been particularly thrilled by one case from what was once "Dutch East Indies", from the Mentawai Islands west of Sumatra, reported by Eichberg[7]. An old Mentawaian reminisces about an episode with a Dutch colonial officer during colonialism:

> "We were really not very happy with him. He had said we should all come with bow and arrow, down to the coast. Everything had been well prepared, they were waiting for us in a big field. We got food and drinks and then they took a cocos nut and said, we should try to hit. So we did, and when someone hit they shouted and cried as if we had hit a monkey and not a cocos nut. At the end we got our rewards and could go home. But what in our opinion was wrong was that we did not get equally much. Some got a lot, others got nothing. Our hearts ached. But what could we do? That is the way they are."

> "Who got most?"

> "That is precisely what we did not understand. Completely at random, regardless of what clan they came from!".

So, the idea of competition and prizes had not arrived, whereas the Dutch colonial officer was convinced it had arrived. And ultimately he was, of course, proven right. Evidently their game was not competitive but served other functions. Many of those functions would be cooperative, togetherness, fun, etc., but *not* winning. They were not (yet) westernized. Which, in turn, does not mean that all competition is done the same way.

To gain some perspective on what competition means in world politics let us now take the six superpowers—three global (United States, European Community/Union and Japan) and three regional (Soviet Union, Peoples' Republic of China, India)—presently taking shape in the new, multi-polar world, and ask, literally speaking, what are their favorite games/sports. They are all competitive, but in very different ways; and the differences may be more important than the similarities:

United States: *golf*, active rather than interactive; short and intense attention-span with periods of relaxation in-between;

Soviet Union: *chess*, intense, long term planning, highly brain-intensive and body-extensive;

European Union: *tennis* (higher class), *soccer* (lower class), highly interactive, very intense, medium term planning;

Japan: *go*, like chess only much more so, with very long term planning and attention-span making the game not only brain- but also body-intensive;

China: *mah jongg*, four-handed (like Chinese linguistic quartet construction), complex, moderately intense, also entertaining; a game with a heavy element of chance, not only skill;

India: *cricket*, low intensity, very long lasting, probably both brain- and body-extensive.

If we should use this list of games/sports as a metaphor for real world behavior of these giants in the coming decades of world politics, and more particularly on their behavior towards each other, what would we arrive at?

The United States would continue setting goals regardless of what other players do assuming that they are striving for the same goals and continue tracing the road from A (actor) to G (goal), forgetting that in the real world the United States is not alone and that goals change by interacting with them, not merely acting on them. Short attention spans make even simple, non-moving goals unattainable.

The Soviet Union might easily err the opposite way, by being so interactive, so filled with speculations of the "if I do this he will do that; but he thinks I will do that hence I do this so that will—", etc. possibly getting lost in too interactive modes; or isolating themselves in order not to fall into that trap.

Japan could be a victim of the same, including the tradition of isolation as defense against that eventuality; but the much longer time perspective and training for extraordinary endurance would probably make Japan not only persevere and overcome, but with considerable distance between them and no. 2, as in today's world. Long term strategies, encircling more than absorbing the Other is the name of the game, not the bloodshed of the chess table.

China would be moderately interactive but less concerned with serious competition with the outside world and with the long haul since it is all to such a large extent decided by chance anyhow, not only by skill like for all the others.

India might go on playing, endlessly, slow pace, benefiting from others becoming so bored that little attention is paid to the possibility of India simply winning, at least in the regional games. The cricket field as a metaphor for a sleepy Indian village. And then there is the (coming) European Union. Letting tennis be the metaphor for the ruling elite alerts the attention to how gentlemanly behavior can be a cloak for darwinian behavior and the well groomed tennis field, not to mention the lawn, a jungle in disguise. Europeans, and indeed the British, have been playing such games with each other for centuries, with the single-minded aim of winning. There is no reason to assume that united they give up such pursuits, only playing on world courts instead of regionally, and not only playing doubles, but dozens.

Is it all a game, then? No, games nations play are as serious as serious can be, unleashing their military, economic, cultural and political resources on the world political arenas and sports fields[8]. The interesting point is only the rather obvious point that they play different games because they have been socialized differently by their national games/sports cultures, or the same game in different ways. They are all competitive so they can all engage in contemporary world politics among nations. They will only play the game very, even *very* differently.

Notice one point: they will all refer to their, sometimes deadly, games as "fair-play". They will invoke the doctrine of equal opportunity, for instance as equal opportunity to enter the battlefield (open for anyone), the market, the struggle for the minds and hearts of all, and the universal political fora, one of them being the set of bilateral inter-state relations. Of course, the assets brought into the competition are vastly different. But so they are in sports; after all, that is what decides who wins.

So, who will win, then? Short term, medium term, long term? Trying to stick to sport as a metaphor, trying to be systematically blind to whatever else I might know about these six actors, blocking out other types of knowledge, let me try some guesses.

In the short term, and we are already there, the United States will not win, and probably not in the medium and longer terms either. The world view is too simplistic, the attention span too short, ways of acting too brain- and body-extensive, leaving brain activity to computers and body activity to other machines and tools. For some time the sheer accumulation of resources and the exhaustion of the rest of the world in their stupid games made the United States look almost like a chess or even go master, as somebody planning it all, reaping the harvest in the end. Not at all. Planning was mainly *post hoc*, and in addition based on simplistic world views that they could enforce as prescriptions, not only descriptions, making them believe they had understood it all. As true golf-players they believed the holes were fixed and did not notice they were not only moving but in addition no longer holes to be filled, some of them shooting back from the most unexpected quarters.

The Soviet Union will continue playing highly complex, short to medium term games, get lost in their complexity, becoming rigid and isolationist, sour and sulky (as will also the United States, but for other reasons, not so easy to come down after basking in the glory at the top). In short, they will shrink, literally speaking, as others come to the fore with new ways of playing. New actors play will focus on less deadly economic games, and non-European, games.

The Europeans will continue their habit of short-term intensive competitions, win some, lose some, rise and fall and rise and fall, integrate and disintegrate and all of that. The game requires tremendous skill and concentration, but is not very subtle. Neither real long term planning, nor intense brain activity is engaged in except by the French who seem to have picked up all the other five games and for that reason may become the most universal players in the world. It belongs to the picture that they win over the others in the internal league, intra-Europe 12, by having longer time perspectives, and by having put more brain work into furnishing that time perspective adequately and in ways only known to themselves. So, to the extent the French, and not the considerably less subtle soccer-oriented Germans, are in command, Europeans will stay on for the medium term.

Of course the Japanese will also stay on, the tenacity and the capacity being overpowering. However, there is a weak point in the picture: the Japanese may be a little bit too clever. They may risk, and right now this is happening, that the rest of the players, the whole field, gang up against them rather than playing each other. The others may not be able to beat the Japanese at go, but they may get at the Japanese with golf, chess, tennis and so on, in all possible ways. Another weakness is singlemindedness, not in the sense of being active instead of interactive, but in the sense of being too focussed on one single goal in a multi-faceted world. This might lead to curves with tremendous amplitudes; great rises and great falls, great dramas, much attention.

So, in the longer term, who are the winners? Depends on definition, of course. But pay attention to some basic aspects of Chinese and Indian games.

The Chinese introduce an element of randomness. Randomness makes for resilience in a world complex enough to present itself as chaotic to the human mind. Pursuits in this world with very complex, long term game plan that is deterministic because it is determined (if he does this, I do that; if he does that I do this; to make him do this rather than that I do that rather than this, etc.) makes for rigidity, albeit at a high level. It is overpowering till that totally unforeseen thing happens that topples the whole game. To see the world merely as random, meeting randomness with randomness, chaos with chaos because that is the only language chaos understands will not bring us very far because it is simply wrong. The world system has a solid deterministic component and a solid stochastic component, like much else. The Chinese combine the two. They will not excel, but will survive.

And so will the Indians, but for an entirely different reason. The basic point about their game plan is its drawn out, boring character that makes spectators yawn, lose attention, except the real *aficionados*, why may or may not be affected by the game. If they are (Sri Lanka) they know what is going on and may shout their watch out to the rest of the world. But chances are that the rest of the world will be much more fascinated with other things going on and lose interest in whatever India does very quickly. The rest of the world will enjoy watching the Americans play golf with themselves, the Russians chess with themselves, the Europeans in their quick-tempered high frequency/low amplitude rises and falls, the Japanese in their slow-tempered low frequency/high amplitude rises and falls. Chinese games with some element of randomness, referred to as "inscrutability" by the true believers in determinism, will generally not attract much attention in a world looking for rises and falls. And India will draw a yawn.

And yet: come back again after 500, 1 000 years. Neither the United States, nor the Soviet Union will be recognizable except to the historians and the archaeologists. The Europeans will continue oscillating between integration and disintegration as it has done the last 2 500 years. Japan will bounce up and down and may one day come in for a hard landing, or declare itself too high up for this world, cohabiting with the Sun Goddess.

But China and India will be there. Both of them. The first so seeing itself as so universal that splendid isolation—with regional control though—is the equally logical answer.

And the rest is sheer speculation. What would happen if cooperative games and sports, not competitive ones and more particularly Western style competitiveness, were dominant, not recessive as today? What would happen if all superpowers, global and regional, were trained in such games? "They would not be superpowers", is the obvious answer. Precisely. And maybe superpowers, like supersport, is a commodity we can do without.

NOTES AND REFERENCES

1. I am indebted to Marc Landry (CAN) for helping me with this information. The concrete breakdown for the summer sports is: Individual, Active: archery, track and field athletics, cycling, equestrian sports, gymnastics, modern pentathlon, shooting, swimming, weightlifting; Individual, Interactive: badminton, boxing, fencing, judo, table tennis, tennis, [both of them both single and double], wrestling; Team, Active: canoeing, rowing, yachting; Team, Interactive: baseball, basketball, [field] hockey, football, handball, volleyball. For the winter sports it is simply ski, luge, skating, biathlon as Individual Active; bobsleigh as Team, Active and ice hockey as Team, Interactive.

2. Michael Shapiro, in Representing world politics: the sport/war intertext. University of Hawaii (1987), tells the story of a captain Neville who brought footballs to the front of the Battle of Somme "and offered a prize to the one of his first platoons which at the "jump-off" cold kick its football first to the German frontline during the "attack". Among the many who failed to survive this attack was the sporting Captain Neville.

3. See Galtung J (1984) Sport and international understanding: sport as a carrier of deep culture and structure. In Ilmarinen (ed) Sport and international understanding. Berlin: Springer-Verlag p 12-19

4. I am indebted to Fernand Landry, the organizer of the symposium, for this highly aggregated information.

5. Take this language as an example (from a xeroxed instruction sheet lying in the xerox room of some place): " [. . .] hit a return directly at him, to his feet. Vary the direction, however, to keep him guessing. Hit a large percentage of your shots crosscourt to prevent him from angling his return sharply from you. Hit down the line occasionally to keep him guessing, and when you think you can make a winning shot [. . .]". Sounds like a war manual; and yet is completely within the logic of an Interactive sport.

6. See the argument by Lenk (1983) in Eigenleistung: plaidoyer für eine positive Leistungskultur. Zurich: Interform; Lenk argues, as for instance buddhists might do, competition with oneself, trying to improve; neither directly, nor indirectly with others. Thus, there is nothing in a critical view of competitive sports against achievement in general. The problem is the structure engendered.

7. Eichberg H (date not given) Legens kulturrelativitet; Ansatser til etnologisk legeforskning. Copenhagen: Institut forkultursociologi

8. See Hoberman J (1982) The Olympic crisis: sport politics and the moral order. New Rochelle: Caratzas for an excellent analysis of the moral and political consequences of "universalism".

Le XXIe siècle: un nouvel âge du sport?
une analyse des changements dans les mobiles,
les attitudes et les valeurs associés au sport

L'auteur caractérise le sport comme une forme d'activité physique structurée de type ludique, fondée sur l'affrontement et la compétition, et accomplie dans des buts précis. Il considère que dans son essence, le sport implique la poursuite et la démonstration de l'excellence, par rapport à soi-même comme en regard des adversaires. Il ajoute que même si la signification donnée à la chose sportive a varié considérablement selon les cultures et les époques, on n'en retrouve pas moins un peu partout les mêmes caractéristiques essentielles. Dans sa présentation, l'auteur montre en quoi les caractéristiques fondamentales du sport expliquent la signification sociale considérable qu'il a revêtue de nos jours. Pour lui, le phénomène socio-culturel du sport moderne tient son importance de trois particularités: il sert de médium à la représentation collective, au plan de la culture; il est générateur de plaisir et d'agrément, au niveau social; enfin, il est une porte grande ouverte, en ce qui a trait à la poursuite de l'excellence individuelle. Au sujet de la représentation collective, l'auteur élabore sur le fait que le sport se fait le plus souvent un miroir fidèle de l'éventail des consensus aussi bien que des conflits qui marquent la vie sociale. En ce sens aussi et paradoxalement, le sport demeure une institution relativement conservatrice qui reflète les systèmes de valeur des groupes dominants et qui tend à renforcer certaines inégalités basées sur l'âge, le sexe, les classes sociales et les groupes raciaux. L'auteur souligne que l'on n'a pas à se surprendre du fait que le sport, en tant qu'instrument si explicite, malléable et populaire, soit ouvertement utilisé par différentes catégories de pouvoir. Au sujet du plaisir que le sport provoque, l'auteur résume l'avis des spécialistes à l'effet que les situations et les spectacles sportifs peuvent servir à libérer les tensions, comme aussi à ce que soient illustrés en pleine lumière des qualités de la personne appréciés par le plus grand nombre, tels que la haute dextérité, la force, l'intelligence pratique, le courage, le contrôle de soi. En ce qui a trait à la poursuite de l'excellence sportive, cette dernière est décrite comme une importante source de motivation; par son étroite association avec l'obtention de la victoire et le succès, elle devient, de l'avis de l'auteur, l'essence même de l'effort et de l'implication athlétiques. Le succès individuel dans le sport prendra ainsi une signification d'autant plus grande que les occasions de se distinguer des autres s'avèrent moins nombreuses, entre autres, dans les sociétés qui tendent vers des valeurs uniformisantes. L'auteur souligne que les mobiles divers qui incitent à la pratique du sport, à quelque niveau que ce soit mais principalement dans le sport d'élite, gravitent autour de deux pôles: l'estime de soi, et le désir de gratification d'ordre sensuel et affectif. Dans la partie suivante de sa présentation, l'auteur traite du sport comme moyen de mériter de l'honneur et de gagner (ou perdre) du prestige, avant tout moral, auprès du public. À son avis l'un des plus puissants mobiles qui gèrent la vie d'un individu serait celui du symbolisme artificiel de l'amour-propre; à cet effet, les aspects les plus disparates des modes de vie expliqueraient en bonne part les efforts consacrés à la protection, au maintien ou au rehaussement de l'estime de soi. Pour l'auteur, les traits et la formation du caractère, et leur corollaire, c'est-à-dire l'image morale que projette un individu au plan de certains attributs tels que le courage, la bravoure, l'intégrité, la sérénité, sont constamment mis à l'épreuve et sujets à critique et à évaluations sociales. Dans la dernière partie de sa présentation, l'auteur souligne qu'à la différence de l'agon dans l'Antiquité grecque, où l'honneur et le prestige d'un athlète découlaient d'abord et avant tout du jugement et de l'estime de ses pairs, la vertu et l'honneur qu'on accorde de nos jours à l'athlète dont on veut reconnaître l'excellence sont devenus le lot de tierces personnes ou d'organismes anonymes. De ce fait, pour l'auteur, le concept même de l'honneur, dans le sport contemporain, pourrait bien être dépassé. L'auteur conclut en suggérant que dans les réflexions sur le bien-fondé de modifier les structures normatives du sport, plus spécialement encore dans la perspective du tournant du troisième millénaire, l'on accorde une attention particulière au fait que la dignité et la vertu se trouveraient aussi bien encouragées et soutenues dans des situations sportives à caractère participatif et humanisant rehaussé.

The 21st Century: a New Age of Sport?
An Analysis of Mutations in Motives, Attitudes and Values Associated with Sport

On the Social Significance of Sport

Sport can be defined "as a structured, goal-oriented, competitive, contest-based, ludic physical activity[1]". As such, sport implies standards of excellence, involves both self-testing and con-testing, and demands a demonstration of physical prowess.

The particular nature and meaning of sport, of course, varies widely according to cultural context and historical moment. Nonetheless, nearly all forms of sport share the identified features to some degree. The critical question is *how* do these intrinsic characteristics of sport account for its social significance.

I propose that sport has come to be considered a significant socio-cultural phenomenon because it: 1– serves as a medium for *collective representation* at the cultural level; 2– generates experiences of enjoyable *excitement* at the social level; and 3– involves the *pursuit of excellence* at the individual level.

Collective Representation

A recent and extensive analysis of sport as a medium for the collective representation is that of Goodger and Goodger. They make the case that "As symbolic systems that reflect the social nature, relations, and identity of the collectivities within which they are generated, sports cultures are capable of stimulating intense emotional involvement and powerful commitments among a wide range of adherents[2]."

I note that as a medium for collective representation, sport expresses both consensus and conflict perspectives of social life. In the majority of cases sport stands as a conservative social institution and, thus, typically reflects the value systems of dominant groups; furthermore, it reinforces social inequalities in terms

1890
1990

John W. Loy, Department of Kinesiology, College of Applied Life Sciences, University of Illinois, Urbana-Champaign, Illinois, USA.

of age, class, gender and race relations. Occasionally, however, sport offers a collective representation of resistance for various oppositional groups[3,4].

Why sport serves so well as a medium of collective representation was discussed by Seppänen in his sociological analysis of the Olympic Games. He showed how sport is a handy tool for external forces, especially foreign policy. Some of the reasons cited were:

> First, it is inherently neutral.
>
> Second, sport is an activity which attracts exceptionally high interest by offering thrilling experiences both to the athletes [. . .] and to spectators [. . .]
>
> Third, sport is a risk-free tool which is socially approved of and highly amenable to societal control over style and content.
>
> Fourth, sport is an easily understood activity, readily comprehensible to the public.
>
> Fifth, sport gives the public an exceptionally good possibility for national identification through athletes representing their own nationality.
>
> Sixth and finally, sport is the only activity in which the measuring and comparison of national achievements is made in an indisputable manner[5].

In sum, as Seppänen concluded: "It would be unfounded to suppose that those in power would have left so malleable, so popular, so risk-free, so easily understood, and so unambiguous a tool unused".

Without going into further detail, one could simply state that sport as a medium of collective representation may be viewed as a cultural system. It may also be defined in the way that Geertz defined religion as a cultural system, namely:

> 1– a system of symbols, which acts to 2– establish powerful, pervasive, and long-lasting moods and motivations in men by 3– formulating conceptions of a general order of existence and 4– clothing these conceptions with such an aura of factuality that 5– the moods and motivations seem uniquely realistic[6].

Quest for Excitement

A second major way in which sport acquires social significance is through its generation of experiences of enjoyable excitement. An excellent treatise on the quest for excitement in sport was that of Elias and Dunning. In brief, they advanced the argument that:

> Within its specific setting sport [. . .] can evoke through its design a special kind of tension, a pleasurable excitement, thus allowing feelings to flow more freely. It can help to loosen, perhaps to free, stress-tensions. The setting of sport [. . .] is designed to stir the emotions, to evoke tensions in the form of a controlled, a well-tempered excitement without the risks and tensions usually connected with excitement in other life-situations, a 'mimetic' excitement which can be enjoyed and which may have a liberating, cathartic effect, even though the emotional resonance to the imaginary design contains, as it usually does, elements of anxiety, fear or despair[7].

There are, of course, many different aspects of sport that create excitement for participants and spectators alike, including: aggression, competition, conflict, physical risk, tactics and strategies, vertigo, and varying degrees of violence. Accordingly, different forms of sport produce varying degrees of excitement.

It should, however, be pointed out that even the gentlest and most passive sporting pastimes are capable of providing a modicum of excitement since they share (in common with all ludic activities) the elements of an "uncertain outcome" and "sanctioned display". Goffman has shown how these two elements in combination constitute the "fun" basis of games. On the one hand, the uncertain outcome of sporting activities maintains the suspense for the full duration of a contest. On the other hand, the sanctioned display gives participants "an opportunity to exhibit attributes valued in the wider social world, such as dexterity, strength, knowledge, intelligence, courage, and self-control[8]".

Representation and Excitement

To this point, only two short accounts have been given of the social significance of sport in terms of collective representation and enjoyable excitement. Recently, John and Brian Goodger have attempted to synthesize these two explanations by demonstrating that excitement enhances collective representation, and collective representation conversely serves as a source of excitement:

> Ultimately, both stem from deeply rooted human desires—for excitement and understanding—and find expression in cultural forms that are shaped by the interplay of these desires with human cognition and the social contexts in which they exist[9].

Although I am in complete accord with their analysis of representation and excitement as two major sociological explanations for the social significance of sport, I think that at least one other explanation needs to be considered, namely, the pursuit of bodily excellence.

Pursuit of Excellence

Although seldom mentioned by social scientists, several humanists, including a few noted philosophers, have pointed to the pursuit of excellence as a primary source of motivation for sport involvement. For example, Huizinga, in his seminal analysis of the civilizing functions of play and contest, emphasized that:

> [. . .] the competitive 'instinct' is not in the first place a desire for power or will to dominate. The primary thing is the desire to excel others, to be first and to be honoured for that[10].

Also Keating, in a comparative analysis of excellence in academia and athletics, forcefully contended that: "The very essence of the athletic endeavor lies in the pursuit of excellence through victory in the contest[11]." Further, in an insightful analysis of modern sport, Weiss made a compelling case to the fact that "Young men are attracted to athletics because it offers them the most promising means of becoming excellent[12]." Putting aside for the moment a seemingly age and gender bias in his pronouncement, I note that Weiss goes to great length to rule out other plausible explanations for the holding power of sport on young men.

Finally, I should like to refer to Lenk's philosophical reflections on the olympic athlete:

> Ideally, the athlete dares to enter a new field of human achievement behavior, namely the field of a symbolic demonstration of strength, not over others but over himself. Athletic achievements also offer adventurous opportunities for gaining distinction in a basically uniform society, which nevertheless emphasizes individual values. The Olympic athlete thus illustrates the Herculean myth of culturally exceptional achievement, i.e. of action essentially unnecessary for life's sustenance that is nevertheless highly valued and arises from complete devotion to striving to attain a difficult goal[13].

Lenk's observations highlight how sport is capable of dramatizing collective representations, generating experiences of enjoyable excitement, and providing contexts for the pursuit of bodily excellence.

Mutations in Motives, Attitudes and Values

Three supplementary points. First, I note that the representation, excitement and excellence theses just outlined are intimately linked to the processes of social bonding, emotional release and self-esteem enhancement. Second, I point out that these three theses are closely connected to the well springs of human motivation. For example, Campbell has asserted that "Virtually all of our human behavior springs from two motives: our desire for self-esteem and/or our desire for sense pleasure[14]." It seems evident that the quest for excitement in sport is related to a general desire for sensual gratification; one may also infer that the pursuit of excellence in sport is related to a general desire to maintain or increase self-esteem. Moreover, it doesn't require much of a conceptual leap to see a connection between the combined consideration of the two major motives and collective representation in sport. Third, I stress that, notwithstanding whatever constraints the intrinsic features and significant foci of sport impose upon human behavior, all forms of sport allow for the expression of a multitude of motives, attitudes and values.

Representation

For example, with respect to collective representation, sport is a *tabula rasa* on which many different values and belief systems can be imposed. One could think of the values and symbols associated with the sacred religious festivals of the ancient Olympic Games on the one hand; and to the values and symbols associated with the secular religious festivals of the modern Games, on the other hand. Or one could compare and contrast the specific codes of fair play associated with the removal of Jim Thorpe's olympic medals in Stockholm in 1912, with the stripping of the olympic gold medal from Ben Johnson in Seoul, in 1988. Without an in-depth analysis of the history of sport in the Western world it is indeed very hard to describe the mutations of values related to sport as a medium of collective representation. I can only state that there is a need for more in-depth case studies of sporting spectacles such as MacAloon's stimulating description of the origins of the modern Olympic Games[15].

Excitement

Similarly, following the lead of Elias and Dunning[16], I suggest that there is a need for detailed sociological analyses of the mutations of attitudes toward aspects of sport such as hostile aggression and violence. Just consider the fact that blood sports were once the norm, whereas today, among Anglo-Saxon social formations, boxing and fox-hunting represent remnants of such sports—and even their survival is a moot matter.

Excellence

Finally, I note that the history of sport in the Western world illustrates that many different sets of "situated actions and vocabularies of motives" as Mills put it[17], have been associated with the pursuit of excellence in sport. Given the fact that several conference papers touch upon the matters of representation and excitement in sport, I shall focus on the pursuit of bodily excellence in the remainder of this presentation. Specifically, I shall proceed as follows. First, I attempt to link the pursuit of bodily excellence to the concepts of moral character and social structure[18]. Second, I offer a quick stretch of the changing vocabulary of motives associated with moral character in sport situations. Third, I make a few speculations regarding the future pursuit of bodily excellence in sport.

Sport, Moral Character and Social Structure

Principle of Self-Esteem Maintenance

As previously mentioned, Campbell has contended that the desire for self-esteem is one of two primary motives of human behavior. In large measure his contention is based on the writings of Becker who formally proposed the Principle of Self-Esteem Maintenance. His principle posits that a "person's entire life (is) animated by the artificial symbolism of self-worth; almost all of his time is devoted to the protection, maintenance, and aggrandizement of the symbolic edifice of self-esteem[19]". Becker asserts that his proposition is an "universal principle for human action akin to gravitation in the physical sciences"; and he contends that it "explains the most disparate life styles as variations around the single theme of self-esteem maintenance[20]".

Pursuit of Prestige

There are, of course, many cultural avenues open to individuals for staging and maintaining self-esteem. But from the perspective of biosocial anthropology, Barkow makes a convincing case that "The major strategy for the maintenance of self-esteem is the pursuit of prestige[21]." Prestige can be pursued in terms of a variety of strategies since it has many sources. Typically, however, individuals seek to gain prestige through either their practical or their moral careers. Practical careers are usually developed in the world of work wherein individuals increase their general social standing by acquisition of greater occupational skills, knowledge, power, wealth, etc. Moral careers, on the other hand, are usually developed in what Harre *et al.* call the "expressive order". This is "[...] the part of life concerned with the pursuit of honour and the public proof of worth[22]".

Quest for Honor

Honor denotes a special type of prestige whereby individuals are accorded varying degrees of moral worth on the basis of the fact that they are perceived to possess valued moral attributes. Thus honor is achieved through the management of a successful moral carreer. Drawing upon the initial ideas of Goffman[23], Harre *et al.* record that "A moral career consists of the stages of acquisition or loss of honour and the respect due from other people as one passes through various systems of hazard characteristic of different social worlds[24]." The end result of moral careers is the development of character. "A moral career creates character: it creates in others the idea that a particular person has attributes and aptitudes of a certain worth[25]." In sum, the concept of moral career refers to "[...] the history of a person with respect to the opinions others have of his qualities and worth[26]".

Character Contests

Moral careers, however, are not easy pursuits and character is difficult to come by. As Goffman[27] pointed out, character can only be developed in the context of "action". By the term action Goffman meant engagement in "[...] activities that are consequential, problematic, and undertaken for what is felt to be their own sake". He stated that "[...] action is to be found whenever the individual knowingly takes consequential chances perceived as avoidable". He further observed that action situations involve character contests, special kinds of moral games, in which contestants' moral attributes, such as composure, courage, gameness and integrity, are displayed, tested and subjected to social evaluation. Goffman had furthermore recognized that: 1– "[...] action in our Western culture seems to belong to the cult of masculinity [...][28]"; 2– moral virtues revealed in action, such as composure, have traditionally been associated with aristocratic codes of conduct[29]; and 3– "Ordinarily, action will not be found during the week-day work routine at home or on the job[30]"; but rather in places like "commercialized competitive sport" and "non-spectator risky sports[31]".

Action and Agon

Goffman's concepts of action and character contest in conjunction with sporting practices reflect what has been termed the *agon motif*[32,33], after the classical Greek word for a system of contests, or an assembly for contests[34]. For example, the concepts of action and agon both direct attention to the notion of virtue. Virtue can be seen as the linchpin which holds the wheels of character and honor to the axle of social structure. The term *virtue* is associated with the Greek word *arete*, an aspect of *excellence*. Thus the pursuit of excellence in a context of action or agon is simultaneously a quest for virtue. Further, *character* is typically described in terms of virtue, and *honor* is always "[...] derived from a concept of excellence [...][35]". The inherent connections among the concepts of character, excellence, honor and virtue are clearly expressed in the literature about the heroic deeds and exploits of aristocratic warriors such as the Homeric Greeks, medieval knights and feudal Samurai. However, a key question is whether action in modern sport represents any true agon, or simply a superficial form of symbolic agon.

Admittedly, modern sport does not have the same strong moral/ethical framework of agon found in archetypal warrior societies. Nor in general does modern sport involve the high degree of physical risk and stringent peer evaluation associated with past agonal contests. Nevertheless, modern sport has a set of ethical imperatives ranging from formal rules and explicit norms of fair play, to implicit peer sanctions and codes of conduct. Moreover, like true agon, modern sport does emphasize physical prowess and can pose life threatening physical risks. Perhaps most significantly, there is more than a metaphorical correspondence between the attitudes, motives and values of the aristocratic warrior and the elite athlete. For example, Donlan's description of the warrior-aristocrat ideal in ancient Greece applies within reasonable bounds to the elite athlete of today:

> We may sum up the Homeric aristocratic ideal by saying that worth or excellence, *arete*, was conceived of in the physical sphere almost exclusively, most specifically in terms of prowess as a warrior. The aim of the high status warrior was public recognition of his ability. The Homeric proto-aristocrat endlessly competed with his fellows for prestige, with the goal of being recognized as "best"; his greatest fear was failure and its accompanying communal humiliation[36].

In short, aristocratic warrior societies and modern sport systems have more than just a symbolic resemblance, in that, both have prestige as their main source of social control[37]. However, there are at least two fundamental differences between the prestige systems of warrior societies and modern sport. First, there is the fact that in the context of true agon prestige in general and honor in particular were conferred only by one's peers, whereas in the case of modern sport, athletes are accorded prestige by a variety of third parties. For example, in the United States, sportswriters elect former professional baseball players into their Hall of Fame; and baseball fans elect current professional players for the annual summer All-Star Game. Secondly, and more significantly, the concepts of excellence, honor and virtue do not hold the depth of meaning (in the context of modern sport) that they did in earlier aristocratic warrior societies. MacIntyre has pointed to this matter, with respect to the Greek term *arete*:

> The concept of virtue or excellence is more alien to us than we are apt at first to recognize. It is not difficult for us to recognize the central place that strength will have in such a conception of excellence or the way in which courage will be one of the central virtues, perhaps the central virtue. What is alien to our conception of virtue is the intimate connection in heroic society between the concept of courage and its allied virtues on the one hand and the concepts of friendship, fate and death on the other.

Courage is important, not simply as a quality of individuals, but as the quality necessary to sustain a household and a community. *Kudos*, glory, belongs to the individual who excels in battle or in a contest as a mark of recognition by his household and his community[38].

MacIntyre's analysis highlights the nexus of character and social structure and illustrates that "The exercise of the heroic virtues thus requires both a particular kind of human being and a particular kind of social structure".

In light of MacIntyre's observations it is not surprising that Berger and his colleagues argued that the concept of honor in modern society, and thus in modern sport, is obsolete. As they so succinctly state their case: "Honor occupies about the same place in contemporary usage as chastity" [...] "At best, honor and chastity are seen as ideological leftovers in the consciousness of obsolete classes, such as military officers or ethnic grandmothers". Their rationale for considering the concept honor as obsolete is that:

> The social location of honor lies in a world of relatively intact, stable institutions, a world in which individuals can with subjective certainty attach their identities to the institutional roles that society assigns to them. The disintegration of this world as a result of the forces of modernity has not only made honor an increasingly meaningless notion, but has served as the occasion for a redefinition of identity and its intrinsic dignity apart from and often *against* the institutional roles through which the individual expresses himself in society[39].

MacIntyre would likely agree with the assertions of Berger and his colleagues as he has acknowledged that "The self becomes what it is in heroic societies only through its role; it is a social creation, not an individual one[40]."

Although Pierre de Coubertin could be appalled, and while it is unlikely to greatly influence the normative structure of sport in the 21st century, I suggest that one had best jettison the usage of the concept of honor in the context of sport. In addition to the rationale offered by Berger and his colleagues, I point out that the close association of the concept of honor with youth, masculinity, expressions of violence, as well as the Victorian notions of nobility, sportsmanship and white supremacy, tend to make the term honor a highly pejorative concept. While I believe in the obsolescence of the concept of honor, I do not propose to throw the baby out with the bath. I am of the opinion that in order to achieve an emphasis on dignity in sport situations, the concept of virtue, in some form, must be maintained. Specifically, I suggest that we consider MacIntyre's ideas of practice as we give consideration to changing the normative structures of sport in the 21st century for purposes of enhanced humanistic participation. By "practice", MacIntyre meant:

> [...] any coherent and complex form of socially established cooperative human activity through which goods internal to that form of activity are realized in the course of trying to achieve those standards of excellence which are appropriate to, and partially definitive of, that form of activity, with the result that human powers to achieve excellence, and human conceptions of the ends and goods involved, are systematically extended[41].

In brief, MacIntyre's conception of practice has two key features, namely, the notions of *internal goods* and *virtue*. He referred to goods as internal for two reasons. First, they can only be identified in terms of what is required to achieve excellence in the practice itself; "and secondly, because they can only be identified by the experience of participating in the practice in question[42]". MacIntyre further distinguished between *external* goods and *internal* goods as follows:

> External goods are [...] characteristically objects of competition in which there must be losers as well as winners. Internal goods are [...] the outcome of competition to excel, but characteristic of them in that their achievement is a good for the whole community who participate in the practice[43].

The second key feature of practice is the concept of virtue which MacIntyre defined as "[...] an acquired human quality the possession and exercise of which tends to enable us to achieve those goods which are internal to practices and the lack of which effectively prevents us from achieving any such goods[44]". He pointed out that every practice 1– has a history and tradition; 2– involves standards of excellence and obedience to rules as well as the achievement of goods; and 3– requires a certain kind of relationship between those who participate in it. Finally, MacIntyre draws a clear distinction between practices and institutions. Although institutions sustain practices, they are concerned with external goods such as wealth; and "they are structured in terms of power and status[45]."

In conclusion, I suggest that there is much merit in giving serious consideration to MacIntyre's moral philosophy as we reflect upon sport as the 21st century draws near. His concept of practice—retains the pursuit of excellence; —places emphasis on the intrinsic motivation of sport involvement; —stresses the communal aspects of participation; —highlights the craft character of sport[46,47], and restores the peer evaluation of sport performance, in that "Those who lack the relevant experience are incompetent thereby as judges of internal goods[48]." Last but not least, if one defines self-esteem as the awareness of internal goods and excellence possessed by self (after Campbell[49]), then we have linked sporting practices to Becker's Principle of Self-Esteem Maintenance.

REFERENCES

1. McPherson BD, Curtis JE, Loy JW (1989) The social significance of sport. Champaign: Human Kinetics p 15

2. Goodger JM, Goodger BC (1989) Excitement and representation: toward a sociological explanation of the significance of sport in modern society. Quest 41 267

3. McPherson BD, Curtis JE, Loy JW (1989) op cit p 23-25

4. Donnelly P (in press) Subcultures in sport: resilence and transformation. In Ingham AG, Loy JW (eds) Sport and social development: traditions, transitions and transformations. Champaign: Human Kinetics

5. Seppänen P (1984) The Olympics: a sociological perspective. International Review for the Sociology of Sport 19 p 116, 117

6. Geertz C (1973) The interpretation of cultures. New York: Basic Books p 90

7. Elias N, Dunning E (1986) Quest for excitement: sport and leisure in the civilizing process. Oxford: Basil Blackwell p 48-49

8. Goffman E (1961) Encounters. Indianapolis: Bobbs-Merrill p 68

9. Goodger JM, Goodger BC (1989) op cit p 270

10. Huizinga J (1955) Homo ludens: a study of the play element in culture. Boston : Beacon Press p 50

11. Keating JW (1965) Athletics and the pursuit of excellence. Education 85 p 429

12. Weiss P (1969) Sport—A philosophic inquiry. Carbondale: Southern Illinois University Press p 17

13. Lenk H (1985) Towards a philosophical anthropolgy of the olympic athlete and/as the achieving being. In Szymiczek O (ed) Report of the Twenty-Second Session of the International Olympic Academy. Lausanne: International Olympic Committee p 166

14. Campbell RN (1984) The new science: self-esteem psychology. New York: University Press of America p xi

15. MacAloon JJ (1981) This great symbol: Pierre de Coubertin and the origins of the modern Olympic Games. Chicago: University of Chicago Press

16. Elias N, Dunning E (1986) op cit

17. Mills CW (1940) Situated actions and vocabularies of motives. American Sociological Review 5 904-13

18. Gerth H, Mills CW (1953) Character and social structure. New York: Harcourt, Brace and World

19. Becker E (1971) The birth and death of meaning. New York: Free Press p 67-68

20. Becker E (1968) The structure of evil. New York: Braziller p 328, 329

21. Barkow JH (1975) Prestige and culture: a biosocial interpretation. Current Anthropology 16 p 555

22. Harre R, Clarke D, De Carlo N (1985) Motives and mechanisms. London: Methuen p 146-147

23. Goffman E (1968) Asylums. Harmondsworth: Penguin

24. Harre R, Clarke D, De Carlo N (1985) op cit p 147

25. Ibid

26. Harre R (1979) Social being: a theory for social psychology. Oxford: Basil Blackwell p 311

27. Goffman E (1967) Interaction Ritual. Garden City: Anchor Books p 185, 194, 239-58

28. Ibid p 209

29. Ibid p 227

30. Ibid p 194

31. Ibid p 195-196

32. Morford WR, Clark SJ (1976) The agon motif. Exercise and Sport Sciences Reviews 4 163-93

33. Loy JW, Hesketh GL (1984) The agon motif: a prolegomenon for the study of agonetic behavior. In Olin K (ed) Contribution of Sociology to the Study of Sport. Jyvaskyla, Finland: University of Jyvaskyla

34. Scanlon TF (1983) The vocabulary of competition: agon and athlos, Greek terms for contest. Arete 1 147-62

35. Speier H (1935) Honor and social structure. Social Research 2 p 81

36. Donlan W (1980) The aristocratic ideal in Ancient Greece. Lawrence: Coronado Press p 23

37. Goode WJ (1978) The celebrations of heroes: Prestige as a control system. Berkeley: University of California Press

38. MacIntyre A (1984) After virtue. South Bend: University of Notre Dame Press p 122-123, 126

39. Berger P, Berger B, Kellner H (1973) The homeless mind. New York: Random House p 83, 93

40. MacIntyre A (1984) op cit p 129

41. Ibid p 187

42. Ibid p 188-189

43. Ibid p 190-191

44. Ibid p 191

45. Ibid p 190, 191, 194

46. Bensman J, Lilienfeld R (1973) Craft and consciousness. New York: Random House

47. Wills GG (1990) Men at work: the craft of baseball. New York: Macmillan

48. MacIntyre A (1984) op cit p 189

49. Campbell RN (1984) op cit p 9

[...] La pratique des exercices sportifs n'égalise pas les conditions mais elle égalise les relations et il est probable qu'ici la forme a plus d'importance que le fond. Après tout, qui oserait se porter garant que l'égalité des conditions sera productrice de paix sociale ? Rien n'est moins certain. Il en va autrement de l'égalitarisme des relations. On peut affirmer que cet égalitarisme là, dans une démocratie, est des plus utiles à pratiquer. [...]

Coubertin P de (1913) Le sport et la question sociale. Revue olympique, août, p 121

[...] La première caractéristique essentielle de l'olympisme ancien aussi bien que de l'olympisme moderne, c'est d'être une religion. En ciselant son corps par l'exercice comme le fait un sculpteur d'une statue, l'athlète antique « honorait les dieux ». [...] J'estime donc avoir eu raison de restaurer dès le principe, autour de l'olympisme rénové, un sentiment religieux transformé et agrandi par l'Internationalisme et la Démocratie qui distinguent les temps actuels, [...] L'idée religieuse sportive, la religio athletae *a pénétré très lentement l'esprit des concurrents et beaucoup parmi eux ne le pratiquent encore que de façon inconsciente. Mais ils s'y rallieront peu à peu. [...] Ce ne sont pas seulement l'Internationalisme et la Démocratie, assises de la nouvelle société humaine en voie d'édification chez les nations civilisées, c'est aussi la science qui est intéressée en cela. Par ses progrès continus, elle a fourni à l'homme de nouveaux moyens de cultiver son corps, [...]*

Coubertin P de (1935) Les assises philosophiques de l'olympisme moderne. Le Sport Suisse, 31ᵉ année, 7 août, p 1

Sport and Esprit de Corps

National and Transnational Logics of Distinctions

Sport et esprit de corps

La logique de la distinction aux échelles nationale et transnationale

Sport et «esprit de corps»:
notes sur le pouvoir, la culture et les politiques du corps

L'auteur utilise l'expression «esprit de corps» dans le sens que le sociologue français Pierre Bourdieu lui accorde, à savoir les pratiques et manières corporelles qui expriment l'identité de corps sociaux. L'examen de la relation entre l'esprit de corps et le sport à la fin du XXe siècle débouche sur un ensemble complexe de problèmes à propos du sport et de l'identité, de l'universalisme et de la différence, de la liberté et de la contrainte, de l'assentiment et de l'auto-détermination, de la cohésion et de la division sociales. Dans une première partie, l'auteur expose brièvement la conception sociale du sport qui prévaut à la fin du XIXe siècle à l'effet que le sport, ainsi qu'une esthétique corporelle particulière, peuvent être des forces positives de la modernité. Dans la vision du sport qui sera proposée universellement, le sport est posé comme un legs du siècle de Périclès plutôt que comme celui de Néron, comme le legs d'Olympie plutôt que comme celui du Colisée Romain. Mais l'auteur souligne que l'émergence du sport «amateur» comme forme dominante du sport moderne n'aura été possible que par la négociation et le compromis entre groupes politiques et sociaux. Il passe ensuite aux critiques radicales de cette vision du sport qui ont prévalu pendant la première moitié du XXe siècle et jusqu'aux années 1960 et 1970. Selon ces critiques, les promesses du siècle des lumières — raison et liberté — qui sont considérées comme une marque de la modernité, ont été transformées en déraison et domination dans les sociétés de masse, qu'elles soient capitalistes ou socialistes. Le sport moderne est vu comme forme de subordination du corps à la logique du rendement caractéristique du processus de travail capitaliste et de la gestion bureaucratique socialiste. La critique radicale du sport en appelle alors au jeu comme seule base d'une esthétique corporelle vraiment émancipatoire. Dans une troisième partie, l'auteur présente les perspectives critiques les plus récentes dans leur capacité d'explication de la relation entre sport et esprit de corps. Il propose que l'acte-même de structurer le sport — en créant une organisation, en spécifiant un réglement, en définissant une pratique légitime ou valorisée, ou en définissant les conditions habituelles de la pratique — est un exercice de pouvoir qui, à la fois, définit et emprunte des capacités, des compétences et des valeurs dans la société. La lutte pour une définition du sport comme un ensemble sain et civilisateur de pratiques culturelles et corporelles, a été menée en privilégiant les ressources matérielles, les compétences culturelles et les croyances d'Européens et de Nord-Américains de sexe masculin et appartenant à une classe donnée. Le consensus a été conquis non par un processus aveugle et abstrait de modernisation, mais par une histoire complexe de négociations, de luttes et de compromis. Au cours du XXe siècle, la conception du sport évolue et puise de plus en plus ses signaux aux sources du grand capital, de la publicité, des media, de l'industrie du spectacle et des stratégies de développement des nations modernes. Cette tendance coexiste avec des alternatives, résiduelles ou émergentes, de structures, d'activités, de pratiques et d'esthétiques, qui ne menacent cependant pas le grand capital, l'hégémonie masculine ou l'Eurocentrisme. L'enjeu de la lutte pour une conception sociale légitime du sport demeure l'obtention d'un consensus large qui favorise (mais ne garantit en rien) les intérêts des groupes dominants. L'auteur conclut en soulignant que le pouvoir est impliqué de manière chronique et inévitable dans tous les processus sociaux, qu'il est un élément-clef des limites et des possibilités du sport moderne, et qu'il est nécessaire d'étudier les relations de pouvoir dans leurs spécificités historiques et ethnographiques.

Sport and "Esprit de Corps": Notes on Power, Culture and the Politics of the Body

Richard Gruneau

The conference organizers have asked me to speak about "Sport and Esprit de Corps". At first sight it seems an unusual topic and I suspect that many of you—upon seeing the topic in the conference program—wondered about exactly what would get discussed in this session. Actually, the source for the title is Bourdieu's outline of a *Program for a Sociology of Sport*, presented in 1987 in Seoul, Korea[1]. Near the end of his paper, Bourdieu offers a number of observations about sport, the body, personal belief, and the reproduction of particular relations of power. "I think that there is a link between the body and what is called in French *l'esprit de corps*", Bourdieu tells us. Organizations such as the church, the army, political parties, or industrial firms "put a great emphasis on bodily discipline [. . .] because a large part of obedience is belief and belief is what the body concedes even when the mind (*l'esprit*) says no[2]". This is a different understanding of the meaning of *esprit de corps* than one is used to in English. Most people understand the phrase to mean something like "team spirit", but here Bourdieu is using the phrase in a deeper sense that carries with it an argument about the literal embodiment of collective beliefs and identities.

To think in this way, Bourdieu continues, leads one to consider the notion of discipline in greater detail. Bodily discipline is a central element in all types of social "domestication" and he cites the example of the Jesuit use of dance in their pedagogy. By extending this logic, he suggests that a key task for the social analysis of sport is to consider the "regulated manipulation" of the body and its means of obtaining "an adherence that the spirit could refuse[3]". The task would then be to analyze the "dialectical relations" that unite bodily practices in sport with a surrounding field of corresponding sentiments.

This is by no means a new idea. Bourdieu reminds us that "it has been known since Pascal", that to take certain positions or postures is to induce or reinforce the feelings they express. The analysis of such positions, postures, and feelings leads one inescapably to consider broader issues of power. In this regard,

1890
1990

Richard Gruneau, Department of Communication, Simon Fraser University, Burnaby, British Columbia, Canada.

Bourdieu notes the adage that "to make people dance" is to "possess" them[4]. Thus, it is no accident that all apparently totalitarian regimes give great priority to collective corporeal practices that "by symbolizing social elements, help to somatize them, and that, by bodily and collective mimesis of social orchestration, aim to reinforce this orchestration[5]".

But totalitarian regimes are only the most extreme case. There is a link between bodily disciplines, beliefs, rituals and power in all societies, not just totalitarian ones. Such a link is a fundamental part of the processes wherein the past is reconstructed and contemporary social relations are rehearsed and reproduced. Arguing along these lines, Connerton has recently suggested that if "there is such a thing as social memory" the obvious place to look for it is in "commemorative ceremonies" such as the opening and closing of rituals of sporting events, flag-raisings, ceremonial dinners and so forth. But when we observe such ceremonies we notice that:

> commemorative ceremonies prove to be commemorative only in so far as they are performative: performativity cannot be thought without a concept of habit; and habit cannot be thought without a notion of bodily automatisms[6].

The precise relations between bodily disciplines and habits, ceremonies, and power, and their various manifestations both in pleasurable social forms and in forms of oppression, will vary from society to society. Such variations will also be found *within* societies as well. Bodily disciplines, habits and ceremonies both constitute and express the relative powers of classes, regions, racial and ethnic groups, men and women. They also constitute and express differences in power between organizational "client groups" and their supervisory or administrative superiors. However, there are important differences between organizations that rely primarily upon ceremonial rituals as agencies of social memory and of social reproduction and those whose routine practices centre upon bodily discipline more directly. Direct corporeal discipline is most obviously central in those organizations that Goffman refers to as "total institutions"—the prison, the convent or the asylum[7]. But we can also find a deep concern for bodily discipline in fitness studios; school, community and professional sports teams; and state-supported sport systems.

I do not want to imply that every organizational setting in sport has parallels with "total institutions" the way Goffman means them. But Bourdieu's comments prompt one to wonder how closely the analogy might hold in certain instances and how best to theorize it. I wonder as well about the extent to which different sporting ceremonies, disciplines and practices actually do "somatize" the dominant cultural elements of our age in various kinds of "bodily and collective mimesis of social orchestration"? When and if they do this, how do they do it? Is "orchestration" even the right metaphor? Should we instead be talking about a bodily and collective mimesis of social struggles?

It is not possible to address all of these questions in this presentation. They are raised only as a point of entry to a consideration of social theory and the politics of the body as part of the broader critique of sport in modernity. First, the social development of sport in the late-nineteenth century will be examined succinctly as a uniquely modernist cultural project centered upon the idea that sport, and a particular bodily aesthetic, can be positive forces in modernity. A discussion will follow of some of the most important "radical" critiques of this view that emerged in the first half of the twentieth century. Finally, more recent critical perspectives on sport and power will be addressed with respect to their utility for theorizing both *l'esprit* and *le corps*.

The Discourse of Sport as a Positive Element
in the Cultures of Modern Societies.

The emergence of self-consciously "modern" sporting practices developed in England during the nineteenth century and quickly took on the character of a totalizing vision to be advanced by its proponents around the world. The ideas of rationality, discipline, health and bodily prowess were fundamental elements in this totalizing vision. The institutional groundwork was provided by the necessary rationalization of sporting structures: the creation of written technical and moral rules and of bureaucratic organizations. But the dominant cultural features of self-consciously "modern" sport centered upon two distinct concepts of discipline: the notion of "self-discipline" through the exercise of a person's supposedly "higher" faculties of reason and the disciplinary bodily mastery achieved through technique. Disciplinary mastery in game-contests, clearly, is an old idea. But in modern sports—especially in the powerful tradition of Victorian athleticism—the two conceptions of discipline were synthesized into a new cultural form.

These two conceptions of discipline coalesced around a growing cultural obsession in nineteenth century Europe and America with cleanliness, health and social improvement. They also tended to be defined within an abstract social contract model of personal and social development—a model that blended the ideas of discipline and health with nineteenth century masculine ideals of mateship and team loyalty. In this model, the pathway to individual advancement, honour and pleasure in sport was seen to lie with voluntary submission to higher rules of authority. Submission to the "rule" tied the ideal of individual cultural and physical development to the social necessity for orderly conduct and regulation.

The objective in all this was not just the pursuit of better sporting performances, it was to participate in a certain kind of culture and to live life in a certain way. In this way of life, the classical Greek notion that nothing should be done in excess corresponded almost perfectly to the cultural impulses of men in the "improving classes" in Europe and North America. The exercise of human reason in sport meant aspiring both to a sense of "stature" and healthy "proportion". The amateur code was to be the organizational and cultural expression of this combined sense of stature and proportion. The "perfectly" proportioned male bodies of Greek athletes revealed in the paintings and sculptures increasingly recovered from classical antiquity at the end of the nineteenth century became its idealized bodily aesthetic.

There was a powerful sense of what Brantlinger calls "positive classicism" to this form of sporting modernism[8]. In order to suggest that modern sport was a legitimate form of Culture it was necessary to differentiate it clearly from other sporting traditions of gambling, drink, and violent spectacle. For that reason, the vision of healthy and socially-improving activity promulgated as the essence of "modern" sport made a claim to the best that the past seemed to offer. Modern sport, in its "ideal" form, came to be signified by its promoters as the legacy of Pericles rather than Nero, of Olympia rather than the Roman Coliseum. More important, it was offered as a testament to the powers of Reason to recreate a civilizing world forum for cultural exchange in modern societies.

Of course, this vision was always contradictory, highly contested and compromised. There were deep tensions, for examples, between the pursuit of disciplinary mastery on the one hand, and a sense of balance and proportion on the other; between the ideals of controlled masculine competence, and masculine competence demonstrated through physical intimidation; between a professed internationalism, and the fuelling of nationalist and colonial rivalries; between the alleged purity of amateurism, and the economic necessities of holding and training for major competitions. We also know that the organizational and cultural "successes" of modern amateur sport tended to push more traditional or alternative forms of folk games, sporting and bodily practices to the cultural periphery. Along these lines, there is considerable literature documenting the struggle to define the female body, or to specify "legitimate" female physicality in sport in ways that excluded women. Similarly, many of the commercial gaming practices common among underclass groups were under continual siege by dominant groups throughout the 19th century.

However, the dominant structures and culture of modern amateur sport—and the associated culture of moral entrepreneurship that sustained them—never fully extinguished opposition or alternatives. And, in many instances, it became necessary to compromise the more puritanical edges of the totalizing vision in order to win consent among groups whose committment to amateur sport did not extend to imbibing the morality, the preferred cultural vision, or the classicist male bodily aesthetic. These groups brought a sense of cultural form and legitimate bodily practice from other places in the social formation—places represented by other classes, by women, or by differing ethnic groups—and adapted these to amateurism's preferred meanings, structures and disciplines.

In other words, the emergence of "amateur" sport as the initial dominant structuring element in modern sport was possible only through negotiation and compromise. Nonetheless, in its negotiated form, the ideology of modern amateur sport proved remarkably successful. The case of the Olympic Movement illustrates this success most graphically. By the nineteen thirties, the Olympic Movement had managed to elevate a Eurocentric, class, and gender-biased culture of amateur sport and the body to a level where it was widely regarded as a valued framework for the pursuit of international understanding and the civilizing process worldwide.

Clearly, however, not everyone bought this idea completely, and many of the claims that sport could be a positive force in modernity were subjected to growing criticism. For example, the argument that modern sport offered little more than "bread and circuses"—despite any pretensions to the contrary—was far from new. Brantlinger notes how, throughout the late nineteenth and early twentieth centuries, conservative critics of liberal democracy and modern industrial life frequently returned to the metaphor of the Coliseum as a way of expressing their concern for cultural decline in the west[9]. Meanwhile, on the other side of the political spectrum, radicals of all types had been quick to view modern sport as a waste of time that embodied martial or predatory instincts, reflected bourgeois values, and distracted workers from politics.

The Rationalization of Sport and the Critique of Modernity

Such criticisms gained momentum in the wake of the Berlin Olympic Games in 1936 and the cold war climate of the immediate post-war period. But one line of critique is of particular interest because of its immense impact on comparatively recent critical analyses of sporting practices and bodily disciplines. In Germany, a small group of self-consciously Marxist writers began to develop a new critical theory of society that polemicised against the seemingly inexorable forces of rationalization sweeping through the modern world. Most notably, Adorno, Horkheimer and Marcuse all argued that the Enlightenment promise of reason and freedom that had been a hallmark of modernity had become transformed into unreason and domination throughout modern mass societies whether capitalist or socialist. By contrast, the social analysis of contemporary times demanded recognition of what Adorno and Horkheimer called "the dialectic of enlightenment[10]".

It is possible to find numerous critical references to sport scattered throughout the work of these influential writers. However, most people in sport studies are far more familiar with the elaboration and extension of their ideas in the critical writing on sport that emerged during the late 1960s and early 1970s. Ingham's groundbreaking critique of the "rationalization" of sport, which synthesizes ideas from Marcuse and Weber, is notable in this regard both for its intelligence and scholarly rigor[11]. But throughout the 1970s arguments drawn from German "critical theory" (although sometimes in caricatured ways) became a staple in the arsenal of nearly every self-professed "radical" western sports critic. Among these critics, Rigauer and Vinnai in Germany, and Brohm in France, gave special emphasis to the subordination of the human body to the logic of efficiency characteristic of the capitalist labour process and of socialist bureaucratic management[12]. Modern sport was seen both as a symbolic representation and physical embodiment of capitalism's insatiable demands for "performance" in the service of profit and the technocratic ideology of science and the machine.

The early 1970s "countercultural" criticisms of sport posed by writers such as Brohm, Vinnai and Rigauer now seem like old hat, and they have been so widely criticized that you might wonder why they are even mentioned here. The answer is that so many of the concerns voiced by these critics seem to have become more pressing than ever and continue to surface again in other guises and in other intellectual traditions. Most notably, the emphasis in late 1960s and early 1970s "countercultural" criticism on consumer culture, on the politics of spectacle, and on the politics of the body, anticipates in fragmentary ways a number of arguments that have recently come back into intellectual fashion with a vengeance in current criticisms of the ideologies of modernism and in debates about the existence of a "postmodern" condition.

Most of the "countercultural" sport criticism noted above, it could be argued, have an anti-modernist slant. The critical theory of Adorno, Horkheimer and their colleagues in the so called "Frankfurt School" of German Marxism was a theoretical hybrid of diverse philosophical and theoretical influences. Yet, throughout this melange of influences, the "Frankfurt School" theorists always saw themselves as extending Marx's critical legacy. Despite their recognition of the "dialectic" of Enlightenment, their rejection of Stalinism, and their pessimism about the forces of contemporary pacification and oppression, they remained largely committed to an Enlightenment vision of universal emancipation. Only Reason itself could interrogate the irrationality of "unreason" in modern mass societies.

But the Frankfurt School writers did not see Reason as something that could ever be concretized in the historical ascendency of the proletariat. The classical Marxian vision of class struggle resulting in the triumph of socialism had been pre-empted by the power of the modern culture industry to create mindless diversion and false consciousness. Modern times required a new "critical theory" of society as a foundation for human emancipation. Adorno, in particular, also suggested the possibility that modern culture might yet maintain a basis for a radical emancipatory aesthetic. The "negative" power of "autonomous art"—for example, certain modernist artistic genres such as surrealism or the atonal music of Schoenberg—kept the promise of liberation alive.

Most of radical critics of sport in the late 1960s and early 1970s essentially adopted the critique of false consciousness and pacification contained within the mainstream of German critical theory. This was accompanied by acceptance of the related idea that classical Marxism required updating and revising. For one thing Marxian categories simply could not readily be stretched to accomodate all of the objects of modern oppression. Sexual oppression, technocratic rationality, bureaucratic domination, scientism, and their manifestations in the seemingly expansive practices of bodily discipline so fundamental to the modern high-performance sporting experience could only be seen within Marxism as expressions of alienation. The problem was that modern sport seemed to involve aspects of domination that existed independent of capital and class.

Marcuse's enthusiasm for Freud was quickly taken up as one possible way to solve these problems[13]. By contrast, there was little support among radical sports critics for the inherent elitism of Adorno's views on the emancipatory potential of a modernist avant-garde. The dominant preference was to shift the emphasis to other potential sources of liberation sometimes noted in German critical theory, again, especially in Marcuse's later work. During the late 1960s and early 1970s, radical criticism of sport became drawn to ideas that figured centrally in the broader wave of countercultural criticism breaking across nearly all western societies. Central among these ideas was the notion that play, or the erotic, were the only real bases for a truly emancipatory aesthetic.

All of this contained residues of the Enlightenment promise of the possibility of universal emancipation but it also featured a retreat from the values of Reason, and of the possibilities of modernity, that went much further than that demonstrated in the mainstream of German critical theory. Communist, trade union, or party politics were all seen to be outmoded, but there was considerable confusion about goals and strategies for effective political opposition. Part of the problem was that most "countercultural" critics in the 1960s and 1970s inevitably found themselves in a theoretical and political halfway house. The source of their anger was never really capitalism, or event the authoritarian technocratic "establishment", it was modernity itself.

We can read this tension between the critique of capitalism and the critique of modernity in the many contradictory tendencies found within many radical critiques of sport published during the late 1960s and early 1970s. In these critiques traditional Marxian language tended to become mixed with an ironically anti-Marxist nostalgia for a utopian individual autonomy, the critique of bureaucratic rationality was expressed in ways that appeared to reject any form of complex social organization altogether, and self-righteous statements of principle typically appeared side-by-side with an unconsciously Nietzschean vision of the all-enveloping character of power in modern life. The fact that sport in communist countries was even more rationalized and oppressive than in capitalist ones merely suggested the hoplessness of any Enlightenment-inspired faith in the power of human reason for social emancipation. The implicit conclusion was inevitable. Modern sport, like modern societies themselves, was inherently totalitarian.

This conclusion always struck me as bloody silly even though I had great sympathy for many of the criticisms raised by radical sports critics at the time. Under its various guises of educative and civilizing cultural practice, forum for international understanding, or socially-valued commercial or non-commercial entertainment, the *dominant* forms of modern sport *had* come to embody a new totalizing vision of bureaucratic organization, and instrumental rationality by the 1960s and 1970s. But was this necessarily totalitarian in any political sense? Did it invade the consciousness and bodies of individuals so totally that sports participants and fans ceased to act as agents, only as mindless carriers of the dehumanizing manifestations of reason gone mad?

I think not. It was only possible to believe the arguments made by countercultural critics if one accepted that the millions of people, who so passionately craved sports either as fans or athletes, had been completely duped by the capitalist culture industry or by socialist technocrats. There was simply no way for countercultural critics of the late 1960s and early 1970s to explore the popularity or the positive possibilities of modern sports, only their socially-produced limits. And there was no way to see that, even in its most commodified and administered form, sport might prove to be a contested area of social life, or that certain practices in sport *might* take on an oppositional or emancipatory character for certain groups in certain times.

Countercultural sport criticism may have intuitively grasped the dialectic of Enlightenment suggested earlier by Adorno and Horkheimer but it forgot about dialectics and contradiction in social life and culture as they are lived in contemporary societies. Instead, the tendency was to see oppression every-where—an oppression "totalized" in the relentless processes of rationalization and instrumentalization literally embodied in the ceremonies, disciplines and bodily practices of modern sport. The result of this decidedly non-dialectical view was an inevitable slide into cynicism and despair. The tacit critique of modern rationalized sport was juxtaposed to a self-consciously anti-modernist solution, the return to simple play. Only in this way would the mechanized and alienated sporting body become liberated and the cycle of ideological indoctrination and social reproduction through sport be broken.

Sport Criticism and the Turn to Gramsci

Through the 1970s and 1980s much of the critical work on sport in western societies struggled to free itself from radical pessimism and the romantic anti-modernism implicit throughout the earlier wave of countercultural sport criticism. An important part of this struggle was restoration of the sense of contradiction and struggle that had always been a hallmark of the Marxian tradition. Another part was to recover Marx's faith in the possibility of human reason moving analysis beyond despair—the part of Marxism that, in Williams' words, has always promised to "make hope practical rather than despair convincing[14]".

In order to do this it was necessary to develop a more adequate understanding of human agency, to reject a totalizing conception of power as constraint, and of ideology as a kind of all-enveloping—and literally embodied— false consciousness. In part, that meant coming to terms with the limitations of German "critical theory", but it did not allow a simple return to classical Marxism. It seemed especially necessary to break from Marxism's logocentric vision of the inevitability of capitalist collapse and its representation of the "interest" of the proletariat as "automatically" equivalent to overall human emancipation. What seemed required was a new theory of power, social practice, and cultural struggle.

I spent much of the late 1970s struggling to develop this kind of theory for the analysis of sport. Most of my inspiration came from the theory of "structuration" championed by Giddens, but I was also influenced by Bourdieu's discussion of "practices" and "rules" in *Outline of a Theory of Practice* and by Willis's analysis of "local groups" and social reproduction in *Learning to Labour*[15]. However, I needed a way to connect up this abstract theorizing about agency, structure and social reproduction with a broader theory of social development. Like many people during the late 1970s, I turned to Gramsci for a possible solution. Gramsci's discussion of "hegemony" in *The Prison Notebooks*, and Williams's discussion of language and ideology in the analysis of "cultural production", provided a framework for bringing these things together[16].

My argument in *Class, Sports and Social Development*[17] was that the act of structuring sport in a certain way—creating an organization, specifying a rule, defining a "legitimate" or valued practice, or the conditions for habitual practice—is an exercise of power that both defines and draws upon different capacities, competencies and values in society. In this formulation I adopted Giddens's argument that power can be viewed as a differential capacity to use resources of different types to secure outcomes. The obvious problem in unequal societies is that the structures which constitute sports as social possibilities are not negotiated equally. Furthermore, once constituted, different structures open up quite different possibilities—social, political and psychological—for various individuals and groups while limiting other possibilities.

The creation of "modern" sport as a coherent and institutionally-distinct field of cultural practice, modelled along the lines of Victorian athleticism, is a powerful example of these varying limits and possibilities. The struggle to define sport as a civilizing and healthy set of cultural and bodily practices conducted by gentleman "amateurs" in the nineteenth century opened up the possibility of standardized orderly sporting competition within and between nations, and it created a powerful new forum for health, bodily expression, recreation, personal achievement and spectator enjoyment. But this only occurred in ways that privileged the material resources, cultural competencies, and preferred beliefs of European and North American males from a particular class. I suggested that the fragile public consensus that briefly emerged around amateur organizations in the late nineteenth and early twentieth centuries, and around the philosophy of civilizing amateur sport, its ceremonies and disciplines was never natural or inevitable—the result of some blind process of modernization. Rather, it was something that was *won* through a complex history of negotiations, struggles and compromises.

Throughout the twentieth century, this earlier dominant "moment" in the institutional structuring of sport, and the dominant social definition of sport that accompanied it, have become increasingly residual in the face of the relentless expansion of capitalism's universal market and challenges from new social movements of various types. Older, more romantic images of "amateurism" still linger in popular memory—indeed, they now provide much of the basis for popular criticism of commercialism in sport—but they are no longer embedded in the structures and meanings of sporting practice in the way they once were nor do they have quite the same degrees of embodiment in sporting ceremonies, bodily practices and disciplines. Today's *dominant* structures and meanings of sport, and the bodily practices they animate, now take virtually all of their cues from Capital, from advertising, commercial media, the entertainment industries, and the development strategies of modern Nations.

Yet, the dominant tendencies in sport today co-exist with a multiplicity of residual, emergent and alternative structures, activities, bodily practices, and aesthetics. Examples include such new (and old) sporting structures as independently organized women's teams, community leagues, Master's competitions, beer leagues and so on; "new" sporting practices ranging from bungee-jumping to snowboarding; and a range of new bodily aesthetics, both for men and women, tied variously to function, performance, or just plain marketing. Bodily prohibitions and ideals based on the popularity of classical athleticized imagery still prevail but in a more fragmentary and diversified way than in the immediate past. The idealized aesthetics of male athletic proportion appropriated from classical Greece stands in contrast to a new array of available bodily aesthetics for men and women—for example, the functionally necessary height of basketball players; the overblown, neckless, bodies of football players; the gaunt body of the marathon runner; the massive muscle development of the pioneers of women's bodybuilding; the countering, more mainstream, sexualization of women's emergent sporting physicality.

We are only now beginning to explore how each of the structures, practices, representations, and aesthetics noted above has a place in contemporary systems of power, how each fits into what Bourdieu has called prevailing "logics of social distinction[18]", and how each offers various degrees of opposition to, or accomodation with, dominant interests. It is tempting to see these differences in the field of sporting practice today as a powerful affirmation of cultural pluralism—a manifestation of the vast range of sites for identity construction, counter-ideological practice and alternative conceptions of the body available in contemporary consumer capitalism. But *difference* alone does not necessarily translate into equality or opposition. Few of the differences noted above are taken up and popularized in media or through State and commercial sponsorship in ways that offer much threat to Capital, masculine hegemony, or Eurocentrism.

I am not trying to suggest that every sporting practice—every contest and every representation of a contest—necessarily has, or ought to have, an overtly political character. MacAloon is fundamentally correct to remind us of the often open-ended metaphoric character of cultural performances of all types[19]. But we are condemned to discuss politics whenever we seek to understand how particular fields of social and cultural practice are constituted, reproduced, and transformed. That is why I have spent much of the last several years exploring ways in which the dominant structures and representational practices in sport today are constituent elements in the ongoing negotiation of cultural and ideological hegemony in capitalist consumer cultures.

Hegemony works best when it concedes to opposition on the margins in order to retain the core principles upon which particular forms of dominance are sustained. And even in the face of contemporary diversity I remain convinced that dominant structures and practices in sport today continue to represent certain class, gender, and Western cultural and bodily practices as if they were universal categories and thereby marginalize many alternative conceptions of sport and the body. There may well be ongoing struggles on the margins to redefine the dominant structuring principles of the field. But, in struggles over "common sense" and public consent, dominant interests are often able to delegitimize alternatives by labelling them as frivolous, unnatural, or archaic. In the meantime, other sources of difference frequently get incorporated in a compromised and nonthreatening manner.

However, none of this should be taken to suggest that sport today is any less malleable and contradictory than in the past. No hegemonic settlement of forces and interests is forever. For instance, there is, clearly, a notable tension in the world today between all totalizing visions of "modern" life and the sweeping forces of social and cultural differentiation now characteristic of contemporary —some people say "postmodern"—consumer societies. But is this tension the result of a new emphasis on, and respect for, cultural, stylistic and aesthetic differences on their own terms? Or is it simply an expression of market segmentation and the transition to what neo-Gramscian political economists call new "post-Fordist" regimes of capital accumulation?

The issue is by no means clear. However, if the latter case is true—and I suspect it is—then we can expect the wide range of structures, beliefs, styles and bodily practices emergent in sport today to continue to be incorporated into the realms of marketing and commerce in a manner that poses the least possible threat to the new bloc of interests that will define the nature of global capitalism in the twenty-first century. I have no way of knowing what the field of sporting practice will look like in the "new times" that lie ahead. However, I suspect that we can take for granted that the commodification of sport in the new global capitalism will continue apace. One thing is certain. In an increasingly international media culture, the sphere of "the popular"—which centrally includes sport—will be more important in the formation of social and political identities than ever before.

This emphasis on "the popular" as a central site for the struggle over hegemony—indeed, over common sense itself—is one of the central insights of a neo-Gramscian conception of social development. But the insights one gets from Gramsci come at a price. First, Gramsci's emphasis on the struggle over common sense in the negotiation of hegemony virtually leaves the body out of account as an object domain. His primary concern is with consciousness and language as central points of struggle in the formation of active political subjects. Even the unconscious and habitual features of common sense are given a markedly cognitive tilt. A neo-Gramscian perspective can certainly accomodate discussion of the *representation* of the body as a bearer of social and political meanings—but it has much greater difficulty discussing how bodies are variously constituted or how the body might provide, in Bourdieu's words, "an adherence that the spirit might refuse". For Gramsci, all people are intellectuals and their capacity to act as conscious agents interests him far more than any unconscious choreography of authority that might be sedimented in the body.

With this in mind it is not surprising that neo-Gramscian perspectives like my own have not really followed up on earlier countercultural criticisms of the regulated manipulation of the body in high performance sport—a system of regulated manipulation that can be viewed as a form of domination in itself and which reproduces that domination. Nor have neo-Gramscians been sufficiently concerned with the precise ways in which particular sporting structures and beliefs have the effect of materializing a logic of social distinction in various sport styles and practices and in their accompanying constitution of the body. To revise Bourdieu's phrase, we might say that the neo-Gramscian critique of sport has emphasized the struggle over "l'esprit" without adequately exploring the issues of embodiment and regulation of "le corps".

There is another problem implicit in neo-Gramscian perspectives that is worth noting. Gramsci did not believe that social identity or political awareness flowed from group membership in any natural or automatic way. For example, he argued that classes do not magically "know" their interests; rather they have to form conceptions of them. They do this through ideas and values found in the language and outlook of their time and culture. This is why he believed struggles over the sphere of "the popular"—over common sense—to be decisively implicated in the formation of active political agents and any alliance of "collective wills" that could be forged into a hegemonic historical bloc.

In analyzing the struggle over "the popular" Gramsci paid considerable attention to the importance of Nationalism in the construction of social consent to particular forms of rule and there is no reason why a Gramscian-inspired framework could not be extended to include struggles over gender, race, ethnicity, or a host of other issues as they surface in diverse areas of cultural life. Nonetheless, Gramsci himself consistently emphasized the role of class agents in hegemonic struggles and the formation of historical blocs. Attendant to this, his concern for the importance of civil society often smacks of Leninist opportunism. One struggles to win consent in the sphere of the popular only to advance the interests of the Party. This lingering vaguardism has been ignored or rejected by most contemporary neo-Gramscians—many of whom even define themselves as "post-Marxists". Nonetheless, the over-riding concern with class continues to dominate Gramsci's legacy and I am not sure it can be so easily wished away simply by piggy-backing a consideration of non-class struggles into the analysis of hegemony.

From Gramsci to Foucault?

Having said this, I still do not believe that the limitations noted above are sufficiently problematic to offset the immense usefulness of *some* of Gramsci's ideas particularly when they are employed as a link between an abstract theory of practice and the more concrete study of social development. However, it is not possible to ignore these limitations either. Is there a more adequate general framework that might be employed to acknowledge the constitution and politics of the body in sport while simultaneously adopting a view of power that readily accomodates the analysis of interests other than those of Capital or the State?

It is sometimes suggested that one way of solving many of these problems is to completely re-orient one's conception of power away from readily identifiable historical agents in order to concentrate on power's abstract and unconscious character. Such a move away from issues of conscious agency "decenters the subject" in a manner that better allows the body to be fully understood as an independent object domain. Similarly, it is argued that a more abstract analysis allows one to see how power operates at all levels of social interaction with no one source of power necessarily privileged over others. This supposedly frees the debate about power from an overly close association with the traditional "universal" subjects of earlier modernist discourse—notably, Man, the Proletariat, the Party or the State. Instead attention is directed to the micro-politics of power implicit in everyday interaction and the "normalized" practices demanded in various institutional settings.

The theorist whose work is most closely associated with these ideas is Foucault. Power for Foucault has little to do with class or gender or any recognizable social group. It is not something wielded by an agent but is a relation of force. As Foucault notes, "power is everywhere; not because it embraces everything but because it comes from everywhere[20]". Giddens has emphasized how this view is declaredly opposite that of Marx. Marx understood power as the noxious expression of class domination capable of being transcended by some progressive moment in history[21]. But for Foucault power is not inherently repressive (a view Giddens shares and one I support as well). It is more, Giddens suggests, than just the capability to say no:

> If this is all power were, Foucault asks, would we really consistently obey it? Power has its hold because it does not simply act like an oppressive weight, a burden to be resisted[22].

On the contrary, Foucault argues, power is actually the means by which things happen. It is productive; "it produces reality; it produces domains of objects and rituals of truth[23]". The individual and an individual's knowledge belong to this production.

So for Foucault the production of things, of knowledge and forms of discourse—even of pleasure—are all instances of power. His classic example is sexuality. Sexuality is often understood in the West as something repressed by external powers—for example, this is a fundamental notion in the Freudian paradigm. But Foucault argues that in actuality sex is a product of power—an historical product produced in discourse through the interplay of power and desire[24]. Furthermore, the case of sexuality demonstrates aptly how power has a "capillary form of existence". Power seeps into the very grain of individuals and the body is the key site where this seepage occurs.

Giddens notes how the concern for bodily discipline in Foucault's discussion of sexuality has "evident connections" with Foucault's account of the origins of the modern prison[25]. Foucault sees the characteristic forms of power in the modern prison to be discipline and surveillance. These he sees as essentially new "technologies of power" that arose in the 19th century. For example, Foucault notes how discipline dissociates power from the body contrary to older traditions of direct corporeal punishment in which the body was marked. In this way disciplinary power has a much less visible character than punishment. With discipline, power is "interiorized". Those who experience it acquiesce and this acquiescence becomes an essential part of the new technology of power[26].

The most visible counterpart to discipline for Foucault is surveillance. Foucault points out how the idea that individuals should be constantly monitered—constantly under observation—is "the natural correlate of discipline, once the latter is manifested externally in the regularity of conduct by "docile bodies[27]". For example, Bentham's Panopticon proposed a model for prison design which would allow for all inmates's activities to be observed from a single central tower. But, as Giddens notes, this is only an "ideal" physical layout for the "discipline/surveillance relationship". Discipline involves the "specified enclosure of space, the partitioning of space according to specialized criteria[28]". And Foucault notes, such spatial sequestration is not limited to the prison. It is also a key feature of factories, schools, offices and other organizations.

Giddens goes on to argue, pursuasively in my view, that if Marx saw the factory, or the site of economic production as the exemplification of our western conception of modernity, for Foucault it is the prison and the asylum[29]. Discipline and surveillance have become such central features of human life that we now take the modern technologies of normalization for granted. Foucault notes the existence of resistence to the forces of normalization in contemporary institutional life but he seems to make resistence into little more than a functionally necessary counterpoint to the omnipresence of power. In my view all of this tends to leave one with a rather pessimistic vision of the docility of the body as a "normalized" condition of modernity.

I have long been struck by the comparative absence of Foucauldian analyses in English language writing on sport. It does not take much imagination to suggest what such an analysis might look like. The emergence of modern sport forms governed by a push for rational organization, discipline and self-improvement could be analyzed as part of the new technologies of power that developed in the 19th century. The values of discipline, health and self-improvement as a source of pleasure could be seen as interiorized in the body in ways that supported powerful new forms of docility and normalization. It would then be possible to study the discourses of sports promoters, health, and physical education professionals as an essential part of the emerging technology of normalization. One could also study the changing nature of training regimes, relationships between athletes and coaches, athletes, and administrators, and spatial arrangements of training locales with respect to the strengthening discipline/surveillance relationship.

It is possible to ask a number of glib questions in the context of this kind of argument. For example, is there any comparison between the coaching observation tower in American football and Bentham's vision of the Panopticon? Is random drug-testing in sport simply another escalation in the discipline/surveillance relationship—a new technology in the move to more complete institutional totalization in sport? The point, of course, would be to move beyond such glibness to sustained analysis but I do not know of a single study published in English where these types of arguments have been developed in any thorough or comprehensive way.

Hargreaves' recent book *Sport, Power and Culture* is the closest thing to an exception[30]. Although even Hargreaves's discussion is by no means a purely Foucauldian analysis. Rather, Hargreaves attempts to weave arguments and ideas derived from Foucault with a Gramscian conception of hegemony and social development. Foucault's presence makes itself known in Hargreaves' definition of power, his attention to the body, and analysis of the discourses of normalization employed by physical education "professionals".

Sport, Power and Culture is a remarkably insightful and extremely ambitious book—perhaps the best book-length piece of sport and social criticism written in the 1980s. But I have reservations about the theoretical compatibility of

Gramsci with a Foucauldian theory of power, and I am not convinced that Hargreaves' ambitious synthesis ever quite comes together. A large part of the problem lies in the difficulty of synthesizing Gramsci's inherently modernist belief in the possibility of emancipatory social transformation with Foucault's Nietzschean vision of the omnipresence and inevitability of power.

In Gramsci, power is grounded in real historical practice—in agency—and its most noxious forms are potentially transformable. But in Foucault discipline and power are characteristically spoken of as if *they* were agents in themselves —the real agents of history. I do not think you can have this both ways. For example, in some instances, Hargreaves speaks of the changing place of sport in a hegemony contested by class and gender agents with a readily-demonstrable historical presence and there is recognition of the possibility of emancipatory oppositional practice. But in other instances, Hargreaves treats power as omnipresent—a Foucauldian technology linking the physical body to the social body in an unmediated way. However, Hargreaves does not provide—I would say cannot provide—any consistent set of principles to allow us to decide when one view of power ought to be employed over the other or when, and in what circumstances, they might be combined.

The virtue of Foucault for the study of sport is that he demands consideration of "administrative power" in the broadest possible range of practices and discourses which impinge on the human body. This encourages one to move beyond discussion of empowerment and disempowerment linked only to class, race, ethnicity or gender. In addition Foucault virtually *forces* one to consider the body by making it the primary site for the deployment of various technologies of power in modernity. He does this without any vague promises of "human" or "social" emancipation overall. On the contrary, he would argue that such conceptions inevitably contain their own technologies of normalization.

There is a great deal that is intellectually intriguing and useful in all this, but I also think there are dangers in swallowing Foucault whole. For one thing, I cannot accept the idea of a history "without subjects". I agree with Giddens, that "history has no subject" if that phrase means a rejection of the view of one "transcendental subject" as either the source or goal of "progressive" social transformation[31]. Similarly, I have little difficulty with the idea of "decentering the subject" if that means one cannot take an originating subjectivity or social identity as pre-given. But any theory that denies the possibility of conscious agency—the possibility that men and women have to make history even if it is under conditions that are not of their own choosing—I find highly problematic.

I also wonder about the inherent limitations of the Foucauldian emphasis on discipline and on the analogy of the prison as something reflected throughout the institutions of modernity. This point has implications for the kind of musing about comparisons between sport and "total institutions" that I raised at the outset of this presentation. If we take the Foucauldian perspective we are drawn to see how technologies of normalization produce docile bodies and we can see how certain forms of sport and fitness pedagogy, or discipline/surveillance relation- ships *appear* to operate like those of "total institutions" in many instances. But we cannot explore the many ways in which varying sporting sites and practices simply do *not* operate in the manner of total institutions. Nor can we adequately explore the different limits and possibilities—forms of freedom and empowerment, oppression and disempowerment—associated with *different* modes of social and political organization in contemporary life.

I think it correct to insist that power is chronically and inevitably involved in all social processes. To recognize this, as Giddens points out, is to say that power and freedom are not inimical and that power is more than outright constraint or coercion[32]. Indeed, this recognition has been a key element of my own work on the limits and possibilities of modern sport. But the elevation of power to a privileged place in action and discourse is something else again. There can be no truth, no set of meanings outside of technologies of power, no values outside of power, and very little sense that some meanings and values are more or less oppressive than others. All one is left with as a guard against radical pessimism is some vague notion of the value of individual and local struggles against institutional power and the abstract forces of "normalization". This latter argument has been taken up with considerable enthusiasm by many recent proponents of "postmodernism" (itself a highly contested concept) but I am not convinced that a politics centred on locality is enough. Furthermore I wonder if the abstract radicalization of power implicit in such perspectives does not have the unintended consequence of displacing criticism away from the unequal powers of collective agents who can actually be *named* (*e.g.*, the class, gender or racial groups assembled into a hegemonic historical bloc).

Concluding Comments

Firstly, a return to Bourdieu's comments about "sport and l'esprit de corps" with which this presentation began. Bourdieu's language sounds Foucauldian at times, especially with respect to its emphasis on bodily discipline, "domestication", and tendency to concede belief "even when the mind (*l'esprit*) says no[33]". But despite these Foucauldian overtones, Bourdieu has something different in mind. He argues that sport, like dance, is an area where teaching bodily discipline, as well as "learning with one's body", is much more clearly evident than in many other areas of cultural practice. But even in sport it is important to study "l'esprit" and "le corps" as a "dialectical relation". He goes on to suggest that through a better understanding of the body in sport or dance "one could possibly contribute to a theory of belief." And a theory of belief is absolutely essential in the world of politics because of the "problem of seizing awareness[34]".

Bourdieu's recognition of the "problem" of the struggle over awareness —over common sense—in contemporary politics is vastly more Gramscian than Foucauldian in its orientation and I have to say that I favour it for that reason. If we want to study the politics of the body as part of the critique of sport in modernity I think there is much more scope for imaginative and useful analysis in Bourdieu than in Foucault. I am particularly supportive of Bourdieu's recognition that the range of meanings attributed to sporting practices is influenced by the various social contexts in which sport is consumed, and I particularly like his analogy of a musical score as a means to theorize the structuring and meanings associated with sport as a field of practice[35].

But I think that even Bourdieu's immensely sophisticated analyses of beliefs and bodily practices are sometimes less sensitive than they ought to be about the centrality of the ambiguities and contradictions of contemporary cultural life. In his *Program for a Sociology of Sport* Bourdieu recognizes that "dominant meanings" in sport are not interpreted in a uniform way and can change historically. But his discussion of what he calls "reversals"—instances where the "logic of distinction" seems to collapse—suggest that ambiguity and contradiction are exceptional conditions rather than the norm. Arguing along these lines, Frow has noted how Bourdieu's work as a whole contains a tendency to view cultural forms and practices as non-contradictory expressive unities rather than ongoing sites of political tension. Commenting on Bourdieu's analysis in *Distinction* Frow notes how for Bourdieu:

> it thus becomes impossible to read, for example, a painting by Goya in terms of contradictions between its functions of cognition and exclusion, or indeed its

changing relation to the art market-place; and, conversely, the kind of political analysis that informs the work of, say, Stedman Jones on the music hall, or Willis on working-class counterschool culture, or Sennet and Cobb on the ethos of self-sacrifice in the American Working class—work which stresses the ideological and political ambiguity of popular cultural forms[36].

To turn Bourdieu's earlier comment about dance around, we might say that to "make people dance" may not be to "possess" them in every instance. The degree of "possession" clearly varies depending upon both the nature of the relationship and the social context with which meaning is attributed to the practice. The dance instructor and the student have a different relationship than the television rock video host and the audience. In most instances of domination in modern societies the possessor and the dispossessed do seem locked into a relationship of endless asymmetry—a relationship where even the criticisms raised by the dispossessed are formed in terms encouraged or defined by dominant discourses (a point Bourdieu makes throughout his work and one which is reminiscent of Foucault). But often the power of this dominant discourse is lost in ambiguity or contradiction, differentially interpreted and transformed in different contexts of use. The point is to attempt to understand how some measure of social reproduction occurs in this dynamic context.

Earlier in this presentation I briefly noted examples of ambiguities and contradictions in the case of the totalizing vision of "amateurism" that briefly operated as a dominant structuring principle in the emergence of modern sport. The case of sport reveals graphically how popular cultural forms are anything but non-contradictory expressive unities. Bourdieu certainly acknowledges this point, but in my view he doesn't take it far enough. In the field of the popular, dominant discourses get ignored, remade, or radically revised on an ongoing basis, and popular support for cultural projects and for particular types of social relationships in contemporary western societies is never automatic. It has to be continually defended, negotiated and revised, because it is always on the verge of breaking apart.

It is difficult to see such things if we concentrate on the structural dynamics—the synchronic study—of relationships of power in the abstract or in the here and now. We need to study such relationships in their historical and ethnographic specificities. It may well be, as Bourdieu argues, that in totalitarian regimes collective corporeal practices do somatize social elements in ways that, through bodily and collective mimesis of social orchestration, aim to reinforce this orchestration. But even here, one might question whether these aims are always met in every totalitarian context. Perhaps a research project is in order which examines sporting practices and beliefs in Eastern Europe in the context of the events of 1989?

In any case, contemporary liberal democracies are different than totalitarian regimes. This does not mean that sporting practices and beliefs necessarily provide the opposite condition to the totalitarian emphasis—bodily and collective mimesis of social struggles—although sometimes this happens. Rather, forces of incorporation and struggle should be seen as an historically shifting and dynamic process. And to do this, if I might be allowed a final statement of preference, it is most useful to link sport and the body to a theory of power, structure and social development that operates with Gramsci in mind.

NOTES AND REFERENCES

1. Bourdieu P (1989) Program for a sociology of sport. In Kang S-p, MacAloon JJ, Damatta R (eds) The Olympics and east/west and south/north cultural exchange: the papers of the first international conference on the olympics and east/west and south/north cultural exchange in the world system. Hanyang Ethnology Monograph no I. Hanyang University: The Institute for Ethnological Studies p 69-83

2. Ibid p 82

3. Ibid p 82

4. Ibid p 83

5. Ibid p 83

6. Connerton P (1989) How societies remember. London: Cambridge University Press p 4-5

7. Goffman E (1961) Asylums. Harmondsworth: Penguin

8. Brantlinger P (1983) Bread and circuses: theories of mass culture as social decay. Ithica: Cornell University Press

9. Ibid Chapters 2 and 4

10. Horkheimer M, Adorno T (1944) Dialectic of enlightenment. New York: Seabury Press 1977 edition

11. Ingham A (1975) Occupational subcultures in the work world of sport. In Ball D Loy JW (eds) Sport and social order. Reading: Addison-Wesley p 333-89. Ingham A (1978) American sport in transition: the maturation of industrial capitalism and its impact on sport. PhD dissertation University of Massachusetts

12. Rigauer B (1969) Sport und Arbeit. Frankfurt: Suhrkamp. Translated by A Guttmann and later published as Sport and work. New York: Columbia University Press (1981). Vinnai G (1970) Fussballsport als Ideologie. Frankfurt: Europaische Verlagsanstalt. Translated as Football mania. London: Ocean books (1973). Brohm JM (1976) Critiques du sport. Paris: C. Bourgeois. Translated as Sport: a prison of measured time. London: Ink Links (1978)

13. Marcuse H (1962) Eros and civilization. New York: Vintage

14. Williams R (1982) Towards 2000. London: Chatto and Windus

15. Giddens A (1976) New rules of sociological method. London: Hutchinson. Giddens A (1977) Studies in social and political theory. New York: Basic Books. Giddens A (1981) A contempory critique of historical materialism. London: Macmillan. Bourdieu P (1977) Outline of a theory of practice. Cambridge: Cambridge University Press. Willis P (1977) Learning to labour. Westmead: Saxon House. Gruneau R (1983) Class, sports and social development. Amherst: University of Massachusetts Press

16. Quentin H, Nowell Smith G (eds) (1971) Selections from the prison notebooks of Antonio Gramsci. New York: International Publishers. Williams R (1977) Marxism and literature. Oxford: Oxford University Press

17. Gruneau R (1983) op cit

18. Bourdieu P (1984) Distinction: a social critique of the judgement of taste. Cambridge: Harvard University Press. Translation of La distinction: critique sociale du jugement. Paris: Éditions de minuit (1979)

19. MacAloon JJ (1984) Olympic Games and the theory of spectacle in modern societies. In MacAloon JJ (ed) Rite, drama, festival, spectacle: rehearsal toward a theory of culture performance. Philadelphia: Institute for the Study of Human Issues Press

20. Foucault M (1980) The history of sexuality. Vol I New York: Random House p 93

21. Giddens A (1982) Profiles and critiques in social theory. London: Macmillan. Chapter 15: From Marx to Nietzsche? Neo-conservatism, Foucault, and problems in contempory political theory.

22. Giddens A (1982) op cit p 219

23. Foucault M (1977) Discipline and punishment. New York: Vintage

24. Foucault M (1980) op cit

25. Giddens A (1982) op cit p 221

26. Ibid p 220

27. Ibid p 221

28. Ibid p 221

29. Ibid p 221

30. Hargreaves J (1986) Sport, power and culture. New York: St Martin's Press

31. Giddens A (1982) op cit p 222

32. Ibid p 226

33. Bourdieu P (1987) op cit p 82

34. Ibid p 82

35. Ibid p 7

36. Frow J (1987) Accounting for tastes: some problems in Bourdieu's sociology of culture. Cultural Studies 1

Sports and "Esprit de Corps":
Systems of Sporting Practices, Relations to the Body, and Production of Identities

In Anglo-Saxon sociology, one tends to attach to the expression *Esprit de Corps* the attribute of *Team Spirit*. In the context of this presentation the author utilizes the term in the specific denotation given to it by French sociologist Bourdieu, that is the bodily practices and manners which express the identity of social entities. In the first part of his presentation, the author proposes a model of analysis with which one can observe how, through the medium of sports, the culture and very spirit of a given social entity imprints on people as corporeal entities. He underlines the impossibility to attach a sport mechanically to a given socio-economic class. Although football (soccer) is generally associated with the lower socio-economic classes and tennis or golf with their upper counterparts, sport ought not be defined in strict social terms. The author contends instead that a sport acquires its distinctive value as part of a spectrum of other activities that constitute and function as a system. With reference to football, the author stresses that it is not obligatorily associated to the social conditions and lifestyle of the working class, for they are indeed not those who practice it the most. A fact remains: football tends to occupy a prominent position in the structure of the sporting activities that the people of the lower socio-economic class engage in. In that perspective, the matter of correspondence between sports and social classes is one of relationship between two spaces: the space of sports; the space of social positions. The author then notes that the above-mentioned relationships are susceptible to change under the combined effect of an increasingly expanding sports market, on the one hand, and, on the other hand, of the transformation of the space that has characterized the various socio-economic classes. Supplementary factors, considered by the author in his model of analysis, are the outcomes of what is generally at stake in the conflicts between genders and generations. Taking as an example the sport of squash, the author shows that the sport in question can be described as a sport for the younger generation. Furthermore, the practice of that sport tends to be associated with the employment situation of the middle socio-economic class. Being a squash player in France, nowadays, is interpreted as being young of spirit and heart, even if one may no longer have the biological fitness associated with the young in age. Referring to golf as a second concrete example, the author explains that it is still a rarity in certain social strata, its practice best described by a bi-modal distribution: the young, and the older category of participants, with most individuals holding advanced degrees or already well engaged in their careers. Typical transfers towards the practice of golf have as much to do with the social aspects of the sport as with the activity proper. In the second part of his presentation, the author deals with the production of sporting heroes in to-day's society. He points out that the present legitimization which is given to the pursuit of sporting excellence constitutes in itself a concealment of the very forces which have been used in the first place to establish the said legitimity. The author contends that no "popular" champion or hero is the true incarnation of the spirit of a people. For him, a given sport acquires symbolism for a collective body only through numerous and prolonged interactions between the circles and groups of leaders, and the social groups of participants and spectators. The media now play a major role in the development of collective opinion and beliefs, as well as in the transformation of an athlete into a symbol of collective identity. Paradoxically, on the other hand, the use of a champion as a symbol or as a bearer of the chances and hopes of a group is a factor which can also re-inforce already existing divisions and even generate exclusions, all in the name of universal values. Particularism (of which nationalism is only a form) and universalism are constituent elements of symbolism in sport. By way of conclusion, the author proposes that the analysis of the general belief in the universality of sporting values and thus of individuals as universal champions or heroes, should start with the study of the work done by national and international bodies that control the various spaces of sport, the sports media and the communications systems.

Sports et «esprit de corps»: système des sports, rapports au corps et production d'identités

Charles Suaud

La richesse de l'expression «esprit de corps» justifie que l'on en fasse un véritable concept, à condition d'en contrôler les usages et les significations qui lui sont couramment attachés. Cette association de mots que l'on effectue dans la pratique quotidienne sans véritablement prendre conscience des enjeux qu'elle contient, invite à rompre avec la logique dualiste dans laquelle certaines philosophies ont décrit les relations entre l'esprit et le corps[1]. La notion d'«esprit de corps» exprime en effet qu'une identité de groupe — autrement dit de corps social — peut se forger et s'affirmer à travers des manières de penser devenues manières corporelles. Toutefois, comme cela se passe chaque fois qu'une expression du sens commun est reprise sociologiquement, celle d'«esprit de corps» demande à être reconstruite théoriquement afin que la part de vérité sur le monde social qu'elle contient ne soit pas détournée par et pour la pratique, dans des sens qui deviennent alors de puissants obstacles à la connaissance scientifique.

Si l'existence de relations entre des sports et des classes sociales de pratiquants est aisément admise, cette vision des choses relève moins d'une connaissance sociologique à proprement parler que d'une sorte de croyance à laquelle le sens commun adhère spontanément, sur la nature des sports d'un côté, des classes sociales de l'autre. On pourrait parler d'*effets idéologiques de corps* chaque fois qu'une relation effective entre un sport et les pratiquants d'une classe sociale (ou d'un sexe) est désignée d'une manière essentialiste qui revient à inscrire dans la nature des corps (ou des sports) la réalité de la relation. Que le football exprime la nature des classes populaires est l'une de ces croyances collectives et tout débordement de violences, comme celui qui est survenu au stade du Heysel en Belgique en 1985, devient une occasion idéale pour dire au grand jour, et en toute légitimité, les préjugés sur ce que *sont* les membres de ces classes. La même logique est à l'œuvre lorsqu'on attache mécaniquement un sport à l'un ou l'autre sexe comme font les insultes sportives lorsqu'elles apostrophent un pratiquant de sport masculin à l'aide d'un nom de sport constitué comme féminin (en traitant par exemple un footballeur de «danseuse»). Ainsi la sociologie du sport conduit à dévoiler les mécanismes les plus cachés, et les plus puissants, de toutes les formes de racisme — de classe, de sexe ou d'âge — que l'on engage le

Charles Suaud, Département de sociologie, Université de Nantes, Nantes, France.

plus souvent inconsciemment à travers les évaluations émises sur les autres à partir de la seule perception de leurs propriétés et attitudes corporelles.

L'exposé qui suit est organisé autour de deux points. Dans une première partie, un modèle est proposé, à partir d'enquêtes empiriques effectuées en France sur des populations de pratiquants[2], modèle théorique à l'aide duquel on peut penser de manière dynamique comment, par la pratique sportive, la culture et l'«esprit» d'un corps social peut informer les corps biologiques. Dans une seconde partie, on s'interrogera sur les transformations des mécanismes de symbolisation qui agissent lorsque les groupes deviennent des communautés de plus en plus vastes et complexes (du village au continent) et que l'«esprit de corps» n'est plus incarné à la première personne, mais à travers le corps des champions.

Sports et «esprit de corps»

Techniques du corps et incorporation des positions sociales

Ce n'est pas sacrifier à la philosophie substantialiste dénoncée plus haut que d'accepter l'idée qu'à travers un sport, un «esprit» particulier vienne à se modeler dans la réalité des pratiques corporelles. L'enjeu principal du concept maussien de *techniques du corps* n'est pas de traiter le sport comme un *fait social total* comme on le trouve rituellement exprimé; il serait plutôt de rappeler que l'usage sportif du corps répond à une *logique pratique* et qu'il engage à ce titre des schèmes culturels et moraux profondément enfouis, clandestinement inculqués à travers des actes apparemment purement techniques et des manières d'être strictement corporelles[3]. La mise en œuvre d'un sport n'est pas d'abord une affaire de représentations mentales mais de montages corporels codifiés et efficaces qui, tout en ayant une logique technique propre, sont des produits culturels engendrés selon des schèmes inconscients, socialement modelés donc largement partagés, à travers lesquels les individus engagent *de manière incorporée* les propriétés fondamentales de leur groupe. Ce qui est vrai de la politesse conçue comme une «mythologie politique réalisée, *incorporée*» pour reprendre l'expression de Bourdieu, devrait l'être *a fortiori* de la pratique sportive où tout ce qui est appris est moins de l'ordre du savoir objectivable que de ce qui contribue à définir l'*identité* de l'individu[4].

Ce rappel de l'aspect corporel et pratique des activités sportives pourrait apparaître comme un truisme si l'on n'apercevait que cette incorporation de la culture était précisément au fondement de l'*illusion de l'autonomie du sport* par rapport au social au point qu'il devient difficile de penser comment des principes culturels agissent sous la forme méconnaissable de manières d'être et de faire sportives. Une théorie conséquente de l'incorporation d'un arbitraire culturel par les pratiques sportives est rendue nécessaire non seulement pour contrer les effets d'une telle naturalisation du social, mais également pour *prévenir toute fausse rupture* comme celle qui propose de voir, au travers des pratiques corporelles, des «volontés pédagogiques» externes exerçant des forces «correctives» sur les corps sans que soient prises en considération les conditions concrètes de réalisation de ces «volontés»[5]. Un tel point de vue intellectualiste qui sous-estime l'inscription corporelle des pratiques sportives, commande en effet de nombreuses études, tout particulièrement lorsqu'elles se fondent sur des analyses de textes. L'histoire des pratiques devient alors une histoire des théories pédagogiques ou politiques dans lesquelles les pratiques corporelles sont décrites comme la réalisation d'idées pré-existantes et les corps ne sont que de simples réceptacles d'un «esprit» explicitement inculqué[6].

En tant que manières corporelles instituées, les pratiques sportives sont l'expression la plus naturelle et par conséquent la plus inconsciente d'une identité individuelle socialement organisée qui acquiert à la fois une grande visibilité pour autrui et une profonde intériorité pour soi-même. Du point de vue d'une sociologie des formes symboliques telle que Cassirer la pensait, elles sont également à considérer de manière dynamique dans leurs fonctions de production pratique de sens. Reprenant la distinction que Sahlins introduit entre structures «prescriptives» et «performatives»[7], on peut penser que les pratiques sportives agissent comme de puissants identificateurs sociaux avec lesquels les individus peuvent jouer pour construire, sans trop le savoir, des personnalités adaptées aux trajectoires qu'ils parcourent dans l'espace social et aux positions qu'ils y occupent. Le caractère *total* de la pratique sportive reposerait plutôt sur son pouvoir d'exprimer simultanément ou successivement suivant les cas ces propriétés indistinctement physiques et sociales que sont le fait d'appartenir à telle catégorie sociale, d'être homme ou femme, d'avoir tel âge, etc. et qui se réalisent sous la forme d'un *rapport durable et généralisé au corps*[8]. Qu'elles soient informelles ou codifiées sous la forme sportive, les pratiques corporelles sont une mise en actes, physiquement éprouvés, des propriétés sociales les plus fondamentales qui, par la magie de la pratique elle-même, se trouvent transmuées du point de vue des agents en différentes facettes d'une réalisation unitaire de leur personnalité.

Le pouvoir d'expression identitaire des sports

La possibilité qu'ont les pratiques sportives d'exprimer simultanément une multiplicité de propriétés socialement significatives et de les inscrire dans des individualités physiquement typées explique la force avec laquelle elles deviennent de véritables symboles sociaux. Pour n'être pas un langage parlé, le langage du corps présente effectivement cette «équivocité expressive» qui, loin de limiter les possibilités d'analyse comme le laisse entendre Vigarello[9], lui confère la puissance d'une expression très ouverte de sens propre à la pensée et à l'action magiques[10]. L'exercice d'un sport permet ainsi à des individus de se réaliser en tant que membres d'un groupe social donné, caractérisés par toute une constellation de propriétés objectives (comme le sexe, l'âge ou le revenu) ainsi que par les mécanismes de classement/déclassement symbolique qui s'exercent sur eux. On a constaté auprès d'une population d'enfants scolarisés dans l'enseignement primaire[11], que la situation scolaire renforçait les effets du milieu social sur les orientations sportives. On peut aisément comprendre que — probablement pour les mêmes raisons — les enfants en retard scolaire pratiquent davantage les sports les plus pratiqués dans les classes populaires. Par exemple 55% des garçons en retard jouent au football contre 44% de ceux qui présentent un âge scolaire normal. Mais ces effets ne font pas que s'ajouter arithmétiquement; ils se combinent pour produire des situations spécifiques. Les sports sont aussi des marqueurs sexuels et leur pouvoir d'expression syncrétique rend possible des *jeux de détournement de sens* par lesquels des décalages de positionnement ou des déclassements prennent la forme d'*inversions symboliques*. C'est ainsi que les filles qui enregistrent un retard scolaire s'adonnent plus au judo que celles qui sont dans la norme (11% contre 5%), le judo étant un sport majoritairement pratiqué par des garçons d'âge scolaire normal et il en irait de même des sports collectifs tels que le basketball, le handball ou le volleyball. On pourrait alors émettre l'hypothèse selon laquelle, à travers la pratique sportive, se jouent des fonctions d'expression par lesquelles des individus en position de décalage social ou institutionnel adoptent des stratégies d'affirmation de *contre-identité* comme celle qui consiste à s'affirmer comme «un garçon manqué» pour une fille confrontée à une expérience scolaire négative. On en trouverait une confirmation dans les attitudes très contrastées que de jeunes judokas ayant entre 10 et 16 ans adoptent en fonction de leur situation scolaire (échantillon construit sur la ville de Nantes en 1986, n=280). Alors que chez les non-redoublants les garçons sont plus nombreux que les filles à faire de la compétition (70% contre 51%) et semblent plus disposés à entrer dans l'«esprit du judo» (54% des garçons contre 46% des filles font un usage systématique des noms techniques japonais), les relations s'inversent chez les redoublants: les filles font alors plus de compétition que les garçons et disent respecter avec plus de rigueur le vocabulaire technique du judo.

On pourrait pousser plus avant l'analyse en montrant qu'une position scolairement et socialement défavorisée des filles se traduit par un rapprochement symbolique assez systématique avec les garçons. Les filles qui prennent les plus grandes distances avec l'univers scolaire (en disant «ne pas chercher à être meilleures en classe») ou le monde ordinaire (elles ne sont pas d'accord pour penser que«le monde est agréable à vivre») s'alignent très souvent sur les attitudes des garçons, qu'il s'agisse de leur façon de penser et de pratiquer le judo, de leurs goûts en matière de disciplines scolaires ou encore des métiers qu'elles aimeraient pratiquer plus tard. Chez les pratiquants de judo qui entretiennent le rapport «le plus heureux» à l'école et au monde social, on enregistre une division traditionnelle des goûts qui, par exemple, portent les garçons à préférer l'aspect «combat» du judo (17% contre 13% chez les filles) ou encore à aimer davantage les matières scientifiques (46% contre 20% chez les filles). Chez ceux qui entretiennent la distance maximale à l'école et au monde, les relations s'inversent. Les filles disent préférer le combat dans une proportion de 21% contre 9% chez les garçons et elles affichent le même intérêt que les garçons pour les disciplines scientifiques (36% dans les deux cas) et littéraires (dans 15% des cas).

Associer ainsi des attitudes très personnelles sur le monde social et une manière de pratiquer un sport cesse d'apparaître comme un rapprochement indu lorsque l'on considère la pratique sportive comme une mise en actes de schèmes corporels inconscients par lesquels les individus incorporent leurs propres conditions de vie et leur rapport au monde social. L'habitus corporel comme principe générateur de perceptions et de comportements multiples explique que l'on puisse dresser des corrélations entre la pratique sportive et un éventail de caractéristiques telles que la perception du corps (comme «gros», «maigre» ou «rond») ou l'usage des techniques d'entretien de celui-ci (comme l'emploi de cosmétiques ou le suivi de régimes alimentaires)[12]. Encore faut-il veiller, comme manquent de le faire les auteurs de l'enquête mentionnée, à ne pas s'en tenir aux propriétés morphologiques objectives des corps (à savoir au poids et à la taille réels) et à considérer que le «corps vécu», impossible à réduire à la simple «image de soi», engage des schèmes d'aperception (grand/petit, gros/maigre, lourd/léger, etc.) qui sont attachés à la distribution inégale des propriétés corporelles entre les classes et à travers lesquels s'expriment de manière méconnaissable les structures fondamentales des groupes d'appartenance.

Système des sports et espace social

Ce mode de construction des relations entre un sport et les propriétés de ses pratiquants prévient déjà contre une interprétation de type essentialiste: le même sport peut être porteur de significations différentes suivant les conditions sociales dans lesquelles il est pratiqué. Cependant le risque d'inscrire la valeur sociale d'un sport dans ses propriétés intrinsèques n'est définitivement écarté qu'à la condition d'effectuer *une double mise en relation*[13]. Un sport ne saurait se définir pour lui-même. Il tire sa valeur distinctive de ses relations avec un ensemble de sports formant système et c'est la raison pour laquelle, dans le sujet proposé pour cet exposé «Sport et esprit de corps», le mot «sport» demande à être pensé au pluriel et de façon relationnelle. Il s'agit à ce niveau d'expliquer la production sociale des affinités qui, à un moment donné, se tissent entre des sports pris avec leurs caractéristiques différentielles et des cultures de classe. Clément a très bien montré comment les règles techniques du jeu sportif qui organisent le judo, l'aïkido et la lutte se trouvent objectivement et subjectivement ajustées aux règles du jeu social des différentes catégories sociales et, plus encore, aux rapports au corps qu'elles engagent[14]. Comment la distance entre les corps, l'évitement de l'adversaire et la valorisation de l'esthétique du geste mettent l'aïkido en accord avec le rapport au corps des fractions intellectuelles des classes moyennes, tandis que le «corps à corps» de la lutte qui fait plus appel à la force et qui présuppose le contact physique direct correspond davantage aux goûts corporels des membres des classes populaires. Mais cette mise en relation qui privilégie les rapports entre les sports et les classes sociales pourrait encore conduire à renforcer les préjugés les plus affirmés. En réalité, la correspondance entre les sports et les groupes sociaux ne se fait pas de sport à classe, selon un rapport immédiat qui ne manquerait pas d'être perçu comme nécessairement inscrit dans la nature des choses (des corps ou des sports). Il ne servirait donc à rien, comme cela se fait fréquemment, d'invoquer une telle construction — taxée à juste titre de «mécaniste» — pour invalider définitivement toute tentative de mise en relation entre les sports et les classes sociales.

Le recours à certaines techniques statistiques formellement irréprochables, mais pas toujours utilisées avec une rigueur suffisante, peut conduire à chosifier les relations entre des sports et des groupes sociaux. S'il est utile et même nécessaire de recourir pour ce faire à la construction de graphiques à l'aide de l'analyse des données, c'est à la condition expresse de ne pas prendre ce que la méthode traite comme des *propriétés structurales* pour des attributs isolés et quasi naturels des classes sociales ou des sports. Placer, par exemple, le football parmi les autres pratiques sportives dans une position homologue à celle qu'occupent les classes populaires dans l'espace social ne signifie pas que le football est attaché de manière immuable aux conditions d'existence des ouvriers et encore moins que les membres de ces classes sont les plus nombreux à le pratiquer (15,8 % des ouvriers qualifiés-contremaîtres disent l'avoir pratiqué au moins occasionnellement durant les douze derniers mois de l'année 1981, contre 19 % de cadres moyens); on exprime ainsi, de manière nécessairement réductrice, que le football occupe une place prééminente, parfois exclusive, dans la structure des sports pratiqués dans les classes populaires.

Un sport est toujours pris dans un réseau de relations d'oppositions avec d'autres sports qui, par delà leurs caractéristiques techniques propres, tirent leur valeur symbolique et leur force d'expression identitaire des correspondances avec les groupes sociaux. Ce sont deux espaces — des sports et des positions sociales — qui se correspondent de sorte qu'une relation entre un sport et une classe sociale, une catégorie d'âge ou un sexe, est toujours *arbitraire*. La notion de *système des sports* qui aide à penser l'ensemble de ces relations ne doit pas figer des affinités particulières; elle a pour fonction, au contraire, de rappeler que ces relations, le plus souvent perçues comme immuables et nécessaires par les agents sociaux, sont à tout moment susceptibles de s'atténuer ou de se déplacer et que ces transformations peuvent avoir des causes multiples et cumulables; par la dynamique de l'offre, le marché des sports s'enrichit sans cesse tandis que la restructuration de l'espace des classes sociales induit d'inévitables déplacements d'affinités avec les sports.

Les lois de restructuration de l'espace des sports

Ce mode de construction rend assez bien compte des restructurations de l'espace des sports durant les quinze dernières années dans une agglomération de l'Ouest de la France (Nantes), en même temps qu'il peut servir de modèle aux transformations futures des pratiques. Le projet n'est pas de dresser le tableau complet des pratiques sportives d'une ville provinciale française mais d'éprouver un système d'hypothèses sur un ensemble limité, bien que significatif, d'activités.

L'intérêt de la diffusion du squash tient en ce que ce sport, tardivement introduit en France, était pratiquement inconnu localement avant les années

1980[15]. Un premier constat s'est imposé auquel la notion de système des sports donne sa véritable signification: le squash s'est diffusé sur la base de ses spécificités techniques de jeu (réclamant de solides qualités d'anticipation, de déplacement, de réflexes et de résistance physique) et non de ses ressemblances (réelles ou supposées) avec les sports les plus proches, en particulier le tennis. On a en effet observé que les propriétaires de salles de sports qui ont voulu faire cohabiter le tennis et le squash — ou qui ont pensé l'aménagement du club de squash sur le modèle du club de tennis — ont échoué, après avoir vérifié que chacun de ces sports avait son propre public et que les transferts escomptés du squash vers le tennis s'effectuaient très mal. Ainsi la diffusion tardive du squash sur le marché des sports a permis à des pratiquants d'exprimer plus complètement et «sur des terrains» différents des goûts corporels qui, dans l'état antérieur de l'espace sportif, ne pouvaient être véritablement satisfaits.

Sport jeune, le squash est un *sport de jeunes* qui porte les marques des transformations survenues cette dernière décennie dans les pratiques sportives des Français. Dans l'échantillon de joueurs de squash enquêtés âgés de 20 ans et plus, 68% ont entre 20 et 30 ans alors que cette tranche d'âge ne représentait que 15% d'un échantillon comparable de joueurs de tennis. Jeunes, les pratiquants de squash sont porteurs d'une culture sportive qui reflète l'état du marché des activités aujourd'hui offertes et les goûts des nouvelles générations qui leur font préférer, entre autres, les sports de glisse au football (pour 31,5% contre 10% d'entre eux). En revanche, il serait vain de mettre en relation les transferts de pratique vers le squash avec une quelconque translation effectuée dans la structure sociale. Si les squasheurs appartiennent eux-mêmes près de deux fois moins aux classes supérieures que les tennismen (25% contre 42%), ils le doivent au fait de se situer, compte tenu de leur âge, en début de carrière et donc d'occuper des emplois de classes moyennes. Par leurs origines, ils s'inscrivent en revanche plus fortement dans les classes supérieures puisque 37% d'entre eux ont un père cadre supérieur contre 28% des pratiquants de tennis. En réalité, les différences les plus significatives s'observent dans les conditions d'existence et plus particulièrement dans les traits constitutifs de leur *style de vie*: 47% des squasheurs sont des célibataires (contre 15% des tennismen) auxquels on pourrait joindre les 6% de personnes divorcées. Sport nouveau qui demande une forte dépense énergétique, le squash se prête tout particulièrement à symboliser, ou mieux, à *jouer la situation* de ces jeunes qui ont à «se battre» pour se faire, tant sur le plan psychologique que professionnel[16].

La force de symbolisation sociale d'un sport se mesure au caractère stéréotypé des propriétés qui lui sont attachées et qui retraduisent dans le registre du langage technique les caractéristiques sociales de ses pratiquants. À la différence du tennis, le squash est reconnu comme étant «d'acquisition facile et rapide». «Le tennis requiert un long apprentissage. Il faut au moins trois ans pour jouer vraiment. Au squash, après trois ou quatre séances, on peut commencer à s'amuser» (homme, 36 ans, président-directeur général). Cette absence supposée de barrières techniques fait du squash un sport «ouvert» qui, joué à un rythme intensif pendant un temps relativement court, apparaît comme un sport «dévoreur d'énergies» particulièrement adapté à des individus qui ont un emploi du temps contraint et «de l'énergie à revendre»: «Au squash, on se surpasse et on se donne à fond jusqu'à l'*overdose*. Au club, c'est sur les courts de squash que le bruit est le plus fort avec le bruit de la balle sur la plaque métallique et les expressions des joueurs. Il y a ceux qui tombent à genoux en exprimant leur désespoir d'une balle loupée, celui qui s'effondre contre le mur et qui se laisse glisser, terrassé, en nage et en criant: 'Non, assez!'» (femme, 28 ans, assistante dentaire). On saisit ici toute la différence qu'il faut introduire entre les *représentations* organisées autour d'un sport et les attitudes profondément enfouies parce qu'enracinées sur les principes inconscients du *rapport au corps* qui résultent de l'incorporation des structures sociales. Le consensus apparent sur les caractéristiques du squash contraste avec la diversité des *produits attendus* qui ne sont jamais formalisés parce que seulement éprouvés à l'état pratique, à travers des sensations kinesthésiques. Alors que 60% des membres des classes populaires pensent que la pratique du squash est «importante pour la forme physique» (contre 26% des membres des classes moyennes et supérieures), la part de ceux qui associent le squash à la recherche d'«une forme physique et psychologique» s'élève régulièrement lorsqu'on passe des classes populaire (23%), aux classes moyennes (35%) puis supérieures (47%).

Par le jeu combiné de ses caractéristiques propres et de sa position dans l'espace des sports, le squash est le moyen d'éprouver physiquement un état d'esprit socialement attaché aux jeunes générations de sorte que le simple fait de s'y adonner offre une preuve que l'on est porteur d'un tel esprit, quand bien même on n'a plus les propriétés biologiques de l'âge. On comprend du même coup que, dans la manière de se définir en tant que joueurs, les squasheurs délaissent les qualificatifs plus techniques (9,5% se disent «tacticiens») et se portent en priorité sur ceux qui désignent indistinctement des qualités sportives, des attitudes professionnelles et des traits de caractère «jeunes» (28% se disent «gagneurs», 14,5% «cool» et 14% «physiques»). La diffusion du squash en France montre qu'un sport est rarement un symbole univoque exprimant la totalité d'un groupe social. Au sein d'une même classe sociale, des concurrences entre sports peuvent toujours se développer, comme celle qui, pour les membres des classes moyennes et supérieures, oppose le squash et le tennis, à travers laquelle s'exprime une opposition de générations corrélative de l'affirmation croissante d'une culture jeune.

Culture de classe, sens du jeu et esprit de club

La théorie du système des sports n'exige pas que les recherches empiriques prennent en compte la totalité des espaces sportifs; elle permet en revanche de dégager le sens d'un sport donné sans risquer de l'autonomiser à l'excès ni d'absolutiser des traits qui lui sont propres. Il faut par exemple partir de la position traditionnelle du tennis dans l'espace des sports en France pour comprendre que sa diffusion n'a pu se faire, du haut en bas de la structure sociale et sportive, qu'au prix de multiples différenciations de la pratique.

Les données sur lesquelles nous nous appuyons révèlent que l'espace de la pratique du tennis, à la dimension d'une ville, est sportivement et socialement structuré[17]. Tout se passe comme si, à un moment donné, les clubs représentaient synchroniquement les *états successifs de la pratique*. Tandis que le club le plus ancien (le SNUC, créé en 1903, porte encore, en raison de ses origines, le qualificatif d'«universitaire») a réussi à conserver un haut niveau sportif tout en exerçant une sélection sociale efficace (il compte 63% de membres des classes supérieures dont 28% de médecins), les clubs municipaux s'ouvrent réellement aux classes moyennes alors que le club privé (la Raquette d'argent), créé vers la fin des années 1970, reçoit plutôt des membres des fractions nouvelles des classes supérieures (ce club accueille 43% de joueurs des classes supérieures dont 21% d'ingénieurs, venus des grandes écoles). Une telle correspondance tiendrait du miracle ou de l'harmonie préétablie si l'on ne voyait qu'elle résulte d'une double intériorisation, de l'espace social et tennistique local, qui rend les pratiquants capables de choisir les clubs dans lesquels ils ont objectivement le plus de chances de bien s'intégrer.

Il n'est pas trop fort de dire que l'intériorisation d'une position dans l'espace social d'un côté, sportif de l'autre, donne un véritable *sens de l'anticipation et du placement* sur l'espace du tennis qui entre pour une large part dans la détermination des choix des clubs. L'attitude de cet ingénieur de 55 ans est significative : tardivement arrivé dans l'agglomération nantaise, il renonce d'entrée de jeu à s'inscrire au SNUC sous prétexte que ce club lui paraît «trop fermé», «trop nantais» et «ressemblant trop aux clubs parisiens de l'après-guerre»; il se tourne alors vers la Raquette d'argent, club nouveau qui, «de manière intuitive», ne lui semblait pas devoir «poser de problèmes». À l'inverse, cette fille d'industriel nantais inscrite pour des raisons de commodité dans un club municipal de la périphérie (Carquefou) pense déjà à quitter «la faune» qu'elle y fréquente pour rejoindre le SNUC où elle est «certaine de retrouver ses amies d'enfance qu'elle n'a pas revues depuis vingt ans».

Les inscriptions dans les différents clubs résultent d'une série d'appréciations et d'actes qui ressortissent moins d'une sélection explicite que d'une élection entre des individus qui se reconnaissent et se choisissent, quand elles ne sont pas le fait de choix négatifs, par élimination des lieux dans lesquels on sait ne pas devoir (ou vouloir) aller[18]. Dans tous les cas, ce sont bien les relations entre les classes sociales et l'espace du tennis qui sont au principe de la composition de chaque club, caractérisé par «un esprit» particulier susceptible de s'investir dans des formes de sociabilité et des styles de jeu. Même si aucun club — y compris parmi les plus sélectifs — ne parvient à imposer une parfaite homogénéité entre ses membres, il n'en reste pas moins vrai qu'il existe des dominantes, statistiquement repérables, qui donnent à chacun son image ou, comme on dit, «sa couleur». L'opposition entre les clubs situés en haut et bas de l'espace du tennis se retraduit en deux types bien différents de sociabilité, l'une organisée selon une logique «interne» conformément à la hiérarchie sportive des classements, l'autre importée de la vie quotidienne et constituée sur la base de relations familiales et amicales entretenues en dehors du club. C'est au SNUC que les joueurs ont en moyenne le plus grand nombre de partenaires différents (51% en ont au moins trois contre 22% à la Raquette d'argent). Si le SNUC est le club où l'on vient le plus au tennis par la famille d'origine, c'est aussi celui où l'on pratique d'abord entre amis et relations que l'on s'y est faites: 57% des membres du SNUC jouent avec un ou plusieurs partenaires «amis» alors que 24% les trouvent dans le cercle étroit de la parenté contre 32% et 41% des joueurs inscrits dans les deux clubs municipaux[19].

Ces deux réseaux de partenaires correspondent à deux modes de production de sous-marchés de joueurs relativement homogènes. L'existence d'une relation familiale crée entre les partenaires une proximité réelle mais la visibilité du rapport social entraîne une disqualification sportive; elle va généralement de pair avec une faible compétence technique. Comparés à ceux qui n'ont que des relations de club comme partenaires, les pratiquants qui ne jouent qu'entre parents «laissent plus filer la partie» quand ils sont dominés (25% contre 5%), savent moins «changer leur jeu» (14% contre 24,5%) et sont moins aptes à adopter des stratégies qui allient la prise de risque et l'exploitation d'un certain bagage technique (3,5% jouent alors «plus vite» contre 16%). Par contre, les joueurs qui sont placés sur un marché sportif «formellement libre» — où les relations ne sont, formellement, que sportives — tirent un surcroît de légitimité du fait d'être engagés dans un réseau d'échanges généralisés dans lequel les propriétés sociales et culturelles n'apparaissent plus que sous la forme de qualités tennistiques individuelles (telles qu'un bon niveau de jeu, un style de jeu «élégant» ou «agréable à jouer»). La force de l'*image de la famille* souvent attachée au club tient précisément en ce qu'elle exprime de manière analogique la force symbolique du club de produire, par le rapprochement d'individus dotés des mêmes dispositions corporelles et sportives, un groupe aussi soudé et solidaire que les membres d'une communauté unie par les liens naturels du sang[20].

Les relations entre les compétences sociales et techniques dans la constitution des marchés des partenaires doivent être établies dans le respect d'une autonomie relative des secondes. Waser montre bien que «plus les joueurs occupent des positions dominées dans l'espace social (d'un club)..., plus la compétence technique est un moyen efficace qui permet d'élargir le cercle des partenaires»[21]. Elle cite en exemple un couple d'enseignants, tard venus au tennis, pour qui «le classement a fait office de passeport» pour entrer dans des réseaux sportifs, mais aussi sociaux, qui leur étaient au début inaccessibles. À l'inverse, il n'est pas rare de constater que c'est sur la base d'un rapport social au jeu que se développent des stratégies particulières pour tenter de réduire d'éventuelles faiblesses techniques. Tel est le cas de cette fille d'industriel que son grand-père avait autrefois initiée au tennis et qui, sentant « son orgueil en jeu » à la suite d'une série de défaites contre des partenaires dernièrement venues au tennis, s'est inscrite pour la première fois, à trente-cinq ans, à des cours particuliers en vue d'améliorer les coups déficients qu'elle n'avait jamais appris rationnellement. En réalité, il existe des relations de dépendance réciproque entre le rapport socialement conditionné au tennis et la maîtrise technique de sorte qu'il faut faire entrer le premier dans la définition exhaustive de la seconde.

Le choix des partenaires s'effectue dans une méconnaissance du social d'autant plus grande qu'il engage des critères en apparence les plus naturels et les plus individuels comme le style de jeu. Waser décrit avec beaucoup de détails techniques comment, au sein d'un même club, le jeu des patrons de l'industrie, basé sur des valeurs de virilité, de courage et de volonté incarnées dans la force physique s'oppose à celui des enseignants davantage fondé sur l'observation de la tactique de l'adversaire, l'anticipation et le recours à la ruse dans un souci d'économie physique. Ses observations rejoignent mes propres constats et s'inscrivent dans le prolongement des hypothèses formulées par Gruneau, selon lesquelles la lutte pour la définition d'un style de jeu s'effectue à partir des ressources que les sportifs importent de la vie sociale et professionnelle[22]. À la question de savoir « quelle tactique ils adoptent lorsqu'ils sont en difficulté » au cours d'une partie, les joueurs du SNUC et de la Raquette d'argent donnent des réponses bien différenciées : 32 % des premiers contre 18,5 % des seconds disent que, dans cette situation, ils « changent » ou « adaptent » leur jeu en fonction de l'adversaire tandis que la part de ceux qui tentent de « casser le jeu » passe de 20 % à 29 %. « Changer de jeu » en fonction du comportement de l'adversaire présuppose que l'on ait à sa disposition une panoplie d'armes techniques substituables, mais aussi que l'on soit apte à analyser le jeu de l'autre et à se mettre à distance de soi afin de modifier rationnellement sa tactique : autant de comportements que l'on est amené à adopter fréquemment dans la vie quotidienne et qui, on le sait par ailleurs, sont constitutifs d'une « expérience bourgeoise du monde[23] ». D'un autre côté, ne peut-on pas voir dans la volonté de « casser le jeu », plus fréquente chez les joueurs de la Raquette d'argent, une disposition particulière de l'habitus du groupe social dominant dans ce club, composé d'individus moins portés par leurs origines, leur formation et leur culture de métier, à euphémiser la violence contenue dans la relation avec l'adversaire et plus enclins à l'exprimer dans le langage d'un rapport de force quasiment mécanique ?

Les luttes pour la définition d'un sport

Les transformations — parfois profondes — qui caractérisent certaines pratiques sportives attestent que la définition d'un sport ne réside ni dans ses propriétés techniques intrinsèques, ni dans les caractéristiques de ses pratiquants à un moment donné, mais bien dans la correspondance entre la position de ce sport dans l'espace des sports et la position d'un groupe de pratiquants dans l'espace social, cette relation n'étant jamais définitive parce que soumise à des luttes incessantes pour la définition légitime de la pratique. Les changements de modalités de la pratique qu'ont connu en l'espace de quinze années la course à pied et le parachutisme sont à ce propos exemplaires[24]. Les mutations par lesquelles le parachutisme sportif naît puis se transforme font apparaître que le pouvoir d'un sport d'exprimer certaines valeurs cristallisées dans un « esprit de corps » ne se réalise pas directement. Il présuppose un travail de *codage symbolique* effectué par un corps de spécialistes — en l'occurrence les dirigeants et plus largement les « encadreurs » — par lequel la pratique reçoit des formes et des significations que les pratiquants sauront reconnaître et s'approprier sur la base de leurs valeurs culturelles. C'est la raison pour laquelle les transformations d'un sport dans le temps ne sont jamais d'ordre purement technique ; les perfectionnements apportés aux matériels utilisés ont certes rendu possible le passage du saut à la « voltige » (réalisation d'une série de six figures en chute libre), puis de la voltige au « vol relatif » (réalisation à plusieurs de diverses figures en chute libre avec un parachute de type « aile ») ; mais c'est à travers les luttes entre catégories de pratiquants — elles-mêmes croisées avec les clivages internes aux groupes des dirigeants et instructeurs — que ces changements se sont réellement produits.

L'histoire du parachutisme retracée par Loirand se présente comme une série de ruptures qui répondent à des logiques différentes. Résultant de luttes internes aux instances dirigeantes, une première mise en forme de la pratique durant la période 1966-1970 qui fait prendre au parachutisme ses distances avec les attaches et les valeurs militaires de ses origines (telles que l'aspect héroïque du saut et la valorisation du risque), sans entraîner de transformations significatives du recrutement social des pratiquants majoritairement issus des classes populaires ; ce faisant, elle lui confère un aspect sportif axé sur l'apprentissage rationnel de la compétition dans le respect croissant des règles de sécurité. Le remplacement progressif des anciens militaires ou héros de la Résistance par des dirigeants appartenant aux classes supérieures qui survient en même temps que le changement de sigle de la Fédération[25] et son rattachement au Ministère de la jeunesse (en 1968), a largement contribué à imposer le modèle sportif toujours fortement ancré dans la vie collective et virile du club, dans lequel les pratiquants des classes populaires vont d'autant plus se reconnaître que le goût pour la compétition leur donne à la fois l'occasion d'une valorisation individuelle et la possibilité d'entreprendre des carrières d'instructeurs. Des changements plus radicaux surviendront avec l'invention du « travail relatif », réapparu en France en 1973[26], et dont le changement d'appellation en « vol relatif » donne la mesure du travail de recodage symbolique qui s'effectue de nouveau. Toujours fondée sur le schème invariant du *survol*[27], la pratique du vol relatif, assez largement diffusée par les médias, va attirer un public nouveau moins assoiffé de compétition que de sensations physiques et émotionnelles, cherchant moins à réaliser l'exploit sportif qu'à ressentir le plaisir de contrôler le corps et ses déplacements dans l'espace[28] ; de poids mort subissant les lois de la chute des corps, le parachutiste devient *pilote*. Dans les clubs qui ont été observés, la base sociale de recrutement se transforme profondément entre 1982 et 1986, en même temps que la part des sauts effectués à 2 500 mètres (hauteur exigée pour le vol relatif contre 2 000 mètres pour la voltige) passe de 15 % à 43 %. La venue de pratiquants appartenant aux classes moyennes et supérieures et porteurs pour la plupart de diplômes de l'enseignement supérieur va permettre l'affirmation de valeurs nouvelles organisées autour d'un certain hédonisme, d'une dévirilisation de la pratique et d'un souci de maîtrise technique. Parallèlement au développement des techniques et à l'utilisation de matériaux plus performants, le renouvellement du corps des instructeurs auquel accèdent désormais des enseignants, des cadres supérieurs et professions libérales, a favorisé l'invention et la diffusion de procédures pédagogiques inédites allant dans le sens d'une individualisation de la pratique. Avec l'initiation directe au saut en chute libre par la « progression accélérée en chute » (PAC) à l'aide d'un parachute de type « aile », le novice est pris dans une relation individuelle avec son instructeur qu'il rémunère lui-même et qui l'introduit directement aux formes les plus recherchées de la pratique parachutiste, sans qu'il soit soumis aux contraintes de l'apprentissage collectif auquel les postulants étaient soumis au sein des clubs[29]. Dans sa forme traditionnelle (initiation à la voltige dans le cadre des clubs), le parachutisme sportif permettait à des individus socialement dominés d'entrer dans des groupes fortement intégrés, à forte sociabilité populaire, dont les membres pouvaient acquérir le sentiment d'appartenir à un corps d'élite à la fois sportif et social. Avec l'apprentissage sur parachute de type « aile », la recherche d'une maîtrise du corps physique et symbolique permet à des individus appartenant aux classes moyennes et supérieures de s'affirmer dans l'excellence de leur personnalité individuelle. À la réalisation de l'individu par la fusion dans un collectif doté d'une excellence sportive dans le premier cas, s'oppose l'affirmation d'une excellence corporelle individuelle, comme expression parfaite et totalement déniée, d'une position sociale dans le second.

Sports, esprit du temps et temps du corps

On reproche fréquemment aux analyses construites dans la logique des systèmes d'ignorer l'histoire et le changement. Parfois justifiées, ces critiques n'atteignent pas la théorie du système des sports en elle-même qui intègre de plusieurs manières les effets du temps. On connaît les transformations que la diffusion du squash en France a entraînées dans les relations entre les sports, les classes sociales et les générations. D'autres actions du temps peuvent être envisagées qui se combinent à de tels effets de structure. En tant que techniques du corps, les pratiques sportives se rapportent à une autre temporalité qui est celle des changements physiques et biologiques subis tout au long d'une vie. La notion d'«esprit de corps» attachée aux sports se charge alors d'un sens nouveau qui permet de rendre compte des transferts de pratique qui s'effectuent avec l'âge.

Il serait aisé de montrer que les raisons, y compris les plus physiques, invoquées pour justifier un changement de sport présupposent des dispositions culturelles très inégalement réparties entre les groupes sociaux. C'est ainsi que bon nombre de golfeurs expliquent leur abandon du tennis par une sorte d'anticipation des effets de vieillissement physique («À quarante ans, au tennis, on finit par se faire mal et se casser») ou encore par une volonté de se ménager une marge de progression que la pratique ancienne ne procurait plus et qu'ils sont d'autant plus portés à valoriser qu'ils ont le sentiment que l'intégrité de leur identité est en jeu. Mais le travail du temps ne fait pas que transformer les corps; il est ce par quoi les carrières professionnelles se réalisent et les positions sociales se conquièrent[30]. La double modalité des venues au golf en France durant les cinq dernières années se comprend à la condition de penser que les espaces relativement autonomes des sports et des positions sociales ne se correspondent qu'en subissant les effets combinés du temps et des âges. Que les 22-25 ans et les 42-45 ans soient les tranches d'âge dont les effectifs s'accroissent le plus (de l'ordre de +40% entre 1986 et 1987[31]) signifie que l'ouverture du marché du golf attire d'une part une proportion de jeunes, le plus souvent hautement diplômés, et d'autre part des individus déjà bien engagés dans la vie professionnelle. Sorte d'anti-squash du point de vue des conditions de jeu et des qualités requises, le golf est un sport qui a conservé sa rareté sociale (du moins en France) et dont l'accès présuppose qu'avec l'action du temps, donc de l'âge, une position sociale se soit affermie. Pour accéder à la pratique, il faut que les nouveaux arrivants laissent agir le temps qui les consacre dans leur situation sociale et professionnelle et, ce faisant, leur permet de faire le travail symbolique sur eux-mêmes nécessaire pour se juger «capables d'entrer dans le milieu». Quand on les rapporte aux trajectoires professionnelles qui très souvent les accompagnent, on comprend que les transferts de pratique sportive du tennis vers le golf soient si souvent décrits comme une recherche de qualités empruntées aussi bien au jeu social qu'au jeu sportif[32].

La production sociale des héros sportifs

Excellence corporelle et domination symbolique

L'existence de pratiques sportives fortement autonomisées contribue à ce que les formes d'excellence corporelle à un moment donné s'imposent en toute légitimité, c'est-à-dire dans une totale dissimulation des rapports de force physiques et sociaux qui les sous-tendent. La spécificité des «situations inaugurales», comme dit Defrance, est de laisser davantage transparaître comment des groupes sociaux dominants ont transmis leur vision du monde et soumis des groupes dominés à leur ordre matériel et symbolique[33], par la mise en œuvre de pédagogies corporelles désintéressées.

La pédagogie déployée par les missionnaires britanniques durant la période victorienne constitue une situation de ce type. On peut la décrire comme une entreprise extraordinaire de *persuasion clandestine*, menée à l'échelle de l'Empire, par laquelle toute une cosmologie, une éthique, une métaphysique, une politique ont été inculquées sous la forme de valeurs faites corps, à travers un apprentissage en apparence purement technique de gestes sportifs[34]. À lire les récits des exploits d'un Pennel (1867-1912) enseignant le cricket aux jeunes Afghans ou de Tyndale-Biscœ obligeant ses élèves Hindous à jouer au football, on comprend toute la force de la phrase de Morris disant de ses compatriotes que «le sport a été leur principale exportation spirituelle». L'efficacité de cette acculturation par le sport reposait sur les principes non pensés pour eux-mêmes qui sont inhérents à tout processus de socialisation des corps. Les missionnaires œuvraient à des fins explicitement morales et religieuses («Athletics created the muscle and skill to fight evil and promote good[35]») et la force de conviction de leur action provenait moins du contenu du message que des modalités de la pédagogie et des conditions sociales de sa transmission. Enseigné par le corps et les jeux, l'«esprit de corps» des public schools pénétrait inconsciemment les élèves; mieux encore, emportés dans les élans de la pratique sportive elle-même, ceux-ci se faisaient les complices actifs de leur conversion.

Le choix des sports anglais contre les jeux indigènes et l'intériorisation des valeurs socialement attachées à ces pratiques sportives (désignées par l'expression «Christian manliness» comme le code de l'honneur, la virilité, l'endurance, etc.), avaient comme enjeu l'intégration à l'empire britannique des jeunes générations des classes dominantes autochtones; ce faisant, cette pédagogie consistait en une entreprise de dépossession de la culture traditionnelle et pouvait susciter à tout moment de fortes résistances comme celles de ces jeunes Brahmanes opposant à Tyndale-Biscœ un premier refus de s'adonner à l'aviron: en sollicitant et développant la masse musculaire, ce sport symbolisait à leur yeux une appartenance inacceptable aux castes inférieures. Mais, faiblement verbalisées, ces résistances étaient facilement contenues. La force d'une telle pédagogie venait en réalité de ce qu'elle agissait en actes, silencieusement, au sein d'institutions dans lesquelles les qualités sportives étaient transmuées en vertus humaines et religieuses par excellence. Les qualités athlétiques que les biographes anglais se plaisent à décrire abondamment chez les missionnaires, n'étaient pas attirantes par elles-mêmes; elles étaient célébrées au titre de symboles incorporés de cette notion tout à fait intraduisible de «muscular christianity» qui désignait à la fois un idéal moral et religieux, un rapport pédagogique et le fondement de la légitimité de cette autorité qui prenait la forme d'une relation enchantée, *charismatique*, dans laquelle les représentants d'un groupe dominant exprimaient le caractère absolu et universel de leurs valeurs, à travers l'excellence de leurs personnes et de leurs corps. On voit toute la force de séduction qui pouvait naître de la rencontre entre un pouvoir d'inculcation dissimulé dans une entreprise parfaitement désintéressée de formation intellectuelle et religieuse, et des individus en situation de vivre leur intégration à la civilisation occidentale comme une expérience de conversion et de réalisation totale d'eux-mêmes. La perfection physique acquise donnait à ces néophytes la preuve irréfutable d'une «complétude d'être» qui les arrachait à l'état d'«enfance» dans lequel leur «nature indigène» était censée les avoir maintenus[36]. L'entrée dans la société britannique pouvait-elle s'effectuer plus complètement que par cette sorte de remise de soi collective à la définition que le groupe dominant imposait de l'homme, corps et âme et âme par le corps? Cette imposition d'un «esprit de corps» consubstantiel à la société tout entière que le groupe dominant voulait légitimer explique l'ambivalence des propriétés et des qualités ainsi prêtées au corps; on comprend en particulier que les sermons des missionnaires aient célébré avec la même ardeur auprès de leurs élèves les vertus de force et d'autonomie d'un côté, de docilité et d'aménité de l'autre. Ne s'agissait-il pas, en se pliant à la discipline sportive, de conquérir «cette force du corps, de l'intelligence et de l'âme» que seule l'intégration à la culture et à l'empire britanniques pouvait donner?

Le peuple et ses champions

C'est à une pareille explicitation des rapports sociaux engagés dans la définition de l'excellence corporelle et sportive qu'il faut procéder pour montrer qu'aucun sport moderne, et partant aucun champion, — y compris ceux auxquels on accorde spontanément le statut de «populaire» — n'incarnent directement l'«esprit d'un peuple»[37]. Un sport ne devient symbole d'un collectif (d'un groupe de salariés, des habitants d'une ville ou des membres d'une nation) que par un travail d'imposition et de mise en forme effectué dans le cadre d'instances d'encadrement spécialisées et qui ne peut réussir socialement qu'à la condition de rencontrer les attentes réelles d'un public potentiel. Par principe, un sport ne devient «populaire» qu'au prix de multiples interactions entre des agents aussi divers que les dirigeants, les journalistes ou les publicitaires, qui organisent la pratique selon des normes particulières et les différents groupes sociaux d'acteurs — pratiquants et spectateurs — qui investissent dans le jeu les principes structurants les plus puissants, parce qu'inconscients, de leurs cultures respectives. Il serait par conséquent tout aussi faux de réduire l'origine des sports «populaires» à des tactiques de pure et simple manipulation symbolique de la part des dirigeants, que de l'inscrire dans une sorte de substrat culturel réifié et prêté au peuple[38].

Une interprétation des sports populaires à l'aide d'une théorie des interactions invite à construire dans la logique des rapports de force et du compromis ce qu'on attribue fréquemment au caractère propre des classes populaires. Ce que Faure rapporte de ce qui se passe sur et autour du terrain de football d'une commune rurale à forte tradition ouvrière (Voutré en Mayenne) n'est fait que de transactions entre les valeurs que joueurs et spectateurs imposent pratiquement et les normes officielles que les dirigeants locaux (en l'occurence l'instituteur-entraîneur faisant office d'intermédiaire culturel) tentent de faire appliquer avec plus ou moins de succès[39]. Une analyse comparative montrerait qu'au fur et à mesure qu'on monte dans la hiérarchie des clubs, les conditions sociales et institutionnelles de régulation du jeu rendent un tel détournement de plus en plus improbable. La logique proprement sportive s'autonomise au point qu'il faut effectuer un travail considérable et difficile pour comprendre comment le «style de jeu» d'une équipe professionnelle de football peut exprimer «l'état d'esprit» d'une agglomération urbaine[40].

C'est lorsqu'il emprunte ses «matériaux» au peuple lui-même, que le travail de production sociale des symboles sportifs susceptibles de devenir objet d'une croyance collective de la part de communautés importantes apparaît pour ce qu'il est, à plus forte raison quand surgissent des significations totalement opposées à celles que les individus-symboles assument subjectivement. La vie et plus encore la mort dramatiques de Garrincha en 1983, cet ancien ouvrier de la banlieue de Rio sacré meilleur joueur de football du monde en 1962 puis tombé dans la déchéance physique, sportive et morale, contraste étonnamment avec l'image que les médias construisirent autour de ce joueur[41]. Les propriétés sociales et culturelles incarnées dans un style de jeu tout en esquives et en spontanéité qui lui valut le surnom de «la joie du peuple», furent probablement aussi la cause de son impossibilité de s'intégrer à l'univers des joueurs professionnels et de conduire rationnellement sa carrière. Garrincha est le cas exemplaire du joueur doté d'un sens inné du «jeu pour le jeu» dont le style, sorte d'habitus fait corps (le dribble était son arme), était de nature à symboliser le mode de vie des classes populaires dont il se disait lui-même resté très proche. Joueur laconique qui était plus parlé par son corps qu'il ne parlait de lui, Garrincha se prêtait tout particulièrement au travail de détournement de sens culturel par lequel les médias firent de lui un symbole identitaire dont la force se mesure à l'ampleur de la mobilisation populaire que provoqua l'annonce de sa mort physique, à un moment où l'heure de sa mort sportive et sociale avait déjà sonné[42].

Les champions : héros de l'universel ?

La grande plasticité de l'expression des corps dans leurs rapports aux groupes sociaux est aussi au principe des enjeux spécifiques, symboliques et sociaux, attachés aux champions sportifs. En autonomisant le temps de la confrontation qui seul a une visibilité sociale, le rituel de la compétition donne une image partielle et absolutisante du champion perçu comme existant en lui-même et par lui-même. Ce serait par conséquent voir les choses telles qu'elles demandent à être vues spontanément que de chercher à comprendre les champions par leurs seules motivations, indépendamment du travail des institutions qui les ont sélectionnés, formés, modelés, entraînés, en bref qui les ont sportivement et socialement produits.

Réaliser une carrière de champion consiste à entrer et à conquérir des positions de plus en plus hautes dans un champ de pratiques fortement structuré, avec le dispositif des clubs, des secteurs amateur et professionnel, des fédérations nationales et internationales ; cela représente d'autre part un engagement total dans une lutte particulière pour le rang sportif qui se déroule selon un calendrier et des modalités institutionnellement établis. C'est dire que le champion est astreint à réaliser un *travail de soi sur soi* dont l'acquisition d'un corps physiquement et techniquement efficace n'est qu'un aspect. Le sportif de haut niveau est aussi tenu d'incorporer des qualités éthiques, psychologiques, intellectuelles, etc., objectivement requises par le fonctionnement du champ sportif et dont on peut faire l'hypothèse qu'elles ne sont pas indépendantes de certaines dispositions mentales inégalement réparties entre les groupes sociaux. D'un autre côté, en tant qu'individu *sélectionné*, le champion est pris dans un jeu complexe de relations sociales qui font de lui un *représentant* qui porte, comme on dit communément, «les chances de son groupe». Ces attentes sociales qui prennent la forme d'une *croyance collective*, placent le champion dans une situation qui, toute choses égales par ailleurs, n'est peut-être pas très différente de celle du magicien vis-à-vis de son public. À la suite de Lévi-Strauss nous expliquant comment le jeune Zuni Quesalid parvint à faire malgré lui des exploits magiques à partir du moment où il intériorisa les attentes de son village à son endroit[43], on peut chercher à savoir dans quelle mesure la force du champion provient, en partie du moins, d'une aptitude à convertir cette tension sociale en une mobilisation individuelle pour atteindre la performance sportive, toujours réalisée pour le compte de son groupe.

Le champ sportif n'est pas le seul à présenter ce paradoxe qui consiste à engager des mécanismes de symbolisation sociale susceptibles de renforcer des divisions existantes et d'engendrer des exclusions (du village à la nation) au nom de valeurs universelles. En tant que système symbolique, la pratique sportive retraduit la réalité sociale sur son propre terrain, avec des règles et des valeurs spécifiques, de sorte que les catégories de la pensée sportive, qui ne sont jamais de simple «images», expriment le monde social et ses divisions d'une manière méconnaissable et positive mais qui peut toujours être dénoncée comme trompeuse dans les moments de crise[44]. Les tensions entre particularisme (dont le nationalisme n'est qu'une forme) et universalisme sont constitutives de la symbolique sportive et c'est une illusion bien fondée que de chercher à inscrire, comme y invite la pratique elle-même, l'aspect universel du sport dans la nature des activités sportives proprement dites. Il s'agit là d'une autre manifestation de la pensée substantialiste qui méconnaît que l'autonomie des valeurs sportives est un produit de l'histoire sociale et que la croyance dans leur universalité a nécessité la création d'institutions nationales et mondiales de plus en plus complexes, formellement indépendantes des pouvoirs économiques et politiques et dotées d'une autorité socialement reconnue; elles ont aussi requis une mobilisation et un travail de mise en forme symbolique de la part d'individus, comme Pierre de Coubertin, dont on peut comprendre, pour des raisons de propriétés et de position sociales, qu'ils avaient partie liée avec les valeurs de l'universel[45].

NOTES ET RÉFÉRENCES

1. Une histoire sociale du couple esprit/corps reviendrait à mettre en perspective la plupart des grandes théologies et philosophies. Elle devrait également prendre en compte toutes les formes d'inculcation — souvent silencieuses, parfois insignifiantes mais toujours efficaces — par lesquelles les rapports entre l'esprit et le corps sont réactivés (comme les règles de politesse, les techniques de correction ou mieux, de redressement, des corps ou encore les simples jeux d'enfants souvent emprunts d'une véritable cosmologie organisée analogiquement autour du corps).

2. L'exposé repose sur une série d'enquêtes réalisées dans l'Ouest de la France entre 1983 et 1988. On trouvera une présentation systématique des résultats dans Suaud C (1989) Espace des sports, espace social et effets d'âge. La diffusion du tennis, du squash et du golf dans l'agglomération nantaise. Actes de la recherche en sciences sociales 79 2-20. Les analyses qui suivent font également une large place aux travaux effectués en sociologie du sport, d'une part dans le cadre du département de sociologie de l'Université de Nantes, et d'autre part, dans le cadre du Centre de sociologie de l'éducation et de la culture (École des hautes études en sciences sociales, Paris) dirigé par P Bourdieu. Les n° 79 et 80 de la revue Actes de la recherche en sciences sociales (septembre et novembre 1989) présentent les recherches les plus significatives conduites ces dernières années par les chercheurs attachés à ce Centre.

3. Mauss M (1968) Les techniques du corps. Sociologie et anthropologie. Paris: Presses Universitaires de France p 365-86. [Je me réfère explicitement d'une part à l'interprétation de Mauss lui-même définissant les techniques du corps comme la mise en œuvre d'un habitus socialement organisé et d'autre part à la théorie de la pratique à l'aide de laquelle Bourdieu pense les pratiques corporelles sous leurs différentes formes (magiques, culturelles, sportives, etc.)] Voir Bourdieu P (1972) Esquisse d'une théorie de la pratique. Paris: Librairie Droz p 189-200 et 211-21, ainsi que Bourdieu P (1980) Le sens pratique. Paris: Éditions de Minuit p 87-166

4. Bourdieu P (1980) op cit p 117

5. Le point de vue intellectualiste est accentué lorsque le sociologue, ayant plus ou moins partie liée avec les professionnels de «l'éducation physique», en vient à autonomiser «les savoirs du corps» moins dans le but d'analyser les pratiques que de légitimer ce corps de spécialistes (et son «esprit de corps»). Voir par exemple, Arnaud P (1983) Les savoirs du corps. Éducation physique et éducation intellectuelle dans le système scolaire. Lyon: Presses Universitaires de Lyon. Ce point de vue est trouvé sous sa forme paroxystique chez les pourfendeurs d'idéologies qui refusent toute réalité pratique au sport pour n'y voir que du discours comme le fait Caillat pour qui «le sport, entendu ici comme activité physique compétitive institutionnalisée, n'est pas seulement gestes, mouvements techniques. Il est avant tout discours». Dans Caillat M (1989) L'idéologie du sport en France. Montreuil: Éditions de la Passion p 12. Une confrontation entre différentes communications faites au symposium ferait apparaître les différences très sensibles que sociologues européens et anglo-saxons attachent aux notions d'«esprit de corps» et d'«excellence corporelle». Il semble qu'«esprit de corps» ne trouverait d'autre traduction que l'expression plus morale de «team spirit».

6. Dans son étude sur l'autonomisation et la formation des pratiques gymniques en France à la fin du XIXe siècle et au début du XXe siècle, Defrance désigne très clairement le risque de glissement d'objet que contient le recours aux textes comme matériaux d'enquête: «La genèse des premières gymnastiques peut être localisée autour des classes cultivées et prendre, entre autres, la forme d'un débat d'idées; cela n'induit pas pour autant la primauté des élaborations intellectuelles, dont décou-

leraient les réalisations pratiques. La recherche peut s'appuyer sur des «textes», sans devenir une analyse d'idées: ces dernières sont considérées comme des instruments, dont on caractérisera le contexte de mise en œuvre». Defrance J (1987) L'excellence corporelle. La formation des activités physiques et sportives modernes 1770-1914. Collection cultures corporelles. Rennes: Presses Universitaires de Rennes p 14-15. De son côté, c'est bien dans un souci de respecter la pratique pugilistique et le rapport au corps qu'elle implique (qui efface la «distinction entre le physique et le spirituel»), que Wacquant justifie l'approche de ce sport par l'observation participante: «Pour se donner quelque chance d'échapper à l'objet préconstruit de la mythologie collective, (la) sociologie [...] doit appréhender la boxe par son côté le moins connu et le moins spectaculaire: la grise et lancinante routine des entraînements en salle, de la longue et ingrate préparation, inséparablement physique et morale [...] Afin donc d'éviter le trop-plein de la sociologie spontanée que l'évocation des combats ne manque pas de susciter, il faut non pas monter sur le ring en pensée avec le champion, mais tâter du sac aux côtés de boxeurs anonymes dans le cadre habituel du gym». Wacquant L JD (1989) Corps et âme. Notes ethnographiques d'un apprenti boxeur. Actes de la recherche en sciences sociales 80 p 34.

7. Sahlins M (1985) Des îles dans l'histoire. Paris: Le Seuil/Gallimard p 40-41

8. Dans son étude sur la pratique rituelle dans laquelle le corps joue le rôle d'un opérateur logique, Bourdieu analyse cette fonction de connaissance pratique comme une «abstraction incertaine qui fait entrer le même symbole dans des relations différentes par des aspects différents ou qui fait entrer des aspects différents du même référent dans le même rapport d'opposition». Bourdieu P (1972) op cit p 217

9. Vigarello G (1982) Le laboratoire des sciences humaines. Esprit 2 90-106. Les principes théoriques engagés par cet auteur s'éclairent lorsque, dans cet article, il inscrit la validité des concepts d'habitus et d'hexis corporelle dans les limites de leurs possibilités d'objectivation. Le concept d'habitus n'étant selon lui «qu'analogie», il refuse le droit à l'objectivation des corps au nom du principe mille fois posé par les tenants de tous les systèmes de croyances selon lequel «rien n'est plus ineffable que les valeurs incorporées». Vigarello G (1982) op cit p 100-01. On peut s'étonner de l'énoncé de telles hypothèses chez l'auteur d'une histoire pourtant très riche de la «rectitude corporelle». Voir Vigarello G (1978) Le corps redressé. Histoire d'un pouvoir pédagogique. Paris: Delarge. Si le projet de faire «une histoire des modèles qui, en gouvernant le fonctionnement des corps, gouvernent par là-même les démarches qui les éduquent» (Vigarello G (1978) op cit p 6), est parfaitement légitime, un glissement se produit lorsque les modèles ainsi construits deviennent le tout de la réalité, y compris de l'expérience de la domestication des corps vécue par les agents sociaux. Ainsi chaque projet pédagogique est présenté comme tirant sa cohérence et sa force d'imposition de lui-même, indépendamment des conditions sociales réelles qui sont désignées, quelle que soit la période considérée, à l'aide des mêmes expressions réifiantes telles que «la démarche redresseuse», «la parole redresseuse», «les énergies redresseuses» ou encore «le geste redresseur».

10. Bourdieu P (1980) op cit p 411-39

11. Enquête réalisée en 1985 auprès de 1 200 enfants scolarisés dans les quartiers Est de la ville de Nantes (Ouest de la France). Voir Suaud C (1988) Les acteurs sociaux dans le champ de l'encadrement de la jeunesse. La Revue de l'économie sociale avril p 158-67

12. Irlinger P, Louveau C, Métoudi M (1990) L'activité physique, une manière de soigner l'apparence? Données sociales. Institut National de la Statistique et des Études Économiques, France p 269-72

13. Bourdieu P (1987) Programme pour une sociologie du sport. Choses dites. Paris: Éditions de Minuit p 203-16

14. Clément JP (1981) La force, la souplesse et l'harmonie. Étude comparée de trois sports de combat (lutte, judo, aïkido). Dans Pociello C (ed) Sports et société. Approche socio-culturelle des pratiques. Paris: Vigot p 285-301

15. La Fédération française de squash-raquettes a été reconnue par l'État comme institution indépendante le 17 janvier 1981. Le nombre de courts de squash en France était de 15 en 1974, 290 en 1980, 600 en 1984 et 725 en 1985. La création du premier court à Nantes remonte à 1980. L'enquête réalisée dans cette ville en 1986, a porté sur un échantillon de 240 joueurs âgés de 20 ans et plus, prélevé dans les six clubs de l'agglomération.

16. «Le corps croit en ce qu'il joue : il pleure s'il mime la tristesse. Il ne représente pas ce qu'il joue, il ne mémorise pas le passé, il agit le passé, ainsi annulé en tant que tel, il le revit. Ce qui est appris par corps n'est pas quelque chose que l'on a, comme un savoir que l'on peut tenir devant soi, mais quelque chose que l'on est». Bourdieu P (1987) op cit p 123

17. L'enquête, réalisée en 1984, a porté sur la population des pratiquants âgés de 20 ans et plus d'une sélection de quatre clubs de l'agglomération nantaise (n=252) : un club associatif, le Stade nantais université club (SNUC), deux clubs municipaux (Carquefou et La Gagnerie) et un club commercial (la Raquette d'argent).

18. Les joueurs du club associatif invoquent spontanément toute une série de justifications de leur choix de club dans laquelle les critères sociaux et sportifs sont intimement mêlés. Par exemple, ce cadre supérieur venu au club dans les années 70 avance successivement le maintien d'un «style» et d'un «esprit» universitaires, le niveau sportif du club et le fait de pouvoir «y rencontrer des cadres».

19. Le réseau de partenaires peut être interprété comme un réseau de sociabilité quand on sait que 71 % des pratiquants du club associatif disent «s'être fait des amis nouveaux» par le club, contre 59 % dans le club commercial et 55 % dans les clubs municipaux.

20. Waser AM (1989) Le marché des partenaires. Étude de trois clubs de tennis. Actes de la recherche en sciences sociales 80 2-21. Par le recours à l'observation directe et participante de trois clubs strasbourgeois, Waser enrichit et confirme les constats statistiques dressés dans l'enquête réalisée à Nantes. C'est dans le club le plus sélectif (qui recrute par parrainage) qu'elle observe les marques les plus évidentes de tolérance et de solidarité dans les gestes de courtoisie dont les membres font preuve les uns à l'égard des autres, ainsi que dans les services qu'ils se rendent, comme celui qui consiste à accepter de jouer malgré une inégalité des niveaux de jeu.

21. Ibid p 12

22. Gruneau R (1983) Class, sports and social development. Amherst : University of Massachusetts Press p 141

23. Bourdieu P (1979) La distinction. Critique sociale du jugement. Paris : Éditions de Minuit p 57

24. Defrance J (1989) Un schisme sportif. Clivages structurels, scissions et oppositions dans les sports athlétiques 1960-1980. Actes de la recherche en sciences sociales 79 76-91 et Loirand G (1989) De la chute au vol. Genèse et transformations du parachutisme sportif. Actes de la recherche en sciences sociales 79 37-49

25. En 1968, on passe d'un Comité directeur national composé d'officiers supérieurs (réservistes, retraités ou en activité), et d'industriels anciens combattants, à un bureau composé de polytechniciens, de médecins et de journalistes. Cette même année, la Fédération nationale des parachutistes français (FNPF) devient la Fédération française de parachutisme (FFP).

26. Après avoir été imaginé en France en 1953, le vol relatif y revient vingt années plus tard, porté par l'«Icarius group» composé de gérants et de directeurs d'entreprises, en bénéficiant cette fois-ci du prestige attaché aux sports californiens.

27. On comprend aisément comment le schème physique du surplomb ou du sur-vol — variante du schème haut/bas — soit particulièrement adéquat pour exprimer l'idée de hauteur sociale qui, en certains cas, peut elle-même servir à désigner une distance sociale ou, comme on dit, une vision hautaine sur le monde social. Tel est le cas de cet ouvrier-carossier cité par Loirand qui, à travers les sensations physiques que lui procure le parachutisme, en vient à décrire le rapport qu'il entretient au monde social et aux membres de son propre groupe en particulier : «Quand je suis pendu et que, dans le soleil couchant, je vois ces colonnes de larves dans les bouchons, je suis bien content d'être au-dessus. Je me sens supérieur à tous ces guignols du dimanche soir qui vont mourir dans les embouteillages. C'est bien une mort de prolétaire, ça!». Dans Loirand G (1989) op cit p 39

28. Pour ces nouveaux pratiquants, il s'agit de «vivre sa chute et non de la subir», Ibid p 45. On retrouve dans le vol relatif la dimension «informationnelle» qui exige des pratiquants des dispositions à l'analyse de l'environnement et à la prise rapide de décisions fondées sur de multiples paramètres, autant de comportements qui se

trouvent fortement liés à la possession d'un fort capital culturel. Voir Pociello C (1981) op cit p 190-93

29. A partir de 1983, les postulants au parachutisme peuvent s'inscrire au Centre-école de la région sans adhérer à un club. Ils se présentent alors comme clients privés demandeurs d'une initiation individuelle à la pratique parachutiste. Avec la «progression accélérée en chute» effectuée dans le cadre d'une formation technique et psychologique spécifique, les premiers sauts se font directement en chute libre, encadrés par deux instructeurs spécialement formés. Le coût de cet apprentissage est sans commune mesure avec celui de l'initiation classique, de l'ordre de 7 000 F environ.

30. On pourrait même s'interroger sur le fait de savoir si l'expérience vécue des changements du corps physique ne procure des schèmes par lesquels on assume les changements psychologiques et sociaux. Ne dit-on pas qu'«avec l'âge», telle personne devient «moins souple», «plus cassante», etc.?

31. En 1987, la part des joueurs de golf s'élève régulièrement au fur et à mesure qu'on monte dans la hiérachie des âges (découpés en périodes quadri-annuelles): les 22-25 ans représentent 4,4 % des pratiquants, les 34-37 ans 9% et les 38-41 ans 12%, les plus de 53 ans en faisant 21%. Les taux d'augmentation des effectifs entre 1986 et 1987 étaient de +41,7% pour les 22-25 ans, de +20,6% pour les 34-37 ans, de 43,9% pour les 42-45 ans et de +11% chez les plus de 53 ans (source: Fédération française de tennis).

32. Le discours que les joueurs tiennent sur le golf est en effet saturé de propositions morales et psychologiques célébrant l'autonomie de l'individu, la connaissance et la maîtrise de soi ainsi que le sens des responsabilités: «Le golf est une grande école de vie. On est toujours puni par là où on est présomptueux. La sanction est immédiate. Je crois que c'est le seul sport où on est responsable de ce que l'on fait. Au golf, on ne peut pas s'en prendre aux autres. On est toujours bon ou mauvais par rapport à soi-même» (médecin, 40 ans, 4 années de pratique, ancien joueur de tennis du club associatif).

33. «Dans le cas où le domaine [des pratiques sportives] et ses éléments sont non encore définis ou mal définis, c'est-à-dire dans les situations inaugurales ou marginales, l'appropriation ne se fait qu'au prix d'un travail de définition; le rôle actif des agents dans la production d'une harmonie entre dispositions et pratiques (ou son échec) est alors accentué, parce qu'ils doivent définir les repères de leur pratique en même temps que leur pratique et que, ne pouvant le faire dans la logique d'un système spécifique symboliquement structuré et délimité, ils s'appuient sur d'autres logiques». Defrance J (1989) op cit p 162

34. Je remercie JM Faure de m'avoir introduit à la sociologie historique anglaise du sport. Comme le rapporte JA Mangan, Tyndale-Biscoe, missionnaire britannique établi au Cachemire de 1890 à 1947, exprime parfaitement la «mission» morale et religieuse qu'il entendait réaliser à travers l'éducation sportive, silencieuse et pratique, de ses élèves: «Etre chrétien est quelque chose qui se vit. Jésus-Christ était à la fois un homme parfait et Dieu; aussi, être chrétien, cela demande-t-il de lutter pour atteindre la perfection de l'homme accompli (perfect manliness) — faite de force du corps et de l'intelligence de l'âme, — tout en montrant que cette force doit être pénétrée de compassion pour le faible [...] Il faut susciter le désir d'idéal, mais cela ne peut se faire en paroles; il convient pour cela de mettre devant les élèves notre meilleur exemple, Jésus-Christ, et de leur demander de nous rejoindre en essayant de vivre cette vie de service». Tyndale-Biscoe CE (1920) Character Building in Kashmir. Church Missionary Society p 13 cité par Mangan JA (1985) The games ethic and imperialism. Aspects of the diffusion of an ideal. Harmondsworth: Penguin Books p 178

35. Mangan JA (1985) op cit p 187

36. De cette étude de cas où l'éducation religieuse et l'éducation sportive sont intimement imbriquées, nous ne tirerons pas la conclusion d'une assimilation entre religion et sport, le plus souvent effectuée à des fins idéologiques de dénonciation de leurs fonctions d'aliénation. Nous y voyons en revanche une extraordinaire preuve empirique que rien n'est plus spirituel (au sens d'«esprit de corps») que le sport, et que rien n'est plus corporel que la religion ainsi que Pascal l'avait déjà parfaitement analysé.

37. Le principe selon lequel il n'y a aucune relation de nécessité entre les caractères intrinsèques d'un sport et les propriétés sociales de ses pratiquants vaut quelle que soit la nature et la dimension des groupes concernés. Comme le fait justement remarquer

Faure, seule l'histoire sociale des communautés, qu'elles soient urbaines, régionales ou nationales, peut faire comprendre — faute d'expliquer — comment des affinités sportives ont pu se créer et devenir de véritables traditions culturelles. Il montre comment il serait par exemple bien difficile, pour ne pas dire illusoire, de chercher dans les caractéristiques internes du football les raisons qui l'ont fait adopter par les milieux populaires dans l'Ouest de la France et par la bourgeoisie dans le Sud-Ouest. Voir Faure JM (1987) Sports, cultures et classes sociales. Thèse de doctorat ès lettres et sciences humaines. Université de Nantes Tome II p 952-953 [non publiée]

38.   Atherton s'interroge sur les raisons qui, au XIXe siècle, ont fait que certains sports en sont venus à exprimer «le génie national américain». Il mentionne que les historiens sont unanimes pour dire qu'une commission nommée en 1907 s'est explicitement chargée de fabriquer de toutes pièces un mythe d'origine du baseball racontant qu'«un certain Doubleday aurait créé le jeu en 1839», doublé d'une seconde légende selon laquelle «le baseball serait l'expression spontanée d'une Amérique pastorale intimement liée à l'image de la préadolescence», dans Atherton J (1988) Sport et culture aux États-Unis. Le sport en Grande-Bretagne et aux États-Unis. Faits, signes et métaphores. Nancy: Presses Universitaires de Nancy p 10-12. Il reste bien entendu à montrer comment et pourquoi le mythe a été cru.

39.   Faure JM (1990) Le sport et la culture populaire. Pratiques et spectacles sportifs dans la culture populaire. Université de Nantes: Les cahiers du Lersco 12. Ce texte regorge de descriptions se rapportant aussi bien au jeu qu'à la sociabilité qui l'entoure dans lesquelles les valeurs de la culture locale l'emportent. Soit, par exemple, cet extrait d'entretien de l'entraîneur du club local Voutré qui est aussi l'instituteur du village: «Je ne vois pas qu'on puisse supprimer la buvette. Il y a des gens qui ne viendraient plus. S'ils ne peuvent plus boire un coup ensemble, ils ne mettront plus les pieds au stade. Ils passent autant de temps à la buvette qu'à regarder le match. Alors on se passe d'autorisation et tout le monde est content», Faure JM (1990) op cit p 45

40.   Tel est le travail réalisé par Bromberger dans une étude comparative de la vie des clubs de La Juve de Turin et de Marseille. Voir Bromberger C, Hayot A, Mariotti JM (1987) Allez l'OM, Forza Juve. La passion pour le football à Marseille et à Turin. Terrain 8 8-41

41.   Leite Lopes JS, Maresca S (1989) La disparition de la «joie du peuple». Notes sur la mort d'un joueur de football. Actes de la recherche en sciences sociales 79 21-36

42.   Dans l'article déjà cité, les auteurs mentionnent que le silence de Garrincha sur lui-même s'est développé en «une abondante littérature interprétive produite par les journalistes, mais aussi par des écrivains à leurs heures [...] des poètes et romanciers [...] Le résultat le plus fameux de l'utilisation de Garrincha comme matière première de l'art reste le film «Garrincha, alegria do povo» Ibid p 25

43.   «C'est en effet dans l'attitude du groupe, bien plutôt que dans le rythme des échecs et des succès, qu'il faut chercher la raison véritable de l'effondrement des rivaux de Quesalid... L'échec est secondaire, et on perçoit, dans tous leurs propos, qu'ils le conçoivent comme une fonction d'un autre phénomène: l'évanouissement du consensus social, reconstitué à leurs dépens autour d'un autre praticien, d'un autre système. Le problème fondamental est donc celui du rapport entre un individu et le groupe, ou, plus exactement, entre un certain type d'individus et certaines exigences du groupe». Lévi-Strauss C (1958) Anthropologie structurale. Paris: Plon p 198-99

44.   Les bouleversements politiques survenus à la fin de l'année 1989 dans les pays de l'Europe de l'Est ont contribué à rendre extrêmement visible la part de croyance/méconnaissance collective d'un peuple dans ses champions. Il a été en effet frappant de constater que la reconnaissance sociale des champions s'est effondrée aussitôt la chute du système politique. En quelques jours, et plus particulièrement en Roumanie et en RDA où plusieurs résidences de nageurs et nageuses ont été saccagées, on est passé de la dénégation par adhésion à des valeurs sportives faisant méconnaître les conditions sociales et politiques qui les produisaient, à la dénonciation, c'est-à-dire à la description des choses telles qu'elles étaient. De tels revirements ont été également le fait des démocraties occidentales. Dès le 11 janvier 1990, le journal français Le Monde publiait un article sur les «Tricheries du sport en Roumanie».

45.   Bourdieu P (1989) La noblesse d'État. Grandes écoles et esprit de corps. Paris: Éditions de Minuit p 548-59 et Saint-Martin M (1989) La noblesse et les «sports» nobles. Actes de la recherche en sciences sociales 80 30-32

Religion et sport :
leur connexité sociale

En guise d'introduction, l'auteur établit que les concepts de religion et de sport varient considérablement selon les attitudes et les antécédents culturels. Pour l'auteur, ni la religion ni le sport ne fonctionnent indépendamment, mais bien et plutôt de concert avec les autres institutions sociales majeures. Dans la première partie de sa présentation, l'auteur décrit les caractéristiques principales des deux institutions, entre autres le rituel et le cérémonial qui ont surtout pour objet de renforcer les systèmes de croyances et de valeurs. L'auteur procède par la suite à l'analyse de la religion et du sport en tant qu'institutions à caractère avant tout social. La religion et le sport sont porteurs de culture : une éthique et une morale, immanente à l'être humain mais surtout étalée extérieurement dans les rites, les institutions hiérarchiques et les manifestations en général. La religion et le sport revêtent la plupart des caractéristiques et des configurations classiques des institutions sociales : idéologies, codes et règles de conduite, écrits ou pas, organisation formelle qui fait aussi office de symbole, enfin, système de mise au point et de contrôle de l'ensemble des activités collectives et des comportements individuels. Il résulte de cela une standardisation des pratiques générales ainsi que des croyances, attitudes et comportements habituels des individus. L'auteur démontre que le sport contemporain peut être défini comme une institution sociale d'importance égale à celles que constituent la famille, la religion, l'économie et la politique. Il avance à ce sujet six éléments explicatifs : 1– l'institution sportive satisfait des besoins humains fondamentaux, tant pour l'individu que pour la collectivité : mouvement, jeu, compétition, loisir, amusement ; 2– l'institution sportive établit et fait respecter ses propres règles d'organisation et de fonctionnement ; 3– elle tend à contrôler les comportements en organisant et en polarisant les rôles sociaux dans ses propres rangs ; 4– elle est utilisée indirectement et directement comme force ou mécanisme de stabilisation et de contrôle social ; 5– l'institution sportive s'inscrit dans un réseau de support mutuel, avec les autres institutions sociales majeures décrites ci-avant ; 6– enfin, l'institution sportive subit l'influence des autres institutions sociales dans le réseau desquelles elle s'inscrit, et elle influence ces dernières à son tour. Une analyse des Jeux olympiques suit, en tant qu'institution modelée sur des valeurs exclusivement occidentales, et dont toutes les facettes, aux plans de l'idéologie, de l'organisation et du fonctionnement, ont de nos jours une influence considérable sur la manière dont le sport s'entrevoit. Dans la troisième partie de sa présentation, l'auteur traite de la question des rituels, en matière de religion comme de sport. Il souligne, entre autres, que lorsqu'une institution acquiert un symbolisme compris et partagé par le plus grand nombre, cette dernière devient du même coup un important mécanisme d'influence et de contrôle social. En quatrième lieu, l'auteur avance que le rituel religieux et le rituel sportif, au fil de l'histoire, ont servi à légitimiser le pouvoir politique. Dans une cinquième partie, l'auteur rappelle et souligne les origines religieuses, partant les influences sociales profondes du sport moderne. À son avis, s'il est vrai que les grandes religions du monde ont été caractérisées par des conceptions différentes de l'être humain, du corps, de l'éthique sociale et de la morale, il semble bien que ce soit l'Occident chrétien qui ait exercé la marque la plus profonde sur le sport, comme d'ailleurs dans les secteurs technique, militaire, économique et scientifique. En sixième lieu, l'auteur pose la question de savoir si les Jeux olympiques modernes, et le fait historique de leur rénovation, ne constituent pas l'invention d'une nouvelle religion, celle d'un *cultus publicus* visant la réforme continue des systèmes éducatifs, la promotion de l'individu et celle d'une nouvelle forme de patriotisme, l'internationalisme. Dans cette perspective, l'œuvre de Coubertin et celle du Mouvement olympique se présentent comme une sorte de religion artificielle, qui symbolise les espoirs du monde laïque d'aujourd'hui. En guise de conclusion, l'auteur revient à l'histoire : la Chrétienté a conquis le paganisme et éliminé les Jeux olympiques de l'Antiquité ; mais l'histoire contemporaine laisse déjà voir qu'une nouvelle forme de paganisme a conquis à son tour la Chrétienté et a rétabli les Jeux olympiques, une institution moderne qui s'apparente plutôt à une quasi religion à caractère somatique.

Religion and Sport:
the Social Connection

Kurt Weis

The concept of religion[1] is used in a variety of ways, depending on attitude, cultural background or scholarly standpoint[2]. The same holds true for sport. Religion and sport are in many ways socially interrelated, interdependent or in conflict. In modern societies, neither is an independent social force, but part of the concert of social institutions.

A textbook makes reference to "a mutual interdependence between religion and sport[3]". It is stated that

> there are many religious values or practices present in sport, including ceremony, ritual, magic, and superstition. These have remained a part of sport because it is commonly believed that they are necessary for the continued institutionalization of a sport, or are somehow related to the outcome of a specific sport event. Moreover, ritual and ceremony, whether in religion or sport, reinforce values and beliefs[4].

Sage wrote: "Sport has taken on many of the characteristics of religion, and indeed it has been argued that sport has emerged as a new religion, supplementing, and in some cases even supplanting, the traditional religious expressions[5]." Sage quoted Rogers that "sports are rapidly becoming the dominant ritualistic expression of the reification of established religion in America" and Edwards, who held that "[. . .] if there is a universal popular religion in America it is to be found within the institution of sports[6]."

There are other connections between religion and sport. In the Federal Republic of Germany, some football supporters, or soccer hooligans, wear badges on their jackets reading: "My football club is my religion", sometimes, unfortunately, right next to the imperial German war flag and to badges reading "Death to . . ." (another city's football club and its supporters). These provocations, however, or the marathon runners' sect of Sri Chinmoy, self-proclaimed meditation guru of the United Nations headquarters, or the religious and philosophical roots of Far Eastern martial arts, which are being increasingly taught in Western countries

1890
1990

Kurt Weis, Institute of Social Sciences, Faculty of Economics and Social Sciences, Technical University of Munich, Munich, Federal Republic of Germany.

as self-defense sports, will, although interesting in their theoretical and practical consequences, not be dealth with here for lack of space.

Coakley[7] lists, aside from differences, the following similarities between sport and religion: "– both are grounded in a quest for perfection; – both are built on asceticism (*i.e.*, discipline and self-denial); – both involve integration of body, mind, and spirit; – both involve strong feelings based on intensive concentration; – both contain established rituals on all levels of participation; – both contain institutionalized symbols related to people, places, procedures, and printed materials; – both are administered through bureaucratized organizational structures."

One may not agree with Coakley's assumptions that both religion and sport are grounded in a quest for perfection or that both are built on asceticism. Religion certainly is not. Simply stated, both are social institutions in the technical sociological sense of the term.

Religion and Sport as Social Institutions

Both religion and sport are social institutions. Religion has for its part many faces and functions: – it is a carrier of culture in its actual historical appearance; – it is radical ethics and morals; – it is theology as theory and dogmatism; – it is inner experience, an often forgotten and unclear but basic residual category for religion's foundation. Religion, as it manifests itself in typical human behavior, in the establishment of churches and administrative hierarchies, in the organization and ritual channelling of religious needs, is one of the basic social institutions. For all societies, tribal or modern, it has been acknowledged as such.

Since Durkheim's definition in 1901[8], sociology has been understood as "the science of institutions, of their genesis and of their functioning". The concept of "institution", its acknowledgment and its use, all have histories of their own. Furthermore, they all vary from country to country (*e.g.*, USA, France, England, Germany) and have been discussed elsewhere[9]. Originally, for American sociology, "institution" was a central concept. In summarizing and concluding the development of the American discussion, Hertzler in 1946 gave the following working definition:

> Social institutions are purposive, regulatory and consequently primary cultural configurations, formed unconsciously and/or deliberately, to satisfy individual wants and social needs bound up with the efficient operation of any plurality of persons. They consist of codes, rules, ideologies, unwritten and written, and essential symbolic organizational and material implementations. They evidence themselves socially in standardized and uniform practices and observances, and individually in attitudes and habitual behavior of persons. They are sustained and enforced by public opinion, acting both informally and formally, through specially devised agencies[10].

Later, the structural-functional theorists lost interest in the concept of *institution*. But the traditional use of the concept of institution remained in the textbooks. In France, too, after Durkheim and his school had introduced the concept, its importance decreased as functionalist, system and critical theorists gained momentum. In Germany, after the Second World War, Gehlen[11] was influential with his sociological anthropology and his rigid new definition of man's basic needs and of a model of institutions to compensate them. In German sociology, however, the concept of institution did not attract much additional attention. As in the United States, it just remained in the textbooks. Sometimes it is criticized for its conservative roots, its idealistic and ideological character and its affirmative use in explaining power structures. For explanation and analysis, the future of the concept is to be less seen in its conservative than in its procedural qualities. The emphasis is on institutionalization. Institutionalization is a way of reducing complexity. It "serves to successfully overestimate consensus[12]." Of primary interest here are the ways in which social institutions are changing, *i.e.*, collecting or losing, functions and influence.

Besides to so-called basic institutions in the areas of family, religion, economics and government, further institutions, including sport, have developed. For our purposes, social institutions will be described and defined with regard to sport. Since the 1970s, in sociological analysis, sport is increasingly referred to as and treated like a social institution[13]. Six essential elements of social institutions are listed below. Sport in to-day society is easily subsumed under these elements of definition[14]:

1– An institution serves to satisfy important human needs in a society. Among others, sport satisfies the need for movement, play and competition, recreation and entertainment. The needs of both participants and spectators are satisfied.

2– For this satisfaction certain patterns of behavior are prescribed. This regulation is especially and clearly seen in organized sport. A time and place for the sports event are set. There are standardized rules of competition and for grading of accomplishments. In place of elemental drive, or regional or native sports, only certain types of sport are admitted in the Olympic Games, or in schools, or by colonial rulers.

3– In social institutions, behavior is organized in social roles. The role players regard this as "duty" or "office". Sport recognizes innumerable types of roles, such as athlete, coach, manager, volunteer, international official, federation president, etc.

4– Institutions as regulatory as sport can fulfill a stabilizing function in society as a whole and thus play a significant role in social control.

5– The institutions in a society act together to a certain degree and also provide mutual support. When important functions of one institution are transferred to another, this is a sign of social change and a certain restructuring of the society. The usual topics of sport sociology (the interplay between sport and economics, politics, the mass media, the educational system, religion...) underline the increasingly important role of sport in these areas, as well as an increasingly dense web of interrelations and dependencies. Some educators believe, and top functionaries of state and church, of party politics and health authorities alike declare, that sport fulfills important functions of socialization and enables people to become happy and healthy, fair and successful, self-disciplined and independent, brave, responsible and law-abiding citizens, proud of their respective democratic, capitalist, socialist or post-modern society—the ideal conformist that no other social institution, be it church or family, state education or media influence, has ever been able to produce.

6– Institutions satisfy important individual and group needs, but their particular character is determined by society as a whole. This last element is merely an extension of the previous one: sport as an institution is shaped by other social institutions as well. In short: society leaves its stamp on sport.

The questions of the extent to which sport as a social institution influences the persons in its sphere, and to what extent it reflects society, pervade every session of this international symposium. One could list all 18 sub-themes and most of the free paper presentations at this conference. This applies to "Sport and the State", "Sports-for-All", "Racial Segregation", as well as to male dominance in the power structure of sport organizations in democratic countries.

The Olympic Games and their development are the culmination of the Western type of sport and the international consequence of the growing significance of sport as an important social institution. There is at this conference a series of contributions on recent controversial developments in the reality and ideology of modern Olympic Games. On earlier occasions Riordan[15] had already described official functions of sport in developing nations and enlarged the number of case studies showing how sport is being saddled with functions that were originally relegated to other social institutions. Others have criticized olympic sport as a variant of neocolonization[16].

The Olympic Games are the culminating event in sport, which has truly become through its own dynamic a social institution on the international level as well—with all its athletes and functionaries, the National Olympic Committees and the IOC, foreign policy implications and dependency on the goodwill of high-level politics, with its extremes from boycotts to glamorous shows with popular appeal, entanglement with and the dependency on the sport industry, the ballyhoo of public relations management and, finally, the now indispensible financial support from and the inescapable dependency on media organizations, especially the giants of the television industry. In Seoul 1988, the journalists and reporters indeed outnumbered the athletes.

The Olympic Games have become a nomadic institution with roots throughout the world and manifesting itself in a given land at a particular time. This is the powerful and impressive concretization of sport as an institution. At the same time, the Olympic Games exert a manifold influence on sport as a social institution in each particular national and cultural context.

Rituals in Religion and Sport

It is usually in ethnological, anthropological and religious writings that cults, rites, rituals and religious ceremonies are described and defined. In the social science literature on sport, especially sport sociology, the term ritual is frequently, sometimes excessively used, but rarely defined or analytically applied[17].

Important in rituals[18]—as in social institutions—are the commonly shared symbolic meaning and social significance of things and events. In sport, the omnipresence of rituals is more obvious than in other secular areas of life. Still, this is often overlooked. Rituals are a part of sport festivals; they create a feeling of community and solemnity; they regulate fights and battles, and prevent them from becoming "serious"; they mark the beginning and end of competitions; they characterize the exchange of courtesies between friends and enemy teams, the presentation of awards, victory celebrations, and also elections and meetings of functionaries. They are part of functioning social control. They steer, permit and limit behavior and treat problem situations symbolically, so that the situation and the appropriate behavior do not have to be contemplated beforehand. One knows what is to be done and how it is to be done. Rituals have to be taken seriously. They make life easier and may even be fun.

Ritual action constitutes and activates the social sense; it makes normative orientations clear. For a long time the attention of sociologists was not drawn to the field of symbolic and ritual actions. They had erroneously believed that rational action is particularly typical of an enlightened and industrial society. The significance and occurrence of ritual action become clear if social action is divided into productive and ritual action. Productive action serves the creation or preservation of utility values. Practically all other action then, including sport, has to be communicative action in the sense of ritual action.

Culturally standardized acts with symbolic significance, which are performed on traditionally prescribed occasions are considered as rituals. Rituals are also more broadly defined by some as simply symbolic behavior which is repeated in a more or less stylized form on certain occasions. The production of symbols, the observance of symbolic meanings, and the (unreflecting) observance of rituals are among the principal occupations of man. This applies particularly to sport, which takes itself and its rituals seriously, even where its rituals do not serve quasi-religious functions. Rituals, like institutions, make us act without thinking.

Thus, rituals handle situations and information symbolically and inform those to whom the symbols are familiar about the given situation and the present status of the event: *e.g.*, the entrance of teams in club colors, exchange of flags, national anthems before games or after an olympic victory, silence before the starts, encouragement from the spectators, vigorous hugs and body contact after a victory or goal, fan aggression rituals, victory celebrations, speeches of high officials, conferences of associations, NOCs and IOC—all "artificial" and "unnecessary" as sport itself, but still inevitable for people as social beings.

All cultures, subcultures and anticultures have their own rituals intended to give encouragement and a sense of identification to their members. All social institutions, all areas of life and all situations have their own rituals which must be carried out and which are tied to role behavior, including consciousness of "office", and which make orderly coexistence and survival at all possible.

Rituals as such are artificial and nonessential products, as sport itself is, but still necessary to coping with everyday life. They are by no means restricted to old tribal societies, even if some elements of the social environment of sport competitions are reminiscent of them. In his book on "The Soccer Tribe" (in the German translation with the subtitle "fascination and ritual of soccer"), Morris[19] went to certain extremes from his cthological, here almost ethnological perspective, to describe and show in pictures the soccer match as "a ritual hunt", "a stylized battle", "a status display", and "a religious ceremony". The "tribal rituals" of football are explained in the ten chapters on "the tribal laws" (rules of the game), "the tribal territories" (stadium), "the tribal taboos" (fouls, misconduct, etc.), "the tribal punishments" (penalties, fines etc.), "the tribal strategies" (formations of attack and defence), "the tribal tactics" (passes, tackles, moves, etc.), "the tribal gatherings" (parades, warm-up, etc.), "the central ritual" (sequence of play), "the ritual climax" (scoring of goals), "the victory celebrations" (awards, lap of honour, homecoming). The book also deals with the "tribal heroes", the "tribal elders" and "witch-doctors", the "tribal followers" with their ritual of violence and many other ritualistic aspects of the hard life of serious football supporters.

To others, the course of a decisive race or some other championship event may resemble a complete transition ritual as is better known from religious initiation rites in truly old or remote tribal societies. Such rites constitute and celebrate the social shift from one state to another, *e.g.*, from childhood to adulthood. They concern the social, not the biological transition. Among our own most familiar initiation rituals are baptism, wedding, examination and graduation. van Gennep in his classic book on *Les Rites de Passage*[20] characterized as initiation rites a class of rituals with three successive and distinct moments in ritual time: separation, margin, aggregation. Turner further elaborated on the central interstructural phase between the two states of having been and becoming. He called it the "liminal period", the time "betwixt and between[21]" full of hope and fear as to whether the neophytes will make it from the previous state to the next. Typically, during the transition period, neophytes are removed from their normal physical and social environment and must sometimes undergo extreme suffering. While this part of the passage ritual is "in the liminal period, structurally, if not physically, 'invisible'[22]", most sport competitions are accessible and visible, and spectators pay to watch and "participate" in the thrill and excitement of the ordeal.

Some people with a religious perspective consider the whole of life on earth as one big initiation or transition ritual. Then a sports final is a ritual of a similar category, though perhaps somewhat less important.

The Politics of Staging Rituals: Sport as Civil Religion

Religious and sport rituals are staged for various reasons and functions. They can both be carried out by those in political power in the hope of bathing in their reflected splendor. Both ritual types occasionally serve the so-called non-political (self-)presentation of the political system.

Theocracies, as well as military dictatorships with a state religion, as especially observed in recent times in Christianity in Spanish- or Portuguese-speaking countries of southern Europe or South America, often employ religious celebrations for the purpose of self-presentation (church services, enthronements, weddings, funerals). In this way the rituals fulfill the aforementioned classic functions. In addition, the legitimization of the powerholders through religion is intended.

Most countries have no state religion. In some, state and church or state, religions and churches are kept separate; others declare themselves atheistic. For all of them, voluminous sport ceremonials provide a vehicle for representation in a non-religious world. This was illustrated by the (in)famous organizational peak performance at the Olympic Games of 1936 in Berlin, when Hitler and the Third Reich showed themselves to participants, spectators and the whole world in large-scale ritual productions as efficient and laudable partners. Through the Olympic Games of 1988 in Seoul, the South Koreans also strove for and achieved the international political recognition that they had hitherto desired or lacked.

In religious rituals, in church services or in other religious ceremonies, the values and content of the religious congregation are symbolized, demonstrated, talked about and preached in compact form. This intensification takes place in a ritual celebration, not in the acts of everyday life.

Similar observations can be made in sport—not so much during the actual sport event as in sport reporting. In the present information society, sport has become ideal material for mass communication. Everyday training routine is not reported upon so much as are, in shortened and condensed form, grand ritualized sport competitions. Society rates highly contents and procedures such as confirmation of the value structure (achievement and reward, defeat and penalty) and entertainment values (excitement, self-presentation and physical struggle of athletes in a fight with fateful overtones, involving victory or defeat). These coincide so directly that they are particularly suited for vicarious experiences and live broadcasting. It would seem as if cultural values were lived out before our eyes, as if social complexity were reduced to a brief, easily comprehensible process. In the case of large ritualized sport festivals, world championships or Olympic Games, the values and contents of the society are symbolized in compact form, performed, talked about and preached. The same was said above concerning religious ceremonial. This is possible in sport particularly through mass communication. Meanwhile, because of the costs involved in staging such rituals, sport with its great competitions, championships and Olympic Games, has become financially dependent on the mass media and television giants.

Rituals promote a feeling of solidarity. This applies more strongly in the religious than the civil area. For this reason state and sport ceremonies[23] are often given a quasi-religious setting. This leads to the establishment of so-called civil religions of which sport has become a prime example. A "civil religion" consists of an institutionalized pattern of symbols, ideas and practices that evokes people's commitment and legitimates the authority of civil institutions in a society. In atheist societies it is used to replace religion and at the same time to utilize the functions of integration and social self-symbolization inherent to religion. The term and the necessity of a *religion civile* was outlined by Jean-Jacques Rousseau (1712-1778) in his *Contrat social* (1762). Emile Durkheim (1858-1917) in his *Les Formes élémentaires de la vie religieuse* (1912), later explained how "the idea of society is the soul of religion[24]." The American discussion started in 1967 with Bellah's paper on "Civil Religion in America[25]". Civil religion mixes church and society, ideology and religious belief and expresses a collective ideal: American "Thanksgiving", the Commonwealth's "God save the Queen", German "Christmas", Poland's "Queen St. Mary", religious rhetoric on American bills and coins ("in God we trust"), in political statements, declarations of war and sport cults. Further on a description will be made of the Olympic Movement as an outstanding case of civil religion.

Religious Roots and Social Influences in Modern Sport

Sport, both as a modern social institution and as actual behavior, is shaped by society. Society is influenced by the underlying culture. Culture is molded by religious and philosophical thought and social developments. Thus there is a connecting line from religion to sport.

All cultures have important religious influences in their historical backgrounds. The manifestations and consequences of these influences are still there, even if the religious factor has lost its impact. Different world religions, even different Christian denominations with their different images of men and women, with their different attitudes toward the body, toward work ethics and worldly success, have led to different social and economic systems, and thus influenced the image of sport and the extent of success or the number of medals achieved.

At a time of both declining religious influence and renewed religious interest, often outside the established churches, the religious roots of sport and other physical behavior should become an important focus of cultural sociology and sport sociology.

The image of God and the image of man influence each other. They are interdependent, and they differ. God can be seen as a hero in the Greeks' olympic family, as dancing Shiva, as Buddha, non-god in a transitory world, as the blood-thirsty Aztec Huitzilopochtli, as Yahweh, warlord of the Old Testament, or as the Lord of peace and love of the New Testament. All these aspects were or are used as reference models for disciplining human behavior in battle or prayer, in physical and spiritual exercises, in sportive competition or breathing techniques. Those, of course, were only overemphasized and simplified qualities, since men in all religions tend to ascribe to their gods and idols the full range of human characteristics.

Man's image or concept of God is the medium through which the more or less religious person encounters his/her God. It depends on his/her religion. Religion is dynamic intercourse with the holy. Religions are living things, namely, human behavior. Human behavior is shaped by time and culture, class, gender, age and situation. This applies also to the area of religion. Religions influence their peoples and believers. Conversely, people form their religions and their concepts of God only within the framework of what they are able to think, to feel and to articulate. In addition, they also project their needs, their hopes and fears and their solutions to problems into this concept. Man at the same time thus reverses the creation story in Genesis and makes a picture of his God in his own image and ideal[26].

Religions reflect, promote or hinder cultural developments. A case in point is the issue of women in sport. The beginning of the three monotheist religions of Jews, Christians and Muslims was marked by the struggle of the people of Israel and their invisible single-person male-patriarch God against the many idols and female goddesses all around. It symbolizes and identifies the mythological and real beginning of patriarchism and male rule in this world, of which we are now facing a late stage.

Christianity always has had Mary, not as a goddess, but as the mother of God, an object of veneration and identification, the outstanding saint and patroness of countless churches and side altars. Islam, with its mixture of Jewish and Christian roots, did not follow the Christian tradition. One knows of the fate of women under today's Shariah, the law of the Koran, in the present fundamentalist interpretation, according to which clothing prescriptions forbid Islamic women to appear in public with bare knees and shoulders, thus practically excluding them from sports. Of course, it is the social context that determines religious practice. The Black Muslims in the US and their women are not submitted to the same Islamic prescriptions and win olympic medals.

The Jewish sport movement, "Makkabi", in Germany and Austria before the Nazi regime may serve as another example. The ancient Jewish faith was opposed to sport as a Greek and Hellenistic, *i.e.*, highly pagan activity. (Herod "the Great" [40-4 BC], however, a friend of the Hellenistic-Roman culture, under whose reign Jesus Christ was born, not only restored and enlarged the temple in Jerusalem and erected the Wailing Wall, but also built several sport arenas in Judaea and financed buildings in Olympia, to be used for the ancient Olympic Games). The Jewish clubs in Germany, founded around and after the turn of last century, were meant to organize the children of Zionism and to promote Jewish identity, "Muskeljudentum" ("muscular Jewdom", probably analogous to the concept of "muscular Christianity") and a psychic and moral revival of Jewish youth. In spite of the ideological differences, the Jewish clubs followed the parallel development of their counterparts, the German sports clubs, in structure and orientation toward competition and achievement. Contrary to anti-Semitic propaganda, Jewish sports clubs were typical products of the German culture and its *bourgeois* middle class[27]. The percentage of Jewish women in Jewish sports clubs was higher than that of German women in German clubs. This was in accordance with their openess for modern and modish developments and the unusually high percentage of female Jewish students in German high schools and universities[28].

Sport for most people means competition. There are, according to religious conditioning, different concepts of competition, achievement and progress in East and West. A short reminder of some roots of today's world religions will suffice. The three monotheist religions have similar or identical roots. They all have typical characteristics: among the Jews, one finds an extreme emphasis on the law and legal technicalities. In Islam there is strong emphasis upon the will of Allah (Kismet, fate). Christianity was originally based on the notions of peace, liberation and freedom.

In the Old Testament, God runs after his people, asks the famous question: "Adam, where are you?", defines himself and his name as the one who is there for his people and to help his people. In the New Testament, which according to christian conviction supplants and fulfils the Old Testament, God becomes man through his Son, incarnates, becomes flesh, thus affirms in this way the earth and humanity, sacrifices himself for his people and opens heaven to them once more. In other religions it seems rather than people run after their god or gods. God does not become man; people want to become god. The earth and human existence is not affirmed and acknowledged. Especially in some branches of Hinduism and the religions growing out of them, people want to leave this earth, leave this world behind them, perhaps to land in the great fulfilled "emptiness" of Nirvana, where all antitheses are resolved.

This affirmation of earthly life, which man may not flee, may be among the many reasons finally contributing to the fact that, in a world of thinking and acting, the christian Occident technically and martially, economically and scientifically—and now also with its Western kind of sport—conquered and colonized the world. The perspective of a religion and of the people it has formed toward this life on earth and the one beyond most probably influences progress in technology, economy and science, even if people have disassociated their thinking from religion.

The evaluation of victory in sport has been in harmony with agonistic features traditional to Western culture since ancient Greek times. Elsewhere, as Seppänen has outlined:

> [...] The tradition of India and China, in the forms of Buddhism and Taoism in particular, emphasizes the vanity of desire and the illusionary nature of the world. Consequently, sport victory in the Western sense of the word is not an important thing in the Orient, but rather an irrealistic demonstration of human action. The invincible Oriental athlete is not one who engages in the escalation of the competition, but one who tries to achieve a kind of mystique and unanalyzable perfection[29].

He later continued: "Although Western civilization has gone through numerous changes and has appeared and continuously appears in a great variety of forms, the most essential in it, belief in progress, a kind of rationality and emphasis on achievements has remained one of the basic characteritics of it[30]."

The idea of progress, of course, is linked to the perception of time. Time may be regarded as being circular (repetitive) as in Hinduism and many other religions of Asian and American Indians, or as being linear, as it is held to be, based on Judeao-Christian theology, in Western cultures. This distinction is probably among the most basic and important points of departure for the different developments in East and West.

In his famous thesis on *"The Protestant Ethic and the Spirit of Capitalism"* (1905), Weber tried to show how the different ethical values internalized by protestants served as an intensifying motivational factor for higher economic achievements. Seppänen used this as a starting point for his studies[31] in which he explained why protestant countries won more olympic medals than catholic countries, and why the combination of protestant ethics and socialist rule and ideology, as in the GDR, beat them all. But after the German Democratic Republic experienced the first successful and peaceful German democratic revolution putting an end to the GDR, all this is a matter of days gone by.

Western ideology, to return to a more global scale, with its emphasis on progress by any means and new records, has had its impact on the olympic idea and is now being copied in the sport arenas of non-western peoples. However, at present in the West, except for the Olympic Games, a slowly growing counter-movement is taking place, rooted in non-european cultures and emphasizing a holistic and hedonistic picture of man. East and West are approaching each other. With a certain amount of oversimplification it could be argued that, while the West is destroying the cultural roots of the East, eastern influence is revitalizing cultural (christian and pre-christian) roots in the West.

It remains to be seen to what extent new social movements, quasi-religious undercurrents like New Age and later trends will influence and change our sport in the post-christian, post-materialistic and post-modern society.

Modern Olympic Games: A Religious Invention?

It was Coubertin's openly admitted intention to restore the Olympic Games and to bestow them with ceremonies, rituals and ideologies in order to literally create in this post-christian time a new secular religion for the youth of France and the youth of the world, a religion which would exercise the socializing influence that the old churches and religions had lost.

Repeatedly, in *Les assises philosophiques de l'Olympisme moderne* for the preparation of the Berlin 1936 Games and elsewhere, he declared: "The first and essential feature of the old as well as the modern Olympism is: being a religion[32]." For this purpose he wanted to refer to the ancient Greeks. He was successful, but many of his reasons were incorrect.

For the ancient Greeks[33], there was no place for rebirth nor life after death in their tragic and pessimistic view of the world. Only the fame attained in the short span of life could survive and distinguish the victor above other members of his tribe, the warrior-athletes of the feudal upper class. Non-Greeks were barbarians and did not count. Thus participation in the olympian competitions was not what it was all about, but rather victory and the victor's wreath or death. Extreme aggression was necessary for this existential self-presentation. Winning was not the most important thing. It was the only thing.

The ancient Olympic Games were religious cult games within the framework of festivals in honor of the gods. They were forbidden by Emperor Theodosius in 394 AD along with other feasts because of their religious character. With ultimatums, two bishops' conferences of the new christian religion had challenged the emperor on this. Christianity was originally, especially in the lower classes, established as a religion of liberation and glad tidings. Followers were to be freed from the rigid rituals of the Jewish faith. Many also yearned to be freed from earthly dominance and foreign political powers. They believed in salvation and life after death. They had a completely new vision of man, which emphasized the worth of every individual, and disapproved of violence. This new religion then underwent a social and political ascent and appropriate modifications. In 312 AD, for the first time, a politically important battle was won under the banner bearing the cross of the christian God: Emperor Constantine defeated his competitor in the battle for power in Rome at the Ponte Milvio. In AD 380/81, Christianity became the state religion. In its name other religions were prohibited and their followers fought against and killed. The christian cult and worldly power, the rituals of the Church and of the Roman Empire and its successors merged in the christian culture into a homogeneous public cult, with which everyone identified—a *cultus publicus*[34].

This Christian *cultus publicus* was ended by the French Revolution in 1789. There were many attempts in France and elsewhere to fill the vacuum that was left with a new cult (*e.g.*, the Cult of Reason, the Cult of the Nation). Coubertin's idea of the modern Olympic Games grew out of this intellectual climate and is one of these attempts. His thinking bore the characteristics of his time: on the one side the conscious new paganism in which the classical philosophy of the Stoa conquered christian concepts and, naturally, on the other the christian elements which had led to the Reformation, the Enlightenment and the social philosophy of the 19th century, Coubertin's century.

Coubertin, a passionate educator, believed that the physical, intellectual and moral qualities of French youth could only be motivated by a new religion. In the post-revolutionary society only sport could accomplish this task as *cultus publicus*. For his purpose, the new religion had to be popularized: the popularization of sport was to be the means of reforming the educational system. And the establishment of Olympism was to be the instrument for popularizing sports.

A religious cult must have a god and content in order not to collapse like an empty husk. Belief in the young and the future, in progress and understanding between peoples were to provide the substance of this new religion. Humanity as God was good rhetoric, but did not attract the public. For this, the nation could serve a subsidiary god. This cult of the nation, nationalism, had in the meantime become a vital force which captured the imagination of whole nations and also of Baron de Coubertin himself. So a *cultus publicus* was already in existence which qualitatively and quantatively was sufficiently concrete in its contents to fill the new Olympic Movement with life.

A religion manifest itself in ritual acts of worship, in religious ceremonial with roleplayers, religious terminology and religious observances. In the spirit of the new "true paganism", Coubertin spoke in his deification of the athletic individual of the "cult of the being 'man', of the human body, of the spirit and the flesh, of feeling and willing, of drives and consciousness[35]." He considered the athlete a "kind of priest and servant of the religion of muscular strength[36]", and spoke of the olympic "priestly council[37]". The solemn oath was to be sworn on the "collected flags of the competing nations[38]". It was supposed to implant unconditional adherence to the rules in the human conscience (thus, in the new god). Then the "priest" was to put his whole strength into the struggle in consummation of the *"religio athletae"*, *i.e.*, the religious act[39]: "The raising of the national flag—the symbol of modern patriotism—as a reward to the victorious athlete—that is to be the continuation of the religious service at the relighted Olympic fire" so that "our secularized century" was thus once again to have a religion[40], which was connected to ancient sources.

Coubertin was successful. But many things turned out to be radically different from what he had intended. The periodical recurrence of festively embellished, regulated competitions are identical in the ancient and modern Olympic Games. The idealized concept of man which Coubertin wanted to take over from the Greeks did not exist even at the time of the ancient Olympic Games. Sport's modern image of man is a diffuse and contradictory mixture. The establishment of Olympism and the popularization of sport did not simply serve as the means to an end, but developed a dynamics of their own. Both became goals in themselves, and did not promote the moral improvement of the educational system. The phrase *"citius, altius, fortius"*, originally used as an encouragement in the mental and moral struggles of monastic life, became the motto of the mania for setting records. This also developed into a goal in itself and into the actual cult of competitive sport.

The Olympic Movement was created as an artificial religion, equipped with all the cultic and ceremonial accessories. As for content, it was bound up to the already existing cult of the nation, even embued with it. This was a post-revolutionary antireligious cult of power and identification. To the extent that this cult may be out of date, seen in an historical perspective, and to the extent that the main educational and ethical concerns of the Olympic Movement have lost much credibility, there remains, nationally and internationally, a fully equipped secular hull. This hull must be refilled in order for it to continue in existence. The Olympic Movement, a modern secular civil religion, is vividly alive. Insofar as today's societies are experiencing a religious reorientation and are presently moving towards religious pluralism, sport and Olympism may follow this development and find themselves filled with many divergent contents, with a potpourri of functions and ideals reflecting the religious and secular needs and hopes of today's world. Christianity conquered the old paganism and therefore eliminated the ancient Olympic Games. The new paganism conquered Christianity and reestablished the Olympic Games. The traditionally christian parts of the world and their current leaders in church and state now support sport and its games.

The Third Millennium...

Although this volume's title might suggest that impression, we do not know in which direction sport and religion will develop in the next decade, century or millennium. This presentation has attempted to show that the modern Olympic Games and sports are festivals of eternal rituals and are staged as and serve as civil religions. They have become international and national social institutions. The shift of functions from one social institution to another indicates social change. In our past, religion and church with their organizations took care of many basic needs of the people beyond the religious ones. Most of these needs are now taken care of by other social institutions. Sport is increasingly being used to fulfill quasi-religious functions. Strangely enough, at least in the (formerly) christian countries of the Occident, not only representatives of states, political parties, educational institutions etc., but also of religions and churches emphasize the manifold values of sport, support it and overburden it with functions which family, state, church, and school no longer seem to be able to fulfill. "Nearly all the great social institutions have been born in religion", wrote Durkheim in 1912[41]. Will sport now be the catchall for them?

With the goal of improving educational content, Coubertin wanted to create a new cult of man. Out of this, only the cult and the concomitant advertising industry, but not the desired educational content evolved and remained. The cult with its image of man was concurrent with post-christian neopaganism.

The present religious world seems to be undergoing drastic changes. The actual influence of the christian churches, officially the largest world religion, is, in most Western countries, still on the decrease. Fundamentalist movements come and go. The waves of so-called new youth religions, sects, destructive cults, of spiritism and occultism, and of New Age have changed some people's attitudes, but they may have had their hey-day.

Sport is concerned with the body. The culture of the new generation, so far mainly a counter-culture, is explicitly somatic. For some time, partly by way of neo-Hinduist guru sects, ideas from the East have been penetrating the West, bringing with them many new techniques for new experiences, consciousness-raising, and self-affirmation *e.g.*, through yoga, meditation and breathing. Their image of man emphasizes the unity of body and mind (often forgotten in Western cultures since Descartes), cosmic unity and the transitoriness of all things. Thus it differs essentially from the christian image of man which, in analogy to the unique occidental judaeo-christian concept of God, also affirmed the dignity of every individual and led to the recognition of human rights. But Mahatma Gandhi, a learned Hindu, is quoted as having said that Christianity is the best religion, but that unfortunately Christians don't live it.

In his latest book on *Europas neue Religion*, Haack[42] discusses the possibility that a "new religion", which he labelled "Western Hinduism", will rise up in the place of the old one. He correctly expects the final decision for Earth's religious future not to take place between Rome and Mecca, symbolic representatives of monotheist religions, but between Jerusalem and Varanasi (Benares), holy cities of the judaeo-christian and the hinduistic belief systems and images of man. Perhaps this process has already begun. But chances are that all religions will take on elements of "civil religions", the "cult of the athlete" being one of them.

NOTES AND REFERENCES

1. This text integrates the contents of two papers, "Religion and sport" and "Sport and the Olympics by sociological definition: a modern social institution and an eternal festival of rituals", presented by the author at the Quebec City International Symposium.

2. In the eyes of some Europeans, *e.g.*, North Americans are judged to have no clear concept of religion, but strict public morals, whereas Latin Americans may appear deeply religious, but lacking in morals.

3. Loy JW, McPherson BD, Kenyon G (1978) Sport and social systems. Reading: Addison-Wesley p 302

4. Ibid

5. Sage GH (1981) Sport and religion. In Lüschen G, Sage GH (eds) Handbook of social science of sport. Champaign: Stipes p 147-59

6. Ibid

7. Coakley JJ (1986) Sport in society. St-Louis: Times Mirror/Mosby p 321

8. Durkheim E (1970) Regeln der soziologischen Methode. Berlin: Neuwied p 100

9. Schülein JA (1987) Theorie der Institution. Opladen: Westdeutscher Verlag p 31-116

10. Hertzler JO (1946) Social institutions. Lincoln: [inc.] p 4

11. Gehlen A (1975) Urmensch und Spätkultur. Frankfurt: [inc.] p 8, 23, 67

12. Luhmann, as quoted in Schülein JA (1987) op cit p 101 ff

13. Edwards H (1973) Sociology of Sport. Homewood: The Dorsey Press p 84 ff; Loy JW, McPherson BD, Kenyon G (1978) op cit p 14 ff, 379 ff; Lüschen G, Sage GH (1981) (eds) Handbook of social science of sport. Champaign: Stipes p 6 f; Weis K (1976) Abweichung und Konformität in der Institution Sport. In Lüschen G, Weis K (eds) Die Soziologie des Sports. Neuwied: Luchterhand Verlag p 296-315

14. Weis K (1990) Sport in society, sociology and journals: missing perspectives and cultural idiosyncrasies in an international social institution. International Review for the Sociology of Sport 25 p 19, 23-25

15. Riordan J (1986) State and sport in developing societies. International Review for the Sociology of Sport 21 287-303

16. Eichberg H (1984) Olympic sport. Neocolonization and alternatives. International Review for the Sociology of Sport 19 97-106

17. Guttmann A (1978) From ritual to record: the nature of modern sports. New York: Columbia University Press

18. Weis K (1991) Ritual. In Reinhold G (ed) Soziologie-Lexikon. München: Oldenbourg Verlag p 486-90

19. Morris D (1981) Das Spiel. Faszination und Ritual des Fussballs. München: Droemersche Verlagsanstalt [translation of Morris D (1981) The soccer tribe. London: Jonathan Cape]

20. van Gennep A (1986) Übergangsriten. Frankfurt: Campus Verlag p 70 ff, 183 ff

21. Turner VW (1979) Betwixt and between: the liminal period in rites de passage. In Lessa WA, Vogt EZ (eds) Reader in comparative religion. New York: Harper & Row p 234-43

22. Ibid p 235

23. Goodger J (1986) Ritual solidarity and sport. Acta Sociologica 29 219-24

24. Durkheim E (1965) The elementary forms of the religious life. New York: The Free Press p 466

25. Bellah RN (1967) Civil religion in America. Daedalus 96 1-21

26. Weis K (1990) Das Gottesbild oder Die Frage: Wer schafft sich wen nach wessen Bilde? In Brauers J (ed) Mein Gottesbild. München: Nymphenburger p 329-45

27. Bernett H (1978) Der jüdische Sport im nationalsozialistischen Deutschland 1933-1938. Schorndorf: Hofmann p 38 ff, 119 ff

28. Pfister G (1989) Die Rolle der jüdischen Frauen in der Turn- und Sportbewegung (1900-1933). In Lämmer M (ed) Die jüdische Turn- und Sportbewegung in Deutschland 1898-1938. Sankt Augustin: Academia Verlag Richarz p 65-89

29. Seppänen P (1988) Competitive sport and sport success in the Olympic Games: a cross-cultural analysis of value systems. Paper presented at the Seoul Olympic Scientific Congress p 2

30. Ibid

31. Seppänen P (1976) Die Rolle des Leistungssports in den Gesellschaften der Welt. In Lüschen G, Weis K (eds) Die Soziologie des Sports. Neuwied: Luchterhand Verlag p 87-100; Seppänen P (1981) Olympic success: a cross-national perspective. In Lüschen G, Sage GH (eds) Handbook of social science of sport. Champaign: Stipes p 93-116

32. Coubertin P de (1966) Der Olympische Gedanke. Reden und Aufsätze. Stuttgart: Olympischer Sport-Verlag p 150

33. Lämmer M (1990) Die Olympische Idee Im Wandel. In Evangelische Akademie Bad Boll (ed) Gold für Olympia—Symposium zu Fragen der Olympischen Idee. Protokolldienst 16/90, p 3-15

34. Herms E (1990) Der religiöse Sinn der Olympischen Idee. In Evangelische Akademie Bad Boll (ed) Gold für Olympia—Symposium zu Fragen der Olympischen Idee. Protokolldienst 16/90, p 26-46

35. Coubertin P de (1966) op cit p 127

36. Coubertin P de (1966) op cit p 153

37. Coubertin P de (1966) op cit p 144

38. Coubertin P de (1966) op cit p 135

39. Herms E (1990) op cit p 36

40. Coubertin P de (1966) op cit p 133

41. Durkheim E (1965) op cit p 455

42. Haack FW (1991) Europas neue Religion. Zürich: Orell-Füssli Verlag p 190

Sport and Educational Values:
New Stakes as the Year 2000 Draws Near

Valeurs éducatives du sport:
les enjeux de l'an 2000

Valeurs éducatives du sport:
les enjeux de l'an 2000

En guise d'introduction, l'auteur explique ce qu'il entend par le concept de valeurs. Il s'agit en l'occurrence des standards à l'aide desquels divers comportements sont observés, comparés, puis approuvés ou désapprouvés comme étant désirables ou pas, corrects ou incorrects, méritoires ou non. Dans cette perspective, tout changement marqué dans un schème de valeurs revêt une importance spéciale en ce sens que les structures sociales et les liens existants entre les sous-ensembles qui les constituent, incluant le phénomène du sport, en sont directement affectés. L'auteur donne par la suite des exemples de valeurs qui sont considérées comme étant intrinsèques au sport, telles que le fair-play, l'honnêteté et l'intégrité personnelle. En rappelant le cas Ben Johnson, l'auteur avance que les valeurs intrinsèques traditionnelles se voient souvent doublées par des valeurs accessoires comme le prestige et le profit personnel. Il souligne que le degré de moralité que l'on accorde à un comportement humain donné dépend par ailleurs dans une large mesure de la conception que l'on a de la formation et de l'éducation des personnes concernées. Les valeurs ne sont donc pas des notions abstraites, mais plutôt des balises qui servent à guider l'activité individuelle et collective dans la vie. L'auteur avance par la suite qu'en cette fin du XXe siècle, des changements importants dans les schèmes de valeurs sont en train de s'effectuer. En gros, l'on semble assister au passage d'une vision ethnocentrique du monde à une autre, fort différente cette fois, que l'auteur qualifie de bio- ou d'égocentrique. Dans la première grande division de son texte, l'auteur brosse un tableau historique des changements qui sont survenus dans l'orientation des schèmes de valeurs : – l'égocentrisme, apparenté à la vision typiquement grecque de faire servir le sport à la poursuite de l'excellence et au développement harmonieux de la personne ; – le biocentrisme, selon lequel le sport et l'éducation physique sont justifiés sur la base de leurs contributions à la croissance et au développement physiques de l'individu ainsi qu'au bien-être et à la santé générale ; – l'ethnocentrisme, selon lequel les schèmes de valeur, principalement dans le sport d'élite, semblent carrément orientés en fonction d'objectifs collectifs ; – l'anthropocentrisme selon lequel on s'occupe de la promotion de valeurs associées aux pratiques sportives avec un souci particulier de protection des ressources et de l'environnement. Dans la deuxième division majeure de sa présentation, l'auteur traite de la neutralité du sport en tant qu'instrument de formation de la personne et de promotion de la culture. Le sport et la compétition, en eux-mêmes, ne sont ni bons, ni mauvais ; ils ont le potentiel de générer des retombées positives, comme aussi d'avoir des effets négatifs. L'auteur présente par la suite quelques-unes des raisons qui sont souvent données pour illustrer les valeurs du sport et de la compétition. Il décrit également ce que plusieurs considèrent comme une place et un pouvoir exagérés qu'a le sport de haute performance à l'échelle internationale. Il souligne au passage le rôle ambigu que les mass media ont joué en permettant d'une part au spectacle de se manifester et d'occuper beaucoup de place dans tous les coins du monde, et de l'autre, en restant en symbiose si étroite avec le pouvoir financier. Dans la troisième partie de sa présentation, l'auteur brosse un tableau des changements qui à l'aube du troisième millénaire se profilent dans les valeurs éducatives associées au sport. Ces derniers gravitent selon lui autour des pôles suivants : – une emphase nouvelle sur les besoins de l'individu ainsi que sur les principes de l'égalité et de l'équité, entre autres en ce qui a trait au favoritisme racial et à la construction sociale des sexes ; – la recherche consciente d'expériences personnelles optimales susceptibles de contribuer au bien-être ; – une évolution des programmes éducatifs et de formation de cadres encore plus axés sur les talents individuels et la créativité ; – enfin, en ce qui a trait au sport d'élite, une diminution du nationalisme primaire et une meilleure appréciation, par les spectateurs en général, des déterminants et des exigences de la haute performance sportive. De l'avis de l'auteur, ces changements progressifs sont susceptibles de contribuer à promouvoir les aspects de l'idéologie olympique qui visent à la promotion du respect mutuel entre pays et nations. En guise de conclusion, l'auteur souligne que toutes les personnes qui forment le tissu social, jeunes, parents, éducateurs, athlètes, entraîneurs, administrateurs et politiciens, ont une part de responsabilité dans l'évolution des schèmes de valeurs vers les expressions et les significations nouvelles décrites. Il invite d'une manière toute particulière les spécialistes de l'activité physique à s'engager dans le processus et à contribuer au mouvement, car l'enjeu, pour l'avenir du sport comme pour celui de leur profession, est lourd de conséquences.

Sport and Educational Values:
New Stakes as the Year 2000 Draws Near

R. Gerald Glassford

In the broadest sense values are considered to be the standards (whether cultural or personal) by which behaviors "are compared and approved or disapproved relative to one another—held to be relatively desirable or undesirable, more meritorious or less, more or less correct[1]". A shift in values is one of the most significant types of societal changes for when systems of values change, societal structures, social systems and therefore sports are impacted.

Fair play, honesty and integrity are examples of intrinsic values that most people associate with the world of sport. The recent coverage of the Ben Johnson case bears evidence that these intrinsic values can be superseded by instrumental ones such as prestige and an external reward system. The use of banned substances by athletes breaches an intrinsic value structure; it strikes at the heart of long-standing values held to be true in sport. One is reminded that moral behaviors are products of systems of training and education. Values, whether intrinsic or extrinsic/instrumental are not simply abstract notions; they are the maps and compasses that guide actions throughout life. Whether sports have intrinsic or instrumental value or both depends in part upon the education and training the participant has received. This point was made by Csikszentmihalyi when he noted that "[. . .] the social context determines which aspects of [sports] are valued and attended to[2]".

As the 20th century draws to a close a shift in values as they apply to sport has become evident. The balance is shifting from what has been fundamentally an ethnocentric world view pervaded by the instrumental values of external reward structures for the athletes and their country (which produced the win-at-all-cost mentality), toward a more individual biocentric/egocentric value orientation focussing on fair-play, honesty, equality, and integrity.

1890
1990

R. Gerald Glassford, Faculty of Physical Education and Recreation, University of Alberta, Edmonton, Alberta, Canada.

Value Orientations: an Historical Context

Shifts in sport value orientation have been chronicled[3] into four broad classes some of which emphasize intrinsic value orientations and some others the instrumental values that can be attributed to sport.

1– *Egocentrism* as a value orientation in sport. Early Greek athletics was based on beauty, harmony, personal excellence, and the totally integrated development of the mind-body unity. Egocentric value orientation places a strong emphasis on these virtues but it also incorporates the intrinsic values of honesty, fair-play and sportsmanship, personal effort, initiative and courage. By definition, the individual is of primary importance. The essence of this value orientation was considered to be at the basis of the sport programs of the English public schools at the end of the 19th century and it was the perceived importance of these principles that Pierre de Coubertin intended to inculcate into his formulated structure of modern olympism.

2– *Biocentrism* as a value orientation. A number of physical education systems which placed an emphasis on the natural developmental/learning processes were created during the 19th and early 20th centuries. Games, play, sport and physical activity patterns were developed to match the naturally occurring growth and development stages as well as the learning readiness of the individual. The promotion of well-being and of health through participation in appropriately structured games, sport and movement programs was central in this value orientation.

3– *Ethnocentrism* as a value orientation. When the salient reason for sport is to promote city, state or nation; where political goals are superimposed over those of the individual athlete, one can consider the ethnocentric value orientation to occupy central stage. The flying of the flags of nations, the singing of national anthems and the publishing of national medal totals is a clear indication of the presence of this value within major sports festivals.

4– *Anthropocentrism* as a value orientation. Within the last few decades people have begun to place a higher value on the protection of the physical environment and to recognize the influence that the human species has had and is having on it. The result has been that we are interpreting and considering the earth more closely in terms of human values, activities and behavior. The values espoused by the Club of Rome and the Greenpeace movement are on the ascendancy. This shift has had only minimal direct impact on the practice of sport but this may change as a heightened concern develops for land, water and air uses and abuses. Already the creation of new ski hills and the scheduling of ski competitions within Canada's national parks has been affected by concerns for the parkland's environmental integrity. Sports, which bring people into touch with nature in environmentally sound ways will be on the ascendancy in the third millennium. From an instrumental perspective, sports will serve to provide a "high touch" counterpoint for a "high tech" society[4].

Sport and Competition: the Good and the Bad

Neither sport nor competition are inherently good or bad. Each contains within it the potential to generate positive, beneficial outcomes or negative, damaging results. Many have been inspired by an outstanding athletic performance, others have stood to applaud as champions received recognition for their accomplishments. Sport can provide appropriate conditions and learning environments for potential talent to be developed. The quest for excellence is unusually well catered to in sport. If sport is stripped to its essence and one asks why people participate in an activity that does not produce direct, economically viable goods, one is left with the following elements: —it is fun, enjoyable, personally satisfying; —it provides a release for the need for movement; —it allows to test the limits of strength, skill, endurance, speed in fair and equitable contest; —it offers a time and space bound opportunity to create and experience aesthetically pleasing movement. These are positive, socially acceptable reasons for valuing sport and competition. But there have been downsides to the ways in which sport has been used. Perhaps it started with rule codification which for most sports occurred late in the 1800s. This evolution, accompanied by greatly enhanced technologies for measuring outcome, helped to move sport to the world stage. Interclub, interschool, interuniversity, international sport competitions became stages on which the best competed. The prestige and recognition that accrued to club, school, university, nation, and political system grew in importance. People came to worship the top level athletes for the reflected glory they brought. Outstanding results yielded outstanding rewards. Increasingly, sport was rationalized. In turn, this led to an international athlete ethos driven by an external reward system. High value was assigned to *the result* and this became a primary reinforcer for nations, coaches, athletes[5]. Psychologist Csikszentmihalyi offered this comment:

> By objectifying incentives into money and status, societies have developed a rational, universal motivational system whereby communities can produce desired behaviors predictably and can allot precisely differentiated rewards to construct a complex, social hierarchy. The standardisation of external rewards, and the general acceptance of their value by most members of society, has created the "homo economicus" responsive to the laws of supply and demand and the "homo sociologicus" who is kept within bounds by the network of social control[6].

In the spirit of self-interest the media have played a role of considerable importance in facilitating the emergence of this powerful ethnocentric value structure. The beautiful yet simplistic drama of the sport spectacle, a drama which purports to produce clear results in superbly contested athletic events, provided the print and electronic media an almost perfect fit. It was time and space bound, there was a high level of uncertainty of outcome and the audiences identified with the contestants by dint of nationalism or as a consequence of careful marketing. Audiences the world over tuned into the media's coverage of major sports events. The quality of sport performances spiralled upward—a rising level of performance being necessary for continuing success[7]—accompanied by a parallel spiral of up-front costs. The media, through a symbiotic gesture, began to provide substantial financial help to offset the rising costs. Some of this money eventually reached the athletes and the external reward system thus took on new meaning. The business world expression, "the bottom line", became a powerful part of the sport value structure. The more money the media invested in elite sport, the more control they commanded and demanded. What had started as a symbiotic relationship increasingly became parasitic, and today, it endangers the host. High performance sport has become a spectacle, a symbol of national/political prestige; it has come to represent a value system that thrives on results. Ethnocentric values have come to dominate the intrinsic values of egocentrism. Athletes are prepared to do whatever is necessary to win. Fair play, honesty, integrity, and equality are de-emphasized.

Today there seems to be a groundswell of change that may move some sports from this instrumental, ethnocentric orientation, back toward the intrinsic values of fair play, honesty, integrity, equality. This shift is being generated by an interactive effect of several factors or forces identified as "megatrends". One of these trends has been labelled a "renaissance in the arts", a spiritual quest where people use their leisure time to "explore what it means to be human[8]", where aesthetic appreciation of the visual and performing arts is esteemed for their intrinsic values. When this trend is for example linked to an increase in spiritual awareness, the rise of women as leaders, and to the growing recognition that it is the individual who is of critical importance[9] (not the bureaucracy or the corporation), it then appears that the stage is set for a significant value reorientation. The term "personal empowerment" succinctly expresses this re-orientation.

Educational Value Shifts—the 3rd Millennium

Individualism/Equality

> The great unifying theme at the conclusion of the 20th century is the triumph of the individual. Threatened by totalitarianism for much of this century, individuals are meeting the millennium more powerful than ever before[10].

It seems paradoxical that at a time when society is moving toward a global economy, the role of the individual is more important than ever. A new era of "mattering" has been entered: "I matter". "What I do matters". "What I say matters".

The choice of the individual to act or not act takes the form of a value statement. Personal empowerment is the phrase used to describe the doctrine of individual responsibility. Embedded in this trend is the value of equality (equity) which carries into the spotlight the current issues surrounding gender equity and racial equity.

Educational Values, Gender and Sport

If the content analysis carried out by Naisbitt[11] is accurate, the 1990s will be a decade during which women will increasingly assume leadership roles. Despite the fact that participation levels by women in sport have been moving upwards, data from both Canada and the United States indicate that women are significantly underrepresented in coaching and administrative roles. Among all divisions in the NCAA, only about 15% of the women's intercollegiate athletic programs are headed by female athletic directors, and there has been a decline in the number of female coaches in the United States since 1972[12]. In Canada, special internship programs for aspiring female sport administrators were created as one part of strategy to address the current inequality, but the situation remains little changed from the early 1980s. Macintosh and Beamish found that, while women were well represented at the lower administrative levels, they were underrepresented at the higher levels[13]. More specifically, their data indicate that among 70 national sport organizations approximately 50% of program coordinators, 23% of technical directors, and less than 10% of national coaches were women. Hall, Cullen and Slack have presented an analysis of the gender structure of national sport organizations in Canada[14]. They have shown how the gender structure of organizations is characterized by power relations which subject and control sexuality in a range of ways. Gender equity and true individual valuation will not come easily to sport or to sport organizations. It has been a male dominated domain virtually since the emergence of modern sport. The broad social trends toward increased involvement of women in leadership roles and the "triumph of the individual" will create an internal pressure for change within the sport subculture[15]. And change will occur. Two additional critical questions: "will current sport leaders value the change and treat it proactively; will our educational system and curriculum be adjusted where gender bias exists?"

Educational Values, Race and Sport

Over the course of the last half century the integration of races (particularly the black in North America) has significantly improved. Unfortunately, racial barriers continue to exist and are resistant to change. In a study released by the Miller Brewing Company[16] only 52% of a sample of 1 300 Americans disagreed that sports were free of racism. Blacks were as likely to disagree as whites. In Canada, aboriginal people also have limited opportunities to participate in sport programs. A major stake which continues to be at risk is the need to create a sport environment where full citizenship and equal opportunity exist for all, regardless of colour or creed. The microcosmic nature of sport suits it to changes in equity of opportunity for women and for minority groups or participants of different races. But is there a genuine will to change from a white, male dominated operation to one which operates on the value of equity?

Personal Empowerment and "Flow"

No sport can shape a person's character in a single direction, for good or for evil. Every sport contains the possibility of being misused, of fostering alienation, competition, aggression, and escape. On the other hand, every sport can provide the ecstatic, growth-producing experience of flow[17].

What is "flow" and how does it relate to sport and educational values as the third millennium draws nearer. The idea of "flow" was developed by Csikszentmihalyi[18] who has coined the term to describe a state of optimal experience. It emerges as a

[...] result of observing and interviewing people who expended much time and energy on activities that provided few extrinsic rewards such as money or recognition [...] Their answer suggested a common set of characteristics that constituted a feeling of enjoyment, well-being and competence which distinguished their particular involvement from the less satisfying events common to most of everyday life. Since the activity usually did not seem to be motivated by external rewards, it is safe to assume that it is *the quality of the subjective experience itself* that motivates the behavior[19].

Sports provide an ideal environment in which these highly individualistic, personally empowering experiences can emerge. In sport, it is relatively easy to match abilities with challenges so that the participant can test their limits and incrementally extend themselves beyond them. The sheer joy of participation, the process of involvement is most important. A second characteristic of flow is that there is a sharp focus on the goal and immediate knowledge of how well one is doing relative to the goal. Because of this close relationship, it is easier for the participant to develop a strongly focussed perspective, to become totally involved, to be at one with the activity. The intensity of this concentration means that the activity becomes the total world, a world within which one's self-concept is allowed to expand. "This momentary expansion of one's being leads to a self-concept enriched by new achievements and a stronger confidence[20]". Once into the flow experience, the athlete has a sense of empowerment, of being in control and the activity becomes intrinsically rewarding.

Sport is an activity where "flow" readily occurs but the strong focus on instrumental values, particularly those applied to elite sport, tends to diminish it. Brettschneider[21] has found that sports which emphasize an immediate physical experience of body and soul awareness, sports involving self-discovery are already on the rise in the German sports clubs which he studied. A means to successfully encourage the intrinsic values of the flow experience may lie in matching the individual's competence level with environmental challenges[22,23]. Wankel and Sefton[24] found that young athletes were most intrinsically motivated when their sport experiences emphasized skill development and where challenges were realistically matched to ability level. While their subjects responded that game outcome was important, it ranked well behind the demonstration of personal ability or competence and a perception that one has played well, as features of a game that were prized. Scanlan, Stein and Ravizza[25] echo the importance of the value of perceived competence in their study of sources of enjoyment among elite figure skaters. The flow experience—the physical act of skating—was ranked highly on the enjoyment scale. Does this suggest that one should dispense with competition? Clearly not. It is not competition per se that is "good" or "bad", it is not what is done but how it is done that is important. The relentless focus upon the outcome of the competition—the win at all costs ethic—has produced major value/ethical stresses. This need not happen. Arnold argues that

> What [...] is needed in the sphere of sport, no less than other areas of the curriculum, is that pupils perceive what is required of them. If [people] are able to see what it is to act honestly, fairly, bravely, resolutely and generously while in competition they are more likely to be impressed by such acts than by a discussion of them[26].

Curricular Changes

The designs of programs of study of sport in its broadest sense will change in the next decade, and the change will be toward the creation of a heightened appreciation of the natural growth and development, learning readiness stages. The fostering of individual talent through appropriately formulated and favourable learning conditions is of critical importance. A thoughtfully presented document entitled *Developing Talent in Young People* extends the case that there is a potential talent in most humans to attain "[...] an unusually high level of demonstrated ability, achievement, or skill in some special field of study or interest" and that "[...] the development of both excellence and standards of excellence in society is dependent on the extent to which there are opportunities and encouragement for individuals to find meaning and enjoyment in one or more areas and fields of development[27]". Some principles for curriculum building to enhance biocentric values would include: – identifying the early, middle and later phases of development and carefully set out the curriculum elements that are best included in each stage; – make the sport curriculum in the early childhood stage child-centered, not content-centered; – help the student/athlete to set goals and to identify what needs to be done to achieve them; – teach values, morals, ethics by example (model), by instruction and reinforcement—they are not acquired by osmosis; – create a positive, supportive environment for each athlete.

An interesting experiment by Traill has been carried out in Australia where "flow" experiences together with a balanced focus on competition, skill development, participation and a stress on the values of fair play and good sportsmanship have been blended into a new sports program called "Aussie Sport[28]". Traill found that by providing all children "[...] with the opportunity to participate in appropriate sporting activities at the right level for each child's stage of development" she was able to increase the levels of participation fivefold in the first year. The response patterns by both boys and girls were similar with respect to levels of enjoyment and perceived success. The empowerment of the individual, attention to "flow" experiences, matching skill requirements to the child's stage of development, permitting competence to enhance self-confidence (in short, a program built on a biocentric value orientation) produced a major change in the responses of 10 to 12 year olds of both sexes. The report by Justice Charles Dubin on the use of banned substances by Canadian athletes will almost certainly focus attention on the importance of the teaching of values, morals, and ethics in sport programs. A draft document *Fair Play for Kids*[29] (the Commission for Fair Play, 1990) has been produced in Canada. In its final form, it is planned to be included in the elementary school curriculum. Similar materials are planned for the coaching certification programs. The importance of moral/ethical education in sports and in school curricula has been made clear in studies by Arnold[30] and Bredemeier[31]. Good moral and ethical behavior results from training in each day's microchallenges that are ideally produced in the play and sport environment. Separate courses on ethics and morality are not necessarily needed. Experiences and models which reinforce ethical behaviors on a daily basis are more appropriate.

Global Economy and Internationalism

Major changes in the international economic structure cannot help but alter the values that affect sport. As the Cold War thaws and the year of the proposed European economic unification approaches, the strident nationalism that has dominated international sport may lose some of its virulence. This does not mean that pride in the performance of athletes from one's country will or should diminish. Rather, the excessive emphasis on outcome could be superseded by a balanced appreciation of what athletes must do to achieve excellence. Perhaps the Olympic Games may more closely approach the ideology proposed by Coubertin. For him the Games symbolized peace among nations; his vision is reflected in the charter which states that one of the purposes of the Olympic Movement is to help building a better and more peaceful world.

Through sport, it is possible to develop a mutual respect among people and nations. This seemed simply a dream but events unfolding now suggest that the world has never been closer to what McLuhan termed "the global village" than it is today. Through heightened awareness, an appreciation of and respect for the individuality and nationality of other athletes can be developed. Tolerance, as an educational value, will be more critical in an era of global economy and internationalism. If this value is ignored, there will be a rise in the level of ethnoviolence. Coubertin's olympic ideology is not hollow musings. Even in the face of political scandals and boycotts athletes surveyed by Denbeck believe that they are at the Olympic Games "[...] to compete and to develop friendships among the athletes of different countries [...] [they] still believe in the original purpose of the Olympic Games [friendship, unity and world peace][32]". Valuing all that is positive in the qualities of the cultures of other countries is equally important. The promotion of education values such as tolerance and empathy for others can be taught through sport. Frey and Allen[33] found that students gained in awareness, tolerance and understanding of Alaskan aboriginal people when native sports and games were taught in the curriculum. In Great Britain a similar strategy has been applied in an attempt to encourage the development of "empathy" among children. Naisbitt has described a trend toward a global economy and a global lifestyle but he also noted the paradoxical need for people to retain traditional cultural linkages. Here in Canada we will continue to value multiculturalism. Québec and the Québécois rightly press on for a status as a distinct society. Sport remains an excellent vehicle through which to teach tolerance and an appreciation of the importance of differences in other athletes, peoples, nations and cultures.

So what is at Stake?

Sport in itself is not value laden but it is an excellent vehicle to teach values. What is taught through sport depends on the emphasis educators, coaches, parents tend to give it. What is emphasized is in turn dependent upon the values society at large holds. And all are cogs in the wheel of this system—everyone from politicians, bureaucrats, educators, coaches, parents and participants contribute to the value orientation which sport enhances. As the millennium approaches, a shift in value orientation appears to have begun. The power of the individual and personal responsibility are on the ascendancy and touch everything from international politics to the economic concerns related to our physical environment. Sport is not immune to this shift. Outcomes/results, no matter how achieved, are not enough any longer. The process counts again. Many athletes have chosen to pursue athleticism within a value system that champions integrity, honesty, fair play. The list is long but the name Dave Steen comes quickly to mind. What is at stake during this decade is sport as sport rather than sport as entertainment, as a profession. Educators must look carefully at curricula and programs offered. If they are not altered to reflect the growing attraction of people to sports which emphasize the "flow" experiences, if they do not include the intrinsic/egocentric values that appear to be dominant in the shift to a new balance, if they are not attuned to the importance of biocentrism and the natural stages of development, program contents then become seriously at odds with what a growing number of participants expect. If that becomes the case, the rationale for services in sport may come into question. In the end one is left with the realization that each person has the responsibility and the power to make of sport what one wills and to take from it what one wants. The values of tolerance, equality, fair play, honesty, courage can be made to be valued above all else. We are attending this conference to pay tribute to the father of the Olympic Games and to honor the hundredth anniversary of his visit to North America. There can hardly be a better concluding statement on values than that made by Coubertin himself:

> The important thing in the Olympic Games is not to win but to take part. The important thing in life is not the triumph but the struggle. The essential thing is not to have conquered but to have fought well.

NOTES AND REFERENCES

1. Johnson HM (1960) Sociology: A systematic introduction. New York: Harcourt, Brace and World p 49

2. Csikszentmihalyi M (1990) What good are sports? Reflections on the psychological outcomes of physical performance. Paper presented at the Commonwealth and International Conference of Physical Education, Sport, Health, Dance, Recreation and Leisure. Auckland, New Zealand p 24

3. Glassford G, Redmond G (1979) Physical education and sport in modern times. In Zeigler EF (ed) History of physical education and sport. New Jersey: Prentice Hall p 103-170

4. Naisbitt J (1982) Megatrends. New York: Warner

5. MacIntosh PC (1983) Universities and sport. Paper presented at the FISU/CESU Universiade Conference. Edmonton Canada

6. Csikszentmihalyi M (1975) Beyond boredom and anxiety. San Francisco: Jossey-Bass p 2

7. Heinilä K (1982) The totalization process in international sport. In Ilmarinen M (ed) Sport and international understanding. Berlin: Springer-Verlag p 21-46

8. Naisbitt J, Aburdene P (1990) Megatrends 2000: ten new directions for the 1990's. New York: Morrow p 63

9. Naisbitt (1982) identified, as a megatrend, the movement from institutional help to self-help which began during the 1970s. After decades of reliance on corporations, bureaucracies and institutions North Americans began to reassert the value of being an individual.

10. Naisbitt J, Aburdene P (1990) op cit p 298

11. Ibid

12. Knoppers A (1989) Coaching: an equal opportunity occupation? Journal of Physical Education, Recreation and Dance 50 38-43

13. Macintosh D, Beamish R (1988) Socio-economic and demographic characteristics of national sport administrators. Canadian Journal of Sport Science 13 66-72

14. Hall MA, Cullen D, Slack T (1989) Organizational elites recreating themselves: the gender structure of national sport organizations. Quest 41 28-45

15. Greendorfer SH (1981) Sport and the mass media. In Lüschen G, Sage GH (eds) Handbook of social science of sport. Champaign: Stipes p 160-80

16. Miller Lite Report on American attitudes toward sports (1983) Milwaukee: Miller Brewing Company

17. Csikszentmihalyi M (1990) op cit p 24

18. Csikszentmihalyi M (1975) op cit

19. Csikszentmihalyi M (1990) op cit p 17

20. Ibid p 21

21. Brettschneider WD (1989) Youth, youth culture and youth sports—a challenge for sport studies. International Journal of Physical Education 26 22-28

22. Traill RD (1989) A national sports program for children—the Australian experience with "aussie sports". International Journal of Physical Education 26 (2) 35-37 and 26 (3) 33-35

23. Wankel LM, Sefton JM (1989) A season-long investigation of fun in youth sports. Sports and Exercise Psychology 11 355-66. The value of linking appropriately tailored sport activity to the individual's natural state of development has long been recognized by many physical educators.

24. Ibid p 364

25. Scanlan TK, Stein GL, Ravizza K (1989) An in-depth study of former elite figure skaters: II, sources of enjoyment. Journal of Sport and Exercise Pschology II 65-83

26. Arnold PJ (1989) Competitive sport, winning, and education. Journal of Moral Education 18 p 23

27. Bloom BS (ed) (1985) Developing talent in young people. New York: Ballantine p 5-6

28. Traill RD (1989) op cit p 35

29. Government of Canada (1990) Fair play for kids: a resource manual. Ottawa: Government of Canada

30. Arnold PJ (1989) op cit

31. Bredemeier BJ, Shields DL, Weiss MR et al (1986) The relationship of sport involvement with children's moral reasoning anf aggression tendencies. Journal of Sport Psychology 8 304-18

32. Denbeck DJ (1986) A comparison of the United States olympic athletes concerning political involvement in the Olympic Games. In Redmond G (ed) Sport and politics. Champaign: Human Kinetics p 181

33. Frey RD, Allen M (1989) Alaskan Native games—a cross-cultural addition to the physical education curriculum. Journal of Physical Education, Recreation and Dance 60 21-24

Gratitude is extended to Jeanine Glassford for her assistance in the preparation of this paper.

Valeurs éducatives du sport:
les enjeux de l'an 2000

En toile de fond de son allocution, l'auteure rappelle les valeurs qui sont au fondement même de l'UNESCO. Ces valeurs ont trait tant au processus d'acquisition et de développement de connaissances qu'aux personnes, aux sociétés, et aux relations internationales concernées. L'approche scientifique de la réalité, le respect de la dignité humaine, le respect des droits de l'homme, le civisme pacifique, la conscience de l'interdépendance des nations sont ainsi évoquées. Dans cet ensemble de valeurs, le respect de la dignité de la vie est posé comme valeur universellement défendable, comme *sine qua non* de toute entreprise éducative. Dans la seconde partie de son exposé, l'auteure souligne les effets que les changements sociaux actuels peuvent avoir sur la qualité de l'éducation morale, par le biais de leur impact sur les institutions traditionnellement en charge de cette éducation: la famille, l'école, l'église, et le sport. À propos de ce dernier, l'auteure mentionne le rôle que la pratique sportive a joué, aux quatre coins du monde, auprès des populations d'acteurs et de spectateurs. Le fair-play, qui incorpore littéralement le respect de la dignité de la vie, devrait être considéré comme le principal message éducatif véhiculé par le biais du sport. L'auteure rappelle ici que l'UNESCO décerne annuellement le trophée international de fair-play Pierre de Coubertin aux individus ou groupes qui méritent une reconnaissance internationale à cet égard. Mais les signaux d'alarme vont croissant en provenance de la scène sportive. La compétition, dit l'auteure, ne peut avoir de valeur éducative — dans la tentative d'explorer ses propres limites — qu'en autant que l'esprit du fair-play soit respecté, sous peine de basculer dans l'excès de la victoire à tout prix. La médiatisation du sport, particulièrement du sport professionnel, est au cœur du problème. L'auteure pose alors la question de la reconciliation difficile entre, d'une part, l'implacabilité du spectacle sportif et, d'autre part, les facettes du sport qui encouragent au respect de la dignité de la vie. L'auteure ne voit de solution que dans l'évolution inéluctable des systèmes économique et médiatique actuels par le truchement de la créativité et de la volonté caractéristiques de l'être humain. La question dc fond, conclut l'auteure, demeure celle de la promotion d'un sport humaniste, par le développement et la transmission de notions d'éthique sportive dans les programmes de formation et d'éducation destinés aux spécialistes de l'éducation, aux dirigeants sportifs bénévoles ainsi qu'aux journalistes de sport.

Valeurs éducatives du sport: les enjeux de l'an 2000

Breda Pavlic

C'est avec joie que j'ai accepté de contribuer à titre personnel aux objectifs du Symposium en proposant quelques réflexions sur les valeurs éducatives du sport. J'aborde néanmoins le sujet en toute modestie. D'abord, parce que je ne suis pas une experte en matière d'éducation physique et de sport; ensuite je ne me reconnais aucun mérite en ces sujets si ce n'est un goût de longue date pour les randonnées, la natation, le ski, le tennis et l'équitation. Ma formation et mes quelques vingt ans d'expérience professionnelle se situent plutôt dans les domaines de la sociologie et de la communication, dont treize ans d'enseignement universitaire. Mais c'est de bon gré et en toute sincérité que je voudrais dire quelques mots sur le sport comme moyen d'éducation — d'éducation morale. Je crois profondément dans les idéaux de l'UNESCO, que j'ai l'honneur de servir actuellement; il me semble donc approprié et utile de revoir les liens qui existent entre le sport et l'éducation morale dans le contexte social actuel et dans la perspective de la décennie qui vient de commencer.

Quelques propos sur les valeurs morales

De façon générale, on peut dire que les valeurs socio-culturelles et morales d'une société (ou, si l'on préfère, les valeurs éducatives au sens large du mot éducation) représentent ce qui est posé comme vrai, beau, bien, d'un point de vue personnel ou selon les vues de la majorité et qui est donné comme un idéal à atteindre, comme quelque chose à défendre. Elles sont transmises par des institutions fondamentales dans chaque société: la famille, l'école, l'église (ou milieu religieux), les institutions culturelles (les livres, théâtres, musées, etc.), le sport et — particulièrement dans la société industrialisée — les médias et le marché. Ces institutions sont d'habitude *complémentaires* dans leurs rôles de transmetteurs de valeurs aux individus, mais elles peuvent être aussi en *compétition* entre elles, voire en *conflit* plus ou moins évident.

1890
1990

Breda Pavlic, Représentante de l'UNESCO au Canada, Bureau de liaison de Québec, Québec, Canada.

Les valeurs morales/éducatives, selon l'UNESCO[1], peuvent se grouper ainsi:

1– *Valeurs sociales*: coopération, droiture, amabilité, piété filiale, justice sociale, respect pour les autres, esprit civique, sens de la responsabilité, respect pour la dignité humaine, les droits de l'homme, la dignité du travail, etc.;

2– *Valeurs se rapportant à l'individu*: véracité, honnêteté, discipline, tolérance, sens de l'ordre, paix de l'esprit, désir de se perfectionner, etc.;

3– *Valeurs se rapportant au pays et au monde*: patriotisme, conscience nationale, civisme pacifique, compréhension internationale, fraternité humaine, conscience de l'interdépendance des nations, etc.;

4– *Valeurs de processus*: approche scientifique de la réalité, discernement, recherche de la vérité, réflexion, etc.

De toutes ces valeurs, les philosophes-humanistes sont unanimes à souligner que la valeur la plus élevée doit être rattachée à la *dignité de la vie*, considérée comme critère universel. Il ne saurait y avoir de valeur plus grande que la dignité de la vie, et «toute tentative, qu'elle soit religieuse ou sociale, de donner une valeur supérieure à toute autre chose conduit obligatoirement à l'oppression de l'humanité[2]». Car la dignité de la vie, faut-il le rappeler, incorpore le respect d'autrui et le respect de soi, le respect de tout ce qui est différent de nous-même et qui, par contre, nous ressemble. C'est le respect de la nature; le respect du patrimoine culturel; le respect de la coopération entre individus et entre nations; c'est le respect du dialogue et de la paix. Bref, c'est la valeur fondamentale, le *sine qua non* de toute éducation au sens de l'épanouissement de l'individu et de la société.

En élaborant davantage cette idée, les philosophes tels que Toynbee et Ikeda soulignent qu'à l'heure actuelle, les gens recherchent une multitude de valeurs; chaque individu s'efforçant de développer son propre système de valeurs:

> Bien qu'il s'agisse là d'une tendance appréciable, car elle permet de libérer le concept de valeur de certains cadres limités tels que le nationalisme, il semble néanmoins que, tout en reconnaissant les mérites d'une diversité de valeurs, nous devons aussi chercher une conception de la valeur elle-même qui puisse servir de base commune à diverses sortes de valeurs. À défaut de cette base commune, il ne saurait y avoir de confiance et de coopération mutuelles entre les hommes. En dernière analyse, la valeur de l'homme et la dignité de la vie répondent aux exigences nécessaires à l'établissement de cette base commune[3].

La perte de la dignité et de l'honneur est, selon ces philosophes, la rançon de la lâcheté morale et physique. Un être humain est considéré avec mépris par ses semblables, et se méprise lui-même, s'il vend sa dignité et son honneur pour acquérir des richesses, pour s'assurer un certain statut social ou même pour sauver sa vie. La dignité est irremplaçable et par conséquent la perte de la dignité est irréparable si la dignité est perdue irrémédiablement. Déjà, le Nouveau Testament posait cette question: «Quel profit, en effet, peut avoir l'homme à gagner l'univers au détriment de son âme? Car que donnera l'homme en échange de son âme?» (Mathieu 16, 26; Marc 8, 36-7).

Les forces sociales qui influent sur le développement des valeurs morales et, par conséquent, sur la qualité de l'éducation morale (sans cependant agir avec la même intensité sur tous les pays-membres) ont été définies en 1978 par la première réunion de l'UNESCO consacrée à l'analyse de la relation entre les programmes scolaires et les valeurs morales:

> (a) le progrès scientifique et technologique, qui risque d'entraîner l'érosion de systèmes de croyances traditionnels et d'obliger l'individu à des choix moraux auxquels il n'est pas habitué;

(b) l'urbanisation, qui bien souvent constitue une menace pour les structures familiales traditionnelles; elle peut développer l'aliénation et favoriser la formation, chez les jeunes, de sous-cultures fondées sur des valeurs concurrentes;

(c) la rapidité de la croissance démographique, qui altère la structure par âge de la population nationale et va peut-être, ainsi, jusqu'à modifier dans la société en cause les sources de l'autorité;

(d) la disparité croissante des richesses entre les nations, qui entretient des sentiments d'exploitation, de colère et de désespoir chez les pauvres et porte les pays riches à une consommation sauvage de leurs ressources ou à l'insensibilité[4].

Il semble nécessaire d'ajouter à cette liste deux autres facteurs, ou forces sociales, qui exercent un pouvoir sensible et qui méritent d'être pris en considération quand on parle du sport et des valeurs éducatives (morales) du sport face à l'an 2000: il s'agit de la logique du marché (ou des impératifs du marché) et l'impact des mass médias. Je reviendrai à ces propos plus avant.

Learning Values through Sport

Recalling the teachings of Pierre de Coubertin, another great man, Philip Noel-Baker, underlined in his 1963 speech at UNESCO that only education can make men free to live the full and noble life that should be theirs, only education can give democracy a meaning, only education can make law and reason the ruling factor in world affairs. Elaborating this further, he pointed out:

> But sport, as the ancient Greeks discovered, is part of education, is an instrument, perhaps as powerful as any, perhaps more powerful than any, in school, in college, in the university, in life, for making people want the things which education alone can give. But the part which sport can play is far greater and will be far greater in the next ten, twenty, thirty years than ever before[5].

Nearly thirty years later one cannot but recognize the lucidity of this statement. Indeed, sport has grown into a very powerful instrument of education. Particularly in those parts of the world where we witness a profound crisis of the nuclear family and the formal educational system, sport—whether practiced out in the street, in clubs or vicariously, via the TV set, may well have become the most important vehicle for the transmission of the values enumerated above. At least two factors seem to have contributed to such a development: —a general decline of the authority of the social institutions which were in the past the main pillars of education, i.e., for transmission of moral values (the family, the church and the school); and—the pervasive presence of the communication media, which exercise an authority at least equal to if not greater than the traditional institutions.

These factors, encouraged further by an overall worldwide trend towards greater democracy and an ever freer flow of persons, ideas and information, have succeeded in making sport a mass phenomenon which is accessible, at least in some of its forms, to practically any person in virtually all modern societies. Sport now plays an important part in the educational system of almost every country, and it provides a stimulating experience for hundreds of millions of people who watch it on the television, or listen to it on the radio, or read about it in the press. It has, moreover, created links among peoples of various nations, thus contributing to better international understanding and, hopefully, to peace.

Beyond and above all this, however, sport has given us *the ethics of sport*: "fair-play on the track, on the playing field, in the dressing room, in the boardroom" as Noel-Baker expressed it. It is precisely fair-play, the ethics of sport, which embodies the ultimate and most complete of all moral values: the dignity of life, which has been referred to above. Fair-play, which expresses the human beings' most noble traits: the sense of understanding and compassion, respect, cooperation and solidarity, should be seen as the main educational message transmitted through sport. It is for these reasons that UNESCO bestows the International Pierre de Coubertin Fair-Play Trophy, the purpose of which is to give international recognition to those individuals and groups who have shown with their behaviour in decisive moments what is indeed most noble in sportsmanship.

One of the basic elements of sport—if not its cornerstone—has been, and remains, the sense of *competition* and the need to surpass the physical and psychological limitations of the others as well as one's own. This basically healthy attitude, which is the driving force of creativity, in arts as well as in other aspects of life, finds its clearest reflexion precisely in sport. It is perhaps logical, therefore, that the warning signals in the form of excesses which have become increasingly visible these past few years—brutal, unscrupulous competition which purports to win, whatever the price—are coming foremost from the sports arena. Looking forward to the year 2000, this is perhaps the moment and the place to ask ourselves: why is this happening? What is the message conveyed by these alarm-signals? What can one do to maintain the positive role which sport has played through centuries as a means to help the individual develop what is best and noble in the human being?

Competition is doubtlessly one of the fundamental postulates—if not *the* main postulate—of our modern world. However, modern societies have developed also on the basis of *cooperation*. The two, go hand-in-hand, paradoxical as it may seem. Competition can be an educational value only insofar as it reflects at the same time the spirit of fair-play, that is, cooperation. Beyond this point, it becomes a destructive force, both for the challenged and the challenger; in terms of ethics, one can even say that it becomes particularly destructive for the winning side, if victory is achieved without due consideration to cost. But these are old truisms that one is almost embarrassed to repeat. They need to be stressed, however, when one considers the changes which seem to be occurring in the appreciation of sport which is increasingly influenced by the penetration of show business criteria, particularly in "entertainment" sport and consequently, through a process of imitation, also in so-called "amateur" and mass sport. Speaking of educational values and sport, one cannot escape the question: Is it possible to reconcile showbusiness criteria with what is fondamental in sportsmanship, i.e., the facets of sports which encourage noble behaviour and the dignity of life? Is the implacable logic of the first compatible with the essence of the latter?

Lorsque l'on tente de répondre à ces questions, il semble évident que le sport, comme toutes les autres activités humaines, subit toujours les influences qui sont dominantes à une époque donnée. L'époque que nous vivons présentement est celle du marché et des médias. On dit aussi que c'est l'époque du triomphe du marché et des grands médias du système commercial. On a sans doute raison. Mais pour ceux et celles qui regardent plus loin que les indices quotidiens du profit et de l'audiomat (audience ratings), le système économique et médiatique actuel ne sera sans doute pas éternel. Il évoluera, c'est certain. Il évoluera en fonction de la créativité, de la volonté de l'être humain qui n'a de cesse d'être à la recherche des meilleures solutions possibles et d'un monde encore plus humain que celui d'aujourd'hui. Mais c'est aujourd'hui même que ce potentiel créatif se manifeste, grâce à l'éducation, grâce aussi au sport et à tout ce que nous y investissons par souci pour la dignité de la vie.

En conclusion, il me semble que c'est dans cette perspective que la réflexion sur les valeurs éducatives du sport doit se situer. La question de fond demeure celle de savoir comment «promouvoir l'esprit de fair-play et le respect des valeurs humanistes du sport, en renforçant la place réservée à l'éthique sportive et dans les programmes de formation et d'éducation, formelles et non formelles, destinés aux spécialistes de l'éducation, aux dirigeants et cadres sportifs et aux professionnels des médias» tel que fut souligné lors de la deuxième Conférence internationale des ministres et haut-fonctionnaires responsables de l'éducation physique et du sport (MINEPS II) organisée par l'UNESCO, et tenue à Moscou en novembre 1988[6].

REFERENCES

1. Rasseker S, Vaideanu G (1987) Les contenus de l'éducation, perspectives mondiales d'ici l'an 2000. Paris: Éditions de l'UNESCO p 163

2. Ibid p 404

3. Toynbee A, Ikeda D (1976) Choisis la vie: un dialogue. Paris: Albin Michel p 403

4. Rasseker S, Vaideanu G (1987) op cit p 161

5. Noel-Baker P (1963) Address to congress: «Baron de Coubertin Centenary». Paris: Éditions de l'UNESCO

6. MINEPS II (1989) Rapport final. La mission humaniste de l'éducation physique et du sport. Deuxième Conférence internationale des ministres et hauts-fonctionnaires responsables de l'éducation physique et du sport. Moscou, 21-25 novembre 1988. Paris: Éditions de l'UNESCO

[. . .] Toute institution, toute création, pour vivante qu'elle soit, évolue conformément aux habitudes, aux passions du moment. Aujourd'hui, la politique pénètre au sein de tout problème. Comment voudrait-on que le sport, le muscularisme, l'olympisme même lui échappent? Mais les ravages qu'elle y peut causer ne sont qu'apparents. En réalité, il y a presque toujours dans une institution deux évolutions: celle du visage et celle de l'âme. La première s'efforce à épouser les contours de la mode et se modifie selon les caprices de cette dernière; la seconde demeure aussi constante que le comportent les principes sur lesquels repose l'institution; elle n'évolue que lentement et sainement, conformément aux lois humaines elles-mêmes. L'olympisme appartient à cette deuxième catégorie.

Coubertin P de (1936) L'olympisme et la politique. La Revue Sportive Illustrée, 32e année, numéro spécial, p 38

Sport and the State

*Allowing for Socio-Politico-Cultural Similarities,
what are the Differences in Sport's Relationships
to the State in Both Capitalist
and State-Socialist Countries?*

Le sport et l'État

*Compte tenu des similarités socio-politico-culturelles,
quelles sont les différences dans les relations
entre le sport et l'État dans les pays capitalistes
et dans des états socialistes?*

From time immemorial, exercise, training and their modern counterparts designated as athletic performance and competitive sport have been supported and used by the State. Although these particular forms of human activity have their own internal structure and logistics, it is evident that they do not exist in a vacuum but rather at the very heart of the fabric of society. Whether as part of education or a constituent of broader programs and services for society in general, the phenomenon of sport cannot escape from morals nor politics. In Ancient Greece, the diverging motives invoked by Athens and Sparta had apparently less to do with the understanding of the fundamental nature of the human being, than they were related to his/her role as a member of society. Already in Sparta, physical fitness and athletic aptitudes were judged to have social (indeed political) usefulness and purposes: readiness and willingness to serve the State. Competition in sporting activities thus has a long and rich past; it stands indeed as a common heritage of humanity. The history of high performance sport since the end of the Second World War has witnessed both an increase and a generalization of governmental interest in the economic and (especially) political outcomes associated with international success in high performance (including olympic) sport. Under many and varied formulas, Governments have stimulated, encouraged, sustained, financed and sponsored the pursuit and attainment of sporting excellence at the international level. Some of the approaches led to well-balanced programs and services, from the standpoint of satisfying the needs and interests of the general population; others have left one in doubt as to equity in the distribution of the overall efforts born at considerable public expense.

It is with a view of providing a descriptive analysis of the current situation of the relationships between *Sport and the State* that the Organizing Committee set up two panels of international experts. In the first, and allowing for socio-politico-cultural similarities, the analyses bore on the differences in sport's relationships to the State in four capitalist countries: United States (USA), Australia-New Zealand (AUS-NZL), Great Britain (GBR), and Canada (CAN), with a commentary by a specialist from a non anglo-saxon country, France (FRA). In the second panel, again allowing for the aforementioned similarities, the presentations were to bear on four socialist countries: Soviet Union (URS), German Democratic Republic (GDR), Peoples' Republic of China (CHN), and Cuba (CUB), with a commentary by a canadian expert (CAN). As the invitations of the Organizing Committee were declined by the GDR, CHN and CUB, the task of describing the changing situation

Depuis les temps anciens, les pratiques corporelles, l'entraînement physique et leurs formes modernes connues sous les appellations de performance athlétique et de compétition sportive, ont eu des raisons d'État. Bien que ces formes particulières de l'activité humaine aient leur propre structure et une logique interne particulière, il est clair qu'elles ne se réalisent pas dans le vide, mais bien et plutôt au cœur même de la société civile. Qu'il s'agisse de projets pédagogiques ou encore de la « société jouante », le phénomène ne saurait échapper ni à la morale ni à la politique. Dans la Grèce Antique, les motifs divergents invoqués à Athènes et à Sparte pour l'encouragement et la promotion de l'excellence athlétique montraient des conceptions sinon différentes de la nature de l'être humain en tant qu'individu, du moins de sa finalité en tant que membre irréductible de la société. Déjà à Sparte, l'aptitude athlétique avait revêtu une raison sociale (donc politique) évidente et marquée : la capacité actualisée et la volonté de servir l'État. Ainsi donc, la compétition sportive a un passé et des racines lointaines ; elle est, en fait, un héritage. L'histoire sportive vécue depuis la fin de la deuxième Guerre Mondiale a vu s'accroître et se généraliser l'intérêt des États envers les retombées économiques et (surtout) politiques associées aux succès athlétiques internationaux (incluant olympiques). En des formules variées, les États ont stimulé, encouragé, favorisé, soutenu, financé ou patronné la poursuite et l'atteinte de l'excellence sportive internationale, parfois selon des formules visant à assurer des services bien équilibrés, du point de vue de la satisfaction des besoins de l'ensemble de la population, parfois aussi selon des formules moins limpides qui laissent place au doute quant à l'équité de la répartition de l'effort général déployé à même les fonds publics.

C'est dans la perspective d'une analyse descriptive de la situation actuelle des relations entre *le sport et l'État* que le Comité d'organisation a invité un double panel d'experts internationaux. Dans un premier temps, et compte tenu des similarités socio-politico-culturelles, les présentations ont porté sur quatre pays capitalistes : États-Unis d'Amérique (USA), Australie-Nouvelle Zélande (AUS-NZL), Grande-Bretagne (GBR), Canada (CAN), avec un commentaire par un expert français (FRA). Dans un deuxième temps, les présentations devaient porter sur quatre pays socialistes : l'Union des républiques socialistes soviétiques (URS), la République démocratique allemande (GDR), la République populaire de Chine (CHN) et Cuba (CUB), avec un commentaire par un expert canadien (CAN). Les invitations du Comité d'organisation ayant été déclinées par la GDR, la CHN et CUB, la tâche de décrire la

in the socialist states of Eastern Europe (excluding URS) was entrusted to a British expert, and that of covering the situation in CHN to an American specialist.

The reader will find in the pages that follow the integral presentations of the nine invited speakers. With the exception of the texts of the two commentators, those of all the panelists focus on the situations which prevail in the selected countries. One should however note that it was not feasible in a book such as this to present in writing the results of the discussions and debates that also took place between the speakers as well as between the speakers and the Symposium participants. The Editors are nonetheless pleased to emphasize that the Discussion-Luncheon of a duration of one-and-a-half hour which was offered by the Organizing Committee as a follow-up to the formal presentations, was very well attended, highly spirited, profitable and appreciated.

Clearly, one can deduce from reading the various texts that in the countries at stake (and notwithstanding an acknowledged willingness to continue to support elite sport at the international level), there is a rising degree of social consciousness and a gradual strengthening of public (if not State) volition and expectation with respect to the desirability of establishing a better balance in the distribution of the national effort and budgets allotted for programs and services likely to contribute to the fitness, health, general well-being, and quality of life of the majority of the citizenry.

situation dans les pays de l'Europe de l'Est (en sus de URS) a été confiée à un expert d'origine britannique, et celle de couvrir la CHN à une experte américaine.

Le lecteur trouvera aux pages qui suivent les présentations intégrales des neuf spécialistes invités. On saisira qu'à l'exception des textes des deux commentateurs, ceux de tous les autres panelistes se limitent aux observations et analyses descriptives de la situation évolutive dans chacun des nombreux pays en cause. On comprendra également que dans le présent ouvrage, il n'a pas été possible de présenter le fruit des échanges et des discussions qui ont eu cours entre les experts eux-mêmes ainsi qu'entre ces derniers et les participants au Symposium. Les éditeurs sont heureux de souligner que le déjeuner-discussion d'une durée d'une heure et demie offert à la suite des présentations formelles par le Comité d'organisation à toutes les personnes intéressées, a été à la fois très suivi, animé, fructueux et apprécié.

Il se dégage clairement de la lecture des textes qui suivent que dans l'ensemble des pays concernés (et nonobstant une volonté de continuer à soutenir le sport d'élite à l'échelle internationale), on assiste à une prise de conscience ainsi qu'à un affermissement nouveau de la volonté populaire (sinon d'État), au sujet du bien-fondé d'établir un juste équilibre, dans le partage des efforts et des budgets nationaux consentis, entre ce qui a trait au sport d'élite et aux programmes et services qui ont pour objectif de contribuer à la santé, au bien-être et à la qualité de la vie de l'ensemble des citoyens.

Sport and the State:
the Case of the United States of America

Laurence Chalip

Scholars have increasingly noted the economic[1], political[2,3] and ideological[4] impact of modern sport. The emerging scholarship has been concerned to discern the relations among sport, culture, ideology, and the state. Current research seeks to illumine those relations, and to specify the social and cultural forces via which they ramify. Studies to date have utilized historical narrative and/or cultural critique as a framework for analysis. This study employs methods of policy analysis[5,6,7,8,9,10,11] to examine the formation of American federal policies for American olympic sports governance. Policy analytic methods clarify the legitimations and frames of reference that steered the course of American sports policy formulation. It is suggested that legitimations, ideological traditions, and frames of reference may provide useful bases for cross-national comparison of sport policies.

In order to render a coherent analysis, this study is limited to olympic sports policies at the federal level. Policy issues in school sport, professional sport, and olympic sports have been relatively distinct[12]. Consequently, policy deliberations focused exclusively on school or professional sports are not included here. Similarly, under the American federal system, sport policies at local and regional levels are relatively independent of federal control, and vary widely among jurisdictions. Therefore, local and regional sport policies are not incorporated into this analysis.

Since American policies for olympic sports were formulated in terms of "amateur sports", the phrases "olympic sports" and "amateur sports" will be used here as if they were synonymous. In fact, both phrases apply only to non-school governance of sports on the Olympic or Pan American Games programs. The discussion draws on a more detailed analysis of the framing and implementation of American policies on olympic sports[13].

1890
1990

Laurence Chalip, Department of Kinesiology, University of Maryland, College Park, Maryland, USA.

The Amateur Sports Act

The provisions for governance of American olympic sports are encoded in the Amateur Sports Act of 1978 (PL 95-606). The Amateur Sports Act confers on the United States Olympic Committee (USOC) policymaking and policy implementing authority for olympic sports. Although encoded in law as the central olympic sports organization for the United States, the USOC is an explicitly non-governmental organization. The only oversight requirement placed on the USOC is that it annually provide a written report to Congress and to the President. However, no Congressional committee nor Executive Branch agency is provided any oversight authority. Indeed, there is no committee or agency that is required to read or evaluate the USOC's annual report. Thus, olympic sports governance is independent of government control.

The primary governance tool of the USOC is its authority to determine which organization will serve as the National Governing Body (NGB) for each sport in the Olympic and Pan American Games programs. The USOC has the authority to select the organization to serve as NGB; and the USOC has the authority to place an NGB on probation or revoke its franchise. However, the USOC is required to be a representative organization in which the NGBs and other organizations with an interest in olympic sports (e.g., the multi-sport organizations like the YMCA, and school sport organizations like the NCAA) have decisionmaking authority via their votes. Thus, although the USOC can determine which organization serves as the NGB for each sport, USOC policies are decided or agreed by the NGBs and the other sport organizations admitted to membership in the USOC.

The Amateur Sports Act specifies 14 "objects and purposes" for the USOC: 1– to establish national goals for olympic sports and to pursue attainment of those goals; 2– to coordinate and develop amateur sport activity; 3– to exercise jurisdiction over United States participation in the Olympic and Pan American Games; 4– to obtain the most competent representation in those games; 5– to promote and support amateur sport; 6– to promote and encourage physical fitness and sport participation; 7– to assist in the development of amateur sports programs; 8– to provide for resolution of conflicts in amateur sports; 9– to foster development of sport facilities for amateur sports; 10– to provide and coordinate technical information on physical training, equipment design, coaching, and performance analysis; 11– to encourage and support sport research; 12– to promote sport for women; 13– to promote sport for the handicapped; 14– to promote sport for minorities.

In addition to their roles in governance of their respective sports, each NGB is also charged by the Amateur Sports Act with responsibility for promoting interest and participation in the sport that it governs. Thus, although the Amateur Sports Act is primarily concerned with sport governance, it also addresses sport development. The Act specifies the governing structure for olympic and pan american sports by placing the USOC at the head of olympic and pan american sports organization, and by requiring the USOC to delegate authority for governance of each olympic and pan american sport to a separate NGB. Sport development is one among the many responsibilities of the USOC and the NGBs.

Two features of the Amateur Sports Act stand out: First, the Act enshrines the USOC as the central sports authority of the United States, and provides no mechanism for participation in sport governance by the federal government. Indeed, beyond the reporting provision of the Amateur Sports Act, there is not even a provision for oversight of the USOC by the federal government. Second, the Amateur Sports Act aims at rationalizing the administration of olympic sports; it is not concerned with guaranteeing sport development or sport-for-all. The Act specifies which sport organizations must report to which others, and how disputes among sport organizations will be resolved; sport development is merely noted in passing as one of the concerns that might be addressed by sport organizations. These features of the Amateur Sports Act contrast with those of other nations[14]. Analysis of the policy debates leading up to the Amateur Sports Act clarifies the bases for these features.

Framing of the Amateur Sports Act

Terms of analysis

An enduring principle of American politics holds that the role of government should remain limited. If the government is to project itself into a particular arena of activity, it must be arguably in the national interest for it to do so, and it should do so in as minimal a fashion as is possible[15,16]. The consequent efforts at legitimation set the boundaries of subsequent policymaking.

Regardless of the pursuasiveness of any legitimation, each policy issue must contend with a surfeit of others if it is to secure a place on American policymakers' agendas[17]. Events that are nationally traumatic can serve to symbolize a policy issue and to focus policymakers' attention on proposals in that policy realm. Kingdon calls these "focusing events". As symbolic representations of the problem at hand, the focusing events help give direction to subsequent policymaking.

Legitimations and focusing events generate the attributions and problem definitions that frame the policy debate. Attributions are the socially ascribed causes of events. Attributions enable policymakers to respond to situations by alleging the underlying bases that must be addressed[18]. Attributions permit problem definitions that specify what there is about an extant situation that requires redress by policymakers[19]. Problem definitions give rise to frames. Frames are abstractions that stipulate the kinds of information and beliefs that are and are not pertinent to a particular policy problem[20]. Frames designate the concepts, categories and realms of knowledge that may appropriately be brought to bear during policy formulation.

The focusing events and their dominant frame combined to distract legislative efforts from explicit provision for sport participation or sport-for-all. The legitimation concerns combined with the dominant frame to keep sport governance out of government hands. In order to see how this occurred, it is useful to review the development of the policy debates.

The legislative agenda for sport

Prior to 1972, there had been no legislation specifying the structure of American olympic sport. However, at the 1972 Summer Olympic Games, a series of fiascoes befell the American olympic team. Four of these were discussed at length in the American press, and became the focus of subsequent policy deliberations[21]: (1) Rick DeMont, an American swimmer, was stripped of is gold medal because his asthma medication contained an ingredient on the International Olympic Committee's list of banned substances. (2) Bob Seagren, an American pole vaulter, was not allowed to use his preferred fiberglass pole, consequently jumping below his world record and finishing second to an East German. (3) The American sprinters Rey Robinson and Eddie Hart were not provided a correct schedule for their competition. Consequently, they were disqualified when they failed to arrive for the quarterfinal heat. A Soviet sprinter won the gold medal. (4) The American basketball team was defeated by the Soviet Union after a disputed ruling by the Secretary-General of the international basketball federation.

In each instance, administrative failures by US team officials were blamed. It was claimed that team doctors did not change Rick DeMont's asthma medication because they had failed to read his medical form. It was claimed that American officials did not adequately defend Bob Seagren's right to use his favored pole. It was claimed that the coach of the American sprinters was never provided an up-to-date competition schedule by team officials. It was claimed that requisite officials of the American team were not present at the basketball game to enter the appropriate protest. The key attributions for these focusing events thus defined the problems in terms of poor administration. By implication, what was required was administrative rationalization of elite sport; sport participation and sport-for-all were not implicated.

In-and-of themselves, these events would probably not have been sufficient to have generated policymaking by American legislators. However, these events occurred against an emerging legitimation for sport policies that invoked American prestige in the face of a Soviet challenge[22]. As early as 1954, Congressman Philip Philbin had wondered:

> What is the meaning of this rapid advancement of Russia in the world of sports? [...] To what extent is superiority in competitive athletics tied in with national success, prosperity, and invincibility in warfare[23]?

Ten years later, as Soviet athletes became increasingly successful, Congress began to reconsider its hands-off policy toward American olympic sport. Congressman Frank Morse explained the reversal of his position against government support of the American olympic team this way:

> The present situation is humiliating for the athletes involved and destructive of team performance and morale. [...] The argument that we do not want to make our athletes political minions or adopt the practices of the Soviet Union does not reflect the realities of the situation[24].

The fact that the American team had for the first time fallen behind the Soviet team in the medal count made the fiascoes at Munich all-the-more salient to policymakers. Nevertheless, the concern that the United States not adopt Soviet methods remained pivotal. Thus, direct federal control of olympic sport was controversial.

On April 16, 1973, Senator Pearson introduced S. 1580. That bill sought to create a five-member US Amateur Sports Association Board to be appointed by the President and approved by the Senate. The Board would function as an agency of the executive branch, and would be empowered to establish rules and regulations for amateur sport. Related bills followed (S. 1690). However, the traditional American preference for minimal government intervention combined with the explicit concern that the Soviet system should not be copied in the American case. Senator Adlai Stevenson opined:

> Several bills to reorganize amateur athletics under federal control have already been introduced [...] I am deeply concerned about the future of amateur athletics and would hate to see the Federal government become involved in this aspect of American life. I urge the President to convene [...] a conference, and I urge the organizations concerned with amateur sports to reconcile their differences and work together for the advancement of amateur sport[25].

White House staff agreed. A staff analysis sent to President Nixon in May of 1973 urged the President to forestall radical legislation by establishing a commission that would examine amateur sports problems and recommend solutions via a reorganization of the USOC (Memo, Jerry Jones to The President, 73/05/24). That analysis also made reference to the long standing disputes between two other amateur sports organizations, the National Collegiate Athletic Association (NCAA) and the Amateur Athletics Union (AAU)[26] as further evidence of the need for rationalization of the administration of amateur sport. The open warfare between those two organizations had already been the subject of extensive government concern[27,28,29]. A subsequent White House memo made the administration's concerns explicit: "This Administration is committed to limiting—not expanding—the scope of Federal Government, and Federal involvement in amateur athletics could well prove counterproductive" (Memo, Ken Cole to Staff Secretary, 73/07/20).

By the end of 1973, the necessary pieces of the puzzle were in place, they merely needed to be assembled. Federal intervention in amateur sport was deemed necessary and legitimate, but a permanent federal involvement was to be eschewed. The problem was framed as one of administrative rationalization, and the USOC had already been explicitly identified as an appropriate vehicle for that rationalization. The focusing events, occurring as they did at the level of olympic competition, reinforced the convergence of attention on elite levels of sport. The legitimation of national prestige in the face of a Soviet challenge combined with the traditional American preference for minimal federal intervention to direct policy proposals toward non-governmental forms of administrative rationalization, with the USOC as a favored option.

Nevertheless, on July 9, 1974, legislation that would bring olympic sports under federal control (S. 3500) was passed by the Senate and referred to the House. White House action to forestall passage of any legislation providing federal control accelerated, culminating in President Ford's signing on December 28, 1974 of an order to create a Presidential Commission to study the problems of olympic sports and to make recommendations. On June 19, 1975, following staffing and funding of the Commission, President Ford announced creation of the President's Commission on Olympic Sports (E.O. 11868). Proposals seeking an active federal role in olympic sport governance were dropped from the legislative agenda.

The President's Commission on Olympic Sports produced two reports. The first report[30] concluded that administrative rationalization would be sufficient to eliminate disputes among sports and enhance participation:

> Based on the Commission's findings so far, it appears that with better organization, management and funding of our amateur sports programs, many of the ongoing disputes can be eliminated; [...] US teams performing in the Olympics and other international competitions will more nearly realize their potential; and, sports participation at home is bound to increase. Therefore [...] there must be a reorganization of amateur sports in this country[31].

The answer, it was suggested, was to create a "highest sports authority":

> Amateur sports in the United States today are fragmented without purpose and are fraught with internal competition for participants, funds and public awareness. A mechanism which pulls together these competing forces and channels their energies toward common goals is sorely needed[32].

The first report thus concludes that the remaining task of the Commission is to propose a structure for the highest sports authority.

The final report of the President's Commission on Olympic Sports[33] urges the United States to establish a "central sports organization" (CSO—renamed from the earlier "highest sports authority"). The new organization, it suggests, should be created by amendment of the USOC's federal charter. Administrative rationalization is explicitly taken to be a panacea:

> Clearly, the establishment of vertical structure and the CSO will provide the sports community with the means to address both inter- and intra-sport problems. [...] The membership requirements of the CSO ensure that all constituents and major programs in each sport belong to and can be coordinated through the national governing body for that sport. Finally, the Board of directors of the CSO is a fully representative forum wherein the priorities, policies and direction of the US amateur sports movement may be decided. Enacting these recommendations will

result in a series of concerted actions to address the prime sports problems enumerated [by the President's Commission on Olympic Sports][34].

In fact, this recommendation, which ultimately became the basis for the Amateur Sports Act, is little more than an elaboration of the suggestions made in White House memoranda four years earlier. This is not coincidental. The legitimations (national prestige), focusing events (American failures at the Olympic Games), and consequent frame (administrative rationalization outside federal control) had remained unchallenged and unchanged. Since sport development and sport-for-all were never considered more than epiphenomena of administrative rationalization, these have never been explicitly addressed by American sport policymakers.

Ramifications of the frame

American fortunes at the Olympic Games have not improved since implementation of the Amateur Sports Act. The exceptional medal tally of the American team in 1984 was substantially due to the absence of every Warsaw pact team except Romania. In 1988, American teams fared less well than the American public had been led to hope. In a move that may have forestalled federal action, the USOC established its own review commission, "The Olympic Overview Commission", as the Calgary Winter Olympic Games were drawing to a close. The USOC's Olympic Overview Commission submitted its report to the meeting of the USOC Executive Board on February 19, 1989. Analysis of that report suggests the degree to which the Amateur Sports Act and the frame of administrative rationalization have continued to dominate American sport policymaking—albeit now in nongovernmental context.

The report references the Amateur Sports Act six times—three times in its first page—and devotes its only footnote to the Amateur Sports Act. The report is devoted to recommendations for further rationalization of the USOC's administrative structure, even if that requires a reduction of democratic forms of decisionmaking. The report asserts:

> In particular, the Commission reaffirms that the USOC is properly designated to serve as the coordinating body for U.S. amateur sport with exclusive jurisdiction to field and finance the best possible United States Pan American and Olympic teams. [...] It has clearly become more important to operate the USOC as an efficient organization than as a perfectly representative form of government. [...] The Commission's purpose is to bring the USOC to a position of efficient management and strength of purpose [...][35]

In putting forward its recommendations for structural and administrative enhancements of the USOC, the report explicitly rejects grassroots sport development in terms of sport-for-all or similar emphases on participation. This is a change, because sport development is no longer argued to be an epiphenomenon of administrative rationalization; it is now said to be contraindicated by the exigencies of administrative rationalization:

> The USOC [...] has drifted into trying to be all things to all people. [...] To be effective, the USOC must focus on its primary purpose, which is the preparation of United States Olympic and Pan American teams. [...] Winning medals must always be the primary goal. The Commission strongly believes that striving for excellence and desiring to win are values that must be encouraged[36].

This assertion was never critiqued by the Congress or the White House. There is currently no prospect that the United States government will seek to assert dominion over olympic sport governance. Meanwhile, the frame that guided legislative and executive deliberations during the 1970's continues to guide policymaking by the USOC today. That frame now legitimizes the eschewing of policies that might promote participation-based sport programs.

Analytic Summary

European programs of sport-for-all were legitimated via the argument that sport is not merely a want, it is a need[37]. No such argument has been seriously asserted in the American political context. Rather, in the American context, sport policies have been legitimated in elite terms as matters of national representation. Even as recently as 1989, the Olympic Overview Commission asserted that "America has always needed heroes". The differences in legitimations for sport policy deliberations explains, in part, the different focus resultant policies have had.

The differing ideological traditions of European and American policy-making also suggest one reason that the degree of government involvement differs cross-nationally. Whereas the American tradition has long been wary of government authority[38,39], many European governments, particularly those with a democratic socialist tradition, have been amenable to projection of government authority into social and cultural services[40]. Thus, although it was ideologically pivotal in the United States that sport governance be independent of central government, that constraint has been less compelling elsewhere.

The concerns for optimal national representation and minimal federal control combined to frame American sports policies as problems of administrative rationalization, preferably outside the sphere of government. Administrative rationalization was thought to require centralization of authority for American olympic sports. The preferred nongovernmental organization to be given that authority was the organization responsible for fielding the American olympic and pan american teams—the USOC. The consequent focus on the concerns of elite sport has served to distance American sport policymaking from the kinds of participative concerns that have emerged elsewhere.

It is useful to go beyond the mere description of sport policies and beyond merely narrative historical accounts of how those policies emerged. Application of methods from interpretive and critical policy analysis to the historical development of sports policies highlights interactions among dominant ideologies, legitimations, focusing events, problem definitions, and frames of reference. These, in turn, provide useful categories for cross-national comparisons of sport policies.

REFERENCES

1. Noll RG (1974) Government and the sports business. Washington: Brookings

2. Espy R (1979) The politics of the Olympic Games. Berkeley: University of California Press

3. Johnson AT, Frey JH (eds) (1985) Government and sport: the public policy issues. Totawa: Rowman and Allanheld

4. Hoberman JM (1984) Sport and political ideology. Austin: University of Texas Press

5. Dery D (1984) Problem definition in policy analysis. Lawrence: University Press of Kansas

6. Dryzek J (1982) Policy analysis as a hermeneutic activity. Policy Sciences 14 309-29

7. Dunn WN (1981) Public policy analysis: an introduction. Englewood Cliffs: Prentice Hall

8. Hambrick RS (1974) A guide for the analysis of policy arguments. Policy Sciences 5 469-78

9. Kaplan TJ (1986) The narrative structure of policy analysis. Journal of Policy Analysis and Management 5 761-78

10. Kingdon JW (1984) Agendas, alternatives, and public policies. Boston: Little Brown

11. Rein M (1983) Value-critical policy analysis. In Callahan D Jennings B (eds) Ethics, the social sciences and policy analysis. New York: Plenum

12. Clumpner RA (1976) American government involvement in sport (1848-1973). Unpublished PhD dissertation University of Alberta

13. Chalip L (forthcoming) The framing of policy: explaining the transformation of American sport

14. Claeys U (1985) Evolution of the concept of sport and the participation/nonparticipation phenomenon. Sociology of Sport Journal 2 233-39

15. King A (1973a) Ideas, institutions and the policies of governments: a comparative analysis: Parts I and II. British Journal of Political Science 3 291-313

16. King A (1973b) Ideas, institutions and the policies of governments: a comparative analysis: Part III. British Journal of Political Science 3 409-23

17. Kingdon JW (1984) op cit

18. Blume SS (1977) Policy as theory: a framework for understanding the contribution of social science to welfare policy. Acta Sociologica 20 247-62

19. Dery D (1984) op cit

20. Rein M (1983) op cit

21. Senate Committee on Commerce (1973) Amateur sports. Washington: Government Printing Office (serial 93-23)

22. MacAloon JJ (1982) Double vision: Olympic Games and American culture. Kenyon Review 4 98-112

23. Congressional Record (1954) p 13763

24. Congressional Record (1964) p 5904

25. Congressional Record (1973) p 16069

26. Flath AW (1964) A history of relations between the National Collegiate Athletic Union and the Amateur Athletic Union of the United States (1905-1963). Unpublished PhD dissertation University of Michigan Ann Arbor

27. Senate Committee on Commerce (1965) NCAA-AAU dispute. Washington: Government Printing Office (serial 89-49)

28. Senate Committee on Commerce (1967) Hearings before the Committee on Commerce. Washington: Government Printing Office (serial 90-27)

29. Senate Committee on Commerce (1968) Sports arbitration board report. Washington: Government Printing Office (serial 90-46)

30. President's Commission on Olympic Sports (1976) First report to the President. Washington: Government Printing Office

31. Ibid p 9

32. Ibid p 50

33. President's Commission on Olympic Sports (1977) The final report of the President's Commission on Olympic Sports 1975-1977 (2 volumes). Washington: Government Printing Office

34. Ibid p 28

35. Olympic Overview Commission (1989) Report of the Olympic Overview Commission. Unpublished report to the United States Olympic Committee Executive Board Meeting. Portland Oregon

36. Ibid

37. McIntosh PC (1974) GOs, NGOs and QUANGOs: from wants to needs. Maxwell Howell Address to the North American Society for Sports History

38. King A (1973a) op cit

39. King A (1973b) op cit

40. Kahn AJ Kamerman SB (1975) Not for the poor alone: European social services. Philadelphia: Temple University Press

Sport and the State:
the Case of Australia and New Zealand

Ian F. Jobling

This presentation was prepared in the wake of the XIVth Commonwealth Games held in Auckland, New Zealand in January 1990. The host city, with a population of approximately one million (about one-third of that of all New Zealand) can be said to be representative of the enthusiasm, almost fanaticism, for sport in that country. Auckland has staged a most successful international athletic festival, but at a financial loss predicted to exceed 20 million dollars AUS. In Australia, the electronic and print media have been ecstatic over the fact that its athletes have merited the most medals of any nation at any Commonwealth Games: a total of 162 (52 gold; 54 silver; 56 bronze). In addition, it has been determined that 39 members of the team from Queensland will receive 5 000 $ AUS from the State Government to cover the cost of their Games preparations.

Government financial support of any significance for Australian athletes has only been available for less than two decades. Indeed, in 1974, Australia's first Minister for Sport at the national level of government, Frank Stewart, stated "Australian sport is among the most unorganised and unco-ordinated in the world... in the past our champions succeeded in spite of our organisation, not because of it[1]". The glorious, golden decade of the 1950s, enhanced by the many successes in international sport since a sole representative won two events in the Athens stadium at the 1896 Olympic Games, had prompted American journalist Wind to write in Sports Illustrated in 1960 "Australia is a sports-playing, sports-watching, sports-talking, altogether sports-minded country such as the world has never known before". Many New Zealanders would consider that this statement equally applies to their country today.

As we have entered the final decade before the third millennium, it is clear that in the liberal democracies of Australia and New Zealand the intervention and involvement of government in the management of sport have now become a most significant aspect of social, political, economic and cultural life within each country.

1890
1990

Ian F. Jobling, Department of Human Movement Studies, The University of Queensland, St-Lucia, Australia.

The Case of Australia

In anticipation of the 1908 Olympic Games in London the following exchange took place in the House of Representatives of the Australian parliament:

> Mr Maloney. Subscriptions are being raised to enable representative Australians to compete in the marathon race in connexion (sic) with the revival of the Olympian [sic] Games. Since the representation of Australia at the carnival would do as much to advertise the Commonwealth as the visits of Australian cricket teams to the Old Country, does the Prime Minister think it would be possible for the Commonwealth government to subscribe, say, half the amount raised by the public for this purpose?

> Mr Deakin. Commencing with an avowal of innocence as to what a "marathon" race may be, but of full confidence in the capacity of Australians to hold their own in that or any other form of competition, I doubt whether it comes within the power of the Commonwealth, strictly interpreting the constitution, to interfere with the rights of the states in that matter. We shall consider that question[2].

Two features of this extract are the sentiments that sport is significant in promoting a national image and that the passing of the responsibility, when it comes to finances or the "buck", from the federal to state governments was then and has remained a problem.

It was not until 1939 that the federal government established the National Fitness movement by providing funds to set up councils in each state. However, financial support was meagre and even in 1968-69 the amount allocated for National Fitness Council purposes was only 416 000 $ for the six states and the Australian Capital Territory: an allocation of 3,4 cents per head of population[3]. But, in the *Australian Labor Party Policy Speech* delivered at Blacktown Civic Centre on November 13, 1972, Mr Whitlam made a statement about the quality of life:

> There is no greater social problem facing Australia than the good use of leisure. It is the problem of all modern and wealthy communities. It is, above all, the problem of urban societies and thus, in Australia, the most urbanised nation on earth, a problem more pressing for us than for any other nation on earth. For such a nation as ours, this may very well be the problem of the 1980s; so we must prepare now; prepare the generation of the 1980s—the children and youth of the 1970s—to be able to enjoy and enrich their growing hours of leisure[4].

In the month following that address (December, 1972) the Australian Labor Party was elected to become the Federal Government, and a Ministry of Tourism and Recreation was created. The Minister, Mr Stewart, and members of this new Department of Tourism and Recreation sought the advice of individuals and bodies associated with recreation, sport and physical education not only from Australia, but from other countries as well. The new Minister then commissioned Professor Bloomfield of the University of Western Australia to prepare a detailed report; ten weeks later, in May 1973, a document entitled *The Role, Scope and Development of Recreation in Australia* was tabled in Parliament. Based on the content, the term "sport" might well have been used instead of "recreation" and, in his statement to Parliament, the Minister indicated that "most of [the] Cabinet submissions and Budget requests would be based on recommendations contained within that report" and that "[. . .] it is our responsibility to recognize for the first time in the history of Australia, that recreation and sport should constitute an integral part of our life and, as such, must receive serious attention and much more than token support from our governments[5]".

In the 1973-74 budget, one million dollars was allocated to assist Australian amateur athletes to participate in national and international teams, giving support to the statement that "our dedicated amateurs have been ignored long enough and we intend to remedy this situation[6]". The total allocation to recreation and sport in 1973-74 was approximately 5,2 million $, a significant increase over previous years but still less than 50 cents per head. However, in comparison, the federal budget provided for expenditure of 14 million $ on programs to be developed by the Australian Council for the Arts—an increase of 7,3 million $ from the previous budget[7].

A key factor in the role and influence the federal government would have on the development of recreation and sport was the relationship and extent of co-operation from the states. Over the years, Commonwealth-state relationships have caused concern in areas other than recreation and sport; it was thus too optimistic of one to presume that the relationship would be free from problems, especially in the early stages. All states now have a ministry of sport recreation and/or recreation but they vary in aims, structure and administration[8]. In 1974 Dr Coles headed a task force to consider an important aspect of sport on Australian culture, that of support for the elite athlete. The Australian Sports Institute report[9] was tabled in the House of Representatives in 1975 but the recommendations were not implemented because, in a unique turn of political events, the Labor government was dismissed by the Governor-General of Australia and was replaced in the subsequent elections by a Liberal-Country Party coalition government. Throughout government by this conservative coalition there was no distinct ministry of sport/recreation as such, but sport was administered through the Ministry of Home Affairs. However, sport—and particularly success in international sport—remained a significant aspect of Australian popular culture. Journalist Keith Dunstan considers that Australians are obsessed with sport: "Sport is the ultimate super-religion, the one thing every Australian believes in passionately [. . .] (it) is wholesome [. . .] it builds stronger Australian men and women, and, best of all, it spreads the fame of Australians overseas[10]". Writer, social commentator and academic, Donald Horne, wrote in his book, *The Lucky Country*, that "to play sport or watch others and read and talk about it is to uphold the nation and build its character. Australia's success at competitive sport is considered an important part of its foreign policy[11]."

The glorious international reputation which Australians had enjoyed in sport, however, seemed to be waning by the mid-1970s. Using olympic gold medals only as a guide to sporting excellence (a spurious measure but of paramount importance to many Australians) one may ascertain the concern from the following results: Melbourne 1956 – 13; Rome 1960 – 8; Tokyo 1964 – 6; Mexico 1968 – 5; Munich 1972 – 8 (3 won by Shane Gould in swimming). At the Montreal Olympic Games in 1976, Australia failed to gain either a gold or silver medal, and there was only one bronze medallist. The print and electronic media reacted strongly to this "failure"—as can be gleaned from the many cartoons pertaining to the "penny-pinching" attitude of the Liberal federal government and, in particular, Prime Minister Fraser, who visited the games village and expressed his desire for "winners". John Daly, track and field coach at those Olympic Games echoed that Australians, shocked by the "poor showing" of their athletes, demanded to know what had "gone wrong".

> A public inquiry was initiated which ultimately resulted in greater governmental funding of Australian sport to bolster the system. For it was not the system itself [which was] at fault. Indeed, the club system of Australian sport still exists but whereas most sports operated on a self-funded, ad hoc basis with volunteer, "kitchen table" administration and untrained coaches and "chook raffles" to fund their efforts before the 1970s and early 1980s. It had to![12]

Prime Minister Fraser officially opened the Australian Institute of Sport (AIS) in Canberra on January 26th (Australia Day) 1980. Athletes at the AIS receive scholarships which may include accommodation, educational allowances, training and competition-clothing and equipment, coaching, domestic and international travel and competition and the support services provided by sports science and medicine. Specialist training and competition facilities were developed for the "institute" sports, as well as a sports science and medicine centre, residential accommodations for scholarship holders, plus accommodations for athletes in residence for short duration, and an administration and information resource centre.

When the Labor Party was returned to government in 1983, the Minister for Sport, Recreation and Tourism, John Brown, while retaining the AIS, proposed that an Australian Sports Commission (ASC) function as a statutory authority. The ASC, established in September, 1984, had three main objectives: to sustain and improve Australia's level of achievement in international sporting competition; to increase the level of participation in sport by all Australians; and to increase the level of assistance from the private sector (which led to the establishment of the Sports Aid Foundation).

In late 1987 the ASC, AIS, and elements of the Department of the Arts, Sport, the Environment, Tourism and Territories (DASETT) were amalgamated to form a new commission under a second Australian Sports Commission Act, May 1989. Chairman Harris of the ASC, stated in the 1988-89 Annual Report:

> With the proclamation of the Australian Sports Commission Act in May this year, the Commission took on the onerous but exciting task of fostering Australian sport. The Government has now provided the legislation, guidance and resources that are essential for the work of the Commission. The Commission's success will depend on its ability to work with national sporting organisations, State sporting institutions, the Australian Olympic Federation, the Australian Commonwealth Games Association, the Confederation of Australian Sport and other bodies and individuals that make up the Australian sports community.

> More than the pursuit of victories in world-wide competition, Australian sport embraces all sport in the community. This includes sport for all age groups and for all groups with special needs and interests, women, children and the disabled in particular. The Commission is promoting sport for the community and increasing the level of sports participation by Australians. Equally, it is seeking to improve the level of performance of Australian athletes nationally and internationally[13].

It is clear that the ASC has assumed responsibility for sport in Australia and its objectives and structure does seek to redress the situation in which the first federal Sports Minister Frank Stewart had found sport in 1970 (*i.e.*, "Australia's sport is among the most unorganized and unco-ordinated in the world").

As the third millennium approaches, it is appropriate to consider some proposed developments of sport in Australia throughout this final decade, especially those pertaining to the ASC. Nine major priorities have been identified by the ASC for its involvement in the development of sport in Australia over the next four years[14]. These are: 1– to raise the international performance of Australian athletes at Olympic and other Games and at world championships; 2– to improve the quality and equity of sporting opportunities and to increase participation in sport for all Australians; 3– to develop sports science and sports medicine to a level of world leadership in those areas which improve international performances and mass participation; 4– to raise the level of coaching expertise available to all Australians at all levels of participation by supporting a major increase in the number and standard of coaches in Australia; 5– to support the education and vocational training of elite athletes for transition to post athletic careers; 6– to improve the quality and level of expertise of sports administration in Australia, in particular that of national sporting organisations; 7– to encourage and work towards the elimination of the use of prohibited performance enhancing drugs in sport; 8– to increase private sector support for the development of Australian sport; and 9– to develop together with States and local government a cohesive plan for the efficient use of government funding of sport and to implement the plan.

It may be considered that there will be "more of the same" from the Australian Sports Commission but it can be noted that priority 1 still endorses "Australia's National Sport—Winning"—which is what Daly[15] wrote nearly two decades ago. It is clear that the government believes that the profile of Australian sport is one which is "populist" and it is noteworthy that Australia's, and perhaps the world's greatest marathon runner (according to many Australians), Robert de Castella, was appointed Director of the AIS in March 1990. In the context of "elite" sport, priority 9 is also worthy of comment because all state governments throughout Australia provide funds for institutes or academies of sport, as there are regionally based structures to facilitate excellence in sport. Indeed also, attention will be given to the other priorities which have to do with the promotion of sporting opportunities for all Australians.

Reference should be made to a relatively recent initiative of the ASC, that of contracting a firm of consultants, Social Impacts Pty Ltd, to study the impact of sport up to the year 2000. The detailed findings of this study are not widely known, but a 26-page synopsis of the study has been published. A significant point underscored is that intrinsic to an analysis of the sports industry and the role of the government is an understanding of the fact that Australia is a federated system, with three tiers of government (national, state and local), all of which do similar things but each of which do some things much better than others[16]. It is acknowledged that one must not, and should not, neglect the fact that sporting associations, sports participants, the corporate sector and professional associations each have a role to play, lest sport shall not be what it could or should be in the third millennium.

The Case of New Zealand

The 1912 Olympic Games were the last in which Australia and New Zealand competed under the combined name of "Australasia", although in World War I the name ANZAC (Australia-New Zealand Army Corps) became indelibly written in the history of both countries. This proud sporting nation of approximately 3 million people has had many sporting tussles with Australia, especially in the imperial sports of rugby, cricket and netball. Therefore, one must be aware of the "politics" of an Australian speaking and writing about New Zealand.

The Hillary Commission for Recreation and Sport was established in New Zealand by an Act of Parliament on April 1, 1987 as an independent and statutory body to replace both the Ministry and Council of Recreation and Sport. Two earlier reviews, which proposed a new and deeper public commitment to sport and recreation, along with guidelines for increasing and making better use of resources compatible with this new vision, pointedly recommended:

> [...] to remove the duplication represented by the Ministry and the Council, to avoid complex bureaucratic processes, to give sportspeople more influence over matters relevant to them, to emphasise the community and social value recommendations of sport, to broaden the discretionary funding base by introducing lotto, to establish the place of recreation, sport and skill learning within the education system, to develop sport science and medicine resources, to encourage wider participation and to recognise sport and recreation as useful resources in dealing with some social issues[17].

In addition to the Commission's central management, there are in New Zealand two operational arms "in the field": RecCorp and SportsCorp. RecCorp supports the wider field of recreation, much of which is loosely structured. The remainder of this presentation will deal more specifically with the function of SportsCorp, although it should be recognised that the objectives and activities of the two operational arms overlap. For example, one of the recently proposed projects of RecCorp was a joint venture between the New Zealand Swimming Pool Managers Association, Local Government and RecCorp, a Swim Project (working titles "Swim for your Life"/"Kiwi Swim") with the goal of increasing long term regular participation in recreational swimming in public pools[18]. Clearly, such a program links in with the SportsCorp which encourages conventional sport at all levels of competence, whether competitive or non-competitive. The Commission is very aware of the contribution which excellence makes to the motivation of those people who may tend to be inactive without sporting heroes and heroines.

Many of the aims and objectives of SportsCorp are based on ideas and the 24 recommendations incorporated in *Sport on the Move* which was the report of the Sports Development Inquiry Committee, published in 1985[19]. [*Editors' note: Some of the most significant recommendations, particularly among those that have to do with the social accountability of the system have been placed under reference # 19*]. One aspect which did become evident throughout this New Zealand inquiry was that most sports governing bodies perceived the role of government ambiguously. The common dilemma is that sports organisations do not have sufficient resources to conduct their activities, they thus look to government as a source of funds—yet at the same time, they want to retain their independence[20].

Under the Hillary Commission a new National Sport Funding Programme has been introduced based on a proposal submitted to the Commission by the New Zealand Assembly for Sport. A major feature of the new program is a contributions approach to funding where the Commission provides grant aid towards the total cost of a project on a case by case basis. In 1988-89 the Hillary Commission distributed nearly 1,5 million $ NZL to 61 national sports governing organisations, much of which was used to improve the management of sport through the employment of administrators and the training of sport volunteers, especially in the area of coaching[21].

Acting on the recommendations of its Regional Sports Trust Task force, the Hillary Commission is currently establishing a network of ten regional sports trusts to encourage and develop sport at a local level. This program was launched in 1988 with an allocation of 200 000 $ to the regional sport trusts with the intention of them representing the regional voice of sport and overseeing the regional delivery of sports services. The trusts are currently responsible for co-ordinating, developing and servicing existing sport delivery systems as well as planning, promoting and managing new programs and services. Consistent with the expressed desire of the Sports Development Inquiry Committee, the functions of the regional sports trusts are fulfilled in co-operation with existing sports bodies and agencies concerned with sport in the various regions. Most of the ten trusts were fully operational at the end of 1989[22].

One of the activities contracted to each regional sports trust in New Zealand is the KiwiSport program, which is a sports education program, with playing areas and equipment scaled down to suit the needs, social skills and abilities of children aged nine to twelve. With the advent of KiwiSport, many codes and schools are now seriously considering modified sports competitions as an alternative to the adult code[23]. Fair play in sport has been identified as a major concern by the Commission; principles drawn from material by international sporting bodies and overseas agencies have been incorporated as an essential component of the KiwiSport Program. Another significant initiative undertaken throughout New Zealand in 1989 was the establishment of a Sport Strategy Group (SSG) which arose from a "futures for Sport Consultation" held in Wellington. The SSG co-ordinates on an on-going basis the planning and goals of all organisations with a major sports interest, including the Department of Education, New Zealand Federation of Sports Medicine, Coaches Association of New Zealand, New Zealand

Assembly for Sport, New Zealand Olympic and Commonwealth Games Association, New Zealand Sports Foundation, regional sports trusts, the Local Government Association and the Hillary Commission[24].

There are many other innovative programs in New Zealand, such as the Task Force on Alpine Sports, Martial Arts Review, Drugs in Sports Review, the Athlete Assessment Board and assessments of the health and fitness industry and deliberations about the sport by tobacco companies; each, in its own right, would be worthy of study by individuals and/or agencies interested and involved in the development of an integrated system of sport.

In 1987 the Hillary Commission had established the International Sports Priority Board (ISPB) with the primary purpose of providing a mechanism for co-ordinating the funding of international sport. The ISPB now has representatives from the New Zealand Assembly for Sport, New Zealand Olympic and Commonwealth Games Association, New Zealand Sports Foundation and the Commission. In total, for the year 1988-89, the Hillary Commission has granted 1,1 million $ NZL aimed at the development of international sport, much of which was targeted to assisting with bids and/or costs of hosting international sports events in New Zealand.

Concluding Remarks

This presentation aimed at providing an overview of sport (mainly "competitive" sport) in Australia and New Zealand, two liberal democracies located in relatively isolated parts of the globe. It has been pointed out that there is much in common about sport in these two countries, both of which are imbued with the British heritage of "athleticism" and competitive sport[25]. The two countries are very different in size. Australia is the largest island continent with a population of 18 million people. New Zealand comprises two main islands with a population of approximately 3 million. As stated earlier, it is clear that in these two liberal democracies, the intervention and involvement of government in the management of sport has become a most significant trend and thus an important aspect of social, political, economic and cultural life within each country. Sport, being manifestly a component of a nation's culture and also because of its immense universal popularity and relative ease of control, can, and is in fact "manipulated" by governments[26].

A recent trend in Australia has been a perceived need to support "elite" athletes. Indeed, in the foreword of *Going for Gold: the first report on an inquiry into sports funding and administration* undertaken by the House of Representatives Standing Committee on Finance and Public Administration, published in March 1989, Chairman Stephen Martin wrote: "Sport today is at the crossroads. The funding under the foreword (sic) estimates does little more than allow Australia's elite athletes to attend residential camps and compete against each other. It implies a withdrawal from international competition. Australians could still be represented at such competitions but it is doubtful if they would be competitive. [. . .] Such a proposal is not acceptable to those, indeed the majority of Australians, who encourage other Australians in their pursuit of excellence in sport[27]."

Clearly, this question of the role of the state in the promotion of "elite sport" as compared to sport-for-all is a matter of continuing preoccupation and debate.

It is hoped that the presentation of information about the role of two national government agencies—the Hillary Commission in New Zealand and the Australian Sports Commission, has provided a basis for comparison and discussion of the relationship of sport and the state in both capitalist and state-socialist countries. The involvement and intervention of government in the promotion and administration of sport, from the international level to mass participation is expected to continue to be fraught with controversy.

NOTES AND REFERENCES

1. Stewart F (1974) Speech at inaugural dinner of Australian Sports Council August 28

2. Hansard of Australia (1908) House of Representatives March 20 p 1330

3. Willee AW (1972) Physical education in Australia. Physical Education Year Book 1971-72. London: Physical Education Association of Great Britain and Northern Ireland

4. Whitlam EG (1972) Australian Labor Party Policy Speech Blacktown Civic Centre p 35

5. Stewart F (1974) op cit

6. Stewart F (1978) Press Release. August 22 p 1

7. The Advertiser (1973) Adelaide August 22

8. For the dates of details of the introduction of the various state government departments with responsibility for sport, see Jobling I F (1976) A ministry of recreation and sport at the national level of government. Report of the British Commonwealth and International Conference on Health, Physical Education and Recreation. Christchurch: New Zealand p 77-81

9. Department of Tourism and Recreation (1975) Report of the Australian Sports Institute Study Group. Canberra: Australian Government Publishing Service

10. Dunstan K (1973) Sports. Melbourne: Cassell Australia Ltd p 1

11. Horne D (1965) The Lucky Country. Melbourne: Penguin

12. Daly J (1985) Structure. Chapter 2 in Department of Sport, Recreation and Tourism/Australian Sports Commission. Australian Sport: a profile. Canberra: Australian Government Publishing Service p 17

13. Harris AE (1990) Letter to the Minister. In Australian Sports Commission Annual Report 1988-89. Canberra: Australian Government Publishing Service p 1

14. Australian Sports Commission (1990) Strategic Plan 1 January 1990 to 31 December 1993. Canberra: Australian Government Publishing Service p 4

15. Daly J (1972) Australia's National Sport – winning. Australian Journal of Physical Education 57 5-14

16. Australian Sports Commission (1987) Sport to the Year 2000. Canberra: Australian Government Publishing Service p 1

17. Hillary Commission for Recreation and Sport (1987) Statement of Intent. Wellington p 2

18. Memo from General Manager, Recreation to RecCorp (November 23 1989) re New Programs/promotions 1990-91 p 1

19. Sports Development Inquiry Committee (1985) Sport on the Move. Wellington: Government Printer – New Zealand [*Editors's note. Examples of specific recommendations of particular significance in terms of the overall social accountability of the sport system*: 1– That the strategy for the development of sport have as its prime emphasis the investment in expertise, that is, people resources, rather than facilities and equipment; 2– That the Recreation and Sport Act 1973 be repealed and replaced with a new Act establishing a government corporation with sole responsibility for the government contribution to sport; and that this corporation, to be called SPORTSCORP, be directly responsible to the Minister of Sport; 3– That an Assembly of Sport be established to fairly represent all organisations with a direct interest in sport; and that this Assembly, though an independent organisation, be accredited by SPORTSCORP as the official voice of sport; 4– That SPORTSCORP be directed by a Board of seven high-calibre ministerial appointees, one of which would be nominated by the Assembly of Sport; 5– That government make a clear and unequivocal commitment to funding community benefits of sport from taxation sources; [. . .]

8– That this Committee supports the National Physical Education Syllabus Revision Committee's intention to improve the quality and status of physical education in all New Zealand schools; 9– That sport should be an integral part of the physical education syllabus at primary and intermediate school level; 10– That at secondary school level, physical education and sports education be recognised as two distinct types of education; 11– That the position of Sports Educators in secondary schools be jointly funded by the Department of Education and SPORTSCORP; [. . .] 13– That a Sport New Zealand promotional campaign be mounted by SPORTSCORP in association with relevant government departments to encourage New Zealanders to participate in health-promoting physical exercise through recreational and competitive sporting activity; [. . .] 17– That a Women's Sport Promotion Unit be established within the proposed SPORTSCORP structure to promote and develop women's sport. That the Unit be established for three years only, and have at least three full-time professional staff, the majority of which may be women; 18– That government assistance to sports associations be fairly distributed between male and female sports; 19– That a programme of promotion of sports participation aimed at ethnic communities be implemented; 20– That a programme identifying and encouraging traditional ethnic sports or emerging sports be implemented; 21– That sport for the disabled be treated in the same way as sport for the able bodied; 22– That SPORTSCORP in association with its Standing Committee on International Priorities direct sufficient funding to international sports and sports players to maintain New Zealand as a significant force in the international arena.]

20. Ibid p 28

21. Hillary Commission for Recreation and Sport (1990) Second Annual Report 1989 p 11

22. Ibid p 13

23. Hillary Commission for Recreation and Sport (1988) KiwiSport takes off! Hillary Highlights (December) p 1

24. Hillary Commission for Recreation and Sport (1990) op cit p 14-15

25. As highlighted in the recent paper by Phillips J (1990) Sons and Daughters of Empire - the meaning of the 1950 Empire Games. Proceedings of the Commonwealth and International Conference on Physical Education, Sport, Health, Dance, Recreation and Leisure. Sport II p 131-141

26. Shuttleworth J (1990) Government sponsorship of sport development. Proceedings of the Commonwealth and International Conference on Physical Education, Sport, Health, Dance, Recreation and Leisure. Sport II p 228

27. The House of Representatives Standing Committee on Finance and Public Administration (1989) Going for Gold: The first report on an inquiry into sports funding and administration. Canberra: The Parliament of the Commonwealth of Australia p i

Acknowledgement: The author is grateful to Mr Perry Crosswhite, Acting General Manager, Australian Sports Commission, for his comments on early drafts of this paper, and to Dr John Shuttleworth, General Manager of the Hillary Commission for his assistance.

Sport and the State:
the Case of the United Kingdom

Michael F. Collins

Sport in the United Kingdom (UK) is managed through a hybrid and fragmented public-private and voluntary system with a quasi non-governmental body, the Sports Council, as leader and coordinator. New challenges face the sports system in both mass participation and excellence programmes at a time when the government is radically changing the rules for public sector operation.

Historical Sketch

A shorthand sketch of phases into which the development of British sport and recreation may be conveniently divided is set out in *Table 1*. As Allison has put it, "by 1890 all the foundations were laid and the building was three quarters of the way up[1]". In this phase and the interwar period local government was a provider of basic facilities and the regulation of sport in general and representative sport in particular fell to the autonomous governing bodies. Under the leadership of the redoubtable Phyllis Colson the concept of a "really active 'umbrella' body with provincial branches but not vested interests[2]" became in 1935 the Central Council for Physical Recreation (CCPR) which within a year had 82 national bodies in membership.

The period of postwar reconstruction perhaps did more for outdoor sport, than when through the opening up of the countryside, the building of schools sports facilities, and the gradual development of a broader curriculum. The growth of affluence, mobility and awareness through television brought a boom of demand in the 1960s and 1970s which coincided with a period of relative economic stability and growth when local authorities, in Stoker's words, became "midwife to the welfare state[3]". After their reorganisation in 1972 to give probably the largest average sized local authorities in the world, over half established leisure departments and developed their portfolio of facilities, and helped thousands of local clubs to obtain their own premises. Except in small areas this provision was

1890
1990

Michael F. Collins, Institute of Sport and Recreation Planning and Management, University of Loughborough, Loughborough, England.

TABLE 1

Phases in the Development of British Sport and Recreation

Periods/Phases	Events/Facilities/Services
Provision Period I	
• Victoriana	• Museums for science • Public baths • Libraries • Parks and gardens for promenading • Founding of sports governing bodies • Golf courses
• Interwar	• Swimming for exercise and safety • Playing fields • 1935 CCPR
• Postwar reconstruction	• Affluence, car ownership, holiday taking, day trips • Playgrounds • Development of school physical education • National Parks
Provision Period II	
• Public response 1960s and 1970s	• Country and water parks • Youth culture and unemployment • 1966 advisory, 1972 chartered Sports Council • 1972 local government reorganisation • Dual use of education, defence facilities
• Consolidation and change 1980s	• Theme parks, fun pools, leisure resorts • Jogging, running and fitness activities • Capital cuts, compulsory tendering, local management of schools, rate increases • Encouragement of private capital and sponsorship, 1986 Local Government Act, 1989 Tenderin regulations

still lower than in several other European countries but Great Britain has developed earlier than any other a structured profession of managers who developed a "high-troughput-low-cost" mode of operation dealing primarily with casual users, and which some other countries are now trying to emulate.

Alongside this, firstly in outdoor adventure sports and more recently in squash, fitness activities and racket sports, a large number of small commercial businesses have developed, as well as a few large chains of sports manufacturers and retailers and developers of sports facilities in hotels, shopping and business complexes and reconstructed docks. The other major development in this period was commercial sponsorship of sports events and individual athletes took off in the UK on a scale only matched in North America, although the same is now happening in other European countries. As this period unfolded, both major political parties in the UK felt that there should be a central body to plan sports provision and to promote its use. In 1966 an Advisory Sports Council was set up, which became executive in 1972 and under a Trust took over from the CCPR nine regional offices and five national sports centres. With a small secretariat, the CCPR became a forum for the sport governing bodies, and an adviser to the new Council.

In this current decade, consumer demand and public and private provision continued to develop, but recently as part of a general call to review and then "roll back the frontiers of the state", severe pressures have been brought to bear on local government—cutting capital allocations in the sector which includes sport by 80% for the next years, requiring 50% of capital receipts to be used to amortise existing debts,—preventing local authorities from taking more than a 20% stake in any development company,—pressing for a greater proportion of costs to be recovered from users rather than all local taxpayers,—and recently compelling all English and Welsh authorities to offer the management of their sports facilities up to tender to private companies. While this falls short of privatisation, it will drive the public direct labour organisations to operate as contractor companies for their own facilities (and those in other areas if they feel able) if indeed they wish to stay in existence. Meantime the Sports Council has had, at best, level funding in real terms and is expected to bring in more private money from sponsorship and partnership deals, and to reduce the subsidy to users of its national sports centres, again by tendering out their management, and bringing in more lucrative lettings.

The Present Structure of Sport

In the present institutional structure of sport in the UK, the Sports Council (SC) is an executive body "at arms length" from government but advising it. A quasi non-governmental organisation or "quango", the CCPR acts as an adviser to the council on behalf of voluntary sport organisations. The British Olympic Association is for its part responsible for organising British representation in that sphere. The decision to have a body independent of government stemmed from the idea of the Macmillan government that followed what Gruneau has called the liberal pluralist view of sport[4] i.e., that sport be not seen as a formal part of the state, but as an expression of a consensus that has developed amongst voluntary actors. With some concerns for protecting voluntary sport, this was done in Britain in the mid 1960s.

The Minister for Sport, the most junior in a team at the Department of the Environment, deals with intergovernmental and parliamentary matters concerning sport, appoints the chairman and members, receives the annual reports and accounts, and argues for sport's share of government budgets, after discussing the Council's forward corporate plans. Although there is weekly contact with top management, Ministers have intervened directly, although relatively infrequently. Some examples have been – insisting on the building of a new stand at Crystal Palace National Sports Centre, but finding only a minority of the money from government sources; – pressing (unsuccessfully) for the Council to boycottt the Moscow Olympic Games; – pressing for the Council to support the Gleneagles agreement; – vetoing the appointment of one applicant invited to be Director General. The Minister, the government auditor or the parliamentary public accounts committee can chastise the Council for its financial conduct, as was for example the case when it gave 400 000 £ to the Sports Aid Foundation at the end of one financial year, or about its financial dealings with the CCPR, yet, they cannot dictate its policy priorities. This arm's length stance partly stems from the fact that like the British Broadcasting Corporation, the Sport Council is established not by parliamentary act but by Royal Charter. One disadvantage of this situation is that on some legislative matters, especially in town and country planning, the Council has no statutory basis for consultation, yet, the Council cannot be abolished or radically changed without a 75% majority vote of the Privy Council. This status has not prevented changes in the format and representation of the Council. Originally, the CCPR could nominate people to 25% of the seats on the Council (numbering over 30); at the present time, it has as of right one seat for its chairperson and an observer on a council of 15 members. For a time, there were three or four of the ten Chairmen of Regional Sport and Recreation Councils on the Council; then, all of them; now, there are none as of right. The present government has now reduced the Council by half, and introduced more people from the business sector. Hargreaves and popular press commentators have seen this as signaling a weakening of the Council's independence[5]. As one who has worked in the system for its first 17 years, I would say that the present trend represents the government flexing its policy muscles to lead the Sports Council through the process of a more market-orientated business-management phase. In this, the sports Council is not singled out; the same process is happening to scores of "quangos" and to local government[6]. This arm's length stance is not very common. The Australian Sports Commission and the Hillary Commission in New Zealand appear to follow a similar path. National Olympic Committees such as those of the USA and Italy are farther from government. The same can be said of sports federations who lead on policy in Norway, Denmark and Sweden. In Germany, the Netherlands and Finland, government takes a lead, alongside active and strong sports federations, in what would seem to be a more hybrid system.

The system which the institutional structure of the UK seeks to serve is very fragmented. This is not an unusual situation if one considers the situation in Australia as reported in its 1987 Strategic Plan[7]. In the UK specifically, the overall partnership in the institutional provision and consumption of sport/recreation services to more than 23 million active participants includes the central government, the local government, the voluntary sector and the commercial sector. In general terms the central government has a large income, mainly from taxes on sports workers' incomes, and on consumers' purchases, but a small expenditure. Local government has a larger expenditure, including at least a 300 million pound sterling subsidy. The voluntary sector is extremely fragmented with 150 000 clubs in 373 organisations recognised by the four Sports Councils. It employs as many workers as the local authorities (a fact not often recognised) as well as involving some 580 000 volunteers. Not surprisingly as a mainly closed production-self consumption system, its income and expenditure are in balance. Then there is the commercial sector about which, because it keeps most of its records private, there is little known for the bulk of the firms in the sports services sector are very small. The commercial sector's contribution has been systematically underestimated in most countries; in the UK, it supports one and a half times as many jobs directly as the state and voluntary sectors together. Commercial operations dependent on sport (some catering, transport, building, media and manufacturing) generate more than as many again[8].

The Thatcher governments have provided grants, advice, training and tax incentives for founding and expanding small businesses, some specifically aimed at tourists but not sporting operations. Research in process at Loughborough University by Randolph and Collins would suggest that few of the 50 000 small firms in the sports sector are aware of or have taken up such offers. But it does seem that this is the sector that governments of both right and left wing persuasions wish to see flourish.

The Sports Council in its 1989 annual report certainly sees itself as both a coordinator/orchestrator of these fragmented forces and as an innovator/leader: "despite its limited financial resources, (the Council) has a crucial role in defining and securing a consensus on the overall strategic direction of British sport, in promoting good practice in the management, marketing and technical development of sport and recreation, in spreading awareness of available opportunities for people to participate in life enhancing activities; and in stimulating both innovative provision of sport-for-all and excellence of personal achievement[9]".

A brief description shall now be given as to how this works itself out with the government and the targets of policy in two areas: elite sport and sport-for-all, since these need to be put in the context of the Government's and the Sports Council's policy aims.

Sport in General

The current Minister for Sport has set out the following aims for government's involvement with sport[10]: – alleviating social deprivation and stress; – imposing health and well-being; – fostering civic and national pride through excellence of international performance; – promoting British influence abroad and trade; – furthering social policies especially for communal harmony (via combatting violence connected with sport); – furthering the stability and unity of the Commonwealth (via sustaining the terms of the Gleneagles agreement); – protecting and increasing the UK interest in intergovernmental and international sports bodies. A similar list might be espoused by most sports ministers, though some would likely add or substitute additional aims, like asserting the success of the political system (as hitherto in USSR, but perhaps no longer), using sport to attract foreign exchange and to support tourism (based for example on skiing, hunting and fishing, or water sports).

Government bureaux and agencies like the Sports Council have to deliver contributions to some of these aims, and increasingly do so through a long term strategy (the Sports Council produced *Sport in the Community* in 1982 and reviewed it in 1987 in *Into the 90s*[11]) and short term corporate plans. The key objectives the Sports Council selected for the period 1990-93 are as follows: – increase womens participation by 38-42%; – increase or maintain number of participants aged 18-25; – target groups outreach programmes and training; – increase public awareness of opportunities; – 200 sports halls and 75 swimming pools; – double intensive use pitches; – promote dual use/joint provision with schools; – specialists' sports facilities; – improve standards, through development programmes (governing body efficiency, NCF, sports science and medicine, increased governing body users of national centres from 56 to 62). Programs of similar range but varying emphasis have also appeared in Australia, the Netherlands and other countries of the OECD with developed economies.

High Performance Sport

Throughout the 20th century, particularly since TV satellites provided global audiences for high performances, international sporting success has been a way to win international recognition and influence, certainly less costly than industrial trade or military means and thus often seized by developing nations. Great Britain has traditionally had a good sprinkling of world champions in minority sports but more recently has had spectacular success in track athletics, field hockey, canoeing and judo. Allison's judgement is that "there is considerable evidence of politicians trying to cash in on sporting success, but very little of them organising sport as a diversion[12]". Government ministers have, like the Royal Family, been pleased to be seen regularly at major sporting events where British teams appear. Hargreaves has several times claimed that the Sports Council gave equal or greater priority to elite sport in the 1970s and 1980s and certainly the major part of its budget[13]. Impriving high level performance is indeed one of the four basic aims of the Council's charter. Throughout its life however, this has not consumed more than a third of its budget and currently, it takes about a quarter (In the 1990-91 planned budget of the Sports Council, the excellence expenditures (net) can be seen to be of the order of 11,2 million pound sterling, that is about 26% of the overall budget). In his analysis of the overall contributions to the cost of excellence in sport, Taylor[14] showed that the effort (164,4 million pound sterling for the year 1985-86) was distributed as follows: sponsorships 67%; private individuals 13%; sport governing bodies 10%; local authorities 6%; sports councils 4%; sport aid funds, negligible; British Olympic Association, negligible.

This emphasises two things. First, the strength of revenue sponsorship centred around events and personalities; in Great Britain, professional and top amateur sport have become an entertainment and advertising vehicle which collectively far outweighs in finance what the sports people and the state put into elite development. Secondly, media influences are increasing, with little control from governments or sport governing bodies. This situation is due to the increasingly multi-national nature of TV distribution networks and of corporate sponsors. For governing bodies, another problem is that as sponsor's agents have become more skilled, the length of contract needed to yield corporate benefits has shrunk to 18 to 24 months, so sponsorship income is neither long term nor assured. This means that British governing bodies have to find a means of increasing income directly from their members by increasing their affiliations and providing better services. This is crucial to British sport, where only one in four sports people and only one in eight of the population are members of a sports club, and where affiliation fees have traditionally been very low as compared to the rest of Europe and North America. Thus far, the only involvement of government in the sponsorship issue has been to draw up a detailed agreement and code of practice with sponsors producing tobacco products to limit the size of advertisement, verbal mentions of sponsorship, the use of logos and so on. The same has not been contemplated yet for any other products. It would appear that the Government will have to consider its stance on sponsorship and advertising through its membership in the European Economic Community.

The financial priority given to elite support in the UK is undoubtedly lower in absolute and relative terms than in some states (including the (former) German Democratic Republic, the USSR, France, to Federal Republic of Germany, or Australia where 75% of the Sports Commission's budget is allocated to high level sport). Certainly neither the British Government nor the Sports Council approaches the situation in Canada where for reasons of national unity and prestige the dependence on finance from the Federal Government and the latter's influence on policy was described by Macintosh as a virtual "stranglehold on elite sport[15]".

Sport-for-All

Since 1972, UK sports opportunities have been transformed by some 1 800 new sports centres, 500 new swimming pools, 500 new golf courses and thousands of new club facilities. There have been over six million new participants in sport, though only a small minority of them joined the clubs in the governing body of their chosen sport. Perhaps the area least developed has been that of high grade competition facilities. The multi-sport open access provision by local authorities as a response to growing demand has undoubtedly enabled many to develop interests in sport which they could not easily have done through private club, but as they develop skills and commitment, indeed seek to do so. Throughout the UK there is still latent consumer demand, and this has continued to express itself; despite attempts by the government to hold down local authority expenditure, it has continued to rise in real terms.

As part of this growth, participation rates have increased amongst women of all ages (though with some substitution of indoor for outdoor sports) and amongst older people. Hargreaves is of the opinion that despite the consumer drive, the ruling groups in British society continue to express their hegemony over what he refers to as subordinate groups—women, the unemployed, the poor in general, the ethnic minorities. Certainly, the difference between these groups and the rest of the population in sports participation has been least affected as part of the market growth. But what Hargreaves' and other analyses do not explain is why, under social democratic governmental or non-governmental-led systems, the same differences persist to similar degrees. Equivalent participant and investment trend data is not available for socialist states, but recent anecdotes would certainly suggest that inequalities were no less, and possibly greater, as a result of the concentration on and heavy investment in elite performers, which Solidarity is for example trying to redress in Poland through its policy of "Common Olympism".

Another trend that transcends politics or institutional systems is a change in the relationship between the government or central sports body and the federations. As corporate managerialism has affected or infected central government or sports councils/commissions, they have demanded more professional planning and service delivery from grant-aided sports federations. This has led to professionalisation of staff and elected officials, to bureaucratisation of methods and to standardisation of procedures which eventually transform sports organisations[16]. This process can be clearly demonstrated in the UK, in the Federal Republic of Germany and Denmark. To some, with its demands for specific outcomes in return for grant aid, this trend threatens the autonomy of the sport governing bodies[17], though the judgement for Western Europe would seem to be that it is strong and resilient, and not currently in any danger[18, 19].

Conclusions

The Sports Council's strategy in the UK has been to push for equality of opportunity through sport-for-all; recent conservative governments, however, have never formally accepted and endorsed its strategy but have given it year-with-year a static or slightly rising budget which did not strangle it either. When in opposition, the Labour Party has said it would provide more resources, but Hargreaves criticised it for having no radical alternative programme "to those articulated in rational recreation and commercial discourse" and so "merely represented a pallid synthesis of the two[20]".

Certainly the British state puts less into sport than some other governments or voluntary led sports systems in Europe[21] (*Table 2*). Nor has its arms-length stance through the Sports Council and the CCPR given it much political strength. The CCPR has had more influence on direct consumer issues (such as loss of access to school sports facilities, the availability of government-produced large-scale maps for countryside sports, etc.) than on fiscal issues (reducing VAT for sport, providing tax incentives for sponsors and investors, extending charitable status beyond youth sports, and relieving sports clubs of their new higher business rates). This may be in part because the organised sports lobby in the UK is small (participation indeed takes place in many sports through pay-as-you-play public or commercial facilities (last column of *Table 2*). The relative strength of the sports federations in the Federal Republic of Germany, the Netherlands, Denmark and Finland is evident. Their strength locally can also be seen in the average size of local sports clubs, already referred to (penultimate column of *Table 2*).

Hargreaves would say that the middle-of-the-road outcome in Great Britain—a state system that supports sport financially but provides very modest resources, seeks association with success, but gets little involved—is an outcome of the intermediate if not ambiguous position of the Sports Council. He would even

TABLE 2

European Sports Data, 1985

| Countries | Expenditures per head of Population ($ US equivalent) | | | | Club Sport | |
	Consumers	State	Gambling	Sponsors	Av. Nos of Members per Club	% Population in Clubs
BEL	106	37	1	2	81	26
DEN	85*	35	n.a.	2	166	43
FIN	106	36	n.a.	7	382	43
HOL	151	38	1	8	115	25
GBR	100	25	36	5	43	12
FRG	125*	n.a.	n.a.	3	312	34

* Including gambling connected with sport
n.a. Details not available

go further and say that the broader hegemonic effects of the British system are such that, together with other cultural interests, they reduce "constestation to a large extent by removing issues from the political agenda[22]".

However, looking at Canada, Australia, the USA and some European nations, while politics and structures make for differences, I argue that they are of degree in outcome rather than of kind. I believe that it would do more for sport-for-all to become a reality in the UK if the sports movement would – affiliate more members, – increase the size and numbers of its clubs, and, through its members – provide a stronger and more unified voice in local government, the media, other social organisations like trade unions, and lobbying to central government, than changing the present Government—Sports Council—CCPR arrangements.

NOTES AND REFERENCES

1. Allison L (1986) Sport and politics. In Allison L (ed) The Politics of Sport. Manchester: Manchester University Press p 3-26

2. Collins MF (1990a) Shifting icebergs: the public, private and voluntary sectors in British sport. In Tomlinson A (ed) Sport in society: policy, politics and culture. LSA Papers 43 1-12 [Brighton: The Polytechnic]

3. Stoker G (1989) Creating a local government for the post-Fordist society, the Thatcherite project. In Stewart J, Stoker G (eds) The future of local government. London: Macmillan p 141-70

4. Gruneau R (1982) Sport and the debate on the state. In Cantelon H, Gruneau R (eds) Sport, culture and the modern state. Toronto: University of Toronto Press p 1-38

5. Hargreaves J (1986) Sport power and culture. Cambridge: Polity Press

6. Stoker G (1989) op cit

7. Australian Sports Commission (1987) Strategic Plan 1986-87 to 1988-89. Canberra: The Australian Sports Commission

8. Henley Centre for Forecasting (1986) The economic impact and importance of sport in the UK. Study 30. London: The Sports Council

9. The Sports Council (1989a) Annual report 1988-89. London: The Sports Council

10. The Sports Council (1989b) Corporate plan beginning 1 April 1989 - 1 April 1990. London: The Sports Council

11. The Sports Council (1987) Into the 90s. London: The Sports Council

12. Allison L (1986) op cit

13. Hargreaves J (1986) op cit

14. Taylor P (1990) The financing of excellence in sport. London: The Sports Council

15. Macintosh D (1985) Sport and the wider goals of government. CAHPER Journal 51 23-26

16. Hinings R, Slack T (1987) The dynamics of quadrennial plan implementation in national sport organizations. In Slack T, Hinings R (eds) The organization and administration of sport. London: Sports Dynamics p 127-51

17. Riiskjaer S (1990 forthcoming) The voluntary sector and the state. In Collins MF (ed) Sport: an economic force in Europe. London: The Sports Council

18. Collins MF (1990b forthcoming) European perspectives on sport 1. Sport as an economic and political force. Leisure Manager

19. Collins MF (1990c forthcoming) (ed) Sport: an economic force in Europe. International Conference Proceedings. London: The Sports Council

20. Hargreaves J (1986) op cit

21. Jones HG (1989) The economic impact and importance of sport: a European study. Strasbourg: The Sports Council

22. Hargreaves J (1986) op cit

Sport and the State:
the Case of Canada

Donald Macintosh

Canada came relatively late, compared to Eastern Bloc socialist nations and certain Western European industrialized countries, to the realization that sport could be used to promote national unity and to legitimize the government of the day. In fact, the Soviet Union's decision shortly after the end of World War II to use sport to promulgate its socialist ideology, both abroad and at home, was a factor that helped bring the Canadian government to this realization. To meet this goal, the Soviets set about to develop a corps of elite athletes; they met with unparalleled success in these endeavours and soon came to dominate many world international sport events, and in particular, the Olympic Games. At the same time, the Soviet national team took over as the premier force in international hockey, a role that Canada had been accustomed to playing ever since the 1930s. Consternation and alarm grew in Canada during the 1950s over the declining fortunes of the country's international hockey representatives. This spilled over to a more general concern over poor international showings of Canadian athletes in the Olympic Games. These events coincided with the growing popularity and importance of sport in Western industrialized nations. International sport became more professionalized and commercialized, and with the advent of television, soon gained access to the living rooms of millions of Canadians who previously had had little exposure to, or interest in, sport. This emerging interest and concern over Canada's international sport performances echoed through the press and the House of Commons, and soon the Canadian government found itself considering ways in which it might help to improve the country's international sport performances. At the same time, there was mounting pressure from physical educators and physical fitness advocates for the federal government to take action on the apparent poor level of physical fitness among Canadians. These two concerns, along with other social and economic forces that were characteristic of the expanding welfare state in Western industrialized nations at that time culminated in the federal government enacting, in 1961, a bill to encourage fitness and amateur sport[1].

1890
1990

Donald Macintosh, School of Physical and Health Education, Queen's University, Kingston, Ontario, Canada.

Early Years

In the first few years following the passage of this bill, the federal government appeared content to play a passive role in the promotion of fitness and amateur sport. It entered into cost-sharing agreements with the provinces, and used the National Fitness and Amateur Sport Advisory Council to discharge its federal responsabilities. This Council recommended grants to national sport organizations (NSOs) on behalf of the federal government in the hopes that such monies would lead to better international sport performances by Canadian athletes. But these measures did little to improve Canada's stature in international sport. On the one hand, other countries were also intensifying their efforts to better their performances. On the other hand, Canadian NSOs did not have sufficient expertise or resources to help their athletes improve their performances significantly. The clamour and outcry in the press and in the House of Commons that had characterized the 1950s continued, unabated. The concerns about Canada's poor international sport showings coincided in the late 1960s with certain larger forces and events in Canadian society. Pierre Trudeau, who had just been elected leader of the ruling Liberal party, was searching for ways to counter what he saw as two strong divisive forces in Canadian society. On the one hand was the growing nationalism and calls for more provincial jurisdiction and independence in Quebec. On the other, was the increasing demand for more autonomy from the other Canadian provinces. Trudeau was a strong advocate of federalism; as such, in the federal election campaign of 1968, he actively sought ways in which he could strengthen Canadian unity. It is significant that the first Canada Games, one of the few initiatives that the federal government took in sport in the 1960s, and which were held in Quebec City in 1967, had as its theme, "Unity through Sport". It was in this context that Trudeau mentioned sport as part of culture and connected it with the national unity theme. He promised, if re-elected, that his government would establish a task force on amateur sport in Canada.

Growing Government Presence

The above mentioned events culminated in a new policy direction for the federal government in sport, in the 1970s. The federal government did not renew the federal-provincial cost-sharing agreements in fitness and amateur sport, in part, because of the continued wrangling with the provinces over jurisdictional matters, and in part, because the federal government was not getting sufficient political mileage from these programs. Instead, the federal government turned its attention to the promotion of what would become known as high-performance sport. It was judged that better international sport performances were essential if sport was to be effective in the promotion of national unity. To this end, the federal government gradually took greater control over high-performance sport from the NSOs.

In the early 1970s, the federal government established the National Sport and Recreation Centre in its national capital city of Ottawa to house the NSOs, and support them. It also created a separate division, Sport Canada, within the Fitness and Amateur Sport Directorate, to deal directly with high-performance sport. The federal government increased greatly its contributions to the NSOs to a point whereby these bodies found themselves largely dependent on the federal government. In the late 1970s, Sport Canada assumed the full responsibility for providing financial aid to high-performance athletes. Under the auspices of the Athlete Assistance Program, it commenced to bypass the NSOs and mail monthly payment cheques directly to Canada's carded athletes. In the early 1980s, Sport Canada introduced the practice of quadrennial planning as a prerequisite for olympic sport NSOs to be funded. This process called for highly structured plans and specific performance objectives in international sport events for each of

Canada's olympic sport NSOs. These measures, along with the gradual relegation of the National Advisory Council to a perfunctory role in the late 1960s, meant that by the 1980s, there was little in the way of independent input in the determination of national sport policy for Canada.

Another feature of government involvement in sport in the 1970s and 1980s was the increasing propensity to use sport as a means of bolstering the image of the government of the day. This involvement was not restricted to the federal government. With the introduction of the Canada Games, provincial recreation and cultural departments were forced to develop a sport arm and devote personnel and public funds to the selection and training of provincial athletes in conjunction with provincial sport organizations. From this modest beginning, provincial governments commenced to support and nurture high-performance sport in their jurisdictions in much the same way and with the same motives as those of federal government. Provincial sport bureaucracies burgeoned in the 1970s and 1980s. In the rush to get on the high-performance bandwagon, the provincial governments abandoned their previously strongly held position as champions of mass sport and recreation programs and commenced to compete with the federal government for the attention and glamour associated with international sport events. This propensity of the provinces to use sport to their own policital ends could be seen in the actions of the Ontario and Quebec governments after Canada's successes at the 1984 Los Angeles Olympic Games. Both these provincial governments followed suit with the federal government by instituting their own "Best Ever '88" programs to provide financial aid to "provincial" athletes to excel in the 1988 Olympic Games[2].

Not surprisingly, the federal government also commenced to use sport in its foreign policy initiatives. The African nations' boycott of the 1976 Montreal Olympic Games brought the federal government to the realization that a similar boycott of the 1978 Commonwealth Games (Edmonton) would have a disastrous impact on these Games. In order to avoid such a boycott, Canada was forced to change its stance towards South Africa from that of compromise to a leadership role among white Commonwealth nations in lobbying for change in the apartheid policies of South Africa[3]. Canada played a prominent role in 1977 in bringing the Commonwealth nations to endorse the *Gleneagles Agreement on Sporting Contacts with South Africa*, a document condemning apartheid and advocating the suspension of all sporting contacts with South Africa. Canada also took a number of concrete measures to prohibit sporting contacts with South Africa. Sport sanctions have since continued to be a prominent part of Canada's leadership role in the Commonwealth in the struggle against apartheid. Secretary of State for External Affairs Joe Clark's current initiatives to provide support to third world Commonwealth nations in developing better sport opportunities and facilities in these countries is the most recent manifestation of the important role that sport plays in Canada's foreign diplomacy initiatives[4].

Another development that is worth noting has been the growing attractiveness (to all levels of government) of providing financial support for the building of massive sport facilities. As financial times in the modern welfare state become difficult, there are few government expenditures that are popular with both the private sector and the general populace. The construction of massive sport facilities is unique in this respect. On the one hand it provides jobs and incentives for profits for the private sector as well as stimulating the local economy by bringing tourists and spectators to the community. On the other hand, such ventures by government satisfies the demand by the general populace for "state of the art" facilities in which to enjoy professional sport and other forms of popular culture. The facilities that were put in place for the 1988 Winter Olympic Games in Calgary, the construction of the Sky Dome in Toronto, and the enthusiasm generated by the prospects of possibly staging the 1996 Summer

Olympic Games in Toronto (with the myriad of new facilities required for such an event) are only the most recent examples of the attractiveness of these enterprises to all levels of government in Canada.

Outcomes and Consequences

These changing motives and both their positive and negative consequences nicely illustrate what Kidd[5] has described as the dilemma of state intervention in sport. On the one hand, there have been some very positive outcomes of government intervention in high-performance sport in Canada. In that respect, the expectations of even the most optimistic of fitness and sport advocates at the time of the passage of the Fitness and Amateur Sport Bill in 1961 have been exceeded. Canada now has a corps of "state" athletes that compete successfully at international sport events. These high-profile international sport figures have served to counter the "North Americanization" of professional sport in Canada and the ubiquitous presence of United States' televised sport. Canadian sport heroes have certainly contributed to a sense of pride and national unity in Canada, and helped make former Prime Minister Trudeau's vision of sport as a unifying force at least partly come true.

The efforts of the federal government have also provided a support system for high-performance athletes that is the envy of most Commonwealth and many other nations in the world: a centralized national sport administration centre and bureaucratic structure; sophisticated sport science, sports medicine, and physical therapy support; a well-developed and wide-spread coaching certification program; a financial support system for high-performance athletes and coaches; and numerous high-performance sport training centres across the country. Federal and provincial government support for the Canada Games over the last two decades has left a legacy of sport facilities in many cities and communities in Canada that have allowed for greater sport and recreation opportunities for citizens. Although the federal government has been less directly involved, there has been a substantial increase over the last two decades in adult participation in sport and fitness activities and a growing awareness of the positive outcomes of a physically active life-style as potentially contributing to the physical and mental health of Canadians[6, 7].

There have also been, however, some negative outcomes of government involvement. In the first place, the penchant of both senior levels of government for reaping the political payoffs of supporting high-performance sport, along with the continuing federal-provincial jurisdictional wrangles, have prevented the development of a truly national plan for sport in Canada. The struggles between the respective provinces and their provincial sport organizations on the one hand, who champion regional development and the *decentralization* of the sport bureaucracy and training centres, and the federal government and the NSOs on the other, whose efforts are directed towards the *concentration* of power and the resources for high-performance sport in a few of Canada's most populated centres, is another powerful obstacle to cooperative planning efforts in sport[8]. As a result, there is confusion and competition over responsibilities and gaps in the high-performance sport system in Canada through which many talented young athletes fall. A truly national plan would provide a blueprint for the delineation of responsibilities, would facilitate cooperation among the two senior levels of government and the two respective levels of sport organizations, and would make provisions to accomodate the aims and aspirations of local sport clubs and municipal governments, who, after all, are fundamental to the successful development of any high-performance sport system. Second, despite consistent rhetoric in federal government sport policy documents over the last three decades about intentions to provide for more equal opportunities in high-performance sport for females, francophones, and people from working-class backgrounds, these claims have not been made good. In spite of specific policies aimed at increasing opportunities in high-performance sport for women and francophones, there is little evidence of such progress in high-performance sport, either in the ranks of athletes or in the sport bureaucracy[9]. In the particular case of equalizing opportunities according to socio-economic class, the limited available evidence suggests that there are fewer athletes from working-class backgrounds in high-performance sport today than there were a few decades ago[10]. Third, the present thrust of the federal government to encourage the private sector to take on more of the financial responsibilities for the promotion of high-performance sport in Canada, a move that is consistent with other government initiatives towards privatizing social services, will only exacerbate existing opportunity inequalities. The private sector appears to be primarily interested in sponsoring only those sports and athletes that will reap a return on their investment. These, for the most part, tend to be high-profile male athletes in sports that attract media and public attention.

The privatization drive and the propensity of government to support the construction of massive sport edifices, which was noted above, illustrate the clear strategy that government has adopted recently in its use of sport in present times of financial uncertainties. Expenditures on sport are increasingly justified according to the extent that they can stimulate the economy and promote private sector interest. Such a focus has resulted in the construction of sport facilities whose operating expense virtually excludes their use by most high-performance athletes or for community-level sport and recreation; they invariably become sites for professional sport and extravagant entertainment spectacles. These powerful economic motives for involvement in sport appear to have been adopted by all levels of government, despite questions such as those that were raised recently by the "Bread, Not Circuses" group in Toronto about the wisdom of large expenditures for olympic facilities in the face of inadequate housing and welfare support for low income families. Such trends serve to illustrate Gruneau's contention[11] that the federal government's change from support of mass fitness and sport programs to the active promotion of high-performance sport is consistent with the interests of capital in that they allow for the private sector to participate profitably in these entreprises. It may also come as a surprise to those who have come to believe that all post-World War II Canadian governments have taken a socialist bent.

Future Directions

The above described developments are ones that many Canadians have on their minds in the light of the "crisis" of purpose and motives in Canadian high-performance sport that has arisen from the Ben Johnson affair and the subsequent Dubin Commission of Inquiry over drug abuse in sport. What is in fact the proper role of government in high-performance sport? Some have argued that a country's international sport performances are important enough to justify government expenditures on the grounds that all citizens benefit in an equal and intangible way from the positive outcomes[12,13]. These intangible "public" goods can be summarized as contributing to national unity (nation-building), attaining international prestige, increased motivation for public participation in sport, and supporting individuals in the development of excellence[14]. But in order for government to get the best value from its investment, it has been necessary to subjugate traditional educational and social values and outcomes of sport to the pursuit of "excellence" and winning performances in international sport events. To what extent, then, is the realization of these so-called "public goods" justifiable in the face of other goals to which both government and the public pay lip service? Should government continue to expend funds on massive spectator sport facilities, given the crisis in social welfare expenditures in today's modern welfare state? What are the alternatives to federal government support of high-performance sport? Is the present trend towards the privatization of sport, letting the free market determine which sports and athletes in Canada will prosper, a desirable one?

One positive outcome of the Ben Johnson affair and the Dubin Commission Inquiry is that it has brought the matter of goals and values in sport for the first time simultaneously to the attention of the sport governing bodies, the government, and the Canadian public. Up to this time, discussions of sport policy have been of interest to and a matter for discussion only among persons concerned with matter in national sport organizations and government agencies, a dialogue, as noted above, that is conducted on an unequal footing. Seldom was the matter of sport policy discussed at Cabinet level. When it was, the issues related mostly to capital expenditures for sport facilities and foreign policy, matters such as Olympic and Commonwealth Games boycotts and sanctions against South Africa. Discussions of sport in the House of Commons and in the media seldom got beyond concern and interest about Canada's international performances. One immediate positive outcome of the Ben Johnson affair has been the establishment of an all-party parliamentary sub-committee to study fitness and amateur sport in Canada, and to review the Dubin Commission of Inquiry Report. The Ben Johnson affair also highlights the difficulty of seeing ethical issues in sport when the focus is primarily on the production of medals. Not that this is the sole responsibility of government. National sport organizations, the Canadian Olympic Association, the sport science community, the media, and, indeed, the Canadian public, have all been caught up in the ever increasing "quest for gold". The revelations at the Dubin Inquiry were the first time that many Canadians were forced to confront questions of the ethical and social costs of high-performance sport. One must now face squarely the question of whether one wants to pay these ethical and social costs in order to have Canada finish "first" in the 1990 Commonwealth Games, and "place among the three leading Western nations (with West Germany and the USA) and to rank among the top 6-8 overall in the 1992 Summer Olympic Games in Barcelona", the goals set in the federal government's recent sport policy document, *Toward 2000*[15]. In the highly commercialized, drug-tainted, and performance-oriented world of international sport, it may be time for Canada to abandon its current international standards for a system that takes far more account of traditional social and educational values, relates more to personal outcomes, and pays more attention to equity and ethical issues[16]. Such a focus might also allow for more input from local sport clubs and organizations, and result in a broadening of the definition of the dominant forms of sport, to include activities such as soccer, a sport that until recently was largely confined to Canada's growing ethnic population.

The publication of the Dubin Commission of Inquiry Report hopefully will serve to push debate about sport policy and the proper role of government into the public domain; as a result, a structure may be established whereby there can be real and effective public input into policy making in sport across a much broader spectrum of Canadian society than has been the case in the past. In a pluralistic society such as Canada, one in which the legitimate concerns of all sectors of society are not equally heard, it is not realistic to expect that a democratization of sport-policy making will resolve all the problems of recent government intervention into high-performance sport. Proponents of government involvement in sport must also realize that the federal government is constrained in its actions by the country's federal structure and by the diversity and power of non-governmental institutions in society.

It is unrealistic as well to expect, given its tendency to seek favour with both the private sector and the general public, that government will always act in a socially-responsible and altruistic manner in matters of sport policy. But the alternative to government support of high-performance sport, that of leaving it to the private sector and the NSOs, is a direction that is likely to lead to even greater gaps in opportunities to participate in sport according to gender, class, and ethnicity, and to a furthering of the negative impact of commercialization and professionalization on values and goals of sport. The federal government has a legitimate and important role to play in fostering opportunities for excellence in sport, just as it does in other areas of culture. A process of cooperation and shared responsibility and decision making among all the legitimate actors and organizations who have an interest in sport will hopefully lead to values and outcomes that are more consistent with those of most sport participants and organizations in Canada.

NOTES AND REFERENCES

1. Government of Canada. An act to encourage fitness and amateur sport. Acts of Parliament of Canada. Fourth Session, Twenty-Fourth Parliament, Part I, Public General Acts, 1960-61, p 421-424. [See also: Macintosh D, Bedecki T, Franks CES (1987) Sport and Politics in Canada. Kingston-Montreal: McGill-Queen's University Press Chapter 2 Origins of Bill C-131 p 10-29]

2. Macintosh D, Bedecki T, Franks CES (1987) op cit p 141-42, 174

3. Olafson G (1986) Canadian international sport policy and the Gleneagles Agreement. In Mangan JA, Small RB (eds) Sport, Culture, Society: International Historical and Sociological Perspectives. London: E and FN Spon p 137-44

4. Franks CES, Hawes M, Macintosh D (1988) Sport and Canadian diplomacy. International Journal XLIII 665-82

5. Kidd B (1981) The Canadian state and sport: the dilemma of intervention. Annual Conference Proceedings of the National Association for Physical Education in Higher Education. Champaign: Human Kinetics p 240-50

6. Canada Fitness Survey (1983) Fitness and lifestyle in Canada. Ottawa: Government of Canada, Fitness and Amateur Sport

7. Stephans T, Craig CL (1990) The well-being of Canadians: highlights of the 1988 Campbell's survey. Ottawa: Canadian Fitness and Lifestyle Research Institute

8. Macintosh D, Whitson D (1990) The game planners: transforming Canada's sport system. Montreal-Kingston: McGill-Queen's University Press [See Chapter 5 for a further development of the subject p 46-58]

9. Ibid Chapter 7 p 81-91

10. Beamish R, Johnson A (1987) Socio-economic characteristics of Canada's current national team, high-performance athletes. Presented at the Annual Meeting of the North American Society for the Sociology of Sport Edmonton Alberta [See also Macintosh D, Albinson J (1985) An evaluation of the athlete assistance program. A report submitted to Sport Canada. Kingston: Queen's University]

11. Gruneau R (1984) Leisure, freedom and the state. In Tomlinson A (ed) Leisure, Politics, Planning and People. Vol I London: Leisure Studies Association p 124-39

12. Gratton C (1988) The production of olympic champions: international comparisons. Presented at the Leisure Studies Association Second International Conference, Brighton

13. Taylor P (1988) The production of sporting excellence in England: a mixed economy problem. Presented at the Leisure Studies Association Second International Conference, Brighton

14. Macintosh D, Whitson D (1990) op cit Chapter 8 p 92-107

15. Government of Canada (1988) Toward 2000: Building Canada's Sport System. Report of the Task Force on National Sport Policy, Ottawa: Fitness and Amateur Sport p 36-38

16. Macintosh D, Whitson D (1990) op cit Chapter 10 p 122-39

Gratitude is expressed to CES Franks, R Gruneau and B Kidd for their assistance in the revision of the text of this presentation.

Le sport et l'État : un commentaire

Nelson Paillou

Monsieur le Président,
Mesdames et Messieurs,

J'ai fait beaucoup de choses dans mon existence, je n'ai jamais été commentateur. Il m'est arrivé, bien sûr, de procéder à des synthèses d'exposés mais «commenter» quatre interventions, c'est pour moi une première. Je me réjouis de cette expérience mais, comme tout néophyte, je revendique votre indulgence.

Qu'il me soit permis de féliciter les organisateurs d'avoir eu l'idée de poser un problème fondamental au-travers le vécu de quatre pays de type politique identique avec leurs différences liées à leur histoire, à leurs racines, à leur culture, à leurs mœurs, à leurs coutumes. L'objet de notre réflexion vise à situer le sport par rapport à l'État ou l'État par rapport au sport. Quel est donc, dans ces démocraties libérales, le rôle de l'État et celui du mouvement sportif?

C'est le problème essentiel et qui est d'autant plus difficile à résoudre que nous assistons, en ce début de la dernière décennie du siècle, à une expansion spectaculaire du sport dans le monde. Expansion quantitative et qualitative qui a provoqué deux réactions très importantes: la médiatisation du sport et ses répercussions déterminantes dans le secteur économique (les marchés du sport représentent, en France, 2% du produit intérieur brut, ce qui est appréciable). Cette importance au plan économique, la place prise par le sport dans les média, augmentent considérablement son importance politique. Les conférenciers s'accordent à constater que l'absence de médailles culpabilise les pays qui estiment que leur rayonnement passe par leur succès dans le domaine sportif, d'où leur souci de populariser, de développer le sport.

Malheureusement, cette expansion entraîne des dérèglements. Pour devenir champion, pour être «le meilleur,» on va vite estimer que la «récupération naturelle» ne suffit plus. On est alors tenté de faire appel aux substances dites dopantes. Ces substances apparaissent indispensables, tout comme si la motiva-

---

Nelson Paillou, Président du Comité national olympique et sportif français, Paris, France.

tion du dépassement de soi n'était pas suffisante pour réaliser ses virtualités. Nous en sommes tous quelque part responsables : les dirigeants politiques bien sûr qui entendent étayer la légitimité de leur régime en «récupérant» les exploits sportifs et les résultats spectaculaires ; mais aussi les dirigeants et entraîneurs sportifs lorsqu'ils veulent asseoir «la permanence» de leurs fonctions sur les titres remportés par leurs athlètes! D'autres dérèglements sont dictés par les fanatismes qui entraînent dans leur sillage l'inquiétant phénomène de la violence. Ces désordres de toute nature sont le revers de la médaille du phénomène expansionnel, sans doute unique, du sport. Il n'existe aucun domaine de l'activité humaine, aucun spectacle qui soit capable, comme cela sera le cas pour les Jeux olympiques de Barcelone, de rassembler plus de 4 milliards de téléspectateurs dans 165 pays du monde. Alors, il ne faut pas s'étonner des hésitations, des interrogations que l'on a vu poindre ici ou là. Qui fait quoi? Qui doit faire quoi de l'État ou du mouvement sportif?

Bien entendu, les reponsables du mouvement sportif que nous représentons, ont quelques raisons de croire à l'importance de leur rôle et peuvent être fiers de leur «indépendance». Cette volonté d'indépendance est-elle légitime? L'indépendance est-elle possible? Légitime, sans aucun doute, parce que les responsables du sport dans tous les pays se sont librement engagés dans cette mission; leur acte est volontaire et conçu comme un *service*. Ils ne «se servent» pas du sport, ils «le servent». Le politique, d'une manière ou d'une autre, «se sert» du sport. L'économique, d'une manière ou d'une autre, lui aussi, et pour d'autres raisons, «se sert» du sport. Pour eux, l'objectif «sport» est au second degré, alors que, pour le militant, le sport est placé au premier degré. Je dirai que, pour le militant sportif, le sport est «sujet», il n'est pas «objet». Le sujet a le rôle noble dans la phrase, car il conduit le verbe. Le complément, l'objet, n'est qu'une conséquence. Le rôle noble, c'est bien le «sujet». En définitive, pour nous le sport est une «fin», ce n'est pas «un moyen».

Si la volonté d'indépendance est légitime, l'indépendance est-elle pour autant possible? Dans la conférence du Dr. Chalip, il m'a paru pertinent d'entendre rappeler qu'aux USA, l'État, tout d'un coup, s'est préoccupé, après 1972 et 1976, des résultats sportifs du pays parce qu'il ne pouvait pas supporter d'être jugé inférieur à l'URSS. C'est bien, pour un pays, d'avoir cette préoccupation. Cela serait naïf de notre part d'ignorer que cela existe, même si nous n'avons pas cette préoccupation, même si notre objectif premier est de nous préoccuper des jeunes et de leur faire aimer le sport. Mais la noblesse de cette mission ne nous autorise pas, pour autant, d'avoir l'apanage exclusif de l'animation du sport. L'État, lui aussi, a son rôle à jouer.

Cela nous ramène à l'excellent propos de MacAloon qui soulignait la tendance à vouloir tout dichotomiser. En France, pays de Descartes, on parle de cette tendance cartésienne à vouloir tout caser dans des schémas bien précis, différents, distincts, alors que les choses beaucoup plus complexes se mêlent plus intimement. MacAloon nous disait, dans sa conférence d'ouverture, «ne faisons pas de dichotomie, le sport ne peut pas se payer le luxe d'être indépendant de la politique». Nous y sommes. Il ajoutait «il faut qu'il y ait une interpénétration croissante» et il a raison de nous dire que le sport ne peut pas être totalement différencié de la politique.

Dans nos pays, qui vote le budget? Ce n'est pas le mouvement sportif, c'est le politique. On a besoin, par conséquent, de ce politique, cette interpénétration existe. N'oublions pas, par ailleurs, que les boycotts des Jeux de Moscou et de Los Angeles en 1980 et 1984, ne sont pas étrangers à la période de guerre froide entre les deux Grands. Ignorer cela serait être naïf! Mais, même dans ce contexte, si on veut avoir une vision globale de l'interférence du politique et du sportif, on a le devoir d'éviter, au maximum, l'ingérence du politique dans le monde sportif. C'est pour éviter cette ingérence que les mouvements sportifs anglais et français, alors que nos gouvernements respectifs souhaitaient qu'on boycotte les Jeux de Moscou, ont décidé librement d'y participer tout de même en pensant qu'en-dehors de toute idéologie politique le sport est un dénominateur commun qui doit dépasser tout le reste.

Nous comptons en France 13 250 000 sportifs, dont je dois me sentir responsable. Je suis convaincu que, dans ces 13 250 000 citoyens, l'éventail des courants de pensée est très largement ouvert. Je n'ai pas le droit de travailler pour un seul courant de pensée, par exemple pour celui qui est au Gouvernement dans l'instant... et qui n'y sera pas demain! Oui, je me dois de travailler pour tous. C'est là que l'on voit qu'il n'est pas possible de dichotomiser «État» et «mouvement sportif» mais qu'en même temps on peut tout de même, dans cet ensemble, conserver son libre arbitre, son autorité, sa lucidité, son indépendance. Il n'est pas question de se laisser récupérer par le politique, et il faut savoir dire non dès lors que l'on est conscient d'une ingérence insupportable.

Il n'est pas question d'unifier les solutions pour l'ensemble des pays. Chacun les trouvera. Mais il me semble qu'il est important d'associer (et je l'entendais dire dans la conférence du Dr. Macintosh) l'État et le mouvement sportif car, en-dehors du phénomène politique, il y a une dimension que nous ne pouvons pas négliger, c'est la dimension économique qui est assez récente et qui est trop lourde de conséquences pour être ignorée. Le sport est à l'origine d'une source de profit économique. Comment le mouvement sportif n'aurait-il pas droit, en retour, à une partie de la manne? Comment ne bénéficierait-il pas d'une partie du profit au terme d'un contrat clair, honnête, librement consenti. Ce n'est pas condamnable, comme le pensaient certains de nos anciens, que le sport traite avec l'économie. Mais, il nous faut être conscients que les partenaires économiques ne poursuivent sans doute pas exactement le même objectif que nous, même si certains partenaires se conduisent en véritables mécènes. N'est-ce pas le cas de ceux qui ont soutenu l'organisation et la réalisation de ce colloque qui n'aurait pas été possible sans eux?

Je pense, en conclusion, qu'il appartient à l'État de s'occuper de l'éducation, de s'occuper du sport à l'école, de le développer, qu'il lui appartient de légiférer, de lutter contre le dopage... On a besoin également de l'État pour éviter que l'on dépende uniquement du secteur économique. Notre indépendance est à ce prix.

Je reviendrai, une dernière fois, aux propos de MacAloon et de Jeu qui nous ont donné une excellente leçon en rappelant que nous devons essayer d'admettre des contradictions apparentes, des ambiguïtés, pour les dépasser. Il ne faut pas dire sport *ou* État, mais sport *et* État. Je ne peux pas dire «je suis contre l'État pour le mouvement sportif». Je préfère déifier le *et* et condamner le *ou*. MacAloon l'exprimait ainsi: «indépendance c'est sûr, mais aussi coopération». Donc, finalement, je crois qu'il va falloir qu'on trouve des solutions qui associent les deux. Jeu ne parlait-il pas de «conservatoire» et de «laboratoire»? Et c'est bien vrai! Soyons à la fois fidèles au «passé», mais, en même temps, préparons «l'avenir». Et ne disons pas «nous sommes pour le passé, pour la vieille conception humaniste du Comité International Olympique» ou bien «nous sommes pour un sport moderne, entièrement placé sous l'emprise de l'argent». Non, nous sommes à la fois désireux de ne pas trahir l'humanisme tout en ne reniant pas l'importance de l'argent.

Permettez-moi, enfin, de dire, au nom du pays de Pierre de Coubertin, que j'apprécie beaucoup ce symposium. Si j'ai tenu à le vivre attentivement tout au long, c'est pour apprendre beaucoup en vue du Congrès du Centenaire du CIO qui rassemblera 2 000 personnes du monde entier à Paris en 1994 pour étudier, lui aussi, «l'Olympisme du 3e millénaire». Au nom de mon pays, je vous exprime donc ma vive gratitude et, vous le savez, mon indéfectible amitié.

Sport and the State:
the case of the USSR with References
to the GDR, Cuba and China

Vladimir Rodichenko

The subject "Sport and the state" proposed by the Symposium organizers takes on a special significance at the present stage experienced by mankind as a whole and the world sports community in particular. But it should be made clear from the start that a thorough analysis of the theme at this particular moment is doomed because of the unprecedented dynamism of the changes occuring. I should like to express gratitude to the Organizing Committee for their kind invitation and for the choice of a very topical subject indeed. My presentation is based on information and data collected from various documental sources in the USSR as well as on personal experiences gained through direct participation in the sports movement in the USSR and through active cooperation within sports and sport sciences organizations in the USSR, the German Democratic Republic and Cuba.

In his inauguration speech of March 1990, the Soviet President Michael Gorbachev said: "The main gain of perestroyka is the democracy and glasnost[1]." Naturally, the latest Soviet events, which have resulted from perestroyka and glasnost, have greatly influenced this report. These processes allow Soviet sports sociology and theory of management specialists to look for a genuine correlation of positive and negative aspects of sport administration. The symposium organizers suggested I make an analysis of differences in sports relationship to the state in the USSR, and make references to GDR, CUB and CHN allowing for their social, political and cultural similarities. In so doing, I have used traditional methods of historico-logical analysis, observation and participant observation. Firstly, terminology. *State*. Historically, and taking into account the specific character of a type of state with only one ruling party, the concept of *State* means a whole complex of the party, state and public (for instance, trade unions) power institutions. Naturally the latest events have brought about some changes in such an interpretation. *Sport*. In this report, the concept incorporates top-level sport, mass sport, physical education within state programmes, and recreation, all of which have common organizational grounds in the countries being considered.

1890
1990

Vladimir Rodichenko, National Olympic Committee USSR, Moscow, USSR.

Two background considerations should be emphasized at this point. The first one refers to Marx who characterized state activity as "the fulfilment of common affairs arising from the nature of any society and specific functions arising from opposition between government and people." The second one is from Weber who considered that "any domination is expressed and functions as management[2]". When referring to domination, Weber meant socio-political power. In that perspective, I shall consider mostly the management aspects of the problem. I should finally like to stress that in such a brief report, I will not insist on the details in which differences or similarities are expressed, but rather on revealed fields of such differences and similarities. I should also stress that I consider only the interrelationship between sport and the state. One more general consideration in assessing interactions between sport and state brings us back to a viewpoint of Pierre de Coubertin who wrote: "The Olympic Movement [. . .] refuses to accept the existence of an educational system which is accessible only to the privileged class because the working class cannot afford it [. . .] It stands for universal and popular sports education[3]." A specific feature of the political power system of the group of states under consideration is that such problems have been solved under conditions of party and government management centralization. The merging of the ruling party with the state was reflected in such general methods of sport movement administration as administrative, economic and ideological. During considerable periods of time the latter influence prevailed.

In those four countries the most important form of strategic management decisions in sport was the adoption of decisions by the central bodies of the ruling parties. For example, the tenth Congress of the Socialist Unity Party of the GDR laid down the following guidelines: "Regular physical training is an important integral part of an individual's all-round development and of the socialist way of life." The general features of the interrelations between state and sport are formulated in approved charters and rules of the highest bodies of sport management in each of the considered countries. The regulation on the USSR State Committee for Physical Culture and Sport, as approved by the Council of Ministers of the USSR, determines that the State Committee is a body of state administration which provides for the guidance and control of the physical training and sports in the country. It bears responsibility for organization and improvement of the public's physical training, as well as for the training of athletes. In addition to that, it pursues a uniform state policy in the assigned field of management. Similar management patterns with insignificant modifications operate in the other socialist countries considered. It can be reasonably assumed that given limited economic resources, the centralized party and government management of sport presents certain advantages. Such a sports management approach in the four countries under consideration was never kept a secret. Moreover, it was acknowledged by the leaders of the international sports and Olympic Movement. One example will suffice. In 1969, Brundage said of the GDR: "Great support rendered by the government to sport can serve as a good example for many other countries [. . .] The state bodies of the GDR fully implement the Olympic principles[4]."

As concerns the occasional criticism of sports organizations of these countries for so-called state professionalism, it should be mentioned that in the whole period of their participation in the international sports movement none of their sportsmen was disqualified for proof of having broken the rules of amateurism. The first such measure was taken by the International Olympic Committee with regard to the Austrian Schranz. It may be that the international community realized the fact that state support is one of the ways of creating the necessary conditions for sportsmen to compete, but not necessarily a means of making profit. It thus appears that such a form of mutual relationship between sport and the state was recognized *de facto* and *de jure* above all because of its efficiency which benefited world sport as a whole.

Does this system of interrelationships between state and sport lead to illegal practices? History has refuted such a standpoint. It will be enough to think of violations which had the strongest resonance, including cheating in measuring long jumps at the world athletics championship and the drugs scandal in Seoul. Concerning the use of top-level sport for politico-ideological purposes, any impartial research shows that it is not the prerogative of a particular socio-economic system.

The sports movement of the countries under study is well integrated into a system of international sports relations. At the same time, political priorities have decisive importance on sports management both within the country and on the international stage as, for example, in a refusal to participate in the Olympic Games. But sportsmen of the socialist countries cannot be considered as the first and the only hostages of political priorities in international sports relations.

After consideration of the similarities, we shall consider some of the differences in the mutual relations between sport and state. Such differences are firstly determined by cultural traditions and social conditions. In the guidelines of the ruling parties and state towards top-level sport, mass sport and recreation, one can see some differences between the constitutional tasks, purposes and possibilities of physical training and sports outlined in the constitutions of these countries. In the constitution of the GDR, amended in 1988, sport is legitimated in three articles[5]: *Article 18:* "Physical training, sport and tourism being the elements of socialist culture provide all-round physical and moral development of citizens." *Article 25:* "[...] For more complete formation of a socialist personality and ever more satisfaction of cultural interests and the requirements of citizen participation in cultural life, physical training and sport is stimulated by the state and society." *Article 35:* "Every citizen of the GDR has the right to health and safety at work. This right is provided by encouraging physical training, school and national sports and tourism."

In the constitution of Cuba: "Each person has the right to physical training and sport. Carring out of this principle is provided by including practical physical training into national education system as well by improving sports equipment and facilities owned by the people[6]."

An article of the constitution of the USSR dealing with the right to recreation says that, together with eight other social conditions, this right is also provided by development of mass physical training, sport and tourism. Today, such a statement no longer corresponds to the social role of sport; yet all the efforts to amend USSR legislation concerning physical training and sport (a draft of which was already produced in 1985, the first year of perestroyka), have so far been in vain. With respect to variations in the organizational structures of sport management, it is emphasized that because of comparable political party and government leadership, the differences are only minimal. For example, there is no essential difference in the forms of interaction and subordination of state and public administrative bodies. In the USSR there is a State Committee of the USSR for Physical Culture and Sport, State Committees in each of the Republics of the Union, and also territorial sports committees. There is in addition a public organization—the Trade Union Society for Physical Training and Sport. Lastly, there exists such state-public organizations as the sport societies "Dynamo" and "Labour Reserves" and a state system of sport in the Armed Forces as well.

In the GDR, there is a public organization known as the "German Sports and Gymnastic Union" (DTSB) with its territorial bodies and a State Secretariat. Besides there are obviously also numerous trade union and state sports organizations in that socialist state.

In the People's Republic of China, two top-level organizations are functioning. They are the State Committee (Commission) for Physical Culture and

Sport and the All-Chinese Sport Federation. In addition, sport is run by trade unions and state bodies.

In Cuba, sport is run by a state administrative body—the National Institute of Sport, Physical Training and Recreation (INDER).

Recently, more specifically in the USSR and GDR under conditions of glasnost, the contradiction between formal government discourse with respect to mass sport and its actual level of development has been subjected to severe public criticism. In both countries, one could see the inequalities between top-level and mass sport. In particular, it was affirmed that top-level sport indeed deprived mass sport of the financial and material support which it so desperately needed.

The four countries in question actually enjoy a high sports rating. However, many believe that this status has never been reached by infringing on mass sport. For them, the inadequate level of mass sports development can be explained by economic reasons, which are not directly connected with elite sport. The background for these reasons lies in the economic weakness of the state. Withdrawal of means from elite sport would not have improved the status of mass sport because of its immense scope. In the last years and months democratic reforms have been taking shape owing to the effect of perestroyka which started in April 1985 in the USSR, and of the new political thinking in both the USSR and GDR. In my opinion, the historic sense of perestroyka for the USSR and the whole world is that it aims to implement those tendencies and interests that are common to all mankind, thus creating the possibility of democratic reforms aimed at eliminating the negative aspects of the interaction between sport and state that have been in existence for decades. In the USSR and GDR, on the basis of the division of the legislative, executive and judicial power in the socio-political sphere, there is search for new forms of combination of state and public organization activity in sport, and a rejection of age-old stereotypes.

In his March 1990 inaugural speech, President Gorbachev stressed that the policy of perestroyka is a transition from an authoritarian and bureaucratic system to a humane, democratic socialist society. However, the changes which are taking place in the USSR under the influence of perestroyka have not yet been adequately reflected in the management of top-level and mass sport[7]. At the same time, as a main effect of perestroyka, we are dismantling the administrative command system, as well as democratizing and decentralizing sports management. State and public federations for sports will be given material and financing resources. The Olympic Movement is broadening by the creation of olympic committees in the Republics. Besides, there is a possibility of broadening the rights of the USSR Olympic Committee by delegating to it powers which are formally assigned to it by the Olympic Charter. More considerable changes, in essence the destabilization of the existing sport structures is taking place in the GDR under the influence of the radical changes in its socio-political system. German sportsmen were the first to feel changes both in the socio-political condition in the country and in existing party and government management structures[8]. Dislike of a considerable number of people with regard to the state was transfered to all its institutions including sport. In the future, there may be a differentiation in this process. In analyzing the efficiency of sports management methods in the USSR and GDR one can see the effect of decreasing ideological methods. We have excluded from the Soviet constitution the thesis about the leading role of the communist party and we have introduced a multi-party system. In the GDR a multi-party system now exists and the communist party has lost its leading role. Notwithstanding, ideological methods of sports management may never wither away completely; one ideology may simply be replaced by another or others. The importance of economic methods of management is also increasing. On the transformation of interaction between state and sport in the GDR, we must consider the process in the context of what President Gorbachev considers to be realization of the Germans' natural right to unity.

In 1988, in the People's Republic of China, the President of the International Olympic Committee, Juan Antonio Samaranch, pointed out that sport in that country had made great progress in terms of the number of sportsmen and the number of events in which they participated in Seoul. He considers that it will contribute to China's transformation into a world sports power in the near future[9]. Regarding relations between sport and state in Cuba, it should be mentioned that as a result of such interaction the Cuban sportsmen won 17 gold medals at 5 Olympic Games and 316 medals at Pan-American Games over the last 30 years. In accounting for such success Cuban experts themselves primarily name such centralized state measures as growing state budget allocations, and a considerable increase in the number of coaches and instructors with higher education levels. While estimating the possibility of changes in existing relations between sport and state, one should take into consideration what Castro said on December 7, 1989: "In Cuba we are correcting mistakes. True social revolution and process of correcting of mistakes are not possible without a strong, disciplined and authoritative party[10]." The international aspect of sport management in the four countries of URS, GDR, CUB and CHN is actually inter-state. In this respect we have joint long-term participation in the international sport and Olympic Movement, and are now establishing the principles of new political thinking which correspond to a well-known, but ignored for many years, statement of Lenin about the priority of interests common to all mankind over class interests. A convincing example of the new political thinking is the USSR participation in the Olympic Games in Seoul.

In conclusion, it should be stressed that it is quite difficult to give a scientific determination of the prospects here because the "sport-state" system is subjected to strong influence from socio-political processes and because of the dynamism of the changes. Today, the most important practical question is what sport and state sport management structures, which actually were the social gains of the people of these countries and which undoubtedly promoted the progress of the sport, should be preserved during the democratization and liberalization taking place in the socialist countries.

REFERENCES

1. Gorbachev M (1990) Rech Prezidenta SSSR M Gorbacheva na wneocherednom tretjem sjezde narodnyh deputatow. Izwestija 16 Marta [Speech of the USSR President M Gorbachev on the extraordinary III congress of peoples deputy]

2. Dewjatkowa RP (1969) Nekotorye aspekty sociologii M Webera (kriticeskii analiz) Awtorefat dissertacii. Leningrad p 11 [Some aspects of M Weber sociology critical analysis. Abstract of dissertation]

3. Coubertin P de (1971) Chetyre storony odnoj medali. Suschestwuft Li "Sportiwnoe chudo GDR?" Drezden p 13 [Four sides of one medal. Does the GDR sportswonder exist?]

4. Brundage A (1971) Chetyre storony odnoj medali. Suschestwuft Li "Sportiwnoe chudo GDR?" Drezden p 15 [Four sides of one medal. Does the GDR sportswonder exist?]

5. The GDR constitution (1988) E Razumowskij. Fizicheskaj kultura i sport W GDR. Moscow p 11 [Physical culture and sports in the GDR]

6. The Cuba constitution. Translation from the archives of all-union sport research institute (VNIIFK)

7. Gorbachev M (1990) op cit

8. Wieczisk G (1990) Kogda wse uwlecheny politikoj. Sovetsky Sport apryl 3 [When everybody enjoy with politics]

9.   Samaranch JA (1989) Jan Wen. Perspektiwy mirowogo sporta. Beseda s prezidentom mok JA Samaranch. Magazin "Kitaj" 1 p 13 [The prospects of world sport. Interview with IOC President JA Samaranch]

10.   Castro F (1989) Socializm ili smert! Izdatelstwo "khose marti", Gawana [Socialism or death! Habana: Jose Marty Publishers]

The Changing Relationship between Sport and the State in Eastern Europe

Jim Riordan

Background to Events

Such is the disorienting *pace of change* in Eastern Europe[1] that the relationships between sport and the state have come to possess quite new dimensions and prospects since the idea for this Symposium was first conceived. This relationship cannot be understood outside the momentous events of late 1989; for they marked a watershed not only in East European history, but in world history too. It was one of the historic moments of modern times, comparable to those of 1848 and 1917. In one country after another the ruling regime yielded to massive popular protest. Poland, Hungary, the German Democratic Republic, Bulgaria, Czechoslovakia and, most dramatically of all, Rumania, all saw their Communist Party leaders driven out, a new government installed and contested elections promised. It is likely that not one of those states will be ruled by a genuine communist party by the end of the 1990s. Stalinism might will be dead (save, for the moment, in Albania), international Leninism indeed has waned. It is tempting to draw parallels with that other recent watershed, in Western history—the year 1968—with its many-sided rebellion against the control, bureaucracy and authority of the state and several of its agencies (including in sport), all for liberation, more democracy and self-expression. Yet, as shall be seen below, such comparisons are misleading, in so far as the struggle today in Eastern Europe is taking place in complex conditions of economic crisis, political bankruptcy and national self-assertion.

There can be little doubt that the popular upheaval in Eastern Europe was accelerated by the policies of *perestroika* and *glasnost* launched since April 1985 when Mikhail Gorbachev came to power in the Soviet Union. Yet while much of the change in the USSR may be attributed to leadership, its achievement, as the eminent US economist and scholar Galbraith has pointed out, "is in bowing to and

Jim Riordan, Department of Linguistic and International Studies, University of Surrey, Guildford, United Kingdom.

1890
1990

not resisting the deeper, more important if less visible forces that were actually in control[2]". By contrast with the Western situation of the late 1960s, the economic, political and social circumstances of Eastern Europe could not be more different. The former planning and command structure of the economy has broken down; bureaucratic sclerosis has set in; the state-controlled economy appears gripped by crisis that deepens by the day. The polity is only slowly emerging from stalinist totalitarianism, while the citizenry clamour impatiently for more voice and participation. Traditionally, it has not been difficult to keep the peasantry silent and subservient; daily toil and survival absorb much of the available energy, and geographical dispersal helps thwart discussion and concerted action. With industrialisation (only the German Democratic Republic and Czechoslovakia can be said to have begun "to build socialism" in an urban-industrial milieu) more and more educated people—workers, managers, teachers, scientists, students, journalists, self-appointed spokespersons for the public interest, even sports scientists or scholars—have come together and demanded to be heard. So in Eastern Europe, as also in many countries of the Western world.

What ought not to be lost sight of in the present turmoil is that socialism, in economic terms, had worked rather well in the Soviet Union and elsewhere. It had built the second greatest industrial economy in the world, provided a much better or certainly a much better distributed living standard than that under the tsars, organised and armed the vast forces that very decisively turned back the Nazi army on its own front. And did quite well in sport too.

Sport at the Barricades

A compelling feature of the turbulent events in Europe's socialist states has been the intense debate about sport. Far from being at the periphery of politics, sport has been right at the centre. In Rumania, sportsmen manned the barricades, with Dinamo Club members defending their patrons, the Securitate, in opposition to the army athletes of Steaua whose olympic gold medallists in shooting were said to have been among those firing on the secret police. Small wonder Dinamo Bucharest changed its name to Unirea Tricolor once the smoke of battle cleared. Rumanian rugby captain Florica Murariu and teammate Radu Dadac were two of the well-known stars who were reported to have fallen in battle. In the German Democratic Republic, sports stars like Katarina Witt, Roland Matthes and Kornelia Ender had their homes and cars vandalised by erstwhile "fans" reportedly angry at the privileges of the stars and their close association with the old regime. The officials of GDR's umbrella sports organisation DTSB, as is well known, resigned *en masse*. In Hungary, Poland and Czechoslovakia several clubs have hurriedly sought a new name, sponsorship and even Western commercial backing (like that of Grundig and Volvo for GDR's teams). In early 1990 Lithuanian and Georgian teams withdrew from all Soviet cup and league competitions and several Soviet republics set themselves to the task of reviving their former National Olympic Committees. With the welling up of hostility and revenge directed against the paramilitary forces that have shored up the former regimes, it was to be expected that their sponsored sports clubs should suffer by association. For since the end of World War II, the East European sports system has been dominated by clubs of the security police and the armed forces: Dinamo (Tirana, Bucharest, Zagreb, Berlin, Dresden as well as Moscow, Kiev, Minsk and Tbilisi—Dinamo Tbilisi was renamed Iveria in 1990) and the clubs of the armed forces such as Dukla Liberec in Czechoslovakia, Legia in Poland, TsSKA in Bulgaria and the Soviet Union, Vorwärts in the GDR, Honved in Hungary, Steaua in Rumania and Red Star in Yugoslavia, to name a few. Such events have demonstrated that sport in these countries has been identified in the popular consciousness with privilege, coercion, pretense, distorted priorities and, in the case of most non-Soviet states, with an alien, Soviet-imposed institution. Some in the West have looked with envy at the successful talent-detection and nurturing system developed in the socialist states. The approach has indeed brought considerable success in world sport—the USSR and GDR athletes and teams have dominated the palmares of the summer and winter Olympic Games of recent years. But many people, East and West of the Oder-Neisse, have abhorred the flag-waving "razzmatazz" accompanying sports success, which was evidently more for the purpose of bringing prestige and recognition to the regime and its ideology than to benefit the ordinary citizen. The elite sports system, by producing medal winners to demonstrate the superiority of communist society, was popularly perceived as being a diversion from the realities of living "under communism". The popular reaction now contains more than passing references to the discipline and dehumanising limitations inflicted on athletes by the requirements of high-performance sport thus highlighting the custodial role the state has played in shaping and controlling people's lives.

Since Mr Gorbachev came to power, however, radical changes have appeared in communist sport. The functionalised, bureaucratic mould has been modified. Until then, not only had the Soviet-pioneered, state-controlled system rendered difficult a true appraisal of the realities beneath the "universal" statistics and "idealised" veneer, it had also hampered concessions to particular groups in the population. The "we-know-what's-best-for-you" syndrome, whereby, for example, men tell women what sports they should play; the fit tell the disabled that sport is not really for them (Soviet disabled athletes—13 blind sportsmen —attended the Paralympics for the first time only in 1988); the political leadership, mindful of the nation's international reputation, has acted as if olympic (*i.e.*, European) sports are the only important forms of the sporting culture.

In the heat of the upheaval, it is tempting to blame stalinists for having neglected "sport-for-all" in their race for state glory. In truth, much effort was made over the years to involve the population in forms of exercise and recreation that were completely free of charge—whether through the national fitness programme, work-based facilities or compulsory sports instruction for all students in their first years at college. But it appears that it was the *coercive* nature of sporting activities, their being part of the plan-fulfilled system (every school, factory, farm and region received a sports quota and conversely incurred penalties if they fell short) that turned people away from mass participation.

In the case of the non-Soviet nations, there was the added irritant of having to put up with a system tailored during the Stalin years and imposed from without, often in contradiction to some of their own traditions: Sokol gymnastics was banned in Poland and Czechoslovakia after 1948; youth organisations involved in recreation, like the YMCA, the Boy Scouts and the Jewish Maccabi, were proscribed; and pre-war National Olympic Committees were disbanded by Moscow. All this despite the long traditions and often superior performance standards. Being part of the USSR meant following Soviet foreign policy, including on olympic boycotts. The Soviet decision to boycott the 1984 Summer Olympic Games in Los Angeles was passed down to the other members of the Warsaw Pact—all indications are that no sports or national Olympic Committee, not to mention athletes, were consulted. Rumania demurred, though hardly because of player-power. Those are thus cogent reasons as to why the relationship between sport and the state is changing swiftly and radically in the Republics of Eastern Europe.

Sport and the State: Some Cross-Cultural Comparisons

The Western pattern of sport has closely followed the idiosyncratic evolution of Western states: from the numerous private single-sport clubs and commercial spectaculars in North America, with minimum intervention by the state; to the amateur-elitist clubs and professional leagues of Britain; and the close links between sport and politics, religion and class in France and the Federal Republic of Germany, all with considerable involvement of the state. By comparison, in Eastern Europe (Russia, Poland, Bulgaria, Czechoslovakia and, to a lesser degree, Hungary and Rumania) organised sports movements had evolved under the direct tutelage of the state, which established and controlled, *inter alia*, National Olympic Committees, even *before* those countries came to socialism. In the case of Russia, for example, not only did the communists inherit the largest nationalised industry in the world, they also took over a centralised state sports system with strong military and utilitarian connections through the tsarist (government) Office for Physical Development in the Russian Empire, headed by General Voyeikov. Just before World War I broke out, a Provisional Committee of representatives from various government departments and sports societies had been established to assist General Voyeikov, giving him effectual control over all sports and quasi-sports organisations in Russia. This centralised state control of sport was primarily intended for mobilising the population for the war effort. The system was to be taken over three years later by the Bolsheviks and turned into the military training organisation *Vsevobuch*. The Russian communists, then, inherited from tsarist Russia an incipient sports movement that had one great advantage: it was largely centrally-controlled. In the United Kingdom and North America, on the other hand, the governing bodies of sports went a different route. They were separate from one another, independent of government, and based for purposes of control and largely of finance on their members. Moreover, many Western clubs tended to specialise in a single sport, whereas Russian and other East European clubs grew up around military training and olympic-type multi-sport organisations (not entirely disimilar to the pattern which also developed in Italy, Spain and Latin America).

Since the October Revolution of 1917 sport has been centrally controlled and employed in the pursuit of specific socio-political objectives. In fact, sport has been a political institution run by the state. The USSR National Olympic Committee, for example and for all practical purposes, is a governmental body appointed by the USSR Sports Committee and run by a member of the sole political party in the USSR—the Communist Party of the Soviet Union. The policy of both the Sports Committee and the NOC has thus been controlled by the Party and Government. Such has also been the case elsewhere in Eastern Europe. The reasons for this "politicisation" of sport, which distinguishes socialist sport from that in the West, but which nonetheless parallels sports development in many other modernising societies, especially in Africa and Asia, can be found in the enhanced role of sport as a social institution and medium of social change, part and parcel of cultural revolutions, also in developing nations.

As far as the Soviet Union is concerned, its leaders, from about 1928 on, would seem to have opted for the following:

– cultivating competitive sport (a leisure-time analogue of the competition between people at work designed to raise work tempos) with—again, as at work—material rewards for victors, the more effectively to improve people's readiness for work and to pre-train soldiers for the Soviet nation-state;

– using sport, specifically, as a means of obtaining the fit, obedient and disciplined work-force needed for achieving economic and military strength and efficiency, in particular in order to: 1– raise physical and social health standards which meant not simply educating people in the virtues of bodily hygiene, regular exercise and sound nutrition, but also overcoming unhealthy deviant, anti-social (and therefore anti-Soviet) behaviour, like drunkenness, delinquency, prostitution, even religiosity and intellectual dissidence; 2– socialise the population into the new establishment system of values; character training, believed to be advanced by sport, in such values as loyalty, conformity, team spirit; 3– encourage people in transition from a rural to an urban way of life to identify with wider communities, that is all-embracing social units such as the workplace, the neighbourhood, the town, the district, the republic and, ultimately, the whole country. By associating sport (like other amenities) organisationally with the workplace, the Party leadership and its agencies were in a position to supervise and "rationalise" efficiently the leisure time activities of the employees;

– linking sport ideologically and even organisationally with military preparedness; the reasons for this "militarisation" of sport can be found in: 1– the leadership's concern for war and its conviction of the need to keep the population primed to meet it; 2– the presence throughout society of the military and the security forces, necessitated by the imposition from above of "socialist construction" (a state of affairs not so odd-seeming in Russian society, since this military presence had also, if for different reasons, been the norm before the Revolution, in sport as elsewhere); 3– the fact that, in a vast country with problems of communication, lukewarm (at best) popular attitudes towards physical exercise, and few sports facilities for most of the Soviet period, military organisation of sport was actually an efficient method of deploying available resources in the most economical way and using methods of direction which were judged more effective coming from paramilitary than from civilian organisations.

Sport, therefore, has since long been associated in Soviet development with hygiene, health (physical and social), defence, patriotism, integration of a multi-ethnic population, productivity, international recognition, even cultural identity and nation building. Sport was regarded as being far too important to be left to the whim of private clubs, or to promoters, commercial entrepreneurs and even rich foreigners—as was the case in most developing countries before the national liberation and regeneration movement. In any case, after liberation or revolution, there is rarely a leisure class around to promote sport for its own disportment. Such has been the case with Russia and most countries of Eastern Europe.

Exporting the Soviet System to Eastern Europe

It was the Soviet state-controlled sports system that was adopted by, or imposed upon (along with other political, social and economic institutions), those countries of Eastern Europe liberated by the Red Army in the period 1945-1949. The eight nations of the Soviet-dominated half of Europe complied with the Soviet system of state control of sport, sports medicine and science, national fitness programme ("Prepared for Work and Defence"), sports rankings pyramid, trade union sports societies, state "shamateurism" (by which athletes claimed full-time employment as army officers or skilled workers, or full-time students, with appropriate remuneration from outside sport, once the USSR (re-)joined the Olympic Movement in 1951), and overall control by the security forces and the army. Such was the extent of the Soviet blueprint being copied that often the Soviet name was retained (however insensitive this may have been to national pride and dignity), as in the case of the KGB's Dinamo clubs, the State Committee on Physical Culture and Sport (*Gosudarstvenny komitet po fizicheskoi kulture i sportu* in the USSR; *Staatssekretariat für Körperkultur und Sport* in the GDR), the monthly journal *Theory and Practice of Physical Culture* (*Teoriya i praktika fizicheskoi kultury* in the USSR; *Theorie und Praxis der Körperkultur* in the GDR; and *Teorie a Praxe Tělesné Výchovy* in Czechoslovakia). In addition, whenever the Soviet sports structure altered, that in Eastern Europe followed suit. It is hardly surprising that such insensitivity to national traditions in that particular domain should have contributed to the mass anger and hatred expressed in the popular uprisings of late 1989.

The domination of sport by the state for political purposes also resulted in deliberate attempts of make-believe and deception aimed at players and public. Foremost was the false status of the amateur athletes. Further, evidence is emerging of long-term state production, testing, monitoring and administering of performance-enhancing drugs, including with young people reportedly as early as age 7-8. In relation to past deceptions, a recent report in the Soviet magazine *Ogonyok* puts the problem bluntly: "From a youngster's first steps in sport he is accustomed to being a parasite, clandestinely assigned to miners, oilers or builders who generously repay his artless "feints" with worldly goods of which miners, oilers or builders can only dream. City apartments, cars, overseas trips, a free and easy life by the seaside—how all that must caress youthful vanity, lifts him above the grey mass of those who have been waiting years for housing, phones and cars, and who have to pay for his seaside and foreign trips out of their own pocket[3]." This suggests a question that was raised frequently in the 1920s in the USSR, yet has rarely been aired since: what price is society prepared to pay for talent? The fundamental question is certainly asked again and now, all over the erstwhile socialist world.

When a number of *émigré* athletes, coaches and sports physicians had previously talked of the widespread use of drugs in Eastern Europe, their testimony carried a whiff of suspicion of "selling out". Even when only recently, in 1989, the one-time East German ski jump champion and now physician Hans-Georg Aschenbach, alleged that athletes used drugs from childhood, he was widely attacked in East and West for sensationalism; yet the substance of what he said was since not successfully undermined. In fact, more evidence has been emerging from the USSR for the last two or three years of just such state-controlled drug administering in the Soviet Union and the GDR. Back in 1986, Yuri Vlasov, then Chairman of the USSR Weightlifting Federation, declared that immense damage had been done to Soviet sport in general, and weightlifting in particular, by the "coach pharmacologist" who worked alongside the sports coach. Not only did Vlasov point to Soviet athletes having used anabolics "for several decades", but he named names—specifically that of a senior coach and Sports Committee official "who was one of the first to distribute anabolic steroids to members of our national teams[4]". A television report made in late 1989 revealed a document, signed in 1982 by two deputy sports ministers, actually prescribing anabolic steroids as part of the preparation for Soviet cross-country skiers. The document set out a programme to test the effects of steroids and for research into ways of avoiding detection[5].

It has long been known by those familiar with communist sport that drug taking was organised *at the top* and that no athlete was allowed overseas unless he or she had a clearance test before departing. At the Olympic Games of Montreal and Seoul, it has now been revealed, the Soviet team had a hospitality boat used as a medical centre to ensure Soviet competitors were at least "clean" at the last moment[6]. Another Soviet coach, Sergei Vaichekovsky, who was in charge of Soviet swimming from 1973 to 1982, has also admitted that the use of drugs was widespread. "From 1974 all Soviet swimmers were using banned substances," he wrote. "I've personally administered the drugs and advised swimmers individually on how to avoid getting caught[7]." He indicated that while the GDR method was to give drugs only during periods of intensive training, which for swimmers usually comes at the start of the year, Soviet competitors took them to within a month of major meetings.

It is this type of deceit by members of the ruling regimes—loudly condemning drug abuse cases in the West as typical excesses of capitalism, while concealing their own involvement in an extensive programme of state manufacture and administering of drugs—that has repelled both the public and the bulk of people involved in sport. The latest revelations are not so much responses to new orders from above; they seem much more to be the result of a "revolution from below", on the part of coaches, athletes, journalists and fans—all of whom obviously would like to see the end of decades of false amateurism, state-manipulation and bureaucratic control of sport[8].

What of the Future?

In their haste to escape from the past state-controlled sports system, there are those sports enthusiasts in Eastern Europe who would clearly like to embrace virtually every aspect of Western sport. Just as those who hanker after an unfettered market economy are often blind to its deficiencies—unemployment, inflation, insecurity, selfishness—so those who wish to install unbridled market sport may stumble upon some unpleasantnesses and, in the process, lose even more of their national traditions, and "socialist gains". The point may be not to throw out the baby with the bathwater. But that is for the people of Eastern Europe to decide for themselves. Some Germans may lick their lips at the prospect of adding East to West medals in a united team again. Others may well be sick and tired of the very high prominence accorded to the winning of victories, the setting of records and the collection of medals and trophies—a fetishisation of sport. For the moment, one thing at least seems clear: the popular mood now favours sport-for-all and sport for fun rather than the elitist sport of the recent past.

NOTES AND REFERENCES

1. Eastern Europe is taken to include the following nine states: Union of Soviet Socialist Republics (pop 284 millions), Polish People's Republic (38 millions), Socialist Federal Republic of Yugoslavia (24 millions), Socialist Republic of Romania (23 millions), the German Democratic Republic (17 millions), Czechoslovak Socialist Republic (16 millions), Hungarian People's Republic (11 millions), People's Republic of Bulgaria (9 millions) and People's Republic of Albania (3 millions)

2. Galbraith JK (1989) Assault on ideology ... Weekend Guardian 16-17 December p 16

3. Petrichenko O (1987) Ne sotvori sebe kumira. Ogonyok 12 March p 15

4. Klaz A (1988) Rekordy po retseptu? Smena 4 May p 3. See also Vlasov Y (1988) Drugs and cruelty. Moscow News 37 p 15

5. Sovetsky sport. 10 October 1989 p 1

6. Gromyko V (1989) Nash styd. Leninskoye znamya 28 March p 2

7. Reported in Corriere Dello Sport. See Page A (1989) Sacked soviet official admits widespread use of drugs. Guardian 2 December p 20

8. For further coverage of drug-taking in Soviet sport, see Dadygin S in Pravda 17 April 1989 p 8; Polonskaya O in Ogonyok no 29 July 1988 p 6-7; Kokurina Y in Meditsinskaya gazeta 4 January 1989 p 4; Toporov S in Sovetsky sport 25 February 1989 p 4 – all reported in English in The Current Digest of the Soviet Press XLI no 16 (1989) p 18-20

The Changing Relationship Between Sport and the State in the People's Republic of China

Susan E. Brownell

China's top leader, Deng Xiaoping, ascended to power in 1977 after the chaotic ten years of the Cultural Revolution. In 1978, Deng initiated the current era of economic reform. The reforms proceeded rapidly, with repercussions in many sectors of Chinese socicty, including sports. The speed of change reached its peak in 1988, during the second period of a research project initiated three years before[1]. In 1989, due to social unrest, the Party attempted to slow the pace of change somewhat; but, in the realm of sport, economic reform seems to have maintained its pace in preparation for the 1990 Asian Games in Beijing.

The 1987 Chinese National Sports Games

The Chinese National Sports Games, held in Guangdong (Canton) province in November and December of 1987, provide an excellent example of the changing relationship between sport and the state in China under the economic reforms. These Games were significant because many new policies were implemented specifically for the occasion. The National Games are a multi-sport event that imitates the Olympic Games and is supposed to be held once every four years; however, the schedule has been repeatedly disrupted by social and economic turmoil. The 1987 Games followed the 13th Party Congress, which convened in November, less than a month before the opening of the Games. Though it was not planned, the timing was perfect for propaganda about the success of the economic policies whose correctness had been reasserted at the Party Congress. The propaganda for the Games made frequent reference to the guidance of the Party and the Basic Road laid out at the Congress. In a very real way, the Games embodied the success of the current reforms, or at least their potential for success. As in other sectors of the economy, sport is being encouraged to rely less on subsidies from the State. It is hoped that sports can eventually be made to generate revenue through better management of existing facilities, corporate sponsorship and advertising, lottery tickets, and other means.

1890
1990

Susan E. Brownell, Department of Anthropology, University of California, Santa Barbara, California, USA.

These practices are expected to supplement the state physical culture budget, which is comparatively small. Today, the state physical culture expenditure stands at around 0,4% of the total budget[2], which is judged inadequate. Zhang Caizhen, deputy director of the State Sports Commission, noted that "even India" spends 1,0% of its annual budget on physical culture. China is in need of more sports facilities and equipment; even the national teams often complain about their lack of facilities[3].

It is widely known that the Los Angeles Olympic Games, held in one of the wealthy capitalist nations in the world and relying on heavy commercialization, turned a huge profit. Less well-known is that the most populous socialist nation in the world sent representatives to learn from the Los Angeles Organizing Committee how to turn sports into a money-making proposition. The head of the Guangdong Sports Commission, Wei Zhenlan, was one of the representatives. As a result of the knowledge he and others gained in Los Angeles, the Sixth National Games in Guangdong were characterized by five new policies: corporate sponsorship (called "society pools its resources") and individual contributions (mostly from wealthy Overseas Chinese); lottery tickets; tour groups; sale of advertising rights to the meet mascot, emblem, and song; and business management of gymnasiums rather than administrative management[4].

Corporate sponsorship has been encouraged since 1984, when Central Document Number 20 called for the "societization" (*shehuihua*—public sector support) of sport. This document is said to have led many enterprises to change their conception of sports and realize the benefits of involvement in sports. The benefits were said to be that sport "brings the competitive spirit into the factories and shops", and that sponsorship increases the name recognition of the enterprise[5].

Corporate sponsorship first reached a large scale in the 1987 National Games, and this was a direct result of the economic reforms of the immediately preceding period. Although this led to some complaints about commercialization, the reception was generally favorable. It was noted that in the past, corporations had not earned enough profit to be able to afford a great deal of advertising. Only under the economic prosperity of the times was it possible, and only under the new policies for the Games was it allowed.

At the National Games, such well-known corporations as Fuji, Kodak, Coca-Cola, Pepsi, Xerox, Boeing, Seiko, Polaroid, Sharp, Olivetti, and NEC, and joint enterprises such as 555 and Gold Lion, prominently displayed logos and billboards all over the city, outside the main sports complex, and inside the arenas along the railings. A total of over 100 enterprises advertised at the Games. Advertising rights for the meet emblem and mascot made a profit of about 20 million yuan (In 1987, the exchange rate was 3,7 yuan to the American dollar). While the largest contributions came from two Chinese companies (Wanbao refrigerators gave 3 million yuan and Jianlibao sports drink gave 2,5), the majority seemed to come from foreign companies. The open-door policy that encouraged foreign investment certainly was a large factor in the financial success of the Games.

In addition, the people of Guangdong contributed 30 million yuan (8 100 000 $ US) through the lottery. Over a three-year period, they bought over 169 million tickets, a remarkable average of 2,5 tickets for each person in Guangdong province[6]. Lottery tickets were a new phenomenon in the People's Republic of China, and the Chinese people's love of gambling was reflected in the lottery's success. This practice, formerly banned as "capitalist", received a warm welcome. It was said that people saw it not only as a way of winning money (5 million yuan for each one-month period), but also they felt if they lost, it went to the good cause of Chinese sports.

Prices of gate tickets were high by Chinese standards: 15 yuan (4 $ US) for opening and closing ceremonies, 5 yuan for key events, and 3 yuan for less popular events like track and field. People from other parts of China were amazed; spectators from the capital joked that at those prices, the stadiums in Beijing would be empty. Even so, the crush was so great that opening and closing ceremonies tickets and soccer final tickets were almost impossible to get, people outside the gates were offering up to 200 yuan with no takers, and fights erupted among the crowds waiting in line to buy the few tickets offered for sale. The gate profits for the opening ceremonies were probably not significant, since the stadium of 60 000 people consisted of a 10 000-member placard section, and also the majority of the tickets were apparently given out to officials and their friends and relatives. The latter was true of the soccer events and closing ceremonies as well. Perhaps the gate profits came to a few million yuan. No information is available on the profits made by gate receipts, nor by tour groups and other sources. In any case, the Sports Foundation felt it could meet all operating costs. Whether or not it turned a profit is not known except by the cadres at the highest administrative levels.

The increasing role of industry in sports was reflected in the presence of several teams sponsored by state industries. The Army has always fielded a strong team outside of the Sports Commission System, but in 1987, for the first time, many industries fielded teams, including the Railway System, the Banking System, the Water and Electricity System, the Petroleum System, and the Coal Mine System. This was hailed as an encouraging development because it provided competition for the state sports system, which has had a monopoly on the organization of sports teams in the past. It was expected that such teams would become more numerous and reach a higher level in the future.

The 1987 Games were also the first in which state subsidies were supplemented by funds from local organizations. Guangdong province built 44 new gymnasiums and repaired 55 old ones; the total cost of building and renovating facilities was 500 million yuan. The operating costs (costs of competitions; the Games committee members' rooms, board, and transportation; the opening ceremonies costs; and apparatus of all kinds) came to 50 million. Together, then, the facilities and operating costs totalled 550 million yuan (149 million dollars US). The State gave a subsidy of 22 million, a little less than half the operating costs. Guangdong province contributed 300 million, and the various localities contributed a total of 200 million. Thus, a total of 522 million yuan came from State, provincial, and local subsidies (See *Table 1* for a breakdown of expenditures and revenue).

TABLE 1

1987 Chinese National Sports Games Expenditures and Revenues*

*Expenditures (in million yuan)***		*Revenue (in million yuan)***	
Facilities	500	*Subsidies*	
Operating costs	50	Guangdong province	300
		Local organizations	200
		State	22
		"Society Pools Resources"	
		Lottery tickets	30
		Corporate sponsorhip	20
		Gate receipts and other	unknown
Total expenditures	**550**	**Partial Revenues**	**572**

* Data from references 7, 8, 9 and 10.
** At 1987 exchange rate, 1 $ US = 3,7 yuan.

Clearly, large sums of money are needed to produce a sports event of this size. Guangdong was able to do it on an unprecedented scale because of local investment in sports facilities and corporate sponsorship, neither of which would have been possible before the economic reforms because localities and Chinese corporations did not have enough funds for that purpose, and foreign companies were not doing intensive business in China.

Guangdong's National Games were a sparkling example of the potential of these new policies. However, Guangdong is a special case. It is a special economic zone with extensive ties to Hong Kong and overseas Chinese. It is also the wealthiest province in China. Whether the same policies could be so successfully implemented in other provinces is another matter. Originally, the next Games were set for Chengdu in Sichuan Province; they were to be the first ever held in an inland province. Shortly after the Guangdong Games, however, a general realization dawned that Chengdu would not be able to live up to the standard set by Guangdong; Chengdu gave up its assignation. The next Games were slated to be held in either Beijing, Shanghai, or Guangdong, the three most advanced cities in China and the only ones to have held a National Games. In summary, the 1987 National Games illustrate some of the concrete changes in the relationship between sport and the Chinese state that resulted from Central Document Number 20 in 1984, which called for the "societization" of sport. One of the goals of this document was to decentralize sport by creating opportunities for public sector support of sports teams and competitions. Decentralization was supposed to encourage progress in high-level sports by creating sports systems that would provide competition for the centralized, state-controlled sports commission system, which until then had a virtual monopoly on high-level sports.

The Implementation of High-Level College Sports Teams

A second important aspect of the societization of sports was the implementation of high-level sports teams in colleges and universities. Under the centralized sports school system, athletes often received an education which was judged inadequate. The sports school system is the main training ground for China's state "shamateur" athletes. English language publications in China call these athletes "professional". The state is now forging a closer link between the sports system and the educational system because parental reluctance to allow children to become professional athletes reached such heights that sports schools could no longer recruit enough students. By 1988 the top-level teams had trouble replacing their aging stars, and many sportspeople felt that China would be unable to continue to improve in international sports. The "education problem", as it is called, is closely linked to another matter, labelled the "exit problem". This refers to the limited career opportunities available to athletes after retirement from sports. In order to discuss these problems, it is first necessary to provide some background on Chinese culture and society.

China has an ancient tradition of education as a means of social mobility. In Imperial China, this tradition was expressed in the state's use of a civil service examination system to select government officials. In modern China, the National College Entrance Examination reproduces the effect of the Imperial Exams. This examination was reinstituted in 1976, at the end of the Cultural Revolution. A college education has become increasingly essential for entering a desirable occupation, because China's modernization requires educated people with scientific and technical skills. The College Entrance Examination is a gruelling, three-day examination that requires a huge amount of memorization. Less than ten percent of middle school graduates are accepted into college, so the competition is very heated. In the intensely competitive atmosphere associated with the examination, schoolchildren who participate in sports are at a disadvantage.

Training takes time and energy away from studies, and they fall behind when they go away for competitions. When an athlete enters a boarding school for sports, he/she may spend only half a day in class, and the academic demands are not very rigorous. Many athletes stop schooling altogether at a young age, some going no farther than the sixth grade. With such a poor educational background, it is impossible for them to score well on the College Entrance Examination, and thus they have in fact sacrificed their education for sports. When they retire from sports, the government will however assign them jobs. The majority will be retained in the sports system as assistant coaches, cadres, office workers, and so on. Coaching a high-level team is considered the best job, but only a limited number of these positions are obviously available. Many of the athletes who receive jobs outside the sports system will be assigned to factories. Most of these job opportunities are not especially appealing, and the transition into the working world is a problematic one. Upon retirement, an athlete may find that he/she not only lacks an education, but also has fewer skills than younger people who have already engaged in the occupation for many years.

In addition, education in itself has a high value in the Chinese culture. Uneducated people are said to "lack culture" and are not well respected. Sportspeople are often said to "lack culture," and are described as "four developed limbs and an undeveloped brain." Because of this prejudice, many parents, especially among the well-educated ones, are unwilling for their children to pursue sports careers. Sociological surveys have shown that people with a lower-middle school level of education value sports most highly, but after that the valuation of sports decreases as educational level increases[11]. Three different polls by the State Sports Commission showed that only 1,2 to 6% of all parents favor sending their children to spare-time sports schools[12].

After the establishment in 1955 of the sports school system, modeled after the Soviet system, China's college sports gradually declined. This trend began to reverse in 1982, when the state established a national collegiate games to promote college sports. Along with the general sports boom, this quadrennial event gained in scale and importance. After 1984, when China's success at the Los Angeles Olympic Games spurred enthusiasm for sports, an increasing number of athletes were recruited onto college sports teams. In preparation for the Second National Collegiate Games in 1986, increasing numbers of regular universities began accepting professional athletes despite questionable academic qualifications. Since the founding of the PRC, outstanding accomplishments in sports have been rewarded with the addition of points to the entrance examination score; but in 1986, some colleges had gone far beyond this point, recruiting athletes who scored hundreds of points below the minimum. In some cases they reportedly had not taken the test at all. At the beginning of the 1985-86 academic year, those universities that had not succumbed to this practice realized they were going to "lose face" in the national college meet. Even such universities as Qinghua and Beijing University, which had high academic standards to uphold, gave in and hurriedly recruited a batch of athletes into the class entering in 1985. Meanwhile, the State Education Commission postponed action, although there were constant rumors that a document was about to "come down" which would restrict the participation of those athletes in the national meet. Finally, only months before the meet, the document appeared. It declared athletes in the entering class of 1985, who had not entered school through the proper testing route, to be ineligible for the National College Games.

There was pressure on all sides for regular colleges to accept former top athletes. The State Sports Commission saw it as a vitally necessary measure to solve the "exit problem" in sports, recognizing that due to this problem, Chinese sports were losing vast numbers of potential recruits. Figures from Liaoning Province are an example of how severe this problem was: the province each year has around 2 000 graduates of spare-time sports schools, but only 500 can be accepted by national, provincial, or municipal teams[13]. It was thought that college teams could take in some of the surplus. As it turned out, not much of the surplus was taken in. Colleges were not interested in recruiting middle school graduates because their level was usually far below that of older professional team athletes. Consequently, colleges were more eager to lure older athletes away from professional teams than to take younger ones. There were many people in colleges and universities who were eager to receive the athletes with the hope of bringing honor to the school in major sports meets. The individual departments were also eager to accept athletes to represent the department in the yearly interdepartmental competitions, which are more heatedly contested than those between colleges.

The problem was not resolved in 1986, and it cropped up again before the Third National College Games in 1988. The situation was complicated by a general uncertainty about the position of the Education Commission on the issue. Schools that recruited athletes were unsure if they would be eligible to compete or not. Finally, in the winter of 1987, the Education Commission gave outright permission to 55 colleges nationwide to create "high-level sports teams" by recruiting former professional athletes. Several options were available to help the athletes catch up in their studies: they could have a year of tutorial classes before they joined the regular students, they could take a longer time to graduate, they could attend middle schools affiliated with the college for a period of time, or they could study special combinations of subjects just for athletes. The "double degree" system was another way for athletes to enter regular colleges. This referred to those who had already earned a degree in a physical education institute, and who then transferred to a related program in a regular university.

Many colleges simply recruited entire teams of professional athletes. China Daily reported that the Tianjin Institute of Finance and Economics "just snapped up the entire Tianjin women's basketball team, even helping them pass the entrance exams. It plans to get a coach from Oklahoma State University, something the Tianjin team would find hard to do[14]."

Conclusions

The state of affairs is changing so rapidly that the system described above will surely be vastly different in the late 1990s. The societization of sport opens up new doors for athletes every year, there are now over 4 000 athletes on college and industrial enterprise teams outside the sports commission system[15]. On the whole, decentralization seems to have benefitted Chinese sports by reducing the monopoly of the State and increasing the involvement of society. However, decentralization has also led to some complications. Because of the linking of enterprise with sport, financial awards and bonuses have become increasingly important. This has led to accusations of greed and even cheating on sports teams. The pressure to win has also led to an increase in the use of performance-enhancing drugs. Many sportspeople are concerned that the commercialization of sport has created problems for the progress of Chinese "socialist spiritual civilization". A second kind of problem is that of college admission for athletes. As in the United States' system, there are now many college athletes who are not truly college students. However, China's experience shows that a centralized sports school system is no better solution to this problem, because athletes in the sports schools often receive an inadequate education as well. Because of the traditional emphasis of Chinese parents on the education of their children, the state will likely continue to promote college sports until the link between education and sports is perfected to a degree that makes sports an attractive career option to athletes and their parents. Otherwise, the future development of both high-level and mass sports will continue to face many and serious obstacles.

NOTES AND REFERENCES

1. Data were gathered during fieldwork in China in 1985-1986 and 1987-1988. The methods included participant observation; review of sport media and sport theory books; discussion with sport scientists; and interviews with sport cadres, coaches and athletes.

2. Guojia tongjiju shehui tongjisi (State Statistical Bureau, Social Statistics Division) (1985) Zhongguo shehui tongji ziliao (China social statistics data) Beijing: Zhongguo tongji chubanshe

3. Qu Guangli (1988) Sporting chance for China. China Daily May 24

4. Cao Yuchun (1987) Yangcheng ban liuyunhui xinzhao (New tricks in Guangzhou's handling of the Sixth Games). Xintiyu (New Physical Culture) November p 14-15

5. Huang Zhenzhong (1988) Qiye weihe yu tiyu 'jieqin' (Why does enterprise get married with physical culture). Renmin ribao (People's Daily) March 4

6. Tiyu bao (Sports News) (1987) Tiyu jiangjuan (Sports Lottery tickets) November 22

7. Tiyu bao (Sports News) (1987) Liuyunhui qishi lu (On the insights of the Sixth Games) December 6

8. Huang He (1987) Yiyi chaoguo tiyu fanwei (The significance surpassed the bounds of physical culture). Tiyu bao (Sports News) December 9

9. Ping Yuan (1987) Jiejue sanda kunnan: changdi zijin huanjing (Solving three big difficulties: sports fields, capital, environment). Tiyu bao (Sports News) November 16

10. China Daily (1988) Guangzhou meet blazed way. February 23

11. Niu Xinghua and Feng Jianxiu (1986) Woguo dazhong chengshi butong chanye tiyu renkou jiegou taishi (Trends in the sports population of different industries in China's large and medium cities). Tiyu shehuixue wenji (Collected Sport Sociology Papers) vol 2 Tianjin: Tianjin Institute of Physical Education Dean's Office p 9-19

12. Shen Yanping (1988) Kids like sports, but parents don't. China Daily, March 17

13. Kang Bing (1988) New look for China's Games. China Daily March 23

14. Ibid

15. Ibid

Sport and the State in Socialist Countries: a Commentary

Peter Donnelly

There is supposed to be a Chinese curse which condemns you "to live in interesting times". These are indeed "interesting times" for social, political and cultural change, particularly in nation states ranging from China, through Eastern Europe, to Central America.

In none of the nations with genuine National Olympic Committees does sport exist completely independent of the state[1]. Thus, where rapid, even revolutionary changes are occurring, those changes will have an inevitable impact on the sport-state relationship. Some of those changes have been described this morning in a set of interesting and insightful presentations. Drs Riordan and Rodichenko have provided us with somewhat different views of the changing relationship between sport and the state in Central and Eastern Europe; Dr Brownell has for her part presented us with invaluable information concerning the relationship between state policy and sport in the People's Republic of China.

I do not claim any special expertise that would permit me to comment accurately on the specific details of the presentations. Nor do I propose, in this brief reaction, to consider the papers in light of theories of the state (a task that should nonetheless be continued[2]). Rather, I would like to react in a general manner to some of the themes common to these papers, and to link this reaction to the last two stated objectives of the symposium, *viz*:

> "4. To examine the *obligations* of society with respect to sport and the *social accountability* of sport.
>
> 5. To consider the *consequences* of possible *destinies* of sport, as the third millennium approaches". (emphasis added)

So, first let me comment briefly on political change, of which we have seen an abundance in the past year in China, South Africa, Europe, and Central and South America; and second, consider some of the limits and possibilities of the sport-state relationship.

1890
1990

Peter Donnelly, School of Physical Education and Athletics, McMaster University, Hamilton, Ontario, Canada.

Social, Political and Cultural Change

One of the more poignant statements that I have heard in this last incredible year came from a man living in what used to be called the German Democratic Republic. He said (and I am quoting from memory here):

> I was born under the Nazis and I have lived my life under the Communists; I am not a guinea pig to be experimented on in a social laboratory; I want to settle down and lead a normal life.

While it is easy to sympathize with his feelings, as a social scientist I know that there is no *natural* or *normal* way to organize a society. Liberal Democracy and market Capitalism are no less experimental than Fascism and Stalinism. The liberal democratic/market capitalist experiment has been rather more successful than Stalinism in making consumer goods available to a larger proportion of citizens, although this does not make it any the less experimental. But the real success of the liberal democratic experiment has been in making itself *seem* natural and inevitable as a means of organizing society—even to many of those who have recently abandoned the Stalinist experiment.

McDonald's hamburgers in Moscow, Rupert Murdoch in Hungary, a government in Warsaw espousing Thatcherite economic measures, and the Sandinista election loss in Nicaragua all appear to support Fukuyama's notion of "the end of history[3]"—the "inevitable" emergence of a homogeneous socio-economic system throughout the world. Helmut Kohl, Margaret Thatcher and George Bush have moved rapidly to claim credit for the failure of the Stalinist experiment, and to attempt to fill the resultant vacuum with their view of the "natural and normal" way to organize society. But, "the end of history" implies the end of ideas, the end of experiments. *Surely* these are not the only choices; *surely* there ought to be workable alternatives to liberal democracy/market capitalism, *and* Stalinism, *and* Fascism. *Surely* one does not have to be condemned to a system which, while nominally democratic[4], is not dissociated from the twin pillars of privilege and exploitation (of people and resources/environment), has little idea how to deal with poverty, bigotry, violence and "the drug problem", and seems to consider unemployment to be a legitimate and appropriate tool to deal with inflation. *Surely* it is possible to envisage a society in which the "best", in whatever field of endeavour (education, work, music, etc.), are encouraged and assisted to achieve their full potential, while the rest are assisted and provided with the opportunity to participate, and to achieve, if one so chooses, one's level of potential (which, in a sense, is what the three papers have been about). Is it possible for the state to intervene to organize sport in a non-exploitative and accessible manner in which *sport-for-all* co-exists with *elite sport*?

Sport and the State

The reasons for state involvement in sport have been well-documented, and professor Riordan has provided us with his view of the motives behind Soviet government sport policy. I am less concerned with *why* states have become involved in sport than with *how* they are indeed involved. The why of state involvement has several features. Firstly, governments do not always say what they mean; and secondly, the reasons why citizens become involved, or avoid involvement in sport often have little to do with government policy. Their involvement may have as many unintended as intended consequences. *How* a government becomes involved often reveals the *real* policy, and has a much more important effect on the opportunities citizens have in fact for participation. Thus, when a government claims to be interested in promoting the fitness, health and well-being of all of its citizens, *but*, 80% of its sport-related budget is diverted toward high performance sport programmes and the development of elite athletes, it is quite clear that international prestige is a more important aspect of sport policy[5].

We have heard here how several goverments have been involved in sport. Dr Brownell has identified the intended and unintended consequences of attempts by the Chinese government to decentralize their sport system; Professor Riordan has identified the pretense behind the success of the Soviet-inspired high performance sports system, and the real concern with sport-for-all that failed because of *how* government policy was implemented (the failure of good intentions); and Dr Rodichenko has described the new democratization process occurring in Soviet sport as a result of the policies of *perestroika*. Apart from the last example, where it is too early to judge, it seems that little common good has resulted from state involvement in sport. In the eyes of many, the prevailing conditions are such that athletes are exploited or encouraged to cheat; governments make ambiguous or hypocritical statements about the reasons for their involvement[6]; sports are differentially funded based on their potential for achieving international success[7], and most citizens, including those who could benefit most from sport involvement, appear to obtain little return indeed from the portion of their tax money which is used to finance sport. In other words, there appears to be fundamental difficulties most everywhere in attempting to combine policies of sport-for-all with high performance sport policies (despite Dr Rodichenko's suggestion that the two are not necessarily related). But this does not make state involvement necessarily bad. There are in my opinion at least two examples where state policy has apparently been successful—the People's Republic of China, in the 1970s, and the Republic of Cuba. It is easy to be cynical about the Maoist policy of "friendship first, competition second". While Chinese sport was developing, and international success seemed unlikely, a policy that did not emphasize the importance of success appeared to be very convenient. But the policy produced what I think is a healthy and inclusive attitude towards athletic competition, and one that is rarely noticed today. Only at events such as the closing ceremonies of the Olympic Games do we now find a sense of proportion about high performance sport—an opponent is not an enemy. State policies where such attitudes prevail are less likely to result in exploitation of the athlete, drug abuse and various forms of cheating.

Cuba has achieved international success in elite sport far out of proportion to its population and economic resources. Cuban high performance athletes, as far as I am aware, have not been accused of cheating; and, despite lucrative contract offers, they have not left their country. Simultaneously, the Cuban government appears to have initiated a successful policy of national fitness and sport-for-all. Has Cuba discovered the philosopher's stone for a successful state sport policy? Theory suggests that a broadly based system of participation can form the base of a pyramid out of which the elite athletes will emerge. This has not been the case in Cuba. Rather, they have modelled the Eastern European system of early identification and specialized training for those with the potential to be high performance athletes. The sport-for-all programme is separate, but the two-tier system appears to approach what many consider to be an ideal system. There are certainly limitations in the Cuban system, not the least of which is the lack of choice of those selected to the elite system, but there are clearly things one can learn from such a system[8].

Concluding Remarks

Pierre de Coubertin once suggested that "sport is a true democracy of ability". Given the differential access to facilities, equipment, sport scientists, and other resources between athletes from less developed and more developed nations, this is no longer true. But even if it was ever true, democracy in sport paradoxically ends with *ability*. Even today, with all of the talk of democratization, sport cannot be considered to be any more *democratized* than other areas of life. The lowest 20% of the population in Canada (in terms of income) is effectively disenfranchised from sport involvement; opportunities for women are still only a fraction of those available to men; and factors such as race, disability, and age can all influence one's access to sport participation[9]. *Of course* we have not come "to the end of history", and *of course* it is possible to envisage a society in which encouragement of the *best* can co-exist with opportunities for the *rest*. If one considers sport to be an important aspect of culture, for whatever complex of reasons, then the state has an obligation to provide opportunities for sport-for-all. If one values the opportunity for talented individuals to achieve their full potential, then the state also has an obligation to make appropriate provision[10].

But this returns us to that significant question posed by Professor Riordan; "what price is society prepared to pay for talent?" Perhaps the luxury of providing both elite sport and sport-for-all is only available to-day in economically successful democracies such as Sweden and Finland[11] (and to Cuba). For other states then, one can ask what priorities should be important. It is clear that a great many states have favoured elite sport at the expense of sport-for-all. A more democratic position would suggest a reversal of priority; that "the popular mood seems to favour sport-for-all and sport-for-fun rather than [. . .] elitist sport", as observed by Riordan, is very encouraging.

NOTES AND REFERENCES

1. The various relationships between sport and the state are insidious and widespread, and often command public interest. Two recent examples reminded me of this: President George Bush recently appointed Arnold Schwarzenneger to head up the President's Council on Physical Fitness and Sports; and, I was in Washington, DC, when the first literal cracks were made in the Berlin Wall. On the front page of the Washington Post there was a photograph of a crowd of happy Berliners sitting on the Wall, while on the sports page was the first instant speculation about the number of olympic medals that would be won by a united Germany.

2. See, for example, Cantelon H, Gruneau R (eds) (1982) Sport, culture and the modern state. Toronto: University of Toronto Press

3. Fukuyama F (1989) The end of history? The national interest: summer. Although it has been widely discredited, the essay continues to influence thinking in right wing circles and in certain Western governments.

4. Recent events provided a series of "democratic moments"—Tienanmen Square before the shooting started; pictures from Roumanian television; rallies in Wenceslaus Square; breaching the Berlin Wall; and even the first two years of Sandinista rule in Nicaragua ["over 40 000 landless farmers were given title to land, more than 1 200 schools were built and illiteracy in over half the population was cut to less than one seventh, malaria was halved, polio, measles, tetanus and diarrhoea were all but eradicated, the death penalty was abolished and infant mortality rate was reduced by a third," Darke N in Guardian Weekly 90/3/11]. Internal and external intervention and economic penalties and realities have ended such moments. But it is tragic to think that these examples of participatory democracy, could, under Western influence, turn into our own current forms of democracy [cynical disenchantment with politicians, low voter turnout, etc.]

5. Similarly, government disinterest in the promotion and support of daily physical activity in schools clearly indicates the lack of importance that is attached to concerns about national health and fitness.

6. The ambiguity or hypocrisy usually involves statements about health, fitness, and sport-for-all while in the end providing the majority of resources for high performance sport; but it can also involve the type of hypocrisy about drugs noted by Riordan [see

also MacAloon JJ (1990) Steroids and the State: Dubin, melodrama and the accomplishment of innocence. Public Culture 2 41-64]; and even the type of private discussions about eugenics occasionally heard among occidental sport officials and sport scientists [such discussions have had a public voice in China: see Mingshan M (1984) The spiritual requirements and satisfaction of a selection of China's top athletes: a survey of 68 national and world champions. Collected Sport Sociology Papers 1. Tianjin, China: Tianjin Institute of Physical Education p 109-17]

7. Available funds tend to be disproportionately provided to the 25 or so "olympic" sports, a situation that tends to result in anomalies such as lacrosse in Canada [once considered Canada's national sport] struggling to find enough money to send a team to the 1990 World Championships.

8. Information from: Sugden J, Tomlinson A, McCartan E (1990) Notes on the relationship between high level performance and sport-for-all in Cuba. ICSS Bulletin 38 5-9

9. Inequalities persist, even at the high performance level and despite efforts by the state to democratize opportunities to achieve elite status [Beamish R (1990) The persistence of inequality: an analysis of participation patterns among Canada's high performance athletes. International Review for the Sociology of Sport 25 143-55]

10. Whannel G (1983) Blowing the whistle. London: Pluto [The author has provided one of the strongest statements to indicate how it is possible to achieve these ends].

11. Finland has recently legislated the provision of sport-for-all opportunities.

[. . .] il importe que l'on ne considère pas les Jeux Olympiques comme une poule aux œufs d'or. Que nos lecteurs ne s'étonnent pas de nous voir aborder ainsi la question mercantile. Il serait bien puéril de croire que les Anciens ne se préoccupaient pas de la prospérité engendrée par les Jeux et que le mouvement des affaires autour d'Olympie ne les intéressait pas! [. . .]

Coubertin P de (1912) Une Olympiade à vol d'oiseau. Revue Olympique, août, p 115

[. . .] Que donnera cette double tendance de l'État et de la famille à se partager l'éducation? [. . .] L'État, à vrai dire, ne rétrograde pas aisément. Ce qu'il a pris, il le restitue rarement: à plus forte raison lorsqu'il s'agit, non d'une conquête violente, mais d'une annexion progressive et consentie sans trop de résistance. [. . .]

Coubertin P de (1901) Notes sur l'Éducation publique. Paris: Librairie Hachette (Chapitre I L'État et la famille p 17)

The Economics of Sport

The Institutions of Modern Sport
as an Area of Economic Competition:
the Law of Supply and Demand.
Sponsorship of Sport and the Olympic Movement:
its Mechanisms and Relationships to Sport's Original Values.
Government, Business and Sport Governing Bodies:
Who are the Decision-Makers?
The North-South and East-West Axes of Development in Sport:
Can the Gaps be Bridged?

Le sport et l'économie

L'institution sportive comme champ de concurrence
économique: la loi de l'offre et de la demande.
Sponsorisation de la culture sportive, ses mécanismes
et ses rapports aux valeurs d'origine du sport
et de l'Olympisme.
L'État, le commerce et les pouvoirs sportifs:
qui sont les décideurs dans le sport?
L'axe Nord-Sud, l'axe Est-Ouest et l'aide
au développement du sport:
les écarts peuvent-ils être réduits?

Sport et économie:
l'institution sportive comme champ
de concurrence économique

L'auteur part de la prémisse selon laquelle le marché et ses lois constituent un mécanisme efficace par lequel les biens et les services peuvent être adaptés aux changements qui sont toujours susceptibles de se produire dans les modes de vie ainsi que dans les besoins individuels et collectifs ou les demandes qui en découlent. Il souligne l'importance de bien comprendre les rouages des mécanismes de l'économie dont les succès et les échecs influent non seulement sur le système des valeurs dans le sport, mais encore peuvent le mettre en danger. L'auteur aborde ensuite la question des liens de toutes sortes qui s'entrecroisent entre l'économie et le sport. Il rappelle que dans les premières décades du siècle présent, on voyait d'un très mauvais œil que l'aide financière et le sponsoring s'approchent du sport et soient progressivement jugés nécessaires à ceux et à celles qui avaient le désir et l'aptitude d'exceller dans le sport amateur de haut niveau. À ce stade évolutif du sport moderne, l'amateurisme était surtout l'apanage des nouveaux riches dont il servait aussi la promotion sociale. Il s'est écoulé aussi un temps considérable avant que les annonces commerciales et le marketing ne deviennent carrément associés au sport en tant que spectacle et forme d'amusement populaire. L'auteur démontre ensuite que l'histoire des relations et des liens entre le sport et l'économie est faite d'un mélange de dissociation et de colonisation. L'establishment du sport tentait à la fois de préserver les idéaux traditionnels et l'autonomie des structures et du fonctionnement de son système, cependant que la rationalité économique et les lois du marché, implacablement, allaient à tout jamais modifier la dynamique d'ensemble et créer de nouveaux rapports de force. Dans la partie suivante de sa présentation, l'auteur souligne sous trois angles la colonisation du sport moderne par les forces économiques. Au plan macro-économique, l'expérience des dernières décades montre clairement que les économies nationales, au moins autant que les politiques sociales et la politique tout court, ont été mises à contribution dans le but de mousser les succès sportifs à l'échelle internationale, plus particulièrement en ce qui a trait aux Jeux olympiques. Au plan méso-économique, l'auteur démontre à l'aide d'exemples de développement et de tendances récentes en matière de formes d'activités physiques et sportives, de catégories de participants ainsi que de production et de consommation de biens et de services, les liens nouveaux entre le sport et l'économie. Au plan micro-économique, l'auteur traite des problèmes d'autonomie et des droits de la société sportive qui surgissent lorsque le sport est utilisé comme moyen de publicité commerciale, sans laquelle, par ailleurs, il ne saurait suffire à ses besoins et encore moins se développer. Par la suite, l'auteur illustre par deux catégories d'exemples les effets de l'économie de marché sur la différenciation et la consommation en matière de pratiques sportives. Dans la dernière partie de sa présentation, l'auteur traite des implications et des conséquences de l'intrusion irréversible de l'économie dans le sport, pour l'avenir de ce dernier. Il souligne que l'économie de marché a favorisé d'un côté l'expansion du sport, mais qu'elle peut aussi lui nuire si en fait elle prend et garde l'exclusivité de l'orientation des objectifs de participation, de l'utilisation des ressources et du contrôle de la qualité des biens et des services. En ce qui a trait au sport d'élite et au sport spectacle, l'auteur souligne les dangers de la montée en spirale des efforts et des investissements qui pour leur part conduisent à une sur-concentration des moyens financiers investis en vue d'une réussite sportive qui se doit de générer des profits. Cet état de chose peut conduire à un tarissement des ressources et à la stagnation du mouvement sportif dans son ensemble, qui lui se doit de demeurer au service de la majorité des citoyens. L'auteur conclut sa présentation en suggérant que la société sportive prenne tous les moyens pour conserver son influence en ce qui a trait à l'orientation des objectifs, des services et des produits, en matière de pratiques sportives, et qu'une façon de parvenir à cet objectif est de résister à l'oligarchisation et à la professionnalisation de ses propres structures. La recherche sur le terrain, l'analyse continue des tendances et la vigilance sont à cet effet des outils indispensables.

The Economics of Sport: the Institution of Modern Sport as an Area of Economic Competition

Klaus Heinemann

The market is in general a particularly suitable institution to adapt a product or service to new life-styles and to changes in individual or group needs, as well as demands. The market can be successful or can fail in fulfilling these requirements. It is thus important to study and understand how the process functions, as the successes or failures of the market are likely to influence the fundamental values of sport and, at times, even endanger them.

Research on Sport and Economy

As early as 1956, Rottenberg published a trailblazing article on "The Baseball Player's Labor Market" in a leading American economic periodical thus laying the founding stone for an economics of sport now well flourishing in the United States[1]. Its main topics had already been established in Rottenberg's article. The host of theoretical and empirical studies in the American literature are devoted to such issues as – the determinants of the demand for spectator sport; – regulations concerning the distribution of player qualities; and, – forms of cooperations between the team owners. In general, they focus on professional team sports organized and supplied by private, profit-oriented enterprises. It is only recently that the managerial problems of commercialized sport suppliers have been focused upon. In addition, there are also some investigations on the links between the economic power of a country and its successes in high performance sport.

Tackling similar issues, an economics of sport has also developed in Great Britain. In the Federal Republic of Germany, however, neither economists nor sport scientists have taken particular interest in the economic aspects of sport. As a result there is a lack of reliable scientific reports on many issues, for example on the economic problems facing sport clubs, that is, on an economics of voluntary associations as well as on the intertwinement of sport and the economy, on the

1890
1990

Klaus Heinemann, Institute of Sociology, University of Hamburg, Hamburg, Federal Republic of Germany.

manifold effects of sponsoring in sport, and on the economic significance of sport for the labor market and for economic growth. My reflections, therefore, are mainly based on assumptions.

Intertwinement of Sport and Economy

Many are well acquainted with the sad story of the American athlete Jim Thorpe who won gold medals in the pentathlon and in the decathlon at the 1912 Olympic Games. But it was revealed that he played minor league baseball in 1909 and 1910, having received a stipend of some twenty-five dollars a week. Great outrage was voiced after the Games, and he was stripped of his olympic medals. This was not a surprising turn of events. As the American social critic and economist Veblen at the turn of the century so astutely described in his book "The Theory of the Leisure Class"[2], sport was performed by a *nouveau riche* upper class as a form of demonstrative consumption, that is as a possibility of vaunting their social status, their wealth and the free time they had at their disposal. Thus, amateur sports, especially those that were relatively expensive to pursue, such as tennis, sailing and golf, were elevated to an ideal by which one could demonstrate that one was in a position to go in for "unproductive" and "purpose free" leisure time activities without the pressures of "serious" aims in life or economic constraints. The defence of amateur sport in the United States therefore served the upper classes as means of downgrading those doing sport for money or requiring financial aid to be able to compete at a high level.

Pierre de Coubertin had recently established the olympic idea by emphasizing "the noble and chivalrous character of sport", a rather ambiguous justification in view of the outlined situation. By using this formulation, he certainly meant to accentuate the educational value of sport. His hope was that sport would lead the individual to self-fulfillment by pursuing and achieving aims that are self-determined and not spurned on by economic interests, for example. However, he also intended or at least achieved a certain social delimitation. Amateur sport helped to hedge the "plebs" off from the gentleman sport of the British upper classes and the demonstrative sport consumption of the American *nouveau riche*.

Jim Thorpe had many fellow-sufferers in the subsequent decades. Although the outrage voiced was not quite so loud when it became known that the ice skaters Kilius and Bäumler had entered into a professional contract prior to the Olympic Games where they won a medal, they were nonetheless stripped of it. The Austrian skier Karl Schranz was not even allowed to participate in the Winter Olympic Games in Sapporo because he had advertised for a coffee brand. At the time, it was strictly forbidden to advertise on tricots or in the stadia, and the clothes had to be changed before television interviews if anything that could be related to a commercial firm was visible on them. It was a long and thorny road before advertising in and with sport gradually became permissible. The amateur status was gradually discarded and sport could then be marketed in the media as part of an attractive entertainment programme.

The history of sport is both the history of *dissociation* and *colonization*. The advancement of an economic rationality and the law of the market, as well as the increasing marketing of sport as a commodity, initially aroused disapproval, opposition and often outrage. However, the borders of what was regarded as permissible were pushed ever farther back. Dissociation was the attempt within the ranks of sport organization to adhere to amateur ideals, to voluntary organizations, to democratic decision-making structures, to honorary work, to equal opportunities against the forces of the market, even if the purchasing power of demand was not present. The theory of dissociation proceeds from the assumption that sport constitutes a counter-world to occupation, work, earning money and rational scheming. Sport was to be based on solidarity, and not on individual self-interest, on honorary work and not on occupations, on voluntariness and not on remunerated work. Colonization, on the other hand, means that sport was increasingly caught up in the maelstrom of a rationally shaped economy and in the laws of the market. Everything became more and more subject to structures characteristic of the economy prevalent in our society, such as the market, professional administration, occupation, profit-orientation, orientation on the purchasing power of demand. Sport thus had to adapt itself in its aims, contents and structures to the rationality of economy.

This process of colonization has largely been completed; an empty shell only stands as a remnant of the original ideals. During the 1984 Winter Olympic Games in Sarajevo, one of the reporters made an interesting slip of the tongue. Instead of saying "in the spirit of sportsmanship" he used "in the spirit of sponsorship". This was nothing more than a coincidental muddling up of two terms, but it rather aptly illustrates who has become Lord of the Rings. It is no longer solely sportive ideals that shape the Olympic Games but rather multifarious economic interests. However, more than the Olympic Games are affected; sport as a whole is developing towards becoming a profit-making business. The marketing of sport has not only opened up new possibilities and sources of financing but also given rise to new dependencies that yesterday's sport officials never even dreamed of or, if they did, banned to an imaginary island that they hoped would never be found.

The initial remarks purported to emphasize – that the increasing intertwinement of sport and economy is a relatively new phenomenon; – that the development was hampered by the manifold ideologies, prejudices and contact fears that are slowly being broken down; – and that as a result, a systematic knowledge of these problems is not yet available, just as experience over time is lacking.

Against this background an attempt will now be made to illustrate to what extent and in what areas the economy has extented its horizon into the field of sport.

The *macro-economic* level. Sport success in international competition is increasingly dependent on the economic performance of a country and its readiness and capability to invest part of its economic power in sport[3]. A country's olympic success is on the one hand determined by the available resources, that is on the size of the population, the economic power, the degree of industrialization, the level of education, and the extent of technical-scientific development. On the other hand, it also depends on the way these resources are used, that is on the political situation, the social structures and the prevalent ideologies. These economic, political and social variables that according to existing investigations influence international top performance sport, are obviously closely interrelated. A country's political system, economic power and social organization are not independent from one another. Investigations show, for example, that given the same per capita income, socialist countries with a planned economy have been more successful in the Olympic Games than capitalist countries with a market economy.

In this context, reference is made to an investigation presented recently by the economist Gärtner[4] who computed the interconnection between the level of income of market economic countries and the number of medals won at the Olympic Games. From this a number or value could be determined which predicts how many medals a country can expect to win, given its present income level. The result: a 1 billion dollar increase in the GNP brings forth 0.17 additional gold medals; in other words: for every additional medal the GNP has to increase by about 6 billion dollars. Gärtner also computed this prediction factor for socialist countries and compared it with the number of medals actually won. This showed that the actual value for the USSR was four times higher than the corresponding expectation value for market economy countries; for the GDR, more than eleven times higher. This illustrates that sport success is not only dependent on the respective economic potential of a country, but also on the efficient, politically controlled, centralized utilization of its resources. Market economic systems and an organization of sport in voluntary sports clubs and associations obviously doesn't constitute the optimum basis in this context. The moral of the story is that sport and economy have entered into a very significant but politically directed alliance.

The *meso-economic* level. The intertwinement of sport and economy also becomes obvious when one considers the significance that sport has with respect to employment and economic growth. Investigations into this matter are rather rare and difficult to effect because in the statistics of population, purchase, consumption and production, the term "sport" does not exist. Sport is not an industry like the building trade or insurance branch. In spite of these difficulties, the Henley Center has managed to carry out an extensive investigation on the importance of economy for British sport. The figures compiled by Krupp and Wagner give a first indication of the economic significance of sport in the Federal Republic of Germany. Both have come to the conclusion that sport constitutes a significant branch of the economy in which about 3% of those gainfully employed are working, which in turn provides for important growth impulses.

The above figures are merely indicators of the fact that sport, to be more exact the numerous forms of an increasing sport consumption, brings forth a multitude of dynamically growing markets. These markets comprise, among others: – the marketing of sport by *commercial sport suppliers* that open up the possibility for bodybuilding, weight reduction, fitness, relaxation, as well as other specific individual objectives; – sport in connection with *tourism*, where sport is provided in a high tech, professionally organized and profit oriented form; – sport as a means of *entertainment*, where sport can be seen to be used in various directions such "as the commercialization of sensations" (such as expectable aggression as in ice-hockey, for example), of risks, even going as far as endangering one's life (in car racing, for example), and tomfoolery, or as the commercialization of entertainment[5]; – the *marketing* of sport articles and equipment which means an expanding market, with sport involvement and just looking sporty becomes a part of individual life-style, and where clothing and equipment increasingly developing into fashionable accessories available for mass consumption.

The *micro-economic* level. The third area of intertwinement of sport and economy concerns the marketing of rights that the sports clubs and associations have at their disposal. The main form of this is the utilization of sport as an advertising medium, especially sport sponsoring[6]. This includes the sale of advertising rights, equipment rights, sponsoring rights, broadcasting rights etc.

If a sports club wants to survive, it must increasingly make use of its economic potential. The main reason for this is the pressure of increasing costs that sports clubs are confronted with. In view of the rising costs of the entire competitive system, it is no longer possible to achieve and present international top performances in sport only with the idealism and devotion of volunteer workers and the annual fees paid by the members. Records must now be produced professionally and at great cost[7]. The club or association is obliged to sell performances to third parties, in this case to profit-oriented enterprises. The sale of these disposal rights is of central significance to the financing of a given sport.

When discussing sport as an area of economic competition, one ought to differentiate between three different types of intertwinement of sport and economy:

1– The performance level of sport which is sustained by the power of the economy but controlled by the state or voluntary associations. An indicator is the number of medals a country wins. In this case we refer to the intertwinement of the *systems* of economy, politics and sport.

2– Commercialized sport consumption and its contribution to economic growth and employment. An indicator is the money spent on sport, leisure-time and tourism. In this case we have an intertwinement of *enterprises* and sport *consumers*.

3– The utilization of the economic potential of sports organizations through the sale of property rights. An indicator is the clubs' and associations' income from advertising and broadcasting. In this case we have an intertwinement of *profit-oriented* enterprises and *sports clubs* as *voluntary organizations*.

These three types of intertwinement of sport and economy have different aspects and thus entail varying consequences and problems. In the first case, one deals with the matter of controlling and making effective use of the wealth accrued in the economic system. In the second, one contends with the consequences of the changes for sport and its providers, on account of an increasing sport consumption and also of sport becoming an economic factor. In the third, one must face the problems that result from the confrontation of two decision-makers with differing structural peculiarities, that is voluntary organizations (with honorary leadership, democratic decision-making structures and obligations to the members' interests), on the one hand, and profit-oriented enterprises, on the other.

The Effects of Supply and Demand: two Examples

From the multifarious intertwinement of sport and economy, two examples will serve to illustrate the effects of the market: – the increasing differentiation of sport as a result of rising consumption; – the "artificial" production of sport as an integral part of entertainment programmes.

To the first example. The market brings forth new types of sport that often become popular overnight but also lose their impact just as quickly. At the same time it also destroys traditional forms of sport. The effects of economic competition are most aptly illustrated in the field of leisure-time sport and sport consumption. In recent years, there has been far-reaching developments in sport: new groups are discovering sport and this leads to changes in motives, demands, and skills on the part of those participating. The desire for relaxation, well-being, fun, health, physical fitness competes with the aspiration for an increase in performance. What is in demand is variety, skilled advisors and a pleasant atmosphere. Increasing material wealth and more leisure time go hand in hand with more sophisticated forms of leisure-time activities.

The rate of commercialization in sport consumption is obviously the expression and result of social change reflected both in the variable but also inconsistent demand for sport. The market tends to react faster than the sports club. The market thus seems to be the more suitable instrument to adapt sport to ever changing life-styles, even though it means hurting those traditional forms of sport that are no longer in line with this demand. In accordance with the laws of the market, sport suppliers quickly adjust to changes in the demand, whether in health needs, in tendencies towards individualization, or in the pursuit of fun, fitness, well-being and identity. Sport indeed changes according to the laws of the market: the industry develops and favors new, profit-oriented, marketable types of activities such as aerobics, squash, surfing, or it systematically markets more traditional types of sport, such as tennis, skiing, golf. The focal point of economic interest is mainly directed towards individual types of sporting activities that often are just fashionable trends popular for only a limited time and may require expensive dress and equipment. Among newly fashionable activities one could cite Seiki and Tai Chi, bodybuilding and ballroom dancing, stretching and calisthenics, kick boxing and somagogics, Thai boxing and anti-terror fighting, Shihatsu and mountain meditation. The borders of various forms of bodily expression and body movement are dissolving into dance and theatre, meditation, yoga, autogenic training, dance therapy etc. In addition, borders are becoming less distinct between other forms of recreational and holiday activities where the individual is looking for recuperation, relaxation, conviviality, entertainment, games and diversions.

To the second example. By means of rules and agreements, the market forces the suppliers to "artificially" produce uncertainty. Rottenberg's central assumption is that professional spectator sports produce uncertainty with regard to the outcome of a match; the longer the outcome is open and uncertain, the greater the attractiveness for paying spectators. Uncertainty, however, presupposes equal performance levels of the teams. No club has an (economic) interest in winning *all the time*. If one team has a (sport) monopoly, that is if there are no serious challengers, the situation becomes detrimental for the quality of the good and thus its sales. Conversely, it is very advantageous for business to have equally strong competitors and frequent changes in the league standings. A football team with no serious rival, a tennis player who is unbeatable will in the long run not succeed in filling the stadia or keeping the viewers glued to the screen. In sport we are therefore dealing with suppliers, who each for himself is striving towards economic profit, yet can only produce the goods necessary to attain this end in cooperation with others. If there is only one winner or loser, economic pressure sets in to change the situation. Uncertainty in sport is produced "artificially". Agreements with one's rivals are necessary. By agreeing on the rules and by shaping the drama, exciting entertainment is "produced". As examples, one can point to agreements on the size of leagues and the determination of entry requirements for new teams, to the rules for carrying out competitions and the distribution of earnings, and, above all, to the rules on the distribution of the talent (labor market regulations). Uncertainty in competition is highest when all teams have an equal amount of good player qualities. The *labour* market and *product* market are thus closely linked with each another.

Market Failure and Sportive Ideals

The long battle of sport against "colonization" outlined above did not stem merely from ideological prejudices; rather it was linked to a fear of the negative consequences of market economic control. Nonetheless, it stands as a good example of the effect of supply and demand on the value of sport. One should not compare market economy and non profit economy on the basic of ideological prejudices—which was to be expected in the long colonization battle but on an understanding of the (often non intended) consequences of the different institutional arrangements associated with the production and the distribution of goods and services.

In general terms, there is little to be argued against sport being controlled by market economic principles in a society where people are to a large extent convinced of the special power of the market or, (if one is not convinced) at least profit from it. The market tends to release new creative impulses, it furthers and commands innovations and progressive development in the expectation that a demand backed by adequate purchasing power can be mobilized. The intertwinement of sport and economy, however, can be disastrous if it comes to a failure of the market that is not associated with a failure of the club. It is not self-evident that voluntary associations in which sport is organized will function adequately where the market has failed. It remains to be substantiated that voluntary associations can provide something the market cannot.

One could say that there is market failure when, firstly, goods that are considered desirable or necessary are not produced and offered on the market on the grounds that there is not a sufficient demand for them backed by a purchasing power that is able to cover the costs, or, because parts of the product have the character of a public good, with the producers not being in a position to record the whole profit from its utilization via the market. Secondly, there is market failure when a long-term utilization of the available resources is prevented because, otherwise, it could result in their exploitation and thus, in their premature exhaustion; and thirdly, when the market alters the type and quality of the products in an undesirable fashion. There are numerous examples of such types of negative effects namely the "tyranny of minor decisions" characteristic of an individualistic conception of the market. If, for example, a great many people decide to do their shopping in discount stores—a rational decision from an individual point of view—the specialist trade with all it has to offer may be eliminated without the individual having a direct say in the matter, even to a point of losing alternative choices. A decision that an individual takes thus seems more attractive than it actually is a situation that becomes evident only after a certain span of time during which other parties also make their choices. To the extent that medicine, for example, becomes a contractual service oriented towards wages or money and the relationship between doctor and patient may become increasingly non-committal, the trust relationship tends to diminish with the consequence that there are more and more complaints about inadequate treatment and, on the other hand, a tendency toward defensive treatment methods that are not open to legal contention[8]. Likewise, if blood is no longer donated but rather bought, this leads, as shown by Titmuss[9], to negative consequences with respect to the quality of the product and the readiness to make it available. If democracy turns into a system of purchasing votes (by means of subsidies or electoral payola), party donations and corruption tend to become run-of-the-mill. Those who regard a satisfaction of needs, (for example in love affairs) as a contractual right of the consumer seem to forgo the possibility of emotional and spiritual experiences. The market restricts possibilities when all or too much depends on money. In as much as commercialization brings about a privatizing of advantages, such as the transition from patronship to sponsorship, assistance, trust, and altruism are reduced to such an extent as to make them not seem worthwhile. The mutual aid as well as the idealism that were characteristic of voluntary activities, automatically take a back seat when performance relationships are increasingly understood in economic terms.

In that perspective three different and non-intended consequences of commercialization will be discussed.

1– The laws of the market can prevent sport from being accessible to everybody and can also prevent every type of sport from being accessible to all. Sport under the laws of the market requires demand that has power to buy. But not everyone who wishes to be involved in sport has such power. Only certain athletes, teams or types of sport have a high advertisement value based on attraction, and only few can use the manifold opportunities to market themselves. Most others have no access to such financial sources. They are therefore disadvantaged or even threatened due to limited financial opportunities, less support for the individual athlete, and generally unfavorable income possibilities. Cultural diversity and the possibility of self-expression according to one's desires are threatened. A self-dynamic *spiral* of preference shifts emerges. Attractive types of sport or teams receive financial support, which leads to better opportunities to discover new talent; they offer good training conditions and favorable financial incentives, and also buy stars, who in turn attract additional spectators. This constitutes a further attraction, which increases the chances to ensure even bigger income, which in turn can be used to become ever more attractive and thus to keep the favor of spectators and of the advertising industry. Preferences of spectators and athletes are shifted in favor of these types of sport. Those sports or teams that are not so effective with respect to spectators obviously lead a more dreary existence. Herewith, one of the fundamental values of sport is endangered: equality of preconditions. Cultural diversity in sport is necessary, if sport is to become or remain open and attractive to all. Commercialization can endanger the cultural diversity of sport in that opportunities for recreational sport and sport-for-all (as well as high performance sport) that promise little profit for commercial enterprises or the sport equipment industry, tend to be neglected.

2– The exploitation of resources can become a problem of market-oriented economic regulation. This can be exemplified through sport as well. One can predict that the physical and psychological demands on athletes will continue to increase. The number of competitions is growing steadily under pressure from commercial interests. Time for rest and recuperation is becoming increasingly shorter. Athletes are at times forced to participate in competitions despite light injuries in order to earn as much money as possible during the relatively short period of his/her optimal form. Nature is overcharged. Micro-injuries do not heal adequately during the phases of rest and rebuilding which are too short. The risk of increased or permanent damage looms over many athletes. When success in sport has increasing financial consequences, the tendency to reach success by all possible means, even illegal, necessarily becomes greater. Herewith controls with respect to means of performance enhancement (such as doping controls) and controls of unfair behavior (through an increase in the number and competence of referees or in the refinement of observation and measurement techniques) are warranted in the eyes of many. At the same time new systems of rules are emerging.

3– The recreational sport and sport-for-all movements, especially within clubs, offer self-expression possibilities to their members. Within a club, members decide on the utilization of the resources, which they themselves brought in order to achieve the best possible realization of this goal. In commercial sport, the club does not produce services for its members, but rather a product geared to the expected interests and desires of third parties. The development of schedules is governed by attractive advertisement times, competition rules and the distribution of players are guided by the principle of increasing suspense and unpredictability, fighting effort is encouraged, various elements of entertainment are added in order to offer suspenseful and diversified entertainment to the layman who is not always familiar with the rules of a given sport. In addition, there are issues that result from a club's structure of resources changing due to commercialization. The basic principle of a club is that it is borne by financial contributions and other commitments of its members, volunteer work in particular, so that it can pursue its aims.

In general terms, it can be argued that changes in the resource structure may become incompatible with some of characteristic variables of the club's traditional financing, if they extend beyond a certain threshold. Structural changes in the resource structure tend to lead to a shift in objectives and a change of product, to favour service orientation on the part of the members, to intensify tendencies towards oligarchization and professionalization, the latter implying an increase in the required skills and a rising proportion of remunerated work.

Furthermore, they result in increasingly bureaucratic structures both for the club (and the association or federation), as well as in a dove-tailing between the goals of the organization and the interests of the members. When these changes exceed a certain threshold, they often necessitate further changes in the structure of resources. This situation may lead to a type of organization that constitutes the exact opposite of the ideal type of voluntary association. The association, its board in particular, become more flexible in the way they fulfill their tasks, and less dependent on the random pool of skills and abilities provided by the members, as well as on their readiness to sacrifice time and money for the sake of the organization, indeed if they do not have to rely on their members' readiness to provide these resources. An effect of this is obviously an increased independence and influence of the board. Changes in the structure of resources can therefore lead to an increasing manifestation of oligarchization tendencies within the club. Research has been carried out on only a few of interfaces between sport and economics. There is an obvious need for more extensive and deeper analysis and treatment of the problems and issues at stake, on the entire spectrum from sport-for-all to high performance and professional sport as well.

NOTES AND REFERENCES

1. Rottenberg S (1956) The baseball player's labor market. Journal of Political Economy 63 242-58

2. Veblen T (1899) The theory of the leisure class. New York: Macmillan

3. Colwell B (1984) Ökonomische Bedingungen des Erfolges im internationalen Spitzensport. In Heinemann K (ed) Texte zur Ökonomie des Sports. Schorndorf: Hofmann p 91-100

4. Gärtner G (1989) Socialist countries' sporting success before perestroika—and after? International Review for the Sociology of Sport 24 283-98

5. Rittner V (1988) Sport als ökonomisches Interessenobjekt. In Diegel H (ed) Sport im Verein und Verband. Schorndorf: Hofmann p 158-59

6. Heinemann K (1989) Sportsponsoring: Ökonomische Chancen oder Weg in die Sackgasse? In Hermanns A (ed) Sport und Kultursponsoring. München p 62-78

7. In the sector of track and field athletics, for example, the athlete's performance is related to the price he is paid.

8. Hirsch F (1982) Soziale Grenzen wirtschaftlichen Wachstums. Reinbeck/Hamburg: Rowolt-Publisher

9. Titmuss RM (1971) The gift relationship. New York: Pantheon

Le gouvernement, le monde des affaires et les organismes de régie du sport: qui prend en définitive les décisions?

En guise d'entrée en matière, l'auteur établit que le développement du sport contemporain est inséparable de celui des économies modernes. Dans les pays de type capitaliste, où le sport a pris racine au siècle dernier, l'accélération de la production industrielle, la création de l'économie de marché et l'expansion du transport, des communications et du commerce international ont servi de toile de fond et ont contribué à l'avènement d'une approche bureaucratique et scientifique du sport d'élite. Le sport moderne, incluant l'olympique, a évolué comme partie intégrante de l'ensemble des transformations qui ont aussi affecté le monde du spectacle et le secteur des mass-media. L'auteur avance que les instances administratives du sport olympique ne jouissent plus aujourd'hui de la même indépendance et de la même latitude décisionnelle que jadis; à son avis, pour le monde du sport, il s'agit moins d'une perte de pouvoir décisionnel que d'un effort conscient d'adaptation à des circonstances et à des institutions nouvelles. L'auteur procède par la suite à une analyse de la situation évolutive en s'appuyant sur un certain nombre d'exemples puisés dans l'histoire et dans l'économie politique canadiennes. Dans la partie centrale de sa présentation, l'auteur décrit trois sortes de changements interreliés qui ont contribué selon lui à l'érosion progressive de l'autonomie dont jouissait par tradition le sport olympique: – la montée des groupements de sociétés industrielles et commerciales (*i.e.*, les grands cartels contemporains); – l'intervention progressive de l'État dans le sport; – la globalisation du tandem sport-mass media. Dans le cas du premier type de changement, l'auteur explique le parallélisme existant entre la montée des cartels commerciaux et celui du sport-spectacle, plus particulièrement en Amérique du nord. En fait, de l'avis de l'auteur, des cartels étaient déjà solidement établis vers la fin de la Grande Guerre, dans le baseball, et vers la fin de la Deuxième Guerre Mondiale, pour ce qui est des grands sports nord-américains du basketball, du football et du hockey sur glace, les media étant devenus des partenaires efficaces de toute l'entreprise. Au sujet de l'intrusion de l'État dans le sport, l'auteur décrit brièvement la situation canadienne des dernières décades. Par tradition, la prise et le partage des décisions se faisait au Canada entre les niveaux de gouvernements provinciaux et fédéral et les organismes de régie du sport. Mais la pression montante que représentait l'expectative du succès sportif sur la scène internationale a eu vite fait, selon l'auteur, de justifier un soutien financier accru de la part de l'État. Paradoxalement, au Canada, on voyait l'intervention de l'État comme une sorte de contre-poids à l'influence et au pouvoir montant des cartels commerciaux dans le sport de haut niveau, là même où s'exerçait lourdement leur influence et où par surcroît la préparation et le soutien des athlètes étaient devenus professionnalisés. Du côté de la globalisation du tandem sport-media, l'auteur décrit trois des facteurs qui dans une très large part ont contribué à l'état actuel de choses: – la montée des investissements de toutes sortes dans le sport, en tant qu'objet de consommation; – la concentration du pouvoir économique dans un nombre sans cesse plus restreint de partenaires; – enfin, en regard de l'opinion publique, une sorte de besoin de faire entrave aux pressions qui ne manquent pas de venir de la part d'organismes ou d'individus qui s'intéressent aux problèmes de consommation, d'environnement ou de questions à caractère nationaliste. Les forces nouvelles qui influent sur la chose sportive, de l'avis de l'auteur, ont largement contribué au fait troublant que le Mouvement olympique en soit venu à consacrer de nos jours une si large part de ses énergies à la production d'un spectacle et du succès. Cette situation rend sans cesse plus difficile, pour les athlètes, la poursuite et l'atteinte des objectifs de développement personnel qui constituaient, dans l'esprit de Coubertin, l'essentiel de l'idéologie olympique. Dans la dernière partie de sa présentation, l'auteur exprime de l'inquiétude sur l'avenir du partenariat entre l'État et l'entreprise privée, au sujet du soutien financier qui sera consenti au sport et qui, du moins au Canada, sera vraisemblablement et de plus en plus associé aux exigences et au succès de la publicité. Il souhaite voir les membres de la famille olympique continuer à poursuivre avant tout les buts de l'Olympisme dans leurs négociations avec les partenaires financiers.

Government, Business and Sport Governing Bodies: Who Are the Decision-makers?

Bruce Kidd

Although one tends to consider them in distinct categories, the development of modern sport has been inseparable from the development of modern economies. In the capitalist countries, where sports were first fashioned and elaborated in the 19th century, the acceleration of industrial production, the creation of an energetic market in urban land and the rapid expansion of international trade created the conditions, furnished the resources, and suggested the meanings. As every student of the "renovation" of the rough and unruled games of early modern Europe and colonial North America into sports well knows, the development of the highly bureaucratized, scientific approach to the athletic competition we know as "sport" would have been inconceivable without the railroad and the social and technological transformations of which it was a part. The amateur code makes no sense without reference to the class struggles and alliances emanating from the transition to a free market, wage labour economy. Nor can we explain the sportsman's discourse on "masculinity" in isolation from the gender tensions exacerbated by the rigid occupational and spacial sexual division of labour perfected by the Victorian bourgeoisie[1,2].

A major part of the process has been the extension of what Braverman[3] called "the universal market", the penetration of commodity production—*i.e.*, production for exchange according to system of wage labour—into ever more spheres of human activity, initially to supplant household production for consumption, then to create new products and services indispensable in the new society. It is no coincidence that historians now contend that the Spalding equipment manufacturers—not the legendary Abner Doubleday—deserve most of the credit for creating the modern game of baseball[4]. The story of modern sports has also been part-and-parcel of the development of commercial entertainment, and the mass media. The same interrelationships can be observed in the socialist countries. As Riordan[5] and Cantelon[6] have argued, the imperatives of rapid industrialization and class conflict in the 1930s led Soviet leaders to initiate their vaunted high performance system—well before they joined the International

Bruce Kidd, School of Physical and Health Education, University of Toronto, Toronto, Ontario, Canada.

Olympic Committee's Games in the 1950s. Throughout the world, the dynamic of economic change continues to shape opportunity and meaning in sports to this very day.

How have the leaders of the modern Olympic Movement responded to the economic forces within which they pursued their ambitions? To what extent have they been able to shape the sports under their nominal control? What other identifiable actors contribute to the process? In this presentation, it will be argued that while the leaders of the olympic sports no longer make decisions with the independence they once enjoyed, the influence of other players represents less a "loss of power" (as is often alleged) than a conscious adaptation to changing circumstances and the willing forging of alliances with more powerful institutions. The perspective that follows stems from an interpretation of history and political economy. Examples will be drawn primarily from Canada. While the Canadian case is unique in several important respects, it is also illustrative of several general patterns.

The Long Reign of the Amateurs

The leaders of olympic sports clubs, associations and federations often look back to an earlier, simpler era when they enjoyed complete independence in sports. This is not entirely romanticization. For most of the long reign of amateurism, the olympic leaders did effectively command the activities they governed and organized. It was in their playgrounds, schools, universities, private clubs and organizations like the YMCAs where sports were played, their associations which conducted major events like national and international championships. In most sports, they were beholden to no one but themselves. They made the rules and determined who could play. Although there was always a measure of resistance to their authoritarianism, most participants accepted the legitimacy of the ideals they espoused. The amateur code they administered kept the time and monies necessary for successful organization to a level which they could manage and finance on a voluntary basis. (It also limited participation to those who could pay their own way, effectively closing the highest levels of competition to the working class.) Clothed in the ideologies of rational recreation, fair play, and selfless nationalism, the amateurs enjoyed the patronage of the most powerful elites, and the support of the mass media and public opinion for many years.

But acknowledging the unrestricted control which the olympic sports leaders exercised during the heyday of amateurism is not to say that they possessed complete "autonomy" from the dominant economic forces. For the most part, their activities were intertwined with them. Most came from the middle and upper classes who fashioned the new sports in step with the rising industrial capitalist economy. To the extent that they were reformers in the wake of Coubertin, seeking to foster a better world through "the making of men" and the reduction of prejudice, ignorance and social tension, they held conservative, not radical, views. While they emphasized the educational benefits of participation, directing it towards individual self-knowledge and productive citizenship, it was nonetheless in the interests of the established order. While they opposed the monetization of training and competition, they actively contributed to the commodification of sports, energetically selling their games and major events.

These characteristics should be kept in mind as consideration will now be given to the alteration of power relations in the olympic sports during the major economic and social transformations of the 20th century. Three interrelated changes which "eroded" the traditional autonomy of the olympic sports governing bodies will be examined: – the rise of the sports cartel; – the intervention of the state; – the globalization of the sports/media complex.

The Sports Cartel

At the time Coubertin visited this City of Quebec a century ago, amateurism was hegemonic. Playing sports for their "use value" of character building and recreation was accepted by most strata of society and legitimized by the mass media. But there were others who sought to enhance the "exchange value" of sports by turning them into profitable entertainments. The sports entrepreneurs continually experimented with the rules to make games more pleasing to spectators, they paid athletes and coaches so that they could train full-time, and they aggressively wooed audiences with audacious public relations. Unlike the directors of professional sport in Britain, Europe and Australia, the North American promoters had no particular loyalty to a given community, moving their operations from city to city whenever greater profits beckoned, buying players and managers wherever they could. By the end of the First World War, in baseball, and by the end of the Second World War, in basketball, football and ice hockey, the entrepreneurs had established powerful cartels which monopolized both the sale of games and the employment of players and coaches. The sports cartels rose with the tide of the US-centred "consumer capitalism". In the 1920s, the movement was often called "Fordism" because the success of Henry Ford in assembly line automobile production both opened up the possibility and necessitated the creation of mass markets for manufactured goods[7]. Investment was increasingly directed towards the production and sale of consumer goods —automobiles, household furniture and appliances, toiletries and cosmetics, and popular entertainments like movies, radio shows, and sports events. The extent of consumer culture has been exaggerated, because real wages rarely increased to permit many beyond the middle class to participate. But growing urban populations expanded the potential markets, while increasing urban densities, along with the accelerating pace of everyday life, added to the attraction of "ready made" entertainments. The media played a pivotal role in this process proclaiming the advantages of the new products and anointing the stars of the new spectacles, while selling readers and listeners to advertisers. In particular, sports broadcasts proved an extremely effective way of assembling affluent male consumers for the promotions of products primarily directed to them. During the 1939 World Series, for example, the sponsors packaged a special "World Series" razor and advertised it during the broadcasts. In just four games, they reportedly sold four million sets, their entire production[8].

The success of the cartels radically altered the balance of power in North American sports. With the growing opportunities for profitable investment presented by sports entertainment, many in the economic elite abandoned the amateurs for professionals. With their vastly superior resources, the sports cartels turned amateur programs into farm systems, reducing the scope of the amateur leaders' control to individual sports such as track and field and swimming. At the same time, their burgeoning partnerships with the mass media—the creation of what Gruneau calls "the sports media complex"—enabled them to overturn the amateurs' ideological hegemony, transforming the dominant connotation of professionalism from "debased" and "dishonest" play to "the best in sport" and of amateurism from "ennobling" to "inexpert". At the same time, the image of the athlete was shifted from self-directed participant to management-directed worker. From my own research, I can argue that the National Hockey League had supplanted the Amateur Athletic Union of Canada as the defining Canadian sports organization by the late 1930s[9]. The net result was to marginalize the Olympic Movement to a few sports and greatly reduce its stature in the public eye. The rise of the sports cartel also contributed to the "symbolic annihilation[10]" of the striking growth in women's sport which characterized the period.

State Intervention

The state must also be considered in any discussion of decision making, economic power and sports. In many parts of the world—the United States is the only major exception—state ministries provide the bulk of resources for high performance training and competition in the olympic sports and they have gained considerable influence over decision-making in return. In the Canadian case, federal and provincial sports agencies determine the goals, set the conditions, and control the most prestigious awards. They even feel a need to control eligibility, as the recent controversy over Ben Johnson's future in international track and field attests. The federal Ministry of Fitness and Amateur Sport seemed intent on withdrawing its annual grant to the Canadian Track and Field Association if Johnson was allowed to compete internationally again. These are not simply "political" decisions, which "interfere" with or "distort" the historic practice of the olympic sports bodies to determine their own course. They, too, are driven by the dynamic of economic change. Most scholars account for the creation of pro-active programs in terms of the "legitimation" function, the effort to justify the social order and/or win international recognition and prestige[11]. In the Canadian case, the new high performance programs of the early 1970s are explained as the Canadian Government's response to the crisis of federal legitimacy occasioned by Quebecois, western Canadian and native people's independence movements, and growing labour militancy, in the context of the welfare state[12]. But these movements, too, had strong economic underpinnings—the devastating effects of uneven development in an country where the dominance of foreign capital and a heavy dependence upon international commodity markets significantly reduced the ability of the federal government to control the pattern of economic development.

The olympic leaders shrewdly exploited these tensions to regain some of their former power and prestige. In large part, the new state programs were suggested and supported by them. They unabashedly saw the State as a source of the resources necessary to combat the influence of the sports cartels and to stay competitive in their own sports in a world where the preparation of athletes was increasingly becoming professionalized. And they have perhaps been the primary beneficiaries, as hundreds of new well-paying jobs have been created at the administrative level. The olympic leaders also won the support of big business for these programs by encouraging the capital accumulation of facility construction and the advertising of popular athletes and teams. They may publicly chafe at the complications created by the layering of state bureaucracies on top of their own organizations, and the necessary sharing of power, but they have never called for their abolition. They are junior partners—not captives—of the State[13].

The Globalization of the Sport/Media Complex

The other major change affecting the olympic sports in recent decades has been the globalization of the sports/media complex. By this is meant the exponential expansion of the web of interests involved in the commodification of sports. It no longer involves just the immediate producers—the sporting goods industry, the North American spectacle-producing cartels like the National Hockey League, and the mass media—but a host of other corporations seeking market share or ideological influence through the rental, production and distribution of sports icons. Many of these promotions are tied to international events and satellite television so they can target the globe. It was as much the lure of new revenue from corporate advertising as the perceived "inequalities" created by the state subsidization of athletes which led the Olympic Movement to repeal all restrictions upon the payment of athletes in the 1970s and 1980s. These developments have been driven – by accelerating investments in the consumer sector, especially the new "food and fun" industries; – by the growing concentration of economic power into fewer and fewer hands, so that successful sales often require increasing market share, rather than opening up new markets; – and by the need to turn public opinion against consumerist, environmental and nationalist pressures[14]. The monies involved—in 1989, Canadian corporations spent an estimated 925 million dollars on advertising promotions[15], more than 15 times what is spent by the federal sports ministry—have given sponsors enormous influence over the setting of goals and the staging of events[16]. But again, one should not characterize the olympic leaders as the "pawns" of commercialization. Some go along reluctantly because they feel they have no alternative in the crunch of underfunding, but most are active partners. The International Olympic Committee has pioneered the creation of global advertising through The Olympic Program (TOP), International Sport Licensing (ISL) and international television. This has been enabled by the IOC's careful recruitement of every major community around the world.

The combined effect of these developments has been to focus more and more of the Olympic Movement's energies on the production of high performance spectacle. Much of this is deeply troubling. The new olympic-state-corporate alliance has constructed a system of underpaid wage labour often as exploitative as any professional sport. Instead of the horizon-expanding search for self-discovery, the heroic ambition of Coubertin, many athletes have been reduced to the raw material for bureaucratic, biophysical and psychological manipulation. In fact, many of them contribute to their own alienation, sculpting and tailoring their bodies to fit the needs of their sports and their sponsors[17]. They have unprecedented opportunity to travel, but engage very little of the cultures they encounter, even at an Olympic Games[18,19]. While the Olympic Movement continues to advance gender equality—still not enough, but at a much, much faster rate than anywhere else in sports—the eradication of other forms of inequality seems more distant than ever before. In Canada, the evidence actually suggests less lower-class participation on national teams than 30 years ago[20]. Most of the sponsors' millions are spent on their own promotions. Very little goes towards the facilities, coaching and training programs used by active athletes, let alone the extension of opportunity. Notwithstanding the IOC's Olympic Solidarity program and other efforts at sport aid, the inequalities are magnified many times internationally with little prospect of significant improvement[21]. These contradictions are as old as the Olympic Movement itself, but they have become more difficult with its expansion into cultures of such diversity. I continue to believe that the olympic project represents a significant plus for humankind. But many olympic leaders contribute to the conditions which undermine the promise of Olympism. They elevate the importance of athletic skill and winning above Coubertin's other aspirations, and they have become masters at the marketing game. They continue to champion *uncritically* the idea that successful athletes are "representative" symbols of community and desirable values. These practices not only complicate the task of healthy self-development and thoughtful intercultural exchange, but they help create the athletic commodities so attractive to governments and corporate advertisers.

The 21st Century

How will the Olympic Movement respond to a future driven even more frenetically by cybernetic changes, instantaneous international capital flows, and transnational mergers and acquisitions, while national governments find it ever more difficult to intervene effectively in the economic sphere? It is difficult to speculate.

Given the scarcity of resources—we can never turn the clock back to the days of self-financing—the olympic sports bodies must continue to pursue their state and corporate partnerships. But the pressure is to restructure more and more of their operations in the direction of commodity production. Given the neo-conservatism which reigns in most western capitals, there will be few additional monies for sports unless the investment can be shown dramatically to improve the prospects for accumulation. The new, post-revolutionary governments in Eastern Europe are already slashing expenditures on elite sport[22]. It will be regrettable—but hardly surprising—if part of the "peace dividend" from the end of the "cold war" will be a world-wide de-emphasis of those olympic sports which do not enjoy a commercial market.

Corporate sponsorship will be increasingly driven by the demographics of advertising, which will mean even less money for more developmental projects, the less visible sports, and women. The Canadian record is very clear in this respect. Even those corporations which have traditionally supported olympic projects out of a sense of philanthropy are cutting back when "the exposure isn't what we wanted". The sports corporations primarily sell male viewers to advertisers, a transaction which continues to exclude many athletically significant female events[23]. In Canada, the only way many women's organizations can get their major events on television is to pay for the coverage[24]. In Toronto, a "reform" city council has passed an ordinance requiring cycling organizers to hold at least one women's race for every men's program and provide equal prizes for women, but several sponsors are threatening to move their races elsewhere because their products are primarily targeted to men[25]. I have argued elsewhere[26] that the olympic leaders need to be much tougher in pursuing the aspirations of Olympism in their negotiations with the corporations. Unless they do, the whole project becomes an advertisement for the multinationals and the future they want us to have. Are we far from the day when olympic teams become like professional cycling teams, marching into the stadium under corporate logos, instead of national flags[27]?

But within and without the olympic family, one can also expect continuing resistance to the developments described. Athletes, the "sweat-suited philanthropists" who donate their underpaid labour to the ambitions of governments and corporations, are becoming better organized, and may well unionize in the interests of higher benefits, better working conditions and a greater share in decision-making. Third-world sports leaders may bargain the legitimacy their participation provides for a real measure of redistribution. Prospective host cities for the Olympic Games may well negotiate collectively with the IOC to ensure a more beneficial combination of activities and legacies. The IOC, NOCs, and some olympic sports associations may reassert their responsibility for the production and distribution of images and meaning on world-wide TV. These prospects will be conditioned by the larger political economy: the limits to unchecked growth so evident from the environmental crisis, the escalating north-south tensions created by the worsening primary producers' terms of trade, and the dramatic rise of the "new Asia".

In such a brief overview, there is always danger that one will suggest closure on the big questions which need to be examined. It is hoped this is not the case here. There is a need to know much more about:

– the production, distribution and consumption of dominant and contestative practices and meanings, and the roles of the major institutions and individuals, including the new intermediaries such as Mark McCormack and Chris Lang;

– the mobilization of capital, the patterns of investment, and the extraction and transfer of surpluses from sports;

– the nature of the new forms of sport-related employment, and its distribution among different sports, classes, genders, regions, and races;

– the social and environmental costs of the rapid commercialization of the olympic sports;

– the patterns of adaptation and resistance.

In particular, scholars must contribute to the process of generating alternative strategies for olympic decision-makers, to help them achieve more of the olympic promise in their negotiations with the sports-media complex. Only one thing is clear: the future of sports will be shaped by the totality of these changes. It will take extraordinarily committed and skilled leadership to intervene in a way which advances the historic mission of the Olympic Movement.

NOTES AND REFERENCES

1. Gruneau R (1988) Modernization or hegemony: two views on sport and social development. In Harvey J, Cantelon H (eds) Not just a game: essays in Canadian sport sociology. Ottawa: University of Ottawa Press p 9-32

2. Hargreaves J (1986) Sport, power and culture: a social and historical analysis of popular sports in Britain. New York: St Martin's Press

3. Braverman H (1974) Labor and monopoly capital. New York: Monthly Review 271-83

4. Levine P (1985) AG Spalding and the rise of baseball. New York: Oxford

5. Riordan J (1977) Sport in Soviet society. Cambridge: Cambridge University Press

6. Cantelon H (1979) Stakhanovism and its influence on the development of international sport in the Soviet Union. In Schrodt B (ed) Proceedings of the 4th Canadian Symposium on the History of Sport and Physical Education. Vancouver: School of Physical Education and Recreation, University of British Columbia

7. Ewan S (1976) Captains of consciousness: advertising and the social roots of the consumer culture. Toronto: McGraw Hill

8. Powers R (1984) Supertube: the rise of television sports. New York: Coward-McCann p 28

9. Kidd B, Macfarlane J (1972) The death of hockey. Toronto: New Press

10. Gerbner G (1978) The dynamics of cultural resistance. In Tuchman G, Kaplan DA, Benet J (eds) Hearth and home: images of women in the mass media. New York: Oxford University Press

11. Panitch L (1977) The role and nature of the Canadian state. In Panitch L (ed) The Canadian state: political economy and political power. Toronto: University of Toronto p 3-27

12. Macintosh D, Bedecki T, Franks CES (1987) Sport and politics in Canada: federal government involvement since 1961. Montreal and Kingston: McGill-Queen's University Press

13. Kidd B (1988) The philosophy of excellence: Olympic performances, class power and the Canadian state. In Galasso P (ed) Philosophy of sport and physical activity. Toronto: Canadian Scholars' Press p 11-31

14. While the extent of "political" sports advertising—*i.e.*, promotions designed to combat public pressures for nationalization, tougher environmental controls, restrictions upon the sale of alcohol and tobacco, etc.—has never been systematically studied, the author's conversations with corporate and advertising executives lead him to conclude that it is substantial. For example, see Laxer J, Martin A (1976) The big, tough expensive job. Don Mills: Press Porcepic

15. The riches of sport. Maclean's April 9 1990

16. As former Canadian national ski coach Currie Chapman has observed: "It's not just (the athletes) going down a mountain, but it's also a bank, a drug store, a car parts chain as well. Then comes, the phone call or the telex and somewhere there is a little note that says politely we'd like to see some results for our money". [Weston G (1987 March) Discovering the flip side of success. Ski Canada p 66]. For the cautions expressed in Canada, see also: Ministry of Fitness and Amateur Sport. Toward 2000: building Canada's sports system: the report of the task force on national sport policy. Ottawa: Fitness and Amateur Sport

17. Beamish R, Kidd B (1990) A brief to Mr. Justice Charles Dubin, Commissioner of Inquiry into the Use of Drugs and Banned Practices Intended to Increase Athletic Performance. Toronto

18. Kidd B (1990) Seoul to the world, the world to Seoul ... and Ben Johnson: Canada at the 1988 Olympics. In Koh Byong-ik (ed) Toward one world beyond all barriers. Keynote speeches, cultural exchange and cultural nationalism. Vol 1. The Seoul Anniversary Conference. Seoul Olympic Sports Promotion Foundation. Seoul: Poong Nam p 434-54

19. MacAloon JJ (1986) Intercultural education and olympic sport. Montreal and Ottawa: Canadian Olympic Association/Olympic Academy of Canada

20. Beamish R, Johnson A (1987) Socio-economic characteristics of Canada's current national team high-performance athletes. Paper presented to the North American Society for the Sociology of Sport. Edmonton, Alberta

21. McIntosh P (1988) Politics and sport: uniformity and diversity. In Broom EF et al (eds) Comparative Physical Education and Sport. Vol 5. Champaign: Human Kinetics p 17-35

22. Starkman R (1990) East German sport in a desperate state. Toronto Star June 2

23. Jhally S (1984) The spectacle of accumulation: material and cultural factors in the evolution of the sport/media complex. The Insurgent Sociologist 12 41-57

24. Olver B (1990) Women cry "no respect". Toronto Sun March 10

25. Duffy A (1990) Organizers oppose bylaw for equality in bike races. Toronto Star April 19

26. Kidd B (1989) The Olympic Movement and the sports/media complex. In Jackson R, McPhail T (eds) The Olympic Movement and the mass media. Calgary: Hurford p 1, 3, 10

27. This situation is already experienced by North American television viewers, who see competing athletes endorsing products in pre-taped commercials inserted into their events. At the Calgary Winter Olympic Games, even the crowds acted as if they were in a commercial. During lulls in the action, they imitated a frequently shown beer promo in which two sides of a stadium shouted competing slogans at each other.

[...] Enfin une troisième période s'inaugure. On a compris les bienfaits de la coopération sportive. [...]

Coubertin P de (1913) L'unification sportive. Revue Olympique, décembre, p 190

Les axes de développement Nord-Sud, Est-Ouest, et le sport: comment combler les disparités?

En guise d'introduction à sa présentation, l'auteur souligne la coïncidence du Centenaire de la visite de Coubertin au Canada avec celui de sa visite à Much Wenlock. Il montre par la suite la convergence des idées de William Brookes et de Pierre de Coubertin en ce qui a trait au bien-fondé des Festivals olympiques, et le respect mutuel que les deux hommes avaient l'un pour l'autre : Coubertin applaudissait aux initiatives de Brookes, au sujet du Festival de Wenlock que ce dernier avait modelé sur les Jeux olympiques de l'Antiquité, cependant que Brookes, de son côté, encourageait Coubertin dans son projet de renouveler les Jeux olympiques à l'échelle internationale. L'auteur mentionne que Brookes et Coubertin étaient tous les deux fort conscients de l'importance de la diversité culturelle dans le sport et du fait aussi que des fossés de toutes sortes existaient entre le Nord et le Sud, plus particulièrement en raison des effets de la colonisation. Il rappelle qu'au cours de la période de la colonisation du continent africain et de l'Asie, les puissances d'Europe exportaient les modèles de sport qui étaient les leurs et qui n'avaient rien à voir avec le développement de la culture locale des pays colonisés. Dans la première grande division de sa présentation, l'auteur donne plusieurs exemples des carences actuelles en matière d'équipements, de personnel et de structures, dans l'axe de développement Nord-Sud. Au sujet de l'axe Est-Ouest, l'auteur décrit le nouveau dialogue qui s'est engagé et le fait que des éléments de la pensée orientale ainsi que des formes de pratiques sportives en provenance de l'Orient ont vu le jour en Occident. Il met en garde contre les explications trop simplifiées qui ont souvent cours dans l'entendement des différences entre les pensées orientale et occidentale, pour ce qui est, entre autres, du concept des affaires et de l'économie ainsi que des forces du marché. Dans la partie suivante de sa présentation, l'auteur dresse une liste des problèmes et des carences de développement ainsi que des besoins spécifiques identifiés au cours des études récentes de la FIAA et des siennes propres effectuées dans plusieurs pays en voie de développement. Il fait aussi allusion aux résultats des enquêtes menées à ce sujet par la Commission du programme du CIO et par le CNO de la Bulgarie, cette fois en ce qui a trait à la participation des pays du tiers monde aux Jeux olympiques. Il rappelle que les Jeux célébrés à Mexico, à Tokyo et à Séoul ont été utiles pour réduire certains des écarts entre les pays concernés et la communauté internationale. Dans la dernière partie de sa présentation, l'auteur aborde la question des approches et des actions spécifiques à prendre pour réduire les disparités dans la communauté sportive internationale. Dans un premier temps, il recommande à ce sujet de ne pas trop attendre du sport, ce dernier ne pouvant en définitive que refléter les conditions du milieu social, économique et culturel où il s'insère. Le plus utile, de l'avis de l'auteur, serait de partager d'abord, sur l'axe Nord-Sud comme Est-Ouest, une approche philosophique et éthique des valeurs fondamentales du sport. Paradoxalement, de l'avis de l'auteur, une modération plus grande dans les objectifs visés et le rejet de toute forme d'abus, entre autres des produits dopants, de la part des pays favorisés, serait susceptible de réduire considérablement les écarts et d'encourager la compétition dans un esprit de fair-play renouvelé. L'auteur ajoute une description des contributions actuelles du monde sportif proprement dit au développement international; allusion est faite aux Fédérations internationales, au Conseil international du sport militaire, au Top Programme du CIO, à Solidarité olympique, à l'UNESCO, à des organismes internationaux, tels le CIEPSS-ICSSPE, enfin, aux accords bilatéraux entre pays et aux initiatives privées d'un certain nombre d'institutions d'enseignement supérieur. En guise de conclusion, l'auteur présente sous forme d'un plan en dix points des suggestions pratiques susceptibles de contribuer directement à la diminution des disparités internationales dans le développement du sport-pour-tous et du sport d'élite, et dans l'accès aux bénéfices divers qui sont associés à leur pratique.

The North-South and East-West Axes of Development in Sport: Can the Gaps Be Bridged?

Don Anthony

This Symposium marks the centenary of Pierre de Coubertin's visit to the United States, to Canada and to this historical City of Quebec. Interestingly, it is also one hundred years since Coubertin was made an honorary member of the Much Wenlock Olympic Society! In his quest for the Olympic equation Coubertin had visited William Penny Brookes in Shropshire, England, to study the movement which Brookes had started in 1850, and which was celebrated annually with an Olympic Festival modelled on the ancient Games. Brookes, medical doctor, magistrate, visionary, and entrepreneur extraordinaire, wished to revive the Olympic Games with Greece as the permanent centre. In an exchange of letters with Coubertin, Brookes stated that Coubertin's idea to have festivals "held in rotation by all nations desirous of joining in the movement", was a "really superb one". He hoped they would lead to "an explosion of interest" in the importance of physical education in schools, that they would reach the masses, that they would lead to international understanding. He thus foresaw many of the elements of the olympic miracle which is celebrated by this occasion. In particular, he predicted that these 'Olympian Festivals' would generate revenue. Any surplus funds "should be divided between all the associated nations and held in trust for this purpose", a brilliant anticipation of "Olympic Solidarity"—the IOC's world bank of sports expertise which is the sharp end of modern-day efforts to bridge the North/South gap in sports.

Brookes's sentiments were close to the heart of Coubertin. Both were highly conscious of the needs of Africa and Asia. In 1912, Coubertin was calling for a "Hindu Games" to be staged in India. In 1923 he championed a "Games for Africa". He recognised the importance of cultural diversity; "Gabon and Polynesia would not require the same regime". Team games like football would perhaps prevail, since they were cheap and easy to organise. Yet, individual sports should not be neglected, and local and traditional sports should be encouraged. But the people of colonised countries should be helped to enjoy what Coubertin boldly called "sports civilisation—this vast sports system which entails rules and regulations, and sports-competitive performances".

Don Anthony, Visiting Fellow, University of London Institute of Education; Adviser IOC's Olympic Solidarity Itinerant School in Sports Leadership. Sidcup, Kent, Great-Britain.

So the matter of gaps in the development of sports has long and strong roots, and the Olympic Movement has more than a century of experience. The sports exported to the South were not designed to meet the needs of that part of the world. The colonisers developed the sports *they* enjoyed the most. In the colonies of the British Empire, replicas of the multi-sport, multi-culture, Hurlingham Club, appeared. Golf, cricket, tennis and swimming could be enjoyed together with cards, dining and dancing. Sports participation was a free choice; an opportunity for voluntary public service. Copies of English private schools appeared in Africa, Asia and the Americas, enabling a small number of local citizens to experience muscular Christianity—and a much larger mass to aspire to the privilege. France for its part exported the centralised system of the metropolis. Ministries of sport and youth were transplanted throughout the French Empire. Martinique was as much France as Paris. Large subventions from the national budget were made for sports development. The Spanish in turn saw the political potential of major sports spectacles, at the local, regional and continental levels. Great infrastructures were gradually created to host Central American, Bolivarian and Pan American Games. Edifices of great beauty were then made over for utilisation to both government and voluntary sports organisations, as headquarters for their work. Yet, below the surface, millions of the indigenous people had little or no access to sport. Such crude thumbnail sketches are extreme generalisations but the broad tendencies are still evident to-day.

The North-South Dialogue

There is one athletics track in Khartoum; there is one indoor sports hall—and that without air conditioning. Yet Sudan has the largest land area of any country in Africa; it is even larger than Western Europe. Zambia has but one inspector of physical education for its schools. He has no car and must make his visits by public transport. Tanzania does not have a national television service. Clearly, the information flow in sports is very much handicapped. In that perspective, if one cannot organise sports well and at all levels in North America—with all its resources—then one should count oneself as an abject failure. If one can organise sport, at all, in the least economically developed countries, one is a genius.

Kuwait demonstrated that if an organization can afford to spend 1 500 dollars a day on each player for six years, it can get a team into the finals of the World Soccer Cup. Peru demonstrated that if 80% of the national sports budget can be targeted into the women's national volleyball team, the latter can be taken into the world top three. Cuba demonstrated that, if sport is made central to social change, the entire nation's perception of sport can be altered and made a part of community and individual lifestyle. Such facts illustrate the dependence of sport on social and economic development.

In 1989, The New York Development Forum reported that people in the Third World find themselves in much the same position as they were before the United Development decades of the last twenty years. The 1989 World Bank Report on the Sub Sahara, showed that this region of 450 million souls had a gross national product equal only to that of Belgium, with 10 million people. Throughout the African Continent, there were inadequacies in investment, school facilities and attendance, employment; there was considerable political instability. Civil wars raged in at least four African countries. Such findings were reinforced by the Organisation of African Unity. The external debt of Africa recently amounted to 230 billion dollars. The 1980s were Africa's "lost decade". We have all failed, said the New York Forum, to "articulate the horror of world poverty". We should not sit around and talk about development—"we should *do* development".

The East-West Dialogue

East/West has a cultural dimension. There is a strong two-way energy to consider. The impact of traditional 'Eastern' philosophies and practices is stronger in the 'West' today, than it was thirty years ago. The East/West transfer of knowledge and techniques fuels such movements as postural education, 'inner tennis', the Californian 'futures' schools typified by the work at Esalen. Breathing, energy, awareness and posture is often seen as a better bet than strength, stamina, speed, and skill. Tai Chi and Yoga are commonplace in the West. In this context E/W can also mean South/North.

At the level of the East/West political dialogue the present is a fascinating period in history. It is already clear that the brutal ideological confrontation will decline. The simplistic Capitalist/Communist thesis/antithesis, has long provided governments and people with a useful comparative tool: one social system in which sport was a commodity to be bought and sold; the other is which it was, in essence, a social service. Like all simplistic models this one was also flawed—but the lack of it would have been puzzling. However the picture is challenging. 'Business' and 'Market Forces' are the global in-words of the day; yet, there are some profound misunderstandings. East Europeans now want to 'market' their expertise; they ask for 'aid' in some areas of sport. This is disturbing. In the first place they will soon discover that in many areas of professional sports skills there is *no* market in the West. Many professions in state-sport, are seen as 'hobbies' in the West! At the aid level they may be assuming a move from sports aid donor, to sports aid recipient. If they are, things are likely to become even tougher for those in real need in the least economically developed countries of Africa and Asia.

Gaps between North and South

The IAAF's recent development survey identified three major North/South 'inadequacies'—development planning, elite programmes, and grass roots programmes. There were also six 'sub inadequacies': scientific medical support; qualified coaches and officials; federation activities; equipment and facilities; competitive opportunities; and a poor 'athletic culture'—including media attention and schools of physical education and sport[1]. My own field studies in eight randomly selected countries in the last five years—in Asia, Africa, and the Caribbean—bear out these findings. Expressed as urgent needs by seminar participants were: planning, elite sport, sport-for-all including the protection of indigenous sports, scientific medical support, federation activities including coaches and officials' education, equipment and facilities, schools of physical education and sport, relations with the media, relations with government, transportation, and finance[2].

At the olympic competitive level, two studies identify the narrow range of sports offered by a majority of countries, and the weak state of some olympic sports vis-a-vis affiliations in developing countries. A study for the IOC Programme Commission showed that only 16 countries entered competitors in 16 or more sports in the Los Angeles Games. Ninety NOCs entered in 5 or less sports. Seventy-eight of these NOCs were from developing countries[3]. A Bulgarian analysis of the Seoul data came up with similar figures. Sixty-three NOCs entered in 10 or less 'events'; only 17 entered in 10 or more 'events'. This study also classified affiliations to international sports organisations. In Africa, archery, fencing, and canoeing had less than five affiliations each. The top affiliations were for athletics (track and field), volleyball, and soccer, in that order. Sixty NOCs did not enter women in any event. Roughly 1% of medals in Seoul were won by Africans. Such facts indeed speak for themselves[4].

There is much to be learned from the South. One needs to understand other cultures so that one can understand and reform one's own culture. Many 'new future' concepts used in the re-design of the societies of the North can be found to be traditionally practised by many in the South[5]. There is also much 'health related exercise' in the day to day life of people in the South. A walking based transportation system executed with exquisite form and posture. Manual work with its own dignity. Traditional dance and sports like wrestling—demonstrating skilled organisation in crowd control, clever matching of opponents, colour and ritual—all reminders that, even if modern sport was no longer resourced as one has come to expect—there *would* still be sport, so refreshing in all its aspects and deep roots.

But there is also South/South. Mexico, Tokyo and Seoul all used the Olympic Games to break out of the 'developing countries' designation. Mexico saw the overall Games investment as a major means of developing its tourist industry. Tokyo, to clearly show that Japan had indeed made it into the ranks of the high-technology industrialised world. Seoul, as a chance to beautifully marry traditional culture with modern technology; a means of sweeping away a lingering sense of inferiority connected with long-term colonialism[6]. All three countries are now able to offer the confidence and expertise they gained in the exercise to interested developing countries. All demonstrated a true capacity to bridge gaps.

Bridging the Gaps

Sport has nonetheless limitations that must be recognized. On the whole, it is a reflection of the society which hosts it. Many advances will depend on the overall social and economic development of the society. A sense of perspective and a set of realistic objectives are necessary. In ten years real advances can be made with respect to creating a fair, and just, and equal, sharing of knowledge and information right across the board in sport. It might however take one hundred years for those millions, caught in the poverty trap of the least economically developed nations, to enjoy the benefits of membership of the global sports family. The perspectives must be far reaching one should *never* say—there is *no* hope.

In the short term, parity should be expected in such matters as ethical behaviour in all sporting situations. In many ways it is possible to recognise the fundamental values of sport more easily in developing countries; many of them are in a sporting time-warp in these matters. Sport is still just *part* of a lifestyle; fairplay is ubiquitous; drug abuse something one only reads about. Indeed, it is a bizarre fact that strict abolition of drug abuse in sport will help to bridge competitive gaps between North and South.

Sport is not only a reflection of its host society. It is also an indicator. It can help people see life as it could be and should be. In all countries it can be the simple and evident living embodiment of equality, fairplay and hard work resulting in success, the full utilisation of mind, body, and soul, chance, luck, and fun. For hundreds of millions of people—a more rewarding and creative experience than what normally passes as 'work'—or 'non-work'.

In a small way, the international sports family *is* bridging the gaps. Some international federations like soccer and basketball have a long standing record of sports-aid projects. Last year, more than 12 international federations reported on their development programmes for Third World countries—conducted in collaboration with IOC's Olympic Solidarity programme[7]. The International Council of Military Sport also has a good curriculum vitae in the matter. So had UNESCO—especially before American, British, and Japanese support was withdrawn. UNESCO affiliated bodies like the ICSSPE-CIEPSS have continued to make specialised contributions. Commercial sports aid is represented at the top end by ISL's "Top Programme[8]", and, at the bottom, by the equipment distribution scheme operated through the World Federation of Sports Goods Manufacturers.

A number of countries have imaginative bilateral programmes. The Scandinavians pool their governmental and voluntary resources and 'target' on Tanzania. The USA had a roving sports ambassador, Mal Whitfield, representing the State Department in Africa—for many years—identifying needs and potential donors. The French look after their 'territories'. The British offer a minor programme through the British Sports Council. China makes a most significant contribution. They have built more than 15 olympic national stadia in Africa. Ecuador is one country to have recently made use of Cuba's expertise in sports coaching and management.

For many years, East/West rivalry in sports aid was embodied in the struggle between Cologne and Leipzig. Who could make the most impact. Are we to witness the end of this struggle? Who will replace the funding for training in physical education, sports management and coaching, sports medicine—which has nourished many cadres in the developing countries? Can Moscow honour its numerous protocol agreements in the sports-help area? One waits to see how the East Europeans will cope; what elements of the former systems will they need to reinvent; what models from the West will they imit; who will assist or advise them? There are grave ramifications for the developing countries in these new international circumstances. Under the banner "A firmer foundation—a brighter future", the Canadian Government presented, last year, proposals for a new Commonwealth Sports Trust. Canada talks of its own pump-priming 'seed corn' of ten million dollars. The Trust would have three major objectives: hosting assistance; travel assistance; sports development. Victoria in 1994 (Commonwealth Games) will try to act as a model in these directions. There will be a drive to place the 1998 Commonwealth Games in a developing country and resource it through aid packages from all member countries.

In the last years, the most dynamic of all the sports aid schemes inside the global sports family has been the "Olympic Solidarity" project. This was given a boost by the financial windfalls sparked off by the commercial success of the Los Angeles Games, the heavy involvement of global television, and imaginative 'new ways' of financing the Olympic Movement. A host of projects are now funded. Training for coaching, administration, medicine, officials, the media, scholarships for promising young athletes, to advance women's competitive sport. Special awards for 'Sport-for-All', to establish sports museums, to organise International Olympic Day, for other worthwhile one-off events. Olympic Solidarity ensures that cost should not prevent any National Olympic Committee from being represented at the Olympic Games. Six competitors and two officials from every NOC are fully funded to travel to and stay at the Olympic Games. It is often said that this representation is mainly symbolic—but symbolism is a modest albeit powerful weapon. Olympic Solidarity's "Itinerant School in Sports Administration" (Leadership) sets out to improve understanding and skill in the management of national olympic bodies. It works on the principle of maximum multiplication of effect—on the postulate that its students will be motivated, informed, and able to transmit what they have learnt on to others. It attempts to inculcate a sense of pride in being a sports administator—paid or unpaid. More than 100 one-week workshops have been held in the last three years in the developing countries of Africa, Asia, and the Americas. This programme meets, head on, the needs expressed by course participants as described above. In 1989, nearly 7 million dollars US was divided between developing countries, through Olympic Solidarity: Africa 2 253 044; Americas 1 703 826; Asia 1 967 642; Oceania 961 392. Europe received 1 308 165 $ US.

In these several ways mainstream sport itself tries to bridge the gaps. Such salami-tactics are slow and obviously not all seeds fall on fertile ground—but, to lean again on a permanent soul sustainer: "No man is more foolish than he who, because he can do only a little, does nothing".

Alternatives

Is there anything more that one can do? Perhaps one or more of the following, offered as a ten-point plan. 1– At the international competitive levels, shared training should become commonplace; a 'mixing' of players in top tournaments to produce an extra day of 'random' teams would do wonders for confidence and skill; the Olympic programme must be ever conscious of what constitutes world sport practice. 2– At the informational level, there are sensational opportunities staring one in the face. Thanks to such networks as CNN and ESPN, one can be at the centre of the sports competitive movement wherever one might be in the world. That potential has yet to be grasped. The IOC's network of sponsored multisystem television players needs substantial software support. World radio is another untapped tool—perhaps even more significant still in the economically poor South. 3– There are exciting opportunities for sport in building new alliances with the great issues-movements of the moment. Sport and the Green movement. Sport and the population-control movement. Sport as an agency in development. And the ongoing role of sport in the promotion of international understanding. Such alliances can help sport to constantly re-think its social role and enhance its value as a change-agent. 4– Commercial opportunities are equally rich. Airlines—especially the giant charter groups could do more for competitive sport. The USOC alliance with 3M—taking in all costs of their three Olympic Training Centres—is a model of excellence. The USOC could also contribute a lot to strategic planning by explaining that commercial sponsorship merely supplements extensive public investment in sport and recreation as is well illustrated by the astonishing 'Californian socialism' of West Coast sport. 5– Academic links are snowballing. The export of such ideas as York University's Certificate in Sports Administration is called for on a larger scale. Such simple and effective ideas are easily adaptable by Universities in developing countries. 6– One has yet to think through the potential of the volunteer sports movement in the light of global changes in work practices. Can the sports group become the new colleges of society? 7– Sport as industry in another topical growth area. No other multi-billion dollar industry is so badly organised. Profits generally creamed off by a short-term-gain elite, while the vast army of participants is left to soldier on in penury. The real need is for sport to demonstrate its capacity to create hundreds of thousands of new job opportunities. As a starter, why not a special tax on the earnings of the elite—dedicated to developing countries—in the same spirit as 'Sports Aid' and the more recent '2000-love' project in tennis? 8– The Tourist industry is a special model. No resort, no hotel, worth its name is complete without lavish health spas and sports facilities. Tourism enables 1st world sports lifestyle to be enjoyed in even 4th world countries. The hotel-sports complex can be an oasis of excellence in a sea of poverty. It can also be used—is being used—as a base for local training of national teams in such sports as tennis. The concept of franchising by international hotel groups also has meaning for improvements in global sports administration, especially as concerns National Olympic Committees and federations. 9– There are other industrial non-models. In some developing countries, the most eager sponsors represent the tobacco and alcohol industries. Heavy tar cigarettes are still being forced on to Third World countries even in spite of the threat of trade sanctions. Alcohol abuse is also rising sharply and proving to be a burden on already meager economic and social resources. 10– The world is poised for the biggest breakthrough ever in world disarmament. Trillions of dollars could be released for sensational human, social, and economic development. Clever persuasion and lobbying could assure sport its due share in the process.

This was the lifelong message of the great Quaker, Olympian, Statesman —Philip Noel-Baker. Son of a Canadian father, one year old when Coubertin was visiting Quebec City. A master of resounding facts. His most pertinent juxtaposition was: "No Olympic Games yet has cost as much as the petrol used by military aeroplanes, in all countries, in one day"! At the 1981 Olympic Congress in Baden-Baden, at the age of 92, he foresaw the following sequence of events: disarmement leading to development; sport playing its part in personal, community, and global peace. If the IOC—with UNESCO—could lead the whole world, especially the developing world, to sports-for-all—both organizations would deserve the Nobel Peace Prize. In the context of our North/South, East/West, debate, this vision-mission is a fine objective to share as the next millennium draws near.

REFERENCES

1. Wangemann B (1989) A report to the IAAF development department. Closed publication by the International Athletic Amateur Federation

2. Anthony D (1986-1989) Field studies. Unpublished notes

3. Smirnov V (1984) International Olympic Committee Programme Commission Report. Lausanne: International Olympic Committee

4. Dimitrov I (1989) Seoul Olympic Games study. Bulgarian National Olympic Committee

5. Ellis WN, McMahon Ellis M (1989) Cultures in transition. What the West can learn from developing countries. The Futurist XXIII 22-25

6. Kim S-g, Rhee S-w, Koo S-c et al (1989) Impact of the Seoul Olympic Games on national development. Seoul: Korean Development Institute

7. Olympic Solidarity report 1989. Lausanne: International Olympic Committee

8. International Sport and Leisure, Lucerne Switzerland

[...] Le sport veut autour de lui une émulation intense et une camaraderie solide. Tous ceux qui ont à cet égard quelque expérience confirmeront notre dire. Il est donc bien basé sur l'entr'aide et la concurrence. Or ces mêmes principes servent d'assises au démocratisme moderne. Les conditions ethniques, économiques, industrielles, scientifiques, dans lesquelles se développent et évoluent les nations d'aujourd'hui leur imposent la pratique d'une concurrence individuelle âpre et perpétuelle. Rien n'indique que la rigueur de ce régime soit près de se relâcher. L'entr'aide y apporte un adoucissement indispensable et sans lequel on pourrait redouter le retour non point à la barbarie d'antan mais à une certaine barbarie qui peut être ne vaudrait guère mieux que l'ancienne. Heureusement l'entr'aide apparait partout. On dirait une herbe qui pousse toute seule à côté du poison auquel elle servira d'antidote. Le sentiment de la solidarité se répand à travers la société qui pressent là une condition vitale d'équilibre et de santé. C'est inconscient et général. Voici donc que le sport nous apparait comme une école excellemment préparatoire à l'existence présente – excellement apaisante aussi. [...]

Coubertin P de (1913) Le sport et la question sociale. Revue olympique, août, p 122

Autour des Jeux Olympiques a commencé une véritable danse des millions : millions imaginaires, millions réels aussi car si les gazettes ont parfois grossi ou inexactement cité les chiffres qui circulaient, ces chiffres pourtant reposaient sur une donnée exacte, à savoir l'effort énorme que gouvernements, municipalités, groupements sportifs se montrent disposés à accomplir pour assurer la célébration des Olympiades. [...] La question qui se pose n'est pas s'ils seront célébrés mais comment ils le seront et à quels frais ? [...]

Coubertin P de (1913) La question d'argent. Revue Olympique, décembre, p 183

The Hosting of Major Games

L'accueil des Jeux d'importance

Editors' note   Note des éditeurs

Nowadays, high performance sport holds a rather prominent position in the interests and in the lives of most peoples and nations. In the last decades, one has witnessed a true globalization of competitive sport as a vast system with national, trans-national and world-wide characteristics and ramifications.

In that perspective, the matter of hosting major games such as the Olympic, Pan-American and Commonwealth Games (as is for example the case with Canada) is a subject of actuality and of many implications and consequences on the sporting, economic, social, political and cultural planes.

For the occasion of the Quebec City Symposium which took place half-way between the celebrations of the Olympic Games of Seoul and of those scheduled for Barcelona, and also in commemoration of the renovation of the Olympic Games, the Organizing Committee had judged it of great importance that a theme such as the *Hosting of Major Games* be made an integral part of the program of the Symposium, and that the subject be treated by persons of international experience and renown.

The Honorable Marcel Danis, Minister of State for Youth and also Minister of State for Fitness and Amateur Sport of the Government of Canada drew from the Canadian service tradition and experience in the hosting of large scale international sporting events and delivered a paper on the subject of the *implications* and *impact* of major games with respect to *domestic sports needs* and *values*, as well as *international influence* and *understanding*. The text of Minister Danis' presentation appears in the following pages in the two official languages of Canada.

The Honorable Park Seh-jik, President of the Organizing Committee of the Seoul Olympic Games, was invited to treat of the *significance* of the acknowledged success of the Seoul Games, as concerns *Korean national identity*, *mutual respect* and *international understanding* between peoples and nations, as well as with respect to the illustration and transmission of cultural values, by and through olympic sport. The complete text of President Park, in the English language, also follows.

Mr. Richard W. Pound, 1st Vice President of the International Olympic Committee, accepted for his part to make a presentation on the matter of the *financing* of major games. Mr. Pound treated his subject from the angles of *capital investment* and *operations costs*, both in terms of the various categories of possible or anticipated *revenues* and *expenses*, due consideration given to the present *financial obligations* and *commitments* of interested parties, and also to the *financial capacities* of the taxpayers, of private enterprise and of various levels of para-governmental and governmental agencies. The text of the paper authored by Vice-President Pound ends the chapter.

Le sport de haute performance occupe de nos jours une place notoire dans la vie des peuples et des nations. On a assisté en fait, au cours des dernières décades, à une véritable planétisation de la compétition sportive en tant que système, aux échelles nationale, transnationale, voire mondiale.

Dans cette perspective, l'accueil des jeux d'importance tels que les Jeux olympiques, Pan-américains ou du Commonwealth (à titre d'exemples, et pour ce qui est du Canada), se présente comme une question d'actualité aux implications nombreuses et interreliées sur les plans sportif, économique, social, politique et culturel.

À l'occasion du Symposium de Québec qui se déroulait dans le temps à mi-chemin entre la célébration de l'Olympiade de Séoul et de celle de Barcelone, en souvenir également de la rénovation des Jeux olympiques, le Comité d'organisation a jugé approprié que le thème de l'*accueil des jeux d'importance* devienne un sujet spécial de réflexion, à la fois rétrospective et prospective, et que le sujet soit traité par des personnages d'expérience et de renommée internationales.

L'Honorable Marcel Danis, ministre d'État à la jeunesse et ministre d'État à la Condition physique et au Sport amateur du Gouvernement du Canada, en s'appuyant sur la longue tradition de service et sur l'expérience canadienne dans la tenue d'événements sportifs internationaux, a traité en détail des *implications* et des *retombées* de tels jeux, aux plans du *modèle sportif national*, de l'*influence* et de la *compréhension internationales*. Le texte de sa présentation apparaît aux pages suivantes, dans chacune des deux langues officielles du Canada.

L'Honorable Park Seh-jik, président du Comité d'organisation des Jeux olympiques de Séoul, a, pour sa part, traité de la *signification* de l'expérience si réussie de Séoul aux plans de l'*identité nationale Coréenne*, du *respect mutuel* et de la *compréhension internationale*, comme aussi à celui de l'*illustration* et de la *transmission* des *valeurs culturelles*, dans et par le sport olympique. Le texte intégral de l'Honorable Park, en langue anglaise, suit également.

Monsieur Richard W. Pound, 1er Vice-président du Comité international olympique, a accepté de traiter du *financement* des jeux d'importance. Il a abordé plus particulièrement le sujet sous l'angle des *coûts* d'investissement et de fonctionnement par rapport aux différentes catégories de *revenus* possibles, le tout dans la perspective des intérêts, des *obligations* et des *capacités financières* des différentes parties intéressées, du payeur de taxe, à l'entreprise privée et aux différents paliers de gouvernement, en passant par les agences gouvernementales et para-gouvernementales. Le texte de la présentation de monsieur Pound termine le chapitre.

Hosting Major Games:
their Implications and Impact with Respect to Domestic Sport Needs and Values, International Influence and Understanding

The Honorable Marcel Danis

It is a great pleasure for me to be in Quebec City this evening to address this conference on *Sport . . . the Third Millennium*. I am especially pleased to be sharing the podium with Mr. Pound and Mr. Park, both of whom are eminent figures in the Olympic Movement.

I have been asked to speak on the subject of "Hosting Major Games". Certainly, Canada can speak with some authority on that matter. Just a few years ago, the 1988 Winter Olympic Games were staged in Calgary—the most successful yet on record. We have also hosted the Summer Olympic Games, in Montreal in 1976, and the City of Toronto is now bidding for the 1996 Summer Games[1]. Aside from our olympic experience, we have hosted many other types of major games—from the multi-sport Commonwealth, Pan-American and World University Games to international single-sport championships. In this regard, we have been very active in the recent past. For example, in 1988, the City of Sudbury hosted the World Junior Track and Field Championships. In 1989, Calgary hosted the World Women's Speed Skating Championships, and Dartmouth staged the World Junior Canoeing Championships. In 1990, Halifax hosted the World Figure Skating Championships, and Ottawa was the host city for the first-ever World Women's Hockey Championships. In August 1990, Edmonton will host the World Baseball Championships, and in 1992 Montreal will stage the World Junior Rowing Championships.

In addition to these international events, the Canada Games themselves must be considered a major sporting event. Our domestic games alternate between winter and summer sports every two years. In 1991, the Canada Winter Games will be hosted by the Province of Prince Edward Island, and it is anticipated that some 2 800 athletes, coaches and officials will participate. This national tradition was launched right here in Quebec City, in 1967. Since then, small urban centres in every province have hosted the Canada Games. Few other countries can claim such an extensive record in the hosting of major games. In fact, it is probably safe to say that in the course of the past 25 years, Canada has hosted more major games

1890
1990

The Honorable Marcel Danis, Minister of State, Youth, Fitness and Amateur Sport, Government of Canada, Ottawa, Canada.

than most other country, and that our success rate in staging these events has been second to none.

To those unfamiliar with sport, a logical question might be "*why*?". More to the point, why does Canada want to *continue* this legacy of hosting major games? There are certainly major financial commitments involved, both from the public and private sectors. And the hosting of major games requires first-rate planning as well as organization; for the Olympic and Commonwealth Games, the preparation literally has to start many years ahead of the actual event. None would argue with any of that—those are the facts. But one should also realize that the benefits of hosting major games—the payback on investment, if you will—is very considerable. When I refer to payback I do not mean in an economic sense, although there are certainly financial rewards to be reaped from a well organized event. I mean payback in terms of enhancing a country's sport system, nurturing national pride and cultural awareness, international prestige and infrastructure development.

From an athlete's point of view, major games provide something to aim for in terms of achievements and performance. This is even more so for athletes in the host country, because they are given the opportunity to compete against the world's best on their own stage. As we have all witnessed from time to time, this can spur athletes on to remarkable performances.

The hosting of a major games may also raise the profile of sport in yet another important way. By increasing the public's awareness of sport, it is often possible to stimulate government financing that can move a country's sport system ahead by leaps and bounds. For example, the awareness that an entire nation will be in the international spotlight through the hosting of a major games often encourages increased expenditures on athlete and coach development. Before the Montreal Olympic Games, the Government of Canada focused additional resources on athlete preparation through a program called Game Plan '76. Similarly, we built up to the Calgary Games and the 1988 Summer Olympic Games in Seoul through the "Best Ever" Program.

A nation's sport infrastructure can also benefit greatly through the hosting of a major games. For example, as a result of staging the 1988 Winter Olympic Games in Calgary, Canada now possesses the world's fastest and safest bobsleigh and luge track. Western Canada has its first ever ski jumping facilities which have been designed for year-round use. We also have the indoor Olympic Oval—the only facility of its kind in the world—and a permanent training centre for our national ice hockey team. As well as these high performance facilities, the Calgary area now boasts expended recreational ski hills, a new day lodge and upgraded lifts.

The hosting of major games can also move a country forward quickly in terms of its non-sport infrastructures. Seoul is an excellent case in point, and I am sure Mr. Park will have something to say on this in his remarks. An event such as the Olympic Games or the Commonwealth Games can accelerate the construction of new and improved transportation systems, additional affordable housing and other services which benefit society as a whole. In fact, a key element in Toronto's bid for the 1996 Olympic Games has to do with bringing much-needed affordable housing onto the market.

Nation building is another important benefit. Major games provide an excellent venue for capturing the imagination and enthusiasm of the public. They are an opportunity to foster national pride, cultivate international understanding, and promote an awareness of national accomplishments and capabilities. Major games can unite a country by centering attention on a popular activity. In countries like Canada, they allow us to bring a widely dispersed and diverse population into focus on a single event. This attention also provides the opportunity for a whole range of festive activities to be arranged around the games themselves. Although major games are primarily a sports event, they are often also a major cultural event, featuring local, national and international performers. They allow the host country and city to, quite literally, entertain the world. Seoul was an excellent example of how a country can stage a successful games while maintaining and showcasing its distinct cultural identity.

The intense media coverage given to major games creates an international awareness not only of a country's sport and organizational capabilities, but also its history, economy, needs and opportunities. This increased awareness can contribute to and enhance mutual understanding among peoples of the world and can enable the host country to extend its sphere of influence.

Significant economic benefits can also result from the staging of a major games. The impact on tourism is immense. People who attend a major international event are committed to spending money, and they usually take the opportunity to travel to different regions of the host country. Calgary and Seoul were certainly not the only cities to gain from the 1988 Games. Major sports events also create jobs for the citizens of the host country. Hundreds of tradespeople and professionals are involved in planning, designing and constructing the facilities required to stage a major games. Others are hired to work throughout the games and, with proper planning, there can be continuing employment at these facilities for many years to come.

There are thus a wide range of potential benefits associated with hosting a major games. But these benefits are not automatic—they are dependent on proper planning, professional management and effective delivery. Poor planning and management can result in embarassing cost overruns and long-term debt problems. Hosting major game can also lead to inflated expectations of the capacities of the host country's own athletes. To avoid this pitfall, host countries should not think in terms of medals alone, but rather of the long-term impact of the games on their sport system. The games should not divert attention away from domestic sport programs, but should be viewed as an opportunity to enhance them.

For our part, Canada has established a solid record of technical competence and organizational capability in the staging of major games. We are very excited with the prospect of hosting the 1994 Commonwealth Games in Victoria. In regard to those Games, my government has already committed 50 million dollars to support the hosting of the event. Canada has a long tradition in hosting the Commonwealth Games, and we have also been very competitive on the playing field. We believe Victoria is particularly well-suited to host the next Commonwealth Games.

We also believe that Toronto has much to offer as a potential host for the 1996 Olympic Games. This cosmopolitan city lives the olympic ideal every day in a spirit of racial and cultural harmony. Toronto offers a safe, clean and attractive environment, exciting entertainment and diverse cultural activities. It has long been a centre of multicultural richness and diversity, with local media coverage in more than 35 languages. The city has an award-winning transportation system, an ideal climate for hosting summer Games, and an extensive communications infrastructure. It also has an excellent record of hosting other types of major international events, as demonstrated through the staging of the May 1988 Economic Summit.

All levels of government are firmly behind the Toronto bid—and it has been demonstrated that this degree of commitment is essential to the staging of a successful games. In fact, governments are contributing 5 million dollars to the bid effort—almost half of which is coming from the federal government. More than 70 corporate sponsors are contributing another 7 million dollars. In addition to supporting Toronto's bid, the Government of Canada is committed to being a partner in the actual hosting and staging of the Games. Our role, in part, will be to provide the essential services required by the International Olympic Committee. This represents a significant financial commitment, but we believe the Games are a sound business investment for Canada.

Prior to 1984 at Los Angeles, the Olympic Games were heavily subsidized by governments, with significant operating costs remaining after the event itself. We had such an experience in Montreal in 1976, as did also other countries before us. To avoid such a problem in Calgary, the continued use of the facilities *after* the Games was a priority consideration during the planning process. Canada Olympic Park was, in fact, designed as an international centre at which athletes from around the world could train at reasonable costs. As its contribution to ensuring a legacy from the Calgary Games, the Government of Canada established a 30 million dollar Olympic Endowment Fund to help cover the post-Games operating costs of Olympic facilities. Proceeds from this fund are now used for operating Canada Olympic Park and the Olympic Oval, as well as for supporting programs and activities at all Olympic facilities. This fund was in addition to a 30 million dollar Endowment Fund established by OCO '88, the Olympic Games Organizing Committee (OCO '88). It should be noted that the finances for these endowment funds were in place *before* the actual staging of the Games. They were not dependent on the Games making a surplus, although I am pleased to say that Calgary was also successful in this regard. I also want to point out that the establishment of such legacy funds were pre-conditions for federal government support for the Victoria Commonwealth Games and Toronto's bid for the 1996 Olympic Games. Organizers in both cities had made a firm commitment to ensure that the hosting process would leave a positive sport legacy for Canada and the world.

The Olympic Torch Relay was also a uniquely Canadian success story. By moving the Torch across the country in the days leading up to the Calgary Games, we were able to build an extraordinary momentum and associate the entire country—and not just the City of Calgary—with the Olympic Games. By merging the Torch Relay with the federal government's Celebration 88 Program, we were able to draw in Canadians involved in recreational level sport in communities from coast-to-coast. Celebration 88 encouraged as many Canadians as possible to get involved in the spirit and values of Olympism. More than 1 700 communities held special pre-olympic events that celebrated and recognized the contribution of individuals to local sport. As a result of Celebration 88, more than 90% of Canadians had the opportunity to share in the olympic experience.

The Calgary Olympic Games also demonstrated the essential contribution that *volunteers* can and do make to the successful hosting of a major games. Nearly 10 000 volunteers assisted in the staging of the 1988 Winter Games. Working in partnership with the organizers, these generous people presented to the world an image of professionalism, discipline, dedication and commitment that had positive effects on all Canadians. Partnerships between governments, and between governments and the private sector, were also a key to success at Calgary. The federal, provincial and municipal governments worked together very closely to ensure the success of the Games. Each level did what it said it would do, and in many cases, it did much more indeed. As well, the close working relationship the Government of Canada established with OCO '88 and the private sector made a number of successful joint ventures possible. For example, more than six million dollars of enhancements in the Canada Olympic Park were provided by private sector sponsors.

On reflection, however, perhaps the single greatest legacy of the Calgary Games is people. Those who are experienced in organizing major international events, and whose experience can be used in the future for the benefit of sport and other sectors of society. People who designed and built world-class facilities. People who made a unique contribution as volunteers. The coaches, who learned so much from and taught so much to their counterparts from other nations. And of course the athletes, who had the ultimate experience of competing. All of these people have been moved and motivated by the olympic experience, and it will always be with them; it will always be an event with which they can proudly identify themselves. Equally as important, this legacy of well-trained people will long be a rich resource upon which Canada can draw.

One thing we often find ourselves doing in the world of sport is looking to the future. I would like now to share some of my thoughts on the problems and opportunities that may arise in the future hosting of major games. I am certain that many share my concern about the widening gap between economically developed and developing countries in terms of their present ability to host and participate meaningfully in major sporting events. The former are winning more and more of the medals, and the enormous costs of staging major games is increasingly putting these events out of the reach of many countries. This is not an easy issue to address but I believe we must turn our attention to it. We made an important move in this direction with the *Jeux de la Francophonie*, held for the first time in 1989 in Morocco, and destined to be hosted alternately by countries of the North and South. The shared expertise and experience that went into the planning and staging of this event could serve as a model for providing many countries with an opportunity to host major sports events. Another route might be for countries that host the Games to use them as an opportunity to transfer some of their expertise to developing nations. This might be achieved through a "live-in apprenticeship program" or by creating central "how-to" files on running major games. It would also be useful to examine ways to keep the costs of hosting major events at a more realistic level, and within the capabilities of more countries. Such initiatives would not put all countries on an even playing field, but they would certainly move us in the right direction.

My second point focuses on the continued use of major games facilities after the big event. As demonstrated by our emphasis on endowment funds, Canada believes strongly in the need to plan for the after-use of these facilities. For future games, perhaps a "legacy clause" should be built into the standard agreement presented by the Games franchise holder and signed by the host country. We should also be establishing better mechanisms for sharing knowledge and experience between a country that has recently hosted a major games and the country that will stage the next event. In this way, one would not have to reinvent the wheel, so to speak, every time the games move to a new country.

In regard to the sport event itself, I believe we should be putting more emphasis on the "pursuit of excellence" as opposed to solely the thrill and glory of victory. We have traditionally focused our attention on the act of "winning", and not on what it takes for an athlete to get there, or on the nature of the sport itself. In enhancing the quality of the competitive sport experience we must address the issue of integrating the disabled athlete's needs and expectations into the mainstream. We must view athletes as "differently-abled", but with the same underlying drive and determination to achieve. We should also devote more attention to underscoring the value system associated with such events as the Olympic and Commonwealth Games. In the future, such values as intercultural understanding and the appreciation of athletic excellence could be more effectively portrayed through the media or special awards programs.

Some people also believe that we have not done as well as we could in terms of building relationships with spectators. We often have a stronger engagement with the television audience than we do with the people actually at the site of a major games. How do we portray to people attending an event the essence of a sport and the athletic experience? How do we provide them with the opportunity to interact with spectators and athletes from other countries and cultures?

I believe we also need a different framework for evaluating major games—a framework that addresses not just the organization but also such things as the cultural impact and the social value of the games. For example, we hardly ever ask athletes whether the games met their requirements or expectations, and I submit we would get some interesting views indeed through such a process. By not seeking the input and evaluation of all the stakeholders, we miss an opportunity to learn from each other and to plan better for the future.

Finally, regardless of which country stages a games, we must preserve the ethical values of sport, including the concept of fair play. The sites of major games should and must change, and we may have to make compromises to ensure that more countries have the opportunity to host. But we cannot compromise our ethics or a level playing field in the sport events themselves. The philosophy of fair play is at the very heart and soul of sport, and this is as true at the international level as it is at the community level. I find the notion of hosting major games to be an exciting and challenging one. It is a challenge that Canada has embraced once again for the 1994 Commonwealth Games, and one that we will eargerly pursue ourselves as well as help others to pursue in the future.

NOTE

1. *Editors' note.* It is in September 1990 that the IOC, at its 96th Session in Tokyo, selected Atlanta (USA) as host city of the Games of the XXVIth Olympiad, 1996.

L'accueil des Jeux d'importance : implications et retombées aux plans du modèle sportif national, de l'influence et de la compréhension internationales

L'Honorable Marcel Danis

Je suis très heureux d'être ici ce soir, à Québec, pour m'adresser à vous à l'occasion de cette conférence qui a pour thème *Sport... le troisième millénaire*. Et je suis heureux, plus particulièrement, de partager le podium avec Messieurs Pound et Park, deux figures éminentes du Mouvement olympique.

On m'a proposé de vous entretenir du défi et des implications que représente la tenue de Jeux importants. Chose certaine, le Canada a une expérience enviable à ce chapitre. L'événement majeur le plus récent, bien sûr, fut celui des Jeux olympiques d'hiver, à Calgary — une réussite sans précédent. Mais nous avons aussi été l'hôte des Jeux olympiques d'été, à Montréal en 1976, et la ville de Toronto est en lice pour les Jeux d'été de 1996[1]. En plus de notre expérience olympique, nous avons été l'hôte de nombreux autres Jeux d'importance, depuis les Jeux pluridisciplinaires du Commonwealth, les Jeux panaméricains et les Jeux universitaires mondiaux, jusqu'aux championnats internationaux dans diverses disciplines. À cet égard, nous avons été très actifs au cours des dernières années. Ainsi, en 1988, la ville de Sudbury a été l'hôte du Championnat mondial junior d'athlétisme. En 1989, Calgary a accueilli le Championnat mondial féminin de patinage de vitesse, et Dartmouth, le Championnat mondial de canotage. En 1990, Halifax était l'hôte du Championnat mondial de patinage artistique, et Ottawa a accueilli le premier Championnat mondial de hockey féminin. En août 1990, Edmonton accueille le Championnat mondial de baseball, et en 1992, Montréal sera l'hôte du Championnat mondial junior d'aviron.

Outre ces manifestations internationales, les Jeux du Canada aussi peuvent être considérés comme une manifestation sportive importante. Ces Jeux, qui se répartissent alternativement en Jeux d'hiver et en Jeux d'été, reviennent tous les deux ans. En 1991, les Jeux d'hiver du Canada se tiendront dans la Province de l'Île-du-Prince-Édouard, et on s'attend à ce qu'environ 2 800 athlètes, entraîneurs et officiels y participent. Et c'est ici même, à Québec, en 1967, que les Jeux du Canada ont vu le jour. Depuis, différentes petites villes canadiennes, réparties dans toutes les provinces, ont été l'hôte des Jeux du Canada. Peu d'autres pays ont à leur crédit

1890
1990

L'Honorable Marcel Danis, ministre d'État Jeunesse, ministre d'État Condition physique et Sport amateur, Gouvernement du Canada, Ottawa, Canada.

autant d'initiatives. En fait, je peux affirmer, sans grand risque de me tromper, qu'au cours du dernier quart de siècle le Canada a été l'hôte d'un nombre plus important de Jeux principaux qu'aucun autre pays. Qui plus est, pour ce qui est de notre performance dans la tenue de ce genre de manifestations, nous ne le cédons à personne.

Pour ceux qui ne connaissent pas bien l'univers du sport, la question qui vient spontanément à l'esprit est sans doute «*Pourquoi?*». On peut en effet se demander pourquoi le Canada veut *poursuivre* cette tradition et continuer de tenir des grandes manifestations sportives. Comme chacun sait, les enjeux financiers, je pense ici aux fonds requis en deniers publics et en fonds privés, sont énormes. Qui plus est, la tenue de Jeux importants nécessite une formidable organisation; des manifestations telles que les Jeux olympiques et ceux du Commonwealth exigent littéralement des années de préparation. Personne ne contestera cet état de choses; cela semble évident. Néanmoins, je pense qu'il faut aussi souligner que les avantages que l'on peut retirer de la tenue de Jeux d'importance — les profits de l'investissement, si vous préférez — sont immenses. Et quand je parle de profits, ce n'est pas aux rétributions financières auxquelles je pense, bien qu'il y en ait certainement à retirer de la tenue de Jeux bien organisés. Non, je pense plutôt à la possibilité que nous avons d'améliorer notre système sportif, de mousser notre fierté nationale et notre conscience culturelle, de rehausser notre prestige à l'échelon international et de développer notre infrastructure.

Du point de vue des athlètes, les Jeux importants représentent un but à atteindre sur le plan de la performance et de la réalisation personnelle. Cette remarque s'applique plus particulièrement aux athlètes du pays hôte, puisque ces derniers ont alors cette rare occasion de se mesurer, sur leur propre terrain et devant leurs concitoyens, aux meilleurs athlètes du monde. Et comme nous avons pu l'observer à quelques reprises, une telle possibilité peut pousser les athlètes à des performances remarquables.

En outre, la tenue de grands Jeux a pour effet de rehausser le prestige du sport d'un autre point de vue important. La sensibilisation du public aux divers aspects du sport se traduit souvent, en effet, par l'affectation de nouveaux fonds publics dans ce secteur, et, en conséquence, par un bond dans l'amélioration du système sportif national. Ainsi, le fait que la tenue de Jeux importants permette à la nation tout entière de jouir d'une attention internationale entraîne souvent une augmentation des sommes affectées aux athlètes et aux entraîneurs. Avant les Jeux olympiques de Montréal, le gouvernement du Canada a investi des fonds dans un nouveau programme, intitulé «Plan des Jeux», destiné à aider les athlètes à se préparer aux Jeux de 1976. De la même façon, nous avons aidé les athlètes à se préparer aux Jeux de Calgary et aux Jeux d'été de 1988 en créant à leur intention un programme, qui s'appelait «Mieux que jamais», lequel fut conçu pour les inciter au dépassement.

Par ailleurs, l'infrastructure sportive d'un pays peut aussi tirer profit largement de la tenue de Jeux d'importance. En effet, les Jeux d'hiver de Calgary ont laissé au Canada la piste de bobsleigh et de luge la plus rapide et la plus sûre au monde. L'Ouest canadien a alors acquis ses premiers tremplins de ski, des tremplins conçus pour être utilisés l'année durant. Grâce à ces Jeux aussi, nous avons maintenant notre Anneau olympique intérieur — une installation unique au monde — ainsi qu'un centre permanent d'entraînement pour notre équipe nationale de hockey sur glace. En plus de ces installations pour manifestations de haute performance, la région de Calgary jouit maintenant d'un nombre plus grand de pistes de ski utilisées à des fins récréatives, ainsi que d'un tout nouveau centre de ski et de remonte-pentes améliorés.

La tenue de Jeux importants peut aussi permettre à un pays d'enregistrer une évolution très rapide de toute son infrastructure, non seulement de son infrastructure sportive. D'ailleurs, Séoul s'avère un bon exemple à cet égard, et je suis persuadé que Monsieur Park y fera allusion dans ses remarques. Il est vrai qu'un événement comme celui des Jeux olympiques ou des Jeux du Commonwealth peut accélérer l'établissement d'un système de transport nouveau et amélioré, ainsi que de nouveaux logements à prix abordable et d'autres services au bénéfice de toute la société. En fait, l'une des raisons qui ont incité la ville de Toronto à poser sa candidature pour les Jeux olympiques de 1996 fut la volonté d'enrichir le marché local d'un nouveau parc de logements à prix abordable, ce dont la ville a grandement besoin.

Ensuite, l'édification de la nation constitue un autre avantage capital. Les Jeux importants sont en effet un excellent moyen de capter l'imagination et de stimuler l'enthousiasme du public. Ils sont l'occasion de rehausser la fierté nationale, de nouer des liens d'amitié et de cultiver des sentiments d'unité, ainsi que de promouvoir la conscience de nos accomplissements et de notre capacité en tant que nation. La tenue de Jeux d'importance peut unifier un pays en attirant l'attention sur une activité populaire. Dans un pays comme le Canada, ils permettent de réunir autour d'un seul événement une population diverse, répartie sur un territoire très étendu. Et grâce à cette attention obtenue à l'échelle nationale, il est possible d'entourer les Jeux de tout un ensemble de festivités. Bien que les Jeux olympiques soient avant tout une manifestation sportive, ils sont aussi un événement culturel important, qui met en vedette des artistes locaux, ainsi que des vedettes nationales et internationales. On peut même dire qu'ils permettent au pays et à la ville hôtes d'être pendant un temps un centre d'attraction pour le monde entier. À cet égard, Séoul est un très bon exemple, puisque les Jeux qui s'y sont déroulés en 1988 ont montré qu'un pays peut être l'hôte de Jeux réussis, tout en conservant et en mettant en valeur son identité culturelle distincte.

L'immense couverture assurée par les médias lorsque des Jeux d'importance se déroulent sensibilise l'opinion mondiale non seulement aux capacités d'un pays sur le plan sportif et organisationnel, mais aussi à son histoire, à son économie, à ses besoins et aux possibilités qu'il offre. Cette sensibilisation peut faciliter et rehausser la compréhension mutuelle entre les peuples et permettre au pays hôte d'étendre sa sphère d'influence.

Sur le plan économique, les avantages à tirer de la tenue de grands Jeux sont substantiels. Quant à l'influence sur le tourisme, elle est énorme. Les gens qui assistent à une manifestation internationale importante dépensent forcément de l'argent, et ils profitent généralement de l'occasion pour visiter les différentes régions du pays qui les accueille. En 1988, par exemple, Calgary et Séoul n'ont certainement pas été les seules villes à profiter des Jeux dont elles ont été les hôtes. Les grandes manifestations sportives ont aussi pour avantage de créer de l'emploi pour les citoyens du pays hôte. Des centaines d'hommes d'affaires et de professionnels doivent participer à la conception et à la construction des installations que requiert la tenue de Jeux importants. Certains sont même appelés à travailler pendant toute la durée des Jeux. Et si la planification est bien faite, les nouvelles installations peuvent, les Jeux terminés, continuer de générer des emplois pendant nombre d'années.

La tenue de Jeux d'importance peut donc entraîner des avantages nombreux et divers. Mais ces avantages ne sont pas automatiques — ils sont le résultat d'efforts de planification, de gestion et de mise en œuvre appropriés et professionnels. C'est donc dire qu'une planification et une gestion de piètre qualité peuvent se traduire par des coûts excédentaires difficiles à justifier et par un problème de dette à long terme. Par ailleurs, la tenue de grandes manifestations sportives peut se traduire par des attentes exagérées à l'endroit des athlètes du pays hôte. Pour éviter ce piège, les pays hôtes devraient s'efforcer de songer moins aux médailles à remporter et davantage aux répercussions à long terme des Jeux sur leur système sportif; car les Jeux ne doivent pas capter toute l'attention au détriment des programmes sportifs nationaux, mais être vus, d'une certaine façon, comme un moyen de promouvoir ces derniers.

En ce qui a trait à l'organisation de Jeux importants, on peut dire que le Canada a acquis au fil des ans un solide bagage de compétence technique et de capacité d'organisation. Nous nous réjouissons d'avoir été choisis comme hôte des Jeux du Commonwealth de 1994, qui se tiendront à Victoria. En ce qui a trait à ces Jeux, mon gouvernement a investi cinquante millions de dollars dans leur préparation. Les Jeux du Commonwealth sont devenus une tradition au Canada, une tradition qui nous enrichit, et nos athlètes font très bonne figure parmi tous les participants à ces Jeux. Nous croyons que Victoria se révèle un très bon choix comme ville hôte des prochains Jeux du Commonwealth.

De même, nous croyons aussi que Toronto a beaucoup à offrir comme ville-hôte candidate pour les Jeux olympiques de 1996. Cette ville cosmopolite applique l'idéal olympique dans la vie de tous les jours, dans un esprit d'harmonie raciale et culturelle. Toronto offre un environnement sûr, propre et attrayant, une panoplie de spectacles de tous genres et des activités culturelles diverses. Et Toronto, où des médias existent en trente-cinq langues différentes, s'est depuis longtemps acquis une réputation enviable comme mosaïque culturelle. La ville est dotée d'un système de transport qui lui a valu une distinction, ainsi que d'une infrastructure très vaste dans le secteur des communications, et les conditions climatiques qui y règnent conviennent parfaitement à la tenue des Jeux d'été. De plus, Toronto a de l'expérience comme ville hôte de manifestations internationales diverses. On se rappellera incidemment le Sommet économique de mai 1988.

Tous les paliers de gouvernement appuient la candidature de Toronto et, comme l'expérience l'enseigne, un tel appui est essentiel à la réussite d'une entreprise comme celle que Toronto souhaite mettre en branle. En fait, la contribution des gouvernements aux efforts déployés pour mousser la candidature de Toronto s'élève à cinq millions de dollars dont la moitié environ provient du gouvernement fédéral. À cette contribution s'ajoute un autre sept millions de dollars en provenance de plus de 70 sociétés commanditaires. En plus d'appuyer la candidature de Toronto, le gouvernement du Canada s'est engagé à jouer un rôle de partenaire comme hôte et organisateur des Jeux. Notre tâche consistera entre autres à offrir au Comité international olympique les services requis. Cette participation représente une dépense importante, mais nous estimons que les Jeux sont une bonne affaire pour le Canada.

Avant les Jeux de 1984 à Los Angeles, les Jeux olympiques étaient des entreprises très largement subventionnées par les gouvernements, et des coûts d'exploitation considérables restaient à éponger une fois les Jeux terminés. C'est l'expérience que nous avons connue à Montréal en 1976, à l'instar d'autres pays avant nous. Pour éviter que la même chose ne se reproduise à Calgary, nous avons décidé, dès l'étape de la planification, qu'il était essentiel que les installations puissent continuer de servir *après* les Jeux. Parc olympique Canada a en fait été conçu pour être un centre international où les athlètes du monde entier pourraient venir s'entraîner à un coût raisonnable. Pour assurer des retombées positives aux Jeux de Calgary, le gouvernement du Canada a créé un Fonds de dotation olympique de 30 millions de dollars pour aider à éponger les frais d'exploitation des installations olympiques après les Jeux. Le produit de ce fonds est affecté à l'exploitation de Parc olympique Canada et de l'Anneau olympique, ainsi qu'au soutien des programmes d'activités qui se déroulent dans toutes les installations olympiques. Ce fonds s'ajoutait à un autre Fonds de dotation de 30 millions de dollars créé par OCO '88, soit le Comité d'organisation des Jeux olympiques. Il importe ici de souligner que ces fonds ont été créés *avant* les Jeux. Et leur création ne supposait pas que les Jeux se terminent par un bilan financier positif. À ce chapitre, je suis heureux de vous dire que les Jeux de Calgary se sont soldés par un tel bilan, positif bien sûr, à la grande satisfaction de plusieurs, vous en conviendrez. Je tiens aussi à souligner que la création de fonds d'héritage est l'une des conditions que le gouvernement avait fixées pour accorder son soutien d'une part à Victoria pour les prochains Jeux du Commonwealth, et d'autre part à Toronto pour les Jeux olympiques de 1996. Dans ces deux villes, les organisateurs s'étaient fermement engagés à veiller à ce que la tenue des manifestations à venir laisse un héritage positif pour le Canada et pour le monde.

Le relais du flambeau olympique est une autre réussite purement canadienne. Cette longue course à travers le pays, dans les jours qui ont précédé les Jeux de Calgary, nous a permis de susciter un vif intérêt pour les Jeux non seulement dans la ville de Calgary, mais dans le pays tout entier. Et en associant le rallye de la flamme olympique au programme fédéral Célébration 1988, nous avons gagné la participation à cet événement des Canadiens qui œuvrent dans le secteur des sports et loisirs, dans nos collectivités d'un océan à l'autre. Célébration 88 avait pour objet d'encourager le plus grand nombre possible de Canadiens à s'imprégner de l'esprit et des valeurs qui font l'Olympisme. Plus de 1 700 collectivités ont organisé des cérémonies préolympiques spéciales au cours desquelles était reconnue et célébrée la contribution de certains citoyens à la vie sportive locale. Grâce à Célébration 1988, plus de 90% des Canadiens ont eu la chance de vivre leur propre expérience olympique.

Les Jeux olympiques de Calgary ont aussi montré que la précieuse contribution de travailleurs bénévoles peut jouer un rôle essentiel dans le succès de ce genre de manifestation, et qu'elle joue effectivement ce rôle. À Calgary, près de 10 000 travailleurs bénévoles ont participé à l'organisation des Jeux. En collaboration avec les organisateurs, ces personnes ont offert au monde entier une image de professionnalisme, de discipline, de dévouement et de sens de l'engagement qui a eu des retombées positives sur l'ensemble des Canadiens. Les rapports de partenariat qui ont existé entre les paliers de gouvernement, et entre les gouvernements et le secteur privé sont un autre élément qui a contribué au succès des Jeux de Calgary. Les autorités fédérales, provinciales et municipales ont travaillé en collaboration très étroite en vue d'assurer le succès des Jeux. Chaque palier a fait ce qu'il s'était engagé à faire, et en a même fait davantage dans bien des cas. Par ailleurs, l'étroite collaboration entre le gouvernement fédéral, l'OCO '88 et le secteur privé a rendu possibles un certain nombre d'entreprises conjointes. Je pense ici entre autres aux six millions de dollars qui ont été investis par des commanditaires privés dans diverses améliorations apportées à Parc olympique Canada.

À la réflexion, toutefois, on peut facilement affirmer que l'héritage le plus important laissé par les Jeux de Calgary constitue l'expérience acquise par les gens qui ont contribué à la réussite de ces Jeux. Ces gens ont en effet acquis de l'expérience dans l'organisation de manifestations internationales importantes, laquelle pourra certainement être mise à contribution pour le bénéfice du sport et d'autres secteurs de la société. Je pense ici aux gens qui ont conçu et construit des installations capables d'accueillir des manifestations internationales. À tous ceux qui ont contribué à la réussite des Jeux par leur travail bénévole. Aux entraîneurs, qui ont énormément appris au contact de leurs pairs de différents pays du monde et qui leur ont fait part de leur expérience. Enfin, je pense aussi, bien sûr, aux athlètes, qui ont connu l'expérience ultime de la compétition. Tous ces gens ont été touchés et motivés par l'esprit olympique, et ils conserveront le souvenir de cette expérience le reste de leurs jours; ils seront toujours fiers d'avoir été associés aux Jeux olympiques. Par ailleurs, et ce facteur est tout aussi important, tous ces gens que l'expérience a rodés demeurent une ressource sur laquelle le Canada peut compter pour la tenue de Jeux futurs ou pour l'organisation d'autres manifestations majeures.

Considérer l'avenir, voilà une chose que l'on est souvent appelé à faire dans le monde du sport. J'aimerais maintenant, à cet égard, vous faire part de quelques-unes de mes réflexions sur les problèmes et les possibilités que nous réserve l'avenir concernant la tenue de Jeux importants. Je suis persuadé que bon nombre d'entre vous partagez mon inquiétude au sujet du fossé grandissant qui sépare les pays riches et les pays en voie de développement. Je pense ici à la capacité de ces derniers pays d'accueillir des manifestations sportives importantes et d'y participer de façon significative. Ces pays, qui pourtant remportent de plus en plus de médailles lors de Jeux, demeurent dans l'impossibilité d'être les hôtes de ce genre de manifestations, parce que les coûts déjà énormes représentés par la tenue de Jeux importants ne cessent d'augmenter. La question n'est pas facile, mais je crois que nous devons nous y attaquer. Les Jeux de la francophonie marquent un pas important dans la bonne direction, car ces Jeux, qui ont eu lieu pour la première fois en 1989 au Maroc, se tiendront alternativement dans un pays du Nord et dans un pays du Sud. Le bagage commun d'expériences et de connaissances qui a été mis à contribution dans la planification et la tenue de cette manifestation offre un modèle sur lequel l'on pourrait désormais se fonder pour permettre aux pays en voie de développement d'accueillir des manifestations sportives de prestige. Une autre solution possible serait que chaque pays qui est l'hôte de Jeux profite de l'occasion pour transférer une partie de son bagage d'expériences et de connaissances aux pays en développement. D'une part, cela pourrait se faire au moyen d'un programme par lequel les agents des pays en développement désireux de tenir éventuellement des Jeux, auraient l'occasion de venir apprendre sur place et participer étroitement à l'organisation des Jeux dans un pays économiquement développé. D'autre part, on pourrait envisager la création d'un fichier central de données sur les façons de mener à bien des Jeux importants. Il serait sans doute utile aussi que nous trouvions des moyens de maintenir les coûts des manifestations sportives importantes à un niveau plus réaliste, et plus en accord avec les possibilités financières d'un plus grand nombre de pays. De telles initiatives n'auraient pas pour effet de mettre tous les pays sur un pied d'égalité, mais représenteraient certainement un pas dans la bonne voie.

Le deuxième point que je tiens à souligner est la nécessité de s'assurer que les installations aménagées pour des Jeux d'importance continuent de servir une fois les Jeux terminés. Comme en fait foi notre insistance sur la création de fonds de dotation, le Canada croit fermement à la nécessité de planifier l'utilisation des installations créées pour des Jeux d'importance une fois la manifestation terminée. Ainsi, pour les prochains Jeux, il serait peut-être indiqué que l'entente type présentée par le détenteur des droits et signée par le pays hôte inclut une clause sur «l'héritage» des Jeux. Dans le même ordre d'idée, il faudrait aussi que nous mettions en place de meilleurs mécanismes pour favoriser le partage des connaissances entre tout pays qui vient d'être l'hôte de Jeux importants et le pays désigné pour accueillir les suivants. De cette façon, on ne serait pas obligé de réinventer la roue, pour ainsi dire, chaque fois que la tenue de Jeux s'annonce dans un nouveau pays.

En ce qui a trait à la manifestation sportive elle-même, j'estime que nous devrions insister davantage sur la «poursuite de l'excellence», plutôt que de simplement rechercher le frisson et la gloire qui accompagnent la victoire. Traditionnellement, nous avons concentré notre attention sur les prouesses des meilleurs, et non sur ce que l'athlète devait subir pour atteindre ce niveau de performance ou sur la nature du sport lui-même. Dans nos efforts en vue de rehausser la qualité de l'expérience de la compétition sportive, nous devons veiller à intégrer les besoins et les attentes des athlètes handicapés à l'ensemble des considérations dont nous tenons compte. Nous devons voir les athlètes comme des gens de «capacité variable», mais qui ont tous la volonté et la détermination d'atteindre des sommets. Il faudrait aussi que nous nous efforcions plus que nous le faisons maintenant de souligner les valeurs qui sous-tendent des manifestations telles que les Jeux olympiques ou ceux du Commonwealth. Nous pourrions à l'avenir veiller à ce que les médias insistent vraiment sur l'harmonie interculturelle, ainsi que sur l'importance de la forme athlétique et de l'esprit sportif, ou même à ce que les prix attribués tiennent davantage compte de ces aspects.

Certaines personnes estiment que nous n'avons pas fait tout ce que nous pouvions pour rejoindre le public qui assiste à de grandes manifestations. Souvent, nous établissons un meilleur contact avec les téléspectateurs qu'avec les gens qui sont là sur place. Ce qui reste à voir, c'est comment communiquer aux gens qui assistent à une manifestation sportive l'essence d'un sport et de l'expérience athlétique. Que pouvons-nous faire pour permettre aux athlètes d'entrer en relation avec les spectateurs et les athlètes qui viennent de l'étranger et ont une autre culture que la leur?

Je crois que nous devons mettre au point un nouveau système d'évaluation des Jeux importants — système qui s'adresse non seulement à l'organisation des Jeux, mais aussi à leur influence culturelle et à leur valeur sociale. Ainsi, nous ne prenons pas soin de demander aux athlètes si les Jeux ont répondu à leurs attentes ou à leurs exigences, et je crois que nous gagnerions à le faire puisque les athlètes nous communiqueraient sûrement des idées intéressantes. En négligeant de faire appel à la participation de tous les intervenants dans le processus d'évaluation, nous nous privons d'une belle occasion d'apprendre les uns des autres et de mieux préparer la manifestation suivante.

Enfin, quel que soit le pays hôte d'une manifestation sportive, nous devons préserver les valeurs éthiques qui sous-tendent le sport, et notamment l'esprit sportif. Il importe que l'endroit où se tiennent les grands Jeux change. Et nous devons, au prix sans doute de certains compromis, veiller à ce qu'un plus grand nombre de pays aient la possibilité d'être l'hôte de Jeux d'importance. Là où nous ne devons pas accepter de compromis, toutefois, c'est là où il est question de valeurs éthiques et de déroulement équitable des épreuves sportives. L'esprit sportif est l'âme même du sport, et cela s'applique autant à l'échelon international qu'à l'échelon communautaire. Être l'hôte de Jeux importants est selon moi une chance et un défi. Une fois encore, le Canada accepte de relever ce défi pour les Jeux du Commonwealth de 1994, et il se dit prêt à le relever de nouveau dans l'avenir, ou encore à aider d'autres pays à le faire.

NOTE

1. *Note des éditeurs.* On se souviendra que ce n'est qu'en septembre 1990 que le CIO, à l'occasion de sa 96e Session, votera en faveur d'Atlanta (USA) comme ville-hôte des Jeux de la XXVIe Olympiade, 1996.

The Experience of Seoul: toward a World without Barriers

The Honorable Park Seh-jik

It is a great pleasure and honor for me to have this chance to address this distinguished gathering. Before I begin however, I would like to thank the Symposium organizers and all those involved who have made us feel so welcome and comfortable here in this beautiful city of Quebec.

But also, I want you to know that the Korean people have a special affinity for the people of Canada—afterall we were both hosts of the 1988 Olympic Games. In fact, I attended the Calgary Games and I must say they were superb. So, since this is my first opportunity to formally thank and congratulate you I tip my hat to all who made the XVth Winter Olympic Games possible.

Some months ago, when I received the invitation to attend this Symposium and had agreed to speak on "The Experience of Seoul: toward a World without Barriers", scores of ideas and thoughts crossed my mind. Before I knew it, in my memory I was back again in my old olympic office calling the shots on the organization and conduct of the 1988 Summer Olympic Games. Each day at the Committee, I was faced with numbers of staggering proportions—hundreds of sporting venues to operate; thousands of sporting and cultural events and receptions to organize; millions of man hours to handle the mountains of paperwork and billions of dollars to spend with efficiency and care if the Games were to work properly. And on top of this, with all of South Korea's 42 million people living within a 4-6 hour drive of our Main Stadium, a ticketing nightmare handle, for even the most daring. So in 1986, when I assumed the Seoul Olympic Organizing Committee Presidency I too was about to become another statistic—one more person to be swept away by the enormity of the task without even seizing-up the great opportunities and outcomes brought about by the Games.

The Spirit

But what lifted my mind above this cloud of numbers was the very strong and pervasive olympic spirit that I detected among most of the Korean people.

The Honorable Park, Seh-jih, President of the Organizing Committee of the Games of the XXIVth Olympiad, Seoul, Republic of Korea.

They were proud indeed of the prospect of the XXIVth Olympiad to be celebrated in their country. And it was not just a superficial spirit. In fact, the olympic fire burned deeply enough, I believe, to help bring about in our nation what many called "The Miracle on the Han"—Korea's economic and political achievements. Certainly, a good part of what was achieved came through effective economic planning and Government guidance but throughout, I thought to myself that what was happening to Korea was because of the sense of commitment and excitement associated with the Olympic Games. I also realized that the success of the Seoul Games depended on the organizers being able to see the "forest fore the trees"—to see the bigger picture of the Games and their significance to us. These guiding themes, as we would call them, would give us the direction, hope and sense of purpose that would allow us to build an olympic city and make the Games of Seoul the best ever.

Peace, Harmony and More

Clue

By now, many of you have heard of the acronym CLUE, —a simple word that we used at the Organizing Committee to assemble and remember the major themes we established for the 1988 Games.

Under this collection of letters, first of all, we put much emphasis on staging an *Olympics of Total Culture*. From the "C" in CLUE. We planned a festival for mankind in which the richness of its cultures from around the globe would be a key ingredient in the Games of Seoul.

Also under "C" we thought the staging of the biggest Paralympics ever just after the conventional Games would allow us to also realize an *Olympics of Compassion*.

Under "L" we hoped that the Seoul Olympic Games would be the *Olympics of a Future Legacy* and serve as an inspiration to other developing nations who may seek to host the Games in the future.

Skipping over "U" we strived to have an *Olympics of a New Era* under "E". We were honored at the opportunity to host the world but also delighted at the chance to properly introduce ourselves to peoples and nations around the globe.

Finally, and I think most relevant to what we are doing here this week, is "U". We sought at every opportunity to make the Seoul Games the *Olympics of Unity*: to tear down every barrier—from race, religion, ideology, nationality to regionalism and more. There were to be no boundaries or walls separating the olympic family in Seoul—only joy, friendship and the desire to participate peacefully in man's largest celebration ever. This is where our work began and this is where the spirit would be such an important tool in barrier busting.

Phase

This brings me to another tool we used to outline the five objectives which were set forth for the Seoul Games—PHASE.

Under "P", was maximum *Participation*. In Seoul we had the greatest number of nations, athletes, officials, journalists and spectators in the history of the Games. As for "H", *Harmony*, we achieved this by finally bringing together East and West, the Soviet Union, the People's Republic of China, the East Bloc and the Western world in Seoul.

Under "A", in the field of *Achievement*, I am proud to say that we had the greatest number of world records set during the Games and what we believe was the most efficient Games operation plan ever. "S" was for *Security*, and area we can be proud of because in the 17-day period of the Games with some 5 million people involved, there was not a single major security mishap. And finally, under "E" or *Efficiency*, we are happy to say that our Games made a profit and that money is being used to help spread sport throughout our nation.

Barrier Breaking—Record Breaking

There is no doubt for us that what happened in Seoul in September and October of 1988 was nothing short of a miracle. A country that was once war-torn and devastated rose from the ashes to welcome the world to its shores. Across the globe, too, a new spirit of peace and cooperation has grown where only recently there was bitter rivalry and distrust. New worlds are opening that were once sealed off and people who previously had no voice are now singing of freedom. Perhaps, the spirit of the Seoul Olympic Games was the spark to the fire.

"Hand in Hand" was the catchy theme song of the Seoul Olympiad and its lyrics sing volumes for the barriers that were crushed by the XXIVth Olympic Games. It is worth examining just what was accomplished by my country diplomatically after the Games of Seoul ended. The Games opened doors for Korea to socialist countries of the world from which we had been isolated for over forty years. Today, only two years after the Games we have consular offices in Moscow. The Soviet Ice Ballet just finished a week's tour in my country's capital and talk of further ties and exchanges continue. Trade between South Korea and the People's Republic of China has now reached nearly 4 billion dollars US. In early 1988, prior to the Games we had agreed to exchange trade offices with Hungary and by January 1989 we had fully functioning embassies. Following the establishment of diplomatic ties with Hungary, Yugoslavia made public its plans to set up trade offices in Seoul and followed that in 1989 with full diplomatic relations. Poland projects that it will establish official diplomatic relations within two years and Czechoslovakia is now about to take the same step. It is difficult to imagine that these amazing developments for my country are not associated with the sporting and diplomatic successes of the Seoul Olympic Games.

Conclusion

If one looks back at mid 1988 and compares the world of then to its current state, there are few who can say that it is not a significantly different place. And few would hesitate to say that it is a better place as well. Whether by design or coincidence, the Seoul Olympic Games indeed brought the world together just as the new peace of the late 20th century was breaking out. The causes of this new world fever are many and intertwined; perhaps only the historians of a later day will sort it all out. But we can say with certainty that a significant part of the vast peace and harmony momentum that was created stemmed from the spirit that the modern Olympic Games have been espousing since their inception less than a century ago.

Let me tell you a brief story that I think summarizes what I have been trying to say to you tonight. It is an anecdote from a book I have just published that is a compilation of a series of stories I wrote for publication in a Korean newspaper during the preparation of our Seoul Olympic Games.[1]. In the final few months before the Games, I made it a point to get out and personally touch base with those people who were on the periphery of the Games. On a particular day, I decided to go and meet those construction workers who were actually building the cauldron that would hold the sacred Olympic flame in our Seoul main stadium. So much came to mind when I envisioned the crew that might be shining and polishing a huge and glimmering stand of silver and gold; I couldn't wait to see it.

When my car finally arrived at the mill, what presented itself before me on that rainy day was a mud puddle, steel, and hats of men hustling and bustling about. To my great horror, I found that what lay before them was the cauldron of the Seoul Olympic Games. One of the workers came forth and told me that their company had turned down all other business orders to specifically prepare the cauldron and that each and every one of the workers had volunteered to work overtime—without pay—to finish this project on time. In addition, and in typical Korean spirit, some of their families and friends engaged in fasting and praying until the immense cauldron was completed. Here, I thought to myself in this muddy field on the outskirts of Seoul, I had found the true meaning of the olympic spirit. The cauldron was indeed in good hands.

In Seoul we tried to provide a proper environment through which this spirit would prevail everywhere and assist us in breaking down the barriers that had put the future of the Olympic Movement in jeopardy. We did this internationally among the 167 nations which have National Olympic Committees and also internally, for our own people. But this was not always an easy job. Our own people were not all and always totally supportive of the Games. Early on, many people had told me that they felt as if the Games belonged only to a few—not to the public. To alleviate this, I had developed a comprehensive public involvement program to bring the people into the Games. This included an annual cross-country speaking tour for me, tours of the Olympic facilities for Koreans from all parts of the country and walks of life arranged by our Committee and public relations campaigns to get the people involved. Just prior to the Games, we held three full rehearsals of the Opening Ceremonies that brought in nearly 300 000 people who would not have seen it live otherwise. And for the actual Opening and Closing Ceremonies we selected 1 200 men and women from such varied professions as street cleaners and hairdressers to very unfortunate people such as disabled veterans and even lepers to join in. And on the banks of our Han River, we placed a large multi-vision screen where some 300 000 people watched the Opening Ceremonies and the River Festival. We tried our very best to make every Korean citizen a member of the 1988 Olympic Family.

For the world, at first, the Seoul Olympic Games was an upbeat news and sports story. But as the flame of the Games went out on October 3, 1988 and unprecedented events began to unfold across the globe, it became clear that in Seoul the people of the world had found a unity of purpose and goal and a spirit that would help all of us play a part in re-shaping a new international system—toward a world without barriers.

In many ways, the Olympic Games are like a large boat steadily making its way to the next port. This came to my mind as we brought the Olympic torch from Cheju-Island to Pusan City by ocean liner. At that time I thought that *first*, everyone on this boat must be an olympic expert and contribute in some way; *second*, I felt we needed solidarity of purpose on the boat; *third*, we must know how to handle a crisis such as severe bad weather or the danger of running aground; *fourth*, the sole purpose of the boat is to make the passengers happy and deliver them to the next docking, and we all must contribute to this; and *finally*, we need the blessing of God and the harmony of Heaven, Earth and Man (as is expressed through our Korean Dae-Dae Cultural Grammar) to make the journey a safe and prosperous one. This is how Seoul and the Korean people safely and unerringly brought the olympic ship to our shores. We hope that in some small way we have cleared the way for smooth sailing for the Olympic Games to come.

REFERENCE

1. Park S-j (1990) The stories of Seoul Olympics. Seoul. [Not for commercial sale]. These stories were first published in *Chosum-Ilbo* from November 4, 1989 to February 4, 1990.

Economic Aspects of Hosting
Major Sports Events

Richard W. Pound

On m'a demandé de vous entretenir des facteurs économiques entourant la tenue d'événements sportifs internationaux tels que les Jeux olympiques. Il est essentiel de bien connaître ces facteurs pour évaluer s'il est souhaitable qu'une ville ou un pays relève le défi que représente l'organisation de tels événements. Au Canada, une expérience considérable a été acquise dans la tenue d'événements internationaux. Nous avons été les hôtes des Jeux olympiques à deux reprises, des Jeux panaméricains à une reprise et des Jeux du Commonwealth plusieurs fois. La ville de Toronto dispute actuellement à cinq autres grandes villes du monde l'honneur d'être l'hôte des Jeux olympiques centenaires de 1996. L'on connait la publicité qui entoure inéluctablement de tels événements et même les efforts qui sont déployés pour les obtenir. Ce qui est moins connu, cependant, ce sont les facteurs économiques que sous-tendent la tenue de ces grands événements. Quels en sont les coûts? Comment peut-on les contrôler? Quelles sont les sources de financement? Quels avantages directs et indirects peut-on tirer de leur tenue? Comment traiter les frais de construction éventuels des installations? Les réponses à ces questions peuvent influencer la décision d'une ville de présenter ou non un dossier de candidature, et si elle est choisie, la façon dont l'événement sera perçu par la population du pays.

What are some of the Economic Issues to be Addressed?

The points which are covered here are far from complete and are intended only to be examples of the types of considerations and questions which come into play.

The Costs

It is important to identify those costs which relate directly to the Games and those which are of a capital or investment nature. This determination will be a

Richard W. Pound, Vice President, International Olympic Committee. Partner, Law Firm of Stikeman, Elliott, Montréal, Québec, Canada.

crucial feature not only in the financing of the Games, but also in the basic decision as to whether or not a city or country will decide to bid. How much has to be built and how much is already in place and needs only fixing up?

Some examples may be helpful. How will such questions as the following be dealt with?

1– A stadium for the athletic events, seating 70 000 spectators, will be required for the Olympic Games. The city has an old stadium which is not suitable. It is proposed to demolish the old stadium and construct a new one at a cost of 200 million dollars. It will be available for a 60 day period before, during and immediately following the Games. After the Games, it will be owned by the city and leased to league teams and used for other purposes. Its estimated life is 50 years.

> Q. *How much of the 200 million dollars should be regarded as costs of the Games?*
>
> (a) 200 million dollars? or
>
> (b) $(1/6 \times 1/50 \times 200\ 000\ 000\ \$) = 667\ 000\ \$$

2– The host city proposes to demolish some old industrial buildings and develop a low-cost housing project which will be used during the Games as the Olympic Village. It will cost 100 million dollars. After the Games, the units will be sold to the public. The city estimates the sale will bring about 400 million dollars.

> Q. *What portion of the cost should be charged to the Games?*
>
> Q. *Should the Games share in the profit on the eventual sale?*

3– The host city has planned for many years, as part of its long range plans, to upgrade its entire road and public transportation system. If it gets the Games, it will not add anything new to the plan, but will accelerate its schedule of work so that everything will be finished in time for the Games instead of being fully finished by 1999—will be moved forward for completion in 1996. This is a major program and will cost 3 billion dollars. It will be financed from taxes and public debt.

> Q. *How much of this expenditure should be regarded as a cost of the Games?*

4– If the projections of the organizers of the Games are correct, the visitors and participants in the Games will spend 1 billion dollars in the host country before, during and after the Games. Such expenditure will include food, accommodation, transport, tourism and purchases from local merchants.

> Q. *Should this be a factor to be considered when deciding whether or not to host the Games?*
>
> Q. *Should the incremental revenues be treated as olympic revenues?*

5– The host city has a perfectly good stadium which is regularly used and which is in a good state of repair. It is big enough for the athletics competition, but needs a new track to be installed. The city would not otherwise install such a track, but is agreeable to do so if it will help attract the Games. The track will cost 3 million dollars.

> Q. *Is this an "olympic" cost?*

The point of these (and many other) questions is that there are many elements of expenditure that occur at or before the time of an Olympic Games. The decision to incur such costs, either at all, or within the particular time frame, may have an impact on the Games or the decision to host them. An understanding of both the nature of the expenditures and their relationship to the Games is essential to a proper appreciation of what the Olympic Games mean to the host city and country.

Some basic operating guidelines could well be adopted by Games organizers, as well as those who direct the bids for any such Games.

Rule 1, therefore, is to separate infrastructure and capital costs from the Games operating costs.

Rule 2, is never forget Rule 1.

Rule 3, is to make sure everyone connected with the Games knows Rules 1 and 2.

Rule 4, is for the organizers to work only with the Games operating budget and costs. The infrastructure is a matter for government or third parties who may be building facilities for their own purposes after the Games. If there are rental or other costs involved for use of the facilities, these should be part of the Games costs.

Rule 5, is to ensure that the infrastructure costs are not portrayed as olympic costs, but as long-term investments which must be amortized over the useful life of each asset.

Rule 6, is that no significant investment should be made in a facility which is only good for the Olympic Games and not thereafter. Host cities should not build white elephants. Perhaps part of the legacy should be a commitment to operate the facilities thereafter as sports facilities.

Rule 7, is to agree from the outset as to the respective responsibilities for expenditure on facilities, as between levels of government, the private sector and the organizing committee. The agreement should be reduced to writing.

Rule 8, is to involve all levels of government and representatives of the community at large in policy decisions which fall within the jurisdiction of the organizing committees. (This is not to suggest that they should *control* the operations, but to ensure that their input is welcomed, collected and considered.)

Rule 9, is to make sure to keep the public at large advised of progress. There will undoubtedly be elements within the media who focus exclusively on problems rather than success and progress, but that appears to be a small, if both predictable and annoying, price for a free press. When the Games are the customary eventual success, one can always send copies of the "gloom and doom" articles to the author.

Rule 10, is to have publicly audited statements so that the record is clear and unambiguous.

The Revenues

The Olympic Games are not all "cost". There is (quite apart from the indirect revenues referred to in Example 4) a great deal of direct income generated by or for the organizing committee of the Olympic Games.

The principal sources (in general order of importance) are the following:

Television rights

The IOC, by agreement with the organizing committees gives a considerable portion of the IOC's proceeds from the sale of television rights it obtains in respect of the Games to the local organizing committee. Television rights to the Games, as well as all intellectual property rights pertaining to the Games, are the exclusive property of the IOC. Until recently, this percentage has been approximately 75%. Starting in 1996 this percentage will decrease to 60%. The total dollars involved for the organizing committees will not, however, decrease. There are many changes occurring in the whole field of television and both the amount of rights and the geographic distribution thereof are likely to undergo significant alterations in the years to come. For 1996, therefore, the host organizing committee might well receive 500 million dollars US.

Sponsorships and Supplierships

In recent years, with increased understanding by sponsors as to the benefits of olympic sponsorship, and with increased understanding of the needs of sponsors, this aspect of financing has become very significant. An organizing committee might expect to generate in excess of 200 million dollars US from such sources.

Tickets

The amount available under this heading is a function of the size of the venues and the enthusiasm of the local population. Almost all tickets for final events can be sold twice over. But there are hundreds of thousands of seats available for preliminary events which, even at Olympic Games, often go unsold. It should be easy for a summer Games to realize 80 million dollars US from ticket sales.

Coin and Stamp Programmes

These depend upon government action and related arrangements with respect to allocation of income. In some cases the profits are used to fund a government contribution, whereas in others the organizing committee benefits directly. This tends to be a function of the form of legislation in the host country relating to the minting of coins. Profits from a well structured and properly marketed coin programme could be up to 50 million dollars US. Poorly conceived programmes are not profitable at all.

Lotteries

Lotteries are an example of programmes (usually requiring enabling legislation) that can provide a source of non-tax base revenues for olympic organizing committees. There is virtually no limit to the amount which can be realized, depending upon the format and duration of the particular lottery. It would not be at all unreasonable to consider revenues in the range of 100 million dollars US from lotteries. The Montreal Olympic Lottery, for example, produced considerably more than this amount.

Licensing

This is difficult money to earn, but a good programme can produce 25 million dollars US or more. It is sometimes doubtful whether it is worth all the effort, but, in the final analysis, there seems always to be a need for souvenirs and similar objects commemorating the Games.

Conclusion

If properly prepared, properly understood, properly accounted for and competently organized, Olympic Games should not be a financial drain on the host city or country. Provided that controls are in place to prevent grandiose schemes and unnecessary construction, it should, in fact, be possible for the Games to produce an operating profit for the benefit, mainly, of the host country.

This is not to say it is *guaranteed* to turn out that way, but recent experience, coupled with the high levels of income, suggest that unless serious errors of judgment are made, there is every likelihood that Games in the 1990s and beyond should at least break even.

Before I sit down, in case there is no opportunity tomorrow, on behalf of the IOC I want to thank our many friends from Laval University for their superb work in making this Symposium such a success.

Behind any success of this magnitude are the efforts of many people whom we thank but in particular wish to express our gratitude to the Rector Michel Gervais for his support, to Symposium Organizing Committee members Magdeleine Yerlès, Michel Bonneau and, of course, to our friend and President of the Symposium Fernand Landry.

The IOC believes that there will be lasting benefits for the Olympic Movement from this Symposium and we hope that it will prove to be the starting point for specific and ongoing contact between the IOC and the academic community on subjects of mutual interest.

La question de l'admission des femmes aux Jeux Olympiques n'est pas réglée. Elle ne saurait l'être dans le sens négatif par le motif que l'antiquité l'avait ainsi résolue; elle ne l'est pas davantage dans le sens affirmatif du fait que des concurrentes féminines ont été acceptées pour la natation et le tennis en 1908 et 1912. [. . .] On le voit donc, la discussion demeure ouverte. [. . .] Il est mieux qu'une discussion trop prompte ne soit pas intervenue et que l'affaire ait traîné. Elle se solutionnera tout naturellement lors de ce Congrès de Paris qui donnera aux Olympiades leur physionomie définitive. Dans quel sens ? Nous n'avons pas la qualité pour le prévoir mais nous ne craignons pas, quant à nous, de prendre parti du côté négatif. [. . .]

Coubertin P de (1912) Les femmes aux Jeux Olympiques. Revue Olympique, juillet, p 109

Olympism, Women and Sport

L'Olympisme, la femme et le sport

Pierre de Coubertin:
a Second Look at his Humanism, his Beliefs
and his Attitudes Concerning Women and Sport

By way of introduction, the author emphasizes that the opus of Coubertin had ideological and moralistic overtones rather than anthropological and historical ones. He invites scholars to read the works of Coubertin directly in the text, rather than through first or second-hand translations, and, more specifically, in the perspective of the social, political and cultural context of Coubertin's times. In the first part of his presentation, the author advances that Coubertin, exposed early to a liberal arts education, familiar with ancient Greek and Latin authors and texts, even comforting himself throughout his life by reading Seneque, more or less consciously became a disciple of the Stoic school of philosophy. Besides, Stoicism was florishing in France in Coubertin's time, which coincided with a difficult period of the country's history and preoccupations with colonial interests. Neo-olympism was a philosophical system characterized by a pursuit of wisdom through a global conception of the world: cosmopolitism. In that perspective, Homo Olympicus is a new conqueror of the impossible who strives with as much abnegation in life as he does in the stadium. In his struggles, the modern athlete aims at reaching an improbable state of eurythmy; for Coubertin, this type of endeavour corresponds to an optimal experience of the cosmos in that it promotes an embodiment of virtue, wisdom and happiness. Bodily and moral asceticism appear to be at the focal point of the stoic ethics of Coubertin's humanistic philosophy. In the author's view, Coubertin was an educator conscious of the destiny of his/her disciples who must become and remain open to and conscious of civic matters and standards. His writings are philosophical teachings or urgings to reflect upon the human condition, that is the individual person, society, the pursuit of self fullfillment and happiness. Over and above his global philosophy befitting the Stoics, Coubertin was a philhellene. But the author emphasizes that Coubertin's Greece was that of the romantics and of the archeologists: a Greece idealized through mental images of democracy and aesthetics, a Greece in essence all masculine; that of the ephebe. Coubertin was also influenced by the ethnocentrism of the Stoics. He saw in Western Man the architect of international goodwill and solidarity, yet who paradoxically remains faithful to his ethnic origin and nucleus. In the next part of his presentation, the author advances that the relative solitude in which Coubertin found himself throughout his life indeed marked him. Coubertin experienced the solitude of a last-born child, of the self-educated, of his political choices, of his understanding and love of anglo-saxon sport, besides having experienced limited contacts with his own children. Olympism in Coubertin's life became the means through which he would attempt to contact and serve his fellow human beings: in a broad perspective of the mutual respect between cultures; in the notion of athletic effort and record which he conceived as an intense moment of communication transcending the human species. In this sense, the author advances that had not Coubertin remained existentially solitary and anguished all his life, perhaps would his neo-olympism never have been born and thus been such a strong force in the century. Finally, the author hinges upon Coubertin's thinking on women and sport. His conception is described as genuinely misogynous, expressed and affirmed until his death. The author then explains the bases of Coubertin's obturate opinion: – the prevailing conception of the social role of women, at the end of the 19th century; – the within-family roles of women which were limited to house management, child bearing and rearing, both in the aristocratic and bourgeois circles to which Coubertin belonged; – the so-called scientific assumption of the time regarding the intellectual potential of women and the role that befitted them best in the household; – the reminiscence of the social roles of women in ancient Greece and Athens; – the fact that there were so few women in the circles frequented by Coubertin; – lastly but not the least, his family and marital experiences. Till the end of his life, Coubertin will refuse any glorification of women; in the author's view, this would have negated, for Coubertin, the very symbolism of the manly sporting hero modeled on the triumphant ephebe. By way of conclusion, the author emphasizes that Coubertin was a powerful and influential creator, deeply committed to what he saw were the strategic battles of his times; yet, he was nonetheless straitjacketed by many of the conservative ideas he had received. A paradigm not to say a paradox to study more deeply, at the dawn of the Third Millennium.

Pierre de Coubertin: un regard neuf sur son humanisme, ses croyances et son attitude à l'égard du sport féminin

Yves-Pierre Boulongne

Dans tout symposium de la dimension de celui auquel nous sommes conviés, les sous-thèmes, appelés à préciser la rigueur du thème ne font très souvent que parcelliser un peu plus la recherche et reculer d'autant les possibilités de synthèse. Ainsi l'écueil se dresse-t-il, quand, abordant l'œuvre et la vie de Coubertin, l'étude se doit d'être centrée sur une partie de l'œuvre, importante certes, mais limitée. Il est à craindre en effet, là comme ailleurs, que focalisant la recherche sur les croyances et l'attitude de Coubertin envers le sport féminin et, plus précisément, le sport féminin olympique, ne soit perdue de vue la globalité de l'œuvre et la complexité de l'homme.

Nous sommes toujours myopes! Certes, nous nous méfions du décentrage, du grossissement anachronique de l'événement. Nous essayons d'envisager «l'avers et l'envers» des faits, et Coubertin nous y invite. Mais, pressés par les médias et une opinion publique sans nuance, nous échappons difficilement à une vision univoque et réductrice de l'histoire: le dogmatisme en est la rançon. Conscients de ces écueils, Théberge, Boutilier, San Giovanni et moi-même proposons une approche pluridimensionnelle, à la fois synchronique et diachronique, singulière et complémentaire, des rapports de Coubertin avec l'Olympisme, la femme, et le sport. Cette démarche transdisciplinaire reste fidèle, autant que faire se peut, au contexte politique et socio-culturel de l'époque, aux croyances philosophiques du rénovateur des Jeux olympiques, aux attitudes qui découlèrent de sa vision du monde hellénistique et des mondes anglo-saxon et français de la fin du XIXe siècle. Ce faisant, nous souhaitons contribuer à une meilleure étude anthropologique de l'œuvre et de la vie de Pierre de Coubertin — étude au demeurant remarquablement engagée par MacAloon[1].

Cette option méthodologique reste malheureusement encore trop isolée. L'épistémologie de la recherche coubertinienne montre en effet que, de 1917, date de la première critique universitaire consacrée à Pierre de Coubertin, par Seillières[2], membre de l'Institut de France, Académie des sciences morales et politiques, section morale — la précision a son importance — jusqu'aux années

1890
1990

Yves-Pierre Boulongne, Unité de formation et de recherche communication et insertion dans la société, Université Paris-Val-de-Marne, Créteil, France.

1970, la mise en question de l'œuvre de Coubertin et de l'Olympisme rénové se caractérise par des mémoires, des monographies, des articles d'ordre hagiographique, au demeurant peu nombreux, et souvent de qualité modeste. Or, ces balbutiements et ces bégaiements sont bien les signes caractéristiques de toute science à ses débuts.

Ainsi l'attitude moralisante et la norme idéologique commencent à peine à quitter le champ des consciences olympiennes. L'arbre olympique, alibi-refuge pour beaucoup, continue de cacher souvent la belle fûtaie pédagogique et culturelle coubertinienne. Aujourd'hui encore, la statue du Commandeur est présentée à l'adoration des fidèles et aux psalmodies des laudateurs, sans souci de trouver, derrière le rituel et le sacré, l'homme de chair et de caractère, et son œuvre vivante.

Nous ne sommes ni le hiérogrammate chargé d'interpréter les textes dans le temple d'Elis, un mois avant l'ouverture des Jeux d'Olympie, ni le sectateur, gardien et sourcilleux de la parole du Maître, décrypteur officiel d'apophtègmes attribués faussement trop souvent à Coubertin. Nous refusons de participer à une seconde mise à mort de Coubertin, en contribuant à l'ensevelir sous le dogme d'une Olympie mythique et béatifiée, aussi bien que sous celui d'un sport angélique.

Pour autant, nous récusons les contempteurs radicaux qui, des deux côtés de l'Atlantique, vouent Coubertin et l'Olympisme aux gémonies. Prisonniers de la catéchèse marxo-réichienne, ils commettent l'erreur d'anachronisme et donc d'irréalité en maniant l'amalgame. Comment, en effet, sentir et comprendre Coubertin et l'Olympisme renaissant, fin du XIXe siècle, en se referant à des valeurs et des comportements de la fin du XXe? Pour autant, ces universitaires — Américains et Français pour la plupart — ont eu le mérite de secouer le monde de la recherche coubertinienne, en l'obligeant à sortir de l'ornière moralisante. Secouant les conformismes et les préjugés, même s'ils en recréaient d'autres, ils ont aidé à mieux situer Coubertin dans le temps bourgeois de l'époque, et à mieux cerner la complexité humaine et sociale de l'Olympisme.

Au même moment, en Europe, vers les années 1960-70, les sciences humaines et sociales étendaient leurs champs d'investigation au domaine du sport et, plus timidement, à celui de l'Olympisme. Bienfaisant questionnement: les drames et les incidents survenant — à Mexico, Munich, Montréal, Los Angeles — les administrateurs du Mouvement olympique, à la demande, après 1980, d'un nouveau président soucieux de secouer la situation léguée par ses deux prédécesseurs immédiats, les journalistes de plus en plus critiques de la désuétude des structures et des mentalités, une opinion publique mieux informée, des athlètes de haut niveau revendiquant leur statut d'hommes et de femmes libres, demandaient et exigeaient des réformes en vue de préparer l'Olympisme à l'inconnu du troisième millénaire. Du coup, Coubertin retrouvait une modernité ignorée ou méconnue. Débarrassée du carcan réducteur du seul paramètre olympique, l'œuvre coubertinienne bénéficiait d'un soudain regain d'intérêt[3,4].

Des textes importants de Coubertin difficiles à trouver, car dispersés dans les multiples revues françaises, américaines, allemandes, ou épars dans plus de 60 000 pages imprimées in-quarto apparaissaient. Certes ces textes, pour importants qu'ils soient, ne sont encore qu'une approche de l'œuvre globale: trop axés à nos yeux sur le fait olympique, leur présentation peut en outre en être discutée. Cette restriction posée, félicitons-nous de leur existence: l'œuvre coubertinienne, en partie dévoilée, est désormais plus accessible. Mais de quel Coubertin s'agit-il, puisque aussi bien aucun choix n'est innocent? Pour autant l'homme et son œuvre sont-ils débarassés des bandelettes dans lesquelles l'ignorance, le conformisme, la mauvaise foi ou la science de l'heure les ont emprisonnés? Le Coubertin que nous interrogeons, est-il encore le guide pieusement vénéré, ou l'homme multiple, passionné, paradoxal, contradictoire, autoritaire, que nous entrevoyons à peine?

Nous devons porter dorénavant sur Coubertin le regard possible et nouveau qui s'impose. Nous devons relire les textes fondamentaux — souvent Coubertin se répète —, investir les archives notariales, si possible familiales, juger encore plus justement de la situation de la famille, de son aisance matérielle, de ses comportements, des idées politiques, culturelles, sociales qu'on y professe ou que l'on méprise, de l'éducation des enfants et pas seulement du jeune Pierre, de l'enseignement des Jésuites, respecté et rejeté, des jeux et des sports qu'il pratiqua effectivement à Mirville, Étretat, Paris, Lausanne, de sa vie quotidienne, des rapports affectifs avec sa mère, sa femme, des drames familiaux que les maladies mentales de ses deux enfants provoquèrent... Et encore, de cette obsession de la question sociale, de son antisocialisme virulent, de ses rapports ambigus avec l'Allemagne par l'intermédiaire de Carl Diem, lié au Reich par l'organisation des Jeux olympiques de 1936. C'est à ce long travail de remise en cause qu'une nouvelle génération de chercheurs est conviée.

Afin de répondre au sous-thème proposé, nous voudrions, aujourd'hui, que notre regard s'attarde plus spécialement sur deux portants de l'homme et de l'œuvre. D'une part, sur l'humanisme de Pierre de Coubertin, ou plus précisément sur les bases intellectuelles et affectives de cet humanisme, durablement influencé durant ses humanités secondaires par les philosophes-pédagogues de la Stoa, puis par un commerce régulier avec l'œuvre de Sénèque, enfin, par les certitudes de sa croyance dans une grécité réifiée. D'autre part, sur la solitude existentielle de l'homme et du créateur, né rebelle, seul toujours dans la lutte, meurtri par la fatalité, qui fut et se donna au monde, parce qu'il sut transcender ses angoisses et celles de sa classe sociale. Nous pensons que ces deux séries causales étudiées, l'attitude de Pierre de Coubertin face au problème du sport féminin en général, et olympique, en particulier, apparaîtra plus logique même si, *aujourd'hui*, nous n'en partageons pas l'esprit et en combattons les conséquences.

Un regard nouveau sur l'humanisme de Pierre de Coubertin

L'homme est généreux et ouvert. Poète et prophète, il a le front dans les nuages. Mais, solidement ancré dans le monde tel qu'il est, philosophe et pédagogue, il s'est donné pour mission de servir sur un front social difficile : celui de l'éducation. Tout ce qui est de l'homme lui est précieux : le corps, l'âme, la sensibilité, le jugement, et les comportements, les rêves de ses contemporains, tous ses contemporains, ceux de France et d'Europe, comme ceux des contrées les plus lointaines. Il n'a de cesse d'inciter au développement de la personne humaine ; à l'accession de chacun à la vertu — par la paix du corps et de l'âme, cette eurythmie grecque recouvrée —, et par le respect des civilisations et l'interpénétration des cultures. Tout son système pédagogique est établi en fonction de la vie. Homme complet, il réclame pour tous des humanités intégrales, qui répondent « à son intégrale humanité[5] », il est le chantre et le grand prêtre de la dernière grand'messe de l'humanité : les Jeux olympiques, cette fête quadriennale, qu'il dédie « au printemps humain ».

Les cheminements de l'humanisme coubertinien

Tant de lyrisme, de foi, de référence et de mesure à l'homme, mérite bien d'être appelé humanisme, selon l'acceptation commune. Mais aux yeux du chercheur, est-il possible de se satisfaire d'une évidence aussi brutale ? Quels sont, plus profondément et cachés, les linéaments culturels et sociaux, les cheminements mal visibles de cet humanisme, qui poussèrent ce rentier nanti à devenir un rebelle et un pédagogue ? La littérature coubertinienne répond mal à cette interrogation légitime, Coubertin lui-même ne fournit pas de clefs — ou très peu — dans son œuvre écrite. Tout au plus, peut-on faire appel aux travaux de deux universitaires qui abordent le problème, l'un est le fait de Seillières, l'autre de Meylan.

Seillières fut le premier universitaire à mettre en lumière l'influence politique et l'œuvre pédagogique de Pierre de Coubertin. Publié en 1917, son mémoire — car c'en est un, dans la forme et dans le fond — est un plaidoyer *pro domo* pour l'armée française et pour tous ceux, tels Lyautey et les «officiers sociaux», qui ont permis cette victoire. L'ouvrage[6] n'est que le panégyrique d'un de ces pédagogues bienfaiteurs sans qui la victoire de Verdun, et l'entrée des Alliés dans Strasbourg, eût été impossible. L'approche de l'œuvre est donc partiale et sélective. Seillières ne retient, pour sa démonstration, que ce qui conforte ses *a priori*. Il voit gros et ne met en valeur que l'appel coubertinien à l'effort et au sacrifice : la France, exsangue, doit se reconstruire. En ce sens, la pédagogie coubertinienne, pourvoyeuse de muscle et de caractère, comble ses vœux, on ne lui demandera pas plus. Inutile d'y chercher plus finement une vision humaniste, Seillières n'en a cure. Pourtant Seillières de par les objectifs pédagogiques qu'il privilégie, révélera le premier l'influence du stoïcisme sur la pensée pédagogique de Coubertin. Ce que Seillières loue en Coubertin, c'est le pédagogue disciple de la Stoa, opposé à Jean-Jacques Rousseau et à Charles Fourrier (dont il dénonce les «petites hordes» anarchiques), qui exige du sportif, et du citoyen, la soumission des instincts à la hiérarchie suprême de «l'impérialisme rationnel[7]». Pour autant, Seillières ne poussera pas son analyse à fond, et ne fera pas du stoïcisme l'une des composantes de l'humanisme coubertinien.

Il faudra attendre près de vingt-cinq ans pour que cet humanisme fasse l'objet d'une étude universitaire. Nous le devrons à Louis Meylan, (1888-1969), professeur d'Université à Lausanne. En plein désarroi de la seconde guerre mondiale (1941), Meylan donne à une revue confidentielle d'étudiants, *La Feuille Centrale de Zofingue*, une courte communication : «L'humanisme intégral de Pierre de Coubertin[8]». Meylan remarque : «Olympie, cette «mine de force vitale», n'avait cessé de lui apparaître comme le lieu très saint d'un humanisme intégral[9]». La formule va connaître un succès étonnant dans les milieux de l'Olympisme, et dispenser d'une réflexion critique. Fils de pasteur, poli au commerce des humanités classiques gréco-latines, Meylan est personnaliste. Représentatif d'un courant intellectuel puissant, illustré en Europe entre les deux guerres par Mouvier (1905-1950), fondateur de la revue Esprit, il est de ces hommes généreux qui, face à la mécanisation et à l'enrégimentement de l'individu — tant par les technologies que par les fascismes politiques —, réclament pour la personne humaine, ce «supplément d'âme» qu'exigeait déjà Bergson.

Meylan demande aux étudiants suisses une prise de conscience du danger, et leur offre en exemple l'œuvre humaniste roborative de Coubertin, où il trouve justification à son engagement philosophique, social, et pédagogique. À ce niveau, émanant à l'époque du maître incontesté de la pédagogie suisse, on attend un exposé critique. Il n'en est rien : Meylan ne définit pas l'humanisme de Coubertin, qu'il qualifie cependant d'intégral. Tout au plus, peut-on imaginer qu'il l'envisage à contrario de sa propre expérience : celle d'un adolescent dont la formation initiale ne s'est faite qu'au contact des textes anciens, sans souci d'une éducation corporelle concomitante, reconnue et assumée. Peut-être peut-on avancer, au vu des publications de l'auteur, que Meylan loue inconsciemment dans l'œuvre pédagogique coubertinienne, les résonnances pestaloziennes, généreuses et populaires, que l'on peut trouver, en effet, dans l'œuvre de Coubertin. Mais de démonstration explicite, point ! Meylan pose un axiome, le mécanisme mis en place va bloquer la critique pendant des décennies. Coubertin ne nous aide pas plus à cerner les fondements de son humanisme. Il nous faut en chercher ailleurs les raisons et les motivations.

Nous avançons que, formé par les textes grecs et latins anciens au cours de ses humanités de collège, conforté, durant sa vie d'homme, par la lecture de l'œuvre de Sénèque et par un commerce mythique avec la Grèce hellénistique, Coubertin fut un disciple de la philosophie stoïcienne. Les humanités classiques du collège Saint-Ignace que fréquente enfant le jeune Pierre, fin du XIXe siècle, sont celles même définies par les Jésuites deux siècles plus tôt. Le pouvoir sur l'homme et sur les hommes, et donc la puissance, est la conséquence d'une longue ascèse : le Roi-Soleil, comme ses commis, doivent subir la rude contrainte des syntaxes grecque et latine. Depuis la création de l'Ordre, rien n'a changé, le *ratio studorium* est le même, les textes choisis prônent à jamais l'honneur du rang et la grandeur du sacrifice : faire face et servir, telle est la loi. Le Père Martin, maître de la classe de rhétorique, ne professe pas d'autre morale, celle même, héroïque et silencieuse, qu'illustrent la vie des hommes illustres et cette vie des saints et des martyrs que lit au jeune Pierre, à la veillée, Marie-Marcelle Gigault de Crisenoy de Catteville, marquise de Mirville, sa mère : « La vie, disait Jésus, personne ne me la prend, je la donne... » Cette éthique sans concession de l'honneur et du devoir, colore tous les comportements, façonne toutes les attitudes de l'élève des Jésuites. Elle est, par voie de conséquence, l'impératif catégorique de la classe sociale des Coubertin, sans doute comparable économiquement à la tranche supérieure de la moyenne bourgeoisie, mais dont elle entend différer par l'excellence et l'élégance de la droiture morale : noblesse ne peut déchoir !

Il y a de la grandeur dans cette tension, de la dignité dans ce comportement, et sans nul doute, conséquence des bouleversements politiques, bien des misères cachées. Coubertin ne déroge pas. C'est l'attitude même d'Étienne de Crussenne, son alter-ego dans *Le roman d'un rallié* :

> La vie est simple parce que la lutte est simple. Le bon lutteur recule, il ne s'abandonne point, il ne cède, il ne renonce jamais. Si l'impossible se lève devant lui, il se détourne et va plus loin. Si le souffle lui manque, il se repose, et il attend. S'il est mis hors de combat, il encourage ses frères de sa parole et de sa présence. Et quand bien même tout s'écroule autour de lui, le désespoir ne pénètre pas en lui[10].

Cet appel au bonheur par l'usage de la vertu, cette image emblématique de l'effort et du courage, résument « la philosophie pratique dont s'inspirent la plupart des écrits de l'auteur[11] » et les attitudes d'une vie. La conscience tranquille, l'esprit libre, dressé contre les malheurs familiaux et les aléas de la vie publique, Coubertin, toute sa vie en effet, poursuivra sa croisade, impavide, sans jamais succomber aux sirènes de l'ambition et de la renommée.

En 1902 (il a trente-neuf ans), dans la Revue du Pays de Caux[12], qu'il vient de créer, il invite les jeunes hobereaux normands à relire un texte de Goethe, traduit d'un auteur anglais : « Tenez-vous bien en selle, et allez de l'avant [...] ». Déjà sa devise est arrêtée : « Voir loin, parler franc, agir ferme ». De même accepte-t-il avec enthousiasme pour le Mouvement olympique, celle du Père Didon : « *Citius, Altius, Fortius* ». Ses amis seront des acteurs de l'histoire : Théodore Roosevelt, Jules Simon, Jules Grévy, Delcassé, nouveaux conquérants de l'espace et du temps, au service de la seconde révolution industrielle et des conquêtes coloniales. Ce qui exige, à hauteur d'homme : effort, sacrifice, souffrances — même si les buts sont contestables.

Rien n'autorise à penser que Pierre de Coubertin soit consciemment un disciple de la Stoa, même si Meylan, le concernant, cite Épictète le Boiteux : « Je ne m'inquiète que des choses qui sont à moi — que nul ne peut contraindre, et qui sont libres par nature ; c'est là qu'est pour moi le bien réel, que les choses soient ce qu'elles sont : j'y suis indifférent[13]. » Nous pensons plutôt qu'il ne fait que refléter l'air du temps, et pas seulement parce que fils de famille, « homme du monde plein de généreuses intentions[14] ». Au même moment, dans les lycées publics, dans les écoles normales d'instituteurs (où jusqu'à la dernière guerre les sonneries de clairon scandaient la vie scolaire), le même humanisme, «dressé», en appelait à une France virile, apte à la revanche et aux conquêtes coloniales. Et il apparaît bien que le stoïcisme soit là, comme au IVe siècle, la réponse adéquate, en tant que philosophie et pratique de l'existence, à une époque troublée de cassure historique. Le stoïcisme est bien alors remède contre les calamités publiques et viatique pour une génération inquiète: «La période présente n'est pas une période de calme, il y a vraiment de la violence dans l'air[15].» Or Coubertin assigne au néo-olympisme d'enseigner le bonheur par le mépris des contingences. Il est donc logique de rechercher, dans la philosophie de l'Olympisme moderne, les linéaments du stoïcisme ancien.

À l'exemple du stoïcisme ancien, le néo-olympisme est une philosophie du tout, et pas seulement un recueil de pratique morale. C'est un système construit, qui se caractérise par un entraînement mental et exprime une conception globale du monde: le cosmopolitisme[16]. L'Olympisme coubertinien est lieu d'exercice et d'entraînement à la sagesse. Il est défini, par son auteur, comme une religion face aux dieux de l'Olympe et/ou au Dieu judéo-chrétien: la réforme proposée de l'éducation de l'adolescence au XXe siècle[17] pose le rapport du profane et du sacré, ainsi que sa position au monde, et devient non seulement indicateur sensible des passions humaines et cadre de leurs résolutions, mais surtout passage obligé vers le divin: l'allégeance à la Grèce antique est patente, l'humanisme de Coubertin, tout comme celui des stoïciens, est un existentialisme. De là, cette vision constante de réalité, vision terrienne, paysanne, s'il en est — et Coubertin est toujours un paysan normand!

C'est évidemment dans son programme de réforme pour l'enseignement secondaire, que se lit le mieux ce souci matériel du concret: des champs objectifs de la connaissance y sont tracés, qui tous ont pour visée (astronomie, géologie, biologie, droit, économie, linguistique, géopolitique, histoire) d'aider l'adolescent à se créer lui-même en créant le cosmos. De ce point de vue, un rôle capital est dévolu à l'histoire et à la longue durée historique. Il y a, dans cet humanisme, une forte influence du paganisme ancien, une sorte de souffle originel qui mêle intimement la nature et la pensée, la matière et la forme, le cosmos et l'individu, l'essence et l'existence. On sent dans la vie de Coubertin, comme dans son œuvre, une tension constante. L'homme est debout, vibrant, frêle et fort, offrant à l'instar de ses ancêtres croisés, une prouesse, une excellence, un chef-d'œuvre toujours remis en question. Le destin guette l'homme coubertinien.

Pour autant, cet homme ne démissionne pas. La liberté, qu'il conquiert durement, n'est pas — comme on l'a reproché aux stoïciens — un esclavage intériorisé. L'*homo-olympicus* est un conquérant de l'impossible, il lutte avec autant d'abnégation dans la vie que sur le stade. Il y a en lui un accord subtil de rupture et de continuité, de discontinuité et de persistance, une dialectique induite, dont la conquête du record, d'essence temporaire, pourrait bien être l'image et le symbole. Prométhée et Sysyphe, l'athlète coubertinien, tendu vers un improbable état d'eurythmie qui l'intègrera au cosmos, est un paradigme de vertu, de sagesse, et donc, de bonheur. C'est cette fusion de l'être avec la nature, cette purgation des passions par l'ascèse corporelle et morale, cet effort volontaire vers un état de vertu, qui fonde l'éthique stoïcienne de l'humanisme coubertinien.

Mais, pour atteindre à cet état, l'individu doit apprendre les règles d'une rhétorique qui définissent les fins et les moyens, et impose les devoirs. Le maître des portiques n'est pas seulement un philosophe, il est également un pédagogue, un guide soucieux du destin de son disciple, mais d'un disciple ouvert aux problèmes de la Cité. Car le but du philosophe-pédagogue est non pas de faire des savants, mais des hommes de bien. Epictète s'insurgeait déjà contre le psittacisme, Coubertin également: «Il en résulte dans le jugement naissant, une sorte d'encombrement qui l'empêche de s'exercer librement[18].»

Coubertin ne se veut rien d'autre que d'être un maître à penser, à la manière des stoïciens. Son Sinaï se trouve Villa Mon Repos (où siège alors le CIO). C'est de là, sur la montagne, qu'il dicte les Tables de la Loi. Ainsi approfondit-il le sillon primordial, sème-t-il avec encore plus de conviction. Il est en Stoïcie aux pires moments du destin, conforté par la lecture des œuvres complètes de Sénèque, qu'il possède en bonne place dans sa bibliothèque[19] et dont on sait par des témoins oculaires (Mme Zanchi, Dr Messerli) qu'il en avait fait son livre de chevet. En miroir de cette somme, les écrits de Coubertin sont à la fois enseignement philosophique et exercices de méditation, réflexion sur l'homme et les civilisations, et guide d'entraînement mental[20] pour la recherche du bonheur individuel dans et par l'action sociale. Coubertin, comme tous les stoïciens, comme Sénèque si évidemment, se veut mentor du citoyen et moraliste de la société.

Mais peut-on réduire au seul paramètre du stoïcisme les fondements de l'humanisme coubertinien? N'est-ce-pas oublier un peu vite le philhellénisme intégral de Coubertin? Car Pierre de Coubertin est toujours le servant d'une Grèce totale et globalisante. Sa Grèce est celle de Missolonghi, et de Byron, de Gœthe, et des Romantiques. Elle est aussi celle d'une Olympie mythique, revisitée et mise à l'honneur par les découvertes d'Abel Blouet, et les fouilles des archéologues allemands[21].

Pour les allemands, en quête de racines culturelles et d'unité nationale, la Grèce est dorienne. Pour la France et pour Coubertin elle ne peut être qu'athénienne: «Sparte n'est qu'un sinistre réduit de la barbarie dorienne[22].» Ainsi l'adolescence de Coubertin est-elle bercée par les chants d'une Grèce mythique et réifiée. Le jeune Pierre a lu Homère dans le texte, traduit Thucidite, pris connaissance d'Hérodote, il écrit le grec ancien. En 1926, dans *Histoire universelle*, au chapitre Hellénisme, il cite peu deux hellénistes contemporains (Reinach, Croiset), mais se réfère aux classiques grecs anciens dont les œuvres sont alors le miel et le lait du collégien français. N'en doutons pas, c'est à ses souvenirs de collège — et qui plus est de collège de Jésuites, où le culte des belles lettres est encore plus poussé qu'ailleurs — que Coubertin se réfère quand il traite de la Grèce antique. Mais il paraît non moins évident que cette Grèce là est a-historique, pétrifiée dans le temps, présentée à l'admiration des fidèles sous une chape ornementale. La Grèce que vénère Coubertin n'est donc pas celle du Ve siècle, mais une icône sacrée, ou plutôt une succession de fresques religieuses, brossées pendant tout le XIXe siècle par les intellectuels, les artistes, et les peuples d'Europe occidentale. C'est une Grèce hellénistique idéalisée, portée à l'empyrée des cultures et des civilisations, mère utopique du «*kalos kagatos*», qui autorise tous les fantasmes de démocratie, d'esthétisme: «de sport, de civisme, et d'art[23]». C'est cette Grèce sublimée, essentiellement masculine, paradis de l'éphèbe, et qui *nie ontologiquement* la femme, l'esclave, le métèque, qui est le lieu de vie et l'espace de rêve de Pierre de Coubertin. C'est le mythe de cette Grèce, qui irrigue l'imagination, fertilise les sens de Coubertin, et fait jaillir le flot puissant de sa création.

Exemple de cet attachement inconditionnel à cette grécitude imaginée: la structure de construction de la philosophie olympique. C'est le panthéisme grec ancien qui compose le corpus religieux du néo-olympisme. C'est à la religion de l'Olympe que le christianisme médiéval européen et l'anglicanisme victorien viennent s'agréger. Et non l'inverse... Et c'est bien en effet à cette Grèce là, imaginaire et romantique, qu'il faut se reférer quand on tente de saisir le climat intellectuel et sensible dans lequel baigna Coubertin durant sa vie entière. Coubertin, en effet, est toujours dans le moindre de ses actes, dans la plus quotidienne de ses démarches, le fils de la pensée grecque, telle qu'on l'enseignait et l'imaginait à son époque. Il l'est tout spécialement par la place qu'il assume à l'âme, au regard du corps, et par son ethnocentrisme. Esprit cosmopolite, tolérant, sceptique, Pierre de Coubertin est l'un des derniers rhéteurs classiques du XIXe siècle. Aristote avance : « L'âme est la forme d'un corps organisé ayant la vie en puissance » — Coubertin entend que le muscle rende partout les armes à l'esprit. Socrate place au sommet des « trois âmes » la raison, laquelle proscrit sentiments et passions — Coubertin précise à l'intention de l'adolescent : « Si le sport lui a fait des épaules larges [...] c'est pour faire taire ses nerfs et le rendre maître de lui[24]. » Faut-il noter ici en outre le « Connais-toi toi-même », éthique et déontologie de l'athlète contemporain.

Un parallèle s'impose par ailleurs entre l'ethnocentrisme des stoïciens, pour qui le savant est l'homme parfait qui maîtrise parfaitement la langue grecque dans un univers réglé « par une raison qui s'apparente à la syntaxe hellénique[25] », et l'ethnocentrisme de Coubertin qui, vingt siècles plus tard, fait de l'homme jeune adulte occidental, le levier et le levain d'une mission mondialiste. L'homme coubertinien, pénétré des lumières d'un certain cosmopolitisme, créateur d'une nouvelle solidarité inter-planétaire, ouvert donc aux « barbares », reste cependant fidèle à son propre noyau ethnique. Il est le maillon final de la ligne évolutive d'un homme occidental, au delà duquel apparaissent quelques nébuleuses, où se situent « des êtres plus ou moins hybrides » (races non-blanches, femmes, ajoutons-nous) « dont l'humanité est moindre[26] ». Ainsi nous semble-t-il possible d'avancer que l'humanisme de Pierre de Coubertin fut profondément le fait d'un stoïcisme induit, d'autant plus réel et puissant qu'il s'inscrivit dans une grécitude rêvée et fantasmatique.

Pour autant, le problème ne saurait être correctement posé, si, conjointement, n'était mise en relief la solitude existentielle de Coubertin. Solitude de l'autodidacte, telle pourrait bien être l'image qui s'impose de Coubertin, cinquante ans après sa mort. En dehors des structures de l'enseignement supérieur français l'homme a pris le temps de réflexion qui sied : le dandy ne se presse pas, il savoure ! Un jeune rentier pourvu n'est pas comptable de sa vie comme un bourgeois affairiste, ou un prolétaire contraint... Mais, rançon de l'éclectisme et de la distanciation de caste, le dandy est seul.

La solitude existentielle de Coubertin

Dès le départ de sa croisade, Coubertin est solitaire. Parce que, dès sa naissance, il est intelligent, sensible, lucide, parce que l'histoire contemporaine le presse et que les grands aïeux l'exigent, il est autre, et se situe ailleurs. Il est ainsi, en marge, en attendant d'être extérieur, puis rebelle. Le collège et sa discipline formelle, militaire d'essence, est une caserne où il étouffe et enrage. Les promenades silencieuses, comme celles des moines de Saint-Wandrille, près de Mirville, les stupides séances de gymnastique suédoise, le manque d'espace et de liberté — partout l'aliénation du corps — l'obéissance passive à une scolastique désuète, vont faire prendre conscience à l'enfant, puis à l'adolescent, du devoir de révolte. Rue Oudinot, dans les salons feutrés du Paris nobiliaire, les sentiments sont écrêtés, les passions dissoutes, dans un climat ouaté de passéisme et de convenance. Pierre est le plus jeune des enfants, le plus avancé dans le temps historique : ses frères, sa sœur, ont été de plain-pied les enfants de la Restauration. Lui, est celui d'un aujourd'hui de la défaite et de la peur. Il est seul, écorché dans sa sensibilité et son patriotisme, hésitant dans ses réactions, encore gauche dans ses comportements. La crise d'identification de l'adolescence ne fait que renforcer son opposition au milieu familial où il est né. Il est l'exception, l'hérétique politique, comme hier le grand-oncle janséniste, dont le souvenir est la tare qu'il importe de rayer de la mémoire familiale.

Certes, le « sang » le guide, cette conscience aiguë d'être et de devoir. Mais il est sans repères, à côté d'un père qui vit dans les conventions d'une mythologie légitimiste et cléricale à peine transposée dans le cadre d'un académisme pictural, et d'une mère pieuse, confite en dévotion dans les œuvres de charité, la tête ailleurs, dans les Saintes Écritures. Seul il se dresse, volontaire, non sans autoritarisme, non sans violence. Comme ses ancêtres vikings, il n'aime rien tant que d'être à la proue du drakkar, face aux vents contraires et aux récifs dangereux. À vingt ans, capitaine courageux, il aborde aux Îles, contre l'opinion anglophobe du milieu politique et culturel qu'il fréquente et subit. Quant au Nouveau Monde, pour lequel il manifeste un enthousiasme tempéré souvent prémonitoire, qui alors, parmi les notables de l'aristocratie terrienne de province, hormis Tocqueville, pourrait s'intéresser à lui ?

Et c'est bien seul, l'enseignement des Jésuites n'y prédispose pas, qu'il se tournera vers l'histoire contemporaine. C'est ainsi, nous semble-t-il, qu'il faut interpréter, à l'âge de ses vingt ans, l'adieu aux armes, au sacerdoce, . . . et à l'université ! L'entrée à l'École libre des sciences politiques est particulièrement significative de ce point de vue. N'y entraient alors que les enfants de la haute bourgeoisie, et fort peu les jeunes aristocrates, traditionnellement destinés aux carrières des armes et de la diplomatie. Or Coubertin, d'un mouvement qui surprend et choque son entourage, se dirige vers cette école peu connue, sans renom particulier, mais qui est le creuset d'une pensée moderne libérale.

Seul encore, dans son milieu, quand il se prend de passion pour le sport anglo-saxon. Car l'image qu'ont du sport Marie-Marcelle, sa mère, et Charles-Louis, son père, n'est rien d'autre que négative. Hormis les promenades au Bois de Boulogne, en coupé, quelques galops au Pré-Catelan, on tient pour vulgaire, voire du plus grand grossier, l'exhibitionnisme du pédestrian ou du leveur de fonte. Pour l'aristocrate catholique et romain, le sport est une invention diabolique de ces pornographes dont on voit les ravages dans le domaine des arts plastiques. Quant à la phtisie qu'il engendre, mieux vaut ne pas en parler ! Coubertin avance seul dans la réflexion et l'action. Autodidacte de l'Olympisme, il rédige des rapports à l'intention des parlementaires et des hommes d'état, écrit des articles multiples dans la presse et dans les revues françaises et étrangères. Certes a-t-il avec lui quelques « ouvriers de la première heure[27] », mais il est « en avant », « en éclaireur », peu souvent compris et suivi. Mais quel charisme !

Dans le secret le plus absolu, il décide, seul, sans consultations préalables, du rétablissement des Jeux olympiques. À la tête du Comité international olympique, son action est celle d'un pionnier solitaire. Épistolier infatigable, il correspond avec de multiples correspondants de par le monde, sans le secours d'aucun secrétaire et d'une machine à écrire, dont il refuse. . . « la dictature ». Seul il vit, près d'une femme originale, autoritaire, qui partage ses intérêts et l'aime vraisemblablement, mais ne peut se fixer, et l'obligera à vivre à l'hôtel toute sa vie. Comme seul, contre l'avis familial, il avait décidé d'épouser « cette protestante » ! Seul encore, déchiré, angoissé, il devra faire face à la solitude murée de ses deux enfants, atteints dans leur équilibre nerveux. Seul, il prend en 1925, à Prague, la décision de se retirer de la présidence du Comité international olympique, surprenant tous ses pairs. Seul, il décide alors de créer l'Union pédagogique universelle, puis le Bureau international de pédagogie sportive. Seul, il lance un Message à la jeunesse américaine[28]. Seul il meurt, anonyme, le 2 septembre 1937, dans un banal parc de la ville de Genève : l'aigle meurt toujours foudroyé.

Seul ? Peut-être moins qu'il ne semble. Coubertin vit dans un rêve façonné à ses rêves, il habite les cultures du monde. Là, en compagnie des plus grands, Lao-Tseu, Jean Huss, Charlemagne, mais aussi Théodore Roosevelt, Pasteur, le Tsar de toutes les Russies, il dialogue sur l'unicité du monde et le progrès humain[29]. Pour lui l'histoire remplace le fatum. L'histoire, qui construit l'homme, est en effet mère de l'angoisse : les civilisations sont fragiles, les famines, les pestes, les guerres, les guettent. L'Europe, qu'il aime tant, n'a-t-elle pas failli mourir récemment par la faute de ses politiciens ? Mais l'angoisse est roborative, il suffit que l'homme le veuille. Alors, passées les affres du doute, les citoyens, régénérés, atteindront à la vérité. L'homme, agent actif des civilisations, à la fois objet et sujet, construira son existence et fera l'histoire. On songe à Kirkegaard: «Par l'angoisse, vers la hauteur...»

Le record, à ce titre, nous paraît exemplaire. Pour Coubertin, le concept de record est l'essence de l'athlétisme (du sport dans la terminologie de l'époque). Le record est croyance dans la recherche de la perfection, mais risque mêlé d'incertitude et de doute. L'idée de record pose un questionnement sans solution de l'existence et de l'essence. C'est un problème de tension et de limite auquel aucune solution ne peut être donnée: le record se situe toujours *a posteriori*. Mais le record fonde l'homme. L'angoisse, qui le sous-tend, met l'homme et l'humanité en situation, dans l'espace et dans le temps. Ainsi l'Olympisme, tension angoissée vers la transcendance, renvoie l'homme à une vision spiritualiste de ses origines. Mais, arrivé trop tard, l'homme coubertinien peine à entrer en contact avec Dieu. Les thèmes fondamentaux de l'angoisse et de l'éternel retour, majeurs dans l'existentialisme, se retrouvent dans l'œuvre de Pierre de Coubertin.

Mais Coubertin ne se veut pas seul au monde. Voyageur sans frontières, esprit fraternel, il recherche passionnément le contact des autres hommes. Il entend que, dans un respect mutuel, les civilisations se reconnaissent: L'Olympisme sera ce vecteur concret de communication dans un siècle de cosmopolitisme, sinon d'internationalisme. C'est par cette perception sensible du monde que l'homme se mettra en situation d'exister. C'est l'histoire qui sera sa richesse, son levain, et son drame. L'eurythmie, et le record, seront les symboles de cette richesse et de cette précarité.

On peut avancer que pour Coubertin, le record, moment intense de vibration interne, de communication avec l'Autre dans la transcendance de l'espèce, crée l'homme. Et que c'est l'angoisse qui permet d'accéder à ce moment, exceptionnel, qu'est l'excellence par le record. Peut-on vraiment penser que si Coubertin n'avait été un créateur solitaire et angoissé, le Mouvement olympique et le néo-olympisme auraient été si forts et si puissants? Les fondements stoïciens de son humanisme et de son philhellénisme mis en relief, la statue du Commandeur mieux éclairée, il paraît possible d'envisager l'attitude de Pierre de Coubertin face au problème du sport féminin olympique.

Coubertin et le sport féminin

Fin du XIXe siècle, en France, à l'âge où Coubertin entre en lice, le mouvement sportif féminin n'est le fait que de quelques originales de l'aristocratie — telle la Duchesse d'Abrantes. Les paysannes et les ouvrières, accablées de travail, usées par les maternités, ont évidemment d'autres soucis. Seule la femme de la haute aristocratie, et à un degré moindre, de la bourgeoisie d'affaires — et parisienne de surcroît, peut s'adonner à quelques sports tolérés: équitation (en amazone), tennis, natation, bicyclette. La mode tolère des défis sportifs pour les femmes, mais seulement en privé. En public, ce serait une irréparable faute de goût.

Le sport n'est alors, pour la femme dans le siècle, qu'un aimable délassement, un passe-temps hygiénique de désœuvrée. Et encore au prix d'une mutilation: le corps de la femme doit rester dérobé aux regards, caché, engoncé dans des jupes amples et des corsages à manches longues; c'est le costume des béguines. Montrer son corps n'est permis qu'aux courtisanes et aux prostituées: une dame bien née ignore l'érotisme et ne saurait éprouver une quelconque jouissance corporelle. La révolte féministe contre ce corsetage physique et moral suscite l'ironie de l'opinion et les brocards des hommes. Car la vie privée de la femme, comme celle de la Cité, appartient à l'homme.

Dans la famille des Crisenoy, et celle des Coubertin, les femmes sont respectées et honorées. Elles ont reçu une bonne instruction, mais à domicile, du fait d'un précepteur, frère des écoles chrétiennes. La mère de Pierre lit Virgile dans le texte, sa grand-mère est cultivée. Pourtant, les convenances veulent qu'elles ne sortent pas du domaine ou de l'hôtel particulier, sauf pour aller à la messe ou rendre visite à leurs pauvres, et toujours accompagnées. Partout, le mari les chaperonne. Quand la famille part en voyage, à Rome, Frohsdorf, ou Étretat, Marie-Marcelle, pourtant Marquise de Mirville, voyage sous la protection de Charles, cachée aux regards indiscrets par les rideaux du phaéton ou du wagon de chemin de fer. Il en est de même dans toutes les familles aristocrates ou bourgeoises: propriétaire du mari, la femme légitime reste dérobée au monde.

Ce n'est qu'à l'intérieur de la maison, au sein du domaine à la fois lieu de civilisation et entité économique que la femme de l'aristocratie et de la haute bourgeoisie, jouit d'une liberté concédée, dans le cadre rigoureux de conventions sociales codées. L'homme lui reconnaît le droit et lui concède le devoir de gérer l'économie domestique, de procréer pour sa descendance, et de veiller à l'éducation des enfants. C'est la loi du patio. Telle est l'image de la femme que le jeune Pierre va intégrer et faire sienne: celle de la mère et de l'épouse, aimée et respectée, mais soumise. Mais c'est également celle que lui renvoie la science française de l'époque: le florilège est révélateur.

Le docteur Broca (1824-1880), père de la craniométrie française, fondateur de la Société d'anthropologie de Paris en 1859, savant reconnu et honoré par la République, écrit en 1861: «Il ne faut pas perdre de vue que la femme est en moyenne un peu moins intelligente que l'homme». Et d'écrire que l'homme se trouve au sommet d'une pyramide, et qu'au dessous se trouvent «les noirs, les femmes, et les pauvres[30]».

Gustave Le Bon, qui fut un chercheur majeur dans le champ de la psychologie sociale, écrit en 1879 (Coubertin a seize ans), que chez la femme «L'infériorité de l'intelligence est trop évidente pour être contestée[31]». Et encore:

> Les crânes des femmes se rapprochent plus par le volume de ceux des gorilles que des crânes des sexes masculins les plus développés [...] Tous les psychologistes qui ont étudié l'intelligence des femmes ailleurs que chez les romanciers et les poètes, reconnaissent aujourd'hui qu'elles représentent les formes les plus inférieures de l'évolution humaine et sont beaucoup plus près des enfants et des sauvages que de l'homme adulte civilisé [...] Vouloir donner aux deux sexes, comme on commence à le faire en Amérique, la même éducation [...] est une chimère dangereuse[32].

Hervé, élève de Broca note, en 1881: «Les hommes de race noire ont un encéphale qui n'est guère plus pesant que celui des femmes de race blanche[33].» Gould, à qui nous empruntons ces citations concluera: «Les racistes et sexistes scientifiques ne réservent pas leur appellation d'infériorité à un seul groupe désavantagé, mais race, sexe et classe vont de pair, et chacun d'eux sert de support aux autres[34].»

Cette image erronée de l'infantilisme féminin, de la femme confinée «aux tâches d'immanence», que dénoncera plus tard Simone de Beauvoir[35] se superposera tout naturellement à celle, révélée et imposée, dès son premier contact avec les humanités classiques. La femme athénienne de la période hellénistique, alors que les Jeux olympiques sont à leur apogée, reste en effet le modèle coubertinien de la femme et de la mère. La femme grecque d'alors, même «citoyenne», reste exclue de toute fonction politique, civique, ou juridique. Tout au plus, occupe-t-elle des fonctions religieuses mineures. Toute la vie, elle reste sous la coupe d'un tuteur *(kurios)*: le père, l'époux, le fils si elle devient veuve, un mâle de la belle famille si elle n'a pas de fils. Elle n'a aucun libre choix en amour, par l'engué, elle devient bien-meuble de la famille du mari. Certes, elle peut divorcer, se plaindre au juge, mais ne peut qu'accepter la conciliation ou la répudiation proposée[36].

Malgré des exemples illustres, mais aberrants, la femme grecque «citoyenne» de la période hellénistique reste une esclave dans une prison dorée. Ce n'est que peu à peu, devenue commerçante par suite de l'enrichissement des domaines, qu'elle acquerra une plus grande mobilité et un statut social plus autonome. «La race des femmes», la «race maudite des femmes» (Hésiode — La Théogonie) est marquée au fer par le mythe de Pandore[37].

En fait, Coubertin intègre cette conception par le détour des théories de Le Play, dont on sait quelles influences elles exercèrent sur son œuvre. La cellule chrétienne de base est la famille patriarcale: Dieu existe qui délègue au *pater familias* l'autorité, garante de l'équilibre humain et familial. Transgresser cet ordre c'est, pour Le Play et pour Coubertin, sombrer dans l'anarchie, c'est-à-dire l'union libre et le socialisme[38]. Coubertin marque l'importance de «l'organisation aryenne de la famille», d'après laquelle, sous la prépondérance de l'homme, celui-ci et son épouse composent avec les enfants un foyer harmonieux et puissant basé sur le respect de la dignité humaine. Et il en déduit qu'il importe d'accorder l'éducation de la femme à sa mission future: «Les matières enseignées seront les mêmes que celles des hommes. Mais l'esprit pédagogique sera différent». La jeune fille sera initiée à l'économie domestique: «architecture morale d'une maison, envisagée elle-même comme la cellule sociale[39]».

La mysoginie de Coubertin s'exprime sans ambiguïté: «La veulerie présente [des parents] est pitoyable. Comment élèvent-ils leurs enfants et surtout leurs filles? Aujourd'hui, dans un grand nombre de pays, c'est la fille qui corrompt les garçons, mais les parents encouragent le garçon lui-même à se montrer précocement flirteur, avisé et roublard, ils s'en amusent [...][40].» Sans doute cette mysoginie, outre ses racines livresques, a pris naissance dans la société sans femmes que fréquente Coubertin: le collège des Jésuites — où l'éducation pédérastique, rapport privilégié entre le maître et le disciple, est vivace[41] le Jockey Club, l'Union sportive française des sports athlétiques (USFSA), les milieux ministériels qu'il approche, plus tard les cercles sportifs, le Comité international olympique. Peut-être, cette mysoginie se fortifia-t-elle inconsciemment par suite de son expérience maritale: on sait combien Madame de Coubertin, pourtant si dévouée à l'ambition de son mari, était une femme de caractère et de forte autorité. Ce qui est patent, c'est l'aversion de Coubertin pour le féminisme, même s'il reconnaît au mouvement d'avoir mis en lumière l'urgence de certaines réformes. Mais le féminisme est coupable à ses yeux d'aider à assouplir et relâcher, un à un, les liens séculaires qui assujettissent le sujet au souverain, les fidèles à l'Église, la famille à son chef, l'ouvrier à son patron.

La cause est une fois pour toute entendue, le sport est une affaire d'hommes. Tout au plus, Coubertin concède-t-il à la femme le pré carré de la culture physique, dans l'intérêt physiologique et moral de cette «race» inférieure, sentimentale, spontanée, infantile, que l'homme, tuteur naturel, doit protéger malgré elle. Car il est fallacieux de penser que le sport puisse la moraliser, la «rebronzer»:

> Cette jeunesse féminine dont je viens de parler avec une cruauté justifiée, n'est-elle pas moralisable par le sport? Je n'en crois rien du tout. De la culture physique sportive, oui, cela est excellent pour la jeune fille, pour la femme, mais cette rudesse de l'effort masculin dont le principe prudemment mais résolument appliqué est à la base de la pédagogie sportive, il faut grandement le redouter pour l'être féminin. Il ne sera obtenu physiquement qu'à l'aide de nerfs mobilisés au-delà de leur rôle, moralement que par neutralisation des qualités féminines les plus précieuses[42].

Les fonctions et les rôles de chaque sexe, conformes à l'ordre naturel, doivent donc être rigoureusement séparés, y compris dans le domaine du sport. Là, comme ailleurs, la femme doit être protégée par l'homme, y compris contre elle-même. En aucun cas, elle ne peut échapper à son statut social minoré.

Dans la *Réforme de la charte sportive*, publiée juste quelques années avant sa mort, la chose est clairement dite : il faut supprimer cette détestable mode d'admettre les femmes aux compétitions réservées aux hommes. C'est non seulement un problème d'ordre hygiénique, c'est un parti-pris de civilisation, une question d'ordre éthique ; « Le sport est une passion qui peut engendrer du grabuge [...] Eh! bien, ce grabuge n'est pas fait pour les femmes [...] la supériorité de l'humanité est accordée au sexe capable de tuer, non à celui qui engendre[43]. »

La motivation militante de Coubertin est donc puissante et agressive : nous le voyons littéralement prisonnier d'une idée qui va de plus en plus se scléroser, aliéner tout esprit critique, voire tout bon sens élémentaire. Au seuil de la mort, Coubertin persiste et signe. Ainsi, navigateur solitaire d'une Grèce mythique, celle du héros de l'épopée et du soldat-citoyen, admirateur inconditionnel d'un arnoldisme conquérant, mysogine par éducation et sans doute par fait de vie, Coubertin ne sera que le chantre d'un Olympisme mâle : « Le seul véritable héros olympique, je l'ai toujours dit, c'est l'adulte mâle individuel[44]. »

Si les femmes, en 1900 (Paris) puis en 1904 (Saint-Louis), entrent par la petite porte dans l'arène des Jeux, et seulement pour le golf, le tennis, puis le tir à l'arc, c'est contre son gré. Si en 1908, à Londres, quarante-trois femmes élargissent la brèche dans trois sports : patinage, tennis, tir à l'arc, c'est encore contre sa volonté. Mais les menaces de désordre, brandis par la suffragette britannique Emmeline Pankhurst ont raison des réticences des membres du Comité international olympique, pourtant totalement dévoués à leur président. En 1912, aux Jeux de Stockholm, Coubertin écrit : « [...] Une olympiade femelle serait impratique, inintéressante, inesthétique, et incorrecte[45]. » En cela, il est suivi par les dirigeants du Comité national olympique américain, opposés à la présence des femmes dans les épreuves de natation, sous prétexte qu'elles ne porteraient pas de jupes.

Petit à petit, pourtant, l'opinion publique évolue, et, péniblement, les femmes, qui ont remplacé avec héroïsme les hommes dans les usines durant le premier conflit mondial, conquièrent droit de cité aux Jeux. Mais la route sera longue ! Seules, treize femmes participent aux premiers Jeux d'hiver à Chamonix (1924). Elles devront attendre trente-deux années pour avoir la permission de s'aligner dans des épreuves de ski nordique, trente-six pour être admises à concourir en patinage de vitesse, et quarante en luge[46]. Ce n'est qu'en 1928, à Amsterdam, qu'elles seront présentes dans cinq épreuves d'athlétisme.

Bravant l'opinion publique de plus en plus favorable, livrant un combat d'arrière garde avec la pugnacité que l'on sait contre des dirigeantes sportives remarquables — telles la française Alice Milliat et la britannique Sophie Elliot Lynn — Coubertin freine des quatre fers. Impavide, il se tient dans le camp de la pire réaction antiféministe. En 1928, il condamne les décisions du Congrès de Barcelone, qui ouvre les Jeux à l'athlétisme féminin. En 1931, confirmant ses positions culturelles, il rappelle les déclarations du Pape Pie XI : « Cette décision [celle de 1928] se trouve avoir coincidé avec la condamnation solennelle prononcée par le Pape Pie XI contre la participation féminine aux concours publics. Déjà, à deux reprises, le Souverain Pontife avait fait entendre de sévères paroles d'avertissement[47]. » Ce n'est un secret pour personne que le rénovateur des Jeux a toujours été un adversaire déclaré de la participation féminine [à ces Jeux], car, précise-t-il, enfonçant une fois de plus le clou, ce serait contraire « au plus grand idéal viril, qui fut, quoi qu'on en prétende, celui de l'athlétisme antique qui triompha complètement à Olympie[48] ». En 1934, il continue de tonner « contre cet athlétisme [...] qui devrait être exclu des Jeux Olympiques[49] ». En filigrane se lit sa certitude: glorifier la femme, c'est nier l'héroïsme viril de l'éphèbe triomphant.

Tant de persévérance dans la foi, tant de passion dans l'idéologie, tant d'innocence dans l'erreur, méritaient bien le long détour auquel nous nous sommes livrés. Coubertin, créateur puissant, donne l'exemple d'un homme de culture engagé dans les combats du siècle, lumineux par ses prémonitions, grand par l'architecture de ses constructions, courageux jusqu'au sacrifice, mais lourdement engoncé dans la gangue des idées reçues et l'imaginaire des fantasmes. Homme d'une carrure historique, sentinelle fragile, contradictoire, à l'interface des civilisations qui tente d'éclairer la marche cahoteuse de l'humanité. Homme debout, présent aux hommes, souffrant, angoissé, et qui, malgré des insuffisances et des erreurs que nous devons nous efforcer de comprendre, reste un paradigme pour le troisième millénaire.

NOTES ET REFERENCES

1. MacAloon JJ (1981) This great symbol: Pierre de Coubertin and the origins of the modern Olympic Games. Chicago: University of Chicago Press

2. Seillières E (1917) Pierre de Coubertin: un artisan d'énergie française. Paris: Didier

3. Müller N, Comité international Pierre de Coubertin (eds) (1987) L'actualité de Pierre de Coubertin. Rapport du symposium du 18 au 20 mars 1986 Université de Lausanne. Niedernhausen/Taunus: Schors-Verlag

4. Müller N, Comité international olympique (eds) (1986) Pierre de Coubertin. Textes choisis. Tome I: Révélation; Tome II: Olympisme; Tome III: Pratique sportive. Zürich: Weidmann

5. Meylan L (1941) L'humanisme intégral de Pierre de Coubertin. Lausanne p 16 [brochure]

6. Seillières E (1917) op cit

7. Ibid p 42

8. Meylan L (1941) op cit p 4

9. Ibid p 5

10. Coubertin P de (1902) Le roman d'un rallié. Auxerre: A Lasnier p 322

11. Reymond A et al (eds) (1933) Anthologie. Aix-en-Provence: Éditions Paul Roubaud. Répertoire des écrits, discours et conférences de Pierre de Coubertin — publié à l'occasion de sa 70e année, par souscription des Comités olympiques d'Égypte, de Grèce, de Lettonie, du Portugal, de Suède et de Suisse, de l'Union pédagogique universelle, et du Bureau international de pédagogie sportive, de la Société fédérale de gymnastique, de l'Association nationale d'éducation physique, de la Société suisse de football et d'athlétisme, de l'Union des sociétés athlétiques de Grèce et de divers groupements universitaires américains.

12. Coubertin P de (1902) Voir loin, parler franc, agir ferme. Revue du pays de Caux 1 p 3-4

13. Meylan L (1941) op cit p 3

14. Audin M (ed) (1896) Extrait de Revue des cours et conférences. Paris: Lecéne, Oudin et Cie p 1

15. Coubertin P de (1899) L'urgente réforme. La Nouvelle Revue 117 p 394 [In Müller N, Comité international olympique (eds) (1986) Pierre de Coubertin. Textes choisis. Tome I. Révélation p 186]

16. Coubertin P de (1912) L'Éducation des adolescents au XXe siècle. II: Éducation intellectuelle. Analyse universelle. Paris: Librairie Alcan [In Müller N, Comité international olympique (eds) (1986) Pierre de Coubertin. Textes choisis. Tome I. Révélation p 276-316]

17. Coubertin P de (1905) L'Éducation des adolescents au XXe siècle. I: L'éducation physique: la gymnastique utilitaire. Sauvetage — Défense — Locomotion. Paris: Librairie Alcan [In Müller N, Comité international olympique (eds) (1986) Pierre de Coubertin. Textes choisis. Tome III. Pratique portive p 481-555]; Coubertin P de (1912) L'Éducation des adolescents au XXe siècle. II: L'analyse universelle. Paris: Librairie Alcan [In Müller N, Comité international olympique (eds) (1986) Pierre de Coubertin. Textes choisis. Tome I. Révélation p 276-316]; Coubertin P de (1915) L'Éducation des adolescents au XXe siècle. III: L'éducation morale. Le respect mutuel. Paris: Librairie Alcan [In Müller N, Comité international olympique (eds) (1986) Pierre de Coubertin. Textes choisis. Tome I. Révélation p 317-50]

18. Coubertin P de (1901) Notes sur l'éducation publique. Paris: Hachette [Publié en partie in Müller N, Comité international olympique (eds) (1986) Pierre de Coubertin. Textes choisis. Tome I. Révélation p 194-273]

19. Catalogue de la bibliothèque du Baron Pierre de Coubertin — La Guilde du livre — Lausanne — 19 et 20 mai 1944

20. Coubertin P de (1912) op cit; et Coubertin P de (1915) op cit

21. Boulongne PY (1975) La vie et l'œuvre de Pierre de Coubertin: 1863-1937. Montréal: Léméac p 141 sq

22. Coubertin P de (1926-1927) Histoire Universelle. Aix-en-Provence: Société de l'histoire universelle

23. Ibid p 40

24. Coubertin P de (1934) Pédagogie sportive. Lausanne: Bureau international de pédagogie sportive p 136 [In Müller N, Comité international olympique (eds) (1986) Pierre de Coubertin. Textes choisis. Tome I. Révélation p 439]

25. Encylopaedia Universalis (1970) vol 15 p 394

26. Leroy-Gourhan E (1970) dans Encyclopaedia Universalis [Anthropologie] vol 2 p 52

27. Coubertin P de (1909) Une campagne de vingt-et-un ans. Paris: Librairie de l'éducation physique p 15

28. Coubertin P de (1934) Message to American Youth. [Version française: Message à la jeunesse américaine. Publié par «Associated Press» lors de la célébration du 40e anniversaire de la renaissance des Jeux olympiques] In Carl Diem Institut (1966) Pierre de Coubertin. L'idée olympique. Discours et essais. Schorndorf: Hofmann p 124-25 [In Müller N, Comité international olympique (eds) (1986) Pierre de Coubertin. Textes choisis. Tome I. Révélation p 488-89]

29. Coubertin P de (1926) op cit p 212

30. Jay Gould S (1983) La mal-mesure de l'homme. Paris: Ramsay 1983 p 70 sq

31. Ibid

32. Ibid

33. Ibid

34. Ibid p 82

35. Beauvoir S de (1949) Le deuxième sexe. Paris: Gallimard

36. Mosse C (1989) La femme dans l'Antiquité. Paris: Fayard

37. Ibid

38. Boulongne YP (1975) op cit p 94 sq

39. Coubertin P de (1926) op cit p 319

40. Coubertin P de (1928) L'utilisation pédagogique de l'activité sportive (I et II). Le Sport Suisse 21 novembre no 1074 p 1 et 28 novembre no 1075 p 1

41. Marrou HI (1948) L'éducation dans l'Antiquité. Paris: Le Seuil

42. Coubertin P de (1928) op cit

43. Coubertin P de (1931) La bataille continue. Bureau international de pédagogie sportive. Bulletin no 5 p 5-7 [In Müller N, Comité international olympique (eds) (1986) Pierre de Coubertin. Textes choisis. Tome II. Olympisme p 292-94]

44. Coubertin P de (1936) Les Jeux à Tokio en 1940? Le Journal 27 août no 16019 p 1 [In Müller N, Comité international olympique (eds) (1986) Pierre de Coubertin. Textes choisis. Tome II. Olympisme p 306-08]

45. Coubertin P de (1912) Congrès de Stockholm. Archives du Comité international olympique

46. Wendl K (1988) La participation des femmes aux Jeux olympiques. Lausanne: Documentation du Comité international olympique

47. Coubertin P de (1931) op cit p 5-7

48. Ibid

49. Coubertin P de (1934) Quarante années d'Olympisme 1894-1934. Le Sport Suisse no 1394 4 juillet p 1 [In Müller N, Comité international olympique (eds) (1986) Pierre de Coubertin. Textes choisis. Tome II. Olympique p. 346-51]

[. . .] Ce n'est pas un secret pour personne, parmi ceux qui touchent aux organisations olympiques, que le rénovateur des Jeux a toujours été un adversaire déclaré de la participation féminine et que, même limitée aux épreuves susindiquées, cette participation lui semblait une concession néfaste à laquelle il regrettait d'avoir dû consentir naguère. [. . .] C'est en fin de compte l'opinion publique qui décidera. [. . .] L'expérience aménera l'opinion à départager adversaires et partisans. [. . .]

Coubertin P de (1930) La bataille continue... Bulletin du Bureau international de pédagogie sportive, no 5, p 6-7

Les femmes et les Jeux olympiques :
considérants sur le changement social, les sexes et le sport

Dans un premier temps, l'auteure retrace brièvement l'histoire de la participation des femmes aux Jeux olympiques contemporains, et dresse un portrait de la sous-représentation actuelle des participantes et des dirigeantes au sein du Mouvement olympique. Après avoir souligné l'importance des changements qui ont eu cours depuis 1896, l'auteure procède à l'analyse du sport comme lieu et milieu de construction et d'interprétation des différences entre sexes. Comme activité apparemment plus libre de choix que d'autres, le sport est un terrain particulièrement fertile pour la construction d'idéologies. Il est aussi compris comme une démocratie d'habiletés, où succès et récompenses vont aux personnes qui les méritent, et où les relations inter-personnelles sont libres d'entraves sociales. Entendu dans ce sens, le sport a longtemps été un milieu privilégié de construction de l'image de l'idéal masculin et de l'identité masculine. Les garçons et les hommes faisaient du sport, les filles et les femmes n'en faisaient qu'au péril de leur propre identité sexuelle. Les préjugés commencent à changer, tant en ce qui a trait à la pratique sportive en milieu civil ou scolaire, qu'en ce qui a trait à la pratique d'activités physiques à visées hygiéniques ou ludiques. Le sport devient maintenant une arène disputée de construction de l'identité sexuelle et de constitution des relations entre sexes. En objectivant les différences quantitatives de performance entre hommes et femmes, le résultat sportif est un « bonus » dans la construction des idéologies à l'égard des sexes et de leurs inter-relations. Il permet de poser comme fait irrécusable l'infériorité sportive des femmes, et place en situation sociale périlleuse les femmes qui s'égareraient au-delà d'une frontière qui les définit comme inférieures. L'auteure insiste sur le rôle que jouent les media dans la construction de l'idéologie d'un sport masculin et d'un sport féminin. Après avoir longtemps trivialisé les performances féminines, et tout en continuant à relativement marginaliser le sport féminin, les media participent actuellement à entretenir une discrimination à l'égard des athlètes de sexe féminin. Si les femmes font partie du discours journalistique, c'est à condition que leurs performances soient de calibre mondial. À preuve, la concentration d'articles portant sur des succès ou exploits inusités. Les media participent aussi à construire deux images distinctes de l'athlète, particulièrement à l'aide de la photographie. Les athlètes de sexe féminin sont souvent immortalisées au moment où elles sont victimes de leurs émotions, les photographies sont nombreuses pour les athlètes dites « de charme », l'angle des photographies et le choix du premier plan participent à présenter l'athlète de sexe masculin en position dominante. Le focus, au sens propre du terme, relève d'une stratégie de pouvoir qui place les femmes en situation d'infériorité. En bref, et en dépit des changements qui se sont produits au cours de ce siècle, le mythe de la fragilité de la femme, fragilité qui était invoquée pour prévenir sa participation en sport, a été remplacé par une idéologie de la supériorité masculine en sport. De l'avis de l'auteure, la devise « *Citius, Altius, Fortius* » demeure une recette de domination masculine. Elle conclut en soulignant la nécessité de déconstruire et de défier le discours dominant, et la nécessité tout aussi actuelle aujourd'hui qu'au début du siècle, de réfléchir aux liens entre l'Olympisme, la femme et le sport.

Women and the Olympic Games: a Consideration of Gender, Sport and Social Change

Nancy Théberge

The Olympic Games may be considered as a playing field for the enactment of important issues in gender relations. These issues concern not only equality of opportunity and participation but also the social construction of gender and the constitution of gender relations. A discussion about Women, Olympism and Sport can be profitably examined as an issue of control: control of access, control of practice and control of the very definitions of sport and gender.

A Brief History of Women in the Modern Olympic Games

There is now a considerable documentation of the historical record of women's involvement in the Olympic Games, beginning with their exclusion from involvement in the ancient Games to their initial exclusion then gradual admission and increased participation in the modern Olympic Movement. Perhaps any account of women and the modern Olympic Games needs to begin with de Coubertin's observation that the Games should be reserved for men. And indeed in their inception that was the case. While change has occurred, this change has been about the form and manner of male and masculine domination. As Hargreaves has written, "the history of the Olympics could be rewritten as a history of power and elitism, obsession and excesses, divisions and exploitation". Concerning gender relations, she continues that "certainly, the modern Olympic Movement has been imbued with male chauvinism and domination over women[1]". Discussion and debate about *whether* women should be allowed to compete has been replaced by issues of *how* women should participate—in what sports and events and in what other capacities including as officials in international and national olympic bodies. No less than at the turn of the century, the key questions now are who is setting the rules and what rules are in operation.

Hargreaves' account identifies three somewhat distinct periods of gender relations in the modern Olympic Games. This framework provides a useful account

Nancy Théberge, Institut Simone de Beauvoir, Concordia University, Montréal, Québec, Canada

of the changing conditions of women's involvement. The years 1896-1928 were an initial period characterized by a tradition of exclusion and some efforts to resist these practices. The admission of women to the first three Olympic Games was "a haphazard and 'unserious' affair[2]" without the official consent of the IOC. And as an indication of their unrecognized status, for their achievements women competitors were not awarded medals but "diplomas". This early participation of women, which took place despite de Coubertin's strong disapproval, was enabled in part by the fact that during these early years control of the organization of the Games was largely in the hands of local organizing committees. As the IOC came to exercise greater power and control, it was necessary to reckon with de Coubertin's stance[3].

The decade of the twenties witnessed one of the most significant and telling chapters in the history of gender relations in the Olympic Games. Struggles were waged over who would control women's international sport and what would be the form and definition of women's participation. The advent of women's sport in the western industrialized countries meant a push for change in women's international sport. A particular focus was athletics or as it is known in North America, track and field. The IOC's refusal to include a program of women's athletics in the Games prompted Alice Milliatt to create the *Fédération sportive féminine internationale* (FSFI) and organize the first Women's Olympics in 1922, held again as the Women's World Games in 1926, 1930 and 1934[4]. The success of these events required olympic organizers to pay attention to women's sport and the public interest it received.

Negotiations over women's participation in the Olympic Games took place against a backdrop of the wider debate about women's involvement in sport[5]. A powerful voice in this debate was that of women physical educators in the United States who were concerned that women's sport would succomb to the problems of men's sport and in particular to the competitive and commercial excesses then (and still) plaguing men's university sport. Also significant were the ideological debates of the times in which the myth of female frailty and its incarnation in the cult of domesticity was continually challenged by the practice of women's sport. Beliefs in women's natural frailty were promoted by the medical wisdom of the day which—despite the lack of evidence bearing on the issue—saw vigorous physical activity as dangerous to women's health and well being.

As histories of this period have shown, the competing positions were resolved by the admission of women's athletics and other sports into the Olympic Games on a limited basis and in line with a model of women's sport that accepted and reproduced the ideal of female frailty. After the now legendary women's 800 metres race at the 1928 Olympic Games in Amsterdam, in which several of the competitors were alleged to be close to exhaustion at the finish line, women were allowed to compete but only at shorter distances in sports such as track and field and swimming. As well, they were excluded from the strength events in athletics and only gradually were women's team events introduced into the Games.

The social and cultural significance of the events of the twenties and thirties was in essence about control: control of the organization of women's sport and of its definition and meaning. The challenge posed by the FSFI and the Women's Olympics and World Games was effectively overcome when women's events were permanently incorporated into the Games. Equally significant, however, was the ideological control exercised in this process. The model of women's sport that emerged in the 1930s, not only in the Olympic Games but also in school sport programs, with its restricted and restricting visions of women's athleticism, acknowledged the ideal of female frailty and signified the "essential difference" between the sexes[6].

This model remained the basis for the organization of women's sport into the 1950s. Hargreaves has described the period between 1928 and 1952 as one of consolidation and struggle. By 1952 women's participation in the Olympic Games was widely accepted but the gains were "conservative"[7]. That is, the model of women's sport conformed to the ideal of feminine athleticism and its cultural significance was to reinforce the myth of female frailty. The years since 1952 have been marked by some amount of challenge to male and masculine hegemony in olympic sport. This challenge has by no means led to a reconstitution of the gender order in olympic sport; nonetheless it has been significant. The challenge initially was posed by developments in the Olympic Movement including the expansion of countries participating in the post World War II era. Particularly significant for women's participation was the entry of the Soviet Union in 1952 followed by other countries in the east bloc. The political and ideological agendas of the east bloc countries' olympic involvement placed a premium on athletic success, with little regard to the gender of medal winners. Moreover, the material and social investment that these countries were prepared to make in pursuit of success also was relatively gender blind. The efforts of the east bloc countries brought visibility to women's olympic sport and forced the western countries out of concern for their own olympic standing to pay greater attention to the participation and performance of women[8].

Further stimulus for change occurred in the 1960s. One of these was the revival of the women's movement in North America and Europe, which brought a rethinking of women's position and a challenge to traditional ideas about gender roles. With this, women's sport participation increased and it was only a matter of time before concern with gender inequality in sport gained prominence. The western countries also were not immune to a consideration of the political and ideological uses of women's sport. In Canada for instance, the expansion of state involvement and interest in high performance sport that occurred in the 1970s yielded gains for women and men alike. Funding for the sport infrastructure, expansion of the government sport bureaucracy and support programs such as athlete funding all benefited the fortunes of men and women athletes and men's and women's programs.

Where do we stand at present? Data on gender imbalance in olympic participation may be presented a number of ways. In all ways, however, the pattern is a familiar one of underrepresentation and fewer opportunities for females. These patterns are found in data for men's and women's sports or disciplines (*Figure 1*); men's and women's events in mixed sports or disciplines (*Table 1*)[9]; and participation rates for male and female athletes (*Table 2*).

> In the 1992 Olympics, there are seven male-only sports [or disciplines], compared to two [disciplines] for women only. Three of the male-only sports are team sports that provide opportunities for large contingents of male participants. Three sports—equestrian, shooting and yachting—have open events for both sexes, but female participation is under 30% in all three and drops to 11% in yachting—the lowest female participation rate in any olympic sport. The fact that these three sports require expensive equipment is no doubt a contributing factor to low female participation. Of the 17 sports with separate events for men and women, women are consistently underrepresented. There is of course a close relationship between the number of women's events and the level of female participation (see, for example, cycling) but even in sports where there are equal events—table tennis and tennis, for example—more than half the participating countries sent no women [to the Seoul Olympic Games] [...] A comparison of the 1968 and 1992 Olympics shows that 12 new sports [or disciplines] and 45 new events have been added for women, and nine new sports and 47 new events for men, so that in terms of actual numbers of participants the gender gap has increased[10].

The underrepresentation of women in the administration of olympic affairs is also extreme. The first women were appointed to the IOC in 1981. Currently the IOC includes 5 women and 89 men. Similar patterns hold on National Olympic Committees. In this regard the Canadian Olympic Association recently made a significant move when a woman was elected President of the Association. For the most part, however, it remains the case that the Olympic Games are organized by men and in considerable measure for men.

In addition to looking at the data on participation and representation of women, it is useful to look at the types of events that have been added in recent years[11]. A review of the events that have been added indicates continuing ambivalence about the meaning of women's sport. The women's marathon, added in 1984, and the women's 10 000-meter race, added in 1988, are distance events. Other additions are multiple events that combine running, jumping, and throwing competitions. In 1964 the pentathlon was introduced; in 1984, it was replaced with the heptathlon. The challenge to the myth of female frailty indicated by the adoption of women's distance and multiple events marks progress. Other additions include team sports. Women's volleyball was introduced in the 1964 Games, women's basketball in 1976, and women's field hockey in 1980. The historical resistance to women's sport participation has been particularly strong in the case of team sports. Traditionally, sports in which it has been acceptable for women to compete internationally and professionally have been individual sports such as tennis, golf, skating, and swimming. The major exception in this regard would appear to be field hockey, which has been organized internationally since the 1930s. Until recently, however, women's field hockey has conformed to the model of restricted sport described earlier. Even at the international level, the structure of tournaments deemphasized competition and winning and focussed instead on the experience of participation[12].

FIGURE 1

Men's and Women's Sports or Disciplines at the 1992 Olympic Games

Female-only	Male-only	Mixed	Open	Demonstration
		Badminton		
		Judo		
		(Female < 1/3)* Canoeing Cycling Fencing Rowing		* 1988 figures
	(Potential for women's events) Baseball Modern-Pentathlon Soccer Water Polo Weightlifting	(Female ≥ 1/3)* Archery Basketball Field Hockey Gymnastics Swimming Table Tennis		Source: 1992 Olympic program, Barcelona. Adapted from Lenskyj, 1990.
Rhythmic Gymnastics Synch. Swimming	(Unlikely to change) Boxing Wrestling	Team Handball Tennis Track and Field Volleyball	Female < 1/3)* Equestrian Shooting Yachting	(Mixed) Tae Kwon Do (Men-only) Jai Alai Roller Hockey

TABLE 1

**Men's and Women's Events in Mixed Sports or Disciplines
1992 Olympic Games**

Sports/disciplines and Gender	Events	
	Men	Women
Gender parity		
Archery	4	4
Badminton	2	2
Diving	2	2
Judo	7	7
Table Tennis	2	2
Tennis	2	2
Gender imbalance		
Basketball	1 (12 teams)	1 (8 teams)
Canoeing	12	4
Cycling	7	3
Fencing	6	2
Field Hockey	1 (12 teams)	1 (8 teams)
Gymnastics	2 (apparatus = 6)	2 (apparatus = 4)
Rowing	8	6
Swimming	16	15
Team Handball	1 (12 teams)	1 (8 teams)
Track and Field	24	19
Volleyball	1 (12 teams)	1 (8 teams)

Source: 1992 Olympic program, Barcelona. Adapted from Lenskyj, 1990.

TABLE 2

**Participation Rates for Female Athletes, in Mixed and Open Sports
1988 Olympic Games**

Sports	Male Athletes	Female Athletes	Total	Female athletes as a % of total
Archery	85	62	147	42
Basketball	144	96	240	40
Canoeing	243	71	314	23
Cycling	391	64	455	14
Equestrian	138	59	197	30
Fencing	247	70	317	22
Field Hockey	192	128	320	40
Gymnastics*	99	142	241	59
Rowing	450	210	660	32
Shooting	294	115	409	28
Swimming**	599	345	944	37
Table Tennis	82	49	131	37
Team Handball	180	120	300	40
Tennis	81	48	129	37
Track and Field	1 148	579	1 727	34
Volleyball	143	96	239	40
Yachting	402	54	456	12
Total	**4 918**	**2 308**	**7 226**	**32**

* Rhythmic Gymnastics included.
** Synchronized swimming and Water Polo included.
Source: Rapport officiel. Jeux de la XXIVᵉ olympiade, Séoul 1988, Vol. 1, p. 284.

Expansion of women's events in the Olympic Games has also included a number of traditionally "feminine" sports. Events introduced in the 1984 Games include synchronized swimming and rhythmic gymnastics. A related development has been the increasing popularity of artistic gymnastics (usually referred to simply as gymnastics). In recent Olympic Games, the stars among women competitors have been gymnasts, including Olga Korbut in 1972, Nadia Comanecci in 1976, and Mary Lou Retton in 1984. The current prominence of "feminine" sports exemplifies the mixed messages appearing in women's sports today. On the one hand, it must be acknowledged that world-class synchronized swimmers and gymnasts (like champions in other artistic sports) are highly accomplished athletes whose performances require remarkable skill and ability. Nonetheless, by their emphasis on beauty, form, and appearance, these sports provide symbolic confirmation of the special nature of women's sport. In this way, sports such as synchronized swimming and gymnastics reaffirm the stigma associated with women's sport participation.

A cursory look at women's participation in the Olympic Movement suggests enormous change since the introduction of the modern Games. And a more careful historical review certainly provides some support for this assessment. That women would compete in the marathon and 10 000 metres or play basketball with the skill, dedication and power of women Olympians of the 1990s was simply unthinkable not many years ago. At the same time, that women would sit on the IOC or head a National Olympic Committee is also remarkable, although the extent of change in the administrative and organizational levels has not been so dramatic as among participants. What though should we make of this increased—if far from complete—equality? What are the social implications of these developments? In this assessment, sport will be considered as a setting for the construction and interpretation of gender and gender differences.

Sport and the Construction of Gender

In recent years the analysis of women and sport has moved past a consideration of relative opportunities and participation—as important as these are—to a consideration of the cultural meaning and significance of this participation. As several writers have demonstrated, sport is a particularly powerful setting for the construction of gender ideology. One of the first and still most astute considerations of this issue is Willis' 1982 essay entitled "Women in Sport and Ideology". Willis[13] notes that sport is a particularly fertile ground for the constitution of ideology because it is apparently more free and voluntary than other activities. Moreover sport is understood to be a democracy of ability, where success and rewards come to those who are deserving. "In some ways", Willis says, "sport provides the morality drama of our electronic age: the ideal expression of unfettered social relations—not worker against manager but player against player[14]."

Sport does more than provide compelling theatre; it is also a setting for the construction and affirmation of identity. And as is now well accepted, most basic to the identities that are constructed in sport is gender. As Connell writes in *Gender and Power*, "images of ideal masculinity are constructed and promoted most systematically through competitive sport[15]". So long as sport was a male preserve, the meaning of sport to the construction of gender identities and gender relations was *seemingly* straightforward: sport is what boys and men did, what girls and women did not do or did at peril to their own gendered identities. All this is of course changing. Not only in the Olympic Games but in school sport programs, in the more popular activities of the "fitness boom" and in recreational sport, women are increasingly taking part and thereby challenging the long cherished beliefs about sport, gender and the connection between the two. As both

Willis[16] and Hargreaves[17] note in respect to gender, sport is now a "contested" arena. What is being contested is not only the meaning and social significance of sport but the construction of gender and the constitution of gender relations. In discussing the power of sport to construct ideology, Willis argues that in addition to the importance of its apparent autonomy and independence, in respect to gender ideology sport offers a further "bonus" in the biological and apparently incontrovertible differences between men and women. He suggests that:

> Ideology can claim biological discrepancy fully for its own: to present cultural legitimations as biological factors [. . .] The fact that no one can deny female difference becomes the fact of female sports inferiority, becomes the fact that females are innately different from men, becomes the fact that women who stray across the defining boundary are in a parlous (sic) state. An ideological view comes to be deposited in our culture as a common sense assumption— "of course women are different and inferior"[18].

An important contingency in the operation of this ideology is the presence of an oppositional ideology. Willis discusses the situation of women who lack a counter ideology. They have, he says, two choices: either immediately collude with the ideological definitions (the female athlete conspiring to be sexy with the news reporter) or take up the challenge within the preferred ideological definition (the angered sportswoman setting out to prove male equivalence in her sport's performance). An example of the latter that Willis offers is Billie Jean King's match against Bobby Riggs. "Either way, men, and what they stand for reign supreme[19]." A major player in the construction of the ideology of women's sport is the media. Willis discusses this in some measure, noting the now familiar practice of stories about women athletes and women's sport making their way into the general "human interest", titillating or unusual category. The trivialization and degradation of women's sport and the performances of women athletes is one of the main ways in which the 'specialness' of their experience is noted and their inferiority to male athletes is signified[20]. Willis' article was presented as an "essay in ideas". At the time of publication it was a landmark and as noted earlier, it remains one of the most astute interpretations of the social significance of sport. Subsequent work has taken up the challenge offered by Willis and provided an increasingly sophisticated account of the construction of gender and the ideology of gender differences.

One of the long standing criticisms of media accounts of women's sport concerns the amount of coverage, which remains far below that of men's sport. Some evidence of this was provided in a recent review done for the Canadian Association for the Advancement of Women in Sport of coverage of men's and women's sport in 13 major daily newspapers from across Canada on one day, Saturday, September 23, 1989[21]. (For those unfamiliar with Canadian newspapers, in most papers the Saturday edition is the largest of the week, comparable to the Sunday edition of most American newspapers). The results of this analysis showed that only a small percentage of coverage was concerned with women's sport. The message conveyed to the reader is that on a typical day in Canada, women's sport for the most part doesn't happen. We know of course that this isn't true; what is true is that in the judgment of newspaper editors and managers, women's sport that is occurring in universities, colleges, schools and communities across the country is not of interest. A similarly long standing concern has been that when women's sport is covered, that coverage trivializes and degrades the activity and participants. This is a practice noted by Willis and also by Boutilier and San Giovanni[22] in their review of media coverage of women's sport published in 1983. Borrowing a term from Gerbner[23], Boutilier and San Giovanni characterized this coverage as a process of "symbolic annihilation".

Research on media accounts of women, gender and sport since the early 1980s, when Boutilier and San Giovanni's review was conducted, has uncovered and exposed this process as a far more complex and layered activity. Media coverage of sport today does not simply exclude women but constructs women and men and the difference between the two in such a way as to present gender and gender differences in sport as both a significant and natural feature of social life. Moreover, differences are constructed as hierarchy. Willis' statement that women who stray across the defining boundary of sport are in a dangerous state is appropriate today. What has occured since Willis made this observation is our more complete understanding of the practices that enforce this condition. Several works published in recent years have been important in this effort. One of these is Messner's article[24] on the "Female Athlete as Contested Ideological Terrain". Messner suggests that there has been a shift in media strategies in portraying female athletes. The explanation for this shift lies in the advances women athletes have made, which have rendered the formerly common practices of marginaliza- tion and trivializiation as apparently too unfair and inappropriate. They have been replaced by another strategy that Messner describes, paraphrasing the media, as "they (women athletes) want to be treated equally with men? Well, let's see what they can do". But as he indicates, given current physiological differences between men and women and the organization of sport around definitions that favour male performance, this strategy is likely once again to reproduce and solidify masculine hegemony. Thus the ideology of equality becomes a means to explain and justify apparently "natural" differences between men and women. This analysis shows that although accounts of women's sport are apparently liberated from the degradations of earlier (but not so distant) times, they nonetheless maintain practices that reinforce ideas about women's physical inferiority and realize their social subordination. And because these accounts have the protection afforded by being apparently fair and equitable, they are a particularly powerful support for hegemonic ideologies and practices.

Support for Messner's thesis is found in an analysis of the print media in West Germany. In a detailed account of sport reports and photographs from four national newspapers, Klein[25] identifies a number of practices that serve to define the anomalous position of women in sport. One of these is a concentration on "unusual achievements and successes". The well known saying that in order to succeed a woman must be better than a man is given an intriguing reality in media coverage of sport. Klein's data show significant differences in accounts of men's and women's competition reported in the media, where coverage of women concentrates more heavily on higher levels of competition and in the more frequent references to success and performance in articles on women's sport. In short, women do enter into the discourse of sport reports but only when they are world class. An additional finding from this analysis concerns the use of metaphors describing women's sport as a battle or fight. Klein argues that this is a historically new phenomenon in which sport is once again constituted as "typically masculine" because of its competitive and fighting nature[26]. Juxtaposed against these findings on the anomaly of women who enter the masculine turf of sport is Klein's analysis of how print media accounts naturalize gender divisions in sport so that they appear to be the outcome of biological differences. This occurs through the use of male standards and norms to evaluate and interpret women's performances, the presentation of a "psychological modality" of the female athlete that is rooted in traditional descriptions of female hysteria (i.e., references to athletes' nerves, dispositions, "mettle", emotions and tears) and, as always, in the sexualization of imagery and accounts of women athletes.

Additional insight is offered in a recent analysis by Duncan[27]. Duncan examined photographs that accompanied sport stories concerning the 1988 Winter and Summer Olympic Games and the 1984 Summer Games in one Canadian and five American magazines. From a sample of nearly 1 400 pictures, she selected for examination 186 pictures that suggested sexual difference. The analysis con- sidered two categories of photographic features as conveyors of meaning: (a) the content of photographs, including physical appearance, subjects' poses and body positions, expressions, emotional displays and camera angles and (b) the context, which includes the visual space, caption, surrounding text and substance of the article. The published account of this analysis presents a number of photos identified in the research, which serve to make clear the major findings. These findings include the continuing association of women's sport and sexuality. Evidence of this appears in several ways, from the expected highlighting of women athletes thought to be glamorous such as Florence Griffith Joyner and Katarina Witt (the Canadian magazine *Macleans's* published five pictures of Witt including two in skin tight jeans, compared to one of the Canadian skater Elizabeth Manley), to the positioning of subjects in sexually suggestive fashion. A further finding of this study which is enabled by the careful textual analysis concerns the representation of sexual difference. Duncan notes that photographs have a particularly powerful capacity to contribute to the construction of ideology. Photographs, she says, "do not simply create images of women or girls, men or boys; they construct differences between females and males and address viewers as though the differences are natural and real[28]."

The analysis of content and context shows convincingly the continuing emphasis on the distinctions between men and women athletes. Women athletes not only are sexualized in a manner to which men are not subjected, they are presented in states of emotion. Women athletes apparently cry quite often; men, the pictures suggest, almost never do. (Recall here Klein's finding that German print media more often present women athletes as victims of their emotions). Camera angles often depict women athletes from below eye level, which suggests a position of inferiority; they present male athletes from an elevated position, suggesting superiority. The positioning of photos also often presents men in dominant positions; examples are a picture in which one man is foregrounded surrounded by a number of women and another in which one man is foregrounded and a woman is presented in a secondary or subsidiary position. There is other evidence. As Duncan concludes, the sports photographs she examined "suggest that women are not like men. The implication is that they can never be like men [. . .] The issue at bottom is one of power. Focusing on female difference is a political strategy that places women in a position of weakness[29]."

Conclusion

As this account has shown, since their inception nearly a century ago the Olympic Games have witnessed enormous change in the participation of women. Although there remains considerable inequality in opportunity, the balance in representation has been redressed somewhat. Distributive questions are however only a part of the consideration of gender in sport and in society. This presentation has also examined developments in the Olympic Movement from the perspective of gender relations. In particular, attention has been drawn to the significance of sport for the construction of the ideology of gender. Again, there has been some change. It is questionable however whether this change should be seen as progress. To be sure, the ideology of female frailty which formed the basis for exclusion in the early years of the modern Olympic Movement has been exposed. But has it been rejected? Has it been replaced; if so, with what?

What we see today is a new incorporation of the ideology of masculine superiority. This is evident especially in media discourse on gender and sport. And because of the power and scope of the modern media, in alliance with the social and cultural positioning of the olympic spectacle, these messages are particularly authoritative. In this discourse, the myth of female frailty has been replaced by a different version of the ideology of masculine superiority. While we should not underestimate the attractiveness and indeed seductiveness to dominant interests of the gendered ideology of an earlier era, it is not unreasonable to argue that the contemporary ideology is equally powerful and equally insidious. In part this is because the contemporary ideology operates in a context of apparent progress and equality or at least relative equality. As Messner suggests, the media seem ready now to give women their due[30]. But on whose terms and by whose definitions of what is "due" or just? In the current definition and social organization of sport, gender equality is illusory. *"Citius, Altius, Fortius"* is a recipe for masculine dominance.

A particularly important aspect of the current discourse on sport is the naturalization of gender and gender differences. And significant here is the unspoken discourse. The spoken discourse tells us that women athletes are attractive and feminine (or at least they can and should be), are composed of different "stuff" or "mettle" than men, and achieve levels of performance that are continually astounding as they approximate but never or rarely equal men's. The more often unspoken discourse asks how is it that women do sport at all? As Willis notes, women in sport must somehow be explained. The attention to sexuality and psychological modalities, to performance in the apparent context of equality all serve to do this by defining the "specialness" of women and locating it in their nature and constitution. In Willis' terms, "ideology has claimed biological discrepancy fully for its own: to present cultural legitimations as biological factors[31]".

The social and cultural significance of this process extends well beyond sport. The ideological struggle of gender is a localized version of a wider social and cultural struggle. We are in a period of enormous change and challenge to entrenched ideologies and patterns of gender relations. The revival in essentialist interpretations of gender and gender differences, both in popular accounts and in the scholarly discourse, indicates the significance of this historical moment. As noted earlier, sport has a particular contribution to make in the ideological contest over gender because of its apparent separateness and the "fact" of biological differences between men and women. It is thus especially critical that we deconstruct and challenge the dominant discourse. A consideration of Olympism, Women and Sport is as timely now as in de Coubertin's day.

REFERENCES

1. Hargreaves J (1984) Women and the olympic phenomenon. In Tomlinson A, Whannel G (eds) Five Ring Circus. London: Pluto Press p 53-70

2. Ibid p 56

3. Ibid p 57-58

4. Ibid

5. Théberge N (1989) Women's athletics and the myth of female frailty. In Freeman J (ed) Women: a feminist perspective. Mountain View: Mayfield p 507-522

6. Ibid

7. Hargreaves J (1984) op cit p 60

8. Ibid p 62

9. Lenskyj H (1990) Sex equality in the Olympics: a report to the Toronto Olympic Task Force. Toronto

10. Ibid p 6

11. See Théberge N (1989) op cit

12. Grant C (1984) The gender gap in sport: from intercollegiate to olympic level. Arena Review 8 40-43

13. Willis P (1982) Women in sport and ideology. In Hargreaves J (ed) Sport, culture and ideology. London: Routledge and Kegan Paul p 117-135

14. Ibid p 121

15. Connell R (1987) Gender and power. Stanford: Stanford University Press p 84-85

16. Willis P (1982) op cit

17. Hargreaves J (1986) Where's the virtue? Where's the grace? A discussion of the social production of gender relations in and through sport. Theory, Culture and Society 3 109-121

18. Willis P (1982) op cit p 130

19. Ibid

20. Ibid p 131

21. CAAWS/ACAFS (1989) Action. Ottawa: Canadian Association for Advancement of Women and Sport

22. Boutilier M, San Giovanni L (1983) The Sporting woman. Champaign: Human Kinetics p 185-86

23. Gerbner G (1978) The dynamics of cultural resistance. In Tuchman G, Daniels AK, Benet J (eds) Hearth and home: images of women in the mass media. New York: Oxford University Press

24. Messner M (1988) Sports and male domination: the female athlete as contested ideological terrain. Sociology of Sport Journal 5 197-211

25. Klein ML (1988) The discourse of women in sports reports. International Review for the Sociology of Sport 23 139-152

26. Ibid p 142

27. Duncan Carlisle M (1990) Sports photographs and sexual difference: images of women and men in the 1984 and 1988 Olympic Games. Sociology of Sport Journal 7 22-43

28. Ibid p 24-25

29. Ibid p 40

30. Messner M (1988) op cit

31. Willis P (1982) op cit p 121

Idéologie, politique et succès des femmes aux Jeux olympiques: analyse trans-nationale des résultats aux Jeux olympiques de Séoul

Les Jeux olympiques, comme spectacle culturel mondial, sont porteurs d'une signification symbolique primordiale pour les femmes, en ce sens qu'ils permettent au monde entier d'être témoin du développement du sport féminin et des performances atteintes, de saisir l'occasion de débattre du sport comme facteur d'émancipation de la femme, de réfléchir sur la construction et la reproduction des idéologies concernant les sexes, et sur la question d'un sport féminin ou d'un sport au féminin. Le cas particulier des Jeux olympiques de Séoul en 1988, avec la participation de la quasi-totalité des pays éligibles, permet de pousser l'analyse du lien entre politiques gouvernementales et succès des femmes aux Jeux olympiques. Dans un premier temps, les auteures soulignent la lenteur de l'accroissement de la participation féminine aux Jeux olympiques, et notent la persistance de la sous-représentation des femmes par rapport à leur poids démographique réel. Que ce soit en termes de nombre d'athlètes, ou de nombre de sports, de disciplines et d'épreuves, la parité entre sexes est loin d'être atteinte. Dans un deuxième temps, les auteures illustrent les différences de participation féminine par pays. Les pays qui n'envoient pas, ou envoient peu, de femmes aux Jeux olympiques tendent à être des pays d'Afrique ou d'Asie, et à religion musulmane. Alors que les pays qui délèguent une forte proportion de femmes dans leurs équipes tendent à être européens, à religion protestante ou catholique dominante. Quant aux pays qui envoient le plus fort contingent d'athlètes de sexe féminin, ils appartiennent au bloc socialiste. Ce sont surtout ces derniers qui remportent la quasi-totalité des médailles allouées aux épreuves, disciplines et sports féminins. Le cas de la République démocratique allemande est un cas exceptionnel en termes de succès, puisque ses athlètes remportent presque le quart des médailles disponibles pour les sports féminins. Les auteures soulignent que la RDA s'est engagée dans une forme de concentration extrême du succès en misant sur quelques sports seulement. Cette concentration suggère une volonté politique d'obtenir une reconnaissance internationale rapide en faisant converger les efforts dans quelques sports. Cette hypothèse est étayée par une analyse corrélationnelle dont les résultats montrent que le type de régime politique, et les indicateurs liés à la santé et au bien-être des femmes, sont étroitement associés au succès national féminin. Cependant, au moment-même où les pays socialistes modifient leurs institutions politiques et économiques, le sport féminin risque de souffrir davantage de coupures budgétaires inévitables que le sport masculin. Les auteures concluent en plaidant pour des efforts accrus afin que les femmes puissent porter, à égalité avec les hommes, la flamme qui symbolise l'idéal olympique.

Ideology, Public Policy and Female Olympic Achievement: a Cross-National Analysis of the Seoul Olympic Games

Mary A. Boutilier
Lucinda F. San Giovanni

The 1988 Seoul Olympic Games are of important historic, symbolic and political value for those concerned with the female olympian, with the role of women in olympic policy-making and administrative functions, and with the direction that Olympism will take in the next century.

Historically, the Seoul Olympic Games are the culmination of almost one hundred years since the revival of the modern Olympic Games in 1896 by Baron Pierre de Coubertin. During this century the degree and nature of women's participation and achievement in the Games has gone through various stages of development[1], each with its unique hurdles and resolutions. As Talbot observes, "[. . .] the power structures and vested interests in the movement, at both national and international levels, have tended to exclude from full participation half the people of the world–women[2]". From the desire by de Coubertin to exclude women from the modern Games, to the expansion of opportunities for women's involvement over the ensuing century, an analysis of female participation in Seoul provides a historical benchmark of how far women have traveled, and still must journey, on the path to full inclusion as olympians.

An evaluation of the Seoul Olympic Games is also important politically because they are the first in sixteen years to include the simultaneous participation of the widest range of eligible countries. One of the aims of Olympism, to promote international harmony and understanding, has been severely jeopardized in the previous three Games by the use of national boycotts. The Seoul Olympic Games provided the first opportunity in almost a generation for the widest possible participation by all countries.

In still another symbolic sense, the Seoul Olympic Games (as do all Games) contain important cultural meanings and messages for women athletes and for those who wish to expand female olympic involvement. If we follow the invitation of cultural studies and feminist theorists to view sport as a cultural performance, we can see that sports embody significant dramatic, expressive

1890
1990

Mary A. Boutilier, Department of Political Science, Lucinda F. San Giovanni, Department of Sociology/Anthropology, Seton Hall University, South Orange, New Jersey, USA.

meanings and messages for the participants and for the larger audiences at these events[3,4,5,6,7,8,9]. In his discussion of cultural performances, MacAloon highlights this symbolic importance of sports: "They are occasions in which as a culture or society we reflect upon and define ourselves, dramatize our collective myths and history, present ourselves and eventually change in some ways.[...][10]".

Indeed, the Olympic Games are the only truly global cultural performance which, once every four years, captures the interest of, it is estimated, one out of every three persons on the planet. It is at these Games, which MacAloon gracefully terms a "feast of interpretation" that "we measure who we think we are by who we think the others are and are measured by them in turn[11]". For women, the Olympic Games are of greater symbolic significance than they are for men as a vehicle for evoking, reflecting and sharing the expressive content and socio-cultural context in which understandings of physicality, athleticism, and gendered experiences are embedded[12,13]. During each Olympiad, elite male athletes have many more national and international championships, with their attend and mass publicity, in which to compete and in which symbolic meanings and messages can be affirmed and explored. For women, by contrast, it is primarily at the Olympic Games that they can witness and become engaged in the symbolic debate over female athleticism and women's place in the larger scheme of national and global life. In his observations on the Olympic Games, Riordan observes that women can be inspired by exposure to female athletes of other nations and that the Games themselves "are significant both as an international arena for demonstrating women's attainments and as a vehicle for promoting women's emancipation throughout the world[14]". It is also important to underscore the symbolic power of the Olympic Games, as the most global of all sporting events, to construct and reproduce dominant notions of gender, gendered athleticism and gender ideologies[15]. It is for these symbolic reasons that the Seoul Olympic Games contain a special significance for women and for scholars.

Finally, due to dramatic challenges to the Communist Party's hegemony in Eastern Europe and the USSR, the Seoul Olympic Games might well be the last ones where sharply delineated ideological and state-institutional differences between occidental countries will have prevailed. Since the post World War II era, the primary political contests waged during the Olympic Games occurred between capitalist and communist countries. As was highlighted in *The Sporting Woman*, Boutilier and San Giovanni[16] point to the general superiority of female olympians from state-socialist countries that has been a consistent, although underplayed, trend for several Olympic Games. This patterned achievement reflects both the desire to gain international prestige and legitimacy and the ideologically-based policy of commitment to female olympic success. Analysis of the Seoul Games provides a chance to further specify the scholarly linkage between ideological and governmental support and women's olympic success.

As we turn to the Seoul Olympic Games, some of our central concerns are: What changes have occurred in the distribution and nature of sports and events available to women olympians between 1972 and 1988? What national patterns of participation were evident at Seoul? Which countries provide the greatest proportion of successful women olympians? What societal factors are correlated with elite female olympic achievement? Finally, we speculate on some of the implications for female achievement of the recent political changes in Eastern European countries and the USSR.

Historical Patterns of Women's Olympic Competition

Surely the history of women's slow and halting inclusion in the Olympic Games confirms a vision that the Games are primarily events among countries and among men. The historic "discrimination against women and their subjugation to male patterns of sport, parallel to the male patterns of industrial capitalist (and state monopolist) production[17]" have been duplicated in the Olympic Games. Eichberg has noted that the Olympic Games are a product of European and North American colonialism, reflect the games of these regions and are not representative of indigenous peoples in the rest of the world. Nor do they do justice to women's sports experience or even the female experience of Western colonial sport itself. *Table 1* summarizes the degree of participation by women from the inception of the modern Olympic Games in 1896 to 1988.

TABLE 1

**Women's Participation in the Summer Olympic Games
1896-1988**

Year	Female Athletes		Female Sports	Female Events	
	n	%*		n	%*
1896	0	0	0	0	0
1900	11	1	2	2	0
1904	8	2	1	1	0
1908	36	2	2	3	3
1912	57	2	2	6	6
1916			World War I		
1920	64	3	3	7	5
1924	136	5	3	10	8
1928	290	10	4	14	12
1932	127	10	3	14	11
1936	328	8	4	14	10
1940			World War II		
1944			World War II		
1948	385	8	5	19	14
1952	518	9	5	24	16
1956	384	11	5	25	17
1960	610	11	5	30	20
1964	732	12	6	33	20
1968	781	14	6	39	23
1972	1,125	14	7	42	21
1976	1,274	21	10	49	25
1980	1,247	23	11	50	25
1984	1,619	23	13	62	28
1988	2,477	26	17	71	30

* Percentages were rounded off

As we can see, between 1972 and 1988 there was a 120% increase in the number of women competing in the Games. Even with this increase, women still constitute only slightly over one-quarter (26%) of all olympic athletes. Women continue to fall far short of their better than 50% representation in the population as a whole. Also women still have far fewer events to participate in at the Games than do the men. Since 1972 women's events have increased by 41%; however their events still account for less than one-third of the total single-sex olympic events.

Examining the sports each competes in reveals some interesting characteristics of women's sport involvement as well. There are seven sports men compete in for which there is no female counterpart: boxing, judo, modern pentathlon, soccer, water polo, weightlifting and wrestling. Boxing, judo, weightlifting and the modern pentathlon tend to emphasize aggressiveness, upper-body strength, pugilistic skills and traditional preparation for hand-to-hand combat. Clearly these are not traditionally associated with stereotyped "feminine" attributes and do not comply with the Olympic Charter regulation that "competitors in sports restricted to women must comply with the prescribed tests for femininity[18]". Ironically, water polo, soccer and judo already have internationally sanctioned world championships for women. Their absence from the Olympic Games may reflect conservatism on the part of IOC members, "the implicit power structures of modern sport and sport organizations" and the commercialization of the Games which make it harder to attract corporate sponsors for elite female athletes who challenge hegemonic images of femininity[19]. The future for sports which lack commercial appeal depends on increasing the participation of women in the IOC and in related sports governing bodies and organizations[20].

There is only one sport (a discipline, acccording to the Olympic Charter) in which women compete for which men do not have a counterpart; it is synchronized swimming. Introduced in the 1984 Los Angeles Olympic Games, this discipline "epitomizes the accepted female physical qualities of grace, precision, and style, and [...] presents a narrow, stereotypical view of the female body[21]". Differences also exist within gymnastics. Both men and women compete in this sport, but the distribution of events complies with the guidelines of the Olympic Charter in that only women perform on the balance beam and on uneven bars, while only the men work the rings, pommel horse, and parallel bars. In addition only the women compete in the decorous and graceful activities of the new event of rhythmic gymnastics. These are important mechanisms for the construction and reproduction of gendered images in sport.

National Profile of Female Olympic Participation

A country's commitment to its women athletes can be evidenced in a number of ways. Perhaps the most basic one is the decision to include female athletes on its national team. There was a total of 2 477 female olympians who participated in the 1988 Olympic Games. Theoretically this could constitute a mean of 15.5 women for the 160 countries who participated in the Games. However, 42 countries sent teams with no women members at all; 85 countries sent teams with at least one woman but less than the mean; and 33 countries exceeded the mean number of female olympians. Thus, there is a dramatic difference among countries in their commitment to female athletic participation.

The 33 countries who exceeded the mean provided the overwhelming majority (88%) of women olympians. Furthermore, there are clear patterns of geography, religion and government that differentiate these countries. Geographically, those countries which did not send even one woman to the Seoul Olympic Games tended to be mainly from Asia and Africa (79%). In terms of religion, predominantly Muslim countries accounted for slightly more than one-half (57%), and Catholic countries accounted for 12% of the countries not sending women to the Games. Regarding the type of government, the overriding fact is—except for Afghanistan which was at that time still counted among the Communist bloc because of the presence of Soviet troops there—none of those countries are in the Communist bloc.

Those countries that had high proportions of females on their teams and comprised almost nine out of ten women olympians were also distributed along identifiable lines relative to geography, religion and government. Almost two-third of these countries (61%) were located in Europe; another 15% were Asian (perhaps partly accounted for by the location of the Games in South Korea). In terms of religion, the pattern is much more varied; 39% were predominantly Protestant; 33% predominantly Roman Catholic and 9% were of the Orthodox faith. These patterns should be viewed with caution, however, because three of the Roman Catholic countries (POL, TCH and HUN) had Communist governments which have had a traditional commitment to women's sports participation. Indeed, the vast majority of Catholic countries, as noted by Biles[22], have weak support for women's athleticism. In terms of governmental forms, 24 of the 33 countries had some form of representative government, the remaining nine were state-socialist governments. This latter group, however, is disproportionaly represented among the countries with high women's participation given the fact that there were few countries designated as communist in 1988.

Women's Contribution to National Olympic Achievement

Before we examine the relative contribution women made to their country's actual performance in the Olympic Games, we should note that for the vast majority of countries, their representation is primarily symbolic and expressive; their athletes are there less as elite contenders for medals than as national ambassadors of good will. This fact is evident in the following data: all the medals awarded at the Seoul Olympic Games went to 52 of the 160 participating countries; that is to say, only about one-third (32.5%) of the countries were "successful" as measured by medal winning; even among these "successful" countries, nearly half (46%) of them failed to win any medals in a women's event. Thus, olympic success, for both women and men, is highly concentrated among select countries.

The reality of the Olympic Games is that they are politically interpreted contests among countries, not solely among athletes. This fact has led scholars, policy-makers and other elites to attempt to evaluate the national success of teams. Most of this literature has assumed that the performance (defined as medals won) of the national team is merely the summation of the results of the male and female representatives of the country. It is our contention that a combined team total count does not adequately address the differences between countries, particularly as they relate to their women's performances. Indeed it is important to distinguish between participation and actual achievement because the two do not necessarily have the same meanings, depend on the same resources nor garner the same rewards. To wit, of the 160 countries only 28 (18%) won any women's medals. The twenty-eight countries were: ARG, AUS, BUL, CAN, CHN, CRC, FRA, FRG, GBR, GDR, HOL, HUN, INA, ITA, JAM, JPN, KOR, NOR, NZL, PER, POL, POR, ROM, SWE, TCH, URS, USA, and YUG. Although these countries had in common the winning of at least one women's medal, the following data in *Table 2* shows the startling and dramatic differences among their medal achievements.

TABLE 2

The Elite Seven: Countries with Most Successful Women Athletes
1988 Seoul Olympic Games

Country	Total Women's Medals		Total Women's gold medals	
	%*	(n)	%*	(n)
GDR	23	(51)	28	(20)
URS	16	(36)	18	(13)
USA	13	(29)	17	(12)
ROM	8	(17)	7	(5)
BUL	7	(16)	4	(3)
CHN	7	(15)	4	(3)
FRG	5	(10)	6	(4)
Total	**80**	**(174)**	**85**	**(60)**

* Percentages were rounded off

Seven countries won virtually eight out of ten (79%) of all women's medals in the Seoul Olympic Games. Each of them garnered the astounding number of at least ten medals thus putting them into a special category that we have labelled the "Elite seven." Their clear dominance in women's competition is incontestable. One should also note that these same seven countries were quite impressive in winning 54% of all the men's medals as well. A final observation, to which we shall return later, centers on the fact that five of the seven countries that dominate women's olympic competition were state-socialist countries in 1988. With respect to gold medals, it is clear that a slightly greater concentration in gold (84% vs. 79%) exists for the "Elite seven". These countries' male athletes accounted for only 60% of the total gold for men.

Let us explore more fully the dominance of the "Elite Seven" by comparing their women's achievement as a percentage of each country gold and total medals won. *Table 3* shows that the women medalists from Romania and from the People's Republic of China accumulated more than half of their country total medals, followed closely by the German Democratic Republic women who won an astounding 51 total women's medals, almost one in every four won by any woman olympian. These data also confirm the trend identified by Boutilier and San Giovanni[23] that Communist countries accrue a great deal of international acclaim through the athletic achievements of their female competitors. At the highest level of medal acclaim, for both individuals and countries, the second column's pattern of gold medal attainment demonstrates again the excellence of these seven countries. While some changes in rank order obtain, Romania, the People's Republic of China and the German Democratic Republic continue to benefit from the highest levels of female olympic achievements. It is precisely the "winning of the gold" that calls forth the most potent national symbols—the raising of the flag, the playing of the national anthem, to say nothing of the massive media attention that prevails worldwide, especially in the gold medalists' home country.

Another consideration when evaluating the success of the "Elite Seven" centers on the range of sports in which women athletes excelled. As we remarked earlier, there has been a slow but steady expansion of both sports and events available for women competitors. At present, women participate in 17 sports and 71 events compared with 24 and 236 respectively for men. It can be assumed that one measure of a country's commitment to female sporting excellence would be to

TABLE 3

Gold and Total Medals won by the "Elite Seven's" Women as a Percentage of their Country's Totals
1988 Seoul Olympic Games

Country	Women's Total as % of Country's Total*	(n)	Women's Gold as % of Country's Gold*	(n)
ROM	71	(17)	71	(5)
CHN	54	(15)	60	(3)
GDR	50	(51)	54	(20)
BUL	46	(16)	30	(3)
USA	31	(29)	33	(12)
URS	27	(36)	24	(13)
FRG	25	(10)	46	(5)

* Percentages were rounded off

make available to its women that range of athletic resources which provides the chance to excel in the broadest scope of competitions sanctioned by the IOC. Indeed, it is important to underscore this difference between IOC sanctioned sports and events and the degree to which national sporting bodies actually avail themselves of these opportunities. One might expect the "Elite Seven's" women athletes to excel in the broadest possible range of sports. The data from *Table 4* examines the extent to which this expectation is not upheld for gold medalists. Clearly, none of the countries' female athletes won gold medals in more than a fraction of the number of sports available to them. Respectable showings by the large teams of Soviet and American women still account for less than half the available opportunities. More telling, however, is the GDR which engaged in an extreme form of sport concentration and subsequent domination of the women's gold. This country won an astounding 20 gold medals in just four sports (track and field, kayaking, rowing, and swimming).

The issue of concentration within sports is less evident when the total medal count is considered. One might expect greater diffusion among sports as the level of excellence is lessened for silver and bronze medals. *Table 5* generally confirms this pattern. The USSR and the USA won medals in more than 50% of the

TABLE 4

**Gold Medals Won by the "Elite Seven's" Women
by Number of Sports, and Percentage of Total Sports Available
1988 Seoul Olympic Games**

Country	Number of Gold Medals	Number of Sports Won In	% of Total Sports Available*
URS	13	6	35
USA	12	5	29
GDR	20	4	24
FRG	5	4	24
BUL	3	3	18
ROM	5	3	18
CHN	3	2	12

* Percentages were rounded off

TABLE 5

**Total Medals Won by the "Elite Seven's" Women
by Number and Percentage of Total Sports Available
1988 Seoul Olympic Games**

Country	Total Number Medals Won	Number of Sports Won In	% of Sports Won In*
GDR	51	6	35
URS	36	11	65
USA	29	11	65
ROM	17	4	24
BUL	16	8	47
CHN	15	7	41
FRG	10	5	30

* Percentages were rounded off

available sports. Bulgaria came very close to this feat. Once again, the GDR stands out as winning the most medals in a far fewer number of sports. Its concentration in track and field, kayaking, gymnastics, rowing, cycling and swimming clearly paid off in terms of the total medal count. The GDR swept five of the six gold medals in rowing (83% of all the gold rowing medals). This country was nearly as dominant in the swimming events as well. Out of the 15 events with a total of 41 possible medals, two events were team events where only one medal per country would have been possible to win. The GDR won 22 medals, or 54% of the total.

One could argue that this represents the ideal benefits of a most efficient return on investment of scarce national resources. One could equally say that this extreme concentration of resources suggests the willingness of some countries to recognize that it is often easier to gain national recognition by deliberately concentrating their efforts on the rapid development of their female athletes in selected sports[24].

National Correlates of Female Olympic Success

The political analysis of the Olympic Games has often compared this international sporting event with a war contested every four years "with medals and team points and international reputation rather than territory as the victor's spoils[25]". Duncan[26] offered a theory of the international social order in which such events were designated as a kind of "status-contesting" in which a country reputation was enhanced or diminished by its team's medal count. Ball writes that the Olympic Games provide a "usefull arena for the production and distribution of the symbols of successful international status-contesting. They become a stage where is played the drama of the politics of symbolic conflict[27]." With such high symbolic stakes it is no wonder that scholars and policy makers have devoted a great deal of effort to determine what factors predict national team success.

We wish to highlight briefly the more widely known research on this topic. Jokl[28] found a high correlation between sporting success and low national death rates, low infant mortality rates and high per capita income. Novikow and Maximenko[29] confirmed the per capita income correlation and added caloric consumption, life expectancy, literacy, urbanization and total size of the population as contributing factors. Lüschen[30] and Seppänen[31] found religious factors to be predominantly important while Pooley et al.[32] focused attention on concrete political decisions. Ball concluded his investigation of this same topic with the statement that:

> [   ] overall the successful nation-state in Olympic competition would appear in a kind of visual factor analysis, to be: stable and homogeneous in population, literate, modern and western, with little institutionalized domestic political competition, economically prosperous, characterized by a strong central government staffed by an elite, and probably a member of the Communist Bloc[33].

There is an assumption made in these studies that one can aggregate a country's olympic success without considering the differential medal contributions of its female and male athletes. The following correlational analysis focuses specifically on national female success to investigate the degree to which the traditional variables posited as predictive of overall national success also serve to explain national female success. This correlational analysis considers fourteen national indicators for 28 countries that differ in their degree of female olympic participation and achievement. Four categories of countries were determined in the following manner: the highly successful "elite seven" were all included; a random sample of seven countries which won at least one women's medal constituted the second category, "some women's medals"; a random sample of seven countries which won no women's medals but did win at least one male medal and which had women on the national team, labeled "no women medals";

and a random sample of seven countries which won no medals nor had any females on their team, designated as "no women". Each country received a score for their women athletes which was computed by weighting the gold medals as three, silver medals as two, bronze medals as one and no medals as zero. *Table 6* presents the list of the twenty-eight countries selected for this analysis along with their female medal total.

Table 7 presents the relationship between the fourteen national indicators and female and male olympic success as measured by medals won. The predictive value of indicators noted in earlier studies of national olympic success were generally similar for female and male athletes. The most important predictor of success for women was governmental system which supports our earlier hypothesis that state-socialist countries promulgate public policies and allocate

TABLE 6

Selected Countries and Female Olympic "Scores"
1988 Seoul Olympic Games

Categories	Countries and Scores						
Highly successful	GDR 97	URS 69	USA 60	ROM 34	BUL 28	CHN 28	FRG 21
At least one women's medal	HUN 8	CAN 7	GBR 5	ARG 2	ITA 2	JAM 2	SWE 2
No women's medal	BRA	CHI	COL	DEN	GRE	FIN	PHI
No women	AND	BRN	IRN	LES	PAK	TOG	SOL

TABLE 7

Correlations Between National Indicators and Medal Scores
by Sex of Athlete†
1988 Seoul Olympic Games

Indicators	Female	Male
Governmental System	.66*	.50*
Gross National Product (GNP)	.56*	.78*
Defense Spending	.52*	.76*
Population Growth	− .38*	− .37*
Per Capita GNP	.35*	.41*
Religious Homogeneity	− .34*	− .35*
Literacy	.31*	.34*
Female Life Expectancy	.31*	.35*
Crude Birth Rate	− .30	− .30
Infant Mortality Rate	− .27	− .28
Population Size 1988	.27	.23
Urbanization	.17	.24
Service Sector Economy	− .12	− .03
Ethnic Homogeneity	.12	− .01

† Only single-sex events were included
* Significant at < .05 level

national resources which reflect their ideological commitment to female athleti-cism. A country's wealth and its budget allocation for military spending were also strong and significant predictors of female success. Negative relationships were found for population growth and religious homogeneity. Female life expectancy and national literacy rates were positive but less strongly related to national female success. The remaining six factors were negligible. Although male and female success rates are highly correlated (.85), there is a noteworthy difference in the rank order of the factors. Specifically, GNP and defense spending are stronger predictors for men than is governmental system which again is suggestive of the greater importance of political ideology and related public policy for women olympians.

The next task was to refine our understanding of those factors that predicated different ranges of female olympic success. We wanted to know what, if any, differences obtain when we compare the "Elite Seven" with a group of countries that sent no women to the Olympic Games. Table 8 presents the correlations for this analysis. We hypothesized that several indicators of special relevance for women would be significantly related to female olympic success. These indicators were population growth, crude birth rate, female life expectancy and infant mortality rate. These four factors are directly tied to female health, physical well-being and reproductive functioning. Furthermore they are intimately connected to governmental policies and national resource allocations. Clearly the data in *Table 8* is suggestive of the potential of this hypothesis for identifying indicators of female olympic participation and success. Countries with lower population growth rates, lower crude birth rates, lower infant mortality rates and higher female life expectancy were significantly more likely to achieve high levels of female athletic success in the Olympic Games than were countries with attributes that have traditionally disadvantaged women.

TABLE 8

**Correlations Between National Indicators and Female Medal Scores:
A Comparison Between National Extremes
1988 Seoul Olympic Games**

Indicators	r
Population Growth	− .76**
Governmental System	.66**
Literacy Rate	.64**
Crude Birth Rate	− .61**
Female Life Expectancy	.61**
Infant Mortality	− .56**
Per Capita GNP	.55*
Religious Homogeneity	− .54*
Gross National Product (GNP)	.52*
Defense Spending	.50*
Urbanization	.49
Ethnic Homogeneity	.33
Population Size 1988	.18
Service Sector Economy	.04

** Significant at < .01 level
* Significant at < .05 level

These preliminary findings suggest the usefulness of future efforts to tease out those national attributes that differentiate male and female olympic achievement and to specify more fully how national policies and priorities impact on female life chances. Nonetheless, it is clear that of all the factors that are related to women's olympic success, the most important is the presence of a state-socialist government. This factor takes on special significance because many countries formerly controlled by the Communist Party are presently open to challenge and transformation.

Concluding Remarks

There are of interest to us several scenarios for state socialist countries that have implications for the future of their women olympians. First, as has been noted above, these countries, to varying degrees, have relied on the Olympic Games as a stage on which to dramatize and proclaim their ideological vigor, their scientific achievements and the personal talents of their citizens. The Games have served as an arena in which to claim and obtain international respect. As these countries experiment with modifications of their political and economic institutions and pursue their own visions of political pluralism and economic vitality, they are likely to engage in international exchanges that become alternative bases of respect, power and recognition in the world community. Advances in their scientific, technical, industrial, economic and cultural institutions, accompanied by enhanced diplomatic and governmental linkages to other countries could reduce their past reliance on the Olympic Games as a source of moral and political legitimacy.

A second and related issue involves the need for these countries to reconsider the present allocation of scarce resources away from certain sectors of the society to others. Clearly, this challenge is already underway in discussions of the re-allocation of resources to military and intelligence sectors. It is conceivable that expenditures for sports would also be re-evaluated and result in a decreased willingness to maintain past resource commitments to athletic endeavors. When food, industry, employment, housing and transportation concerns, among others, become focal citizen concerns, one wonders whether the goal of continued athletic and olympic dominance can be justified or will be well-received. If this should happen then elite athletes, both male and female, might not remain among the beneficiaries of scarce resources. The relative impact of this choice for female athletes is, we believe, more deleterious than for male athletes.

A third scenario centers on the dynamics of national gender ideologies and images. As walls come down, both in concrete and symbolic ways, between previously opposed countries, women in athletically dominant Eastern Europe countries, in the USSR and in the People's Republic of China will be exposed to a wider range of discourses on sex, physicality, gender identity, gender systems and gender ideologies. It is not implausible to propose that, given the power of white, Western, Anglo-European countries to convey convincingly attractive images of women as individualistic, narcissistic, sexualized consumers of the goods and services of more privatized economies that these portrayals may challenge the present gender conceptions and gender ideologies that prevail in state-socialist countries. We are not suggesting that women in these countries will uncritically adopt these images and options; rather, we wish merely to call attention to this possibility which has, in our opinion, played a substantial role in producing and maintaining relatively lower levels of female athletic achievement evident in the United Kingdom, Canada, Australia, France, Italy, Switzerland and Belgium to name but a few examples. In the USA, for example, a country of considerable wealth, political opportunity, economic resources, leisure, reproductive freedom, scientific knowledge, the level of female olympic achievement is much less than one might expect or desire.

We wish, then, to end our paper with a call for women, at all levels and forms of athletic involvement—as athletes, coaches, administrators and policy makers—to remain alive to the critical crossroads at which we find ourselves. We need to shape the discourse on female athleticism, each in our own voice, as citizens, scientists, scholars, feminists, physical educators, media representatives, athletic sponsors and government leaders. We must insist on creating opportunities, resources, laws, organizations and policies that bring women into the Olympic Movement as equal bearers of the flame that symbolizes the ideals that the Olympic Games proclaim.

NOTES AND REFERENCES

1. Hargreaves J (1984) Women and the olympic phenomenon. In Tomlinson A, Whannel G (eds) Five Ring Circus. London: Pluto Press

2. Talbot M (1988) Women and the Olympic Games. Action 19 10-12

3. Birrell S (1988) Discourses on the gender/sport relationship: from women in sport to gender relations. Exercise and Sport Science Review 16 459-502

4. Donnelly P, Young K (1985) Reproduction and transformation of cultural forms in sport: a contextual analysis of rugby. International Review for the Sociology of Sport 20 19-38

5. Hall M (1985) How should we theorize sport in a capitalist patriarchy? International Review for Sociology of Sport 20 109-13

6. Hargreaves J (1982) Sport, culture and ideology. London: Routledge and Kegan Paul

7. Harris J (1987) Moving toward sociocultural sport studies. Sociology of Sport Journal 4 133-36

8. Lenskyj H (1986) Out of bounds: women, sport and sexuality. Toronto: The Women's Press

9. Théberge N (1985) Toward a feminist alternative to sport as a male preserve. Quest 10 193-202

10. MacAloon JJ (1984) Rite, drama, festival, spectacle: rehearsals toward a theory of cultural performance. Philadelphia: Institute for the Study of Human Issues

11. MacAloon JJ (1988) Double visions: Olympic Games and American culture. In Seagraves J, Chu D (eds) The Olympic Games in transition. Champaign: Human Kinetics p 279-94

12. Rintala J (1988) Women and the Olympics—making a difference. Journal of Physical Education Recreation and Dance 3 p 34

13. Talbot M (1988) op cit

14. Riordan J (1985) Some comparisons of women's sport in East and West. International Review for the Sociology of Sport 20 117-25

15. Willis P (1982) Women in sport and ideology. In Hargreaves J (ed) Sport, culture and ideology. London: Routledge and Kegan Paul p 117-35

16. Boutilier M, San Giovanni L (1983) The sporting woman. Champaign: Human Kinetics

17. Eichberg H (1984) Olympic sport—neocolonization and alternatives. International Review for the Sociology of Sport 19 97-105

18. Spears B (1988) Tryphosa, Melopomene, Nadia, and Joan: the IOC and women's sport. In Segrave J, Chu D (eds) The Olympic Games in transition. Champaign: Human Kinetics p 365-73

19. Talbot M (1988) op cit p 11

20. Davenport J (1988) The role of women in the IOC and IOA. Journal of Physical Education Recreation and Dance, March p 42-45

21. Talbot M (1988) op cit p 11

22. Biles F (1984) Women and the 1984 Olympics. Journal of Physical Education Recreation and Dance May-June p 62, 65, 72

23. Boutilier M, San Giovanni (1983) op cit

24. Ibid p 233-34

25. Ball D (1972) Olympic Games competition: structural correlates of national success. International Journal of Comparative Sociology 13 186-200

26. Duncan H (1962) Communication and social order. New Jersey: Bedminster Press

27. Ball D (1972) op cit p 188

28. Jokl E (1964) Health, wealth and athletics. In Jokl E, Simon E (eds) International Research in Sport and Physical Education. Illinois: CC Thomas

29. Novikow A, Maximenko A (1972) The influence of selected socio-economic factors on the level of sports achievement in various countries. International Review of Sport Sociology 7 27-44

30. Lüschen G (1967) The interdependence of sport and culture. International Review of Sport Sociology 2 127-39

31. Seppänen P (1970) The role of competitive sports in different societies. Paper presented at the 7th World Congress of International Sociological Association. Varna (Bulgaria) September

32. Pooley JC et al (1975) Winning at the Olympics: a quantitative analysis of the impact of a range of socio-economic, politico-military, growth rate and educational variables. A paper presented at the annual Conference of APHPERA, Charlottestown (Prince Edward Island, Canada) November

33. Ball D (1972) op cit p 198

[. . .] les femmes ont sans doute prouvé qu'elles étaient à la hauteur de presque tous les exploits dont les hommes sont coutumiers, mais elles n'ont pas réussi à établir qu'en ce faisant, elles soient demeurées fidèles aux conditions nécessaires de leur existence et dociles aux prescriptions de la nature [. . .]

Coubertin P de (1902) Le tableau de l'éducation physique au XXᵉ siècle. Revue Olympique, octobre, p 61

UNIVERSITÉS

TRANSATLANTIQUES

PAR

PIERRE DE COUBERTIN

PARIS

LIBRAIRIE HACHETTE ET Cⁱᵉ

79, BOULEVARD SAINT-GERMAIN, 79

—

1890

**Quelques institutions universitaires visitées
par de Coubertin... (1889-1890)**

Cornell

Boston College

Michigan

M.I.T.

Amherst

Princeton

Chicago

West Point

Columbia

Tulane

John Hopkins

Yale

Wellesley

Washington U.

Virginia

Cath. U. of Washington

Harvard

Georgetown

Washington-Lee

Pennsylvania

McGill

Laval

Collège de Montréal

Ottawa

Toronto

1890
1990

Canada

Québec

UNIVERSITÉ
LAVAL

Play, Sport-for-All, Elite and Olympic Sport, and the Social Construction of Gender

Le jeu, le sport-pour-tous, le sport d'élite et olympique, et la construction sociale des sexes

La participation des femmes au Mouvement olympique :
progrès, obstacles, et conditions d'accroissement

L'auteure, elle-même ex-athlète olympique et membre du Comité international olympique, rappelle en introduction le lourd tribut imposé par Coubertin au développement du sport féminin, puis procède à l'esquisse des progrès effectués au cours du siècle dans l'accès des femmes aux Jeux olympiques. Le rôle des fédérations internationales y est mentionné, à la fois comme facteur de progrès et de frein, puisque ce sont ces fédérations qui proposent au CIO les disciplines et épreuves, autant masculines que féminines, à porter au programme des Jeux. La Fédération internationale de natation aura été la première à promouvoir le sport féminin en votant pour l'inclusion féminine au programme. Les autres fédérations internationales suivirent, mais très lentement. Le cas de l'athlétisme en est un exemple, à propos duquel l'auteure souligne, d'une part, la durée des affrontements entre la Fédération sportive féminine internationale et l'International Amateur Athletic Federation et, d'autre part, le rôle des media dans l'entretien des stéréotypes à l'égard du sport féminin. En athlétisme, il aura donc fallu 60 ans, des Jeux olympiques de 1928 à ceux de 1988, pour que les femmes atteignent la presque parité avec les hommes en termes de nombre d'épreuves. Pendant ce temps, la différence de performance quantitative entre hommes et femmes aura été considérablement réduite, notamment en ce qui concerne les épreuves controversées de courses de longue distance. Plusieurs paradoxes demeurent, dans d'autres sports, notamment dans les compétitions de tir aux Jeux olympiques, où la différence réglementaire dans le poids des armes prive les femmes de l'utilisation d'armes dont l'avantage technique est manifeste. Dans la seconde partie de son exposé, l'auteure relie directement les problèmes de règlements inappropriés ou de restrictions dans les occasions de compétition à l'absence de femmes dans les postes décisionnels aux plus hautes instances des sports nationaux et internationaux. D'après l'auteure, une enquête-maison, menée par les soins de l'Amateur Athletic Foundation of Los Angeles, indique que 5 % de femmes seulement occuperaient les quelque 13 000 positions décisionnelles disponibles en sport tout autour du monde. Pourtant, de l'avis de l'auteure, le vécu compétitif est souvent décisif dans l'accès aux postes de décision. En conclusion, l'auteure suggère un certain nombre de conditions qui seraient favorables à l'accroissement de la participation féminine en sport. Elle suggère qu'à l'avenir : – les femmes soient encouragées à la pratique sportive en y étant formées tout autant dans le rôle d'entraîneure que dans celui d'athlète ; – les quelques femmes qui exercent actuellement un leadership soient utilisées comme modèles de rôle ; – le recrutement de femmes à des postes décisionnels soit accompagné de lignes directrices pour que ces femmes fassent l'expérience du succès. L'auteure conclut en souhaitant que la décade des années 1990 permette aux femmes d'occuper la place qu'elles méritent au sein du système sportif, de manière à ce qu'elles participent à l'infléchissement des trajectoires du sport au troisième millénaire.

Progress made, Pitfalls and Conditions for further Advancement of Women in the Olympic Movement

Anita L. DeFrantz

Sport belongs to all human beings. It is unique to the human species. Other animals, like humans, engage in play. Other animals, like humans, engage in setting aside and protecting their territory. But only the human species take part in sport. We are the only ones on Earth who set up barriers and try to jump over them and to see who can get to the finish line first. We are the only ones who compete for the sheer satisfaction of winning.

Sports is our birthright. Sport provides an opportunity for individuals to set their own goals and accomplish those goals, whether it is to run a mile in four minutes or to jump eight feet. It allows a person to take on a personal challenge and to succeed. And yet, at the revival of the most enduring and important sporting event, the Olympic Games, 51% of humanity was excluded.

The father of the modern Olympic Games, Pierre de Coubertin, was not in favor of women participating in the Olympic Games, or in sports in general. Coubertin defined the Games as "[...] l'exaltation solennelle et périodique de l'athlétisme mâle avec l'internationalisme pour base, la loyauté pour moyen, l'art pour cadre et l'applaudissement féminin pour récompense[1]." According to Leigh, "Coubertin felt a women's glory rightfully came through the number and quality of children she produced, and that as far as sports were concerned, her greatest accomplishment was to encourage her sons to excel rather than to seek records for herself[2]." With such strong feelings on the part of Coubertin, it is not surprising that women were excluded from the first modern-era Olympic Games in 1896 in Athens.

Even though women were excluded from the 1896 Games, a woman named Melpomene, trained secretly for weeks and asked to enter the marathon. Despite being denied access by olympic officials, she ran the distance from Marathon to Athens, with followers on bicycles to chronicle the event, in four and a half hours. But things were changing. At the end of the 19th century and during the beginning of the 20th century, industrialization and the impact of social reform

1890
1990

Anita L. DeFrantz, Member of the International Olympic Committee, President of the Amateur Athletic Foundation of Los Angeles, Los Angeles, California, USA.

through the women's movement changed the passive role of women to an active one, which also involved sports. In the Paris Olympic Games in 1900, 12 women did compete in tennis and golf. But it was not until 1912 that the women's movement in sports found any kind of a champion within the Olympic Movement.

While the International Olympic Committee decides the program of the Games, the IOC has always looked to the international sports federations to propose the events. Unless a sports federation supports women's sports, the IOC will not act on inclusion. The *International Swimming Federation* was the first to promote women's involvement and voted to include women on the Olympic Games program in swimming. This opened the way for other international governing bodies to follow. But they followed extremely slowly.

The story of track and field is very enlightening in this regard. In response to the exclusion of women from track and field in the Olympic Games, Alice Milliat of France founded the *Fédération féminine sportive de France* (FFSF) in 1917 to oversee national women's athletic competition. Four years later she established the *Fédération sportive féminine internationale* (FSFI) to include international competition. The FSFI conducted the first Ladies Olympic Games in 1922 in Paris. The FSFI conducted similar Games every four years until 1934, and the schedule of athletic events rose as high as 15, with 19 countries participating in the program of the 1934 Games in London. In fact, the 1924 Women's International and British Games were attended by 25 000 spectators.

When it became apparent that the Ladies Olympic Games were successful in terms of competition and participation, the men's international governing body, the International Amateur Athletic Federation (IAAF), became interested in absorbing the FSFI. The struggle between the IAAF and FSFI went on for 14 years. During the struggle, the IAAF decided to offer women an opportunity to compete in the 1928 Olympic Games in Amsterdam. But the women were offered only five events, and the press (still a male-dominated institution) was decidedly against participation by women in the Games.

At the center of the 1928 controversy was the women's 800 meter run. The male administrators, members of the IOC and the all-male media had apparently pre-determined that women were too frail to compete in a race as long as 800 meters. As a result, the reports from the 1928 Games not only distorted the results of that race, but in some cases completely fabricated facts to support their viewpoint. The tragic result was that the event was removed from the Olympic program and not reinstated until 1960. John Tunis, a prominent sportwriter of the day, portrayed the 800 meter event as follows: "Below us on the cinder path were 11 wretched women, 5 of whom dropped out before the finish, while 5 collapsed after reaching the tape [. . .][3]." Unfortunately for Mr. Tunis, the camera had been invented by 1928, and photographs, as well as Olympic Games records, clearly indicate that only 9 women started the race, *not 11*, and all nine of them finished the race. The winner, Lina Radke of Germany, set a world record. She and a few of the other competitors were understandably spent after racing at world-record pace. Some of them laid down beside the track, but none of them dropped out or collapsed from exhaustion. This report was made by Dr. Messerli, one of the officials of the race: "[. . .] the journalists believed them to be in a state of exhaustion [. . .] I can certify that there was nothing wrong with them, they burst into tears betraying their disappointment at losing [. . .][4]." And in Bill Henry's book *An Approved History of the Olympic Games*, he writes: "[. . .] to the majority of seasoned spectators the women seemed overcome by disappointment rather than exhaustion[5]". And yet, members of the press chose to write what would suit the purpose of the male-dominated administration, and effectively prevented women from competing in any race longer than 400 meters in the Olympic Games for the next 32 years.

It is interesting to compare a report on men's events from earlier Games. The men's 800 meter race from the 1904 Olympic Games was described as follows: "Thursday afternoon at the finish of the 800 meter run, two men fell to the track, completely exhausted. One man was carried to his training quarters helpless. Another was laid out on the grass and stimulants used to bring him back to life[6]." Apparently the men are allowed to collapse following 800 meters, but the women are not. Interesting that no one used this race to prevent men from running that distance in subsequent Olympic Games. Nor did anyone react at the spectacle of Roger Bannister as he crossed the finish line in breaking the four-minute mile, collapsing in a state of exhaustion into the arms of officials.

The point, of course, is that anyone, man or woman, has the right to be fatigued as a result of giving their all in a race. But in that 1928 women's 800 meter race fatigue was used as a means of controlling the events in which women would participate in future Olympic Games. Of course we know today that the decision-makers were wrong in denying women equal athletic opportunities to those enjoyed by men. We also know today that given the opportunity to participate, women will excel and improve.

The 1928 800 meter event challenged the ability of women to excel. Women have met that challenge. In fact, the improvement in women's athletic achievements since then has been remarkable. The gender gap is shrinking rapidly in terms of competition in athletic events shared by men and women. For example, the women's world record in the 800 meters set by Lina Radke in the 1928 Olympic Games was 26 seconds slower than the men's world record. Today that gap has shrunk to a mere 12 seconds. In the marathon, the current women's world record of 2:21.06 by Ingrid Kristiansen would have defeated all of the men in Olympic Games competition up to 1960, including the legendary Emil Zatopek by four minutes. She would have beaten the male winner of the 1928 marathon by a full 12 minutes. That was the year the women were considered too frail to run 800 meters.

And yet the growth of women's participation in track and field in the Olympic Games following the 1928 incident was painstakingly slow. By 1936 the IAAF had managed to absorb the women's organization completely. The IAAF promised increased participation and support for women's sports at all levels. The record suggests they have been slow to fulfill that commitment. It was not until 1960 when the women were once again permitted to race at 800 meters. In 1964 the 400 meters was added, and in 1972 the 1 500 meters. By 1984 in Los Angeles the women had successfully lobbied for inclusion of the 3 000 meters and marathon, and finally in 1988 the 10 000 meter race gained acceptance on the program. There is still no 5 000 meter run, although there will be a 10 000 meter race walk event for the first time in Barcelona. It has taken 60 years since that 800 meter race, for women to approach parity with men in terms of the number of events on the Olympic Games track and field program. From just 5 events in 1928 to a slate of 18 events in Seoul.

In sports other than track and field, the shrinking gender gap comparisons are even more remarkable. For example, in swimming, the 800 meter world record held by Frenchman Jean Taris in 1930 was a full two minutes faster than Yvonne Goddard's women's record. But in 1989, the diminutive Janet Evens' world record trails the men's time by only 27 seconds, and her time of 8:17.12 is more than two minutes faster than Taris' 1930 world record. In speed skating the margin in the 1 500 meters has shrunk from 42 seconds as recently as 1960, to just 8.6 seconds at the Calgary Games, in 1988.

But the injustices heaped on women are not confined to track and field. In the shooting competition of the Olympic Games, for example, women are not given the same advantages as the men because there is a weight limit placed on the women's weapon. The reasoning is that women are not strong enough to support a heavier weapon which would contain many of the technical advantages enjoyed by the men. And in the sport of rowing, when women's events were added to the Olympic Games program in 1976, the women's eights rowed 1 000 meters while the men rowed 2 000 meters. Actually, the shorter distance rowed by the women is harder and more demanding because it is a sprint and doesn't allow for pacing like the 2 000 meter race does. Fortunately, rowing has changed so that everyone races 2 000 meters now.

Most of the problems surrounding lack of competition opportunities for women and inappropriate rules relate directly to the lack of input from women at the administrative level. Women are conspicuously absent from the upper level management positions where policy is determined worldwide. In a recent informal survey taken by the Amateur Athletic Foundation of Los Angeles staff, some disturbing evidence was found: of the nearly 13 000 positions available worldwide in sports and decision-making capacities, a mere 5 percent were held by women. This is in stark contrast to the fact that women comprise more than 51% of the world's population.

It is disturbing for me to admit that, of the 167 presidents of National Olympic Committees worldwide, only six are women. And only four of the 167 secretaries general for those same NOCs are women. The six presidents are: Sophia Raddock, (FIJ); HRH Princess Salote Pilolevu Tuita, (TGA); Princess Nora, (LIE); Carol Anne Letheren, (CAN); Lia Manoliv, (ROM); and Vera Caslavska, (TCH). The four secretaries general are: Eileene L. Parsons, (IVB); Nour El Houda Karfoul, (SYR); Gunilla Lindberg, (SWE); and Myriam Margarita Quezada De Rodriguez, (ESA). Even in the United States of America the record is not excellent. Since 1976 there had been one female officer of the United States Olympic Committee. But for the current quadrennial leading to the Barcelona Games in 1992, not one woman was elected. There are many who could serve as excellent officers, but none were proposed on the slate of officers.

And perhaps more important is the membership of the International Olympic Committee. There are only six women among the 92-member IOC. But prior to 1981 there were none. President Samaranch has been a strong advocate of women in the Olympic Movement. He has insured that women have become involved in the decision-making process. Now it is up to us to provide opportunities for women to take responsibility at every level of sport. There are examples of progress being made however. The election of Carol Anne Letheren as president of Canada's National Olympic Committee is one example. But such examples are all too rare.

The proving ground for upper level management in sports is often the playing field. The future of women in leadership roles begins with today's young girls. They need to be encouraged to participate in sports and learn how to coach as well as play. To encourage women to seek leadership roles, we need role models or examples for them to emulate. But without women in positions of responsibility, we have no role models. Certainly we must make every effort to take advantage of the few examples of successful women that we do have in sports leadership. Women must be allowed to move from the field of competition to the upper levels of management. They must be encouraged to do what Ms. Letheren and others are doing in an effort to ensure the rights of equal and fair competition for women worldwide.

Sports belong to us all, and women will and must continue to fight to take part in sport. If in fact only 5% of all available leadership positions are held by women, that means there are still 95% of them available to women. Sport and the Olympic Movement has long been held in high regard for its ability to appreciate and celebrate human excellence. The Olympic Movement has been responsible for bringing together nations of the world. We must now become the leading force in making the world a better place for everyone by including women at all levels of sport.

It is not difficult to do. It is much like training an athlete. We each need to find women who are interested in serving sport, and provide them with the encouragement and guidance for them to be successful. This is not such a difficult task. There is a slogan used by athletes in the United States, "Just Do It!"

I hope that in 10 years, when I look back on the 1990s, I and other women can refer to it as the decade that saw us take our rightful place alongside men at the helm, guiding sports and athletics into the 21st century.

REFERENCES

1. Coubertin P de (1912) Les jeunes aux Jeux Olympiques. Revue Olympique p 109-111. In Müller N, Comité international olympique (eds) Pierre de Coubertin. Textes choisis. Tome II. Olympisme. Zürich: Weidmann p 705-06

2. Leigh MH (1974) The evolution of women's participation in the summer Olympic Games, 1900-1948. PhD Dissertation. Physical education, Ohio State University. Ann Arbor: University Microfilms p 72

3. Gerber EW, Felshin J, Berlin P, Wyrick W (1974) The American women in sport. Menlo Park: Addison Wesley p 148

4. Leigh MH (1974) op cit p 333

5. Henry B, Yeomans PH (1984) An approved history of the Olympic Games. Los Angeles: Southern California Committee for the Olympic Games p 136-37

6. Leigh MH (1974) op cit p 333

Lobby féministe et pouvoir de décision à propos des politiques nationales, des programmes et des services en activité physique et sport: le cas du Canada

Dans sa présentation, l'auteure utilise le concept de féminisme dans un sens large, incluant égalité entre sexes, mais aussi acquisition de pouvoir et changement social pour tous et toutes. Le lobby féministe en sport au Canada, d'après l'auteure, a tenté de changer les structures du sport pour s'assurer que chaque personne, homme ou femme, garçon ou fille, puisse bénéficier d'équité, de pouvoir de décision, de liberté de choix et de contrôle dans sa vie sportive et récréative. Dans une première partie, l'auteure brosse une toile de fond des mouvements féministes canadiens durant les années 1960 à 1980 et souligne quelques aboutissements concrets et majeurs en termes de retombées. La création de la Commission royale d'enquête sur la situation de la femme en 1967, et son rapport publié en 1970, conduisent à un nouvel agenda féministe. En 1973, le Conseil consultatif canadien de la situation de la femme est créé avec pour mandat de conseiller le gouvernement fédéral et d'informer le public sur les questions permettant d'améliorer la condition féminine dans la société canadienne. Les ramifications provinciales de ce conseil permettront la répercussion des pressions exercées au niveau fédéral auprès des instances gouvernementales et législatives provinciales. Cependant, durant les années 1970, le lobby féministe en activité physique et sport est exercé par des femmes impliquées en sport ou en sciences de l'activité physique et qui adhèrent individuellement à des organismes féministes, plutôt que par les entités gouvernementales responsables de l'activité physique et du sport. La seconde partie de l'exposé est consacrée à la perspective féministe des années 1980 et aux actions gouvernementales entreprises. Un programme consacré aux femmes est créé au sein du ministère de la condition physique et du sport amateur, programme destiné à développer et à promouvoir la participation primaire des femmes en activité physique et sport. En 1981 était créée l'Association canadienne pour l'avancement des femmes et du sport, une organisation non-gouvernementale mais subventionnée par les fonds publics, à perspective féministe avouée, en quête d'un modèle non-sexiste de sport, et avec quatre aires d'activité: la défense politique de la cause féministe; la recherche; le développement du leadership et les communications. Grâce à cette association, l'égalité d'accès à la pratique d'activités physiques et sportives fait partie de l'agenda féministe des années 1980 et, parallèlement, la communauté sportive prend progressivement conscience des problèmes associés à la masculinité du sport. Mais l'impact de cette association comme groupe de pression sera atténué par le bassin réduit de ses membres. En 1986, Sport Canada, l'entité gouvernementale responsable du sport amateur au sein du ministère canadien de la condition physique et du sport amateur, produit un énoncé de politique concernant les femmes et le sport — une stratégie féministe de changement visant à l'égalité d'accès à la pratique et à l'administration du sport. Cet énoncé de politique est suivi d'une stratégie d'application et exerce une pression sur le système sportif canadien, notamment sur les fédérations nationales, pour que les besoins des femmes soient pris en compte. Même s'il est trop tôt pour évaluer l'impact de cette politique, dit l'auteure, la stratégie envisagée pose des problèmes plus complexes aux fédérations que leur simple planification quadriennale. Finalement, l'auteure souligne que la législation canadienne a également été saisie, lors d'un certain nombre de cas, du problème difficile de la ségrégation ou de la mixité dans la pratique sportive compétitive, en utilisant la Charte canadienne des droits et libertés qui interdit toute discrimination sexuelle. Cette question, dit-elle, est au cœur de l'égalité des hommes et des femmes en sport et de l'équité dans l'allocation des ressources et des équipements. En guise de conclusion, l'auteure souligne que, bien que le lobby féministe en sport ait été efficace, le droit des citoyens et citoyennes à la pratique d'activités physiques et sportives demeure un objectif à atteindre.

Feminist Lobbying and Decision-Making Power in Fitness and Amateur Sport National Policies, Programs and Services: the Case of Canada

Mary E. Keyes

In the working meaning of feminism used in this presentation, feminism is understood as a philosophical framework that embodies equality, empowerment, and social change for women and men. Certain goals for women are inherent in this framework: to make visible women's power and status, to redefine existing societal structures and modes of existence, and to enable every woman to have equity, dignity, and freedom of choice through power to control her life and body, both within and outside the home[1]. Feminism seeks to give women, as well as men, the opportunity to be what they can best be. Thus the sport feminist lobby has sought to change the structure of sport in Canadian society—in national sport organizations (NSOs), international sport organizations, and Sport Canada—to ensure that everyone, women and men, girls and boys gain equity, empowerment, and freedom of choice and control over their sport and recreation lives. The problems facing women have been real: *e.g.*, few women in leadership roles within the NSOs and international sport organizations, a sexist media image of women as sport and recreation participants, fewer female competitors in international sport competitions.

This presentation will discuss from an historical perspective, feminist lobbying to improve the sporting environment for women in Canada from 1961 to the present, including the impact of Canadian legislation, the women's movement, catalytic conferences, the persuasive influence of significant women sport and physical activity leaders, fitness and amateur sport national (government) policies, programs, and services, and finally, to consider the significance of this complex movement for sport and for women.

Canadian Legislation

Two important pieces of legislation have significance for our exploration of women and sport in the past three decades. First is the enactment of Bill C-131

1890
1990

Mary E. Keyes, Department of Physical Education, McMaster University, Hamilton, Ontario, Canada.

An Act to Encourage Fitness and Amateur Sport. The Honorable JW Montieth, then Minister of National Health and Welfare introduced this bill in the House of Commons on September 18, 1961 and stressed how pleased he was to introduce this measure relating to "a matter which is wholly dedicated to the greater benefit and enjoyment of the people of Canada[2]." Although the provision of the Act were expressed in vague, general terms, leaving room for interpretation of the government's intention during the early years of its implementation its purpose was to provide access to sport and fitness for *all* Canadians. The immediate effect was felt in the form of unprecedented stimulus to the agencies active in the field of fitness, recreation, and sport across the nation. Between 1961 and 1989 while the budget increased from 5 million dollars to more than 55 million dollars *per annum* and Canada successfully hosted international competitions—Pan-American Games, Summer and Winter Olympic Games, the Commonwealth Games and the FISU Games—provided research monies, initiated innovative arms length organizations such as the Coaching Association of Canada and PARTICIPaction, many women in the sport and physical activity field began to believe that the implementation of the Act left much to be desired in providing access in sport and fitness activities for at least half of the Canadian population. This disquieting recognition that all was not well in fitness and amateur sport will be discussed in greater detail later. The second important piece of legislation—the *Constitution Act 1982*[3]— resulting in the *Canadian Charter of Rights and Freedoms* needs to be examined in its relationship to the second wave of the Women's Movement which coincidentally also gained momentum in the early sixties across our country.

The Canadian Women's Movement: The Second Wave

To understand the ideologies and the strategies employed by women in sport and fitness to make the original intent of the Fitness and Amateur Sport Act a reality, it is essential to discuss the women's liberation movement in Canada since the sixties because it was in this environment that sport and fitness leaders began to seek change. The organization known as the *Voice of Women* begun in 1960 marks the beginning of the second wave of feminism in Canada[4]. It was formed in response to a newspaper column by Lotta Dempsey[5] asking whether women could not do something to deal with international conflict and the threat of war. Married women initially organized the *Voice of Women* and concentrated their efforts on protection of family well-being but also championed a safe and peaceful world. Also in Quebec, in 1966 after celebration of the twenty-fifth anniversary of full enfranchisement, the *Fédération des femmes du Québec* was formed by women's groups called together by suffragist Thérèse Casgrain who gave leadership in this organization and provided a link with the *Voice of Women*[6,7,8].

Increased media urgings, the development of feminist groups in most major cities, and support from volunteer and professional women's groups spearheaded by energetic Laura Sabia led to the organization of a *Committee on Equality of Women of Canada* which called for a royal commission and incorporated their request in a brief to the prime minister. When the brief-approach brought no response Laura Sabia used the press, threatening to march two million women on Ottawa, and finally convinced the government to establish a royal commission. During the 1960s, although women in larger numbers were in the work force and education, the government seemed to underestimate their dissatisfaction, it rationalized a royal commission as a plausible way to examine women's role in the labour force and perhaps at the same time diffuse the feminist criticism.

The *Royal Commission on the Status of Women* established in 1967, reported in 1970. A Toronto Star columnist told his readers that this report was nothing less than "a bomb already primed and ticking [...] packed with more explosive potential than any device manufactured by terrorists [...] a call to revolution [...][9]." Its report spelled out four principles: 1–women should be free to choose whether or not to take employment outside their homes; 2–the care of children is a responsibility to be shared by the mother, the father, and society; 3–society has a responsibility for women because of pregnancy and childbirth, and special treatment related to maternity will always be necessary; and 4–in certain areas women will, for an interim period, require special treatment to overcome the adverse effects of discriminatory practices[10]. As will be discussed, interestingly, sport has become an area of "special treatment". The Report containing 167 recommendations became a national best-seller and set the agenda for the second wave of feminism in Canada.

When the government did not act on the commission's report as quickly as feminists wanted, again it was impatient and persistent Laura Sabia who led the *Committee on Equality for Women* as it evolved into the *National Ad Hoc Committee on the Status of Women in Canada* in 1971. The *ad hoc* committee presented a substantial brief to the government, incorporating three priority goals: expansion of day care, insertion of "sex" as a prohibited basis of discrimination under Canadian human rights provisions, and decriminalization of abortion[11]. Early in 1972, the *ad hoc* committee became the continuing umbrella organization, the *National Action Committee on the Status of Women (NAC)*[12]. NAC dropped the *ad hoc* from its title because the government would not otherwise supply the money essential first for the "Strategy for Change" conference held April 1972 in Toronto, and then for continuing funding. In 1973 the federal *Advisory Council on the Status of Women*[13] was accordingly established with the mandate to advise the government and inform the public on issues of improving women's position in society and councils were organized in several provinces across the country. But although some progress was seen many feminists felt that progress was too slow.

All the time some women were striving for change through organizations and pressuring the government, sometimes called "institutional feminist"; ordinary women, "grass-roots feminist", were demanding change in their own environment. As so often happens in any movement there were different analyses and strategies for change within the women's movement and in hind-sight we are able to recognize during the late 1970s and early 1980s at least three currents of feminism—radical feminists focused on violence against women as their main issue, while social feminists concentrated on various aspects of women's work, and liberal feminists continued to lobby the government for legal changes[14]. When the federal government decided to patriate the Canadian constitution and to add to it a *Charter of Rights and Freedoms*, many women's groups made presentations and the Constitution is stronger than it might have been because of their determination, persistence, and extraordinary methods and effort. Two sections illustrate the impact of the women's lobby:

Section 15

1. Every individual is equal before and under the law and has the right to the equal protection and equal benefit of the law without discrimination based on race, national or ethnic origin, colour, religion, sex, age or mental or physical disability.

2. Subsection 1 does not preclude any law, program or activity of conditions of disadvantaged individuals or groups including those that are disadvantaged because of race, national or ethnic origin, colour, religion, sex, age, or mental or physical disability.

Section 28

Notwithstanding anything in this Charter, the rights and freedoms referred to in it are guaranteed equally to male and female persons[15].

As has been demonstrated women involved in the second wave of the women's movement in Canada 1–joined together in groups to change society, to gain equality; 2– they met together in conferences and study sessions; 3– they researched and studied issues, wrote briefs and presented them to the government; 4– they reasoned, planned, cajoled, threatened, resigned, used the media, lobbied with letters, telegrams, and personal presentations, and they effected changes in Canadian society through legislation. And women disagreed with each other about the agenda and the appropriate strategies for change, as well some became tired, discouraged and disenchanted. It was in this Canadian environment that women in sport and recreation approached their concern for equality in sport and benefitted directly from the *Royal Commission* and the *Charter of Rights and Freedoms*, in addition to a more enlightened attitude generally in Canadian society—at least equality of women since the 1960 beginning was a recognized Canadian issue. And, if as Eichler has suggested, we should expect attitudes to change first and then behaviour change to follow[16], the environment was fertile for behavioral change in sport.

Equality in Sport and Recreation

During the period 1960 to 1980, women active in sport and physical activity participated individually in feminist organizations but there was no visible sport or fitness organizational involvement in the women's movement. However, in the *Report of the Royal Commission on the Status of Women* of 1970, two recommendations addressed the issue of female participation in sports programs:

> Recommendation 77: We recommend that the provinces and territories (*a*) review their policies to ensure that school programmes provide girls with equal opportunities with boys to participate in athletic and sports activities, and (*b*) establish policies and practices that will motivate and encourage girls to engage in athletic and sports activities.

> Recommendation 78: We recommend that, pursuant to section 3(*d*) of the federal Fitness and Amateur Sport Act, a research project be undertaken to (*a*) determine why fewer girls than boys participate in sport programmes at the school level and (*b*) recommend remedial action[17].

These published recommendations provided the stimulus in the early 1970s for Fitness and Amateur Sport (FAS) bureaucrats to question inequities in the sport and recreation system but it is interesting that at this time there was not a ground swell of women athletes, coaches and administrators, or physical educators demanding more opportunities to participate in the system which had expanded considerably following the passage of the Act to Encourage Fitness and Amateur Sport in 1961 and was greatly strengthened under the Honorable John Munro's leadership in the early seventies.

To explore the issues raised by the Royal Commission recommendations, FAS in March 1974 sponsored a National Conference on Women and Sport in Toronto. As the forward of the report suggested:

> [...] [this conference] provided an opportunity for delegates to exchange information in an attempt to gain a better understanding of the situational and attitudinal factors which often constrain the participation of girls and women in physical recreation; formulate recommendations regarding the role of girls and women within the existing sport structure and develop programs directly affecting the opportunity and status accorded to women in sport and recreation[18].

Significant recommendations were targeted to governments, sport agencies, educational authorities, status-of-women groups, and individuals. In addition to the recommendations made and forwarded, this conference was important to women because for the first time they communicated as administrators, athletes, and coaches about their common experiences. It was a positive forum because most women in attendance were positive about their own sporting experience and were committed to increasing these opportunities for more and more girls and women at every level of sport across the country. But it would be stretching the truth to suggest that a feminist perspective permeated the conference even though spirited Laura Sabia, Chairperson of the *Ontario Status of Women Council*, delivered the keynote address to open the conference. She tried to clear up some misconceptions about the women's movement and attacked directly the feelings of many women in the sport field: "Some women say to me, I wouldn't be a women's libber for anything; don't talk to me of Women's Lib. What is Women's Lib? [she asked] Let's take just one minute to look at it. Women's Lib is nothing more than equality of opportunity, responsibility, and choice[19]."

Although the 1974 conference must be seen as the beginning of the women's movement in sport and fitness, between 1974 and 1979 only one person was hired by the Sport and Fitness Directorate to improve the status of women in sport and substantive change did not take place even when Iona Campagnolo became the first Minister of State Fitness and Amateur Sport and spent time defining the mandate of the Ministry. And the recommendations, which had been sent to so many authorities and jurisdictions, lacked impact because there was no person or agency monitoring to see that they were considered or implemented. The *shotgun* approach was found not to be effective. At the level of the Canadian provinces, for example in Ontario and Quebec, the Status of Women Councils were particularly active and addressed the issues of the place of women in the domains of leisure and sport[20].

In its report *What's Been Done* the Canadian Advisory Council on the Status of Women (CACSW), listed the accomplishements of the FAS Branch of the Ministry of Health and Welfare in achieving the recommendations from the Royal Commission. In summary these included:

> [. . .] hiring one women's consultant responsible for defining the problems facing women in sport and designing programs to alleviate these problems. Programs have included (1) educational programs to ascertain the reason behind the lack of female participation and programs to alleviate the problem areas; (2) coaching programs for increasing the quality and quantity of women coaches, (3) promotional programs such as symposia, films and printed materials on women and sport; (4) establishment of an information retrieval center collecting and distributing needed materials on women in sport; (5) development of women officials for the 1976 Olympics and beyond[21].

Feminist Perspective

1980 is a watershed year in the history of women and sport. First, in March 1980 a Female Athlete Conference was held in Vancouver, co-sponsored by FAS and the Institute for Human Performance at Simon Fraser University. In the rationale the organizers established the conference's focus:

> In order to eradicate the misconceptions and inequities which have prevailed regarding women and sports, it is necessary to first recognize that women are unique to the sports arena. They do not wish to emulate their male counterparts, nor should they be compared. Female athletes are not only those women participating in competitive sports at the provincial, national or international level, but rather include all women and girls who participate in physical activity regardless of their skill level. Many of these women share mutual concerns and face similar barriers to their continued and expanding interest in sport and recreation, and a greater understanding of these barriers is necessary to enhance their opportunity to express their physical being. Therefore it is important to examine a multitude of factors which affect women's sport participating in the Canadian sports structure[22].

If the 1974 Toronto conference had been important in getting women sport leaders together to meet and communicate, the 1980 Vancouver conference was significant because those in attendance realized that even though they had been working hard individually to improve the sport scene for girls and women not much had been accomplished since 1974—the same kind of problems were identified and the same kind of recommendations were coming forward from the delegates, but also there were specific ideas about the problems that existed and explicit strategies proposed to break down the barriers. Just as had happened in the women's movement ten years earlier, different ideological perspectives and strategies for change were evident among the delegates. The women's movement in sport and recreation was maturing and just talking about change was no longer adequate; action, therefore, became the rallying call. Sportswomen were beginning to examine the structural inequities in the sport system and to appreciate that although individual effort had increased the number of female participants appreciably, women still lacked power and resources within the sport system—the goal of the Act to Encourage Fitness and Amateur Sport for *all* Canadians was not being realized—the Canadian model of sport was the male model of sport. If women were to have the opportunity to be the best they could be in the sport of their choice, then the structure of sport had to change. As a point of interest, it should be said that in the 1970s there had already been specific initiatives to bring the thoughts of sports scientists to bear upon women's issues. At the Olympic Scientific Congress held in Quebec City on the occasion of the Montreal Olympic Games in 1976, for example, one of the main themes chosen for the Congress was *Sport, Women's Emancipation and Feminity*[23].

A second important event occurred in 1980, a "women's program" within FAS[24] was established to develop and promote ways of involving more women in sport and fitness activities. Originally 250 000 dollars to fund research in the area of women, physical activity and lifestyle was set aside and several projects were launched that have had an on-going influence on many areas that had been identified by women leaders as needing seed money for study, implementation, and emphasis. The research, including a leadership survey and a talent-bank feasibility study, indicated that women in leadership positions tended to be concentrated in the middle and lower levels of all type or organizations surveyed. The results stimulated the development of two major components of the FAS Women's Program: an internship program designed to provide on-the-job training for national-calibre female athletes and ex-athletes; and the National Association Contributions Program (NACP). The NACP, by providing contributions to national sport and recreation associations, aimed to encourage women and girls to participate more actively in sport and fitness activities. Several provincial and local initiatives were also funded—a fitness program for inner-city women in Halifax; a post-mastectomy exercise program in Vancouver; and several promotional projects, including the publishing of a book of biographical sketches of outstanding Canadian women athletes.

Several individuals working with the Sport Canada consultant in planning these initiatives began to discuss the need to move past the recommendation stage of conferences to establish a national organization whose rationale would be the eradication of inequities for women in sport. A planning workshop with the specific mandate "to explore the need for an organization concerned with women and sport" was held at McMaster University in Hamilton, in March 1981 and the major outcome was the establishment of the *Canadian Association for the Advancement of Women and Sport* (CAAWS)[25]. Wide-ranging discussions reviewed the status of women in sport, what the sources of inequity were, and what feminism was and how it is related to sport. There was an appreciation of the under representation of women as participants, organizers, and administrators in all levels and types of sport involvement. A turning point in the conference occurred when the fifty in attendance endorsed a series of statements asserting that there was inequity in sport based on sex, the sport system was sexist, and an understanding of sex roles and sexism in sport was the starting point for an analysis of sport. Equality was a goal within a non-sexist sport environment. These statements were called a "feminist perspective on sport[26]". This was the first time many women in attendance considered their concerns with sport as feminist concerns and were willing to call themselves feminists.

Another significant debate occurred about whether the organization should be called women *and* sport rather than women *in* sport. Women *and* sport was adopted because first, the group felt the advancement of women in sport would be achieved only when the status of women in general improved; and secondly, there was consideration of the need for a new model of sport—a non-sexist model—different from the prevalent male model which emphasized commercialism, violence, and performance rather than participation. Although sport was viewed as being patriarchal and a male-oriented institution, those in attendance at the CAAWS founding meeting believed the benefits of access to sport and fitness for all Canadian women was so important that change was essential. The delegates developed a statement of the association's purpose: "to advance the position of women by defining, promoting, and supporting a feminist perspective on sport and to improve the status of women in sport[27]." Toward this end, four activity areas were identified: political advocacy, research, leadership development, and communication both within and outside the association. The CAAWS executive committee and provincial representatives began work building membership, publishing a newsletter, and conducting research.

Because the membership base was small the organization needed to come to grips with funding sources. Many argued that if CAAWS was to advocate against government sport and fitness policies and programs that it should not accept funds from government agencies. The majority, on the other hand, were convinced that government support was necessary and acceptable. CAAWS subsequently received funding from the Secretary of State and from FAS. Since 1981 CAAWS introduced sport into the agenda of feminism and increased the awareness of the sport community to the problems inherent in the maleness of sport. Its research has been instrumental in examining and evaluating Canadian sport and making connections between sport and gender issues. Because CAAWS' membership has been slow to increase and it has not received the full support of Canadian women in sport and physical activity fields, as would have been expected, its impact as a feminist lobby has been diluted and its potential for effecting change within the sport system has not been fully realized.

During the 1980s another feminist influence was making an impact. Feminist scholars and writers were beginning to be heard, read, and discussed. Although Dr Ann Hall from the University of Alberta spoke about the need for "a conceptual framework for the investigation of female involvement in sport[28]" at the National Conference in 1974, and was an influential participant at the CAAWS founding meeting at McMaster University in 1981, the feminist perspective in sport became more widely discussed when she co-authored with Dorothy Richardson *Fair Ball Toward Sex Equality in Canadian Sport* a book about women and sport written from the feminist perspective[29]. The Canadian Advisory Council on the Status of Women commissioned and published *Fair Ball* and following its publication made six recommendations aimed at removing inequities for women and sport. These included requirements that national sport governing bodies, lotteries, agencies and publicly funded sport organizations as well as the Canadian Radio-Television and Telecommunications Commission work towards equitable funding and representation of women in sport. It also recommended a stronger role for the FAS Women's Program in monitoring organizations in this regard.

The same year speaking at the 3rd Annual Conference of the North American Society for the Sociology of Sport in Toronto, in November, Hall explored her own work in the sociology of sport and how it had been influenced by feminism and feminist scholarship. She said:

> There can be no separation of feminism as analysis, feminism as theory, and feminism as political practice. Feminism is all three, and more importantly, analysis and theory are interconnected with practice. In the context of our discussion about gender inequality in sport, I have argued elsewhere [. . .] that we could go on indefinitely showing that structural equality does not exist within the sports world, but we have failed to take account of the origins and causes of women's oppression (or male supremacy) which have produced the societal sex structure and inequality in the first place. To do so would mean we must recognize, use, and contribute to feminist social theory in one or more of its forms[30].

Hall has been the most prolific and influential in Canadian feminist sport research. During this period scholars in addition to Hall, such as Théberge at the University of Waterloo, contributed to the growing feminist sport literature. Feminist analysis has become an accepted research perspective as demonstrated by the quantity and quality of presentations given at conferences and a growing body of literature. But the impact of these scholars has not solely occurred through their writings, also of importance has been the rippling effect of their teaching and research mentoring with graduate students and faculty colleagues.

After a decade of funding conferences, research and promoting programs within the government Sport Canada in 1986 established a *Policy on Women in Sport*—a philosophically based feminist strategy for change. Sport Canada's goal with respect to women in sport as published in the policy statement appears straight forward:

> To attain equality for women in sport. Equality implies that women at all levels of the sport system should have an equal opportunity to participate. Equality is not necessarily meant to imply that women wish to participate in the same activities as men but rather to indicate that activities of their choice should be provided and administered in a fair and unbiased environment. At all levels of the sport system, equal opportunities must exist for women and men to compete, coach, officiate or administer sport. The purpose of this goal is to create an environment in which no one is forced into a pre-determined role or status because of gender[31].

The Sport Canada Policy identified a two-pronged, action-oriented approach to achieving their goal of equality for women in sport: 1–initiatives through their Women's Program and 2–through its financial support and program services. A strategy of implementation was developed for thirteen activities including policy and program development, sport stratification, sport infrastructure, leadership development, high performance competition, participation development, resource allocation, liaison, research, education, promotion, advocacy, and finally monitoring and evaluation. But what does this policy really mean? It means, for example, that if a National Sport Organization accepts funding from FAS that in the leadership development activity it will ensure developmental needs of female administrators, coaches, and officials.

The Sport Canada Policy on Women and Sport represented the first government initiative to change the sport system rather than addressing and solving, through programme initiatives, each problem faced by women desiring to participate in sport. Sport Canada attempted to persuade, challenge, motivate, or withhold funds to make the sport system comply with the law of the land. In place now for only four years, it would be premature to evaluate its success or failure. However, an important consideration, when examining the policy on women and sport is its initial impact. Is the policy changing attitudes about equality in sport? Are there more opportunities for girls and women to participate or administer sport? NSOs appear to give higher priority to Sport Canada's high performance goals. Medal performance objectives are allocated more dollars and are given more attention than increasing opportunities for girls and women at all levels within the

NSOs. Does this situation exist because Sport Canada has not priorized and publicized its goals? Or is it because NSOs believe the goals for high performance rank higher than the goals to improve the status of women and sport? Is it unrealistic to suggest these goals could be complementary? More and accurate information is needed about the attitudes of NSO Boards and employees to suggest that they are not supporting the Policy of Women and Sport but it is curious that little concrete improvement has been achieved. In a comparison of women in leadership positions it is noted that betwen 1982 and 1988 only minimal improvement has occurred—in 1988 fewer than 30% of the Executive Directors of NSOs were women[32]. The policy is voluntary, approximately 500 000 $ per annum is allocated for this program, is the goal of a non-sexist sport system viable under these conditions? Is it unrealistic to expect more women coaches, executive directors and international competitors when women's role in every sphere of society remains inequitable. Although the problems have persisted, committed women have given leadership within the Women's Program. Mention must be made of the guiding influence of the Director General of Sport Canada Abby Hoffman. It has been under her leadership that the federal government has developed and supported the women's program and has established a policy for women's sport that has been so innovative and far-reaching. It will be her responsibility to evaluate any change which this program has made and to chart the FAS strategies for the future—including compliance strategies.

A final issue to be discussed in this presentation is the nature of sport competition and its relationship to human rights legislation in Canada. Lenskyj[33,34] who has added much to our understanding of sport for girls and women, at the 1984 CAAWS Conference reviewed the situation for girls and women at all levels and in all sporting contexts across Canada and developed a detailed analysis of the strengths and weakness of the various models of integration, separate-but-equal, and combined approaches to competition[35]. The complex issue of integrated *versus* segregated sport will be debated for years to come as women try to define equality of opportunity for girls and women in the world of sport.

The issue came to a head in the courts in 1985 when the Ontario Hockey Association denied Justine Blainey the opportunity to become a regular member of a minor hockey team (a boys' team). Justine Blainey first turned to the Ontario Human Rights Commission for help but was advised they could not assist her because of Section 19(2), which specifically protected the continued existence of single-sex sports[36]. She turned to the court and challenged the validity of Section 19(2) of the Ontario Human Rights Code. She challenged in terms of sex equality, arguing that Section 19(2)—that is, the single-sex sports team law—violated her right to sex equality under Section 15(1) of the Charter of Rights and Freedoms. After an unsatisfactory lower court decision Justine fought her case before the Ontario Court of Appeal and was finally successful. The Ontario Hockey Association immediately sought leave to appeal the decision of the Ontario Court of Appeal to the Supreme Court of Canada. In June 1986, however, the Supreme Court of Canada refused to hear the case. Justine once again turned to the Ontario Human Rights Commission when the Ontario Hockey Association again refused to allow her to play. It took 18 months for the Human Rights Commission to rule that first she was eligible to play on a boys' team and secondly, that girls' hockey was a special program under sub-section 13(1) of the Humans Rights Code because the program is designed to assist disadvantaged persons or groups to achieve equal opportunity.

Although Justine was allowed to play on a boys' hockey team the questions arising from this case are very complex and run to the heart of equality of girls and women in sport. Does sex equality mandate integrated sports teams? Are all girls' teams in Ontario classified as "special programs"—for disadvantaged persons or groups or was only girls' hockey protected by the Blainey decision? Will every sport that wishes to be separate-but-equal (if separate ever is equal) need to seek special status through the Human Rights Commission—does that give the perception of second-class sport—is that what equality means? Will answers to questions about leadership roles, about equitable budgets and the use of scarce facilities by female participants, and about systemic under-representation by women in leadership roles in sport organizations be resolved by court challenges? The implications for school, university and amateur sport are mind-boggling.

Although the women's movement in sport followed the Canadian women's liberation movement by more than a decade, the knowledge and strategies for change learned from this Canadian movement have been significant. It was the recommendations from the Royal Commission on the Status of Women which initiated government attention to the inequities in sport for women. It has been feminist sportswomen who it has been demonstrated, employed methods used so successfully by the women before them, and convened conferences, conducted research, wrote briefs, lobbied the government, established policies and programs within the government, and finally challenged in the courts. The feminist struggle to redefine equal opportunities for girls and women in sport is an interesting episode in Canadian history.

But a cautionary note in conclusion, it is apparent that although the feminist lobby in sport has been effective in organizing an advocacy organization such as CAAWS; feminist researchers have examined sport from many disciplinary dimensions; feminist administrators within the government have designed and implemented a policy to promote equality of women in sport; and finally with the support of CAAWS an athlete used the court to seek equality; the mainstream of sport has changed very little.

If sport in the third millenium is to be equitable for all women and men in Canada the strategy of system reformation begun with the 1986 Policy on Women and Sport has greater potential than has yet been realized. The government of Canada through Sport Canada not only has a social responsibility to implement the intent of the Act to Encourage Fitness and Amateur Sport for *all* Canadians, it has policy formulation and financial allocation authority to expect NSO compliance. But at the same time all of Sport Canada's policies need to be rationalized, priorized, and promoted consistently and resources needed to be allocated in compliance with stated policies. To date there is still the perception among NSO's that winning gold medals is more important than providing opportunities for all Canadians. Until this attitude changes, behavioural changes which promote equality will not be evident within the national sport system.

REFERENCES

1. Bunch C (1985) Bringing the global home. Denver: Antelope Publications

2. Government of Canada (1961) House of Commons Debates Official Report Fourth Session twenty-fourth Parliament Volume VIII 1960-1961 Introduction to Bill C-131 28 September 1961 p 8461

3. Government of Canada (1982) Constitution Act 1982. Ottawa: C44 29 March—Loi constitutionnelle de 1982. Ottawa: c 44 29 Mars; The Canadian Charter of Rights and Freedom—la Charte canadienne des droits et libertés

4. Morris C (1980) Determination and thoroughness: the movement for a Royal Commission on the Status of Women in Canada. Atlantis 5 1-21

5. Dempsey L (1960) Private line. Toronto Star 21 May

6. Black N (1988) The canadian women's movement: the second wave. In Burt, S et al (eds) Changing patterns: women in Canada. Toronto: McClelland & Stewart p 80-101

7. Casgrain T (1971) Une femme chez les hommes. Montréal: Éditions du jour

8. Fournier F (1977) Les femmes et la vie politique au Québec. In Lavigne M, Pinard Y, (eds) Les femmes dans la société québécoise. Montréal: Les Éditions du Boréal Express p 169-90

9. Westall A (1970) Report is more explosive than any terrorists' time bomb. Toronto Star December 8

10. Black N (1988) op cit

11. Adamson N et al (1988) Feminist organizing for change. Toronto: Oxford University Press p 51

12. National Action Committee for the Status of Women—Comité canadien d'action sur le statut de la femme (NAC-CCA) In Adamson N et al (1988) op cit p 53

13. Canadian Advisory Council on the Status of Women (1974) What's been done? Assessment of the federal government's implementation of the recommendations of the Royal Commission on the Status of Women—Conseil consultatif de la situation de la femme (1974) Où en sommes-nous?

14. Adamson N et al (1988) op cit p 53

15. Constitution Act 1982 op cit

16. Eichler M (1983) Families in Canada today. Toronto: Gage

17. Report of the Royal Commission on the Status of Women/Rapport de la commission royale d'enquête sur la situation de la femme au Canada (1970) Ottawa: Information Canada p 406

18. Report National Conference on Women and Sport (1974) Toronto May 24-26 p 2

19. Ibid p 11

20. Gouvernement du Québec, Conseil du statut de la femme (1978) Pour les Québécoises: égalité et indépendance. Québec: Éditeur officiel du Québec p 280-92; Hoffman A (1976) About face: towards a positive image of women in sport. Toronto: the Ontario Status of women Council

21. Canadian Advisory Council on the Status of Women (1974) op cit p 15

22. Pompa A (ed) (1980) The female athlete. Proceedings of a national conference about women in sports and recreation. Vancouver: Simon Fraser University p 3

23. Govaerts F (1978) Sports, émancipation des femmes et féminité; Sherif CW (1978) Women's emancipation, feminity and sports: a psychologist's viewpoint; Stone RE (1978) Caveat emptor!; Gummel M, Bierstedt H (1978) Participation in sports and women's emancipation. In Landry F, Orban WAR (eds) Physical activity and human well being/L'activité physique et le bien-être de l'homme. Quebec and Miami: Éditeur officiel du Québec, Symposia Specialists p 445-89

24. Government of Canada (1980) Annual report 1980-81. Ottawa: Fitness and Amateur Sport p 6

25. Advancement of women and sport - a planning workshop (1981) report. Hamilton: McMaster University (mimeographed); this workshop resulted into the establishment of the Canadian Association for the Advancement of women and sport (CAAWS) —L'Association canadienne pour l'avancement des femmes et du sport (ACAFS)

26. Ibid p 9

27. Ibid p 11

28. Report National Conference on Women and Sport (1974) op cit p 23

29. Hall MA, Richardson DA (1982) Fair ball: towards sex equality in canadian sport. Ottawa: The Canadian Advisory Council on the Status of Women—Franc-Jeu: vers l'égalité des sexes dans les sports au Canada. Ottawa: Conseil consultatif canadien de la situation de la femme

30. Hall MA (1984) Toward a feminist analysis of gender inequality. In Theberge N Donnelly P (eds) Sport and the sociological imagination. Fort Worth: Texas Christian University Press p 87-88

31. Government of Canada (1986) Sport Canada policy on women in sport. Ottawa: Fitness and Amateur Sport p 14—Politique de Sport Canada sur les femmes dans le sport. Ottawa: Condition physique et sport amateur

32. Government of Canada (1986) Women in sport leadership: summary of national survey. Ottawa: Fitness and Amateur Sport—Les femmes dans le leadership sportif: résumé de l'enquête nationale. Ottawa: Condition physique et sport amateur

33. Lenskyj H (1986) Out of bounds: women, sport and sexuality. Toronto: The Women's Press

34. Lenskyj H (1988) Women, sport and physical activity: research and bibliography. Ottawa: Fitness and Amateur Sport

35. Lenskyj H (1984) Female participation in sport: the issue of integration versus separate-but-equal. Paper presented to CAAWS Conference, April

36. Ontario Human Rights Commission Board of Inquiry Decision Justine Blainey Complaint against the Ontario Hockey Association et al (1987)

[. . .] le féminisme n'est autre chose qu'un des aspects du vaste mouvement d'émancipation qui transforme la société moderne et qui relâche et assouplit, un à un, les lieux séculaires par lesquels les sujets tenaient au souverain, les fidèles à l'Église, la famille à son chef, les ouvriers au patron [. . .]

Coubertin P de (1901) Notes sur l'éducation publique. Paris: Hachette p 282 (Chapitre XVII L'éducation des femmes)

L'émergence de la sous-culture du triathlon et son impact sur le changement dans la définition des rôles sexuels dans la société nord-américaine

L'expansion de la pratique sportive des plus de trente ans peut être considérée comme l'un des indicateurs de changement social aux États-Unis pendant les années 1980. Dans la diversité des nouvelles pratiques sportives, la popularité du triathlon — qui combine natation, cyclisme et course à pied — est à souligner avec, notamment, la naissance d'une compétition particulièrement exigeante, le *Hawaiian Ironman Triathlon*. L'accroissement de la participation à ce sport semble être exponentiel, et il est indiqué de manière tangible par la création d'une fédération internationale en 1989. À partir d'une enquête menée par observation participante et par entretiens, enquête menée pendant plusieurs années au sein d'un club local de triathlon en Californie, l'auteure s'efforce de dégager le processus de socialisation qui conduit à la pratique de ce sport et de décrire l'influence de cette pratique sur la conception de l'identité et du rôle sexuels. Elle identifie, dans les trois premières phases de socialisation, les facteurs-clé suivants: – le désir d'être en bonne condition physique; – l'influence de la famille et des amis; – la volonté de la municipalité de promouvoir les sports d'endurance; – l'organisation d'épreuves locales de triathlon. La socialisation au rôle de triathlète est achevée, d'après l'auteure, lorsque la personne prend part au Hawaiian Ironman et arrive à bout des distances, performance qui nécessite un investissement considérable de temps, d'argent et d'énergie. La participation à cette compétition exige que l'entraînement soit hissé au rang de priorité, parmi les priorités familiales et occupationnelles. Cette priorité, nouvelle pour les femmes beaucoup plus que pour les hommes, influence la conception de l'identité et du rôle sexuels. Les femmes-triathlètes développent notamment, d'après l'auteure, un sentiment d'identité distinct de la relation à autrui, accompagné d'un sentiment accru de compétence personnelle et d'une plus haute estime de soi. Un groupe nouveau de référence prend de l'importance — celui des femmes ayant adopté le même style de vie. À cause des attentes traditionnelles à l'égard des rôles sexuels, il semble que les relations de type marital soient mise à l'épreuve. De fait, avec le style de vie des triathlètes, nous assistons à la naissance d'une nouvelle réalité culturelle, qui reflète la transformation des rôles sexuels dans la société nord-américaine. En conclusion, l'auteure suggère que la promotion efficiente du sport-pour-tous, basé sur la participation plutôt que sur le classement de la performance, passe par des études d'impact d'un nouveau style de vie sur l'ensemble des relations sociales des participants.

Tri-ing for Life: the Emergence of the Triathlon Sport Subculture and its Impact upon Changing Gender Roles in North American Society

Jane Granskog

One of the hallmarks of social change in the United States of America within the last decade has been the multifaced burgeoning of athletic participation particularly by individuals over thirty. One of the relatively new and increasingly popular sports to emerge out of this "fitness revolution" is the triathlon, a continuous athletic event with three legs consisting of swimming, biking and running. Even more recently, its "step-sister" the biathlon (or "duathlon", now the new official term for a running and biking event—although some also refer to such as "bi-sports") has also gained in popularity. Although the beginnings of the sport of triathlon go back to the very first event held in San Diego, California (the *Fiesta Island Triathlon*) in 1974, most view the emergence of the ultradistance *Hawaiian Ironman Triathlon* (consisting of a 2,4 mile ocean swim, 112 mile bike, and 26,2 mile marathon run), first held in 1978, as the real beginning of the sport. Twelve men finished that first "Ironman" in 1978; fifteen, including one woman, finished it in 1979. The 1979 race was written up in *Sports Illustrated*; a year later, ABC began its coverage of the race on "Wide World of Sports".

Since then the sport has literally exploded in popularity. By May of 1987, in an evaluation of the state of the sport conducted by *Triathlete Magazine*[1], there were an estimated 1 000 000 individuals around the world who had competed in triathlons of varying lengths—ranging from sprint triathlons with a 200 yard swim, 15 km bike and 5 km run and the popular olympic distance events (1,5 km swim, 40 km bike, and 10 km run) to the ultradistance Ironman length events. The number of participants as well as the level of participation in the sport (measured by the yearly average number of races individuals complete) continues to grow exponentially. Within the past year, efforts to establish the legitimacy of the sport on an international level have resulted in the establishment of the International Triathlon Union, the first World Championship olympic distance event (in Avignon, France, August, 1989), and imminent olympic recognition. Many now view the triathlon as *the* sport of the 1980s as well as the decade to come.

1890
1990

Jane Granskog, Department of sociology/anthropology, California State University, Bakersfield, California, USA.

The individuals (and their families and friends) who train for and participate in these multisport events share a culture of their own that has emerged along with the growth of the sport. This paper analyses the impact of participation in the triathlon sport culture upon its members by examining the process by which individuals, and women in particular, are socialized into the sport culture and establish a triathlete identity. It also argues that for the majority of triathletes (most of whom are in their thirties or older), participation in the triathlon culture has transformed their lives. There is a correlation between level of involvement in the sport and the re-defining of one's gender roles and identity. This is particularly true for older women, many of whom began with little or no athletic background. Given the burgeoning popularity of the sport of triathlon, as noted above, examination of the nature of the impact of participation shall contribute to a better understanding of the transformation of gender roles that is taking place within American society today.

The description and analysis presented herein is based on my own participation and involvement in triathlon and duathlon/biathlon (bi-sport) activities since the fall of 1984[2]. Over the last five years, I have been able to conduct a number of informal interviews with participants at varying levels—from first timers to professionals—as well as with race directors, organizers, and volunteers in different parts of the country. I have also gathered extensive field notes based on my observations and informal discussions with members of the triathlon community with whom I train and interact on a regular basis. Most importantly, however, because I share my research observations and analysis with my fellow triathletes, my insights into the character of this lifestyle and its impact upon individuals are not solely mine. This is, for the most part, a collaborative effort—an analysis of experiences and perceptions shared by and with fellow multisport enthusiasts. The research methodology employed herein, therefore, is one of participant observation, but from an insider's viewpoint. It is thus perhaps better defined as a dialectical approach within the interpretive tradition delineated by Geertz[3] and others.

The Triathlete Identity and the Emergence of the Triathlete Culture

There is a considerable amount of literature that focuses on the gender roles and identity manifested by participants in competitive individual and team sports[4,5,6,7,8]. Particular attention in this literature is given to the psychological characteristics of female athletes and their differences from non-athletic females. Although there are some problematic issues with the measures employed, and despite the fact that most of this literature is based on the examination of high school and/or college-age students (young adults), the general psychological profile of such individuals is fairly well defined. Male athletes tend to rank high in masculinity (as measured by the Bem Sex Role Inventory and other similar indices); female athletes tend to be either androgynous or masculine in their gender role identity. Both male and female athletes also rank higher than non-athletes in levels of self-esteem, self-respect, and self-acceptance. Based upon discussions and informal interviews with triathletes, including a number who have completed the Hawaiian Ironman, as well as my own experiences, triathletes characteristically portray a similar psychological profile. Nonetheless, there are a number of limitations inherent in the research that has been carried out on the gender role identity and socialization of athletes and the impact of sport participation that need to be elucidated.

First, in terms of the primary characteristics attributed to athletes, it should be noted that triathletes are, for the most part, older athletes who are usually fairly affluent and settled in their careers. Based upon a survey conducted by the Triathlon Federation/USA (the national governing organization) of its members, the average triathlete is 35 years old (29% are between 18-29, 40% are 30-39, and 22% are 40-49). Seventeen percent have at least some college education; 45% are college graduates and 33% have a post graduate degree. The average family income is 50 000 $ a year (24% make over 70 000 $ per year; 19% make between 50 000 $-70 000 $; 30% make between 30 000 $-50 000 $ and 27% make 30 000 $ or less). Slightly more than half (54%) are married; 77% are male and only 23% are female[9]. The "typical" triathlete, in sum, is a married, white-collar professional male in his mid thirties who often makes over 50 000 $. The women who participate in this lifestyle have similar traits (or are married to men who do). It is a sport of the middle class. Participation in athletic endeavors thus (with the exception of the professionals) tends to be defined as leisure activity that is carried out on one's own time and an activity that must be balanced with occupational and familial priorities. Nonetheless it is a leisure activity that, for committed triathletes, takes up a considerable amount of free time. According to the Tri-Fed survey, the typical triathlete spends an average of 16,5 hours per week in training and competes in 6 triathlons and between 1-2 bi-sport races per year[10].

In contrast to the leisure time, athletic activities of most triathletes, participation in athletics for college and high school students (the focus of most of the research, as noted above), is structured within an educational setting that places high status value upon such participation (particularly for males) and that therefore may not require the same level of balancing priorities. The motivation and commitment to participation in athletic activities will therefore be structured somewhat differently for triathletes than for student athletes. This is particularly true for those older female triathletes, who began with little or no athletic background and whose lives have been profoundly affected by their participation in the triathlete lifestyle. Correspondingly, it may also be argued that the importance of athletic participation for triathletes, and especially female tri-athletes, as measured by their commitment to the sport role identity and its attendant impact upon their gender role identity, is greater than that which may be characteristic of student athletes, precisely because of the significance of the impact of the triathlete culture upon the lives of its members.

Curry and Weaner's[11] discussion of the positive relationship between the salience of the sport role identity and degree of involvement of self in that identity on the one hand, and commitment to the sport role identity on the other, lends support to this argument. They note that commitment to a role identity, as measured by the number and importance of the interpersonal relationships associated with that role identity, is the critical factor determining the extent to which the role identity will be maintained[12]. For triathletes, then, the level of commitment to a triathlete identity depends, in part, on the characteristic structure and organization of the triathlete sport culture to which they are exposed and within which they are socialized. It is the triathlete sport culture that provides the necessary context in terms of appropriate role models and support networks for the development of interpersonal relationships essential to the establishment of a triathlete identity. Moreover, the well developed structure and organization of the triathlete sport culture centered in Bakersfield, California, the primary focus of this study, may, in fact, be one reason for the significant number of elite age group triathletes found within the community. I will return to this point later.

A second limitation of much of the research that has been carried out lies in the analysis of the processes by which individuals are socialized into sport. There is a tendency to look at the process of socialization into sport as a mechanism by which individuals are molded to fit the dictates of societal mores; sport participation is a means for learning the appropriate roles as they are defined by society. As Théberge[13] notes, however, this approach places too much emphasis upon the capacity of the social system to determine the behavior of compliant, conforming individuals. The ability of individuals to creatively define their own roles in dynamic interaction with others and to actively construct a new gender role identity in the process has not been sufficiently examined.

The research carried out by Donnelly and Young[14] on the stages of the socialization process that underlie the construction and confirmation of sport role identities, however, does provide a useful framework for analysis. They propose a four-stage contingency model with each stage playing an important role in the development of the sport role identity: presocialization, selection and recruitment, socialization, and acceptance/ostracism. Presocialization refers to all of the knowledge and information obtained about the sport subculture prior to actual participation in the sport. Selection and recruitment refers to the process of actually becoming a member of the sport subculture. Socialization is the ongoing period wherein an individual learns the appropriate role behavior and values of the group; role modeling of established members is an important component of this stage. While these first three stages deal with identity construction, the final stage—acceptance/ostracism—provides the critical confirmation of the sport identity by other established members of the sport subculture[15]. This model will be used as the basis for the analysis of the socialization of triathletes into the triathlete sport culture that follows.

Becoming a Triathlete

The primary focus of this study, as noted above, is upon the process by which individuals—more specifically, women who are active participants in the local triathlete sport culture to which I belong—have attained and maintain a triathlete identity and the impact that doing so has had on other aspects of their lives. The information used as a basis for this discussion was derived from informal interviews and discussions with twenty local female multisport enthusiasts (including myself). Four of the women are between 28 and 30 years old, seven are in their mid to late thirties, six are between 40 and 48, and three are 50 to 52 years old. Thirteen are married (including two who have co-habitated with their significant other for more than four years), two are divorced, and five are single. All but four have careers outside the home, and eighteen have at least some college education. The typical characteristics of triathletes noted above (with the exception of gender) thus also apply here.

All twenty women reflect a number of common patterns in the first three stages of socialization—presocialization, selection and recruitment, and socialization—that involve the construction of a triathlete identity as discussed above. All but two of us (myself and one other woman who came primarily from a cycling background) began their athletic involvement with running, and then extended that to incorporate cycling and finally (for all but one) swimming. Likewise, the initial motivation and stimulus for participating in athletic activities reflects a similar pattern. We all started exercising out of a desire to become more fit—lose weight—and because we were influenced by close friends and/or family doing likewise. Most of us also began participation in athletic activities (running, biking, and swimming) on a consistent regular basis when we were in our thirties or early forties and therefore did *not* have an established history of participation as would normally be the case with males and younger females. It should also be noted, however, that only two of the four women in their late twenties to early thirties, and one woman in her mid-thirties participated in sports during their adolescence and college years.

The cultural context has also played an important role in shaping the nature of our involvement in multisports. Bakersfield is a mid-sized city located in the southern portion of the central valley of California (a state long touted as the mecca for triathletes). We have had strong running and cycling clubs in the area since the 1970s as well as one of the most active, dedicated local parks and recreation districts in the country—the North Bakersfield Recreation and Parks District (NBRPD)—which works with the local clubs and promotes sporting activities in the region. Within the last three years the city itself has also begun to develop a reputation as a leader in the promotion of endurance sports with the establishment of the Endurance Sports Citizen's Advisory Committee (ESCAC). The ESCAC works with NBRPD and the local sports clubs to coordinate the variety of triathlon, bi-sport (run/bike) events as well as running and cycling events that are held within the county each year.

There are two triathlon events that the NBRPD puts on that have played a key role in the socialization process for triathletes. First, since 1982, the NBRPD has conducted a winter and summer series of time trial triathlons. Each series consists of six time trials held two to three weeks apart. Each time trial has three separate events—a 10 mile time trial bike race followed by a 3,1 mile (5 km) run and a 600 yard pool swim in the winter (400 yards in the summer). Individuals do as many of the events as they wish. The emphasis of these time trials is to help individuals, especially those with little experience, prepare for participating in a triathlon. In most cases they are used as a means of preparation for the *Bakersfield Bud Light Triathlon* (BBLT)—the major event of the year—that has been held on the outskirts of the city since May, 1981. Up until this year, the BBLT consisted of a 2 km swim, a 40 km bike, and a 15 km cross country run and was one of six regional qualifying races for the prestigious ultradistance Ironman Triathlon in Hawaii. In 1990, in order to retain its status as one of three regional qualifying races for the Hawaiian Ironman, the bike event was lengthened to 80 kilometers. The BBLT has also gained a national reputation for being one of the best run events in the country as well as one of the toughest races in the region (because of the heat and nature of the hilly run course). It is considered by local triathletes to be one of the most important if not *the* most important race of the year. Participating in this race marks one's confirmation as a "real" triathlete and a *bonafide* member of the triathlon community.

Although a number of us began running first (jogging and doing a few 5 and 10 kilometer races), we all began our multisport activities with the time trials. Several women (4) began in 1982-83, the majority (10) in 1984-85, and the remainder since then. It was through our participation in these time trials that most of us met one another and, in turn, developed training networks with one another. DL is a good example of this process. She started running because of a friend with whom she played racketball thought it would be a good idea. (She began to play racketball primarily because the facility where she played provided childcare services). Another friend that she met had gone over to Hawaii and watched several triathletes from Bakersfield complete the Ironman; she had also watched friends complete the local BBLT. Both decided that they wanted to do the BBLT and proceeded to do the time trials in preparation. Both also had small children that rode around with them on their bicycles. When they proceeded to do the 10 mile bike time trial, they received considerable teasing—especially from male cyclists—about leaving the baby baskets on their bikes. DL borrowed a bicycle from a local bike shop in order to do the BBLT that year and was just happy to finish. In 1988, using a much more sophisticated racing bike, she came in second in her age group at the BBLT and qualified for and later completed the Hawaiian Ironman.

While the process of constructing a triathlete identity is similar for all twenty women, and although each of these women is an active participant in the triathlete culture, their status within the triathlete community and their level of involvement as measured by the number and difficulty of the triathlons and bi-sport events in which they have participated as well as the nature of their participation (*i.e.*, their commitment to a triathlete identity) varies considerably.

For several, completing the BBLT (even on a team) defines the extent of their commitment; they do not have the time nor the desire to do more. For the majority, however, like most triathletes everywhere, the ultimate goal is to be able to complete the Hawaiian Ironman. Completing the Ironman represents the highest status one can achieve as a triathlete, one which reflects a total commitment to the triathlete identity (particularly when one considers the amount of time, money and energy needed to prepare for such ultradistance events).

Three of us (all in the Masters—over forty—category) who had started to participate about the same time (1984-85) qualified for and completed the Ironman in 1987. In 1989, seven of us (including four over forty) completed it. Among the twenty triathletes, nine have completed Ironman distance events at least once; eight have qualified for and completed the Hawaiian Ironman. When one considers that only slightly over 100 women over forty in the world have completed the Hawaiian Ironman, this is no small feat. It may perhaps best be viewed as a testimony to the strength of the triathlete community and the mutual reinforcement and support that we, as women, give each other in particular. It also illustrates the significance of the impact that participation in this lifestyle has for committed female triathletes.

When Masters Ironwomen were asked if participation in the Hawaiian Ironman changed their life, the most common response were along these lines. As one woman said "it gave me a dose of self confidence like I've never experienced before, and my self respect is at an all time high". Another said "I'm more self confident, therefore more self directed, better able to problem solve, more risk taking, and less afraid to face failure in life". And finally, as one woman noted in an interview when discussing the significant amount of time it took to train for competing in such an ultradistance event:

> Training for the Ironman gave me the opportunity to be good to myself; it taught me how to pace myself in life, how to be more patient with myself and with others, how to manage my life better. Before, I had low self-esteem and sought to define myself in terms of my husband and children. I never felt that I was good enough as a mother or as a wife. Now I have learned how to balance my own priorities (what's good for me) with those of significant others more. Learning how to put myself first is still my greatest weakness but now I know who I am—I am strong and can do anything that I set my mind to do.

Perhaps the most telling comment about the significance of participation in the triathlete lifestyle for women, however, was made by a 52 year old woman, two time Ironman finisher. When asked whether participation in this lifestyle changed her life in terms of her sense of self as well as her relationships with others, her response was an emphatic yes. As she noted:

> It has been revolutionary. It has brought such a sense of joy and empowerment to my life, [...] one that simply intensified after finishing the Ironman. Participating in this lifestyle has given me the courage to do some inner homework, to change inside. I see the major benefit of participation in the whole person development —mental, physical, emotional, and spiritual—that I have achieved. I continue to grow more every day. It's simply wonderful.

Needless to say, when asked if she could ever give it up, her response was "Heavens no! I want to be one of the first to start a new age group category when I'm ninety".

The Impact of the Triathlete Lifestyle on Changing Gender Roles

The impact of participation in the triathlete lifestyle is not the same for women as it is for men. The impact of this lifestyle on women, as indicated above, is generally much more significant. The impact it has on men may be more aptly measured in terms of their reaction to the new gender identity of the female triathletes in their lives. This is partly due to the fact that participation in sports, in general, is, still and yet, much more acceptable for men than it is for women. Males in our society are socialized to view athletic activities as a way of asserting themselves as "real men". Women, on the other hand, (particularly those over 30) have been traditionally socialized to view athletics as a male defined and dominated sphere; participation in sports and all that it entails was (and is) not a traditional feminine activity. Multisports like the triathlon and, more recently, the bi-sport (run/bike) events, in one sense, then, provide a vehicle for expressing the essential traditional character of the male gender identity that presently may be more difficult to achieve in the workplace (especially considering that the majority of triathletes are white collar professionals as noted earlier).

Based upon discussions and interviews with fellow triathletes, including a number who completed the Hawaiian Ironman, and my own experiences, the key attributes of the gender identity developed by female triathletes include a sense of personal competence, higher self esteem and self respect, and *above all*, an acceptance of oneself and one's athletic capabilities as legitimate dimensions of self separate and distinct from one's relationships with significant others. Male triathletes also report an increased sense of personal competence, self esteem and self respect as a result of their participation in the triathlete lifestyle. However, as noted earlier, the traditional socialization of males includes an emphasis upon participation in athletic activities; the traditional socialization of females stresses just the opposite. Herein lies the particular significance of athletic participation for women. It also underscores one of the significant differences between female and male triathletes.

Once women become involved in this lifestyle—even though they may have to curtail some of their training and/or racing from time to time because of injury or other responsibilities—they will not give it up. None of the female athletes I interviewed would even consider doing so. This is particularly true for those women who start later in life and may not have had any significant athletic experience beforehand. Once they get "hooked" in terms of what it does for their sense of self esteem, self confidence, and self respect, they cannot give it up. As DL noted:

> It's such a high to be able to define oneself for the first time in terms of one's own capabilities, the sense of growth and confidence in oneself. It is something that is you and it's something that is really tangible—like work is for men. To go back to being subordinate, to defining oneself in terms of others, in terms of relationships, you just can't do it. You're much more likely to take another look at the relationship first.

Having a support group, the triathlon family—the core of which centers on women participating in the same lifestyle—also is important.

In contrast, there have been a number of male triathletes—including one who did the Hawaiian Ironman back in 1982—who have given up participating in triathlons and in the triathlete lifestyle for the most part. They may participate intermittently in one or more of the component sports, but not all three on a regular basis. As indicated in the above quote, men can give it up easier because they have their work to fall back on. Their sense of identity (ego involvement) perhaps does not hinge so critically upon their physical activities. After all, men are socialized to participate in athletic endeavors from childhood on; it is an expected, normal component of self identity, not a radically new or different activity as it is for many women. They are also perhaps more individualistic in orientation—there is an underlying competitiveness in relations between male triathletes that is not evident (at least to the same extent) among the female triathletes that serve as one's support group.

As noted above, the impact of participating in the triathlon lifestyle for men is different than it is for women. One of the more difficult aspects for many men—particularly if they are not active athletically—is dealing with the change in the sense of identity that the women triathletes in their lives have attained. Because of traditional gender role expectations, it is often difficult for men to accept the new independence and strength of such women. (It is even more difficult for men to accept being passed up in a race by women—especially if they are of similar age. This is also something that most female triathletes relish doing). Female triathletes, by virtue of their athletic abilities alone, are often perceived as a threat to the traditional male identity which is based on the presumed inferiority of women. If the men are participants in the triathlete lifestyle as well, it is sometimes easier—especially if the male is the better triathlete. If the wife or girlfriend is a better triathlete, it often is another story. One female triathlete I talked with noted that her first husband was not at all interested in her athletic activities when she began to train for and participate in triathlons; he wanted a more traditional woman who would have supper on the table when he came home instead of juggling work and family schedules with ongoing training activities. The relationship ended in an amicable divorce. Her next boyfriend, however, was a fellow triathlete who was very supportive at first but became jealous and resentful over the period of several months because she became a better athlete than he was. That relationship too, ended. The man she finally married was a fellow triathlete who was secure enough in his own sense of self so that he did not feel threatened by her success; their relationship is egalitarian and mutually supportive.

To summarize, the gender identity and corresponding gender roles expressed by female and male triathletes are, in my view, significantly affected by two interactive processes. First, and perhaps most importantly, one's sense of self (gender identity) is critically affected by one's evaluation of her/his performance in triathlon activities. This is measured not only by one's level of performance in competitive events (in relation to others of the same gender within one's age group and adjacent age groups as well as, on a secondary level, to those of the opposite gender) but also by the reinforcement and support one receives from training partners and others within the community. As noted above, this process is more significant for women than it is for men. Secondly, one's sense of self is predicated upon the nature of the relationships one maintains with significant others—particularly within the family context. If one's spouse is supportive and/or a participant, the level of commitment to the lifestyle will be reinforced. If one's spouse is not supportive, continued participation will put a strain on the relationship and, depending on the strength of the commitment to triathlon activities versus the relationship, either the relationship will be terminated (which often occurs) or participation in triathlon activities will be curtailed or will cease.

Generally speaking, in most instances, the men who are involved with female triathletes are supportive and share in their lifestyle. In some instances, where the men could not or would not accept the changes in the women's identity—as noted in the example given earlier—the relationship was terminated. Likewise, most of the male triathletes I know as a rule, have less traditionally defined gender identities, (those who have more traditional identities are more likely to have non-athletic or less-athletic wives). This is not surprising when one considers the characteristics and athletic abilities of the female triathletes with whom most male triathletes associate. Nor is it surprising when one considers the significance of the wider "triathlon family" in reaffirming and supporting one's identity as a triathlete. The triathlete lifestyle itself thus represents the creation of a new cultural reality; one that reflects the transformation of gender roles that is taking place within our society today.

Concluding Remarks

One final point needs to be made regarding the significance of the emergence of the triathlon sport culture for the future of sport participation by women and men of all ages and backgrounds. Considerable attention has been given by researchers to some of the more problematic issues of modern organized sport: the role of the media and its impact upon sport; the growing commercialization and professionalization of sport including amateur sports within educational settings; and the attendant emphasis upon competition and "winning at all costs" with the awards and glory going only to the successful few. Relatively little attention, in contrast, has been given to the study of sports that have emerged within the last decade as a result of the fitness revolution. Yet if we wish to evaluate the prospects for promoting "sport-for-all" with all of its attendant benefits, it is precisely this area that needs to be explored. Herein lies the value of investigating multisports such as the triathlon and duathlon. Unlike most more traditional mono-sports where primary attention is given to those who win with the fastest times or best scores, all individuals who complete a triathlon or duathlon are winners by virtue of the fact that they finished; participation itself is a primary goal. And as I have argued in this paper, although individuals (and women in particular) may begin participation in such multisports for a variety of reasons—to lose weight and become more physically fit or for the challenge of doing something different—they continue to do so because of the significant impact that participating in the lifestyle has on their lives overall. In sum, ethnographic research on the triathlon sport culture serves as an important vehicle for examining the ways in which sport participation affects individuals within our rapidly changing society, thereby helping to illuminate the meaning that such participation plays within their lives.

NOTES AND REFERENCES

1. Triathlete Magazine (1987) The state of the sport. May 61-79 111

2. Since its inception in early 1985, I have been an active member of the local triathlon club which serves as a primary data resource for this research. Within the last five years, I have participated in over fifty triathlons and duathlons/biathlons of varying lengths ranging from sprint triathlons (the shortest consisting of a 3,1 mile run, 9 mile bike, and 75 yard pool swim) to the ultradistance Hawaiian Ironman event (2,4 mile swim, 112 mile bike, 26,2 mile run) which I qualified for and completed in October of 1987, 1988 and 1989. In 1988 and 1989, I also participated in 11 of the *Coors Light Biathlon Series* events (each consisting of a 5 km run followed by a 30 km bike and another 5 km run). Although most of the events I have participated in have been in California, I have raced in eight other states from Kansas to Hawaii as well.

3. Geertz C (1973) The interpretation of cultures. New York: Basic Books

4. Colley A, Roberts N, Chipps A (1985) Sex-role identity, personnality and participation in team and individual sports by males and females. International Journal of Sport Psychology 16 103-12

5. Del Rey P, Sheppard S (1981) Relationship of psychological androgyny in female athletes to self esteem. International Journal of Sport Psychology 12 165-75

6. Marsh HW, Jackson SA (1986) Multidimensional self-concepts, masculinity, and feminity as a function of women's involvement in athletics. Sex roles 15 391-415

7. Myers AM, Lips HM (1978) Participation in competitive amateur sports as a function of psychological androgyny. Sex Roles 4 571-78

8. Uguccioni SM, Ballantyne RH (1980) Comparison of attitudes and sex roles for female athletic participants and nonparticipants. International Journal of Sport Psychology 11 42-48

9.   Triathlon Federation/USA (1989) Who are the triathletes? Triathlon Times June 4-7

10. Ibid p 6

11. Curry TJ, Weaner JS (1987) Sport identity salience, commitment, and the involvement of self in role: measurement issues. Sociology of Sport Journal 4 280-88

12. Ibid p 280-81

13. Théberge N (1984) On the need for a more adequate theory of sport participation. Sociology of Sport Journal 1 26-35

14. Donnelly P, Young K (1988) The construction and confirmation of identity in sport subcultures. Sociology of Sport Journal 5 223-40

15. Ibid p 224-26

Bio-Ethics, Social Ethics and Sport Ethics

Aspects and Implications of the Olympic Motto Citius, Altius, Fortius and of the Expectation of Ever-Increasing Levels of Athletic Performance

Bio-éthique, éthique sociale et éthique du sport

Problématique du Citius, Altius, Fortius et de l'expectative d'un accroissement indéfini de la performance

High Performance Sport in Present-day Context:
Considerations for an Ethical Analysis

The author first establishes that the close ties between high performance sport and ethics had been recognized and debated long before present-day problems associated with the use or misuse of doping substances. In Ancient Greece, the educational and other contributions of athletics to individual development and citizenship had been lauded by many thinkers. On the other hand, as early as the 5th century B.C., reputed philosophers and moralists were already criticizing the attitudes and behavior of certain athletes as well as state intervention in the field of sport. It should thus be of no surprise that diverging viewpoints as to the virtues of sport and the behavior of athletes have persisted through the centuries. A description follows of the ethical model used in the presentation. The author acknowledges the current ideological pluralism and proceeds to base his model on the present bioethics movement characterized by thoughts and analyses aimed at establishing the spectrum of conditions which would be most likely to ensure that the new powers derived from knowledge in the biological sciences will be kept or put at the service of humanity. It is pointed out that the rapid and extensive developments in the biological and life sciences are uncovering unprecedented possibilities for the transformation of the human being. This situation is not without triggering reflexions and debates among scientists and scholars concerned with scientific, social and moral responsibility/accountability. The author stresses that new knowledge and techniques compel society to make choices that commit not only the present, but the future as well. In his opinion morals and ethics do not have ready-made answers to the spectrum of questions and problems raised. Only through dialogue and deliberations, as has been the case for the last 25 years in the field of bioethics, can consensus be achieved and decisions made that will have humanizing consequences. The author then proceeds to discuss sport ethics in the perspective of high performance sport, more specifically from the angle of the sporting spectacle. He advances that most of contemporary ethical problems in high performance sport are linked with sport's henceforth inseparable spectacle/entertainment dimension. The ethics of high performance sport are then discussed under three specific aspect: – the social, political, and economic context in which sport is nowadays indulged in and offered to the public as a consumer good, especially in the technologically advanded cultures; – the concepts of progress and limits, the requirements of sporting excellence, and the personal significance and consequences of its attainment, in contemporary society, as compared to that of the Ancien Greeks; – three conditions through which high performance sport could remain an area of endeavour and of service conductive to humanization. With respect to the latter, the author emphasizes that a first condition should be a recognition of the fact that high performance sport (including the Olympic Games) belongs to the culture of the 20th century; as such the cultural framework and ethics through which sport should be judged be those of the present times. A second condition has to do with the challenge of avoiding a run-away situation as concerns the technological context and its impact on the quest for a type of excellence in sport which would remain commensurate with humanism. A third condition would be for scientists and scholars to try and propose, with respect to the development of high performance sport, sets of guiding principles based on an objective vision of sport rather than on national pride. The author concludes by inviting the international community of scientists and scholars and the IOC to cooperate and muster their energies and competences in a genuine attempt at developing guiding principles which would have international applicability.

La performance sportive en contexte contemporain: jalons pour une analyse éthique

Hubert Doucet

Lorsque ces dernières semaines, j'abordais avec quelques collègues la question qui est au centre de nos débats aujourd'hui, leur figure exprimait au premier abord scepticisme et surprise. Les uns disaient mi blagueurs mi sérieux: «L'éthique, c'est le mot à la mode.» «Voilà qu'après l'éthique des affaires, on se met à l'éthique du sport!» D'autres gardaient silence puis tout d'un coup disaient: «Bien sûr, il y a la question du dopage!» Cette dernière réaction a le mérite d'exprimer la déception actuelle de certains citoyens à l'égard des grandes compétitions sportives. Et la première réaction nous met en garde contre l'effet de mode qui s'attache aujourd'hui à l'éthique et risque de la dénaturer. Mais ces deux réactions passent cependant sous silence le fait que sport et éthique ont noué des relations profondes bien avant la survenue du problème particulier que représentent les produits dopants et bien avant que le goût de nos contemporains ait remplacé la morale par l'éthique.

Le sport est depuis longtemps objet d'une attention particulière de la part de la morale. Celle-ci, par exemple, a loué le rôle social et pacificateur des Jeux dans la Grèce antique. Elle a aussi célébré la fonction éducative et civique du sport dans la cité grecque. Les moralistes, cependant, s'en prennent dès le Ve siècle av. J.C., aux premières manifestations du sport étatisé. À la même époque, Solon, législateur et philosophe athénien, critique les athlètes en quête d'une gloire qu'il juge méprisable. L'opposition de certains philosophes se fait sans merci à l'égard du sport alors que d'autres continuent d'en reconnaître les vertus. Cette double attitude (positive et négative) que l'on retrouve en Grèce antique existe tout au long de l'histoire du sport, du moins en Occident. Pour un Jean Giraudoux qui affirme que «le sport consiste à déléguer au corps quelques-unes des vertus les plus fortes de l'âme: l'énergie, l'audace, la patience[1]», un autre répond: «Vaillance n'est pas la qualité du corps mais de l'âme, fermeté non des bras et des jambes, mais du courage. Roideur des jambes et des bras est qualité de portefaix[2].»

Cette remarque d'introduction oriente déjà le propos. En effet, l'éthique n'est pas une nouvelle instance qui s'introduirait aujourd'hui dans le sport pour le juger. Sport et éthique ont toujours été en dialogue l'un avec l'autre. La tâche

Hubert Doucet, Faculté de théologie, Université Saint-Paul, Ottawa, Ontario, Canada.

consiste, dans ce contexte, à faire voir le type de dialogue qui aujourd'hui doit se nouer entre ces deux dimensions de l'expérience humaine. À cette première précision s'en ajoute une seconde, qui particularisera encore davantage l'analyse proposée. Le thème de cet atelier n'est pas sport et éthique mais plus précisément la «problématique du *Citius*, *Altius*, *Fortius* et de l'expectative de l'accroissement indéfini de la performance». D'où le titre du présent exposé: La performance sportive en contexte contemporain: jalons pour une analyse éthique.

La réflexion qui suit cherchera à montrer la contribution de l'éthique aux débats sociaux sur l'accroissement indéfini de la performance sportive. Pour y parvenir, deux préalables doivent d'abord être examinés. Le premier concerne le modèle éthique qui sera utilisé. Le second précisera le concept de sport qui a servi à la présente analyse. Une fois posés ces préalables, le thème principal de l'exposé sera développé.

Le modèle éthique

L'éthique peut être abordée de multiples façons. On peut partir de la question de la sémantique: l'éthique est-elle identique à la morale? Ou des multiples écoles morales: utilitarisme, conséquentialisme, eudémonisme, téléologie, déontologie, etc. Dans ce cas, l'accent est placé sur le pluralisme éthique. Pour ce propos, le modèle éthique retenu est ce mouvement actuel que l'on appelle *la bioéthique*. Celle-ci se présente comme un effort de réflexion visant à dégager les conditions qui permettent aux nouveaux pouvoirs issus des sciences biologiques de servir l'humanité. Le modèle, en raison tant de ses objectifs que de sa méthodologie, apparaît tout à fait approprié dans le contexte actuel.

Dans son origine tout au moins, au milieu des années 1960, la bioéthique se propose à la fois comme une solution de remplacement ou de complémentarité devant l'indifférence ou l'incapacité de la morale (ou des morales) d'entrer en dialogue avec les sciences de la vie. Les Américains, puisque c'est chez eux que cette histoire commence, prennent alors conscience des problèmes nouveaux que pose l'extraordinaire entreprise de transformation humaine qu'est la biomédecine. Les nouvelles prouesses techniques suscitent de profondes inquiétudes et d'intenses réflexions tant sur la nature de la vie et de la mort que sur la responsabilité des scientifiques en tenant compte de celle de la collectivité. Comment, dans un contexte de pluralisme idéologique et de développement des sciences biologiques qui remettent en cause les idées les plus fermes sur la réalité de l'être humain, dégager les conditions d'une action humanisante? L'interdisciplinarité s'est révélée l'instrument privilégié pour y parvenir. La méthode ne cherche pas tant à atteindre un consensus minimal qu'à établir, à travers un dialogue où nulle discipline ne doit dominer, les conditions d'une prise de décision qui privilégiera le respect et la dignité de l'être humain.

Les vingt-cinq ans de travail et de dialogue bioéthique n'ont pas mis fin aux inquiétudes ni apporté de réponses définitives à toutes les questions de fond soulevées par la biologie moderne. Cependant, à travers le dialogue souvent ardu et les débats parfois houleux, on apprend à mieux poser les questions, à percevoir avec plus de clarté les enjeux, à cerner avec une plus grande précision les implications des décisions à prendre. L'on sait maintenant que la morale ne donnera plus de réponses toutes faites: il n'y a pas de science de la morale. D'autre part, le savoir et les techniques obligent à des choix qui engagent le présent tout autant que le futur. Quels seront donc les fondements de ces choix s'il n'y a pas de science de la morale? Seules les délibérations permettront d'en arriver à des décisions qui auront ou non des conséquences d'humanisation. La responsabilité s'accroît à mesure que les choix se multiplient d'où l'importance de préciser les méthodes de travail en morale et d'approfondir la réflexion sur ce que l'humanité veut devenir.

Le concept de sport

Le concept de sport est tellement vaste qu'il importe, au départ, de préciser le sens dans lequel on entend l'interpréter. Il ne s'agira ici ni de la notion de jeu, ni même de celle de sport en général. La réflexion éthique se construit généralement à partir de ces deux notions. Le contexte présent de l'organisation sportive oblige cependant à faire des distinctions supplémentaires importantes. Le sport-loisir s'identifie mal au sport-travail ou au sport-spectacle. Entre le jeu de l'enfant et la performance d'un athlète d'élite, il y a un fossé qu'il n'est pas facile de combler. En partant du jeu en soi ou du sport en général, le philosophe contemporain arrive mal à intégrer de juste façon l'élément compétition et l'élément spectacle qui sont pourtant caractéristiques de nombreuses pratiques sportives. Cela étant, le sens de ce «sport» sera limité dans le présent exposé à celui de la «haute performance» telle que pratiquée dans le cadre des grands jeux internationaux. L'athlétisme d'élite en serait un exemple patent.

La question du sport telle qu'entendue ici mérite d'être abordée *à partir* du spectacle sportif puisque ce dernier est devenu inséparable des sports de performance pratiqués dans le cadre des grands jeux et que les problèmes d'ordre éthique qui sont aujourd'hui soulevés dans le sport le sont dans une large mesure en raison même de cette dimension du sport.

Les sports de performance pratiqués dans le cadre de jeux organisés, qu'ils soient professionnels ou amateurs, soulèvent encore aujourd'hui de nombreuses critiques. À lire certains écrits, l'observateur est tenté de conclure que ces pratiques iraient à l'encontre de la nature même du sport; elles en seraient la négation. En réaction contre cette présumée dégénérescence, s'est dessiné un mouvement centré sur la participation, le développement de la santé et le bien-être. Les témoignages de profanes sont souvent à cet effet très éloquents. Dans *Le Devoir* du 23 février 1990, une lectrice se disait profondément déçue d'apprendre que le marathon de Montréal aura finalement lieu.

> [...] Oui je condamne la course, ce sport qui est pour moi le reflet d'une société qui n'est justement pas bien dans sa peau. Un monde qui comme le nôtre, où tout n'est que rapidité, performance et exigences a-t-il besoin d'un marathon pour amateurs qui pousse une fois de plus les gens à se surpasser?[3]

Cette lettre me semble faire écho à certains passages de *Scènes de la vie future* parus il y a 60 ans sous la plume de Georges Duhamel:

> Cette comédie du sport avec laquelle on berne toute la jeunesse du monde, j'avoue qu'elle me semble assez bouffonne.
>
> Dans la mesure où il participe de l'hygiène et de la morale, le sport — acceptons le terme puisqu'il a forcé notre vocabulaire — devrait être, avant tout, une chose personnelle, discrète, ou même un jeu de libres compagnons, une occasion de rivalités familières, [...] et surtout une récréation, comme disait le mot avant ses aventures modernes, un plaisir, un amusement, un thème de gaieté, de récréation.
>
> [...]
>
> Dès que les compétitions perdent leur gracieux caractère de jeux purs, elles sont empoisonnées par des considérations de gain ou de haines nationales. Elles deviennent brutales, dangereuses; elles ressemblent à des attentats plutôt qu'à des divertissements[4].

Il est peut-être vrai d'une part, qu'il y a quelque chose d'antisportif dans la commercialisation du sport ou dans les comportements de certains athlètes et de certains organismes nationaux de régie du sport. D'où, pour certains, la nécessité de moraliser le sport et le sportif. Le sport, cependant, serait-il lui-même s'il n'était que promotion de la santé et du bien-être du sportif? Cette interrogation se retrouve chez un certain nombre d'auteurs pour qui le sport est aussi une forme de compensation contre les méfaits de la civilisation[5].

D'autre part, il faut reconnaître la fascination qu'exercent les grands événements sportifs sur toutes les catégories de citoyens. Cet intérêt dit quelque chose d'important sur l'être humain dont il importe de souligner le sens. Il affirme, semble-t-il, le désir profond d'excellence qui habite l'être humain. Le philosophe américain Paul Weiss a bien résumé le sens de cette fascination: «Unlike other beings, we men have the ability to appreciate the excellent. We desire to achieve it. We want to share it[6].» Les athlètes désirent atteindre l'excellence; et les spectateurs, par personnes interposées, participent de cette quête. Les athlètes renvoient aux spectateurs leur idéal du corps. Ils sont en quelque sorte un portrait idéalisé de ces derniers. D'où la grande déception lorsque l'excellence et les moyens utilisés pour y parvenir relèvent de la duperie.

Dans la visée de l'excellence que poursuit l'athlète, il y a quelque chose de commun avec de nombreuses autres activités humaines, tel l'art, la science, la religion. À la source de ces différentes activités, se trouve le désir d'atteindre «l'idéal», «la perfection». En même temps, elles sont une rencontre avec soi-même en raison des exigences quotidiennes que requiert la quête d'excellence. C'est dire comment, au plan d'une anthropologie philosophique, l'excellence sportive ne doit pas être vue comme une espèce de dégénérescence humaine: elle est au contraire un des hauts lieux de l'humanité puisqu'elle *dit* la corporalité, «le mode spécifique humain d'agir et d'être au monde[7]». La quête de l'excellence n'est pas le tout du sport, on en convient facilement. Elle est cependant un élément essentiel de sa dynamique et c'est à partir de cet élément, qu'il devient possible d'analyser et d'évaluer, au plan éthique, la performance sportive.

La performance sportive

La question de la performance sportive sera abordée sous trois aspects. Le premier aura trait au sens de la performance dans le contexte social, politique et économique où se pratique le sport contemporain. Le deuxième portera sur des points de comparaison entre la performance contemporaine et la performance à des époques précédentes. Enfin, le troisième traitera d'un certain nombre de conditions pour que la performance sportive demeure un des hauts lieux d'humanisation de la personne et de la collectivité.

Quel est le sens de la performance dans le contexte social, politique et économique où se pratique le sport d'élite contemporain? Le désir incoercible du record paraît être un des éléments caractéristiques du sens contemporain de la performance. La perfection relative ne serait-elle pas qu'à chaque représentation un record soit abaissé? Il ne s'agit pas tant de se mesurer avec ses collègues d'un jour que de dépasser la marque établie. Est-ce l'athlète qui compte ici ou le record qu'il abaisse? Pour parvenir aux grandes prouesses, la machine-corps doit de toute évidence se faire de plus en plus performante. Sans doute, l'exténuant travail quotidien de l'athlète garde-t-il son importance mais n'est plus suffisant. S'y ajoutent des éléments extrinsèques à l'athlète lui-même. Que l'on pense ici aux équipes de spécialistes qui appuient et contrôlent le travail des athlètes engagés dans la compétition. Que l'on pense aussi aux possibilités ouvertes par le développement des sciences biologiques (biologie moléculaire, pharmacologie, génétique, etc.). Tout est organisé en vue de «faciliter la chasse aux points, aux secondes, aux centimètres, aux kilogrammes[8]». Et que seraient les sports de haute compétition s'il n'y avait pas le record à abattre? L'obsession du record trouve une explication dans le fait que dans le monde occidental, tout est mesuré, calculé ou traduit en chiffres. Dans le sport on accumule aujourd'hui les statistiques d'une façon phénoménale. La précision dans la quantification est telle que le centième de seconde arraché au record précédent est loué comme un progrès de l'humanité. On se souviendra qu'aux Jeux olympiques de Montréal, en finale du concours multiple individuel, gymnastique, Nadia Comaneci avait mérité une note précisée au millième de point: 79.275. Cette place donnée au quantitatif n'est qu'une image des multiples statistiques nécessaires à la démarcation des athlètes et dont certains raffolent dans nos sociétés.

La primauté donnée au record s'explique aussi par la place qu'occupe la politique dans les grands Jeux. Celle-ci a toujours été présente dans les stades en raison de la nature du sport. Ce dernier, en effet, reproduit le système social qui l'engendre. Malgré, par exemple, les importantes différences d'organisation entre les sociétés capitalistes et les sociétés socialistes, «le sport capitaliste américain et le sport socialiste soviétique témoignent apparemment d'un même souci d'exploitation rationnelle et de valorisation exacerbée de la compétition sportive au profit des intérêts économiques, sociaux, politiques et culturels du pouvoir de chacun de ces grands États[10].» Le système de production dans le sport est comparable au système de production industrielle. Ce qui fait dire à Parlebas: «Le corps du sportif de compétition est un corps-machine appartenant à un collectif-machine[11].» La performance sportive appartient ainsi à l'ordre de la production. «Il s'ensuit que le corps se trouve à être réduit à un ensemble de processus biologiques, à une pure donnée susceptible d'être manipulée, contrôlée et soumise aux principes de la production rationnelle[12].» Dans cete perspective, le sport de compétition peut être vu comme appartenant à la sphère de l'efficacité et du rendement et non plus à celle du jeu. Le sport moderne est donc incompréhensible en dehors de la culture qui le fait naître. Et de fait, les problèmes d'ordre éthique que soulève le sport de compétition sont à toutes fins utiles les mêmes que ceux auxquels notre société est confrontée à presqu'à tous le niveaux. Trois exemples dans le domaine de la santé. Il existe des techniques de plus en plus sophistiquées pour prolonger la vie, on rêve même d'une sorte de progrès indéfini de la vie. Pourtant l'inquiétude monte en ce qui a trait au type de vieillesse et de mort que la biomédecine est en train de fabriquer. Dans les hôpitaux pour enfants, plusieurs soignants s'interrogent sur le sens de l'action qui consiste à sauver des bébés extrêmement prématurés ou sévèrement handicapés dont la vie sera une lutte sans relâche contre la souffrance. Qui en retire le plus grand bénéfice? Le médecin qui augmente l'âge de survie des prématurés ou l'enfant malade chronique pour qui le vie sera minimale? La thérapie génétique se développe aussi de plus en plus. Le succès de ce type de thérapie ouvre la voie à l'utilisation de la génétique pour l'amélioration de certains caractères chez des humains vulnérables. Devrait-il y avoir des limites à cette transformation? Les problèmes nouveaux que pose la haute performance dans le sport contemporain sont du même ordre que ceux posés par la biomédecine. Il convient donc qu'ils fassent l'objet d'une analyse semblable.

L'interprétation faite ci-avant de la performance dans le sport de compétition ne se comprend qu'à l'intérieur du contexte d'une culture technologique. Le fondement de cet aspect de la culture occidentale est le rêve du progrès. La modernité est construite sur l'idée d'une capacité indéfinie de l'être humain de dépasser les limites. Le record n'est qu'une conséquence et une expression de ce mouvement. D'autre part, en cette fin du deuxième millénaire, l'angoisse et la déception semblent habiter cette culture. On devient inquiet. Il y a l'échec du côté de la nature et de l'environnement: c'est la crise écologique. Il y a l'échec du rêve de la santé parfaite pour tous et toutes; la qualité de la santé varie inéluctablement selon la condition socio-économique et l'accès aux soins de santé se fait plus coûteuse et plus difficile. Il y a l'échec de la distribution équitable des biens: c'est l'appauvrissement continu d'un grand nombre de personnes au profit d'un petit nombre. Dans le vocabulaire courant, un nouveau mot tend à remplacer celui de *progrès*, c'est celui de *limite*. Au rêve de l'illimité succède la prise de conscience de la finitude. Dans cette perspective, les concepts de la haute performance et du record apparaissent sous un autre jour: ils ne sont ni univoques ni négatifs.

On peut dire que les Grecs ont donné beaucoup de place à la performance car les Jeux antiques ont été des activités de haute compétition qui engageaient le prestige des individus et des cités. L'objectif n'était pas de supprimer l'autre comme à la guerre mais justement de se mesurer à lui[13]. La mesure n'était cependant pas quantitative, elle était qualitative. Il s'agissait d'être le meilleur de tous les concurrents qui aspiraient, pour eux-mêmes et leurs cités, à la gloire et la renommée. Pour atteindre l'objectif poursuivi, le gagnant devait s'être mesuré à tous les autres participants qui, eux aussi, avaient déployé leurs capacités au maximum. Chacun, après s'être sérieusement préparé, devait donner le meilleur de lui-même sinon la gloire du stade perdait son éclat. La performance qui donnait la gloire de la couronne de laurier avait une fonction éthique. En effet, les Jeux antiques permettaient aux Grecs divisés entre-eux, de développer un sens ethnique et national. Ils ont ainsi développé une sorte d'unité morale du pays. L'esprit de compétition — Ἀγών (l'*agôn*) — qui engageait le prestige des individus et de leurs cités revivifiait à chaque reprise des Jeux l'unité de cette civilisation[14]. L'esprit de compétition, était un facteur de construction de la paix sociale. La performance a donc occupé dans les Jeux grecs une place centrale. Elle ne se mesurait cependant pas de manière quantitative. Le temps nécessaire à parcourir le stade ne paraît pas avoir été mesuré. La distance variait d'ailleurs d'un stade à l'autre. La couronne était l'un des symboles de la gloire du vainqueur. Guttmann, dans *From ritual to record* se demande pourquoi les Grecs n'ont pas cherché à chronométrer les activités. Est-ce dû au fait qu'ils n'avaient pas les instruments adéquats? Sa réponse est la suivante: «Les Grecs n'avaient pas de chronomètres précis parce qu'ils ne se préoccupaient tout simplement pas d'établir le temps pris par les coureurs[15].» On ne mesurait pas non plus la distance parcourue par le javelot ou par le disque dont on ne sait d'ailleurs pas s'ils étaient toujours comparables d'un jeu à l'autre. Les mesures quantitatives n'avaient guère d'importance.

D'une culture à l'autre les performances se mesurent de façons fort différentes. Aujourd'hui, la mesure se prend par rapport à l'objet définissant ou caractérisant tel ou tel sport, d'où la quantification. La science moderne a pris son essor au moment où l'esprit humain a commencé à abstraire l'objet de son contexte et à le considérer pour lui-même. Sport moderne et science appartiennent au même univers culturel. Dans la civilisation grecque, la mesure se prenait par rapport aux participants rassemblés dans le stade. C'est entre eux que les hommes se mesuraient. De nouveau, nous sommes renvoyés à la confrontation entre le thème du *progrès* et celui de la *limite* comme l'a déjà fait remarquer Ulmann[16]. Pour lui, la gymnastique grecque est inséparable d'une conception du corps qui est elle-même conditionnée par une métaphysique de la *finitude*. Le sport moderne, au contraire, est liée à une tout autre philosophie, à la fois diffuse et cohérente, celle de la théorie du *progrès*.

Les remarques qui précèdent permettent d'en venir aux *conditions* nécessaires et suffisantes pour que la performance sportive demeure un des hauts lieux d'humanisation de la personne et de la collectivité. La première condition exige de reconnaître que les sports de compétition pratiqués dans le cadre des grands Jeux doivent être évalués, au plan éthique, à l'intérieur du cadre culturel qui est le leur, *i.e.*, le cadre de la modernité. Si les Jeux olympiques modernes trouvent leur origine et leur inspiration en Grèce, leur pratique est contemporaine. Nier ce fait serait nier le réel et la démarche éthique qui consiste à écouter la réalité dans toute sa complexité serait alors confuse. La première tâche éthique est de se libérer des illusions pour reconnaître les données totales et souvent contradictoires d'une situation. Les grands Jeux modernes appartiennent à la culture du 20ᵉ siècle, et c'est à partir de la culture d'aujourd'hui qu'il faut les évaluer.

La seconde condition concerne l'analyse même de la haute performance. Cette dernière, en contexte contemporain, est louée par les uns, décriée par les autres. Pour les premiers, elle est le signe même de la modernité, pour les seconds, elle témoigne d'un délaissement des valeurs humaines fondamentales. Pour être juste, une analyse de la haute performance exigerait d'en reconnaître d'une part le sens humain naturel et d'autre part les risques que certaines formes de pratique entraînent. La performance *i.e.*, l'obtention d'un résultat optimal appartient à l'être humain. Depuis toujours ce dernier a cherché à rendre meilleure son existence. Cela s'est produit non seulement en améliorant les conditions du réel mais aussi par le truchement de l'auto-transformation planifiée[17]. Rahner, dans son essai théologique, donne des exemples très simples de cette manipulation : café comme stimulant, modification de l'aspect corporel, méthodes pédagogiques pour accélérer le processus d'apprentissage, etc. Il s'agit évidemment là de gestes élémentaires pour améliorer l'être humain. Aujourd'hui les possibilités ont été décuplées et elles effraient parfois. Malgré les inquiétudes qui lui viennent du constat des nouveaux pouvoirs à sa disposition, l'être humain demeure toujours en quête de perfection, la haute performance sportive est certes un des moyens pour y parvenir. Le défi auquel l'on fait face n'est pas de choisir ou non la voie de la performance sportive mais plutôt de réussir à l'intégrer à notre dynamisme pour qu'elle soit humanisante. Ce défi est d'autant plus réel et exigeant qu'approche une nouvelle croisée des chemins. En effet, la technologie créée par l'homme semble lui échapper de plus en plus pour suivre sa propre logique. Quel type de performance voudra-t-on développer dans le contexte technologique de demain ? Telle est la question fondamentale à laquelle la société se trouve confrontée.

La troisième condition concerne plus directement la mise en oeuvre de la haute performance dans le cadre des Jeux organisés. Une question d'importance a trait aux possibilités nouvelles offertes par la génétique. On se référera au texte de Bouchard (dans ce volume), pour saisir les multiples avenues qu'ouvre la génétique. L'homme possède maintenant des pouvoirs extraordinaires. Comment seront-ils utilisés ? À des fins purement thérapeutiques ? À d'autres fins ? L'analyse exige sans doute de considérer les implications de ces pouvoirs nouveaux sur le sport de compétition mais aussi de faire porter le regard critique sur les implications de ces connaissances au niveau de la vie en société. Au nom du sport, va-t-on développer une classe spéciale d'individus ? Ne poussera-t-on pas trop loin la spécialisation des individus ? N'y a-t-il pas ici quelque chose de semblable à l'eugénisme ? Ces questions ne peuvent être balayées du revers de la main puisqu'elles concernent l'humanité dans son devenir. Dans l'ensemble, la société semble favorable à utiliser la génétique à des fins thérapeutiques. Elle est cependant inquiète lorsqu'on propose qu'elle soit utilisée pour d'autres fins. Les spécialistes ne peuvent se permettre de perdre de vue cette perspective globale. Dans le contexte présent, il y aurait lieu d'établir des lignes directrices pour guider le développement de la performance. Ces lignes directrices ne doivent pas servir de paravent à l'orgueil national mais plutôt exprimer une vision objective du sport. Depuis 40 ans maintenant, malgré bien des conflits d'intérêts et de valeurs, la communauté scientifique a réussi à développer des lignes directrices concernant la recherche sur les sujets humains. Des principes ont été reconnus, des limites ont été posées, des méthodes d'analyse ont été développées. Dans le développement du sport, de semblables lignes directrices devraient être développées par la communauté internationale. Impossible défi? Peut-être pas, dans le présent contexte international.

Il serait particulièrement intéressant que le CIO, comme l'ont fait d'autres organismes internationaux, mette sur pied un comité d'éthique largement interdisciplinaire qui étudierait ces questions. La rencontre régulière de spécialistes engagés dans le sport et d'autres personnes dont la formation est philosophique, théologique, sociologique et autre ne pourrait qu'aider le sport olympique à mieux définir les lignes directrices nécessaires pour que le développement de la haute performance sportive demeure une belle expression d'humanité. Par l'entremise de la haute performance sportive, quelle sorte d'humanité veut-on établir? Les techniques disponibles permettent toutes sortes de changements et de transformations. Quels critères utiliser pour évaluer les choix à faire? Dans un article récent Gaylin, fondateur du *Hastings Centre for Ethics* écrivait:

> Acknowledging that one of the primary aspects of our humaness is the capacity to modify ourselves, I would hold that the guidelines necessary to test the value of change would be the degree to which those changes encourage or discourage the emergence of the other noble and human qualities[18].

La question fondamentale à laquelle l'éthique convie à réfléchir et à débattre garde toute son étendue: à quelles conditions, le sport de haut niveau peut-il vraiment servir à rendre ce village global meilleur, plus convivial?

NOTES ET RÉFÉRENCES

1. Giraudoux J (1977) Le sport. Paris: Grasset p 14 [Ce texte est d'abord paru en 1928 dans une collection de «Notes et Maximes»]

2. Parienté R (1985) Sport. Histoire du sport. Dans Encyclopaedia Universalis Vol 17 Paris: Encyclopaedia Universalis p 115

3. Lavigueur C (1990) Être bien. Le Devoir 23 février p 9

4. Duhamel G (1930) Scènes de la vie future. Paris: Mercure de France p 184-87

5. Csepregi G (1988) Le sport a-t-il un sens? Science et Esprit 40 p 219

6. Weiss P (1969) Sport: a philosophical inquiry. Carbondale: Southern Illinois University Press p 3

7. Volant E (1976) Le sport: perspectives théologiques. Dans Boutin M et al. (eds) L'homme en mouvement: le sport, le jeu , la fête. Montréal: Fides p 62-64

8. Csepregi G (1988) op cit p 210

9. Guttmann A (1978) From ritual to record: the nature of modern sports. New York: Columbia University Press p 47-49

10. Bernard M (1985) Sport. Le phénomène sportif. Dans Encyclopaedia Universalis Vol 17 Paris: Encyclopaedia Universalis p 124

11. Parlebas P (1975) Jeu sportif, rêve et fantaisie. Esprit 5 p 794

12. Csepregi G (1988) op cit p 212

13. Couturier F (1976) Interprétation: réduction et création de distance. Dans Boutin M et al. (eds) L'homme en mouvement: le sport, le jeu, la fête. Montréal: Fides p 93

14. Parienté R (1985) op cit p 111

15. Guttmann A (1978) op cit p 49

16. Ullmann J (1971) De la gymnastique aux sports modernes. Paris: Vrin p 336

17. Rahner K (1970) La manipulation de l'homme par l'homme. Dans Rahner K Écrits théologiques: Problèmes moraux et sciences humaines. Tome XII. Tours: Desclée de Brouwer/Mame p 126

18. Gaylin W (1990) Fooling with mother nature. Hastings Center Report 20 p 21

Some Thoughts on the Advent of Biotechnologies in Sport

The author comments on the widespread attractiveness of the motto *Citius, Altius, Fortius,* The benefits that can be derived from success in high performance sport and the present-day requirements on the human organism, however, have become such that it should be of no surprise to anyone that certain principles and practices are incompatible with those that have prevailed up to now, more specifically as concerns what is judged ethically or legally acceptable. The author's thoughts are then exposed under three sub-themes: – consideration of the positive as well as of the negative aspects of the contributions of biological sciences to contemporary sport; – consideration of the potential impact on sport of the most recent developments in the biological sciences; – consideration of the new and even more complex ethical problems to which sport will be confronted at the turn of the century, on account of the current developments in cellular, molecular, and reproductive biology, and human genetics. The biological sciences have provided an unprecedented knowledge and understanding of the workings of the human organism as well as of the effects of exercise and training, from the angles of systems and organs to those of complex cellular and molecular processes. The author stresses that the current body of knowledge pertaining to regular and well balanced regimens of physical activity unequivocally points to potential benefits of significance with respect to fitness, risk reduction, health promotion and individual well-being. Conversely, knowledge in the biological sciences has been used by scientists and technicians, indeed with the encouragement and approval of a number of sport administrators, in avenues and circumstances that are questionable as concerns individual well-being, health, and current sport and/or social ethics. Analgesics, ergogenic aids, blood-doping, weight reducing techniques are cited as examples. The author then proceeds to describe some of the recent advances in the biotechnologies that have to do with the understanding of control and regulation of specific tissular and cellular processes. He emphasizes the fact that biologists can nowadays even successfully proceed to cellular transfection of foreign genes and produce transgenic organisms. These technological advances bring up questions and problems of unprecedented and enormous implications. It is pointed out as an example that molecular biologists are moving ahead with the task of sequencing the ADN of the 24 chromosomes of Homo Sapiens. In parallel, recent and rapid advances in the biology of reproduction have rendered possible the in-vitro fertilization of gametes from donors selected on the basis of given phenotypic criteria or desired genetic polymorphisms. In the author's view, there is little doubt that the very existence of these biotechnologies will, sooner rather than later, have repercussions on the matters of talent detection, selection and development in high performance sport. Eventually, embryo selection will also become a reality in the world of sport performance. The author concludes his presentation by sketching seven areas in which repercussions of the continuing advances in cellular, molecular and reproductive biology and in human genetics may further be felt in the near future. Eight questions are raised with respect to ethics in sport and a suggestion is made to sport governing bodies at the international level not to leave informed scientists and scholars outside of the debate on the ethical issues confronting modern sport.

Quelques réflexions sur l'avènement des biotechnologies dans le sport

Claude Bouchard

Tous savent que les records sportifs sont constamment améliorés. Ce qui semblait impossible dans le saut en hauteur, en course de fond ou en haltérophilie au début du siècle est maintenant atteint et dépassé par des centaines d'athlètes lors de séances régulières d'entraînement. Aux quatre coins du monde, on a donc bien répondu à l'exhortation du *Citius, Altius, Fortius*. Dans la poursuite des honneurs ou du défi que représentent le dépassement, la satisfaction de faire encore plus, de devenir le meilleur, les athlètes consentent des investissements considérables et sont l'objet d'attentions qui semblent bien au delà des pratiques des autres époques. Il n'est pas surprenant, dans ce contexte, que des gestes incompatibles avec le concept de compétition loyale et des pratiques jugées illégales dans plusieurs sociétés soient devenus monnaie si courante. Le monde du sport est, et sera d'ailleurs toujours, un peu en retard dans son agenda, ses énoncés politiques, sa législation en ce qui concerne l'attention à accorder aux pratiques sportivement ou socialement déloyales. Sous cet aspect, l'agenda des dirigeants locaux, nationaux et internationaux est déjà fort rempli. Qui plus est, ils ne soupçonnent généralement pas que les problèmes d'éthique du présent apparaîtront minimes par rapport aux dossiers complexes et lourds de conséquences qui pointent à l'horizon.

Dans l'exposé suivant, celui d'un scientifique impliqué dans l'étude des fondements biologiques de la performance physique humaine ainsi que dans l'étude des liens entre activité physique et santé, trois thèmes ayant trait aux relations entre le sport et la bioéthique sont proposés à la réflexion: – quelques unes des contributions positives et négatives des sciences biologiques au monde du sport contemporain; – quelques développements récents dans les sciences biologiques qui sont susceptibles d'avoir éventuellement des répercussions sur le monde du sport; – quelques-uns des problèmes d'éthique auxquels le monde du sport sera confronté au début du troisième millénaire en raison principalement de la révolution présente en biologie cellulaire et moléculaire et en biologie de la reproduction.

1890
1990

Claude Bouchard, Laboratoire des Sciences de l'activité physique, Université Laval, Québec, Canada.

Les sciences biologiques et le sport contemporain

La biologie du sport et de l'activité physique est un domaine d'étude et de recherche bien jeune qui était et demeure tributaire des progrès réalisés au sein des disciplines mères telles que la physiologie, la biochimie, la pharmacologie et plusieurs autres. En dépit de cette relative jeunesse, les sciences biologiques appliquées au sport ont exercé une certaine influence sur le développement et la gestion du sport au cours du présent siècle, et plus particulièrement encore depuis le début des années soixante. Si certaines de ces contributions des sciences biologiques ont été heureuses, d'autres, en revanche, paraissent l'avoir été moins.

Par ailleurs, un observateur avisé perçoit également que la biologie du sport a des réalisations considérables dans ses archives de recherche mais aussi que bon nombre de ses acquis scientifiques n'ont pas encore été absorbés en pratique par le monde du sport. Qui plus est, l'avancement des connaissances sur la biologie de la personne active semble avoir servi autant le développement de pratiques qualifiées d'illégales ou de frauduleuses que l'enrichissement de la pratique du sport à des fins socialement et éthiquement acceptables. Aux yeux d'un bon nombre, cela est inquiétant et augure mal pour l'avenir. Sera-t-on capable de sagesse et de modération en présence de développements scientifiques et technologiques dont la portée risque d'être beaucoup plus considérable ? Au stade ou en sont les choses, la réponse à cette interrogation n'est pas forcément positive.

Parmi les acquis du monde du sport et de l'activité physique qui n'auraient pu survenir sans les progrès réalisés en sciences biologiques, il faut noter une compréhension croissante des conséquences de l'effort physique sur l'organisme, des effets de l'entraînement et des mécanismes de l'adaptation à un régime élevé d'exercices physiques, et ce sous les plans des divers systèmes et organes, de l'utilisation des substrats énergétiques, de la thermorégulation, de la régulation hormonale et des principaux tissus impliqués dans l'exécution des divers types d'effort physique. La biologie du sport a également permis d'en apprendre davantage au plan des exigences biologiques de la performance dans une variété considérable de sports. Elle a permis d'en savoir plus sur les conditions qui permettent d'optimiser le rendement à l'entraînement et sur les conditions d'exercice d'un contrôle biomédical suivi. La biologie du sport a mis en lumière les ressemblances manifestes, aussi bien que les différences qui existent entre l'homme et la femme dans la tolérance à l'effort physique et l'adaptation à l'entraînement. Ces études ont par ailleurs indiqué qu'il fallait prendre des précautions pour une pratique sécuritaire du sport par grande chaleur ou grand froid et en présence de conditions géoclimatiques variables. Ces mêmes sciences biologiques appliquées au sport ont également permis de réaliser des progrès substantiels dans les connaissances sur la prévention du surentraînement et des blessures et dans le traitement de ces dernières.

Il convient de souligner que la contribution la plus importante des sciences biologiques appliquées au sport, au cours des dernières décennies, est probablement celle qui a trait à la « réhabilitation » de l'activité physique et du sport en tant que moyens de rehausser le capital santé de l'individu. Le sport des élites nationales et internationales est un phénomène bien particulier dont la principale caractéristique demeure le dépassement de soi, la performance, la poursuite de l'excellence, bref, le *Citius, Altius, Fortius*. À ce niveau, les préoccupations de santé et de bien-être sont généralement marginales, les compétiteurs étant jeunes et plutôt en bonne santé. Par ailleurs, il y a les autres, ceux et celles qui n'ont pas ou n'ont plus le désir d'être parmi les élites nationales ou mondiales. Les résultats de la recherche montrent sans équivoque que la pratique régulière d'une ou de plusieurs activités physiques se traduit par une diminution des facteurs de risque associés aux maladies dégénératives communes ainsi que par une réduction de la morbidité et de la mortalité, et une plus grande sensation de bien-être.

Ces acquis et contributions de la biologie du sport sont dans l'ensemble considérables surtout lorsqu'on prend en considération la jeunesse relative du champ de recherche. Cette dimension du bilan ne doit cependant pas faire oublier que les sciences biologiques appliquées au sport ont également un passif. Si les développements scientifiques ont permis de développer des techniques thérapeutiques et des médicaments dont l'effet est de réduire la douleur associée à une blessure, il se trouve par ailleurs qu'ils soient souvent utilisés afin que des athlètes reviennent prématurément à la compétition avant guérison de la blessure. Ces mêmes sciences biologiques ont également à leur crédit le développement de substances dites illégales en raison de leurs effets transitoires ou chroniques présumés ou démontrés sur l'organisme. Il semble bien que les biologistes du sport n'aient été qu'indirectement associés aux travaux des pharmacologistes et autres scientifiques qui sont parvenus à isoler ou à synthétiser des composés ayant des effets ergogéniques. Ce sont toutefois les premiers qui ont mis en lumière le rôle de ces substances lors de l'effort physique et leurs propriétés dans le contexte de l'entraînement et de la compétition. Ces scientifiques ont également été impliqués dans l'identification de composés qui permettent de masquer certaines substances dopantes, les rendant ainsi difficiles à détecter aux contrôles anti-dopage. On pourrait ajouter que c'est la biologie du sport qui est responsable du développement du «blood doping». Ce développement est associé au fait que certains de ses meilleurs scientifiques s'intéressaient au rôle de la capacité de transport de l'oxygène dans la performance aérobie par rapport aux limites imposées par les mécanismes périphériques musculaires d'utilisation de l'oxygène aux fins de régénération de l'ATP. À des fins de recherche, ils utilisèrent les techniques de cryogénisation des globules rouges, la conservation de ces derniers, et leur réinfusion, en temps utile, chez le donneur afin d'augmenter la quantité totale d'hémoglobine. De là, on est vite passé à leur utilisation au sein des activités physiques les plus exigeantes au plan du métabolisme aérobie en vue d'améliorer la performance. Un autre secteur où des excès ont été observés est celui des méthodes employées pour perdre rapidement du poids, et parfois beaucoup de poids, en vue de parvenir aux normes pondérales requises dans certaines activités sportives individuelles (*e.g.*, la boxe, la lutte, l'haltérophilie, etc.). Là encore, les données accumulées par les biologistes au fil des ans sont exploitées dans des conditions qui peuvent, dans certaines circonstances, comporter des risques pour les participants.

Les biologistes du sport ont donc eux aussi contribué à rendre possible des pratiques qui comportent des dangers potentiels ou sont jugées moralement répréhensibles. Par ailleurs, il faut bien le reconnaître, ces pratiques ont souvent été encouragées ou tolérées par les dirigeants du sport eux-mêmes. Mais au fond, ce sont toutefois les athlètes qui en assument les conséquences, quelles qu'elles soient, au plan de leur bien le plus précieux, la santé.

Des changements dramatiques en vue

Les excès et les abus qui s'observent présentement dans le sport et qui posent des problèmes d'éthique sérieux, sont en fait relativement simples par rapport aux crises auxquelles le monde du sport devra faire face dans l'avenir en raison des développements continus dans les sciences biologiques. Le dopage par substance proscrite par l'establishment sportif, le «blood doping», le retour prématuré à la compétition après blessure, les méthodes de perte rapide de poids qui comportent des dangers, la sollicitation grandissante de la jeunesse sportive par des intérêts commerciaux, entre autres de la part des compagnies de tabac et d'alcool, et un certain nombre d'autres pratiques du genre sont certes sources de préoccupations. Ces pratiques posent des problèmes d'éthique dans le sens où elles heurtent certaines des valeurs personnelles et celles dont s'enorgueillit le monde du sport au sein de ses instances les plus hautes. Mais, il faut faire face à ces difficultés et les surmonter avec succès dans les meilleurs délais, car les problèmes qui pointent à l'horizon sont beaucoup plus complexes et sont susceptibles d'être encore plus préjudiciables à l'institution du sport. Avec la présente réduction dans les tensions politiques entre l'Est et l'Ouest, il semble que les conditions sont devenues meilleures pour que soient avancés des correctifs scientifiquement et moralement acceptables ainsi que pratiquement réalisables. Ce qui pointe toutefois à l'horizon sera d'une tout autre complexité qui obligera à déployer des ressources encore plus considérables pour parvenir à contrôler leur impact éventuel sur le sport.

On tient généralement pour acquis que le développement d'un sport donné passe par une large base de participants qui progressent dans la pyramide en fonction des succès obtenus au sein de l'activité elle-même. En ce sens, la structure des participants dans un sport est plutôt darwinienne. On progresse en fonction de ses performances. Tous peuvent tenter d'y exceller et les combinaisons de talent et d'effort qui permettent d'émerger parmi les meilleurs sont nombreuses. Les athlètes d'élite qui parviennent au sommet de la pyramide de participants obtiennent généralement la plus grande partie des ressources des organismes qui régissent le sport. Dans certains cas, ces athlètes bénéficient du support d'équipes médicales et scientifiques. Plus tard, après une carrière en haute compétition, bon nombre d'athlètes rejoignent les rangs des autres participants et s'insèrent à nouveau dans le réseau au sein des ligues pour adultes et vétérans. Dans ce contexte, les stratégies qui sont présentement déployées afin de détecter les jeunes talentueux pour la performance dans un sport donné ont une importance certaine. La pratique la plus répandue est de ne rien faire pour perturber la sélection qui résulte du passage à travers les diverses strates de la pyramide. Ainsi donc, on tient pour acquis que ceux qui en émergent sont les plus talentueux et les efforts de développement intensif des élites portent alors surtout sur ceux-ci. D'autres procèdent différemment en partant du principe qu'il existe au départ des individus plus doués que d'autres pour parvenir aux performances les plus élevées dans chacun des sports ou des catégories de sports. À cet effet, on a développé des systèmes dans le but de repérer les jeunes doués pour une activité sportive particulière. Ces systèmes utilisent, en des combinaisons variables, des données anthropométriques, des mesures de force et de puissance musculaires, des évaluations d'habiletés motrices, des indications sur les capacités aérobies et anaérobies de travail, des informations sur le niveau de maturité biologique atteint par l'enfant et d'autres données de ce type. De telles informations sont généralement obtenues auprès des enfants âgés de 9 à 14 ans. Il est facile de se rendre compte qu'un système basé sur des données de cette nature ne peut avoir qu'un faible pouvoir de discrimination entre ceux qui sont exceptionnellement doués et les autres. Et voilà exactement le secteur où les progrès actuels et prévisibles dans les domaines des bases génétiques de la performance, de la biologie de la reproduction et en biologie cellulaire et moléculaire sont susceptibles de changer radicalement les choses avec des répercussions sur l'ensemble de la structure du monde du sport.

La révolution en cours dans les sciences biologiques

Il n'est pas exagéré d'affirmer que, depuis une dizaine d'années, les sciences biologiques ont effectué des virages importants et des gains majeurs. De fait, il se passe une révolution dans ces sciences au plan des méthodes d'étude, des questions posées, des occasions offertes et des implications des travaux pour l'individu, le couple et la société. La révolution en cours dans les sciences biologiques semble être particulièrement importante à évaluer dès maintenant par le monde du sport; quatre raisons sont avancées.

Les méthodologies nouvelles

Il s'est produit un développement considérable de méthodes permettant d'évaluer avec précision les niveaux de substances biologiques qui font l'objet de régulation dans les cellules et les tissus; cela permet d'envisager la mise au point de trousses simples pouvant être utilisées sur de grandes populations, avec des ressources matérielles et humaines relativement modestes. À cet effet, la capacité des biologistes à marquer, identifier et quantifier des molécules qui sont sous le contrôle des gènes, mais font également l'objet d'une régulation principalement en fonction des besoins des cellules et tissus de l'organisme, s'est accrue considérablement au cours de la dernière décennie. Le développement phénoménal de la recherche, et des secteurs de l'industrie qui en sont le prolongement, au plan de la production des anticorps polyclonaux et monoclonaux, des méthodes immunologiques de détection et de quantification, des techniques de séparation des protéines et des ARN, et des méthodes de marquage et de comptage d'isotopes radioactifs et naturels, pour ne donner que quelques exemples, a eu un impact considérable sur le pouvoir d'étudier des molécules de toute provenance, in vitro et in vivo. Ainsi, les progrès récents dans les méthodes faisant appel à des isotopes non radioactifs et à la résonnance magnétique nucléaire ont grandement amélioré la capacité d'étude de la régulation biologique chez l'individu normal et en bonne santé.

À un niveau plus fondamental, l'avènement des techniques de la transfection cellulaire et de la production d'animaux transgéniques permet d'envisager des investigations sur les problèmes de régulation biologique qui n'auraient pas été possibles auparavant. Et les progrès dans ces domaines s'effectuent à un rythme qui dépasse les prévisions les plus optimistes des biologistes informés. Il est difficile de décrire quelles seront les conséquences des nouveaux acquis et des progrès attendus dans ce secteur sur le monde du sport. Il est par ailleurs évident que dans l'avenir de telles méthodes et, nul doute, d'autres en voie de développement rejoindront le secteur de la biologie du sport afin de permettre un contrôle toujours plus précis de l'état d'entraînement, voire même d'affiner le pouvoir d'identification de ceux et celles qui répondent bien à l'entraînement et qui sont en mesure de bien réguler les mécanismes biologiques fondamentaux de l'adaptation à l'exercice et à l'entraînement physiques.

Les différences innées au niveau de l'ADN

La révolution dans les sciences biologiques a rendu possible le développement d'outils (sondes) permettant de définir les différences inter-individuelles innées au niveau de l'ADN (donc du matériel génétique) de nos cellules. Les biologistes ont en effet appris à isoler, amplifier, séquencer et immortaliser l'ADN de nos cellules et à en établir l'individualité par l'étude de la variation de séquence. Sous ce dernier aspect, l'approche la plus répandue qui consiste à couper l'ADN en fragments avec une variété d'endonucléases et à mettre à profit les propriétés de l'hybridation hautement spécifique ADN-ADN afin d'établir s'il existe un polymorphisme de séquence pour un gène ou un fragment d'ADN à l'aide d'une sonde, et en utilisant la technique du «Southern blotting», a permis de démontrer que les différences inter-individuelles dans le matériel même de l'hérédité ne sont pas rares. De fait, environ une base d'ADN sur 100 serait variable entre deux personnes prises au hasard si l'on s'appuie sur les données fragmentaires actuellement disponibles. À mesure que le nombre de gènes ou de fragments d'ADN clonés augmentera, nul doute que la capacité de comprendre la variation génétique deviendra meilleure. Déjà, les généticiens disposent de plus de 5 000 de ces sondes et leur nombre croît de jour en jour. La technique du polymorphisme de longueur des fragments de restriction, mieux connu sous le sigle RFLP, est en ce sens fort utile et a d'ores et déjà permis d'améliorer considérablement la compréhension de l'importance de la variation génétique humaine mais également de son rapport avec un bon nombre de maladies héréditaires dont on ignorait les bases moléculaires jusqu'à tout récemment[1].

Mais il y a plus encore. Le projet de séquencer complètement les 3 milliards de paires de base d'ADN des 24 chromosomes de l'Homo Sapiens est déjà en marche aux USA à l'instigation du «National Institutes of Health» et du «Department of Energy»[2, 3]. La tâche devrait être complétée dans environ 15 ans, *i.e.*, autour de l'an 2005 ; on estime qu'elle coûtera 3 milliards de dollars en valeur constante de 1990. Plusieurs équipes sont déjà à l'œuvre. En 1990, on a consacré à ce travail un budget d'environ 90 millions de dollars, aux USA seulement. Connaître la séquence complète du matériel génétique d'un être humain permettra très rapidement de déterminer, d'une manière claire, l'importance de la variation génétique humaine plus particulièrement celle des variations entre les groupes humains et les «races»[4]. Une fois cette tâche complétée, la question des différences innées et des différences raciales dans la performance devrait pouvoir s'aborder avec des critères plus objectifs, et le débat pourrait ultérieurement devenir caduque. De tels progrès dans les connaissances au sujet de l'individualité du matériel de l'hérédité, et le pouvoir de vérifier chez une personne ou un groupe la présence des polymorphismes d'intérêt, ne seront pas sans répercussions sur le sport d'élite.

Gamètes de donneurs sélectionnés et la fécondation in vitro

Les développements récents ont rendu possible la mise au point de méthodes en biologie de la reproduction qui permettent d'envisager la fécondation in vitro de gamètes provenant de donneurs sélectionnés sur des critères phénotypiques ou la présence des polymorphismes génétiques désirés. Les progrès dans ce domaine de la biologie de la reproduction, combinés avec ceux de la génétique moléculaire et des bases génétiques de la performance, auront sans doute des répercussions choc sur le monde du sport. Il n'est pas impensable que ce pouvoir donne lieu à des abus outrageants, aux yeux de la majorité des citoyens. Comme le monde du sport n'y échappera probablement pas, mieux vaut commencer à y réfléchir tout de suite.

L'avènement des techniques de fécondation in vitro, de l'insémination de l'embryon dans l'utérus d'une mère porteuse, de l'amniocentèse, de la cryopréservation des gamètes mâles (et bientôt sans doute, des ovules), de traitements permettant des ovulations multiples, et d'autres encore, rendent possible l'établissement de protocoles de reproduction qui n'auraient pu être envisagés il y a quelques années. Ces approches, utilisées de concert avec les techniques de prélèvement de cellules *in utero* (voire même d'une cellule sur un embryon fécondé *in vitro*), celles d'amplification de l'ADN à partir d'une seule copie des séquences d'intérêt, et des connaissances actuelles et prévisibles sur la cartographie des gènes au sein de chacun des chromosomes, rendraient théoriquement possible non seulement de féconder *in vitro* à partir de gamètes provenant de donneurs triés sur le volet, mais également de sélectionner parmi les ovules fécondés ceux qui portent les polymorphismes génétiques jugés désirables avant leur insémination dans l'utérus de mères porteuses. Un tel pouvoir des biologistes ne sera pas sans conséquences dramatiques sur la société, les couples et, bien entendu, le monde sportif qui valorise tant le *Citius, Altius, Fortius*.

Les implications de ces acquisitions des sciences biologiques ainsi que des développements en cours ou envisagés sont énormes pour le monde du sport. Comme les conséquences les plus dramatiques sont susceptibles de se faire sentir d'abord en regard du processus de la détection ou de la sélection des plus doués, puis, plus tard sans doute, au plan de la fécondation *in vitro* et de la planification de la fécondation de zygotes porteurs de caractéristiques jugées désirables, les considérations qui suivent seront limitées à ces questions.

Coup d'oeil sur l'avenir

Fort probablement avant la fin du présent millénaire, mais certainement tôt dans le troisième, la révolution esquissée plus haut (et toujours en cours) en biologie cellulaire, en biologie moléculaire, en biologie de la reproduction et en génétique humaine aura des implications percutantes pour le monde du sport. Il est difficile de prévoir ces implications d'une manière détaillée. Néanmoins, on ne risque pas de se tromper beaucoup en avançant que ces répercussions incluront au moins celles dont l'énumération suit.

– Les bases génétiques de la performance au sein de chacune des grandes familles d'activités sportives, *i.e.*, ces activités qui ont des exigences physiques, physiologiques, métaboliques et comportementales relativement semblables, seront mieux comprises. Le déterminisme génétique de la performance physique humaine ne saurait être absolu. Il faut cependant reconnaître que le génotype, l'individualité biologique, explique une fraction importante des différences individuelles dans la performance[5,6,7].

– Les bases génétiques de la réponse de l'organisme aux divers types d'entraînement physique auront également été élucidées et l'on comprendra mieux le rôle de la variation génétique dans le phénomène de la trainabilité[8,9].

– Pour chacune des familles d'activités sportives, une batterie de sondes sera éventuellement disponible en vue de permettre la définition des polymorphismes de l'ADN pour des gènes importants[10].

– Les biologistes du sport, sous la pression des entraîneurs, des athlètes, des parents, et sans doute de certains dirigeants sportifs, feront appel à des batteries de sondes génomiques et mitochondriales, particulièrement celles qui s'avèreront des marqueurs solides de la performance et de la sensibilité à l'entraînement.

– Comme les études de dépistage des polymorphismes génétiques ne requièrent qu'un faible prélèvement sanguin, elles seront étendues aux jeunes enfants, tôt après la naissance.

– Sous la pression de parents ambitieux, le dépistage des polymorphismes génétiques ayant le pouvoir de discriminer au plan du talent pour des performances physiques pourrait éventuellement être effectué sur l'ADN de fœtus prélevé *in utero*.

– Dans une phase ultérieure, il peut même être envisagé que les techniques de la biologie de la reproduction soient exploitées afin de sélectionner et implanter dans un utérus receveur des embryons d'un sexe donné possédant les polymorphismes génétiques désirés pour une catégorie donnée de performances sportives.

Il va sans dire que de telles pratiques ne seront pas l'apanage uniquement du monde du sport. On peut en effet anticiper que dans les sociétés de haute technologie qui valorisent tant la compétition et le succès, le recours à ces techniques fera également partie des luttes contre les maladies héréditaires, des efforts en vue d'accroître la longévité et l'espérance de vie active, de la détection des individus doués pour la musique, la création littéraire ou scientifique, etc. En dépit de cela, le sport devrait être particulièrement touché pour la simple raison que les particularismes génétiques associés au rendement devraient être plus faciles à identifier dans ce laboratoire naturel et constant d'observation que constituent les affrontements du stade. De fait, l'univers du sport pourrait être, avec celui de la médecine génétique, l'un des domaines qui sera le plus marqué par les nouveaux pouvoirs de la biologie.

Conséquences pour le sport

Les nouvelles technologies font déjà, dans une certaine mesure, partie de nos sociétés[11]. Qu'on l'accepte ou non, qu'on le veuille ou non, les pratiques brièvement esquissées ci-avant affecteront le monde du sport. Elles sont susceptibles d'entraîner des bouleversements majeurs autant dans la pyramide des participants que dans les règles et conventions qui régissent les conduites sportives. Inutile de souligner que le Mouvement olympique lui-même sera alors soumis à des tensions intenses qui pourraient mettre son existence même en cause. Il y a donc un risque sérieux de déstabilisation de l'appareil international du sport. On ne saurait cependant effectuer des progrès réels sur la question de fond en se campant dans des attitudes pro-sciences ou anti-sciences. Il faudrait également se méfier des formules simplistes en cette matière. La force déployée par la révolution dans les sciences biologiques est trop considérable pour qu'on puisse l'écarter ou la maîtriser avec un simple slogan, une simple formule. Les interrogations sont déjà, et demeureront nombreuses.

– Est-ce que les dirigeants des grands organismes internationaux de régie du sport sauront s'adapter à la présence des nouvelles biotechnologies?

– Quelles seront, à ce sujet, l'attitude et les politiques du Comité International Olympique?

– Comment la société dans son ensemble réagira-t-elle, face à l'introduction des biotechnologies dans le monde du sport?

– Les gouvernements nationaux seront-ils tentés d'intervenir et de légiférer en la matière, au-delà des lois existantes?

– Comment réagiront les athlètes, les entraîneurs et les scientifiques du sport aux prises avec un nouveau pouvoir?

– Quel sera l'impact des pratiques envisagées sur la traditionnelle pyramide des participants? Auront-elles comme effet d'accroître la proportion des jeunes qui ne feront pas de sport et demeureront sédentaires?

– Est-ce que les développements à venir nuiront aux efforts consacrés à l'augmentation de la participation des citoyens aux activités physiques en vue de leur santé et de leur bien-être?

– L'impact des nouvelles technologies aura-t-il comme conséquence de détourner les gens d'une vie active, de les décourager même d'essayer?

Au fond, ce dont il s'agit dans le débat présent et à venir (et dont le foyer est le sport à l'échelle planétaire) c'est le grand thème des «conséquences sur l'homme et la société de la révolution biotechnologique que nous vivons à l'heure actuelle[12]». Dans ce domaine comme dans les autres, le vrai débat ne pourra avoir lieu et des solutions concrètes ne sauraient émerger tant que les décideurs du monde du sport, les participants et les autres citoyens demeureront peu ou mal informés.

Et l'éthique?

La révolution biotechnologique aura des implications d'importance pour l'éthique. Ces dernières feront nul doute l'objet de nombreux débats, car le questionnement sur les implications des pouvoirs nouveaux de la biologie pour le sport est également celui de la science et de la société. Les valeurs présentes seront mises à épreuve plus rude encore à mesure que les biotechnologies feront leur entrée dans le stade. Les applications des connaissances en génétique de la performance, en biologie moléculaire et en biologie de la reproduction pourraient même survenir dans la présente décennie ou au plus tard, au début du troisième millénaire. Mais, on ne saurait les éviter. Que peut-on faire d'ici là?

En tout premier lieu, il conviendrait d'évaluer la moralité, l'acceptabilité de pratiques comme celles décrites ci-avant pour le monde du sport, bien sûr, mais également pour la société dans son ensemble. L'exercice ne devrait épargner personne, car tous, athlètes, parents, entraîneurs, médecins du sport, biologistes du sport, dirigeants sportifs et autres ont une part de responsabilité à cet égard. La contribution des philosophes, des scientifiques, des juristes et des autres citoyens sera également requise si l'on souhaite parvenir à une éthique du sport vraiment adaptée à ces temps nouveaux.

En second lieu, on doit s'interroger sur un aspect particulier de l'éthique. Il s'agit en l'occurence des conséquences que peut avoir sur l'individu, sa vie et ses choix de carrière, le fait d'être informé en bas âge qu'il possède ou non dans ses noyaux cellulaires une combinaison favorable de polymorphismes génétiques pour un ou des types particuliers de performances sportives. À bien des égards, apprendre que l'on est en quelque sorte «détenteur» d'une combinaison favorable sera plus anxiogène et potentiellement dérangeant que la situation inverse. Comment concilier le droit d'être informé avec celui de ne pas l'être dans le contexte des législations sur l'accès aux dossiers qui concernent l'individu dans les sociétés démocratiques?

En troisième lieu, il faudrait prévoir l'encadrement de ceux qui auront l'information biologique et qui pourraient ainsi exercer des pressions considérables sur les participants afin de les motiver ou de les dissuader de continuer, selon le cas. Les législations actuelles sur les libertés individuelles, les droits de la personne, les biotechnologies, la protection des sujets humains, et autres lois promulguées en plusieurs pays sur des thèmes apparentés, seront nettement insuffisantes.

Si les défis du présent semblent énormes et énergivores, ceux qui apparaîtront au tournant du millénaire seront comparativement démesurés. Les difficultés qui vont surgir ne sauraient être surmontées sans une réflexion soutenue sur les dimensions morales et éthiques de ces biotechnologies et de leur insertion progressive dans le monde du sport. Le Comité international olympique et les autres grands organismes de régie du sport à l'échelle mondiale devraient prendre action à brève échéance dans ce secteur. Le leadership devrait préférablement être assumé par le Comité international olympique lui-même qui sera, de toute manière, appelé à jouer un rôle central dans le dossier dès l'instant ou le pouvoir biotechnologique commencera à envahir le monde du sport. Dans un premier temps, le Comité international olympique, serait bien avisé d'inviter des spécialistes en biotechnologies et en biologie de la reproduction à faire partie intégrante des équipes de scientifiques et autres savants qui pourraient donner des avis sur les problèmes qui affligent aujourd'hui et confronteront demain le sport d'élite et le Mouvement olympique.

Conclusions

Le *Citius, Altius, Fortius,* dans le contexte de la fin du présent siècle est loin d'avoir les mêmes implications que celles qui pouvaient être envisagées par de Coubertin et ses disciples à la fin du siècle dernier. Les ressources scientifiques et technologiques qui peuvent maintenant être mises au service de la performance maximale sont telles qu'elles ont même le potentiel de détruire les fondements originaires de la compétition sportive entre les nations et peut-être le Mouvement olympique sous sa forme présente. Il est sans doute possible d'envisager des scénarios moins apocalyptiques pour le sport dans le troisième millénaire, des scénarios où le sport continuerait à croître en popularité et où la majorité des citoyens pourrait apprécier les joies et les bénéfices d'une vie active. À la limite, on pourrait concevoir un scénario dans lequel le sport ne serait pas touché par les progrès dans les sciences biologiques. Mais, un tel scénario ne serait pas réaliste et serait d'une naïveté impardonnable. Il faudra convier au débat sur les biotechnologies et le sport d'élite les plus avisés de nos concitoyens de tous les coins de la planète car le défi sera vraiment de taille. Pour ma part, sans vouloir être indûment pessimiste, je crois que l'incorporation progressive des nouveaux pouvoirs de la biologie dans l'univers du sport présente des risques énormes pour la survie de celui-ci.

REFERENCES

1. Scriver CR, Beaudet AL, Sly WS, Valle D (eds) (1989) The metabolic basis of inherited disease. Vol I et II. New York: McGraw-Hill

2. Watson JD (1990) The human genome project: past, present and future. Science 248 44-49

3. Cantor CR (1990) Orchestrating the human genome project. Science 248 49-51

4. Cavalli-Sforza LL (1990) Opinion: How can one study individual variation for 3 billion nucleotides of the human genome? American Journal of Human Genetics 46 649-51

5. Bouchard C (1986) Genetics of aerobic power and capacity. Dans Malina RM, Bouchard C (eds) Sport and human genetics. Champaign: Human Kinetics p 59-88

6. Bouchard C (sous presse) Genetics determinants of endurance performance. Dans Shephard RJ, Astrand PO (eds) Encyclopaedia of sports medecine: the olympic book of endurance in sports. Oxford: Blackwell Scientific

7. Bouchard C, Dionne F, Simoneau JA (1990) Les bases génétiques de la performance. Interface 11 28-37

8. Bouchard C (1986) op cit

9. Bouchard C, Boulay MR, Simoneau JA et al (1988) Heredity and trainability of aerobic and anaerobic performances: an update. Sports Medecine 5 69-73

10. Bouchard C (sous presse) op cit

11. Bernard J (1990) De la biologie à l'éthique. Paris: Buchet/Castel

12. Gros FG, Huber G, Kahn A et al (1990) La biologie, l'homme et la société. Médecine/sciences 6 125-51

[...] *Un travailleur intelligent vise à fournir le plus de besogne possible dans le moins de temps et avec le moins de fatigue possible. Le sportsman demeure étranger à toute préoccupation utilitaire. La tâche qu'il accomplit, c'est lui-même qui se l'est assignée et, comme il n'est pas obligé pour gagner sa vie de la recommencer le lendemain, le souci de se ménager lui est épargné. Il peut ainsi cultiver l'effort pour l'effort, chercher les obstacles, en dresser lui-même sur sa route, viser toujours un degré au-dessus de celui qu'il doit atteindre. C'est ce qu'exprime si bien la devise* [...] citius, altius, fortius*: «Plus vite, plus haut, plus fort!»* [...] *De sorte qu'on en peut tirer cette conclusion, qu'aujourd'hui comme jadis, la tendance du sport est vers l'excès; il vise plus de vitesse, plus de hauteur, plus de force... toujours plus. C'est son inconvénient, soit! au point de vue de l'équilibre humain; mais c'est aussi sa noblesse – et sa poésie.*

Coubertin P de (1901) Notes sur l'Éducation publique. Paris: Librairie Hachette (Chapitre X, La psychologie du sport, p 171-173)

Citius, altius, fortius et la problématique de l'éthique sportive: point de vue d'un philosophe

En lançant les trois superlatifs citius-altius-fortius, le Dominicain Henri Didon venait non seulement de fixer de façon superbement lapidaire les caractéristiques essentielles de l'Olympisme moderne, mais encore le célèbre religieux venait-il de faire en sorte que le concept de record sportif ait désormais, selon l'expression même de Coubertin, «sa glorification en style classique». Dans un premier temps, l'auteur procède à une explication des contrastes existant entre, d'une part, le contexte de réalisation des Jeux antiques où les éléments rituels et une culture orale prévalaient, et, d'autre part, le contexte des Jeux modernes où le record, par le truchement des écrits, agit comme une force motrice en fixant dans la mémoire collective les événements, les exploits et les acteurs. Il souligne par la suite les difficultés et les risques qu'il y a à superposer ou à comparer des concepts d'éthique dont les points d'ancrage sont d'époques et de cultures différentes. L'auteur décrit comme un penchant regrettable ou un parti-pris le fait que l'on s'attende des athlètes d'aujourd'hui qu'ils/elles aient des attitudes morales et des comportements en tous points identiques à ceux que l'on dit avoir prévalu dans le passé. Selon l'auteur, la dynamique de ce qui conduit aux records sportifs contemporains ne saurait être la même que celle que devait provoquer, du moins selon l'espoir de Coubertin, l'essor d'une «chevalerie». La notion de chance, celle des succès en fonction du mérite, et celles aussi des motivations intrinsèques et de l'avantage que l'athlète s'efforce d'avoir sur l'autre en mettant à contribution tous les facteurs et toutes les énergies qu'il/elle peut contrôler, sont par la suite analysées dans une perspective élargie du fair-play. L'auteur montre également qu'il y a eu une mutation progressive du sens profond de la règle dans le sport d'élite moderne. Il souligne que ce sont les motivations personnelles, les enjeux économiques, les attentes de la société et l'influence des media, qui déterminent en fait les marges de manœuvre et les comportements qui sont qualifiés ou pas de fair-play. Dans une telle perspective l'auteur se dit d'avis qu'il est justement contraire à l'éthique d'imposer de l'extérieur aux athlètes un code rigide et abstrait d'éthique comportementale. En guise de conclusion, l'auteur exprime le souhait qu'en matière d'éthique sportive – on tienne mieux compte des avis des athlètes eux/elles-mêmes, à titre de partenaires centraux du Mouvement olympique; – on reconnaisse et fasse meilleur cas des effets de brouillage causés par les personnes qui, de l'extérieur, portent des jugements hâtifs ou superficiels sur des comportements sportifs complexes dont les résultantes sont loin d'être indépendantes des facultés supérieures (le mètis, chez les Grecs); – on reconnaisse enfin que les formes égocentriques de moralité, telles que l'on peut facilement les observer dans le sport d'élite contemporain, peuvent contribuer positivement aussi bien que négativement à la mosaïque des valeurs culturelles.

Citius – Altius – Fortius
and the Problem of Sport Ethics:
a Philosopher's Viewpoint

Gunter Gebauer

It was the rhetorical gesture of a headmaster, the Dominican Henri Didon, that became for Coubertin the motto of the Olympic Games and the most succinct inscription of the Olympic Movement: "Henceforth, the record had its glorification in classical style[1]." But just as Latin rhetoric was grafted onto the Greek games, so the principle of records was grafted onto the ritual events of the modern Olympic Games. Two sharply contrasting cultures are overlaid. The Greeks were not familiar with the principle of *Citius – Altius – Fortius*; the Ancient Olympic Games were part of a culture that did not write down records. It was an *oral* culture.

Thanks to breakthroughs achieved by the Canadian researcher Havelock, the special characteristics of the *oral* culture in ancient Greece have been brought out and contrasted with those of the *written* culture[2]. The oral features of the Greek Games are the rituals and ceremonies, the situational context, the coincidence of fortunate circumstances, the here and now, the dependence of achievement on the human body, and the presence of spectators. By contrast, the principle of records implies and demands that performances be measured, written down, recorded and handed down. It draws on essential features of the written culture: lists, accounts of past events, written descriptions of athletes, competitions and performances in the form of biographies, stories, comparisons, and interviews. Written records constitute an accessible evidence or a memory of the past and of the very identities of events and persons[3].

Superimposing two types of culture in the modern Olympic Games —which were originally an oral event, yet whose principles, results, past, and identities have been preserved in writing—inevitably brings up an issue that has been analyzed in detail by Havelock, Goody, and Watt. It is the point that oral culture is often distorted, misrepresented, and even falsified when codified in writing; it becomes saddled with a system of logic that does not necessarily reflect the nature of the oral culture. This issue dominates the question of the ethics underlying olympic competition. The concept of ethics is normally reserved for a

1890
1990

Gunter Gebauer, Philosophy and Sociology of Sport Department, Institute of Sport Sciences, Freie Universität Berlin, Federal Republic of Germany.

theory and doctrine of normative principles of action; but in sports, only *practical* action is what really counts[4]. In that perspective, can one perhaps speak at least of the *morals* with which athletes govern their individual actions?

However, event morals are usually formulated in the form of principles and on the basis of general concepts. Morals represent an attempt to "translate" the specifics of the oral situation into something written. The very feasibility of such a translation is doubtful. A different level of discourse would be useful in the discussion of the morals of to-day's athletes. Present approaches may well be biased in the sense that one tends to remonstrate athletes to-day about some inherent ethical or moral qualities of competition that are presumed to have prevailed in the past or to have been realized at a given point in time. Coubertin, in 1935, proposed the term *chevalerie* for the kind of elitism he propagated; he also wrote "Trying to subject athletics to obligatory restraint is to seek a utopia. Its adherents need the 'freedom of excess'. That is why we have given them the motto *Citius, Altius, Fortius*, ... the motto of those who dare to aspire to break records![5]"

There are serious difficulties in comparing the dynamics of "the record" to those of the "chevalerie". The latter is a written codification of the past, whereas sports are pursued in the here and now of practice. If one wants to extrapolate from the physical, sensuous, immediate situation inherent to sport and derive from it positive morals that are *more* than only the formal principle of competing, one would have to codify them in writing, and that act alone may lead to typical and systematic misrepresentations of what was originally oral. We will see that the way in which competition is engaged in is characterized by the fact that it is not distinct, that it cannot be pinned down to concepts, and furthermore that it is ambiguous by nature and constantly changing[6]. Competition in sport is absolutely no realm in which morals can flourish, let alone ethics. Penetrating it and developing a sense for its incessantly changing conditions demands sets of ideas or mental tools other than those fixated on the written documents.

What the athlete seeks in the competitive situation is *his/her chance*. The French word *chance* contains an ambiguity. One of its meanings is "coincidence" of "happenstance". As a fortuitous accrual of positive opportunity, Caillois has contrasted chance with the principle of 'Αγών (*Agon*), warranted success in competition[7]. Accordingly, chance is that which threatens the meritorious aspect of achievement by either nullifying its result or allowing gain to fall, unearned, to just anybody. Another meaning of chance, which Caillois does not treat at all—much to the detriment of his theory of games—denotes the possibility of influencing competition in one's favor by summoning all of one's capabilities, both physical and mental. Gaining the advantage is of central interest to all athletes. They pursue this objective to the finest detail in their preparation for competition by enduring extensive physical conditioning, acquiring proper attitudes, learning from and acting on experience, applying knowledge, and, in the competitive situation itself, mobilizing all their physical and mental energies and abilities. The quest for one's chance determines the "internal perspective" that one has on the competitive situation as an athlete and the manner in which one organizes the related events.

But are there not generalized statements about behavior in play, that is about the rules of a game? And is it not a moral dimension of sports that athletes contribute to, when they take rules seriously and thus guarantee that they work? These ethical dimensions of play and sport have recently been the object of a number of penetrating analyses and discussions[8]. What do the rules of a game really do? It is difficult, if not impossible, to say. It is easier to state what they do *not* do. In fact, they neither regulate what does happen in a game nor do they indicate what *can* in fact happen[9]. Aside from a few constitutive rules and regulations dealing with material conditions, they simply draw a line between what is allowed and what is not.

This demarcation or boundary brings up three problems. First, it is often unclear and thus leaves a wide gray area. Second, it is not always respected even by the referees themselves in certain characteristic cases, with the result that in actual play situations, the line indeed diverges from the one set forth in the standard formulation. Third, the line can be interpreted as offering choices between an acceptable course of action (following the rules strictly) and one that is unacceptable (breaking the rules) but nonetheless *possible* at the price of certain sanctions. The latter option is neither prohibited nor "formally unfair". The rules of the game thus allow for different consequences of action to be weighed. Ever since soccer became professionalized, for example, players appear to have adopted this calculating attitude toward the rules. Should it be concluded that they have changed the old, stricter attitude toward the rules because they have become less moral and more brutal? Such a presumption illustrates the distortion mentioned earlier. When one makes allowances for the "internal perspective" of the players themselves, one then recognizes that the game has fundamentally changed. Professionalism implies that players are better-trained, more athletic, and faster than they used to be. This development clearly favors the attackers, who, in addition, are surer in exploiting their chances. In the new systems of play, the team members are spread further apart than they used to be and the individual defender bears a far greater responsibility than was previously the case. Behind him, the path to the goal is free. Teams today are better at protecting a lead for an entire period of play; a goal scored can thus mean an invaluable advantage. In addition, there is the pressure of competition between the players and the financial loss incurred by defeat. In short, the changed situation confronting defenders in quick and athletic play forced them to seek new ways to regain advantages. One of them that used to be shunned is physical aggression. It has never been banned from soccer. Quite the contrary, it has always been valued as an element of man-to-man struggle and has typically been acknowledged as such by referees, within limits of course. In this manner, a new balance between attack and defense has been arrived at, but *a different kind of soccer*, a different *game*, is being played. The rules are interpreted in a different way; the defense has acquired an additional weapon. Much the same thing has happened in team handball. It began when the game was moved from large playing fields to smaller indoor courts. Here, too, the defense was put at a comparative disadvantage in relation to the attackers, who could throw the ball at short range. In response to this situation, huge and extremely hard-playing defenders were positioned in front of the circle, producing a new balance insofar as a great amount of violence was henceforth tolerated in the game.

These internal developments of games have as little to do with morals as do the punches thrown by boxers. The aforementioned examples show that there is a certain latitude afforded by the rules themselves and shaped by the athletes. It is within this fair amount of latitude that participants decide which kind of game is being played. Thus, whether the label be soccer, handball or long distance running, it is indeed possible to play *at* quite different games. The rules of the game just do not define the "spirit of the game", or its "essence", that ostensibly guides the actions of the players[11]. What was earlier referred to as "chance" consists in seeking a kind of game that gives one the advantage, and then forcing it upon the opponent. The athlete's "chance" thus lies in *defining the game*. Competitions are full of uncertain, fluctuating situations in which even the most successful athlete interacts with opponents who momentarily seem stronger. Experience, tactical and psychological know-how, patience, confidence in one's own superiority, the ability to size-up the antagonist, every available mental capacity and skill is played out in the moment of encounter in order to gain the upper hand. Hopefully, the opponent is surprised, fatigued, deceived, given a false sense of security; every athlete brings all his/her mental powers to bear so that he/she can play *his/her* game.

The latitude that is possible becomes much wider when the entire range of methods of preparation for competition is brought to bear upon a game. Indeed, sport is partially defined by the amount and quality of medical, biological, psychological, biomechanical knowledge, materials development, and other scientific expertise involved in the preparation for and unfolding of competition. The history of athletics brims with examples illustrating blatant redefinitions of games. Some of these redefinitions were brought about by technical innovations like the O'Brien and Fosbury styles, others by new training methods. Still others were prompted by new materials like the fiberglass pole. In a formal sense, the athlete is operating under the same conditions as his/her competitors, but in his/her individual view he/she egocentrically seeks the most favorable game conditions and situations.

What Coubertin meant by *chevalerie* is an ideology by which one willfully refrains from exploiting the very latitude allowed by the rules. It purported to hold the definition of the game constant. Coubertin's proposal not only runs counter to our present-day convictions of how competition should be managed, but it virtually precludes the astucious use of knowledge about the game. It prevents the activation of mental abilities and thereby thwarts precisely what Coubertin enthusiastically described as "a largely intellectual atmosphere" of athletics and what its progress encourages[12]. That very progress would be impeded if one were to harp upon an essentialism of rules that ostensibly would guide the actions of all athletes. It is unfair and intellectually dishonest to hold up to athletes today a rigid code of virtues. Athletes, confronted with many competitors who are nearly their equal, are increasingly called upon to optimize their mental possibilities.

Why is this situation not recognized? Could it be that too few attempt to understand sport from the athlete's "internal perspective"? In fact, sport ideologists and scientists often indulge in idealistic constructs at the level of general concepts, principles, and maxims. International as well as Olympic sport may have fallen under the sway of the written. Whoever controls the access to the media of the printed word, journalists, associations, or functionaries, has a symbolic power over the perception of the manner in which athletes engage in competition. The view of the competitors, their interests, do not appear to have permanent advocates in the printed media. The fiction of rules according to which the actions of athletes are expected to be guided robs them of a considerable amount of latitude for intellectual and creative activity.

Instead of clouting athletes with accusations of unethical conduct, one can turn the argument around. One conclusion to be drawn is the *ethical* demand that the views of the athletes be brought out in the media, with the intent to foster a better understanding of the material and symbolic reality of sport and of the Olympic Games. Athletes should be brought to play a more genuine role in the printed media. Their involvement ought to go beyond merely formal representation and toward dialogue with associations, journalists, and the public. This fundamental ethical demand, a dictate of fairness toward the most important partner in the Olympic Movement, has gone unfulfilled in principle thus far.

A second conclusion could be a word of caution against the written culture. Distortions may result when the views of athletes become codified in conceptual language and systematic, scientific thinking. The *quest for one's chance*, which I regard as the main feature of the "internal perspective", would gain at being studied and described on a much broader plane. One would then be in a better position to recognize the moral claim that athletes themselves raise with respect to their own conduct. That athletes do in fact pursue a higher aspiration in their activity than just making sure a game continues to function, is shown by the fact that they also strive for a personal style: a commitment to an impressive performance, plus a participation in the aesthetic staging of the competition, as is the case, for example, in the Olympic Games.

What has been described so far, concerns as the mental attitudes, characteristics, and abilities involved in a competitive context, amounts to realizing that one can theorize only with great difficulty about them. This problem is not new. Detienne and Vernant have described in classical Greek thought a "great category of mind" that also subsumes the quest of the ancient athletes for the "advantage". It is a "game of social and intellectual practices" that are bound to the conditions of place and time, embedded into conduct, and inseparable from it. It is a covert type of behavior "that docs not openly reveal itself to be what it is", the Μῆτις (*Mètis*), the Greek designation for "wits[14]".

Mètis is the category in which thinking, knowledge, and recognition are melded into a complex whole that is applied to a fleeting and ambiguous reality that cannot be grasped by logic, concepts, and argumentation[15]. *Mètis* appears particularly in situations of confrontation and competition. It defies straightforward definition in terms of characteristics and always relates to the perspective of the athletes. *Mètis* occupied a significant place in Greek thought, as shown not only by Detienne and Vernant's studies but also by philological studies on ancient athletic contests. It was quite obviously the taste of Greek Antiquity to have competitions decided in a game of cunning, deception, even trickery so as to express that pure physical strength is not what wins but rather the capacity to define the game, of leaving nothing to chance, the ability to master things at just the right moment, the Καιρός (*Kairos*).

Mètis prompts athletes to execute the most favorable motion successfully at the right instant and makes it appear as though one's physical abilities transcend human powers and attain the quality of the unique. If one sees a modern athlete suddenly rise to the occasion with spectacular artistic perfection after periods of mediocrity, coasting, cheap victories, and perhaps dickering over the slightest advantages, then one can get the impression that the hidden morals of sport and of Olympism lie in trying, daring, on the spur of the moment, to perform an inimitable act that sets itself apart from all others by virtue of its aesthetics, assurance, boldness, surprise, energy, or of the pure pleasure it gives. It is the aspiration of athletes themselves to act according to their imaginations, internal scenarios, and wishes for immortality. This goes beyond a mere desire for perfection or excellence. It deals with the individualistic morals of achieving distinction through action. It is the wish of genuine athletes to be remembered in sports, that is, to go down in its written history. Such egocentric morals can create cultural values but can also threaten them[16]. They can be judged trivial, but can also enrich the image of the human being. Recognition of such morals depends on the extent to which having wits is judged of value and on the extent to which the aims of sport and the goals of the Olympic Movement appear desirable. High performance sports constitutes a system of innerly sharing in the achievements of athletes; conversely, it is also a process of sharing in the morals of athletics. Those morals are expressed in the popular wish "to do it like" the athletes do. To attempt that in practice obviously requires very great commitment; but to experience it vicariously requires only the power of one's desires, wishes, and empathy.

NOTES AND REFERENCES

1. Coubertin P de (1929) Citius, altius, fortius. Bulletin du Bureau international de pédagogie sportive. Lausanne 4 p 13. In Müller N (ed) (1986) Pierre de Coubertin Textes choisis Tome II Olympisme. Zürich: Weidmann p 454

2. The reader is invited to read the works of E Havelock as well as those of M McLuhan. The thoughts of the latter are known to have influenced those of the former.

3. With respect to the language-impregnated character of competition in sport, the reader is referred to Lenk H, Gebauer G (1988) Sport and sports literature from the perspective of methodological interpretationism. Aethlon: the Journal of Sport Literature 2 73-86. In this presentation what is referred to as "interpretive constructs" belongs in fact to the written language.

4. Gerhardt V (1990) Die Moral des Sports. Sportwissenshaft (in press)

5. Coubertin P de (1935) Les assises philosophiques de l'Olympisme moderne. Le Sport Suisse 31 1. In Müller N (ed) (1986) Pierre de Coubertin Textes choisis Tome II Olympisme. Zürich: Weidmann p 436

6. This is a characteristic of social practice in general; for this reason it is not a theoretical reconstruction of the "sens pratique" (the practical sense). Cf Bourdieu P (1980) Le sens pratique. Paris: Minuit

7. Caillois R (1958) Les jeux et les hommes: Le masque et le vertige. Paris: Gallimard

8. Recommended readings: Herms E (1986) Ist Sportethik möglich? In Deutscher Sportbund (ed) Die Zukunft des Sports. Schorndorf: Hofmann 84-111. Franke E (1988) Etische Fragen im Sport. In Schwenkmezger (ed) Diagnostik, Intervention und Verantwortung. Köln: Bps-Verlag 40-65. Lenk H, Pilz G (1989) Das Prinzip Fairness. Zürich: Interform. Heringer HJ (1990) Regeln und Fairness. Woher bezieht der Sport seine Moral? In Grupe O (ed) Kulturgut oder Körperkult? Sport und Sportwissenschaft im Wandel. Tübingen: Attempto 157-171. Gerhardt V (1990) op cit

9. The reader is referred to the Wittgensteinian account of the concept of rule published earlier by the author of this presentation: Gebauer G (1983) Wie regeln Spielregeln das Spiel? In Grupe O Gabler H Goehner J (eds) Spiel, Spiele, Spiele. Hofmann: Schorndorf 154-61

10. Recommended reading, with respect to the concept of "fairness": Lenk H, Pilz G (1989) op cit

11. Elias N (1986) An essay on sport and violence. In Elias N, Dunning E (eds) Quest for excitement. Sport and leisure in the civilizing process. Oxford: Blackwell 150-74. "If one tests current theories of society, one discovers strong tendencies to regard norms and rules in the succession of Durkheim — almost as if they had an existence independently of persons. One often speaks of norms or rules as if they were data which account by themselves for the integration of individual persons in the form of societies and for the particular type of integration, for the pattern of structure, of societies. In short, one is often given the impression that norms or rules, like Plato's ideas, have an existence of their own [...]" p 153
It is an illusion to think "that norms or rules have a power of their own, as if they were something outside and apart from the groups of people, and could serve as such as an explanation for the way in which people group themselves as societies" p 154. It is one of Elias' discoveries "that a game may reach in the course of its development a peculiar equilibrium stage. And when this stage has been reached, the whole structure of its further development changes. For to have reached its mature form, or however one cares to call it, does not mean that all development stops; it merely means that it enters upon a new stage" p 156. "[...] it is useful to enquire whether changes in the game-pattern are due to what are felt to be deficiencies in the game-pattern itself at times when the conditions for playing the game in society at large remain largely unchanged, or whether changes in the game-pattern are due to felt deficiencies which arise largely from changing conditions of the game in society at large. A sport-game, in other words, particularly when it has reached maturity, can have a degree of autonomy in relation to the structure of the society where it is played; hence, the reasons for changes can lie in the game-pattern itself" p 158

12. Coubertin P de (1939) Les sources et les limites du progrès sportif (IV). Olympische Rundschau 5 1-2. Dans Müller N (ed) (1986) Pierre de Coubertin Textes choisis Tome II Olympisme. Zürich: Weidmann p 75

13. Detienne M, Vernant JP (1974) Les ruses de l'intelligence, la mètis des Grecs. Paris: Flammarion

14. Detienne M, Vernant JP (1974) op cit p 9

15. Detienne M, Vernant JP (1974) op cit "La mètis est bien une forme d'intelligence et de pensée, un mode de connaître; elle implique un ensemble complexe, mais très cohérent, d'attitudes mentales, de comportements intellectuels qui combinent le flair, la sagacité, la prévision, la souplesse d'esprit, la feinte, la débrouillardise, l'attention vigilante, le sens de l'opportunité, des habiletés diverses, une expérience longuement acquise; elle s'applique à des réalités fugaces, mouvantes, déconcertantes et ambigües, qui ne se prêtent ni à la mesure précise, ni au calcul exact, ni au raisonnement rigoureux" p 10

16. This is the point of view which Lenk and Grupe expose in their book: Lenk H (1985) Die achte Kunst: Leistungssport—Breitensport. Zürich: Interform. Grupe O (1987) Sport als Kultur. Zürich: Interform

[. . .] Maintenant quelles seront les limites de ce progrès [sportif] ? Ces sources que nous avons passées en revue ne vont-elles pas s'user, s'épuiser ? Tout se transforme et, dans notre temps, plus encore en raison de la hâte générale, du goût de la vitesse et des moyens qui s'offrent de satisfaire ce goût. [. . .]

Coubertin P de (1938) Les sources et les limites du progrès sportif. Olympische Rundschau [Revue Olympique], no 4, p 1

One Year After
the Dubin Commission:
where Do we Stand
with Respect to the Use
of Antidoping Substances
and the Development of Antidoping
Strategies in International Sport?

Un an après la Commission Dubin :
où en sommes-nous en matière
d'utilisation des dopants
et d'endiguement du problème
dans le sport international?

Editors' Note

Note des éditeurs

The Organizing Committee had given this Sub-theme the title *One Year after the Dubin Commission: where do we stand with respect to the use of antidoping substances and the development of antidoping strategies in international sport?*

The original intent was to have three panel presentations and an open discussion period which would focus on the latest legal, ethical and technical considerations, data, trends and strategies having to do with the complex phenomenon of doping in contemporary cultures and societies of which sport is a part.

Judge **Dubin** (CAN), Dr **Fost** (USA) and Dr **Dugal** (CAN) had kindly accepted to make presentations. Circumstances, however, prevented Judge Dubin to be present at the Symposium, as the final report of his Commission of Inquiry was to be released in the very weeks that followed the May 1990 Quebec City Conference. It became perfectly understandable that Judge **Dubin**, with respect to the substance of his forthcoming report, owed confidentiality and priority to the Canadian Government from which he had received a mandate.

Having judged that the individual paper presented by philosophers **Schneider** and **Butcher** (CAN) was most pertinent to the central topic, the Editors have placed it in the present section, immediately after those of Drs **Fost** and **Dugal**.

Full reference to Judge **Dubin**'s report released in June 1990 is given hereunder:

Dubin CL (1990) Commission of inquiry into the use of drugs and banned practices intended to increase athletic performance. Ottawa: Government of Canada Publications Catalogue No. MAS CP32-56/1990F.

Le Comité d'organisation avait choisi comme titre du présent sous-thème: *Un an après la Commission Dubin: où en sommes-nous en matière d'utilisation des dopants et d'endiguement du problème dans le sport international?*

L'intention originale était d'offrir un panel suivi d'une séance de discussion ouverte sur les aspects juridiques, éthiques et techniques des données de la recherche ainsi que des tendances et des stratégies qui ont cours en matière de doping dans le sport en tant que sous-phénomène de société et de culture.

Le Juge **Dubin** (CAN), le Dr **Fost** (USA) et le Dr **Dugal** (CAN) avaient aimablement accepté d'agir comme panelistes. Les circonstances ont toutefois empêché le Juge Dubin d'être présent au Symposium. Le Rapport de la Commission d'enquête qu'il présidait ne devant être rendu public que peu après la date de tenue du Symposium international dc Mai 1990, le Juge **Dubin** se trouvait alors dans l'obligation de confidentialité, en ce qui a trait à la substance de ce rapport, auprès du Gouvernement du Canada qui lui avait confié son mandat.

Par ailleurs, les Éditeurs ont jugé que la substance de la communication individuelle présentée au Symposium de Québec par les philosophes **Schneider** et **Butcher** (CAN) était pertinente au thème central du panel; ils ont donc placé leur texte à la présente section du rapport, immédiatement à la suite des conférences des Drs **Fost** et **Dugal**.

La référence complète du Rapport du Juge **Dubin** qui a été publié en juin 1990 est la suivante:

Dubin CL (1990) Commission d'enquête sur le recours aux drogues et aux pratiques interdites pour améliorer la performance athlétique. Ottawa: Centre d'édition du Gouvernement du Canada, No de catalogue CP32-56/1990F.

Questions d'ordre social et éthique en jeu
dans les stratégies anti-dopage dans le sport

D'entrée en matière, l'auteur pose la question de savoir si l'athlète qui utilise des substances susceptibles d'améliorer sa performance viole des principes de morale autres que le devoir simple et évident de respecter les règlements de la compétition sportive. La tâche d'analyser les bases éthiques sur lesquelles repose l'interdiction des substances réputées dopantes se trouve compliquée, selon l'auteur, par un manque flagrant de rigueur dans le raisonnement qui a servi à l'établissement des règles mêmes qui président aux efforts qui ont cours présentement en vue d'endiguer le problème. Par surcroît, les recensions des écrits ne font guère état de discussions serrées sur les fondements éthiques de la question en cause. C'est dans la perspective de ce qui précède que l'auteur a choisi délibérément de se faire l'avocat du diable et d'examiner au plan de l'éthique sociale et de l'éthique tout court les arguments avancés pour justifier l'interdiction de l'usage de substances réputées dopantes dans le sport. Les arguments les plus couramment invoqués en faveur de l'interdiction sont résumés sous quatre chefs : – les substances dopantes procurent à celui ou à celle qui en fait usage un avantage indu par rapport aux adversaires qui s'en abstiennent ; – les drogues qui sont couramment utilisées, notamment les stéroïdes anabolisants, sont nuisibles, ce qui amène l'obligation de protéger les athlètes contre eux-mêmes ; – l'usage des substances dopantes par un/une athlète donné/e force en quelque sorte les adversaires à agir de la même façon ; – enfin, l'usage de substances dopantes va contre nature et constitue de ce fait une perversion de l'essence même du sport. L'auteur procède par la suite à l'analyse de chacune des catégories d'argumentation. Au sujet de l'avantage indu, l'auteur avance que l'objectif même de la préparation à la performance est justement celui de faire en sorte que l'on obtient un avantage sur l'adversaire ; par surcroît et de toutes façons, l'argument de l'avantage indu se trouve déjà contredit par l'existence, au départ, des différences inter-individuelles associées au patrimoine génétique de chacun. L'auteur juge donc que le fait de tenter d'ajouter un avantage au-delà de ce que la nature a bien voulu accorder ne constitue pas, en soi, une intention ou une action intrinsèquement immorale. Il donne ensuite plusieurs exemples tirés des annales sportives et qui montrent qu'il y a eu clairement tendance à considérer un « avantage » de moins en moins « illégitime » dans la mesure où l'accès à l'avantage en question devenait de plus en plus facile et répandu. Il souligne également comme paradoxal le fait qu'on ait fait si grand état de l'avantage indu acquis par Johnson, cependant qu'on a passé sous silence l'usage au grand jour d'équipements sportifs et de techniques poussées d'entraînement, dont on vante qu'ils procurent justement un avantage, sans être pour autant facilement accessibles aux athlètes moins fortunés. Du côté des effets ou conséquences nuisibles, l'auteur avance que pour que les arguments soient fondés sur une morale et une éthique solides, il conviendrait que les résultats de la recherche scientifique soient moins ambigus et plus convaincants. Il ajoute que la problématique scientifique de la causalité en matière d'effets délétères du doping demeure entière et que les résultats de la recherche, pour intéressants et utiles qu'ils soient, se trouvent encore loin de satisfaire aux critères des études rétrospectives de cas-contrôles et ceux des études prospectives dont les schèmes expérimentaux relèvent de l'épidémiologie. À nouveau, l'auteur souligne la situation paradoxale d'une société qui bannit, sans plus, une pratique dont on ne sait trop encore quels en sont les vrais effets, alors qu'elle se refuse à être tout aussi répressive pour une gamme de pratiques et d'habitudes de vie dont on sait fort bien, évidence épidémiologique à l'appui, qu'elles sont effectivement délétères. Pour ce qui est de l'effet coercitif, l'auteur argumente que l'usage de produits dopants par un athlète ne constitue pas en soi une pression ou une invitation au conformisme différente de celles qui comportent aussi des risques certains dans la poursuite indéfinie du *Citius, Altius, Fortius*. La dernière partie de la présentation porte sur la question des aides naturelles ou non-naturelles mises à contribution. Il se dit d'avis qu'il n'y a pas plus en ce cas de base éthique ou morale pure pour justifier, sans plus, une prohibition. En guise de conclusion, l'auteur se dit d'avis que les infractions aux règles dans le sport ne sauraient être soumises à des critères d'analyse éthique et de jugement moral différents de ceux qui prévalent dans la société globale.

Ethical and Social Issues
in Antidoping Strategies in Sport

Norman C. Fost

My purpose, in this presentation, is to question the claim that athletes who use performance enhancing drugs, such as anabolic steroids, violate moral principles other than the obvious duty to obey the rules of competition. I will conclude that the prohibition of such drugs is based on no apparent moral principles, and must therefore serve some other purpose. Finally, I will suggest that the extreme outrage and vilification cast on the Canadian sprinter Ben Johnson is so disproportionate to whatever offense he may have committed, as to raise questions as to the true source of the campaign to discredit him. The task of analyzing the moral basis of prohibiting performance enhancing drugs is complicated by the virtual absence of any strict rationale in the rules governing the subject. Neither has there been much discussion of the moral basis of these rules in the voluminous and raucous literature on the subject over the past decade. I must begin therefore by taking the opponent's view and offering whatever moral arguments might be proposed as a basis for prohibiting drugs in sport.

As best as I can infer from reading commentaries on the subject, there seem to be four moral or quasi-moral concerns:

1– Such drugs provide users with an *unfair advantage* over opponents.

2– The drugs commonly used, particularly anabolic steroids, are *harmful* and there is a duty to protect athletes from harming themselves.

3– The use of such drugs forces competitors to use them, placing them in a situation of *coercion.*

4– Such drugs are *unnatural*, and constitute a perversion of the essence of sports in which they are used.

The problems associated with each of these claims will be examined in turn.

1890
1990

Norman C. Fost, Department of Pediatrics and Hospital Ethics Committee, Medical School, University of Wisconsin, Madison, Wisconsin, USA.

The "Unfair Advantage" Claim

It should be obvious that merely seeking or gaining an advantage over an opponent is not *implicitly* unfair. It is the essence of sport that athletes have or seek to gain an advantage over their opponents. The most obvious advantages are those created by different genetic endowments. We do not say it is unfair that one runner is faster than another, or a wrestler stronger than his opponent, if these differences are due to natural *endowments*. Questions of morality arise only when humans choose certain courses of action. But simply trying or succeeding in gaining an advantage beyond what nature confers is not implicitly immoral. Most athletic training and preparation is indeed guided by the very desire to gain an advantage over one's opponents. Sometimes these efforts are as simple as routine practice and training procedures. But since the first Olympiad, both ancient and modern, athletes have explored an infinite variety of natural and unnatural advantages, ranging from better shoes or swimsuits, to better coaches or training equipment, or better diets or nutrition advisors. The mere seeking of an advantage is not implicitly unfair, nor is the gaining of an advantage implicitly unfair. To label it unfair, and prohibit such a practice on the basis of that claim, requires more argumentation than simply showing that an athlete seeks or indeed gains an advantage. Conversely, seeking an advantage by a practice which, in fact, confers no advantage, would not be judged clearly immoral, nor would a ban on such practice seem appropriate. To facilitate discussion of the moral issues I will thus assume for this discussion that anabolic steroids *do* confer an advantage in that they allow some athletes to improve their maximum performance over that which they could have achieved without using steroids. I believe it has been clearly demonstrated that some athletes in some events, particularly weightlifting, can improve upon their previous best performance by adding anabolic steroids to an already intensive training regimen. Whether or not this advantage extends to sprinters, and whether or not Ben Johnson himself in fact was able to run faster *because* of the use of steroids, is less clear. But let us assume for the purpose of this discussion that he was, in fact, able to run faster as a result of using steroids so that we can get to the question of whether he would have violated any moral rule by so doing, and whether officials have a moral basis for prohibiting such a practice.

One factor which might constitute a moral claim that a given practice confers an *unfair* advantage would be unequal access. In the 1972 Olympic Games, for example, the American pole vaulter Seagren sought to gain an advantage by using a fibreglass pole, a clear improvement on the traditional poles made of other materials. Because his opponents had not had the opportunity to obtain or practice with the new device, it was prohibited. Four years later, when access had been "equalized", the use of that device was permitted. Thus far, I have seen no claim that access to steroids is unequal. On the contrary, it is acknowledged that they are nowadays readily available and widely used. Indeed, it is also widely acknowledged that Johnson is distiguishable from many of his competitors not because he *used* steroids but because he was *caught*. The sophisticated athlete and/or his managers know that the use of such drugs must be scheduled in such a way as so that hormonal balance is restored at the time of testing; *i.e.*, it is necessary to use the drugs on a schedule that is coordinated with testing, which heretofore has been rather predictable, since it was done primarily at the time of championship events.

In the eyes of many, it is ironic, at least, and hypocritical, at worst, that Johnson was punished and castigated beyond punishment for a practice that had little unfairness (of accessibility), while others publicly boasted of achieving medals by using other types of unnatural assists to victory in ways that appear more clearly unfair. The American swimming coach, for example, gleefully displayed a "greasy" swimsuit which allowed the women swimmers to improve upon their previous best times with the marginal advantage of reducing friction between the swimsuit and the water. He acknowledged that this small differential might well have been the difference between victory and defeat. Similarly, the American volleyball team claimed they had substantially improved their leaping ability with the assistance of expensive computer analyses of their movements and consultation with experts in kinesiology and biomechanics. These advantages, *if* real, could by the same token be judged unfair in that they were *intended* to be kept secret so that opponents would *not* have access to the same technology, even if they could afford it. If there is a rational basis for the ubiquitous steroids to be considered unfair, and the secret greasy swimsuits to be considered objects of praise and admiration, it has not yet been explained.

The "Harmful" Claim

Most published discussions of the steroid controversy emphasize the health hazards and medical harms. A list of dangerous side effects has become a virtual mantra—liver cancer, heart attacks, sterility, hirsutism, psychopathic behavior and others. But good ethics starts with good facts and the first question is whether, in fact, there is unambiguous evidence that steroids, in the doses and duration commonly used by world class athletes, have been shown to cause such harm and, if so, in what incidence.

Much of the data published thus far is anecdotal and of little scientific use. A case report of even a rare event, such as liver cancer in a young adult who had used anabolic steroids, does not prove *causation* or even statistically significant association. Either longterm prospective studies are needed, or at least better retrospective case control studies with careful design and analysis by expert epidemiologists. Many adverse effects which are unquestionably caused by anabolic steroids—such as hirsutism and infertility—are reversible for the vast majority of individuals. But as with the "unfair advantage" argument we can get to the moral question by stipulating the facts. Let us assume, for the sake of discussion, that steroids do in fact, cause serious, irreversible longterm physical harm, including perhaps death, in some users. What would follow from such a finding? It would not follow that such consequences would justify prohibition among competent adults. Approximately two-thirds of premature mortality in the United States is attribuable to personal behavior: smoking, heavy drinking, high fat diets, lack of exercise, inadequate use of seat belts, and so on. For skeptics who would dispute this, there are simpler examples: skiing, sky diving, or automobile racing, to name a few. Indeed, sport itself carries *per se* a substantial risk of death and permanent disability. The majority of professional football players who play for five years or more develop permanent disability. Far more deaths have been attributed to football than to steroids. Quite obviously, it does not follow from these observations that such sports should be banned, or that officials would be morally justified in prohibiting individuals from pursuing these activities. Such paternalism is generally opposed on philosophical and political grounds in western society, particularly in North America. As stated by John Stuart Mill, the dealings of society with the individual should be governed by "one very simple principle":

> [...] that the sole end for which mankind are warranted, individually or collectively, in interfering with the liberty of action of any of their members, is self-protection... [...] His own good, either physical or moral, is not a sufficient warrant. He cannot rightfully be compelled to do or forebear because it will be better for him to do so, because it will make him happier, because in the opinion of others, to do so would be wise, or even right. These are good reasons for remonstrating with him, or reasoning with him, or persuading him, or entreating him, but not for compelling him, or visiting him with any evil in case he do otherwise[1].

Even proving that an activity is harmful is therefore not a sufficient reason for preventing a *competent* person from pursuing that activity. While there are some exceptions to the general prohibition against paternalism, the burden is on those who would practice it to justify their intrusion into the liberty of those athletes who choose to pursue whatever risks are entailed in exchange for the benefits of athletic success.

The claim that the ban on steroids is justified by concern for the well-being of the athletes is not only paternalistic without justification, but disingenuous. In sports such as football and hockey, where disability and mayhem are ubiquitous, it is implausible that a drug with few proven harms is singled out as part of a beneficent program to protect athletes from physical harm. If the consequence of roughing the passer were a three point penalty, the practice would disappear and far more disability would be prevented than has been attributed to steroids by even their most severe critics. Similarly, illegal violence in ice-hockey, with its attendant risks, could be dramatically reduced with harsher penalties. The failure of leaders to curtail these clearly dangerous activities suggests that protecting athletes from harm is obviously not the highest priority; presumably, it is balanced with the entertainment objectives, and therefore the economic value, associated with violence. If the health of the athletes were truly the concern and responsibility of the leaders of organized sports, then screening athletes for evidence of heavy smoking and drinking would seem a more justifiable or efficient program.

In summary, the proposition that steroids *are* harmful claims too little and too much. There is little evidence that whatever harms they cause can match numerous other self-destructive activities of world class athletes, including sport itself. And further, the demonstration that any of these behaviors are harmful does not justify, in and by itself, coercive interference with the liberty of competent adults. The concern for liberty would certainly support better research and education on the potential benefits as well as the potential harms of steroids. A competent person remains not truly free to make an informed choice if the data essential for such a choice are not available. A beneficent concern for the well-being of athletes would clearly support expenditure of funds for the development of better scientific and clinical data as well as information.

The "Coercion" Claim

In one of the few attempts to provide a philosophical rationale for the prohibition of anabolic steroids, Murray has argued that their use creates a coercive environment in which use by one or some athletes "forces" others to use them lest they be disadvantaged[2]. Murray's argument, in my view, rests on a wrong use or a misunderstanding of the *meaning* of coercion, which implies restraint "by force, especially by law or authority[3]". I am not aware of any instance or proposal that athletes be forced to use steroids. I believe what Murray means is that an athlete who *chooses* to compete at the highest levels believes, perhaps correctly, that since his/her opponents are using steroids, he is less likely to win unless he too uses steroids, even though he/she might *prefer* not to use them. But this pressure to "pay the price" comes with the territory in many other ways. Competing and winning at the highest levels requires sacrifices and risks imposed by the activities of competitors. Olympic competition requires years of arduous training, involving many risks and discomforts. The ever-increasing intensity, training and performance of other athletes in some sense "forces" one to also seek higher levels, and endure more risk than one otherwise might have wished. In gymnastics, for example, the new "tricks" which one's opponents develop in some sense "forces" current competitors to match or exceed these tricks. Newer maneuvers are always more difficult than older ones. They require more training, and often more risk, either because of the time of exposure on already hazardous equipment, or because of the complexity of the maneuver and the greater possibility of a dangerous slip. It is certainly the case that a modern gymnast is required to make these sacrifices as a condition of competing at the highest levels. But we could not properly say that the success of the competitors coerces or forces the gymnast into making the choice to compete. At least in the western world, athletes remain free to walk away from the arena or the sport. Yet, such athletes appear to be driven by their own internal desires, not by the threats or physical force of others.

It may be that the enormous financial rewards awaiting some winners may constitute a strong part of their motivation. A decision to forego competition, including the risks of preparing for competition, whether it be hours of practice on a balance beam or the use of anabolic steroids, may therefore constitute a decision to forego enormous and most tempting rewards and opportunities. But these rewards are discretionary pursuits. They are not requirements for living. If, in fact, an athlete could not provide for the necessities of life other than by competing and succeeding in international competition, and that steroids were essential for success, then the word coercion might indeed be applicable. But that does not seem to be the case.

There is another moral issue which may be involved, namely *exploitation*, by which we mean taking unfair advantage of someone's need for the money or other rewards which competition brings. It is certainly the case that many athletes are driven to pursue risky athletic careers because of the lack of other opportunities for comparable wealth or success. It is not coincidence that most professional athletes in North America come from classes or conditions of poverty. Nor would I dispute the claim that the enormous economic rewards available to a small proportion of young athletes entices them only because of the otherwise bleak prospects they face for rising out of poverty. But it does not follow that the fair solution to this problem of unequal opportunity is to close one of the few opportunities available. All blue collar work is exploitative in the sense that it attracts workers who primarily have limited options for choosing and pursuing careers. The just solution to this problem is to strive for a society in which everyone has the same opportunity to be either a lawyer or football player, based on his ability rather than his race, gender, or social class. But while we must wait for that "city on a hill", I doubt those whose options are limited would appreciate or support policies which in fact would limit their opportunities even further.

It may be that athletes who are willing to endure the substantial risks inherent in many sports would prefer not to add to these risks those associated with steroids. That is, if the athletes could make their own rules, a majority might prefer steroid-free competition. Yet it is not clear that such is the case, since professional athletes have the means to negotiate the rules of their employment and they have not heretofore asked for the kind of testing which would be necessary to eliminate the use of such drugs. If they did choose such a system it would not clearly be based on any moral claim, but would appear to be the expression of a preference to endure some kinds of risks—such as those associated with roughing the passer, or more difficult tricks on the balance beam—while foregoing others.

In summary, the claim that the use of steroids is coercive seems to constitute a wrong use of the word. Steroid usage does indeed create pressure on others to conform, but it does not differ in this regard from other pressures implicit in sports which continually require sacrifices and risks on the open-ended continuum of the *"Citius, Altius, Fortius"*.

The "Unnatural" Argument

The most obscure of the claims that use of steroids is immoral is the one based on the distaste for *unnatural* means of assisting performance. Like the other claims, this one lacks internal coherence. Athletes have used unnatural means of improving performance since the first Greeks started training for athletics. Today's training approaches and performances are pervaded by unnatural technologies, from greasy swimsuits to computerized exercise machines to scientifically concocted beverages prepared and packaged in laboratories and factories. To add to the confusion, substances which are completely *natural*, such as testosterone or marijuana, are prohibited as *unnatural*. There does not appear to be coherent principles behind the decisions to allow some performance enhancing chemicals or devices and disallow others. Nor is there an apparent moral issue involved in the claim that some assists should be banned merely because they are unnatural. What moral principle would be involved in allowing a shotputter to lift rocks as part of his training but not manufactured weights or a Nautilus machine? What moral principle is involved in allowing runners to ingest some natural substances, such as vitamins or Gatorade, but not others such as steroids? Some claim that certain unnatural assists (such as steroids) change the essential nature of the sport. But has sport an essence? Sports are games, invented by men and women, with constantly changing rules. Is pole-vaulting *inherently* something that must be done with a bamboo, rather than a fibreglass pole? Has not the forward pass changed the fundamental nature or essence of football more than steroid usage? But such comparisons are, I hope, patently irrelevant, for no sport has an inherent nature or essence. The simplest race requires man-made rules regarding its distance, the width of the lanes, the number of false starts allowed, and I suppose, even the diets or drugs the competitors may or may not use in the hours, days, weeks or years before an event. I certainly do not dispute the right of the athletes and organizers or of the entire sporting community to make whatever rules they wish. I simply dispute the claim that some rules are more "natural" than others, or have an inherent moral basis.

Conclusion

Something is surely amiss in sports. If amateurism means competing for the "love of the thing", it seems to have faded as the sole basis of athletics and of olympic competition long before the present time. Exploitation, politics, and economic considerations increasingly dominate sports throughout the world, as the third millennium draws near. In the face of these complex and seemingly intractable problems, it is perhaps understandable that scapegoats would be sought as a distraction. The extent and intensity of the vilification cast on Ben Johnson would lead one to believe he has violated some moral principle that is at the bedrock of society. I fail to see what, if any, purely moral principle he violated. He *broke* a rule and most assuredly risked losing (and indeed lost) his medal as a consequence. But the rule is not based on any coherent moral principle the demonstration of which has been offered by those who had promulgated the rules. And whatever moral principles might be involved, such as gaining unfair advantage, or preventing harm, are most everywhere violated in far more obvious and worrisome ways, with little comment or apparent effort at correction.

REFERENCES

1. Mill JS (1970). On liberty. Columbus: Neridian Books, World Publishing

2. Murray TH (1983). The coercive influence of drugs in sports. In Gaylin W. Feeling good, doing better, but using drugs. The Hastings Center Report, 13: 24-30.

3. Webster's New Collegiate Dictionnary (1953). Springfield: GC Merriam Publishing

Recent Developments in the Antidoping
Strategies on the International Scene

In the first part of his presentation, the author stresses that modern competitive sport can no longer be explained in terms of a simple tendency of human nature to excell. The sporting phenomenon has for all practical purposes been recuperated by economics and politics. In that perspective, the individual pursuit of excellence, in the author's opinion, no longer appears to be the supreme criterion of the intrinsic value of sport. The social and economic benefits to be derived from success in high performance sport have become such that a great many athletes find themselves tempted and are often even encouraged to utilize all means possible in order to attain success. It should then be of no surprise, in the author's view, that once the standard approaches to training have been put to full use, one be tempted to have recourse to other methods with a view of raising performance levels still higher. In the panoplies of means used to enhance physiological processes and psychological states, various drugs and related pharmaceutical products have risen to the forefront in recent years. The author then proceeds to describe some of the anticipated objectives and outcomes associated with the use of certain drugs in sport which have nothing to do with standard pharmacologic or therapeutic justification. He also stresses the fact that drug use carries with it the risk of behavioral and/or health outcomes that may eventually prove to be serious or difficult to reverse. The 1963 definition of doping by the Council of Europe is then given as an example of the kind and commented upon by the author with a view of pointing to the difficulty of judging intentionality in matters of drug use and/or abuse. The author also alludes to the difficulties encountered when one wishes to weigh the scientific evidence concerning the efficacy of drug regimen in association with sport, and likewise that which relates to various categories of deleterious effects. The data are at best and all too often controversial. In the next part of his presentation, the author describes the approach, procedures and justifications put forth by the Medical Commission of the IOC with respect to the doping phenomenon in sport. Reference is then made to some recent antidoping initiatives and strategies, both on the national and international scenes. Examples of such strategies, conventions and/or charters are given with respect to Canada, the United States, the Council of Europe. In the last portion of his presentation, the author comments on the most recent initiative aiming at the harmonization of international efforts against doping in sport: the IOC's International Charter Against Doping in Sport.

Tendances et développements récents dans la lutte contre le dopage athlétique sur le plan international

Robert Dugal

Il est difficile d'imaginer un secteur d'activité qui suscite plus de ferveur, dans l'imagination populaire, que celui de l'activité sportive. Le sport, pour autant qu'il constitue l'une des manifestations les plus spectaculaires des tendances naturelles de l'homme à atteindre de nouveaux sommets, englobe des fonctions qui vont de l'affrontement au spectacle, en passant par le simple besoin de dépassement personnel. Selon les situations dans lesquelles elle s'exerce, l'activité sportive revêt des significations différentes: si un match de tennis est souvent l'expression que prend l'amitié entre deux hommes, certaines compétitions internationales vont jusqu'à donner l'impression d'être des substituts de la confrontation armée.

Dans le contexte du sport moderne tel que nous le connaissons, le souci de dépassement a débordé les motivations personnelles et est devenu économiquement ainsi que politiquement soutenu et organisé. Les grandes compétitions internationales, et les Jeux olympiques en particulier, conçus pour attirer et réunir les meilleurs éléments de la jeunesse du monde, sont avec le passage du temps devenus des prétextes de sensibilisation de l'opinion à des idéologies politiques ou, ce qui est plus sérieux, ont contribué à cristalliser de vieux antagonismes. Le retrait de plusieurs pays africains des Jeux de Montréal (1976) et les problèmes diplomatiques créés par l'inscription de Taiwan à ces mêmes Jeux, les boycotts successifs des Jeux olympiques de Moscou (1980) et de Los Angeles (1984), sont des exemples patents de ces types de crises.

Et l'athlète, dans ce capharnaüm? L'aspiration naturelle à être champion est devenue, elle aussi, non plus un simple besoin, mais pour un grand nombre, une nécessité. Cela procède de plusieurs facteurs. En premier lieu, la sophistication croissante de la technologie et de l'informatique, doublée de la rapidité avec laquelle on véhicule l'information présente et passée, transforme graduellement l'athlète en machine à briser des records. En d'autres mots, une excellente performance sur le plan individuel n'est plus le critère suprême de la valeur

Robert Dugal, Institut national de la recherche scientifique-santé, Université du Québec, Pointe-Claire, Québec, Canada; membre de la Sous-commission Dopage et Biochimie du sport, Commission médicale du Comité international olympique.

intrinsèque de l'activité sportive. Parallèlement, les bénéfices sociaux et financiers souvent démesurés que retire l'athlète d'une victoire dans sa discipline le poussent, sinon le contraignent, à utiliser le plus de moyens possible en vue de l'amélioration de sa performance, compte tenu de l'impitoyable concurrence qui règne dans le sport d'élite international. Le prix à payer pour devenir héros sportif est souvent d'avoir été au préalable une victime plus ou moins consciente ou tacite de la commercialisation.

Dans une certaine mesure, il est compréhensible qu'un record à briser revête un caractère obsessionnel et puisse engendrer des problèmes psychologiques, aussi bien dans la victoire que dans la défaite. Il n'est pas surprenant, de la même manière, qu'une fois épuisées les techniques d'entraînement (musculation, préparation psychologique, relaxation, alimentation et diètes spéciales, etc.), on soit tenté de recourir à d'autres méthodes pour accroître encore le niveau de la performance. Parmi les moyens les plus simples et les plus accessibles d'arriver à ces fins, on trouve certains médicaments dont les propriétés pharmacologiques sont aptes à potentiellement améliorer les fonctions physiologiques et psychologiques reliées à l'exercice musculaire de haute intensité. Cette préparation médicamenteuse à la compétition figure à la liste des méthodes de « dopage ». Les objectifs recherchés ainsi que les classes de médicaments et pratiques qui ont été et sont encore les plus utilisés figurent au *Tableau 1*.

TABLEAU 1

Exemples d'objectifs poursuivis selon certaines classes de médicaments prohibés dans la lutte antidopage dans le sport

Objectifs	*Produits, médicaments ou pratiques*
Augmentation de la masse et de la capacité musculaires	Stéroïdes anabolisants* Hormone de croissance humaine*
Augmentation du rendement cardiaque	Digitaliques
Conditionnement du système nerveux central	
—Suppression des symptômes psychologiques de la fatigue	—Stimulants psychomoteurs*
—Diminution de la nervosité et des inhibitions	—Anxiolytiques, barbituriques, bloqueurs B-adrénergiques*
Prévention des perturbations métaboliques	
—Déficit d'oxygène tissulaire	—Inhalation d'oxygène, stimulants respiratoires
—Acidose lactique	—Breuvages alcalins
Prévention de la douleur et/ou contrôle de l'inflammation	Analgésiques narcotiques* Corticostéroïdes*
Perte de poids et/ou manipulation en vue de diluer un spécimen urinaire	Diurétiques*
Augmentation de l'endurance	Transfusions sanguines autologues et hétérologues* Erythropoietine*

L'utilisation des classes de substances suivies d'un astérisque (*) est actuellement prohibée par le Comité International Olympique et les Fédérations Internationales de sport.

La performance sportive est, en situation compétitive classique, la résultante globale de l'intégration optimale des capacités physiques et psychologiques de l'individu. Ces capacités ont chacune un niveau limite qu'il est possible d'approcher lentement par un entraînement physique soutenu et rationnel, ainsi que par une préparation psychologique appropriée. On peut dire que la performance-limite est la plus haute performance dont chaque individu est théoriquement capable. Dans cette perspective, sur l'axe du temps, la performance optimale est donc susceptible d'être sans cesse haussée, même si elle a tendance à plafonner à des moments précis. Dans cette perspective, les dépassements au-dessus de «la normale» apparaissent donc comme des interruptions des mécanismes régulateurs qui limitent, dans l'intérêt même de l'organisme, les performances plus élevées dont on est momentanément «capable». Il semble cependant que les mécanismes régulateurs puissent être sublimés par une motivation extraordinaire, de nature endogène, par la suggestion hypnotique, ou encore par des médicaments. C'est surtout dans ce dernier cas qu'est utilisé le terme «dopage».

Des athlètes utilisent certains médicaments dans une perspective qui n'a rien à voir avec leur justification pharmacologique ou thérapeutique ordinaire. Comme l'activité sportive fait appel aux grandes fonctions physiologiques et physiques reliées au rendement musculaire, on en est venu à songer à utiliser plusieurs types de médicaments susceptibles d'augmenter la performance. Ainsi, des médicaments conçus pour le traitement de certaines pathologies musculaires et osseuses (les stéroïdes anabolisants) sont utilisés dans l'espoir d'augmenter la force et la puissance musculaires, pendant que des stimulants psychomoteurs, longtemps utilisés pour leur propriété anorexigène, sont également utilisés pour faire reculer le seuil d'apparition de la grande fatigue en situation compétitive. Parallèlement, les cardiotoniques sont utilisés en vue d'augmenter l'endurance, les vasodilatateurs périphériques pour augmenter l'irrigation sanguine aux muscles et les anxiolytiques comme inhibiteurs du trac. Cette «malutilisation» des médi-caments—qui dégénère souvent en abus—soulève ainsi des questions et problèmes d'ordre clinique et éthique, tant sur le plan individuel que social. De plus, il semble que des athlètes s'administrent des médicaments de toutes sortes non seulement avant ou durant les événements sportifs eux-mêmes, mais également durant des périodes d'entraînement. L'utilisation périodique peut se transformer en usage permanent et ensuite en abus, ce qui est susceptible de résulter en l'établissement de schèmes comportementaux difficilement réversibles. Finalement, l'activité sportive étant avant tout basée sur une saine rivalité entre deux ou plusieurs individus «normaux» faisant appel à des forces qu'ils ont développées par une discipline rigoureuse d'entraînement, la majorité des organismes et associations scientifico-médico-sportives estiment que la perspec-tive éthique et la valeur foncière du sport comme élément culturel perdent une bonne part de leur signification si les athlètes tentent d'augmenter leurs chances de vaincre en ingérant des produits dopants de façon systématique. Il existe plusieurs définitions du dopage, toutes controversées. Par exemple, le Conseil de l'Europe, réuni à Strasbourg en 1963, avait à l'époque défini le dopage comme suit:

> L'administration à un athlète ou l'utilisation par lui de toute substance *étrangère* à l'organisme ou de toute *substance physiologique* prise en quantités *anormales* ou par une voie d'administration anormale, dans la *seule* intention d'augmenter *artificiellement* et *injustement* son rendement dans une situation compétitive. Quand une situation clinique exige un traitement *médical* avec une substance qui, à cause de sa nature, sa posologie ou son mode d'application, est susceptible d'augmenter la performance d'un athlète artificiellement et injustement en compétition, cela *doit* être considéré comme *dopage*.

Cette définition, discutable à plusieurs niveaux, mettait l'accent sur l'*intention* qui motive l'utilisation d'une ou plusieurs substances. Il est cependant difficile d'évaluer l'intention et de faire le partage entre l'utilisation de médi-caments à des fins thérapeutiques d'une part, et comme moyens de dopage d'autre part. Il est non moins difficile de définir adéquatement le dopage pour d'autres raisons. D'abord, l'évidence scientifique concernant l'efficacité des médicaments utilisés par rapport aux objectifs recherchés porte, au mieux, à controverse. Les amphétamines, par exemple, ont été parmi les drogues les plus couramment utilisées dans le monde athlétique. Or, quelques études semblent indiquer qu'elles sont efficaces pour augmenter le niveau de la performance sportive pendant que d'autres infirment cette hypothèse. Le même principe tient pour l'efficacité présumée des stéroïdes anabolisants. Les contradictions relevées dans les études cliniques de ces médicaments peuvent être attribuées, entre autres facteurs, aux difficultés méthodologiques inhérentes à leur exécution et à l'impossibilité de recréer, en laboratoire, l'atmosphère de compétition qui caractérise un événement sportif donné. On peut, en second lieu, penser qu'un athlète prenne un médicament dans une intention justifiable, à savoir pour lui permettre de donner le maximum de lui-même dans une situation compétitive. L'intention n'est pas à ce moment nécessairement celle d'augmenter la performance au-dessus de ses propres limites mais de situer ou de rétablir un niveau de fonctionnement analogue à celui de l'entraînement, lequel peut de toute évidence diminuer à la faveur d'une nervosité incontrôlable, face à l'exposition aux foules, par exemple. Certains auteurs estiment, en troisième lieu, que l'utilisation, par un athlète, d'un médicament qui n'a pas d'effet adverse décelable sur sa santé ne peut être considérée plus immorale que celle de faire appel à des techniques mécaniques, comme le massage, populaires dans les milieux athlétiques. Face aux difficultés inhérentes à la tâche de formuler une définition adéquate du dopage, le Comité international olympique et les Fédérations internationales ne tiennent plus compte des définitions proposées et estiment maintenant suffisante la publication dans leurs règles et procédures d'une liste de médicaments dont la Commission médicale du CIO suggère d'interdire l'utilisation durant l'entraînement et la compétition. L'interdiction du dopage sans le définir, sauf sous la forme d'un règlement d'une association sportive à laquelle un athlète est censé adhérer volontairement, présente l'avantage que lors de contestations, devant les tribunaux d'athlètes révélant des résultats positifs, les arguments ne peuvent porter sur une définition dont la clarté et la justification peuvent être aisément mises en cause.

La réaction des organismes sportifs et de certains gouvernements au problème du dopage ne semble s'être matérialisée qu'au cours des années 60, suite aux pressions exercées par l'opinion publique devant un phénomène dont on ne soupçonnait pas vraiment l'ampleur mais que l'on estimait être d'une envergure suffisante à justifier une action concrète. La première Fédération internationale de sport à se doter d'une réglementation antidopage a été l'Union cycliste internationale en 1965. Le Conseil de l'Europe, l'organisme qui regroupe les 22 démocraties parlementaires du continent européen, adoptait pour sa part, en 1967, une résolution ferme contre le dopage et invitait les États membres à se doter de règlements à cet effet. À la même époque, quelques pays ont légiféré contre le dopage dont, notamment, la France et la Belgique en 1965, et l'Italie en 1971. Le Comité international olympique, pour sa part, formait une Commission médicale en 1967, qui instituait les premiers contrôles de dopage aux Jeux olympiques d'hiver de Grenoble l'année suivante.

À cette époque, les actions entreprises étaient basées sur quatre principes:

1– Dissuader de l'usage de médicaments réputés dopants et qui peuvent présenter un danger pour la santé de l'athlète.

2– Éviter l'usage abusif de certains médicaments réputés dopants tout en n'interférant pas avec un traitement justifié par une condition clinique particulière.

3– Interdire l'usage de médicaments réputés dopants et pour lesquels existe une méthodologie qui permette leur identification formelle à partir d'un exemplaire urinaire exigé de l'athlète.

4– Bannir des classes de médicaments sans tenter de dresser une liste exhaustive, ce qui sur le plan international serait de toutes façons pratiquement impossible. Encore aujourd'hui, les listes de substances bannies contiennent seulement des exemples et chaque énumération est suivie d'une annotation à l'effet que des composés apparentés, sur le plan chimique et pharmacologique, aux médicaments cités en exemple sont également prohibés.

L'application de ces principes a posé certains problèmes. Par exemple, on soupçonnait depuis le début des années 60, que les stéroïdes anabolisants étaient utilisés dans certains sports où la masse et la puissance musculaires sont les éléments déterminants de la performance. Cependant, aucune méthode de détection et d'identification fiable n'existait à l'époque de sorte qu'il a fallu attendre jusqu'en 1975 (année où une méthode de détection est devenue disponible) avant que la Commission médicale du Comité international olympique fasse figurer ces substances à sa liste des substances bannies. En 1985, cette politique a été modifiée par l'inscription des transfusions sanguines à la liste des pratiques interdites, même si des méthodes fiables n'existent toujours pas à l'heure actuelle pour la détection des transfusions autologues.

Au cours des années 70, plusieurs fédérations sportives ont formulé des réglementations antidopage. En 1983, le Canada adoptait une politique nationale et instaurait des contrôles, suivi du Comité national olympique des États-Unis en 1984. À cet égard, la période 1965-1984 a été marquée par des efforts soutenus de la part des associations sportives internationales ou des gouvernements, mais il est permis de douter de l'efficacité des systèmes proposés. Par exemple, durant cette période, les listes de substances prohibées ont différé selon les sports. Les sanctions imposées aux athlètes n'ont pas été identiques pour des offenses équivalentes. Pendant qu'une fédération imposait une suspension de deux ans à un athlète trouvé «positif» à un stéroïde anabolisant, une autre ne le suspendait que pour trois mois pour une offense analogue. Il est devenu évident que pour assurer une lutte antidopage efficace, il serait essentiel d'harmoniser les actions et d'uniformiser les règlements et leurs modalités d'application.

L'une des premières tentatives dans ce sens a émané du Conseil de l'Europe, via la Charte Européenne contre le dopage, un document qui a résulté de la synthèse des travaux antérieurs de cet organisme ainsi que des partenaires concernés (gouvernements, associations sportives, scientifiques et médicales du sport) de manière à élaborer une stratégie aussi globale et uniforme que possible. La Charte, adoptée en 1984, décrivait certains principes généraux et offrait des informations de caractère pratique en ce qui a trait aux politiques et stratégies de la lutte antidopage. Ce document avait le statut de «recommandation», et non celui de «convention»—ce qui aurait constitué un accord juridiquement contraignant. La même année, le Comité international olympique et l'Association générale des fédérations internationales de sport ont adopté des résolutions soutenant la Charte Européenne, ce qui lui apportait un appui moral important et constituait une invitation à d'autres pays à souscrire aux principes énoncés. Cette Charte est devenue, en 1989, la Convention Européenne contre le dopage et a été ratifiée par plusieurs états membres. Une particularité intéressante de la Convention est qu'elle est ouverte à la signature par des états qui ne sont pas membres du Conseil de l'Europe et certains de ces derniers, notamment la Hongrie, l'ont ratifié. En 1986, le ministre canadien de la Condition physique et du sport amateur, s'adressant à la 5e Conférence des ministres européens responsables du sport, a fait des propositions visant à élargir l'impact de la Charte Européenne sur le plan international. Ce geste a donné le coup d'envoi à un effort qui a conduit, en juin 1988, à la première Conférence mondiale sur la lutte contre le dopage tenue à Ottawa. Cette conférence a adopté une série de déclarations, dont une charte internationale contre le dopage dont les dispositions reposent largement sur celles de la Charte Européenne de 1984. Ce document a été plus tard endossé par le Comité international olympique et est subséquemment devenu la *Charte internationale olympique contre le dopage dans le sport*. Bien que non contraignante sur le plan juridique, la Charte internationale olympique constitue une première initiative visant à uniformiser et harmoniser les actions entreprises par les gouvernements ct/ou lcs fédérations sportives, dans la lutte contre le dopage sur le plan mondial. Le document décrit les responsabilités respectives de la communauté sportive (v.g. les règlements d'application, comme l'adoption de la liste des substances prohibées par le Comité international olympique, celle des mécanismes et procédures pour la collecte des spécimens urinaires et l'imposition de sanctions adéquates) et celles des gouvernements (mcsurcs législatives et financières, financement de laboratoires accrédités compétents et prévention du trafic des substances dopantes). La Charte définit également les responsabilités qui doivent être partagées par les principaux intéressés (éducation et information) de même que des stratégies de prévention et de répression.

La Charte contient en outre six annexes qui fournissent une description détaillée de ses éléments fondamentaux. On y trouve notamment :

– Les conditions requises par le Comité international olympique pour l'accréditation des laboratoires de contrôle analytique du dopage, de même que les normes requises sur le plan technique.

– La liste des classes de substances dopantes et les méthodes de dopage prohibées actuellement par le Comité international olympique.

– Un modèle détaillé d'un programme antidopage national.

– Des procédures type pour les contrôles de dopage.

– Les principes et lignes directrices pour la réalisation des contrôles antidopage hors compétition.

– Les droits et responsabilités des athlètes et de leur entourage.

– Les sanctions et les mesures disciplinaires envisagées.

Un des éléments, à savoir les contrôles hors compétition, vaut qu'on s'y arrête. Il est devenu assez clair, au cours des dernières années, que les contrôles exercés lors des compétitions avaient une efficacité relativement limitée. Bien que ces contrôles aient contribué de façon significative à réduire la consommation de drogues qui, comme les stimulants psychomoteurs, sont administrées en relation directe avec une compétition, leur effet dissuasif en ce qui a trait aux «drogues d'entraînement», comme les stéroïdes anabolisants, a été à juste titre remis en question. Un consensus international s'est maintenant développé à l'effet que le seul moyen efficace de contrôler l'usage d'anabolisants est d'organiser des contrôles hors compétition, sans préavis à l'athlète. Plusieurs fédérations internationales et certains pays semblent avoir dominé les obstacles constitutionnels et légaux qui s'opposent à des actions de ce type. En Suède, par exemple, la très grande majorité des contrôles (de 80 à 85 %) est exécutée hors compétition. La Fédération internationale d'athlétisme et la Fédération internationale d'haltérophilie ont pour leur part formé des équipes itinérantes qui peuvent, par exemple et à tout moment, faire des contrôles dans un camp d'entraînement dans un pays particulier. On espère ainsi que la menace constante d'un contrôle éventuel éloignera les athlètes du dopage à long terme aux stéroïdes anabolisants. Il est enfin utile de signaler que la Charte internationale olympique contient une autre disposition, à savoir l'élaboration d'accords bi- ou multilatéraux qui prévoient que des athlètes d'une nation qui s'entraînent dans une autre soient soumis à des contrôles par le pays-hôte. Ce principe s'est concrétisé et même élargi dans un accord bilatéral intervenu entre les Comités olympiques des États-Unis et de l'URSS à la fin 1988. Cet accord prévoit notamment que les contrôles seront exécutés conformément aux dispositions de la Charte olympique. Chaque Comité national olympique peut désigner les athlètes de l'autre CNO qu'il souhaite voir contrôler, avec un préavis maximum de 48 heures. L'accord est basé évidemment sur le principe de la vérification mutuelle—les contrôles analytiques devant être faits dans le laboratoire national, sous la supervision d'un scientifique de l'autre pays. Ainsi, à titre d'exemple, les États-Unis pourrait demander que soient contrôlés, dans les 48 heures, les 5 meilleurs haltérophiles soviétiques et les analyses seraient réalisées en Union Soviétique sous la supervision d'un expert américain. Des accords de cette nature, mais où la composante de vérification mutuelle est atténuée, sont également intervenus entre les pays scandinaves et, plus récemment, entre le Canada, la Grande-Bretagne et l'Australie.

L'expérience passée a démontré que les tentatives de suppression d'un phénomène social complexe comme le dopage ne sont pas nécessairement réglées par des mesures répressives, comme celles sur lesquelles on met l'accent depuis maintenant plus de 25 ans. Il y a de fortes indications à l'effet que les mesures coercitives mises en œuvre par certains gouvernements et organismes sportifs internationaux auraient eu pour effet de repousser les actions dans la clandestinité. On pourrait citer comme exemple la mainmise du trafic des stéroïdes anabolisants par le monde interlope et la mise sur pied apparente d'usines de fabrication clandestines. Il y a probablement des athlètes qui demeurent convaincus que des performances sportives de niveau international ne sauraient être réalisées qu'avec l'aide d'adjuvants ergogéniques. Il reste à espérer que les mesures éducatives récemment mises en place par plusieurs gouvernements et associations sportives nationales et internationales contribueront, avec les mesures nécessaires de contrôle, à ce que la génération montante d'athlètes de haut niveau, les organismes régisseurs du sport et la société tout entière se questionnent en profondeur sur la nature et les valeurs du sport dans le monde d'aujourd'hui.

Idéal olympique et doping:
une mésalliance et un divorce en vue

Les auteurs rappellent que l'utilisation de substances susceptibles d'améliorer la performance athlétique est un phénomène de longue date. Le monde du sport canadien et le Mouvement olympique tout entier, depuis les événements de Séoul et comme conséquence de l'enquête Dubin sur le dopage dans le sport, se sont trouvés tout de go plongés dans un état de crise. Un premier constat fut celui de réaliser l'éventail considérable d'avis sur la question. Les données de la recherche cumulées au cours des années 80 ont en effet montré que le degré de permissivité à l'égard du doping dans le sport variait de manière significative en fonction de la distance où l'on se trouve du feu de l'action et du groupe social dont on pouvait faire partie: entraîneurs, journalistes, athlètes, administrateurs de sport, médecins ou scientifiques, public en général. Les auteurs font porter l'interrogation sur les raisons invoquées pour proscrire l'utilisation de substances ou d'approches méthodologiques susceptibles d'améliorer la performance sportive de haut niveau, incluant l'olympique. Les auteurs procèdent ensuite à une analyse serrée des arguments avancés en matière d'interdiction du recours aux substances ou aux pratiques réputées dopantes, dans une perspective d'amélioration de la performance athlétique. Les arguments sont présentés sous quatre chefs: – la tricherie simple, ou le non-respect d'un règlement de la société sportive; – la possibilité ou le fait de nuire à la santé de l'athlète (en tant que citoyen adulte et en principe libre ou indépendant); – les prémisses à l'effet que l'utilisation de substances dites ou jugées dopantes pervertit la nature même du sport; – enfin, le concept à l'effet que l'usage de substances ou de pratiques dopantes déshumanise celui ou celle qui s'y prête. Pour chacune des catégories d'arguments qui précèdent, les auteurs décrivent les raisonnements qui sont le plus couramment faits et ils exposent le pour et le contre. Dans le cas de l'argument de la tricherie, les auteurs insistent sur le fait que l'obtention, par un athlète, d'un avantage décrété illégitime ne saurait, au plan de la logique, être utilisé comme seul soutien du «pourquoi» et doit en être ainsi. Au sujet du danger de nuire à la santé, les auteurs se disent d'avis que l'argument tient mal devant plusieurs sortes d'objections: – les résultats de la recherche scientifique, dans l'état actuel des choses, ne sont pas concluants sur le tort réel subi à court, à moyen ou à long terme par les usagers de substances dopantes, incluant les stéroïdes anabolisants; – l'objectif avoué de protéger l'athlète des effets délétères possibles a des relents de paternalisme et ne semble guère dans la ligne de l'argumentation qui évolue de nos jours fort rapidement en matière d'éthique médicale et scientifique plus particulièrement en ce qui a trait aux contraintes associées aux risques d'ordre professionnel et au principe de la liberté individuelle; – le problème de l'équité et de l'égalité des chances dans la poursuite de l'excellence sportive vient paradoxalement en conflit avec les fins mêmes de l'entraînement athlétique et la boucle ouverte du *Citius-Altius-Fortius*; – la question du rôle de modèle social qu'est censé jouer l'athlète de haut niveau ne mérite pas d'être plus contraignante pour ce dernier qu'elle ne semble l'être pour d'autres catégories de citoyens qui ont une visibilité publique comparable. Enfin, pour ce qui a trait à la question de la déshumanisation du sport, les auteurs se disent d'avis que face aux exigences mêmes du rendement sportif de haut niveau ainsi que du recul constant des frontières du possible, il n'est guère logique d'établir *a priori* et sans le moindre consensus, ce qui est «humain» et ce qui ne l'est pas, comme aussi ce qui est une pratique «naturelle» et une autre qui ne le serait pas. Les auteurs insistent dans la dernière partie de leur présentation sur le fait que s'ils partagent l'avis général à l'effet que l'usage de substances dopantes n'a guère sa place dans le sport, ils n'en cherchent pas moins la justification philosophique et scientifique de cette conviction. En guise de conclusion, ils soulignent que dans l'état actuel des choses, les arguments utilisés dans les stratégies de répression du doping dans le sport ne sont ni bien articulés ni convaincants.

The Mesalliance of the Olympic Ideal and Doping: why they Married, and why they Should Divorce

Angela J. Schneider
and
Robert B. Butcher

Performance enhancing substances have played a part in the Olympic Games since the very beginning. Yet until the relatively recent past their use was not considered to be an issue worthy of much attention; certainly, their use was for long of far less importance than the issue of amateurism. This is not the case today. Canadian sport and indeed olympic sport (as evidenced by the Dubin inquiry and the International Olympic Committee's [IOC] efforts to clarify the fundamental principles at stake in the Olympic Charter) are in a state of turmoil, as doping appears to be a most pernicious problem, one that has indeed triggered a crisis of values. Why is it that so many sports administrators and politicians are so quick to decry the use of performance enhancing substances while so many people and athletes appear to take a different stand? Surprisingly, data reported by Vuolle[1] and Heinilä[2] has clearly shown that interest groups differed significantly in their "permissiveness" with respect to doping in sport. Whereas there was almost unanimity against doping in sport when "youth was concerned", there was far greater laxity in the case of top level sport and competitive sport in general. The percentages of those of the opinion that doping be "not permitted in any circumstances" in association with top level sport were lower than expected and varied considerably indeed: coaches, 53%; sport journalists, 54%; athletes, 60%; sports leaders, 62%; sport physicians, 81%; public at large, 82%. Why is it then that one ought to ban performance enhancing substances in the first place? It is our contention that the answers to these questions are all linked together. It is no longer sufficient to simply blame a few deviant athletes for bringing sport into disrepute. It is also our contention that no amount of enforcement of regulations against "banned substances" will ever suffice to eradicate their use. What is required is rather a reaffirmation of the fundamental values of sport and the clarification of the mixed messages the olympic sports hierarchy currently sends out. There is a dire need for clarifications as to why performance enhancing substances *should* be banned, and as to why *"Citius, Altius, Fortius"* cannot be allowed to stand alone. Part of the explanation of the current situation is doubtless that in this field, as in many others, technology has outrun the moral intuitions. Just

1890
1990

Angela J. Schneider and Robert B. Butcher, Department of Philosophy, the University of Western Ontario, London, Ontario, Canada.

as there are outstanding unsolved moral questions about the use of reproductive technology, there are indeed also outstanding questions about the use of performance enhancing substances in the field of sport. In this presentation, we will lay out and examine the justifications that are standardly given for banning performance enhancing subtances. We will then argue that in our judgment, none of them are very convincing.

The philosophical arguments that are advanced in the literature and which purport to justify the banning of performance enhancing substances in sport can be reduced to four main categories. We shall treat each of these four main types of argument in turn and examine their validity. We will then turn to an examination of the way in which one part of the "olympic ideal" itself may have indirectly fostered and encouraged the use of banned substances. Finally we will discuss the most promising line of argument open to justify a ban and suggest that perhaps rather than viewing the issue as a problem to be "solved", it would appear more promising to view it as an opportunity for choices, a chance for the Olympic Movement to state its fundamental values clearly, coherently and with conviction.

Arguments For Banning Performance Enhancing Substances

Cheating

One set of arguments purported to show just what is wrong with the use of substances such as steroids in high performance sport is that their use is "against the rules" and is therefore cheating. It is advanced that athletes should not use substances because their use gives them an "unfair advantage" over other athletes who play "by the rules". This, of course, is true as far as it goes. If steroids are banned, then any athlete who uses them is a cheat and has done something wrong. But that is not the question of central interest in this paper. Rather, we are concerned with the justification for banning the use of performance enhancing substances in general, and anabolic steroids in particular. The assertion that their use is currently cheating is of no help as one attempts to determine whether or not they should be proscribed in the first place. With this in mind it is easy to see that a great deal of the current literature simply begs the question about *why* substances should be banned, concentrating as it does on the fact that such substances are currently banned and on the consequences of that ban for contemporary athletics. Assertions that drug use is unfair, or cheating can hardly serve as an *a priori* justi-fication for banning the substances in the first place.

The Argument from Harm

The argument from harm is probably the first one that comes to mind when one seeks the justification for banning substances. It usually comes in two forms. The first is based on the harm that performance enhancing substances are *believed* to cause their users. In its simplest form, the scenario goes something like this: 1– drug "x" *harms* its user; 2– its user *needs* to be protected; 3– the user can be protected by *banning* the drug; 4– therefore the drug *should* be banned.

If one considers this general argument with respect to adult competent athletes using steroids, we can see that it fails in three quite different ways. In the first place, the assertion that steroid use harms the user is, as yet, questioned. At best, the scientific/medical evidence is inconclusive. Much of the evidence concerning harm appears not to be derived from case studies of athletes using very high doses in uncontrolled conditions, which is generally the practice. Abhorrence of the practice has prevented the gathering of hard, scientifically validated evidence. For premiss one of the argument to be fully acceptable, one would expect more data.

The second premiss also fails but for different reasons. The desire to protect some other adult from the consequences of his or her own actions appears rather paternalistic. (We should make it clear at this point that the argument from paternalism operates specifically in the case of competent adults; different considerations come into play when the people one seeks to protect are children or persons deemed not to be competent to make their own decisions). Generally speaking, people tend to foster and value independence and the right to make the important choices that effect one's own life. Much of the thrust of modern North American medical ethics has been directed precisely against medical paternalism in medicine and/or science. To ban steroids to protect adult competent athletes can be viewed as treating them as children or persons unable to make the choices that most effect them. This is morally wrong. It is also inconsistent, as there are many training practices and indeed many sports that carry a far greater likelihood of harm to the athlete than does the controlled use of steroids. For instance, recent anecdotal evidence indicates that there is a very high probability of suffering an injury requiring surgery if one is a member of the Canadian Alpine ski team for five years. Other sports and other countries fare no better. If the reasons for banning drug use in sport really were a genuine concern for the health and well-being of athletes, then there are many sports and many more practices that should also be banned.

Finally, the third premiss fails because there is no evidence to suggest that banning steroids really will protect athletes. When in a sub-culture there are indications that steroid use brings benefits and that this constitutes an occupational hazard of high level competitive sport, athletes will continue to use them, even in clandestine, unsanitary and uncontrolled ways. There is therefore little if any justification for banning steroids on the basis of the harm they may cause to their users.

A second form of the argument from harm is based not on the harm that the steroids may cause to their users but on the harm their use causes to others. The "others" in this argument vary. They can be other "clean" athletes, the sports establishment, the general sports-watching public or society at large. This argument is more difficult to discuss. The same liberal tradition that prohibits paternalistic intervention in fact permits interventions designed to prevent harm to others. The crucial questions concern how great the harm is to others and how severe the limitation is on personal action. The argument runs like this: 1– drug "x" causes harm to people *other* than its users; 2– *those* people need protection; 3– banning drug "x" will protect *those* people; 4– therefore drug "x" *should* be banned.

In assessing this argument, one needs to look at exactly who the "others" are that may be or are being harmed, and consider whether or not that harm outweighs the infringement on the liberties of athletes that is caused when a drug is banned. One possible group of others is "clean athletes". They are harmed, so the argument goes, because drug users "up the ante". If some competitors are using steroids, then all competitors who wish to compete at that level will need to take steroids to keep up. Elite level competitive athletics is already a very high stakes game. In order to compete effectively, one has to dedicate oneself totally and sustain a minutely controlled training regimen that will dictate almost all aspects of one's life. Why is the upping of the ante caused by the use of steroids qualitatively different from the upping of the ante caused by the increasing professionalization of athletes and coaches and the mechanization of athletes that elite level competition now requires? There is no very convincing answer to this question. Some suggestions have included attempts at a distinction between "natural" and "unnatural" training methods and aids. These distinctions, however, are quite difficult to make scientifically as well as philosophically. The feeling that somehow steroid use in association with the scientific control of anabolism or of recuperative metabolic processes is worse than ever longer and ever more specialized training, just begs the question of *why* it is or should be judged worse.

A second potential group that could be harmed by steroid use by athletes is the general public, in particular children. People look up to athletes and many view them as role models. If they take steroids, they are judged no longer suitable as role models and the general public has lost a potentially significant benefit. One could first examine just why it is that steroid use should disqualify one from acting as a role model. A quick response might be that those who use steroids are cheats and of course cheats cannot pose as role models. This is true as far as it goes, but interestingly, it begs the very question one is trying to answer! A further response to the suggestion that athletes should be role models asks just why that should be so. Generally speaking, widely varying things are expected of public figures. No-one seriously expects musicians or actors and actresses to be moral role models, why then should athletes be singled out for that special purpose? There is apparently quite widespread use of Beta-blockers by concert musicians; yet, there has not been with the latter the hue and cry and media circus that followed the revelations of drug use by athletes. It is rather unreasonable to expect athletes in the public eye to be moral role models when we do not, as a society, lay the same burden on other categories of public figures.

One other group of "others" that has appeared in the literature is the sports-watching public. These people are said to have been harmed because they have been cheated. They expected to see drug-free athletes battling it out in fair competition and they were denied this. This situation can be remedied in one of two ways. The first is to do away with the expectation that athletes are drug free. If one does not expect them to be drug free, then one cannot be harmed if they are not. The feeling of being cheated is thus dependent on the idea that what was expected was "fair" competition. But as was discussed above, the fact that steroid use is now judged cheating, and therefore "unfair" competition, is no overwhelming reason justifying *why* it should be considered as cheating.

It should be reiterated at this point that none of the arguments currently presented have any bearing on the enforceability of a ban. If one decides to ban a drug or practice, one should then also decide how one will enforce that ban and how one will punish infractions. Clearly the methods required to police and enforce a ban on, for instance, anabolic steroids will have a serious and negative impact on the freedom of individuals to go about their daily lives in freedom and with dignity.

Drug Use Perverts the Nature of Sport

The third argument stems from the idea that drug use is *essentially* antithetical to the "true" nature of sport. The suggestion is that there is something special about the nature of sport that renders drug use in the pursuit of sporting excellence an abhorrence: if one thinks that one can pursue sporting excellence through the use of potentiating substances, then one has misunderstood something fundamental about the nature of sport. On the face of it the argument looks promising; there certainly do seem to be elements of sport and sporting values that are contravened by the use of substances. The arguments appear in two forms. One version suggests that the use of substances perverts the nature of sport in general. In this form of argumentation, sports are held as essentially related to games in that both are rule-governed activities[3]. Being excellent at a sport is being excellent at some game, where the game is defined by its rules[4]. If one breaks the rules, then one is no longer playing *that* game and so, obviously, one should not be judged excellent at it[5]. It is instructive to compare how this argument works with two games one of which is played with a referee, the other of which is not. If one cheats in golf (for instance if the ball is kicked from the rough into the fairway), it matters little whether or not one is playing against an opponent who is being cheated, or one has changed the game[8]. When one has cheated, then the score is no longer an accurate representation of one's play on that round. On the other hand if one consistently cheats, then the game of golf has been adapted and changed to suit one's own purposes. Breaking the rules implies stepping outside the game; changing the rules implies changing the game. Playing that game is thus intimately tied to the rules of the game. The situation is slightly different for a game that relies on a referee or umpire to call penalties. There it can be argued that what is acceptable as playing the game is what the referee allows or fails to see. Some would propose that in a game like this the rules do not define the game but rather the referee defines it using the rule book as a guide. In effect, the argument here is that the defining rule of the game is that the referee's interpretations and rulings constitute the game.

In both cases the central argument is that a game or sport is essentially related to its rules, somehow defined, and if one breaks those rules, one is then no longer playing that game. Unfortunately this argument can hardly be used to justify banning steroids in sport. All it does (and in this respect it is similar to the cheating argument) is to show that if a drug or practice is banned in a particular sport then if one wants to play that sport one must stick to its rules.

The second form of the "perversion of sport" argument works not at the level of sport in general but rather in respect to particular sports. Here the suggestion is that if sportsmen are allowed to compete with the aid of substances, they have then changed, or worsened that particular sport. The argument operates from a question. Would the introduction of this modification to the sport improve or diminish the sport? So, for example, would the acceptance of "U" groove clubs in golf improve or diminish golf? The answer seems to be that while "U" groove clubs improve the scores of those who use them, the introduction of such clubs would tend to compress the range of scores making it less easy to tell the exceptional golfer from the one who is merely good; and this is judged "bad" for the game[7]. Obviously, questions about whether or not a certain innovation would be "good" for a particular sport are difficult and the answers will contain a number of factors which may well be different for each sport and event and for each innovation. Let us consider just one event, the 100 metre dash, and one innovation, the use of steroids as a training aid. The 100 metre dash is a nice, simple event. The purpose is to propel the human body, without mechanical aid, from a standing start 100 metres in the shortest possible time. It is difficult to see how steroid use perverts the very nature of this event. One could argue that steroids are a mechanical aid (like using a bicycle, a wheelchair or articicial limbs). This is rather unconvincing. Alternatively, one could argue that the use of steroids changes the "human" body into something else, that their use is thus "dehumanizing". This argument however is a change from the previous position that steroid use should be banned because it is a "perversion" of sport; it has now become an argument that steroid use should be banned because it is "dehumanizing".

Doping Substances are "Dehumanizing"

This argument has it that sport is a human activity, one which challenges people as humans; consequently, any practice which dehumanizes the athlete necessarily detracts from the sport as well as the person. To continue with the example of the 100 metre dash, that would be a different event if people with extremely powerful mechanically powered artificial legs were allowed to take part. The 100 metre dash would no longer be a sporting event between two or more people, but rather a competition between two engineering design teams. At the intuitive level this argument strikes a chord. One could describe the essence of sporting competition and excellence as the drive to perfect one aspect, the *physical*, of what it is to be *human*. Anything that detracts from the competitors' humanity detracts from that sporting event or game. But the argument as it stands also has some gaps. A great many "legal" training practices can in fact be said to already "dehumanize" the athlete, systematically removing from him or her control over what he or she eats, and does, and thinks. The price of success in the current competitive environment is absolute total dedication, often the relinquishing of most other aspects of one's life, and often total subjection to the dictates of a battery of coaches, physiologists, pharmacologists, physicians and dieticians. An even more glaring gap is left by the fact that there may not be a good, perfectly defensible, and consistent view of what it is to be "human" anyway. If one cannot define what it is to be truly human, the task of labelling something as "dehumanizing" becomes all the more difficult.

Many are tempted to postulate a distinction between "natural" and "unnatural" substances and training or performance "enhancers". If such a distinction would clearly exist, then perhaps those that were "unnatural" could be used to define the practices which were "dehumanizing". Unfortunately, none of the purported distinctions between "natural" and "unnatural" appear to work. This ought not to be surprising, "natural" and "unnatural" mean "natural" or "unnatural" *for us*, as human beings. If we don't have a consistent view of what it is to be human, we will then be in an uncomfortable position to define what is "natural" or "unnatural". Deciding what it is to be human thus appears as a prerequisite to determining what is or is not an "unnatural" practice.

In the foregoing, we have taken a brief and somewhat sketchy tour of the arguments designed to show that steroids should be banned. Unfortunately those arguments have proved to be not very convincing. We nonetheless share the general conviction that steroids have no place in sport; yet, we still are actively seeking a solid justification for that conviction. At the outset, we indicated that we would draw attention to one way in which the olympic ideal itself may have contributed to the use of performance enhancing substances. "Faster, higher, stronger" refers directly to the goal of creating the fastest human being, or the strongest. Canadian newspaper headlines after Ben Johnson's win and before the scandal broke indeed heralded him as the "Fastest Man Alive". If the goal is to be the fastest person over some distance, without mechanical aids, it is easy to see why the ban on steroids can be seen as an unnecessary and indeed arbitrary restriction. In seeking to be the fastest, what appears to have been lost is the idea that the olympic ideal really entails being the best person at "some" game. The "game" in question here is the olympic 100 metre dash complete with all the other arbitrary rules that it implies. So Ben may well have fulfilled one part of the olympic ideal, *he was* the fastest man alive but he *was not*, indeed could not have been, even if undetected, the winner of *"that"* game as its rules then stood.

To return to the original olympic ideal we need to re-emphasise the "game" element in the Olympic Games. To the philosopher, distinctions between "games", "sports", and "play" are indeed possible, yet, the source of much debate. One thing is clear: games have rules even if at times those rules appear rather arbitrary (but not necessarily absurd). To be excellent at a game requires playing by its rules, even the arbitrary ones. To the non-philosopher the word "game" also has important connotations, not the least of which is that games should be fun. With respect to that element of play, using performance enhancing substances appears absurd. Playing involves an attitude that should normally value the activity for its own sake and not for the sake of extrinsic rewards[8]. If one uses a performance enhancing substance in play, one is then circumventing the point of playing that game and one's attention becomes directed towards some goal external to the game.

Much confusion remains in this domain. The values inherent in any particular game as well as those inherent in the Olympic Games need to be clearly articulated and perhaps eventually shown to be incompatible with the use of performance enhancing substances. In the case of the Olympic Games that articulation will continue to be unconvincing unless the play and game elements of the Games become emphasized to the point where they are given more importance than the quest for records and the desire for *Citius, Altius, Fortius*. It is realized that this emphasis is not likely to gain universal acceptance, as many feel that this would weaken the commitment to excellence. The goal of faster, higher, stronger is a laudable and very human quest; as it now stands however, it does not specify or preclude means. If this really is one of the prime goals of the Olympic Movement, then we feel that there is, at present, no convincing reason for banning the use of performance enhancing substances without further a do. As we remarked at the outset, there is a choice to be made, a difficult choice and one that will inevitably leave many unsatisfied. But that is no reason not to make the choice, for if it is not made consciously it will be made by default. Our intention has not been to make that choice but rather to throw it into sharper relief, for we firmly believe that those called upon to make this decision have an obligation to the athletes who are the first people concerned, who will live it and thus have a right to know what the socially acceptable commitment to olympic excellence entails.

REFERENCES

1. Vuolle P (1982) Doping-tutkimus (Research on doping) In Siukonen M (ed) Doping. Jyväskylä p 69-100

2. Heinilä K (1988) Social research on sport in Finland. Sportwissenschaft 1 9-28

3. Suits B (1988) Tricky triad: games, play and sport. Journal of the Philosophy of Sport XV 1-9. See also Meier K (1988) Triad trickery: playing with sport and games. Journal of the Philosophy of Sport XV 11-30

4. Meier K (1985) Restless sport. Journal of the Philosophy of Sport XII 64-77

5. Pearson K (1973) Deception, sportsmanship and ethics. Quest 19 115-18

6. Adapted from Suits B (1988) op cit p 1-9

7. Gardner R (1989) On performance enhancing substances and the unfair advantage argument. Journal of the Philosophy of Sport XVI 59-73

8. Meier K (1985) op cit p 11-30

[. . .] l'internationalisme sportif qui se développe autour de nous d'une manière si heureuse est basé sur le sens des rivalités et sur l'esprit d'émulation, nullement sur l'espèce de cosmopolitanisme et d'amour de l'humanité dont certains politiciens escomptent l'avènement. Dans ces conditions, autant les rencontres sont populaires, autant l'ingérence étrangère dans l'administration des sports nationaux paraîtrait vite intolérable à ceux qui devraient la supporter. [. . .] L'ère qui s'ouvre est bien plutôt l'ère des « traités de commerce » appliqués aux sports. C'est aux fédérations elle-mêmes à s'aboucher entre elles, à conclure des ententes qui faciliteront les rencontres, et dont les clauses, d'ailleurs, pourront toujours être dénoncées en temps opportun ou modifiées selon les besoins du jour. Cela et l'unification raisonnable des règlements de jeux et de concours, voilà le but à poursuivre. [. . .]

Coubertin P de (1903) L'organisation olympique. Revue Olympique, juillet, p 35

Legitimacy and Legality of International Structures in Sport

Infranational and International Aspects
and Implications of Deviant Behaviors in Sport,
of Arbitration and Sanctions in International Sport

Légitimité et légalité des structures du sport international

Des aspects infranationaux et internationaux
des comportements sportifs déviants, de l'arbitration
et des sanctions dans le sport international

Legitimacy and Legality
of International Structures in Sport:
Background Considerations

The author recalls that it is thanks to the concepts and efforts of Pierre de Coubertin if the international structures of sport have known such a decisive development. For the renovator of the Olympic Games, the first important task of a sport federation was to organize itself properly and solidly, from a legal standpoint. A necessary consequence of the expansion of the sporting movement has been the proliferation of sport governing bodies and thus the increasing complexity of structures at all levels. The very fact of sport's enormous and ubiquitous successes has made it a target of economic and political interests. A large number of modern States now have laws, indeed even articles of their constitutions that have to do with sport. The double-barrel question of the legitimacy and legality of the international structures of sport is intimately connected to the proper identity of the sporting institution itself within the overall political and economic configurations of power structures. The said identity can best be understood through an analysis of the relative objects and functions of the constituent parts of the national, transnational and international sport structures. In principle, the international organizations of sport are non-governmental (NGOs) as well as non-profit organizations which group natural and/or juristic persons that adhere willingly and freely to its objects. According to the author, the legal framework within which sport governing bodies operate is that of the law of the state, in principle that of the territory in which the organization's headquarters are situated physically. But the NGOs, in their charters or constitutions typically never make reference to state laws. The case indeed applies also to the International Olympic Committee, which presents itself as a lawful international association with legal status. The evident absence of reference to national law bears witness to the acknowledged intent of sports governing bodies to be of service on a world scale. In this respect, most states tend to have a very tolerant and even generous attitude. He further explains that in fact, the international glitter and influence of sport itself, by feedback, indeed provides protection to its NGOs. Reference is made to the prescription of rights and mandates which are typically invested through the mechanism of cooptation, thus on the basis and in principle according to the wishes of the sporting movement itself. Exclusivity within sports governing bodies constitutes a mechanism of protection with respect to the identity and independence of sport. In addition, the processes and acts of investiture which are typical of sport governing bodies are given legitimacy by sovereign states in that they recognize as a matter of fact the existence of international agreements between NGOs and in turn seek visibility and recognition through international sport. At this point in time, the sporting movement finds itself in an order of values which is basically different from that in which typical states conduct economic and political matters. In the second part of his presentation, the author deals with the roles of the international sport governing bodies which are to make and enact rules and to judge accordingly. International sport governing bodies have *de facto* placed themselves in a difficult position since, in order to exercise their authority, they can hardly come into opposition with sovereign states. An evident difficulty has to do with the matter of nationalities: there has been numerous instances whereby the "sporting nationality" has been at odds with the notion of "civil nationality". The author comments that for the sporting movement to protect its own future, it ought to make use of every opportunity to illustrate and defend the primacy of the principle of world-wide sporting rules and regulations. One can easily observe that sovereign states give only limited consideration to the sanctions imposed by international federations upon their citizens, and at times even have argued that athletes can only be sanctioned by their own national federation. In that perspective, the author refers to the International Tribunal of Sport as an example of the kind which presents an image of expertise and credibility in matters of legalistic concerns in international sport. The author concludes his presentation by emphasizing that the legitimacy of international structures in sport is not a matter of degrees; it will either be won or lost, yet it remains the key to the true autonomy of sport's structures.

Légitimité et légalité
des structures internationales du sport:
une toile de fond

François Alaphilippe

À l'occasion de la célébration du centième anniversaire de la rencontre de Pierre de Coubertin avec le nouveau continent il m'a été demandé de «brosser une toile de fond» sur un sujet bien impressionnant: les structures internationales du sport, au développement desquelles le Baron a donné un élan décisif. Dans les dernières décennies, elle a vraiment beaucoup changé, cette vaste constellation du mouvement sportif: l'expansion considérable de l'activité sportive a provoqué la prolifération des organes dirigeants et, fatalement, l'alourdissement des structures. Et la question se pose: quelle place ont prise, quelle place peuvent prendre les structures internationales du sport dans l'ordonnancement juridique et institutionnel du monde où elles évoluent?

C'est à cette question *d'identité institutionnelle* que se ramène, je crois, le thème qui m'a été confié: *Légitimité* et *légalité* des structures internationales du sport.

L'interrogation première, celle qui va au fond des choses porte sur la *légitimité*. Il est difficile de définir la légitimité. Disons qu'elle s'apprécie par rapport à des principes ou à des valeurs reconnus comme découlant de l'ordre des choses, ou de la raison: la référence est une sorte d'ordre naturel dont on sait bien qu'il n'est pas immanent; dont on sait bien qu'il est lié à tout un ensemble de facteurs contingents: le poids de l'histoire, l'évolution des mentalités, voire, parfois, la stature de telle ou telle personnalité. Si bien que je me contenterai de reprendre la formule de Ferrero pour dire que la légitimité se trouve entre les mains des «*génies invisibles de la cité[1]*». La cité ici est vaste puisque le sport est universel: c'est dans cette dimension que doit s'apprécier la légitimité des structures internationales du sport. On dira déjà que les valeurs humanistes sur lesquelles reposent les principes olympiques sont naturellement porteuses de légitimité; mais que, s'agissant ici d'apprécier les structures qui les diffusent, ce premier argument ne suffit pas. Il faut aller plus loin.

1890
1990

François Alaphilippe, Centre de droit et d'économie du sport, Faculté de droit et des sciences économiques de Limoges, Limoges, France.

L'autre question, celle de la *légalité*, paraît plus simple : la légalité étant la conformité à un ordre établi, à une loi positive, il suffit de trouver l'ordre juridique de référence. Mais c'est là précisément que gît la difficulté.

D'un côté les instances sportives sont là pour établir un ordre interne qui, discipline par discipline, doit être le même pour tous si l'on veut que puisse se dégager à chaque fois le champion du monde ou le champion olympique. *Cette légalité là ne peut venir que d'en haut, c'est à dire des structures internationales qui se trouvent ainsi dotées d'une puissance de communication juridique remarquable* puisque leur message doit atteindre même les rouages les plus discrets de la machinerie institutionnelle, des clubs les plus reculés.

D'un autre côté, chaque État a ses lois qu'en toute souveraineté il impose sur son territoire. Et depuis que, par son succès, l'activité sportive se trouve au milieu d'enjeux politiques et économiques, bon nombre d'États ont même des lois, voire des articles de leur constitution spécialement destinés au sport.

Il faut faire avec les deux légalités : toutes deux doivent composer entre elles. C'est dire que le tissu juridique du sport mêle dans sa trame *ordre sportif* et *ordre d'État*, toujours. L'équilibre varie, on s'en doute, suivant les pays et les régimes politiques. Mais s'il fallait esquisser des repères, j'avancerais volontiers ce que j'appelle la *loi des trois zones* :

– Il y aurait d'abord *zone de la logistique*, celle qui se rapporte à l'administration des moyens économiques du sport. Cette zone est le lieu d'élection du droit administratif, du droit fiscal, des finances publiques, du droit civil, commercial ou du travail. Bref c'est la zone où la légalité de l'État occupe toute la place ou presque : la densité sportive y est minimale.

– À l'opposé, il y aurait la *zone de densité sportive maximale*, là où l'ordre sportif aurait le monopole : cette zone est celle du terrain sportif, de l'affrontement, enfermé dans son unité de temps, de lieu et d'objectif. La règle sportive y règne de façon exclusive ; elle a un caractère fondateur : sans elle, pas de compétition, le vainqueur gagne toujours de par le règlement et son adversaire, d'une certaine façon est vaincu par le règlement. La légalité de l'État n'a pas à s'en mêler.

– Enfin, entre les deux, il y a la *zone de l'institution sportive*, zone complexe, hétérogène, où se meuvent précisément les structures internationales. Chaque *unité élémentaire* — fédération, CIO, ACNO, association continentale de CNO, AGFIS et regroupement de fédérations internationales — y a sa place : elle s'organise et fonctionne en prenant pied matériellement et juridiquement sur le territoire d'un État. Mais la *composition d'ensemble* est en mesure d'exercer, comme on l'a dit, sa propre pression juridique, de mettre en œuvre *cette force de communication institutionnelle* qui dépasse chaque rouage puisqu'elle est indispensable à la cohérence du système et à la réalisation de ses objectifs. Dans cette zone, quelle légalité s'impose ? L'ordre d'État ou l'ordre sportif ?

On sent bien ici que, quelque part, la réponse sera inspirée par les « génies invisibles de la cité » ; qu'elle est étroitement liée à un autre débat : celui de la légitimité.

En réalité, derrière la double question, légitimité et légalité, se profile bien *l'interrogation fondamentale* pour les structures internationales du sport ; la question d'aujourd'hui et de demain aussi : celle de *l'identité de l'institution sportive*. Devant pareil sujet, le juriste incline à beaucoup de prudence ; le sportif militant vers une certaine passion. Nouveau dilemme qui me vaudra, j'espère, votre indulgence.

S'agissant d'une question d'identité, ce que l'on est largement déterminé par ce que l'on fait : surtout quand ce que l'on fait est tellement important pour la solidarité de l'ensemble. Et c'est là que l'expression structures internationales du sport est si pertinente : une structure, c'est en effet *un ensemble formé de phénomènes solidaires*, tel que *chacun d'eux dépend des autres et ne peut être ce qu'il est que dans et par sa relation avec eux*.

On ne peut trouver meilleur terme pour le mouvement sportif. L'identité institutionnelle de ce mouvement doit se rechercher à la fois dans les *organes* qu'il regroupe et dans les *fonctions* qui les rassemblent.

Les organes internationaux du sport

Il s'agit en toute logique du chapitre qu'il convient d'aborder en premier, car il traite des éléments corporels, de la partie la plus visible, la plus tangible des structures. Deux propositions rendent compte de leurs caractéristiques : ce sont des organisations *non gouvernementales* ; elles ont reçu une *investiture sportive*.

Des organisations non gouvernementales (ONG)

À ce titre, les organes internationaux du sport font partie du bon millier d'ONG dont la définition est simple : ce sont des organismes créés par une initiative prévue, regroupant des personnes — physiques ou morales — de nationalités diverses et qui toutes ont adhéré volontairement, et poursuivent un but non lucratif. La catégorie est vaste : elle rassemble des institutions aussi diverses que la Croix Rouge, Greenpeace, Amnesty International, les Églises, les fédérations socialistes, communistes, libérales, des fédérations syndicales et j'en passe. Toutes ont en commun *un régime* juridique qui relève de la loi d'un État (en principe celui sur le territoire duquel se trouve leur siège).

Pour une fédération internationale, une union continentale ou toute autre instance internationale du sport, on peut difficilement imaginer qu'elle puisse se créer en se conformant strictement à la loi d'un État ou même en lui faisant référence. Le CIO, lui-même, se présente dans la règle 11 de la Charte comme « une association de droit international ayant la personnalité juridique » : le moins que l'on puisse dire est que cette formule dénie toute référence — toute révérence — à une légalité nationale.

Cela témoigne, pour le moins, d'une volonté d'éviter toute allégeance incompatible avec un rayonnement universel[2]. D'autres organisations non gouvernementales ont la même attitude ; par exemple, l'Institut de droit international fondé à Gand en 1873 et dont les promoteurs ont eu la même intention, pour ne pas compromettre leur indépendance, d'éviter d'afficher une soumission à l'ordre d'un État. Si l'on revient au sport qui se trouve aujourd'hui aspiré par tant de stratégies politiques ou économiques, il est parfaitement légitime que la même volonté s'affirme pour préserver ses valeurs et ses structures.

Reste que, même dans ces conditions, les États ont tendance à considérer les ONG comme de simples associations internes. Cette analyse constitue un handicap sérieux dans la mesure où la présence de dirigeants étrangers incitera à soumettre l'organisation au régime moins favorable des associations étrangères. Il est vrai que certains États — ceux, en général où ces instances ont leur siège — ont tendance à être plus généreux. Leurs tribunaux admettent sans difficulté qu'une fédération internationale, par exemple, puisse agir en justice et jouir d'une « personnalité juridique fonctionnelle », même si elle n'a pas satisfait à toutes les exigences légales requises pour la constitution d'une association. En France, par exemple, la théorie dite « de la réalité des personnes morales » autoriserait — elle a autorisé — de telles solutions.

En plus, il arrive que des dispositions légales ou réglementaires *ad personnam* accordent à telle instance sportive internationale un statut privilégié.

C'est ainsi qu'en 1981, un arrêté du Conseil fédéral suisse a fait bénéficier le CIO de tout un ensemble de mesures dérogatoires. Il s'agissait bien d'une décision unilatérale de l'État et non de l'accord du siège demandé pour le CIO dans des termes comparables à ceux qu'aurait utilisés une organisation interétatique.

En droit, la différence est sensible, car un État est toujours maître de modifier ou d'octroyer l'une de ses décisions. De ce point de vue, la situation des ONG est toujours précaire car elle est subordonnée au maintien de l'acte favorable; de cette façon, elle est précaire aussi parce que, sortie des limites de l'État, l'ONG perd son statut protecteur. En fait, dans la situation du CIO, ces risques sont pour ainsi dire inexistants. D'une manière générale, d'ailleurs, on doit reconnaître que le rayonnement du sport fournit une protection non négligeable à ces structures internationales: c'est dire l'importance de leur investiture sportive.

Une investiture sportive

Totalement indépendante de la volonté des États, cette investiture marque, à la fois, la naissance de l'ONG et son entrée dans les structures sportives. Parfois les deux vont de pair. C'est le cas par exemple, à l'aube de notre sport moderne, de l'acte fondateur du CIO en 1895 ou, plus tard, de l'AGFIS, par exemple. Parfois, ils sont séparés dans le temps, en ce sens que l'investiture est progressive et que, par étapes successives, l'instance internationale se trouve de plus en plus intégrée au sein de l'institution sportive: ainsi l'agrément d'une fédération internationale déjà établie par une association de fédérations internationales, puis sa reconnaissance par le CIO en tant qu'instance régissant un sport figurant, ou non, au programme des Jeux olympiques.

Je passe sur les procédés, les mécanismes techniques de cette investiture sportive — acte-fondateur, acte-condition, possession d'État aussi — pour insister sur le fait que l'investiture sportive est susceptible de degrés; il y a en quelque sorte, un *cursus honorum*: des grades dans les structures internationales du sport, des grades d'autant plus qualifiants qu'ils sont proches de ce noyau dur, de ce centre de gravité que constitue le CIO.

Quel que soit son degré, l'investiture par le mouvement sportif marque l'entrée dans un système universel et exclusif: hors du système pas de salut — de salut sportif s'entend. Ce principe est important à une époque où beaucoup d'intérêts sont tentés de se combiner pour organiser des compétitions qu'ils utiliseront ensuite afin de promouvoir des produits, des idéologies, ou de vendre du spectacle tout simplement. De telles organisations marchandes peuvent bien se créer: elles n'obtiendront le label sportif que par la volonté du mouvement sportif. Et cette cooptation, les structures internationales du sport ne peuvent que veiller à l'exercer avec la plus grande vigilance si elles veulent préserver et promouvoir leur identité. Faute de quoi, le sport serait vite pris dans le tourbillon des intérêts marchands et politiques.

Cette investiture par cooptation est donc une véritable légitimation à l'égard de l'institution sportive. Elle est aussi porteuse de légitimité pour l'extérieur: à l'égard des États, aussi? C'est peut-être paradoxal: comment une investiture émanant d'un milieu privé pourrait-elle s'imposer à des États souverains? Pourtant, qu'on en juge: 3 preuves:

– Nombre d'États, dans leur loi-même, accordent considération aux règles techniques édictées par les fédérations internationales: des fédérations dont la consécration institutionnelle leur échappe complètement!

– De même, bon nombre d'actes internationaux montrent que les États ou leurs organisations ont enregistré l'existence et la consistance internationale des instances sportives: qu'il s'agisse du traité de Nairobi sur la protection des emblèmes olympiques ou encore d'accords de coopération comme celui établi, en 1984, entre le Président du CIO et le directeur de l'UNESCO; qu'il s'agisse également des proclamations du principe en faveur du respect de l'autonomie du mouvement sportif, comme celles émanant, ces dernières années, de l'UNESCO ou du Conseil de l'Europe.

– De même, comment expliquer que des populations, désireuses d'apprécier leur indépendance nationale, appuient leur démarche en revendiquant la consécration internationale de leurs structures sportives?

Il est donc vrai de prétendre que l'investiture sportive est sensible aux génies invisibles de la cité; qu'elle est bien porteuse de légitimité. On aura beau contester le système, reprocher à certains organismes leur recrutement aristocratique; à d'autres, le caractère inégalitaire de leurs formules représentatives; revendiquer un nouvel ordre sportif international, c'est reconnaître qu'un ordre sportif international existe. Et si, autre réserve, cet ordre est impuissant à constituer les structures internationales du sport en sujets du droit international, c'est seulement parce que dans leur propre communauté internationale, les États n'admettent que leurs semblables, ou les institutions qu'ils créent eux-mêmes et que, d'une certaine façon, ils maîtrisent.

Au fond, n'est-ce pas mieux ainsi? Le sport se place dans un ordre de valeurs autre que celui des États, où se disputent et se règlent rapports politiques et relations marchandes. Que ces structures internationales soient des personnes privées ne soulève pas de difficultés insurmontables à partir du moment où, reposant sur la défense d'un humanisme universel, leur solidarité les dote d'un dynamisme protecteur. Encore faut-il qu'elles s'appliquent à bien faire passer le message; mais c'est là un impératif qui s'attache à l'exercice de leurs fonctions.

Les fonctions des structures internationales du sport

Des fonctions remplies par les structures internationales du sport, seules nous intéressent ici les aspects en rapport avec les notions de légalité et de légitimité, c'est-à-dire les aspects institutionnels, ceux qui illustrent la puissance de communication juridique du mouvement sportif.

De ce point de vue, on retrouve les deux genres majeurs qu'ont en commun toutes les institutions: établir une réglementation et trancher les différends, *légiférer* et *juger*. Légiférer et juger: les autorités sportives ne sont pas les seules à le faire dans le domaine du sport; les États s'en préoccupent aussi, chacun sur le territoire où il exerce sa souveraineté. Du coup, la question est toujours la même: mesurer ce que pèsent, par rapport à la légalité des États, les structures internationales du sport dans l'exercice de cette double fonction institutionnelle.

Légiférer d'abord

Légiférer est la tâche de tout groupement pour définir son ordre et son fonctionnement internes. Chacun, de sa propre initiative, met en place son ordre réglementaire qualifié souvent de «droit spontané». Et ce droit spontané s'applique, en général, sous réserve de sa conformité à l'ordre de l'État. Il n'est pas légitime qu'il en soit autrement: ce principe vaut pour les associations, le syndicats, les groupements privés, en général. Seulement voilà: il n'est pas sûr que les structures internationales du sport puissent se plier à ce schéma. En effet, par hypothèse, leur autorité est universelle: comment peut-elle s'exercer si elle vient buter, à chaque fois, sur les souverainetés des États? Je ne prendrai qu'un exemple, celui de la nationalité ou plutôt des nationalités.

On ne peut pas admettre que des sportifs se conduisent comme des mercenaires et se vendent à de multiples pavillons. Pour organiser des rencontres internationales, il faut bien que les critères de rattachement national soient partout les mêmes. De là, les règles définies par les fédérations internationales qui instituent des critères universels de la «nationalité sportive». Au contraire, la nationalité civile — la vraie — est définie en pleine souveraineté, distinctement, par chaque État qui fixe ses propres critères et choisit les bases à partir desquelles il entend reconnaître ses propres sujets. Critères universels d'un côté, nationaux de l'autre, la contrariété est inévitable.

Qui doit l'emporter? Le problème s'est posé surtout à un niveau sportif moindre, à propos des règles (sportives nationales) par lesquelles les fédérations nationales veulent protéger leurs sélectionnables. Pour cela elles doivent «brimer» les autres qui peuvent avoir la même *nationalité civile*. Que va-t-il se passer? L'État dira peut-être «mon ordre public interdit qu'on distingue entre mes nationaux»[3]. En Europe, une question identique se rencontre à propos du principe communautaire de libre-circulation des personnes entre États membres de la Communauté[4]. La jurisprudence montre qu'en général, et même si c'est avec des nuances, les règles étatiques ont, sur ce point, barre sur des règlements sportifs.

Je voudrais proposer une réponse. Ce n'est pas celle qui a vraiment cours, en ce moment, auprès de nos tribunaux: celle que de ce côté-ci de l'Atlantique une Cour d'appel, celle de Los Angeles a donnée, sur un sujet voisin: «Nous hésitons beaucoup à appliquer une loi nationale qui pourrait altérer une épreuve à laquelle participent des athlètes du monde entier, suivant les règles de cette convention»[5]. C'était en 1984. Et il s'agissait de la réglementation des épreuves des Jeux olympiques de Los Angeles. Mais cette préférence reconnue à la règle sportive universelle devrait donner à réfléchir: elle est certainement vitale pour l'avenir du mouvement sportif; il est important qu'il s'attache à la défendre. Elle est, sûrement aussi à considérer pour les États auxquels les structures internationales du sport offrent un terrain privilégié de communication, parce que la diplomatie peut s'y exercer en dehors de ses chemins habituels.

Puis, juger

Juger, les structures du sport ont également ce rôle. Pour elles il est même primordial: il s'exprime essentiellement, mais pas exclusivement, dans l'application d'une discipline interne, inévitable condition de survie juridique des institutions. Gardienne des règles, protectrice de l'éthique, cette discipline est garante de la solidarité qui unit les membres de la fédération.

Pierre de Coubertin, lui-même, le constatait: «La première, la plus utile des tâches qui incombent à une fédération sportive, c'est de s'organiser judiciairement. Elle doit être à la fois un Conseil d'État, une Cour d'appel et un Tribunal des conflits[6].» Tout un programme qui vaut plus encore pour les fédérations internationales dont, bien souvent, les statuts font référence à la discipline parmi les buts et les principes de l'organisation. Que pèserait en effet une institution si elle était incapable de résoudre les tensions qui la traversent? C'est peut-être là le point le plus délicat, on ne peut pas dire en effet que la confiance règne toujours.

Côté justiciables d'abord: car d'une manière générale, les instances disciplinaires devant lesquelles ils comparaissent sont à la fois juges et parties. Elles sont en effet constituées par ceux-là mêmes qui détiennent le pouvoir politique, qu'il s'agisse du congrès — organe souverain de la fédération internationale — ou d'une instance spécialisée. Cet inconvénient fréquent est parfois aggravé en ce que les droits de la défense ne sont pas ménagés d'une manière satisfaisante, ou par l'absence de recours possible (je schématise beaucoup). Et puis, si par bonheur pour lui, le condamné trouve à l'extérieur un tribunal qui annule une sanction contestable, l'annulation n'aura qu'une portée réduite, limitée au territoire de l'État où siège le tribunal.

Il se pourrait bien, d'ailleurs, que le doute règne aussi du côté des fédérations internationales elles-mêmes. Un peu de mauvais esprit suffirait pour expliquer de cette manière les dispositions réglementaires qui interdisent fréquemment tout recours devant une instance extérieure. Sans doute s'agit-il surtout de protéger l'ordre sportif contre les intrusions d'un pouvoir extérieur. Mais quelle peut être la légitimité de règles aussi contraires au principe de libre accès à la justice, unanimement consacré aujourd'hui?

Alors, côté États, la réserve est grande. D'abord les États n'admettent pas, en principe, d'autre justice que la leur. Voilà pourquoi ils considèrent que les décisions disciplinaires n'ont pas de valeur juridictionnelle. Pour eux, ce sont de simples actes privés que leurs destinataires peuvent toujours contester devant un tribunal. Resterait d'ailleurs à définir lequel. De toutes façons, les États n'accordent qu'une considération limitée aux sanctions prises par les fédérations internationales. Certains vont même jusqu'à affirmer qu'un licencié ne peut être sanctionné que par sa fédération nationale ; et lorsque celle-ci ne fait qu'appliquer une mesure décidée par une fédération internationale, ils estiment qu'elle n'a pas respecté les droits de la défense ; pourtant la fédération nationale n'aura fait que se conformer aux règles internationales qui s'imposent à elles.

On serait encore loin du compte sur ce terrain juridique s'il n'y avait de sérieux facteurs d'amélioration. D'un côté l'élaboration d'un système uniforme de répression du dopage met l'accent sur l'importance des garanties procédurales. D'un autre, un tribunal arbitral du sport a été créé, voici quelques années, par le CIO. Parce que ses juges sont indépendants, parce que sa procédure est équitable, parce que sa justice est consentie, donc reconnue, il propose, à bien des égards, un modèle dont il faut s'inspirer. Sans doute, sa compétence est différente ; mais justement elle s'étend à l'ensemble des litiges se rattachant au sport — moins d'ailleurs à ceux de l'institution qu'à ceux de la logistique sportive ; et elle offre aux partenaires du sport, et au monde sportif lui-même, l'image d'une justice sportive plus convaincante.

Il est temps de conclure. On comprendra que je le fasse sur des convictions fortes qui sont celles d'un militant sportif. Je crois que les structures internationales du sport sont à leur place parmi les ONG ; qu'il est bon qu'elle soient établies en un réseau privé, extérieur à la communauté internationale des États. Cet écart offre la marge d'autonomie utile, le cas échéant, pour une diplomatie — ou une pression — discrète et souple, donc efficace. À ceux que cela surprend ou choque, on répondra que c'est tout de même cet espace de liberté qui a permis au talent des hommes de remporter, à Séoul, une victoire éclatante sur les boycott d'avant ; occasion d'avancer «vers un monde meilleur et plus pacifique» — ce sont les termes mêmes de la charte olympique.

Je crois aussi que les structures internationales du sport doivent veiller à occuper totalement leur place ; sinon — et c'est l'enjeu des temps futurs — elles risqueront de la compromettre. Leur légitimité ne se dose pas, elle se gagne ou elle se perd. Elle est la clé de leur autonomie. Pour la mériter, il ne suffit pas de résister aux contraintes de la politique ou de la finance, et de vouloir récupérer les tentations qu'elles font venir d'ailleurs. Il est au moins aussi important de chasser «les démons de l'intérieur» pour tendre vers une légalité plus juste, qui s'impose plus sûrement parce qu'elle rendra plus légitime encore une institution qui se réclame de valeurs humanistes. C'est bien là, affaire d'identité.

NOTES ET RÉFÉRENCES

1. Ferrero G (1942) Pouvoir: les génies invisibles de la cité. Montréal: Valiquette

2. C'est sans doute cette préoccupation qui a fait que les organisations internationales du sport ont évité toute démarche en vue de se faire reconnaître le statut « consultatif » auprès des différentes instances interétatiques, alors que la plupart des ONG sont très friandes de telles consécrations qu'ils ne manquent pas lorsqu'elles les obtiennent, de présenter comme des « labels de crédibilité internationale ». Du même coup, les organisations internationales du sport sont fréquemment « oubliées » par les nomenclatures des ONG. Ainsi, un récent ouvrage collectif édité en France sous la direction de Bettati et Dupuy ne cite pas même les structures internationales du sport dans les développements très importants qu'il consacre au sujet des ONG (Les ONG et le droit international — Collection droit international — Economica 1986).

3. En France, dans un premier temps, le Conseil d'État avait paru laisser une certaine place à la règle sportive: il avait admis qu'elle porte atteinte au principe d'égalité, dès l'instant où ces atteintes n'excédaient pas, par leur importance, celles que pouvait justifier le fait d'assurer le perfectionnement des joueurs formés en France (CE 16 mars 1984, Broadis c/ Fédération française de basket-ball). Plus récemment, il a refusé à la Fédération tout pouvoir de distinguer entre joueurs titulaires de la nationalité française (CE 23 juin 1989).

4. La Cour de justice des communautés européennes estime que le droit communautaire n'a pas prise sur les dispositions purement sportives; toutefois, « en tant qu'opérateur économique » le sportif peut se voir appliquer les règles qui imposent la libre circulation dans la CEE, des ressortissants d'États membres (Cour de justice des Communautés européennes, 12 décembre 1974 — Walrave et Koch c/ Union cycliste internationale; 14 juillet 1976 — Dona c/ Mantero; voir Recueil 1974 p 1405 et 1976 p 1333

5. Cité par Samuel Pisar, Les Jeux olympiques et le droit. Message olympique 1985 n° 10 15-21

6. Coubertin P de (1907) Le rôle des fédérations. Revue Olympique, mars, p 231. In Müller N, Comité international olympique (eds) Pierre de Coubertin. Textes choisis. Tome III. La pratique sportive p 355

[. . .] Le Comité International représente au sein de l'olympisme rénové la permanence de l'institution; il est le gardien de sa charte fondamentale; il est aussi l'agent directeur de son perfectionnement continu. On peut discuter la valeur théorique de la constitution du Comité, mais la valeur pratique en est au-dessus de toute contestation. [. . .]

Coubertin P de (1920) A Messieurs les membres du comité International Olympique. Circulaire. Décembre p 1

Légitimité et légalité
des structures internationales en sport:
aspects et implications de l'arbitration
et des sanctions en sport international

Le contexte de la pratique sportive a considérablement changé avec l'augmentation de la visibilité du sport par le biais des médias, ainsi qu'avec l'augmentation des coûts et des enjeux financiers associés à l'organisation de compétitions internationales. Dans ce contexte, les parties concernées par des intérêts financiers substantiels sont particulièrement attentives et exigeantes à l'égard de leurs droits. Dans une première section, l'auteur traite des litiges en sport. Il constate que la frontière entre les règlements sportifs et les normes légales est de plus en plus difficile à tracer, et ce, essentiellement à cause des conséquences des décisions qui sont prises. En premier lieu, les décisions rendues par les instances arbitrales d'une fédération peuvent causer de lourds préjudices financiers, et il arrive alors que ces décisions soient renversées par des tribunaux ordinaires. Par ailleurs, certains types de litige ne peuvent être tranchés que si l'instance saisie du cas possède l'expérience et les connaissances des technicalités du sport en question, et ceci n'est pas nécessairement vrai de la part de juges locaux. Finalement, à cause de la visibilité médiatique de certains athlètes, les décisions rendues à leur encontre peuvent porter préjudice non seulement à leur réputation, mais aussi à leurs droits et libertés, comme dans le cas d'une exclusion à vie. De fait, la variété, la portée, la magnitude des intérêts impliqués est plus qu'impressionnante. En conclusion de cette section, l'auteur définit le litige en sport comme tout conflit surgissant des actes relevant du sport. Certains de ces conflits peuvent porter sur des questions de principe. D'autres peuvent concerner tout autant des problèmes comme celui de l'éligibilité de l'athlète, que des problèmes financiers, des conflits d'autorité et de compétence, des bris de contrat, des actes de violence, des problèmes de réputation et d'honneur, de droits et de libertés. Dans la seconde partie de son texte, l'auteur traite de la résolution des litiges, tant par les institutions sportives que par les tribunaux ordinaires. De fait, de plus en plus de conflits sont d'abord soumis à l'attention des instances sportives concernées pour être ensuite portés à l'attention des tribunaux. Les fédérations nationales et internationales ont toutes instauré des instances arbitrales qui ont l'autorité de trancher les litiges dans leur propre sport. Mais, dit l'auteur, la force exécutoire de décisions prises par ces instances varie d'un pays à l'autre, selon le système légal du pays. Sur la scène internationale, la situation est encore plus complexe, et la légitimité de l'autorité des instances fédérales n'y est pas toujours claire, d'un stricte point de vue légal. Cependant, ces instances tranchent des milliers de litiges de manière efficiente. Il reste certains litiges difficiles, où l'instance arbitrale, elle-même une émanation de la fédération, peut être considérée comme juge et partie. Habituellement, les tribunaux ordinaires interviennent dans trois types de situation: – dans les cas de violence jugée criminelle, ou d'accidents impliquant les spectateurs, comme en course automobile; – lorsqu'à la demande de l'une des parties, les tribunaux estiment avoir une juridiction claire sur les actes concernés; – lorsque les tribunaux sont sollicités en appel d'une décision prise par une instance sportive. Mais, souligne l'auteur, alors que les tribunaux offrent un recours à des juges légalement qualifiés, indépendants et intègres, ces juges n'ont pas nécessairement les connaissances requises à propos du sport concerné. L'auteur conclut que le tribunal arbitral du sport, instauré en 1983, et composé d'environ une soixantaine d'arbitres, constitue une solution plausible à un ensemble de problèmes. D'après l'auteur, ce tribunal, où les parties peuvent choisir leur arbitre, où la procédure est simple et peu onéreuse, permet de trancher rapidement les litiges liés à la pratique du sport ou aux intérêts financiers qui y sont associés.

Legitimacy and Legality of International Structures in Sport: Aspects and Implications of Arbitration and Sanctions in International Sport

François Carrard

In recent years, the world of sports, whether amateur or professional, has undergone dramatic changes which may be characterized as follows: – the *exposure of sports to the public* at *large* has substantially increased through the growing interest shown by all media, taking more particularly into account the coverage of more and more events by TV; – whether one likes it or not, *money* plays a key role in the development of all sports activities. This particularly spectacular development is best illustrated by quoting some figures relating to television rights fees paid by US TV networks for the Olympic Games. In 1964, the rights fees for the Winter Games in Innsbruck amounted to 597 000 $ US. For the Innsbruck Winter Games 1976—twelve years later—, ABC paid 9 000 000 $ US. In 1980, ABC paid 15 000 000 $ for the Lake Placid Games. In 1984, the fee for the Sarajevo Games amounted to 91 000 000 $ US and, for the 1988 Games in Calgary, ABC payed 309 000 000 $ US. Consequently, in the period of just twelve years, Winter Olympic rights have increased thirty-three times.

Apart of the growth of the fees collected from TV, the organizers of major events have also been able to rely more and more on sponsorships, the amount of which have become quite substantial. Individual athletes have also seen the amount of the contracts binding them to sponsors or organizers grow in dramatic proportions.

The natural and obvious consequence of such an evolution is that, among others, all parties concerned by sports activities, and more particularly those parties which have substantial financial interests involved, are more and more careful and demanding when their rights are concerned.

Sports Litigation

In earlier days, there was a feeling that the world of sports was one of fair play and loyalty. Whilst there is no doubt that a most sincere ambition of many

1890
1990

François Carrard, Directeur général du Comité international olympique, Lausanne, Suisse.

athletes and sports administrators still is to promote such virtues, the fact remains that the world of sports is neither better nor worst than the rest of the world. Therefore, litigations and disputes are not absent from sports. The evolution described above inevitably results into an increase of the number of disputes and conflicts relating directly or indirectly to sports activities. The following characteristics of such litigation may be emphasized:

The "border" between the provisions which can be characterized as mere sports rules and regulations and those which should be defined as legal norms is more and more difficult to trace. Such difficulty essentially arises in connection with the consequences attached to decisions taken. Let us quote an example which illustrates how such "border" can be crossed: if, in an ice hockey game, a referee negligently allows a team to play with one more player than provided in the rules and if such referee fails to impose a penalty on the "guilty" team, the only provisions involved or breached are obviously, at this stage, the rules of the game and not the law. At first sight, the same seems to apply if, during that period of time, the "guilty" team scores a goal. Let us now assume that both teams involved are professional teams playing the last playoff game in the finals of a major professional league and that the goal thus irregularly scored enables the "guilty" team to obtain victory and be declared champion, with very substantial financial benefits and rewards for the winning "guilty" team and its players. Let us also assume that the losing team files the necessary appeals and procedures within the competent institutions of the body governing professional ice hockey. Let us further assume that the said institutions finally reject the appeal of the losing team in a way which the said team considers to be either irregular or such that it causes to the said team a huge prejudice. Let us assume, at last, that the losing team decides to challenge in an ordinary court the so-called final decision of the body governing professional ice hockey and sues the said body for damages. In such an event, the conflict obviously began by being a mere problem of rules of the game; it further involved and "crossed the border" to become a true legal issue beyond the authority of the body governing the concerned sport. As one shall immediately understand, it may be very difficult to determine the exact moment and points at which the so-called "border" was crossed. The question which could arise in front of such an issue is: when do ordinary courts begin to have jurisdiction over such matters?

A recent authentic case illustrates such difficulties: at the 1990's world championship in Vienna, Austria, the International Ice Hockey Federation took some decisions relating to the fact that one of the players of the Federal German national team had irregularly taken part in some games because he had previously played with the Junior Polish national team in official competition, which was in breach of international regulations. The Federation decided in substance that the games won by the German team with that player were to be considered as lost, with the subsequent changes in the classification. The Germans immediately filed for and obtained from a civil judge in Vienna an injunction reversing the Federation's decision which was allegedly causing to the German team a prejudice which could not be remedied. One immediately understands that such a situation is highly unsatisfactory and most detrimental to the sport concerned and its spirit.

Certain types of disputes relating to sports activities can only be resolved if the body empowered to settle them has a broad experience in the sport concerned as well as a good understanding of its technicalities. Let us quote another example to illustrate this: it is well known that Formula 1 racing is a professional sport which involves highly advanced technology. One of the characteristics is that under the regulations governing such sport, the weight of the cars has always been defined according to strict norms so that, among others, the weight of the cars competing in a race should not be below a specific figure upon departure. An imaginative constructor invented a system under which its cars were complying with such regulations by using a tank filled with water allegedly necessary or useful for technical purposes; in fact, as soon as the race would begin, the drivers of such cars could empty such tank on the track, the result being that their cars would be lighter than those of their competitors during the race. Depending where such races take place, it may well be that the local judges are not the most qualified persons in order to decide on such matters.

With the increasing public exposure of sport in the media, a growing number of decisions taken against teams, clubs or athletes affect not only their own status or position within the sport considered, but also their economy (in a world of growing professionalism), and, as far as individual athletes are concerned, their reputation (as a consequence of spectacular public exposure) as well as possibly their freedom, liberties and human rights (in the event of life exclusion). Let us quote another example: an amateur weightlifter has been found "guilty" of doping. The competent national and international federations governing that sport decide that the said athlete shall be excluded for lifetime from all competitions. Apart from the doping offence, the record and background of the concerned athlete were excellent. Furthermore, the investigation had revealed that the athlete had not been acting wilfully but by negligence. The federations concerned consider that it is most important, for the future of sport, that a spectacular example be made through a harsh decision. On the other hand, the athlete's career—even as an amateur—is ruined for ever. Is it fair? Who shall decide?

The examples quoted above are only three of a huge list of actual disputes relating to sports activities. The variety, scope, magnitude and importance of the interests involved is more than impressive.

Sports litigation may be defined, in general words, as all kinds of disputes arising from all activities pertaining to sports. Some of these disputes may bear on questions of principle. Others may concern numerous different interests such as personal eligibility of athletes, financial problems, conflicts of authority and competence, performance or breach of contract, tortious interference, violence, reputation, honour, freedom and human rights, such list being certainly not exhaustive.

Resolving Disputes Relating to Sport

In the world of sport, apart from arbitration which will be examined below, the parties, clubs, teams, organizations, athletes, sponsors, employers, employees, agents, etc. concerned by sports litigation presently only have one alternative if they do not settle their disputes amicably: – the first option is to let their disputes be resolved by the institutions established by the relevant national or international federations or other bodies governing the sport concerned; – the second option is to submit such disputes to the ordinary courts, provided that such courts do have jurisdiction over such matters.

In fact, there are more and more examples of disputes in which the parties—or one of them—begin by submitting their dispute to the institutions established by the federations or other bodies governing the concerned sport, in compliance with the regulations of such institutions. If a party is not satisfied with the decision taken by such institutions, it then continues by taking the matter to the ordinary courts which, apart from their own possible direct authority, happen to sometimes act as some form of a court of appeal reviewing, according to its own legal norms, the decisions taken by the bodies governing the sport concerned.

Sports disputes resolved by sport institutions

Throughout the world, the vast majority—if not all—of the national and international federations or other organizations governing sports have established specific institutions such as institutional arbitral tribunals, commissions, commissioners, panels and other bodies empowered with the authority to resolve disputes relating to the sports which they govern. The authority and legal status of these numerous institutions is sometimes difficult to determine. As far as national sports organizations or federations are concerned, their status very much depends upon the legal system of the countries in which such institutions are established and exercise their activities. In many countries, there are laws which grant specific powers and authorities to such national organizations or federations. In other countries, such organizations are totally independent from the governments and have received no delegation of any competence from the public authorities. Therefore, the enforceability of decisions taken by such institutions may well vary from country to country.

On the international scene, the situation is even more complex and delicate. In most cases, the international federations or organizations governing major sports on an international level are non-governmental international organizations. The legitimacy of their authority, attributions and powers is not always clear, from a mere legal standpoint. Thus, the question of the enforceability of the decisions taken by such institutions and organizations is delicate and complex.

The fact remains that the very many institutions established by national and international sports federations and organizations do actually settle thousands and thousands—if not more—conflicts and disputes relating to sports activities in the world. In most of the cases, the decisions taken by such institutions are adequate. They are usually taken within the framework of procedures which may be questionable from a formal legal procedural standpoint but which usually have the great advantage of being quick and cheap. The persons empowered with such authority are, in most cases, rather familiar with the sports concerned, their practice and regulations. On the whole, this system works rather efficiently.

There remains, however, certain disputes—usually not minor ones —which cannot be settled satisfactorily by the institutions established by the national or international sports federations or organizations. In such cases, the weaknesses of the system can be summed up as follows:

Nearly all national or international sports organizations or federations want the decisions of the institutions which they have established for the purpose of resolving disputes to be final and binding. The constitutions, articles and by-laws of nearly all national or international sports federations or organizations include provisions specifically setting forth that all decisions taken by them are "final", "binding", "without appeal", etc. In fact, in many countries, such clauses are in conflict with constitutional or other legal rights granting to all parties concerned specific guarantees such as the right to appeal to ordinary courts. Thus, there are many instances in which the authority of the decisions taken by institutions established by national or international sports federations or organizations may be challenged in courts.

One of the arguments which may be successfully invoked is that the institutions established within sports federations or organizations are not independent from the said organizations. Quite often, the disputes submitted to such institutions concern, directly or indirectly, the sports organizations themselves. Thus, such organizations appear to be to a certain degree simultaneously "parties" and "judges". Whilst the issue of jurisdiction established by sports organizations is already delicate on a national level, it becomes even more complex, when international organizations are involved. The existing uncertainties as to the legal status and authority of some international sports organizations raise a number of difficult legal questions when it comes, among others, to the enforceability of their decisions. One answer to such a problem is to offer, to the world of sports, an arbitration institution which is independent, qualified, and legally organized in such a way that its decisions may be reasonably considered as final and enforceable. As will be seen below, the Court of Arbitration for Sport provides a reasonably adequate answer.

The intervention of ordinary courts in the world of sports activities

The first type of situation is rather exceptional—or at least should be very exceptional: it involves the intervention of public criminal or penal courts. There may well be, in sports activities, acts which may be characterized as penal or criminal ones. Let us quote two examples: violence acts in certain sports by certain athletes are sometimes characterized as falling under penal or criminal laws. In such cases, the public authorities such as prosecutors may well take action, *ex officio* or upon application from another party, resulting iato penal judgements against athletes or other participants. Another example is to be found when accidents take place in motor car or motor cycle racing, for instance when spectators are hurt. In such a case, the persons involved are not only the drivers or racers but also the organizers or officers of organizations governing the sports. Normally, nothing can be done which could prevent the competent public authorities of a country from taking legal action of that kind if they so decide.

Another situation in which ordinary courts may take action is when, usually upon application from a party having an interest, they find they have direct jurisdiction over a specific matter relating to the sports activities concerned. The ordinary courts then tend to consider that the issues at hand involve norms of civil law more than rules or regulations governing the sports concerned.

A third situation occurs when ordinary courts act as some form of "courts of appeal". A party dissatisfied with the decision rendered by a sports organization applies to an ordinary court in order to have such decision reversed. Many systems of law know provisions granting specific rights to that effect.

Whilst the ordinary courts normally offer the best standard and degree of integrity, independence and legal qualification, the fact remains that in many situations involving sports activities, one may question whether ordinary courts are indeed the most appropriate forum for resolving specific disputes. For instance, is it really appropriate that a civil judge in Vienna decides whether the German national ice hockey team has won or lost a couple of games in a world championship? Using another example, was it normal that a Swiss civil judge should decide what could be the flag of the Chinese Taipei delegation at the Winter Olympic Games of Lake Placid? In spite of all their qualifications and diligence, do such magistrats really have the experience and knowledge of the very specific issues at hand in order to resolve them?

In such instances, it may be extremely important for the parties concerned to have the opportunity to select their judges and to ensure that such judges have the necessary knowledge and experience relating to the world of sports. There is no such choice available when applying to ordinary courts. One solution to such a problem lies in arbitration, provided that such arbitration is organized in such a way as to serve the cause and world of sports. Such an answer is offered by the Court of Arbitration for Sport.

The Court of Arbitration for Sport

The situation described above and the numerous problems relating to it called for creative and imaginative action. The idea of establishing a new arbitration institution specialized in disputes relating to sports activities came from Juan Antonio Samaranch, the current President of the International Olympic

Committee. Thus, the Court of Arbitration for Sport was established in the spring of 1983[1]. The Court of Arbitration for Sport (CAS) is not but one more institution for arbitration. It has been established in order to fill a specific gap in the world of sports, by providing cheap, quick and adequate solutions to disputes through the arbitration of learned and skilled arbitrators having broad experience in the fields of law, arbitration and sports. The CAS has its seat in Lausanne, Switzerland. Its present Executive President is Keba Mbaye, Vice President of the International Court of Justice.

The CAS is composed of a list of approximately sixty arbitrators, most of them well-known lawyers who also have a good knowledge of sports. Any individual or legal entity may submit a case to the CAS. CAS arbitration may take place in any dispute arising from all activities pertaining to sport, whether amateur or professional. The statutes and regulations of the CAS provide procedural rules which are essentially precise and flexible enough so that decisions may be taken and enforced quickly and at low cost. The disputes involved may be national or international. Apart from arbitral awards, the CAS is also entitled to issue advisory opinions on legal matters relating to all activities pertaining to sports.

The administration of the CAS is ensured by its Secretary General under the direction of the Executive President. Its administrative offices are in Lausanne where the CAS also offers adequate facilities for holding hearings. Although its operational costs are presently covered by the International Olympic Committee, which thus wants to contribute to the settlement of sports disputes within the sports world itself, the International Olympic Committee exercises no influence of any kind over the members of the CAS who are entirely independent. The ties between the International Olympic Committee and the CAS are of a merely administrative nature. The awards rendered by the CAS may be characterized as similar to awards rendered by other independent arbitral tribunals. The parties may select their arbitrators. The procedure is simple enough so that it may be adjusted for each particular case. The costs are very low. The deadlines are short.

It will be the purpose of another speaker to describe how the CAS operates. Let it suffice to state that the CAS may be defined as a precious institution for the rapid resolution of all disputes relating to the practice of sports and all economic or financial activities linked to it.

NOTE

1. See Court of Arbitration for Sport/Tribunal arbitral du sport (1987). Practical Guide of the Court of Arbitration for Sport (CAS). How to resolve disputes arising from sports activities. Lausanne, Tribunal Arbitral du sport.

Issues Related to Racial Segregation in International Sport

Problématique de la ségrégation raciale dans le sport international

L'universalisme olympique
et la question de l'apartheid

En guise d'introduction, l'auteur exprime son étonnement devant le temps considérable qui s'est écoulé avant que le Mouvement olympique ne prenne officiellement position contre le racisme en général et l'Apartheid Sud-africain en particulier. Il avance qu'on ne saurait guère expliquer ce fait sans admettre la co-existence d'une forme de pensée à la fois internationaliste et raciste, chez ceux qui ont guidé le Mouvement olympique à ses origines. Il n'y a pas à se surprendre, selon l'auteur, que le sens de la supériorité raciale qui impreignait les classes instruites européenne et américaine, ait déteint sur Pierre de Coubertin et dans la mise en pratique de l'Olympisme. La première partie de la présentation, porte sur les faits et les influences historiques qui à l'époque ont rendu un alliage d'internationalisme et de racisme possible. Dans la seconde partie, l'auteur fait allusion aux facteurs historiques et aux personnes qui auraient contribué au maintien d'attitudes racistes au sein du Mouvement olympique, au cours des trois premiers quarts de siècle de son existence, cette période s'achevant selon lui avec la fin de la présidence d'Avery Brundage. Au sujet de son premier thème, l'auteur fait une analyse commentée des vues de Coubertin sur les relations raciales et le colonialisme. Il souligne, compte tenu du contexte des attitudes raciales qui prévalaient en Europe à l'époque, que certains des écrits de Coubertin n'étaient pas exempts de paternalisme racial, plus spécialement en ce qui a trait au continent africain, et nonobstant le fait que son attitude devenait progressivement plus libérale à l'égard des colonisés et des colonisateurs. L'auteur avance que le cosmopolitisme racial de type anglo-saxon qui prenait naissance au tournant du siècle allait graduellement faire contre-poids au racisme plus manifeste qui avait eu cours auparavant. Le rêve d'une grande famille mondiale n'en demeurait pas moins une abstraction. Par ailleurs, le Mouvement olympique moderne, même s'il conservait à son origine une vision implicitement hiérarchique de l'humanité, avait suffisamment de substance et d'attrait pour servir de nouveau projet internationaliste. Dans l'imagination euro-américaine, le nouvel âge d'une unité psychique de l'humanité se faisait jour. Ce type d'idéal, de l'avis de l'auteur, s'accommodait cependant fort bien de la croyance par laquelle toutes les races n'avaient pas la même aptitude à l'atteindre. Il rappelle à titre d'exemple les exhibitions grotesques d'unité et de diversité qui eurent cours sous formes de journées anthropologiques aux Jeux olympiques associés à l'Exposition de St-Louis, en 1904, et qui reflétaient la vieille habitude européenne de classifier les peuples, leurs qualités ou leurs aptitudes en termes de hiérarchie raciale. L'auteur explique par la suite que l'intérêt marqué des allemands à l'égard du Mouvement olympique s'explique en fonction d'une mémoire historique, d'une nostalgie et d'un rêve ancien d'hégémonie. À ce sujet, l'expérience vécue au moment des Jeux olympiques de 1936 est vue par l'auteur comme un exemple du fait que l'idéologie internationaliste olympique s'était facilement accommodée de motifs et de visées carrément nationalistes et racistes. Un parallèle est fait avec le mouvement du Scoutisme international de Baden-Powell qui de l'avis de l'auteur a conservé pendant de nombreuses décades des facettes impérialistes et ségrégatrices. Au chapitre des événements et des personnes qui à son avis ont contribué au maintien d'attitudes réputées racistes au sein du Mouvement olympique, l'auteur énumère : le système de cooptation des membres du CIO ; la présence au CIO d'une élite franco-allemande et son influence, surtout au cours des années 1920 et 1930 ; la culmination de la discrimination et du racisme aux Jeux Nazis de 1936 ; la longue amitié entre Coubertin et Diem, et le fait que ces derniers aient été associés à l'establishment nazi dans l'organisation et le déroulement des Jeux de 1936 ; enfin, le conservatisme et la tolérance que l'auteur impute à Avery Brundage ; sont vus par lui comme indicateurs d'attitudes tacitement raciales chez des personnes pourtant chargées de l'orientation d'un mouvement présumément pluri ou multi-racial. En guise de conclusion, l'auteur montre que la montée des mouvements internationalistes, vers la fin du XIXe siècle, n'était pas le fruit de politiques impérialistes, mais bien et plutôt des extensions de nationalismes qui se donnaient l'allure de cosmopolitisme. Ancré dans les vieilles mythologies racistes européennes, le nouveau cosmopolitisme ne pouvait guère avoir un agenda multi-racial chargé. À cet effet, l'auteur souligne l'utilité des méthodes d'analyses comparatives qui permettent de mettre en lumière, au plan historique, les faits aussi bien que les paramètres du possible à une période donnée. L'auteur cite des paroles récentes du Président Samaranch comme faisant augure d'un meilleur avenir multi-racial pour le Mouvement olympique.

Olympic Universalism and the Apartheid Issue

John M. Hoberman

The purpose of this paper is to propose an approach to the study of a neglected historical problem: Why did it take the multiracial Olympic Movement so long to embrace the cause of anti-racialism in general, and the international campaign against South African apartheid in particular? This question is related in turn to Guttmann's observation that: "Of all the family of man, the last major group to be integrated into the Olympic Movement were the black peoples of Africa[1]". An answer to this question must account for the fact that racialistic thinking played an important role in the modern Olympic Movement for many years after its founding in the 1890s. I will argue, in fact, that the racialistic phase of the Olympic Movement did not actually conclude until the retirement of Avery Brundage from the presidency of the IOC in 1972.

The historical "problem", which was referred to, concerns the coexistence —indeed, the integration—of internationalist doctrine and racialistic thinking. While this combination appears paradoxical to us, it appears that it did not to Pierre de Coubertin, his European and American colleagues and the many others who guided and influenced the Olympic Movement during its early period of development. Given the official status of racial egalitarianism in the postwar world, as exemplified by the UNESCO "Statement on Race" issued in 1950[2] and by other United Nations documents, it is difficult for us to grasp in its full sense the effortless sense of racial superiority which came naturally to most Europeans and Americans, prominently including the educated classes, at the turn of the century. This is the cultural world in which the Olympic Movement was formed, and it is not surprising that its racial attitudes found their way into the thinking of Coubertin and of other historical actors who formulated the theory and practice of Olympism during its early years. More interesting than this unproblematic historical fact are the two questions this paper will attempt to address. First, which historical factors made a synthesis of internationalism and racialism possible then? Here it is useful to adopt the comparative approach to internationalist movements routinely neglected by olympic historiography. Second, which historical factors and

1890
1990

John M. Hoberman, Department of Germanic Languages, University of Texas at Austin, Austin, Texas, USA.

personalities preserved the influence of *fin de siècle* racial thinking within the IOC for three-quarters of a century? Of special interest here are links between right-wing circles in France and Germany during the 1920s and 1930s and the long career of the philogermanic Avery Brundage. As we shall see, it is the persistence of a certain racialistic tradition within the Olympic Movement which best accounts for the IOC recalcitrance toward Black African appeals about apartheid which lasted well into the 1960s.

A full-scale analysis of *fin de siècle* European racial doctrines is beyond the scope of this paper. For our purposes, it is nonetheless appropriate to examine Coubertin's views on race relations and colonialism in the larger context of European racial attitudes. Coubertin's view of colonialism in Africa combined the conventional racial paternalism of his day with a more progressive emphasis on developmental possibilities[3]. "Colonies", he wrote in 1902, "are like children: it is relatively easy to bring them into the world; the difficult thing is to raise them properly. They do not grow up by themselves, but need to be taken care of, coddled, and pampered by the mother country; they need constant attention to incubate them, to understand their needs, to foresee their disappointments, to calm their fears[4]." When King Leopold of Belgium asked Coubertin to draw up plans for a "colonial preparatory school", he was only too happy to oblige, although this project was never actually realized[5].

In 1912 Coubertin published his advice to colonial regimes on how they could best make sport an instrument of administration. It is a great mistake, he said, to assume that a victory achieved by a "dominated" race over the dominating one constitutes a dangerous temptation to rebellion. On the contrary, he argues, the example of British India shows that such incidents actually legitimize colonial rule in the eyes of the "winners". Political common sense, he adds, will rule out attempts to spread jiu-jitsu in the Far East or to promote native gymnastics associations with militaristic overtones[6]. In summary, Coubertin's managerial intentions vis-à-vis colonized peoples were at the time rather evident. It is therefore interesting that in his *Mémoires olympiques* (1931) Coubertin appeared to adopt a more liberationist attitude toward colonizers and colonized. He blamed the failure of his "African Games," planned for 1925 and then 1929, on "the struggle of the colonial mind against movement in the direction of emancipating the natives[7]". Yet only a few pages prior to this progressive remark, Coubertin had quoted without embarrassment what appear to be his own words spoken at the 21st IOC session held at Rome in 1923. He spoke of bringing sport to "a retarded continent [*un continent retardataire*], to populations still deprived of basic culture [*culture élémentaire*]" and invoked the stereotype of the "lazy" African who requires reform[8]. Yet even today we may note how difficult it can be to advance beyond a colonialist vocabulary. For example, when Pope John Paul II visited Zaire in May 1980, he, too, ascribed to Africa an underdeveloped "personality and culture[9]", a phrasing which reminds us that Western international institutions in general have retained more 19th-century mental habits than one tends to admit. This bifurcated attitude toward indigenous Africans, improving and infantilizing them simultaneously, exemplifies the conflicted—almost schizoid—racial cosmopolitanism of the turn-of-the-century period during which the Olympic Movement and analogous internationalist projects came into being. This racial cosmopolitanism, of which Joseph Conrad's novel *Heart of Darkness* (1899) remains a much-celebrated cultural monument in the Anglo-American world, stood in stark contrast to the straightforward racist imperialism against which he and others protested at this time. (The term "humanitarian imperialism[10]" makes a useful distinction between Conrad's outlook and that of more rapacious types.) Yet here, too, the schizoid attitude toward African humanity is evident[11]. For Conrad's inspired attempt to integrate the inhabitants of the Belgian Congo into the human family clearly failed by modern standards; his natives remained insubstantial specimens rather than fully human beings, and his own thinking advanced no farther than a "suspicion of their not being inhuman[12]". The family of man remained, then, an inspiring abstraction. At the same time, however, the European mind endowed the notion of a family of man—this implicitly hierarchical version of humanity—with enough substance to serve as a charismatic vehicle for internationalist projects like the modern Olympic Movement.

The enlightened Euro-American racial imagination of this period was thus able to promulgate an ideal of "the psychical unity of mankind[13]", as some anthropologists called it, while preserving traditional racial distinctions and rankings and pursuing researches meant to document a wide range of racial differences. This purported "psychic unity" referred to a capacity to exercise reason presumably shared by all races, but in the last analysis this did not mean assigning those races equal status. The evolutionary model of human development which posited this "psychic unity" easily accommodated the contemporary anthropological view that some races had evolved farther than others. Thus the American anthropologist Brinton could acclaim the discovery of the "psychical unity of man, the parallelism of his development everywhere and in all time", while declaring at the same time that "I must still deny that all races are equally endowed [...] None, I maintain, can escape the mental correlations of its physical structure[14]." In *The Descent of Man* (1871), Darwin himself had resolved the problem of racial differences in an equally ambivalent fashion. One "can hardly fail to be deeply impressed", he wrote, "with the close similarity between the men of all races in tastes, dispositions and habits", and he credits the various races with "similar inventive or mental powers". Yet Darwin was less impressed by these apparent similarities than by the racial differences he described at greater length and in some detail[15].

This ostensibly paradoxical combination of human unity and diversity could be displayed in a conspicuous public forum which preceded—and on three occasions[16] actually annexed—the early modern Olympic Games, namely the universal expositions which were held in France and the United States during the second half of the nineteenth century. Few cultural productions of that period are more vulnerable to modern and critical eyes than these anthropological shows, which featured what MacAloon has called "this cross-cultural voyeurism in the name of science and the colonial march of Western civilization[17]". Writing of the colonial exhibits at the 1889 Paris exposition, Ory has argued that it was precisely French confidence in their domination of colonial peoples which permitted colonialist discourse at the *exposition coloniale* to take the form of racial paternalism rather than downright hostile assessments of these lower races. The racism which framed these exhibits, he says, requires nothing less than a "typology of condescension[18]".

The most interesting (and grotesque) of these exhibitions from the standpoint of olympic history were the so-called "Anthropological Days" at the 1904 Games, which were attached to the Louisiana Purchase Exposition held at St. Louis. In these mock competitions Blacks, Chinese, Philipinos, Turks, Mexican *mestizos*, Eskimos and Indians "competed among themselves in track-and-field events and then in their native sports[19]". The Hungarian member of the IOC, Ferenc Kémény, reported the obscene spectacle to Coubertin[20], whose reaction to this overtly racist entertainment took the form of an ironic detachment from American vulgarity[21]. In a word, Coubertin's response must be distinguished from the more visceral disgust of a Joseph Conrad. Yet one should also note that this assessment of the interracial (but wholly non-white) athletic spectacle at St. Louis was not shared by the Chief of the Department of Anthropology of the Exposition. In fact, Professor McGee, president of the American Anthropological Association, offered an impeccably Coubertinian rationale for the anthropological dimension of the fair: "for it is the lesson of experience that personal contact is the best solvent of enmity and distrust between persons and peoples". It is the anthropological exhibits alone, he argued, which provided "the moral motive" of the entire Exposition. It is therefore not surprising that Professor McGee referred approvingly to "the Inter-Racial Athletic Contest of August 12", during which an elderly Patagonian chief had shown himself to be "so well preserved that he captured the prize for accurate ball-throwing[22]". The impact of these events on the popular imagination can well be imagined. As Guttmann has noted: "Watching pygmies engaged in a mud-fight, American, British, French, and German spectators might well have felt that their nations were morally right to bring modern sports (as well as the rest of civilization) to the Philippines, to East Africa, to Indo-China, and to the islands of the Pacific[23]." I would suggest, in addition, that this forcing or inducing of nonwhites to engage in Anglo-American athletic exercises can be compared to the practice of certain European visitors to Africa, who turned Africans' unfamiliarity with Western technology into occasions for practical jokes[24].

On a level distinct from that of "popular ethnography[25]", however, this anthropological exhibition provided opportunities for the scientist to draw ostensibly nonracialistic conclusions about purported human differences. Indeed, it was professor McGee who facilitated the psychophysiological researches at the Exposition of Robert S. Woodworth, a professor of psychology at Columbia University, whose report was published in the journal *Science* in 1910. Having performed cross-racial studies of vision, hearing, smell, touch, pain thresholds, and mental skills, Woodworth advised his readers in no uncertain terms that the conventional assumptions about racial differences were both spurious and antiscientific. What is more, Woodworth understood that discrediting these racialistic misconceptions meant confronting coexisting myths of nonwhite inferiority and superiority which were, in fact, wholly compatible within the framework of Eurocentric racial thinking. Regarding the human senses, he said: "The point of special interest here is whether the statements of many travellers, ascribing to the 'savage' extraordinary powers of vision, hearing and smell, can be substantiated by exact tests. The common opinion, based on such reports, is, or has been, that savages are gifted with sensory powers quite beyond anything of which the European is capable [...]". From a European perspective, however, these were ambiguous "gifts"; for as Woodworth pointed out, Herbert Spencer (among others) had argued that the sensual superiority of the "savage" led directly to intellectual inferiority[26].

It is a short step from this sort of racial physiology to analogous investigations of athletic aptitudes. But while correlating specific athletic abilities with certain racial types has become today a persistent (if also poorly defined) public issue, it does not appear to have been of concern to Coubertin or his Olympic colleagues. In a way this lack of interest in racial differences is surprising; for as the "Anthropological Days" of the St. Louis Exposition had so clearly demonstrated, athletic competition and the exploration of racial differences, real or imagined, were wholly compatible activities. What is more, nineteenth-century European anthropology offered theories of racial differentiation which postulated differences more profound than the merely external features—skin color, hair texture, and bodily dimensions—which had been so evident to early European visitors to Africa, Australia, and other remote places. The more "scientific" racial physiologies distinguished between races—and primarily between Negroes and Caucasians—in terms of reactions to drugs, sensitivity to pain, reaction time, glandular chemistry, acuteness of the senses, muscle strength and composition, physical dexterity, brain size and structure, perceived body odor, and even the structure and functioning of the nervous system. Although several of these variables are clearly related to athletic potential, racial sportive aptitude remained an entirely peripheral issue for many years. This lack of serious interest in the athletic potential of nonwhites may have been one result of the physical assessments of nonwhites, made by European anthropologists, which suggested their physical inferiority to Caucasians[27].

In any event, black Africans did not even enter Olympic competition until 1952[28], suggesting that Coubertin's interest in Black African participation in the Olympic Movement, whatever its intensity, did not become a priority for the IOC leadership which followed him. This lack of interest in Africa raises in turn the fundamental question of why Europeans long accustomed to ranking the peoples of the earth in terms of a racial hierarchy (which always assigned black Africans the lowest ranking) conceived of and campaigned for an ostensibly multiracial sport movement at all. To a considerable degree, this initiative was a natural extension of the imperial impulse. Such a conflation of athletics and Empire was evident, for example, in the proposal for a Pan-Britannic Festival which received considerable attention during the 1890s[29]; and it is worth noting that the originator of this failed idea referred disparagingly even to the very limited race-mixing which occurred at the 1896 Athens Games, which amounted to a virtual Pan-European Festival. In a similar fashion, German interest in the Olympic Movement—which today probably exceeds that of any other single nation—must be understood in relation to Germany's complex memories of and nostalgia for the Holy Roman Empire [*das römische Reich der deutschen Nation*] and the dream of German hegemony over the civilized world. In this respect the 1936 Berlin Olympic Games represented, if not a Pan-Teutonic Festival, then a re-enactment of the centuries-old fantasy that Germans would someday be "the natural lords of the universe (*weltherrschendes Volk*)[30]". The fact that the Nazi spectacle received the enthusiastic support of a Euro-American elite within the IOC is only one example of how nationalistic motives could accommodate and absorb an essentially theatrical olympic internationalism for which race relations was a public relations problem rather than a moral issue.

A comparative approach to the internationalist movements which came into being around the turn of the century can help to explain why the men who initiated and led them for decades did not specifically promote multiracialism for many years after their founding. The Boy Scout movement of Lord Baden-Powell (1857-1941), started officially in 1907, is comparable to the Olympic Movement in many important respects. Both movements proclaimed their universal, apolitical, nonracial and nonmilitary nature; both claimed to be classless movements but were in fact intended as strategies to deal with domestic social instability in general and the class issue in particular; both claimed to be "educational" enterprises; both incorporated aspects of a European chivalric ethos which provided a male character ideal; both have cultivated "creation myths" about themselves and hagiographical institutional memories of their founders; and both mobilized young people in ways many societies have found useful enough to adapt for social or political purposes[31]. It is hardly necessary to point out that both movements have exercised an enormous and virtually global appeal for almost a century. Less noted, perhaps, is that both of these ostensibly nonracial movements remained racially segregated for decades. In both cases, the views of the founders shaped policy for years to come. If Coubertin may be described as an enlightened colonialist, Baden-Powell can be viewed as an imperialist and, at least during his colonial career, an out-and-out racist who had served the British Empire in South Africa and India. "Given Scouting's ostensible commitment to equality, brother-hood, and other respectable pieties concerning the oneness of mankind", one historian has written, "it is at first glance astonishing to find Baden-Powell's thought laced with a full range of racial stereotypes. Starting with blacks and moving without self-consciousness through diverse racial and ethnic groups, Baden-Powell exhibits a virtuosity of contempt for other breeds that is rather startling in its purity". In 1936 Baden-Powell stated in private correspondence that Scouting was to be "open to all, irrespective of class, colour, creed or country". But long before the Olympic Movement agonized over the eligibility of white-ruled

South Africa, Baden-Powell had given in to political pressures and opted for apartheid within the South African scouting movement[32], even if he appears to have suffered conscience pangs at having done so[33]. At the same time, and expressing himself in language almost identical to that of Coubertin, he was convinced that this European import would benefit "the uncultured races who are only now emerging from primitive savagery into civilization". And, like Coubertin, Baden-Powell congratulated himself on having taken a progressive stand on behalf of the rights of "the Non-Europeans[34]". This self-exculpating rhetorical strategy, and the canny determination of Coubertin and Baden-Powell not to commit racially discriminatory language to paper, must be regarded as important elements of the common strategy which effectively ruled out genuine multiracialism within these international organizations[35].

Yet even if one concedes the formative influence of colonialist thinking on the Olympic Movement, this factor alone cannot account for the support enjoyed by the South African regime within the IOC during most of the 20th century; nor can it explain how Avery Brundage could have occupied the presidency of the IOC until 1972. The IOC's persistent loyalty to the Pretoria regime, and the concomitant toleration of its racial policies, requires a description of a network of important relationships which extends from Coubertin to Avery Brundage. The (necessarily brief) historical analysis which follows suggests how racialistic thinking was able to persist within the Olympic Movement over a long period of time. The ideological continuity within the IOC was related, of course, to its self-recruiting procedure as well as to who joined the movement and the motives which drew them to Coubertin's brand of internationalism in the first place. In 1908 European nobility composed 68% of the IOC membership, a figure which had declined to 41% by 1924[36]. It is a truism to suggest that this constituency did not put multiracialism on its olympic agenda. More interesting, however, than the ideological constraints imposed by this elite is the Franco-German relationship within the Olympic Movement which extended four decades, from Dr. Willibald Gebhardt's acceptance as a "provisional" IOC member in March 1896 to the Berlin Olympiad celebrated in 1936 and even beyond. Despite the frictions, rooted in nationalism, which made the early years of this relationship a difficult one[37], it eventually flourished and reached its culmination in the Berlin Games of 1936, which have been widely misunderstood as an isolated, and perhaps lamentable, lapse on the part of the Olympic Movement as a whole. This interpretation of the Berlin Games overlooks the fact that Coubertin's potent combination of sport, international competition, pagan ritual, and body cultism had long appealed to sports-minded German males for whom *völkisch* nationalism and a right-wing military outlook were wholly compatible with devoted service both to the Olympic Movement and to the Nazi regime. The Olympic career of Carl Diem, which stretched a half-century from the 1912 Stockholm Games to his death in 1962, is a case in point. Diem's posturings as a German humanist and olympic internationalist went hand-in-hand with a longing for the German *imperium* promised by Hitler, including an Olympic Movement to be administered by the Nazis[38]. A devoted disciple of Coubertin, Diem served the Nazi regime from the beginning to the end of the Third Reich. Diem's friend Walter von Reichenau had traveled with him to the United States in 1913 to study American sport. As one of Hitler's most powerful generals, and renowned for his sporting prowess, von Reichenau became an IOC member in 1938. As Field-Marshall and commander-in-chief of the German Sixth Army "during the Russian campaign of 1941 he was to issue a notorious order of the day condoning a stupendous massacre of Jews which the SS conducted at Kiev[39]". It is quite possible that his death in 1942 saved the IOC from the disgrace of seeing one of its members stand trial at Nuremberg. Karl Ritter von Halt, a member of the IOC from 1929 to 1964, was Hitler's last *Reichssportführer* and a member of the SA[40]. When the Winter Olympic Games were held in Oslo in 1952, the Norwegians would not even let him into the country.

These case histories point to the larger historical context in which the
Olympic Movement remained an expression of that "European idea" which, from
1940 to 1945, took the form of a Nazi "New Order" in Europe. Like analogous
servants of the Nazi empire assigned to literature or music, Carl Diem labored to
bring about "the reorientation of European sport[41]" within the new *imperium*.
After 1945 he continued his mission within the larger context of an Olympic
Movement which was now beyond Hitler's control. Despite the pioneering
research[42] of the West German historian Hans Joachim Teichler, which is largely
unknown outside of Germany, the Franco-German axis which controlled the
Olympic Movement during much of the 1930s remains poorly understood. At the
center of this relationship was Coubertin himself, courted and deceived by German
operatives, including Carl Diem, yet genuinely drawn to his own idea of the new
Germany and the spectacle of the Berlin Olympiad. It was Hitler's Foreign Office
which proposed Coubertin for the Nobel Peace Prize, Hitler's government which
gave him 10 000 Reichsmarks, and Hitler himself who received Coubertin's letter of
thanks[43]. But the Berlin Olympic Games must be understood as only the most
dramatic episode within a larger political scheme pursued throughout the 1930s by
Nazi agents like Otto Abetz, later a German ambassador to occupied France, in
partnership with French fascists and other right-wing elements which looked
forward to a New Order in Europe. For this Franco-German network, the Berlin
Olympiad was both the political and aesthetic fulfillment of an inchoate Fascist
International and the hottest VIP ticket in Europe. By the time of his death in 1937,
Coubertin had attained iconic status for the *Comité France-Allemagne*, a principal
front group managed by Abetz[44]. A year later, the Comité and its German
counterpart dedicated a bust of Coubertin at a "cultural congress" held at Baden-
Baden[45]. This ceremony capped a decade of efforts by Otto Abetz and others to
promote their own brand of "Franco-German reconciliation" in the interests of
German foreign policy. This "fraternal" campaign sponsored bilateral student
festivals and reunions of war veterans [*anciens combattants*]. Dedication to sport
and "a cult of outdoorsy muscularity[46]" became defining characteristics of this
movement and of French fascism itself. What is more, this sportive style had
attracted an international caste of adherents to the Olympic Movement since the
turn of the century. Although he did intuit the charismatic potential of high-
performance sport, Coubertin could not foresee the consequences of this auto-
recruitment, including the cooptation of the Olympic Movement by fellow-tra-
vellers like Carl Diem, his own public (and publicized) endorsement of the "Nazi
Olympics", and the recruitment of a germanophilic American named Avery
Brundage—friend of Carl Diem and Karl Ritter von Halt—into the Nazi propaganda
apparatus[47]. The Berlin Olympiad demonstrated that four decades of recruitment
into the Olympic Movement had preserved Eurocentric thinking about race within
the IOC. In this respect the multiracial dimension of the Berlin Games, featuring
the victories of Jesse Owens, was and remains profoundly misleading. No
assessment of the Olympic Movement during the 1930s can overlook the
enthusiastic reception accorded to Olympism by internationalists like Carl Diem,
Otto Abetz, and Avery Brundage, all of whom existed on comfortable terms with
the Nazi movement. What is more, any assessment of the racial policies of the
Olympic Movement after the Second World War must take into account the
prehistory of Avery Brundage's twenty-year presidency of the IOC (1952-1972) and
the re-emergence of his friend Carl Diem who co-founded the International
Olympic Academy in Greece, in 1961. The leadership roles of such people within
the Olympic Movement after 1945 demonstrates that the affinity group of insiders
which planned and defended the Berlin Games remained intact—and was accepted
by other olympic insiders—for many years after the event. The mere fact that Nazi
associations were not viewed as disqualifying after 1945 within the closed circle of
the IOC speaks volumes about the tacit racial views of people charged with
administering this multiracial movement. And it was the essentially colonialist

racial attitudes of this affinity group which preserved South African membership in the Olympic movement until 1970.

The purpose of this narrative has been to illuminate the historical origins of racial conservatism within the IOC. But it is also appropriate to ask whether the performance of the Olympic Movement in this regard has been typical or atypical of Western internationalist movements in general, and here is where a comparative methodology can help us understand the Olympic Movement better than it has been understood before. As has been observed, the Olympic and Scouting movements dealt with the race issue in strikingly similar ways; the same observation applies to relations with Nazi Germany, although Baden-Powell seems to have entertained suspicions about Hitler in a way Coubertin did not appear to but might have, had he lived longer[48]. Even the Esperanto movement, which is of European but noncolonialist origin, made similar adjustments to accommodate its German membership and the political outlook of the Nazi state. The difference is that this policy of appeasement encountered significant resistance within the Esperanto movement itself, deriving from a supranationalist faction which has never had an olympic counterpart[49]. Yet today, unlike the Olympic Movement, the Esperanto movement has only a handful of registered members in Black Africa[50]. It was the antiracialism and (anticapitalist) anticolonialism of the socialist Second International (1889-1914) which represented the real alternative to colonialist internationalism, and we should recall the socialist Olympiads of the 1920s and 1930s as analogous alternatives to "bourgeois" Olympism. In the last analysis, however, one must concede that an often invisible, and therefore powerful, eurocentrism has shaped the premises as well as the practices of most Western internationalisms, and especially those which derive from the turn-of-the-century period.

Today the "Olympism Against Apartheid" statement, issued in Lausanne on June 21, 1988, appears to be the IOC's definitive repudiation of racialism in sport, and recent developments confirm this trend in IOC policy. This paper has addressed certain historical factors, inherent within the olympic subculture, which delayed the development toward a more equitable multiracialism within the Olympic Movement. In closing, it is perhaps appropriate to acknowledge the role Africa's olympic athletes have played in promoting the cause of greater racial equity. And here, too, one may return to the early years of this century to find the sources of change. "Whether [...] the total mental capacity of all races is essentially equal", an American professor wrote in 1911, "is not here the question. Achievement of any valid kind, whether by individuals or by racial groups, is bound ultimately to command respect[51]." The rule of *Citius, Altius, Fortius* is cold and unforgiving, and it is not an ideal basis for racial progress. But this is the rule Coubertin proclaimed, and Black Africa has answered the call.

In conclusion, I would like to expand on the comparative approach I have proposed and add some historical evidence which confirms the value of this methodology. Far better than the study of a single internationalist movement, comparativism shows what actually happened and suggests what was actually possible given the parameters of the historical period in question. The problem of what kinds of internationalisms were actually viable at that time prompts us to examine our own ideas about internationalist organizations, shaped at least in part by the founding of the United Nations in 1945, which are easily—but inaccurately—projected back onto previous epochs. As I have argued earlier, the eurocentric internationalisms of the turn of the century, and in particular their potential for genuine multiracialism, were severely limited by colonialist attitudes. At the same time, one must look at other historical factors which are less directly related to racialistic thinking per se.

The accelerated formation of internationalist movements and organizations during the last decades of the 19th century was not simply the result of imperialist politics or advancing technologies, although these were certainly important factors. A separate point is that certain ostensibly international projects of this period were not negations of nationalism but rather extensions of nationalism employing cosmopolitan[52] vocabularies. A variety of internationalist initiatives, including the Olympic Movement, both included and disguised nationalist and even cultic themes which could be presented as cosmopolitan projects within the European context. Rooted in racialistic European mythologies, such idealistic cosmopolitanisms could not possibly accommodate a multiracial agenda. Olympism, Wagnerism and the Salzburg [music] Festival are three such cosmopolitanisms rooted in cultic reappropriations of the European past. Their respective ideological sources are the myth of ancient Hellas, Germanic mythology, and a myth of Austria's baroque cultural heritage, and there is evidence which suggests they once constituted a single festival metagenre in the minds of some observers. In his *Olympic Memoirs*, Coubertin reports that a visit to Bayreuth, and the "passionate strains" of Wagner's music, assisted him in seeing the "Olympic horizons" before his mind's eye[53]. In 1918 an Austrian cultural critic wrote that the Salzburg Festival was the first "total aesthetic realization (*Durchbildung*) of the festival character" since the revival of the Olympic Games[54]. What is more, historians of both Wagnerism[55] and the Salzburg Festival have shown how these cultural productions—in effect, nationalistic cults—were successfully marketed to international audiences. "The tact and success of the pan-European Salzburg propaganda came from the fact that this nationalist program could be expressed as a cosmopolitan ideal that in turn would seem like pure internationalism to the English and the French[56]." Suffice it to say that the Olympic Movement has achieved much of its international prestige from precisely this sort of misunderstanding. In all three cases—Olympism, Wagnerism, and Salzburg—the "European idea" proved to be a politically viable replacement for nationalistic ideas, until the African revolt against eurocentric Olympism broke the mold.

In January 1990, the racial implications of eurocentrism were acknowledged, if somewhat obliquely, by the president of the IOC. On a visit to Melbourne, Juan Antonio Samaranch stated: "Australia presents a good opportunity to make it clear that the Olympic Games concern, not only Europe, but the entire world[57]". Mr. Samaranch's identification of a Commonwealth country as a part of the non-European world would appear to confirm my original point about our stubborn eurocentric orientation. But his remark also points forward to a more genuinely multiracial future for the Olympic Movement.

NOTES AND REFERENCES

1. Guttmann A (1984) The Games must go on: Avery Brundage and the Olympic Movement. New York: Columbia University Press p 230

2. On the origins and politics of the UNESCO "Statement on race" see Stocking GW (1960) American social scientists and race theory: 1890-1915. Ann Arbor: University Microfilms p 6-13

3. In an article which appeared in 1900, Coubertin predicted the spread of sport to "the black continent" and "the yellow empire", calling sport "a purely international phenomenon" apparently unrelated to nationality [race] or inheritance [hérédité]. See Coubertin P de (1900) La psychologie du sport. Revue des Deux Mondes 1 Juillet 167-68

4. Coubertin P de (1909) Pages d'histoire contemporaine. Paris: Plon p 4

5. Coubertin P de (1931) Mémoires olympiques. Lausanne: Bureau international de pédagogie sportive p 73

6. Coubertin P de (1912) Essais de psychologie sportive. Paris: Payot [Les sports et la colonisation] p 235-36, 238

7. Coubertin P de (1931) op cit p 188 [«Mais au fond des choses, il y avait le conflit essentiel, la lutte de l'esprit colonial contre la tendance à émanciper l'indigène, tendance pleine de périls au regard des états-majors de la métropole.»] According to Pascal Ory, this emphasis on "le rôle libérateur et modernisateur de la métropole" was a standard claim regarding recently occupied French colonies. See Ory P (1989) L'Expo universelle. Paris: Éditions Complexe p 96

8. Ibid p 186 [«Et peut être paraîtra-t-il prématuré de songer à implanter dans un continent retardataire, parmi des populations encore dépourvues de culture élémentaire, le principe des luttes sportives—et singulièrement présomptueux d'attendre de cette extension un renfort propre à accélérer dans ces contrées la marche de la civilisation. Réfléchissons pourtant à ce qui tourmente l'âme africaine. Des forces inemployées—de la paresse individuelle et une sorte de besoin collectif d'action— mille rancunes, mille jalousies contre l'homme blanc et l'envie cependant de l'imiter et de partager ainsi ses privilèges—les soucis contradictoires de se soumettre à une discipline et de s'y soustraire—au milieu d'une douceur qui n'est pas sans charme, la subite poussée de violences ancestrales... tels sont, parmi plusieurs autres, quelques traits de ces races vers qui se dirige l'attention de nos nouvelles générations.»]

9. The full quotation reads: "This nation has a long way to forge its unity, develop its personality and culture, realize its potential and actively insert itself in the concert of nations. And for this, Africa needs independance and it needs peace". See Hanson EO (1987) The catholic church in world politics. Princeton: Princeton University Press p 258

10. Woodruff Smith D (1986) The ideological origins of nazi imperialism. New York: Oxford University Press p 258

11. This "schizoid" quality is especially evident in an essay published in 1911 by one Professor UG Weatherley of Indiana University. This author's racial stereotyping does not rule out his own disapproval of "[n]egrophobe critics" more prejudiced than himself. See Weatherley UG (1911) A world-wide color line. Popular Science Monthly November p 475

12. Conrad J (1899) Heart of darkness; Conrad J (1978) The secret sharer. New York: Bantam Books p 59

13. George W Stocking calls the "psychic unity of mankind" thesis at this time "the major assumption underlying evolutionary theory and the comparative method in ethnology". See Stocking GW (1960) op cit p 431

14. Ibid p 451

15. Darwin C (1871) The descent of man, and selection in relation to sex. Princeton: Princeton University Press [1981] p 232, 233; 216, 217, 247

16. Paris (1900), St-Louis (1904), London (1908). On the 1900 Paris Olympic Games see Mandell RD (1981) Paris 1900: the great world's fair. Toronto: University of Toronto Press p 69-70

17. MacAloon JJ (1981) This great symbol: Pierre de Coubertin and the origins of the modern Olympic Games. Chicago: University of Chicago Press p 136

18. Ory P (1989) op cit p 94-95

19. Guttmann A (1984) op cit p 19-20

20. Blödorn M, Nigmann W (1984) Zur Ehre unseres Vaterlandes und zum Ruhme des Sports: Über die Anfänge des Olympismus unter besonderer Berücksichtigung des deutschen Beitrags. In Blödorn M (ed) Sport und Olympische Spiele. Rheinbek bei Hamburg: Rowohlt p 32-33

21. Coubertin P de (1908) Une campagne de vingt-et-un ans. Paris: Librairie de l'Éducation Physique p 161

22. McGee WJ (1904) Introduction. In Buel JW (ed) Louisiana and the fair: an exposition of the world, its people and their achievements. St Louis: World's Progress Publishing Co, V, p ii, p v

23. Guttmann A (1984) op cit p 20

24. Adas M (1989) Machines as the measure of men. Ithaca: Cornell University Press p 40

25. MacAloon JJ (1981) op cit p 134

26. Woodworth RS (1910) Racial differences in mental traits. Science February 4 174-75. An analogous argument had appeared in an earlier, and racially biased, study of reaction time in relation to the boxing aptitudes of whites and blacks. See Meade Bache R (1895) Reaction time with reference to race. The Psychological Review II 475-86. On the St Louis tests see also Stocking GW op cit p 545-46

27. See for example, Waitz T (1863) Intoduction to anthropology [Anthropologie der Naturvölker] London: Longman Green Longman and Roberts p 109

28. Baker WJ (1987) Political games: the meaning of international sport for independant Africa. In Baker WJ, Mangan JA (eds) Sport in Africa: essays in social history. New York: Africana Publishing p 275

29. See Krüger A (1980) Neo-Olympismus zwischen Nationalismus und Internationalismus. In Ueberhorst H (ed) Geschichte der Leibesübung. 3/1 Berlin: Bartels und Wernitz p 539-40; MacAloon JJ (1981) op cit p 167-68; Hoberman J (1986) The olympic crisis: sport, politics and the moral order. New Rochelle: Aristide D Caratzas Publisher p 91-93; Moore K (1988) The pan-britannic festival: a tangible but forlon expression of imperial unity. In Mangan JA (ed) Pleasure, profit, proselytism: British culture and sport at home and abroad 1700-1914. London: Frank Cass p 144-62

30. Poliakov L (1977) The aryan myth: a history of racist and nationalist ideas in Europe. New York: New American Library p 82

31. On the Boy Scout movement see Rosenthal M (1984) The character factory: Baden-Powell and the origins of the Boy Scout movement. New York: Pantheon p 7, 253, 115; 57, 191 sq; 59, 108, 280; 10; 55, 60, 106, 120, 174-75; 280; 12; 280-81. On this final point see also Jeal T (1990) The boy-man: the life of lord Baden-Powell. New York: William Morrow p 550

32. Rosenthal M (1984) op cit p 254, 261, 260-63. Jeal T (1990) op cit p 491-96

33. Jeal T (1990) op cit p 494

34. Rosenthal M (1984) op cit p 263

35. It is worth noting that racial segregation predominated within the Boy Scouts of America until after the Supreme Court Brown vs Board of Education decision of 1954. "The boy Scouts of America never drew a color line, but the movement stayed in step with prevailing mores". See Peterson RW (1984) The Boy Scouts: An American adventure. New York: American Heritage p 99

36. Blödorn M, Nigmann W (1984) op cit p 42

37. Ibid p 26-35

38. Diem C (1941) Weltspiele? In Olympische Flamme: Das Buch vom Sport. Berlin: Deutscher Arkiv Verlag p 244-45 [1942]

39. Reitlinger G (1957) The SS: alibi of a nation 1922-1945. New York: Da Capo Press [1989] p 135. For the English text of von Reichenau's statement, see Dawidowicz LS (1975) The war against the Jews 1933-1945. New York: Holt, Rinehart and Winston p 124. For a part of the German text, including a reference to "Jewish subhumans" [jüdischen Untermensch[en]tum] see Teichler HJ (1987) Der Weg Carl Diems vom DRA-Generalsekretär zum kommissarischen Führer des Gaues Ausland im NSRL. Zeitschrift für Sozial-und Zeitgeschichte des Sports I p 1 [47ftn]. A recent apologistic account of von Reichnau's career emphasizes his athleticism and refers only obliquely to his notorious statement of 1941. See Görlitz W (1989) Reichenau. In Barnet C (ed) Hitler's generals. New York: Grove Weidenfeld p 209-219

40. For a brief—and apologetic—survey of von Halt's political and olympic career, see Scherer KA (1974) Der Männerorden: Die Geschichte des Internationalen Olympischen Komitees. Frankfurt: Limpert p 74-77. For a more detailed and reliable account of von Halt's contributions to Nazi sport see Krüger A (1972) Die Olympischen Spiele und die Weltmeinung. Berlin: Bartels und Wernitz KG. While Scherer [p 76] dispels a false rumor that von Halt had belonged to the SS, Krüger [p 128] confirms that he had been a member of the SA and the NSDAP.

41. Teichler HJ (1987) op cit p 70

42. Teichler HJ (1982) Coubertin und das Dritte Reich. Sportwissenschaft XII 18-55

43. See also Hoberman J (1986) op cit p 42-44

44. See, for example, Draper T (1939) Nazis spies in France. The New Republic August p 72; Sternfeld W (1942) Ambassador Abetz. The Contempory Review p 85-90; Ory P (1976) Les collaborateurs 1940-1945. Paris: Éditions du Seuil p 13-15

45. Abetz O (1953) Histoire d'une politique franco-allemande 1930-1944. Paris: Librairie Stock p 69. See also Ory P (1976) op cit p 19

46. Paxton RO (1972) Vichy France: old guard and new order 1940-1944. New York: Alfred A Knopf p 33

47. See, especially Guttmann A (1984) op cit p 62-81

48. Jeal T (1990) op cit p 545. On the matter of relations with contemporary dictators Tim Jeal comments: "Not to be able to recognize evil in a national ruler is a grievous fault in a prime minister or a foreign secretary, but in the leader of a world-wide youth movement dedicated to international friendship it is not a fatal flaw" p 552. Presumably, this biographer of Baden-Powell would have applied the same dubious judgement to Coubertin.

49. See Forster PG (1982) The esperanto movement. The Hague: Mouton Publishers p 215-219

50. Pasporto servo (1988) (Budapest: Hungara Esperanto-Asocio p 11, 23, 35, 52, 66, 69)

51. Weatherly UG (1911) op cit p 484

52. Cosmopolitanism and internationalism have been (properly) defined as different ideals. Marcel Mauss, writing in 1919-1920, regarded these terms as opposites: "Internationalism worthy of the name is the opposite of cosmopolitanism. It does not deny the nation. It situates it. Internation is the opposite of a-nation. Thus it is also the opposite of nationalism, which isolates the nation". Mauss defines cosmopolitanism as a doctrine which tends toward "the destruction of nations, to the creation of a moral order (morale) in which they would no longer be the sovereign authorities, creators of the law, nor the supreme ends worthy of future sacrifices to a superior cause, namely humanity itself". Mauss derides this ideal as "an ethereal theory of the monadic human being who is everywhere identical". See Mauss M (1969) Nation, nationalité, internationalisme. In Mauss M (1969) Oeuvres 3. Paris: Éditions de minuit. In his study of the Salzburg Festival in its European context, Michael P Steinberg has offered a useful distinction especially applicable to Germany and Austria: "Cosmopolitanism, in the Kantian sense of the word, is therefore a transcendental principle. Just as conciousness exists and comes to know the world from the central vantage point of the individual, the nation, as a theoretical consistent extension of the individual, comes to know and judge the world from the vantage point of its own national language and counsciousness. Cosmopolitanism is therefore distinct from internationalism, which posits no a priori subject or center. What for the Germans is internationalism is cosmopolitanism for the French and the English". See Steinberg MP (1990) The meaning of the Salzburg Festival: Austria as theater and ideology 1890-1938. Ithaca: Cornell University Press p 97. I would argue that Coubertin's use of the myth of ancient Hellas makes Olympism a cosmopolitalism in this sense, possessing an "a priori subject or center". And this is why Olympism was absorbed so easily by German "national cosmopolitanism" (Steinberg)

53. Coubertin P de (1931) op cit p 64

54. Steinberg MP (1990) op cit p 60

55. Large DC (1984) Wagner's Bayreuth disciples. In Large DC, Weber W (eds) Wagnerism in European culture and politics. Ithaca: Cornell University Press p 95

56. Steinberg MP (1990) op cit p 69

57. (1990) "Samaranch: Melbournes Bewerbung 'perfekt' ". Frankfurter Allgemeine Zeitung January 29

[. . .] C'est au loin du reste et chez les peuples jeunes (jeunes du point de vue de leur organisation moderne) que l'on est porté à nous suivre avec le plus de spontanéité et le moins d'arrière-pensées. En Occident on a des visières. Les uns sont des myopes du spécialisme. Dans les Jeux ils n'aperçoivent que le côté championnat, – et encore chacun pour la catégorie qui l'intéresse: n'allez pas parler des lutteurs à qui ne veut entendre parler que des coureurs à pied ni des gymnastes à qui ne regarde que les escrimeurs. D'autres sont des presbytes de l'idéalisme. Chaque fois qu'on prononce le mot: olympique, ils entonnent le couplet pacifiste: leurs regards, plongeant extatiquement au fond des âges, y cherchent la vision du champ de bataille définitivement remplacé par l'arène sportive. Si la guerre, un jour, doit se raréfier, ce ne sera que par la diffusion générale de la culture, notamment de la culture historique. [. . .] En attendant, bornons-nous à souhaiter que, grâce aux Jeux Olympiques, se répande parmi la jeunesse virile de tous les pays cet esprit sportif par lequel prennent l'habitude de s'unir le muscle et la réflexion, le calme et la passion, l'ambition et la modestie! [. . .] trop nombreux sont encore ceux qui n'envisagent pas l'olympisme sous cet angle, [. . .]

Coubertin P de (1924) Autour des Jeux de la VIIIᵉ Olympiade. La Revue de Genève, 5 septembre, p 263-64

Apartheid et Olympisme:
sur l'abolition de la discrimination institutionnalisée
dans le sport international

En guise d'entrée en matière, l'auteur présente le sport comme l'une des activités humaines dont la nature et les valeurs ont le plus fait l'objet de commentaires élogieux. La notion du sport transcende en principe les notions d'injustice et de préjudice. Mais l'histoire du sport contemporain a montré de plus d'une manière qu'il en fut autrement, même dans le sport olympique. Dans la première partie de sa présentation, l'auteur fait un rappel de l'origine européenne aussi que de certains événements des premières célébrations des Jeux olympiques modernes. Il souligne entre autres comme des exemples de préjudice et de discrimination d'ordre racial: – les «journées anthropologiques» associées aux Jeux de St-Louis, en 1904; – l'entrée en scène olympique de l'Afrique du Sud, en 1908; – l'affaire Thorpe, aux Jeux de Stockholm de 1912, laquelle eut connu selon l'auteur un autre dénouement si le grand athlète américain avait été de descendance raciale européenne; – l'attitude ambiguë et tolérante du CIO en regard des Jeux olympiques de 1936, du nazisme et du traitement indigne fait aux juifs. Dans la deuxième partie de sa présentation, l'auteur trace les grandes lignes des relations de l'Afrique du Sud avec le Mouvement olympique. Au plan historique, il souligne l'origine du lien institutionnel entre l'Apartheid et le sport en montrant que la discrimination raciale qui se retrouvait dans le sport n'était en fait qu'une suite logique et incontournable d'une politique gouvernementale que les organisations sportives nationales, voire même internationales prenaient bien garde de confronter. L'auteur décrit ensuite la montée progressive des protestations de la communauté noire Sud-africaine, ainsi que la création de premiers organismes formels de coordination et d'expansion de la résistance. Dans la partie suivante de sa présentation, l'auteur fait l'histoire de la montée de la coordination et du succès de l'action internationale contre la présence et la participation de l'Afrique du Sud au Mouvement olympique. Il souligne de nouveau l'attitude tiède du CIO, au cours de la longue histoire du combat en question, et diverses manœuvres de diversion et d'actions de freinage exercées selon lui par l'ancien président Brundage. Il est fait état de la Rhodésie dont la politique raciale était semblable à celle de l'Afrique du Sud. L'auteur rappelle la crise des Jeux de Munich laquelle, bien qu'elle fut de moindre notoriété que l'attentat terroriste contre la délégation olympique d'Israël, a conduit directement à l'expulsion de la Rhodésie de la famille olympique, en 1975. L'auteur situe également au cœur du combat contre l'Apartheid le boycott des Jeux de Montréal par quelque 22 CNOs. Dans la dernière partie de sa présentation, l'auteur traite de la question de l'inévitabilité de l'ingérence politique dans le sport international et dans le Mouvement olympique. Il souligne que dans la vision occidentale des choses, laquelle a dominé historiquement et domine encore, il ne pouvait guère en être autrement: la discrimination raciale dans le sport reflétait typiquement l'attitude d'un pouvoir politique qui n'a surtout pas été exempt, au cours du siècle, de préjudice et de discrimination, surtout de type racial. À l'aide d'exemples puisés dans le déroulement des Jeux de 1960, 1968, et 1972, l'auteur montre que les Jeux ont aussi été utilisés pour illustrer à la face du monde la discrimination qui existait dans le Mouvement olympique lui-même et celle aussi que subissaient dans leur propre pays des athlètes issus de classes défavorisées. En guise de conclusion, l'auteur fait l'éloge du Mouvement olympique présent qui s'est ressaisi et même rattrapé, en matière d'équité internationale et de traitement accordé aux éléments et forces minoritaires qui le composent. Il souligne à cet effet le rôle marquant joué par le président actuel du CIO, Son Excellence Juan Antonio Samaranch, lequel a su composer admirablement bien avec la contiguïté du sport et de la politique, au bénéfice et à l'avancement du Mouvement olympique et du sport en général.

Apartheid and Olympism: on the Abolishment of Institutionalized Discrimination in International Sport*

Sam Ramsamy

Very few human activities have their virtues so continuously and repeatedly praised as sport. Overtly, sport represents clean-living, fairness and righteousness. When it comes to colour and race, sport is the only aspect of life that is said to provide equality of opportunity. Sport is supposed to transcend all notions of prejudice. Sport epitomises utopia on earth. The International Olympic Committee, the very custodian of internationalism in sport, has reiterated this notion:

> Olympism seeks to create a way of life based on the joy of effort and respect for the fundamental principles of universal ethics. Its aim is to place sport at the service of man in order to bring about a world of peace in respect for human dignity. This ideal was proclaimed with fervour at the festivals celebrated every four years by the ancient Greeks at the Olympic Games, in which they devoted themselves to the pursuit of harmonious development, not only the body and the moral sense, but also of man's cultural and artistic qualities.

The ancient Greeks proclaimed this ideal and the modern world proclaims it with great fervour. How close are we to this ideal? Do sport and sports participation provide respect for human dignity?

Race and the Olympic Games

The modern Olympic Games were revived chiefly by people of European origin. The first record of people of non-European origin participating in the modern Olympic Games was in 1904 at St. Louis, United States. There is vague reference to one or two "Kafirs" (derogatory term for Blacks in Southern Africa) having participated in the marathon. Whether these "Kafirs" were from the USA or

Sam Ramsamy, International Campaign Against Apartheid Sport, London, England; Advisor, Apartheid and Olympism Commission, International Olympic Committee.

* *Editor's Note.* Standard and full references requested for the quoted material used by the author in his text were not provided before going to press. The reader is thus cautioned against the fact that words and/or statements quoted may or may not be in direct and/or full correspondence with the bibliographical material provided by the author.

1890
1990

elsewhere is still unclear. Race prejudice and racial discrimination were quite blatant then in the state of Louisiana. It may well be that some local Blacks tried to circumvent obstacles by entering as overseas competitors. There is no record of any African country having sent competitors to the St. Louis Games. Yet, the St. Louis Games recorded a most undignifying aspect of race humiliation in sport. During the Games, two days were set aside as "Anthropological Days". Ethnic groups from Africa, Asia and the two Americas were rounded up to parody events in running, jumping, throwing, climbing and shooting. Pierre de Coubertin was not present himself at the Games but when news of these events reached him, he found himself embarrassed, and he is reported to have said: "as for that outrageous charade, it will of course lose its appeal when black men, red men and yellow men learn to run, jump and throw, and leave the white men behind them".

The London Olympic Games of 1908 recorded the entry into and support for institutionalized racism in the Olympic Movement, when South Africa participated. The Stockholm Olympic Games of 1912 saw the participation of Jim Thorpe of American Indian extraction. Thorpe, 24 years old then, was hailed as the greatest athlete in the world after he won two of the most demanding olympic events—the pentathlon and the decathlon. The 15 events required a great diversity of skills and Thorpe excelled in most of them. No one else has since won a pentathlon-decathlon double. Thorpe's feats were later erased from the olympic records because it was established in 1913 that he had taken part in semi-professional baseball matches before the Stockholm Games. Thorpe did not deny the fact, as he did not believe he had done something wrong. "I did not play for the money. I did it because I liked to play ball. I was not very wise in the ways of the world [. . .] and did not know I was doing wrong", Thorpe said. Philip Noel-Baker, who was a member of the British Government for 23 years and who also competed in the 1912 Games in Stockholm said he remembered the indignation he felt when on pure technical grounds Thorpe was disqualified. It was only recently that the Thorpe affair was redressed by the International Olympic Committee. It was believed then and is still believed now that if Thorpe had been of European descent, the matter would have been overlooked.

There were other incidents of a similar nature which were not brought to public notice. In 1972, Schüller, of the Federal Republic of Germany, took the Olympic oath at the opening ceremony after she had charged photographers for taking a picture of her in the preceding days. This was during the term of office of Avery Brundage, one of the greatest proponents of the amateur status and the leader of the Olympic Movement until 1972. Avery Brundage's entry into the IOC was preceded by a race controversy about the 1936 Berlin Olympic Games and the Jews. In his resolve to celebrate the Olympiad every four years irrespective of circumstances, he was accused of supporting Nazism and thus what it stood for. Brundage used every argument to hit back at the forces which lobbied for American withdrawal from the 1936 Olympic Games. Sadly, this included his personal vituperation against the Jews.

An Olympic Committee for Human Rights (OCHR), was formed to lobby for a black American boycott of the 1968 Olympic Games, openly accusing Brundage of being a racist. The Committee demanded the removal of Avery Brundage from his post as President of the International Olympic Committee. The OCHR exposed the fact that at the terme Brundage owned the Montecito Country Club in Santa Barbara, California which in fact excluded Jews and Blacks from membership. Brundage also displayed sympathy for the white South African National Olympic Committee.

South Africa and the Olympic Games

South Africa first competed in the Olympic Games in London, in 1908, although the constitutional entity of South Africa only came into being in 1910. Its early competitors were of British origin. Since then it participated in every Games up to 1960. It is important to note that while the IOC accepted the South African Olympic and Empire Games Association (SAOEGA—as it was called then) as representing the whole of the country, it represented, in fact, only its white population which made up less than 20% of its citizens. The non-whites (hereafter referred to as Blacks) were excluded from representing the country. The South African association was renamed the South African Olympic and National Games Association (SAONGA) after South Africa's membership in the Commonwealth was terminated in 1961. Thereafter it became known as SANOC (South African National Olympic Committee).

Racial Discrimination in South African Sport

In South Africa it was a combination of accepted colonial policy and the general constitutional practices in the other facets of life that determined discrimination in sport. Racial discrimination in sport was only a social practice. In effect it was the national governing bodies themselves which enforced race and colour discrimination. Only after 1948, when the present ruling group, the Nationalist Party, came into power, were specific legislations in relation to sport promulgated. Even these only came into effect in the late 1950s.

The Struggle for Recognition by Black Sportsmen and Women

Whenever black sportsmen and women sought membership in the so-called establishment (white) sports bodies, their applications were repeatedly refused on the grounds that "government policy" prohibited the mixing of races on the sports field. Frustrated by the blocking procedures of the Whites, black sports organisations and individuals appealed to international and Commonwealth associations for help. They were not successful in the early years. Many national and international associations were unsympathetic to their pleas. For instance, the British Amateur Weightlifters Association replied:

> [. . .] we cannot bring any pressure on the South African Weightlifting Federation to force them to recognise you. Their rules, as with all national sports associations in South Africa, will not permit of mixed contests between White and Coloured athletes. This is also a condition of the South African Olympic Council. Therefore non Coloured man could be chosen to represent South Africa [. . .]

The only alternative left to black South Africans was to go abroad. Because of prohibitive costs, only a handful could leave South Africa. The few that did go were greatly successful. In 1947, Ron Eland, who by far exceeded the total weight lifted by any white South African in his division, left South Africa where he was completely ignored. By 1948, he was representing Britain at the Olympic Games in weightlifting. Jake N'Tuli, who could not be rated in South Africa, became the British and Commonwealth flyweight boxing champion in 1952.

Internal Resistence and Protests

The first black sports body to publicly challenge white sport was the South African Soccer Federation (SASF) which represented 82% of South Africa's footballers. In 1956, the black South African Table Tennis Board obtained affiliation to the International Table Tennis Federation (ITTF).

A year earlier, the Co-ordinating Committee for International Recognition was formed. This soon collapsed and the South African Sports Association (SASA) was founded in October 1958 "to co-ordinate non-white sport, to advance the cause of sport and the standards of sport among non-white sportsmen, to see that they and their organisations secure proper recognition here and abroad, and to do this on a non-racial basis". The new organisation which represented more that 70 000 sportsmen was seeking recognition and representation in South African teams. Although SASA did not succeed in obtaining recognition for non-white sport, it nevertheless succeeded in arousing international attention about the plight of Blacks. Its attempts to seek affiliation for black sports failed because international bodies could not affiliate more than one body from a given country. Voting distribution in most international bodies was then heavily loaded in favour of European or ex-British Empire members, whose relations with South Africa were traditionally close.

SASA soon realized that pressure could be brought to bear upon white sports organisations if it created focus on the olympic front. This effort resulted in the formation of the South African Non-Racial Olympic Committee (SAN-ROC) in 1963. SAN-ROC's successes in arousing public opinion soon attracted police attention. Its officials were frequently intimidated. Its offices were even raided. As a consequence, SAN-ROC was forced to remain dormant for a while until some of its officials left the country and set up offices in London, England. SAN-ROC then continued its campaign abroad. Its activities not only changed the balance of power between white and black sportsmen and women but it also severely damaged white South Africa's image abroad. SAN-ROC chalked up a series of successes against apartheid sport by co-ordinating the international boycott which was backed up diplomatically by African countries and had won support from most parts of the world.

International Action Against South Africa's Olympic Participation

International protests at South Africa's participation in the Olympic Games only began in the 1950s. In 1955, Reverend (now Bishop) Huddleston criticized the IOC for accommodating apartheid sport:

> The Olympic Games are open to competitors from the whole world—with the exception of the non-white peoples of South Africa. South African teams to these Games have so far been selected only from the white population of the country although the other sections have produced men of olympic status [. . .] By accepting these colour-bar teams, the Committees of the Games have also supported the colour-bar, and made it impossible for non-white South Africans to compete as South Africans. We wish to urge that in the future both committees [the IOC and the South African NOC] make it a condition of South Africa's participation that the teams be chosen without regard to race.

More than 500 protestors turned up at Cardiff Arms Park, Wales, the venue for the 1958 British Empire and Commonwealth Games, to demand that the South African team be excluded if it were not mixed. The British Empire and Commonwealth Games Federation then conveniently side-stepped the issue by ruling that non-white bodies which were not affiliated to international federations could not compete at the Cardiff Games.

It was only in 1959 that lobbying took place within the IOC for the exclusion of South Africa. With no African member on the IOC at that time, the issue was raised by Alexei Romanov of the Soviet Union at the IOC session in Rome. Reg Honey, the South African IOC member, said that they had governmental guarantees that all South African athletes entered by their NOC would be supplied with passports. Avery Brundage, the then IOC President, guaranteed white South African participation at the 1960 Rome Olympic Games on the unsubstantiated assurances of Honey.

In 1961 South Africa became a Republic outside the British Common-wealth and it soon strengthened its racial legislation. On February 4, 1962 the

South African Minister of Interior, de Klerk, publicly contradicted the assurance given by Honey. De Klerk's policy statement was rather clear:

> South African custom is that within the boundaries of the republic, whites and non-whites exercise their sports separately and this custom must be adhered to, that is; that within our boundaries, whites and non-whites must not compete with each other, either in individual teams or in teams or as members of teams. Participation of mixed teams as representatives of South Africa as a whole in world sporting tournaments or competitions cannot be approved.

But the IOC, or at least President Brundage, was not convinced. The IOC Executive Board meeting in March noted that assurances given in Rome in 1960 were not effected, and that the IOC would communicate with the South African NOC (SANOC) to obtain an explanation. Despite South Africa's blatant racism, its friends within the IOC managed to preserve the *status quo* at the Moscow meeting of the IOC in 1962. Although it was confirmed that Honey's assurances were not carried out, there were only five votes for South Africa's immediate suspension. The IOC, instead, decided to give South Africa until its next session in October 1963 to abolish sports racism. Again, the issue was further postponed by the IOC which merely called upon the South African NOC to publicly oppose racial discrimination in sport and competition. When the IOC met at the 1964 Winter Games in Innsbruck, it finally decided to withdraw the invitation to South Africa to participate in Tokyo as its request had not been met.

South Africa has not taken part in any Olympic Games since, but the campaign to expel the country from the Olympic Movement, nevertheless, proved most arduous. South Africa's white sports officials soon manoeuvred to ensure that their country's team would be present at the 1968 Mexico Olympic Games. South Africa had enough friends within the IOC to support its reinstatement; however, a respectable formula for team selection was still to be found. Meanwhile the African countries established the Supreme Council for Sport in Africa (SCSA) in 1966, and declared that they would consider a boycott of the 1968 Games if South Africa were indeed invited to participate. But at the 1966 IOC Session in Rome, President Brundage tempered the tone of the IOC demands for immediate suspension by pointing out that the South African NOC risked sanctions if it violated its government's legislation on apartheid. He said that the issue must be re-examined realistically. "If we suspend them immediately, this could cause the arrangement that they are desperately trying to make with their government to miscarry". He thus appears to have wanted no decision to be taken at that session.

It was generally felt that South Africa's exclusion would be formulized at the IOC's May 1967 Session in Tehran. However, the African countries were dismayed to learn that several IOC members, in collaboration with the white South Africans, were formulating a series of compromises to ensure the latter's presence at the Mexico Olympic Games. Just prior to the Tehran meeting, the then South African Prime Minister, Vorster, announced, not coincidentally:

> The Olympic Games is a unique event in which all countries of the world take part, and our attitude in respect of that event was that if there were any Coloured or Bantu who were good enough to compete there, or whose standard of proficiency was such that they could take part in it, we would make it possible for them to take part.

Vorster's statement, although not spelling out how team selection would be effected, seemed magnanimous enough, and was therefore useful ammunition for the pro-South African lobby within the IOC. Frank Braun, President of SANOC, tried to push the IOC into immediate acceptance of South Africa's participation in the Mexico Games by announcing several concessions. He promised some form of mixed team, but reiterated that there would be no mixed trials. Braun asked for an immediate decision because, if he went home without it, those opposed to concessions in the first place would want them rescinded.

Ethiopia immediately announced that it would boycott the Games if South Africa was present. But President Brundage told those NOC's present in Tehran that the decision on South Africa would be taken at the next IOC Session scheduled for Grenoble in February 1968. First, an IOC Commission would visit South Africa and table a report. With such a clear-cut case, it was difficult to understand why the IOC was continuously delaying any decision on South Africa. The IOC Commission was led by Lord Killanin of Ireland, who was later to become the sixth President of the IOC. The other two members were Sir Ademola of Nigeria and a white Kenyan, Reginald Alexander. The commission carried out its brief, with Sir Ademola, the only black member, undergoing several humiliating experiences. The report was presented to the Grenoble session of the IOC. Apparently the meeting was not well-attended although 50 IOC members were present, many more than there had been in Moscow in 1962. So a postal vote was in the end taken to settle the apartheid issue. Although the Killanin Commission report clearly indicated that "South Africa was not subscribing to Olympic rules and principles", the strong Western bias within the IOC caused the vote to be taken in favour of South Africa's participation in the Mexico Games.

This decision unleashed the first major confrontation between the African countries and the IOC. The SCSA, supported by SAN-ROC, mounted a campaign to boycott the Mexico Olympic Games if South Africa was allowed to participate. Ethiopia and several other African countries announced that they would not be participating in Mexico. By April 1968, the number increased to more than 40, with the majority coming from Africa. Soon several Caribbean and Asian countries joined in. President Brundage was also under pressure from the Mexico Organizing Committee, which had earlier assured the Africans of its support. Black American athletes announced that they would also join the boycott. Brundage was reluctantly compelled to call a meeting of the IOC Executive in Lausanne. Just prior to the meeting, President Brundage spent four days in South Africa, apparently for a visit to the Kruger National Park games reserve. Whether his purpose was to gather more information to retain South Africa's participation or to ask the South Africans to decline the invitation, remains to this date unknown. After two days of deliberations, the IOC decided on a U-turn: it decided to recommend that the invitation to South Africa be withdrawn "because of the international climate" and would request a postal ballot from its members for endorsement. The executive's recommendation was eventually supported by 47 votes to 16. The fact that the decision was based on the then international climate indicated in no uncertain terms that the IOC did not feel racial discrimination was in violation of its fundamental principles.

The SCSA and SAN-ROC continued their campaign against South Africa. At the 1968 session of the IOC held in Mexico City, the Africans presented a joint resolution calling for the expulsion of South Africa from the Olympic Movement. At the same time, South Africa's sporting position was becoming more untenable. South Africa was being refused participation in several international competitions. African and black American athletes were even refusing to compete against athletes who competed in South Africa. In March 1970 the United Nations Secretary General, U Thant, called on all member-countries to cease sports exchanges with South Africa.

The scene was now all set for the great debate at the session of the IOC held in Amsterdam in May 1970. The African countries presented their case and charges. Seven related to discrimination and one pertained to the unauthorised use of the olympic symbols. SANOC, as expected, contradicted the charges; but this was made in such an inflammatory speech, attacking both Brundage and the IOC, that its fate was finally sealed. By a vote of 35 to 28 with 3 abstentions, the IOC voted to expel South Africa from the Olympic Movement. The narrowness of the vote margin again indicated the relative support South Africa had within the IOC.

Rhodesia

Rhodesia, with a racial policy similar to that of South Africa, escaped African scrutiny in 1964 because it was still a British colony. In 1965, white Rhodesians, refusing to share political power with the country's black population, announced their unilateral declaration of independence (UDI). International condemnation followed, and the United Nations declared the Rhodesian regime illegal. The world community, with the exception of South Africa, did not recognize Rhodesian travel documents. Mexico announced that in keeping with the United Nations resolutions, it would not admit Rhodesian passport holders entry into the country. Rhodesia did not participate.

In March 1971, Rhodesia received an invitation to compete in the 1972 Olympic Games in Munich. The Federal Republic of Germany (FRG), then not being a member of the United Nations, had no obligation to comply with its resolutions. To facilitate Rhodesian participation in Munich, the IOC agreed that Rhodesia should march behind the same flag it used in Tokyo and not the new "independent" flag; and would use British travel documents. Some African countries raised the issue of racial discrimination but the International Amateur Athletic Federation (IAAF) acted as if discrimination in sport did not exist. It was thereafter reported that a compromise, agreed to by the Africans was reached. The IOC obviously felt that there would be less opposition to Rhodesian participation. A racially mixed Rhodesian team soon arrived in Munich. The Africans, on learning that the Rhodesians were already housed in the village, threatened a boycott. Although not publicly stated, it was assumed that the East European and some Asian and Caribbean countries would support the Africans. Guyana announced that it would join the African boycott. Some black American athletes also stated that they would join in solidarity.

On August 20th, not long before the opening ceremony, the Africans presented the IOC with a petition stating that the Rhodesians had not conformed to an earlier agreement. The Rhodesians had entered the FRG on olympic identity cards and not with British passports. It was speculated that the German Government, not to damage relations with African countries, pressured the IOC to annul Rhodesia's participation. It became soon evident that mass withdrawals would seriously affect the Games. The IOC, in a close vote—36 for, 31 against and 3 abstentions—withdrew the invitation to Rhodesia. The decision raised controversy in some quarters, but the subsequent terrorist attack on the Israeli delegation at the Olympic Village permanently buried the Rhodesian controversy.

Rhodesia was eventually expelled from the Olympic Movement in 1975; after independence, Zimbabwe was readily accepted into the olympic community. The Zimbabwe Olympic Committee now plays a very prominent role in militating so that apartheid South Africa remains out of olympic sport. With the exclusion of South Africa and Rhodesia it can be said that the Olympic Games became at least free of institutionalized racism. This does not mean however that racism is no longer present in the Olympic Movement.

Montreal and After

Most observers felt that the exclusion of South Africa and Rhodesia from the Olympic Movement might result in no further problems from African countries. But another boycott emerged. This time it was the result of the New Zealand national rugby team touring South Africa. Although rugby was not an Olympic sport and had no direct bearing on the Games, the tour, nevertheless, caused great international concern and 22 countries, all African with the exception of Iraq and Guyana, withdrew from the Montreal Olympic Games. Robert Muldoon, who had been elected as New Zealand's Prime Minister in early 1976, had reversed the previous government policy of discouraging sports contacts with South Africa. He had openly ignored appeals to retain the old government policy. It was not surprising that African countries were incensed, as rugby in South Africa has for long had the aura of being the national sport of the apartheid regime.

My personal view is that a compromise might have been ironed out had the IOC kept abreast of developments and understood the magnitude of the problem and the concerns of the Africans. Sadly, this did not happen. A similar situation developed in 1980, when a combined British and Irish rugby team toured South Africa just prior of the Moscow Games. However, this issue became submerged in the President Carter initiated boycott of the Moscow Games after the Soviet Union had sent its troop into Afghanistan in late 1979.

Sport and Politics

Whenever some form of controversy arises regarding the staging of international sports competitions, the word "politics" is inevitably mentioned. Blaming politics for all the problems in international sport is part of modern-day phraseology; and this concept has been so successfully bandied around by many, that it has become most difficult to discuss the issues clearly and objectively. Indeed, it is not unusual to blame "politics" for most, if not all, of the woes of present-day international sport. On the eyes of many, politics has been used as a glorified cover for racism in sport. This has certainly been the case with South Africa.

The modern Olympic Movement, strongly influenced by countries from North America and Europe, until recently reflected Western political ideology and prejudices. Until the exclusion of South Africa from the Olympic Movement, the Games provided overt respectability for institutionalized racism. Those who protested were accused of bringing "politics" into sport. In other words, it was acceptable that sport reflect the established political and racial values of Western countries. What was not tolerated were political and racial principles and values seen to be antagonist to the Western way of life. The IOC's inclination to and maintenance of Western values was made evident when the racial issues of South Africa and black America were brought to the forefront of the Olympic Games.

The United States, in the eyes of many, has used its film industry and sport to create the myth that there is racial equality and tolerance within its borders. As a result of media propaganda and the disproportionally high visibility of the black athlete, millions of blacks have been led to believe that sport provides unique opportunities for upward mobility out of the conditions prevailing in the black ghettos of the United States. The feats of Joe Louis, the heavyweight boxing champion, and the world renown Jesse Owens were used as role models to flog this notion. Harry Edwards, American sociologist and civil rights activist, noted that: through the character of their sports involvement, Black people may be unwillingly contributing to the perpetuation of their own oppression as well as personal and institutional under-development. After the termination of the black athlete's competitive life there were no opportunities for coaching or administrative posts.

The manner in which the IOC handled the black American protests at the Mexico Olympic Games was also evidence of existing prejudices. At the victory ceremony of the 200 metres, Tommie Smith (gold medallist) and John Carlos (bronze medallist) bowed their heads and defiantly thrust their gloved fists skyward in a black power salute to protest against race discrimination in their country. The United States NOC reprimanded the two athletes and issued an official apology. That did not satisfy the IOC which warned about drastic sanctions against the United States team, including possible expulsion from the Games, unless stronger action was taken against Smith and Carlos. Under pressure, the United States NOC suspended the two athletes and ordered them expelled from the Olympic Village.

This contradicted the IOC position at the 1960 Rome Games. The IOC had then decided that as the Olympic Committee of the Republic of China (ROCOC) [Formosa] did not represent the whole of China, its name should be changed. The Taipei committee was told to enter the Games in Rome under the name "Formosa". At the opening ceremony, as the Formosa team passed the presidential box they unfurled a banner with the words, "Under Protest". This was evidently also a breach of the IOC rules forbidding political demonstrations in the arena. But the IOC took no action. This was not surprising since there was a general feeling that President Brundage's views were not at variance with those of the US State Department, which at the time did not recognize mainland China [The People's Republic of China (CHN)].

Black Americans also made individual protests at the 1972 Munich Games. One demonstration was staged by two track stars, Vince Matthews and Wayne Collett. They appeared on the victory stand casually dressed, moving about nonchalantly and not facing the flag. Avery Brundage, President of the IOC sent a letter to the President of the United States NOC which stated, *inter alia*:

> This is the second time the USOC has permitted such occurrences on the athletic field. It is the Executive Board's opinion that these two athletes had broken Rule 26, Paragraph 1, in respect of the traditional spirit and ethic, and are, therefore, eliminated from taking part in any future Olympic competition.

Where then were the IOC's "traditional spirit and ethic" when the issue of South Africa was raised? It was interesting to note that George Foreman waved an American flag after winning the heavyweight boxing title in 1968; in 1976, Bruce Jenner also waved an American flag after he won the decathlon. One must believe that such behaviours may be regarded as acceptable patriotic gestures within IOC norms.

As far as apartheid was concerned, President Brundage's view was that it was a political question, totally removed from sport, and that the South African NOC need not be sanctioned as the IOC had no jurisdiction over a government's actions. This was in sharp contrast to a statement Brundage made in 1953 to the fact that indeed not much can be done if a government dictates to its Olympic Committee, but the world should "refuse to play with countries which are in violation of Olympic principles." In the long debate over apartheid the IOC appeared in fact to have deliberately bamboozled the world into believing that the whole issue was solely political. Consequently, race discrimination in South African sport remained for long a peripheral issue in the whole debate. Brundage, by conveniently side-stepping the South African racial issue, kept alive the hopes of apartheid within the IOC until its expulsion in 1970. In 1972, after his retirement as President of the IOC, during an address he gave to the Afrikaans press, Brundage said that South Africa should be re-admitted in the Olympic Movement and undertook to help achieve that end.

Whither Apartheid and Olympism

The present power base and the international respect that the IOC now commands is undoubtedly due largely to the foresight of Juan Antonio Samaranch. He is in the habit of confronting the problems facing international sport rather than shying away from them. The success of the 1988 Seoul Olympic Games was to a large extent the result of Samaranch's untiring efforts. Although South Africa is no more a part of the Olympic Movement, the issue of apartheid could still create concern as was noticed at the 1986 Commonwealth Games when more than half the countries, which intended participating, withdrew at the last minute. After a historic meeting convened in Lausanne in June 1988, the IOC established the Apartheid and Olympism Commission to monitor developments in South African sport and intensify the isolation of apartheid sport. Actions initiated by the IOC as a result of recommendations from the Commission has certainly assured African countries that the Olympic Movement will not again tolerate or accommodate overt racism. The IOC's position is now absolutely clear. As far as South Africa is concerned it will take its cue from the African NOC's.

The interesting and certainly more encouraging aspect of IOC activities in relation to South Africa now is its willingness to make a positive contribution to eliminating racism in South Africa and to provide assistance to the disadvantaged section of South African sport. This is an aspiring and promising move. A move that will ensure equality when apartheid is finally eradicated. This gratifying result is owed in good part to the IOC at last understanding the realities of the situation in the present day world. Moreover the IOC, or at least President Samaranch, not only accepts the contiguousness of sport and politics but translates this into a positive and a favourable environment for the benefit and advancement of the Olympic Movement in particular and international sport in general.

BIBLIOGRAPHY

Archer R, Bouillon A (1982) The South African game. London: Zed Press

Associated Press and Grolier (1979) Pursuit of excellence: the olympic story. Danburry: Grolier Enterprises

Baker WJ (1986) Jesse Owens. New York: The Free Press

Bunting B (1986) The rise of the South African Reich. London: International Defence and Aid Fund

Brohm JM (1978) Sport – a prison of measured time. London: Ink Links

Edwards H (1983) Race in sport. Berkeley: University of California Press

Edwards H (1970) The revolt of the black athlete. New York: The Free Press.

Espy R (1979) The politics of the Olympic Games. Berkeley: University of California Press

Fredrickson GM (1981) White supremacy. New York: Oxford University Press

Killanin Lord (1983) My olympic years. London: Secker and Warburg

Killanin Lord, Rodda J (1976) The Olympic Games. New York: MacMillan

Lapchick R (1975) The politics of race and international sport. Westport: Greenwood Press

Lipton M (1985) Capitalism and apartheid. Aldershot: Gower

Lowe B, Kane D, Strenk A (1978) Sport and international relations. Champaign: Stipes

Lucas J (1980) The modern Olympic Games. New York: Barnes

Ramsamy S (1982) Apartheid the real hurdle. London: International Defence and Aid Fund

Tomlinson A, Whannel G (1984) Five ring circus. London: Pluto Press

The Future of Sport: Athletes and Coaches Take the Floor

L'avenir du sport : la parole est aux athlètes et aux entraîneurs

Editors' Note

Note des éditeurs

In its intent and proposition to look at sports prospectively, as a cultural phenomenon, as a social phenomenon, and as a fundamental right of every human being, the Organizing Committee had judged it essential to take into account the opinions of the persons most directly involved in elite sport: the athletes and the coaches. For that purpose, two international level athletes and one coach were invited to speak on the future of sport.

The presentations by athletes **Ann Peel** (Athletics, CAN), and **Pierre Harvey** (Nordic Skiing, CAN), and by coach **Richard Chouinard** (Athletics, CAN), were followed by a panel co-chaired by **Jean-Marie DeKoninck**, professor at Laval University and former national level coach (Swimming, CAN) and by **Yves Dion** (Gymnastics, CAN), presently Chairman of the Athletes' Commission of the Canadian Olympic Association. Thanks to the cooperation and assistance of the Olympic Torch Scholarship Fund of Petro-Canada, a number of Canadian athletes of the two sexes were invited to attend the presentations and to also take part in the bilingual discussion period which took place during the luncheon panel.

The texts of the presentations made by **Ann Peel** and **Richard Chouinard** follow.

Un regard prospectif sur le sport comme phénomène de culture, comme phénomène social, et comme droit fondamental de tout être humain (en tant qu'objectif central du Symposium), n'aurait su être porté sans qu'il soit tenu compte de l'avis des personnes les plus directement intéressées et impliquées: les athlètes et les entraîneurs. À cet effet donc, deux athlètes d'élite et un entraîneur de haut niveau furent invités à prendre la parole sur l'avenir du sport.

Les présentations des athlètes **Ann Peel** (Athlétisme, CAN), et **Pierre Harvey** (Ski de fond, CAN), ainsi que de l'entraîneur **Richard Chouinard** (Athlétisme, CAN), ont été suivies d'un panel bilingue dirigé par monsieur **Jean-Marie DeKoninck**, professeur à l'Université Laval, et ex-entraîneur national (Natation, CAN) et par monsieur **Yves Dion** (Gymnastique, CAN), président de la Commission des athlètes de l'Association olympique canadienne. Ont bénéficié de ces activités des athlètes canadiens des deux sexes, grâce à la collaboration d'un Fonds particulier, le Fonds de bourses d'études du flambeau olympique de Pétro-Canada.

Les textes des communications et des interventions de **Ann Peel** et de **Richard Chouinard** sont présentés ci-après, sous forme condensée.

The Future of Amateur Sport: an Athlete's Viewpoint

Ann Peel

As an athlete, and that is the point of view I have been invited to express today, I am optimistic about the future path of amateur sport. The source of my optimism is that I see developments in the structure and decision-making processes of amateur sport which are opening sport up so that it truly belongs to all who participate. And by that I mean, principally, that athletes are taking a more active role in the decision-making processes of amateur sport, on both the national and the international level, and, I believe, sport is benefitting tremendously.

But, while I am optimistic about our future, there are certain issues which sport must confront. The issue that has occupied so much of our time and energy in Canada since Seoul is the use of banned substances by athletes (and coaches). To restore the integrity of sport in the eyes of its public and its participants we must deal with this issue effectively while, at the same time, we must not allow it to preoccupy us unduly since there are other issues of great importance to which we must also turn our minds. One of these is the ever growing commercialism of sport which, although in many ways is a positive development, may also lead to confusion and corruption in the minds and deeds of athlete and administrator. The final issue I would like to discuss is the necessity to encourage and promote the participation of women in sport, not only as athletes, but as coaches and administrators, since sport cannot be a legitimate expression of our society and culture unless and until both sexes participate fully at all levels.

Of course, we can, and will, deal with these issues to the benefit of sport. And I would like to suggest that they can be dealt with most effectively by encouraging an ethical and inclusive approach to decision-making in sport.

One of the difficulties many athletes face in their participation in sport is the paternalistic attitude taken to the athlete by coaches and administrators. The tendency has been to treat athletes as overgrown children incapable of dealing with anything but the daily training routine. This tendency, I believe, helps to create an athlete who becomes incapable of making reasonable decisions and who is ill-equipped to deal with life. We can see this quite clearly in relation to the issues

1890
1990

Ann Peel, national-international athlete in Athletics; Barrister, Toronto, Ontario, Canada.

I raised earlier: For instance, the use of banned substances is, I believe, in many ways a microcosm of the problems our society confronts—the impatience to get results; the money, media attention and other external rewards to be gained by winning; and a decline of ethics, honour and integrity in a society which rewards (or at least seems to condemn only mildly) unethical behaviour.

And what has been the response of sports administrators? Condemn the athlete who is caught. Devote more resources to increase the chances of catching delinquent athletes. And where has the athlete been in this? Whereas the athlete's goal is the same as that of the administrator—that is, a "clean" sports world—the athlete has become the pawn. Subject to increasingly frequent and strict testing procedures for an ever-increasing number of banned substances; condemned for speaking out if affronted by these procedures; and suspicious both of fellow athletes and of administrators who many athletes perceive to be acting without developing comprehensive frameworks to deal with a problem which is much deeper than just "catching the cheat". Why has our moral outrage been visited on the athlete? Aside from the pressures athletes face to win, which pressures *do not* excuse the use of banned substances by athletes, any more than they excuse the business person who accepts a bribe; should we not also blame ourselves for the failure of sport to treat athletes as competent human beings with integrity? Sport has supported a "win at all costs" attitude. We tolerate the use of performance enhancing substances in professional sport whose athletes are also employed as role models—why do we then not understand the confusion of the young athlete engaged in amateur sport who seeks reasons not to emulate his or her heroes. Of course, society should not tolerate such behaviour in pro sport any more than in amateur, but that is another issue.

I would suggest that in many ways we have failed our athletes and that is why amateur sport has been in danger. When the problem could no longer be swept aside we turned instead to blaming the athlete. Only now are we beginning to recognize the need for education of both coaches and athletes. But this is not enough. We need to develop a comprehensive framework to restore integrity to sport linking education with ethics in a rational and broad approach to a complex problem.

Similar problems exist with respect to commercialism in sport. I would argue that very little of the money to be made in sport filters down to the athlete, but, in a sense that does not disturb me because that is the way the market works and we, as athletes, are in the end responsible for developing ways to enhance our incomes. What does disturb me, however, is that what income an amateur athlete does make (above whatever limit each sport sets, which for example now stands at 350 $ US as per IAAF rules) must be "laundered" through a trust fund managed by the athletes sports federation—almost as if it were "dirty" money. I believe that this type of structure unfortunately encourages unethical behaviour in the same way many people tend to cheat on their income tax. The process is so inefficient and differs so much among different sports that athletes will risk their amateur status or decline to participate in a process which makes a mockery of the simple and real need to make a living from sport. It is not a truism to say one simply cannot compete any longer at an elite level and also hold down a job—I know, my personal athletic performances have certainly suffered now that I work! Why do we not recognize that athletes are entitled to a decent, reasonable income? Why was it somehow perceived as unjust that Ben Johnson bought a Ferrari Testarosa when Wayne Gretsky owns a Rolls Royce and any number of other business people own whatever car their hearts desire?

It has been postulated that the concept of *amateurism* was developed in Victorian times to keep out of sport anyone who had to *work* for a living. Now that we all have to work for a living let us recognize it as a dated concept. Of course, this may create visions in the heads of many athletes who, by demanding million dollar salaries will kill "amateur" sport. But that need not happen—sports administrators still hold the power to make the rules of the game. I am simply arguing that these rules must adapt to economic *reality* and must be *consistently* applied across sports.

My final point is a discussion of the role of women in sport and here amateur sport must also face a new reality which can only be to its benefit. We must encourage women to participate in sport both as athletes and in leadership positions or sport will lose. I think the reasons for this are self-evident—an endeavour which takes its players from only one half of the population effectively loses the ability to use the talents and abilities of the other half. This makes no more sense in sport than it does in business and the professions.

Now that I've described a few of the issues which I believe amateur sport must deal with to prosper, let me also discuss a process-oriented solution. Let me qualify this by stating that a good process does not, of course, always lead to good decision-making but, I think, it is a start. I would suggest that the decision-making process in sport must make increasing efforts to be credible and, to do so, must become more inclusive and must be founded within a clear ethical framework.

We must recognize that the competitive athlete wants to win (and, hopefully, support himself or herself financially in doing so), and will devote his or her competitive life to increase the chances of success in this object. Let us recognize this as a valid objective and seek to ensure that it is both facilitated and pursued in an atmosphere of ethical and fair conduct which incorporates the sometimes differing needs and viewpoints of athletes, coaches and administrators, male and female.

We have begun, already, to incorporate athletes in the decision-making process as is evident in the growing legitimacy of various athletes' councils; in my sport, by the request from the IAAF Racewalk Committee that the athletes report on possible changes to the Grand Prix; and by the presence here today of athlete panelists. Perhaps athletes could also be involved in creating a rehabilitation program for athletes who have used banned substances (including those who may not have been caught); in reviewing and/or developing testing procedures which protect athletes' rights without detracting from the effectiveness of those procedures; in working with the sports federations to develop a new concept of amateurism which recognizes present economic realities (this may become even more important on an international level for athletes from the socialist countries who, accustomed to state subsidies, will have to look elsewhere for an income); in developing programs to encourage female athletes, who have few role models, to become coaches and administrators; and in creating a Code of Ethics for athletes and coaches. A start may be to provide athletes' councils with a budget and staff as a recognized operating division of each federation so that athletes can be more effective players in the process and take on the responsibility of contributing to the success of amateur sport.

Let me just repeat that sport is not an "us vs. they" proposition—we are all in the same game, quite literally. So let us think about involving all the players at all levels of decision-making.

[. . .] La direction des groupements sportifs est trop souvent aux mains de professionnels de l'administration ou de la politique, en tout cas de gens personnellement étrangers à toute activité sportive. Le danger a été maintes fois dénoncé. [. . .] que les groupements sportifs tiennent résolument écarté l'arriviste qui s'offre à les diriger et ne songe, en réalité, qu'à utiliser les muscles d'autrui pour échafauder sa propre fortune politique ou faire prospérer ses affaires personnelles. [. . .]

Coubertin P de (1920) Discours du Président du CIO prononcé à la séance d'ouverture de la XVIIIᵉ session plénière du CIO tenue à l'Hôtel de Ville d'Anvers, août 1920

L'avenir du sport: point de vue d'un entraîneur

Richard Chouinard

La société en cette fin du XXe siècle est grandement bouleversée. Le sport international, miroir fidèle de cette société, n'échappe pas aux bouleversements. L'esprit olympique est grandement secoué. L'idéologie de Pierre de Coubertin, selon laquelle l'important n'était pas de gagner, mais de participer, devient certes controversée. Nous sommes loin dc l'attitude ludique dans la simple pratique sportive. Le sport est incontestablement régi par le principe de rendement. L'athlète est évalué en fonction de records, de compétitions, d'entraînement, de sélections, de classement.

L'essence même de la compétition devient la victoire. La victoire, mais à quel prix? Le souci de pureté dans le sport n'existe presque plus. Des aberrations de toutes sortes sont mises à jour. L'usage des substances réputées dopantes n'est qu'un exemple, les pressions politiques et les enjeux financiers en sont d'autres.

La pratique du sport de compétition et ses incidences à divers niveaux, dont celles que nous venons de signaler, inquiètent de très nombreux militants à tous les niveaux de la hiérarchie sportive: les athlètes, les entraîneurs, les administrateurs, les scientifiques, les personnages politiques ainsi que les partisans ou les simples spectateurs, sont souvent perplexes. Ainsi par exemple, les autorités sportives se sont engagées dans une lutte acharnée contre le dopage chez les athlètes de haut niveau.

L'entraîneur, pour sa part, doit transiger chaque jour avec les exigences de la rivalité sportive: la relation athlète-entraîneur est centrée non seulement sur le travail et le succès sportifs, mais elle doit également tenir compte des questions de prestige national, des pressions politiques, de la reconnaissance sociale et des avantages pécuniaires. De plus, ces différents aspects occasionnent de fortes tensions entre le couple athlète-entraîneur aussi bien qu'entre le couple et le système tout entier. Ainsi, ce couple perd souvent son autonomie et se retrouve intégré, bon gré mal gré, dans un vaste système. Lorsque, pour différentes raisons, l'intervention de l'entraîneur demeure centrée strictement sur le résultat et ses

1890
1990

Richard Chouinard, entraîneur national d'athlétisme, Département d'éducation physique, Université Laval, Québec, Québec, Canada.

incidences, et non sur le développement global de l'individu, les valeurs éthiques du sport risquent à ce moment d'être mises à l'écart. Le développement de la technologie, le raffinement de la technique, la préparation mentale, la physiologie de l'effort, les méthodes d'entraînement, la médecine sportive, la recherche scientifique, la pharmacologie et les manipulations génétiques peuvent, il est vrai, supporter un corps performant, mais ils n'assureront pas, à eux seuls, le développement d'un être humain. Une mise au point s'impose donc sur l'importance excessive souvent accordée au succès sans un souci réel de la qualité des moyens utilisés pour y parvenir.

Ainsi l'entraîneur, en plus d'assumer un rôle d'expert de sa discipline dont l'objectif est d'obtenir la performance optimale de l'athlète, se doit-il d'opter pour une approche humaniste. Il ne doit pas se soucier exclusivement du développement physique et biologique de l'athlète, mais également du développement personnel de l'individu pour que ce dernier devienne un être sociable, autonome et responsable. Dans cette optique, il faut recruter et former des entraîneurs-éducateurs qui seront compétents et enthousiastes et qui auront le souci constant d'intervenir à la fois sur le corps, le caractère et l'esprit en vue de l'épanouissement global de l'individu. Le sport se doit d'être une école de discipline personnelle et cette discipline doit se transposer dans les actes de la vie. Concrètement, en cette dernière décennie du XXe siècle, nous nous devons de susciter des transformations majeures de notre système. Donnons-nous comme mission de rénover le sport que les jeunes et les athlètes consommeront au cours du troisième millénaire. Sinon, l'histoire du sport risque de tomber de rêve en cauchemar, avec de moins en moins de chance d'en sortir.

Jetons maintenant un regard sur notre société canadienne et considerons les conditions de travail dans lesquelles évolue l'entraîneur professionnel, dont on s'attend à ce qu'il favorise à la fois la haute performance et l'apprentissage des valeurs fondamentales de la vie.

Dans les faits, nous exigeons de lui des qualifications d'expert et lui demandons du même coup d'accomplir des tâches fort exigeantes dans un contexte maintes fois paradoxal. Le style de vie dans lequel il assume son travail est insolite. Il n'a pas, du moins dans notre société, la reconnaissance habituelle d'un professionnel, sa rémunération est minimale et les bénéfices sociaux qui pourraient se rattacher aussi à sa profession sont pratiquement inexistants. Les contrats de travail sont reportés (en de nombreux cas laborieusement) d'une année à l'autre, les horaires de travail sont interminables, les voyages nombreux et parfois prolongés éloignent de la famille, lorsqu'en fait elle peut exister! Le support des organismes et des bénévoles, même avec la générosité et la bonne volonté qui les caractérisent, n'est pas toujours suffisant. Parfois, les idéologies se confrontent. Les discours sur l'excellence sportive ne sont pas tous de même niveau, et cela provoque beaucoup de malentendus et de frustrations. Les clubs, souhaitant maximiser le développement de l'élite, sont constamment inquiets de leur situation financière. Nous sommes à une époque où la recherche et l'obtention de financement consomment énormément de temps et d'énergie. Mais fort heureusement, malgré tout, la plupart des entraîneurs se satisfont de peu et trouvent leur motivation ultime dans les succès de leurs athlètes, leur reconnaissance et parfois leur contribution aux succès sportifs canadiens.

Si le désir de préparer une élite sportive au sens profond du terme est sincère pour les autorités politiques et sportives du Canada et même du Québec, des choix et des orientations s'imposent. Il faut légitimer le statut d'entraîneur et assurer à ceux et à celles qui l'exercent un avenir professionnel décent. Dans les délais, il faudra en faire des employés permanents au même titre que ceux qui ont cours dans d'autres professions dispensant de la formation.

Compte tenu de notre culture sportive relativement jeune, le milieu sportif ne peut compter exclusivement sur le support de l'entreprise privée. Les différents niveaux de gouvernements devront contribuer davantage, à l'aide d'une taxe spéciale peut-être (loterie par exemple), et de façon continue. Si les moyens demeurent limités, on devra de toute évidence prioriser certains sports. Les tenants principaux du système devraient s'associer à des partenaires du milieu, par exemple à des institutions scolaires avec protocoles d'entente officiels. On pourrait ainsi, encore mieux institutionnaliser le sport afin de dispenser efficacement le support et le soutien logistique nécessaires au développement de l'élite sportive et à la réalisation des différentes tâches des entraîneurs. De cette manière, on pourra évaluer le rendement général de ces derniers sur un ensemble de critères et non plus uniquement à partir des résultats. Une telle démarche s'accommoderait mieux de l'éthique sociale dont on tend à faire de nos jours grand état sans pour autant en favoriser le contexte de réalisation.

Actuellement, nous observons un manque de profondeur quantitatif et qualitatif d'entraîneurs nationaux car nous n'avons pas de système formel pour identifier les personnes talentueuses, les recruter, les encourager à œuvrer dans la profession. Jusqu'à ce jour, nous n'avons pas encore réussi à leur offrir une formation continue, ni à leur assurer de l'emploi permanent. Cependant, dans notre système politique, ce ne sont pas que les structures mais aussi le climat social global qui détermineront un avenir plus prometteur à nos entraîneurs et au sport.

En terminant, une pensée de Umberto Eco, tirée du *Bavardage sportif*; elle reflète bien l'esprit des lignes qui précèdent: «S'il est vrai qu'une révision globale de nos rapports humains est en jeu, il faut qu'elle touche le sport».

[. . .] Il y a deux façons de comprendre l'internationalisme. [. . .] La seconde est celle des hommes qui observent sans parti pris et tiennent compte de la réalité, plutôt que de leurs idées préférées: ceux-là ont noté, dès longtemps, que les caractéristiques nationales sont une condition indispensable de la vie d'un peuple et que, loin de les affaiblir, le contact avec un autre peuple les fortifie, les avive. Pas plus que les individus, les peuples ne sont faits pour vivre dans la solitude; il leur est bon de se connaître et de se comparer: mais cette comparaison même est propre à leur faire mieux prendre conscience d'eux-mêmes, à leur donner un sentiment plus net des qualités qui les distinguent et des besognes auxquels ils sont enclins. [. . .]

Coubertin P de (1901) Notes sur l'éducation publique. Paris: Hachette p 262-63

Societal Megatrends

*An Assessment of the Influences Shaping the Future
of 21st Century Social Institutions*

Tendances sociétales

*Une analyse des courants majeurs qui vont transformer
les institutions sociales du 3ᵉ millénaire*

Mégatendances:
une analyse des courants majeurs
qui vont transformer les institutions sociales
du 3ᵉ millénaire, y compris le sport

D'entrée en matière, l'auteur établit que le cours de l'histoire a été marqué par des changements profonds dans la manière dont on percevait et faisait l'expérience du temps. Au cours de la longue période du développement de l'agriculture, l'orientation du temps était sur le passé. Pendant la période plus récente de la révolution industrielle, l'orientation du temps fut sur le présent. Dans le nouvel âge de l'information où nous entrons, l'orientation du temps se trouve carrément axée sur l'avenir. Dans la perspective d'un concept illimité du temps, il ne saurait y avoir de restrictions, selon l'auteur, à conjecturer sur l'avenir de la société globale en se basant sur l'analyse des données et des tendances qui sont présentement connues. La présentation porte par la suite sur une description de huit grandes tendances (ou megatrends) dont l'influence se fait déjà sentir et qui, selon l'auteur, ne manqueront pas d'imprimer un mouvement nouveau aux diverses formes de relations déjà existantes entre les personnes, les nations et les peuples, ainsi que les États, grands et petits, au cours du troisième millénaire. L'auteur souligne que ces huit grandes tendances ne manqueront pas d'avoir de l'impact sur la conception du mode de vie, et partant, sur les loisirs et le sport. Mégatendance 1 – Les arts remplaceront progressivement le sport, comme forme populaire et dominante d'activité de loisir. À l'appui de l'énoncé, l'auteur démontre qu'il y a à la fois une désaffection graduelle à l'égard du sport spectacle dont les mass media sont de nos jours saturés, une montée de l'éducation populaire en regards des arts, de la littérature et de la spiritualité, enfin et par surcroît, un déplacement de l'intérêt des commanditaires vers le monde des arts. Mégatendance 2 – Nous assistons à un déclin de l'État-providence et à l'émergence d'un nouveau socialisme de type libre-échange. Des exemples concrets de cet état de choses sont donnés pour plusieurs pays économiquement développés, pour les pays socialistes dans le sillage des événements politiques récents, particulièrement ceux qui se sont fait sentir en URS. Mégatendance 3 – La tendance actuelle à l'uniformisation du mode de vie se trouve contrebalancée par la montée du nationalisme culturel. Des exemples sont donnés par l'auteur en ce qui a trait, entre autres, aux habitudes alimentaires offertes par une nouvelle ubiquité des produits et une uniformisation progressive des marchés et des prix, au marketing international des vêtements, et de nombreux produits culturels dont font partie les langues, les arts et même le sport, le tout conduisant paradoxalement à l'uniformisation autant qu'à la différenciation. Mégatendance 4 – Au plan de l'influence économique et culturelle, nous assistons à son déplacement du centre de gravité de l'Atlantique vers le Pacifique. La tendance est décrite par l'auteur des points de vues du pouvoir et du momentum économique, de l'affirmation des concepts et valeurs culturels et religieux, enfin, de l'ampleur des engagements dans l'éducation. Mégatendance 5 – L'anglais est devenu la langue universelle des communications. La tendance est soulignée dans les avenues du commerce, du transport et des communications, de l'informatique, de la science, et des rapports entre les jeunes. Mégatendance 6 – Le triomphe de l'individu dans une économie devenue planétaire. L'auteur explique qu'en contrepoint à la mondialisation, l'individu et les associations libres de personnes prennent plus de poids que jamais. La communauté supplante l'individualisme. Mégatendance 7 – L'aube du libre échange entre toutes les nations. Il est démontré par l'auteur que dans l'économie planétaire, les considérations économiques l'emportent de plus en plus sur les considérations politiques. Mégatendance 8 – Les années 1990 seront aussi caractérisées par la croissance économique. À cet effet, et malgré les problèmes et les entraves, l'auteur se dit d'avis que les alliances économiques et l'efficacité sans précédent des réseaux de communication sont des forces motrices suffisamment puissantes pour assurer la mondialisation et le succès éventuel du libre échange.

Megatrends:
an Assessment of the Influences Shaping the Future of 21st Century Social Institutions with Reference to Sport

John Naisbitt

There is a very good reason why there is so much talk today about the future, about vision, about the year 2000 and the next millennium. It is because we are experiencing a profound shift in *time-orientation*.

The time-orientation during the long agricultural period was to *the past*. We learned from the past how to plant, how to harvest, how to store (and I say this as someone who grew up on a small sugar beet farm in southern Utah. Everything we knew about farming in those days, we learned from those before us).

The time-orientation in the industrial era was *the present*: get it out, get it done, bottom-line.

The time-orientation in our new global information era is *the future*. Things are rushing past us with such speed and complexity that we cannot grasp them. So we create pictures—visions—of the future to instruct us how to get there: what we want to look like in 1995 or in the year 2000, and these visions shape the way for us.

So there is no end to the talk about the future, about visions, about the year 2000. And that year 2000, that great symbol of the future, is now only 10 years away. To get a sense of how near the next millennium is, let me invite you to think back 10 years. It was not so long ago. Think of what was going on in your own life in 1980. It sometimes seems like just the other day...

– 1980 was the year that Solidarity was born—outlawed later—and finally at the end of the decade it overthrew Communist rule in Poland.

– 1980 Andrei Sakharov was exiled to the city of Gorky, later to emerge as figure of Perestroika in the Soviet Union, dying just days before the 1980s ended.

– 1980 was the year of the Three-mile Island debate augmenting environmental concerns, and followed later by Tchernobyl.

– 1980 was the year of the boycotted Moscow Games, the year Eric Heiden won five gold medals at the Lake Placid Winter Games, and the year Jesse Owens died.

1890
1990

John Naisbitt, The Naisbitt Group, Washington, DC, USA.

– And 1980 was the year that Ronald Reagan was elected President of the United States by a landslide, setting the tone for the decade.

These decade-signaling events are still green in memory... That is how many years forward the next millennium is. It is just around the corner. So what are some of the global trends in the 1990s that will impact on sports as we move toward the next millennium? What are the most important global tendencies as we move toward the Millennium Games?

I propose eight such megatrends.

The Arts are Replacing Sports as the Dominant Leisure Activity of Society

This is occurring in all post-industrial societies. It is not that sports are going away. But their growth, for the most part, is flat. Whereas the fine arts are everywhere growing dramatically. Paradoxically, premier sports events, like the Olympic Games, are assuming more importance because of the globalization of television.

The big story of the 1990s will not be high technology, but a renaissance in the *arts* and *literature*, and *spirituality*.

I know that up until now almost all the talk you hear and the books you read about *the 1990s* and the dawning of the 21st century, focus on high technology: space travel, lasers, robots, superconductivity, artificial intelligence. The accelerating pace of technology is tipping our balance—and we seek to regain our balance by re-examining and experiencing our humanity. Science and technology do not tell us what life means. It is mostly through the arts and literature that we examine and re-examine the nature of humanity.

There is an unprecented interest in the visual arts today. In the United States, new art museums are opening at a rate greater than any time in its history. During the past decade, 300 new art museums opened in the Federal Republic of Germany[1]; 220 during the same period in Japan. New museums are opening at the rate of one every 18 days in Great Britain[2]. There is a similar unprecedented interest in poetry, dance, theatre, and in the high art of opera. From the United States and Europe to the Pacific Rim, wherever the affluent information economy has spread, the need to re-examine the meaning of life through the arts has followed.

It may be of interest to know that today more Americans go to arts events than sports contests. And the number of people attending arts events is going up, while the number of people attending sports events and watching on television is going down. Taking a long view, this makes a certain amount of sense. During the industrial period the popular form of entertainment of the industrial workers (and they were all men) were the gladiators. The most popular sport in the United States in the 1920s and 1930s and 1940s was boxing. When Joe Louis had a championship bout, the whole country would stop and listen to it on the radio. This was followed by the quintessential industrial sport of American football with its 22 gladiators on the field, each a precision part of the football machine.

The industrial period is now behind us. The workforce in the mature economies are loaded with women (more likely arts fans than sports fans), and the education level is the highest it has ever been. More sophisticated entertainment for the workers is required. At the same time individual interest in exercise and nutrition is increasing. Highly developed information societies have become nations of clerk, so to speak: sedentary information workers in contrast, say, to agricultural workers. Farmers working 10 to 12 hours a day in the fields and eating food fresh from the ground or a cow had little use for fitness studios or nutrition charts. The industrial era was also very physical for worker (in the USA about 85 percent) there is widespread interest and participation in all forms of exercise and nutrition. It is that perhaps we are moving toward a modern version of the ancient Greek ideal of a balanced development.

Two decades ago, in 1970, Americans spent twice as much money going to sports events as arts events. The arts caught up with and passed sports about three years ago. In 1988, Americans spent a billion dollars more on arts than sports events[3]. The crossover will continue, and sometime in the 1990s—probably sooner than later—arts events will take in double the dollars that sports events do. Also, many corporate sponsorships are beginning to shift from sports to the fine arts. Yet, the shift from Monday-night football to the "Marriage of Figaro" (Monday-night ballet!) will not occur overnight. But as many of us will be dealing with the nature of our humanity against the onslaught of technology, a new emphasis on the arts and literature and spirituality, will become part of the context for the 1990s. While Barcelona will host the 1992 Olympic Games, Madrid, designated the cultural capital of Europe for 1992, will host major ballet and opera companies and other cultural activities[4]. This, of course, fits right in with and olympic program, which must include exhibitions and demonstrations of fine arts. Perhaps will the Millennium Games carry this aspect of the olympic celebrations to new heights.

The Decline of the Welfare State and the Emergence of Free-Market Socialism

The welfare state is being privatized in all economically developed countries: in England, France, Canada, Germany, and in Sweden, which carried it the furthest. Today everyone is re-thinking, re-conceptualizing, re-inventing a society's responsibilities to its citizens, especially those who are not in a position to help themselves. This process of working out what will replace the welfare state, the privatization of the welfare state will surely continue for the years left in this century. More than 100 countries in all parts of the world—Mexico, Malaysia, Brazil, India, Turkey, and now, even the Soviet Union—are turning government-provided goods and services over to private hands[5].

And Britain has been the leader. Almost half of Britain's huge nationalized workforce has been transferred to the private sector, and those newly privatized workers own stock in their companies. An interesting benchmark was reached last year: for the first time, more citizens owned stock in companies than were members of trade unions, a symbolic crossover indeed. During the floatation of British Telcom stock, the trade union movement mounted a campaign to try to persuade employees of British Telcom not to buy stock in the company. But 96 percent bought stock anyway. Britain is now privatizing its social security system, and may become the first nation to privatize its postal system[6].

In Spain, Felipe Gonzales and his so-called Socialist government are positioned in the political center, pushing privatization and entrepreneurism, becoming champions of capitalism. In France, Socialist President Mitterand never mentions the word "socialism" any more. The Prime Minister of France Michel Rocard, is a self-described "Free-market Socialist". Bob Hawke, the Prime Minister of Australia, calls himself a "Market-driven Socialist". In Italy, Gianni De Michelis, the Foreign Minister told me: "It is not left vs. right anymore. It is old vs. new". And, "We are all"—said this socialist minister—"for privatization[7]".

The *old* is centrally-planned socialism; the *new* is free-market socialism; this is the larger context for the extraordinary changes happening in Eastern Europe today. During the past three years I have made six trips to the Soviet Union, the last in October 1989 to Estonia. You can image the excitement and chaos. Meeting with the reformers there was an invigorating and instructive experience. A little story about my trip to Estonia. I was to give a lecture in Helsinki, and it struck me that that would be a good time to visit Talinn, the capital of Estonia, it being only about 40 miles over the Baltic Sea from Helsinki. It seemed to me that the best thing to do was to charter an airplane for what would be a flight of just a few minutes. I called my friend Seppo in Helsinki to make arrangements. He assured me that in entrepreneurial Finland there was no shortage of planes and pilots, but that I would have to get a landing permit from the Soviet authorities, and that would take about a year. I took the four-hour ferry. On my trips to Moscow, I have met with scores of officials and members of the intelligentsia, and with members of the Central Committee. During one of my stays, I met with President Mikhail Gorbachev in the Kremlin. I had the occasion to ask him what he thought his chances of success were. He said he didn't know. He said he didn't know if the chances were 50/50 or 1 in 100, but he added, "We have no choice. We must do something or our economy will continue to go down, down, down, and we will fall further and further behind the rest of the world[8]." And I wondered how they could rationalize their free-market experimentation when central to their ideology was that the state must own the means of production and distribution. It appears that the state will now lease the means of production to individuals and cooperatives. The leases are from 50 to 90 years, and in some cases may be inherited. The idea is that the entire economy could be a vast network of leased means of production and distribution.

As the 1990s begin, the indications are that perestroika is slowing down, the economy is getting worse, and ethnic unrest is increasing. President Gorbachev's power remains relatively intact, but it appears that he will need all the help he can get if he is to bring off the miracle of rescuing the Soviet economy. A large irony in the making is that Hungary and Poland, who could never have started their revolutions without Gorbachev, may find straighter paths to the free market. The privatization of the welfare state and the transformation of socialism by market mechanisms is one of the really extraordinary stories of our time. The context for sports in the 1990s is thus unparalleled global political change.

The Trend toward a Global Lifestyle and its Countertrend, a Backlash of Cultural Nationalism

Increased trade, travel and telecommunications have laid the groundwork for an unparalleled exchange of cultures. Every year one billion people fly from one place on the planet to another. But by the year 2000, it will double to 2 billion[9]. The consideration here is: the integrations of economies and lifestyles vs. maintaining one's own cultural values, arts, literature, and spirituality. *Lifestyles* —what we eat, what we drink, what we wear, where we vacation, are coming together, blending. We are borrowing from each other, playing in each other's back yards. But this does not mean we are melding culturally. *Indeed*, the more our lifestyles are blurred, the more each country insists on its cultural identity.

In the lifestyles direction McDonalds has 11 000 restaurants in 44 countries including 600 in Japan[10]: *Japan* has more American food franchises than any other country[11], including 611 Kentucky Fried Chicken outlets[12] and 4 000 7-Elevens[13]. *Indeed* the popularity of American fast foods is spreading over the planet like some kind of contagious disease. There are now 40 truly world brands: IBM, Coke, Sony, Porsche, Honda, Nestlé: 17 of the 40 are American; 14 European; 9 Japanese[14]. Harrods, the great department store in London, does 40% of its sales to overseas customers . . . in every country in the World. In the vegetable section, at Harrods in London, one can buy French peaches, Dutch radishes, English strawberries, California asparagus, Russian button mushrooms and East African lemon grass.

Harrods, which operates shops in Japan and West Germany, is owned by Egyptians[15]. One can buy a Benetton sweater in any one of 4 500 outlets in 70 countries[16]. International retailing *is* at the center of the globalization of life styles. Benettons... Esprit... Laura Ashley... Ikea... High fashion early lead the way... and now is leading the way in the globalization of price.

We welcome this exchange of food and fashion because it increases options. It is delightfully superficial and threatens no one. But, cultural exchange grows more sensitive in the areas of film and television, where the United States is criticized for exporting too aggressively. Americans, who are appalled by the violence in the entertainment produced in their own country, cringe when it is shipped abroad as representative of "American culture". With entertainment one ventures into the deeper areas of language, values and tradition. Dallas is seen in 98 countries[17]. In Shangai, every Wednesday night, 70 percent watch "Hunter"[18]. In France, 50% of films released in 1987 were American[19]. No wonder French Prime Minister of Culture, Jack Lang spoke about American cultural imperialism. When American cultural exports dominate, especially in developing countries whose sense of identity is vulnerable, the result is anti-American backlash often with a conservative, even fundamentalist component.

Sports will also reflect the global lifestyle. Professional sports will see an increase of players going to different countries to play on foreign teams[20]. Decisions about food, clothing, and entertainment remain psychologically relatively superficial decisions; but cultural values are in the bones. In sorting this out, the trick—of course—is to figure but what is becoming universal and what is remaining distinctive. The great battles of the 1990s will be *cultural*—language, tradition, religion—rather than strictly political. When Salman Rushdie was judged to have blasphemed the Prophet, the Ayatollah imposed a death sentence upon him. As Turkey petitions to join the common market, the influence of Islam grows, University women are again wearing the Islamic scarf, even though it has been outlawed since the secular reforms of the 1920s[21]. In the Soviet Union, demonstrations against the state of the economy are rising. But many ethnic groups are also asserting their culture and religion. Estonia's first act of defiance was to inform the Central Committee in Moscow that henceforth Estonian, not Russian would be the official language[22].

Amid economic crisis and political reforms in the Soviet Union, sports authorities are straining to preserve the costly sports system. Officials admit that success at the international level is too important to the Soviet people to allow the system to degenerate[23].

At the dawn of the millennium the great challenge is how to maintain one's cultural heritage amidst the growing tide of homogenization. The unfolding paradox is that a new emphasis on the importance of the individual in the entire world will be accompanied by a rise in cultural nationalism, with implications for the Olympic Games.

The Shift from the Atlantic to the Pacific

The Pacific Rim—bounded by Los Angeles, Sydney and Tokyo—is taking over from the formerly dominant Atlantic—with its New York - Paris - London industrial culture. Five hundred years ago, the world's trade center moved from the Mediterranean to the Atlantic... Today it is shifting from the Atlantic to the Pacific. The Pacific is now a 3 trillion dollars market... growing at the rate of 3 billion dollars a week[24].

The Pacific Rim region is twice as large as Europe and the United States combined. The Pacific Rim today has half of the world's population. By the year

2000, it will have two-thirds of the world's population, while Europe will have only six percent[25]. The Mediterranean—with its Greece and Rome, and later Spain and Portugal—was the sea of the past; the Atlantic is the ocean of the present; the Pacific is the ocean of the future. The 5 most important things to understand about the Pacific Rim are:

1– The Pacific Rim shift is *economically-driven* (not politically driven: Taiwan does business with 120 countries many of which do not even give it political recognition) and at a pace that is without precedent globally or historically. The economic expansion of the Pacific Rim is growing at about five times the growth rate during the Industrial Revolution[26].

2– The shift is not only economic but *cultural* as well. And the countries of the Pacific Rim speak more than 1 000 languages... and have the most varied religious and cultural traditions in the world.

3– Although Japan is the region's undisputed economic leader today, the *East Asia region*—China, and the four economic tigers—South Korea, Taiwan, Hong Kong, and Singapore—will eventually dominate.

4– The Pacific Rim's economic thrust is being re-inforced with a commitment to *education*. As early as 1985, a higher percentage of young Koreans attended institutions of higher learning than young Britons[27]. Korea's and Taiwan's commitment to education exceeds or matches that of every developed country in the world except the United States and Japan. South Korea has the highest number of PhDs per capita in the world[28].

5– In a global economy the rise of the Pacific Rim need not signify the *decline of the West*... unless the West ignores the significance of this phenomenon and fails to react to it. The Pacific's growing economic muscle is clearly visible in trade patterns. As far back as 1983, the United States for the first time began to trade more with the Pacific community than the Atlantic[29]. That difference has widened greatly since: in 1988, it was 50% more[30]; in 1991 or so, it will be twice as much.

Today, the United States exports more to South Korea than to France; more to Taiwan than to Italy and Sweden combined. Taiwan has become the United States' 6th best trading customer[31]. Canada's British Columbia trades more to the Pacific than to the United States[32].

There is much excitement about the decade of the 1990s. The number of new consumers in the European Economic Community will increase by some 10 million. By comparison, the increase in the richest nations of the Pacific Rim will be about 100 million[33]. The four economic Tigers and others are quickly becoming consumer-driven economies as rising wages translate to discretionary consumer-spending. The new, great opportunities for the balance of this century and into the 21st will be in the Pacific Rim. A whole new culture and new center of economic gravity beckons us. That is the context for the 1990s. It is not difficult to imagine a rise of Asian interest and participation in the Olympic Games.

English is Emerging as the First Truly Universal Language

The worldwide spread of English is remarkable. There has been nothing like it in history. Today, about 330 million people throughout the world speak it as a mother tongue. That is of course less than half the 750 million who speak Mandarin Chinese. But about 400 million people speak English as a second language, and another 350 million have reasonable competence in English as a foreign language[34]. All that adds up to more than one billion English speakers.

English is also the language of international shipping and air travel. It has become the language of the international youth culture. It is certainly the language of science—two-thirds of all scientific papers are now initially published in English[35]. And it is clear that English has become the language of the Information Age: 80% of all the data in the more than 100 million computers in the world is in English[36]. Sixty percent of all films, worldwide, are in English including most made in India and Hong Kong.

But English is not replacing other languages... it is supplementing them. For example, one-fourth of China's 1,1 billion people is engaged in studying English[37]. Interestingly, there are more people studying English in China than the entire population of the United States. In Paris there is a company called Alcatel. It is the second largest telecommunications company in the world, and it is Very French. Yet if one calls their headquarters, the operator answers in English, "Alcatel, good morning". And English will be the language of *Single Market Europe 1992*. One has come to think of English in a different perspective, that of a strategic asset in the global marketplace.

The Growing Individualization in a Global Economy

We hear and read a lot about globalization, but simultaneously—as we globalize—individuals are becoming more important and more powerful. An analog for this is the simultaneous globalization and individualization of electronic media. The globalization of television is a fact: two billion people watched the Olympic Games in Seoul; the whole world watched the incredible political upheavals in Eastern Europe. We will soon be able to tune into all the other networks of the world. At the same time we have the phenomenon of video cassettes: the ultimate in narrowcasting, where the individual is the broadcaster.

Globalization and individualization: the ultimate in broadcasting and the ultimate in narrowcasting. Personal computers moved the power of the computer to the level of the individual, and now we are beginning the process of linking PCs globally, much as telephones are linked globally, creating powerful networks of individuals. Also, just as a truly global system of 1 billion stationary telephones —with direct dialing among them—is getting in place, we have begun a process of mobile cellular telephone technology that will link individuals directly—without going through national systems. Just as with the launching of the first satellites, the launch of cellular technology begins a new state in the development of the Information Age. Within a few years, any person will have *instant access* to on-line information in the world, no matter where he or she is on earth. One will be able to call anyone else who has a portable phone anywhere in the world—directly—from wherever one might be in the world... without knowing... call *person*; not *place*. Cellular and satellite technology will help fashion people into some sort of global family. It will have social and political implications that are as profound as those which came with the introduction of the telephone. Interestingly, greater *individualization* is also a phenomenon of the Information Age.

Moving Toward World-Wide Free Trade

Moving toward a world where there is free trade among all countries is the large over-arching trend, beneath which are the smaller counter-trends of protectionism. The emerging global economy should be understood not merely as more and more trade among 160 countries, but as the world moving toward a single, unitary global economy. One economy. One market. Europe 1992 as a single market is but a step to the entire world as a single market. For a global economy—one market place—to work, there must eventually be completely free trade among nations, just as there is within nation-states themselves. We do not know (no one does) what the imbalance of trade is between Montreal and Toronto; between Tokyo and Osaka; between Denver and Dallas; nor will we (in-time) be trying to keep track of what it is between countries.

And the free-trade world is beginning to take shape. The free-trade zone between the United States and Canada went into effect some years ago; Mexico is expected to join in soon. The prominent year 1992 will see Europe become a single market, to be joined later by other countries who are now queuing up, perhaps even Eastern European countries before the decade is out. Australia and New Zealand became a free-trade zone more than two years ago. Brazil and Argentina are working on a free-trade agreement, perhaps the beginning of a South American common market. The Baltic States have also created a common market. Over the past years there has been talk about a free-trade zone between Japan and the United States; completely unthinkable not so long ago. Other regional agreements will follow; regions will join other regions. Before the 1990s are over, it is likely that North America, Northeast Asia, and Europe will link up as a golden triangle of free-trade. The whole world moving toward a single market is our destiny: that is the larger context for today's short-term, protectionist hysteria. As trade barriers come down, other barriers will follow. And economic interdependence will work for peace in the world. Pierre de Coubertin's dream of world peace is beginning to come true[38].

The Global Economic Boom of the 1990s

As we enter the last decade of the century, the world is entering a period of economic good times. There is no single factor behind economic booms, but instead an extraordinary confluence of factors. The economic forces of the world are surging across national borders, resulting in more democracy, more freedom, more trade, more opportunity, and greater prosperity. The first of the many factors is the movement toward worldwide free-trade just discussed. It is as if the 50 American states were economically self-sufficient with little trade among them, and then were suddenly integrated into a single economy; the economic explosion is easy to imagine. Inflation will be contained because of the global competition for price and quality, a new phenomenon. Interest rates will be contained because there is plenty of capital in the world today, and there is now world-wide competition in the renting of money. Business cycles are waning. They were a phenomenon of the industrial era with its self-contained economies. We now live in the information era of the global economy. Old concepts apply less and less. Very helpful has been world-wide de-regulation, first in financial services and now spreading through many sectors. There are now no limits to growth. Agricultural foodstuffs, natural resources are now oversupply. There will be no energy crisis to impede the 1990s global boom. There is almost no chance of another oil shock, simply because we are using less, producing more, and discovering new reserves that are awesomely greater than we ever imagined.

Taxes are expected to down everywhere, even in England, even in Sweden. It is a world-wide tax reform revolution. This is of course a trend complementary to that of entrepreneurism, reducing as it does disincentives to creating wealth. In the past few years 55 countries have reduced the top tax on individual income. Among the most dramatic reductions is the reduction of the top tax in the United States which in just seven years dropped from 75 percent to today's 28 percent. We have begun to attend our global environment in the only way feasible: globally. Indeed there is now a kind of competition of leadership in the global effort. George Bush wants to be the environmental president. Mikhail Gorbachev mentioned his concern for the environment at least 20 times during his last speech at the United Nations. The world's preoccupation with defense and the cold war, is being replaced by genuine concern about the natural environment, now our most common problem.

Authoritarian regimes all over the world are shifting toward democracy, laying the political groundwork for global economic growth. The 1980s saw democracy grow in Brazil, Argentina, Chile, Pakistan, Philippines, South Korea, Taiwan, and Mexico. The democratization of Spain and Portugal has meant that for the first time ever, all of western Europe is governed by democracies. There is detente between the Soviet Union and the United States. There have been no wars among the world's 44 wealthiest nations in 45 years. The world has never even come close to that before[39].

The cold war is over. The post-war period is over. A new era has begun. This new era will see the development and full realization of a single global economy. It will be the era of Globalization. And that will include the true globalization of sports. The millennium is only 10 years away, and a millennium is a powerful, powerful thing. The last time around, in the 990s, as humanity approached the year 1 000: 997, 998, 999, people went a little nuts. Many thought that *surely* the world would end in the year 1000. Prophets of all sorts were saying it, and people were getting ready. Others at the time thought that perhaps the year 1000 would usher in a golden era.

The year 2000, as we start our countdown, will have a powerful gravitational pull on the 1990s that will exaggerate everything we are doing. Intensify, amplify everything we are doing. The 1990s will be a fantastic decade: may be the most exciting decade of our lives.

NOTES AND REFERENCES

1. Number of new museums in the Federal Republic of Germany from: "Museum Mania grips the Globe" Los Angeles Times May 23 1986

2. New museum openings in Great Britain from: "Begone you old glass boxes" The Times (London) June 21 1988

3. Amounts spent by Americans attending sports and arts events from: "Research Division note # 30 November 30 1988. The Arts in GNP revisited and revised: for the third consecutive year consumer expenditures for performing arts events exceed spectator sports". National Endowment for the Arts, Washington, DC

4. Business America August 28 1989 p 2

5. Countries privatizing government goods and services from the following sources: "Governments put themselves out of business" The Christian Monitor May 26 1990; The Economist June 9 1990 p 11; Asiaweek March 23 1990 p 57; "Teetering on the high wire" The New York Times May 20 1990; "Turkey to start long promised program" The Wall Street Journal August 25 1987

6. Data on privatization in Britain from: "Governments put themselves out of business" The Christian Monitor May 26 1990; and "Privatization: irreversible" The Financial Times March 25 1987

7. Quote by Gianni De Michelis from a conversation with the author

8. Quote by Mikhail Gorbachev from a conversation with the author

9. Global airline travelers from the International Air Transport Association, Washington DC. Worldwide air travel in 2000 from the International Civil Aviation Organization, Montreal, Canada

10. McDonald's information from interview with media relations associate at McDonald's Corporation, Oak Brook, Illinois

11. American food franchises in Japan from "Tokyo takeout" The Wall Street Journal March 3 1987; and "Franchising in the economy 1986-1988" International Trade Administration. US Department of Commerce February 1988

12. Kentucky Fried Chicken in Japan from interview with Richard Detwiler of Kentucky Fried Chicken February 9 1988

13. 7-Elevens in Japan from 1988 Corporate Profile Southland Corporation

14. World brands from "Coke, IBM put their brands on the world" USA Today November 15 1988

15. Harrods' overseas sales and description of produce section from: "Harrods is shopping center for the whole world" The Denver Post August 2 1987

16. Benetton information from interview with Jeremy Weithas, media contact at Benetton Service Corporation, New York February 14 1989

17. "Dallas" reported in The Harpers Index Book. New York: Holt 1987

18. Hunter in China from: "China's appetite for US TV" The New York Times May 28 1988

19. American films in France from: "France" International Film Guide 1987 p 155

20. Insight November 27 1989 p 8

21. Islamic scarf ban from "Rise in Islamic fundamentalism" The Washington Post April 4 1989

22. Soviet nationalism, described in various sources, including "Resurgent nationalism" The Washington Post August 9 1987; and Christian Century January 25 1989 p 81. Language law in Estonia reported in "Estonia votes to make its own official language" The New York Times January 19 1989

23. "Tides of change lap at soviet sports" The New York Times April 16 1990

24. Size and growth of Pacific market from: World Trade Commission. Sacramento, California, April 6 1989

25. Estimated percentage of world population for Asia and Europe from: Europe May 1986 p 30

26. Pacific Rim's fastest growth rate from: Department of State Bulletin June 1987 p 80

27. "More Koreans than Britons in schools of higher education" from: The Economist June 20 1987 p 9

28. PhDs in South Korea from "Hyundai vs Honda" The Christian Science Monitor March 16 1987

29. Pacific trade exceeding Atlantic in 1983 from: Department of State Bulletin April 1989 p 33

30. US trade in 1988 from: US Export and Import Fact Sheets. December 1988 Commerce Department Trade Reference Room

31. US exports (1988) to South Korea, France, Taiwan, Italy and Sweden, from: Country desks US Commerce Department

32. British Columbia's trade with the Pacific "How not to say 'trade bloc'" The Financial Times (Canada) November 6 1-2 1989

33. New consummers by 2000 in Europe and Pacific countries computed with figures from: World Population Profile: 1987 WP-87 Bureau of the Census Commerce Department December 1987

34. Numbers who speak English as a second language and with some knowledge of English cited in: US News & World Report February 18 1985 p 49

35. English scientific papers from: Newsweek November 15 1982 p 99

36. English-language information in computers is from: Robert McCrum, William Cran and Robert MacNeil in The Story of English (New York: Viking 1986) p 20. Number of computers worldwide is from interview with Lloyd Cohen of International Data Corporation May 25 1989

37. Number of Chinese English students from: US News & World Report February 18 1985 p 49

38. "Modern Olympics organized to encourage world peace" from: The World Book Encyclopedia 1987 p 565

39. No wars between the world's wealthiest nations, based on GNP per capita, figures from: The World Bank Atlas 1989

Free Papers

Communications individuelles

Universality of Sport:
Problems and Promises

L'universalité du sport:
problèmes et promesses

Droits de l'homme et idéologie sportive

Frans de Wachter

L'année 1990, riche en commémorations mais aussi pleine de promesses, nous invite à penser les liens entre l'idée des droits de l'homme et l'idéologie sportive. Une approche éthique du sport consistera pour plusieurs en l'application de certaines règles morales externes. Une « éthique appliquée » semble référer pour sa part à une application de principes venant d'une extériorité éthique. C'est tout comme si le sport était une donnée pré-morale, voire une jungle immorale de cupidité et d'ambition, attendant d'être civilisée par l'éthique. Ce n'est pas le cas. Dans chaque domaine culturel (aussi bien dans l'art, dans la science, que dans le sport) il y a un élément spécifique d'humanité et d'humanisation, une pesanteur et une grâce propres, qui nous rendent meilleurs, qui nous humanisent, avant toute intervention explicite moralisante. Penser le lien du sport avec la moralité, ne veut pas dire l'ensevelir sous un discours externe moralisant. Penser son lien avec la moralité, c'est penser sa dynamique morale intrinsèque. Humaniser le sport ne veut pas dire le maîtriser ou le domestiquer, mais lui rendre justice. Il ne s'agit donc pas d'appliquer les exigences des droits de l'homme aux sports comme à un champ extérieur. Il s'agit plutôt d'une autre question, celle de savoir quels éléments de l'univers sportif sont porteurs d'une signification relationnelle humaine du même type que celle envisagée par les dits droits de l'homme. Je propose trois éléments à cet effet: le procéduralisme, l'inclusion et le jeu de rôles.

Procéduralisme

Accepter les droits d'un individu comme individu (comme homme) implique l'acceptation de la différence, de la multiplicité des sujets, ou, comme dit Lefort, de la béance de la société: « Dans tous les rapports se circonscrivent des lieux d'où les hommes perçoivent d'autres hommes, à distance et différents, porteurs d'une autre finalité sociale[1]. » Le système totalitaire par contre « est régi par la représentation de la non-division, par le phantasme de l'Un, il requiert, à

1890
1990

Frans de Wachter, Institut de philosophie, Université catholique de Louvain, Louvain, Belgique.

distance, la figure de quelqu'Un, une figure qui assure la société de son identité, de ses contours, de son homogénéité[2]».

Mais comment arriver à des décisions collectives quand il n'y a pas d'homogénéité dans le corps social, et quand on veut respecter les divergences? La solution démocratique est celle du *procéduralisme*. Les décisions publiques ne sont pas légitimées de façon substantielle ou cognitive, mais de façon formelle ou procédurale. Le fait qu'un parlement prévoie le vote, signifie l'acceptation du fait que l'on ne sera jamais parfaitement d'accord. Mais si l'on donne son adhésion à des procédures (par exemple, droit de vote, liberté d'opinion), on donne par le fait même son adhésion aux résultats de ces procédures, même si on peut les critiquer dans leur contenu.

Ce respect de la division sociale, et donc de la procédure, est représenté formellement dans le jeu sportif. Dans la présence de l'adversaire se constitue, dans toute sa pureté, la non-identité ou la béance. Les procédures s'appellent règles de jeu, leur respect s'appelle le fair-play. Les décisions sont respectées, non en raison de leur vérité, mais en raison de la légitimité du pouvoir auquel on a octroyé contractuellement la compétence de la décision. Si la démocratie est, en un mot, l'acceptation de l'opposition, le jeu sportif est sa représentation parfaite. Parce qu'ici l'opposition, l'existence d'un adversaire, constitue le sens même, et la joie, du jeu. Le respect de l'autre dans son altérité, même là où ses intérêts s'opposent aux miens, même là où il me résiste, n'est donc pas un discours édifiant plaqué sur le sport par des zélateurs moraux, mais touche au cœur même de la réalité sportive. Le philosophe et sociologue Aron l'avait compris, quand il écrivait à la veille des championnats du monde de football en Espagne en 1982: «Ne boudons pas à cette grande fête, non d'amitié, mais de compétition entre les nations. Une compétition soumise à des règles, contrôlée par des arbitres, n'est-ce pas, en dernière analyse, l'image de la seule réconciliation entre les peuples compatible avec la nature des collectivités et peut-être de l'homme lui-même[3].» Coubertin avait déjà exprimé la même idée quand il disait à la radio de Berlin en 1935: «[...] Demander aux peuples de s'aimer les uns les autres n'est qu'un enfantillage. Leur demander de se respecter, n'est point une utopie, mais pour se respecter, il faut d'abord se connaître[4].».

Inclusion

Toutefois, la perspective précédente ne suffit pas. Les droits n'y sont enracinés que dans l'individu, ce qui pourrait faire supposer une dissociation des individus au sein de la société, une société atomisée. Mais le droit est une catégorie relationnelle. Pour pouvoir parler de droit, il faut au moins être deux (comme pour l'amitié). La naissance des droits de l'homme au XIXe siècle n'a pas marqué la victoire de l'individu souverain, mais plutôt un nouveau type de rapport entre les hommes, et un nouveau mode d'accès à l'espace public. De quel nouveau type de rapport s'agit-il?

Dans la période prémoderne, la personne est intégrée, avec toutes ses fonctions vitales, dans un sous-système unique, par exemple une classe. À l'intérieur d'un tel sous-système, des jonctions diffuses s'établissent entre les fonctions vitales, c'est-à-dire entre les sphères familiale, religieuse, économique, politique ou juridique. Des pays aussi se sont déjà unis par un mariage, le pouvoir politique étant alors lié à une descendance familiale, une situation économique ou une délégation divine. Dans la différenciation fonctionnelle qui est au cœur de la modernité, les fonctions vitales vont former des sous-systèmes relativement indépendants: commerce, politique, église, droit, sciences, famille, récréation, éducation, entre autres. Il y a toujours interaction, mais chaque sous-système a tendance à délivrer des performances systémiques particulières, grâce à une rationalité spécifique au système. L'on assiste donc à une émancipation de chaque fonction, laquelle implique en même temps l'abandon d'une ambition plus englobante (par exemple, du politique ou du religieux), et un gain de performance spécifique.

On peut dire que c'est seulement maintenant, au seuil de la modernité, que le sujet s'est constitué comme individu. En effet, dans un système fonctionnellement différencié, l'identité d'un sujet ne peut plus reposer sur une seule position sociale ou sur un rôle social unique. Personne ne vit à partir d'un sous-système clos; tout le monde doit pouvoir remplir plusieurs fonctions et jouer des rôles variés (principe de l'*inclusion*): fonder une famille, recevoir ou donner une éducation ou un traitement médical, participer à la vie économique, aux décisions politiques ou à la célébration religieuse. Je ne suis qu'individu, individu nu, parce que je dois être en mesure de porter tous les habits, de jouer tous les rôles. Si les sujets sont tous différents, en relation avec le système ils sont tous égaux: rien qu'individu, mais possibilité de remplir tout rôle social.

Le principe de l'inclusion est donc et par surcroît un principe de non-discrimination. Avoir un mode d'accès individuel à un sous-système signifie que mon fonctionnement ne devrait aucunement y être compromis par ma position dans un autre système, par exemple par mon ascendance raciale, religieuse ou familiale. Cette idée cruciale de la modernité est aussi représentée idéalement dans le jeu sportif. La raison en est bien évidente. La pointe du jeu sportif réside dans l'intention d'établir et de désigner un vainqueur, c'est-à-dire de célébrer la personne qui se révèle comme la plus capable ou performante dans l'univers clos du jeu. Pour cette simple raison, toute interférence d'éléments non-ludiques externes, toute interférence donc d'autres sous-systèmes, doit être interdite. On aura saisi pourquoi l'idéologie olympique doit s'ériger contre toute forme de discrimination. Une fois de plus, il ne s'agit pas d'un discours ou d'une volonté externe à l'idéologie elle-même, ni même d'une stratégie inventée par des groupes dans la lutte pour le pouvoir. L'on touche ici à la condition intrinsèque même qui permet l'existence d'une chose comme le jeu sportif. L'égalité des chances, et l'égalité des droits, voilà un postulat interne du jeu. Un ancien président du CIO a déclaré un jour à bon droit: «In the Olympic Games victory is based on merit. Everyone is entitled to equal rights and to equal opportunities, and if so, the race will be won by the fastest man regardless of colour, creed or political affiliations. This is the kind of world we all see[5].» Brundage avait bien raison. Dans le jeu sportif, le principe d'inclusion ou de non-discrimination est pratiqué de façon première, par la force des choses, qu'on le veuille ou non. Mais c'est là aussi une faiblesse: l'inclusion vécue n'est pas encore ou nécessairement une conscience morale explicite, et la transition vers une telle conscience n'est pas de l'ordre d'un transfert automatique; cette transition exige, selon nous, une intervention pédagogique explicite.

Jeux de rôles

Le système moderne de différenciation fonctionnelle n'a pas uniquement besoin d'un principe d'inclusion. Il a besoin aussi d'une certaine protection de l'autonomie de chaque sous-système. C'est précisément dans la mesure où le système politique, économique, scientifique ou autre préservera son autonomie, qu'il sera capable de régler les problèmes qui se posent en son sein. La crise de conscience d'un roi n'équivaut pas à une crise politique; de même un problème économique se doit-il d'être résolu par des techniques économiques et non par l'intrusion d'éléments politiques ou éthico-religieux. La différenciation doit donc être sauvegardée contre toute tendance de dé-différenciation, contre tout retour à une déliquescence des domaines, contre leur effacement diffus, comme ce pourrait devenir le cas, par exemple, si le système politique, ou le système religieux, dépassait ses bornes. C'est à quoi peuvent et doivent servir les droits de l'homme. C'est une institution sociale qui doit garantir le maintien de la différenciation. Mes droits n'expriment donc pas un individualisme, mais ma possibilité d'entrer dans un nouveau réseau de rapports, comme parent, comme scientifique ou comme artiste. La Charte 77 a commencé comme mouvement de support pour des musiciens emprisonnés.

La signification du sport devient plus claire si on réalise que la dite autonomie des sphères s'accompagne, dans l'expérience vécue, d'un *jeu de rôle* permanent. Je rencontre l'autre seulement dans un rôle limité, faisant abstraction des rôles qu'il joue dans d'autres sous-systèmes. Un industriel a plutôt affaire à des travailleurs ou des clients, qu'à des pères de famille ou à des membres de partis politiques ou de dénominations religieuses. L'on se sent même obligé de changer de rôle à tout moment. Dans l'espace d'un jour, je dois jouer au moins un rôle familial, un rôle économique, un rôle scientifique, parfois aussi un rôle politique.

Le jeu sportif est le jeu de rôle de ce jeu de rôle. Comme l'ont souligné Huizinga et Caillois, chaque jeu est mimétique. C'est un univers clos, bien séparé des autres systèmes sociaux par une multitude de conventions et de règles, et même par une ritualité et une théâtralité impressionnantes. Une fois de plus, l'exigence d'un jeu de rôle n'est pas une exigence externe; elle concerne l'essence même du jeu sportif. J'y suis contraint à une théâtralité fictionnelle qui ne se rencontre nulle part ailleurs: face à l'autre, je remplis le rôle d'adversaire, tout en étant son ami. C'est la fiction par excellence. Le fair-play n'est donc pas seulement le respect des règles internes du jeu. C'est aussi la volonté de ne pas dépasser les bornes qui séparent le jeu du monde dans lequel il s'inscrit, de ne pas exporter l'antagonisme au dehors des limites de jeu, et de ne pas transformer la fiction en réalité.

La logique totalitaire apparaît de la façon la plus brutale là où il y a confusion des rôles. Quand le politique atteint la vie familiale, et que des enfants se croient obligés de trahir leurs parents. Quand un psychiatre quitte son rôle médical pour sombrer dans un rôle politique. Quand la religion se confond avec la critique littéraire ou avec la cour de justice. Mais nulle part la confusion des rôles n'a-t-elle paru plus absurde, que lorsqu'un dictateur essaya de falsifier les résultats d'une compétition de football. Le jeu est tellement univers clos, qu'il est intrinsèquement subversif envers les intentions englobantes. Mais tout système totalitaire, par définition, abusera du sport parce qu'il cherche toujours à intégrer comme instrument du politique ce qui est (comme le jeu et le sport) univers autonome *(Eigenweltlichkeit)* par excellence.

Le sport est éloge de l'opposition, donc de la démocratie. Il est éloge de l'égalité des chances, donc de la non-discrimination. Il est éloge du jeu de rôle, donc de l'autonomie des domaines sociaux. Ces trois aspects des droits de l'homme sont au cœur même du jeu sportif, avant toute intervention morale explicite. Dynamique interne et logique immanente du sport font que la lutte contre toute forme de discrimination, d'une part, et contre toute forme de confusion entre le politique et le ludique, d'autre part, restera un des buts prépondérants de l'idéologie olympique. Toutefois, comme il a été signalé plus haut, l'inclusion vécue dans l'univers clos du jeu n'est pas encore une conscience morale explicitée. La socialité de l'univers ludique, socialité *an sich* dirait Hegel, n'est pas encore la reconnaissance consciente, *für sich* de la communauté des hommes. Un tel transfert n'est pas automatique; il requiert une intervention pédagogique continue et explicite. Peut-être l'Olympisme sera-t-il cette intervention. L'Olympisme peut utiliser la dynamique interne du jeu sportif pour éduquer la jeunesse à un universalisme des droits de l'homme, qui sera, chacun l'espère, la caractéristique fondamentale du lien social dans le troisième millénaire.

NOTES ET RÉFÉRENCES

1. Lefort C (1974) Un homme en trop. Paris: Du Seuil p 194

2. Lefort C (1981) L'invention démocratique. Paris: Fayard p 126

3. Aron R (1982) Confession d'un fan. L'Express 16 avril p 67

4. Coubertin P de (1935) Les assises philosophiques de l'Olympisme moderne. Le Sport Suisse, 31e année, 7 août, p 1. In Müller N, Comité international olympique (eds) Pierre de Coubertin Textes choisis. Tome II. Olympisme. Zürich: Weidmann p 439. Lire aussi: Coubertin P de (1915) L'Éducation des adolescents au XXe siècle. III L'Éducation morale. Le respect mutuel. Paris: Librairie Alcan. In Müller N, Comité international olympique (eds) Pierre de Coubertin Textes choisis. Tome I. Révélation. Zürich: Weidmann p 317-350

5. Brundage A (1964) Speech by the President of the International Olympic Committee. Bulletin du Comité international olympique p 63-65

La planète sportive

Borhane Erraïs

La planète sportive. Ce titre pour le moins insolite participe au constat de la mondialisation du sport[1]. Dès lors que le présent symposium s'interroge sur le sens de la culture sportive, sur l'expression plausible de normes ludiques nouvelles à l'approche du troisième millénaire, il paraît important de porter attention, dans une vision macroscopique, sur l'état sportif du monde et sur l'Olympisme.

On ne peut que rendre grâce au Mouvement international olympique pour sa performance relative à la diffusion et à l'organisation du sport à l'échelle planétaire. À l'actif de ce mouvement, sa capacité d'organiser et de spectaculariser les compétitions sportives et de mobiliser, grâce aux média une large partie de la population mondiale. Jeux olympiques et Coupe du Monde de Football figent devant leurs téléviseurs des milliards d'individus. Réplique et prolongement des Jeux Olympiques, les Jeux sportifs régionaux participent à un véritable quadrillage planétaire par le sport et témoignent de son universalisation[2]. Soulignant l'universalité du Mouvement olympique, Boulongne note que «le CIO reconnaît 166 Comités nationaux olympiques, 16 Fédérations sportives internationales, 38 organisations sportives [...] Il y a plus de nations adhérentes au CIO qu'à l'ONU. Toute nation culturellement reconnue peut-être membre du CIO[3].» Il importe aussi d'observer les arborescences qui se dessinent à partir des milliers de structures sportives nationales, régionales et locales renforçant le processus du contrôle ludique de la planète.

Entre le Mouvement olympique et les États, il y a une véritable collusion dont l'enjeu est la diffusion et la promotion du sport dans l'enclos terrestre. Dans un processus de légitimation mutuelle, le Mouvement olympique cherche à élargir le nombre des États-adhérents, tandis que les États en quête de reconnaissance investissent ces organisations non gouvernementales. Il faut reconnaître qu'aujourd'hui l'humanité aidée par les média et les associations caritatives a pris conscience de sa communauté. Mais, paradoxalement, cette prise de conscience aiguise les nationalismes, comme si chacun voulait asseoir son identité, renforçant ainsi les antagonismes entre États. Or le sport, malgré les discours lénifiants des

Borhane Erraïs, Unité de formation et de recherche en sciences et techniques des activités physiques et sportives, Université de Franche-Comté, Besançon, France.

instances qui le coordonnent, se nourrit de ces antagonismes. Il les attise en déplaçant leurs lieux d'expression des champs de bataille ou des tribunes politiques aux stades, ce qui est déjà, il faut l'admettre, une conquête sur le plan de l'humanisme.

Mais Dupuy observe avec pertinence que «l'État se nourrit de la violence de la Nation. Même contenue, elle dresse ses hommes à l'exclusivisme, voire à la xénophobie car l'Autre est concurrent. L'État est fondamentalement rival, il est fait pour gagner[4].» L'ère des nationalismes est loin d'être révolue et l'alerte que déclenche Julien relative aux réveils des nationalismes dans le Monde n'est pas faite pour nous rassurer: «Combinées aux frustrations économiques et sociales, les identités nationales constituent un mélange explosif qui à tout instant, peut rallumer d'inextricables conflits de souveraineté et de frontières[5].» On peut dire que la lune de miel du sport et du nationalisme est encore loin de s'éteindre. L'endémie nationaliste du Monde ne manquera pas d'alimenter durant de longues décennies la dynamique sportive. Le Mouvement olympique international aura encore le loisir de reconnaître et de légitimer des États nations en construction. En tant «qu'ordre strict, logifié et logistique[6]», il soutiendra ces nations-fœtus dans leur gestation, étayant ainsi son universalité.

Procès sportif mondial et illusion démocratique

Au-delà du caractère interactif de la dynamique sportive et du nationalisme qui entache le projet d'universalisation du sport dans lequel est engagé le Mouvement olympique international depuis un siècle, l'aventure sportive planétaire trouve ses limites à travers l'ensemble des contradictions qui la traversent. Le sport qui a baigné, dès sa naissance, dans la tradition démocratique sécrétée par la bourgeoisie anglaise des XVIIIe et XIXe siècles, s'est trouvé immergé au cours du XXe siècle dans l'idéologie olympique qui se nourrit elle-même des principes de la déclaration universelle des droits de l'Homme. Il faut voir dans la Charte internationale de l'éducation physique et du sport proclamée en 1978 par l'organisation des Nations Unies pour l'Éducation, la Science et la Culture (UNESCO), la consécration de cette idéologie humaniste et égalitariste. L'article premier de la Charte revendique la pratique de l'éducation physique et du sport comme un droit fondamental pour tous[7].

Ces vœux et déclarations d'intention prennent une toute autre signification lorsqu'ils sont confrontés aux réalités de la pratique sportive mondiale. La distribution de celle-ci est fondamentalement inégale. Les taux de pratique concernant les activités sportives hors de l'école varient considérablement entre les pays industrialisés (un peu plus de 40 % en France[8]) et les pays en voie de développement (3 % et 5 % respectivement pour la Tunisie et l'Algérie[9]). Les disparités concernant les moyens financiers et humains engagés par les États au service de la promotion du sport sont criardes. À un sous-développement économique se superpose un sous-développement sportif, faisant du sport véritablement une culture de l'abondance. Ces inégalités se trouvent accentuées dans les pays en voie de développement par cette tendance signalée par une récente enquête internationale, réalisée par le groupe de recherches en sociologie des loisirs de l'Association internationale de sociologie[10], tendance qu'ont les gouvernements «à recentrer leur intérêt sur le sport de haut niveau qui est supposé contribuer au prestige des nations». Une autre enquête conduite par nos soins corrobore cet état de fait. Certains pays africains qui comptent moins de 250 escrimeurs, disposent d'une fédération nationale et d'une équipe nationale dans cette discipline; ainsi que des représentants nationaux au sein de la fédération internationale correspondante.

Autre signe des inégalités qui affectent le procès sportif mondial, celui de l'impossibilité, pour certains pays d'organiser des grandes compétitions internationales. Si les Jeux olympiques apparaissent comme une véritable fête planétaire associant tous les pays, il y a lieu cependant de constater que les grandes manifestations se concentrent dans un petit nombre d'États. L'écrasante majorité des compétitions sportives, remarquent Mathieu et Praicheux, a lieu dans les pays développés, pays de l'OCDE et du CAEM, une trentaine d'États rassemblent à eux seuls 96 % du total, et les dix premiers plus de 63 %. Le reste du monde, soit quelque 150 pays, appartenant presque tous au Tiers-Monde, n'est pratiquement pas concerné par les compétitions internationales[11].

À ces disparités régionales se superposent des inégalités d'ordre qualitatif. Alors que le Nord, opulent, connaît une diversification de ses pratiques sportives, le Sud essaye par élites nationales interposées d'absorber les «surplus» de la culture sportive occidentale. À l'accentuation de la tendance vers l'individualisation des choix des consommateurs sportifs dans les pays riches correspond une tendance à la reproduction des pratiques sportives «traditionnelles» et principalement olympiques dans les pays les plus démunis. Telles sont les premières contradictions qui traversent la réalité sportive mondiale. L'illusion démocratique que sécrète le pouvoir olympique en est l'aspect le plus marquant. Celui-ci «se situe en apparence au-dessus de la Société des États et des Nations et des intérêts particuliers, mais il reste l'organisateur des inégalités et des hiérarchies principales selon lesquelles est ordonnée cette société mondiale[12]».

Le sport: un modèle ludique dominant

Malgré les disparités signalées précédemment au niveau des consommations de pratiques on peut dire que le sport s'est infiltré dans les coins les plus reculés de la planète surtout comme spectacle. Il a particulièrement profité du développement de la communication de masse et en tant que spectacle il s'est massifié. Véritable culture de masse, au sens où l'entend Morin, c'est-à-dire «comme une culture produite en fonction de sa diffusion massive et tendant à s'adresser à une masse humaine», le spectacle sportif enveloppe la planète. L'immédiateté du spectacle sportif produit par les «retransmissions en direct» donne son caractère attractif et fascinant à l'événement sportif. Les images sportives peuvent être fabriquées à profusion compte tenu du caractère répétitif et quotidien de la compétition.

Ces images acquièrent, grâce aux moyens audiovisuels, une force d'irruption et une présence diffuse inconnues jusque là. Balandier explique que «Les média contribuent surtout à provoquer l'imitation, à susciter et à glorifier la conformité[13].» Or il ne faut pas oublier que la diffusion des pratiques sportives modernes à l'échelle planétaire s'est étendue des aires économiquement développées vers les aires économiquement faibles. Dans ce processus diffusionnel, les puissances industrielles ont joué à l'égard du Tiers-Monde, le rôle de modèle prestigieux et attractif tandis que les instances internationales déclenchaient une mise en état de résonnance de l'ensemble de la planète, relayées en cela par les États, soucieux à travers une quête de succès sportifs, d'une plus grande légitimité et représentatitvé à l'échelle mondiale. Les élites nationales, détentrices du quatrième pouvoir, celui des média, participent à l'extension du modèle sportif dominant. Car il faut l'admettre, le sport fondamentalement européo-centré est associé à des valeurs telles que le libéralisme démocratique, l'esprit de compétition et de performance, le fair-play, l'esprit d'équipe et parfois un certain ostracisme et chauvinisme. Au-delà de ces valeurs considérées comme intrinsèques au sport, d'autres normes et valeurs inhérentes à son environnement sont ainsi propagées.

En effet, l'extension planétaire du sport participe non seulement à accroître le pouvoir des langues dominantes comme l'Anglais ou le Français reconnues langues officielles par les instances sportives internationales, mais aussi à valider universellement un système de mesure, le système métrique. Le sport occidental contribue par ailleurs à modeler l'espace urbain en installant dans toutes les aires culturelles ses arènes modernes réalisées à partir du modèle olympique. Le stade devient aujourd'hui un édifice banalisé de l'espace urbain. Le sport interfère aussi sur le temps, il le rythme en occupant les moments de non travail. Il induit les grandes transhumances hebdomadaires et affecte l'individu à la fois dans son langage, dans ses choix culturels, dans sa motricité et son rapport au corps et enfin dans ses lectures et ses modes vestimentaires qui se sportivisent. Par les symboliques et imaginaires qu'il suscite, le sport s'insinue au plus profond de l'être.

Culture ludique mondiale en péril et solidarité olympique

Ce modèle hégémonique, l'un des fers de lance de la culture occidentale, parce qu'il prétend à l'universalité, risque de figer l'humanité dans un modèle corporel unique et de la sorte contribuer au dessèchement de l'imaginaire. Avec la planétisation de la culture sportive on entre dans une ère de banalisation de la culture au sens où l'entend Balandier «c'est-à-dire la formation de cultures devenant plus homogènes parce que d'avantage communicantes, plus similaires, donc appauvries par l'effacement progressif des différences[14]».

Ce risque est réel pour la culture ludique mondiale, car le Mouvement olympique international, véritable holding s'affirmant comme la plus grande société médiatique du Monde, détient le monopole de la gestion du sport à l'échelle de la Terre. En outre, dans ce processus d'acculturation sportive planétaire, c'est l'espace culturel occidental et ses foyers les plus actifs, États-Unis et Europe, qui produisent les nouvelles formes de pratique construites selon la logique interne du système sportif. Parce que ces foyers ont l'initiative et le plus souvent le monopole de la production du nouveau et compte tenu de l'impact «des processus modernisants par le jeu, des imitations, ou plus brutalement des dominations exercées par les nouvelles industries de la culture[15]», on est en droit de penser à une accélération du phénomène de sportivisation planétaire.

Ne risque-t-on pas de déboucher sur la clôture du système sportif international, c'est-à-dire sur l'achèvement d'un système dont les promoteurs auraient réussi la gageure de contaminer l'ensemble de la planète par le virus du sport. On ne peut adhérer à cette vision idéalisée et humaniste de l'universalisation des pratiques sans penser qu'elle puisse engendrer une fossilisation de la culture et un dessèchement de l'imaginaire ludique. Que penser d'un gouvernement mondial de sport qui aurait conduit des groupements humains aussi différents que Franciliens, Bushmans, Lapons ou Malinké, Mozabites ou Cingalais, à s'adonner à des formes identiques de pratiques ludiques dont les codes et normes auraient été définis dans une capitale occidentale, et qui participerait conjointement à la désagrégation des pratiques ludiques en vigueur au sein de ces entités ethniques? On crierait au génocide culturel? Et pourtant, c'est à un tel processus de gommage de cultures ludiques que l'on assiste depuis un peu moins d'un siècle, car, et il faut bien l'admettre, l'Occident est prédateur. La planète subit effectivement, et avec l'assentiment des occidentaux, un phénomène d'acculturation sportive auquel s'associe un effet de déculturation ludique. Il ne s'agit pas d'un mécanisme de substitution directe des pratiques ludiques ancestrales par les pratiques sportives modernes, mais plutôt d'un processus plus diffus d'érosion de ces cultures corporelles traditionnelles, suite aux désarticulations économiques et structurelles que subissent les pays économiquement faibles sous l'impact des économies dominantes.

On ne peut certes pas arrêter le cours de l'histoire, une histoire qui conduit à la perte du sens de l'Humain comme l'observe Parlebas:

> Une activité physique qui se veut universelle, peut-elle encore illustrer l'originalité personnelle de chaque culture? Le paradoxe du sport est bien là: en accédant à la mondialisation, cette pratique motrice institutionnalisée favorise les confrontations entre des représentants de tous les pays. Le sport devient l'activité commune de toutes les nations: il offre un langage corporel partagé. Mais en devenant l'Esperanto du corps, le sport ne risque-t-il pas de perdre les singularités des langages corporels propres à chaque culture? [. . .] Aux originalités ethniques correspondent des originalités ludiques. Le «Je» de chaque culture s'exprime par ses jeux: on peut parler d'une véritable techno-motricité, au sens où chaque pays et chaque région possèdent leur propre motricité liée à leur coutume[16].

Sans sombrer dans un passéisme nostalgique, on peut stigmatiser cette dérive de la culture corporelle mondiale, mais aussi souligner la richesse ludique de l'humanité. Des centaines de jeux et sports de traditions ont échappé au rouleau compresseur de l'histoire. Certains sont moribonds, d'autres résistent encore aux agresssions de la modernité: luttes africaines, arts martiaux asiatiques, fantasia marocaine ou algérienne, crosse québécoise ou égfa tunisienne, bouskatchi afghan, lutte russe, joutes à cheval danoises ou espagnoles, luttes indiennes ou turques, boomerang australien, etc. Ces formes jouées déjà recensées sont fort nombreuses. Elles font partie du patrimoine ludique universel qui, nous pouvons le dire, est aujourd'hui en péril. Fait paradoxal, les réservoirs de la planète en jeux se situent logiquement dans les aires culturelles qui ont subi avec une moindre intensité les effets déculturants de la modernité. Or, c'est précisément ces derniers pays qui paraissent les moins bien nantis pour préserver et revivifier ce patrimoine ludique universel.

À l'ère où s'ébauchent, face aux grands déséquilibres économiques mondiaux, certaines formes de solidarité planétaire, il faut poser le problème de jeux traditionnels en termes de solidarité et de soutien aux cultures corporelles locales. «La solidarité olympique», heureuse et généreuse initiative du CIO, ne pourrait-elle pas s'étendre aux jeux et aux sports traditionnels, contribuant de la sorte à la sauvegarde du patrimoine culturel ludique de l'humanité? Plaidant en faveur d'un soutien du CIO à la préservation de cette forme culturelle en péril, Sala écrit: «Arts et sports modernes ont une dette importante envers ces jeux de tradition qui, le plus souvent, leur ont donné naissance[17].» Le Mouvement olympique international peut-il aujourd'hui se satisfaire de son universalité en ignorant la situation ludique qu'il a partiellement provoquée dans les aires culturelles dominées? Ici le politique rejoint le culturel car, note Balandier:

> [. . .] c'est justement parce qu'il y a banalisation des cultures que les revendications de reconquête des identités culturelles accompagnent celles de caractère plus politique et parfois prévalent sur elles, se retrouve ici un processus déjà signalé: à une culture extensive résultant d'une modernité généralisée et en voie d'universalisation, réplique une culture intensive, localisée, provocatrice de différences[18].

On peut observer et regretter que certains intégrismes se trouvent sous-tendus par de telles logiques.

Dès lors, comment le sport, cette culture ethno-centrée, peut-il contribuer à la sauvegarde de la culture ludique mondiale en péril? Seul un élan de solidarité sportive dépassant le cadre étroit du développement du sport «traditionnel» et prenant en compte les incessantes injures faites à l'homme, pourra raviver une culture ludique micro-localisée. Le Mouvement olympique peut se glorifier de nombreuses actions humanistes: croisades contre l'Apartheid et pour la paix, lutte contre le dopage et pour le respect de la dignité de l'athlète et du sport. Le mouvement sortirait ennobli s'il consentait à développer un nouvel humanisme qui prendrait en compte le patrimoine ludique universel en participant à sa sauvegarde. Nous n'avons pas ici l'intention de nous substituer à des organismes comme le FIDEPS pour proposer des actions. Signalons cependant que cette structure de l'UNESCO a déjà réalisé ou soutenu certaines manifestations visant à faire connaître les jeux de traditions, malheureusement faute de moyens, certains projets, comme le « 1er printemps des Jeux et des Sports de traditions de l'Europe du Sud », n'ont pu voir le jour. Des expériences et démonstrations de jeux à l'instar de celles réalisées parallèlement aux Jeux olympiques de Montréal pourraient être réitérées. Une action systématique pour identifier, localiser, répertorier les jeux dans le monde à l'aide d'enquêtes de terrain, films, photos, mériterait d'être entreprise.

Mais c'est à la réactivation de certains jeux qu'il faut donner la priorité. Des expériences d'auto-développement économique et ludique pourraient être conduites dans des zones économiquement défavorisées. Plutôt que de développer à l'infini une liste d'actions ponctuelles, il nous paraît plus pertinent de sensibiliser les plus hautes autorités du sport mondial à l'urgence de la mise en place d'un programme de sauvegarde de ce patrimoine culturo-ludique en péril. «La proximité nouvelle des Nations dans l'enclos planétaire, multiplie entre elles les causes de conflit en même temps qu'elle leur interdit de s'ignorer[19].» Ce constat de Dupuy sur la clôture du système international, c'est-à-dire, sur cette nécessité pour les hommes de vivre ensemble, devrait conduire la communauté sportive internationale à une réflexion distanciée à l'égard du procès mondial du sport et à un changement d'expectative intégrant l'idée de la pluralité de la culture ludique mondiale.

NOTES ET RÉFÉRENCES

1. Nous utilisons volontairement le mot sport au singulier car nous considérons celui-ci comme une entité culturelle et institutionnelle.

2. Errais B, Fates Y (1989) Les Jeux régionaux, témoins de l'universalisation des sports. Mappemonde 2 26-28

3. Boulongne YP (1990) De Pierre de Coubertin à Juan Antonio Samaranch. Où en est le Mouvement olympique? DIRE en APS 34 p 16

4. Dupuy RJ (1989) La clôture du système international. La cité terrestre. Paris: PUF Collection Perspectives Internationales p 20

5. Julien C (1990) Alerte: Nationalismes. Le monde diplomatique (Janvier p 1)

6. On consultera à ce sujet Lefebvre H (1977) De l'État, le mode de production étatique. Paris: Union générale d'éditions, Coll 10/18 p 104

7. Cette charte a été proclamée le 21 novembre 1978 à l'occasion de la tenue à Paris de la Conférence générale de l'UNESCO. UNESCO (1979) Charte internationale de l'éducation physique et du sport. Paris.

8. Le taux de pratique sportive en France est estimé à 41,2%. Voir Irlinger P, Louveau C, Metoudi M (1987) Les pratiques sportives des Français. Paris: Institut national du sport et de l'éducation physique, Tome I, p 54

9. Institut national de l'éducation physique et du sport (1978) Sport et sous-développement. Paris: document non publié p 4

10. «Trends in sports, a multinational perspective» est une publication de l'Association internationale de sociologie. Ces tendances du sport mondial ont été dégagées à partir des contributions d'experts nationaux des activités sportives concernant quatre continents et quinze pays. Association internationale de sociologie (1989) Trends in sport, a multinational perspective. Voorthuizen, Netherlands: Giordano Bruno Publishers.

11. Ces auteurs montrent que les régions les plus indigentes en matière d'organisation des grandes compétitions internationales sont: le Sud-Est asiatique, l'Amérique centrale, la

Péninsule arabique et surtout l'Afrique. Voir à ce sujet Mathieu D, Praicheux J (1989) L'espace mondial des grandes manifestations sportives internationales. Mappemonde 2 7-13

12. Balandier G (1985) Le détour — Pouvoir et modernité. Paris: Fayard, Coll L'espace du politique p 93

13. Ibid p 107

14. Ibid p 167

15. Ibid

16. Parlebas P (1988) Le paradoxe des Jeux et des sports. In UNESCO, Fonds international pour le développement de l'éducation physique et des sports, Sports et traditions. Paris, texte non paginé

17. Sala G (1987) Sports et beaux arts, dialogues ou monologues. In Szymiczek O (ed) Rapport de la vingt-sixième session de l'Académie internationale olympique. Lausanne: Comité international olympique p 185-94

18. Balandier G (1985) op cit p 220

19. Dupuy RJ (1989) op cit p 162

L'« Empire » olympique

Jean Praicheux

Manifestation sportive la plus importante du monde, les Jeux olympiques ont réussi la gageure de regrouper la presque totalité des États ou régions du monde (167). Les quelques absents sont des pays de très petite taille et peu peuplés. Signe des temps, le boycott de la célébration d'une Olympiade prend une signification plus lourde de sens qu'une participation! Ce phénomène est d'autant plus remarquable que dans un domaine à l'origine mineur, le sport, ce quasi-unanisme a été obtenu assez rapidement et selon un rythme croissant.

Les renseignements recueillis auprès du Comité international olympique permettent l'analyse géographique de ce phénomène sous trois de ses aspects: – la dynamique de l'adhésion des différents États; – la représentativité politique du CIO à travers l'origine de ses membres et à travers eux, la date d'entrée des nationalités dans cet organisme; – la géographie de la décision à travers les lieux où se tiennent les principales sessions du CIO.

La dynamique des adhésions au mouvement olympique

Le Comité international olympique, organisme exécutif du Mouvement olympique, étend son influence sur la presque totalité des pays du monde. On a coutume de qualifier les Comités nationaux olympiques de représentants des États. Si c'est la cas de figure très majoritaire, il n'est pas exclusif. Un Comité national olympique peut représenter un État mais aussi une région géographique «qui a bénéficié d'un gouvernement stable pendant une période raisonnable». Certaines entités territoriales, qui n'ont pas le statut d'État, sont ainsi représentées de plein droit au sein du CIO; c'est le cas par exemple des Bermudes ou de Porto Rico. Lors de sa 96ᵉ session, en septembre 1990, le CIO devrait modifier ces dispositions statutaires dans le cadre d'une révision de la Charte olympique.

1890
1990

Jean Praicheux, Laboratoire de géographie humaine et régionale, Université de Franche-Comté, Besançon, France.

L'œcuménisme olympique

En 1990, le CIO regroupe 167 Comités Nationaux Olympiques. La *Figure 1* montre que les vides sont rares. Parmi les pays d'une certaine étenduc géographique on ne note guère comme absents que l'Afrique du Sud et le Cambodge. Les autres nations non représentées sont, pour la plupart, des États insulaires (Caraïbes, Océanie) n'ayant accédé à l'indépendance politique que depuis peu. En moins d'un siècle, le Mouvement olympique a été reconnu dans la quasi totalité du monde. Le CIO est devenu une institution internationale de première importance : – par le poids des décisions prises dans son domaine de compétence ; – par l'importance populaire, médiatique et économique de ses manifestations ; – par le rôle de vitrine politico-économique des États que ses succès ont suscité.

Les reflets des grandes transformations politiques

Pour rapide qu'elle fut, l'extension de l'audience du CIO s'est faite par vagues successives qui témoignent étroitement des bouleversements contemporains de l'échiquier politique mondial. La *Figure 1* souligne les cinq grandes étapes de la mondialisation du CIO. Encore faut-il parfois la lire avec prudence. Certains pays, naguère membres du CIO en ont été exclus (Afrique du Sud), parfois réintégrés (Chines, Allemagnes) ou politiquement assimilés dans un cadre politique plus large (Pays Baltes). Les dates qui figurent sur la carte ne sont pas toujours celles de la première entrée des territoires dans le Mouvement olympique mais celles de leur adhésion sous leur forme politique ou territoriale actuelle (le cas des deux Allemagnes en est un exemple).

Les créations de Comités nationaux olympiques relèvent de trois grands critères : – L'éco-politique : les premiers pays participants regroupaient l'essentiel du pouvoir économique, et, partant, politique mondial ; – Le genre de vie : en particulier celui des élites d'une nation qui véhicule des idéaux résultant d'un transfert où la colonisation a joué un rôle décisif (Inde, Amérique du Sud) ; – Les transformations politiques : la plus importante est l'accession à l'indépendance qui trouve dans le Mouvement olympique une occasion extraordinaire de s'affirmer sinon juridiquement du moins publiquement. On constate d'ailleurs que les reconnaissances de certains Comités nationaux olympiques sont en phase directe avec ceux d'une reconnaissance politique de droit (Chine et Taiwan par exemple).

Une diffusion en plusieurs étapes

Les cinq étapes de l'expansion du Mouvement olympique décrites ici, montrent une grande cohérence dans le cadre d'une lecture géopolitique.

De 1894 (création du CIO) à 1915, des CNOs de 22 pays obtiennent leur adhésion : on constate que ces derniers représentent le cœur du pouvoir mondial autour de l'Europe occidentale ct de ses grandes zones de peuplement outremer (Amérique du Nord, Australie). La présence du Japon (dès 1912) montre clairement la relation entre sa formidable montée en puissance et la volonté d'accéder au mode de représentation occidental.

Entre les deux guerres mondiales, la diffusion se fait dans deux directions essentielles ; la totalité de l'Europe est maintenant concernée par l'adhésion des dernières nations du Sud et de l'Est (à l'exception de l'URSS) ; l'Amérique latine entre massivement dans le Mouvement olympique, conséquence probable d'une indépendance politique précocement acquise, mais aussi sans doute de l'origine et de la culture européennes de ses classes dirigeantes.

Après la Seconde Guerre Mondiale, les nouvelles vagues d'adhésions sont le double résultat des bouleversements politiques dus à la guerre dans les pays développés et des vagues de décolonisation qui ont affecté les anciens Empires coloniaux. De 1946 à 1959, 42 Comités nationaux olympiques vont être créés. Les derniers grands européens s'intègrent ou se réintègrent au mouvement (Allemagne, URSS). Mais l'Olympisme pénètre largement le continent asiatique (Moyen-Orient, anciennes zones d'influences britanniques et néerlandaises) et aborde l'Afrique : les anciens protectorats français d'Afrique du Nord et les anciennes colonies britanniques représentent dorénavant un continent où seule l'Égypte figurait dans les nations olympiques (depuis 1910). L'Amérique centrale et les Caraïbes complètent la précocité de la participation américaine.

De 1960 à 1969, le mouvement d'intégration est presque exclusivement africain et témoigne de la seconde grande vague de décolonisation (française, belge, espagnole).

Enfin depuis 1970 et l'accession à l'indépendance des dernières parcelles d'Empires, 44 adhésions ont permis au CIO d'être implanté dans presque tous les pays. Le règlement du problème chinois intervient en 1979. À l'exception de l'Afrique du Sud, les derniers grands pays africains affirment leur participation et l'adhésion des micro-États de l'Océanie et de l'Océan Indien se généralise.

Géopolitique de la décision olympique

Le Comité international olympique «chargé [...] du contrôle et du développement des Jeux Olympiques modernes» est un «organisme permanent» qui coopte ses membres par «l'élection de personnalités qu'il juge qualifiées, sous réserve que celles-ci [...] soient des nationaux résidents d'un pays doté d'un CNO reconnu par le CIO[1]». Leur pouvoir, dans leur domaine, est d'autant plus important qu'ils «sont ses représentants [du CIO] auprès de leurs pays respectifs et non les délégués de leurs pays au sein du CIO[2]».

À la veille de la Première Guerre Mondiale, 30 pays étaient représentés au CIO. Outre les pays riches qui avaient été à l'origine de la rénovation des Jeux, on note la présence des plus grands États d'Amérique latine : ceux où l'émigration européenne est importante par son poids démographique et économique (ARG, CHI, BRA). Entre les Deux Guerres Mondiales, le CIO ne change guère de visage à l'exception notable d'une importante pénétration asiatique avec la cooptation de représentants indiens (1920) et chinois (1922) et d'un renforcement de l'Europe avec l'entrée des états nouvellement créés (POL, YUG). L'immédiat après guerre entérine les bouleversements politiques (arrivée de la RFA et de l'URSS), mais il faut attendre les années soixante et la décolonisation pour voir le CIO accueillir des pays d'Afrique et de l'Insulinde. Aujourd'hui 76 pays sur les 167 pays-membres sont représentés dans l'instance suprême du CIO qui compte 84 membres. Ou, à l'inverse, 91 nations ou régions géographiques, dont le Comité national olympique a été reconnu par le CIO ne sont pas représentés au sein de cette instance.

La *Figure 2* montre que ces entités ne sont pas dispersées au hasard. Sans que ces remarques aient un quelconque caractère systématique, ces «exclus» relatifs sont manifestement plus nombreux dans le groupe des pays pauvres, d'accession récente à l'indépendance politique ou de très faible étendue (en particulier les micro-États insulaires). Géographiquement ces trois thèmes trouvent leur concrétisation en Afrique, en Asie du Sud-Est et Proche-Orient, dans la zone Amérique Centrale — Caraïbes et Pacifique. Huit États qui ont eu, à un moment donné, un ambassadeur du CIO dans leur pays, ne sont plus présents au sein de l'instance décisionnelle du CIO. La majorité d'entre eux sont de toute évidence des États marqués par une instabilité politique : ARG, CHI, LIB, IRQ, ETH.

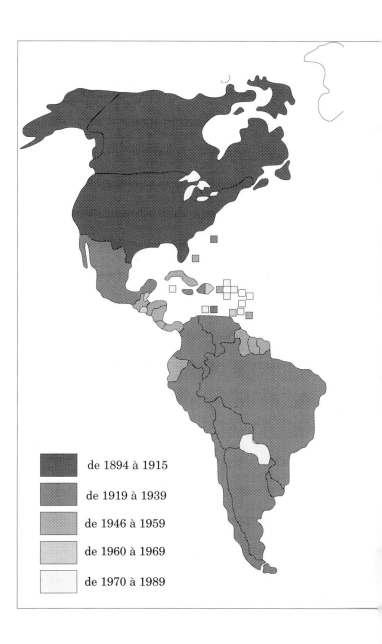

de 1894 à 1915

de 1919 à 1939

de 1946 à 1959

de 1960 à 1969

de 1970 à 1989

FIGURE 1
Période d'adhésion au CIO

0   5000 km

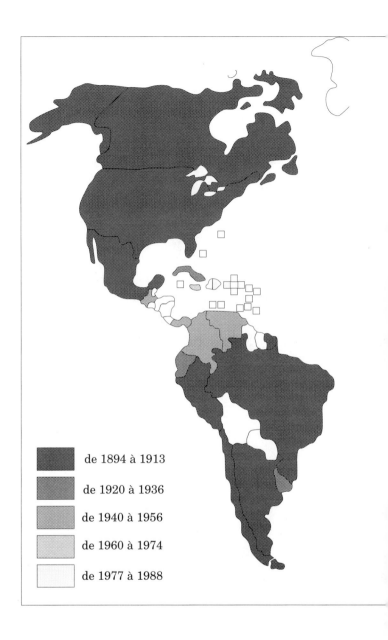

de 1894 à 1913

de 1920 à 1936

de 1940 à 1956

de 1960 à 1974

de 1977 à 1988

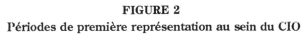

FIGURE 2
Périodes de première représentation au sein du CIO

0   5000 km

Enfin un certain nombre de pays (16) bénéficient de deux représentants au CIO : cette sur-représentation est prévue dans la Charte olympique, qui peut d'ailleurs, en tant que de besoin, permettre une interprétation assez large : « Il ne sera nommé qu'un seul membre par pays, exception faite pour les plus grands, ceux où le Mouvement olympique est très répandu et ceux où ont eu lieu des Jeux olympiques. Le maximum pourra être de deux[3]. »

On retrouve inévitablement dans ce groupe le noyau originaire des pays occidentaux fondateurs, ceux dont les villes ont été hôtes des Jeux olympiques mais pas tous. Il ne fait guère de doute que la majorité des nations restera longtemps écartée de cette sur-représentation faute d'avoir les capacités techniques et surtout financières pour organiser des Jeux.

Les lieux symboliques et techniques de la décision olympique

Les lieux des sessions du CIO, annuelles depuis 1905, bi-annuelles les années olympiques depuis 1936, soulignent de façon ostentatoire la localisation du centre de gravité de la décision olympique. Si 167 pays ou régions participent au Mouvement olympique, 35 seulement d'entre eux ont accueilli une session sur leur territoire. Deux phénomènes sont à la base de cette disparité : l'avantage reste encore aux pays promoteurs de la rénovation des Jeux, les nations occidentales. Le caractère récent de l'adhésion d'un nombre très important de nations ne leur a pas permis, à ce jour, de manifester publiquement l'éclat de leur participation par l'accueil d'une session. L'Europe occidentale demeure le centre symbolique de la décision olympique, accompagné par la participation des pays développés de l'Est ou de l'Ouest (URS, BUL, POL, TCH d'un côté, JPN, CAN de l'autre).

On constate pourtant un glissement géopolitique si l'on considère séparément les deux grandes périodes qu'individualise la Seconde Guerre Mondiale. De 1894 à 1939, 20 pays seulement ont accueilli une session, 18 sont européens, 1 est américain. Une seule session s'est tenue dans un pays pauvre, l'Égypte, dont il faut souligner la précocité de l'adhésion, dès 1910. Le rôle de l'Europe est écrasant. Deux critères contribuent à faire émerger quelques pays. La France, initiatrice de la rénovation des Jeux, est le pôle symbolique. La Suisse, terre d'accueil du CIO est le pôle technique. La Grèce est l'inévitable référence mythologique. La Grande-Bretagne affirme sa place prépondérante dans le développement du sport moderne et sa puissance économico-politique. L'Allemagne enfin, qui en 1936 accueille deux sessions du CIO, affiche son rôle de grande puissance et inaugure l'utilisation de l'image des Jeux à des fins de propagande idéologique.

Après la Seconde Guerre Mondiale, le paysage change sensiblement. Toujours prépondérante, la place de l'Europe se dilue partiellement dans l'ensemble des pays industrialisés. Sur les 30 pays organisateurs, on ne compte plus que 20 nations européennes. Quoiqu'en relative régression l'Europe conserve le leadership et regroupe encore les deux-tiers des lieux de décision. La distribution y est un peu différente que dans la période précédente. En particulier le rôle de la France devient plus discret : le poids politique de son initiative pèse moins lourd qu'auparavant. Les pays organisateurs sont répartis d'une manière plus homogène dans l'Ouest et le Sud européens. Les pays industrialisés du bloc de l'Est sont assez faiblement représentés (ils organisent 7 sessions sur 60), le Japon surtout et l'Amérique du Nord confortent leur présence (13 sessions organisées contre 1 seule dans la période précédente) : il est vrai qu'avec le développement des moyens de transports modernes, la distance au centre n'a plus le même sens. Les pays du Tiers-Monde ne font qu'une apparition bien timide (3 sessions) et encore le sens de leur présence est-il bien particulier : on ne s'interroge guère sur les mobiles de prestige ou de caution politique que représentent l'acceptation des propositions de l'Iran du Shah en 1967 et de l'Uruguay en 1979.

Dans l'ensemble et sans vraies entorses, la symbolique du pouvoir olympique reste l'apanage des pays riches, la tradition laissant à l'Europe un poids encore très lourd. Les lieux de réunion entre le CIO et les Fédérations internationales, où se prennent de multiples décisions lourdes de conséquences pour le sport d'élite, confirment les remarques précédentes. La représentation de l'Occident libéral est renforcée avec un poids écrasant pour la Suisse (organisatrice de 19 réunions sur 42), pays d'accueil du CIO.

Ces trois approches restent bien sûr très globalisantes. Il conviendrait de les affiner pour dégager des éléments plus pertinents. Telles quelles, elles soulignent combien le sport, à travers le Mouvement olympique, est un traceur efficace du système politique mondial. L'analyse géographique de la performance olympique elle-même, déjà abordée par plusieurs auteurs doit aussi contribuer à une meilleure lisibilité de ce phénomène complexe.

RÉFÉRENCES

1. Comité international olympique (1990) Charte olympique 1990. Lausanne [article 12] p 9

2. Ibid

3. Ibid

In Quest of Excellence: Development, Problems, and Values

La quête de l'excellence sportive : développement, problèmes et valeurs

Tradition and Science
in the Training of Athletes:
1870-1914

Roberta J. Park

As several published studies have shown, "modern" structures for and attitudes regarding agonistic games and competitive athletics had become well-established by the mid-1800s[1]. On both sides of the Atlantic, during the middle decades of the 19th century, sports flourished and became increasingly organized, routinized, and commercialized. Elaborate sets of rules and codes specific to a given sport were promulgated, and athletes became more specialized. Codified rules were ultimately needed to define and legislate the matter of *amateurism* as contests grew in numbers, intensity, and popularity. By the 1890s, what had been phenomena unique among English-speaking nations, had gained footholds in France, Germany and elsewhere[2].

In 1869, American interest in international sports became manifest and was given considerable impetus by the boat race between Oxford and Harvard crews on the course between Putney Bridge and Mortlake before a crowd estimated to be 750 000[3]. In 1870, *The Illustrated London News* was filled with pictures and stories of Oxford-Cambridge boat races, Thames Rowing-Club Athletic Sports, King's College School Athletic Sports, and similar activities. *Baily's Magazine of Sports and Pastimes* that same year extolled the virtues of the London Athletic Club, University Athletic Sports, cricketer WG Grace, and MCC. The rapid growth of amateur athletics, it declared, had led, among other things, to an increased interest in more rational and "scientific" training procedures. Although this statement was more style then substance, the beginnings of a modern approach to athletic training (and a few scientific studies of intense muscular exertion) was beginning to emerge[4].

In 1867, William Wood, proprietor of New York City's Wood's Gymnasium, had included a lenghty section on "training" in his popular *Manual of Physical Exercise*. Training, he observed: speeded the removal of waste products; increased the size and power of voluntary muscles; and enhanced respiration, thereby promoting health and strength of the whole body. Although he had little to say

Roberta J. Park, Department of Physical Education, University of California, Berkeley, California, USA.

about diet, Wood did include a table of digestion rates derived from data that the American Army Surgeon William Beaumount had gathered in 1837[5].

Benjamin W Dwight examined current practices in "Intercollegiate Regattas, Hurdle-Races and Prize Contests" in 1876 and concluded that the new modes of training college teams absorbed "altogether too much of their time and thought and zeal". Instead of maintaining health and strength, the aim was rapidly becoming to push body, mind, and even morals beyond natural bounds. "Science" was invoked in an effort to support the claims of both supporters and critics, but most training theories remained substantially rooted in practices which could be traced back to Sir John Sinclair's *Code of Health and Longevity* (1807) and Walter Thom's *Pedestrianism* (1813)[6].

By the 1870s, several members of the medical profession became interested in conducting scientific investigations of "[...] the vital phenomena connected with muscular effort, notably simple 'the laws of waste and nutrition'. The American physician Austin Flint, Jr. analyzed urine collected during one of EP Weston's pedestrian performances". Weston agreed to be a subject for another series of "physiological investigations bearing on the waste of tissue". These were conducted by Dr. FW Pavy, FRS, Physician to Guy's Hospital, especially on behalf of the *British Medical Journal*. Pavy published his results in the February 26, 1876 issue. As these did not seem to agree with the results that Flint had obtained, the results of Pavy's more comprehensive analyses of 48- and 75-hour performances were awaited with particular interest[7].

Dr. John Morgan's longitudinal study of the health and longevity of men who had rowed in Oxford and Cambridge crews between 1829 and 1869 brought forth quite different facts about athletics than the health reformer Benjamin Ward Richardson had claimed. This lengthy book, accompanied by 270 pages of testimony and appendices, appeared in 1873. The journal *Nature* immediately published a three-part discussion of the work, written by Archibald MacLaren (Director of the Oxford Gymnasium). An oarsman at both Shrewsbury and University College, Oxford, Morgan had both a medical and an athletic interest in his topic. Of the 251 men who responded, 162 believed that their exertions had no negative effect, and 115 reported benefits. In 1876, Boston's EH Bradford, MD, published the results of his own study of Harvard crews between 1852 and 1870, reaching the same conclusions as had Morgan. Substantially the same results were reported by Dr. George Meylan in 1904[8].

The same month that MacLaren's commentary appeared in *Nature*, the author of an anonymous article entitled "Scientific Athletics" declared in the *British Medical Journal* that several members of the medical profession had become concerned about the need to "[...] Inquire in an impartial and scientific manner into the subject of exercise in its influence on health". While the writer may have had Morgan's book in mind, the specific reference was to Dr. RJ Lee's *Exercise Training, and Their Effects Upon Health* (1873), and the "[...] desirability of a scientific inquiry into the whole subject of exercise[9]".

Interest in scientific understandings of athletic performance was by no means confined to Britain. In 1892, Dr. George Kolb, with the help of a Glasgow friend, prepared an English translation of his *Beitrage zur Physiologie maximaler Muskelarbeit besonders des modernen Sports* (1887) *Physiology of Sport: Contibutions Toward the Physiology of Maximum Muscular Exertion, Especially Modern Sport*. Both a sportsman and a physician, Kolb insisted that only those who had experience in both sports and medicine were qualified to research athletic subjects. Medical men could not fully comprehend the enormous strain of a race unless they had endured it; sportsmen were apt to "shut out" physiologists who approached research on athletes as they would on animals. Interested in examining the "physiological effects of maximum exertions", Kolb reported data on men like Paul Wolff, Germany's rowing champion and the distance runner GP Mills. He insisted that development could be achieved only by means of *maximum* muscular exertion; and in a declaration that reflected evolutionary ideas and recent "Social Darwinistic" tendencies, Kolb wrote: "[. . .] only those beings have a right to live, develop and multiply, that can compete best and are better organized than the more significant rest[10]."

French physiologists and physicians also had developed considerable interest in exercise and athletic performance. Fernand Lagrange published *Physiologie des exercises du corps* in 1888. This was quickly translated as part of Appleton's International Scientific Series, which had already issued an English version of Marey's *Animal Mechanism* in 1874[11]. The *Revue des Deux Mondes* published such articles as "The Reform of Physical Education" in which Lagrange declared that physical education was on the verge of becoming a "positive science" thanks to developments in hygiene and physiology[12]. In 1894, Phillippe Tissié reported his investigations of physiological measures taken of the bicycle champion Stéphane during a twenty-four hour, 400 mile endurance performance, concluding that the body needed greater quantities of hydrocarbons as muscular work became prolonged and that there was no correspondence between fatigue of the muscles of locomotion and fatigue of the heart. A Congress of Physical Education formed part of the 1900 Paris International Exposition, and an international committee of hygienists, physiologists, and physicians was appointed to study the effects of the athletic events that were to be held in connection with the Exposition[13].

Among those selected to attend the Congress were Tissié, Henry G Beyer, Dudley Allen Sargent, and also George Fitz, who in the early 1890s had been instrumental in establishing the first research-oriented physical education Bachelor of Science degree program in the United States[14]. Italy's Angelo Mosso, one of the six foreign Vice Presidents of the Congress, spoke cordially of the physical education he had seen during a visit to the United States. A physiologist of high standing among contemporaries, Mosso authored, among other things, various papers in support of physical education, an influential book on fatigue, and the results of his extensive high altitude experiments on respiration, circulation, fatigue of the heart, diet and fasting, muscular force, vital capacity, training, and other functions[15].

Americans were also interested in bringing scientific attitudes and techniques to bear on "Popular Fallacies Regarding Athletes and Athletics". In an article for the April 27, 1889 issue of the *Journal of the American Medical Association*, Dr. Irving Rosse had observed that the whole question of athletics, (which had "[. . .] for its object the bringing of man to a greater state of perfection [. . .]") should be of the greatest interest to the medical profession. Ranging widely from the Columbia Club's 450 members, to Sargent's anthropometric work that had recently attracted the attention of West Point, to the introduction of physical culture at the United States Naval Academy, to conflicting opinions regarding the influence of athletics on hernia, aneurism, and heart disease, to Royer-Collard's *Organoplastie hygiénique* (which declared athletes and circus performers to be remarkably healthy), Rosse concluded that "[. . .] healthy exercise of the physical powers is one of the necessary pastimes "[. . .] healthy of a mainly and vigorous race; and that next to food and sleep, athletics has the largest share in advancing the human race[16]."

Not all physicians were as exuberant or as convinced of the merits of intense muscular exercise as Rosse, however. Discussing "Exercise and Disease" for the *New York Medical Journal* in 1898, Dr. E Palier declared: "Physical exercise, when judiciously used, is a most valuable prophylactic and therapeutic agent; misused, it is productive of great harm". Drawing from Morgan's *University Oars*, from Foster's *Textbook of Physiology*, Lagrange's *Exercise Physiology*, the

French neurologist Charcot's studies of hysteria and chorea, the German physiologist Du Bois-Reymond, and other contemporary sources, Palier presented a much more cautious assessment of the merits of exercise and training for heart, gastro-intestinal system, nervous system, venereal diseases, and rheumatism[17].

Questions of whether—and if so, what kinds of—structural and physiological changes might occur in connection with *training* attracted increased attention from investigators in the 1890s and early 1900s. The Harvard Athletic Committee invited Dr. Eugene A Darling to investigate physiological changes that occurred during severe training, specifically with the hope of shedding light on the much-debated question of "over-training". "Over-training" was an amorphous term that referred to a decline in performance after an athlete had reached what appeared to be his maximal level. It was widely held that this was due to the fact that a man could "[...] not repair the waste"; but what mechanisms were involved was unknown[18].

Darling examined heart, kidneys, weights, and temperatures of men on the Harvard crew in May and June 1899. Investigations were made on the football team in autumn of the same year, resulting in findings similar to those obtained in the rowing study. Since the research had to be designed so as not to interfere with the technical aspects of training, data collection was difficult. It was found that the average daily weight of the varsity crew dropped from 171.4 lbs on May 18 to 166 lbs on June 29—and that the average loss on the last race day was 4.25 lbs. This was not considered injurious, however, as laboratory experiments on animals had already show "[...] that during active exercise the energy is largely if not wholly derived from the oxidation of fat and glycogen, and that the muscles themselves are not used up". This, Darling observed, conformed to the general experience of athletes who, it was said, typically lost weight in the form of superfluous fat during the early stages of training, but upon reaching what was referred to as "weight in training" experienced lassitude and were unable to sustain prolonged exertion if they lost more weight. This particular form of "over-training" was known as "stateless"—and was believed to be due to a deficiency of reserve fuel in the form of fat and carbohydrates stored in the body[19].

Darling's attempts to study the effects of training on body temperature proved to be inconclusive, neither confirming nor refuting recent observations that Williams and Arnold had made on men who had run a twenty-five mile Boston marathon. As had Williams and so many others at the turn of the century, Darling also studied effects of exercise on the heart; but the issue of whether the "enlargement" that was found was due to hypertrophy and/or to dilation remained unresolved, and was a constant source of disagreement among physicians and trainers for many years[20]. The most useful deduction to be made, Darling concluded, was that "[...] the heart is a muscular organ and that it shows with the other muscles both the fatigue due to violent and prolonged exertion and also the increase in size and power due to proper exercise and nutrition [...]. As with other muscles, not size but quality tells in the long run." Darling criticized the crew's practice—which was typical of the period—of eating large quantities of roast beef as rapidly as possible, noting the excreted urea indicated that much of the proteid material had been unassimilated and was probably a major cause of the indigestion and diarrhea that plagues the crews, especially in the hot summer months[21].

Shortly before Darling's second study appeared, the United States Department of Agriculture published Atwater and Bryant's study of nutrition and energy production. These two investigators also had conducted dietary studies on Harvard and Yale crews in 1898 and of the Harvard four-man crew in 1900[22]. According to the *Boston Medical and Surgical Journal*, Darling, Atwater, Williams, and Arnold had been the chief contributors to scientific physiological research conducted under actual competitive conditions where the "[...] uproar and excitement which surrounds both start and finish [. . .]" might influence the body's responses. Blake, Larrabee and associates published the results of their extensive physiological investigations of runners in the Boston Marathon for the years 1900, 1901, and 1902. Significantly, their paper closed with a section devoted to "physical characteristics" and a recitation of the anthropometric characteristics of the winners who, it was claimed, were of medium height and resembled "[. . .] privates of the French and Austrian rather than the English or German armies [. . .]" or the "long, lanky Yankee greyhound". It was marvelous, the authors concluded, that the human body could be trained to withstand so much[23].

The reference to anthropometry reflected another late 19th century preoccupation: the *form* of the body. Addressing Manchester's Royal Institution in 1880 on "The Relationship of Anatomy to the Fine Arts", SM Bradley, F.R.C.S. had declared the two to be "[. . .] like brother and sister." He argued that "natural law" had established the harmony of proportions governing the human form, and set forth the example of the Apollo Belvedere as the standard to be attained. The gymnasium and athletics, Bradley maintained, had afforded the Greeks a "[. . .] unique field for studying the human figure in action and in repose". If the entire body was taken as 1 000, the lower half should be 618.033 and the upper half 381.966. Bradley and his contemporaries, however, were not content with studying the "law of proportion" as it was displayed in static poses. They were keenly interested in *action* and the meanings that action conveyed. The artist, therefore, "[. . .] must also have a knowledge of the disposition of the muscles [. . .] and the shapes they assume in contraction and extension [. . .][24]."

The frontispiece of Richard Proctor's *Strength: How to Get Strong and Keep Strong With Chapters on Rowing and Swimming, Fat, Age, and the Waist* (1889), was one of those late 19th century books which bore a representation of the Apollo Belvedere. A decade earlier, Harper and Brothers had embossed the cover of William Blaikie's *How to Get Strong and How to Stay So* with brawny arms and flexed biceps[25]. Blaikie dedicated his book to Oxford Gymnasium Director Archibald MacLaren, who had included drawings of sunken-chested young men and boys who had not had proper exercise in his influential *A System of Physical Education, Theoretical and Practical* (1865). Blaikie used similar representations in his own book. Charles Woodhull Eaton, who included long passages taken directly from MacLaren in his *Things Young Men Should Know. A Manual of the Anatomy, Physiology and Hygiene of the Sexual System* (1884), insisted that it was the duty of colleges to turn "[. . .] flat-chested, spindle-shanked [. . .] half-developed [. . .]" boys into virile men[26]. According to many contemporary sources, the athlete provided the anatomical, biological, social, and moral ideal that other men should strive to emulate—even if they could never attain his perfection.

HH Griffin stated in the preface to *Athletics*, one of the "All-England Series" handbooks:

> We live in an Athletic age, and the man who is not an athlete in some shape or form is pretty sure to be not only written down as a nincompoop, but to prove himself one, even in the more serious battles of life; for, unless a man has the pluck and determination to succeed in whatever branch of sport he adopts, he is not likely to win his way to fame and fortune in whatever occupation or profession may fall to his lot [. . .].

Participation in athletics was not solely for pleasure, therefore; it was a duty to oneself, to one's country, and to the "rising generation[27]".

Across the ocean, De Pauw University's John Bigham uttered similar sentiments, stating that football was America's most important game as it required of a man superior skill, strength, endurance, regular habits, suppleness, scrupulous care in diet, obedience, self-restraint, mental alertness, and cooperation. Walter Camp and Lorin Deland's popular book *Football* (1896) equated the physical and moral courage the game instilled in players with the qualities of the Civil War's best men. Not only were football players superior to other men in height, weight, and lung capacity, enthusiasts maintained; they were almost certain to be superior in courage, fortitude, pluck, and "sand[28]".

Not content to speculate about the benefits and evils of athletics, in 1894 Henry G Beyer, surgeon at the United States Naval Academy, called for factual studies regarding the effects of football on participants rather than the continued war of words between enthusiasts and critics. Beyer had analyzed the height, weight, lung-capacity, and strength of cadets engaged in football, rowing, and gymnastics between 1892 and 1894, concluding that both systematic gymnasium drill and rowing were productive of better results than was football. With regard to the hotly debated question of whether athletics benefitted mental and moral development, he insisted that this should be studied by psychologists; however, he was certain that any measurable changes would require generations, not merely a few afternoons practice at football[29].

Beyer's attitudes were among the more forward-looking. The movement toward a more scientific attitude in both medicine and physiology that had begun before 1870 would be in full force when the University of Pennsylvania's famous coach Michael Murphy wrote *Athletic Training* (1914)[30]. Murphy had coached American athletes for both the 1908 and 1912 Olympic Games. By the Stockholm Games of 1912, athletes in many nations had learned the value of carefully prescribed, systematic training. With the advent of sport sciences, including sports medicine, in the 1920s and 1930s, thanks to precedents set largely by German physicians[31], and American scientists, athletic training would begin to take on new and more modern dimensions.

NOTES AND REFERENCES

1. For example, Haley B (1978) The healthy body and the victorian culture. Cambridge: Harvard University Press; and Adelman M (1986) A sporting time: New York city and the rise of modern athletics 1820-1870. Urbana: University of Illinois Press

2. For example, Weber E (1986) France, fin de siècle. Cambridge: Harvard University Press; Arnaud P (ed) (1987) Les athlètes de la République française: gymnastique, sport et idéologie républicaine 1870-1914. Toulouse: Bibliothèque historique Privat; Langerfeld H (1988) Auf dem Wege zur Sportwissenschaft: Mediziner und Leibesübungen im 19 Jahrhundert. Stadion 14 125-48; Mangan JA (1988) (ed) Pleasure profit, proselytism: British culture and sport at home and abroad 1770-1914. London: Frank Cass

3. Durick WG (1988) The gentleman's race: an examination of the 1869 Harvard-Oxford race. Journal of Sport History 15 41-63

4. Sports, past and to come. Baily's Magazine of Sports and Pastimes 18 (1870) 191-204

5. Wood W (1867) Manual of physical exercises. New York: Harper and Brothers

6. Dwight BW (1876) Intercollegiate regattas, hurdle-races and prize contests. The New Englander 35 251-79; Radford P (1986/87) From oral tradition to printed record: British sports science in transition 1805-1807. Stadion 12 295-304; Sinclair J (1807) The code of health and longevity or a concise view of the principles calculated for the preservation of health and the attainment of long life. Edinburgh: Arch Constable and Co; Thom W (1813) Pedestrianism or an account of the performances of celebrated pedestrians during the last and present century. With a full narrative of captain Barclay's public and private matches and an essay on training. Aberdeen: Chambers

7. Flint A (1878) On the source of muscular power. New York: D Appleton and Co; Pavy FW (1876) Report of analyses of urine during severe exercise in the case of Mr Weston. British Medical Journal (February 26) 271-72

8. Morgan J (1873) University oars. London: Macmillan; MacLaren A (1873) University oars. Nature (March 27) 397-99, (April 3) 418-21, (April 17) 456-60; Richardson BW (1878) Diseases of modern life. New York: Appleton; Bradford's study is referred to by Meylan p 363. Meylan G (1904) Harvard University oarsmen. American Physical Education Review 9 362-76, 115 [sic]-552

9. Reviews and notices. British Medical Journal (March 24 1873) p 589; Lee RJ (1873) Exercise and training: their effects upon health. London: Smith, Elder

10. Kolb G (1893) Physiology of sport. London: Krohne and Sasemann; Langenfeld H (1988) op cit

11. Lagrange F (1889) Physiology of bodily exercise. London: Kegan Paul, Trench; Marey EJ (1874) Animal mechanism: a treatise on terrestrial and aerial locomotion. New York: Appleton

12. Lagrange F (1892) La réforme de l'éducation physique. Revue des deux mondes 112 338-74

13. Demeny G (1900) Procès-verbaux sommaires. Congrès international de l'éducation physique. Paris: Imprimerie nationale; Address of M Georges Demeny (1900) American Physical Education Review 5 291-300

14. Park RJ (forthcoming) The rise and demise of Harvard's BS program in physical education: a case of scarce resources and conflicts of interest.

15. Mosso A (1898) Life of man in the high alps. [translation Klesow EL] London: T Fisher Unwin

16. Rosse I (1889) Popular fallacies regarding athletes and athletics. Journal of the American Medical association 12 577-79

17. Palier E (1898) Exercise and disease. New York Medical Journal (July 13) 109-15

18. Darling E (1899) The effects of training: a study of the Harvard University crew. Boston Medical and Surgical Journal 141 229-33

19. Ibid; Darling E (1901) The effects of training: second paper. Boston Medical and Surgical Journal 144 550-59

20. Medical report on marathon runners. American Physical Education Review 5 (1900) 176-78

21. Darling E (1899) op cit

22. Darling E (1900) op cit; Atwater WO, Bryant AP (1900) Dietary studies of university boat crews. Washington: Government Printing Office

23. Blake JB, Larrabee RC (1903) Observations upon long-distance runners. Boston Medical and Surgical Journal 148 195-203

24. Messenger Bradley S (1880?) The relationship of anatomy of fine arts: a lecture delivered at the Royal Institution, Manchester

25. Proctor RA (1889) Strength: how to get strong and keep strong. London: Longmans, Green; Blaikie W (1879) How to get strong and how to stay so. New York: Harper and Brothers

26. MacLaren A (1865) A system of physical education. Oxford: Clarendon Press; Eaton CW (1884) Things young men should know. Des Moines: Miller, Girton and Walters

27. Griffin HH (1893) The all-England series: athletics. London: George Bell and Sons

28. Bigham J (1897) The football question. Depauw Palladium 1; Camp W, Deland L (1896) Football. Boston: Houghton, Mifflin

29. Beyer HG (1894) Foot-ball and the physique of its devotees from the point of view of physical training. American Journal of Medical Sciences 108 306-22

30. Murphy MC (1914) Athletic training. New York: Charles Schribner's Sons

31. Hoberman J (1988) The development of high performance sports medecine in Germany. Paper presented at the 1988 North American for Sport History Conference, Arizona State University

Ethical Implications
of Expert Systems in Sports Training:
a Plea for Ethical Limits to Striving

William H. Freeman

Expert systems have great potential for coaching sports and for increasing opportunities for every athlete as a potential elite performer[1,2]. When sport-specific expert systems are developed, *every* athlete can then have the equivalent of an olympic-level coach. However, the process of developing such advanced training systems requires that the ethical implications of sport training programs be carefully considered and weighed.

The Function of Expert Systems

Expert systems are an outgrowth of artificial intelligence research. They are software programs that contain the knowledge and decision-making processes and rules that an expert in a given field uses and that can, therefore, make the same judgements that an expert would make, if given the same information. Thus these programs can make an expert's counsel easily available to any user. While early systems were rule-based, knowledge-based systems may have greater potential for sport applications.

Originally, the function of expert systems was to make up for the limited number of real experts available in some fields. During the last two decades such programs have been expanding into many new realms. While specialists may not agree on the potential of these systems[3], many useful ones have been produced for "real-world" applications. Their degree of development may indeed be overstated; nonetheless, computers themselves are now used extensively in most workplaces. The technology used in today's physical and biological sciences will gradually move into sport settings, at least as research and diagnostic tools.

A standard expert system has three components: – a *knowledge base* (database), with the known facts about the subject; – a *rule base*, the rules that an expert follows in solving problems; and, –a *rule interpreter, which interprets the rules based on the facts in the knowledge base.*

William H. Freeman, Department of Physical Education and Sport Management, Campbell University, Buies Creek, North Carolina, USA.

When an expert system is developed, a programming specialist, called a *knowledge engineer* works with one or more other specialists in the given subject area to determine the problem-solving process that the expert uses. They work together to identify the rules used to make decisions in that field. It is a process of learning that *if* this is the situation, *then* we shall follow procedure A, or *else* we shall follow procedure B (which may be yet another if-then-else structure).

What complicates the programming logic, is that people do not think like computers. A computer sees only two choices, "yes" or "no". In this sense, a computer program is simply a series of yes-no decisions. For humans, the procedure is more complicated, because humans think with what is called "fuzzy logic". *Fuzzy logic* uses approximations and rough rules of thumb[4,5]. One tends to say: *if* this is approximately the situation, *then* one *may* (but not always) follow procedure A.

An expert has many rules of thumb that suggest what to do in different situations or conditions. Those rules of thumb based on experiential knowledge are sometimes called *heuristics*. Heuristics includes a type of expert knowledge that is sometimes called *intuition* or *insight*. An expert may have a "feel" for a solution, based on a number of loosely defined factors, combined with personal knowledge and experience gained over the years. Thus, an heuristic approach may lead to solving a problem that an ordinary computer program would be unable to solve.

Potential Applications of Sport-Specific Expert Systems

What types of tasks can expert systems perform? The major kinds include interpretation, prediction, diagnosis, design, planning, monitoring, debugging, repair, instruction, and control. These represent activities such as predictive modeling; providing answers for various problem solutions; testing out various hypotheses or options; evaluating new approaches and strategies; "remembering" policies, opinions, previous strategies used, and other key information that can be used for further study and analyses; and training[6].

The methods used to train elite athletes are changing incessantly and are becoming increasingly complex[7]. But fortunately, expert systems can provide the benefits of computer technology. A sport-specific expert system has the potential of at least six basic applications. It should be capable of, and thus able to: – maintain the training records; – monitor the progress of the training program; – answer training questions; – train coaches; – design the basic training program; and – apply and refine the training model. The last four of those applications have ethical implications.

The philosophical foundation that underlies such a training system is critical. There is a need to be concerned about the philosophical foundation because ethical and philosophical questions are a fundamental and growing issue in sport training. Many training actions are possible that one may not consider proper, and which thus should perhaps be made illegal (such as the use of performance enhancing substances). If one wishes to set boundaries on how an athlete can be properly trained, there must then be an ethics or a philosophy that helps to set those limits.

Sport Philosophy and Ethical Concerns: Focused on Competition

The philosophic discourse on sport generally deals with the contest setting, rather than the training scene. This implies ignoring the time-consuming process, focusing instead on the product. For example, in a single-periodized program of sport training, the year or macrocycle tends to be divided into six phases[8]. Only three of those phases may include any competition at all, and the total competition phases in a year typically last only about three months. This leaves 75% of the athlete's year largely ignored by the sport philosopher. Athletes do not develop their personal philosophies of sport *after* they go to an Olympic Games. Competition *is* the test: it demonstrates what they have learned and what they can do. It is indeed during the training phases that learning occurs.

Most texts on the philosophic study of sport over the last two decades have focussed on competition rather than training. Morgan and Meier's text has a number of readings on "Sport and Ethics", but all of them deal with competition[9]. Fraleigh's book on applied ethics for the athlete deals strictly with the competitive setting[10]. McIntosh's work on fair play also focuses on competition[11]. Indeed, the typical book on sport philosophy gives only passing mention to the process of athletic training. In eighteen pages of suggestions relative to proper conduct for athletic programs, Lapchick and Slaughter suggest only one rule (limit the number of practice hours) relating to training itself[12]. It is as if the training process has no ethical bounds. Indeed, it is as if the training process were of no philosophic concern.

Weiss has proposed a departure point for many sport philosophers. He describes training as "using the mind to dictate what the body is to do", the imposing of mind on body for self-mastery. This process "requires [the athlete] to give up, for the time being, any attempt to allow his mind to dwell on objectives that are not germane to what his body is, what it needs, and what it can or ought to do[13]". Weiss hinges on striving for excellence when he writes that "Young men should try to push the limits of their capacities, and there court failure again and again. When they stay within the limits set by others, because these had been the limits which other men accepted, they are not tempted to make full use of their abilities[14]."

Many philosophers have discussed sport as an opportunity for the pursuit of excellence. Mihalich argues that "sports and athletics provide the greatest opportunity for the greatest number of people to achieve and to witness human excellence[15]." He suggests that other forms of excellence (the scholarly and the spiritual, for example) may be impossible goals for most people and for the young, while sport offers a more realistic hope for a sense of satisfaction and recognition. Thus, the pursuit of sports excellence is judged a worthy goal. Fraleigh echoes this point of view by maintaining that sport serves the educational purpose of self-actualization, in this case "the realization and use of physical abilities[16]". While he puts the activity into an educational context, it is no less true applied to a wholly athletic endeavor, such as striving to reach the level of setting a world record. By contrast, Vanderzwaag's contends that "the very nature of sport is such that the participant does not subject himself to long and gruelling training; if he does, he has taken a step along the continuum from sport toward athletics. Sport is for fun, enjoyment, pleasure, diversion[17]." For Vanderzwaag, apparently, the pursuit of excellence has little place in sport, for it cannot be a source of pleasure or joy to the athlete. But for many, this would appear strange. In discussing elite sport as a former Canadian olympic participant, Kidd has noted that "all Canadian athletes in the olympic sports have trained and competed under specific material and ideological conditions [. . .] without independent means, none of us could devote all our energies to perfecting what we were best at[18]".

It is difficult to really understand the motives behind the early rules of amateurism. Were they written to provide a level playing field, or a segregated one? Were they written to give everyone an equal chance, or to limit their writers' risk of losing in competition? As has been shown, the athletes were not always the force behind rising professionalism. In fact, one can argue that it is the forces of nationalism and commercialism that pressed for greater levels of excellence; the "professional amateur" has simply been the recipient of this twinned boon and curse. Kretchmar has pointed to the need for more work in the ethics of sport:

> 'moralizing' on paper can have considerable value and, in truth, some good work in the ethics of sport has been produced. But such progress has been the exception, rather than the rule. In very fundamental ways, this literature remains critically undeveloped[19].

Thomas has for her part discussed intent and training. Just as Kretchmar noted the paucity of work on sport ethics, she suggested that

> the two most overlooked aspects of sport are the intent and preparation stages [...] little attention has been paid to the training, or preparation, stage of sport as it involves player choices and the relationships of preparation, or training, to intent and eventually to contest outcomes[20].

Lemay has argued that because "training is a chosen activity" the athlete "may choose how well he is to play[21]". On this point, Thomas has argued that the argument that undertraining has ethical undertones (a failure to live up to the intent to contest as a worthy opponent) may be equally true for overtraining, depending on the athlete's intent[22]. In short, she argues that "to fail to train in accordance with intent becomes an act of 'bad faith', a breach of sportsmanship[23]." One might say that setting limits to the act of striving is a form of "throwing" the contest, or failing to try to perform to the best of one's capabilities. Nonetheless, I suggest that we need to do so.

A Plea for Ethical Limits to Striving

The crux of my concern is a growing belief that we *should* set ethical limits to striving. That is, we must agree that sport success should not be simply a matter of who can spend the greatest amount of money and time to train, nor of who is willing to take chances with one's future health by abusing one's body with overtraining, performance enhancing substances or drugs, or with questionable psychological techniques that may affect one's emotional stability[24].

Suggesting ethical limits to striving may seem to be in opposition to the noble olympic motto *"Citius, Altius, Fortius"*. From at least two angles, in my opinion, this is not the case. First, there is wide agreement as to the personal and social values in sport indulged-in as a pastime, as compared to an avocation or an obsession. Second, there is equally wide agreement that sport indulged-in as an obsession does not have redeeming personal and social values. Success in 21st century sport should mean more than victory for whoever devoted the most time and money to sport. This obsessive approach to sport lessens the meaning of the achievement, because society is neither surprised nor uplifted by the success of one who strives only in a single arena of life.

Focal Questions before Developing Sport-Specific Expert Systems

The potential benefit of a sport-specific expert system as part of an integrated and balanced system of services in sport is easy to see: it offers opportunity and high quality programs for all categories of citizens. The development and availability of sport-specific expert systems would be a giant step toward the goal of sport-for-all, toward equality of sporting opportunities for every man and woman, every boy and girl. That goal of universal opportunity is reachable and indeed expected in any advanced society.

However, we must not forget the risks that we take in developing a rather universal model of training. Because any training model is built on a foundation of beliefs regarding what constitute appropriate or ethical training methods and work loads, the process by which that model is developed is critical. Thus, at least three focal questions about the model ought to be answered before the developmental process begins or accelerates.

A first focal question is, *Who develops the training model.* While there is a standard approach to developing an expert system (having a knowledge engineer work with a field expert), two things have a major impact on the design of the system when it is completed: the expert who is chosen, and the financing of the program's development and implementation.

An expert is selected for his/her practical experience and factual knowledge. However, experts disagree on many aspects of training, such as the training limits that should be set for athletes. Those limits are ethically critical, whether they are limits on training time, or training methods, or what substances an athlete can properly utilize. Thus, the matter of *which* expert is charged with developing the model is a critical issue, for that expert's ethical sensibilities are most likely to be woven into the training model.

Developing an expert system is costly, so one must decide who will be the system's patron. Will a sport body pay for the development? Will it be produced with corporate sponsorship? This question is also of importance since "He who pays the piper, calls the tune". Few groups will indeed sponsor something that comes in conflict with their ethical sensibilities. At the same time, the sponsor usually has the power to select the expert, thus increasing his power to promote or impose his own set of ethical values or norms before the system is developed.

A second focal question is, *Who controls, interprets and refines the training model?* Again, sponsorship is a factor. As has become obvious, sport governing bodies are affected by politics. Regardless of the organization, one is dealing with human beings, and humans act in a political manner. Recognition of this human factor is of consequence since the group that controls the training model is the one responsible for modifying and improving it. That group will judge whether or not the model is ethically sound, and they will make that decision based upon their own group and personal ethical standards. Thus, the choice of the sponsor is of personal as well as social consequence.

A third and no less important focal question is, *What are the moral and ethical limits set for training?* When one formulates the rules, one is making ethical judgements having to do with matters of fairness, of justice and propriety in an imperfect world. Our rules set our boundaries, the limits to our striving. They tell us what training is considered fair or unfair, reasonable or unreasonable. The olympic maxim of *Citius, Altius, Fortius* sets no limits, so we must decide that ultimate question in sports, as well as in life: "What shoudn't we do to win?" Should there be limits? What is proper and what is improper in our striving for that distant, shining peak of olympic success?

Why Are Ethical Limits Important?

There is a need for ethical limits because those limits help determine whether olympic athletes will truly meet on a "level playing field". Those limits affect whether an athlete's success is more dependent upon his true ability and potential than upon an obsessive investment of time and money toward achieving success in sport. Ethical limits and standards help the athlete determine if he/she will make sport the focus of existence rather than simply one facet of a well-rounded life. If there are no ethical limits, then it becomes indeed difficult not to accept professionalism in olympic sport or the use of performance enhancing substances and/or methods as part of training approaches and programs.

If expert systems can someday provide wide spread quality coaching for the common man and woman, then the goal of *Everyman as a potential olympian* becomes attainable. The lack of means (indeed the lack of wealth) would no longer be a major handicap to any person's olympic aspirations. Then *any* citizen who would wish can chase an olympic dream. A net effect would be a considerable increase in the number of participants in the sport system. When large numbers of people are part of a system, that system's obligation to be ethically bound becomes particularly heavy as core value systems of the participants are powerfully affected by both example and practice within that system. Just as people expect their schools to foster ethical standards and behaviors, so should they expect also of the sport system. Otherwise, the latter acts like a loaded gun in our midst, threatening the very fabric of what we claim to believe in.

REFERENCES

1. Freeman WH (1987) Physical education and sport in a changing society. New York: Macmillan p 273-75

2. Freeman WH (1990) The potential of expert systems for sport coaching. New Studies in Athletics 5 (in press)

3. Hillman DJ (1985) Artificial Intelligence. Human Factors 27 p 22

4. Van Horn M, The Waite Group (1986) Understanding expert systems. New York: Bantam p 143-50

5. Minasi M (1990) Putting expert systems in their place. AI Expert 5 13-14

6. Hsu J, Kusnan J (1989) The fifth generation: the future of computer technology. Blue Ridge Summit: Windcrest p 157, 160-62

7. Teich M, Weintraub P (1985) Ultra sports. Omni 9 p 39-40, 42, 44, 96-97, 100-01

8. Freeman WH (1989) Peak when it counts: periodization for american track and field. Tafnews p 23-34

9. Morgan WJ, Meier KV (1988) Philosophic inquiry in sport. Champaign: Human Kinetics

10. Fraleigh WP (1984) Right actions in sport: ethics for contestants. Champaign: Human Kinetics

11. McIntosh P (1979) Fair play: ethics in sport and education. London: Heinemann

12. Lapchick RE, Slaughter JB (1989) The rules of the game: ethics in college sport. New York: American Council on Education and Macmillan p 205

13. Weiss P (1969) Sport: a philosophic inquiry. Carbondale: Southern Illinois University Press p 40-41

14. Ibid p 45

15. Mihalich JC (1982) Sports and athletics: philosophy in action. Totowa: Littlefield, Adams p 49

16. Fraleigh WP (1990) Different educational purposes: different sport values. Quest 42 84-86

17. Vanderzwaag HJ (1972) Toward a philosophy of sport. Reading: Addison-Wesley p 104

18. Kidd B (1988) The elite athlete. In Harvey J Cantelon H (eds) Not just a game: essays in canadian sport sociology. Ottawa: University of Ottawa Press p 287-307

19. Kretchmar RS (1984) Ethics and sport. An overview. Journal of the Philosophy of Sport 10 p 21

20. Thomas CE (1984) Thoughts on the moral relationship of intent and training in sport. Journal of the Philosophy of Sport 10 p 84

21. LeMay S (1979) Sport and training: some preliminary philosophic considerations. In Morgan WJ (ed) Sport and the humanities. Knoxville: University of Tennessee Press p 59

22. Thomas CE (1984) op cit p 87

23. Ibid p 90

24. Williams JM (1986) (ed) Applied sport psychology. Mountain View CA: Mayfield p 320-21

The Value of Failure in Athletics

Carolyn E. Thomas

The object of any athletic contest is to demonstrate superiority, to win, to be the best. Even the conscious intent to pursue individual excellence requires that some standard be used against which the effort is measured. However, if the sole value of the athletic contest was seen as the objective establishment of superiority, then this single benefit of participation would be achieved by very few. While it is possible to identify numerous benefits unrelated to contest outcomes, this presentation will emphasize the potential value of failure in the athletic contest. It is not a matter of advocating failure, but simply of attempting to examine how one can make the most of an outcome which, sooner or later, becomes inevitable. Selected components of the sport contest (intent, preparation, commitment, effort, and resolution) will be examined as necessary but perhaps not sufficient conditions for the proposition that failure may be as valuable *i.e.*, meaningful and authentic an experience as winning is typically portrayed.

Sport and athletics represent one of many life forums to which individuals are drawn by their need to test the limits of human ability[1]. It has been established in previous writings that it is possible to consider the sport world as a separate, non-utilitarian area in the inevitable human existential searches for commitment to a cause, fulfillment of potential, a sense of purpose or even a sense of immortality and acceptance by others[2,3]. Although these motives may be partially explained in the context of some hierarchy of psychological needs, it nonetheless remains that sport can be *one medium* for the acting out or playing out of the individual's search for self, for the fulfillment of goals, or for a sense of purpose and meaning in life. Some existential philosophers have emphasized the moral necessity for man to commit himself by choosing a project and assuming the responsibilities for choices, successes, and failures[4]. Ortega has expanded on the ethical ideal of men who live under the bondage of *self-imposed* tasks and imperatives, who devote

1890
1990

Carolyn E. Thomas, Department of Physical Therapy and Exercise Science, State University of New York at Buffalo, Buffalo, New York, USA.

their lives to higher ideals insisting that this alone can give meaning to their existence. Fraleigh spoke to this point relative to the sport world when he said:

> [...] And it is in entering such a world (sport) that man may know himself symbolically as a powerful agent in being since, in that world, he literally uses externally controlling necessities [...] to serve his own purposes[5].

It is in this context of using sport as a test of self and as a search for purpose that an examination of *failure* follows.

To claim unilaterally or uncritically that failure has value is unwarranted. However, in meeting *at least* the following and perhaps other additional criteria, one may be able not only to recognize value in failure but to utilize such understandings in preparation for future contests in sport or non-sport settings.

Intent

The primary focus of any intent in sport is related to what the performer plans to accomplish. This plan involves the setting of some goal, the strategy for achieving this goal and the evaluation of the outcomes. Establishment of such goals should be realistic and grounded in *actual* capabilities. The philosophic concept of authenticity is instructive in setting the stage for the true agon to occur. Authenticity, which is "the excellence of being what one is, fulfillment of one's particular functions, and true self-realization in the sense of self-disclosure and self-fulfillment[6]" applies to the development of authentic intent and subsequent authentic outcome in sport from the standpoint that winning, *i.e.*, the demonstration of clear superiority over the opponent becomes an authentic intent *only* when there is sufficient ability, preparation, and commitment to legitimize the possibility of superiority.

The element of unpredictability and each contestant having an even chance to win is an essential *component* of a genuine or authentic contest. To be required to or to choose to compete against a far superior opponent leads to an expectation of failure and does not yield a value which stems from the tension of an evenly matched struggle. Morford saw the true agon as embodying

> [...] the concepts of struggle, toil, hardship, risk, and the *nike*. This latter was the qualitative victory embodied by the triumph of the cause, of the struggle within oneself and against one's competitors, even unto death. To merely overcome was not enough, for one must internally *deserve* the victory if there was to be a true agon[7].

It can be inferred from this that to beat an underdog is simply actualizing a predetermined superiority. To lose to an underdog may have some tertiary meaning or value but the prerequisites of preparation, effort, and desire were probably not met in such a failure. Hence, we have not only a failure as outcome but a failure in the preparation and presentation of self as a "worthy" opponent.

Preparation

Preparation is the second aspect of sport occurring prior to "the" actual contest. It is an essential foundation for the sport encounter to carry its full meaning. Although it is possible to come to the contest with minimal preparation, this negates the spirit of the commitment to be a "worthy" opponent. There must be a willingness to prepare optimally for the encounter through training, to develop the required expertise, and, through the commitment of time and other resources, to become all one is capable of becoming. This is the "getting ready" stage that few people see or care to see. It is the hours of training, of pain, fatigue and of trial and error which are often discouraging, physically stressful, and psychologically dissonant. But it is a requirement for a performance of even less than 10 seconds to carry its full potential for self-understanding. For the agon to take on authentic and meaningful dimensions, the athlete must be prepared to the extent that technique and training become the background over which the figure is free to move. To fail when one has not prepared to the best of his/her ability presents failure more as an expectation than as the outcome of one's best effort. Le May[8] has pointed out that training (preparation) requires a decision not only that one *will* train but how *well* one will train. The choice to train with dedication or half-heartedness can give the athlete insight about his/her willingness to endure hardship and about the basic significance they see in their own involvement.

To arrive at a contest with less than the best preparation negates both the agonistic value and meaning of both victory and defeat. One has not brought one's best; hence, what has been demonstrated to be superior? It is very unclear except that a score or a time is posted for a particular event on a particular day. I argue then that for success *or* failure to achieve any personal significance, or to have any value, preparation must be optimal and one must make as much of a commitment to that aspect of the contest as one does when that contest starts.

Commitment and Effort

It would appear that the athlete is largely responsible for defining the dimensions, quality, and potential meaning of the sport experience. Commitment and effort represent two major elements over which only the athlete has control. Sometimes one intends to make an all-out effort and knows only in retrospect that one did not: one became distracted, lost concentration and could not keep one's head inside the ropes as the golfers say. Sometimes the performers are just tired or don't feel well or a nagging little injury subconsciously plays a larger role than anticipated. As a result the effort is less than one's best and, like non-optimal preparation, does not represent a given performer as the best potential opponent. Another feature of effort is related to the ethical aspect of effort. What kind of effort is one wholeheartedly making? If the efforts violate the letter and /or spirit of the contest, then one should admit that both victory and defeat are meaningless descriptors.

A dimension of commitment which goes beyond the obvious one the athlete makes to even bring himself/herself to the point of taking the field, has to do with "becoming one" with the act. Sartre's examination of mountain climbing and moving beyond the preparation stage explains this:

> He no longer thinks of his shoes to which an hour ago he gave such great attention, he "forgets" the stick that supports him [. . .] He "ignores his body" which he trained. For only by forgetting [. . .] his plans and his body, will he be able to devote himself to the laborious task that has to be performed[9].

Such a commitment puts the player "in" the game and beyond the influence of audience distractions; indeed, above the influence of his/her own analytic thought patterns. It is a union of performer and action that allows the athlete the essential unity which is a prerequisite to the kind of "knowing" that later serves as the basis for self-understanding and reflection. Lack of such a commitment keeps the athlete at a critical distance when it comes to examining the values of either victory or defeat.

Resolution

Given then that the athlete's intent is realistic and his/her goals are achievable, given also an appropriate and optimal preparation and a commitment that focuses the contest as the only action of consequence at a given moment and one's best effort, one must face not only the contest *per se* but still the resolution of one's endeavor. The nature of any contest involves an inevitable clash of strong wills, skill, the desire to dominate, and the certainty that only one contestant or team will prevail. The desire to win cannot be excluded as one of the determinants of action. This desire requires a considerable emotional investment on the part of the athlete from the onset, and the events of the contest which serve to build dramatic tension only compound the emotional involvement. Eventually, in the Western approach to competitive sport, resolution is a necessity. It seems that in some respects it is this need to "give all and see what you get back" which separates the trite and mundane drama of many athletic contests from those true agons which reveal not only the actions and motives at the moment but the quality of the human spirit which traditionally one sees played out on theatrical and literary pages rather than playing fields. The player defines the contest through his/her own acts and must then accept the consequences of those acts as the context drama is resolved. The dramatic resolution may be manifest in either fulfilled or unfilled intent, and the consequences will be success or failure.

There is intent, a willingness to do whatever is necessary, and a total reliance on self. There can be an integrity and clarity in sport for the athlete who is not the victim of the elements or external fates *and* whose shortfall is directly attributable to simply "not being good enough" on a particular day. Whether this means a tactical error or a skill deficiency, it seems possible to look at failure with a lucidity uncharacteristic in many other "life projects".

When an athlete has truly given all because he/she wanted to, because it was important and necessary to do it, then one is "on the line". When an athlete cannot retreat anywhere to hide his/her ignorance or incompetence in a "world" uncomplicated by the outside world, perhaps then there exists a true test and one of the cleanest confrontations of man, will, and fate. No time to be phoney. No time to think and cover up. Perhaps it is on this kind of "stage" that the athlete may come to realize that it is not the fates, the consequences of one's choices or one's failure, but one's *reaction* to these things and the ability to deal with them that make the real difference in how he/she assesses existence.

The Value of Failure

It is fairly well documented by research in the social sciences that competitive behavior is learned and that the achievement orientation characteristic of Western society is the chief causative factor explaining high levels of competitive behavior. Even a casual observation by a casual observer would reveal that most "play" is for the prize and that the agon is alive and well. Winning is not a moral question, it is the object of a game. There will be losers. Yet we are *taught* to believe that failing will bring us and those close to us nothing but shame, obscurity, and discredit. Heroes and winners are recognized and rewarded. Goats and losers are ignored and punished in both subtle and overt ways.

Ermler[10] has written that failure in sport is a form of symbolic death because defeat brings about the collapse of an athlete's "world" as a result of the performer's unsuccess in actualizing his/her goal. She maintains that this "death" in sport can be viewed one of two ways by the athlete. It is either a motivation to set new goals, to re-assert commitment or, more characteristically, it is a tragedy in that the athlete gives up hope and symbolically dies. As Kostenbaum writes, "[...]

to be a failure means not to exist, it means to cease to *be* in any significant and concrete sense[11]." One ceases to be (or feel) significant or see significance in one's world. Failure is experienced not so much because one is in reality insignificant, but because one comes to believe that failure makes one less significant than one is.

The athlete chooses to enter the arena, to step onto the stage and unlike thinking or cognitive skills whose deficits can be hidden by silence or disguised by rhetoric, kinetic acts leave no place to hide. To swim or to drown; and there is no way to talk a good game. One enters the unspoken contract to make the best choices that can be made, to persist, and to demonstrate the best of skills and to be the best contestant one can be for a given period of time. This contest, this series of acts being played out, is of some intrinsic value; it is by its nature self-validating; it is by its demands self-defining; it is in its outcome potentially self-realizing.

It would be poor logic to suggest that simple reflection is a guarantee of self-realization or even that failure brings one closer to an authentic perspective of self. Yet the admonitions of writers, playwrights, and philosophers to look to one's soul for the answer, to create "life projects" that demand complete solitary commitment, and to look to successes and failures as dynamic rather than static should not be ignored. I suggest that for many participants, sport has the potentiality to be a life project in the human search for purpose, commitment, or identity. Failure in sport whether it results from error, incompetence, or unpreparedness can have the epistemic revelations one seeks in the many dimensions of daily life. Perhaps in defeat one can come to understand that striving rather than achievement may be the ultimate preoccupation of man. In one of his more eloquent observations Schaap noted:

> And who knows [. . .] perhaps the only goal on earth to which mankind is striving lies in the incessant process of attaining, in other word, in life itself, and not in the thing to be attained[12].

Failure, despite commitment, effort and preparation need not be negative. Failure may be an excellent medium for the insight which allows one to see and understand one's *reactions* to failure as well as one's failure. To thine own self be true *and* to thine own self be truthful. There is in sport the inevitability of outcome. The "common man" performing a common non-utilitarian act against another who seeks the same common goal. Perhaps one will fall down. Perhaps one will fail. The value lies in the decision one makes whether to get up and try again and in honestly examining such a decision.

REFERENCES

1. Metheny E (1968) Movement and meaning. New York: McGraw-Hill p 74

2. Thomas CE (1983) Sport in a philosophic contest. Philadelphia: Lea and Febiger

3. Thomas CE (1979) The sportman as a tragic figure. In Morgan WJ (ed) Sport and the humanities. Knoxville: Bureau of Educational Research and Service College of Education University of Tennessee

4. Sartre JP (1956) Being and nothingness. New York: Pocket Books

5. Fraleigh W (1973) The moving I. In Osterhoudt RG (ed) Philosophy of sport. Springfield: Thomas p 5

6. Heidegger M (1962) Being and time. Toronto: SCM Press

7. Morford WR (1973) Sport: whose bag? Is sport the struggle or the triumph. Quest 19 83-87

8. LeMay S (1979) Sport and training: some preliminary philosophic considerations. In Morgan WJ (ed) Sport and the humanities. Knoxville: Bureau of Educational Research and Service College of Education University of Tennessee p 59

9. Sartre JP (1956) op cit p 107

10. Ermler KL (1980) The relationship of existential freedom to symbolic death. PhD dissertation State University of New York at Buffalo, New York, USA

11. Kostenbaum P (1971) The vitality of death. Westport: Greenwood Publishers p 29

12. Schaap D (1976) The Olympics. New York: Ballantine p 290

Analyse de la fonction
et de la structure des règles du jeu

Shinji Morino

Là où existe une société, existent des règles; cette affirmation vaut aussi pour le monde du sport. Le jeu sportif ne peut se dérouler dans le cadre d'un «état naturel» tel que décrit par Hobbes, par exemple. Le déroulement du jeu nécessite un mécanisme de contrôle qui permette d'y mettre de l'ordre. Dans le cas du sport, il s'agit tout simplement des règles du jeu, d'où leur raison d'être fondamentale. Cependant, certains éducateurs physiques et certains chercheurs ont tendance à accorder aux règles du jeu une signification beaucoup plus large. L'image qu'ils se font des règles du jeu est, si l'on ose dire, celle d'une loi idéale où se cristallisent les principes du comportement de l'homme, et dont l'apprentissage contribue tant au développement de la personnalité des athlètes qu'à la démocratisation de la société à laquelle appartiennent ces derniers. Avant que d'approuver ou rejeter cette thèse il faut examiner objectivement les caractéristiques des règles du jeu. L'objectif de cette étude est de clarifier la fonction et la structure des règles du jeu[1].

Fonction des règles du jeu

Les règles sont comprises de deux manières différentes. La compréhension de leur contenu exact est indispensable non seulement aux athlètes et aux entraîneurs mais aussi aux arbitres. Ces acteurs doivent saisir ce que les règles permettent ou interdisent aux joueurs. Par ailleurs, les chercheurs doivent en saisir la finalité, finalité qui ne réside pas dans leur contenu.

Trois fonctions des règles du jeu

Quels rôles jouent les règles sportives? À cette question, on pourrait répondre de différentes manières. On peut dire que les règles assurent que les jeux se déroulent suivant un ordre établi préalablement par l'autorité dans une discipline concernée. Ce faisant, les règles rendent possible la comparaison des performances des athlètes à des époques et dans des lieux différents. Dans ce cas, le rôle des règles est de spécifier les conditions qui doivent être remplies pour

1890
1990

Shinji Morino, Faculté d'éducation physique, Université Chukyo, Toyota, Japon.

qu'une performance puisse être comparée à d'autres. Ou encore, peut-on même dire que les règles existent pour que le sport puisse faire l'objet de paris. Comme l'a dit Caillois, «toute rencontre qui possède les caractères d'une compétition réglée idéale peut faire l'objet de paris[2]». En effet, sans parler de la valeur morale du pari (ceci est après tout le problème de l'homme et non pas celui des règles), les règles permettent le déroulement des jeux dans les conditions où se tient le pari. Dans ces deux rôles que joueraient les règles, on ne trouve aucun aspect d'ordre éthique ou moral. À partir de ces considérations, sont proposées trois fonctions des règles du jeu : – assurer la certitude légale (legal certainty) ; – garantir la justice ; – rendre le jeu intéressant. De ces trois fonctions, la dernière est la plus importante. Si une règle, exerçant bien les deux premières fonctions, n'assure plus la troisième pour une raison ou une autre, elle doit être modifiée ou même remplacée complètement.

Assurer la certitude légale

On ne saurait survivre quotidiennement si la société n'indiquait à ses membres ce qui est permis ou interdit dans leurs comportements. Les lois et règlements se chargent de maintenir et d'assurer la certitude légale des actes. Il va de soi que les règles du jeu exercent la même fonction dans le domaine compétitif. Or, ce qui est permis ou interdit par les règles diffère selon les sports. C'est justement ce fait qui nous interdit d'analyser la fonction des règles à partir de leur contenu ou de considérants éthiques. Prenons comme exemple deux faits très simples : bien que «ne pas frapper des poings» soit une loi morale très fondamentale pour presque toutes les disciplines sportives, cela n'est certainement pas le cas de la boxe. Ou bien, le plaquage au rugby qui est tout à fait légal dans ce sport, ne l'est point dans le cas du football où il sera sûrement condamné comme conduite extrêmement anti-sportive. Ces deux exemples montrent qu'il est impossible de parler du rôle que jouent les règles tant que l'on fixe les yeux sur leur contenu, étant donné que la valeur et la signification d'une même conduite diffèrent selon les sports.

D'après Vinogradoff[3], professeur anglais bien connu d'histoire de la législation, l'élément de base qui constitue la loi n'est pas un simple ordre donné unilatéralement aux membres d'une communauté, mais l'expression d'un consentement accepté par eux ; ainsi la loi en est-elle la déclaration officielle. De la même manière, on peut considérer que les règles du jeu sont aussi la déclaration faite par l'autorité d'une communauté sportive de ce à quoi ses membres ont donné leur consentement soit d'eux-même, soit par l'intermédiaire de leurs représentants. C'est la raison pour laquelle une règle du jeu doit être respectée à tout prix par les intéressés, d'autant plus qu'ils y ont consenti. De sorte que la communauté sportive prépare tous les moyens nécessaires pour défendre l'effet des règles, depuis la sanction légère jusqu'à l'expulsion, en passant par l'exclusion temporaire ou la disqualification. Il est donc tout à fait naturel qu'une règle dans un sport donné puisse être incompatible, ou même contradictoire, avec celles des autres sports. L'important, c'est de formuler le plus clairement possible le consentement en question et d'assurer ainsi la certitude légale. Dans ce but, une règle du jeu doit avoir les caractéristiques techniques suivantes : – être explicite – une règle dont le contenu est obscur et imprécis ne mérite pas ce nom ; – ne pas faire l'objet de modifications trop fréquentes – cela ne cause que des ambiguïtés qui portent atteinte à la certitude légale ; – être applicable — une règle dont le contenu est excellent comme idée mais inapplicable dans les faits, ne contribue pas au maintien de l'ordre, ni par conséquent à la certitude légale ; – être compatible avec les intentions des athlètes, puisque ceux-ci sont, au premier chef, concernés par le consentement à la règle.

Garantir la justice

Lorsqu'il est fait mention ici de justice, il s'agit de la notion des sciences du droit telle qu'elle a été décrite par Aristote il y a plus de deux mille ans dans son ouvrage « Éthique à Nicomaque ». Une règle qui ordonne aux joueurs de faire ou de ne pas faire telle ou telle chose, est une norme de conduite destinée aux joueurs. En même temps, elle est une norme de conduite destinée à l'arbitre dans ce sens qu'elle l'oblige à infliger une punition aux joueurs dont la conduite ne se conforme pas à ce que les règles ordonnent. Cela implique que les règles du jeu assurent une deuxième fonction la garantie de la justice. Or, on distingue deux sortes de justice dans le domaine du droit. Premièrement, la justice dite rectificatrice ou arithmétique qui ordonne de traiter en égaux ceux qui sont égaux ; deuxièmement, la justice dite distributive ou géométrique qui ordonne de traiter en inégaux ceux qui ne sont pas égaux.

La justice rectificatrice est très importante dans notre vie civile parce qu'elle règle les différends concernant les avantages et désavantages entre les deux parties intéressées, de telle sorte qu'elles se trouvent quittes. C'est la justice qui s'applique aux affaires civiles mais qui n'a rien à voir avec le monde sportif, puisque cette justice n'interviendra qu'après qu'une requête aura été adressée par l'intéressé qui a été lésé. Or, dans le domaine du jeu, les règles de n'importe quelle discipline sportive interdisent catégoriquement aux joueurs de faire une telle démarche auprès de l'arbitre, même s'ils sont réellement victimes de la mauvaise conduite des adversaires. De sorte que l'on peut dire que, dans le domaine du jeu, les joueurs n'ont pas le droit de demander à l'arbitre l'application de la justice rectificatrice.

C'est donc la justice distributive, justice du domaine du droit public, qui s'applique dans le domaine de la compétition. Il s'agit de la justice dont la pertinence d'application est jugée uniquement par l'autorité qui détient le pouvoir de juridiction sur l'affaire, indépendamment de la plainte adressée de la part des victimes. Dans le cas du sport, c'est l'arbitre seul qui se prononce souverainement sur la violation des règles, et toute discussion de l'intervention de l'arbitre de la part des joueurs est nulle et sans effet selon les règles. Ainsi, l'arbitre enlèvera le ballon à l'auteur d'une violation des règles pour le donner à la victime, mais ce n'est pas du tout pour dédommager cette dernière par l'application de la justice rectificatrice. C'est pour traiter celui qui a désobéi aux règles de manière autre que ceux qui ne l'ont pas fait, en suivant la justice distributive qui ordonne de traiter en inégaux ceux qui ne sont pas égaux. Il est à noter, en passant, que dans ce sens même, la lutte professionnelle n'est pas un sport, puisque l'arbitre n'a aucunement l'intention d'y appliquer une telle justice.

Rendre le jeu intéressant

Après avoir examiné ces deux fonctions des règles, il faut ensuite poser une question plus fondamentale : pourquoi les règles s'efforcent-elles ainsi d'établir un tel ordre et permettent-elles de prendre des mesures contre leur violation ? Lorsqu'on essaie d'y répondre, on parvient à reconnaître cette troisième fonction, à la réalisation de laquelle contribuent les deux premières fonctions : rendre le jeu intéressant. Il s'agit de la fonction la plus importante, et dont pourtant personne n'a parlé jusqu'ici à notre connaissance. Quel que soit le contenu d'une règle, tant qu'il est présenté de façon explicite, la certitude légale et la justice sont assurées. De sorte que si les règles n'exercent que ces deux fonctions, on n'a pas du tout besoin de les modifier. Mais en réalité, elles font souvent l'objet d'une modification. Cela montre que lorsqu'une règle, exerçant bien les deux premières fonctions, ne le fait plus suffisamment quant à la troisième, elle est destinée à être modifiée. L'évolution des règles du volleyball (surtout la modification récente selon laquelle le contre ne compte plus comme un contact) et du baseball (celles concernant la distance entre le lanceur et le frappeur) en sont la preuve. On ne saurait chercher le motif de leur modification nulle part ailleurs que dans l'intention de rendre le jeu plus intéressant. Ce faisant, on a réussi à établir un nouvel équilibre entre les forces d'attaque et de défense; ce qui a permis d'assurer un échange plus long dans le premier cas, et une nouvelle parité des chances de succès entre le lanceur et le frappeur dans le second cas. En somme, on a rendu ainsi ces sports plus intéressants. On comprendra l'importance de cette troisième fonction qui surpasse de loin celle des deux autres.

Structure des règles du jeu

Reclassement des règles selon leur raison d'être

Comme mentionné auparavant, ce que les règles permettent dans un sport ne l'est pas forcément dans un autre (le plaquage, le coup de poing, par exemple). De plus, une règle qui est considérée comme indispensable dans un sport ne l'est pas nécessairement dans un autre; la règle fixant la durée de temps d'un match n'existe pas dans le volleyball, ou bien la règle de hors-jeu (off-side) du type football n'existe pas dans le basketball ni dans le handball. Ainsi, il est impossible de clarifier la structure des règles tant qu'on fixe les yeux sur le contenu lui-même des règles pour en extraire les éléments composants. Ce serait tomber dans une situation inextricable, du fait-même qu'il y a autant d'espèces d'éléments que de contenus de règles. Ici encore, le seul moyen de tirer au clair la structure est de classifier les règles selon leur raison d'être.

Ainsi, on parvient à les classifier en cinq groupes comme suit. Une règle ne peut appartenir qu'à un seul de ces cinq groupes:

Règles obligeant les bonnes manières. Règles qui précisent la nature et la limite du contact personnel comme «tenir», «pousser» ou «charger». En fait, ce que l'on entend par «charger» diffère entre le basketball et le football, mais la raison d'être de la règle qui l'interdit est commune — le maintien de bonnes manières. À ce groupe, appartiennent aussi les règles qui interdisent les mauvaises conduites verbales émanant tant de joueurs que des entraîneurs.

Règles exigeant l'attaque. Sait-on pourquoi le basketball comporte la règle de «30 secondes»? C'est justement pour exiger de l'équipe possédant le ballon et ayant marqué plus de points que l'adversaire, d'attaquer le plus activement possible. Cependant, on ne parle pas beaucoup de la raison d'être de règles comme celle des «5 secondes», ou encore celle des «10 secondes», ou de la règle interdisant le «retour du ballon en zone arrière», lesquelles exercent toutes le même rôle que celui de la règle des «30 secondes». Faute de quoi, le jeu deviendra somme toute peu intéressant du fait que l'équipe gagnante, à un moment donné, ne tente plus d'attaquer et se contente de faire circuler le ballon entre les équipiers. Le tennis de table a une règle typique de ce genre depuis 1953. Il en va de même pour les sports de combat (boxe, judo, lutte, etc.) dont le joueur n'attaquant pas avec intention perdra le match.

Règles délimitant l'espace jouable. La règle de hors-jeu du football en est le cas typique. Pourtant, toute les disciplines ont en réalité des règles de ce genre; la règle de «3 secondes» du basketball en est l'exemple. En effet, dans le cas du football ou du rugby, la ligne de hors-jeu se déplace selon la position du ballon, mais dans le cas du basketball, cette ligne est fixée à l'avance par celle délimitant le couloir des lancers-francs, et dans le cas du volleyball, par le filet et les lignes marquées sur le terrain. Il en va de même pour le tennis et même pour les sports de combat comme le judo et la lutte où l'espace jouable est délimité d'une façon explicite. Ainsi, dans tous les sports, les règles délimitent d'une façon ou d'une autre les lignes de hors-jeu.

Règles indiquant la formalité de jeu. Il y a des règles dont le contenu ne peut être justifié d'une façon raisonnable. Ainsi, on ne comprend pas, au bout du compte, la raison pour laquelle la rotation des joueurs de volleyball se fait dans le sens de l'horloge et non pas dans le sens inverse. On ne comprend pas non plus pourquoi le coureur au baseball doit toucher le deuxième but après le premier et non pas après le troisième. En somme, ces règles ont un tel contenu tout simplement parce qu'on les a fixées ainsi. À cet égard, on ne peut trouver de fondement objectif soutenant ce que les règles indiquent comme tel. Elles ordonnent la façon formelle dont on joue et permettent ainsi d'assurer essentiellement la certitude légale.

Règles fixant les conditions d'organisation du jeu et de décision du gagnant. Dans le cas du basketball, il est dit à l'avance qu'un panier réussi du terrain compte 2 points, sauf s'il est tenté au-delà de la ligne des 3 points. Ces règles sont indispensables pour décider laquelle des deux équipes aura gagné le match à la fin. C'est par la même nécessité que l'on fixe les règles concernant la durée du temps, les lignes délimitant le terrain, la position des panneaux, etc. Les caractéristiques des règles de ce groupe se trouvent dans le fait qu'elles ne sont pas des règles de conduite. En d'autres termes, elles n'ordonnent aucunement aux joueurs de faire ou de ne pas faire telle ou telle chose.

La structure des règles du jeu

La discussion sur la raison d'être des règles conduit tout d'abord à une division en deux groupes: d'une part, les règles qui ordonnent la façon d'agir, c'est-à-dire celles qui indiquent aux joueurs de faire (ou de ne pas faire) telle ou telle chose pendant le match (règles 1, 2, 3 et 4 mentionnées plus haut) et d'autre part, les règles qui ne donnent aux joueurs aucune indication de ce genre (règles 5). En ce qui concerne les dernières, il s'agit de règles que les joueurs ne peuvent transgresser. En somme, elles sont semblables aux lois fixant le régime parlementaire par exemple, selon lesquelles les Chambres se composent de celles des représentants et des conseillers; le peuple tout au moins ne peut transgresser une telle institution. De la même façon, un joueur de basketball ne saurait violer, par exemple, les règles fixant la durée du temps du match ou la position des panneaux. Nous appelons donc ces règles, *les règles du type « loi organique ».*

Or, les règles qui ordonnent quelque chose aux joueurs peuvent, bien entendu, être violées par eux. À l'égard de ces règles, on peut aussi les diviser en deux: d'une part, celles dont la violation porte atteinte à la liberté ou à la dignité humaine des adversaires (règles 1) et d'autre part, celles dont la violation ne cause de dommages physiques à personne (règles 2, 3 et 4). Les premières sont semblables au droit pénal dans ce sens qu'elles interdisent le manquement à la morale qui causera une atteinte à l'intégrité physique des autres; il s'agit de la faute qui est équivalente au crime. De sorte qu'on peut les nommer *les règles du type « droit pénal ».* On doit y ajouter les règles semblables au droit naturel; ce sont les règles qui accusent aussi le manquement à la morale, mais leur particularité se trouve dans le fait que leur indication ne peut être présentée d'une façon explicite et concrète. Il s'agit par exemple des règles ordonnant le « fair-play » ou le « sportsmanship » dont le contenu différera selon les cas et ne sera surtout pas présenté dans une phrase écrite. Ainsi, lorsque l'adversaire est tombé par terre, le joueur de tennis doit-il renvoyer une balle rapide ou une balle lente pour être conforme à la règle du fair-play? Personne ne pourra répondre avec assurance à cette question qui n'a pas de réponse correcte au bout du compte. On ne peut dire préalablement quel acte se conforme à la notion dite de « sportivité » ou de « loyauté sportive » bien que cela ne signifie point que le monde sportif n'en ait pas besoin. En tout cas, comme la nature de ces règles diffère un peu de celles du type « droit pénal », nous les appelons *les règles du type « droit naturel ».*

Quant aux règles dont la violation ne blesse personne, elles sont analogues au droit administratif; la violation duquel ne signifie la désobéissance qu'aux ordres purement formels. Si l'on prend comme exemple le chauffeur qui tient sa gauche au lieu de la droite, son acte lui-même ne donne aucun fondement permettant de lui reprocher sa «moralité», sinon les Anglais et les Japonais qui sont obligés de tenir la gauche sur la route devraient être considérés inconditionnellement comme immoraux. En ce qui concerne ce chauffeur-là, ce qu'on peut lui reprocher, ce n'est pas du tout sa moralité, mais son «ignorance» ou «inattention» à l'égard du code routier qui établit la certitude légale dans un pays où il prend le volant. Dans le cas du sport, on peut dire la même chose à l'égard de la violation des règles telles que celles des 3 secondes, des 10 secondes, du «marché», du hors-jeu, etc. Pour cette raison, nous les appelons *les règles du type «droit administratif»*.

La *Figure 1*, résumant la discussion ci-dessus, indique la structure des règles du jeu et les quatre éléments de base qui la constituent. Si l'on tient compte de la relation réciproque de ces éléments, la structure des règles peut être présentée comme la *Figure 2*. Le cercle de gauche contient les règles à dominante légale, tandis que le cercle de droite contient celles à dominante morale. On comprendra ainsi la particularité des règles du type «droit pénal» qui sont à cheval sur deux cercles.

FIGURE 1

Représentation de la structure des Règles du Jeu

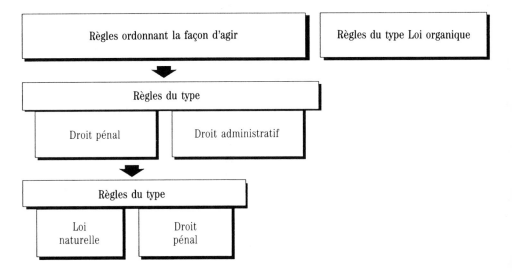

On se souviendra peut-être ici des termes proposés par Searle dans son ouvrage «Les actes de langage»: règles normatives et règles constitutives. Selon lui, «les règles normatives gouvernent des formes de comportement pré-existantes ou existant de façon indépendante; les règles de politesse, par exemple, gouvernent les relations interpersonnelles qui existent indépendamment des règles», tandis que ses règles constitutives, «n'ont pas une fonction purement normative, elles créent ou définissent de nouvelles formes de comportement[4]». En somme, dans les règles normatives de Searle sont comprises à la fois nos règles du type «loi naturelle» et du type «droit pénal»; et dans ses règles constitutives nos règles du type «droit pénal» et du type «droit administratif». On ne saurait lui reprocher cette équivoque, car il n'avait aucune intention d'analyser la structure elle-même des règles du jeu.

FIGURE 2

Représentation des relations entre les composantes des Règles du Jeu

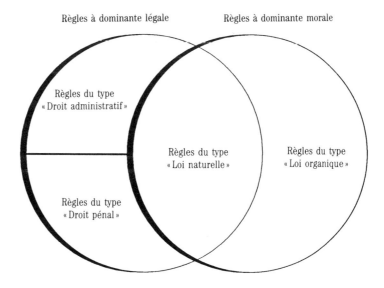

Règles à dominante légale   Règles à dominante morale

Règles du type « Droit administratif »

Règles du type « Loi naturelle »

Règles du type « Loi organique »

Règles du type « Droit pénal »

Conclusion

Quelle signification accorder à la réflexion sur la fonction et la structure des règles du jeu? En appliquant cette réflexion, on peut expliquer la structure des règles de tous les jeux et sports, depuis les jeux pratiqués par des enfants dans le quartier jusqu'aux sports compétitifs des Jeux olympiques ou des championnats mondiaux. En même temps, cette réflexion permettra de comprendre non seulement la raison pour laquelle telles ou telles règles ont été modifiées, mais aussi la nécessité de ce que les joueurs eux-mêmes modifient les règles lorsqu'ils jugent bon de le faire. Quelle est la finalité de la loi? Au bout du compte, c'est la réalisation de l'idéologie de ceux qui l'ont créée. Cela peut être la réalisation des idées dictatoriales dans le cas où le pouvoir est accaparé par une poignée d'hommes, ou bien cela peut être la réalisation des idées démocratiques dans le cas où le peuple détient le pouvoir. Dans le monde sportif, cette idéologie doit être toujours marquée par le souci de rendre le jeu plus intéressant. Si une loi est incompatible avec l'idéologie du peuple, elle doit être modifiée ou abolie. Il en va de même pour le sport; si une règle n'assure plus la fonction qui est de rendre le jeu intéressant, elle doit être modifiée ou abolie, car un sport qui n'est pas intéressant ne mérite pas d'être joué. Ainsi, l'apprentissage lui-même du contenu des règles ne donne peut-être pas d'effet d'ordre éducatif aux joueurs. Mais lorsqu'ils apprennent leur contenu avec leur raison d'être, ils peuvent apprendre ce que c'est que la vie civile et sociale qui est administrée par les lois. On n'en saurait minimiser l'effet. Notre réflexion sur la fonction et la structure des règles permet aussi d'aborder sous un angle différent les problèmes divers qui entourent le monde sportif: argent, fanatisme et chauvinisme sportifs, intervention politique, etc. Mais, ce n'est pas le but de cette communication que de les discuter[5].

NOTES ET RÉFÉRENCES

1. Pour cette étude, nous avons consulté plusieurs livres en sciences du droit. Ces livres étant écrits en langue japonaise, il n'est pas fait ici mention du titre.

2. Caillois R (1967) Les jeux et les hommes. Paris: Gallimard p 58

3. Vinogradoff P (1959) Common sense in law. London: Oxford University Press

4. Searle JR (1972) Les actes de langage. Paris: Hermann p 72. Il faut mentionner le nom de Weiblen J qui a écrit sa thèse sur les règles en appliquant largement les idées de Searle: Game rules and morality. University of North Carolina at Greenboro (1972). Cependant, à notre avis, il s'agit d'une thèse à dominante spéculative et peu convaincante.

5. Ces sujets sont traités dans: Morino S (1984) Sport to rule no shakaigaku. (Sociologie du sport et ses règles) Nagoya: Presses de l'Université de Nagoya (en japonais)

Socialization into and Through Sport

Socialisation vers et par le sport

Sports in Higher Education:
a Means toward Maturity or Enculturation?

Yiorgos Apostolopoulos and Stella Leivadi

Throughout its history, the institution of education has known periodical crises and reforms having to do with its values aims, purposes and programs. Due consideration given to a broad spectrum of purposes stated in various cultures, some contend that education (bureaucratic education) has been created by governments to serve either or both of two purposes: "as a selection device for recruiting persons to governmental or other positions, or as a means of socializing and disciplining the masses in order to win their political compliance[1]". The debate in the literature has been extensive regarding the actual goals of education and whether schooling ought to place greater emphasis on maturity and the individual development of each person or on fitting individuals into existing cultural patterns and social systems to ensure the normal functioning of the system itself[2,3,4].

These two perspectives approach the purpose of education from two polar points of view. The first perspective, an approach with long tradition in American education[5,6], holds that education is designed for enculturation. According to this perspective, young people learn and internalize the prevailing patterns and values accepted by the dominant ideology. Matters such as loyalty to the nation authorities, traditions and adjustments to various societal roles are some of the standard guidelines. Questioning, individuality, change, innovation, controversal subjects such as concentration of wealth, ownership, involvement of high finance and real estate interests in urban blight, ethnic and racial minority viewpoints, control of mass media, military budgets, viewpoints of underdeveloped nations and so on, tend to be avoided[7]. Curricula in schools foster a kind of learning and knowledge which ensures marketable skills generally useful to the establishment. There is an overt as well as a covert teaching of those values which the present system accepts and everyone has to do his/her best to preserve the system's stability. This perspective has its roots in the functionalist theory which explains education by citing its contribution to the integration or productivity of a given society.

The alternative view holds that educational systems should help individuals become independent and effective decision makers. This approach

Yiorgos Apostolopoulos, Department of Sociology, Stella Leivadi, Department of Sport, Leisure and Exercise Science, University of Conncticut, Storrs, Connecticut, USA.

purports that education should promote creativity, intellectual inquiry, and positive human growth. It does not foster ideological conformity to dominant beliefs, autonomous personalities are reinforced, and the challenge and critique of the establishment is not avoided. This process aims to reinforce and support personal maturity and awareness. One is given access to information, all dimensions of even "difficult" topics can be discussed, inequalities and social injustices are explained and experimentation is encouraged. For this perspective, self is the end and not the means to another end. Self worth, personal identity, lack of external control (if it is possible), evaluation of established values, are some of the elements of this model.

Sports in Higher Education

Given the above dichotomy, and the fact that sport is an integral part of the educational process, the following questions were raised: Do American sports and especially collegiate sports, develop, reinforce or perpetuate the "maturity" or the "enculturation" model? Do collegiate sports have an innovative and progressive influence or are they a conservatizing and integrating factor? Do collegiate athletics contribute to an adjustment to formal organizations and develop an apolitical stance toward social problems? Does contemporary sport perform a social control function in capitalist societies by acting as a vehicle of political socialization employed by political and media elite within the dominant class[8]?

Rigauer has stated that sports functions as a sector of social conformity to industrial, bureaucratic social relationships[9]. He also has claimed that under these conditions the human person becomes a commodity exchanged in the market for an equivalent value expressed in money. In a similar vain, Brohm has purported that sports reproduces vertical and hierarchical models which perpetuate alienated labor. Work, continuous effort[10], cults of suffering and self-denial, performances records, remind of the driving forces of bureaucratic professional organizations. In addition, claims have been made that participation in sports will enhance one's acceptance of and socialization into the traditional, idealized values of a particular society[11]. In the same context, Rehberg and Cohen have argued that the socializing experience of sports, exerts a conservative influence on the athlete[12]. Petrie maintains for his part that sport "provides a means of underlining and exhibiting the major elements of the ideological base of the power structure of the society[13]".

Prisuta, in a study on the impacts of televised sports events on the political values of individuals, concluded that heavy viewing of televised sports was one of the best predictors of conservative values. Specifically, he stated that "the behavioral and cognitive impact on young viewers with emphasis on property and competition, male domination, ethnocentric entertainment themes and authoritarian structures operate as a means of mass propaganda sustaining social institutions and life styles[14]". Moreover, Roszak[15] argued that American mainstream sport education has as its objective to fit youth into already prescribed ways through the development of marketable skills, and the maintenance of *status quo* by constellation of actions, thoughts, and feelings.

Two studies which took place in Chile (1972) and Greece (1990), dealt with socialization through organized athletics. Stern surveyed more than 1 500 male high school students in Santiago and concluded that participation in sports indeed appears to be linked to general acceptance of the society's authority structure and ideology[16]. On the other hand, Apostolopoulos and Leivadi, in a study conducted in Athens, Greece, established that there are some connections between conservative social and political learning and the extent of socialization and participation in organized sports[17].

As concerns the organizational structure of sports, Frisby[18], Naison[19], and Schafer[20] presented clear frameworks which support the fact that sport organizations function like business bureaucracies. According to Frisby, most athletic organizations pursue their goals in a business-like manner. They emphasize directly or indirectly: – reduction of personal autonomy, – the concentration of means on producing winners instead of an emphasis on the personal and emotional growth of the athlete, – depersonalization of relationships, – and subordination of the athlete to the major decision makers. According to Naison[21] and Tompson[22], the sports industry has served as a safety valve for social discontent; it functions as a major means for assimilation into the mainstream of American society and it also operates as an instrument of political control and even repression. In the same context, Apostolopoulos and Leivadi[23,24,25], on the basis of a random sample of 1 021 subjects from two different campuses (New England area) found that participation in varsity interscholastic athletics was the best predictor of the development of conservative values, attitudes, beliefs, and behavior among college students. These studies also revealed that athletes as a group were generally against change and mostly in favor of stability and acceptance of established ideas, and that the intensity of sport involvement was the most important predictor of a conservative stance towards various social issues.

Study purpose and methodology

The purpose of the study on which this report is based was twofold: first, to investigate whether interscholastic sports serve as a socializing means for sport participants in order to incorporate them into the mainstream of American life through the teaching of appropriate attitudes, norms, values and behavior patterns; second, to examine the possible relationship between fundamental social issues and intensity of practice, type of sport, and social class. Specifically, the study addressed the following questions: – Are athletes more religious than non-athletes? – Are non-athletes more progressive than athletes? – Do athletes discriminate against sex, color, ethnicity? – Are athletes in favor of traditions and conventions? – Are athletes different from non-athletes with respect to sexual mores? – Are athletes politically conservative? – Are athletes opposed to female social equality? – Do athletes support people's equality of rights?

A questionnaire consisting of 27 items was distributed to 503 varsity athletes and non-athletes randomly selected from the University of Connecticut. The instrument was a fixed choice questionnaire which was designed, developed, and tested for validity and reliability by the authors[26,27]. The items of the questionnaire were derived from the seminal works of Adorno[28], McClosky[29], Rokeach[30], and Wilson[31], but the final version also included issues and problems of contemporary life. To test the reliability of the instrument, the Alpha Cronbach method was used; the values ranged from $\alpha = .75$ to $\alpha = .87$. The construct validity of the instrument was established by conducting a factor analysis on the data obtained from 954 students from the University of Connecticut and Springfield College. Eight constructs were derived from the factor analysis, and on each construct a cluster of attitudes was established. The most significant loadings on a particular factor were then matched with the appropriate category of various social issues. Demographic information such as age, gender, type of sport, intensity of practice, and social class were also collected. The results were analyzed using two- and three-way cross-tabulations and stepwise discriminant analysis. A stepwise multiple regression was also used to determine the best predictors for the "enculturation" or "maturity" model.

Results and Analysis

Across all eight categories of social issues, significant differences were found between athletes and non-athletes (*Table 1*). Non-athletes seem to be less religious (chi square = 65.17, p < .001) and more progressive towards various social issues (chi square = 134.20, p < .001). Non-athletes were also against discriminatory stance towards color, ethnicity, and expression of ideas (chi square = 127.02, p < .001), while athletes were found to prefer traditional/conventional institutions, (chi square = 29.31, p < .001). Athletes tended to be more politically more conservative (chi square = 5.37, p < .05), and they were against egalitarianism (chi square = 15.64, p < .001). In addition, athletes believe less in sex equality (chi square = 24.52, p < .001) and more of them tended to have negative views for issues like abortion and pre-marital sex (chi square = 16.29, p < .001); see also *Figure 1*.

When the above results were collapsed into sex groups, male athletes differed significantly from male non-athletes in seven out of the eight social issues categories. The only issue where male athletes and male non-athletes did not differ significantly was political ideas (chi square = .662, NS; data not shown). The same pattern appeared to be the case with females. Female non-athletes seemed to be less influenced by the system and their attitudes tended to be more liberal than those of female athletes.

TABLE 1

**Differences between Athletes and Non-Athletes
in Eight Categories (Factors) of Social Issues[1]**

Factors	Athletes		Non-Athletes		Chi Square	Probability Level
	Low %	High %	Low %	High %		
F1 Religious dogmatism	33.2	66.8	69.9	30.2	65.17	.001
F2 Stance on progressive social issues	39.6	60.4	89.9	10.1	134.20	.001
F3 Discrimination	42.4	57.6	90.8	9.2	127.02	.001
F4 Preference for traditions and conventions	35.6	64.4	60.1	39.9	29.31	.001
F5 Sexual mores	52.8	47.2	70.6	29.4	16.29	.001
F6 Right wing political orientation	26.8	73.2	36.6	63.4	5.37	.05
F7 Female social equality	78.0	22.0	93.7	6.3	24.45	.001
F8 Egalitarianism	31.6	68.4	49.1	50.9	15.64	.001

[1] Percentages represent the proportion of subjects classified in the lowest or highest portion of the distribution for each category or social issues

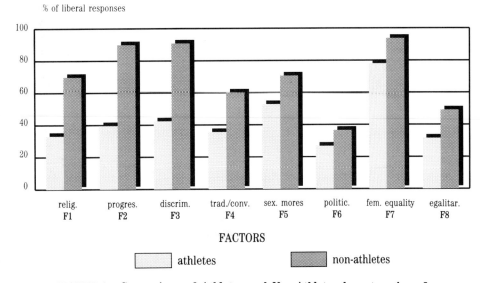

FIGURE 1. **Comparison of Athletes and Non-Athletes by categories of social issues. A higher percentage implies a greater proportion of subjects expressing a liberal response for any guion social issue**

The relationship between the eight different social issues and the intensity of practice was also important. As the intensity of involvement in organized athletic activities increases, the responses of the participants become more conservative and they seem to have internalized to a greater extent the value system of the mainstream. The only issue where no significant difference was found between athletes and non-athletes, with respect to the intensity of practice, was the matter of traditions and conventions (*Figure 2*).

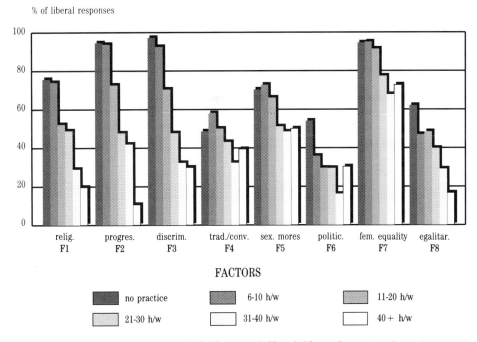

FIGURE 2. **Comparison of Athletes and Non-Athletes by categories of social issues on the basis of intensity of practice or involvement in sport in terms of hours per week**

In order to illustrate the relationship between the eight social issues and type of sport, sports were collapsed into low and high visibility ones. Participation in high visibility sports seems to go hand in hand with the expression of more conservative attitudes in most of the social issues examined in this study (*Figure 3*).

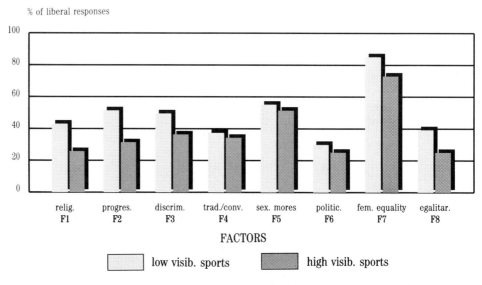

FIGURE 3. **Comparison of low- and high-visibility sports in terms of the percentages of participants manifesting liberal attitudes**

No significant relationship was found between three socio-economic classes (low, middle, and upper) and the social issues under consideration. Sexual mores was the only factor where significant differences were found among the three levels of socio-economic class. The responses of athletes on stance on progressive social issues and sexual mores indicate that the higher the socio-economic class, the more liberal the responses tend to be with respect to these two issues.

Furthermore, the stepwise discriminant function analysis revealed that religious dogmatism, stance on progressive social issues, discrimination, and traditions and conventions, significantly discriminated athletes from non-athletes at the .001 level of significance (*Table 2*).

Discussion

The results support most of the initial hypothetical statements. Sport, as a social phenomenon which extends into education, politics, economics, and the mass media, has been a very politicized phenomenon. The rationalization and professionalization of collegiate sports has led to the adoption of characteristics that are ideologically compatible with the features of society and the values of the dominant ideology.

Althuser, examining the ways in which "the ruling class ensures its domination over the privileged elements of society[32]", argued that certain institutions "function as effective vehicles in the realm of socialization and social control". Thus, in sports' context, the socializee is exposed to, and ultimately accepts the ideology and the cultural values espoused by the dominant social group of the specific society.

TABLE 2

**Sub-Scale C-Scores for Athletes and Non-Athletes
(Stepwise Discriminant Function Analysis)**

Sub-Scale	Mean Score			Lambda	F	Coefficient
	Total	Athletes	Non-Athletes			
F2 *Stance on progressive social issues*	2.80	4.05	1.51	0.69	221.56*	.74
F3 *Discrimination*	1.19	1.90	0.44	0.58	87.14*	.59
F4 *Preference for traditions and conventions*	1.78	2.14	1.40	0.56	19.12*	.29
F1 *Religious dogmatism*	4.39	5.42	3.31	0.54	16.76*	.28
F8 *Egalitarianism*	.66	.77	.54	—	NS	.10
F5 *Sexual mores*	1.26	1.48	1.03	—	NS	.01
F6 *Right wing political orientation*	3.46	3.63	3.28	—	NS	.08
F7 *Female social equality*	.23	.38	.08	—	NS	.01

Degrees of freedom = 10 992
* p ≤ .001
NS = not significant.

Specifically, the data presented above suggest that participation in varsity sports "constructs" personalities who in fact accept the values of the mainstream. Furthermore, type of sport and intensity of practice seem to be the most influential elements of this enculturation process. However, there is no proof or indication as to whether "conformers" are attracted by athletic activities or whether organized athletics reinforce and perpetuate already existing conservative attitudes, values, and beliefs, or both. However, as one interprets the characteristics of the maturity-enculturation model, it becomes obvious that participation in organized collegiate sports in the United States, results in the construction of young people who appear not to accept neoteric views and ideas, who are religious, and who prefer traditional and conventional ways of thinking and behaving. They discriminate more than non-athletes against color, sex and ethnicity and they feel less comfortable in accepting progressive or innovative social ideas and issues. In the same vein, Smith[33] stated that it is generally the ruling class that has control over the Universities because this is a way to ensure the continuity of the capitalist order and the stability of its system. Edwards[34] as well as Scott[35] said that athletic institutions in the United States are resistant to change and function as typical dictatorships. Moreover, Berlage[36] suggested that attitudes, values and skills inculcated in the training of team athletes clearly mirror the values and the ethic of the corporate world. In the same context, Yiannakis[37] argued that institutionalized sports prepare the participants to function effectively in corporate settings.

Schafer[38] stated that athletics are strongly supported by the state because they emphasize loyalty to authorities, they function as social control mechanisms, and contribute to the internalization of values and beliefs such as hard work, postponement of gratification, obedience and respect of the established order. McLaren believes that schooling serves to reproduce the technocratic and corporate ideologies that characterize dominant societies, and that education programs are designed to create individuals who operate in the interests of the state, whose social function is primarily to sustain and legitimate the *status quo*. Teachers have been "reduced to what Giroux calls 'clerks of the empire', whose dreams, desires, and voices are often silenced in order to remove any distractions to industry's call for more entrepreneurial savvy among its future workers, and its desire for a more compliant, devoted, and efficient work force[39]". Thus, the enculturation model functions as a pessimistic doctrine in that tradition and order are judged vital for controlling social behavior. Religion, hierarchy, nationalism, and respect for authority are some of the major building blocks of this type of society; these are also values that organized sports seem to perpetuate and reinforce.

REFERENCES

1. Sanderson SK (1988) Macrosociology: an introduction to human societies. New York: Harper and Row p 363

2. Reich CA (1970) The greening of America. New York: Random House

3. Schafer WE (1971) Sport, socialization and the school: toward maturity or enculturation? Paper presented at the 3rd International Symposium on Sociology of Sport, Waterloo, Ontario

4. Schafer WE (1976) Sport and youth counterculture: contrasting socialization themes. In Landers DM (ed) Social Problems in Athletics. Urbana: University of Illinois Press p 43-75

5. Collins R (1977) Some comparative principles of educational stratification. Harvard Educational Review 47 1-27

6. McPherson BD, Curtis JE, Loy JW (1989) The social significance of sport—an introduction to the sociology of sport. Champaign: Human Kinetics

7. Harris M (1987) Cultural anthropolgy. New York: Harper and Row

8. Helmes RC (1981) Ideology and social control in Canadian sport: a theoretical review. In Hart M, Birell S (eds) Sport in the sociocultural process. Dubuque: WC Brown p 207-32

9. Rigauer B (1981) Sport and work. New York: Columbia University Press

10. Brohm JM (1978) Sport: a prison of measured time. London: Ink Links

11. Cozens FW, Stumpf FS (1974) The role of the school in the sports life of America. In Sage GH (ed) Sport and the American society. Don Mills: Addison-Wesley p 104-31

12. Rehberg RA, Cohen M (1976) Political attitudes and participation in extracurricular activities. In Landers DM (ed) Social problems in athletics: essays on the sociology of sport. Urbana: University of Illinois Press p 201-11

13. Petrie BM (1977) Examination of a stereotype: athletes as conservatives. International Review of Sport Sociology 2 p 12

14. Prisuta RH (1979) Televised sports and political views. Journal of Communication 29 p 94

15. Roszak T (1969) The making of a counter culture. New York: Anchor

16. Stern BA (1972) The relationship between participation in sports and the moral and political socialization of high school youth in Chile. Unpublished PhD dissertation, Stanford University, Los Angeles, California, USA

17. Apostolopoulos Y, Leivadi S (1990) Professional sports in Greece and the development of conservative attitudes. Paper presented at the XIIth World Congress of Sociology, Madrid, Spain

18. Frisby W (1982) Weber's theory of bureaucracy and the study of voluntary sport organizations. In Dunleavy AO, Miracle AW, Rees CR (eds) Studies in the sociology of sport. Forth Worth: Texas Christian University Press p 53-71

19. Naison M (1972) Sports and the American empire. Radical America 6 95-120

20. Schafer WE (1987) Some social sources and consequences of interscholastic athletics: the case of participation and delinquency. In Yiannakis A et al (eds) Sport sociology: contemporary themes. Dubuque: Kendall-Hunt p 108-23

21. Naison M (1972) op cit

22. Thompson RW (1978) Sport and ideology in contemporary society. International Review of Sport Sociology 13 81-94

23. Apostolopoulos Y, Leivadi S (1988) Participation in collegiate sports and conservative attitudes—a preliminary study. Unpublished manuscript. The University of Connecticut

24. Apostolopoulos Y, Leivadi S (1989) Socialization effects from participation in collegiate athletics and the development of conservative attitudes. Paper presented at the Xth meeting of the North American Society for the Sociology of Sport, Washington DC

25. Apostolopoulos Y (1990) Participation in organized athletics and conservatism. Unpublished Master's thesis, University of Connecticut, Storrs

26. Apostolopoulos Y, Leivadi S (1988) op cit

27. Apostolopoulos Y, Leivadi S (1989) op cit

28. Adorno TW et al (1950) The authoritarian personality. New York: Harper

29. McClosky H (1958) Conservatism and personality. The American Political Science Review 52 27-42

30. Rokeach M (1960) The open and closed mind. New York: Basic Books

31. Wilson GD (1973) The psychology of conservatism. London: Academic Press

32. Althuser L (1971) Lenin and philosophy. London: New Left Books

33. Smith DN (1974) Who rules the universities? An essay in class analysis. New York: Monthly Review Press

34. Edwards H (1973) Sociology of sport. Homewood: Dorsey Press

35. Scott J (1971) The athletic revolution. New York: The Free Press

36. Berlage IG (1982) Are the children's competitive team sports socializing agents for corporate America? In Dunleavy AO, Miracle AW, Rees CR (eds) Studies in the sociology of sport. Forth Worth: Texas Christian University Press p 309-324

37. Yiannakis A (1979) Socio-political socialization and the function of organized sport in America. Arena Review 3 29-33

38. Schafer WE (1987) op cit

39. McClaren P (1989) Life in schools. New York: Longman p 2

Characteristics of Competitive Older Adults: Insights for the 21st Century

Robert Gandee, Bruce Hollering, Karen Peracchio, and Mark Peracchio

Over the past 10-15 years older adults have demonstrated significantly greater interest in sport participation and competition. This is evidenced by the emergence of many local, regional and state senior competitive sporting events. Additionally, in 1987, the first United States National Senior Competition was held in St. Louis, Missouri, then repeated in 1989, and is to be held again during the summer of 1991 in Syracuse, New York. These competitions have attracted thousands of older adults from across the United States. Such sporting events at the local, regional, state and national levels are found exciting, colorful, and thus have much appeal to aging individuals. The purpose of the study which is now the object of this presentation was to identify major characteristics of the aging competitors who participated in the 1987 Ohio Senior Games State Finals. These individuals had qualified previously for the state competition at various local/regional games throughout Ohio.

Methods and Procedures

Approximately 385 local and regional finalists qualified for state competition in 1987, and 155 of these individuals volunteered during the Games' registration to answer a self-reported questionnaire. There were 48 questions addressing matters relative to demography, health status, competitive and recreational interests, smoking habits, training sites, event selection, and reasons for participation in the Senior Games. The responses of the volunteer subjects were subgrouped by gender and reported as a percentage of their respective total. The gender distribution of the sample was as follows: 58 females (37%); 97 males (63%). The racial composition of the subjects was essentially caucasian, except for 13 black males.

1890
1990

Robert Gandee, Slippery Rock University, Slippery Rock, Pennsylvania, USA; Bruce Hollering, Karen Peracchio, and Mark Peracchio, University of Akron, Akron, Ohio, USA.

Results

　　　　The survey responses indicated that 62% of the females and 86% of the males were married. Twenty-one percent of the female subjects were widows, as compared to only 4% of widowers in the male subjects. The employment status responses of the subjects revealed that 69% of the females and 63% of the males were fully retired, while only 12% and 18%, respectively, of females and males had full-time employment (*Table 1*).

TABLE 1

Senior Athletes: Retirement Status

Status	Female		Male	
	%	*n*	%	*n*
Fully retired	69	40	63	61
Semi retired	16	9	20	19
Works full-time	12	7	18	17
No answer	3	2	0	0

　　　　The most represented income range of the females 19% and males 21% was 20 000 to 24 999 $ US. Incomes of the subjects ranged from less than 5 000 $ to over 50 000 $ for both sexes. The living environments of these athletes are depicted in *Table 2* as primarily metropolitan areas and small cities.

TABLE 2

Senior Athletes: Living Environments

Living Sites	Female		Male	
	%	*n*	%	*n*
Rural farm	9	5	7	7
Rural nonfarm	5	3	2	2
Small town	16	9	9	9
Small city	22	13	21	20
Suburbs	28	16	28	27
Large city	21	12	25	24
No answer	0	0	8	8

　　　　The subjects' perception of their health status was very positive. As shown in *Table 3*, 88% of the females and 87% of the males identified their health as excellent or good. The subjects' use of medications substantiated their perception of health. Forty-three percent of the females and 62% of the males reported that they did not make use of medications. Of those individuals using medications, blood pressure and circulatory drugs were most common among both females (45%) and males (44%).

TABLE 3

Senior Athletes: Self-Reported Health Status

Status	Female		Male	
	%	n	%	n
Excellent	40	23	53	51
Good	48	28	34	33
Average	9	5	8	8
Fair	3	2	5	5
Poor	0	0	0	0
No answer	0	0	0	0

Smoking patterns of these athletes also reflected the positive health practices by the fact that 69% of the females and 65% of the males never smoked. The smoking status of the Senior athletes is further described in *Table 4*.

TABLE 4

Senior Athletes: Cigarette Smoking Habits

Smoking Habits	Female		Male	
	%	n	%	n
Current	7	4	5	5
Used to smoke	24	14	30	29
Never	69	40	65	63
No answer	0	0	0	0

The age decade in which the majority of the senior athletes were found was the 60-69 years for both males and females. The competitors age groups are shown in *Table 5*.

TABLE 5

Senior Athletes: Age Group Distribution

Age Group Distribution	Female		Male	
	%	n	%	n
50-59	17	10	17	16
60-64	28	16	22	21
65-69	26	15	28	27
70-74	16	9	19	18
75-79	10	6	11	11
80-84	2	1	3	3
85-89	2	1	1	1

The majority of athletes came to the Senior Games with prior sport experience, for 78% of the males and 64% of the females indicated that they participated in sports during their youth. However, further analysis of the data demonstrated that only 26% of the females' spouses and 10% of the males' spouses participated in the Senior Games. The senior athletes of both genders became aware of the games primarily through friends (25-30%) and local newspapers (20-25%).

The subjects' event selection for the Senior Games are presented in *Table 6*. The most popular event for both males and females was track and field. Golf ranked next in preference for the females, while tennis was the second choice of the males.

TABLE 6

Senior Athletes: Event Selection*

Event	Female		Male	
	%	n	%	n
Track & field	59	34	48	47
Tennis	24	14	29	28
Softball throw	17	10	24	23
Golf	28	16	26	25
Swimming	14	8	21	20
Basketball free throw	22	13	14	14
Bowling	12	7	14	14
Football throw	14	8	13	13
Table tennis	16	9	10	10
Horseshoes	14	8	7	7
Shuffleboard	2	1	3	3

* Multiple event selections influence *n's* and percentages

Approximately 75% of both the males and females indicated that they had engaged in some type of *ad hoc* training prior to the Senior Games. These individuals trained in a variety of locations. The various types of training locations are listed in *Table 7*. The most frequently reported training sites for males and females were facilities of the local parks and recreation departments.

TABLE 7

Senior Athletes: Training Locations

Training Sites	Female		Male	
	%	n	%	n
Local high school	11	5	24	17
City parks	32	14	32	23
Local golf course and bowling alley	20	9	13	9
City streets	20	9	11	8
Spa	7	3	8	6
YMCA	5	2	6	4
Bike club, etc.	5	2	6	4

The senior athletes engaged in competitive activities for a variety of reasons as presented in *Table 8*. Physical fitness and enjoyment ranked first and second for both males and females. With respect to awards, recognition is also a motivating factor for these individuals as shown in *Table 9*. Nearly 80% of the females and males felt that awards were of important value to them.

TABLE 8

Major reasons for Senior Games Participation*

	Female		Male	
Reason	%	[*Rank*]	%	[*Rank*]
Physical fitness	55	[1]	53	[1]
Enjoyment	36	[2]	47	[2]
Mental relaxation	3	[4]	14	[3]
Social	3	[4]	11	[4]
Weight control	5	[3]	10	[5]

* Multiple rankings influenced the percentages

TABLE 9

Senior Athletes: Value of Awards

	Female		Male	
Value	%	*n*	%	*n*
Very important	52	30	36	35
Important	31	18	44	43
Not important	17	10	20	19

Discussion

The senior athletes participating in this survey were predominantly white, married males in their 60s, fully retired with an annual income of 20 000–25 000 $ US, and living in the major metropolitan areas in the State of Ohio. They perceived their health status as good/excellent and approximately 50% of the group were not using medications. Additionally, about two-thirds of the survey respondents were non-smokers. A majority of the athletes had been active in sports during their youth. Track and field events, golf and tennis were the sports most often selected for participation and competition in the Senior Games. Seventy-five percent of the competitors trained specifically for their events. The most popular training site was local city parks. Primary motivational factors for these senior athletes were physical fitness, enjoyment and recognition through awards.

Contributions

Although the senior athletes surveyed appear remarkably healthy and independent, society continues to perceive older adults as frail or debilitated. This perception may be appropriate for a percentage of aging individuals, but a great many individuals live productive lives. Athletic competition among healthy older adults provides recognition for their active lifestyle and gives encouragement to those who are less physically active[1]. Senior competition contributes to the well being of the elderly by:

Promoting the positive acceptance of aging

The development of positive attitudes towards senior athletes, and making certain that they are given adequate credit for their competitive abilities in the public arena is a major concern and implication. Public and private administrators and managers, however, of course without ill-intendedness, reinforce negative myths concerning the elderly by perpetuating images of decrepitude and dependency, and by giving disparaging advice concerning people over age 60 participating in sport activities[2]. Older athletes at all levels of competition often refute the stereotypes of aging persons depicted in these myths, in the media and in public policy.

While receiving limited public recognition, older athletes continue to compete in events mostly designed for younger athletes and in so doing find gratification within themselves. Although many senior athletes have won medals and ribbons at innumerable senior athletic competitions in local, state, national and international arenas, their efforts and achievements are ignored by all but a few, even in their home communities.

With the development in recent years of the World Veterans Games, World Masters Games, and United States Senior Games, international competition for aging athletes had a fragmented focus. Slowly, sporting competition among older persons is gaining visibility and prestige. Future senior athletes will have more arenas in which to demonstrate their outstanding abilities. The national and international electronic and print media were urged by Rosenberg[3] to publicize and legitimatize these accomplishments. Sports Illustrated has taken a significant first step[4], and ESPN is scheduled to broadcast the 1991 United States National Senior Sports Classic in Syracuse, New York. Through sport and exercise achievement, the public perception and acceptance of aging individuals will be better focused upon their capacities, capabilities, and independence, not only upon the fears of frailty, disease, dependency, and long term care facilities as so often portrayed in the insurance, medical, and governmental communities.

It is the creative achievement of older adults in all endeavors, sport, art, dance, theatre, that will generate their identity and validation to themselves and others [5,6,7,8]. In this manner, senior sport events contribute to society's acceptance of this ever increasing segment of our population in the third millennium.

Recognizing the importance of regular exercise
in maintaining health and independence

Twentieth century technological/industrial development resulted in lesser physical activity demands in most occupational and social settings. In turn, the elderly of today tend to adopt sedentary lifestyle[9]. Few of the older citizens were exposed to a type of education and motivation which was conducive to an active lifestyle[10]. Atrophy of inactivity was purported to account for about 50% of the ravage of aging[11]. Regular exercise was shown to influence not only the physiological aspects, but also the cognitive functions and personality characteristics of older individuals[12]. Physical activity is indeed required for the maintenance of functional abilities that are necessary for the elderly to lead an independent lifestyle[13-17].

During the 1970s and 1980s there emerged organized competitive sporting events to promote physical activity amond elderly persons. Often these events were viewed with pessimism and ridicule by members of the traditional sport and athletic community, but perceptions by the older population were for their part very positive. Upon observation of the physical feats of their peers, many were motivated to challenge their own lifestyles and physical fitness levels, and a significant number eventually tested their abilities in the athletic arena. These competitive individuals may still represent a minority among aging persons. They do, however, personify the potential of many aged individuals, for a majority of those persons over age 65 tend to live independently, in both the United States and Canada[18,19].

In the face of the accomplishments and surprising physical well-being of senior athletes, a variety of agencies were prompted to promote physical activity programs for the elderly in shopping malls, health spas, and city parks and recreation facilities[20]. Official programming of vigorous exercise for older members of the community sanctions the importance of physical activity for all elderly, and clearly underscores the potential of the aged. The societal recognition and value of those elderly individuals who demonstrate high physical fitness and ability levels provides encouragement to their peers.

Enhancing socialization among the elderly

Society's standard expectations of older adults are a less active lifestyle and social disengagement[21,22,23]. This is even symbolized in the character's reactions of amazement and surprise to grandfather's dancing in Act I, Scene II of the Nutcracker[24]. As aging individuals experience negative labelling, identity loss, lack of a productive daily routine, skill atrophy, and retirement itself, new social networks may facilitate and foster independence[25,26,27]. Through sport training and activities new opportunities appear for maintaining and developing friendships, status, and purpose to one's days[28,29]. The multidimensional nature of sport participation can be of great usefulness in periods of transition[30]. The competitive network of senior athletes provides for social interaction and reciprocal relationships at the local, state, national, and international levels. The sociability of competition involves laughter, companionship, and caring among and for senior athletes[31]. Life satisfaction is enhanced by these behaviors. In turn, sport socialization contributes to the positive morale and well-being of aging individuals[32,33]. The preparation, travel, public appearances, training and competition itself promotes the social integration and independence of older athletes in the same manner as the Olympic Games tend to do for younger athletes. Social integration stifles dependency and depression often observed among the aging.

Implications

The implications of this survey for organizations promoting competitive activities for aging athletes in the 21st century are:

Expansion of organizational structures to advance
Senior Games at the local and state level

In both the economically developed and developing countries, there are limited opportunities for older citizens to exercise and engage in sport activities. It is everywhere that a city recreation department or school district provides facility time on a regular basis for the older members of the community to exercise and train for health and sport competition purposes. Society's traditional attitude towards these independent, healthy individuals has been one of lack of interest or concern.

The focus at the local and state Senior Games is the encouragement of aging individuals to become involved in a variety of regular activities emphasizing participation and social interaction with peers. The implementation of sporting competition indeed enhances motivation and combats boredom.

The YMCAs, YWCAs, city recreation departments, public schools and universities ought to provide facility time for older community members to exercise routinely and train for competition. Coaching is also necessary to give proper instruction and counselling to the older athletes and assist them in improving their skill and performance levels safely. These procedures would update the senior athletes in current training practices. Every community would gain in providing regular instructional and exercise opportunities for its older citizens. The public and private money invested in promoting the positive physical and psychological well-being of aging individuals is also potentially very cost effective.

Organizational and funding structure for the senior athletes' competition

Cohesive structures are needed to promote the continuity of governance and funding. A cohesive, national governing body would be useful. Organizational fragmentation causes confusion among potential corporate sponsors, and among the athletes in the interpretation of the rules of competition from one governing body to another. One organization at the pinnacle of senior sport competition within each nation would provide a singular and strong voice for this sports movement. Such efforts would ensure success in developing a national senior olympics movement and tend to decrease rules, title, and territorial conflict, and attract better financial support.

As sport competition evolves for aging individuals, there will be increasing demand for competition at the international level

This trend points to the need for the implementation of an international umbrella organization to provide coordination, promotion, and recognition for the Senior Games and international senior athletes. In the face of the current organizational and funding problems, it becomes imperative that a strong international umbrella organization evolves with representative officials from participating countries. The primary function of such an organization would be the development of leadership and the enhancement of the visibility of the senior sports movement throughout the world, and the provision of guidance for those countries seeking to develop senior competition among their older citizens. A secondary emphasis would be the development of a funding basis to promote international competition, support member countries' promotional activities, and to assist developing countries in creating and promoting exercise and sport competitions among their older adults. A model for this eventual international body already exists, the International Olympic Committee. Under a similar type of structure, the basic theme and voice of the senior olympic movement would be visible from the local competition to the state and national, and up to the crowning of international champions. This would lead to as well as result in a common effort for the coordination, promotion, and recognition of senior sporting competition throughout the world in the 21st century.

REFERENCES

1. Gandee R, Campell T, Knierim H et al (1989) Senior Olympic Games: opportunities for older adults. Journal of Physical Education Recreation and Dance 60 72-76

2. Gandee R, Layfield R (1981) University network model for statewide senior olympics. In Wittels IG, Hendricks J (eds) Proceedings of the seventh annual meeting of the Association for Gerontology in Higher Education. St-Louis: University of Missouri, Center for Metropolitain Studies p 201-06

3. Rosenberg E (1986) Sport voluntary association involvement and happiness among middle-aged and elderly Americans. In McPherson BD (ed) Sport and aging. Champaign: Human Kinetics p 45-51

4. Moore K (1989) The time of their lives. Sports Illustrated 7 44-47

5. Ebersole P, Hess P (1990) Toward healthy aging. St. Louis: CV Mosby

6. Riker HC, Myers JE (1990) Retirement counseling: a practical guide for action. New York: Hemisphere

7. Simonton DK (1990) Does creativity decline in the later years? Definition, data, and theory. In Perlmutter M (ed) Late life potential. Washington: The Gerontological Society of America p 83-112

8. Viney LL, Benjamin YN, Preston C (1989) Mourning and reminiscence: parallel psychotherapeutic processes for elderly people. International Journal of Aging and Human Development 28 239-49

9. Heikkinen E (1989) Medical and biological research: a global approach. In Harris R, Harris S (eds) Physical activity, aging and sports. Albany: Center for the Study of Aging p 145-50

10. Ostrow AC (1984) Physical activity and the older adult: psychological perspective. Princeton: Princeton

11. Smith EL (1981) The interaction of nature and nurture. In Smith EL, Serfass RC (eds) Exercise and aging. Hillside: Enslow p 11-17

12. El-Naggar AM, Ismail AH (1986) Cognitive processing, emotional health, and exercise in middle aged men. In McPherson BD (ed) Sport and aging. Champaign: Human Kinetics p 205-09

13. Muir-Gray JA, Bassey EJ, Young A (1985) The risk of inactivity. In Muir-Gray JA (ed) Prevention of disease in the elderly. New York: Churchill Livingstone p 78-94

14. Payne VG, Isaacs LD (1987) Human motor development; a lifespan approach. Mountain View: Mayfield

15. Pohjolainen P, Heikkinen E (1989) A longitudinal study of the physical activity of retired people. In Harris R, Harris S (eds) Physical activity, aging and sports. Albany: Center for the Study of Aging p 219-24

16. Walker SN (1990) Promoting healthy aging. In Ferraro KF (ed) Gerontology: perspectives and issues. New York: Springer p 266-82

17. Willott JF (1990) Neurogerontology: the aging nervous system. In Ferraro KF (ed) Gerontology: perspectives and issues. New York: Springer p 58-86

18. Canada's senior (1990) National Advisory Council on Aging. Ottawa: Minister of Supply and Services, Canada

19. Perlmutter M (1990) Introduction: individual and societal potential of late life. In Perlmutter M (ed) Late life potential. Washington: The Gerontological Society of America p vii-x

20. Palmore E (1970) Health practices and illness among the aged. Gerontologist 10 313-16

21. McPherson BD (1986) Sport, health, well-being and aging: some conceptual and methodological issues and questions for sport scientists. In McPherson BD (ed) Sport and aging. Champaign: Human Kinetics p 3-23

22. Schaie KW, Willis SL (1986) Adult development and aging. Princeton: Princeton

23. Sterns H, Matheson N, Schwartz L (1990) Work and retirement. In Ferraro KF (ed) Gerontology: perspectives and issues. New York: Springer p 163-78

24. Ostrow AC (1984) op cit

25. Kuypers JA, Bengston VL (1973) Competence and social breakdown: a social-psychological view of aging. Human Development 16 37-49

26. Lohman N (1977) Correlations of life satisfaction, morale, and adjustment measures. Journal of Gerontology 32 73-75

27. Schrock MM (1980) Holistic assessment of the healthy aged. New York: Wiley & Sons

28. Fasting K (1986) The effect of recreational sports on the quality of life of the unemployed. In McPherson BD (ed) Sport and aging. Champaign: Human Kinetics p 53-59

29. Rosenberg E (1986) op cit

30. Dixon MJ (1986) Participation in physical activity and male adult development. In McPherson BD (ed) Sport and aging. Champaign: Human Kinetics p 73-77

31. Beran J (1986) Exercise and the elderly: observations on a functioning program. In McPherson BD (ed) Sport and aging. Champaign: Human Kinetics p 117-23

32. Ismail AH, Young RJ (1977) Effect of chronic exercise on the personnality of adults. Part XI. Psychological consideration of long distance running. Annals of the New York Academy of Sciences 301 958-69

33. Meusel H (1986) Health and well-being for older adults, through physical exercise and sport: outline of the Giessen Model. In McPherson BD (ed) Sport and aging. Champaign: Human Kinetics p 107-15

Social Patterns and Sports Participation among Female Students in India

Kiran Sandhu

Modern sport cuts across countries, nations and peoples. It also has a strong bearing on the physical, psychological and social aspects of human development and existence. Within a given culture, and as is the case for all social institutions, sport is subjected to the influences of traditions, existing structures, resources, individual and collective aspirations and goals. In the domain of individual lifestyle and social life, traditional and newly emerging values are sometimes at odds and thus have implications and consequences. In that perspective, sport participation is not free from social factors, pressures or reinforcements. A study was conducted on a sample of women at Delhi University, India, to determine the patterns of social characteristics or factors which could best account for participation in sports.

Two hundred sportswomen (SW) were selected among the college students who represented Delhi University in interuniversity championships during the year 1985-86. The subjects included SW who participated in team games or individual/dual games. The team games included basketball, cricket, field hockey, handball, kabaddi, kho-kho, and volleyball. The individual/dual games were badminton, crosscountry, chess, gymnastics, rifleshooting, lawn tennis, swimming, table tennis, and track and field. Another group of two hundred non-sportswomen (NSW), was selected amongst the college students on the basis of the same age group and educational level as that of the sportswomen.

An adapted version of Kapoor's S.E.S.S. questionnaire was used to obtain detailed information on – personal lifestyle, – demographic pattern of family, – economic status, – social and – cultural status as well as some psycho-social components for functional assessment. The scale was divided into five main categories: upper, upper-middle, middle, lower-middle and lower.

The questionnaire was administered to the sportswomen in small groups. At a later time, the same procedure was followed with the non-sportswomen, exactly as per the procedures outlined in the standards manual. The data were collected, verified and then computer-analyzed.

1890
1990

Kiran Sandhu, Indira Ghandi Institute of Physical Education and Sports Science, University of Delhi, Delhi, India.

The fundamental hypothesis was that there were statistically significant differences between the sportswomen and the non-sportswomen in terms of social characteristics or patterns. Measures of central tendency and dispersion were computed. The *t* and *Chi Square* tests were used to determine statistical significance at the chosen levels of $p \le .05$ and $p \le .01$.

An admitted limitation of the study was that the entire sample of subjects (both sportswomen and non-sportswomen) were of the same educational level. Their reading comprehension, however, was not controlled. In addition, the quality of the data may have been affected by the degree of cooperation, just plain honesty, or ulterior motives that some subjects may have had in describing themselves, their family or their social environment. The fact that some sportswomen were participating in more than one type or category of sporting activity may also have had an effect on their responses and thus on the interpretation of the data.

Differences between SW and NSW on Some Social Factors

Statistically significant differences were found between the SW and the NSW on seven of the ten social factors of the S.E.S.S. questionnaire ($p \le .05$). In general terms, the observed differences had to do with type of urban area lived in (urban or semi-urban), previous schooling (government or public school system), living or not with the parents, and amount of money at one's personal disposal.

Comparatively, sportswomen tended to come from families the members of which had lower educational and income levels. By comparison, the non-sportswomen tended to have better housing conditions and household articles, an indication of higher economic means and/or stability. In addition, sportswomen belonged to families which tended to spend comparatively less money on goods and services associated with or indicative of social and cultural awareness or interest, such as newspapers, magazines, books and the like.

There were indications that sportswomen were less *progressive* than non-sportswomen with respect to various social issues. However, there were no differences between the two groups of women as concerns membership and/or participation in associations or clubs, professional aspirations, or concept of social prestige.

The relative distributions of SW and NSW according to the four chosen social categories or clusters of social factors (*i.e.*, upper, upper-middle, middle, and lower-middle) are illustrated in *Figure 1*. It can be seen that among the sportswomen, 1.5% were classified in the upper-middle, 77% in the middle, and 9.5% in the lower-middle class. By contrast, among the non-sportswomen group, 33% (10% upper, 23% upper-middle) were classified in the two top classes, 60.5% in the middle and only 6.5% in the lower-middle.

A value of 15.0 for the Chi-square ($p \le .01$) pointed to the significance of the differences in the percentages of SW and NSW in the four social categories described. There were thus clear indications that, in the sample of Indian college women studied, there were indeed significant differences in the social pattern of living between sportswomen and non-sportswomen. The majority of SW tended to be classified in the middle class, with none in both the lower and upper classes. On the other hand, a greater proportion of NSW were classified in the upper-middle and upper classes, with the majority in the middle class.

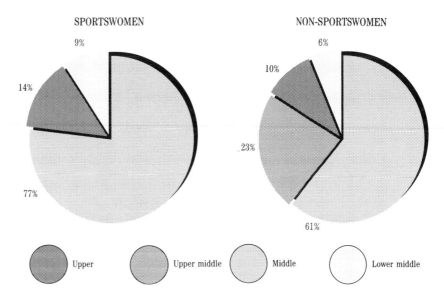

SPORTSWOMEN

NON-SPORTSWOMEN

9%

14%

77%

6%

10%

23%

61%

Upper   Upper middle   Middle   Lower middle

FIGURE 1. **Relative distribution of *Sportswomen* and *Non-sportswomen* on the basis of Kapoor's classification by categories of socio-economico-cultural characteristics.**

Differences Between SW Indulging in Team Games and Individual-Dual Games

Out of a total of 200 sportswomen, 129 (65%) were indulging mainly in team games, and 71 (35%) in individual-dual games or sports. On eight of the ten social factors of the S.E.S.S. questionnaire, significant differences were found between the two sub-groups. This tended to indicate that sportswomen of the latter sub-group (individual-dual games) had been educated in the public schools, and were coming from family circles with higher per-capita income and educational level, including better housing, more household goods, and better access to and use of reading materials. In addition, the sub-group of SW indulging in individual-dual sports and games had parents who tended to mingle more through social, political, and religious interaction as well as through membership in clubs and/or associations. The SW in that sub-group were also found to be issued from more progressive environments and to have generally higher social aspirations, in comparison to team game SW.

The percentage distribution of SW in team games and in individual-dual games, according to the four chosen social categories is shown in *Figure 2*. Among the SW practicing team games, 9.3% were classified in the upper-middle, 76.7% in the middle, and 14% in the lower-middle class. By comparison, with the SW practicing individual-dual sports and games, 21.1% were classified in the upper-middle class, 77.5% in the middle, and only 1.4% in the lower-middle class.

A Chi-square value of 14.6 ($p \leq .01$) also pointed to significant differences in the proportions of SW in one or the other social category, on the basis of whether they indulged in team, or individual-dual games and sports.

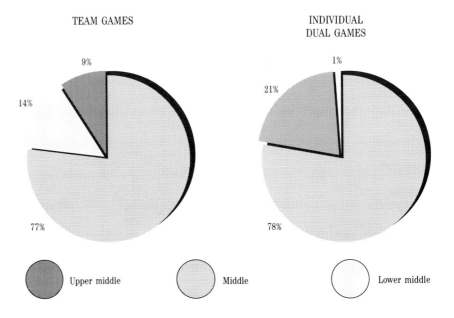

FIGURE 2.   **Relative distribution of *Sportswomen* indulging in team-games as compared to individual-dual games on the basis of Kapoor's classification in three of the categories of socio-economico-cultural characteristics.**

Summary and Conclusion

In the current socio-economic and cultural context in India, college sportswomen differ significantly from their non-sportswomen counterparts in a number of social characteristics, which pertain to personal lifestyle, demographic pattern of family, type of household, material possession in general, information materials, and opinion on the usefulness of the caste system in Indian society. The fact that non-sportswomen scored significantly higher on all above mentioned factors is indicative of a relatively more favorable socio-economic background and environment than what was the case for sportswomen. Participation in social activities and professional as well as social aspirations, however, were not useful in discriminating between the two groups.

With respect to category of socio-economic class or status, the majority of both SW and NSW were classified in the middle class, while NSW were clearly more numerous in the upper middle and upper classes combined.

Among the sportswomen, a supplementary finding was that there was a significantly higher proportion of them who indulged in individual-dual sports (as compared to team sports and games) while being classified in the upper-middle social class.

A general observation and conclusion can be that with the present sample of Indian college women, the individuals classified in the middle social class appeared particularly attracted to sports participation. It may be that sport is viewed as an excellent means through which one channels energies, learns to interact, to cooperate, and to socialize. The results presented above also support the notion that sport is judged by the middle class stratum of society as a means to satisfy the urge for achievement, to gain social prestige and to feel socially accepted. The existence of relationships between social patterns and category or type of sport chosen confirms that among the college level sportswomen studied, such variables as income and educational levels, parental occupation or profession, residential area, social interaction among (and of) family members, and the associated constraints of life, were important determinants of choice.

BIBLIOGRAPHY

Carron AV (1980) Social psychology of sports. Ithaca: Movement Publication

Clausen JA (1968) Perspective on child socialization. In Clausen JA (ed) Socialization and society. Boston: Little, Brow & Co

Cowell C, Ismail AH (1960) Relationship between selected social and physical factors. Research Quarterly 31 40-43

Dyer KF (1976) Social influences on female athletic performance. Journal of Bio-Social Sciences 8 123-29

Famaey L, Hebbelinck M (1979) Team sports and individual sports. International Review of Sport Sociology 14 37-47

Greendorfer SL (1978) Social class influence on female sports involvement. Sex Roles 4 619-25

Harris DV (1973) Involvement in sport. Philadelphia: Lea and Febiger p 6

McPherson BD (1978) Success in sports: the influence of sociological parameters. Canadian Journal of Applied Sport Sciences 3 51-57

McPherson BD (1972) Socialization into the role of sports consumer: a theory and casual model. PhD Dissertation, University of Wisconsin, USA

Oglesby CA (1978) Epilogue: the reality. Women and sport from myth to reality. Philadelphia: Lea and Febiger p 255

Sack AL, Robert T (1979) College football and social mobility: a case of Notre Dame football players. Sociology of Education 52 60-66

Sohi AS (1981) Social status of Indian elite sportsmen in perspective and social stratification and mobility. International Review of Sport Sociology 16 61-78

Verma KK (1975) A comparative study of anxiety difference within the sports groups of women and with those of non-sports women. KUEJ-Arts and Humanities 4

Wightman BJ (1965) Extracurricular physical activity of entering university freshman as a function of social class and residence location. Master's Thesis, University of Wisconsin, USA

Sport:
Organizational
and Service Prospects

Sport:
perspectives d'organisation
et de services

Sport et économie: l'émergence de nouveaux acteurs en France, les collectivités territoriales

Le sport français traverse une crise de croissance: l'augmentation soutenue des effectifs de sportifs s'accompagne de nouveaux modèles de gestion. Ces mutations engagent le mouvement sportif vers une clarification et une redéfinition des enjeux, ainsi qu'un renforcement des initiatives et des pouvoirs locaux sportifs. C'est dans ce contexte sportif qu'émergent de nouveaux acteurs, les collectivités territoriales.

Trois constats fondamentaux

L'analyse du système sportif français révèle, depuis 1980, l'importance et l'incidence de trois caractéristiques: – l'essor de la pratique sportive s'affirme au travers d'indicateurs quantitatifs: le nombre de licenciés et le nombre de fédérations. En 1980, on dénombrait 10 millions de licenciés, 23 fédérations olympiques et 38 fédérations non olympiques. En 1988, ces indicateurs avaient pour valeur: 13 millions de licenciés, 26 fédérations olympiques et 53 fédérations non olympiques; – le budget de l'État en matière de sport stagne et plafonne à moins de 1 % du budget national; – les lois de décentralisation de 1982 n'évoquent pas le sport et n'opèrent, en conséquence, aucun transfert de charge dans ce domaine.

Composante sociale et culturelle, qui remplit des fonctions d'intérêt public, le sport est placé dans une situation paradoxale: *engagement* des citoyens et *désengagement* de l'État. Ce constat a poussé le mouvement sportif à rechercher de nouveaux partenaires. Parallèllement à une ouverture vers le secteur privé, les agents sportifs ont intensifié leur demande auprès de leurs interlocuteurs naturels, les collectivités territoriales. Les communes, au centre du dispositif, consacrent en moyenne de 3 à 8 % de leur budget au sport et ont atteint un seuil critique de financement. De façon massive, à partir de 1982-1983, les départements et les régions sont sollicités par les associations sportives et les instances sportives locales pour apporter leur aide et leur soutien financier et logistique.

Charles Pigeassou, Unité de formation et de recherche en Sciences et techniques des activités physiques et sportives, Université de Montpellier I, Montpellier, France.

L'introduction de nouveaux partenaires, les départements et les régions, crée une situation nouvelle. Le sociologue, intéressé par les changements sociaux, s'attachera à comprendre les effets de cette demande et la nature des réponses apportées en analysant les processus et les stratégies développées. Dans le cadre de cette communication, l'analyse portera sur les départements.

Les politiques départementales en matière de sport

À l'exception de quelques départements[1], les aides apportées au sport par les Conseils Généraux se sont développées à partir de 1983. Un premier état de la situation a été accompli en 1986. Il mettait en évidence les faits suivants[2]:

– la présence systématique d'un budget conséquent consacré au sport réparti en crédits d'investissement et en crédits de fonctionnement;

– une grande disparité entre les départements dans le soutien apporté au sport: l'aide ramenée au nombre d'habitants s'étend dans une fourchette de 1 à 30;

– l'impossibilité de faire apparaître des critères différenciateurs de l'importance de l'aide allouée: richesse du département, urbanité ou ruralité, densité du réseau sportif, aire géographique, particularismes locaux, parenté politique ne constituent pas des opérateurs efficients;

– de profondes différences dans la forme d'organisation des services ou structures gérant le sport au niveau des Conseils Généraux. Ces différences portent sur le statut juridique adopté (service intégré, service associé, organisme associé) et sur le degré de structuration du service ou de l'organisation (différenciation ou non différenciation des tâches, effectif, etc.).

L'absence de logique apparente renvoyait à une explication en termes de stratégie politique ce qui laissait présager des évolutions possibles. Cette hypothèse a été le point de départ d'une réflexion et d'une recherche qualitative sur les stratégies des départements en matière d'aide et de soutien au développement du sport. À ce jour, vingt-cinq départements ont été analysés sur leur politique en matière de sport.

La montée en puissance du sport dans les politiques départementales

Paradoxalement, alors que rien n'oblige les Conseils Généraux à soutenir le développement du sport, on observe un intérêt croissant pour le sport. Ce phénomène se matérialise par une montée en puissance des budgets affectés au sport et la mise en place de prestations de services. À titre d'exemple, les évolutions observées dans les départements du Gard et de l'Hérault sont symptômatiques. La croissance soutenue observée entre 1983 et 1986 devient littéralement explosive à partir de 1987. De la même façon, les moyens humains suivent. Ils correspondent au développement et à la structuration des services. À des tâches de gestion administrative de dossiers s'ajoutent des tâches de conseils et de gestion des actions (conception, assistance, etc.). Ces nouvelles actions impliquent la mise en place d'une logistique propre à répondre aux demandes du mouvement sportif.

Du point de vue du soutien, on assiste à une *diversification des actions* prises en compte en réponse à la *multiplication des demandes*. Les actions se répartissent en six grandes catégories:

– le soutien au fonctionnement administratif des instances représentatives locales du mouvement sportif;

– l'aide au développement de l'action éducative entreprise par les comités et les associations sportives (stages, écoles de sport, manifestations à caractère départemental);

– l'aide à l'implantation et au développement des activités nouvelles, plus particulièrement les activités de loisir de pleine nature;

– l'aide au développement de la pratique par l'achat de matériels distribués aux comités départementaux et/ou aux associations;

– l'organisation ou la collaboration à l'organisation de manifestations départementales, régionales, nationales ou internationales;

– la distribution de récompenses.

Tous les départements ne sont pas homogènes du point de vue du niveau d'intervention et de structuration des services. Mais l'évolution, constatée sur les quatre dernières années, trace le cheminement des procédures d'intervention. La démarche plus tardive, la mise en place plus lente des procédures ou le report dans le temps ne représentent que des épiphénomènes d'une même logique.

La constitution d'un secteur d'intervention

L'action départementale dans le domaine du sport est érigée progressivement en secteur d'intervention. Trois étapes décrivent la mise en place d'un processus.

Première étape. Au caractère informel de la demande répond un engagement au coup par coup. L'élargissement de la demande amène une instruction et un examen des dossiers. À ce stade, il n'y a pas de définition de politique départementale en matière de sport, seuls des objectifs limités sont avancés, collant à la réalité de la demande.

Deuxième étape. L'abondance de la demande amène une régulation des procédures de demande. Formulaire, instance centralisatrice, délai de dépôt sont les repères d'une formalisation et de la mise en place d'une gestion organisée. À ce stade, la réflexion précède l'action et l'action départmentale en matière de sport s'appuie sur des objectifs coordonnés.

Troisième étape. L'évolution de la demande ne faiblit pas mais s'amplifie par la nature des actions proposées. Face à cette multiplication, des options politiques s'imposent afin d'adopter des modes de gestion appropriés. À ce niveau pointe une élaboration et une définition implicites ou explicites de la stratégie. Qu'il s'agisse du développement d'un service ou d'une organisation du département, ou encore d'un renforcement des moyens appropriés à la demande, l'engagement impose des moyens supplémentaires et des arbitrages politiques.

L'évolution du processus n'est pas, pour autant, achevée; deux orientations s'affirment : – l'évaluation des actions engagées; – la valorisation politique des actions menées par le moyen de la communication. La perspective gestionnaire se déploit : – dans l'établissement de règles et de règlements; – dans la réalisation de bilans qui objectivent les coûts. L'intérêt pour le sport se combine avec des actions de communication à travers le sport. Le sport tend à devenir un support de communication au service de l'instance départementale. L'évolution décrite par les trois phases traduit le passage d'une logique externe — la logique sportive — à une logique interne de développement d'un secteur d'intervention du Conseil Général.

Sport et communication

Le développement rapide des crédits affectés au sport doit être mis en relation avec les actions engagées en matière de communication. En effet, les premières actions de communication ont pour objet le sport: il s'agit de promouvoir la pratique, l'événement sportif. Très vite des actions de communication par le sport se combinent avec les précédentes. Par le sport, il s'agit de promouvoir l'image du Conseil Général et/ou l'image du département. Cette perspective, dans laquelle se sont engouffrés les départements les plus engagés en matière de politique sportive, traduit l'intérêt de développer les actions dans le domaine sportif, mais aussi, la nécessité de les maîtriser pour valoriser l'action du département.

En aidant le mouvement sportif, le Conseil Général développe un secteur d'intervention relativement nouveau. La mise en place de ce secteur se caractérise par trois phases qui traduisent, au fil du temps, un changement de logique, le passage d'une logique externe à une logique interne: favoriser le développement du sport mais en rapport avec des objectifs politiques externes au sport.

NOTES ET RÉFÉRENCES

1. On peut citer la Loire-Atlantique en 1972, le Gard en 1975, l'Hérault en 1980.

2. Crédits départementaux consacrés aux APS en 1986. Nice: Université de Nice.

Politique sportive et stratégie économique: les nouveaux décideurs en France

Alain Michel

La décentralisation décidée en France en 1982, fut vraiment effective à partir de 1985. Le transfert de compétences dans le domaine législatif s'accompagna à cette date d'un transfert de moyens budgétaires. Dans les faits, cela se traduisit par une prise de conscience des communes, des départements ct des régions du rôle important qui pouvait être le leur. Mais surtout, ces régions retrouvaient, près de deux siècles plus tard, un début d'autonomie perdue dans le centralisme du code napoléonien. Dès lors, il s'est agi pour les grandes villes, les départements dynamiques et les régions renaissantes de faire la différence. Il fallait se singulariser soit par des actions retentissantes ou des événements spectaculaires, soit par des politiques originales dans des secteurs jusque là délaissés et ainsi faire la preuve d'un particularisme notoire.

Un certain nombre d'études furent entreprises dans ce domaine par l'entremise de la Direction générale des collectivités locales. La première, en 1979, concernait l'impact des activités physiques et sportives dans le budget de fonctionnement des collectivité locales dans l'un des 95 départements français: l'Yonne[1]. La seconde, en 1983, portait sur la politique municipale d'équipement sportif et le rôle des associations sportives, pour une dizaine de communes réparties dans trois régions différentes: Rhône-Alpes, Normandie et Pays de la Loire[2]. Dans un domaine quelque peu différent, d'autres recherches furent conduites en 1984, sur l'analyse des retombées économiques d'une épreuve internationale de planche à voile: la Coupe du Monde de Fun Board (professionnelle) et sur la quatrième Semaine Internationale de Vitesse à la Voile dans l'ouest de la France[3,4]. Mais c'est à partir de 1985, que des audits de villes permirent de déceler une réelle demande des élus et un changement significatif des politiques municipales[5,6,7].

Plusieurs analyses permettent de dégager les éléments qui aident à élaborer une politique sportive locale. L'étude quantitative passée auprès de 1 000 pratiquants sportifs dans chaque ville et une série d'entretiens avec des élus,

Alain Michel, Unité de formation et de recherche en économie appliquée, Université Paris Dauphine, Paris, France.

dirigeants, responsables et personnalités locales conduisent: – d'une part, à proposer l'évaluation d'une politique sportive qui nécessite l'analyse de la pratique sportive; – d'autre part, à élaborer une stratégie à moyen et long terme en définissant un schéma directeur avec un contrat d'objectifs ainsi qu'une prospective du sport, du loisir et du tourisme. En outre l'étude budgétaire comporte l'examen des comptes administratifs sur une période de dix années en analysant les sections de fonctionnement et d'investissement. Finalement, l'analyse des dépenses d'investissement est complétée par le taux de réalisation des équipements, traduisant l'écart entre les investissements prévus et ceux effectivement réalisés, et la part du financement extérieur (État, région, emprunts).

En bref, ces analyses montrent que: 1 – la croissance des dépenses de fonctionnement est régulière entre 1976 et 1985, alors que les dépenses en matière d'investissement sont relativement faibles; 2 – le rapport des dépenses directes (personnel, matériel, subventions) sur les dépenses indirectes (transport, hébergement, administration) demeure de 1 à 3 pour les 10 ans concernés; 3 – le pourcentage des subventions allouées aux différentes activités sportives est sujet à des disparités que ne justifient ni les effectifs, ni les résultats, ni la qualité de l'encadrement; les ressources consacrées aux équipements sportifs en matière d'investissement sont marquées par d'amples variations annuelles.

À l'examen de toutes ces données, les décideurs purent dégager les activités à privilégier à moyen terme compte tenu: – de la demande de la population et de l'évolution de sa composition socio-professionnelle; – de la progression de nouveaux secteurs de sport ou de loisir; – de leur nouvelle approche davantage tournée vers une pratique hygiénique que vers la compétition; – du cadre de pratique exigé, à savoir plus de confort par rapport au passé spartiate, c'est-à-dire des équipements d'un nouveau type; – de l'encadrement compétent à engager, à former et à indemniser; – des charges financières à consentir tant en fonctionnement qu'en investissement.

Il faut souligner que les grandes lignes qui semblent conditionner le succès d'un programme dynamique dans ce domaine, consistent à: – disposer d'une équipe soudée et stable dans le temps; – consacrer des ressources substantielles; – définir un cadre d'action pluriannuel; – créer un groupe de réflexion sur les impacts à venir en anticipant les changements; l'installation d'un tel «suivi» est déterminante.

Ainsi les grandes lignes d'une politique sportive et de loisir purent être préconisées dans les diverses villes étudiées. À Brest, à l'ouest de la France, ont été conseillés: – le renforcement de sports comme le football ou le basket-ball qui offraient l'avantage d'être des sports de plein-air ou de salle; – le développement du centre nautique où se tiennent annuellement des manifestations internationales de vitesse sur divers engins tels que le catamaran ou la planche à voile; – la poursuite des efforts pour le hockey-sur-glace et le judo; – l'ouverture au loisir et au tourisme sportif. À Villepinte, commune située au nord de la région parisienne, d'autres facteurs devaient être pris en considération: – les actions prioritaires visant deux sports collectifs à savoir le football et le handball, un sport de loisir en l'occurence le tennis; – le particularisme local lié à la demande spécifique en sports de combat tels que le judo, le karaté et le *viet-vo-dao*; – l'encouragement à deux disciplines dynamiques à savoir le *roller-skate* et le tennis-de-table. À Vernon, ville de Normandie à l'environnement privilégié, aucune définition de politique sportive n'existait, l'étude permit de proposer: – le développement de la gymnastique réputée sur un plan national, la poursuite des efforts pour le handball et le basketball proches du haut niveau et une aide particulière pour le canoë-kayak et l'haltérophilie; – la mise en valeur d'une zone verte de cinq hectares jusque là laissée sans aucune activité, qui pouvait devenir un parc de loisir idéal.

Mais de ces trois audits, il ressort quelques points communs à renforcer, voire à créer, dans le domaine de l'organisation et de la gestion tant des ressources financières que des ressources humaines. Il s'agit de: – la création d'une information en direction des responsables et la présentation du budget consacré à ce secteur par les élus; – la mise en place d'une communication afin d'utiliser tous les médias modernes: vidéo-clips, panneaux d'affichages mobiles, émissions radiophoniques, presse écrite et publications ciblées; – l'organisation d'un service des sports opérationnel, autonome et disposant d'une réelle capacité de gestion, l'ensemble implique l'existence d'un directeur des sports compétent; – le nouveau mode de répartition des subventions au sein des divers clubs sportifs tenant compte d'une grille d'évaluation; – enfin, la mise en place d'une structure de concertation offrant l'avantage de réunir régulièrement toutes les parties en présence.

Pour l'arbitrage de toutes ces composantes, l'analyse stratégique a été utilisée et, parallèlement, quatre critères ont été retenus: – les activités à «radiographier» et le budget afférent à chacune; – le personnel d'organisation et d'encadrement indispensable; – la structure juridique dans laquelle évolue l'ensemble; – le financement.

Pour la dernière décade de ce XXe siècle, la tâche des responsables de toute nature en général, et du secteur sportif en particulier, consistera à intégrer plusieurs facteurs déterminant les conditions d'optimisation de la qualité de vie de leurs semblables. Tout d'abord, il s'agira de concilier l'exigence d'équipements à grande capacité de spectateurs, dotés d'un haut niveau de technologies nouvelles et parallèlement de répondre aux attentes d'une population tournée de plus en plus vers le sport-loisir, hygiénique et régénérateur. Les dirigeants nationaux et internationaux des diverses instances sportives se trouveront dans l'obligation de concilier l'intérêt particulier d'une élite sportive minoritaire et exigeante avec l'intérêt général d'un nombre croissant de pratiquants moyens. Le corollaire de cette harmonisation qui reste à trouver, se situe dans les domaines de la normalisation des règlements et d'une compensation financière des instances citées ci-dessus qui devraient se traduire par une recherche de la polyvalence des installations nouvelles et un accueil élargi. Ensuite, la différence essentielle et originale consistera dans la présentation de nouvelles activités particulièrement attractives tant au plan de la faisabilité que de leur promotion. En d'autres termes, l'accueil et l'environnement compteront autant que leur pratique effective. Elles devront satisfaire les différentes classes d'âges, libérer davantage les jeunes couples avec notamment la création de halte-garderies et élargir l'éventail des services. La résultante de ces obligations se situe dans la nécessité de disposer d'un personnel compétent et disponible et d'un encadrement qualifié et à l'écoute du pratiquant/consommateur/contribuable, voire du contribuable/électeur. Ceci étant posé, il faudra en outre que la concurrence qui ira grandissante entre le secteur public — les municipalités — le secteur privé — les divers centres — se passe dans de bonnes conditions.

Le sport comme le loisir se trouveront être la «cible» de financiers en tout genre. À l'alternative: équipements publics et activités sportives ou de loisir mis à disposition et structures privées organisées, accueillantes et encadrées, devra succéder une complémentarité nécessaire, indispensable et salutaire pour les deux parties. Dans le cas contraire, on pourrait assister à un clivage de pratiquants par catégories sociales et une rivalité insoutenable à terme, voire ingérable. Les financeurs ne parlent-ils pas du risque-sport? L'harmonisation des multiples centres sportifs et de loisir ou de parcs récréatifs qui se développent semble souhaitable tant dans le domaine du choix des espaces, de l'équilibre des pouvoirs, de la souplesse d'organisation ou d'innovation des parties en présence. Nous abordons ici la capacité d'adaptation à la demande. Le secteur public a toujours tenu compte de celle-ci avec un temps de latence plus ou moins long. L'anticipation n'est pas de son fait. Il en résulte que son offre s'accompagne souvent d'un décalage qui va de cinq à dix ans avec les attentes de la population. On peut tenir le même raisonnement avec les différentes fédérations sportives qui acceptent avec beaucoup de réticence et après une longue procédure tout changement. Les exemples abondent, ainsi avec le ski artistique à côté du ski alpin, de la natation synchronisée à côté de la natation sportive, ou de la gymnastique rythmique sportive à côté de la gymnastique sportive.

Les «corps constitués» que sont les organismes olympiques et nationaux freinent souvent toute nouveauté avec force; leur conservatisme dans bien des cas est la règle. Ce n'est que contraints et forcés qu'ils acceptent les exigences du monde économique ou les impératifs des médias. Dans le premier cas, on a assisté à la disparition du terme «amateur» dans la Charte olympique, dans le second, à la modification des règlements de certains sports. Cette rigidité constatée depuis plusieurs années peut expliquer le désintéressement, le détournement, voire le rejet de la «chose» sportive, codifiée, réglementée, chronométrée, ...imposée, en réalité institutionalisée. Cette rupture due également à l'apparition de nouvelles activités liées aux éléments naturels: air, eau, neige ...a fait s'engouffrer vers de nouvelles pratiques une quantité de sportifs assoiffés de liberté, d'aventure et de découverte et enfin libérés d'entraves artificielles.

Les nouveaux décideurs se retrouvent désormais à l'échelon des collectivités locales. Il s'agit des élus, des partenaires financiers et des pratiquants. Les élus locaux, confrontés désormais à ces nouvelles demandes, devront tenir compte de ces évolutions. Il s'ensuivra des politiques originales à proposer qui intègreront ces divers paramètres. Plus que jamais l'adéquation de l'offre et de la demande apparaîtra comme un impératif nécessaire à l'équilibre du climat local et à l'harmonisation des lieux de vie. Des efforts indispensables, d'adaptation et d'innovation s'imposeront pour protéger les espaces, rééquilibrer le déphasage entre l'urbain et le rural, miser davantage sur la complémentarité que sur la concurrence. Au premier rang des élus on rencontre les maires qui sont dorénavant davantage concernés par ces nouvelles responsabilités. Ils prennent conscience de leur poids dans le choix budgétaire tant dans les équipements à concevoir qu'en dépenses de fonctionnement à prévoir. Ils mesurent aussi le nouvel impact du secteur sport-loisir dans la population. Les présidents des régions, provinces ou départements s'efforcent depuis deux à trois ans de mettre en place un projet dans ce secteur avec une politique clairement définie. La notoriété qui accompagne souvent une telle initiative mérite le détour. Puis on trouve les financeurs, commanditaires en provenance du monde de l'entreprise surtout. Ils interviennent avec de plus en plus de poids dans les décisions des élus locaux. Leur présence initiale dans le sport se limitait à des sommes mises à disposition sans contrepartie. Désormais, ils penchent pour influer sur telles activités, privilégier tels objectifs, favoriser tel développement. Leur pouvoir décisionnel est proportionnel à leur participation. Enfin les nouveaux acteurs que sont tous les pratiquants font basculer ou non la décision en répondant largement à l'offre ou en s'abstenant d'y participer.

Ainsi, la politique sportive établie verticalement, du haut vers le bas, fait apparaître souvent des décalages considérables avec la demande sur le terrain. Tout projet dans ce secteur en constante mutation nécessite des études de motivation. Les changements intervenus depuis les deux dernières décennies annoncent une période de grandes mutations aussi bien dans la pratique des activités traditionnelles ou nouvelles que dans leur nature, c'est-à-dire la compétition ou le loisir. Le coût des installations, le prix des pratiques, le changement des comportements impliquent une remise en question des décideurs d'antan: les dirigeants de fédérations ou de clubs «sclérosés» qui imposent trop longtemps leur autocratie à des pratiquants «ignorés». On assiste depuis peu à une pratique «zappée» d'un sport à un autre, d'un lieu à un autre. Fidéliser une clientèle devient le nouveau leitmotiv des anciens dirigeants face à une population qui essaie beaucoup d'activités mais ne reste pas longtemps dans une seule. Une des solutions qui peut être avancée se situe dans la constitution d'une véritable recherche/développement et d'une stratégie transversale qui intéresseraient les différentes générations, les familles qui participeraient à l'élaboration des décisions. Mais surtout, il reste à favoriser un encadrement de qualité, formé et disposant d'un potentiel d'innovation et d'une aptitude au changement. Ce dernier point nous ramène à l'importance de la formation. Le succès du secteur privé dans le sport et le loisir provient du fait de l'exigence de ses décideurs en ce qui concerne la qualité des hommes, qu'il s'agisse des administrateurs ou des techniciens. Suivant que l'attention sera ou non portée à cet aspect, la réussite s'ensuivra ou l'échec en résultera.

Nous abordons enfin, avec cette dernière remarque, le développement de la pratique individualisée. Celui-ci peut s'expliquer de différentes façons: saturation d'équipements normalisés, inadaptation d'organismes conservateurs, augmentation de l'indépendance et de l'autonomie des individus dans leurs déplacements, exigence des emplois du temps ou des plannings d'utilisation et soif de redécouverte de l'environnement naturel. Il semble que la modernisation effrénée du monde actuel a fait prendre conscience à l'homme de la nécessité de retrouver ses rythmes biologiques. Avec celle-ci, on a assisté à l'apparition du sport à domicile et de tout l'équipement qui l'accompagne comme l'appareillage de musculation et les divers soins du corps: la diététique sportive, les UVA, sans oublier l'inévitable renforcement de substances «dynamisantes» qui permettent un dépassement de soi. Le sport-santé devient l'objectif sinon la règle, en même temps qu'il justifie le sport «chacun pour soi».

NOTES ET RÉFÉRENCES

1. Michel A (1981) Impact socio-économique des activités physiques et sportives dans le budget de fonctionnement des collectivités locales — subventions — dans le département de l'Yonne. Paris: Université Paris Dauphine

2. Michel A (1984) Politique municipale d'équipement sportif et rôles des associations sportives. Paris: Université Paris Dauphine. L'étude porte sur 6 à 8 collectivités locales réparties dans trois régions différentes.

3. Michel A (1984) Retombées économiques de l'épreuve internationale de Planche à voile (fun board) La Torche, Mai. Enquête – Quimper. Paris: Université Paris Dauphine

4. Michel A (1984) Impacts économiques de la semaine internationale de vitesse à la voile. Octobre. Enquête – Brest. Paris: Université Paris Dauphine

5. Michel A (1986) Étude socio-économique de la pratique des activités physiques Étude – Brest. Paris: Université Paris Dauphine

6. Michel A (1987) Analyse socio-économique du sport et détermination des choix de politique sportive. Étude – Villepinte. Paris: Université Paris Dauphine

7. Michel A (1988) Diagnostic et prospective de la politique sportive municipale. Étude – Vernon. Paris: Université Paris Dauphine

Paradigm Lost:
Crisis in the Development of Sport-for-All

Dan G. Tripps

During the past decades, development has been universally considered an imperative. Leaders around the planet were determined to guide their nations to the future through better use of their own resources or as a result of increased international cooperation. This imperative was based on three assumptions which may not serve as adequate underlying principles for development activities.

First, development has traditionally been viewed through a mechanistic and linear concept of history. Such a concept assumes that every society must go through the same phases until it reaches a stage similar to those of countries at present considered developed.

Theories of modernization tend to be culturally loaded with Western perceptions of the world. Those perceptions include a deterministic view of progress, an idea resulting from the discoveries and contributions of 18th century European science. As Western nations colonized the developing world in the last centuries, they imposed the same deterministic standard to the belief that all peoples want change, should have change and that it was their moral duty to help them obtain change[1].

But openness to change, and thus to progress, varies widely from culture to culture. Western colonial nations such as England, for example, confident from events of the Enlightenment, were open to the energy and uncertainty of change and the resulting march to the future. Eastern societies such as China, then and still now, seek greater stability, continuity and tradition resulting in a resistance to change and a slower time-table for development[2]. Indigenous peoples may welcome new ideas while rejecting at the same time the cultural implications of progress itself thus wandering about within a labyrinth where a path toward progress is difficult to trace[3].

Further, there is a problem with time itself. To construct an imaginary future worth working towards, one must evoke some images of a past. In this view,

1890
1990

Dan G. Tripps, School of Physical Education and Athletics, Seattle Pacific University, Seattle, Washington, USA.

the future thrives on values which are endangered by conflict, nourished by integration and which are imaginatively accessible to all who have located themselves in a tradition[4]. It can be argued that for a colonial culture there is no memory for [it is] a political entity which has been brought into existence by the actions of an external power; [it is composed of] a population consisting of the descendants of conquerors, of slaves and indentured laborers and of dispossessed aboriginals; [it uses] a language in the courts and schools which has been imported like an item of heavy machinery; [there exists] a prolonged economic and phychological subservience to a metropolitan center a great distance away [...]. Such conditions make it extremely difficult for the population to develop a vital, effective belief in the past as a present concern and in the present as a consequence of the past's concerns[5].

Second, development has been based on a paternalistic theory. This theory assumes that the basic goal of any society is to achieve the values that characterize the economically developed societies namely, enterprise, competition and material security. Societies which had not reached these goals or which did not share them were not considered different but were generally considered primitive or under-developed. But modern societies are built around a culture of production-con-sumption; quite a contrast to those cultures of efficiency often labelled primitive or underdeveloped. Primitive cultures by their very nature have exercised controls over population growth, food production, energy consumption and pollution[6]. In the Kalahari desert, one of the most non-productive areas of the world, people still have enough to feed and live. Bantu tribes of central Africa only use those foodstuffs considered surplus to trade. Production and consumption are local and prudent rather than external and excessive. The loss of such an efficient use of nature and resources as well as the failure to manage consumption have forced many of today's modern societies into massive import requirements and frightening ecological problems. The United States' overwhelming trade deficit and highly petroleum dependent energy system threaten to bring an enterprising, competitive and materially secure nation to its knees.

Finally, development has traditionally been based on an economic approach which contends that adequate management of funds and finances was sufficient to maintain any country on the road to development. Foreign investment in the third world, however, has arrived on colonial terms, that is with a view to extract more money for the investor than to develop economic resources of the receiver[7]. Major projects produce revenue primarily for the technologically advanced society proposing and managing the project. Moreover, such projects often require the adoption of personnel, policies and procedures aimed at introducing new types of economic and social dependencies with little intention to promoting the growth of local investment and local leadership. More sadly, foreign investment has focused all too often on centralized and expensive projects which do not necessarily benefit the masses. Large hospitals in a capital city capable of scientific procedures such as CATSCAN, or huge stadia available for a megaevent do not effect the entire population; the elite may indeed acquire new opportunities for health or entertainment while the masses may remain malnourished and fragmented socio-economically. Typical assumptions about development—linear progress, modernistic paternalism and economic panacea—often ignore the host culture entirely, failing to examine and build upon the collection of values, aspirations, beliefs, patterns of behavior and interpersonal relations, established or predominating within the society. Development, for long, has thus essentially been a mechanism to transfer the preferred culture from industrialized countries to third world countries, a process most obvious in the colonization of Africa. Lessing wrote, in a review of The Lost World of the Kalahari, that beyond the white man's more obvious crimes in Africa was an unforgivable one; namely, that even the "best of [white men] use Africa as a peg to hang [their] egos on[8]".

Crisis in Development

After 45 years of efforts geared toward development, peoples of the third world find themselves in much the same position as they did before the effort inspired by the United Nations at the close of World War II[9]. That much of humanity still finds itself living in dire poverty bears witness to the failure of the development paradigm. The crisis is one of information and agenda. If not for infrequent media reporting, few people in the economically developed nations would be aware of the hardships experienced by millions of human beings in the third world who forge only a marginal existence. Sealed off from visions of acute deprivation, the industrialized world preoccupies itself with consumption, fashion and leisure. The reality of conditions in the third world must also be brought home to the professions of physical education and sport. While one should not overdramatize the crisis, there is a need to realize that the subject matters of sport and physical education are indeed concerned with human lives impacted by inadequate nourishment, shelter, clothing and medical care. This reality is not always apparent in the profession's strategies for development.

Development specialists gloss over distasteful facts, preferring to talk in terms of modernization, capitalization, construction. Emotional responses must be returned to decision making. Indeed moral reactions to these phenomena quite correctly define the current international condition as unjust. But description itself brings no remedy for the conditions that persist. The problems, of course, are more easily stated than solved. These conditions appear beyond individual grasp and as practitioners, too many devolve into pessimistic nihilism that is non-prescriptive and fruitless[10]. Referring back to the emotive level, sport teachers need to define their subject matter at the grassroots. The bottom line for all practitioners should be that development is about people, not gross domestic product or economic models, or international athletic reputation. If third world nations are to build their own future, it is time for foreign advisors and local planners to take into account the needs and culture of the beneficiaries; that is the needs and culture as actually felt by the people directly concerned instead of a representation of those needs which local planners and foreign experts propose on their behalf. This requires integrating the target population into the planning and implementation and taking into account qualitative aspects of human life as well as the material aspects.

It is in this context of culturally defined development activities that the future of sport-for-all ought to be examined. In such a context, traditional models as seen in North America and Europe are not appropriate. There is a need for new thinking, fresh ideas, imaginative experiments and, perhaps, new or adapted forms of sport itself. To that end, it is proposed that development strategies for sport seek to reach five major objectives: 1– To develop an ideology about sport which influences governmental plans also in public health and social development; 2– To draft a systematic plan for utilization and maintenance of appropriate technology and facilities; 3– To design programs that accommodate local conditions, traditions, facilities and needs of the masses as well as the elite; 4– To establish procedures whereby sport connects with the local economy; 5– To prepare sports leaders with attitudes and skills which will enable them to work collaboratively to benefit all participants.

A New Paradigm

Ideology. In third world countries, sport must be viewed in the given social-cultural context. People in developing countries are concerned with problems that have to do with health, demography, employment, distribution of goods, services and wealth. Sport, which often functions as an escape from such problems, must function as a social force which can contribute to the resolution of these problems. Pierre de Coubertin was aware of this potential of sport when he founded the modern Olympic Movement. He saw sport as a means of social and universal education, as a "training grounds for citizens of tomorrow[11]". National leaders in sport must echo these hopes through an ideology which attempts to foster community and national development while it attempts to predispose individuals towards change and innovation. Moreover, given the magnitude of social-economic problems in developing countries, sport must be put in perspective with respect to its importance. No amount of physical activity is going to help children to become physically fit if they are under- or malnourished. Food plays such a basic role in the personal and social dimensions of life in developing countries that it is the responsibility of leaders in sport to establish proper linkages between nutrition, training and performance, and thus to forge the initial step in the process of community nutritional improvement. Sport can be a useful means to teach ethics. Properly conducted and managed, sport can be made to encourage those who participate and those who watch to conduct themselves in a manner which is commensurate with fraternization, respect for life and the dignity of all persons.

Facilities. Development has been contested most frequently in terms of construction of public projects and modernization of services, often accelerated by the dynamism of championship sport events. The Olympic Games, the Pan American, and the Caribbean Games, to name a few, have required substantial facility construction. But, large sums of money invested in modern structures do not guarantee their subsequent use and, alone, will not necessarily provide for the health, fitness and social consciousness needed by the society concerned for its existence and development. Throughout the developing world, dysfunctional, ill-used or empty stadia stand as white elephants from an era of momentary sport excitement. Lack of appropriate management interest and skill, insufficient funds and complex and serious difficulties in programming doom such facilities to misuse and decay. Moreover, priority given to the expenditures to build such enormous sport facilities or hire the renown athletes and coaches often reflects a displacement of values, namely the development of those goods or services which would make a significant difference for the most people across the nation. Such situations occur throughout the third world. Opportunities to combat polio with Salk vaccine were reported to have been ignored by government officials in an African country so that funds might be spent to build stadia and support services needed for the 1974 World Championship Fight between Mohammed Ali and George Foreman. Similarly, decisions in New Delhi, India, are reported to have caused resources required for flood control and deforestation projects to be redirected to complete stadia requirements for the 1983 Asian Games.

Developing countries may desire stadia which serve as symbols of geopolitical parity, but they need also parks and play areas for the community as well as community pride and involvement in the care and management of existing facilities and spaces. Sport leaders in developing nations who seek to foster national pride would be well advised to redirect the activities away from the momentary and artificial drama of an expensive stadium complex or world championship competition. Indeed important are long range objectives such as hundreds of simple community play and sports centers with programs which aim to improve the quality of life. A healthy nation at play is a concept which is susceptible to provide a more profound, longer lasting sense of national pride among the people and, in due time, accrue the desired status and recognition from other nations.

Programs. Third world leaders in sport often provide top-quality instruction only to the talented few rather than fundamentals to as many as possible. Those responsible for sport development must strike a balance between elite sport and sport-for-all. Improvements in fitness and health for all people are more important in a national effort to develop vibrant, capable and committed citizens, are of more consequence than inter-scholastic or inter-city victories gained by a select few. Leaders ought to recognize the need for training and cooperation at a local and regional level as a high order priority to create a sense of community identity; a localized approach is a prerequisite to international considerations.

Programs must reaffirm traditional games and music. Indigenous activities tend to encourage shared purposes and mutual respect between the old and the young and add much needed cultural color to a sports world in danger of universal grayness. Further, they capitalize on the spontaneity and joy in living and enable participants to express themselves in the energy of the local culture.

Economy. Issues surrounding third world debt will dominate international economic activities for years to come. According to the World Bank's tables, total third world debt in 1989 reached a record high exceeding 1,3 trillion dollars[12]. Each year developing countries debt payments exceed their monetary receipts, thus freezing economic growth in its tracks. In order to spur growth, a cooperative framework among economically developed nations is needed to reduce third world debt, just as local strategies are needed to enhance economic activity. Fundamentally, there are economic returns available through better utilization and improved maintenance of existing facilities and development of tourist services based on or associated with sport.

The reasons for poor utilization and maintenance are many and costs-benefits analyses are critical if change is to occur. At the policy level, leaders need to recognize the costly long-term consequences of deferring necessary maintenance, against the gains of small expenses required of continuous upkeep. Administrators should become aware of the benefits associated with a structured information system, accurate recordkeeping, clear lines of responsibility, greater accountability and standardization of procedures, against the expense and waste caused by erratic management.

A regular, annual tourism calendar designed around sport would be useful as a strategy for a destination point economy, that is, using local culture and geography to attract short-stay visitors and foreign currency. Such a calendar could include festivals to illustrate local history and culture as well as its pageantry or its unique indigenous games. Government sponsored tourism programs centered around native canoe and sailing craft are said to have netted economic and cultural gain throughout the Pacific. Sport activities such as fishing, hiking, climbing, river adventures, land or animal safari, and others, have enabled areas in Central Asia, Africa and Latin America to prosper in spite of a difficult economic climate.

Leadership. A new approach to sport implies new directions in decision making. The first priority is social-cultural. Future leaders must grasp the significance of the anthropology of play; namely the ethnic, aesthetic and historical relationship between play and a community's culture. So too, leaders must understand the socio-psychological dynamics of group behavior and participation to foster the social cohesion and communication required of a new ideology and which lead to a more unified and purposeful community. Administration theory is the second element necessary for well prepared leadership. The management of sport programs encompasses finances, public relations, promotion, office protocol, evaluation, program planning and communication. These skills are essential at all levels if one is to have coordination among the ministry of education, office of home affairs, teacher colleges, schools, community agencies, military, voluntary organizations, interest groups, churches, sport organizations and individual sport clubs.

Conclusion

Amidst a world of high tech communications systems, architectural wonders, genetic engineering, and other important achievements, the people themselves often end up last and become lost in the maze of development plans. Putting people first in development strategies nurtures healthy, educated and resourceful citizens who will tend to initiate, create and implement innovative ideas and policies essential to a nation's economic, political and social dynamism. Human rights and social justice have been and remain guiding principles. As we develop a global paradigm for sport for the next millennium, we must aim to improve the material and spiritual standard of living of all peoples; we must connect our effort to programs which combat illiteracy, hunger, poverty and unemployment; all citizens are encouraged to participate in defining their nation's future. Development must be inherently people oriented. Development projects devoid of human considerations ultimately worsen conditions for the very people they are intended to benefit. Strategies which fail to consider the accountability aspect of development will result in long term economic, political and social instability and will continue to operate as a paradigm lost.

NOTES AND REFERENCES

Ideas and suggestions presented in the paper represent the results of project experience, observations, and interviews. Several theses and selected quotes were derived or supported by the following:

1. Kiggundu MN (1989) Managing organizations in developing countries. Hartford: Kumerian Press

2. Bonavia D (1982) The Chinese. Harmondsworth: Penguin Books

3. Burger J (1987) Report from the frontier: the state of the world's indigenous peoples. London: Zed Books

4. Gordimer N (1960) The english novel in South Africa. In The novel and the nation. Cape Town: National Union of South African Students

5. Jacobson D (1971) Introduction to Schreiner O (1971) The story of an african farm. Harmondsworth: Penguin Books

6. Denslow JS, Padoch C (1988) People of the tropical rainforest. Berkeley: University of California Press

7. Ward PM (1989) Corruption, development and inequality. London: Routledge

8. Lessing D (1958) Desert child. New Statesman 15 November

9. Berthelot (1989) Wanted: a strategy for the 1990s. Development Forum July-August

10. Desmond C (1971) The discarded people. Harmondsworth: Penguin Books

11. Purposes, principles and contradictions of the Olympic Movement. Proceedings of the United States Olympic Academy VI Malibu: Peperdine University 1983

12. United Nations Department of Public Information for the joint UN Information Committee. (1989) The 1989 world economic survey. New York: United Nations

Valeurs, préférences et comportements d'adeptes francophones et anglophones du ski de randonnée au Nouveau-Brunswick, Canada

Hermel Couturier

Le ski de randonnée est l'une des activités physiques populaires auprès des Canadiens. Statistique Canada rapporte qu'en 1987, plus de 2,5 millions de ménages canadiens *possédaient* de l'équipement de ski de randonnée soit une augmentation de 44 % comparativement à 1980, alors qu'un million sept cent quatre-vingt ménages canadiens avaient déclaré posséder de l'équipement de ski de randonnée[1]. Par ailleurs, l'enquête Campbell sur le mieux-être des Canadiens et des Canadiennes montre que le taux de *participation* au ski de randonnée a connu ces dernières années une baisse de 2 %, passant de 18 % en 1981 à 16 % en 1988[2]. Le ski de randonnée se situe au treizième rang parmi les activités physiques pratiquées par les Canadiens. Cet intérêt marqué pour le ski de randonnée mérite d'être considéré avec attention par ceux et celles qui offrent des produits et des services *ad hoc*, ainsi que par les chercheurs dans le domaine de l'activité physique et des sports.

Malgré la popularité de ce sport, très peu d'études ont été faites à son sujet. Selon Chevalier et al., la majorité des études de marché antérieures «[...] nous informait sur le marketing réalisé, la consommation, les salaires des intervenants, la fréquentation des sites, et certaines données socio-démographiques [...][3]». La recherche de Chevalier et collaborateurs sur le profil et les motivations des skieurs de randonnée du Québec, est l'une des rares études faites auprès des skieurs de randonnée au Canada. Leur étude est cependant de nature descriptive; elle n'aborde pas le sujet de la causalité des motivations et des comportements des skieurs de randonnée. Des chercheurs américains ont aussi étudié les motivations des skieurs de randonnée[4-9]. Cependant, ces études étaient elles aussi de nature descriptive et on n'y a pas tenté d'explorer la causalité des motivations et des comportements des skieurs.

Comme le Canada est composé principalement de deux communautés linguistiques distinctes et que la province du Nouveau-Brunswick reflète de façon particulière cette dualité, il fut jugé utile d'établir si les membres de deux groupes

1890
1990

Hermel Couturier, École d'éducation physique et de loisir, Université de Moncton, Moncton, Nouveau-Brunswick, Canada.

ethniques distincts, pratiquant le ski de randonnée, avaient ou pas des valeurs, des motifs et des comportements différents. Selon la théorie d'ethnie en loisir proposée par Washburn[10] et les théories des valeurs proposées par Rokeach[11] et par Kluckholm et Strodtbeck[12], les membres de différents groupes ethniques à l'intérieur d'une société globale possèdent un héritage culturel distinct qui influence leur système de valeurs, leurs motivations et leurs comportements.

Le but de notre recherche était d'identifier la relation entre l'ethnie (définie par la langue d'usage des répondants), le système des valeurs, les préférences et le comportement auprès de skieurs de randonnée francophones et anglophones du Nouveau-Brunswick. Cette présentation visait trois objectifs:

– présenter le profil des skieurs de randonnée dans la province du Nouveau-Brunswick en tenant compte des valeurs, des préférences et du comportement;

– montrer s'il existe ou non une relation entre l'ethnie des répondants et leur système de valeurs, leurs préférences et leurs comportements;

– mettre en lumière les implications des résultats de la recherche pour les gestionnaires de centres de ski de randonnée, les pouvoirs publics, les éducateurs et les chercheurs dans le domaine de l'activité physique.

L'étude visait principalement à vérifier l'hypothèse de l'existence de différences significatives entre les skieurs de randonnée de langue française et de langue anglaise en ce qui a trait au degré d'importance qu'ils accordent à:

– différentes valeurs terminales. Selon Rokeach[13], une valeur « terminale » est « une croyance durable à l'effet qu'une fin d'existence spécifique est personnellement et socialement préférable à son opposée ou à sa contrepartie ». Selon le même auteur, une personne n'admet qu'une quantité restreinte de valeurs, qu'elle organise dans un ordre préférentiel les unes par rapport aux autres. Les valeurs qui collent du plus près à la personnalité jouent un rôle déterminant par rapport à la motivation, aux attitudes et au comportement de l'individu.

– différentes préférences intangibles. Les préférences intangibles se définissent comme étant les bénéfices ou résultats d'ordre immatériel ou psychologique recherchés en préférence par les adeptes de ski de randonnée. Cinquante-deux items furent utilisés pour mesurer 19 préférences intangibles.

– différentes préférences tangibles. Les préférences tangibles se définissent par l'aménagement des installations et des équipements ainsi que par les différentes catégories de services préférés ou désirés par les skieurs. Quarante-six items furent utilisés pour mesurer 8 catégories de préférences tangibles.

– leurs comportements de skieurs.

Méthodologie

L'étude visait un échantillon aléatoire de 1 000 skieurs de randonnée âgés de 13 ans et plus et membres des 25 clubs de ski de randonnée reconnus officiellement dans la province du Nouveau-Brunswick. Le total des skieurs de randonnée inscrits dans ces clubs étaient de 3 961. Pour des raisons diverses, l'échantillon final fut réduit à 952 sujets. Au total, 496 questionnaires (53 %) furent retenus comprenant 369 (74 %) répondants de langue française et 127 (26%) répondants de langue anglaise.

La saisie des données a été effectuée au moyen d'un questionnaire bilingue expédié par voie du courrier suivant la méthode de Dillman[14]. Le questionnaire contenait quatre parties visant à obtenir de l'information au sujet des comportements des skieurs; – de leurs préférences (tangibles et intangibles); – de leur système de valeurs; – de leur profil socio-démographique. Les valeurs furent mesurées au moyen du questionnaire préparé par Rokeach[15] et les préférences intangibles furent mesurées au moyen de l'instrument préparé par Driver[16]. Le questionnaire et sa traduction furent validés par la méthode de test/re-test auprès d'un échantillon de 30 skieurs bilingues.

Dans un premier temps, des analyses descriptives furent faites pour établir les profils des réponses pour chaque question. Ensuite, des analyses corrélationnelles furent utilisées pour choisir et regrouper les variables les plus propices à vérifier les hypothèses. Quatre variables socio-démographiques furent retenues pour les analyses multivariées : la langue d'usage, le niveau de scolarité, l'âge et le niveau d'habileté perçu. Les préférences tangibles furent regroupées en huit domaines sur la base des 46 items utilisés, et les préférences intangibles en 19 domaines à compter des 52 items du questionnaire. La fidélité des domaines fut établie au moyen du coefficient alpha de Cromback. Par la suite, les tests appropriés de tendances centrales et de dispersion (test-t ou Chi-carré) ainsi que les tests de régression multiple pas à pas et les tests d'analyse statistique discriminante furent utilisés pour vérifier les hypothèses établies.

Résultats et discussion

Profil des skieurs de randonnée au Nouveau-Brunswick

L'analyse descriptive des données a montré que les skieurs de randonnée ont en moyenne un statut socio-économique plus élevé que celui de la population en général. Leur niveau moyen de scolarité est de 12,6 années d'éducation formelle. Plus de 50 % d'entre-eux ont un revenu familial de plus de 30 000 $ alors que 35 % occupent un emploi à caractère professionnel ou semi-professionnel. Soixante-dix pourcent sont mariés et sont en moyenne âgés de 36,3 ans. Ils ont en gros 6 ans d'expérience dans la pratique du ski, dépensent très peu pour pratiquer leur sport, et plus de la moitié (58 %) font du ski de randonnée moins de 15 fois par saison. Ils se déplacent en moyenne 7 km pour se rendre à un centre de ski, et parcourent en moyenne 9,7 km par sortie. Très peu voyagent à l'extérieur du Nouveau-Brunswick pour faire du ski (7 %) ; la plupart préfèrent skier pendant le jour (83 %) et les fins de semaine (54 %). Une grande proportion des skieurs (48 %) skient en famille et 62 % n'ont jamais suivi de cours dans ce sport.

Dans l'échantillon concerné, on accorde de l'importance aux valeurs suivantes : la santé (bien-être physique et mental), la sécurité familiale (prendre soin de ses proches), la paix dans le monde, le respect personnel (estime de soi), la liberté (indépendance, liberté de choix) et l'amitié véritable (camaraderie intime, proches). Les motivations principales des skieurs sont la santé physique, la fuite des pressions physiques, l'harmonie avec la nature, le repos physique et la fuite des tensions sociales et personnelles. Les préférences tangibles les plus affichées sont : des sentiers entretenus, la sécurité, l'information, les programmes d'instructions et l'aménagement de sentiers intéressants.

Des différences significatives ont été notées entre les deux groupes ethniques (*Tableau 1*). À cet effet, les skieurs anglophones tendent à être plus âgés que les skieurs francophones, avec une moyenne d'âge de 38 ans comparativement à 35,7 ans, et ils surestiment leur niveau d'habileté par rapport aux francophones. De plus, les skieurs anglophones ont un niveau de scolarité plus élevé que les skieurs francophones.

TABLEAU 1

**Différences socio-démographiques entre les adeptes francophones
et anglophones de ski de randonnée au Nouveau-Brunswick**

Variables socio-démographiques (moyenne)	Échantillon N = 496 (100%)	Francophone N = 369 (74%)	Anglophone N = 127 (26%)	p
Âge (années)	36	36	38	0.07[a]
Niveau d'habileté perçu (%)				
Novice	27	28	22	
Intermédiaire	63	63	62	0.06[b]
Expert	11	9	16	
Niveau de scolarité (Nombre d'années)	13	13	13	0.09[a]

[a] Test-*t*
[b] Chi-carré

Relation entre l'ethnie, les valeurs, les préférences et le comportement des skieurs de randonnée

L'objet de l'étude était de vérifier l'effet de l'ethnie sur les valeurs, les préférences et le comportement des skieurs de randonnée au Nouveau-Brunswick. Les répondants devaient mettre en ordre de priorité les 18 valeurs terminales en utilisant le formulaire G du Rokeach Value Survey. De plus, ils devaient indiquer le degré d'importance qu'ils accordaient aux 52 items du Driver's Item Pool (pour exprimer leurs préférences intangibles ou psychologiques) et aux 46 items utilisés (pour exprimer leurs préférences tangibles, *i.e.*, attributs physiques et services), sur une échelle Likert de six points de « pas important » jusqu'à « extrêmement important ». Finalement, les participants étaient invités à répondre aux 13 questions reliées aux comportements de skieurs de randonnée.

Dans un premier temps, l'application du test-*t* révéla qu'il existe des différences significatives entre les skieurs de randonnée francophones et anglophones au niveau de 8 des 18 valeurs mesurées. Les skieurs de randonnée anglophones accordent plus d'importance aux valeurs « sécurité familiale », « salut », « amitié véritable » que les skieurs de randonnée francophones. Par contre, ces derniers accordent plus d'importance aux cinq autres valeurs décrites au *Tableau 2*. Par la suite, l'analyse de régression multiple pas à pas (*Tableau 2*) a démontré que l'ethnie est une variable explicative pour 7 des valeurs à un niveau de probabilité de .05 et à un niveau de probabilité de .10 pour la valeur « un monde en paix ».

Même si les résultats montrent que l'on ne peut pas attribuer les différences dans les valeurs des skieurs de randonnée francophones et anglophones uniquement à l'ethnie, ils supportent néanmoins l'hypothèse à l'effet que les skieurs des deux groupes ethniques accordent une importance différente à différentes valeurs terminales.

TABLEAU 2

**Coefficients de régression multiple pas à pas relatifs à l'effet
de l'ethnie sur certaines valeurs terminales des skieurs de randonnée**

Valeurs terminales	Ethnie	Âge	Scolarité	Niveau d'habileté perçu
Une vie confortable (une vie prospère) $R^2 = .04$ p = .001	.097*	− .104*	− .102*	.012
Un monde en paix (libre de guerre et conflits) $R^2 = .11$ p = .001	− .076**	.036	− .306*	− .058
Sécurité familiale (prendre soin de ses proches) $R^2 = .04$ p = .000	.144*	.071	− .112*	.004
Santé (bien-être physique et mental) $R^2 = .05$ p = .000	− .191*	.110*	− .035	.042
Plaisir (une vie agréable, de plaisir) $R^2 = .09$ p = .000	− .107*	− .218*	− .122*	.091*
Salut (une vie éternelle, sanctifiante) $R^2 = .09$ p = .000	.088*	.269*	− .022	− .079**
Reconnaissance sociale (respect, admiration) $R^2 = .04$ p = .001	− .139*	− .124*	− .033	.029
Amitié véritable (camaraderie intime, proches) $R^2 = .02$ p = .08	.092*	− .094*	.028	− .035

* p ≤ .05
** p ≤ .10

Pour ce qui est de l'hypothèse ayant trait à l'existence de différences entre les deux groupes ethniques au plan de leurs préférences, l'analyse du test-*t* révèle des variations significatives au niveau de 13 préférences intangibles et de 4 préférences tangibles. L'analyse de régression multiple pas à pas (*Tableau 3*) montre que l'ethnie est une variable explicative pour 12 des préférences intangibles.

TABLEAU 3

Coefficients de régression multiple pas à pas relatifs à l'effet de certaines préférences intangibles des skieurs de randonnée

Préférences intangibles	Ethnie	Âge	Scolarité	Niveau d'habileté perçu
Réussite $R^2 = .11$ p = .000	− .106*	− .206*	− .126*	.183*
Leadership/Autonomie $R^2 = .07$ p = .000	.112*	.124*	.124*	.173*
Risque $R^2 = .08$ p = .000	− .130*	− .162*	− .152	.067
Montrer son équipement $R^2 = .04$ p = .001	− .097*	− .128*	− .064	.104*
Être avec d'autres gens $R^2 = .04$ p = .001	.122*	− .079	− .137*	.049
Être près de la nature $R^2 = .02$ p = .124	− .090**	.094**	.024	.034
Réfléchir sur valeurs personnelles $R^2 = .03$ p = .001	− .163*	− .036	.018	− .023
Créativité $R^2 = .04$ p = .001	− .142*	− .044	− .105*	.058
Repos physique $R^2 = .05$ p = .000	− .220*	− .016	.059	− .012
Fuir les pressions personnelles/ sociales $R^2 = .04$ p = .000	− .123*	.061	.143*	− .017
Sécurité $R^2 = .04$ p = .005	− .131*	.108*	− .091**	.084*
Fuir la famille $R^2 = .06$ p = .000	− .064	− .217*	− .047	.017
Solitude $R^2 = .09$ p = .000	.273*	.009	.108*	− .002

* p ≤ .05
** p ≤ .10

L'influence de l'ethnie sur les préférences intangibles est assez convainquante pour accepter l'hypothèse à l'effet qu'il existe des différences significatives entre les skieurs francophones et anglophones pour la majorité des variables étudiées. Au *Tableau 4* on voit que l'ethnie a un effet significatif sur les 4 préférences tangibles auxquelles les skieurs francophones accordent plus d'importance que les skieurs anglophones. À l'exception de la variable «programmes de ski» où le niveau d'habileté perçu a un effet plus accentué, les résultats indiquent que l'hypothèse ayant trait à l'existence de différences significatives entre les préférences tangibles des skieurs francophones et anglophones se trouverait acceptée.

Au sujet des différences entre les comportements des adeptes francophones et anglophones du ski de randonnée, les analyses statistiques (tests de tendances centrales et analyse discriminante) nous ont obligés à rejeter l'hypothèse. Ce résultat peut être associé au fait que nous avons utilisé un nombre de variables assez restreint (13 variables) pour mesurer les comportements des skieurs de randonnée. Les variables retenues étaient: la fréquence de sorties, les sorties à l'extérieur du Nouveau-Brunswick, les leçons suivies, le montant d'argent dépensé, les moyens d'information utilisés, la possession d'équipement, la distance entre la demeure et le centre de ski, le nombre de kilomètres parcourus lors d'une randonnée, le type de sentier utilisé, le nombre d'heures sur les sentiers lors d'une sortie, les jours de la semaine et le temps de la journée où l'on pratiquait le ski de randonnée, et enfin, la nature du groupe avec lequel on s'adonnait à ce sport.

TABLEAU 4

Coefficients de régression multiple pas à pas relatifs à l'effet de l'ethnie sur certaines préférences tangibles des skieurs de randonnée

Préférences tangibles	Ethnie	Âge	Scolarité	Niveau d'habileté perçu
Programmes d'instruction (novice, intermédiaire, expert, entraîneur, conseil sur l'équipement, l'habit, le fartage) $R^2 = .02$ $p = .06$	− .092**	− .040	− .091**	.067
Programmes de ski (marathon, excursion, compétition) $R^2 = .06$ $p = .000$	− .107*	− .109*	.055	.173*
Programmes sociaux (party, pique-nique, excursion à la belle étoile, activité pour dames) $R^2 = .02$ $p = .02$	− .121*	− .014	− .014	.065
Installations et services de soutien (hébergement, salle licenciée, location d'équipement, stationnement, route d'accès, pro shop, camping, hutte de fartage) $R^2 = .03$ $p = .004$	− .124*	− .111*	.032	.062

* $p \leqslant .05$
** $p \leqslant .10$

Conclusion et implications

L'étude révèle plusieurs similarités entre les skieurs de randonnée francophones et anglophones du Nouveau-Brunswick; elle montre aussi des différences significatives au niveau de leurs valeurs et de leurs préférences. Les résultats soutiennent la théorie de l'ethnie proposée par Washburn[17] et la théorie des valeurs de Rokeach[18]. L'étude confirme l'existence de différences entre les valeurs et les préférences tangibles et intangibles des skieurs de randonnée francophones et anglophones du Nouveau-Brunswick, mais par contre elle infirme l'existence de différences au niveau de leur comportement. Par surcroît, l'étude a permis de développer un profil global des skieurs de randonnée au Nouveau-Brunswick: il possède un statut socio-économique plus élevé que l'ensemble de la population, il a un niveau d'habileté moyen, il se déplace très peu et dépense peu aussi pour pratiquer son sport préféré. De plus, il valorise beaucoup la santé, le milieu naturel, la liberté et veut échapper aux tensions de la vie quotidienne. Il cherche des sentiers intéressants mais sécuritaires avec de bons programmes d'instruction et d'information. Les différences significatives entre les deux groupes ethniques en matière de caractéristiques socio-démographiques, valeurs et préférences, ont certes des implications pour les gestionnaires des clubs de ski de randonnée, les pouvoirs publics, les intervenants et les chercheurs dans le domaine de l'activité physique.

Les gestionnaires du ski de randonnée auraient avantage à tenir compte des différences qui existent entre les deux groupes ethniques dans l'élaboration des politiques de gestion ainsi que dans la planification et l'aménagement des services et des ressources affectés à l'intention de ceux et celles qui pratiquent le ski de randonnée. Entre autres, on devrait voir à ce que l'environnement propice à la pratique de cette activité physique soit en premier lieu sécuritaire, paisible et offre un panorama à la fois esthétique et intéressant. On devrait aussi offrir plus d'activités familiales ou de groupes, ainsi que prévoir plus de programmes d'instruction sur divers aspects de la pratique de l'activité physique en question.

Pour les anglophones, on devrait faciliter les activités familiales et les rencontres amicales. Pour les francophones, les gestionnaires de clubs devraient aussi offrir un environnement sécuritaire (panneaux d'information, pistes moins dangereuses et plus courtes, abris le long des pistes, programmes d'instruction) tout en leur permettant de satisfaire leur goût de s'affirmer, de s'auto-déterminer et d'élever leur niveau d'habileté. À cet effet, on devrait offrir plus de programmes d'instruction et de compétition dans les clubs francophones de la province en tenant compte bien sûr des niveaux d'habileté perçus chez eux comme étant inférieurs à ceux des anglophones. Sur ce point, le gouvernement provincial devrait faire plus d'efforts pour former des instructeurs francophones et offrir plus de cours de formation dans les régions francophones du Nouveau-Brunswick.

Devant le fait que les skieurs de randonnée francophones au Nouveau-Brunswick semblent plus préoccupés que les anglophones par la qualité des équipements et des installations, les gestionnaires des clubs de ski de randonnée dans les milieux francophones devraient porter une attention particulière à l'amélioration des infrastructures et des programmes d'instructions et d'activités sociales offerts aux francophones. En milieu anglophone, les gestionnaires de clubs de ski de randonnée devraient s'intéresser davantage à créer un milieu qui favorise les relations familiales et l'harmonie avec la nature. De manière générale, on peut dire que les skieurs de randonnée sont préoccupés par leur santé, un environnement sain et serein; ils désirent aussi pratiquer le ski de randonnée à faible distance de leur résidence et préfèrent des activités peu structurées. Pour les chercheurs dans le domaine de l'activité physique, l'étude souligne plusieurs besoins, entre autres: – le besoin de recherches multi-culturelles dans d'autres sphères de l'activité physique et du loisir en général; – la nécessité d'ajouter des

variables géographiques ainsi que socio-culturelles dans le modèle de recherche ;
— le besoin de techniques statistiques avancées pour l'analyse des relations
cause/effet entre l'ethnie, les valeurs, les motivations et les comportements ; – le
besoin de renseignements complémentaires sur l'environnement physique et social
relatif au lieu où l'activité physique est pratiquée ; – le besoin d'instruments de
recherche toujours mieux standardisés dans le domaine de l'activité physique et
des loisirs en général.

RÉFÉRENCES

1. Statistique Canada (1988) Touriscope. Le tourisme au Canada. Résumé statistique. Catalogue 87-401. Ottawa : Statistique Canada

2. Stephens T, Craig CL (1990) Le mieux-être des Canadiens et Canadiennes : faits saillants de l'Enquête Campbell de 1988. Ottawa : Institut canadien de la recherche sur la condition physique et le mode de vie, Tableau 6, p 56

3. Chevalier N, Garnier C, Girard A (1985) Profil et motivation des skieurs de fond canadiens. Revue de l'ACSEPL 51 34-38

4. Rollins R (1986) Perceived motives for nordic skiing : an application of attribution theory. Outdoor Recreation Research Journal 1 26-30

5. Rosenthal DH, Driver BL (1983) Managers' perceptions of experiences sought by ski-tourers. Journal of Forestry (February) 88-90

6. Ballman G (1980) Operationalizing the cross-country skiing opportunity spectrum. In Proceedings of the North American Symposium on Dispersed Winter Recreation. Agricultural Extension Service. Educational Series 2-3. University of Minnesota, St-Paul p 31-35

7. Hass GE, Driver BL, Brown PJ (1980) A study of ski touring experiences on the White River National Forest. In Proceedings of the North American Symposium on Dispersed Winter Recreation. Agricultural Extension Service. Educational Series 2-3. University of Minnesota, St-Paul p 25-30

8. McLaughlin WJ, Paradise WEJ (1980) Using visitor preference information to guide dispersed winter recreation management for cross-country skiing and snowmobiling. In Proceedings of the North American Symposium on Dispersed Winter Recreation. Agricultural Extension Service. Educational Series 2-3. University of Minnesota, St-Paul p 64-72

9. Mills AS, Hodgson RW (1980) Cross-country skiers at Tahoe downhill resorts. In Proceedings of the North American Symposium on Dispersed Winter Recreation. Agricultural Extension Service. Educational Series 2-3. University of Minnesota, St-Paul p 105-109

10. Washburn RF (1978) Black-participation in wildland recreation. Alternative explanations. Leisure Sciences 1 175-89

11. Rokeach M (1968) Beliefs, attitudes and values. A theory of organization and change. San Francisco : Jossey Bass

12. Kluckholm FR, Strodtbeck FL (1961) Variations in value orientation. New York : Row-Peterson

13. Rokeach M (1968) op cit p 160

14. Dillman DA (1978) Mail and telephone surveys : the total design method. New York : Wiley & Sons

15. Rokeach M (1968) op cit

16. Driver BL (1977) Item pool for scales designed to quantify the psychological outcomes desired and expected from recreation participation. Unpublished report. USDA Rocky Mountain Forest and Range Experiment Station. Ft Collins, Colorado

17. Washburn RF (1978) op cit

18. Rokeach M (1968) op cit

The Relationship of Job Satisfaction to Leadership Behavior and Other Selected Variables, among Chief Executive Officers of National Sport Organizations

Daniel MacDonald

One of the challenges facing any organization is how to take a group of people with different capabilities and different desires and to involve them in activities that will lead to the success of the organization and bring satisfaction to the individuals involved in it. A person's satisfaction, with different facets of his/her work, is an important variable which may have an influence on the effectiveness of an organization. Motowildo[1] stated that studies show that people who report high levels of job satisfaction are more likely to behave in ways that are important to the organization, even though their actions might not necessarily contribute directly to higher levels of their own job performance or productivity. Job satisfaction is one of the variables of the quality of work life that many researchers are studying today. This report deals with the results of a study the purpose of which was to investigate the relationship of job satisfaction of Chief Executive Officers (CEO) of National Sport Organizations (NSO) in Canada, with their leadership behavior, age, education, administrative experience, athletic experience and the size and type of the organization[2].

Locke[3] and Pinder[4] have identified a great number of studies relating to job satisfaction. Different motivation theories form the foundation for its study. Lawler[5] has described four different approaches, and basically, job satisfaction refers to the affective notions one has toward the job or occupation. Smith, Kendall and Hulin defined job satisfaction as "the feelings a worker has about his job; furthermore, they hypothesize that these feelings are associated with a perceived difference between what is expected as a fair and reasonable return and what is experienced[6]". This is a discrepancy theory approach to job satisfaction. In brief, job satisfaction is a complex concept, it has thus been difficult for researchers to develop a precise definition because it depends on how one perceives and values the different facets of work.

Much of the early job satisfaction research has dealt with the relationship of job satisfaction to job performance, by examining the hypothesis that higher levels of job satisfaction will produce better job performance. Due to the

1890
1990

Daniel MacDonald, École d'éducation physique et de loisir, Université de Moncton, Moncton, Nouveau-Brunswick, Canada.

complexity of this relationship, researchers have judged that job satisfaction is not a reliable predictor of job performance but that it may be related to other job factors such as absenteeism, job withdrawal or other factors of quality of work life[7].

The majority of the leadership studies relating to job satisfaction have used the factors of *consideration* and *initiating structure*, which have produced varying results. In general terms, certain studies have shown a positive relationship between the two leadership dimensions of supervisors and job satisfaction of their subordinates. Motowildo[8] found that managers' satisfaction correlated positively with their *consideration* rating score. Leadership behavior does correlate with facets of job satisfaction but other factors may moderate these relationships.

Individual personal variables, such as *age, length of service (tenure)* and *experience* have been studied in relation to job satisfaction. In reviewing the literature relating to age, one can see that it has positive relationships with job satisfaction, but there appears to be no consensus as to the form of the relationship. For example, Hulin and Smith[9] described it as a monotone relationship whereas Kalleberg and Loscocco[10] have shown a third order polynomial representation for men and a linear relationship for women. Similar findings were reported as to the relationship of *tenure* to the facets of job satisfaction. Several different explanations were advanced in interpreting these results, such as the varying family life cycle stages, people adjusting their expectations with experience, different generations with different values or other factors.

Education is another variable that has been studied in relation to job satisfaction. One would think that education is positively related to satisfaction because it would seem that better educated workers tend to have more interesting and challenging jobs. Different studies have led to a variety or results ranging from positive through negative relationships. Glenn and Weaver[11] explained the lack of a strong positive relationship, in that education can have a negative or a positive effect on satisfaction to the extent that education may increase job expectations and aspirations more than it does increase one's ability to attain satisfaction. Job satisfaction research relating to the size of the organization has also produced inconclusive results.

In reviewing the literature, no job satisfaction studies were found relating to amateur sport administrators but several were identified relating to physical educators and/or athletic administrators. Again these studies produced inconclusive findings. Daniel found a significant correlation between *salary level* and *satisfaction* with the work itself, with *pay* and the *job in total*. He also reported that the number of *university degrees* correlated negatively with *satisfaction of supervision* and positively with *pay* and the *job in total*[12]. Other studies reported similar results[13,14]. *Situational differences* from one organization to another can have a major influence on the job satisfaction of the workers. Thus, it is important to study a variety of organizations because it is indeed difficult to generalize the results from one type of organization to another.

Method

The subjects were the chief executive officers of the NSOs which are located at the National Sport and Recreation Centre, Ottawa, Canada; 55 NSOs were eligible for the study. The data were obtained through three written questionnaires which were distributed to the CEOs and other personnel of the NSOs, in May 1987. The CEOs completed a personal information questionnaire and a second questionnaire involving four of the *satisfaction* facets of the Standardized Job Descriptive Index (JDI) and the Job in General (JIG)[15]. The third questionnaire was completed by the subordinates of the CEOs, it was a shortened version of the Leadership Behavior Descriptive Questionnaire–Form XII[16] which provided the data for the leadership dimensions of *consideration* and *initiating structure*. Both the JDI and JIG and the LBDQ–Form XII questionnaires have been validated and used extensively in research. Descriptive statistics, one way analysis of variance and backward multiple regression techniques, were used to test the 15 hypotheses of the study.

The collection of the data was done according to standard survey research procedures with follow up to non respondents. The response rates from the two groups were high: 84.7% for the CEOs and 80% for the leader behavior analysis by the subordinates. The *leadership scores* for both dimensions were the average of the responses received for each CEO. A minimum of two scores for each dimension was used, as suggested by Stogdill. The following definitions are presented in order to clarify the technical terms used in the text:

Consideration is leader behavior that regards the comfort, well-being, status and contribution of followers[17]. The behavior fosters two-way communication; the subordinate is involved in the decision-making process.

Initiating structure is leader behavior that clearly defines one's own role, and lets followers know what is expected[18]. It would involve such behavior as establishing rules, procedures, and specific directions to subordinates so that they may accomplish their tasks.

Job satisfaction refers to the feelings a worker (CEO) has about his/her job. Job satisfactions are feelings or affective responses to facets of the situation. The different facets of job satisfaction included in the study were satisfaction with the work itself, satisfaction with pay, satisfaction with superordinate supervision, satisfaction with co-workers, and satisfaction with the job in general.

Supervision is the amount and the type of direction or guidance that one receives from the person or persons to whom he/she is responsible to. In this study supervision or superordinate supervision refers to the supervision that the CEOs receive from their president, executive committee, and/or board members of their organization.

Job performance is the degree of effectiveness to which one accomplishes the tasks and assumes the responsibilities of their job.

The following hypotheses were tested:

H_1:   The *consideration* facet of leader behavior will have a significant positive relationship with the facets of *job satisfaction*.

H_2:   The *initiating structure* facet of leader behavior will have a significant positive relationship with the facets of *job satisfaction*.

H_3:   Chief executive officers who are *high* in *consideration* and *initiating structure* leader behavior will have *high* satisfaction with the facets of their job.

H_4:   Chief executive officers who are *low* in both *consideration* and *initiating structure* leader behavior will be *low* in job satisfaction.

H_5:   *Satisfaction* with the facets of the job will *increase* significantly with *age*.

H_6:   The higher the level of *education* of the CEOs, the higher the level of *job satisfaction*.

H_7:   The educational *major area of study* of the CEOs will not differ significantly with their *satisfaction* with the facets of job satisfaction.

H_8:   *Satisfaction* with the different facets of the job will increase significantly as the number of *years of experience* in sport administration increases.

H_9:   The *number of years* of other administrative experience of the CEOs will not create any significant differences with the facets of *job satisfaction*.

H_{10}:   *Tenure* (the number of years in the present job) of the CEOs will not produce any significant differences in relation to the facets of *job satisfaction*.

H_{11}:   The higher the *level of salary*, the greater the CEOs' *satisfaction* will be with the different facets.

H_{12}:   The CEOs' *satisfaction* with the different job facets will not differ significantly with the *size of the NSO*.

H_{13}:   There will be no significant difference between the *type of NSO* and the CEOs' *satisfaction* with the facets of the job.

H_{14}:   The level of past *athletic experience* of the CEOs will not differ significantly with their *satisfaction* of the different job facets.

H_{15}:   Athletic participation on a *national team* by the CEOs will not significantly increase the CEOs *satisfaction* with the different facets of the job.

Results and discussion

To begin, a descriptive profile of the CEOs is presented. They were relatively young, with 72% of the executives being 39 years of age or younger and 86% were 49 years or less. Also, they were well educated, with 90% having completed an undergraduate university degree and 44% having completed a graduate degree. The median salary range for the CEOs was 30 000 $ to 39 999 $ (51%). It was found that 60% of the CEOs had been in their present position for three years or less and 90% for six years or less, which indicated a high turnover rate for the position. Their mean scores for the leadership dimensions of *consideration* (34.65) and *initiating structure* (36.78) were comparable to those reported by Stogdill[19] for several different groups of people.

The four JDI and the JIG scales mean scores are presented in *Table 1*.

TABLE 1

Means, Standard Deviations, Medians and Range for Job Satisfaction Scales

Satisfaction facets for JDI and JIG	Mean	S.D.	Median	Range
Work itself	38.88	7.85	40.00	11-49
Pay	31.22	13.02	32.00	0-54
Supervision	34.47	16.96	40.00	0-54
People on the job	44.69	9.16	48.00	9-54
Job in general	44.56	9.95	48.00	10-54

In general, the CEOs were satisfied with the different facets of their job and they were most satisfied with their relations with the other people on the job and the job in general. The satisfaction with pay was the lowest of the five scales, which is similar to findings of other studies[20,21]. The satisfaction with superordinate supervision mean score of 34.47 and a large standard deviation (16.96) indicated a wide discrepancy between the CEOs on this facet of satisfaction.

One way analysis of variance was used to test the hypotheses along with backward multiple regression for some of the hypotheses. A summary of the significant variances found between the job satisfaction scales and the other variables is presented in *Table 2*. In qualifying these findings, it is acknowledged that the majority of the variances were only statistically significant at the 0.10 level. These low common variances may be due to the small sample size ($N = 55$) available for the study.

TABLE 2

Significant F Values for the Analysis of Variance Between Satisfaction Scales and Other Variables

Variables	Work on present job	Pay	Supervision	People on the job	JIG
Consideration			3.50*	6.03**	
+ IS + CON			3.18*	3.17*	
Age	2.22*				
Education (level)			2.43*	3.55**	
Other administration experience				3.75**	
Tenure			2.88*		
Size					4.70**
Type	2.91*				3.21*
Athletic Experience			2.32*		
National Team	2.91*				

* p ⩽ .10
** p ⩽ .05

In the case of the leadership dimensions, it was found that the CEOs who were high in *consideration* were significantly more satisfied with their relations with the people on the job and somewhat more satisfied with the superordinate supervision they received. Similarly, those that were high for both *initiating structure* and *consideration* behavior were more satisfied with the same facets.

The backward multiple regression summaries relating to the job satisfaction facets and the leader behavior of initiating structure and consideration are presented in *Tables 3* and *4*. The equation in each table encompasses all the facets of job satisfaction that were included to determine the total R^2 for each leader behavior facet. As each job satisfaction facet is removed (step by step) from the equation in order of least importance, the equation is continued until the removal of one facet creates a significant change in the variance (R^2) and ends the equation. Thus, the job satisfaction facet or facets remaining in the equation are the most important facets that account for the variance in the leader behavior in question.

Multiple regression analysis showed that the *work itself* and the *Job in General* (JIG) scales ($R^2 = .178$) were the two facets that accounted significantly at the .05 level for the variance in *initiating structure* behavior (*Table 3*), whereas the *supervision* facet accounted for 10.2% of the variance of *consideration* behavior (*Table 4*). But, *initiating structure* ($R^2 = .23$) behavior (*Table 3*) was more useful than *consideration* ($R^2 = .13$) (*Table 4*) in predicting the variance in satisfaction. These findings were in agreement with the results of other studies, in that the leader must provide some structure to the staff and yet be considerate of their needs and task autonomy.

TABLE 3

**Job Satisfaction Facets that Attempt to Explain the Variation
in the Initiating Structure Behavior**

Order of removal	Facets removed	R	R^2	Change in R^2
All variables entered		.481	.231	
Step 1	Pay	.474	.225	.006
Step 2	Co-workers	.468	.219	.006
Step 3	Supervision	.422	.178	.031
	End of equation			

Work itself ** Remain in the Equation
Job in General **

** p $\leqslant$ .05

TABLE 4

**Job Satisfaction Facets that Attempt to Explain the Variation
in the Consideration Behavior**

Order of removal	Facets removed	R	R^2	Change in R^2
All variables entered		.359	.129	
Step 1	Pay	.355	.126	.003
Step 2	Work itself	.350	.122	.004
Step 3	JIG	.345	.119	.003
Step 4	Co-workers	.319	.102	.017
	End of equation			

Supervision ** Remain in the Equation

** p $\leqslant$ .05

The study showed that the degree of *satisfaction* of the CEOs did not vary significantly with *age*. Only a low positive relationship (p $\leqslant$ .10) was indicated between the *work itself* and *age*. Thus *age* was not a useful variable to predict *satisfaction* of the CEOs. This may partly be explained by the fact that the CEOs were relatively young.

The results of this study also point to an inverse relationship between the *level of university education* and the CEOs *satisfaction* with co-workers relations (p $\leqslant$ .05). Similarly, a moderate negative relationship (p $\leqslant$ .10) was found for satisfaction with supervision. These results are somewhat different from those of other studies[22,23] possibly due to a difference in the perception of the role of the CEOs and the type of supervision they wish to receive. No significant differences were found between the major educational area of study of the CEOs and their satisfaction with the different facets of the job.

The number of years of experience was another variable studied in three different ways: total years of sport administration experience, years of other administrative experience and the number of years in present position (tenure). Only two significant variations were found. The CEOs who had one to five years of other administrative experience were significantly (p $\leqslant$ .05) more satisfied with their relationship with co-workers than the executives who had six or more years of other administrative experience. Secondly, the number of years in the present position produced only a moderate U shaped relationship for satisfaction with supervision ($p \leq .10$). CEOs with four to six years of tenure were significantly less satisfied with superordinate supervision than CEOs with seven or more years in their present position. This could be a possible indicator as to why 90% of the CEOs had been in their present position for six years or less. The findings relating to experience and job satisfaction supported those of other researchers in that there exists a complex relationship between the two factors.

No significant relationship was found between salary level and satisfaction with the facets of the job. This was contrary to Daniel[24] and Vazquez[25] who found a significant positive relationship between *salary* and several facets of *satisfaction* for physical education faculty and athletic directors, respectively. This divergence may be due to the fact that the CEOs salaries were within two levels and/or the sample size was too small.

The variables of the *size* and *type* of organization produced some significant relationships with at least one facet of *satisfaction* as indicated in *Table 2*. It was found that CEOs of larger organizations, based on the budget of the NSOs, and CEOs of multi-sport organizations were significantly more satisfied with their job in general than those who directed smaller or single sport organizations. Osborn and Hunt[26] reported similar results between size of the organization and overall satisfaction. It is plausible that the findings of the present study may be due to the availability of more resources (both financial and human) in larger NSOs, and to the fact that the majority of the multi-sports organizations were classified as larger NSOs.

The last group of variables studied was in relation to the past athletic experience of the CEOs to their job satisfaction. The author was interested to see if the level and type of the CEOs past athletic experience was significantly related to their satisfaction with the job. The CEOs who reported their level of past athletic experience as being at the provincial or national level were significantly ($p \leq .10$) more satisfied with their superordinate supervision than CEOs who were local or international athletes. It is possible that CEOs with only local athletic experience may have felt that they did not receive enough or adequate supervision, whereas the CEOs with international athletic experience may have felt that they received too much supervision from their boards or presidents. This result was not replicated when studying the difference between CEOs who were either a member or non-member of a national team; therefore, it is difficult to indicate for sure the reasons for these variations. CEOs, who were former members of a national team, were significantly ($p \leq .10$) more satisfied with the work itself than non-member CEOs. There could be a number of possible explanations for this difference, one being that CEOs with past national team experience may have developed a greater commitment to or appreciation of the pursuit of excellence in amateur sport.

Conclusion

The results of the study showed that the CEOs of the national sport organizations in Canada were fairly satisfied with the different facets of their job. The executives, who were rated high on both leadership dimensions of *consideration* and *initiating structure*, were more satisfied with their job. These leadership dimensions may assist the CEOs in developing a positive work environment within the organization and in turn, produce greater satisfaction for them. The CEOs satisfaction with the *superordinate supervision* that they received produced the greatest number of significant relationships with the variables studied. Similarly, the *satisfaction with the people on the job* produced a number of significant variances. The relationships for the two facets were both positive and negative in nature. Both these facets deal with the people involved in the organization, the CEOs co-workers and the people, generally volunteers, who supervise or direct the CEOs. The findings point to the need for a more in-depth study to determine the *causes* for these relationships as well as the reasons for the high turnover rate of CEOs found in this study. It is realized that other situational and organizational variables not selected for the study or controlled may have had an effect on the results. National sport organizations are dynamic organizations which are continually changing their structures, financial base, programs, and staff. This dynamic environment may also influence the CEOs perception of their job. It may also explain why 60% of the CEOs had been in their present position for as few as three years or less.

As a group, the CEOs were young, well educated executives who were fairly satisfied with the different facets of their job, yet, they remain mobile. These findings may indicate to the CEOs that by developing a leadership style that is high in both *consideration* and *initiating structure* behavior will provide them with a greater feeling of job satisfaction. Also by increasing their organization's resources, the CEOs will contribute to the growth and the effectiveness of the organization and in turn to their own job satisfaction. The results of the study indicate another area of concern for the NSOs and their executive committees which relates to the type and the degree of supervision that they provide to their CEOs. It is imperative that the NSOs provide the appropriate guidance to their CEOs which will permit them to do their jobs ever more effectively. This approach may help to decrease the voluntary turnover rate of the CEOs, a situation which in turn would decrease the NSOs expense in replacing their own executive officers.

REFERENCES

1. Motowildo SJ (1984) Does job satisfaction lead to consideration and personal sensitivity? Academy of Management Journal 24 910-16

2. Macdonald DH (1988) The relationship of job satisfaction of chief executive officers of national sport organizations to leadership behavior and other variables. Unpublished PhD dissertation, Ohio State University, Columbus, Ohio, USA

3. Locke EA (1976) The nature and causes of job satisfaction. In Dunnetee MD (ed) Handbook of industrial and organizational psychology. Chicago: Rand McNally p 1297-1349

4. Pinder CC (1984) Work motivation: theory, issues and applications. Glenview: Scott, Foresman & Co

5. Lawler EE (1973) Motivation in work organizations. Monterey: Brooks/Cole p 65-74

6. Smith PC, Kendall LM, Hulin CL (1969) The measurement of satisfaction in work and retirement: a strategy for the study of attitudes. Chicago: Rand McNally p 6

7. Pinder CC (1984) op cit

8. Motowildo SJ (1984) op cit

9. Hulin CL, Smith P (1965) A linear model of job satisfaction. Journal of Applied Psychology 49 209-16

10. Kalleberg AL, Loscocco KA (1983) Age differences in job satisfaction. American Sociological Review 48 78-90

11. Glenn ND, Weaver CN (1982) Further evidence on education and job satisfaction. Social Forces 61 46-55

12. Daniel JV (1983) Job satisfaction of physical education faculty in Ontario. CAHPER Journal 49 19-21

13. Vazquez JH (1982) An analysis of the relationship of athletic director job satisfaction and leadership behavior in the three divisions of the NCAA and NAIA. Unpublished PhD dissertation, Florida State University, Tallahassee, Florida, USA

14. Perry JL (1976) Job satisfaction as it relates to similarity in philosophical view between physical education faculty members and their department chairperson. Unpublished PhD dissertation, University of Illinois at Urbana-Champaign, Illinois, USA

15. Smith PC, Kendall LM, Hulin CL (1969) op cit (revised 1985)

16. Stogdill RM (1963) Manual for the leader behavior descriptive questionnaire-form XII. Columbus: Bureau of Business Research, Ohio State University, Columbus, Ohio, USA

17. Ibid p 3

18. Ibid

19. Ibid

20. Daniel JV (1971) Differentiated roles and faculty job satisfaction in departments of physical education and athletics in Ontario universities. Unpublished PhD dissertation, University of Illinois at Urbana-Champaign, Illinois, USA

21. Daniel JV (1983) op cit

22. King M, Murray MA, Atkinson T (1982) Background, personality, job characteristics and satisfaction with work in a national sample. Human Relations 35 119-33

23. Daniel JV (1983) op cit

24. Ibid

25. Vazquez JH (1982) op cit

26. Osborn RN, Hunt JG (1975) Relationship between leadership, size, and subordinate satisfaction in a voluntary organization. Journal of Applied Psychology 60 730-35

Historical Aspects
of the Olympic Movement

Aspects historiques
du Mouvement olympique

For Such Olympic Games:
German-American Turnfests as Preludes
to the Modern Olympic Games

Robert K. Barney

In just a few years the modern Olympic Movement will celebrate its centennial anniversary. Obviously, at the time and place of that celebration, in Atlanta, and also in the other candidate cities for 1996 as well as in all olympic Cities since Athens, there will be cause to pause and reflect on the various historical events that have articulated to produce a vast olympic family of some 170 countries, located in every corner of the world. Though it is generally believed that the penetrating modern phenomenon of Olympic Games rose from the zealous efforts of Pierre Fredy, the Baron de Coubertin, it has been established that before Coubertin was even born, various attempts had been made to establish sporting festivals based on the known and understood legacy of the Olympic Games in Greek Antiquity. Coubertin did not acknowledge such festivals in full or sufficiently, leaving the impression that his genius and inspiration alone led to the great modern masterpiece of sport festival.

A few scholars have been successful in penetrating the mist surrounding some of the prelude attempts at establishing athletic festivals based wholly or partially on inspiration drawn from the ancient olympic legacy. For example, Redmond has reported on the 19th century sporting rites of Highland Scots and the extension of those rites overseas to the United States and Canada[1]. Rühl has researched the Cotswold and Much Wenloch festivals held in England dating from the 17th and 19th centuries, respectively[2]. Each was embellished by an "olympic-like" atmosphere. One also knows of attempts by Scandinavians to establish a festival of athletics in the first half of the 19th century for people living in the Nordic countries[3]. And, here in Quebec, an athletic festival referred to as *Jeux Olympiques* was indeed held in Montreal in 1844[4]. (*Figure 1*). Finally, though remaining largely unknown outside of Greece proper, a national olympic festival was established in Athens in 1859[5]. Again, in 1875, 1879 and 1889, the Greeks repeated their Zappian Games, modern renditions of ancient olympic festivals. Indeed, such Greek attempts to recreate the glory of sport in Hellenic antiquity left an indelible mark on greater Greek sporting culture in the late 19th century, a mark admired by Coubertin on the occasion of his visit to Athens in 1894 to "check out

1890
1990

Robert K. Barney, Faculty of Physical Education, University of Western Ontario, London, Ontario, Canada.

the grounds" for the first international modern Olympic Games scheduled to be held in Athens in 1896[6].

Oddly enough, however, perhaps the most sophisticated, elaborately organized, multi-event olympic-like festival that drew at least part of its organizational inspiration from knowledge of sport in antiquity has passed hardly noticed by olympic historians: the German-American *turnfest* phenomenon.

The first German-American turnfest of "national" consequence was organized in 1851. They continue to be held in our time, the next quadrennial edition to be celebrated in Indianapolis in 1991. By 1860, three years before Coubertin's birth, *Turners* referred to them as "Olympic Games[7]". By the time of the Sorbonne Conference in 1894, these olympic-like national festivals showcased many qualities that took many years for the modern Olympic Movement to develop. Did Coubertin know of them? Did they play any role in stimulating the Baron's quest to establish the modern Olympic Movement? We may never know the definitive answers to such questions, but the evidence suggests that the history of German-American turnfests before 1896 identifies them as an extremely important member in the pantheon of olympic-like sport festival occurrences established well before Coubertin's 1896 inaugural.

Although the typically German practice of *turnen* (literally, "to do gymnastic exercises") first appeared in the United States in the 1820s[8], it was not until the arrival of thousands of German Forty-Eighter political refugees from the failed revolutions of 1848-1849 in Europe that gymnastic societies called *Turnvereins* were established in America. The first of such entities was founded in 1848[9]. By 1850 the growth in the number of individual turnverein societies in America prompted the establishment of a National *Turnerbund*. The Turnerbund's initial concerns focussed on political, educational and social issues related to Germans living in a new land. The Turner creed, *Mens sana in corpore sano* (borrowed from the Roman poet, Juvenal), prompted the Bund to place high priority on both intellectual and physical development, especially for youth, both male and female. Obviously, a natural extension of teaching and practice of turnen was the development of competition, some of the earliest manifestations of which occurred at turnfests sponsored and organized by local turnvereins and the National Bund.

The historic inaugural of national turnfest tradition in America, a legacy that continues in only slightly modified fashion to the present day, occurred in September 1851 in Philadelphia. The first issue of *Turn-Zeitung*, the Turnerbund's national newspaper, reported that almost 700 Turners attended and that the historic fest had been "a complete success[10]". In order to enhance participation by decreasing the travel burdens imposed on Turners scattered throughout America, the Turnerbund implemented a model for staging two annual turnfest celebrations, one in the East and one in the West[11]. Subsequently, in September 1852 the eastern edition of Turnfest II was presented in Baltimore, while in the west, Turners from thirty different societies convened in Cincinnati to participate in athletics and gymnastics competition. In 1853 the dual turnfest scheme continued. New York City hosted the eastern aspect of Turnfest III and Louisville, Kentucky, provided the site for the western meeting. From the pages of the *Louisville Anzeiger*, the thriving Ohio River city's first daily German-Language neswpaper, one learns first hand of the flamboyant events surrounding a turnfest celebration. The *Anzeiger's* descriptions of formidable welcoming ceremonies, parades, gymnastics and sports competitions, banquets, speeches, and a gala ball render a graphic picture of the exciting and festive atmosphere prevalent at such meetings. Noting that 1 400 Turners attended the competitions, the *Anzeiger* triumphantly reported the wisdom of awarding the festival to Louisville: "The gathering for competitive gymnastics exercises shows the high esteem accorded the Louisville Turners by other societies in the United States[12]."

LA MINERVE

VOL. XIII.
IMPRIMÉE ET PUBLIÉE
PAR LUDGER DUVERNAY.

NO. 105.
MONTREAL, BAS-CANADA,
LUNDI SOIR 5 AOÛT 1844

JOURNAL POLITIQUE, LITTÉRAIRE, AGRICOLE, COMMERCIAL ET D'ANNONCES.

JEUX OLYMPIQUES
DE MONTRÉAL
SOUS LE PATRONAGE DE SON EXCEL:
Le Gouverneur Général

SURINTENDANT - C.F. CLARK

DIRECTEURS:

Son Honneur le MAIRE.	M.J. HAYES, Ecr.,
Président,	J. DYDE, Ecr.,
J. BOSTON, Ecr. Shérif,	C.H. CASTLE, Ecr.,
Hon. Col. GORE,	Hon.L.H. LA FONTAINE
Hon. C.C.S. DE BLEURY,	Major KENDALL,
Lt.Col. W. ERMATINGER	L.T. DRUMMOND, Ecr.,
J.B. FORSYTH, Ecr.,	M.P.P.
Col. BOUVERIE,	Lt. et Ajt. MACDONALD,
Col. WETHERALL,	93eRégt.
B.HOLMES, Ecr.	Capt. HIGGINSON/A.D.C.

AUX COURSES ST.PIERRE,
Le 28e et 29e jour d'Août.

Les divertissements commenceront chaque jour à MIDI précis, et auront lieu dans l'ordre suivant :

PREMIER JOUR

Tir à la carabine, de 100 à 180 verges
Sault, sans courrir
Sault saut en course
Jeter des marteaux légers et pesants
Longue course à pieds, 400 verges
Jetter la boule du jeu de crosse
Monter en grimpant au haut d'un mat
Marcher un mile.

SECOND JOUR

Jeu du disque
Courses (steple chase) par dessus de barrières de 4 pieds, 200 verges
(Patting light and heavy Ball)
Sault (hop, step and leap) en courant
Sault (hop, step and leap) sans courir
Courte course à pieds, 100 verges
Long sault à la course
Longue course à pieds, un mile
etc. etc. etc.

A l'exception du tir à la carabine (qui ne sera ouvert qu'à ceux qui souscriront 10s) les autres divertissements seront ouverts à tous. Ceux qui souscriront 10s auront droit à un Billet d'admission à la Station du Club.

Ceux qui remporteront les principaux prix recevront des médailles d'argent ou leur valeur en argent à leur choix.

Ceux qui se proposent d'entrer dans la lice doivent inscrire leurs noms à la loge du Secrétaire et du Trésorier avant que le jeu auquel ils se proposent de prendre part soit commencé.

Les Directeurs, les Trésorier et le Secrétaire recevront des souscriptions et livreront les billets pour les stations.

MYER SOLOMONS,
Secrétaire et Trésorier.

Montréal, 1 août 1844.

Montreal Gazette.

THURSDAY MORNING, AUGUST 29, 1844

MONTREAL OLYMPIC GAMES

UNDER THE PATRONAGE OF HIS EXCELLENCY
THE GOVERNOR GENERAL

FIRST DAY

These sports commenced yesterday at noon, and were attended by a large number of competitors, and a considerable assemblage of our citizens. The day was exceedingly favorable, and the arrangements admirable — reflecting great credit on the gentlemen who assumed the management of the games.

1. RIFLE SHOOTING

Six competitors entered their names — Bertram carrying off the prize.

2. STANDING HIGH VAULT

Four competitors appeared, and the vaulting was considered excellent. The prize was won by Mr. Wm. Boyd, Montreal Gazette Office. The following are the names of the parties, and the height of their respective vaults:

* W. Boyd, 6 ft. 6 in.
* F. Duclos, 6 ft. 3 in.
* J. Cushing, 6 ft. 3 in.
- Meagher, 5 ft., 10-in.

3. RUNNING HIGH LEAP

Eight competitors keenly contested this game, and the leaping was admirable, exciting intense interest among the spectators. The prize was won by Mr. Augustus Lamontagne, hotly pressed by Sergent McGillivray of the 93rd Highlanders, and Private A. McPherson of the same Regiment. The winner cleared 5 ft.1/2 inch, and McGillivray 5 feet. This game was very protracted.

4. THE STANDING LEAP

Was contested with great spirit by six gentlemen, who acquitted themselves very creditably; C. Burroughs, Esq., winning the prize, after a hard struggle — height 4 ft. 5 in. — Ross of the 93rd, and Mr. Boyd, cleared within half an inch of the winner.

5. THROWING LIGHT HAMMER - 8 LBS.

This prize was won clearly by Mr. Wm. Shaw, of Chichester, England, from 8 competitors, most of whom acquitted themselves creditably. The distances thrown were:

. Shaw, 124-feet.
. Sergt. McGillivray, 118 ft, 10 in.
. Prvt. Peter McDonald, 93rd Regt., 118ft, 9 in.
. John McDonald, 117 ft, 9 in.

6. THROWING HEAVY HAMMER - 15 LBS

This prize was won, after a severe struggle, by Sergent McGillivray, 93rd Regt., who threw the hammer 80 feet 6 inches, Mr. Shaw contended for the prize, followed. Six competitors contended for the prize, and the throwing was very good throughout.

7. FOOT RACE - 400 YARDS

Nineteen persons started, several of them being Indians — the contest, however, terminating in favor of the white man. Mr. C. Burroughs won the prize cleverly, followed by an Indian glorying in the mellifluous name of Onasateka, and the winner of the running high leap, Mr. Lamontagne.

8. GAME OF LA CROSSE

The race was followed by the Indian game of la Crosse, much resembling the game in Scotland termed «shinty». A purse of $ 10 was made up for the winners among the spectators, who appeared highly gratified by the agility displayed.

9. THROWING CRICKET BALL

F. Duclos won this prize, after a hard struggle, from 20 competitors - distance 96 yards.

10. WALKING MATCH - 1 MILE

Next followed a walking match of one mile, which was not decided, on account of alleged irregularity on the part of the two foremost competitors. The match will come off again to-day.

Great amusement was afforded by the two last matches viz., Climbing the Pole and a Wheelbarrow Race. Private McPherson of the 93rd, won the latter; and an Indian, named Jacques, the former, after the most eager contest we ever witnessed.

This closed the amusements for the day, to be resumed to-day at 12 o'clock, when excellent sport is anticipated. The greatest harmony prevailed throughout, and the gentlemen who directed the games manifested much commensurable urbanity in their department and impartiality in their decisions.

N.B. - Those marked with an asterisk are members of the Olympic Club.

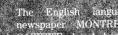
Adapted from: Rendez-vous 76 Montréal.
Bulletin officiel publié par le COJO-76. Numéro 1, août 1973, p 4-5.

The Turnerbund's annual dual turnfest scheme was however shortlived. At their annual convention in Cleveland, in October 1853, the Turnerbund membership voted to revert to a single annual celebration alternately held in an eastern and a western city. Accordingly, Turnfest IV was awarded to Philadelphia, where, for the first time, both free and turning gymnastics competitions were held for division classifications (junior, active and senior)[13].

By the end of the first decade of the national turnfest experience in the United States the annual festival had taken on many of the characteristics which, in time, the modern Olympic Games would also reflect, including: a varied program of athletic competitions, a model for awarding prizes, a formula for staging the event in sharply defined periodic intervals, a scheme for making the festival ambulatory across America, and finally, a place for women in the active exercise proceedings.

The program of athletic events included a military division which featured target shooting, fencing with sabre and foil, and bayonet thrusting. A so-called "free turning" classification provided for competitions in wrestling, weightlifting, sprint running, hurdles racing, high jumping, javelin throwing, stone putting, swimming and stilt walking. Whereas the "blue ribbon" sport of the modern Olympic Games has always been track and field, the highlighted activities of the turnfest were competitions in the apparatus turning classification, specifically, work on the horizontal and parallel bars, the swinging rings, vaulting horse and rope climbing (*Figure 2*).

There were other similarities between mid-nineteenth century German-American national turnfests and the modern Olympic Games established much later. At the outset of the turnfest experience small trophy mementos in the form of medallions, silver cups and jewelry items were given to winners of the various events. By 1857 the character of prize awards changed. In fact, strong sentiment existed that prizes be eliminated altogether, it being argued by some that "it would be unworthy of Turners to come to a turnfest because of prizes only[14]". The Turnerbund's final deliberations on the subject of prizes to be awarded at the great national fest resulted in a decision whereby the top competitors in each classification would receive a tastefully decorated diploma and a laurel wreath. In order to be eligible for a prize in the apparatus or free turning classifications the competitor was obligated to participate in each of the individual exercises[15]. It was judged that to be a specialist in a single event denied the Turner creed of all-around development.

By the end of the first decade of the Bund's experience solutions to other organizational problems were found. Originally, a single annual national turnfest had been the plan. By 1860, it had become obvious to all that the expense incurred by the host turnverein kept that organization in debt for several years, a phenomenon not without parallel in modern olympic history. Then too, individual turnvereins which sent large delegations of competitors to the annual turnfest met with considerable financial debt resulting from the burden of travel expenses. These two factors prompted the Bund to organize the national turnfest on an every-other-year basis[16]. After the Civil War, during which no turnfests were held, the national turnfest was celebrated without interruption in event-numbered years until 1881 (Turnfest XIX). By the late 1870s and early 1880s the Bund's national membership increased in staggering circumstance[17], prompting the Bund to stage its national turnfest in quadrennial fashion. The first edition of the Bund's quadrennial games occured in 1885 (Turnfest XX). Since 1885 the Bund's national turnfest has been celebrated at regular four year intervals, except during the years of World Wars I and II (as was the case with the modern Olympiads).

Right from the start the Bund had planned the national turnfest to be ambulatory in character, that is, the great athletic festival would be held in

Figure 2. Turner Competitions on the horizontal bar during Turnfest XXII (Milwaukee-1893). From the author's private collection.

different cities of the United States. The American cities which hosted the festival up to the time of Coubertin's first Olympic Games were:

1851	Turnfest I	Philadelphia		1867	Turnfest XII	Baltimore
1852	Turnfest II	Baltimore/Cincinnati		1869	Turnfest XIII	Chicago
1853	Turnfest III	New York/		1871	Turnfest XIV	Williamsburg (now
		Louisville				Brooklyn, NY)
1854	Turnfest IV	Philadelphia		1873	Turnfest XV	Cincinnati
1855	Turnfest V	Cincinnati		1875	Turnfest XVI	New York
1856	Turnfest VI	Pittsburgh		1877	Turnfest XVII	Milwaukee
1857	Turnfest VII	Milwaukee		1879	Turnfest XVIII	Philadelphia
1858	Turnfest VIII	Belleville (Illinois)		1881	Turnfest XIX	St. Louis
1859	Turnfest IX	Baltimore		1885	Turnfest XX	Newark, New Jersey
1860	Turnfest X	St. Louis		1889	Turnfest XXI	Cincinnati
		Civil War		1893	Turnfest XXII	Milwaukee
1865	Turnfest XI	Cincinnati				

There remains two points of discussion which demonstrate that the German-American National Turnfest phenomenon was decades ahead of developments achieved by the modern Olympic Movement. One point concerns the participation of women. Coubertin, as is well known, was adamant that women should not compete in the Olympic Games. In effect, except for exhibition notations that evolved slowly in the first quarter of the 20th century, women were not accorded official status until after Coubertin's retirement from the IOC presidency in 1925, and even then, not without much controversy. Female Turners had been a part of turnverein gymnastics programs almost from the outset of the "American experience". By the 1870s Turner ladies were performing in mass drill and exercise formations at national turnfest celebrations, even though they did not compete for individual prize awards until 1921[18]. The final point concerns the number of participants in the national turnfests. In the same year that Coubertin first visited the United States and Canada (1889), the great national turnfest held in Cincinnati showcased the athletic activities of 1 179 individual turners. Four years later, when Coubertin once again journeyed to North America (1893), 3 380 Turners competed in the national fest hosted by Milwaukee[19]. The question again poses itself. What of all this did Coubertin know? His memoirs reveal few reflections acknowledging olympic-like festivals organized prior to his own international project. Only the Much Wenlock Games seem to have aroused the Baron's interest, partial description and comments[20]. Even though the Baron's memoirs are silent on the Zappian Games, it can be seen through his voluminous writings and some analyses by MacAloon and Young that Coubertin knew about the 19th century Greek attempts to establish a modern sports festival based on antiquity's legacy. Of German-American turning and turnfests, Coubertin also had knowledge, though there is no trace of it in his memoirs. He certainly knew much about turnen in Germany. Exercises of the turnplatz had even been received and acclaimed in France. When Coubertin made his first visit to North America in the autumn of 1889, he attended the now noted Boston Conference in the Interest of Physical Training, convened on the campus of the Massachusetts Institute of Technology, November 11 and 12. At the opening session the Baron listened to a paper written by Heinrich Metzner, principal of the New York Turnverein's school for training teachers of German gymnastics[21]. Metzner, of course, extolled the German system of exercise as the best for developing general rather than specialized physical fitness. Alluding to the Turner's quest for pursuit of all-around development of fitness and skill, Metzner made specific reference to turnfest athletic events. Wrote Metzner: "The contests among the Turners (turnfest events) are thus arranged, that exercises in all the different branches must be performed[22]."

From reactions to Metzner's paper, Coubertin learned still more about German-American gymnastics activity in late 19th century American sport and exercise culture. Following Metzner's paper, Edward M. Hartwell, one of America's preeminent physical educators at the time, enthusiastically reaffirmed the value of German gymnastics in the greater scheme of contemporary American physical education theory and practice. In fact, Hartwell called the German system the most comprehensive and effective in the entire United States[23]. Coubertin and his conference colleagues were thus informed of the facts and the statistics Hartwell presented in the process of concluding his remarks. Noted Hartwell, "The North American Turnerbund numbers 30 000 members, owns property free from debt worth more than 2 000 000 \$ including 160 gymnasium halls [...][24]." Following Metzner's paper and the reaction it generated from the convention floor, an exhibition of German gymnastics class exercises was given by twenty boys under the direction of Emil Gröner of the Boston Turnverein.

At the last of the conference's four sessions Coubertin was invited to speak about the development of physical education in France. He had come to North America "[...] commissioned by the French Government to visit the universities and colleges, not only with reference to the subject of physical training, but with reference to other branches, [...][25]". Yet, in the preface of his speech, Coubertin is referred to as "Secretary of the French Educational Reform Association". The Baron spoke briefly and commented on American education. Said Coubertin: [...] "I was asked the other day what, in my opinion, American education was like, I answered that in some respects it looked like a battlefield where English and German ideas were fighting. While I fully acknowledge that from the physical point of view nothing can be said against the German system, I believe, on the other hand, that from the moral and social point of view no system, if so it can be called, stands higher than the English athletic sport system as understood and explained by the greatest of modern teachers, Thomas Arnold of Rugby[26]." Yet, Coubertin gave high praise to the German approach to "the primary school question which our government has lately settled, as I believe, in the best way. In such schools a systematic course of physical training is needed, and the experiments that have been tried in France have proved so successful that there is no reason why we should try anything else. The German methods have now only to be developed in all our primary schools and made the general rule[27]." Clearly, Coubertin knew the fabric of German gymnastics.

It remains coincidental, indeed ironic, that glorious editions of that sport festival most approximating what in time Coubertin's Olympic Games would become, occurred in those years coinciding with the Baron's visits to the United States. In 1889, some three months after the National Turnfest celebrated in Cincinnati, Coubertin visited nearby St. Louis, a river city of significant German population and culture featuring two thriving Turnvereins, each of which, by the way, played prominent roles in the gymnastics segment of the Olympic Games of 1904. Few things about "new places" escaped the Baron's sharp eye for "sizing things up," particularly if they related to his main interests, general education, sport and physical education. Did he learn about or come in contact with elements of St. Louis German turnverein activity that might have complemented what he had learned in Boston? In 1893 Coubertin visited the United States again. Two months after the Milwaukee Turnverein had hosted the largest national turnfest ever, the Baron arrived in Chicago, Milwaukee's Lake Michigan sister city. There he stayed at the Chicago Athletic Club while visiting the World Columbian Exposition. Subsequently, he journeyed to San Francisco and New Orleans. All three cities harbored enclaves of pronounced German ethnicity. And each could demonstrate an almost half-century old turnverein tradition. It is difficult to believe that Coubertin could have left such experiences without having had his Boston-induced German-American turnverein and turnfest knowledge furthered. Except for a scanty allusion to the American Turnverein phenomenon and the expression (in his 1890 book "Universités transatlantiques") of a certain uneasiness about what he felt was a strong germanic influence at the Boston Congress[28], Coubertin thereafter remained silent on the subject and/or influence of the Turnfest. But then, history has shown that Coubertin appeared not eager to mention or to give proper acknowledgement to many of the phenomena which contributed directly and unequivocally to the coming of age of the International Olympic Movement.

The record of the German-American turnfests stands. By the time that Coubertin's dream was being assembled in real terms on the launching pad at the Sorbonne in 1894, German-American Turners already had in place a well-established blueprint for the operation of a sporting festival celebrated every four years and rotated among American cities. The festival encompassed a variety of athletic sports, featured women's participation, and awarded wreath-prizes of ancient olympic symbolism. This is not to say that the fact should belittle or denigrate Coubertin's role in establishing the modern Olympic Games. Rather, when the subject of precursors to Coubertin's "noble crusade" is addressed, more consideration ought to be given to one of sporting history's outstanding example, the 19th century German-American National Turnfest phenomenon.

NOTES AND REFERENCES

1. Redmond G (1971) The Caledonian Games in nineteenth century America. Rutherford: Farleigh-Dickenson University Press; and Redmond G (1982) The sporting Scots in nineteenth century Canada. Toronto: Associated University Press

2. Rühl J (1985) The Olympic Games of Robert Dover, 1612-1984. In Müller N, Rühl JK (eds) Sport History Official Report, 1984 Olympic Scientific Congress. Niederhausen: Schors-Verlag p 192-203; Rühl J (1988) Pierre de Coubertin und William Penny Brookes. In Proceedings: ICOSH Seminar Sarajevo p 243-64; and Rühl J (1985) William Penny Brookes and the Much Wenlock Games. In Proceedings: XI HISPA International Congress Glasgow p 89-91

3. Redmond G (1988) Toward modern revival of the Olympic Games. The various "pseudo" Olympics of the nineteenth century. In Segrave JO, Chu D (eds) The Olympic Games in transition. Champaign: Human Kinetics p 71-78

4. La Minerve (Montreal) vol 8 no 105 Août 5 1844. The announcement in La Minerve trumpeted the patronage of the Governor General and, more importantly, outlined two

days of athletic events which included running contests of 100 yards, 400 yards, one mile, and a hurdles competition of 200 yards. Other events included putting the light and heavy ball, the hop-step-leap, running and standing long jumps, and rifle competitions at both 100 and 180 yard distances.

5. Young DC (1987) The origins of the modern Olympics: a new version. The International Journal of the History of Sport 4 p 271-300

6. For Coubertin's memoir impressions of his first visit to Athens in November 1894, originally published in Une Campagne de vingt-et-un ans (1887-1908), see Müller N, Comité international olympique (1986) (eds) Pierre de Coubertin: Textes Choisis. Tome II. Olympisme. Zürich: Weidmann p 131-38. For an excellent synthesis of the Baron's 1894 visit to Greece, written in English, see MacAloon JJ (1981) This great symbol: Pierre de Coubertin and the origins of the modern Olympic Games. Chicago: University of Chicago Press p 184-85

7. Turner expression of the term "Olympic Games" was first enunciated at the National Turnerbund Convention held in Rochester, New York, in 1860. The correlation between the Bund's national turnfest and a sporting festival, olympian-like in character, was prompted by discussion debating the time of the year that the fest should be held. A by-law statute set the month of September as the best time of the year for such "Olympic Games". See "Minutes of the National Turnerbund Convention", recorded by the National Executive Committee, Rochester, New York, 1860. From the outset of the evolutionary process of the National Turnerbund organization, Turners were sensitive to the fact that the minutes of the annual conventions were, in effect, the basic historical record of the organization. Recorded in German until 1872, the minutes of the annual National Turnerbund Conventions were recorded in English beginning in 1873. In 1873, too, Turner Henry W. Kumpf was directed to execute an English translation of each of the National Convention minutes previously recorded in German (1854-1872). A complete set of Kumpf's translations is located at The Centre for Olympic Studies, The University of Western Ontario, London, Canada.

8. For a treatment of the early history of German gymnastics in America, see Geldbach E (1976) The beginnings of German gymnastics in the United States. Journal of Sport History 3 236-72

9. Barney RK (1984) America's first turnverein: commentary in favor of Louisville, Kentucky. Journal of Sport History 11 134-37

10. Turn-Zeitung, November 15 1851 as cited by Metzner H (1974) History of the American Turners. Rochester: National Council of American Turners p 10

11. Metzner H (1974) op cit p 10

12. Louisville Anzeiger, May 31 1853

13. Juniors were youths, aged 12 to 17. Actives were individuals between 18 and 35 years of age. Seniors were those over 35.

14. Minutes of the National Turnerbund Convention. Recorded by the National Executive Committee, Detroit, 1857

15. Minutes of the National Turnerbund Convention. Recorded by the National Executive Committee, Indianapolis, 1858

16. Minutes of the National Turnerbund Convention. Recorded by the National Executive Committee, Rochester, 1860

17. Between 1877 and 1885, for example, the Bund's membership grew from 167 societies, encompassing 11 653 members, to 213 societies and 21 809 members. See Leonard FE, Affleck GB (1947) The history of physical education. Philadelphia: Lea & Febiger p 300

18. Metzner H (1974) op cit p 29

19. Ibid

20. Coubertin visited Brookes at Much Wenlock in 1890. The Baron's memoirs, almost entirely silent in mentioning olympic-like festivals occurring before 1896, did, however, comment on the Much Wenlock festival, which fascinated him. For Coubertin's original comments on his visit to Much Wenlock, published originally in La Revue Athlétique (December 1890), see Müller N, Comité international olympique (1986) (eds) Pierre de Coubertin: Textes Choisis. Tome II. Olympisme. Zürich: Weidmann p 78-84. For his

appreciation of Brookes, the Much Wenlock Games and Olympic Festivals in England, see Coubertin P de (1897) A typical Englishman: Dr. W.P. Brookes of Wenlock in Shropshire. The Review of Reviews XV p 62-65

21. For the full text of Metzner's paper see The german system of gymnastics. In Barrows IC (ed) (1890) Physical training: a full report of the papers and discussion of the Conference held in Boston in November, 1889. Boston: Press of George H Ellis. Metzner was not present at the Boston proceedings; his paper was presented in his absence by Carl Eberhard, a Boston Turnverein official who was also superintendent of the Boston Athletic Club Gymnasium.

22. Ibid p 24

23. Ibid p 28

24. Ibid p 31

25. Coubertin P de (1890) Athletics and gymnastics. In Barrows IC (ed) op cit p 112-15

26. Ibid

27. Ibid

28. Coubertin P de (1890) Universités transatlantiques. Paris: Hachette p 346-49

Actions of the IOC, the ILTF, and the USLTA Regarding Tennis as an Olympic Sport, from 1896 to 1988

Joanna Davenport

For the first time since 1896, tennis was not included in the official program of events when the 1928 Olympic Games were held in Amsterdam. This absence of tennis as a full fledged olympic sport continued for 64 years until the recent 1988 Games in Seoul. This presentation deals with the reasons why tennis was discontinued as an olympic activity, and with the efforts over the years to have it reinstated. It involves many issues and the underlying causes are varied and intricated. Tennis as an olympic sport caused much controversy over the years between the International Olympic Committee (IOC), the governing body of the Olympic Games; the International Lawn Tennis Federation (ILTF/FILT), the international governing body of tennis; and many tennis associations, one of the more powerful being the United States Lawn Tennis Association (USLTA). For a fuller understanding of the situation, a brief history of tennis in the Games until 1924 will be discussed as well as the power struggle between the IOC, the ILTF and the USLTA.

When the Modern Olympic Games were instituted, tennis was included as part of the program.Tennis was a customary activity for the upper classes in the 1890s and the men who were members of the IOC for the first Modern Games of 1896 in Athens were from this stratum of society. As a matter of course, tennis was easily selected to become an olympic event. In the succeeding years it was not the most popular sport but it nonetheless attracted top ranked players as will be discussed shortly.

As the 1896 Athens Games were only for men, the tennis competition consisted of Men's Singles and Men's Doubles. The two tournaments were of limited scope, with only four players in the Singles and six teams for the Doubles. The stories about the Singles winner, John Boland from Ireland, illustrate the casual approach to the event. It has been reported that he was there only as a spectator and when he heard there was a tennis match, quickly bought a racket, entered and subsequently won the gold[1]. The next Olympic Games in Paris

1890
1990

Joanna Davenport, Department of Health and Human Performance, Auburn University, Auburn, Alabama, USA.

featured not only Men's Singles and Doubles but also women's Singles and Mixed Doubles. Women's Doubles was not on the Olympic Games program until its last year, 1924[2]. Again, the competitions had a slim draw averaging around four- eight entrants. However, the caliber of play was outstanding featuring in every event former or future Wimbledon champions of the times[3]. At the 1904 Games in St. Louis, even though women were in some events, there was only tennis competition in Men's Singles and Doubles which, incidentally, had as entrants only American players. An unusual situation occurred in tennis at the next two Games, 1908 in London and 1912 in Stockholm. Several months before each Games began, indoor tournaments were held and the winners were without further a do declared olympic champions. It is speculated that these earlier indoor competitions might have been a regularly scheduled tennis tournament which somehow received olympic sanction[4].

After World War I, when the 1920 Olympic Games were held in Antwerp, the number of tennis competitors had increased considerably with 41 men and 18 women in the respective singles tournament[5]. It is ironic that in 1924 when tennis appears for the last time in the Games in Paris, the competition drew not only the best players in the world but the events were the largest ever held. For example, in Men's Singles, there were 82 competitors representing 27 countries and the Women's Singles had 31 players from 14 countries[6].

Given the steady growth of tennis as an olympic sport, what were the factors that led to its discontinuation? Not suprisingly, the issue revolved around the question of who was to control tennis in the Olympic Games. It certainly is understandable that the IOC is the overall controlling body for the Olympic Games. The IOC was then (as is now) a powerful body that is self appointing and self perpetuating. It recognizes only the National Olympic Committees (NOC) of each country who, in cooperation with the sports governing body of each activity, select the teams for the Games.

Unlike some sports where the Olympic Games are the epitome and ultimate of competition, the tennis world had many other tournaments each year, which to some believers were more important and prestigious than the Olympic Games events held only every four years. Perhaps, a brief examination of the USLTA in regard to the Olympic Games over the years will illustrate the situation. First of all, the USLTA which was established in 1881 had a full schedule of important tournaments every year before the Olympic Games were re-instituted in 1896. An examination of the written records of the USLTA revealed no mention of the Olympic Games, until 1908 when a resolution was passed that the Association "should take no part in the Olympic Games[7]". However, the USLTA did enter some players in the 1904 Games at St. Louis. An editorial concerning this event revealed that since tennis was on the St. Louis program, there was no other course at the time but for the USLTA to enter the contest[8]. The USLTA did not send players in 1908 and in 1912 and of course the 1916 Games were cancelled due to World War I. The 1920 Games marked the beginning of friction between the USLTA and the International Olympic Committee. In November, 1919, the USLTA accepted an invitation by the American Olympic Committee to participate in the 1920 Games at Antwerp, Belgium. Shortly after, it was discovered that the dates for the tennis events conflicted with the scheduled United States National Championships. The USLTA asked the Belgian authorities to change the olympic tennis events to July. When the Belgian Committee replied that they were unable to make such a change, the USLTA simply withdrew from the Games. This 1920 schedule of the Olympic Games at the same time as important tennis tournaments was not a first for such an occurence. In the 1912 Games the level of play in the tennis matches had not been of the highest level as the world's best players were at the Wimbledon Championships which were scheduled at the same time[9].

Furthermore, it was not the first time the USLTA had had problems with other governing bodies. It might be helpful to briefly refer to the chief organization, the ILTF. In 1913, delegates from the major tennis countries of the world, except for the United States, met in Paris and founded the ILTF[10]. The nations represented were Australasia, Austria, Belgium, Denmark, France, Germany, Great Britain, Netherlands, Russia, South Africa, Spain, Sweden and Switzerland[11]. The USLTA would not join this international body for nine years. One explanation for this absence is as follows. The purpose of the Federation was to increase international tennis, to make the laws of the game more uniform throughout the world, and to hold world championships. At the very first meeting the constitution and by-laws were established and a world's championships tournament to be held thereafter every year was awarded to England[12]. Due to these entitled world's championships, the USLTA declined membership. The Association felt that the Davis Cup matches which they had inaugurated in 1900 were the epitome of international tennis supremacy and it did not wish to back any tournament that might take the place of Davis Cup play. Negotiations between the USLTA and ILTF were held yearly on this question of membership but the results were nearly always the same. The USLTA would not affiliate as long as the Federation's constitution gave perpetual award of world's championships to any one country. The USLTA was in fact adhering to a resolution passed at its annual meeting in 1914 which stated "[. . .] that the Davis Cup contest should be the sole international team contest of the World[13]". In March, 1923, the ILTF met and made some noteworthy decisions: it abolished the world's championships from the constitution, it adopted international playing rules, and it recognized the National Championships of England, France, United States and Australia[14]. Consequently, the USLTA became a member of this international body for tennis.

The same year, 1923, when the American Olympic Committee asked the USLTA to enter players for the 1924 Paris Games, much discussion over the matter occurred at Association meetings. Again the inclination towards the Games was lukewarm and some officials were heartily against the participation of the United States. Similar to the Federation controversy it was recorded that "[. . .] by getting tied up with this Olympic organization you are going to lessen interest in the Davis Cup contest[15]". However, the USLTA did send a team to Paris where every gold medal in tennis was won by an American[16]. But, as mentioned before, these Games were the last ones to have tennis events on the program. There had been troubles even before the Games had begun. The crux of the matter was that the USLTA and the ILTF felt that the tennis tournaments should be run by tennis people and not by the Olympic Committee[17]. The Olympic Committee would not give-in to the tennis associations and "disturbances" and "rows" marked the events. After the Games, the USLTA sent a resolution to the ILTF which in essence stated the following: that an ILTF representative be on the IOC and that tennis in the Olympic Games be managed by ILTF members[18]. Subsequently, the ILTF approved the USLTA resolution and added further stipulations that the olympic tennis events not conflict with major tennis championships and that the "Olympic Games not be regarded as a championship of the world in [. . .] tennis[19]". The ILTF sent the full resolution to the IOC and stated that if the requested demands were not met, tennis would then withdraw from future Games. The IOC would not accept the demands and tennis thus withdrew from the Olympic Movement. In the ensuing years different countries suggested to the ILTF that perhaps a compromise could be reached but the proposals were always turned down by the Federation[20].

It is a matter of history but the tennis world was not affected by the IOC ruling. The sport grew tremendously and many of the Grand Slam tournaments, plus the Davis Cup for men and the Federation Cup for women, were to many people the equivalent of the olympics of tennis. Furthermore, many authorities did not want tennis to be in the Olympic Games because they felt that the well established tournament schedules would be drastically affected if there was a conflict of dates. Moreover, as indicated above, tennis had many events of an international nature and not being in the Olympic Games did not seem very important.

In the 1960s with tennis competition becoming open to both amateurs and professionals, and each olympic sport being governed by the International Federation of that sport, brought a complete change of opinion. In the end, with most of the national tennis associations' support, the ILTF formally applied to the IOC to be again recognized as an olympic sport[21]. It was indeed a blow when the IOC announced that tennis would not be taken back into the olympic family[22]. The request to be an exhibition sport was half heartedly approved, and at the 1968 Games in Mexico City a small tennis tournament designated as a demonstration event with little publicity was held as far as 200 miles away[23].

One could speculate as to why the application of the ILTF was denied, for it is well known the IOC is not in the habit of explaining its rulings. One reason could be the same one that had caused controversy for years, *i.e.*, the ILTF would have had to give up some of its authority, and perhaps the IOC felt that this situation would cause many difficulties. Another theory was that the IOC in general, and the then President Avery Brundage in particular, disapproved of the excessive expenses received by the top tennis players of the times and consequently, that they were not as amateur as the competitors in the other olympic sports.

But the tennis-Olympic Games impasse changed due to many factors in the 1980s. Firstly, Juan Antonio Samaranch in 1980 was elected President of the IOC. He agreed with the contention of the pro-Olympic tennis enthusiasts to the fact that tennis, as a highly international sport, should be included in the olympic program. Next, there was the election of Philippe Chatrier as President of the ITF. In 1977, he made it the Federation's main thrust as well as his own personal mission to see tennis become an olympic sport once again[24,25]. Furthermore, the line between the so called terms "amateur" and "professional" were no longer clear as it had become obvious that athletes were making money due to their accomplishments in sport. In fact, the IOC, cognizant of this change, recently removed the word "amateur" from its charter which since 1896 had been the main eligibility requirement for participation in the Olympic Games. Also, each international Federation has its own eligibility requirements for the Olympic Games and evidently, some allow *bona fide* professional athletes while others do not.

Thus, the above mentioned events paved the way for tennis to once again be part of the olympic family. Finally, in 1981 it was announced by the IOC that tennis would be a demonstration sport in the 1984 Games in Los Angeles and a full fledged sport for the 1988 Seoul Games. There was an addendum to the 1988 ruling that stipulated it would be on a trial basis[26]. In other words, if all went well and there were no difficulties, tennis would be a sport also in the 1992 Games of Barcelona. Some brief remarks should be made of tennis at the 1988 Seoul Olympic Games. The competitions were very well attended and there were no problems either with the ITF or IOC or the Seoul Organizing Committee. As a consequence, tennis is on the program for the 1992 Games in Barcelona.

Before concluding, two issues must be mentioned. First, if tennis as an olympic sport is to achieve prominence, then the top players, particularly the men, will have to support it. In Seoul only one of the top five male players in the world entered the competition and the finals were between Number 10 and Number 12 in international rankings. The Number 1 player in the world at the time, Mats Wilander, declined playing saying "it would be just another stamp in my passport[27]". Even Martina Navratilova bypassed the competition with these remarks: "The most important thing for me is becoming Number 1 again. The Olympics won't help me. It would be like going back to the amateur days[28]". Hopefully, over time, this attitude held by some will be changed to that of highly ranked Tim Mayotte who stated that "the Olympics will be the greatest sporting event of my life[29]". Second, and a much bigger issue than the support and attitude of players, is the problem of South Africa. It has not been well publicized that tennis is again "under the gun", so to speak, and is scheduled for the 1992 Olympic Games on a "conditional" basis[30]. This "conditional" label is because some IOC members feel that "tennis hasn't gone along with international sanctions against South Africa and its policy of apartheid[31]". The IOC, in exchange for re-admitting tennis to the Games, is reported to have insisted that the ITF drop South Africa as a member of the Federation, suspend the country from Davis Cup play and not sanction any tournaments played in South Africa[32]. The IOC had previously issued a warning that any tennis player who competed in South Africa after August 31, 1989 would be ineligible to play in the Olympic Games beginning with the 1992 Barcelona Games[33]. The USTA, also, sent a resolution to the ITF supporting the idea of suspending South Africa from ITF membership until it abandons its apartheid policy[34]. Nevertheless, who knows whether future olympic tennis competitions will ever gain the prominence of a Wimbledon championship or the other Grand Slam tournaments? But as a well known tennis writer observed, tennis is for the moment back in the Olympic Movement "and the Olympics—and tennis—may never be quite the same[35]."

REFERENCES

1. Mandell R (1976) The first Olympics. Berkeley: University of California Press

2. Wallechinsky D (1984) The complete book of the Olympics. New York: Penguin

3. Ibid

4. Ibid

5. Ibid

6. Olympic Games (1958) Colliers encyclopedia p 156

7. Davenport J (1966) The history and interpretation of amateurism in the United States Lawn Tennis Association. Unpublished doctoral dissertation, Ohio State University p 110

8. Editorial (1920) American Lawn Tennis. XIV p 480 (October 15)

9. Wallechinsky D (1984) op cit

10. Davenport J (1966) op cit

11. Tingay L (1973) Tennis. New York: Putnam's Sons p 43

12. Davenport J (1966) op cit

13. Ibid p 119

14. Ibid

15. Ibid p 112

16. Wallechinsky D (1984) op cit

17. Reviving the Olympic Games (1945) American Lawn tennis 39 p 15

18. Davenport J (1966) op cit

19. Olympic Games Demands (1931) ILTF annual meeting (mimeographed)

20. Davenport J (1966) op cit

21. Ibid

22. Ibid

23. Fabricus E (1984) Tennis. The Olympian 10 p 56

24. Flink S (1988) Chatrier calls the shots. World Tennis 35 p 24

25. USTA (1977) The official United States tennis association yearbook and tennis guide with the official rules. Lynn: Zimman Inc

26. Higdon H (1988) Will tennis and the Games change. Tennis 24 p 130

27. Deford F (1988) Serves return. Sports Illustrated 69 p 116 (October 10)

28. Who's playing, who's not (1988) Tennis 24 p 139

29. Ibid

30. Doherty D (1989) (ed) South Africa is in the news again. Tennis 25 p 11

31. Ibid

32. Moore R (1989) A race against time. World Tennis 36 p 95

33. Doherty D (1989) op cit

34. Markin D (1989) Challenges met. Tennis USA 11 p 2

35. Higdon H (1988) Tennis goes for the gold. Tennis 24 p 126

Olympism and Dance:
the 1990 Coubertin Connection

Elizabeth A. Hanley

The 1990s have been proclaimed "The World Decade for Cultural Development", by UNESCO, the United Nations Educational, Scientific, and Cultural Organization. One cannot help but be excited at the prospect of what this decade may hold for the relationship between Olympism and Dance. We are all aware that Olympism is a philosophy which embraces the arts and that dance is often referred to as the mother of the arts; hence, there exists a nurturing relationship between the two.

Nearly one hundred years have elapsed since the great humanist Pierre de Coubertin formulated his philosophy of social peace and equality of opportunity, two basic elements of Olympism. Coubertin was concerned about the society of his time, its moral standards, its uncertain future. In 1894, during a lecture at the Parnassus Club of Athens, Coubertin poignantly stated his worries:

> If we begin to study the history of our century we are struck by the moral disorder produced by the discoveries of industrial science. Life suffers an upheaval, people feel the ground tremble continually under their feet. They have nothing to hold onto, because everything around them is shifting and changing: and in their confusion, as though seeking some counterpoise to the material powers which rise like Cyclopean ramparts about them, they grope for whatever elements of moral strength lie scattered about the world. I think this is the philosophic origin of the striking physical renaissance in the XIXth century[1].

As a pedagogue and historian, Coubertin believed he could recapture the ancient Greek ideal of educating the total person—body, mind, and spirit—and thereby achieve that "harmony of proportion", or balance called "eurythmy", an avowed objective in Hellenistic society centuries ago[2]. Coubertin was single-minded in his quest of reviving the ancient Olympic Games, those great festivals of athletics, art and religion, as one way to spread his olympic philosophy. He emphasized that the revived Olympic Games must provide the opportunity for the

Elizabeth A. Hanley, Department of Exercise and Sport Science, Pennsylvania State University, University Park, Pennsylvania, USA.

youth of the world to experience "[. . .] a happy and brotherly encounter, which will gradually efface the peoples' ignorance of things which concern them all, and ignorance which feeds hatreds, accumulates misunderstandings and hurtles events along a barbarous path toward a merciless conflict[3]". Coubertin's goal was to serve mankind in striving for one of its highest levels of perfection, known by the ancient Greeks as *areté*.

After the first modern Olympic Games were hosted by the city of Athens in 1896, Coubertin experienced with both admiration and criticism. The heavy task of shaping future Olympic Games within the context of his broad olympic idea had now only commenced in earnest. In 1918, Coubertin referred to Olympism as "a state of mind borne of the twofold cult of effort and eurythmy[4]", once again clinging to the ancient Greek ideal. It was not until 1935 that he formulated a fuller, more sophisticated definition of his philosophy, emphasizing three essential characteristics that embraced both ancient and modern Olympism. The first essential element was religion, since it was a prominent aspect of athletic festivals in ancient Greece. The second characteristic was that of an aristocracy—an elite, the origin of which, however, was egalitarian in nature. The last element he termed "Beauty, through the participation in the Games of the Arts and of Thought[5]."

Coubertin's descriptions of Olympism has been reworded and re-evaluated by many since 1935, but the basic tenets have tended to remain the same. His genius in realizing that to appreciate beauty to its fullest one had to participate in the arts, was made evident by their inclusion from the onset in the modern Olympic Games. Most ancient festivals included music, poetry, and the dance, and to the ancient Greeks all three were facets of the same art, *mousiké*—the art of the Muses[6]. During the ancient Games held at Olympia, for example, parades, processions and sacrifices to the gods marked both the beginning and the end of each festival. "Throughout the entire sacrifice", according to Poole and Poole, "hymns of praise to Zeus, and other gods, were sung and recited by poets and trained choirs. Strong men, singly or in groups, danced around the altar, much as Greek men today are inspired to dance on the spur of the moment in 'tavernas' [. . .][7]." The inclusion of the arts as part of the Olympic Games was not necessarily in the form of competitions, but rather as an unofficial on-going accompaniment to the festivities. Athletic competitions continued each day of the Olympic Games, and although the Games were officially concluded on the fifth day, "throughout the night, the green, luscious valley of Olympia was alive with singing and dancing[8]". Coubertin believed that every modern Olympic Games should also be a spiritual and artistic event with "the presence of the genius of the nations, the collaboration of the muses, the cult of beauty, all the apparel which befits the potent symbolism which the Olympic Games embodied in the past and which they must continue to represent today[9]".

If one studies dance separately from the other arts, one quickly realizes that it is as old as life itself. According to anthropologist Royce, "The human body making patterns in time and space is what makes dance unique among the arts and perhaps explains its antiquity and universality[10]." Dance critic Martin noted that basic dance is identical throughout the world, in all times and all cultures, and is a fundamental element of our behavior. From internal physiological mechanisms to outward conduct, "movement is the medium in which we live our lives[11]". There is no single definition for dance, but in its simplest form it is called by most anthropologists and historians "rhythmic and patterned movement". Because of its all-inclusive nature and ultimate significance in the daily life of humans from earliest civilizations, dance historian Sachs related that "[. . .] dance in its essence is simply life on a higher level[12]".

Dance has existed in every ancient civilization of which there are records. The Egyptians, Assyrians, Hebrews, Hindus, Greeks, and Romans all participated in dancing, but no nation appears to have held it in higher esteem, or cultivated it for its moral and aesthetic values more than the ancient Greeks[13]. In fact the Greeks considered dance as a proper medium for the expression of lofty motives, and "[...] great-minded artists chose it as a career; not in spite of a public condescension to it, but with the support of a profound public respect[14]". Every important event in ancient times was accompanied by dance: birth, courtship, marriage, and death; sowing and harvesting; preparation for combat and victory in battle; and many other reasons that humans have used to express themselves.

Dance, however, has evolved through the ages. There is no universal form; there are many forms. Dance can be divided into two broad categories of practices: – for the emotional release of the individual dancer without regard for potential spectator interest; – for the specific enjoyment of the spectator[15]. In Coubertin's days, the ballet had emerged as a distinct form of dance. A century later, there is a wide variety to behold, including the ballet, ballroom dance, character and folkloric dance, jazz, and modern dance, plus a host of other activities which are very much dance-like in nature: aerobic dance, ice dance, rhythmic gymnastics, and water ballet or synchronized swimming.

Although each has its own special characteristics and appeal, it is the folkloric dance that, in the author's opinion, best illustrates the "1990 Coubertin Connection". When the ballet became accused of stiffness and artificiality during the half-century ending around 1908, these years were "[...] saved from complete sterility by the dances that are rooted in the soil. 'Jigs' and 'Reels', 'Hornpipes' and 'Tarantellas' held their own like hardy wildflowers in a garden of weeds [...][16]". Folkloric dance exists in every culture of the world. In its pure and unspoiled form, it is simply the dance of the people; in its stylized form, it becomes the dance of the trained elite. Folkloric dance appeals to all: participant and spectator, young and old, experienced and neophyte.

In 1938, one year after Coubertin's death and in honor of his colleague's wishes, Carl Diem proposed to the Greek Minister of Education and to the Hellenic Committee that an Olympic Academy be established near the site of ancient Olympia. Included within the teaching plan of the program was time allotted specifically for games and folk dancing, along with other artistic endeavors[17]. Coubertin's plan to put Olympism on a scholarly basis had gained a strong foothold in the Olympic Academy idea. He would have been pleased to know that multi-cultural "social evenings" would become an integral part of International Olympic Academy sessions each year. In 1986, Professor Nissiotis, then president of the IOA, instituted dance and painting workshops for the participants which culminated in a wonderfully creative presentation, not only of folkloric dance and painting, but modern interpretive dance, poetry, and music.

Dance, therefore, clearly deserves a place under Olympism's umbrella of Sport-for-all. Nearly every modern Olympic Games has produced an artful opening opening and closing ceremony, many of which have included elaborate folkloric dance presentations—the most recent examples being Moscow, Sarajevo and Los Angeles, and Calgary and Seoul. The 1980 Olympic Games in Moscow were the site of unparalleled dance festivities: the 15 union republics demonstrated their diverse art, costumes, and culture in a brilliant spectacle of dance during the opening ceremony, while highlights of the closing ceremony occurred when "Immense Matryoshka dolls rolled into the stadium on lorries. A Russian festival—merry, lively, and full of inventiveness—began. Young lads playing Russian accordions pranced dashingly about the field, and girls in folk costumes swirled about them in a round dance[18]." Anyone who viewed these ceremonies appreciated the undefinable sense of well-being that dance imparts to its audience: the aim of all great art.

In Sarajevo, site of the 1984 Winter Olympic Games, the author was privileged to be an eyewitness at the impressive opening ceremony, resplendent with the colorful presentation of hundreds of folk dancers performing to Westernized renditions of traditional Yugoslav folk music. Opening ceremonies at Los Angeles provided over three hours of spectacular entertainment, with countless dancers woven into the heart of the festivities to display the role of dance in the United States. Similar performances, once again linking dance and sport in age-old tradition, were seen during the closing ceremony when dozens of "break dancers" put on displays of athleticism[19].

The 1988 opening ceremony at the Winter Olympic Games in Calgary recognized Canada's cultural diversity, from the aboriginal tribes of Alberta in their brightly colored native dress to the hundreds of dancers in Western garb whirling through a lively "two-step" while the audience clapped in time to the music[20].

The City of Seoul, in the Land of the Morning Calm, created the theme "Peace, Harmony and Progress" which was embraced by the world during the 1988 Seoul Olympic Games. From bustling cities to rural villages, the world watched as opening and closing ceremonies reached out in dignified splendor to bridge the gap of culture and tradition between East and West. The Seoul Olympic Organizing Committee (SLOOC) has put its heart and soul into preparing for these ceremonies, drawing attention to the task of removing cultural, racial and ideological barriers experienced throughout the world today, in an attempt to have the world become one. By weaving its philosophy of harmony between heaven, earth, and people into the opening and closing ceremonies, SLOOC's goal was to have all mankind share emotions and feelings about the Korean people long after the Seoul Olympic flame had been extinguished[21]. "Beyond All Barriers", a videotape produced in 1989, created that very effect, keeping alive the essence of Olympism that Coubertin so longed to share with the world. The exceptional display of traditional Korean dance, with its special characteristics of calmness, discipline, and dignity; the well-chosen narration to explain elements of Korean culture and symbolism; the blending of Korean and Greek dance to commemorate the origin of the Olympic Games in Greece; and the merging of the Barcelona troupe with the Korean dancers are but fragments of the glorious ceremonies in Seoul which evoked memories of an ancient past reaching toward the future.

In recent years the cultural program at the Olympic Games have also expanded greatly and virtually every program has highlighted performances by international folkloric ensembles. One of the most memorable cultural festivals was Mexico City's "Fiesta of the Whole Man". This festival was a colorful part of the 1968 Olympic Games, and the program lasted for an entire year. Visitors were able to sample cultural events of the whole world, and one of the most popular aspects of the cultural program was in the area of folk arts: folk dance, folk music, and crafts. The cultural program pervaded the city and performances occurred in nearly every available space, in addition to the formal theatre performances[22]. After Mexico City's successful and comprehensive "Fiesta of the Whole Man", each succeeding Olympic Games responded with an ever-widening range of cultural programs, all of which included folkloric dance: Sapporo and Munich, Innsbruck and Montreal, Lake Placid and Moscow, Sarajevo and Los Angeles.

The year 1988 signaled the largest olympic arts festivals in Olympic Games history, both at Calgary and at Seoul. Calgary's fine theatres, concert halls, galleries, and museums provided the physical resources necessary for a successful cultural program. The performing arts component included native participation by Canada's aboriginal peoples as well as folkloric dance ensembles highlighting Canada's diverse ethnic population[23]. The city of Seoul was literally transformed into an artistic venue to promote the olympic ideal of universal peace and harmony, with artists invited from over 80 countries, providing an opportunity for

Editors' Note:

Fan Dance by designer Kim Hyun. One of the twelve official Cultural Posters of the Games of the XXIVth Olympiad. Fan Dance is a typical folk dance of Korea, and a woman performing fan dance is rendered here to signify the festive mood of the Seoul Olympic Games. The close-up of her face and fan provides a modern touch.

the fusion of world cultures. The dance program featured both traditional and modern Korean dance, as well as an international folklore festival highlighting dance ensembles from 12 other nations. Athletes and officials at the olympic village were also treated to daily performances in order to promote better understanding of Korean lifestyle and culture[24].

If the olympic ideal is to be pursued, with the goal of mutual respect for one another throughout the world, one should first begin to understand one another. The olympic arts festival has emerged as one bridge to international understanding and mutual respect, and dance has played an ever-increasing role in it.

The most recent Seoul Olympic Games provided the world with the opportunity to savor the sacred character and ancient tradition of Asian dance, an art form central to the culture. The West possesses nothing comparable, except for the American Indian heritage. Too often, dance is seen as only peripheral to the culture—a secular amusement, an entertainment. The origin of dance, as noted earlier, is sacred, magical, and ritual. Korean dance still embodies these characteristics even at the onset of the 21st century. The Korean dancer is not focussing on external aspects of physical movement but rather on expression a deep sense of ecstasy, a metaphysical joy[25]. It is in this perspective that folkloric dance adds a unique dimension to Olympism.

Folkloric dance includes not only the physical skill of dance steps indigenous to a country, but it provides an opportunity to study a people's music and art, customs and traditions, politics and religion, geography and history. It also serves to develop an understanding and appreciation for the diverse peoples of the world, as we approach the 21st century. The beginning dancer, as well as the elite performer, can be challenged to strive for personal excellence, an underlying element of Olympism. Classes, family-oriented camps, and workshops are becoming more numerous each year to satisfy the recreational dancer. Performing ensembles, from amateur to professional, exist for the trained dancer. International folklore festivals have virtually blossomed throughout the world during recent years, notably in the United States and Canada.

The International Council of Organization of Folklore Festivals, or CIOFF, was founded in France in 1969 and has grown from an organization of 11 countries to one of over 30 countries, with many nations hosting more than one festival. The USA and Canada both host multiple CIOFF-sanctioned festivals, including one in Drummondville, just 150 kilometers west of this City of Quebec. Every summer the city of Drummondville extends a welcome to thousands of visitors who attend the festival and enjoy the camaraderie they find there. Most of the international festivals, if not all, include both participation in dance as well as the opportunity to observe some of the best ensembles in the world. The cities, towns, and villages throughout the world that host these festivals promote the olympic spirit by opening their hearts and homes to visitors from foreign lands. Perhaps this is the most important human aspect of folkloric dance: the sociability, the feeling of togetherness that is created whether during participation or by being a spectator.

Dance needs neither common race nor common language for communication; it always has been a natural means of communication. Is this not the same in sport? Who would not marvel at the strength and beauty of the Greek Tsamiko dancer as he jumps and twirls in the air? And who could not feel exhilaration in the daring athletic feat of the Ukrainian dancer, of the incredible toe dance of the Georgian man, and of the rapid footwork of the Serbs and Bulgars? Can one not also appreciate the grace and beauty of Korean dance, and of the world's many courtship dances? Let us therefore look forward to the "cultural decade" of the 1990s and a continuing relationship between Olympism and dance.

REFERENCES

1. Coubertin P de (1894) Athletics in the modern world and the Olympic Games. In Carl-Diem-Institut (ed) Pierre de Coubertin. The Olympic Idea. Schorndorf: Hofmann (1966) p 8

2. Coubertin P de (1929) Olympia. In Carl-Diem-Institut (ed) Pierre de Coubertin. The Olympic Idea. Schorndorf: Hofmann (1966) p 110

3. Coubertin P de (1894) Athletics in the modern world and the Olympic Games. In Carl-Diem-Institut (ed) Pierre de Coubertin. The Olympic Idea. Schorndorf: Hofmann (1966) p 9

4. Coubertin P de (1918) Olympic letters. IV. In Carl-Diem-Institut (ed) Pierre de Coubertin. The Olympic Idea. Schorndorf: Hofmann (1966) p 55

5. Coubertin P de (1918) The philosophic foundation of modern Olympism. In Carl-Diem-Institut (ed) Pierre de Coubertin. The Olympic Idea. Schorndorf: Hofmann (1966) p 133

6. Lawler LB (1964) The dance in ancient Greece. Middletown: Wesleyan University Press p 12

7. Poole L, Poole G (1963) History of ancient Olympic Games. London: Vision Press p 93

8. Ibid p 97

9. Coubertin P de (1918) Mens fervida in corpore lacertoso. In Carl-Diem-Institut (ed) Pierre de Coubertin. The Olympic Idea. Schorndorf: Hofmann (1966) p 92

10. Peterson-Royce A (1977) The anthropology of dance. Bloomington: Indiana University Press p 3

11. Martin J (1946) The dance. New York: Tudor Publishing p 7

12. Sachs C (1937) World history of the dance. New York: WW Norton p 5

13. Sharp CB, Oppé AP (1924) The dance: an historical survey of dancing in Europe. London: Halton and Truscott Smith p 11

14. Kinney T, West Kinney M (1924) The dance: its place in art and life. New York: FA Stokes p 17

15. Martin J (1946) op cit p 24

16. Kinney T, West Kinney M (1924) op cit p 120

17. Carl-Diem-Institut (ed) (1969) Carl Diem. The Olympic Idea. Discourses and essays. Schorndorf: Hofmann p 112

18. Moscow '80: Games of the XXII Olympiad. Moscow: Fizikultura i Sport, 1980, first US release 4/81

19. Schaap D (1984) The 1984 Olympic Games: Sarajevo/Los Angeles. New York: Random/House p 110, 284

20. Robertson L, Johnson BD (1988) The official commemorative book: XV Olympic Winter Games. Calgary: Key Porter Books p 25-26

21. Kim U-y (1990) The greatest Olympics: from Baden-Baden to Seoul. Seoul: Si-sa-young-o-sa p 223

22. ben Avram R (1968) The Olympics in Mexico. In Olympics '68. New York: ABC and Rutledge Books p 10-13

23. XV Winter Olympic Games Organizing Committee (1988) XV Olympic Winter Games: Official Report. Calgary: Calgary Olympic Development Association p 271-75

24. Seoul Olympic Organizing Committee (1988) Seoul olympic arts festival. Seoul: Oricom

25. Seoul Olympic Organizing Committee (1987) Korean art guide. Seoul: Yekyong Publications p 171-72

Contrasting Giants of the Olympic Movement: Pierre de Coubertin and Juan Antonio Samaranch

John Lucas

The modern Olympic Games and the Olympic Movement were the direct creations of the French educator, Coubertin (1863-1937)[1]. The startling growth of the Games and Movement during the decade of the 1980s is directly attributable to the Catalonian diplomat Samaranch. Both men consecrated their entire public careers to the perpetuation of a kind of symbiotic "sacred cause", that of energizing the quadrennial festival to universal proportions and at the same time underscoring, for all to see, to learn from, and to enjoy the Games' educational, cultural, and festive dimensions. Coubertin and Samaranch differed not at all in these olympic aspirations. But, in at least three major expressions of their personal psyches, they differed: – in individual idealist-realist configurations; – in attitudes toward athletic amateurism and professionalism; – in contrasting styles of personal and world-wide olympic administration. As a prelude to this exercise in contrasting these two olympic "giants", one is obliged to repeat the theme of this Quebec City international symposium—to recognize the significance to Olympic Games history of the young 26-year-old Baron Pierre de Coubertin's first visit to North America... one hundred years ago.

In 1887, the second year of young Pierre de Coubertin's illustrious publishing history, the 24-year-old Parisian had just returned from a British Isles visit resulting in a small essay titled " 'Toynbee Hall'. Le patronage social à Londres et les étudiants anglais." "Our French school masters", he said, "look with disdain at the kind of education taught at this London institute. But I firmly believe that Toynbee Hall builds character, helps relieve the foolishness of excessive academic over-loading, strengtens moral values, and emphasizes wholesome physical activity. En France, Toynbee Hall serait vite devenu une petite église[2]". The same enthusiasm and insight would continue for another half century of writing and publishing. Two years later he came to North America and in a marathon train pilgrimage visited 25 universities as well as a number of colleges and institutions, and wrote a book about his insights[3]. He worked unceasingly in the next decade, a vague dream at the start, but that gained greater shape and form as it culminated

1890
1990

John Lucas, Department of Exercise and Sport Science, Penn State University, University Park, Pennsylvania, USA.

on Easter Sunday 1896 with the Opening Ceremonies of the Games of the first Olympiad in Athens' old-new Panathenaic stadium. Coubertin stood transfixed with joy: [...] "Les Jeux olympiques n'ont plus d'ennemis"—The Olympic Games no longer have ennemies[4].

A great many essays and biographies have been written about Coubertin in the century that has passed since his first North American visit. One of the most recent analyses of Coubertin's contribution appeared in Saint Martin's 1989 "La noblesse et les 'sports' nobles", which emphasized the fundamental role of nobility, and of Coubertin, in the establishment and development of modern sport[5]. So very much of that transcendental voyage began one hundred years ago in Canada and the United States. With hindsight we thank McGill and Laval universities; we are indebted to Harvard, Yale, and Princeton and other fine North American institutions[6].

One of Coubertin's dearest friends—a charter member of the IOC and his literary colleague—was William Milligan Sloane (1850-1928). He was Coubertin's senior by more than a dozen years but unabashedly admired the Frenchman and said so many times in his 65 letters to the IOC president written between 1897 and 1924. "My dearly beloved Pierre", he wrote in the midst of the First World War cataclysm:

> God's grace has not been withheld from you and your efforts. [Do not join the French army] if only you could see that as an even higher duty than to go to the front! Some lives are so infinitely more precious than others! [...]. It seems as if Europe were committing suicide [...]. We long for a fair and honorable peace [...]. Once more, dear Pierre au revoir, not adieu. And if you can see your way honorably do cross the Atlantic and take up the preliminary peace work for the games. Love to you and your dear ones[7].

Yet, one must avoid making a demigod of Coubertin. His place is fixed historically as the most important (but not the only) architect of the modern Olympic Games. I doubt that Madame Coubertin's memory had failed her in a 1960 interview. I asked her about her husband; she hesitated a moment and then this remarkable 102-year-old lady, a half smile on her face, said in a quavering French language whisper: "My God, he was difficult. Not only did he spend every franc on his olympic passion, but he spent all of my own monies on this obsession[8]." So be it, their life together was two full generations before olympic television and ISL-TOP sponsorship!

Contrasting Idealist-Realist Configurations

At the outset it must be stated without equivocation that I am talking about *degrees* of difference, for both men were (at various times in their long olympic careers) idealistic and realistic. Although the book is not yet closed on President Samaranch, the extant evidence is strong that this Spaniard, recognized here this week by Laval University with an honorary doctorate, is a consummately practical man, a realist of the first order. Always the careful diplomat, Samaranch directly, with gentle forcefulness and with utilitarian mind-set, goes about his business of olympic problem solving. Beneath the mask, always, as interviewer Clive Gammon saw, was "Juan Antonio Samaranch, carrying the Olympic torch, bearing the Olympic spirit[9]". I have always known, Mr. Samaranch observed, "that sport and politics did not live on separate planets[10]". He warned that he would fight all divisive forces from within as well as outside the Olympic Movement that would attempt to upset the delicate balance of support for both the international sport-for-all movement as well as healthy elite sport on all six continents[11].

MacAloon, in his always guarded way, told an audience at the 1986 Olympic Academy of Canada that on the subjects of cosmopolitanism and true internationalism, Coubertin "not only had worthwhile things to say, but his message ought to make many sports officials who claim to be carrying on his legacy extremely nervous[12]." Coubertin floated on an ether of idealism, both at the beginning of his career and even more so in the last years of his illustrious life. In 1887, the young baron, strongly influenced by the French sociologist-economist Frédérick Le Play (1806-1882), lectured and then wrote: "Sport and games offer peace of mind and strengthen the body and the will. . . Sports education provides the foundation of ethical education[13]." Far from being frivolous, play and honorable competitive sport were for Coubertin and fellow intellectual Paul Adams not mere escapism. "On the contrary", said Charles Rearick, in his *Pleasure of the Belle Époque*, for them, play was "fundamentally utilitarian and serious, essential to national survival[14]".

Underscoring this seering seriousness about play, the young Coubertin's stratospheric idealism touched on sport as a dynamic social force with extraordinary possibilities; and, as Himmelfarb said of many late nineteenth century Victorians and French aristocrats, they possessed "a compelling, almost obsessive faith in morality[15]". At the end of his life, having been nominated for the 1936 Nobel Peace Prize, Coubertin wrote from Geneva on July 29, 1937, only a long month before his death, a hand-written letter to a member of the organizing committee of the abortive Games of the XIIth Olympiad in Tokyo 1940:

> Thank you for your very nice visit to Geneva [. . .] The task of celebrating these next Olympic Games will be the greatest ever given to a country, for it does not mean merely to pursue the Olympic Torch through the universe and to unite the whole of Asia with modern Olympism, but also to combine Hellenism, the most precious civilization of ancient Europe, with the refined culture and art of Asia. It is a most enjoyable thought to me to be able to promote the rapproachment of world interest[16].

This is not to say that, at times, Coubertin could not also be extremely down-to-earth. He was, if only for the survival of the Olympic Movement. But at the core, the marrow of the man was transported by some kind of soaring, not always perfectly clear idealism. Samaranch, on the other hand, is rarely vague and represents the *summun bonum* of cool rationality in most things olympic. But take away the mask and you will find in Samaranch something akin to Coubertin's passion, only couched in today's 1990s vernacular[17].

Contrasting Views on Athletic Amateurism

Coubertin was warm to the idea of pristine-pure, amateur athletes alone as participants in his new Olympic Games, but he was cool and vague about the implementation of older, restrictive English upper-class customs which forbade the "good" amateurs from mingling with the working class professionals. The anglophile Coubertin and some of his well-to-do continental sporting colleagues kept intact the whole "amateur rules" and appended them to the first olympic eligibility regulations. But Coubertin paid a price in doing so, for aside from finding money to fund these early Olympic Games, the most vexing problem facing him during his tenure as IOC president (1896-1925) was the problem of amateurism. . . that "same old tired subject", he moaned in his 1931 *Mémoires Olympiques*[18]. Surrendering his IOC leadership on May 29, 1925, Coubertin warned his colleagues that the "lust for money is threatening to rot to its marrow" the athletic code of amateurism[19]. Coubertin wanted the poor in his Olympic Games; but he wanted them to abide by a set of rules that were socially and, just as importantly (psychologically) from an alien world. Right from the beginning Coubertin recognized the ambivalence; right to the end he was unable to settle the unstable ideological ship[20].

One cannot detect any criticism by Samaranch about the founder's hesitations regarding the thorn of athletic amateurism. No such unsureness exists with Samaranch. Slowly at first, but always in a straight line, he moved in the direction of eventual "open" Olympic Games where all the world's eligible amateur and professional athletes (with three exceptions) might come together. Beginning in the mid-1980s, Samaranch finished what IOC President Killanin started in 1974—another revision of Olympic Charter Bye-Law 26. The triple Olympic Games "boycotts" of 1976, 1980, and 1984 were behind him and Samaranch said with greatest candor: "For us, a professional athlete is the same as an [Eastern bloc] state athlete". And by extension then, American, European, and world professional athletes are hereafter (1986) eligible to participate in the Olympic Games[21]. At last the Olympic Movement has released itself from that phantom boogey man—the professional athlete—and all well-intentioned men and women can offer to all eligible humankind the opportunity to participate in the Olympic Games. This is the Samaranch message, a call somewhat similar to Coubertin's circular of seventy years earlier... but with a difference.

Contrasting Styles of Administration

This is a difficult one, for almost nothing about the ambiance in which Coubertin moved during the early years of this century resemble the world in which Samaranch has worked for the full decade of the 1980s. Differences can be detected in administrative styles, however, the result of deeply personal constitutional traits as well as a thousand times a thousand profound changes that have occurred in the world from, let us say 1910 to 1990. The evidence is large and irrefutable: Pierre de Coubertin was unprogressive regarding women as athletes and women as sport administrators. He lumped them together, placed them on some vague idealized pedestal... and left them there. This good and great human being was the consummate Victorian-Edwardian gentleman and found it impossible to encourage women as participants in the arena or as coaches, trainers, and sport administrators. He was full prisoner of his age, no better nor worse than those in the circle in which he moved[22].

Juan Antonio Samaranch has taken a different track and in an instinctive and emminently practical mind-set has quietly determined to utilize the brain power and athletic talent that exists in women, that 52% of all humanity. The picture today is a bit uneven and puzzling. Within the Château de Vidy, the proportion of women in the personnel is greater than that of men, the result of work begun by former IOC director, Monique Berlioux. Samaranch continued and accelerated this central administration tradition of recruiting women of ability. The doyenne of olympic administrators is the dignified, low-key feminist, Nadia Lekarska. Her nearly 55 years of Olympic Games watching and her present position as a member of the IOC Programme Commission give her sound historical footing to point out the Olympic Movement's dismal record of female administrators in the Olympic Games' early years. But the most recent dozen years, she said, have been "a period marked by the unprecedented advance of women's sports on an international scale, due mainly to the IOC[23]". In an entire *Olympic Message* issue devoted to women, Samaranch pointed out the obvious regarding women's rightful place in the world, and in that of olympic sport. "An irreversible trend is under way", he said, regarding female athletes and also women "in the ranks of sports administration[24]". The "die is cast"; the role of women will increase within the olympic framework, and although it borders on being a silly statement, I am of the opinion that Baron de Coubertin, were he alive today, would cast aside his ancient prejudices and join in the logical trend of men and women together celebrating this greatest of all humanity's paeceful get-togethers: the international Olympic Games.

Conclusion

In a revealing statement of several months ago, Samaranch admitted that "the last nine years that I have been in Lausanne I have had the happiest times of my life[25]". Never in the history of olympic leadership has there been anyone to match Samaranch's physical energy, his understanding of the olympic tripartite, his deep, almost instinctual comprehension of the political mind-set of national leaders. Because of these obvious skills it is not always, at first glance, evident that Samaranch has also an abiding sympathy for the athletes—an attitude that is matched by his quiet, unobtrusive devotion to the ideological basic tenets that were so dear to Pierre de Coubertin and successive IOC presidents. Above all, this present IOC leader is patient. When his biography is written (and there surely will be several), the authors will be faced with scores of examples of patience inside the private IOC chambers, with olympic administrators around the world and with many of the most powerful politicians and diplomats during the decade of the 1980s and 1990s. This privileged opportunity of mine today is not an appropriate one for a "bottom line" and definitive biography of Samaranch. It would be premature. He has several more years of work remaining. . . until 1993. So what must one say at this penultimate stage in the career of the IOC's seventh president? Samaranch has seen more, done more, visited more people in ways that would be unrecognizable to predecessors like the redoubtable Avery Brundage. Juan Antonio Samaranch has advanced Lord Killanin's Bye-Law 26 legislation to a point of absolutely no return. He may indeed also have broken the vicious trend of olympic "boycotts". Samaranch's "Athlete's Council" adds a new dimension to olympic sensitivity, as does his quantum leap expansion of the "solidarity" funds. He has in mind the impossible—the participation by athletes in the Olympic Games from every single member nation in the world. If Samaranch and his people could consummate a peaceful and successful Olympic Games in Albertville and Barcelona, then I am convinced that he will be deserving and will be seriously considered a candidate for highest olympic honors and also summit recognition by world leaders. If he were to receive such richly deserved honors, a veritable army of support people at Château de Vidy, inside NOC's, and sport federation offices everywhere would have to take silent bows. May I be one of the first to congratulate this vast and invisible and peaceful olympic army. When these precious and fragile Winter and Summer Olympic Games take place nearly perfectly (we have not yet seen that), they will take on a dimension larger than that of a sporting world championship. These festivals have the capacity someday of putting on a universally accepted "coat of many colors", and to become transformed from a unique sporting festival to a cultural concept of the mind acceptable to all of humanity, a binding force. As philosopher Whitehead said: "Culture is activity of thought, and receptiveness to beauty and humane feeling[26]." Despite nightmarish pitfalls everywhere, I do firmly believe that the Olympic Movement is moving in that direction—thanks be to that unseen peaceful army out there, worldwide, that has made, are making, and will make this cultural concept a reality. And hail to and special thanks to our two olympic bookends facing one another from conjoining centuries, but men who never knew one another personally. . . the Baron Pierre de Coubertin and His Excellency Juan Antonio Samaranch.

NOTES AND REFERENCES

1. See MacAloon JJ (1981) This great symbol: Pierre de Coubertin and the origins of the modern Olympic Games. Chicago: University of Chicago Press; Lucas J (1980) The modern Olympic Games. New York: AS Barnes; Ullrich K (1982) Coubertin. Sportverlag; Lenk H (1964) Werte Ziele Wirklichkeit der Modernen Olympischen Spiele. Stuttgart: Hofmann; Müller N, Comité international Pierre de Coubertin (eds) (1987)

L'actualité de Pierre de Coubertin. Niedernhausen-Taunus: Schors-Verlag; Navacelle G de (1987) Pierre de Coubertin: sa vie par l'image. Zürich: Weidmann; Eyquem MT (1966) L'épopée olympique. Paris: Colmann-Lévy; Callebat L (1988) Pierre de Coubertin. Paris: Fayard; and Boulongne YP (1975) La vie et l'oeuvre pédagogique de Pierre de Coubertin 1863-1937. Montréal: Léméac. Müller N, Comité international olympique (eds) (1986) Pierre de Coubertin Textes choisis. Tome I. Révélation. Tome II. Olympisme. Tome III. Pratique sportive. Zürich: Weidmann

2. Coubertin's essay on Toynbee Hall was originally published in La Réforme sociale 1er septembre, 1887 p 227-33, and reproduced in his *L'Éducation en Angleterre-Collèges et Universités*, 1988. Paris: Hachette p 271-91. The paraphrase and the direct quotation used in this essay are found in his book, pages 268 and 283

3. Coubertin P de (1890) Universités transatlantiques. Paris: Hachette. For excerpts see Müller N, Comité international olympique (eds) (1986) Pierre de Coubertin Textes choisis. Tome I. Révélation. Zürich: Weidmann p 113-39

4. Coubertin's letter from Athens reproduced and translated in Bill Henry Yeomans P (1984) An approved history of the Olympic Games. The southern California committee for the Olympic Games. Los Angeles, California. Sherman Oaks: Alfred Pub p 34 [original edition 1948]; see also Coubertin P de (1897) Lettres olympiques I. In Müller N, Comité international olympique (eds) (1986) Pierre de Coubertin Textes choisis. Tome II. Olympisme. Zürich: Weidmann p 148

5. Saint-Martin M de (1989) La noblesse et les sports nobles. Actes de la recherche en sciences sociales 80 30-32

6. Amongst others: McGill; Laval; Toronto; Ottawa; Collège de Montréal; Michigan; Boston College; West Point; Virginia; John Hopkins; Washington University (St-Louis); Cornell; Amherst; Columbia; Wellesley; Tulane; Chicago; Harvard; Yale; Princeton; Georgetown; Catholic University of Washington; Pennsylvania; MIT; and Washington-Lee Universities.

7. Sloane to Coubertin; letter dated March 15, 1916; IOC Archives

8. Personal interview with Madame de Coubertin in Geneva, August 1, 1960

9. Gammon C (1984) Still carrying the torch. Sports Illustrated July 16 63 p 67

10. Ibid p 57

11. Miller D (1990) Sport-for-all not an ideal cherished by Olympic bureaucrats. The Times of London April 23 p 50

12. MacAloon JJ (1986) Intercultural education and olympic sport. The 1986 challenge address to the Olympic Academy of Canada p 9. A 50 page pamphlet, in french and english, published by the Royal Bank of Canada, the national sponsor of the Canadian Olympic Academy

13. An essay by Pierre de Coubertin "Le surmenage" and which appeared in Le Français (30 avril 1887) is discussed in Lauerbach E (1973) The propagation of olympic principles in schools. In Hellenic Olympic Committee (ed) Report of the twelfth session of the International Olympic Academy at Olympia. Athens: Grafiki EPE p 102. Coubertin's speech titled "Un programme: Le Play" was delivered on November 14, 1887, à la Société nationale française à Londres, and published in La Réforme sociale, 7e année, 2e année, Tome IV, 15 décembre 1887, p 621-22. In Müller N, Comité international olympique (eds) (1986) Pierre de Coubertin. Textes choisis. Tome I. Révélation. Zürich: Weidmann p 543-59

14. Paul Adam's book *La Morale des sports*. Paris: La Librairie mondiale, 1907, was widely read in France. Also see Charles Rearick's (1985) reference to both Adam and Coubertin in *Pleasure of the belle époque*. Entertainment and festivity in turn-of-the-century France. New Haven: Yale University Press p 213

15. Himmelfarb G (1986) Marriage and morals among the Victorians. New York: Alfred A Knopf p 78-79

16. Coubertin correspondence dated July 29, 1937, and located in Report of the Organizing Committee on its work for the Games of the XXIIth Olympiad 1940 (Tokyo: 1940 Olympic Organizing Committee, 1940) p 13. See also "Olympic reviver suggested for Nobel Peace Prize". The Boston Globe (1936) July 30 p 23

17. There are scores of Samaranch biographies (no book ...yet). In the past two years and only in the English language, see The Independent [London], August 27, 1988 p 12; The Times [London], September 15, 1988, p 10; Sports Inc, 2 (March 13, 1989), 15-22; Olympic Message, 23 (March, 1989), 6-15; Observer [London], September 18, 1988, p 17; The Olympian [USOC], 15 April 1989, 28-29; The Times [London] December 16, 1988, p 40; Olympic Review, 262 (August 1989), 376-79; and The Samaranch Era, in Oympic Magazine Tribune, ACNO, 1 May 1990, p 17

18. Coubertin P de (1931) Mémoires olympiques. Lausanne: Comité international olympique 65-68

19. Coubertin P de (1966) Address delivered at the opening of the Olympic Congress 1925. In Carl-Diem-Institut (ed) The olympic idea. Schorndorf: Hofmann p 97. See also Coubertin P de (1925) Discours prononcé à l'ouverture des congrès olympiques à l'hotel de ville de Prague le 29 mai 1925. Brochure spéciale. Prague: Imprimerie d'état. In Müller N, Comité international olympique (eds) (1986) Pierre de Coubertin Textes choisis. Tome II. Olympisme. Zürich: Weidmann p 404-10

20. Lucas J (1988) From Coubertin to Samaranch: the unsettling transformation of the olympic ideology of athletic amateurism. Stadion XIV p 67

21. Olympic Charter 1990 Bye-Law 26, in convoluted language states that an athlete may receive payments, sign contracts for sponsorship or for advertising equipment, and be eligible for Olympic Games participation, provided that his or her international federation, national federation, and NOC give permission and hold in trust all such monies earned. Samaranch's views on all this are unequivocal. See Los Angeles Times, February 13, 1986, Part III, p 8; Los Angeles Times, August 31, 1989, Part III, p 8; Olympic Review 262 (August, 1989) p 377; Olympic Review 263-264 (September-October, 1989) p 431

22. My own presentation at the 1990 International Olympic Academy (IOA) at Olympia, Greece is entitled "Female competitors in the early years of the Olympic Games and a modern day 52 percent solution". The 15-day IOA session dealt with Women and the Olympic Movement.

23. Lekarska N (1990) The entry marathon of the second sex. Olympic Review 275-276 (September-October) p 458. Lekarska made a thoughtful presentation on a related topic at the 1990 IOA session.

24. Samaranch JA (1985) Women and sport. Olympic Review 12 (December) p 5. Other contributors to this landmark issue are Ruth Guy, Donna de Varona, Svetla Otzetova-Guenova, Nadiejda Lekarska, Carla Giuliani, Jean-Loup Chappelet, Edwige Avice, Flor Isava Fonseca, and Mary Alison Glen-Haig.

25. Samaranch JA (1990) as quoted in the Olympic Review 267 (January)

26. Whitehead AN (1929) The aims of education. New York: Mentor p 13

Sport, Culture and Society:
New Analyses in the Making

Sport, culture et société :
vers de nouvelles analyses

Technologie post-moderne et culture: un regard sur le sport médiatisé

Geneviève Rail

Le terme «post-moderne» a été maintes fois utilisé pour décrire la société nord-américaine actuelle. Non plus basée sur une économie qui cherche à subvenir aux besoins engendrés par la modernisation, elle est basée sur une économie de surplus qui exige la création continue de nouveaux désirs[1,2,3]. La société post-moderne est une société de capitalisme «avancé», de besoins qui paraissent illimités, de sur-consommation et qui tend à transformer en marchandise tout ce qui tombe sous la coupe de son champ hégémonique d'influence, y compris la connaissance[4,5]. La post-modernité se distingue par une mercantilisation de l'information et transcende l'ère littéraire[6] pour reposer principalement sur le signe, l'image, le spectacle[7,8]. Grâce à la technologie nouvelle, les mass-média fabriquent, interprètent et distribuent des images et révolutionnent ainsi les modes de connaissance et d'appréhension de la réalité. En fait, les mass-média sont tellement présents dans la culture nord-américaine, qu'ils tendent à être perçus comme substituts de la réalité. La nature se meurt et la culture prend le dessus: c'est la représentation, et non plus l'expérience directe, qui détermine la signification.

De telles tendances expliquent en partie l'importance que prend le sport médiatisé dans la société post-moderne. L'intérêt, l'émotion et le plaisir n'étant plus souvent vécus dans la routine quotidienne, le sport médiatisé permet une excitation de type «mimétique[9]» qui ressemble à celle dont on pourrait faire l'expérience dans des situations réelles, sans toutefois les risques qui lui sont habituellement associés[10].

Le sport médiatisé a subi une véritable explosion dans l'ère post-moderne et, pour atteindre un auditoire toujours plus important, on a fait appel à des technologies nouvelles permettant de créer un spectacle sportif plus dramatique, plus excitant, plus attrayant[11]. Ce qui est suggéré ici, c'est que cette technologie de pointe, particulièrement celle utilisée pour la télédiffusion d'évènements sportifs, est non seulement anti-médiatique, mais qu'elle modifie notre expérience du temps

1890
1990

Geneviève Rail, École de l'activité physique, Université Laurentienne, Sudbury, Ontario, Canada.

et de l'espace et contribue ainsi à l'esthétisme populaire, la fragmentation, le manque de profondeur et l'effacement de l'histoire qui caractérisent l'espace culturel des sociétés capitalistes avancées[12].

Le modèle anti-médiatique du sport médiatisé, ou la technologie comme instrument d'oppression

Anti-médiation

La technologie employée pour télédiffuser le sport est anti-médiatique en ce sens qu'elle ne permet pas la communication. Le téléspectateur, en position passive d'écoute et d'observation, n'a plus que la liberté de consommer ou de rejeter le spectacle sportif. En fait, pour reprendre les termes de Baudrillard, on pourrait avancer que les média sportifs sont:

> [...] anti-médiateurs, intransitifs, qu'ils fabriquent de la non-communication — si on accepte de définir la communication comme un échange, comme l'espace réciproque d'une parole et d'une réponse [... les média] sont ce qui interdit à jamais la réponse, ce qui rend impossible tout procès d'échange (sinon sous des formes de simulation de réponse, elles-mêmes intégrées au procès d'émission, ce qui ne change en rien l'unilatéralité de la communication)[13].

Même si plus récemment, les média sportifs ont permis une certaine réversibilité des circuits (e.g., via le courrier des lecteurs, l'intervention téléphonique des auditeurs, les sondages, la logique des cotes d'écoute), ils n'ont toutefois pas laissé place à une réponse et n'ont rien changé à la discrimination entre les rôles d'auditeur et de producteur. Dans la culture post-moderne, si l'audience peut influencer la production ou la programmation, c'est seulement de la manière la plus réifiée qui soit. Par exemple, des enquêtes détermineront si plus de gens écoutent le «Roller derby» ou la «Soirée du hockey» et les résultats pourront influencer l'éventuel abandon de l'un de ces programmes. Mais il reste que ces deux programmes sont faits pour une élite spécialisée qui n'a que des liens ténus avec les auditeurs et leur vie de tous les jours. Ces programmes ne contribuent pas vraiment à la communauté; au contraire, ils jouent souvent contre elle[14].

L'impact culturel du sport médiatisé et de la technologie post-moderne qui lui est associée ne repose pas tant sur la diffusion d'images et de messages, que sur l'imposition de modèles à travers lesquels la signification des événements sportifs est encadrée, organisée et interprétée[15,16,17]. Ces modèles sont tels qu'ils incitent le téléspectateur à croire que ce qui lui est présenté constitue la version naturelle et universellement acceptée du sport. Dans les faits, cependant, les modèles médiatiques sont sous-tendus par une idéologie qui transparaît non seulement au niveau du choix des programmes et du narratif, mais également au niveau des technologies et des techniques de production. Par exemple, le modèle incite à croire que le sport professionnel masculin est le plus important et le mérite plus de visibilité, en dépit du fait qu'il a peu à voir avec la réalité. Et encore, les matériaux, les techniques et les styles d'édition sont utilisés de façon à transformer le sport télédiffusé en événement dramatique auquel l'auditeur est invité à s'attacher[18]. Les analyses d'avant-match, les angles de caméra, les *close-ups*, les ralentis, l'attention donnée à certains athlètes, la description du jeu, le sommaire du match, les reprises et les faits saillants sont autant de pièces du modèle orientées vers la production d'émotion, de drame et d'héroisme et centrées sur la signification de l'issue de la compétition pour les acteurs présents[19,20,21,22].

Fétichisme

Les modèles médiatiques utilisés pour diffuser le sport ne permettent pas d'échange réel. Le téléspectateur ne participe pas et ne fait que consommer un spectacle sportif déjà analysé, interprété, mâché, digéré, régurgité. À l'aide des technologies post-modernes, les média sportifs entretiennent en plus une sorte de « fétichisme[23] » ou fascination pour le spectacle, qui incite à la consommation du sport. Des fétiches ou objets de fascination sont créés lorsque les athlètes et leurs actions sont transformés en commodités, en marchandises à être consommées. Les commentateurs récitent les statistiques personnelles des athlètes et comblent les temps d'arrêt par leur évaluation des performances. Les descriptions de jeu et commentaires multiples incitent le spectateur à fixer son écran. La rapide succession des images est unifiée par la technologie des reprises, des ralentis, des *close-ups*, des super-imposés, des écrans divisés et des fenêtres télévisuelles. Ces moyens permettent de soutenir une fascination pour le spectacle et un confort dans la non-participation à sa production.

Voyeurisme

Il existe également une coupure entre le téléspectateur et l'objet de production lorsque les média sportifs offrent des moments de « voyeurisme[24,25] », c'est-à-dire des opportunités de regarder à l'écran un acteur et son action mais avec l'impression de ne pas y avoir été invité. Les télédiffusions en direct contiennent souvent de telles opportunités: une image furtive et « illicite » du décolleté d'une nageuse, d'un entraîneur qui montre le doigt, d'un gymnaste qui pleure, etc. Les jeux de distance focale, les microphones à distance et les autres techniques modernes rendent le voyeurisme plus facile. La technologie permet même de transformer certains moments de voyeurisme en spectacle: par exemple, la faute commise discrètement par le basketteur peut être vue encore et encore grâce aux *close-ups*, aux reprises et aux ralentis.

Reproduction culturelle

Les modèles médiatiques du sport impliquent donc une coupure réelle ou symbolique entre l'auditeur et le producteur ainsi qu'une communication à sens unique. Le spectacle sportif télédiffusé devient idéologie et encourage la négation de la vie réelle et la servitude des consommateurs. Les média sportifs recréent le sport et transmettent des valeurs qui produisent et reproduisent une culture[26]. Des valeurs telles que le succès, la victoire à tout prix, le progrès, la supériorité masculine, l'individualisme, le conformisme, le nationalisme, la science, la technologie, la quantification et la spécialisation sont autant de clefs permettant de décoder le sport médiatisé et d'en appréhender la signification véritable[27,28,29,30,31]. Les modèles du sport médiatisé et la technologie qu'ils nécessitent contribuent également à la culture post-moderne en entretenant l'esthétisme populaire, la fragmentation, le manque de profondeur et l'effacement de l'histoire.

Esthétisme populaire

Dans la post-modernité, la capacité technologique de fabriquer des images sportives favorise la production de signes de plus en plus divorcés de leur épistémologie. Cette dissociation des signes et de leur signification apporte une esthéticisation que l'on retrouve aussi dans les autres types de média[32,33]. Cette esthéticisation se traduit par un mode de discours vide où le social devient un objet de contemplation plutôt qu'un champ de pratique[34,35]. L'analytique et le critique sont déplacés en faveur des plaisirs associés à la consommation des signes. Les média doivent faire appel aux effets-choc de nature esthétique pour mobiliser ou motiver la population. L'importance de l'aspect esthétique en sport fait que les média sportifs sont avantagés par de telles conditions. Mais les média sportifs eux-mêmes doivent recourir au spectaculaire et créer de toutes pièces des effets esthétiques afin de satisfaire leur auditoire. Les images brillantes, les collages, les assemblages, les ralentis, les super-ralentis, les sur-imposés, les cadrans, l'arrangement des couleurs: tout est fait pour en « mettre plein la vue ». Le sport médiatisé actuel est orienté vers la consommation des images, des formes esthétiques, des signes.

Fragmentation et manque de profondeur

La post-modernité se distingue par la fragmentation du temps, de l'espace, du sujet et de la société elle-même[36,37]. Les modèles médiatiques sportifs contribuent à cette fragmentation de plusieurs façons. Par exemple, le principe fondamental de la télédiffusion sportive est de choisir des éléments d'un seul ou de plusieurs événements sportifs, de les isoler de leur contexte global, puis de les juxtaposer à d'autres fragments isolés et de leur donner ainsi une signification nouvelle. Ce principe de «montage[38]» présuppose une fragmentation de la réalité et une perte de signification.

Les télédiffusions sportives nord-américaines sont également interrompues par les publicités, les reprises, les commentaires, les reportages spéciaux, etc.[39]. En fait, pour plusieurs spectacles sportifs, le pourcentage de temps de jeu réel représente moins de 10 % du temps de la télédiffusion globale[40]. De plus, le spectacle sportif est fragmenté par l'utilisation des écrans divisés, des fenêtres télévisuelles, des reprises, des ralentis, des faits saillants et des simulations de jeu par ordinateur. Quant à l'équipe, comme entité sportive, elle est fragmentée par la recherche constante de héros, d'individus sur lesquels porte toute l'attention, l'information et les statistiques.

La fragmentation du sport et de sa représentation est inextricablement liée au manque de profondeur qui les caractérise. Le discours des commentateurs sportifs qui apporterait une certaine connaissance est simplement absent. Le narratif superficiel s'harmonise avec la succession rapide des images et la capacité de concentration réduite des téléspectateurs qui en résulte. Le spectacle et ses acteurs sont constamment réifiés en statistiques abstraites qui brisent leur lien avec la réalité profonde du vécu et empêchent tout effort épistémologique.

Effacement de l'histoire

Finalement, la société post-moderne est marquée par un effacement de l'histoire que le critique américain Jameson[41] associe aux tendances vers le «pastiche» et la «schizophrénie». La pratique du pastiche, ou l'imitation des styles morts, indique l'incapacité à se centrer sur le présent. Quant à la schizophrénie, elle se traduit par l'expérience de faits significatifs isolés, non-reliés, qui ne se rejoignent pas dans une séquence cohérente et ne permettent donc pas l'expérience du temps.

Les modèles du sport médiatisé contribuent à ces deux tendances de multiples façons. Par exemple, le principe du pastiche peut être vu dans les films nostalgiques sur les héros sportifs du passé; films que l'on découpe et colle, puis recolle et recolle encore dans les productions télévisuelles de spectacles sportifs actuels. L'incapacité de se localiser dans le présent se remarque dans l'utilisation des reprises et des ralentis. L'usage successif des caméras isolées, des grands angles, des *close-ups*, des écrans divisés et des sur-imposés transforme aussi le spectacle sportif en brisant le rythme temporel de la compétition. Le temps est manipulé avec les ralentis, les arrêts ou les reprises, de façon à dramatiser l'action. Encore, on utilise les fenêtres télévisuelles qui concentrent des événements diffus dans l'espace et on synthétise l'action en «faits saillants» qui concentrent des événements diffus dans le temps[42]. Le sport médiatisé défie la localisation et participe donc à l'effacement de l'histoire.

Hégémonie culturelle

Cette dernière caractéristique, comme l'anti-médiation, l'esthétisme populaire, la fragmentation et le manque de profondeur, fait partie de l'idéologie des modèles médiatiques du sport. Dans nos sociétés post-modernes, cette idéologie étant plus diffusée, connue, intériorisée, elle catalyse un type d'uniformité qui suggère l'hégémonie culturelle[43,44].

Cette conclusion n'est pas nouvelle: il y a plus de 40 ans que les théoriciens de la gauche tels qu'Adorno et Marcuse soutiennent que la télévision est un instrument hégémonique du grand capital, qui vise à susciter toujours plus de consommation de la part des masses spectatrices. Depuis, cette perspective a été maintes fois remise en question par les théoriciens de la droite. D'autres perspectives et d'autres concepts ont aussi été utilisés comme contre-arguments[45,46]. Plus récemment, Fiske[47] a introduit le concept de «polysémie» pour parler de la capacité de chacun d'interpréter le texte à sa façon. Ce concept implique la possibilité d'interprétations multiples dont certaines pourraient dévier des formes dominantes. Ce concept implique également la possibilité que les téléspectateurs soient imperméables aux constructions de la réalité des média et donc à l'impact idéologique de ces derniers.

Il s'avère donc envisageable que la technologie post-moderne utilisée pour médiatiser le sport ne soit pas fondamentalement une structure de pouvoir hégémonique. Bien sûr, les arguments conservateurs et la notion de polysémie pourraient être utilisés pour défendre cette thèse. Toutefois, les perspectives sur lesquelles ils reposent ne remettent pas en question la structure actuelle des média et c'est justement elle qu'il faudrait bouleverser. Toute tentative de modifier les contenus, de les subvertir ou de les contrôler est sans espoir si n'est pas brisé le monopole de la parole, et ceci, non pas pour la donner individuellement à chacun, mais pour qu'elle puisse s'échanger, se donner et se rendre. À la limite, ce qui doit disparaître, c'est la notion de medium, d'intermédiaire. Comme l'a si bien dit Baudrillard: «on rencontre enfin ses voisins quand on contemple avec eux son immeuble en feu[48].»

Le potentiel anti-hégémonique du sport médiatisé, ou la technologie comme instrument d'émancipation

Il est donc possible de démontrer que la technologie post-moderne des sports médiatisés n'est pas essentiellement un instrument hégémonique: il suffit de discuter de la possibilité d'utiliser les média pour une communication véritable. Le cas des Inuits du Canada, par exemple, illustre parfaitement le potentiel des média en termes d'émancipation sociale et de consolidation culturelle[49]. Les Inuits ont d'abord reconnu le danger posé par la technologie des communications. En fait, plusieurs communautés l'ont rejetée jusqu'à ce qu'elles soient assurées d'une station inuite. La Société de télédiffusion inuite ou IBC a été établie au début des années 1970. Actuellement, elle possède trois centres principaux de production et plusieurs unités secondaires à travers les communautés de l'Arctique. La Société produit une émission de nouvelles et des documentaires en Inuktutut. Ces documentaires sont une réflection de la vie inuite et portent, entre autres, sur les activités culturelles, les danses, les jeux et les techniques de chasse et de pêche. Ce qui est particulier aux Inuits, c'est la relation intime entre leur vie culturelle et la façon dont ils se sont approprié la technologie post-moderne. L'utilisation de cette technologie n'a pas nécessairement contribué à l'érosion du style de vie traditionnellement inuit. Au contraire, la technologie avancée a été utilisée par les Inuits pour consolider leur culture et leur économie[50]. De plus, et paradoxalement, la résistance à l'assimilation technologique et culturelle est devenue plus efficace en utilisant la technologie.

Certains avanceront que l'utilisation de la nouvelle technologie correspond automatiquement à une subordination à la logique du système dominant et que, même lorsque cette technologie est utilisée pour la résistance, elle n'en correspond pas moins à une perte stratégique cruciale. Mais si les Inuits ont adopté une stratégie politique qui ne change en rien le pouvoir hégémonique de la technologie post-moderne des communications, il n'y a cependant rien d'inhérent dans cette technologie qui empêche que la forme des nouveaux messages soit changée. Et cette stratégie semble avoir été celle des communautés inuites. D'abord, la division entre l'auditeur et l'acteur, qui marque les modèles médiatiques de nos sociétés, n'existe pas. À la télévision inuite, il n'y a pas d'artiste, seulement des producteurs: producteurs et téléspectateurs sont parties prenantes de la communauté. Ce type de télévision interactive est déterminé aux niveaux de la production, de la distribution et de la consommation par une relation intime avec la communauté dans laquelle il est produit. Il en résulte des documentaires au sein desquels le langage visuel permet à la communauté de se voir dans ses propres termes. Les documentaires démontrent aussi une absence de prédisposition concernant ce que la télédiffusion «devrait» être. Par exemple, un documentaire montre un Inuit installé au-dessus d'un trou dans la glace[51]. Son bras est levé, il tient une lance. Le film est fait à distance et on peut voir l'homme au complet. Le moment est dramatique et on en attend impatiemment l'issue. L'homme est debout, la caméra ne bouge pas. L'intensité du moment n'est pas produite par un *close-up*, des coupures ou des additions. On devient ennuyé, mais on attend toujours. L'intensité revient occasionnellement: on anticipe le phoque, le mouvement soudain, l'action. Mais l'action ne vient pas. On attent 5 minutes, 10 peut-être, avant de réaliser que l'on attend que le chasseur frappe et que lui attend le phoque et donc, que l'on attend tous deux le phoque et que cette attente est peut être la même. On commence à comprendre que la chasse au phoque n'est pas l'utilisation d'une lance ou le moment soudain de la frappe, mais plutôt l'anticipation, l'ennui, l'intensité, la fatigue, l'attente. Après quelque 15 minutes, le reportage se termine sans que l'on ait vu la frappe.

Par contraste, dans n'importe quel programme suivant la logique médiatique des sociétés post-modernes, ces images auraient probablement été éditées comme suit. On aurait pris une première prise à distance pour établir le contexte; puis, un *close-up* pour établir l'identité; ensuite, une prise de l'arme, puis du trou, le tout avec un narratif et une musique établissant l'aspect dramatique; finalement, une prise ralentie du mouvement de la lance et du phoque mourant, afin d'intensifier le point culminant. Nous n'aurions pas été ennuyés ou forcés d'attendre longtemps, mais nous aurions été manipulés par les producteurs: nous aurions vu tous les aspects essentiels de la chasse au phoque, mais nous n'aurions fait l'expérience d'aucun d'entre eux.

L'exemple inuit nous fait comprendre que la technologie post-moderne des communications n'est pas en soi une structure de pouvoir hégémonique et, qu'en fait, elle contient un potentiel émancipatoire. Bien sûr, il n'y a plus de culture inuite «pure» mais ce qui demeure distinctement inuit dans cette culture hybride, c'est une communauté qui est assez forte pour briser la logique du spectacle et utiliser la technologie post-moderne de façon radicalement subversive, c'est-à-dire comme communication qui met au défi le modèle émetteur-récepteur et organise des discours avec des réponses.

L'exemple inuit peut paraître extrême. Pourtant, un peu partout au monde et même ici en Amérique du Nord, des stratégies similaires sont utilisées présentement pour munir les auditoires de réponses contre-hégémoniques aux messages encodés dans les produits de culture de masse[52]. La prolifération des vidéo-cassettes et des réseaux de cablo-diffusion en marge des réseaux officiels permettent aux voix longtemps censurées de se faire entendre[53]. Des média à buts non-lucratifs, des organisations culturelles activistes telles que «Pacifica Radio» et

«Alternative Views» et des média alternatifs émergent de toutes parts. Mais qu'en est-il des pratiques sportives et de leur médiatisation? Comment bouleverser la structure actuelle des modèles médiatiques sportifs afin que le sport télédiffusé corresponde à la réalité de nos communautés et contribue à leur bien-être?

Conclusion

En guise de conclusion, il est possible d'esquisser une réponse et ainsi, de souligner le potentiel des technologies post-modernes de communication quant à l'émancipation des pratiques sportives du troisième millénaire. Il semble que la solution se situe dans la restitution d'une pratique dialectique. L'exemple inuit est révélateur à ce sujet et il faudrait peut-être le suivre pour arriver à dépasser la logique actuelle de l'émetteur et du récepteur. La solution se trouve dans la possibilité d'une communication immédiate, non filtrée par des modèles bureau-cratiques. La spontanéité, l'échange original, des gens qui se répondent. À la rigueur, il faudrait qu'il n'y ait plus de message, c'est-à-dire d'information à décoder de façon univoque sous l'égide d'un modèle. Il faudrait briser l'univocité du message, restituer l'ambivalence du sens.

Cette stratégie est-elle possible dans les sociétés post-modernes? Il semble que oui. Déjà les masses spectatrices commencent à revendiquer un rôle plus important dans la programmation et la production des événements sportifs. La prolifération extraordinaire des vidéo-caméras et des réseaux locaux de télédif-fusion permet une représentation plus réaliste du sport qui remet en question les modèles hégémoniques des puissants média sportifs nord-américains. Les tech-nologies nouvelles ont des effets comparables. Par exemple, on peut aujourd'hui utiliser des appareils informatiques qui permettent d'annuler automatiquement les publicités insérées dans les programmes sportifs. Encore, les nouveaux téléviseurs permettent au spectateur de jouer au producteur dans son salon en sélectionnant simultanément les caméras placées sur un ou des sites sportifs ainsi que les fenêtres télévisuelles correspondantes. La dissolution des polarités qui caractérise les sociétés post-modernes devrait permettre un rapprochement encore plus grand entre les rôles de producteur et de récepteur. Si cette prédiction s'avère véridique, le troisième millénaire aura au moins apporté une solution au piège de la communication dirigée et, ainsi, indirectement contribué à l'émancipation des pratiques sportives des citoyens et citoyennes de l'ère post-moderne.

RÉFÉRENCES

1. Bataille G (1976) Œuvres complètes. Vol VII. Paris: Gallimard

2. Jameson F (1984) Postmodernism or the cultural logic of late capitalism. New Left Review 146 53-92

3. Kroker A, Cook D (1986) The postmodern scene. New York: St-Martin Press

4. Baudrillard J (1970) La société de consommation. Paris: Gallimard

5. Baudrillard J (1988) America. New York: Verso

6. Guiraud P (1975) Signification: form and substance of the sign. In Semiology. London: Routledge & Kegan Paul p 22-44

7. Debord G (1983) Society of spectacle. Detroit: Red and Black

8. Kuhn A (1985) The power of the image. London: Routledge & Kegan Paul

9. Elias N, Dunning E (1986) Quest for excitement. Oxford: Blackwell

10. Goodger JM, Goodger BC (1989) Excitement and representation: toward a sociological explanation of the significance of sport in modern society. Quest 41 257-72

11. Coakley JJ (1990) Sport and the mass media. In Sport in society. St-Louis: Mosby p 277-301

12. Jameson F (1984) op cit

13. Baudrillard J (1976) Pour une critique de l'économie politique du signe. Paris: Gallimard p 208

14. Rader B (1984) In its own image: how television has transformed sports. New York: Free Press

15. Baudrillard J (1980) The implosion of meaning in the media and the information of the social in the masses. In The myth of information: technology and post-industrial culture. Madison: Coda Press p 137-148

16. Gamson WA (1989) News as framing. American Behavioral Scientist 33 157-61

17. Wenner LA (1989) The Super Bowl pregame show: cultural fantasies and political subtext. In Wenner LA (ed) Media, sports, and society. Newbury Park: Sage p 157-79

18. Cantelon H, Gruneau R (1988) The production of sport for television. In Harvey J, Cantelon H (eds) Not just a game. Ottawa: University of Ottawa Press p 177-94

19. Clarke A, Clarke J (1982) Highlights and action replays: ideology, sport and the media. In Hargreaves J (ed) Sport, culture and ideology. London: Routledge & Kegan Paul p 62-87

20. Cantelon H, Gruneau R (1988) op cit

21. Coakley JJ (1990) op cit

22. Gruneau R (1989) Making spectacle: a case study in television sports production. In Wenner LA (ed) Media, sports, and society. Newbury Park: Sage p 134-56

23. Duncan M, Brummett B (1989) Types and sources of spectating pleasure in televised sport. Sociology of Sport Journal 6 195-211

24. Duncan M (1990) Sports photographs and sexual difference: images of women and men in the 1984 and 1988 Olympic Games. Sociology of Sport Journal 7 22-43

25. Duncan M, Brummett B (1989) op cit

26. Gruneau R (1988) Modernization or hegemony: two views on sport and social development. In Harvey J, Cantelon H (eds) Not just a game: essays in canadian sport sociology. Ottawa: University of Ottawa Press p 9-32

27. Bryant J (1989) Viewers' enjoyment of televised sports violence. In Wenner LA (ed) Media, sports, and society. Newbury Park: Sage p 270-89

28. Cantelon H, Gruneau R (1988) op cit

29. Duncan M, Hasbrook CA (1988) Denial of power in televised women's sport. Sociology of Sport Journal 5 1-21

30. Signorelli N (1989) Television and conceptions about sex roles: maintaining conventionality and the status quo. Sex Roles 21 341-60

31. Vandeberg LR, Trujillo N (1989) The rhetoric of winning and losing: the American dream and America's team. In Wenner LA (ed) Media, sports, and society. Newbury Park: Sage p 204-24

32. Faurschou G (1987) Fashion and the cultural logic of postmodernity. Canadian Journal of Political and Social Theory 11 68-82

33. Paoletti JT (1985) Art. In Trachtenberg S (ed) The postmodern moment. Westport: Greenwood p 53-80

34. Lucaites JL, Charland M (1989) The legacy of liberty: rhetoric, ideology, and aesthetics in the postmodern condition. Canadian Journal of Political and Social Theory 13 31-48

35. Kroker A, Kroker ML (1987) Theses on the disappearing body in the hyper-modern condition. Canadian Journal of Political and Social Theory 11 p i-xvi

36. Hassan I (1987) The postmodern turn: essays in postmodern theory and culture. Columbus: Ohio State University Press

37. Lyotard JF (1984) The postmodern condition: a report on knowledge. Minneapolis: University of Minnesota Press

38. Sarup M (1989) Totality or fragmentation. In Post-structuralism and postmodernism. Athens: University of Georgia Press p 134-38

39. Zoglin R (1990) The great TV takeover. Time 135 66-68

40. Meier KV (1984) Much ado about nothing: the television broadcast packaging of team sport championship games. Sociology of Sport Journal 1 263-79

41. Jameson F (1984) op cit

42. Birell S, Loy JW (1981) Media and sport: hot and cool. In Loy JW, Kenyon G, McPherson BD (eds) Sport, culture and society. Philadelphia: Lea & Febiger p 296-307

43. Cantelon H, Gruneau R (1988) op cit

44. Mosco V, Wasko J (1988) The political economy of information. Madison: University of Wisconsin Press

45. Jensen KB (1990) The politics of polysemy: television news, everyday consciousness and political action. Media, Culture and Society 12 57-77

46. Peters JD (1989) Satan and savior: mass communication in progressive thought. Critical Studies in Mass Communication 6 247-63

47. Fiske J (1987) Television culture. New York: Methuen

48. Baudrillard J (1976) op cit

49. Kulchyski P (1989) The postmodern and the paleolithic: notes on technology and native community in the far North. Canadian Journal of Political and Social Theory 13 49-62

50. Kulchyski P (1989) op cit

51. Kulchyski P (1989) op cit

52. Lazere D (1988) American media and mass culture: left perspectives. Berkeley: University of California Press

53. Beyer L (1989) Subversion by video. Time 134 66-74

Le sport en France :
de l'utilité publique à l'utilité ludique

Alain Loret

Le sport moderne a souvent été considéré comme une activité possédant en propre un certain nombre de caractéristiques censées favoriser l'accès à la société de ceux qui s'adonnaient à sa pratique. Ce point est remarquablement présent dans les écrits des tenants du sport comme Pierre de Coubertin, mais aussi, et cela est plus étonnant, dans les discours des hommes politiques français depuis le XIXᵉ siècle. L'idée générale qui sous-tend ces prises de positions revient à considérer que le sport rassemblerait sur son nom les grandes valeurs de la société française égalité, solidarité, respect de la règle et de l'autre, goût de l'effort, vigueur et santé, idéal moral, gratuité de l'engagement personnel, respect du drapeau et volonté de réussir. Ainsi, la pratique du sport ne serait pas autre chose qu'un résumé de la pratique sociale « la plus pure ». Bref, le sport serait utile à la construction d'une société harmonieuse. Une telle conception traverse l'histoire du sport moderne en France et, partant, le détermine en tant que support didactique propre à permettre une meilleure intégration des individus au sein de l'organisation sociale.

Dans ces conditions, on comprendra aisément que le sport relève aujourd'hui de ce que nous appelons en France le domaine de « l'utilité publique ». De fait, de nombreuses fédérations sportives françaises ont reçu un label institutionnel en devenant des organisations reconnues d'utilité publique par l'État. Elles relèvent donc, dans une certaine mesure, d'une forme de « service public » des activités sportives[1].

Il s'avère pourtant que depuis le milieu des années soixante-dix le sport a revêtu des formes bien différentes de celles que nous lui connaissions depuis un siècle. L'aventure, la recherche de « l'extrême » et du vertige, du « hors limite » ou de « nouvelles sensations », le rejet des stades et de leurs réglementations contraignantes, ont fait basculer des activités « sportives » inédites dans une certaine forme de marginalité sociale. Loin de l'utilité publique traditionnelle, celles-ci s'inscrivent alors dans ce que nous pourrions appeler le domaine de

1890
1990

Alain Loret, Unité de formation et de recherche en sciences et techniques des activités physiques et sportives, Université de Caen, Caen, France.

«l'utilité ludique». Il apparaît, en effet, que le jeu participe de manière souvent ostentatoire des motivations des adeptes de ces nouvelles pratiques que sont le parapente, le planche-à-voile, la «course à pied en autosuffisance», le *snowboard* ou bien encore le saut en *benji*, le *base jump*, le *delta-plane* ou le *canyoning*... Cette liste n'est bien entendu pas limitative tant la créativité de nos contemporains semble inépuisable dans le domaine de la recherche et de l'invention de jeux avec la nature.

Dans son livre «Des jeux et des hommes[2]», Caillois a magistralement montré en quoi certains jeux valorisant le «hors limites», autrement dit le vertige, la peur ou la recherche de sensations voluptueuses, pouvaient apparaître comme l'antithèse de la société. Il n'est donc pas surprenant de constater que l'utilité ludique qui imprègne les pratiques «sportives» les plus récentes ait pu générer des discours, des comportements, des attitudes et, surtout, des symboles propres à engendrer une forme inédite de critique sociale. Ce qui est plus étonnant, par contre, c'est que cette nouvelle culture sportive — que j'ai appelé ailleurs la «culture sportive analogique[3]» — pille ouvertement, comme pour mieux s'opposer au sport traditionnel, les éléments symboliques issus des mouvements d'avant-garde, de contestation sociale et de contre-culture, nés aux États-Unis dans les années soixante.

Ainsi pourrions-nous émettre l'hypothèse que certaines pratiques sportives contemporaines s'inscrivant dans un système de valeurs de nature alternative, loin de faciliter l'intégration sociale comme ce fut le cas depuis un siècle, permettrait, au contraire, une certaine forme d'opposition à la société.

Les exemples sont nombreux, qui illustrent le point de vue selon lequel une forme de contre-culture sportive existe bel et bien aujourd'hui. Celle-ci puise une partie de son inspiration dans ce que les américains ont appelé *the counter culture* dans les années soixante. Autrement dit, un mouvement de mise en question de la culture bourgeoise traditionnelle (en particulier dans les domaines de la peinture, de la poésie, du roman et de la musique) qui connut son apogée en Mai 1968 au sein de la société occidentale.

Ainsi, les couleurs «fluo», qui ont envahi ce qu'en France nous appelons le monde de la «glisse», ne sont pas autre chose que les couleurs emblématiques et psychédéliques (le violet, le jaune, le vert pomme, le rose et le rouge vif) d'un mouvement pictural d'avant-garde des années soixante connu sous le nom de pop'art. Le leader de ce mouvement, Andy Warhol, inspire d'ailleurs nettement certaines publicités françaises récentes valorisant des produits liés au *funboard*. *Gotcha*, une marque de *surfwear*, exploite notamment des photographies américaines des années cinquante qu'elle retouche dans le plus pur style du pop'art tel qu'il fut remis au goût du jour de manière provocante, en France, par les Bazooka, un groupe de créateurs particulièrement extrémiste sur le plan du graphisme. Dans ce domaine, la nouvelle vague du *sportwear* s'inscrit résolument dans l'avant-garde la plus débridée. Ainsi, la société de vêtements *Oxbow* a obtenu son premier succès commercial en créant un blouson à damier reprenant le sigle Ska, un mouvement *new wave* anglais des années soixante. Le fabricant de *sportwear Poivre Blanc* utilise pour sa décoration des inclusions de bandes dessinées; une technique graphique proche des conceptions de Roy Lichtenstein, un peintre pop' américain des années soixante. La marque *Quiksilver*, pour sa part, fut un temps représentée par un logo simulant une tête osseuse aux yeux proéminents et aux dents très apparentes, extrêmement proche des dessins de Jean Michel Basquiat, le leader de «l'underground new-yorkais». Or, Basquiat affirmait être «un enfant du pop'art» et avait Warhol pour «père spirituel». De son côté, *Wind Magazine*, la principale revue française de planche-à-voile s'est plu également à utiliser des formes et des éléments issus du pop'art pour sa maquette. Elle copia aussi de manière très significative un groupe de peintres français particulièrement provocateurs liés à la «Figuration Libre»: le «Groupe Finir en Beauté», qui rassembla notamment des peintres comme Boisrond, Di Rosa et Combas. Ceux-ci rejettent toute tradition picturale pour peindre «avant de penser». Un peu à la manière des surréalistes qui inspirèrent les tenants de la *beat generation* américaine en la personne de Jack Kerouac le leader du mouvement *beatnick*. Il faut d'ailleurs noter que de nombreux points communs existent entre la «route» américaine que décrit Kerouac dans ses livres et la «glisse» telle qu'a pu la définir Bessas en France[4].

Les «glisseurs» n'hésitent pas à puiser leurs références symboliques dans des mouvements de contestations américains particulièrement violents. Ainsi, la société Quiksilver fut à l'origine d'un concept original en matière de décoration *fun*: les *warpaints*. Autrement dit, des «peintures de guerre» qui viennent agrémenter la présentation des vêtements de la marque. Cette fois l'inspiration vient des *Hell's Angels*, qui décoraient leurs blousons de cuir de cette façon, à la manière des pilotes américains durant la seconde guerre mondiale. Certains termes de vocabulaire utilisés en planche-à-voile comme *run* ou *baston* sont d'ailleurs issus du langage des *Hell's Angels*. D'autre part, Roby Naish, le leader charismatique du *funboard* qui se plaît à poser pour les photographes sur une motocyclette de marque *Harley Davidson*, épouse la philosophie *Hell's* qui consiste à «vivre vite, à mourir jeune et à faire un beau cadavre». N'affirme-t-il pas, en effet, dans une revue comme *Wind Magazine*: «Je veux mourir avant d'être vieux (...) j'ai envie de faire des trucs dangereux[5].»

L'escalade dite «libre» illustre également cette propension à exploiter des symboles liés aux *Hell's Angels*. En France, certaines voies ont été baptisées *Easy Rider*, «Les anges de la rue 27», *Overcoolbabadose*, «La rage de vivre», «Orange mécanique», «J'irai cracher sur vos tombes», ou bien encore, «Septembre noir» ou «Ossuaire».

De son côté, la revue française *Nouvelles Sensations* cultive l'ambiguïté en traitant l'activité «sportive» des *gangs* de *snowboard* (le *surf* des neiges) comme s'il s'agissait de *Hell's Chapters* (des bandes Hell's) et en prévenant lors de la saison 1987: «*Place les touristes, les tribus débarquent!*[6].» Cette revue persiste dans la comparaison en commentant de manière très particulière les exactions d'un groupe de *surfers* des neiges, les *Bootleggers Connection*: «Privés de spots permanents les Boots errent de station en station, de course en course, jalonnant çà et là leurs passages de quelques graffitis, ne laissant derrière eux que la pagaille semée [...] salissant tout et tout le monde, un bootlegger ne reculant devant rien pour saloper son voisin[7].» Il est significatif, dès lors, que les *Boots* utilisent largement la profession de foi des *Hell's Angels*: l'expression «fuck off». Ainsi leur cri de guerre annonce-t-il: «Bootleggers are the best, fuck the rest!».

Le *skate-board*, ou la planche à roulettes, a généré, pour sa part, un graphisme très particulier de nature spontanéiste à l'image de la Figuration Libre et que certains n'hésitent pas à qualifier de *street art*, reprenant ainsi un terme dont use déjà le peintre américain Karel Appel, l'un des précurseurs du graffiti urbain. Le *free style* que revendiquent les *skaters* se conjugue ainsi parfaitement avec la liberté que veulent exprimer les «graffiteurs» en s'appropriant par le dessin certains sites urbains quelque peu marginaux. Ainsi, trois éléments sont nécessaires pour créer un «stade» de *skate-board*: une usine désaffectée, des *skaters* «fous» et des «bombeurs», autrement dit des «peintres» dont la spécialité, le bombage des murs des villes, est nettement prohibée par la société. Si l'on considère que les adeptes du *skate-board* sont des enfants d'âge scolaire, on mesure la distance qui existe entre des pratiques sportives traditionnelles qualifiées d'éducatives par l'école et une activité qui se plaît à valoriser des sites parfaitement surréalistes, des comportements «fous», donc anormaux, et des «qualités» picturales que, justement, la société cherche à brider. Là encore nous constatons que le risque, le déguisement, la recherche de sensations liées à des figures acrobatiques, autant de paramètres comportementaux que promeuvent les *skaters*, sont bien, comme le suggère Caillois, des modèles d'attitudes qui se positionnent aux marges sociales. Il semble normal, dans ces conditions, que les adeptes du *skate-board* plébiscitent le graffiti urbain; un mouvement pictural lui même marginalisé.

Ce processus latent de contestation, est largement relayé par des mazagines français spécialisés dans la planche-à-voile, le *surf*, le *skate*, ou encore la «grimpe», et que cherchent à mettre en évidence de façon ostentatoire les leaders d'opinion des sports de glisse, peut être de nature à entraver le développement futur des fédérations sportives «d'utilité publique». En effet, nombreuses sont celles qui cherchent à inclure ces activités nouvelles au sein de leurs structures pour tenter de capter ces pratiquants inorganisés et que l'on dit «sauvages». Dès lors, une question ne manque pas de se poser: comment une organisation ayant reçu une mission de «service public» peut-elle intéresser ou séduire des acteurs qui rejettent si ouvertement certaines normes sociales en créant leur propre système de valeurs contre-culturelles?

À l'évidence la réponse n'est pas simple si l'on considère les multiples difficultés rencontrées par des fédérations sportives françaises cherchant à intégrer, qui le vélo-tout-terrain (VTT), qui la planche-à-voile, qui les coureurs sur route, qui les grimpeurs ou les adeptes du *snowboard*. On mesurera l'ampleur de la tâche si l'on envisage qu'un tel problème ne pourra être résolu en conservant l'identité culturelle attachée au sport traditionnel[8].

Les fédérations sportives d'utilité publique doivent admettre que le sport est entré dans une ère nouvelle. En effet, outre les multiples symboles contre-culturels que nous avons évoqués dans cette communication, les nouveaux pratiquants de ce que nous appelons en France les «sports californiens» valorisent nettement des paramètres comme le libre-arbitre, la nature, la connaissance de soi, l'émotion ou la connivence avec l'autre. Ils rejettent, par contre, de plus en plus manifestement les paramètres sportifs traditionnels que sont l'arbitre, le stade, la reconnaissance de soi, la raison et la domination de l'autre. L'avenir des organisations sportives traditionnelles semble donc bien devoir passer par une véritable révolution culturelle qui fera la part belle au jeu et à l'irrationnel pour mieux rejeter la règle et la mesure qui constituent depuis un siècle les éléments fondateurs du socle doctrinal sur lequel le sport s'est construit.

RÉFÉRENCES

1. Houel J (1983) Règles de droit et culture sportive. Actes du VIIIe symposium de l'ICSS. Paris INSEP p 109

2. Caillois R (1977) Des jeux et des hommes. Paris: Gallimard

3. Loret A (1987) Culture sportive «analogique» et structures sportives «digitales». In Sport et changement social. Bordeaux: Société de sociologie du sport

4. Bessas Y (1982) La glisse. Paris: Fayard. Voir également Loret A (1990) Les organisations sportives françaises au risque de la culture californienne. In Actes du congrès "Géopolitique du sport". Université de Besançon

5. Wind Magazine 93 p 40

6. Nouvelles Sensations 6 p 46

7. Nouvelles Sensations 5 p 34

8. Loret A (1987) op cit

The Dissolution of Polarities as a Megatrend in Postmodern Sport

Geneviève Rail

As a means of expression and identification, sporting practices are deeply rooted in everyone's individuality. However, they are also influenced by impersonal factors such as the media and the rapid evolution of technological societies. In a multiplicity of forms and in its most complex ramifications, sport is interwoven with the world of education and health, work and leisure, communications and business, art and culture and, of course, politics and international relations[1]. Sport, especially the high performance sport discussed here is marked by the transformations and innovations specific to a period that could be described as "postmodern".

In 1970, Kavolis defined the postmodern personality as one "characterized by the sense that both polarities of a great many [. . .] dilemmas are contained [. . .] within one's experience[2]". Almost two decades later, deconstructions of such dilemmas have been noted in many areas. In the arts, pure ecclecticism and pastiche are the prevailing styles[3]; in architecture, the ancient and the modern are mixed and traditions, superimposed[4]; in fashion, the abstract mingles with the concrete, the artificial and the natural are blended together[5]; in religion, dogmas crumble and rapprochements are operated[6]; in politics, systems are amalgamated and traditional divisions are disappearing[7]; in the media, facts and fictions are merged[8]; and finally, in social theory, structuralisms seen in the modern period, be they DeSaussurian, Lévi-Straussian or Parsonian, are abandoned in favor of deconstructionist and pragmatic approaches[9,10,11,12].

What is suggested in the following pages is that, as a cultural production, sport is also imprinted with this general impulse toward a dissolution of polarities. It is suggested that further this megatrend is directly linked to the ethical crisis facing high performance sport today. In order to better understand this problematic, it is situated in the line of dissolutions affecting postmodern sport; dissolutions which mainly concern dualities such as male versus female, work versus leisure, universal versus particular, and self versus body.

Geneviève Rail, School of Human Movement, Laurentian University, Sudbury, Ontario, Canada.

Male and Female

When various societies began to tolerate sporting practices among women, the latter had no choice but to integrate a world of sport already built by men, for men. Some criticized this world and attempted to change it so that it would better correspond to women's experiences[13,14,15], but without much success. An "androcentric[16]" value system is invading women's high performance sport and women athletes are giving more and more emphasis to traditionally masculine attributes such as power and strength and values such as specialization and productivity. In postmodernity, a blurring of the genres is taking place and male and female athletes come to exercise, train, and compete quantitatively and qualitatively in the same ways. It is also in the same ways that they dress for sport and prepare their bodies for competition.

From the popular movement of sport and fitness is emerging a new ideal-type of body for the woman. This ideal-type combines several cultural antitheses: strength with beauty, muscularity with slimness, firmness with softness of the curves. Women are "rebuilding their bodies out of muscle[17]" and their power and hardness prepare them for sporting experiences similar to that of their male counterparts. For example, women reach the top of Mount Everest; they have their own rugby, ice hockey, and soccer teams; they belong to professional volleyball, basketball or football clubs; and they earn a living as tennis players, golfers, cyclists, boxers or bodybuilders.

Leisure and Work

A second duality that tends to disappear is that of work and leisure. In modernity, work strengthened the conscience while leisure practices facilitated impulses[18]. In postmodern life, however, not only the concept of leisure society becomes a utopia (according to Harris and Trotter[19] leisure time is decreasing instead of increasing), but leisure itself becomes work.

In the sport "industry", training machines become labor-making devices and impulses are harnessed into endless repetitions. Work value such as standardization, taylorization, impersonality, rationality, efficiency and productivity have invaded the world of sport[20]. Sport becomes alienated labor[21] or commodity[22]. The athletic body is bought, molded, exploited, exchanged, sold or discarded. The body becomes a means of production that can be sacrificed for the product. The human machine is appropriated by the political-economical system and the search for solutions to such problems as stress, violence or injuries in sport is granted to the scientific and medical communities. In that perspective, when the athletic body is damaged, efforts are not geared to change the sport or the attitudes of those who participate in it, but to quickly repair the body and return it on the production line. Furthermore, when this human machine becomes obsolete, it is replaced by less-human, high-tech versions of the body made possible by postmodern technology (*i.e.*, drugs, diets, hormones, prostheses, implants, transplants, plastic surgery, etc.).

This obliteration of the work-leisure opposition entails a gradual disappearance of another distinction: that made between amateur and professional athletes. In postmodern societies, the concept of amateurism vanishes and high performance athletes come to see themselves as workers entitled to a minimum of social benefits in exchange for the services they offer[23].

Particular and Universal

A third polarity which is dissolving is that of the particular versus the universal. Simply, the particular becomes universal through communications and mass media. In the global village which our planet is becoming, the sporting news, fashions, techniques and practices are transcending geographical frontiers. For example, professional sport is following international market laws and Americans are playing basketball in Italy or practicing baseball in Japan. Sweden has its own American Football League and Russians come to play hockey in Canada. In traditionally amateur sport, there is a genuine "planetization[24]" of competition. International sport federations are consolidating themselves and multiplying in number; international committes and multi-sport organizations are increasing in strength; and international games as well as world championships are growing in scale.

The universalization of sporting practices is also translated by the gradual disintegration of barriers such as those relative to race, ethnicity, age or handicap. More and more individuals from ethnic or racial minorities are excelling in sports which they could not practice before. High performance sport is not the exclusive privilege of the youth anymore, as age categories are rapidly increasing in number at national and international competitions[25]. Similarly, on a world scale, the wall separating high performance sport and physically or mentally challenged individuals is starting to collapse[26].

To summarize up to now, the postmodern era and the trend toward the dissolution of polarities which characterizes it, have brought an enhanced value on leisure and sporting practices of women as well as a great number of particular groups. Paradoxically, it is the newly found fascination for such practices which is leading them to disappear or, at least, to lose their identity. Indeed, the "male" sport model is absorbing the "female" one, work values are imposed during leisure time, and the ideology of the economical, technological and athletic elite is shaping the sporting practices of the particular groups making up our planetary village. This type of paradox is also present in the postmodern situation of the human entity. As distinctions fade between the self and the body, the body becomes so important that the self attempts to appropriate it.

Body and Self

The self had been lost in the structures of modernity, but it struggles to return in postmodernity. As for the body, it is more and more engulfed in the field of social power. The next paragraphs provide brief examples from epistemology, ideology, technology and semiology, which speak to such subordination of the body to the postmodern apparatus of power.

Epistemologically, the postmodern body moves at the center of subjectivity. The self in touch with the body, the self caring for the body, that is what sport is said to offer. Through sport, the self becomes conscious of the body, the self is embodied, exteriorized. Not only bodily practices, but the body itself becomes a sign of the self. Enhancement of the outside is undertaken in the service of the inside, and the body image becomes not only a symbol of physical health, but of mental health as well[27]. By conveying the idea that spirit can shape matter, postmodernity tends to reduce surface and depth to a relative sameness. The postmodern self is only skin deep.

Ideologically, the "body to excess[28]" becomes the perfect analogue to the general economy of excess structuring postmodern societies[29]. The body is inscribed by the signs of the fashion industry and the arts. Skin itself becomes clothing for the body, and body parts become artistic creations. The body, especially the impossibly ideal athletic body, holds a signal position in the somatic culture as locus for billions of dollars of commercial exchange and a site for moral action[30]. In publicity and marketing, the glorification of the perfect body condemns the natural body to be shattered in parts that are bought, sold, exchanged, replaced, molded, trained and reified. Sports media provide a particularly compelling example of how body parts (*e.g.*, arms of pitchers, legs of runners, feet of soccer players, etc.) undergo alienation and commodification to excess. The orgy of body parts which floods our societies reveals how media present the plastic-fantastic body as a reality, and the natural body as a fraud of the second order[31].

Technologically, the natural body becomes an object superfluous to the operation of a postmodern sport system. The natural body is covered with aerodynamically designed clothes; shaved for speed; locked into ankle, knee, arm, and neck braces; invaded by diuretics, growth hormones, high-calory foods, vitamins, carbohydrates, "pure" blood and multiple drugs; divided in parts to be separately trained and shaped with computerized machines; and divided in pieces that are sometimes thrown away (*e.g.*, plastic surgerie) or replaced by artificial versions (*e.g.*, teflon articulation). The natural body disappears. In modern times, the image was modelled after the human body. In postmodernity, the reverse is true: the human body is modelled after the image. Consequently, the type of body which is glorified is the one that looks inhuman. For example, an athlete recently confided: "You should see my calves since I took up triathloning. People behind me in supermarket checkout lines whisper: 'They must be implants'. It's incredibly gratifying[32]." In postmodern societies, high performance sport is more and more contingent upon computer-revealed genetic potentialities, absorption of chemical substances, and individualized diet and training. Technologically, the reality of the natural body becomes that of "ultra-refuse[33]".

Semiotically, the body constitutes a sign system that is processed through the imperatives of postmodern social power. Mediatization of the body, publicization of the skin, and exteriorization of body organs match a social system that depends on the outering of body functions (we need only to think of walkmans as ablated ears, *in vitro* fertilization as alienation of the womb, or computers as external memory). In our civilization of signs, objects are consumed in their sign form and their meaning is derived from their position in a system of differentiation[34]. In postmodern somatic culture, the body is seen as a sign of the self: it constitutes identity. The body experiences its immersion in nature when it grows old or sick. Nature mercilessly contradicts the human dream of self-mastery, freedom or infinitude. If, as a sign, the athletic body fascinates, it is because it signifies this dream. The perfect body fabricated and glorified by the sport institution and the media symbolizes infinitude and self-mastery: a body that belongs not to nature but to a self. However paradoxical, it is in this vision of a "rational self" controlling bodily existence that enters the computerization, medicalization, and pharmacologization of the athletic body. In such vision, the alienating power of nature is replaced by a power that is not only technical, but which requires the infrastructure of an entire social, economic, and political system[35,36]. In many ways, this corresponds to what Heinilä[37] has described as the nightmare of "totalization".

Ethical and Unethical

Extrapolating the analysis presented so far, the dissolution of the self-body, particular-universal, leisure-work, and male-female polarities are but a few of the multiple dissolutions taking place in postmodern sport. Indeed, one could argue that such a megatrend is reflected in the ethical crisis affecting postmodern societies. The emergence of totalization for instance, means the transformation of political, economical, medical and scientific systems in what Foucault calls a "government of the body[38]". By taking over bodily ethics, this government brings it on shaky grounds. For example, the definition of what is life, death, health, normal, natural, or ethical depends on the political group in power, the economy, technology and medical discoveries. The prolongation of life is questioned in period or recession; the workers' consumption of cafeine, fluoride, aspirin, vitamins, hormones, antibiotics, or synthetic food is considered normal when the goal is increased production; and the rent or sale of one's own organs (*e.g.*, uterus, kidney) is considered ethical when medical science reduces the negative consequences usually associated to these practices.

Such a dissolution of the line separating the ethical from the unethical in the general domain of the body has obvious repercussions in the domain of sport. The same political, economical and medical considerations come into play, justify even, the technological modifications of the body or certain forms of cheating, doping, or violence in sport. The typically postmodern "everything goes" ideology invades sport. For example, athletes can access an increasing number of performance enhancing chemicals and violent incidents are multiplying even in traditionally non-contacts sports.

With regards to the particular problems of violence, cheating and doping in sport, what makes them specifically postmodern is not their existence, since historians have demonstrated their presence in the Games of Antiquity. But *firstly*, it is their epidemic proportions. There is a clear difference between the modern and postmodern periods with respect to the frequency of known incidents of doping, violence and cheating[39,40]. *Secondly*, it is their mediatization: while in pre-modernity the sport institution managed to mask these problems, nowadays they are publicized (in most cases) and even at times used for commercial purposes. *Thirdly*, it is the attitude of tolerance which postmodern citizens have adopted toward them. For example, the number of spectators continues to increase at an important number of sport spectacles, despite the fact that they are more and more violent. Similarly, there have already been a few serious proposals concerning universalization of access to performance enhancing drugs[41], as opposed to universalization of their prohibition. *Fourthly* and finally, it is their recuperation by the government of the body, and the transformation of the ethical discourse which concerns them into a discourse that is commercial, medical, technological and scientific. The result? Problems of violence and injuries in sport, for example, are tackled by granting money to agencies responsible for designing safer equipments. Or, attempts to solve the problems associated to doping in sport are centered on high-tech research regarding detection.

By taking over sport ethics, the government of the body gives legitimacy to the technological and scientific discourse relative to the body as well as to the ideology of a "plastic" somatic culture. This ideology incites the technological transformation of the natural body, which catalyses its disappearance. As for the "plastic" athletic body, its efficiency allows for better performances and records that are crucial to postmodern capitalist societies, where the capacity for consumption of records grows by an arythmetic ratio[42]. In fact, the conspicuous consumption which afflicts postmodern societies weighs on sporting practices and ethics in that professionalization of athletes, violence, drugs, or technological modifications of the body come to be considered as legitimate means of production and overproduction in sport. In that perspective, the natural body disappears and the athletic body is sacrificed for the spectacle, the performance, the record[43].

Conclusion

In this *fin-de-millennium*, high performance sport is witness to the dissolution of several cardinal polarities of experience which existed in modern society. The body-self distinction, for example, is attenuated in the process of constant comparisons with ideal images in the media. The borders between male and female, young and old, amateur and professional, particular and universal founder as well. While some of these dissolutions may be seen as potentially progressive, the general trend toward collapsing oppositions and the "everything goes" ideology associated with it have contributed to the blurring of ethical and unethical practices in sport, and the transformation of the ethical discourse into a commercial, medical and scientific discourse. This has had devastating consequences for the athletes and the sport institution, particularly in terms of their subordination to a totalitarian apparatus of power: the "government of the body". It should be mentioned that the sociological understanding of postmodern sport is not exhausted, but only started by identification of its tendency to dissolve polarities. Nevertheless, such an effort serves to situate what would otherwise be viewed as mere fad or fancy, as a constituent part of the ongoing process of culture production.

REFERENCES

1. Landry F (1985) Les Jeux olympiques et le sport de compétition en tant que système à l'échelle mondiale: coup d'oeil sur les rapports de force. In Szymiczek O (ed) Rapport de la vingt-quatrième session de l'Académie internationale olympique 4-19 juillet 1984. Lausanne: Comité international olympique p 163-75

2. Kavolis V (1970) Post-modern man: psychological responses to social trends. Social Problems 17 435-48

3. Paoletti JT (1985) Art. In Trachtenberg S (ed) The postmodern moment. Westport: Greenwood p 53-80

4. Frampton K (1986) Some reflections on postmodernism and architecture. In Appignanesi L (ed) Postmodernism. London: ICA Documents p 26-29

5. Faurschou G (1987) Fashion and the cultural logic of postmodernity. Canadian Journal of Political and Social Theory 11 68-82

6. Mitchell E (1989) Hands across the sees. Time 134 p 96

7. Hebdige D (1986) Postmodernism and the other side. Journal of Communication Inquiry 10 78-98

8. Zoglin R (1989) TV news goes Hollywood. Time 134 75-76

9. Baudrillard J (1987) Forget Foucault. New York: Semiotext

10. Jameson F (1984) Postmodernism or the cultural logic of late capitalism. New Left Review 146 53-92

11. Lyotard JF (1984) The postmodern condition: a report on knowledge. Minneapolis: University of Minnesota Press

12. Kellner D (1988) Postmodernism as social theory: some challenges and problems. Theory, Culture and Society 5 239-69

13. Birell S, Richter D (1987) Is a diamond forever? Feminist transformations of sport. Women's Studies International Forum 10 395-409

14. Boutilier MA, San Giovanni L (1983) The sporting woman. Champaign: Human Kinetics

15. Hult JS (1989) Women's struggle for governance in US amateur athletics. International Review for the Sociology of Sport 24 249-61

16. Blinde EM (1989) Participation in a male sport model and the value alienation of female intercollegiate athletes. Sociology of Sport Journal 6 36-49

17. Lingis A (1988) Orchids and muscles. In Morgan WJ, Meier KV (eds) Philosophic inquiry in sport. Champaign: Human Kinetics p 125-36

18. Kavolis V (1970) op cit

19. Harris TG, Trotter RJ (1989) Work smarter not harder. Psychology Today (March) 33-38

20. Laguillaumie P (1968) Pour une critique fondamentale du sport. Partisan 43 27-46

21. Beamish R (1988) The political economy of professional sport. In Harvey J, Cantelon H (eds) Not just a game: essays in canadian sport sociology. Ottawa: University of Ottawa Press p 141-57

22. Gruneau R (1988) Modernization or hegemony: two views on sport and social development. In Harvey J, Cantelon H (eds) Not just a game: essays in canadian sport sociology. Ottawa: University of Ottawa Press p 9-32

23. Sport and Leisure Studies Research Group (1988) Workshops for Canada's high performance athletes. Kingston: Queen's University

24. Landry F (1985) op cit

25. McPherson BD (1984) (ed) Sport and aging. The 1984 Olympic Scientific Congress Proceedings. Champaign: Human Kinetics

26. Sherill C (1986) Sport and disabled athletes. The 1984 Olympic Scientific Congress Proceedings. Champaign: Human Kinetics

27. Glassner B (1989) Fitness and the postmodern self. Journal of Health and Social Behavior 30 180-91

28. Kroker A, Kroker M (1987) Theses on the disappearing body in the hyper-modern condition. Canadian Journal of Political and Social Theory 11 p i-xvi

29. Bataille G (1976) Oeuvres complètes. Vol VII. Paris: Gallimard

30. Crawford R (1984) A cultural account of 'health'. In Issues in the political economy of health care. London: Tavistock p 198-214

31. Kuhn A (1985) The power of the image. London: Routledge & Kegan Paul

32. Murphy A (1989) Another view. Sports Illustrated 71 14-16

33. Kroker A, Kroker M (1987) op cit

34. De Wachter F (1988) The symbolism of the healthy body: a philosophical analysis of the sportive imagery of health. In Morgan WJ, Meier KV (eds) Philosophic inquiry in sport. Champaign: Human Kinetics p 119-24

35. Becker MH (1986) The tyranny of health promotion. Public Health Reviews 14 15-25

36. De Wachter F (1988) op cit

37. Heinilä K (1982) The totalization process in international sport. Jyväskylä: University of Jyväskylä

38. Cited in Turner BS (1984) The body and society: explorations in social theory. New York: Blackwell

39. McCallum (1988) Disorder on the court. Sports Illustrated 68 72-76

40. Montville L (1987) Where fouls are fair. Sports Illustrated 67 66-69

41. Brown WM (1980) Ethics, drugs, and sport. Journal of the Philosophy of Sport 7 15-23

42. Turner BS (1984) op cit

43. Crawford R (1984) op cit

Accompanying Activities

Activités complémentaires

Editors' Note

Note des éditeurs

The present section of the Official Report of the Symposium purports to describe a number of accompanying activities provided by the Organizing Committee. An avowed aim was to have the event of the Symposium and its activities serve the needs and interests not only of the scholars, scientists, athletes and sport specialists, but also those of representatives of governments, the media, and the public in general.

In this fashion, the Organizing Committee intended: – to celebrate appropriately the centennial of Pierre de Coubertin's visit to Canada (1889); – to evoke the forthcoming centennial of the historical decision to restore the Olympic Games (1894), and the ensuing centennial of the celebration of the First Olympic Games of the Modern Era (1896); – to bring thoughts to the approaching end of "... this strange century of sport" (François Mauriac); – to associate its efforts to those which are systematically deployed to analyze and illustrate the aims and aspirations of the modern Olympic Movement.

In the pages that follow, descriptions are made: – of an historical feature of the Official Opening Ceremony of the Quebec City Symposium (the interpretation of the **First Delphic Hymn to Apollo**); – of the homage paid by Laval University to the President of the International Olympic Committee for his commitment to the cause and spirit of Olympism, and thus, to coubertinian internationalism (the Honorary Doctorate in Physical Activity Sciences bestowed upon His Excellency **Juan Antonio Samaranch** on May 22, 1990); – of the public lecture on the person, life, and works of Pierre de Coubertin, delivered at the Musée de la civilisation de Québec on May 22, 1990, by **Geoffroy de Navacelle**, a relative of Pierre de Coubertin and currently President of the Pierre de Coubertin International Committee; – of the important public exhibition on Pierre de Coubertin and his educational philosophy, as well as on the historical, technical and artistic aspects of sport and of the Olympic Games (the International exposition *Sport-Olympism* featured at the **Musée de la civilisation de Québec** from May 8 to August 12, 1990); – of the graphic symbol, logo and other memorabilia of the Quebec City Symposium created in the ways and customs of the academic, sporting and olympic circles (the official Commemorative Medallion produced by **Royal Canadian Mint**, and the Fist-day cover bearing a special postal cancellation mark produced by **Canada Post Corporation**).

Note des éditeurs

La présente section du Rapport officiel du Symposium porte sur un certain nombre d'activités complémentaires prévues par le Comité d'organisation. L'objectif visé était celui de voir l'événement et les activités du Symposium servir, au-delà de la population-cible des scientifiques, des athlètes et des spécialistes du sport, les représentants de l'administration publique, du monde journalistique et des media, enfin, le public en général.

De cette manière, le Comité d'organisation entendait non seulement souligner le centenaire de la visite de Pierre de Coubertin au Canada (1889), mais encore: – évoquer l'approche du centenaire de la décision de rénover les Jeux olympiques (1894) et de celui des 1ers Jeux de l'Ère moderne (1896); – faire réfléchir à la fin prochaine de «... cet étrange siècle du sport!» (François Mauriac); – enfin, collaborer aux initiatives d'éducation populaire qui ont cours de par le monde, en vue d'une réflexion élargie sur les aspirations du Mouvement olympique contemporain.

Dans les pages qui suivent, le lecteur trouvera des renseignements sur – un aspect historique du cérémonial de l'Ouverture officielle du Symposium (l'interprétation du **1er Hymne Delphique à Apollon**); – l'hommage rendu par l'Université Laval au président actuel du Comité international olympique pour son dévouement et sa contribution à l'œuvre et à l'esprit olympique et partant, à l'internationalisme coubertinien (le Doctorat honoris causa en Sciences de l'activité physique décerné à Son Excellence **Juan Antonio Samaranch**, le 22 mai 1990); – la conférence publique ayant trait à la personne, à la vie et à l'œuvre de Pierre de Coubertin, conférence prononcée au Musée de la civilisation de Québec le 22 mai 1990 par Monsieur **Geoffroy de Navacelle**, petit-neveu de Pierre de Coubertin et président actuel du Comité international Pierre de Coubertin; – l'importante exposition ayant trait à Pierre de Coubertin, à sa pensée pédagogique, ainsi qu'aux aspects historiques, artistiques et technologiques du sport et du Mouvement olympique (l'Exposition internationale *Sport-Olympisme* tenue au **Musée de la civilisation de Québec**, du 8 mai au 12 août 1990); – enfin, l'utilisation graphique et la description du logo du Symposium de Québec, ainsi que des objets iconographiques et memorabilia créés spécialement pour l'événement historique, le tout dans les traditions des façons de faire qui ont cours, en pareilles occasions, dans les sphères académique, olympique et sportive (le médaillon-souvenir créé par **Monnaie royale canadienne**, et le pli premier-jour avec cachet postal spécial créé par la **Société canadienne des postes**).

Hymn to Apollo

Hymne à Apollon

Editors' Note

Note des éditeurs

The International Symposium held to commemorate the centenary of Coubertin's visit to North America, Canada and Quebec City was open to the sounds of the *Delphic Hymn No. 1 to Apollo*, sung by barytone **Michel Ducharme** accompanied by harpist **Danielle Abel**.

The intent of the Organizing Committee was to bring thoughts back to the 1894 International Congress of Paris staged by Coubertin in view of the revival of the Olympic Games on an international scale. Coubertin had arranged for the official opening ceremony of the Sorbonne Congress to end with the performance of the Delphic Hymn on a music created especially for the occasion by the renowned French composer **Gabriel Fauré**, a first public audition on that very occasion.

It is pointed out that the First and Second Delphic Hymns to Apollo (~138-128 B.C.) had been discovered only very shortly before the Paris Congress, more specifically during the 1893 French archeological explorations near the south wall of the Treasury of the Athenians, at Delphi. Although only incomplete fragments were found, the Delphic hymns nonetheless allowed specialists to decipher the Greek musical notation for voices and instruments.

In 1896, on the occasion of the celebration of the First Olympiad of the Modern Era, Coubertin specifically recalled the opening ceremony of his 1894 Congress with these words:

> [. . .] The opening ceremony which took place with great solemnity on Saturday the 16th of June in front of an audience of nearly two thousand persons, and which was concluded by the playing of the *Hymn to Apollo* gave to the congress its true character. The Olympic Games were being transferred to the first place. [. . .]

Le Symposium international marquant le centenaire de la venue de Coubertin en Amérique du Nord, au Canada et à Québec a été ouvert aux sons de l'*Hymne Delphique No 1 d'Apollon*, chanté par le baryton **Michel Ducharme** accompagné à la harpe par **Danielle Abel**.

L'initiative se voulait un rappel du Congrès International de Paris pour le rétablissement des Jeux olympiques, en 1894, où Pierre de Coubertin avait fait en sorte que la séance solennelle d'ouverture à la Sorbonne se termine par cet hymne sur une musique du compositeur français **Gabriel Fauré**, une première audition à l'époque.

On se souviendra que le Premier et Deuxième Hymne Delphique à Apollon (~ 138-128 av. J.-C.) avaient été découverts peu de temps auparavant, en 1893, lors des fouilles archéologiques françaises à Delphes, près du mur sud du trésor des Athéniens. Bien qu'incomplets, les hymnes de Delphes ont permis aux spécialistes de décoder la notation musicale grecque pour les voix et les instruments.

Rappelant en 1896 à Athènes la séance d'ouverture du Congrès de 1894, Coubertin, philhellène et grand amateur de musique, écrivit à ce propos

> [. . .] La séance d'ouverture qui eut lieu en grande solennité le samedi 16 juin devant un auditoire de deux mille personnes et qui se termina par l'exécution de l'*Hymne à Apollon* donna au Congrès son véritable caractère. Les Jeux olympiques passaient en première place. [. . .]

[École française d'Athènes (1893) Bulletin de correspondance hellénique n° 17.
Paris: Thorin et Fils Pl. XXI bis].

Text of the
First Delphic Hymn
to Apollo

*by an Athenian composer,
possibly Limenios*

Hear me, you who possess deep-wooded Helicon, fair-armed daughters of Zeus the magnificent! Fly to beguile with your accents your brother, golden-tressed Phoebus who, on the twin peak of this rock of Parnassus, escorted by illustrious maidens of Delphi, sets out for the limpid streams of Castalia, traversing, on the Delphic promontory, the prophetic pinnacle.

Behold glorious Attica, nation of the great city which, thanks to the prayers of the Tritonid warrior, occupies a hillside sheltered from all harm. On the holy altars Hephaestos consumes the thighs of young bullocks; mingled with the flames, the Arabian vapour rises towards Olympus. The shrill rustling lotus murmurs its swelling song, and the golden kithara, the sweet-sounding kithara, answers the voice of men.

And all the host of poets, dwellers in Attica, sing your glory, god, famed for playing the kithara, son of great Zeus, beside this snow-crowned peak, o you who reveal to all mortals the eternal and infallible oracles. They sing how you conquered the prophetic tripod guarded by a fierce dragon when, with your darts you pierced the gaudy, tortuously coiling monster, so that, uttering many fearful hisses, the beast expired. They sing too, how the Gallic hordes, in their sacrilegious impiety, when trying to cross... Let us go, son, warlike scion...

Texte du
premier hymne delphique
à Apollon

*par un compositeur athénien,
possiblement Liménios*

Écoutez, vous à qui l'Hélicon aux bois profonds échut en partage, filles, aux beaux bras, de Zeus le magnifique! Accourez pour charmer de vos accents votre frère Phébus, à la chevelure d'or qui, sur la double cime de cette roche du Parnasse, escorté des illustres Delphiennes, s'achemine vers les flots limpides de Castalia, parcourant, sur le promontoire de Delphes, le faîte prophétique.

Voici la glorieuse Attique, la nation à la grande ville, qui, grâce aux prières de la guerrière Tritonide, occupe un col à l'abri de toute atteinte. Sur les saints autels Héphaestos consume les cuisses des jeunes taureaux; mêlée à la flamme, la vapeur d'Arabie s'élève vers l'Olympe. Le lotus au bruissement perçant murmure sa chanson modulante, et la cithare d'or, la cithare au doux son, répond à la voix des hommes.

Et l'essaim tout entier des artistes, habitants de l'Attique, chante ta gloire, dieu célèbre par le jeu de la cithare, fils du grand Zeus, auprès de ce faîte couronné de neiges, ô toi qui révèles à tous les mortels d'éternels, d'infaillibles oracles. Ils disent comment tu conquis le trépied prophétique que gardait un dragon farouche, quand de tes traits tu perças le monstre bariolé aux replis tortueux, tant que la bête, poussant de nombreux, d'effroyables sifflements, finit par expirer. Ils disent aussi comment la horde gauloise, dans son impiété sacrilège, quand elle voulut franchir... Mais allons, fils, rejeton belliqueux...

Reference/référence: Paniagua G. Musique de la Grèce Antique. Atrium Musical de Madrid. Harmonica Mundi, nº 1,015

Honorary Doctorate   Doctorat *honoris causa*

The Organizing Committee wishes to acknowledge the cooperation and support of the University and Executive Council, of Rector **Michel Gervais**, of the Public Relations Department and staff, particularly the Director, Mr. **Jacques Duguay** and Assistant-Director Mrs. **Nicole Toffoli**.

Le comité d'organisation du Symposium tient à exprimer sa reconnaissance au Conseil de l'Université Laval, au recteur **Michel Gervais**, à son Conseil Exécutif, et particulièrement aussi à monsieur **Jacques Duguay**, directeur des Relations publiques et à madame **Nicole Toffoli**, adjointe au directeur, ainsi qu'au personnel du Service des Relations publiques de l'Université Laval, pour leur bienveillante collaboration.

Speech by the President of Laval University

Allocution du Recteur de l'Université Laval

Michel Gervais

Monsieur le Président,
Madame et messieurs les Vice-recteurs,
Monsieur le Secrétaire général,
Madame la Doyenne de la Faculté des sciences de l'éducation,
Madame la Directrice du Département d'éducation physique,
Distingués invités,
Mesdames, Messieurs,

L'événement qui nous réunit aujourd'hui revêt une *portée symbolique* hors du commun.

Il y a cent ans, dans le cadre d'une tournée nord-américaine, Pierre de Coubertin venait ici à Québec pour visiter le Séminaire de Québec et l'Université Laval. Un rêve l'habitait: celui de voir le sport devenir, partout à travers le monde, une voie par excellence d'éducation et de promotion de la personne en même temps qu'un puissant instrument de rapprochement entre les êtres et entre les peuples.

Aujourd'hui, cent ans plus tard, l'Université Laval est heureuse et honorée d'accueillir le témoin par excellence de la réussite du rêve que Pierre de Coubertin était venu lui faire partager et l'un des plus grands artisans de cette réussite, l'actuel président du Comité international olympique.

Excellence, l'université qui vous accueille et qui veut vous honorer aujourd'hui a bien changé depuis la visite du rénovateur des Jeux olympiques. D'un établissement de petite taille n'accueillant qu'un groupe restreint d'étudiants dans les facultés traditionnelles des arts, de la théologie, de la médecine et du droit, la plus ancienne université française d'Amérique est devenue un établissement gigantesque, qui accueille plus de 36 000 étudiants, dont les programmes jouissent d'une excellente réputation à travers le monde comme en témoigne la proportion croissante de ses étudiants étrangers, qui brille par l'importance de ses activités de recherche, notamment dans les domaines scientifiques de pointe, et qui est particulièrement active au plan de la coopération internationale. Le baron de Coubertin n'en croirait pas ses yeux. Lui qui, lors de sa visite, regrettait l'état de sous-développement de l'éducation physique et des sports chez le jeunes Canadiens-français serait particulièrement frappé de constater que le campus de l'Université Laval est le site d'un des plus importants complexes sportifs au Canada, que le sport de compétition et le sport-pour-tous y sont des réalités bien vivantes et que l'enseignement et la recherche dans les domaines de l'éducation physique et des sciences de l'activité physique y ont atteint des niveaux très élevés de qualité.

Mais la cérémonie d'aujourd'hui n'a pas pour but d'évoquer le passé ou de retracer l'évolution des cent dernières années. Nous sommes surtout réunis pour célébrer une réalité éminemment actuelle, celle d'un idéal qui motive les individus et réunit les peuples et d'un mouvement qui est l'un des plus importants mouvements sociaux de notre époque, et pour honorer la personne qui incarne cet idéal et qui préside ce mouvement, son Excellence monsieur Juan Antonio Samaranch.

Plutôt que de retracer, dans un ordre chronologique, la carrière extrêmement brillante et féconde de Juan Antonio Samaranch, j'attirerai l'attention sur certaines dimensions de sa personnalité si riche en l'illustrant par quelques-unes de ses manifestations.

Le président Samaranch est lui-même un sportif. Dès son jeune âge, son père lui a inculqué une véritable passion pour le sport qu'il a pratiqué et pratique toujours avec enthousiasme. Sans doute faut-il voir là une des sources profondes de la motivation qui l'anime et de l'infatigable vitalité qu'il manifeste à la direction du Mouvement olympique. D'ailleurs, on s'explique mal autrement qu'un homme de soixante-neuf ans puisse déployer une telle énergie et répondre aux exigences surhumaines d'une telle tâche : des journées de 15 heures de travail, le poids d'une organisation ayant des assises dans 167 pays, les voyages incessants (depuis son accession à la présidence en 1980, monsieur Samaranch a parcouru plus de 6 millions de kilomètres, soit l'équivalent de 150 fois le tour de la planète).

Le président Samaranch est en outre et initialement, devrais-je dire, un homme d'affaires avisé. Il a dirigé avec succès une entreprise familiale de textile et il est toujours président de La Caixa, la plus importante banque d'épargne d'Espagne. Ses qualités de « manager » se sont avérées d'une importance décisive dans son succès à la présidence du CIO. Notamment, d'une entreprise dont le financement était précaire et dépendait trop exclusivement des droits de la télévision américaine, il a fait une organisation rentable, aux assises financières solides, grâce à l'adoption d'un audacieux plan de « marketing » et de diversification des sources de financement. Le but visé n'était cependant pas la rentabilité pour elle-même, mais plutôt l'acquisition par le CIO de la marge de manœuvre requise pour l'atteinte de ses objectifs.

Ces ressources lui permirent notamment, pour reprendre les termes du président, « d'assurer une plus grande égalité entre tous les membres de la famille, en permettant à chacun d'être présent et de faire entendre sa voix dans les forums olympiques » et de faire en sorte « que le contrôle du sport par le sport reste réel, en lui donnant les moyens de mieux défendre son indépendance et son autonomie ».

Juan Antonio Samaranch est passé, avec une étonnante facilité, du monde des affaires à celui de la diplomatie. En 1977, le roi Juan Carlos le nommait, en effet, Ambassadeur à Moscou avec la mission de normaliser les rapports entre l'Espagne et l'Union soviétique. Il s'acquitta de sa tâche avec brio. On ne s'en étonne pas quand on porte attention aux extraordinaires qualités de diplomate qu'il manifeste depuis son accession à la présidence du CIO : un sens politique aigu, une habileté consommée de négociateur, une capacité sans borne de bâtir des consensus à travers la discussion et le dialogue.

Si l'on juge l'arbre à ses fruits, force est de reconnaître en Juan Antonio Samaranch un des grands de ce siècle. Qu'on en juge par le bilan qu'il traçait lui-même en 1988 de son action à la présidence du CIO en faisant modestement reposer ces résultats positifs sur l'engagement personnel de chacun des membres du Mouvement olympique.

> Beaucoup a été fait en un laps de temps relativement court et dans des conditions extérieures qui furent loin d'être toujours idéales. Pour m'en tenir aux grandes lignes, aux grands principes auxquels nous nous sommes finalement toutes et tous ralliés, permettez-moi de citer pêle-mêle : l'apparition des femmes au sein du CIO ; la prise en charge systématique par le Mouvement olympique d'une représentation minimum de chacun de ses membres aux grandes manifestations olympiques, que ce soient les Jeux eux-mêmes ou les principales réunions olympiques ; l'adaptation nécessaire de nos règles au monde d'aujourd'hui ; la reconnaissance de l'indépendance et de la maturité de chacun des piliers qui forment notre mouvement ; l'apparition indispensable mais contrôlée de la commercialisation ; la prise en compte du nouveau statut de l'athlète de haute compétition et la reconnaissance parallèle des autres formes de sport, comme le sport de masse ou le sport pour tous ; le renforcement et la réaffirmation de notre attitude face à l'apartheid et la convocation pour la première fois d'une réunion spécifique sur ce sujet ; l'association du sport et de l'Olympisme avec d'autres activités humaines comme l'art, la science, la culture, la médecine etc. ; le développement de la Solidarité olympique ; le renforcement de la lutte contre le dopage ; le souci de collaboration avec toutes les organisations gouvernementales ou non qui s'intéressent au sport et la conclusion d'accords de coopération avec elles ; la construction de notre siège à Lausanne et les plans prêts à se réaliser d'un véritable Musée et Centre d'études olympiques.

Et l'on pourrait, aujourd'hui comme alors, ajouter longtemps à cette énumération qui illustre le leadership, le dynamisme, la puissance et l'extraordinaire efficacité du président Samaranch.

Il est toutefois un événement qui a révélé ces qualités mieux qu'aucun autre. Je veux parler des Jeux de Séoul. D'avoir réuni, après trois boycotts successifs des Jeux olympiques, 160 pays — un record ! — dans une capitale avec laquelle 28 nations n'avaient aucune relation diplomatique, et d'en avoir fait un événement rentable (dimension à laquelle les Québécois sont naturellement assez sensibles après l'expérience des Jeux de Montréal), bref, d'avoir fait de Séoul un tel succès tient du prodige.

Mais, par-delà toutes ces merveilleuses réalisations, ce que l'Université Laval veut surtout honorer chez vous, Excellence, c'est l'homme, l'homme attaché à des valeurs fondamentales, celles-là même qui sont à la base du mouvement olympique, qui ont animé Pierre de Coubertin et qui inspirent toujours votre propre action.

Ces valeurs, vous n'avez cessé de les évoquer, de les défendre et de les exalter dans vos innombrables prises de parole. Je me contenterai d'une seule citation, extraite d'une allocution que vous avez prononcée en 1984, à la Sorbonne, en la salle même où se déroula en 1894 la séance d'ouverture du Congrès pour le rétablissement des Jeux olympiques.

> Les Jeux de l'Olympiade et les Jeux d'hiver sont devenus les plus grands rassemblements pacifiques de la planète. Ils ne s'opposent à aucune croyance, à aucun idéal, à aucune activité normale, à aucune conception. Au contraire ! Et c'est là le secret de leur appel. Ils apprennent à chaque participant, à chaque délégation, d'accepter et de comprendre la foi d'autrui, son système de vie, sa civilisation, sa position et ses espoirs, sans aucune discrimination.
>
> À se retrouver ensemble au sein du village olympique, toutes races et nationalités confondues, à se mesurer en joutes loyales, à se dépasser soi-même, à ressentir l'honneur et la responsabilité d'appartenir à l'élite mondiale du sport et de représenter son pays, athlètes et dirigeants acquièrent presque immanquablement

l'esprit olympique. C'est une éthique très simple et pleine de lumière. C'est la célébration de la concorde humaine. La fête olympique devient celle de l'humanité.

Excellence, je vous invite à recevoir votre doctorat «honoris causa» en Sciences de l'activité physique de l'Université Laval, à revêtir l'épitoge et à signer le livre d'or de l'Université.

Speech by the President of the International Olympic Committee

Discours du Président du Comité international olympique

Juan Antonio Samaranch

L'événement qui nous réunit ici aujourd'hui confirme de façon officielle et éclatante l'importance du Mouvement olympique et de l'Olympisme dans cette ville et ce pays qui eurent une grande influence sur le rénovateur des Jeux olympiques, le baron Pierre de Coubertin.

Permettez-moi, Monsieur le recteur, en vous remerciant chaleureusement de cette initiative, de déclarer qu'elle honore le Mouvement olympique tout entier, c'est-à-dire les millions d'hommes et de femmes, dans 167 pays du monde, qui le défendent, l'illustrent et le servent tous les jours au mieux de leurs capacités. En rendant au Mouvement olympique cet hommage, vous démontrez en fait que nous avons sans doute commencé d'atteindre un des buts pour lesquels nous travaillons et luttons, c'est-à-dire de promouvoir le sport, l'éducation physique et la culture comme moyens de communication, de maîtrise de soi et de respect d'autrui. En me décernant cette distinction, vous soulignez l'importance de l'action du Mouvement olympique dans le rapprochement entre les peuples.

Créé en 1894 — nous allons d'ailleurs en célébrer le centenaire dans quelques années — le Mouvement olympique moderne se caractérisait dès ses débuts par sa force conciliatrice, son humanisme et ses objectifs moraux ambitieux. Un des grands soucis de ce grand pédagogue et humaniste qu'était Pierre de Coubertin était de réformer l'éducation de son pays qu'il jugeait désuète et inadaptée aux réalités du monde moderne. L'éducation, selon le fondateur de l'Olympisme moderne doit être une préparation à la vie, et non un entassement de connaissances sans conscience : elle doit être globale et elle ne doit négliger aucun aspect de la personnalité. L'éducation doit donner à la jeunesse le goût de la découverte, le sens des grandes actions en faveur de la société, ainsi que de l'histoire en éternel mouvement. L'éducation, d'après Coubertin, doit aider les jeunes à s'abstraire des difficultés quotidiennes en élevant leur esprit à la hauteur des principes, en s'appuyant sur une force morale et une énergie physique acquises entre autres par la pratique du sport et l'éducation physique. Ceci aiderait à rapprocher les peuples. L'éducation doit aider les hommes et les femmes à reconnaître dans les autres par l'expérience, la confrontation amicale, ce qui est identique pour toute l'humanité, ce que nous partageons tous; admettre comme naturel qu'il existe des différences de constitution, de caractère, de pensée comme il existe des différences de relief, d'hydrographie ou de climat. Le respect mutuel ne s'acquiert que par la connaissance, à la fois intellectuelle, morale et physique de «l'autre». Telle est la mission première de l'éducation.

C'est cette mission que notre fondateur, Pierre de Coubertin, a donnée à notre mouvement. À l'aide d'une discipline librement consentie imposée par la pratique du sport et le respect de ses règles et des Jeux olympiques, il a tenté de faire prendre conscience à la jeunesse du monde entier de son identité de fait, de sa similitude de fonction et de sa convergence d'intérêt en dépit de toutes les différences.

En dépit de tous les problèmes, de toutes les difficultés, de toutes les incompréhensions et de toutes les oppositions, notre devoir à tous, et en particulier celui du Comité international olympique est d'essayer de rendre la vie meilleure sur notre Terre, de la rendre plus paisible, d'essayer d'éduquer les hommes dans un esprit de franche camaraderie et de loyauté mutuelle qui n'exclut pas la compétition à condition que celle-ci se réalise dans un esprit de fair-play. Dans cet effort universel, le Mouvement olympique a joué et n'hésitera jamais à jouer un rôle particulier. De par notre position à l'écart des gouvernements, des philosophies et des religions, nous sommes le point de rencontre idéal de cette nouvelle conception de l'humanité.

Monsieur le recteur, la reconnaissance qu'a voulu nous donner aujourd'hui l'Université Laval, en nous décernant ce prestigieux diplôme, constitue pour nous une reconnaissance du travail accompli et un encouragement à continuer dans notre tâche, avec l'aide et le soutien de tous ceux qui partagent nos idéaux et notre foi en l'homme. Permettez-moi, au nom du Comité international olympique et de tout le Mouvement olympique, de vous remercier pour ce geste qui justifie notre action depuis près d'un siècle.

Les Jeux olympiques ont été rétablis pour l'homme de notre époque, d'où qu'il vienne, quel qu'il soit. La haute opinion que notre fondateur, le baron Pierre de Coubertin, avait à propos du Mouvement olympique doit être un défi pour nous, les adeptes de ses idéaux. Notre devoir est d'être à la hauteur des qualités morales de notre mouvement.

Speech by the Chair of the Physical Education Department of Laval University

Allocution de la Directrice du Département d'éducation physique de l'Université Laval

Michelle Fleury

Excellence,
Monsieur le Recteur,
Madame la Doyenne,
Monsieur le Président du symposium,
Mesdames, Messieurs,

Arnold et Thring ont défini respectivement l'éducation comme une *partie d'échecs* et *comme une œuvre d'observation, de travail et d'amour*.

Votre contribution au monde du sport, Excellence, est teintée de ces deux définitions. Stratège, diplomate et éducateur, vous l'avez été et vous l'êtes toujours. Adhérer à une cause, sans exclure les opposants, est une mission ingrate et difficile que le Département d'éducation physique et l'Université Laval partagent avec vous et dont ils comprennent parfaitement l'ampleur.

Des liens entre les Lettres, les Arts et les Sports, de Coubertin mentionnait en Sorbonne que, dans ce «ménage à trois» subsiste encore un peu de dédain de la part des lettres, un peu de gaucherie de la part des arts et une naturelle timidité de la part des sports. À l'Université Laval, comme dans bien d'autres universités de par le monde, j'ose affirmer qu'existe actuellement un «ménage à quatre», intégrant les sciences. Le doctorat honorifique en Sciences de l'activité physique qui vous est octroyé aujourd'hui, de même que la tenue du symposium sur le passé, le présent et l'avenir du sport, contribuent à estomper la timidité qui pourrait subsister de la part des Sciences de l'activité physique, ainsi que le peu de considération des autres sciences à l'égard du sport comme objet d'études. De Coubertin mentionne que l'université moderne travaille à redevenir ce qu'elle fut en d'autres temps: *une cité intellectuelle autonome*. Et il ajoute: «Nulle part l'esprit de tradition et l'esprit de nouveauté ne se combinent plus volontiers». C'est ce jumelage de la tradition et de la nouveauté que le doctorat en Sciences de l'activité physique qui vous a été conféré, veut exprimer.

Au Comité que dirigeait de Coubertin et où siégeaient les représentants de 42 nationalités sont venus s'ajouter 125 états membres et actuellement, Excellence, vous présidez ce Comité. L'internationalisme progressif dont parlait le Baron est donc d'autant plus tangible aujourd'hui et nous comprenons bien que les conflits que vous devez affronter sont nombreux. Nous vous souhaitons beaucoup de courage et de succès dans cette charge qui ne cesse de s'alourdir. Et de Coubertin qui disait déjà en 1922, «quand j'ai voulu rétablir les Jeux olympiques, on m'a pris pour un fou». La question qui peut nous venir à l'esprit est la suivante: «quels seront les commentaires de ceux qui feront l'analyse des énergies que vous investissez dans l'organisation, le contrôle et l'universalisation des jeux?»

D'une «petite tribune des nations unies», comme le qualifiait Coubertin, le Mouvement olympique est devenu une tribune encore plus importante que les Nations unies, du moins quant aux nombres de représentants. Cet internationalisme fut et demeure le garant de la pérennité du Mouvement olympique. Et si la sportivité d'un peuple est une «plante artificielle et délicate», c'est aussi, comme le propose l'un des objectifs du Symposium que nous vivons actuellement, un droit de l'être humain.

Ce *droit*, notre Université et notre département l'ont à cœur. Nous œuvrons dans ce sens et notre support vous est assuré. Comme de Coubertin le prétendait, les siècles sportifs dans l'Histoire furent brefs et rares. Soyez assuré de notre constant appui pour que le XXIᵉ siècle en soit un.

Le monde de la culture est également un support sur lequel il faut compter. Coubertin, mentionnait en 1919 que l'Institut olympique de Lausanne, toujours préoccupé du progrès de l'éducation, s'attaqua à l'ensemble de la question sportive. Aujourd'hui, le Musée olympique de Lausanne, en collaboration avec le Musée de la civilisation de Québec et le Département d'éducation physique de l'Université Laval, ont marqué de façon tangible leur support à la cause olympique. Et ceci est d'un excellent augure pour autant d'appuis sur lesquels, Excellence, vous pouvez dorénavant compter.

En terminant, permettez-moi, Excellence, de vous réitérer notre gratitude d'avoir été présent aujourd'hui parmi nous.

Pierre de Coubertin: His Life Through Pictures, Ideas and the Written Word

Pierre de Coubertin: sa vie par l'image, l'idée et la plume

Editors' Note   Note des éditeurs

The presentation of Mr. **Geoffroy de Navacelle** on Pierre de Coubertin's life and works took the form of a public lecture at the Musée de la civilisation de Québec. The Organizing Committee had urged Mr. **de Navacelle** to make use of the abundant photographic documents he possesses on his illustrious relative as a result of his own research and publication.

In proceedings such as these, it is unfortunately not feasible to do justice to the excellent pictures and visual materials used by the author throughout his presentation and diaporama, which indeed led participants and guests to a better understanding of the "sympathetic, prophetic, exceptional and above all deeply human person" whom Coubertin was.

The public lecture of Mr. **de Navacelle** hinged upon:

– the aims and itinerary of Pierre de Coubertin's visit to the United States and Canada, in the fall of 1889;

– the places where he lived most of his life, and the familial, educational, social, professional, and cultural environments in which he grew and developed;

– Pierre de Coubertin, the educator;

– Pierre de Coubertin, the historian;

– Pierre de Coubertin, the artist and the promoter of artistic and cultural activities and events;

– Pierre de Coubertin, the impassioned individual and citizen committed to the social and political issues of his time;

– Pierre de Coubertin, the patient and astute tactician and propagandist endowed with strong persuasive powers;

– and, in terms of social and moral consciousness, Pierre de Coubertin as a generous human being, a person who loved life and struggling for the cause of humanism and internationalism, unshakable in his conviction that the Olympic Games ought to be renovated on an international basis and that the Olympic Movement would eventually succeed in this century.

Bearing in mind not only the occasion of the centennial of Coubertin's visit to Quebec City, but also the forthcoming celebration of the first century of existence of the modern Olympic Movement, the Editors have judged it useful to refer the interested persons to some relatively recent publications which bear directly upon the life and

La présentation de monsieur **Geoffroy de Navacelle** sur Pierre de Coubertin a pris la forme d'une Conférence offerte au grand public; elle eut lieu en soirée du 22 mai 1990, au Musée de la civilisation de Québec. Il avait été prévu que la conférence aurait un caractère aussi visuel que possible. A cet effet, l'auteur a puisé dans l'abondante documentation photographique qu'il possède, d'après ses recherches et à sa publication sur la vie et l'œuvre de son illustre parent.

Dans le présent rapport officiel, il n'est malheureusement pas possible de reproduire les excellentes images projetées et qui ont permis aux personnes présentes de mieux saisir encore « ce personnage sympathique, visionnaire exceptionnel et particulièrement humain » que fut Pierre de Coubertin.

La conférence de monsieur **de Navacelle** et son diaporama ont porté, entre autres, sur les sous-thèmes suivants:

– la visite de Pierre de Coubertin aux États-Unis d'Amérique et au Canada, à l'automne de 1889;

– les lieux où il a vécu, et les milieux familial, éducatif, social, professionnel et culturel où il a grandi et s'est développé;

– Pierre de Coubertin comme pédagogue;

– Pierre de Coubertin comme historien;

– Pierre de Coubertin comme artiste et promoteur d'art;

– Pierre de Coubertin comme citoyen passionné et fortement engagé en matière d'affaires sociales et politiques;

– Pierre de Coubertin comme un tacticien rusé et patient et comme un propagandiste doté d'un pouvoir de persuasion étonnant;

– enfin, au plan de la conscience et de l'engagement social, Pierre de Coubertin comme un être humain généreux, aimant la vie, la lutte pour les causes de l'humanisme et l'internationalisme, persuadé en son for intérieur du bien-fondé de sa vocation de rénovateur et d'éclaireur comme aussi de la réussite éventuelle du Mouvement olympique à l'échelle internationale.

Les Éditeurs ont jugé à propos, en raison même de l'événement historique du centenaire de la visite de Coubertin à Québec, et aussi de la célébration prochaine du premier siècle d'existence des Jeux olympiques modernes, de référer les personnes intéressées à des ouvrages publiés

opus of Coubertin as well as to an international organization the purpose of which is in fact the study, analysis and criticism of his ideas, philosophy and realizations:

• De Navacelle G (1986) Pierre de Coubertin, sa vie par l'image. Zürich: Weidmann, 96 p
[Nota: The monograph, written in the french language, contains more than 200 photographs and/or illustrations]

• Müller N, Comité international olympique (eds) Pierre de Coubertin. Textes choisis. Tome I. Révélation. Zürich: Weidmann, 666 p

• Müller N, Comité international olympique (eds) Pierre de Coubertin. Textes choisis. Tome II. Olympisme. Zürich: Weidmann, 760 p

• Müller N, Comité international olympique (eds) Pierre de Coubertin. Textes choisis. Tome III. Pratique sportive. Zürich: Weidmann, 836 p

[Nota: The 3-volume series contains some 3 000 pages of Coubertin's writings in the original text, and not through first or second-hand translations. The texts were carefully selected from an *opus* of more than 20 books, 1 000 essays and some 13 000 pages of texts produced by Coubertin and printed during his lifetime. The series represents a unique collection of primary documentation for scientists and scholars]

• International Pierre de Coubertin Committee
Head Office, P.O. Box 2546, CH-1002, Lausanne, Switzerland

assez récemment et qui portent justement sur la vie et sur l'œuvre écrite de Pierre de Coubertin ainsi qu'à un organisme international dont les objectifs sont l'étude, l'analyse, la critique et la diffusion de la pensée et de l'opus coubertiniens:

• De Navacelle G (1986) Pierre de Coubertin, sa vie par l'image. Zürich: Weidmann, 96 p
[Nota: La monographie comprend plus de 200 photographies et clichés]

• Müller N, Comité international olympique (eds) Pierre de Coubertin. Textes choisis. Tome I. Révélation. Zürich: Weidmann, 666 p

• Müller N, Comité international olympique (eds) Pierre de Coubertin. Textes choisis. Tome II. Olympisme. Zürich: Weidmann, 760 p

• Müller N, Comité international olympique (eds) Pierre de Coubertin. Textes choisis. Tome III. Pratique sportive. Zürich: Weidmann, 836 p

[Nota: La collection de trois volumes contient près de 3 000 pages de textes originaux. Ces derniers ont été choisis par une équipe d'experts à même l'opus de quelque 20 livres, 1 000 articles et essais et 13 000 pages publiées par Coubertin au cours de sa vie. Les textes choisis constituent une source unique de documentation primaire pour toute personne intéressée à lire Coubertin «dans le texte» plutôt que par le truchement de traductions].

• Comité international Pierre de Coubertin
Siège social Case postale 2546, CH-1002 Lausanne, Suisse

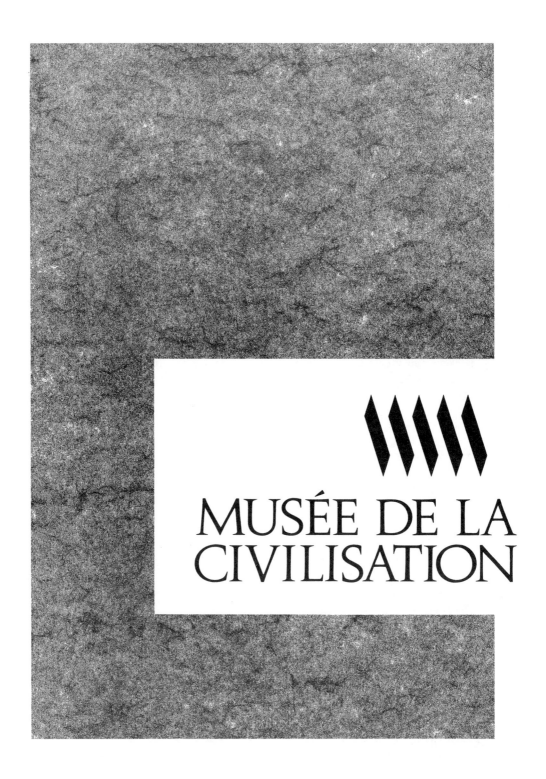

MUSÉE DE LA
CIVILISATION

Editors' Note

Note des éditeurs

The Museum made a most valuable contribution to the cultural objectives of the International Symposium *Sport ... The Third Millennium*, particularly in the area of olympic education for the general public.

The associative program of the Museum was comprised of two main parts: – participation-oriented activities; – an international exposition on the theme *Sport and Olympism*.

A central objective of the first part of the program was to inform the general public on the aims and purposes of Olympism and on the origin and development of the modern Olympic Games. The following were included among the activities scheduled for the general public:

– Sunday, May 6, 1990, meeting **Pierre Harvey** nordic skier and cyclist, the only Canadian athlete to have competed in both the Winter and the Summer Olympic Games in the course of a given Olympiad. The theme of the meeting was *On Becoming a Quebec Athlete of International Caliber: The Two Sides of the Coin*. The interview and discussion was conducted by Quebec City journalist **Jean St-Hilaire**; the public also took part in a free and open discussion period with the athlete.

– During the week of the Symposium, May 21 to 25, a series of film projections highlighting historical and controversial aspects of sport and of the Olympic Games was presented free of charge to the general public: *The Origins of Sport; The Olympic Games and Cultural Exchange; The Olympic Games of Berlin, 1936*, and *The Olympic Games of Mexico, 1968; Pierre de Coubertin and Montreal, 1976; Sport and Economics: The Games of Los Angeles, 1984; The Olympic Games of 1992: Candidatures to become the host city; Sports and Posters.*

– A public lecture on *Pierre de Coubertin: His Life Through Pictures, Ideas and the Written Word* was presented May 22 by **Geoffroy de Navacelle**, a relative of Coubertin and currently President of the International Pierre de Coubertin Committee.

– Production of a video on Pierre de Coubertin. Actor **Paul Hébert** personified the renovator of the Olympic Games. The scene represents Coubertin at age 62, working at his desk. He writes, reads aloud, corrects and reads again the text of his last speech as President of the IOC which he has been heading for 29 years. This particular speech deals with the grandeurs and miseries of sport as well as with the educational and cultural values he believes should be promoted through the Olympic Games. Couber-

Le Musée de la civilisation de Québec a contribué de façon marquante aux visées culturelles du Symposium international *Sport... le troisième millénaire*, tout particulièrement en ce qui a trait à l'information du public et à l'éducation populaire.

Inscrit en marge du Symposium, le programme du Musée comportait – des activités d'animation ; – une exposition internationale proprement dite.

Dans le cas du programme d'animation, l'objectif fut de familiariser le grand public avec les fondements de l'Olympisme et avec l'évolution des Jeux de l'Ère moderne. Au nombre des activités offertes on trouvait :

– Dimanche, le 6 mai 1990, une rencontre avec **Pierre Harvey**, fondeur et cycliste, le seul athlète canadien à avoir participé aux Jeux olympiques d'hiver et aux Jeux d'été, au cours d'une même Olympiade. Le thème de la rencontre : *Devenir athlète québécois de calibre international : l'endroit et l'envers de la médaille*. L'entrevue fut menée par le journaliste **Jean St-Hilaire** et le public a pu converser à loisir avec l'athlète.

– Du 21 au 25 mai, en matinée et pour la durée complète du Symposium, une série de projections de films portant sur les faits saillants et controversés du sport et des Jeux olympiques. Parmi les thèmes abordés se trouvèrent : *Les origines du sport; Les Jeux olympiques, lieux d'échanges culturels; Les Jeux de Berlin, 1936 et Les Jeux de Mexico, 1968; Pierre de Coubertin et Montréal 1976; Sport et économie : les Jeux de Los Angeles, 1984; Les Jeux olympiques de 1992 : les villes candidates; Les affiches et le sport.*

– Une Conférence Grand Public : *Pierre de Coubertin : sa vie par l'image, l'idée et la plume* prononcée en soirée du 22 mai par **Geoffroy De Navacelle**, petit neveu du Baron Pierre de Coubertin et président actuel du Comité international Pierre de Coubertin.

– Production d'un vidéo sur Pierre de Coubertin. L'homme de théâtre **Paul Hébert** personnifiait Pierre de Coubertin. La scène représente Coubertin âgé de 62 ans; assis à sa table, il travaille, lit à haute voix, corrige et relit le texte de son dernier discours en tant que président du Comité international olympique qu'il dirige depuis 29 ans. Ce discours traite des grandeurs et des misères du sport ainsi que des valeurs éducatives et culturelles qu'il souhaite toujours voir proner par le moyen des Jeux olympiques; Coubertin prononça le discours en question quelques

tin delivered the speech a few weeks later, 29 May 1925, at the opening session of the Olympic Congress held at the Prague City Hall.

– At the intention of children who were to visit the international exposition, and also of those of the entire provincial school system, a game-type questionnaire focussing on general knowledge of the Olympic Games and Movement was produced and widely distributed [Reference: *À vos marques, prêts, partez!* (in) Le Musée Amusant, Volume 3, No 3, June 1990, p 6-7, 14-15].

– In addition, on June 16, a 10-kilometer run was staged in the vicinity of the Museum. There were eight categories of participants on the basis of age, sex and fitness levels. Refreshments were served at the Museum, followed by a guided tour of the International Exposition for all those present.

The International Exposition *Sport and Olympism* was the focal point of the Museum's contribution to olympic education. It was open to the general public from May 9 to August 12, 1990. During the Symposium, all participants could visit the Exposition at will. Free access was graciously given to those who wore the Symposium name-badge.

The International Exposition occupied a surface of some 205 square meters. The phenomenon of sport was presented to the public under three main sub-themes:

– the distant origins of sport and its continuing association with the civilization process;

– the revival of the Olympic Games, and the educational aspects of Coubertin's modern Olympic Idea;

– the international aspects of the modern Olympic Games, presented as a forum favoring relations and exchanges between peoples, nations and cultures.

In order to facilitate the association of the three sub-themes, the spatial organization of the exposition was divided into three adjacent zones. In that fashion, the visitor could perceive the continuing presence and importance of sport through the ages, from Antiquity to the 20th century.

Visitors would enter and circulate through the exposition just as an athlete does in a modern stadium. The entire room was given the shape of an oval track on which visitors proceeded from the entrance to the exit; the objects, texts and documents were mounted in sequence, both inside and outside the four-lane track made of genuine material.

The specific topics treated within each zone included the following:

Zone 1

– The origins of sport (pre-historic times; Ancient Greece);

– Sport and art (plastic arts, literary works).

Zone 2

– Pierre de Coubertin and his time (Coubertin, the educator, the sportsman, the reformer), details of his visit and study-

semaines plus tard, le 29 mai 1925, lors de l'ouverture du Congrès olympique à l'Hôtel de Ville de Prague.

– À l'intention des enfants qui allaient visiter l'exposition et aussi de ceux du milieu scolaire à l'échelle du Québec, production et distribution d'un jeu-questionnaire sur les connaissances générales du phénomène olympique [Référence: *À vos marques, prêts, partez!* (dans) Le Musée Amusant, Volume 3, Numéro 3, juin 1990, pp 6-7, 14-15].

– Enfin, le 16 juin, une activité de participation sportive: un 10 kilomètres en périphérie du Musée de la civilisation, avec quatre catégories de participation selon l'âge et le degré d'aptitude physique, pour chacun des deux sexes, le tout suivi de rafraîchissements et d'une visite guidée de l'exposition internationale *Sport et Olympisme*.

L'Exposition internationale *Sport et Olympisme* a constitué, pour sa part, le nœud de la contribution du Musée de la civilisation aux objectifs d'éducation populaire. L'exposition a été ouverte au grand public du 9 mai au 12 août 1990. Les participants et participantes au Symposium ont pu s'y rendre à volonté, le port de la carte d'identité du Symposium servant de titre d'admission.

L'exposition occupait une superficie de quelque 205 mètres carrés. En gros, elle traitait de trois dimensions principales du phénomène du sport:

– ses racines et ses liens avec le processus de civilisation;

– la rénovation des Jeux olympiques et l'importance de la visée éducative de l'œuvre coubertinienne;

– enfin, la dimension internationale des Jeux modernes, vus comme lieu et milieu de relations et d'échanges entre les peuples, les nations et les cultures.

Afin de lier les trois axes proposés, l'organisation spatiale de l'exposition comportait trois grandes zones contiguës. Le visiteur qui y cheminait pouvait saisir la place et l'importance continuelle du phénomène sportif à travers les époques, des civilisations antiques jusqu'à aujourd'hui.

Le visiteur entrait et circulait dans la salle d'exposition comme l'athlète dans un stade contemporain. La salle avait pris forme d'une véritable piste ovale sur laquelle le visiteur cheminait du début à la fin de l'exposition. Les objets, textes et images étaient montés de part et d'autre de cette piste.

Les thèmes traités dans chacune des trois zones furent les suivants:

Première zone

– Les racines du sport (coup d'envoi; préhistoire du sport; la Grèce Antique);

– Le sport et les arts (l'univers plastique; l'univers littéraire).

Deuxième zone

– Pierre de Coubertin et son temps (un milieu fécond; Coubertin éducateur, sportif, réformateur), détails sur sa visite de quelque trente-sept institutions nord-américaines d'enseignement supérieur, à l'automne de 1889;

tour of some thirty-seven North-American institutions of higher learn, in 1889;

– A major and fruitful project (renovation of the Games on an international basis; the celebration of the first Olympiad of the modern era; the Olympic Games as an heritage).

Zone 3

– Sport as a world-wide reality (the Olympic Movement; its actors, its symbols and impact);

– The modern Olympic Games (100 years of celebration; a complex and large-scale organization; the Games of the Olympiad; the Olympic Winter Games; the Games and art; olympic rewards and memorabilia);

– The other side of the coin (truce and boycotts; women and the Olympic Movement; doping, a complex problem; the requirements of modern athletic training);

– The athletes (our first Olympians; star athletes of the Summer and Winter Games; heroes; honor list of all Canadians and Quebecers having participated in the Olympic Games).

The experts of the Musée de la civilisation de Québec had mustered the cooperation and support of the Olympic Museum of Lausanne and of his Director, **Jean-François Pahud**, as well as of a number of institutions and private collectors; the Royal Canadian Mint and Postal Archives, the Canadian Amateur Sports Hall of Fame, the Royal Ontario Museum, and the University Museum, University of Pennsylvania, amongst others.

The Organizing Committee wishes to express its deep gratitude to the Director of the Musée de la civilisation de Québec, **Roland Arpin**, to the Head of International Relations, **Henri Dorion**, as well as to the project director, **Yvan Chouinard** and producers **Lucie Daignault**, **Martin Leblanc** and **Hélène Daneau**, and indeed also to the Public Relations Department and museum staff, for their prompt endorsement of the objectives of the Symposium and for such a concrete and successful contribution to sport appreciation and olympic education at the Quebec, Canadian and international levels.

– Un travail fructueux (les germes de la rénovation des Jeux; la célébration de la première Olympiade moderne; l'héritage).

Troisième zone

– Le sport, un mouvement planétaire (le Mouvement olympique; des symboles éloquents);

– La tenue des Jeux olympiques (cent ans de célébration; une organisation élaborée; les concours d'art; les Jeux d'été; les Jeux d'hiver; relever le défi; les récompenses olympiques);

– L'envers de la médaille (la trève: quelle trève?; la place des femmes; le doping; les exigences de l'entraînement moderne);

– Des athlètes d'ici (nos premiers olympiens; personnalités d'été et d'hiver; des héros en capsules; tableau d'honneur des olympiens et des olympiennes canadiens et québécois).

Les équipes d'experts du Musée de la civilisation de Québec ont demandé et obtenu la collaboration empressée du Musée olympique de Lausanne et de son directeur **Jean-François Pahud**, ainsi que d'un certain nombre de collectionneurs privés et d'institutions canadiennes et américaines, entre autres, le Musée de la Monnaie et les Archives Postales canadiennes, le Canadian Sports Hall of Fame, le Royal Ontario Museum et The University Museum, University of Pennsylvania.

Le Comité d'organisation du Symposium tient à remercier d'une façon très particulière le directeur du Musée de la civilisation de Québec, **Roland Arpin**, le responsable des relations internationales, **Henri Dorion**, ainsi que le chargé du projet, **Yvan Chouinard**, et les réalisateurs **Lucie Daignault**, **Martin Leblanc** et **Hélène Daneau**, enfin, les membres de la direction et du service des Relations publiques du Musée, pour leur bienveillante et efficace collaboration aux visées du Symposium et pour une contribution si concrète et si réussie à l'éducation populaire québécoise, canadienne et internationale.

 Royal Canadian Mint   Monnaie royale canadienne

Editors' Note

Note des éditeurs

Since its very beginnings, and indeed at the initiative of Pierre de Coubertin himself, the modern Olympic Movement has fostered the periodical staging of scientific and cultural activities in association with its events. In the sporting and olympic circles, it has thus been a tradition to produce specific memorabilia of major events and identification objects for the participants.

In the case of events that have a particular historical significance, it is customary to strike a souvenir medallion, which is given to those persons who have participated fully in the program. As concerns the Quebec City International Symposium, Royal Canadian Mint, in cooperation with the Organizing Committee, conceived and struck two collection pieces of high quality:

– a *metallic pin* which was given to every participant at the time of registration. Among those wearing the official pin, the following categories of participants were easily recognizable as follows: plain pin: participants; with *white* ribbon: IOC members; with *green* ribbon, invited speakers; with *blue* ribbon: dignitaries, guests, co-presidents; with *yellow* ribbon: accredited media representatives; with *red* ribbon: members and staff of the Organizing Committee;

– a *souvenir medallion* bearing on the adverse and reverse the components of the Symposium logo and, in letters, the identification of the historical occasion as well as the signature of Pierre de Coubertin, the acknowledged initiator of the modern international Olympic Games.

The numismatic object, finished in toned bronze, was remitted to every registered participant and guest. The medal bearing the special series number #001, gold plated, was bestowed upon His Excellency **Juan Antonio Samaranch** by **Maurice Lafontaine**, President of Royal Canadian Mint, at the issue of the Opening Ceremony of the Symposium, May 21, 1990. The text of the speech which Mr. **Lafontaine** pronounced for the occasion is reproduced hereafter in the two official languages of Canada.

Sincere gratitude is expressed to the President and to the higher administration of Royal Canadian Mint for their generous support. The special cooperation of **Jack Julien**, Vice President, Marketing, of **Michael Francis**, Director of Communications and of **Louise Millette**, Sales Representative, Medals and Refinery, is also acknowledged with thanks.

Le Mouvement olympique inclut depuis ses tous débuts, et par surcroît à l'initiative de son fondateur, Pierre de Coubertin, des activités scientifiques et culturelles périodiques. Il est de tradition que soient produits en ces circonstances des memorabilia de l'événement ainsi que des objets d'identification des participants et des participantes.

Pour les événements qui revêtent un caractère historique particulier, il est également de bonne coutume que soit produit un médaillon-souvenir que l'on remet, à titre de pièce de collection, à ceux et celles qui se sont associés à part entière à l'événement. Dans le cas du Symposium international de Québec, Monnaie royale canadienne, en collaboration avec le Comité d'organisation, a conçu et frappé deux objets de collection soignés:

– une *épinglette métallique*, remise à chaque personne au moment de l'inscription. Les catégories de participants étaient reconnaissables comme suit: épinglette seule: participants(es); à ruban *blanc*, membres du CIO; à ruban *vert*, conférenciers et conférencières sur invitation; à ruban *bleu*, dignitaires, invités(es), co-présidents(es); à ruban *jaune*, représentants des media; à ruban *rouge*, membres et personnel du Comité d'organisation.

– un *médaillon-souvenir* portant à l'avers et au revers les composantes principales du logo officiel du Symposium international de Québec, et, en lettres, l'occasion historique et la signature de Pierre de Coubertin, rénovateur des Jeux olympiques.

L'objet numismatique, en bronze avec fini antique, entièrement poli à la main par les artisans de Monnaie royale canadienne, a été remis à chaque personne dûment inscrite au Symposium. Le médaillon portant le numéro hors-série 001, plaqué or, a été remis à Son Excellence **Juan Antonio Samaranch** par le président de Monnaie royale canadienne à l'issue de la Cérémonie d'ouverture du Symposium, le 21 mai 1990. Le texte de l'allocution prononcée à ce moment par le président **Maurice Lafontaine** est reproduit ci-après dans les deux langues officielles du Canada.

Des remerciements spéciaux sont adressés au président, à la direction ainsi qu'au personnel de Monnaie royale canadienne, entre autres à **Jack Julien**, vice-président du Marketing, et **Michael Francis**, chargé des Communications et à **Louise Millette**, représentante du secteur Médailles et affinerie, pour le rôle particulièrement actif qu'ils ont joué dans le présent dossier.

Speech by the President of the Royal Canadian Mint

Maurice Lafontaine

Excellency;
Ladies and Gentlemen;

It is a great pleasure and an honour for me to join you today representing the Royal Canadian Mint.

As you have heard, the Organizing Committee has called upon us to craft a medallion commemorating this very special anniversary. Mint staff have taken a great deal of pride in this type of project. Indeed, the spirit of Pierre de Coubertin's constant quest for excellence is present in the ethic which drives the Royal Canadian Mint in its endeavours.

One of Coubertin's maxims, in particular —"Success is not a goal in itself but a means to aim even higher"—is of special significance to the Mint and to our people. It is, in our case, particularly appropriate since it appeared as a legend on the medal that was created to celebrate the 100th anniversary, in 1963, of de Coubertin's birth.

The Royal Canadian Mint is not new to the coin and medal business. In fact, our history dates back almost as far as de Coubertin's modern day Olympic Games, to 1908. In recent years we have had the privilege of creating commemorative olympic coin sets for the 1976 Montreal Olympic Games, and the 1988 Calgary winter Games. As well, the athletes' medals for the Montreal Games were a creation of our engraving and medals staff. Samples of these are on display at our exhibit in the hall as well as a unique collection of coins relating to Pierre de Coubertin.

The Mint has enjoyed great success with these programs in the past, yet de Coubertin's credo continues to apply to us, more than ever – Our success gave us the occasion to aim even higher!

Ladies and gentlemen, Dr Landry has already unveiled the photographs of the most recent endeavour of our engraving and medals staff, the commemorative medal for this Symposium. It now gives me great pleasure to present the first medallion of gold to a person who, beyond having a broad and distinguished background, is known by most people around the world as a brilliant propagandist of Olympism—His Excellency Juan Antonio Samaranch.

Allocution du Président de Monnaie royale canadienne

Maurice Lafontaine

Excellence,
Mesdames et Messieurs,

C'est un plaisir et un honneur pour moi de me trouver parmi vous aujourd'hui et de représenter Monnaie royale canadienne.

Comme vous le savez sans doute déjà, le Comité d'organisation du Symposium a fait appel à nous pour frapper un médaillon commémorant cet anniversaire très spécial. Monnaie royale canadienne éprouve de la fierté à réaliser de tels projets; en fait, l'esprit qui nous anime dans ce genre d'entreprise s'inspire de l'idéal olympique de Pierre de Coubertin.

Il est une maxime du célèbre rénovateur que notre équipe a fait sienne: «Le succès n'est pas un but en soi mais un moyen de viser toujours plus haut». Elle est d'ailleurs celle qui ornait la médaille créée en 1963 par la Fonderie d'art de Coubertin pour célébrer le centenaire de sa naissance.

Ce n'est pas d'hier que Monnaie royale canadienne fabrique des pièces de monnaie et des médailles. Son histoire remonte à presque aussi loin que celle des Jeux olympiques modernes, soit à 1908. Pour parler de nos réalisations récentes, nous avons eu le privilège de créer des ensembles de pièces olympiques commémoratives à l'occasion des Jeux de Montréal en 1976, puis à ceux d'hiver de Calgary en 1988. Les graveurs et le personnel de notre Service des médailles ont aussi conçu et produit les médailles qui ont été remises aux athlètes lors des Jeux olympiques de Montréal en 1976. Des exemplaires de ces médailles sont exposés ici-même dans le hall, avec une collection unique de pièces ayant pour thème Pierre de Coubertin.

Monnaie royale canadienne a connu beaucoup de succès avec ces programmes dans le passé; et le credo de Pierre de Coubertin s'applique à nous aujourd'hui, et encore plus que jamais: notre succès nous a fourni l'occasion de viser toujours plus haut.

Mesdames, Messieurs, Dr. Landry a déjà dévoilé les photographies de la plus récente réalisation de nos Services, le médaillon commémoratif du Symposium. J'ai maintenant le grand honneur de présenter le tout premier médaillon-or à une personne qui, en plus d'antécédents aussi brillants que diversifiés, est connu partout dans le monde comme un inlassable propagandiste de l'Olympisme, Son Excellence Juan Antonio Samaranch.

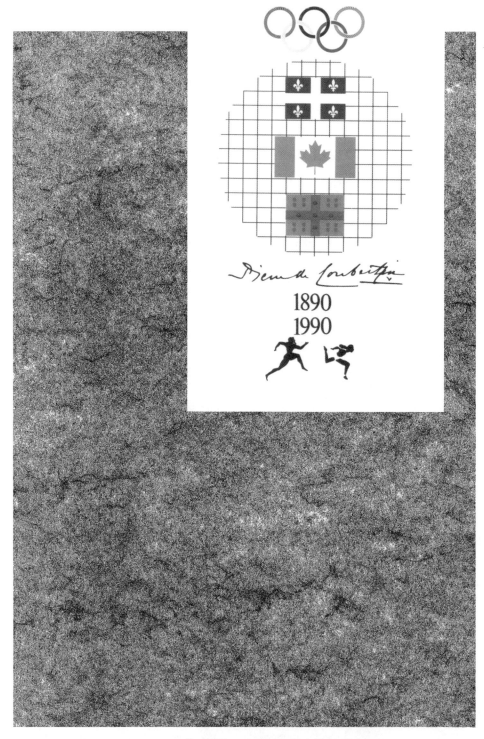

Conception graphique: Jean-Pierre Labeau.
Texte: Exécutif du Comité d'organisaiton.

The Symposium Logo

THE CIRCLE

represents both the world and unity of the Federation-based and olympic sports movement and its globalization. The circular line is absent, alluding to the continuing development of the sporting phenomenon.

THE GRID

the background contains 166 squares representing current membership in the olympic family with the Canadian flag symbolizing the 167th National Olympic Committee. The squares have equal areas to indicate the identity in principle of NOC mandates as well as the efforts aiming at international coherence in executing them.

THE FLAG

of Canada, Quebec, and l'Université Laval pinpoint, among the places and institutions in North America visited by Coubertin a century ago, the site of the International Symposium: *Sport . . . The Third Millennium.*

THE SIGNATURE

of Pierre de Coubertin, the dates "1890-1990", and the olympic symbol, by vertically framing the heart of the Symposium's distinctive logo, allude to the historical role of the renovator of the Olympic Games, the centennial of his visit to Canada and, finally, the International Olympic Committee's leadership in the globalization of sports.

FINALLY . . . THE ATHLETES

one from Ancient Greece and the other from the 20th century, both running in the same direction, symbolize the perennial quest for excellence and transcendence as well as the question of their potential directions.

Logo du Symposium

LE CERCLE

représente à la fois l'universalisation et l'unité du mouvement sportif fédéré et olympique. La ligne circulaire est absente, une allusion à l'expansion continue du phénomène.

LE QUADRILLÉ

de fond comporte 166 cases représentant les membres actuels du rassemblement olympique, le drapeau du Canada symbolisant le 167e Comité national olympique. Les surfaces équivalentes des carreaux soulignent l'identité de principe des mandats des organismes de régie du sport, ainsi que les efforts de cohésion internationale dans l'exécution de ces derniers.

LES DRAPEAUX

du Canada, du Québec et de l'Université Laval identifient, parmi les lieux et les institutions visités en Amérique du Nord par Coubertin il y a un siècle, la scène du Symposium international: *Sport . . . Le troisième millénaire.*

LA SIGNATURE

de Pierre de Coubertin, les dates « 1890-1990 », et le symbole olympique, en encadrant à la verticale le coeur du signe distinctif du Symposium, rappellent le rôle historique du rénovateur des Jeux olympiques, le centenaire même de sa visite au Canada, enfin, le leadership du Comité international olympique dans le processus d'universalisation du sport.

ENFIN . . . LES ATHLÈTES

celui de la Grèce antique et celui du XXe siècle symbolisent, en courant tous deux dans la même direction, la quête pérenne de l'excellence et du dépassement ainsi que la question de leurs destins possibles.

POSTE MAIL

Société canadienne des postes ╱ Canada Post Corporation

Editors' Note

Note des éditeurs

Canada Post Corporation, in cooperation with the Organizing Committee, produced a special occasion envelope for all participants and guests. The philatelic object bears on its front the logo of the Quebec City International Symposium as well as a cancellation mark commemorating the site and dates of the event. A full description of the logo is given at the back of the envelope in the two official languages of Canada.

The 50¢ CAN stamp affixed on each envelope was chosen from the series on Masterpieces of Canadian Art. It depicts *"The West Wind"* painted in 1917 by the celebrated artist Tom Thomson.

With respect to the translation of culture, there are indeed many who consider the modern olympic phenomenon as illustrating, first and foremost "western" values or standards. From an historical standpoint, some take this state of affairs for granted whilst others see and criticize hegemonic tendencies in the movement.

In that perspective, Canada Post Corporation and the Organizing Committee chose not only to contribute to international sport philately, but at one and the same time to bring the thoughts on the paradoxes between professed universalism, on the one hand, and continuing cultural imprinting from the "West", on the other.

The Organizing Committee wishes to express its special gratitude to the higher administration of Canada Post Corporation, particularly to **Donald B.R. Murphy**, Director of Special Events, Exhibits and Corporate Identity, Ottawa, as well as to **André Villeneuve**, General Director, and to **Gilles R. Drolet**, Director of Sales and Services, Quebec Division.

La Société canadienne des postes, en collaboration avec le Comité d'organisation, a bien voulu produire à titre gracieux et à l'intention de tous les participants et participantes du Symposium de Québec une enveloppe de type pli premier-jour. L'objet philatélique porte à sa partie antérieure le logo du Symposium international de Québec ainsi qu'un cachet spécial d'oblitération commémorant le site et les dates et l'événement. La signification des composantes du logo est décrite au dos de l'enveloppe dans les deux langues officielles du Canada.

Le timbre de 50¢ CAN apposé à chaque enveloppe a aussi été choisi pour l'occasion. Il s'agit en l'occurrence du timbre de la série «Art Canada» qui représente, en reproduction-couleur miniaturisée, l'œuvre du célèbre peintre canadien Tom Thomson *«Le Vent d'Ouest»* (1917).

Or, l'on sait qu'au plan de l'illustration et de la transmission des valeurs culturelles, le phénomène olympique moderne est vu ou qualifié par un bon nombre comme de nature et à visées avant-tout *«occidentales»*. Sous l'aspect historique, certains tiennent cet état de choses pour acquis cependant que d'autres, aux plans de la conception de l'être humain, de la société et de la culture, voient et critiquent des formes d'hégémonie dans l'ensemble du mouvement.

C'est dans cette perspective que la Société canadienne des postes et le Comité d'organisation ont choisi de contribuer au patrimoine de la philatélie sportive mondiale, et du même coup d'évoquer l'image de flux et de reflux persistant autour de l'imprinting culturel occidental et d'un internationalisme nouveau et en principe désintéressé.

Le Comité d'organisation tient à exprimer sa gratitude à la haute direction de la Société canadienne des postes, entre autres à **Donald B.R. Murphy**, Directeur des Événements marquants, expositions et identité générale, Ottawa, ainsi qu'à mssieurs **André Villeneuve** et **Gilles R. Drolet**, respectivement Directeur général de la Division de Québec, et Directeur des ventes et des services, Québec.

Authors and Symposium Administration

Auteurs et administration générale du Symposium

Subject index   Index des matières*

---

* Les mots-clef des textes présentés en *français* ont été traduits en *anglais* et paraissent sous cette forme à l'index des matières.

Participants   *Les participants*

Aguilar Franco Javier
Proyecto Deporte Para Todos
Villa deportiva Nacional
Av del Aire s/n Casilla postal 41-0034
Lima 41
PERU

Alaphilippe François
Centre de droit et d'économie du sport
Faculté de droit et des sciences
économiques
4, Place du Présidial
87031 Limoges Cedex
FRANCE

Alexandrakis Ambrose
1387 North Cleveland Ave
St. Paul MN 55108
USA

Allard Raymond
Régie de la sécurité dans les sports
du Québec
100 Laviolette
Trois-Rivières QC G9A 5S9
CANADA

Allison Gary
1st Century Project
1300 North Alexandria Ave
Los Angeles CA 90027
USA

Anthony Don WJ
Itinerant School for Sports Leaders
IOC Olympic Solidarity
15 Elm road
Sidcup Kent DA14 6AF
GREAT BRITAIN

Apostolopoulos Yiorgos
181-C Foster Drive
Williamantic CT 06226
USA

Arpin Roland
Directeur Général
Musée de la civilisation de Québec
85 rue Dalhousie
Québec QC G1K 7A6
CANADA

Asselin Marie-Claude
105-936 des Prairies
Québec QC G1K 8T2
CANADA

Auclair Renée-Claude
7140 ave Ouellet
Charlesbourg QC G1H 5Y1
CANADA

Bambuck Roger
Secrétaire d'État
Ministère de l'éducation nationale
Jeunesse et Sports
110 rue de Grenelle
75700 Paris
FRANCE

Bani Lorenzo
c/o UISP
Largo Nino Franchelluci 73
00155 Roma
ITALY

Bard Chantal
Laboratoire de performance motrice
humaine
Département d'éducation physique
Université Laval
Ste-Foy QC G1K 7P4
CANADA

Barney Robert K
Centre for Olympic Studies
University of Western Ontario
London ON N6A 3K7
CANADA

Barr John M
Director
Corporate Sponsorships & Events
Communications & Public Affairs
Eastman Kodak Company
343 State Street
Rochester NY 14650
USA

Beauregard Gaston
Senior Vice President
Eastern Region
Petro-Canada
PO Box 2844
Calgary AL T2P 3E3
CANADA

Beckhouse Lawrence S
College of William and Mary
107 Harbin Court
Williamsburg VA 23185
USA

Bédard Michel
Directeur
Condition physique Canada
Gouvernement du Canada
365 ave Laurier Ouest
Ottawa ON K1A 0X6
CANADA

Bedecki Thomas
Executive Director
Canadian Association for Health
Physical Education and Recreation
1600 Naismith Drive
Gloucester ON K1B 5N4
CANADA

Benjelloun Hadj Mohamed
Membre du CIO
2 rue des Cols-Bleus
Casablanca
MAROC

Bennett John H
Senior Vice-President
VISA USA Inc
PO Box 8999
San Francisco CA 94128
USA

Bernier Sylvie
Petro-Canada Olympic Scholarship Fund
Olympic Scholarship Fund
c/o Christopher Lang and Associates
2 Bloor Street West
Toronto ON M4W 3E2
CANADA

Bérubé Gilles
Département d'éducation physique
Université Laval
Ste-Foy QC G1K 7P4
CANADA

Bigras Guy
Régie de la sécurité dans les sports
du Québec
100 Laviolette
Trois-Rivières QC G9A 5S9
CANADA

Boileau Roger
Département d'éducation physique
Université Laval
Ste-Foy QC G1K 7P4
CANADA

Bonneau Michel M
Directeur
Extension de l'enseignememt
Université Laval
Ste-Foy QC G1K 7P4
CANADA

Borg Vincent
Ontario Olympic Secretariat
5320 Whitney Block
99 Wellesley Street West
Toronto ON M7A 1W3
CANADA

Bouchard Claude
Laboratoire des sciences de l'activité
physique
Département d'éducation physique
Université Laval
Ste-Foy QC G1K 7P4
CANADA

Boucher Gaétan
Bureau Laitier du Canada
1981 ave McGill College
Montréal QC H3A 2X9
CANADA

Boulongne Yves-Pierre
UFR Communication et insertion dans
la société
Université Paris Val de Marne
200 avenue du Général de Gaulle
94010 Creteil Cedex
FRANCE

Boulonne Gérard
Chef de division/Sports
Ville de Montréal
415 Ouimet
Montréal QC H4L 3N6
CANADA

Boutilier Mary
Department of Political Science
Seton Hall University
South Orange NJ 07079
USA

Bradley Jim
Manager Sport Technical Section
Ministry of Tourism and Recreation
77 Bloor Street West
Toronto ON M7A 3R9
CANADA

Brand William W
Vice President
Marketing & Development
Petro-Canada
PO Box 2844
Calgary AL T2P 3E3
CANADA

Brodeur Jacques
9587 Martigny
Québec QC G2B 2M6
CANADA

Brownell Susan E
Department of Sociology/Anthropology
Middlebury College
Middlebury VT 05753
USA

Buist André
Régie de la sécurité dans les sports
du Québec
100 Laviolette
Trois-Rivières QC G9A 5S9
CANADA

Caissie Alphonse A
École d'éducation physique et de loisirs
Université de Moncton
Moncton NB E1A 3E9
CANADA

Callaghan John
Director
Sports Studies Program
University of Southern California
725 W 27th Street
Los Angeles CA 90007
USA

Cantelon Hart
Graduate Coordinator
School of Physical and Health Education
Queen's University
Kingston ON K7L 3N6
CANADA

Carrard François
Directeur général
Comité international olympique
Château de Vidy
Ch-1007 Lausanne
SUISSE

Chalip Laurence
Department of Kinesiology
HLHP Building, room 2351
University of Maryland
College Park MD 20742
USA

Choi Soo Ho
42-70 79th Street
Elmherst NY 11373
USA

Chouinard Richard
Département d'éducation physique
Université Laval
Ste-Foy QC G1K 7P4
CANADA

Chouinard Yvan
Musée de la civilisation de Québec
85 rue Dalhousie
Québec QC G1K 7A6
CANADA

Chu Charles Fook-wing
Recreation Management
Hong Kong Sports Development Board
10/F Harbour Centre
25 Harbour Road
Wan Chai
HONG KONG

Collins Michael F
Director
Institute of Sport & Recreation Planning
& Management
Department of Physical Education
& Sports Science
Loughborough University of Technology
Loughborough Leicestershire LE11 3TU
GREAT BRITAIN

Comte-Offenbach Pierre†
Président
Comité Pierre de Coubertin France
23 rue D'Anjou
75008 Paris
FRANCE

Couturier Hermel
École d'éducation physique et de loisirs
Université de Moncton
Moncton NB E1A 3E9
CANADA

Crosswhite Perry
Executive Director
Australian Sports Commission
Leverrier Crescent
Bruce Act
Belconnen Act 2616
AUSTRALIA

Crowell Lee
Executive Director
Canadian Olympic Association
2380 ave Pierre Dupuy
Montreal QC H3C 3R4
CANADA

Daignault Lucie
Musée de la civilisation de Québec
85 rue Dalhousie
Québec QC G1K 7A6
CANADA

D'Amboise Gilles
Directeur
Services des activités sportives
Université Laval
Ste-Foy QC G1K 7P4
CANADA

Danis Marcel
Ministre d'État a la jeunesse et
ministre d'État à la condition physique
et au sport amateur
Gouvernement du Canada
Place du Portage
Hull QC K1A 0J9
CANADA

Davenport Joanna
Department of Health and Human
Performance
Auburn University
2050 Joel H Eaves
Auburn AL 36849
USA

Defrantz Anita
Member of the IOC
President
Amateur Athletic Foundation of Los Angeles
2141 West Adams Blvd
Los Angeles CA 90018
USA

de La Sablonnière Marcel SJ
Président directeur général
Centre Immaculée Conception
4265 Papineau
Montréal QC H2H 1T3
CANADA

Delpy Lisa
805 Wellesley Dr. NE
Albuquerque NM 87106
USA

De Koninck Jean-Marie
Département de mathématiques
et de statistiques
Université Laval
Ste-Foy QC G1K 7P4
CANADA

de Moragas i Spà Miquel
Director
Centre d'Estudis Olimpics
Universitat Autonoma de Barcelona
08193 Bellaterra
Barcelona
ESPAGNE

de Navacelle Geoffroy
Président
Comité international Pierre de Coubertin
60 rue de Montreuil
Versailles 78000
FRANCE

De Wachter Frans
Institut de Philosophie
Université Catholique de Louvain
Kardinaal Mercierplein 2
B-3000 Louvain
BELGIQUE

D'Hellier Florence
89 rue St-Martin
Caen 14000
FRANCE

Diarra Lassina
150 Boulevard St-Cyrille est
Québec QC G1R 4Y3
CANADA

Dickson David
Director of sports
Melbourne Olympic Candidature 1996
Old Treasury Building
Spring Street
Melbourne
Victoria 3000
AUSTRALIA

Dion Yves
Président Conseil des athlètes
Association olympique canadienne
2380 ave Pierre Dupuy
Montréal QC H3C 3R4
CANADA

Dior Diouf Marie Henriette
Centre national d'éducation populaire
et sportive
BP 191
Thiès
SÉNÉGAL

Dohrmann Ruediger
Proyecto Deporte Para Todos
Villa deportiva Nacional
Av del Aire s/n Casilla postal 41-0034
Lima 41
PERU

Donnelly Peter
School of Physical Education and Athletics
McMaster University
1280 Main Street West
Hamilton ON L8S 4K1
CANADA

Dorion Henri
Directeur de la recherche
Musée de la civilisation de Québec
85 rue Dalhousie
Québec QC G1K 7A6
CANADA

Doucet Hubert
Faculté de théologie
Université Saint-Paul
223 Main
Ottawa ON K1S 1C4
CANADA

Doyle Marie-France
745 du Château 24
Ste-Foy QC G1X 3P4
CANADA

Doyon Jean
2100 B Chemin Ste-Foy 3
Ste-Foy QC G1V 1R6
CANADA

Driega Alexander
848 Thorndale Drive
Ottawa ON K1V 6Y3
CANADA

Drolet Gilles R
Directeur ventes et service
Société canadienne des postes
1305 chemin Ste-Foy
Québec QC G1S 2A0
CANADA

Duchesne Denis
16375 Bourdages Sud
St-Hyacinthe QC J2T 3R4
CANADA

Duerkop Diana
Vice President
Canadian Olympic Association
2380 ave Pierre Dupuy
Montreal QC H3C 3R4
CANADA

Duffin Megan
National Coalition on Television Violence
PO Box 2157
Champaign IL 61820
USA

Dugal Robert
Institut national de la recherche
scientifique-santé
Université du Québec
245 boulevard Hymus
Pointe-Claire QC H9R 1G6
CANADA

Duplessis Suzanne
Députée de Louis-Hébert
Gouvernement du Canada
2406 des Quatre-Bourgeois
Ste-Foy QC G1V 1W5
CANADA

Duval Johanne
3014 chemin St-Louis
Ste-Foy QC G1W 1R2
CANADA

Echard Denis
Rédacteur de la Revue Olympique
Comité international olympique
Château de Vidy
Ch-1007 Lausanne
SUISSE

El Farnawani Mahmoud
a/s Toronto Ontario Olympic Council
707 Queen's Quay west
Toronto ON M5J 1A7
CANADA

Erraïs Borhane
UFR-STAPS
Université de Franche-Comté
25030 Besançon
FRANCE

Escobar F Patrick
Vice President Communications
Amateur Athletic Foundation of Los Angeles
2141 West Adams Blvd
Los Angeles CA 90018
USA

Ethier Ghislaine
99 Bellerive
L'Annonciation QC J0T 1T0
CANADA

Fernandez Luis
Laboratoire de psychologie
Institut national du sport et de
l'éducation physique
74 ave du Marronnier
Favières 77 220
FRANCE

Fleury Michelle
Laboratoire de performance
motrice humaine
Département d'éducation physique
Université Laval
Ste-Foy QC G1K 7P4
CANADA

Fost Norman C
Department of Pediatrics
Medical School
University of Wisconsin
H4/442 Clinical Science Center
600 Highland Avenue
Madison WI 53792
USA

Foster Mary E
Ontario Commission on Interuniversity
Athletics
130 St. George Street
Toronto ON M5S 2T4
CANADA

Foulkes Robert
Vice President Public Affairs
Petro-Canada
PO Box 2844
Calgary AL T2P 3E3
CANADA

Fowler Bill
School of Physical Education and Athletics
McMaster University
1280 Main Street West
Hamilton ON L8S 4K1
CANADA

Francis Michael
Chargé des communications
Monnaie royale canadienne
320 promenade Sussex
Ottawa ON K1A 0G8
CANADA

Freeman William
Department of Physical Education
and Sport Management
Campbell University
Buies Creek NC 27506
USA

Gagnon Jean-Pierre
Directeur
Module Sciences de l'activité physique
Université du Québec à Chicoutimi
555 Boulevard de l'Université
Chicoutimi QC G7H 2W7
CANADA

Galtung Johan (NOR)
College of Social Sciences
University of Hawaii
Honolulu HA 96822
USA

Gandee Robert
University of Akron
580 Northwood Drive
Akron OH 44313
USA

Garger Elizabeth
ISL Marketing USA Inc
645 5th ave
New York NY 10022
USA

Gaudet Eugène
École d'éducation physique et de loisirs
Université de Moncton
Moncton NB E1A 3E9
CANADA

Gebauer Gunter
Institut für Sportwissenschaft
Freie Universität Berlin
Rheinbabenallee 14
1000 Berlin 33
FEDERAL REPUBLIC OF GERMANY

Gervais Michel
Recteur
Université Laval
Ste-Foy QC G1K 7P4
CANADA

Glassford R Gerald
Dean
Faculty of Physical Education
and Recreation
University of Alberta
Edmonton AL T6G 2H9
CANADA

Glen-Haig Mary Alison
Member of the IOC
66 North End House
Fitzjames ave
London W14 0RX
GREAT BRITAIN

Goulet Claude
Régie de la sécurité dans les sports
du Québec
100 Laviolette
Trois-Rivières QC G9A 5S9
CANADA

Goyette Bernard
Directeur
Service des sports
Université de Montréal
Montréal QC H3C 3J7
CANADA

Granskog Jane
Department of Sociology/Anthropology
California State University
9001 Stockdale Highway
Bakersfield CA 93311
USA

Gravel Yves
Association de natation Région de Québec
1050 Louis Hébert
Cap-Rouge QC G1Y 3C6
CANADA

Grenier Jean
Secrétaire/trésorier
Association olympique canadienne
2380 ave Pierre Dupuy
Montréal QC H3C 3R4
CANADA

Gruneau Richard
Department of Communication
Simon Fraser University
Burnaby BC V5A 1S6
CANADA

Grupe Ommo
Institut für Sportwissenschaft
Universität Tübingen
Wilhemstrasse 124
7400 Tübingen 1
FEDERAL REPUBLIC OF GERMANY

Hanley Elizabeth
Department of Exercise & Sport Science
Pennsylvania State University
105-E White Building
University Park PA 16802
USA

Harvey Pierre
123 du Marais
St-Féréol-des-Neiges QC G0A 3R0
CANADA

Hébert Daniel
Services aux étudiants
Université de Montréal
Montréal QC H3C 3J7
CANADA

Heine Michael
Faculty of Physical Education
University of Alberta
Edmonton AL T6G 2J9
CANADA

Heinemann Klaus
Institut für Soziologie
Universität Hamburg
Allende-Platz 1
D 2000 Hamburg
FEDERAL REPUBLIC OF GERMANY

Henderson Paul F
President and Chief Executive Officer
Candidature Committee
Toronto Ontario Olympic Council
707 Queen's Quay West
Toronto ON M5J 1A7
CANADA

Hendren Gordon
Senior Vice-President
Christopher Lang and Associates
2 Bloor Street West
Toronto ON M4W 3E2
CANADA

Hérisset Jacques
Club de tennis Avantage
1080 rue Bouvier
Québec QC G2K 1L9
CANADA

Hillmer Ann
Relations internationales, sports
et Jeux olympiques
Affaires extérieures Canada
Édifice LB Pearson
125 promenade Sussex
Ottawa ON K1A 0G2
CANADA

Hite Gary
Vice President International Sports
Coca-Cola Plaza
PO Drawer 1734
Atlanta GA 30301
USA

Hindmarch Robert G
Vice President
Association olympique canadienne
2380 ave Pierre Dupuy
Montréal QC H3C 3R4
CANADA

Hoberman John
Department of Germanic Languages
University of Texas
Austin TX 78712
USA

Hoffman Abby
Director General
Sport Canada
Government of Canada
365 Laurier ave West
Ottawa ON K1A 0X6
CANADA

Hrycaiko Dennis
Faculty of Physical Education
and Recreation Studies
University of Manitoba
Winnipeg MA R3T 2N2
CANADA

Hynes Mary
Canadian Broadcasting Corporation
365 Church Street
Toronto ON M5B 1Z9
CANADA

Inschauspé Annie
Comité international olympique
Château de Vidy
CH-1007 Lausanne
SUISSE

Isava-Fonseca Flor
Member of the IOC
Quinta Shangri-La
Avenida Principal
Country Club
Caracas 1060
VENEZUELA

Jacques Claude
Polyvalente des Appalaches
135 boulevard Lessard
Ste-Justine QC G0R 1Y0
CANADA

Janzen Henry
Faculty of Physical Education
University of Manitoba
Winnipeg MA R3T 2N2
CANADA

Jeu Bernard†
Faculté de philosophie
Université de Lille III
Lille
FRANCE

Joannisse Robert
Faculté des sciences de l'éducation
Université de Genève
CH-1211 Genève 4
SUISSE

Joblin Douglas
Department of religious studies
Huntington College
116 McNaughton Street
Sudbury ON P3E 1V1
CANADA

Jobling Ian F
Department of Human Movement Studies
The University of Queensland
St Lucia Brisbane
Queensland 4067
AUSTRALIA

Kang Shin-pyo
Director
Institute for Ethnological Studies
Department of Cultural Anthropology
Hanyang University
Ansan 425-791
KOREA

Keyes Mary E
School of Physical Education and Athletics
McMaster University
1280 Main Street West
Hamilton ON L8S 4K1
CANADA

Kidd Bruce
School of Physical and Health Education
University of Toronto
320 Huron Street
Toronto ON M5S 1A1
CANADA

Kirsch Kerstin
University of Düsseldorf
Universitätstrasse 1
D-4000 Düsseldorf
FEDERAL REPUBLIC OF GERMANY

Konnor Paul C
Vice President
International Amateur Boxing Association
744 N 4th Street
Milwaukee WI 53203
USA

Kouame N'Guessan (CIV)
2463 Jean Durand 2
Ste-Foy QC G1V 4L2
CANADA

Kreiner Kathy
Petro-Canada Olympic Scholarship Fund
Olympic Scholarship Fund
c/o Christopher Lang and Associates
2 Bloor Street West
Toronto ON M4W 3E2
CANADA

Labadie Michael James
4350 Curé Drolet
Cap-Rouge QC G1Y 2H3
CANADA

Labelle Denis
6 Moussette
Hull QC J8Y 5J1
CANADA

Laberge Suzanne
Département d'éducation physique
Université de Montréal
Montréal QC H3C 3J7
CANADA

Lachance Gilles
Chef de la division des programmes
municipaux
Le service des loisirs et des parcs
de la ville de Québec
1595 rue Mgr Plessis
Québec QC G1R 4S9
CANADA

Laferrière Thérèse
Doyenne
Faculté des sciences de l'éducation
Université Laval
Ste-Foy QC G1K 7P4
CANADA

Lafontaine Maurice
Président
Monnaie Royale Canadienne
320 Promenade Sussex
Ottawa ON K1A 0G8
CANADA

Lagacé France
Directrice des communications
Communauté urbaine de Québec
399 St-Joseph est
Québec QC G1K 8E2
CANADA

Lamarche Pierre
Coordonnateur
Service des loisirs
Ville de Ste-Foy
1020 route de l'Eglise
Ste-Foy QC G1V 4E1
CANADA

Lamprecht Markus
Forschungsstelle Sportsoziologie
Winterthurerstrasse 143
CH-8057 Zürich
SWITZERLAND

Landry Fernand
Département d'éducation physique
Université Laval
Ste-Foy QC G1K 7P4
CANADA

Landry Marc
1140 Desjardins
Cap-Rouge QC G1Y 2B3
CANADA

Lang Christopher
2 Bloor Street West
Toronto ON M4W 3E2
CANADA

Laplante Laurent
Journaliste et écrivain
BP 1228
Ste-Croix QC G0S 2H0
CANADA

Larson James F
School of Communications, DS-40
University of Washington
Seattle WA 98195
USA

Lastel Arnauld (FRA)
Pavillon Moreau no 2414
Université Laval
Ste-Foy QC G1K 7P4
CANADA

Lasuncion F Xavier
Director
Sports Quality International
ED Brafa Artesania 75
Barcelona 08033
SPAIN

Leblanc Christine
École d'éducation physique et de loisirs
Université de Moncton
Moncton NB E1A 3E9
CANADA

Leblanc Martin
Musée de la civilisation de Québec
85 rue Dalhousie
Québec QC G1K 7A6
CANADA

Leclerc Carolle
Service des activités sportives
Université Laval
Ste-Foy QC G1K 7P4
CANADA

Lee Jong
1231 29th Street 103
Greeley CO 80631
USA

Lee Nancy
Canadian Broadcasting Corporation
365 Church Street
Toronto ON M5B 1Z9
CANADA

Letheren Carol Anne
Membre du CIO
Présidente
Association olympique canadienne
2380 ave Pierre Dupuy
Montréal QC H3C 3R4
CANADA

Levesque Martin
2006 Richer
Ste-Foy QC G1V 1P1
CANADA

Loret Alain
UFR STAPS
Université de Caen
Boulevard Maréchal-Juin
14032 Caen CEDEX
FRANCE

Loy John W
Department of Kinesiology
University of Illinois
906 South Goodwin Avenue
Urbana IL 61801
USA

Lucas John
Department of Exercise & Sport Science
College of Health and Human Development
Pennsylvania State University
University Park PA 16802
USA

Lynch John C
972 Galinee
St-Bruno QC J3V 3W4
CANADA

MacAloon John J
Social Science Graduate Division
University of Chicago
5845 South Ellis Ave
Chicago IL 60637
USA

Macdonald Daniel
École d'éducation physique et de loisirs
Université de Moncton
Moncton NB E1A 3E9
CANADA

Macintosh Donald
School of Physical and Health Education
Queen's University
Kingston ON K7L 3N6
CANADA

MacMillan Susan
216-10045 83th Ave
Edmonton AL T6E 2C3
CANADA

Mainguy Pierre
Conseiller municipal
Mairie de la ville de Québec
2 des Jardins
Québec QC G1R 4S9
CANADA

Mallen Patrick
Technical Program Co-Ordinator
Ministry of Tourism and Recreation
77 Bloor Street West
Toronto ON M7A 2R9
CANADA

Marcotte Gaston
Département d'éducation physique
Université Laval
Ste-Foy QC G1K 7P4
CANADA

Mason Suzanne
Director of Sport
Departement of Tourism, Recreation
& Heritage
PO Box 12345
Fredericton NB E3B 5C3
CANADA

McDermott Lisa
School of Physical and Health Education
Queen's University
Kingston ON K7L 3N6
CANADA

McKenzie Lorraine
Relations internationales, sports
et Jeux olympiques
Affaires extérieures Canada
Édifice LB Pearson
125 promenade Sussex
Ottawa ON K1A 0G2
CANADA

McMillan Peter
Manager, Special Projects
Canada Post Corporation
Station 480
Ottawa ON K1A 0B1
CANADA

Métot Alain
Directeur
UFR STAPS
Université de Caen
Boulevard Maréchal-Juin
14032 Caen CEDEX
FRANCE

Michel Alain
UFR Économic appliquée
Université Paris IX Dauphine
Place du Maréchal-de-Lattre-de-Tassigny
75775 Paris Cedex 16
FRANCE

Millette Louise
Monnaie royale canadienne
320 promenade Sussex
Ottawa ON K1A 0G8
CANADA

Morino Shinji
Faculté d'éducation physique
Université Chukyo 6-8 Umemori, Koshido
Toyota 470-03
JAPON

Moujane Mohammed (MAR)
Pavillon Parent no 9680
Université Laval
Ste-Foy QC G1K 7P4
CANADA

Murphy Donald BR
Director, Special Events
Canada Post Corporation
Station 480
Ottawa ON K1A 0B1
CANADA

Murray Sandra
School of Physical and Health Education
Queen's University
Kingston ON K7L 3N6
CANADA

Mzali Mohamed
Membre du CIO
a/sComité International Olympique
Château de Vidy
CH-1007 Lausanne
SUISSE

Nadeau Georges A
Département d'éducation physique
Université Laval
Ste-Foy QC G1K 7P4
CANADA

Naisbitt John
Megatrends Ltd
1601 Connecticut Ave
NW Suite 201
Washington DC 20009
USA

Ndiaye Antoine Diahère
Secrétaire Général
Conférence des Ministres de la jeunesse
et des sports
des pays d'expression française
26 rue Huart
Dakar 51204
SÉNÉGAL

Neill Susan
Chief of Policy, Planning and Evaluation
Sport Canada
Government of Canada
365 Laurier Ave West
Ottawa ON K1A 0X6
CANADA

Paal Gounnar
IAK Estonian Broadcasting
and TV Center
21 Lomonossovi Street
200100 Tallinn
ESTONIA

Pagé Joseph L
Conseiller pédagogique
Conseil des écoles publiques d'Ottawa-
Carlton
12 Promenade Glen Park
Gloucester ON K1B 3Z2
CANADA

Paillou Nelson
Président
Comité national olympique et sportif
français
23 rue d'Anjou
75008 Paris
FRANCE

Palmason Diane
Women's Program
Fitness and Amateur Sport
Government of Canada
365 Laurier Ave West
Ottawa ON K1A 0X6
CANADA

Paquet Denis
Ministère du Loisir, de la Chasse
et de la Pêche
Gouvernement du Québec
150 Boulevard St-Cyrille est
Québec QC G1R 4Y3
CANADA

Parent Claude
Directeur général
Fédération québécoise du sport étudiant
4545 Pierre de Coubertin
Montréal QC H1B 3GS
CANADA

Parés I Maicas Manuel
Centre d'Estudis Olimpics
Universitat Autonoma de Barcelona
08193 Bellaterra
Barcelona
ESPAGNE

Park Roberta J
Department of Physical Education
200 Hearst Gymnasium
University of California
Berkeley CA 94720
USA

Park Seh-jik
President
Seoul Olympic Organizing Committee
Olympic Center
CPO Box 1988
Kangdong-Gu
Seoul
KOREA

Paton Garth
Faculty of Physical Education & Recreation
University of New Brunswick
Fredericton NB E3B 5A3
CANADA

Pavlic Breda
Directrice
Bureau de liaison de l'UNESCO
56 rue St-Pierre
Québec QC G1K 4A1
CANADA

Peel Ann
a/s Goodman & Goodman
Barristers & Solicitors
20 Queen Street West
Toronto ON M5H 1V5
CANADA

Percic John
Petro-Canada Olympic Scholarship Fund
Olympic Scholarship Fund
c/o Christopher Lang and Associates
2 Bloor Street West
Toronto ON M4W 3E2
CANADA

Pigeassou Charles
UFR-STAPS
Université de Montpellier I
700 avenue du Pic St-Loup
34090 Montpellier
FRANCE

Pittenger Baaron
2802 Country Club Drive
Colorado Springs CO 80909
USA

Pleau Gaby
1024 ave Dijon
Ste-Foy QC G1W 4M1
CANADA

Plourde Gaston
Sous-ministre adjoint
Ministère du Loisir, de la Chasse
et de la Pêche
Gouvernement du Québec
150 Boul. St-Cyrille est
Québec QC G1R 4Y1
CANADA

Poirier Paul
2982 Gentilly
Ste-Foy QC G1W 1C4
CANADA

Porcellato Lorna
School of Physical and Health Education
Queen's University
Kingston ON K7L 3N6
CANADA

Poulin Guylaine
Centre de santé Hydro-Québec
2625 LeBourgneuf
Québec QC G2C 1P1
CANADA

Pound Richard W
Vice-Président du CIO
a/s Stikeman-Elliott
Barristors ë Solicitors
1155 Boulevard René Lévesque
Montréal QC H3B 3V2
CANADA

Praicheux Jean
Laboratoire de géographie humaine
et régionale
UFR des sciences de l'homme, de langage
et de la société
Université de Franche-Comté
32 rue Mégevand
25030 Besançon Cedex
FRANCE

Pyves Rick R
Vice President Marketing
VISA Canada Association 40 King Street W
PO Box 124
Toronto ON M5H 3Y2
CANADA

Quanz Dietrich R
Institut für Sportdidaktik
Deutsche Sporthochschule Köln
Carl Diem Weg 6
5000 KÖln 41
FEDERAL REPUBLIC OF GERMANY

Rail Geneviève
École des sciences de l'activité physique
Pavillon Montpetit
Université d'Ottawa
Ottawa ON K1N 6N5
CANADA

Ramsamy Sam
Executive Director
International Campaign Against
Apartheid Sports
PO Box 235
London NW3 5T5
GREAT BRITAIN

Rémillard Gil
Ministre de la Justice,
Procureur général et
Ministre délégué aux Affaires
intergouvernementales
canadiennes
Gouvernement du Québec
1200 route de l'Église
Ste-Foy QC G1V 4M1
CANADA

Riordan James
Department of Linguistic
and International Studies
University of Surrey
Guildford Surrey GU2 5XH
ENGLAND

Rivenburgh Nancy
School of Communications, DS-40
University of Washington
Seattle WA 98195
USA

Rivet Daniel
97 rue de l'anse
St-Rédempteur QC G0S 3B0
CANADA

Rodichenko Vladimir
National Olympic Committee USSR
Luzhnetskaya nab 8
Moscow 119270
USSR

Rose Murray (AUS)
Coordinator-North America
Melbourne Olympic Candidature 1996
401 S Prairie Ave
Los Angeles CA 90301
USA

Royer Guy
Directeur Affaires publiques
Laurentienne Vie
500 Grande-Allée est
Québec QC G1R 5M4
CANADA

Saganash Diom
Grand Conseil des Cris
1215 ave Royale
Beauport QC G1E 2B3
CANADA

Saleh Al-Sayyar
Technical Affairs
Saudi Arabia Olympic Committee
PO Box 6040
Riyadh 11442
SAUDI ARABIA

Samaranch S.E. Juan Antonio
Président
Comité international olympique
Château de Vidy
CH-1007 Lausanne
SUISSE

Samson Jacques
Vice-rectorat ressources humaines
University Laval
Ste-Foy QC G1K 7P4
CANADA

Sandhu Kiran
Indira Gandi Institute of Physical Education
and Sport Science
University of Dehli
61/36 First Floor, New Rohtak Rd
New Delhi 11005
INDIA

San Giovanni Lucinda F
Department of Sociology/Anthropology
Seton Hall University
South Orange NJ 07079
USA

Savola Jorma
Strategic Planning Officer
Finnish Central Sports Federation
Radiokatu 20
00240 Helsinki
FINLAND

Schneider Angela
Faculty of Philosophy
University of Western Ontario
London ON N6A 4K7
CANADA

Scott John
International Relations
Fitness and Amateur Sport
Government of Canada
365 Laurier ouest
Ottawa ON K1A 0X6
CANADA

Scott-Pawson Samantha
School of Physical and Health Education
Queen's University
Kingston ON K7L 3N6
CANADA

Shears Jerry
COA Board of Directors (Boxing)
CP 521
Saint-Laurent QC H4L 4Y7
CANADA

Shuttleworth John
General Manager Sport
Hillary Commission for Recreation & Sport
Investment House
Cnr Featherston and Ballance Streets
Wellington
NEW ZEALAND

Silvestrini Simon Florentino
Comite Olympico Argentino
Juncal 1662
Buenos Aires 1062
ARGENTINA

Sinclair Heather
Christopher Lang and Associates
2 Bloor Street W
Toronto ON M4W 3E2
CANADA

Smith Michael D
Department of Sociology, Exercise
and Sports Sciences
York University
4700 Keele Street
North York ON M3J 1P3
CANADA

Smyth John
Box 23 The Citadel
Charleston SC 29409
USA

Sobers Marc
1422 Harris Street
State College PA 16803
USA

Stasynec Candice B
Director
Sports & Recreation
City of Edmonton Parks & Recreation
Edmonton AL T5J 2R7
CANADA

Stevens Julie
School of Physical and Health Education
Queen's University
Kingston ON K7L 3N6
CANADA

Stewart Dianne
School of Physical and Health Education
Queen's University
Kingston ON K7L 3N6
CANADA

Suaud Charles
Département de sociologie
Université de Nantes
Chemin de la Sensive du Tertre
44036 Nantes CEDEX 01
FRANCE

Sumu Cyriaque (BUR)
Pavillon Lemieux no 6595
Université Laval
Ste-Foy QC G1K 7P4
CANADA

Taillibert Roger
Architecte en chef
des bâtiments civils et
Palais nationaux
163 rue de la Pompe
75116 Paris
FRANCE

Terenzio Umberto Maria
c/o UISP
Largo Nino Franchelluci 73
00155 Roma
ITALY

Tessier Jean-Guy
Directeur du sport
Ministère du Loisir de la Chasse
et de la Pêche
Gouvernement du Québec
150 Boul St-Cyrille est
Québec QC G1R 4Y3
CANADA

Tétrault André
Secrétaire exécutif
Comité international des Jeux
de la Francophonie
800 Maisonneuve est
Montréal QC J4L 3S5
CANADA

Théberge Nancy
Institut Simone de Beauvoir
Concordia University
Montréal QC
CANADA

Thomas Carolyn E
Department of Exercise Science
School of Health Related Professions
Faculty of Health Sciences
410 Kimball Tower
State University of New York
Buffalo NY 14214
USA

Thomas Raymond
UFR STAPS
Université de Paris X Nanterre
200 Avenue de la République
92001 Nanterre Cedex
FRANCE

Thompson March
Canadian Broadcasting Corporation
365 Church Street
Toronto ON M5B 1Z9
CANADA

Tibi Jean-Pierre
Sport Canada
Gouvernement du Canada
365 Laurier ouest
Ottawa ON K1A 0X6
CANADA

Toner Vance
École d'éducation physique et de loisirs
Université de Moncton
Moncton NB E1A 3E9
CANADA

Toor Daljit Singh
Department of Physical Education
Panjab University
Chandijarh
INDIA

Tossini Massimo
c/o UISP
Largo Nino Franchelluci 73
00155 Roma
ITALY

Tripps Dan G
Associate Dean
Director of Academic Programs
School of Physical Education and Athletics
Seattle Pacific University
Seattle WA 98119
USA

Tsarik Anatolii
National Olympic Committee USSR
Luzhnetskaya Nab 8
Moscow 119270
USSR

Tshimpumpu Wa Tshimpumpu
4195 route de Matadi-Ngaliema
BP 3626
ZAIRE

Turner Sylvie
Régie de la sécurité dans les sports
du Québec
100 Laviolette
Trois-Rivières QC G9A 5S9
CANADA

Ueberhorst Horst
Fakultät für Sportwissenschaft
Ruhr Universität Bochum
Postfach 102148
4630 Bochum
FEDERAL REPUBLIC OF GERMANY

Vagliani P
Coordonateur, Jeunesse et sport
UNESCO
7 Place de Fontenoy
75700 Paris
FRANCE

Värri Kyösti
Head of the HRD Division
Finnish Central Sports Federation
SVUL Radiokatu 20
Helsinki 00240
FINLAND

Vigneault Michel
11470 Drouart
Montréal QC H3M 2S5
CANADA

Villeneuve André
Directeur général divisionnaire
Division de Québec
Société canadienne des postes
1535 chemin Ste-Foy
Québec QC G1S 2P0
CANADA

Viru Atko
Tartu University
18 Ylikooli
Tartu 202400
ESTONIA

Walker Leroy T
Treasurer
United States Olympic Committee
1208 Red Oak Ave
Durham NC 27707
USA

Wall Edward A
Department of Physical Education
McGill University
475 Pine ave West
Montreal QC H2W 1S4
CANADA

Walsh Jean
Director of Communications
Melbourne Olympic Candidature 1996
Old Treasury Building
Spring Street
Melbourne
Victoria 3000
AUSTRALIA

Weis Kurt
Institut für Sozialwissenschaften
Fakultät für Wirtschafts- und
Sozialwissenschaften
Technische Universität München
Lothstrasse 17
D-8000 München
FEDERAL REPUBLIC OF GERMANY

Wigmore Sheila
School of Leisure & Food Management
Sheffield City Polytechnic
Totley Hall Lane
Sheffield S17 4AB
ENGLAND

Woodward Roger
President
VISA Canada Association
40 King Street West
Toronto ON M5H 3Y2
CANADA

Worrall Jim
Member of the IOC
c/o Ontario Sports Center
1220 Sheppard Ave East
Willowdale ON M2K 2X1
CANADA

Yerlès Magdeleine
Département d'éducation physique
Université Laval
Ste-Foy QC G1K 7P4
CANADA

Young David C
Classics Department
College of Liberal Arts & Sciences
University of Florida
Gainesville FL 32611
USA

Zerguini Mohamed
Membre du CIO
8 rue Mustapha Khalef
El Biar Alger
ALGÉRIE

Geographical Distribution of Participants
Répartition géographique des participants

Country/Pays		Province/State							N
ALG									1
ARG									1
AUS									5
BEL									1
BUR									1
CAN		AL	BC	MA	NB	ON	QC	SK	
		7	2	2	8	54	83	1	157
CIV									1
ESP									3
FIN									2
FRA									20
FRG									7
GBR									6
HGK									1
IND									2
ITA									3
JPN									1
KOR									2
KSA									1
MAR									2
NOR									1
NZL									1
PER									2
SEN									2
SUI									7
USA	West	CA	CO	NM	WA				
		7	2	1	3				
	Central	IL	MN	TX	WI				
		3	1	1	2				
	East	AL	CT	DC	FL	GA	MD	NC	
		1	1	1	1	1	1	2	
		NJ	NY	OH	PA	SC	VA	VT	
		2	3	1	2	1	1	1	41
URS									4
VEN									1
ZAI									1
TOTAL									277
[IOC/CIO]									[13]
CAN	57‰								
USA	15‰								
OTHER	28‰								[♂75‰ ♀25‰]

Achevé   Imprimerie
d'imprimer Gagné Ltée
au Canada Louiseville